Jeff Herman

GUIDE TO
BOOK
PUBLISHERS,
EDITORS,
& LITERARY
AGENTS

2009

**Who they are!
What they want!
How to
win them
over!**

D1314574

19TH EDITION

JEFF HERMAN

THREE DOG PRESS

Published by Three Dog Press. Distributed to the book trade by Watson-Guptill, a division of Random House.

For all other inquiries, including individual orders or details on special quantity discounts for groups or conferences, contact:

Three Dog Press
c/o The Jeff Herman Agency, LLC
3 Elm Street, POBox 1522
Stockbridge, MA 01262
Jeff@jeffherman.com
413-298-0077

Printed in the United States of America

04 05 06 07 08 09 10 11 12 13   10 9 8 7 6 5 4 3 2 1

Publisher's Cataloging-in-Publication Data
(Prepared by The Donohue Group, Inc.)

Herman, Jeff, 1958-
    Jeff Herman's guide to book publishers, editors, & literary agents : who they are! what they want! and how to win them over! / Jeff Herman.—2009 ed.

        v. ; cm.
    Annual
    ISSN: 1548-1344

1. Publishers and publishing—United States—Directories.   2. Publishers and publishing—Canada—Directories. 3. Editors—United States—Directories. 4. Editors—Canada—Directories. 5. Literary agents—United States—Directories. 6. Literary agents—Canada—Directories. 7. Authorship—Periodicals. I. Title: Guide to book publishers, editors, & literary agents II. Title: Book publishers, editors and literary agents.

Z475 .H47
070.5/025/73

ACKNOWLEDGEMENTS

I did not get this book done all by myself, nor would I have been able to (nor would anyone else be able to). A number of wonderful and talented people gave the best of themselves for the purpose of creating the 19th Edition of this book. In no particular order, I shall happily thank them below.

Deborah Herman, Thank you for everything until now, and I'm grateful knowing that more will follow.

Susan Hessler, From Columbus, OH, hessler.susan@gmail.com, who is a friend and the most gifted book production person I could imagine.

Carrie Lyon, From Housatonic, MA, CarrieLyon@gmail.com, who is an outstanding writer and researcher.

Cassie Lynch, From Amherst, MA, cassielynch@gmail.com, who is an excellent free-lance editor.

Wilkie, I'm sure you'll be the one to discover teachable ways to travel though time and space.

To the memories of Boney The Whippet, and Curley The Mugwump, two of the original Three Dogs, RIP. To Blossom The Spitz, who doggedly carries on for the pact and never looks back. And to Gracie, The New Whippet, for her eagerness to hit the ground running and learn the tricks of the trade.

DEDICATION

I hereby dedicate the 19th edition (2009) of this book to people who share their blessings, knowledge and wisdom with others.

PUBLISHERS, EDITORS, AND LITERARY AGENTS

ADVICE FOR WRITERS

INDEPENDENT EDITORS

RESOURCES FOR WRITERS

INTRODUCTION

Dear Writer,

This is the 19th edition of a book that has sold several hundred-thousand copies since its first incarnation about 19 years ago. The idea for this book came to me in a moment of inspiration. I came to this business as a young man still in my 20s with little experience, and probably no right to call myself an agent. But I was just innocent enough not to know what I didn't know and shouldn't try. Youth gives us that special air pocket in which what we want to do fuels us into action, without the suffocations of logic or reason.

To succeed, an agent needs to know editors, and I didn't know any. I looked for a book that listed who these people were and what types of work they acquired, but no such centralized source existed. So I compiled my contacts the old-fashioned way, cold-calling.

I discovered that some editors, certainly not all, had disdain for hungry unproven writers. It surprised me that they actually did not want to have any contact with these people, unless they could somehow be "pre-certified" as someone that the editor might likely want to publish. It seemed as if some editors wanted to be cloistered within the chambers of a secret society, to which membership would only be offered to a select few. This web of legacies, pedigrees, and "secret handshakes," disqualified admission to too many people who had too many important ideas to share. And so I had the idea for this book. I envisioned it as a way for writers to have a little more information; a little more power; a little more of an opportunity to maybe get their words published.

I was with my original publisher for more than a decade, but then they were abruptly taken off the map by one of the international "gigantors". I had a nice run with my second publisher, but then they unilaterally deleted themselves from the trade publishing market. I dreaded the tedium of having to now sell my own book all over again. Instead, I decided to publish it myself. It was my dogs who told me to do it, so my publishing firm is named for them, Three Dog Press.

I encourage you to stay in touch with me about your ideas for this book and your experiences (whether negative or positive).

Thank you, and may you realize all the success you seek.

Best wishes,

Jeffrey H. Herman
THE JEFF HERMAN AGENCY, LLC
P.O. Box 1522
Stockbridge, MA 01262
Jeff@jeffherman.com
413-298-0077

ABOUT THE AUTHOR

Jeff Herman is the founder of The Jeff Herman Literary Agency, LLC, based in Stockbridge, Massachussetts. One of the most innovative agents in the book business, he represents more than 100 writers and has sold more than 500 titles in the United States and internationally. Herman has been extensively written and talked about in numerous print publications and broadcast programs, and he speaks at writer's conferences around the country. He is the coauthor with Deborah Levine Herman of *Write the Perfect Book Proposal*. Be sure to visit his high-content Web site at www.jeffherman.com.

CONTRIBUTORS

Deborah Herman, Chairman of the Board, The Jeff Herman Literary Agency, Stockbridge, MA, deborah@jeffherman.com, blog: www.spiritualwritingagent.com

William Hamilton, Publisher, University of Hawaii Press

Greg Ioannou, Editorial Director, Colborne Communications, Toronto, Ontario, gregg@colcomm.ca

Jerry Gross, Freelance Editor & Book Doctor, Croton-on-Hudson, NY, GrosAssoc@aol.com

Mr. Jamie Forbes, 212-924-0657

Toni Robino, President of With Flying Colours Literary Services, Conifer, Colorado, ToniRobino@Yahoo.com

Carrie Lyon, author of Working Dogs, creator of Web sites including MyMamaDoneToldMe.com, and founder of Honeyland Press, CarrieLyon@gmail.com

Gerald Sindell, Independent Publishing Consultant, ThoughtLeadersINTL., www.thoughtleadersintl.com, 415-789-9040

SECTION ONE

THE PUBLISHING
CONGLOMERATES

THE MULTINATIONAL CONGLOMERATED PUBLISHING ENTITIES

JEFF HERMAN

A long time ago, the U.S. book publishing business consisted of hundreds of mom-and-pop companies. Each was generally named for the individual(s) who founded the firm, and their respective catalogues reflected their own special tastes and sensibilities. Separately, none of these entities or individuals had the power to dictate the contemporary status or future direction of publishing. They were a thriving community of several hundred distinct pieces. Collectively, they comprised our nation's entire book publishing structure.

The revolution came and happened quickly. Some of us complained, but it didn't make any difference. It was a funny revolution in that it reversed the usual dynamic. Unlike the breaking away of exploited tribes from masters of conquest, which is revolution in its most romantic form, we watched as faceless and formless conquerors wrapped themselves around most of our precious tribes and soundlessly absorbed them into a small number of obese oceans. Perhaps those who might have cared the most saw gold before they saw the cost. Can we blame them? Should we even judge the result? Perhaps it is wiser to simply adjust.

We have consolidated the largest multinational publishing properties into their own section. It seemed right to do so, since consolidation has been their most striking feature. These companies possess the brand names of the firms they have acquired over the past three decades. While some of the firms may be led by high-profile individuals or greatly influenced by multigenerational families that control large blocks of non-traded stock, it is also safe to say that these firms are greater than any one person or any unified collection of people. At the end of the day, it is the various pension funds and institutional investment firms that must be satisfied.

There are two other key features of multinational publishers. 1) Most of them are controlled by foreign interests. 2) The book publishing programs are an extremely small part of a much larger agenda, which includes movies, magazines, broadcast and cable channels, newspapers, music, and the Internet.

Do not let my irreverent or ominous tone chase you away. At all of these firms you will find hard-working, dedicated editors who want nothing more than the ability to publish good books. And they manage to achieve that. So join with them and adjust to the system as it is. The best thing you can do is get your book published.

This section is followed by a large number of independent and small houses, each of which is capable of doing as much, or more, than the big houses. The independent houses are not vestiges from a dead past. To the contrary, they keep the current publishing climate vibrant, and help create the future with their entrepreneurial and innovative ways. Don't ever think twice about joining them.

I have asserted my discretionary powers to place a few houses in the Independent Section that could also fit into the Corporate Section. Obviously, not all corporations are the same. Some are the equivalent of Jupiter while others are more like Mercury (I'm actually referring to size, not "personalities"). When the book division is not a mere asterisk within its corporate envelope, but is instead a crucial piece, you will find it with the independents.

BERTELSMANN AG

A global media firm based in Germany, Bertelsmann AG is comprised of publishing, music, and broadcasting operations in nearly 60 countries; these include Random House, the world's largest English-language general trade book publisher. Bertelsmann is a privately held company, owned by the Mohn family and their foundation.

Corporate acquisitions—including Watson-Guptill, The Monacelli Press, BBC Books, Multnomah, and Triumph Books—have helped Bertelsmann achieve growth in recent years.

RANDOM HOUSE, INC.

BANTAM DELL PUBLISHING GROUP

CROWN PUBLISHING GROUP

DOUBLEDAY PUBLISHING GROUP

KNOPF PUBLISHING GROUP

RANDOM HOUSE CHILDREN'S BOOKS

RANDOM HOUSE INFORMATION GROUP

RANDOM HOUSE PUBLISHING GROUP

1745 Broadway, New York, NY 10019

212-782-9000

www.randomhouse.com

Random House is the largest English-language general trade publisher in the world. The span of this house's titles runs both wide and deep, including a broad array of categories in fiction and nonfiction.

Founded in 1925, Random House has grown into an intricate and shifting web of divisions, publishing groups, and imprints, which includes well-known names like Knopf, Pantheon, Vintage, Anchor, Schocken, Bantam, Dell, Dial, Delacorte, Doubleday, Broadway, Nan A. Talese, Random House, Ballantine, Villard, Crown, Clarkson Potter, Shaye Areheart, Three Rivers Press, Fodor's Guides, Living Language, Delacorte Press, WaterBrook, Multnomah, Watson-Guptill, and Golden Books. Random House is based in New York City.

Random House was acquired by Bertelsmann in 1998. Random House's major publishing groups include Bantam Dell Publishing Group, Crown Publishing Group, Doubleday Publishing Group, Knopf Publishing Group, Random House Children's Books, Random House Information Group, and Random House Publishing Group.

The company was founded when Bennett Cerf and Donald Klopfer purchased The Modern Library, an imprint that reprinted classic works of literature, from publisher Horace Liveright. Two years later, in 1927, the publisher decided to broaden its publishing activities, and the Random House colophon made its debut.

In recent years, Random House revenues have continued to grow, despite a sluggish international marketplace. The international nature of the company tends to attract a global audience, with operations in Asia, South Africa, South America, and the UK, to name a few. In 2007, Random House launched Insight, a US book and audio search and browse service that operates as a widget inside Web browsers. If you have online access, be sure to explore the Random House Web site; it's chock full of information, including blogs, podcasts, and newsletters. Random House had a new CEO appointed in 2008, Markus Dohle, who previously ran Arvato Print for Bertlesmann in Germany.

Random House editors prefer to accept manuscripts submitted by literary agents. They do not accept unsolicited submissions, proposals, manuscripts, or submission queries via e-mail at this time.

Markus Dohle, CEO, Random House

BANTAM DELL PUBLISHING GROUP

BANTAM

DELACORTE PRESS

DELL

DELTA

THE DIAL PRESS

SPECTRA

1745 Broadway, New York, NY 10019

212-782-9000

www.randomhouse.com

Bantam Dell Publishing Group publishes a broad spectrum of adult fiction and non-fiction, including frontlist commercial category, literary works, specialty titles, and genre fiction. It is the largest division of Random House, Inc, which includes books published under the following imprints: Bantam Hardcover, Bantam Mass Market, Bantam Trade Paperback, Spectra, Delacorte Press Hardcover, Dell Mass Market Paperback, Delta Trade Paperback, The Dial Press Hardcover and Dial Press Trade Paperback.

BANTAM

Established in 1945, Bantam is one of the most successful publishers of adult fiction and nonfiction. In addition to being the nation's largest mass market paperback publisher, Bantam publishes a select yet diverse hardcover list, which includes the best-selling novelists Dean Koontz, Tom Robbins, Elizabeth George, Iris Johansen, Tami Hoag, Diane Mott Davidson, George R.R. Martin, Michael Palmer, and Luanne Rice.

Recent nonfiction titles include *7 Deadly Scenarios: A Military Futurist Explores War in the 21st Century* by Andrew Krepinevich; *The Much Too Promised Land: America's Elusive Search for Arab-Israeli Peace* by Aaron David Miller; *The Almanac of Political Corruption, Scandals, and Dirty Politics* by Kim Long; *Seinlanguage* by Jerry Seinfeld; *Super Crunchers* by Ian Ayres; and *Getting to 50/50: How Working Moms and Dads Can Have It All by Sharing It All* by Sharon Meers and Joanna Strober.

Bantam's fiction list includes commercial novels, mysteries, thrillers, suspense, science fiction and fantasy, romance, women's fiction, and select literary works. The hardcover fiction list includes such novelists as Dean Koontz, Tom Robbins, Elizabeth George, Iris Johansen, Tami Hoag, Diane Mott Davidson, George R.R. Martin, Michael Palmer, and Luanne Rice. Bantam mass market and trade paperback authors include Louis L'Amour, Maya Angelou, Jean Auel, Sandra Brown, Pat Conroy, Nora Roberts, Tom Wolfe, Kay Hooper, Lisa Gardner, and Rita Mae Brown.

Recent fiction titles include *Moon Women* by Pamela Duncan; *The Secret Lover* by Julia London; *Loose and Easy* by Tara Janzen; *Blood Sins* by Kay Hooper; *The Spy's Bedside Book* by Graham Greene and Hugh Greene; *The Geometry of Sisters* by Luanne Rice; *The Treasure* by Iris Johansen; and *Your Heart Belongs to Me* by Dean Koontz.

Irwyn Applebaum, President

Toni Burbank, Vice President and Executive Editor, Bantam Dell—Self-help, spirituality and health

Kate Miciak, Executive Editor, Bantam Dell—Mysteries, thrillers, other fiction and narrative nonfiction

Juliet Ulman, Senior Editor—General fiction, science fiction, fantasy

Shauna Summers, Senior Editor—Women's fiction, romance, erotica

John Flicker, Editor—Nonfiction, including history, politics, war and current events; and historical & time travel fiction

Caitlin Alexander, Editor—Fiction including debut fiction, mysteries

Molly Boyle, Assistant Editor—Commercial fiction and mysteries, particularly for women, as well as memoir, narrative, and pop culture nonfiction

DELACORTE PRESS

Delacorte Press focuses on hardcover frontlist releases in the categories of self-help, self-actualization, popular psychology, child care, politics, true crime, and current issues and events. Delacorte's fiction includes commercial novels, romance, historical, mystery, and futuristic works.

Recent nonfiction titles include *Do Gentlemen Really Prefer Blondes?: Bodies, Behavior, and Brains—the Science Behind Sex, Love, and Attraction* by Jena Pincott; *Flights of Fancy: Birds in Myth, Legend, and Superstition* by Peter Tate; *The Smart Cookies' Guide to Making More Dough: How Five Young Women Got Smart, Formed a Money Club, and Took Control of Their Finances* by The Smart Cookies and Jennifer Barrett; and *Lang Lang: Playing with Flying Keys* by Lang Lang.

Recent fiction titles include *Echoes from the Dead* by Johan Theorin, translated by Marlaine Delargy; *Company of Liars* by Karen Maitland; *My Husband's Sweethearts* by Bridget Asher; *Fractured* by Karen Slaughter; and *The Garden of Evil* by David Hewson.

Irwyn Applebaum, President

Kate Miciak, Executive Editor, Bantam Dell—Mysteries, thrillers, other fiction and narrative nonfiction

Kerry Buckley, Editor—Fiction, including women's fiction, debuts, and coming-of-age

DELL

A leading publisher of adult fiction and nonfiction for the past seven decades, Dell is home to the best-selling female novelist of our time, Danielle Steel, who is published in Delacorte hardcover and Dell paperback. Dell also publishes the biggest-selling male novelist of the last decade, John Grisham, as a Dell paperback author.

Other writers who are published in mass market by Dell include Sophie Kinsella, Thomas Harris, Sara Paretsky, Belva Plain, Perri O'Shaughnessy, Harlan Coben, and Homer Hickam.

Recent titles include *The Devil's Due* by Jenna Black; *Dreaming the Bull* by Manda Scott; *Simply Perfect* by Mary Balogh; *Veil of Midnight* by Lara Adrian; *Getting Old is a Disaster* by Rita Lakin; *The Complete Book of Food Counts* by Corinne T. Netzer; *The Appeal* by John Grisham; *The Darkest Touch* by Jaci Burton; and *The Invasion of Privacy* by Perri O'Shaughnessy.

Danielle Perez, Senior Editor—Fiction

Philip Rappaport, Senior Editor—Nonfiction

DELTA

Delta publishes literary fiction and nonfiction. This imprint includes works by Alice McDermott, Allegra Goodman, Justin Cronin, Marie Arana, Patrick Ryan, Elizabeth McCracken, Ian Caldwell, Dustin Thomason, and Sting.

The fiction list includes reprints of best-sellers as well as steamy romances, thrillers, and mysteries—and the popular *Outlander* series by Diana Gabaldon.

Recent titles include *Sexile* by Lisa Lawrence; *The Might Following* by Morag Joss; *Mad Dogs and an Englishwoman: Travels with Sled Dogs in Canada's Frozen North* by Polly Evans; *Lord John and the Hand of Devils* by Diana Gabaldon; *Your Body's Red Light Warning Signals: Medical Tips That May Save Your Life* by Neil Shulman, Jack Birge, and Joon

Ahn; *See You in a Hundred Years: Discover One Young Family's Search for a Simpler Live. . . Four Seasons of Living in the Year 1900* by Logan Ward; and *Firmin: A Tale of Exile, Unrequited Love, and the Redemptive Power of Literature* by Sam Savage.

Danielle Perez, Senior Editor—Fiction

Philip Rappaport, Senior Editor—Nonfiction, including history, humor, parenting

Shauna Summers, Senior Editor—Women's fiction, romance, erotica

THE DIAL PRESS

The Dial Press, an imprint of Bantam Dell Publishing Group, publishes literary fiction and nonfiction. This imprint includes works by Sophie Kinsella, Allegra Goodman, Justin Cronin, Marie Arana, Patrick Ryan, Elizabeth McCracken, Ian Caldwell, Dustin Thomason, and Sting.

Recent titles include *The Slide* by Kyle Beachy; *Lima Nights* by Marie Arana; *The Good Thief* by Hannah Tinti; *The Guernsey Literary and Potato Peel Pie Society* by Mary Ann Shaffer and Annie Barrows; *The Answer is Always Yes* by Monica Ferrell; *Turning Tables* by Heather & Rose MacDowell; and *The Opposite of Love* by Julie Buxbaum.

Direct queries and SASEs to:

Susan Kamil, Vice President and Editorial Director

Beth Rashbaum, Senior Editor—Nonfiction, memoir, health

SPECTRA

Spectra's slogan is "Speculative Fiction, Speculative Fact." This imprint of the Bantam Dell Publishing Group publishes science fiction and fantasy books in trade paperback, mass market paperback, and, occasionally, hardcover.

Recent titles include *Blood and Ice* by Robert Masello; *Hope's Folly* by Linnea Sinclair; *Made to Be Broken* by Kelley Armstrong; *Black Blood* by John Meaney; *Palimpsest* by Catherynne Valente; *The Republic of Thieves* by Scott Lynch; *Spell Games* by T. A. Pratt; *Flight into Darkness* by Sarah Ash; *Iron Angel* by Alan Campbell; and *The Map of Moments: A Novel of the Hidden Cities* by Christopher Golden and Tim Lebbon.

Anne Lesley Groell, Editor

Juliet Ulman, Senior Editor

CROWN PUBLISHING GROUP

CLARKSON POTTER

CROWN BUSINESS

CROWN FORUM

CROWN PUBLISHERS, INC.

HARMONY BOOKS

SHAYE AREHEART BOOKS

THREE RIVERS PRESS

WATSON-GUPTILL

1745 Broadway, New York, NY 10019

212-782-9000

www.randomhouse.com

The Crown Publishing Group originated in 1933 and is known today for the broad scope of its publishing program and its singular market responsiveness, qualities that are reflected in its savvy selection of authors and books and in its aggressive efforts to market them.

Acquired by Random House in 1988, Crown incorporates a number of Random House imprints and acquisitions that together make up the Crown Publishing Group. Crown imprints include Clarkson Potter, Crown Business, the Crown imprint, Harmony Books, Shaye Areheart Books, Three Rivers Press, and Watson-Guptill.

CLARKSON POTTER

POTTER CRAFT

POTTER STYLE

Clarkson Potter is a leader in beautifully illustrated nonfiction books on cooking, parenting, pets, crafts and hobbies, decorating, self-help, and other lifestyle topics. Clarkson Potter authors include Rachel Ray, Martha Stewart, Mario Batali, Chris Casson Madden, and Ina Garten.

Imprints include Potter Craft, which has been very successful with knitting and crafting books, and Potter Style, which also publishes in spiral-bound and deck editions.

Recent titles include *The New Terrarium: Creating Beautiful Displays for Plants and Nature* by Tovah Martin and Kindra Clieneff; *Knitting and Tea: 25 Classic Knits and the Teas That Inspired Them* by Jane & Patrick Gottelier; *The Crafty Chica's Guide to Artful*

Sewing: Fabu-Low-Sew Projects for the Everyday Crafter by Kathy Cano-Murillo; *Mix, Match, or Clash Deck: The Ultimate Compatibility Test for Love, Friendship, and Career Success* by Dewey Sadka; *Sex Checks: 60 Checks for Maintaining Balance in the Bedroom* by Potter Style; *The Paper Architect: Fold-It-Yourself Buildings and Structures* by Marivi Garrido and Ingrid Siliakus; *Together We Go: Extraordinary Family Journeys to Discover and Remember* by Anita Kaushal; *Dessert FourPlay: Sweet Quartets from a Four-Star Pastry Chef* by Johnny Iuzzini and Roy Finamore; and *Born-Again Vintage: 25 Ways to Deconstruct, reinvent, and Recycle Your Wardrobe* by Bridgett Artise and Jen Karetnick.

Direct query and SASE to:

Lauren Shakely, Publisher—High profile lifestyle titles

Doris Cooper, Editorial Director—Lifestyle, relationships

Rica Allannic, Senior Editor—Cookbooks

Judy Pray, Senior Editor—Parenting, lifestyle, advice

Aliza Fogelson, Editor—Decorating, style, cooking, food

Rosy Ngo, Editor—Potter Craft; especially knitting, felting, quilting

Melissa Bonventre, Editor—Potter Craft, including sewing, needle crafts, paper crafts

CROWN BUSINESS

Crown Business is one of the leading publishers of business books, producing titles by authors such as Charles Schwab, Suze Orman, Ram Charan and Michael Hammer. Crown Business looks to publish both traditional and cutting-edge business books.

Recent titles include *Real Leaders Don't Do PowerPoint: How to Sell Yourself and Your Ideas* by Christopher Witt; *Cracking the Growth Code: How Ordinary Managers Become Extraordinary Catalysts* by Jeanne Liedtka; *The CEO's Boss: What Wall Street Knows That Top Managers Don't* by Anne-Marie Fink; *Magic Moves: 32 Lessons on How to Be an All-Star in Business* by Earvin Magic Johnson; and *The First Billion is the Hardest: Reflections on a Life of Comebacks and America's Energy Future* by T. Boone Pickens.

Direct queries and SASEs to:

John Mahaney, Executive Editor

CROWN FORUM

Crown Forum serves a conservative readership; its list includes several best-selling titles from Ann Coulter, Tammy Bruce, and Kenneth Timmerman.

Recent titles include *10 Big Lies About America* by Michael Medved; *The New Ann Coulter* by Ann Coulter; *Hamilton's Curse: How Jefferson's Arch Enemy Betrayed the American Revolution—and What It Means for Americans Today* by Thomas Dilorenzo; *The Failure Factory: How Unelected Bureaucrats, Liberal Democrats, and Big Government Republicans are Undermining America's Security and Leading Us to War* by Bill Gertz; *Behind Every Successful Man: A Woman's Guide to Having It All* by Megan Basham; and *Real Education: Four Simple Truths for Bringing American Schools Back to Reality* by Charles Murray

Direct queries and SASEs to:

Jed Donahue, Senior Editor

Mary Choteborsky, Assistant Editor—Nonfiction, including memoir

CROWN PUBLISHERS, INC.

Crown publishes a hearty list of fiction and nonfiction. Nonfiction encompasses popular titles in biography, history, art, pop culture, contemporary culture, crime, sports, travel, popular and literary science, languages, spirituality, cookbooks, self-help, how-to, and antiques and collectibles, as well as popular reference works. Fiction titles focus on literary and popular works in hardcover.

Recent bestsellers include *The Billionaire's Vinegar* by Benjamin Wallace and *The 4-Hour Workweek* by Timothy Ferris. Other recent Crown titles include *Positivity: Master your Emotions to Broaden Your Mind and Build Your Best Future* by Barbara Fredrickson; *No Angel: My Harrowing Undercover Journey to the Inner Circle of the Hells Angels* by Jay Dobyns and Nils Shelton-Johnson; *The Peachgrower's Almanac* by Elaine Dirollo; *13 Is the New 18: And Other Things My Children Taught Me—While I Was Having a Nervous Breakdown Being Their Mother* by Beth J. Harpaz; *In Search of Our Roots: How 19 Extraordinary African Americans Reclaimed Their Past* by Henry Louis Gates Jr.; and *The 6-Week Cure for the Middle-Aged Middle* by Michael R. Eades and Mary Dan Eades.

Direct queries and SASEs to:

Rick Horgan, Executive Editor—Nonfiction, business, politics, current affairs, popular culture, historical narratives, humor

Heather Jackson, Executive Editor—Nonfiction, memoir, humor, popular culture

Rachel Klayman, Executive Editor—Politics, pop culture, memoir

Allison McCabe, Senior Editor—Nonfiction, memoir, fiction, including debut and historical

Sean Desmond, Senior Editor—Politics, history, political thrillers

Lucinda Bartley, Associate Editor—Social and cultural studies, science, narrative nonfiction

Julian Pavia, Associate Editor—Fiction, including mysteries

Mary Choteborsky, Assistant Editor—Politics, pop culture, memoir

HARMONY BOOKS

Harmony Books is a market leader in the area of mind, body, and spirit, as well as biography/memoir, science, and general narrative nonfiction. Its critically acclaimed and best-selling authors include Cesar Millan, Stephen Jay Gould, Caroline Myss, Deepak Chopra, and Suzanne Finstad.

Harmony's bestsellers include *Why is God Laughing?: The Path to Joy and Spiritual Optimism* by Deepak Chopra; *Anatomy of the Spirit: The Seven Stages of Power and Healing by Caroline Myss; *Emotional Alchemy* by Tara Bennett-Goleman; *Bhagavad Gita* translated by Stephen Mitchell; and *Loving What Is: Four Questions That Can Change Your Life* by Byron Katie and Stephen Mitchell.

Recent titles include *Freak Nation: How I Discovered That No One is Normal* by Dawn Prince-Hughes, PhD; *God Stories: Inspiring Encounters with the Divine* by Jennifer Skiff; *The Inheritance: The Global Challenges to American Power* by David E. Sanger; *Reinventing the Body, Resurrecting the Soul: How to Create a New Self* by Deepak Chopra; and *Magnificent Mind at Any Age: Natural Ways to Unleash Your Brain's Maximum Potential* by Daniel G. Amen, MD.

Harmony Books does not accept manuscripts without agent representation. Direct queries with SASEs to:

Shaye Areheart, Vice President and Publisher—Fiction and nonfiction, including memoir, debut fiction, coming-of-age novels, and how-to

John Glusman, Executive Editor—Fiction and nonfiction, including history, science, current events, health, and thrillers

Julia Pastore, Editor—Nonfiction, memoir

Kate Kennedy, Associate Editor—Narrative nonfiction, biography, memoir, spirituality, self-help

Anne Berry, Assistant Editor—Narrative nonfiction, biography, memoir, spirituality, self-help

SHAYE AREHEART BOOKS

Shaye Areheart Books is devoted to contemporary literary and commercial fiction. Authors include Chris Bohjalian, Craig Nova, Jeanne Ray, John Smolens, Sheri Reynolds, and Maggie Estep. Shaye Areheart Books embrace a typically vanguard literary tone.

Recent titles include *Kissing Games of the World* by Sandi Kahn Shelton; *Time of My Life* by Allison Winn Scotch; *The Sweet In Between* by Sheri Reynolds; *Fidel's Last Days: A Novel* by Roland Merullo; *The Grift* by Debra Ginsberg; *Tethered* by Amy Mackinnon; *Murder at the Bad Girl's Bar and Grill* by N. M. Kelby; and *How Far Is the Ocean From Here* by Amy Shearn.

Shaye Areheart Books does not accept manuscripts without agent representation. Direct queries and SASEs to:

Shaye Areheart, Vice President and Publisher—Fiction and nonfiction, including memoir, debut fiction, coming-of-age novels, and how-to

John Glusman, Executive Editor—Fiction and nonfiction, including history, science, current events, health, and thrillers

Kate Kennedy, Associate Editor

Anne Berry, Assistant Editor

THREE RIVERS PRESS

Three Rivers Press publishes trade and hardcovers as well as reprints of books issued initially in hardcover by the other Crown imprints. Categories include humor, popular culture, music, and other nonfiction. A recent best-seller was *The Audacity of Hope* by Barack Obama.

Recent titles include *Godmother: The Secret Cinderella Story* by Carolyn Turgeon; *In the Ring: The Trials of a Washington Lawyer* by Robert S. Bennett; *Sit, Ubu, Sit: How I Went from Brooklyn to Hollywood with the Same Woman, the Same Dog, and a Lot Less Hair* by Gary David Goldberg; *How to Sleep Alone in a King-Size Bed: A Memoir of Starting Over* by Theo Pauline Nestor; *Doing What Matters: How to Get Results That Make a Difference—The Revolutionary Old-School Approach* by James M. Kilts, Robert Lorber, and John F. Manfredi; and *Kitty Grub: Easy, Wholesome Home Cooking for Your Cat* by Rudy Edalati.

Carrie Thornton, Publishing Manager—Pop culture, music, humor, gay and lesbian, dating/relationships, fiction and film

Lindsay Orman, Editor—Nonfiction, especially business

Julian Pavia, Associate Editor—Fiction, including mysteries

WATSON-GUPTILL

Random House purchased Watson-Guptill in 2008, making it a stand-alone imprint in the Crown group. With a backlist of over 1,000 titles, Watson-Guptill's list of nonfiction reference books focuses on art, photography, craft, and performing arts titles. Imprints include Amphoto Books for photography subjects, Back Stage Books for the performing arts, Billboard Books for music and entertainment titles, and Lone Eagle for subjects of interest to entertainment industry professionals. Watson-Guptill is now under the supervision of Clarkson Potter publisher, Lauren Shakely.

Recent titles include *Classic Human Anatomy: The Artist's Guide to Form, Function, and Movement* by Valerie L. Winslow; *Collage Journeys: A Practical Guide to Creating Personal Artwork* by Jane Davies; *Girligami: A Fresh, Fun, Fashionable Spin on Origami* by Cindy Ng; *Beginner's Guide to Animation: Everything You Need to Know to Get Started* by Mary Murphy; *Baby Beanies: Happy Hats to Knit for Little Heads* by Amanda Keeys; and *Jewelry Techniques: The Essential Guide to Choosing and Using Materials, Stones, and Settings* by Anastasia Young.

Lauren Shakely, Publisher

DOUBLEDAY PUBLISHING GROUP

BROADWAY BOOKS

DOUBLEDAY

SPIEGEL & GRAU

WATERBROOK MULTNOMAH

1745 Broadway, New York, NY 10019

212-782-9000

www.doubleday.com

A division of Random House, the Doubleday Publishing Group is known for its strong commercial lists in both fiction and nonfiction. Among the group's bestselling authors are John Grisham, Dan Brown, Suze Orman, Bill O'Reilly, Tina Brown, Sara Gruen, Bill Bryson, Pat Conroy, Ian McEwan, Chuck Palahniuk, Margaret Atwood, Gore Vidal, Jeffrey Toobin, E. Lynn Harris, Pope Benedict XVI, Jonathan Lethem, Hampton Sides, David Bach, Thomas Cahill, Barbara Delinsky, and Frances Mayes.

Formerly Doubleday Broadway Publishing, the group was rebranded in 2008 and now comprises four divisions: Doubleday, Broadway, WaterBrook Multnomah, and Spiegel & Grau, along with associated imprints like Nan Talese, Doubleday Business, and Flying Dolphin.

President Steve Rubin said in the announcement that with so many divisions "we have outgrown the Doubleday Broadway name. By simplifying our name and implementing a fresh, bold look, we are able to preserve the strong brand equity of the name 'Doubleday' while ensuring that our publishing group maintains a clear, forward-looking identity in the marketplace."

BROADWAY BOOKS

Broadway generates a variety of nonfiction, including celebrity autobiography and biography; historical, political, and cultural biography and memoirs; politics and current affairs; multicultural topics; popular culture; cookbooks, diet, and nutrition; consumer reference; business; personal finance; and popular psychology, spirituality, and women's issues. The house also provides selective commercial/literary frontlist fiction, primarily by established or highly promotable authors. Broadway's emporium strategy involves publishing unique, marketable books of the highest editorial quality by authors who are authorities in their field and who use their credibility and expertise to promote their work.

Broadway has established many long-running best-sellers, including *Saving Graces: Finding Solace and Strength from Friends and Strangers* by Elizabeth Edwards; Frances Mayes's *Bella Tuscany* and *Under the Tuscan Sun*; Bill Bryson's *In A Sunburned Country, A*

Walk in the Woods, and *I'm a Stranger Here Myself*; Bob Costas's *Fair Ball*; and Bill O'Reilly's *Who's Looking Out For You?*

In addition to narrative nonfiction, Broadway publishes a highly successful range of self-help, mind/body/spirit, business, and cooking books.

Recent Broadway titles *The Man Who Owns the News: Inside the Secret World of Rupert Murdoch* by Michael Wolff; *Why We Make Mistakes: How We Look Without Seeing, Forget Things in Seconds, and Are All Pretty Sure We are Way Above Average* by Joseph T. Hallinan; *A Date You Can't Refuse* by Harley Jane Kozak; *Vegan Soups and Hearty Stews for All Seasons* by Nava Atlas; *The Ties That Bind: A Memoir of Race, Memory, and Redemption* by Bertice Berry; *Are You Ready!: Take Charge, Lose Weight, Get in Shape, and Change Your Life Forever* by Bob Harper; and *Feeling Good Together: The Secret to Making Troubled Relationships Work* by David D. Burns MD.

Broadway does not accept unsolicited manuscripts; only agented works are considered.

Bill Thomas, Editor-in-Chief—High-profile fiction and nonfiction

Charles Conrad, Vice President and Executive Editor—New nonfiction projects, including popular culture, social history, and literary nonfiction; contemporary literary and quality fiction; also in charge of trade-paperback reprints

Stacy Creamer, Executive Editor and Deputy Director, Editorial—Nonfiction, including science, narrative nonfiction, and memoir

Gerald Howard, Executive Editor-at-large—Narrative nonfiction and unusual literary fiction

Jennifer Josephy, Executive Editor—Cookbooks and general nonfiction

Kristine Puopolo, Senior Editor—Literary nonfiction, self-help, spirituality, health, fitness

Ann Campbell, Editor—Narrative nonfiction, women's history, women's fiction, health, fitness, spirituality, armchair travel, and politics

Becky Cole, Editor—Nonfiction including reference, how-to, and narrative nonfiction

Andrew Corbin, Editor—Biography, nonfiction, fiction, religion

Christine Pride, Editor—Narrative nonfiction, fiction

Dan Feder, Associate Editor—Science, popular culture, narrative nonfiction

DOUBLEDAY

DOUBLEDAY BUSINESS

DOUBLEDAY RELIGION

FLYING DOLPHIN

NAN TALESE / DOUBLEDAY

Doubleday, with more than a century in the publishing business, remains one of the world's most renowned houses. Perhaps best known for its strong commercial list in fiction and nonfiction, Doubleday continues to be a dominating force in mainstream popular nonfiction, in addition to publishing books of literary note.

Recent titles from Doubleday fiction include *Shatter* by Michael Robotham; *Terminal Freeze* by Lee Child; *Living in Perhaps* by Julia Widdows; and *While My Sister Sleeps* by Barbara Delinsky.

Doubleday nonfiction categories include biography and autobiography, art and photography, current affairs, political science, public affairs, philosophy, ethics, family, marriage, sports and recreation, health, history, home and garden, and self-help.

Recent nonfiction titles include *How to Believe in God (Whether You Believe in Religion or Not)* by Clark Strand; *The Yankee Years* by Joe Torre and Tom Verducci; *Lost in the Meritocracy: The Undereducation of an Overachiever* by Walter Kirn; *The Lost City of Z: A Tale of Deadly Obsession in the Amazon* by David Grann; *The Wisdom of His Compassion: Meditations on the Words and Actions of Jesus* by Joseph F. Girzone; *Get Motivated!: Unlocking the Secrets to Our Motivational DNA* by Tamara Lowe; and *The Next 100 Years: A Forecast for the 21st Century* by George Friedman.

Direct query letters and SASEs to:

Bill Thomas, Editor-in-Chief

Jason Kaufman, Vice President and Executive Editor—Thrillers, action adventure, sports, biography, true crime and narrative nonfiction

Alison Callahan, Executive Editor—Fiction, including fantasy and debut

Phyllis Grann, Senior Editor—Nonfiction including biography, current affairs

Kristine Puopolo, Senior Editor—Literary nonfiction, self-help, spirituality, health, fitness

Dan Feder, Associate Editor—Science, popular culture, narrative nonfiction

Andrew Corbin, Senior Editor—Biography, nonfiction, fiction, religion & spirituality

Darya Porat, Assistant Editor—Nonfiction, including religion & spirituality

Melissa Danaczko, Associate Editor—Fiction

DOUBLEDAY BUSINESS

Formerly named Currency, Doubleday Business publishes hardcover business books in a variety of categories, including business narrative, biography, general business, marketing/sales, careers, personal finance and investing, leadership, and entrepreneurship.

Recent titles include *House Lust: How Americans Turned a Basic Necessity Into an All-Consuming Obsession* by Daniel McGinn; *The Necessary Revolution: How Individuals and Organizations Are Working Together to Create a Sustainable World* by Peter M. Senge, Bryan Smith, Nina Kruschwitz, Joe Laur, and Sara Schley; and *The One Minute Entrepreneur: The Secret to Creating and Sustaining a Successful Business* by Ken Blanchard, Don Hutson, and Ethan Willis.

Send query letters with SASEs to:

Roger Scholl, Executive Editor

Sarah Rainone, Editor

DOUBLEDAY RELIGION

Doubleday Religious Publishing produces select titles in hardcover, as well as makes some books available as e-books. Categories cover spirituality and religion, including Christianity, Buddhism, and Judaism.

Representative titles include *Sexless in the City* by Anna Broadway; *The Last Secret of Fatima* by Cardinal Tarcisio Bertone; *Moving Up* by Suzan Johnson Cook; *God in the Wilderness* by Jamie Korngold; *To Bless This Space Between Us* by John O'Donohue; and *We Plan, God Laughs* by Sherre Hirsch.

Trace Murphy, Editor-in-Chief

Andrew Corbin, Senior Editor

Darya Porat, Assistant Editor

FLYING DOLPHIN PRESS

Flying Dolphin Press focuses on popular culture and fiction titles. Great emphasis is placed on the quality of the writing as well as finding subject matter that examines people and ideas central to contemporary culture. A small imprint, it releases six new titles per year with plans to grow.

Recent titles include *Mr. Fooster Traveling on a Whim* by Tom Corwin and Craig Frazier; *Chasing Windmills* by Catherine Ryan Hyde; *Three Bags Full: A Sheep Detective Story* by Leonie Swann; *The Time of My Life: Writers on the Heartbreak, Hormones, and Debauchery of The Prom* by Rob Spillman; *Walking on Eggshells: Navigating the Delicate Relationship Between Adult Children and Parents* by Jane Isay; and *BORAT: Touristic Guidings to Minor Nation of U. S. and A. and Touristic Guidings to Glorious Nation of Kazakhstan* by Borat Sagdiyev.

Suzanne Herz, Publisher—Flying Dolphin Press

NAN A. TALESE / DOUBLEDAY

Formed in 1990, Nan A. Talese / Doubleday is committed to publishing quality fiction and nonfiction, both in terms of its authors and the production of its books. This literary trade paperback imprint is known for its new authors of fiction and nonfiction, as well as for the authors Nan Talese has published for many years.

Among its writers are Peter Ackroyd, Margaret Atwood, Pinckney Benedict, Thomas Cahill, Kevin Canty, Lorene Cary, Pat Conroy, Jennifer Egan, Mia Farrow, Antonia Fraser, David Grand, Nicola Griffith, Aleksandar Hemon, Thomas Keneally, Alex Kotlowitz, Robert MacNeil, Ian McEwan, Gita Mehta, George Plimpton, Edvard Radzinsky, Mark Richard, Nicholas Shakespeare, Barry Unsworth, and Gus Van Sant.

Former publisher at Houghton Mifflin, Janet Silver, joined Nan Talese in 2008. Very well-respected in the literary community, she has edited authors including Monique Truong, Peter Ho Davies, John Pipkin, and Philip Roth, some of whom are expected to follow her to Nan Talese.

Recent titles include *The Wilderness* by Samantha Harvey; *Ayn Rand and the World She Made* by Anne Conover Heller; *Poe: A Life Cut Short* by Peter Ackroyd; *Land of Marvels* by Barry Unsworth; *It Seemed Like a Good Idea at the Time: My Adventures in Life and Food* by Moira Hodgson; *Searching for Schindler: A Memoir* by Thomas Keneally; *The Implacable Order of Things* by Jose Luis Peixoto, translated by Richard Zenith; and *Twenty Fragments of a Ravenous Youth* by Xiaolu Guo.

This imprint does not accept unagented or unsolicited submissions.

Nan Talese, Senior Vice President, Publisher and Editorial Director; ntalese@randomhouse.com

Janet Silver, Editor-at-large—Fiction and memoir

Lorna Owen, Senior Editor; lowen@randomhouse.com

Ronit Feldman, Assistant Editor; rfeldman@randomhouse.com

Luke Hoorelbeke, Editorial Assistant; lhoorelbeke@randomhouse.com

SPIEGEL & GRAU

1745 Broadway, New York, NY 10019

212-782-9000

www.randomhouse.com

A new publishing division from Broadway, Spiegel & Grau was launched in 2007 by former Riverhead co-publishers Cindy Spiegel and Julie Grau. This house focuses on literary fiction and quality nonfiction and will eventually publish about 30 hardcovers and 40 trade paperbacks per year.

The publishers seek to realize and enhance each author's vision, by bringing to each publication—from the editorial process to the book's physical packaging to its launch into the world—the same level of energy, creativity, and ambition that authors put into their craft. They further state they aim to create a list of books that share the potential to transform us and unite us in a common experience, in fiction and nonfiction.

Most recent titles include *Coal Into Diamonds* by Beth Ditto; *No Certain Place: Nine Lies, Two Epic Storms, and a Lost American Outpost* by Dan Baum; *The Local News* by Miriam Gershow; *American Rust* by Philip Meyer; *Against the Machine: How the Web is Reshaping Culture and Commerce—and Why It Matters* by Lee Siegel; *Blindspot* by Jane Kamensky and Jill Lepore; and *American Buffalo: In Search of a Lost Icon* by Steven Rinella.

Spiegel & Grau only accepts manuscripts submitted by an agent.

Julie Grau, Senior Vice President and Publisher, Spiegel & Grau

Cindy Spiegel, Senior Vice President and Publisher, Spiegel & Grau

Christopher Jackson, Executive Editor—Popular culture, science, narrative non-fiction, memoir

Tina Pohlman, Senior Editor, Hardcovers, and Editorial Director, Paperbacks—Humor, fiction, narrative nonfiction

Michael Mezzo, Editor—Fiction, including debut

Ms. Kirk Reed, Assistant Editor

Hana Landes, Editorial Assistant

Mya Spalter, Editorial Assistant

WATERBROOK MULTNOMAH

MULTNOMAH

WATERBROOK PRESS

12265 Oracle Boulevard, Suite 200, Colorado Springs, CO 80921

719-590-4999 fax: 719-590-8977

www.randomhouse.com e-mail: info@waterbrookpress.com

Based in Colorado, WaterBrook Multnomah is headed by WaterBrook publisher Steve Cobb. This division is the result of the integration of Random House Christian imprint WaterBrook with evangelical publisher Multnomah, which was purchased by Random House in 2006.

MULTNOMAH

Multnomah is an evangelical Christian publisher with imprints including Multnomah Books, Multnomah Fiction, Multnomah Gifts, and Multnomah Kidz. Multnomah publishes nonfiction books on such topics as Christian living, prayer, devotions, evangelism, parenting, women's issues, and marriage. Multnomah Fiction editors look for well-crafted fiction that uses the power of story to change lives. Multnomah Gifts looks for books on substantive topics with beautiful, lyrical writing.

Multnomah is the publisher of *The Prayer of Jabez: Breaking Through to the Blessed Life* by Bruce Wilkinson, an eight million copy best-seller that spawned a fruitful franchise of abundance titles.

Recent titles include *Experiencing the Spirit* by Henry & Mel Blackaby; *The Fight of Your Life* by Jeffrey Dean; *It's Not Easy Being Green (Diary of a Teenage Girl)* by Melody Carlson; *Kingdoms at War: Points of Tension Between Islam and Christianity* by Ravi Zacharias; *Outlaw Marshall (Return of the Stranger)* by Al Lacy and Joanna Lacy; *The Late Great United States: What Bible Prophecy Reveals About America's Last Days* by Mark Hitchcock; and *Death at a Discount (Bargain Hunters Mystery Series)* by Sharon Dunn.

Steve Cobb, Publisher

Ken Peterson, Vice President, Publishing Director for Multnomah Books

David Kopp, Executive Editor

WATERBROOK PRESS

WaterBrook Press was launched in September 1996 as an autonomous evangelical religious publishing division of Random House. Since the release of the first books in February 1998, the publishing program has grown dramatically, and now includes such best-selling and well-respected authors such as Joanna Weaver, Kay Arthur, David Gregory, Jane Kirkpatrick, Liz Curtis Higgs, and Charlie Peacock.

Recent titles include *Hero: Becoming the Man Women Want* by Fred Stoeker, Jason Stoeker, and Mike Yorkey; *Rules of Contact* by Kristin Heitzmann; *The Echo Within: Notes on Calling and Vocation* by Robert Benson; *Intimate Issues: Twenty-One Questions Christian Women Ask About Sex* by Linda Dillow and Lorraine Pintus; *Aurora: An American Experience in Quilt and Craft* by Jane Kirkpatrick; and *The Friends We Keep: How Women Navigate the Delights and Wounds of Friendship* by Sarah Zacharias Davis.

WaterBrook Multnomah accepts unsolicited manuscripts only from literary agents. Direct queries and SASEs to:

Steve Cobb, Publisher

David Kopp, Executive Editor

Ron Lee, Editor—Leadership, business, family

Shannon Hill, Editor—Inspirational fiction

Jeanette Thomason, Editor—Nonfiction, including inspirational memoir

KNOPF PUBLISHING GROUP

ALFRED A. KNOPF

ANCHOR BOOKS

EVERYMAN'S LIBRARY

PANTHEON BOOKS

SCHOCKEN BOOKS

VINTAGE

1745 Broadway, New York, NY 10019

212-782-9000

www.randomhouse.com

Alfred A. Knopf was founded in 1915 by Alfred and his wife, Blanche. Knopf (sound the k: k'nupf), is recognized as a publisher of distinguished hardcover fiction and non-fiction, and is also well known by its logo, the running dog, officially referred to as a "coursing Borzoi." Knopf was quoted as saying, "The coursing Borzoi has always been our trademark... From the very beginning we have frequently been asked the meaning of the word Borzoi and what it has to do with books. When I started in business, the publisher I admired most was London's William Heinemann, and the sign of a Heinemann book was a windmill. Since a windmill obviously had nothing to do with books, I saw no reason why we could not adopt the Borzoi as our mark."

This Random House group is comprised of six imprints: Alfred A. Knopf, Anchor Books, Everyman's Library, Pantheon Books, Schocken Books, and Vintage.

ALFRED A. KNOPF

One of the most respected publishers of fiction, Knopf attracts literary stars and commercial hit-makers. Knopf nonfiction categories include biography, history, nature, travel, cooking, and select poetry. The house also publishes nature guides and travel guides including *National Audubon Society Field Guides*, *Sibley Field Guides*, *Knopf MapGuides*, and *Knopf City Guides*.

Recent titles include *Heart and Soul* by Maeve Binchy; *Joseph P. Kennedy Presents: His Hollywood Years* by Cari Beauchamp; *Try to Tell the Truth: A Memoir* by David Thomson; *Angels and Ages: Lincoln, Darwin, and the Making of the Modern Age* by Adam Gopnik; *Confession* by Lee Gowan; *Lark and Termite* by Jayne Anne Phillips; *Fundamentals of Photography: The Essential Handbook for Both Digital and Film Cameras* by Tom Ang; *The Private Patient* by P.D. James; *Somebody: The Reckless Life and Remarkable Career of Marlon Brando* by Stefan Kanfer; *The Age of Entanglement: When Quantum Physics Was Reborn* by Louisa Gilder; *In Spite of Myself: A Memoir* by Christopher Plummer; and *A Mercy* by Toni Morrison.

Send query letters and SASEs to:

Sonny Mehta, Editor-in-Chief—Fiction, narrative nonfiction, high-profile memoir

Robin Desser, Senior Editor—Fiction, memoir

Ann Close, Senior Editor—Literary fiction, geography, social and cultural history

Jonathan Segal, Vice President and Senior Editor—Twentieth-century history, contemporary events, biography and health

Edward Kastenmeier, Executive Editor—Nonfiction, history, biography, fiction

George Andreou, Senior Editor—Nonfiction, narrative nonfiction, history, biography, fiction

Victoria Wilson, Senior Editor—Nonfiction, history, popular culture

Andrew Miller, Senior Editor—Narrative nonfiction, history, current events

Marty Asher, Editor-at-Large

Carole Baron, Editor—Fiction, her authors include Maeve Binchy and Poppy Adams

Jordan Pavlin, Editor—Fiction, including debut novels, and memoir

Gary Fisketjon, Editor-at-Large—Fiction, literary thrillers, debut novels

ANCHOR BOOKS

Anchor Books is the oldest trade paperback publisher in America. It was founded in 1953 by Jason Epstein with the goal of making inexpensive editions of modern classics widely available to college students and the adult reading public. Today, Anchor's list includes award-winning history, science, women's studies, sociology, and quality fiction.

Authors published by Anchor Books include Susan Sontag, Natalie Angier, Thomas Cahill, Ian McEwan, Anne Lamott, and Margaret Atwood.

Representative titles include *On Chesil Beach* by Ian McEwan; *Black & White* by Dani Shapiro; *The Opposite House* by Helen Oyeyemi; and *The Diana Chronicles* by Tina Brown.

Recent titles include *The Palace of Illusions* by Chitra Benerjee Divakaruni; *The Almost Archer Sisters* by Lisa Gabriele; *Killer Heat* by Linda Fairstein; *ABC* by David Plante; *Karnak Café* by Naguib Mahfouz; *The Science of Leonardo: Inside the Mind of the Great Genius of the Renaissance* by Fritjof Dapra; *The World According to Bertie* by Alexander McCall Smith; and *The Gift of Stones* by Jim Crice.

Direct queries with SASEs to:

Anne Messitte, Publisher, Vintage/Anchor

LuAnn Walther, Senior Vice President, Editorial Director—Literary fiction

Edward Kastenmeier, Vice President, Executive Editor—Fiction and nonfiction, science, sports, history, narrative nonfiction

Lexy Bloom, Senior Editor—Fiction, memoir

Jennifer Jackson, Senior Editor—Fiction, including debut

EVERYMAN'S LIBRARY

Everyman's Library was founded in 1906 by London Publisher Joseph Malaby Dent, who sought to put out literature that would appeal to "every kind of reader: the worker, the student, the cultured man, the child, the man and the woman." These beautiful editions feature original introductions, up-to-date bibliographies, and complete chronologies of the authors' lives and works. The series has grown to hundreds of volumes and includes sets such as *100 Essentials*, *Children's Classics*, *Contemporary Classics*, and *The Great Poets*.

Titles include *The Blue Flower* by Penelope Fitzgerald; *A Handful of Dust* by Evelyn Waugh; *Dickinson* by Emily Dickinson; *Rabbit Angstrom* by John Updike; *Book of Nonsense* by Edward Lear; *The Periodic Table* by Primo Levi; *The Talented Mr. Ripley* by Patricia Highsmith; *Crime and Punishment* by Fyodor Dostoevsky; and *Things Fall Apart* by Chinua Achebe.

PANTHEON BOOKS

Pantheon handles nonfiction books in categories such as current events, international affairs, contemporary culture, literary criticism and the arts, popular business, psychology, travel, nature, science, and history. The house has a strong list in contemporary fiction, poetry, and drama. Pantheon also offers the Fairytale and Folktale Library.

Pantheon was founded in 1942 by Helen and Kurt Wolff, refugees from Nazi Germany. "Building on its tradition of publishing important works of international fiction in translation and groundbreaking works of social policy, Pantheon now publishes quality fiction and nonfiction in a wide range of areas."

Representative titles include *Microcosm: E.coli and the New Science of Life* by Carl Zimmer; *Ask for a Convertible* by Danit Brown; *Still Waters* by Nigel McCrery; *Mind's Eye* by Hakan Nesser; *Broccoli and Other Tales of Food and Love* by Lara Vapnyar; and *Netherland* by Joseph O'Neill.

Recent titles include *Sum: Forty Tales from the Afterlives* by David Eagleman; *Brothers: A Novel* by Yu Hua; *Saviors and Survivors: Darfur, Politics, and the War on Terror* by Mahmood Mamdani; *The Elsewhere Society: How We Got to Where We're Not* by Dalton Conley; and *Victor Fleming: The Life and Work of an American Movie Master* by Michael Sragow.

Direct query letters and SASEs to:

Errol McDonald, Vice President, Executive Editor

Daniel Frank, Editorial Director—Nonfiction

Deborah Garrison, Senior Editor—Fiction, memoir

Victoria Wilson, Senior Editor—Nonfiction, history, popular culture

SCHOCKEN BOOKS

Schocken publishes books of Jewish interest in the following areas: history, biography, memoir, current affairs, spirituality, religion, philosophy, politics, sociology, and fiction.

Founded in Berlin in 1931 by Salman Schocken, a department store magnate, bibliophile, and ardent Zionist, Schocken Verlag was closed down by the Nazis in 1938. Salman Schocken founded Schocken Books in the U.S. in 1942. The company became a division of Random House in 1987.

Recently published books include *A Pigeon and a Boy* by Meir Shalev; *The Jewish Body: An Anatomical History of the Jewish People* by Melvin Konner; *How to Raise a Jewish Child: A Practical Handbook for Family Life* by Anita Diamant; *The Book of New Israeli Food: A Culinary Journey* by Janna Gur; *Benjamin Disraeli* by Adam Kirsch; and *Laish* by Aharon Appelfeld.

Direct queries with SASEs to:

Altie Karper, Editor

VINTAGE

Vintage is the trade paperback arm of the Knopf Publishing Group and consists of Vintage Books and Anchor Books.

The Vintage Books publishing list includes a wide range, from world literature to contemporary fiction and distinguished nonfiction, featuring such writers as William Faulkner, Vladimir Nabokov, Albert Camus, Ralph Ellison, Dashiell Hammett, William Styron, A. S. Byatt, Philip Roth, Richard Ford, Cormac McCarthy, Alice Munro, David Guterson, and Arthur Golden. Vintage Crime / Black Lizard titles focus on crime and suspense. Spanish-language titles are released through Vintage Español.

Recent Vintage titles include *Our Ancestors* by Italo Calvino; *Revelation* by C.J. Sansom; *Christ the Lord: Road to Cana* by Anne Rice; *His Illegal Self* by Peter Carey; *Judas Horse* by April Smith; *The Reserve* by Russell Banks; *The Sexual Paradox: Extreme Men, Gifted Women and the Real Gender Gap* by Susan Pinker; *The Soul Thief* by Charles Baxter; *The Thing About Life Is That One Day You'll Be Dead* by David Shields; *The Way Through Doors* by Jesse Ball; and *The Exchange-rate Between Love and Money* by Thomas Leveritt.

Send query letters and SASEs to:

Anne Messitte, Publisher, Vintage/Anchor

LuAnn Walther, Senior Vice President, Editorial Director—Literary fiction

Edward Kastenmeier, Vice President, Executive Editor—Fiction and nonfiction, science, sports, history, narrative nonfiction

Lexy Bloom, Senior Editor—Fiction, memoir

Jennifer Jackson, Senior Editor—Fiction, including debut

Lisa Alpert, Publisher, Libros en Español

RANDOM HOUSE CHILDREN'S BOOKS

ALFRED A. KNOPF BOOKS FOR YOUNG READERS

BANTAM

BEGINNER BOOKS

CROWN

DAVID FICKLING BOOKS

DELACORTE PRESS

DISNEY BOOKS FOR YOUNG READERS

DOUBLEDAY

DRAGONFLY

FIRST TIME BOOKS

GOLDEN BOOKS

LANDMARK BOOKS

LAUREL-LEAF

PICTUREBACKS

RANDOM HOUSE BOOKS FOR YOUNG READERS

ROBIN COREY BOOKS

SCHWARTZ & WADE BOOKS

SESAME WORKSHOP

STEP INTO READING

STEPPING STONE BOOKS

WENDY LAMB BOOKS

YEARLING

1745 Broadway, New York, NY 10019

212-782-9000

www.randomhouse.com

The home of Dr. Seuss, Madeleine L'Engle, Judy Blume, Swimmy, and the Magic Tree House, Random House Children's Books is the world's largest English-language children's trade book publisher. Creating books for preschool children through young adult readers in all formats—from board books to activity books to picture books and novels—Random House Children's Books brings together world-famous franchise characters, multimillion-copy series, and top-flight, award-winning authors and illustrators.

Random House Children's Books publishes Barbie and other well-known licensed characters, such as Arthur, the Berenstain Bears, Disney, Sesame Workshop, and Thomas the Tank Engine. The house also publishes many of children's favorite authors, including Judy Blume, Robert Cormier, Madeleine L'Engle, Leo Lionni, Mary Pope Osborne, Gary Paulsen, Tamora Pierce, Philip Pullman, Faith Ringgold, and Jerry Spinelli.

In August 2001, Random House acquired all the book-publishing properties of Golden Books Family Entertainment, which produces storybooks, coloring and activity books, puzzle books, educational workbooks, reference books, novelty books, and chapter books. The Golden Books publishing program features *Blue's Clues*, *Rugrats*, *Bob the Builder*, and *Barbie*; and the Little Golden Books series publishes classic favorites such as *Pat the Bunny* and *The Poky Little Puppy*.

Disney Books for Young Readers features a wide array of books based on Walt Disney live-action and animated films; titles include coloring and activity books, storybooks, novelty books, and early readers.

Random House has a number of book series specifically designed for young readers, including the *Stepping Stones* first chapter book series: *Marvin Redpost*; *A to Z Mysteries, the Magic Tree House*; *Junie B. Jones*; *Replica*; *Dinoverse*; and Francine Pascal's *Sweet Valley High Senior Year*, a popular series aimed at middle-grade and young adult readers.

In addition to series, Random House Children's Books publishes popular fiction including *Anne of Green Gables*, *Where the Red Fern Grows*, and *The Phantom Tollbooth*, as well as Newbery Honor and Medal winning books such as *The Watsons Go to Birmingham 1963*, *Lily's Crossing*, *Holes*, *A Wrinkle in Time*, *The Giver*, *The Dark-Thirty* and *Shabanu*. The Random House list also features Caldecott Honor- and Medal-winning books, including *Tar Beach*, *Time Flies*, *Song and Dance Man*, and the late Leo Lionni's *Frederick*, *Swimmy*, and *Alexander and the Wind-Up Mouse*.

Recent releases include *Madlenka's Music* by Peter Sis; *The Princess and the Unicorn* by Carol Hughes; *Bones of Faerie* by Janni Lee Simner; *Baby Nose to Baby Toes* by Vicky Ceelen; *The Seven Keys of Balabad* by Paul Haven, illustrated by Mark Zug; *Loose Leashes* by Amy Schmidt and Ron Schmidt; and *Magic Tree House #40: Eve of the Emperor Penguin* by Mary Pope Osborne, illustrations by Sal Murdocca.

Alfred A. Knopf Books for Young Readers (BFYR) publishes quality books for children of all ages, toddlers to young adults. The imprint publishes between 60–70 new hardcover books each year, ranging from board books to picture books to novels to nonfiction. Known for both the caliber of its authors and artists and the high quality of its book design and production, Alfred A. Knopf BFYR publishes books intended to entertain, inspire, and endure. The imprint is deeply committed to its authors and illustrators, and believes that by working closely with them, they can create books that children, and adults who read to children, will love for years to come. Authors and illustrators published by Alfred A. Knopf BFYR include Marc Brown, Robert

Cormier, Leo and Diane Dillon, Carl Hiaasen, Leo Lionni, Christopher Paolini, Philip Pullman, Eric Rohmann, Judy Sierra, and Jerry Spinelli.

In addition to books for adults, Knopf Trade Paperbacks publishes paperback editions of novels for middle and young adult readers originally published by Alfred A. Knopf Books for Young Readers. The imprint, established in 2002, publishes authors such as Carl Hiaasen, Christopher Paolini, Philip Pullman, Jerry Spinelli, and Wendelin Van Draanen.

Recent titles for children from Knopf include *I'm Your Peanut Butter Big Brother* by Selina Alko; *Same Difference: A Novel in Four Summers and One Winter* by Brent Runyon; *The Anatomy of Wings* by Karen Foxlee; *Scat* by Carl Hiaasen; *Sneaky Weasel* by Hannah Shaw; *Perpetual Check* by Rich Wallace; and *The Gecko and Sticky: Villain's Lair* by Wendelin Van Draanen, illustrations by Stephen Gilpin.

Bantam Books publishes highly commercial paperbacks in both rack and digest-size formats with a focus on movie and television properties as well as original paperback series.

David Fickling Books is dedicated to bringing the best of England's children's books to the young readers of America. The David Fickling Books team loves American stories and thinks that Americans will love British stories in return. The imprint is very small, but its editors would like it to be a little-big publisher and believe that it can be. David Fickling Books publishes just 12 books a year, all of which are chosen and edited in their small offices in Oxford, England. Titles include *Catcall* by Linda Newbery; *Bog Child* by Siobahn Dowd; *Time's Chariot* by Ben Jeapes; and   by Jeremy De Ouidt.

Delacorte Press Books for Young Readers publishes literary and commercial novels for middle-grade and young adult readers, as well as nonfiction that crosses both educational and general interest categories. Among the many best-selling authors published by Delacorte Press Books for Young Readers are David Almond, Ann Brashares, Libba Bray, Caroline Cooney, Robert Cormier, Lurlene McDaniel, Phyllis Reynolds Naylor, Joan Lowery Nixon, Louis Sachar, Zilpha Keatley Snyder, and R. L. Stine.

Delacorte Press Trade Paperbacks publishes literary as well as commercial novels originally published in hardcover for middle-grade and young adult readers. Many Delacorte Press Trade Paperbacks are part of the Readers Circle publishing program and include exclusive content such as author interviews and reading group discussion questions. In addition to reprints, the imprint also publishes original paperback books, including highly entertaining young adult fiction as well as some nonfiction that crosses both educational and general interest categories.

Doubleday Books for Young Readers, the country's oldest children's book publisher, strives to create accessible, joyful, and child-friendly picture books for young readers, as well as beautifully illustrated gift books for an audience of all ages.

Dragonfly introduces children to talented and award-winning artists and writers through affordable paperback picture books. These inspiring and imaginative full-color books range from first concept books to read-together stories to books for newly independent readers. Through the variety of writing and illustration styles, children reap the rich rewards that Dragonfly's paperback picture books offer. Authors and illustrators include Leo and Diane Dillon, Jarrett J. Krosoczka, Grace Lin, Leo Lionni, Anita Lobel, Jack Prelutsky, Raffi, Faith Ringgold, Lizzy Rockwell, Eric Rohmann, Judy Sierra, Peter Spier, Meilo So, Nancy Van Laan, and more.

Laurel-Leaf is a paperback imprint committed to providing teens with quality literature in an accessible, mass market format. Laurel-Leaf offers reprints of contemporary and classic fiction, mystery, fantasy, romance, suspense, and nonfiction appropriate for ages 12 and up. Laurel-Leaf is the young adult paperback home of such best-selling and beloved authors as Judy Blume, Caroline B. Cooney, Robert Cormier, Lois Duncan, S.E. Hinton, Lois Lowry, Scott O'Dell, Gary Paulsen, Philip Pullman, and Jerry Spinelli.

Established in March 2005, Schwartz and Wade Books is the newest addition to Random House Children's Books' family of imprints. Schwartz & Wade Books is co-directed by Anne Schwartz and Lee Wade, who take a unique approach to the creative process and believe that the best books for children grow from a seamless collaboration between editorial and design. The imprint launched its first list in spring 2006 with four picture books and continues to publish approximately 20 hardcover books a year. Authors and illustrators include Tad Hills, Deborah Hopkinson, James E. Ransome, Ronnie Shotter, Giselle Potter, and Valorie Fisher.

Yearling Books is celebrating 40 years of providing parents, teachers, and children ages 8–12 with distinguished paperback books in an affordable digest format. The Yearling imprint features a wide variety of books: beloved classics, Newbery award winners, first-rate contemporary and historical fiction, fantasy, mystery and adventure. The Yearling brand is recognized by generations of readers as representing quality. Yearling is the middle-reader paperback home of such beloved authors as Judy Blume, Christopher Paul Curtis, Patricia Reilly Giff, Norton Juster, Madeleine L'Engle, Lois Lowry, Gary Paulsen, Philip Pullman, and Louis Sachar, and classic characters such as *Encyclopedia Brown*, *Harriet the Spy*, *Nate the Great*, and *Sammy Keyes*. Recent titles include *100 Cupboards* by N. D. Wilson; *Toby Wheeler: Eighth Grade Benchwarmer* by Thatcher Heldring; *Pee Wee Scouts: That Mushy Stuff* by Judy Delton; *Hattie Big Sky* by Kirby Larson; and *Brendan Buckley's Universe and Everything in It* by Sundee T. Frazier.

Wendy Lamb Books, established in 2002, focuses on innovative middle-grade and young adult fiction by award-winning writers such as Christopher Paul Curtis, Peter Dickinson, Patricia Reilly Giff, Gary Paulsen, and Graham Salisbury. The imprint also seeks new talent and publishes many first novels. Recent titles include *Calvin Coconut in Trouble Magnet* by Graham Salisbury; *Jolted: Newton Starker's Rules for Survival* by Arthur G. Slade; *Sunny Side Up* by Marion Roberts; *10 Lucky Things That Have Happened to Me Since I Nearly Got Hit by Lightning* by Mary Hershey; and *Harmless* by Dana Reinhardt.

Recent Schwartz & Wade titles include *This Little Bunny Can Bake* by Janet Stein; *The One and Only Marigold* by Florence Parry Heide and Jill Mcelmurry; and *Princess Baby, Night-Night* by Karen Katz.

Random House Children's accepts unsolicited manuscripts only through their contests, The Delacorte Press Contest for a First Young Adult Novel and the Delacorte Dell Yearling Contest for a First Middle Grade Novel. You may request the rules and guidelines at the Random House address, attention Contests, or view them online. All other submissions should come from a literary agent.

Query letters and SASEs may be directed to:

Chip Gibson, President & Publisher, Random House Children's

Mallory Loehr, Vice President and Associate Publisher, Editor-in-Chief, Random House Children's Books

Schuyler Hooke, Senior Editor, Random House Children's—Middle grade, young adult

Chris Angelilli, Editor-in-Chief, Golden Books

Naomi Kleinberg, Editorial Director, Sesame Street Publishing

Jennifer Arena, Executive Editor, Random House Children's Books

Robin Corey, Vice President and Publisher, Robin Corey Books

Diane Landolf, Editor, Random House—Middle grade

Heidi Kilgras, Editor, Random House—Picture books

Alice Jonaitis, Senior Editor, Random House

Jodi Kreitzman, Associate Editor, Random House

Beverly Horowitz, Vice President and Publisher, Bantam/Doubleday/Dell Children's/Yearling

Wendy Lamb, Publisher, Wendy Lamb Books

Wendy Loggia, Publishing Director, Random House Children's / Delacorte

Nancy Hinkel, Publishing Director, Knopf Children's

Michelle Poploff, Vice President and Editorial Director, Children's Paperbacks

Ann Schwartz, Editorial Director, Schwartz & Wade

Francoise Bui, Executive Editor, Delacorte

Nancy Siscoe, Executive Editor, Knopf/Crown Books for Young Readers

Michelle Frey, Executive Editor, Knopf Children's Books—Young adult

Stephanie Lane, Senior Editor, Delacorte

Claudia Gabel, Editor, Random House Children's / Delacorte

Krista Marino, Editor, Random House Children's / Delacorte

Krista Marino, Editor, Delacorte

Erin Clarke, Editor, Knopf Children's

Ann Kelley, Associate Editor, Schwartz & Wade

RANDOM HOUSE INFORMATION GROUP

FODOR'S TRAVEL PUBLICATIONS

LIVING LANGUAGE

PRIMA GAMES

THE PRINCETON REVIEW

RANDOM HOUSE PUZZLES & GAMES

RANDOM HOUSE REFERENCE PUBLISHING

SYLVAN LEARNING BOOKS

1745 Broadway, New York, NY 10019

212-782-9000

www.randomhouse.com

A division of Random House, the Information Group publishes a well-developed list of consumer reference and dictionary titles, language study courses, and academic test preparation titles. The newest imprint is Sylvan Learning Books, with titles focusing on building academic skills for elementary through high school students.

FODOR'S TRAVEL PUBLICATIONS

www.fodors.com

Fodor's Travel Publications is a unit of Fodor's LLC, a subsidiary of Random House. It is the world's largest English-language travel information publisher, with more than 440 titles to destinations worldwide. Fodor's publishes niche market travel guidebooks, as well as more traditional guides that offer practical information on popular destinations. Fodor's publishes over 14 different series to address every type of travel experience. These series include the flagship *Gold Guides series, Fodor's FYI, Escape, Around the City with Kids, To Go,* and *Fodor's Road Guides USA.*

Recent titles include *Fodor's Morocco, Fodor's Amsterdam's 25 Best; Fodor's Cape Cod, Nantucket & Martha's Vineyard 2009; Fodor's Exploring California;* and *Fodor's See It France.*

Send book proposals or queries to the attention of the Editorial Director. For more information about Fodor's, visit its Web site at www.fodors.com. Information on researcher writer positions is also available online.

Linda Cabasin, Editorial Director

Paul Eisenberg, Editorial Director

LIVING LANGUAGE

Living Language is one of the most well-known names in both foreign-language and English-language instruction, and publishes courses that meet a variety of needs. Living Language offers a wide range of programs, including *Complete Basic Courses; the All-Audio, Ultimate, In-Flight,* and *English for New Americans series;* and the popular *Daily Phrase & Culture Calendars.* The Living Language line includes books, cassettes, CDs, and DVDs in 23 languages including sign language.

Query with SASE to:

Tom Russell, Vice President and Publisher, Princeton Review, Living Language, RH Reference, Sylvan Learning

PRIMA GAMES

3000 Lava Ridge Court, Suite 100, Roseville, CA 95661

916-787-7000

www.primagames.com

Prima Games publishes strategy guides for PC and console games and has more than 90 million strategy guides in print. Located near Sacramento, CA, Prima Games continues to dominate the niche it created in 1990. They publish about 140 new titles per year.

Recent titles include *Left 4 Dead: Prima Official Game Guide* by Prima Games; *Codes & Cheats Winter 2009: Prima Official Code Book* by Prima Games; and *Tom Clancy's Splinter Cell Conviction: Prima Official Game Guide* by Prima Games.

Prima Games welcomes submissions from experienced strategy guide authors or expert gamers who love to write. Send a query letter with resume and writing samples to:

Debra Kempker, Publisher

THE PRINCETON REVIEW

1745 Broadway, New York, NY 10019

The Princeton Review imprint publishes books that help students sharpen their academic skills, prepare for standardized tests, and gain entrance into college and graduate school. Representative titles include *Cracking the SAT, The Best 331 Colleges,* and *Word Smart,* the flagship title of The Princeton Review's "Smart" series. A new series, *Ahead of the Curve,* focuses on K-12 education.

Recent titles include *1,296 ACT Practice Questions* by Princeton Review; *Guide to College Majors, 2009 Edition* by Princeton Review; *1,014 GRE Practice Questions* by Princeton Review; and *Cracking the ACT with DVD, 2009 Edition* by Princeton Review.

Query with SASE to:

Tom Russell, Vice President and Publisher, Princeton Review, Living Language, RH Reference, Sylvan Learning

RANDOM HOUSE PUZZLES & GAMES

Random House Puzzles & Games publishes crossword puzzle books, including those drawn from the pages of the *Los Angeles Times*, the *Boston Globe*, and the *New York Times*. The imprint also has a line of Dell Crossword puzzle books, as well as trivia books on baseball by Jeffrey and Doug Lyons.

Recent titles include *Random House Casual Crosswords, Volume 6* by Mel Rosen; *Modern Chess Openings, 15th Edition* by Nick De Firmian; *Quotable Cryptograms: 500 Famous Quotes to Decipher* by Terry Stickels and Sam Belotto, Jr.; *Los Angeles Times Sunday Crossword Puzzles, Volume 27* by Barry Tunick and Sylvia Bursztyn; and *Treasure Chess: Trivia, Quotes, Puzzles, and Lore from the World's Oldest Game* by Bruce Pandolfini.

Helena Santini, Editor

RANDOM HOUSE REFERENCE PUBLISHING

Random House Reference Publishing is a leading publisher of reference works in both print and electronic formats. Its lexicography program is highly regarded for its inclusion of new words in the English language earlier than most other reference publishers.

Other classic titles include *Random House Webster's College Dictionary*; *Random House Webster's Unabridged Dictionary*; *Random House Roget's College Thesaurus*; and *Random House Historical Dictionary of American Slang*.

Random House Reference also publishes a line of trade reference titles including, most recently, *Random House Webster' Compact American Sign Language Dictionary* by Elaine Costello, PhD.; *You and Your Aging Parents: The American Bar Association Guide to Legal, Financial, and Health Care Issues* by The American Bar Association; *Random House Webster's Rhyming Dictionary* by Random House; and *Random House Reference Timetables of History* by Random House.

Direct queries with SASEs to:

Tom Russell, Vice President and Publisher, Princeton Review, Living Language, RH Reference, Sylvan Learning

Helena Santini, Editor

SYLVAN LEARNING BOOKS

Sylvan Learning Books is a publishing partnership established in 2007 by Random House and Sylvan Learning, Inc. Initial titles focus on supplemental learning for elementary school-aged children, with an eventual expansion into titles for children in grades K-12, and their parents.

Recent titles include *Fourth Grade Reading Comprehension Success* by Sylvan Learning; *Fourth Grade Spelling Success* by Sylvan Learning; and *Third Grade Spelling Success* by Sylvan Learning.

Query with SASE to:

Tom Russell, Vice President and Publisher, Princeton Review, Living Language, RH Reference, Sylvan Learning Books

THE RANDOM HOUSE PUBLISHING GROUP

BALLANTINE BOOKS

THE MODERN LIBRARY

THE MONACELLI PRESS

RANDOM HOUSE

RANDOM HOUSE TRADE PAPERBACKS

READER'S CIRCLE

VILLARD BOOKS

1745 Broadway, New York, NY 10019

212-782-9000

www.randomhouse.com

The Random House Publishing Group was formed in 2003, uniting the two divisions formerly known as the Random House Trade Group and the Ballantine Books Group. Publishing in all formats—hardcover, trade paperback and mass market—it encompasses the following imprints: Ballantine Books, Ballantine Reader's Circle, Del Rey, Fawcett, Ivy, Modern Library, One World, Presidio Press, Random House, Random House Trade Paperbacks, and Villard.

Gina Centrello, President and Publisher, Random House Publishing Group

BALLANTINE BOOKS

  DEL REY / LUCASBOOKS

  ONE WORLD

  PRESIDIO PRESS

Ballantine Books publishes commercial fiction and general nonfiction, including health, diet, psychology, history, and biography. Founded in 1952, Ballantine was acquired by Random House in 1972. Its imprints include Ballantine Books, Ballantine Reader's Circle, Del Rey, Del Rey / LucasBooks, Fawcett, Ivy, One World, and Wellspring.

The mass-market list includes such best-selling authors as John Case, Robert Crais, Fannie Flagg, Sue Grafton, Kristin Hannah, John Irving, Jonathan Kellerman, Richard North Patterson, Anne Perry, Anne Rice, Edward Rutherfurd, and Anne Tyler. Fawcett and Ivy are mass-market imprints that are currently fallow.

Recent titles include *The 33-Year-Old Rookie: How I Finally Made it to the Big Leagues After Eleven Years in the Minors* by Chris Coste; *Birth Day: A Pediatrician Explores the Sci-*

ence, the History, and the Wonder of Childbirth by Mark Sloan, MD; *The Bulletproof Spirit: How to Bounce Back from Life's Hardest Hits* by Azim Khamisa and Jillian Quinn; *Cape Disappointment: A Novel* by Earl Emerson; *Everyone is Beautiful* by Katherine Center; and *Chemical Cowboy: The DEA's Secret Mission to Hunt Down a Notorious Ecstasy Kingpin* by Lisa Sweetingham.

Libby McGuire, Publisher

Marnie Cochran, Executive Editor—Nonfiction, lifestyle, parenting, advice, diet

Linda Marrow, Vice President and Editorial Director—Women's fiction, thrillers and suspense

Bruce Tracy, Executive Editor—Nonfiction, sports

Susanna Porter, Executive Editor—Fiction, nonfiction

Anika Streitfeld, Senior Editor—Fiction

Mark Tavani, Editor—Thrillers, memoirs, true crime

Kate Collins, Senior Editor—Women's fiction, romance, suspense

Rebecca Shapiro, Editor—Nonfiction

Charlotte Herscher, Senior Editor—Women's fiction, romance

Laura Ford, Editor—Fiction, including debut novels

Christina Duffy, Editor—Nonfiction, including business and investing

Paul Taunton, Associate Editor—Thrillers

Tricia Narwani, Editor—Fiction, including graphic novels & short stories, and memoir

DEL REY / LUCASBOOKS

Del Rey publishes manga, science fiction, fantasy, graphic novels, and alternate history in hardcover, trade paperback, and mass-market paperback formats. Del Rey is also home to LucasBooks, publishing *Star Wars* novelizations, spin-off novels, and nonfiction books.

Recent titles include *Iron Man Original Novel #1* by Ballantine; *The Better to Hold You* by Alisa Sheckley; *Buyout* by Alexander Irvine; *The Caryatids* by Bruce Sterling; *Dorothy 1* by Alesteir Gilgrim; *Kasumi 2* by Surt Lim and Hirofumi Sugimoto; *The Dreaming Void* by Peter F. Hamilton; and *Sayonara, Zetsubou-Sensei 1: The Power of Negative Thinking* by Koji Kumeta.

Betsy Mitchell, Editor-in-Chief

Liz Scheier, Senior Editor

Chris Schluep, Editor

ONE WORLD

In 1991, Ballantine launched One World and became the first mainstream publisher to create an imprint devoted to multicultural titles. Its list encompasses subjects of African American, Asian, Latin, and Native American interest across all categories and formats. Its best-selling backlist titles include *The Autobiography of Malcolm X* as told to Alex Haley and *Dreaming in Cuban* by Cristina Garcia.

Current and forthcoming authors include the best-selling novelist Pearl Cleage, the film historian Donald Bogle, and one of the stars of "street lit," Nikki Turner.

Recent titles include *Lemon City* by Elaine Meryl Brown; *Seen It All and Done the Rest: A Novel* by Pearl Cleage; *Numbers* by Dana Dane; *Hitting the Bricks: An Urban Erotic Tale* by Noire; *Trouble Man* by Travis Hunter; *A Woman's Worth* by Tracy Price-Thompson; *Jackson Park* by Charlotte Carter; *Meant to Be* by Rita Coburn Whack; and *Cubicles* by Camika Spencer.

Melody Guy, Senior Editor

PRESIDIO PRESS

The military history publisher Presidio Press was acquired by Ballantine in 2002. Presidio publishes about 25 new titles per year, fiction and nonfiction. Formats include mass market, paperback, and hardcover.

Most recent titles include *The Culture of War* by Martin Van Crevald; *Brothers in Arms: Hell's Highway* by John Antal; *Firefight: Inside the Battle to Save the Pentagon on 9/11* by Patrick Creed and Rick Newman; *Still Broken: A Recruit's Inside Account of Intelligence Failures, from Baghdad to the Pentagon* by A. J. Rossmiller; and *The Changing Face of War: Combat from the Marne to Iraq* by Martin Can Crevald.

Direct queries and SASEs to:

Ryan Doherty,

THE MODERN LIBRARY

The Modern Library, one of the most beloved lines of American classics, celebrated its 75th anniversary at Random House in 2000 and has continued to thrive. In 1999 it generated spirited debate with its published lists of the 100 Best Novels and the 100 Best Nonfiction Books published in English in the 20th century. The year 2000 saw the introduction of *Modern Library Chronicles*, short histories by the world's great historians, including *Islam* by Karen Armstrong and *The Age of Shakespeare* by Frank Kermode. That same year the Modern Library introduced its first line of paperback classics, a list that has grown to more than 300 titles. Twenty-two leading writers and intellectuals, including A. S. Byatt, Joyce Carol Oates, Edmund Morris, Shelby Foote, and Maya Angelou, make up the Modern Library Editorial Board, which continues its unique role of providing editorial counsel to the Modern Library and its editors.

Recent titles include *The Essential Writings of James Weldon Johnson* by James Weldon Johnson; *A Short History of Medicine* by Frank Gonzalez-Crussi; *The Canterbury Tales* by

Geoffrey Chaucer; *Paradise Lost* by John Milton; *Hamlet* by William Shakespeare; and *Les Miserables* by Victor Hugo.

Direct queries and SASEs to:

Jane Von Mehren, Senior Vice President & Publisher, Trade Paperbacks and Modern Library

Judy Sternlight, Editor

THE MONACELLI PRESS

The Monacelli Press, acquired by Random House in 2008, is a leading publisher of books on architecture, fine arts, interior design, landscape architecture, photography, and graphic design. An independent imprint within Random House, Monacelli has relocated to company headquarters at 1745 Broadway.

Recent titles include *A History of the Future* by Donna Goodman; *The Philip Johnson Tapes: Interviews* by Robert A. M. Stern; *The Colors of Nature: Subtropical Gardens* by Raymond Jungles; *Counterpoint: Daniel Libeskind in Conversation with Paul Goldberger*; *Monochrome* by Paula Jackson and John Saladino; and *Bringing Paris Home* by Penny Drue Baird.

Gianfranco Monacelli, Publisher

RANDOM HOUSE

Random House publishes distinguished trade fiction and nonfiction covering a broad scope of literary and commercial appeal. Since 1995, it has published four of the best-selling books of all time: *My American Journey* by Colin Powell, *Midnight in the Garden of Good and Evil* by John Berendt, *The Greatest Generation* by Tom Brokaw, and *Seabiscuit* by Laura Hillenbrand.

This group has also become a showcase for fiction and nonfiction authors publishing for the first time. Particularly notable titles include *The Dante Club* by Matthew Pearl; *Reading Lolita in Tehran* by Azar Nafisi; *Shadow Divers* by Rob Kuraon; and *The God of Small Things* by Arundhati Roy.

Recent titles include *Honeymoon in Tehran: Two Years of Love and Danger in Iran* by Azadeh Moaveni; *Oh, Johnny: A Novel* by Jim Lehrer; *Perfectly Imperfect: Notes on a Marriage* by Lee Woodruff; *Barbara Cartland's Etiquette Handbook: A Guide to Good Behaviour from the Boudoir to the Boardroom* by Barbara Cartland; *Cartoon Marriage: Adventures in Love and Matrimony by The New Yorker's Cartooning Couple* by Liza Donnelly and Michael Maslin; *Banquet at Delmonico's: Great Minds, the Gilded Age, and the Triumph of Evolution in America* by Barry Werth; *Water Dogs: A Novel* by Lewis Robinson; and *The Well-Dressed Ape: A Natural History of Myself* by Hannah Holmes.

Direct queries and SASEs to:

Kate Medina, Associate Publisher, Executive Editor—Fiction, nonfiction, thrillers

Bob Loomis, Executive Vice President, Executive Editor—Fiction, nonfiction

Will Murphy, Executive Editor—Nonfiction, business, science, history, politics

Jennifer Hershey, Editorial Director—Nonfiction, memoir, popular culture

Susan Mercandetti, Senior Editor—Nonfiction, memoir, humor

Millicent Bennett, Editor—Nonfiction, memoir

Susanna Porter, Senior Editor—Fiction, romance, mysteries

Tim Bartlett, Senior Editor—History, politics, narrative nonfiction, biography

Jonathan Jao, Editor—History, politics, current events

David Ebershoff, Editor-at-Large—Fiction, memoir, including debut novels

Peter Gethers, Editor-at-Large—Fiction, film projects (President of Random House Films)

RANDOM HOUSE TRADE PAPERBACKS

First launched in 2001, Random House Trade Paperbacks is the paperback imprint of Random House, with an emphasis on serious nonfiction and literary fiction.

The nonfiction list includes the best-seller *The Audacity of Hope: Thoughts on Reclaiming the American Dream* by Barack Obama.

Random House Trade Paperbacks also has a line of mysteries and thrillers called Mortalis, comprising both originals and reprints. Recent Mortalis titles include *The Hidden Man: A Novel of Suspense* by Anthony Flacco; *Fatal Lies* by Frank Tallis; and *Havana Bay* by Martin Cruz Smith.

Other recent titles include *The Folded World* by Amity Gaige; *Gardens of Water* by Alan Drew; *Condoleeza Rice: An American Life* by Elisabeth Bumiller; *The Living Cosmos: Our Search for Life in the Universe* by Chris Impey; *The Logic of Life* by Tim Harford; *The Second World: Empires and Influence in the New Global Order* by Parag Khanna; and *Twilight at Monticello: The Final Years of Thomas Jefferson* by Alan Pell Crawford.

Jane Von Mehren, Senior Vice President & Publisher, Trade Paperbacks and Modern Library—Humor, fiction, including romance and debut novels

Jill Schwartzman, Senior Editor, Trade Paperbacks—Nonfiction, business, reference, history, current events

Lea Beresford, Asst. Editor, Trade Paperbacks

READER'S CIRCLE

The Reader's Circle is a select line of leading paperback originals and reprints marketed specifically for reading groups. This was the first imprint to bind a discussion guide into the back of each book—featuring author interviews, discussion questions, author biographies and excerpts from reviews.

The Reader's Circle list encompasses both literary and commercial fiction, with such best-selling authors as Fannie Flagg, Lorna Landvik, Sue Miller, Jane Smiley, Adriana Trigiani, Anne Tyler, and Alice Hoffman. In recent years, the imprint has added distinguished nonfiction as well, including Karen Armstrong's *The Battle for God*,

Laura Hillenbrand's *Seabiscuit*, and Mary Pipher's *Reviving Ophelia*.

Other recent titles include *The River Wife* by Jonis Agee; *Summer Reading* by Hilma Wolitzer; *The Difference Between Women and Men* by Bret Lott; and *Anything for Jane* by Cheryl Mendelson.

Jane Von Mehren, Senior Vice President & Publisher, Trade Paperbacks and Modern Library—Humor, fiction, including romance and debut novels

VILLARD BOOKS

Villard Books was founded in 1983 and named after the Stanford White brownstone mansion on Madison Avenue that was the home of Random House for 20 years. It publishes a general nonfiction and fiction list that has positioned itself on the leading edge of popular culture. Among the best-selling authors it has published are Jon Krakauer, Eve Ensler, Jesse Ventura, and the "Travel Detective," Peter Greenberg. Villard is also known for its titles in the areas of humor, graphic novels, personal narrative, and new-voice fiction, including the books of Laurie Notaro and Jon Katz.

Recent titles include *New York, New York: The Mets, the Yankees, and Me* by Emma Span; *When You Lie About Your Age, the Terrorists Win: Reflections on Looking in the Mirror* by Carol Leifer; *Girl on the Couch: Life, Love, and Confessions of a Normal Neurotic* by Lorna Martin; *Under Their Thumb: How a Nice Boy from Brooklyn Got Mixed Up with the Rolling Stones (and Lived to Tell About It)* by Bill German; *The Big Skinny: How I Changed My Fattitude* by Carol Lay; *Rejected: Tales of the Failed, Dumped, and Cancelled* by Jon Friedman; *Life with Mr. Dangerous* by Paul Hornschemeier; and *In the Flesh* by Koren Shadmi.

Bruce Tracy, Editorial Director

Jill Schwartzman, Senior Editor, Trade Paperbacks

CBS CORPORATION

The CBS Corporation was formed in 2005, when Viacom Inc. split into two publicly traded companies: Viacom and CBS Corporation. Based in New York, CBS Corporation holds assets in television, radio, digital media, outdoor advertising, and publishing, including the distinguished house of Simon & Schuster.

SIMON & SCHUSTER

SIMON & SCHUSTER ADULT PUBLISHING GROUP

SIMON & SCHUSTER CHILDREN'S PUBLISHING

1230 Avenue of the Americas, New York, NY 10020

212-698-7000

www.simonsays.com

Simon & Schuster was founded in 1924 by Richard L. Simon and M. Lincoln Schuster. Their initial project was a crossword puzzle book, the first ever produced, and it was a runaway best seller. From that, the company has grown to become a global, multifaceted publishing house releasing more than 1800 titles annually. Simon & Schuster titles have won 54 Pulitzer Prizes, 15 National Book Awards, 14 Caldecott and 18 Newbery Medals.

Simon & Schuster today is wholly focused on consumer publishing. Its seven divisions—the Simon & Schuster Adult Publishing Group, Simon & Schuster Children's Publishing, Simon & Schuster Audio, Simon & Schuster Online, Simon & Schuster UK, Simon & Schuster Canada, and Simon & Schuster Australia — are home to many distinguished imprints and recognizable brand names, including Simon & Schuster, Scribner, Pocket Books, The Free Press, Atria, Fireside, Touchstone, Atheneum, Margaret K. McElderry, Aladdin Paperbacks, Little Simon, and Simon Spotlight.

The newest Simon and Schuster imprints are Howard Books, a religious and inspirational publisher; Threshold Editions, a Pocket imprint for conservative readers; a Hispanic/Latino publishing line in its Atria imprint; and Simon Scribbles, a coloring and activity imprint for children. Recent bestselling titles included *The Secret* by Rhonda Byrne, *The Spiderwick Chronicles* by Holly Black and Tony DiTerlizzi, and *Duma Key* by Stephen King.

Simon & Schuster policy is to not accept unsolicited manuscripts; its editors recommend working with a literary agent.

SIMON & SCHUSTER ADULT PUBLISHING GROUP

ATRIA BOOKS

THE FREE PRESS

HOWARD BOOKS

POCKET BOOKS

SCRIBNER

SIMON & SCHUSTER

SIMON SPOTLIGHT ENTERTAINMENT

STREBOR BOOKS

THE TOUCHSTONE AND FIRESIDE GROUP

1230 Avenue of the Americas, New York, NY 10020

212-698-7000

www.simonsays.com

The Simon & Schuster Adult Publishing Group includes distinct publishing units that offer books in several formats. Each unit has its own publisher, editorial group, and publicity department. Common sales and business departments support all the units. With the exceptions of Howard Books in Louisiana and Beyond Words in Oregon, all imprints are housed in the Simon & Schuster New York headquarters.

ATRIA BOOKS

BEYOND WORDS

WASHINGTON SQUARE PRESS

Atria Books, established in 2001, publishes a mix of fiction and nonfiction—especially biography and celebrity memoirs. The imprint is the home of several best-selling authors including Jennifer Weiner, Jodi Picoult, Judith McNaught, Vince Flynn, and Jude Deveraux. It is the hardcover imprint for Pocket Books, a commercial publishing house pledged to bring the world a wealth of timely, important, and entertaining publications. Atria releases trade paperbacks under the Washington Square Press imprint.

In recent years, Atria has placed an emphasis on publishing for diverse audiences and has launched a Hispanic/Latino line and entered a co-publishing deal with Beyond Words—now an imprint—that gives Atria world rights to that company's titles, mostly in the mind/body/spirit and self-help categories. A hugely successful Beyond Words title is *The Secret* by Rhonda Byrne.

Recent Atria titles include *The 90 Second Weight Loss Solution* by Pete Cerqua; *Baldwin's Harlem: A Biography of James Baldwin* by Herb Boyd; *The Book of Unholy Mischief* by Elle Newmark; *Young, Rich, and Dangerous: The Making of a Music Mogul* by Jermaine Dupri and Samantha Marshall; *In the Convent of Little Flowers* by Indu Sundaresan; *You're Not Who You Think You Are: A Breakthrough Guide to Discovering the Authentic You* by Albert Clayton Gaulden and James Redfield; and *The Rose Labyrinth* by Titania Hardie. Recent releases from Beyond Words / Atria include *Huna: Ancient Hawaiian Secrets for Modern Living* by Serge Kahili King; *Animal Talk: Interspecies Telepathic Communication* by Penelope Smith; and *The Gabriel Method* by Jon Gabriel.

Direct query letters and SASEs to:

Judith Curr, Publisher—Significant mystery and suspense novels

Emily Bestler, Vice President and Executive Editorial Director—Commercial fiction and nonfiction, especially thrillers with some debut novels

Greer Hendricks, Senior Editor—Literary and commercial fiction, narrative nonfiction, memoir, and lifestyle

Malaika Adero, Senior Editor—Literary fiction, narrative nonfiction, health and fitness, spirituality, memoir, biography, African American interests, art and culture

Peter Borland, Senior Editor—Nonfiction, memoir, reference, true crime

Johanna V. Castillo, Senior Editor—Hispanic-Latino and Spanish language publishing program

Sarah Branham, Editor—Mysteries, thrillers, chick lit, and memoir

Amy Tannenbaum, Editor—Fiction, including debut novels

Wendy Walker, Editor—Nonfiction, including sports, narrative nonfiction, true crime, pop culture, entertainment, history and memoir

Hannah Morrill, Editor—Nonfiction, including humor, narrative nonfiction

Krishan Trotman, Associate Editor—Nonfiction, including pop culture, hip hop

Cynthia Black, Editor-in-Chief, Beyond Words, 20827 NW Cornell Road, Suite 500, Hillsboro, OR 97124; www.beyondword.com—Mind/Body/Spirit especially the power of the mind, self help, healing

THE FREE PRESS

The Free Press has a distinguished history of publishing cutting-edge nonfiction works in social thought, politics, current affairs, history, science, psychology, religion and spirituality, music, and a broad business list. It has recently begun to publish fiction, as well. Titles are produced in hardcover format.

The 2006 Free Press release, *YOU: On a Diet* by Michael F. Roizen, M.D., and Mehmet C. Oz, M.D., was the fastest selling book in Simon & Schuster history and a continued bestseller.

Other recent releases include *Appetite for Self-Destruction: The Rise and Fall of the Record Industry in the Digital Age* by Steve Knopper; *Bluegrass: A True Story of Murder and*

Family in Small-Town Kentucky by William Van Meter; *Embracing the Wide Sky: A Tour Across the Horizons of the Mind* by Daniel Tammet; *Your Call Is (Not That) Important To Us: Why Customer Service Is Broken* by Emily Yellin; *The Great Crash of 2010: How to Survive and Thrive in the Coming Hard Times* by Harry S. Dent; *Hope Endures: A Sister's Story of Leaving Mother Teresa and Losing Faith* by Colette Livermore; *The Man Who Created Sherlock Holmes: The Life and Times of Sir Arthur Conan Doyle* by Andrew Lycett; and *The Book of Dahlia: A Novel* by Elisa Albert.

Direct query letters and SASEs to:

Dominick Anfuso, Editor-in-Chief—General nonfiction, history, politics, business and careers

Liz Stein, Senior Editor—Current events, history, serious nonfiction

Emily Loose, Senior Editor—Nonfiction, including history, business, parenting, sports

Ms. Hilary Redmon, Senior Editor—Nonfiction, including memoir, history, politics, affairs, science

Martin Beiser, Senior Editor—Nonfiction, sports, history, current affairs

Leslie Meredith, Senior Editor—Animals, spirituality, health, and pop science

Wylie O'Sullivan, Editor—Fiction, narrative nonfiction, memoir, history

Amber Qureshi, Editor—Narrative nonfiction, fiction (including debut), current events, memoir

HOWARD BOOKS

3117 North 7th Street, West Monroe, LA 71291

318-396-3122 / 800-858-4109   fax: 800-342-2067

www.howardpublishinng.com   e-mail: query@howardpublishing.com

Howard Books was founded in 1969 and has grown into an award-winning publisher of more than 45 titles per year in Christian living, inspirational, gift, fiction, devotional, and youth books. Simon & Schuster acquired Howard Publishing in 2006 and renamed Howard Books. It is officially an imprint of The Touchstone and Fireside Group, operating out of its own headquarters in Louisiana.

Not affiliated with any religious group or denomination, Howard Books maintains an objective editorial independence, which allows for a broad base of authors and subject matter. Its titles promote biblical principles for Godly living as expressed by qualified writers whose lives and messages reflect the heart of Christ. Howard authors include Point of Grace, Andy Stanley, Sandi Patty, Big Idea's VeggieTales, Ed Young, David and Claudia Arp, Tony Campolo, Dr. Ken Canfield, Calvin Miller, and Bill Bright.

Recent titles include *Expectant Prayers: Praying for Your Child's Development, Body and Soul* by Maria Taviano; *Grandmother, Another Name for Love: Celebrating the Special Bond Between a Grandmother and a Grandchild* by Alice Gray and Susan Wales; *Tea Parties with a Purpose: 10 Simple and Fun Party Ideas for Kids of All Ages* by Bobbie Wolgemuth; *A Love that Heals: Letting God's Love Give You Hope in Times of Grief* by Angie Winans; *Small Things and Secret Places: Art, Scripture, Prayers, and Reflections to Inspire Your Awe of God* by Carolyn Blich; and *Unpretty: A Novel* by Sharon C. Rogers.

Howard Books is open to unsolicited queries, do not send manuscripts until invited to do so. Send queries with SASEs to:

Denny Boultinghouse, Editor—Nonfiction, especially religion, true crime, advice

Philis Boultinghouse, Editor—Fiction and nonfiction, including memoir, parenting, relationships

POCKET BOOKS

DOWNTOWN PRESS

G-UNIT

MTV BOOKS

STAR TREK BOOKS

THRESHOLD EDITIONS

VH1 BOOKS

Pocket Books, founded in 1939, was America's first publisher of paperback books. Today, Pocket is producing general-interest fiction and nonfiction books in mass market and trade paperback formats. Pocket Books is also the publisher of the Star Trek novels, MTV and VH1 Books, Threshold Editions (politics and current events), Downtown Press (Chick Lit), and G-Unit (50-Cent's line of street fiction).

Representative titles include *Big, Bad & Barbaric* by Jaid Black; *A Rush of Wings* by Adrian Phoenix; *Dead Broke* by Trista Russell; *A Flat Stomach ASAP* by Ellington Darden; *Past Secrets* by Cathy Kelly; *The Cholesterol Counter: 7th Edition* by Annette B. Natow, Ph.D., R.D. and Jo-Ann Heslin, M.A., R.D.; *Smoke, Mirrors, and Murder: And Other True Cases* by Ann Rule; *Marked by Moonlight* by Sharie Kohler; and *What You Can't See* by Allison Brennan, Karin Tabke, and Roxanne St. Claire.

Recent releases include *The After Wife* by Lexi Davis; *Not That Innocent* by Sherrilyn Kenyon, Kresley Cole, and Gena Showalter; *Mirror Image (Serenity)* by Keith R. A. DeCandido; *Fat Chance* by Rhonda Pollero; *24 Hours as a Sex Vixen* by Lisa Cach; *The 6 Sacred Stones* by Matthew Reilly; *Delia's Heart* by V.C. Andrews; *A Consumer's Guide to Psychiatric Drugs* by John Preston; and *The Complete Food Counter, 3rd Edition* by Annette B. Natow and Jo-Ann Heslin.

Pocket Books only accepts agented submissions. Guidelines for Star Trek novels are available on the Simon & Schuster Web site, www.simonsays.com, or by written request with SASE to the Star Trek Editorial Department.

Louise Burke, Publisher—Memoir, current affairs, pop culture

Anthony Ziccardi, Associate Publisher—Threshold Editions, politics, current events

Lauren McKenna, Executive Editor—Women's and YA fiction, memoir, including MTV Books and G-Unit

Margaret Clark, Executive Editor—Star Trek, Threshold, current events

Abby Zidle, Senior Editor—Fiction, especially women's fiction

Jennifer Heddle, Senior Editor—Fiction, including young adult and manga

Kathyrne Sagan, Senior Editor—Fiction and nonfiction, for trade paper, mass-market and hardcover programs, including Threshold

Maggie Crawford, Editor—Pocket, Threshold, and Downtown Press

Jacob Hoye, Editor—MTV and VH1 Books, includes fiction, popular culture

Micki Nuding, Editor—Women's fiction, thrillers

Edward Schlesinger, Editor—Fiction, graphic novels

Brigitte Smith, Editor—Fiction, including young adult

SCRIBNER

Scribner was founded in 1846 by Charles Scribner and Isaac Baker, and initially focused on religious books. As Charles Scribner's Sons, and under legendary editors such as Maxwell Perkins and John Hall Wheelock, the house published many of the giants of nineteenth and twentieth-century American literature, including Henry James, Edith Wharton, Ring Lardner, Ernest Hemingway, F. Scott Fitzgerald, Thomas Wolfe, and Marjorie Kinnan Rawlings. Many of these authors and their classic works remain in print today as a mainstay of the Scribner list.

Today, Scribner produces fiction and nonfiction titles in hardcover format. Categories include general fiction, history, military, social science, popular culture, and self-help. Scribner authors include Annie Proulx, whose novel *The Shipping News* (1993) won both the Pulitzer Prize and the National Book Award; Frank McCourt, whose memoir *Angela's Ashes* (1996), became a mainstay of the *New York Times* bestseller list, was awarded the Pulitzer Prize and the National Book Critics Circle Award, and was followed by the bestselling *'Tis* and *Teacher Man*; and Don DeLillo's *Underworld* (1997). Scribner is also the home bestselling authors Stephen King, Kathy Reichs, and Linda Fairstein, and to the *Joy of Cooking*, revised in 2006 for a 75th Anniversary edition.

Recent releases include *Without Fidel: A Death Foretold in Miami, Havana and Washington* by Ann Louise Bardach; *The Devil's Punchbowl: A Novel* by Greg Iles; *Just Past Sunset* by Stephen King; *Bakewise: The Hows and Whys of Successful Baking with Over 250 Magnificent Recipes* by Shirley Corriher; *Warren Buffett and the Interpretation of Financial Statements* by Mary Buffett and David Clark; *Fidali's Way* by George Mastras; *The Mercy Papers: A Memoir of Three Weeks* by Robin Romm; *NoVA: A Novel* by James Boice; and *The Ultra Mind Solution: Automatically Boost Your Brain Power, Improve Your Mood and Optimize Your Memory* by Mark Hyman, M.D.

Send query letters with SASEs to:

Nan Graham, Editor-in-Chief—American literary fiction; fiction about clashing cultures, Third World and European; nonfiction interests include contemporary social and political issues, women's studies, historical and literary biography, and biographies of artists

Beth Wareham, Director of Lifestyle Publishing—Cookbooks, food, pets

Brant Rumble, Senior Editor—Biography, memoir, sports, current events

Colin Robinson, Senior Editor—Serious nonfiction, memoir, international narrative nonfiction

Anna de Vries, Editor—Fiction, including thrillers, debut novels, short stories, graphic novels

Colin Harrison, Senior Editor—True crime, narrative nonfiction, thrillers

Samantha Martin, Associate Editor—Nonfiction, including memoir, international narrative nonfiction, parenting

Alexis Gargagliano, Assistant Editor—Fiction, memoir, international narrative nonfiction, debut novels

SIMON & SCHUSTER

Simon & Schuster publishes fiction and nonfiction in hardcover format. It is the publisher of nonfiction authors Bob Woodward, David McCullough, Taylor Branch; and fiction authors Mary Higgins Clark and Larry McMurty, among many, many others.

Titles representative of this list include *Swimming in a Sea of Death: A Son's Memoir* by David Rieff; *Might: How America Will Thrive in an Era of Big Powers* by Nina Hachigian and Mona Sutphen; *KIA: A Dr. Kel McKelvey Novel* by Thomas Holland; *The Sex-Starved Wife: What to Do When He's Lost Desire* by Michele Weiner Davis; *The Great Experiment: From Tribes to Global Nation* by Strobe Talbott; *The Mutineer: Rants, Ravings, and Missives from the Mountaintop, 1977-2005* by Hunter S. Thompson; *Blue Goose* by Nancy Tafuri; and *Domestic Partners* by Anne Bernays.

Recent titles include *American Thighs: The Sweet Potato Queens' Guide to Preserving Your Assets* by Jill Conner Browne; *The Best Life Diet* by Bob Greene; *I Am Not a Cop* by Richard Belzer; *Desire: Where Sex Meets Addiction* by Susan Cheever; *Jack London in Paradise: A Novel* by Paul Malmont; *Night of Thunder: A Bob Lee Swagger Novel* by Stephen Hunter; *Old Dogs Are the Best Dogs* by Gene Weingarten and Michael S. Williamson; and *Queen Takes King: A Novel* by Gigi Levangie Grazer.

Send query letters and SASEs to:

David Rosenthal, Publisher—Fiction and nonfiction by high-profile authors

Alice Mayhew, Editorial Director—Politics, current events, contemporary biographies, memoirs

Robert Bender, Vice President, Senior Editor—Nonfiction, especially history, current affairs, biography, and narrative nonfiction

Sydny Miner, Vice President, Senior Editor—Cookbooks, memoir

Amanda Murray, Senior Editor—Hardcover nonfiction, both narrative and practical; subjects include memoir, women's issues, popular reference, beauty, inspiration, entertainment and mind/body/health.

Denise Roy, Senior Editor—Fiction and nonfiction, including debut fiction and narrative nonfiction

Dedi Felman, Senior Editor—Nonfiction, including politics, current events, and related fiction

Colin Fox, Senior Editor—Memoir and fiction, including mystery, debut, historical fiction

Roger Labrie, Editor—Nonfiction, history, military

Sarah Hochman, Editor—Fiction, memoir, humor, including debut novels

Kerri Kolen, Editor—Narrative nonfiction, humor, memoir, and commercial fiction

SIMON SPOTLIGHT ENTERTAINMENT

Simon Spotlight Entertainment (SSE) launched in September 2004 with *He's Just Not That Into You: The No-Excuses Truth To Understanding Guys* by Greg Behrendt and Liz Tuccillo, which became an instant national bestseller, hitting the number one spot on the *New York Times*, *USA Today*, *Publishers Weekly*, and *Wall Street Journal* best-seller lists. Officially an imprint of Pocket Books, SSE continues to publish original nonfiction, fiction, and media tie-ins, including, most recently, *Note to Self* by Andrea Buchanan; *The 30-Day Heartbreak Cure: Getting Over Him and Back Out There One Month from Today* by Catherine Hickland; *The Cardio-Free Diet* by Jim Karas; *Passport to Pleasure: Secret Sealed Seductions for Fun-Loving Couples* by Laura Corn; and *Sunset Stripped* by Mark Ebner.

Direct query letters and SASEs to:

Jennifer Bergstrom, Publisher—Health, celebrity memoir, relationships

Carl Raymond, Associate Publisher—Cooking, lifestyle

Tricia Boczkowski, Senior Editor—Humor, celebrity memoir, pop culture, narrative nonfiction

Patrick Price, Senior Editor—Humor, sex, relationships, parenting, pop culture

Jeremie Ruby-Strauss, Senior Editor—Celebrity memoir, humor

Terra Chalberg, Associate Editor—Fiction and reference

Emily Westlake, Editor—Relationships, celebrity, health, humor

Cara Bedick, Editor—Nonfiction especially relationships and memoir

PUBLISHING CONGLOMERATES

STREBOR BOOKS

Strebor Books is the company originally founded in 1999 by author Zane to publish her first three books; it was purchased by Simon and Schuster in 2005 and is now an imprint with a focus on popular fiction and nonfiction by African American writers. It releases 48 new titles per year in hardcover and paperback. As a publisher, Zane is committed to finding and developing the careers of cutting-edge authors. Strebor Books is on the outlook for the next big thing.

Recent titles from Strebor include *Diary of a 12-Inch Brotha* by Dante Feenix; *The Precious Life* by Che Parker; *Beneath the Bruises* by Dwayne Birch; *Make it Last Forever: Official Guide for a Gay Relationship with Staying Power* by J. L. King; *Caged Innocence* by A.P. Ri'Chard; *A Bona Fide Gold Digger* by Allison Hobbs; and *Decoys, Inc.* by Shonda Cheekes.

Direct query letters and SASEs to:

Zane, Publisher—Commercial fiction and nonfiction from African American authors

THE TOUCHSTONE AND FIRESIDE GROUP

The Touchstone and Fireside Group was created at Simon and Schuster in 1970 to publish books in trade paperback, although the changing marketplace resulted in the addition of hardcover books in 2003. The two imprints share an editorial staff and have separate small, focused lists.

Touchstone publishes fiction and serious nonfiction books in all categories of history, politics, military, political science, biography, and autobiography. They publish almost exclusively original trade paperbacks and hardcovers as well as reprints from other houses in the industry. In 2007, the imprint launched Touchstone Faith, to release religious and spiritual titles, like *God Wants You to Be Rich: How and Why Everyone Can Enjoy Material and Spiritual Wealth in Our Abundant World* by Paul Zane Pilzer.

Titles representative of Touchstone's list include *Girls Only: Sleepovers, Squabbles, Tuna Fish and Other Facts of Family Life* by Alex Witchel; *Gotta Keep Trying: A Novel* by Virginia DeBerry and Donna Grant; *Harriet and Isabella* by Patricia O'Brien; *Looks to Die For: A Lacy Fields Mystery* by Janice Kaplan; *Oscar Wilde and a Death of No Importance: A Mystery* by Gyles Brandreth; and *Be In It to Win It: A Road Map to Spiritual, Emotional, and Financial Wholeness* by Kirbyjon H. Caldwell and Mark Seal.

Recent releases include *The King's Pleasure* by Norah Lofts; *General Psychological Theory: Papers on Metapsychology* by Sigmund Freud; *Fallen Skies* by Phillipa Gregory; *Cruel Intent: A Novel of Suspense* by J. A. Jance; *What Doesn't Kill You: A Novel* by Virginia DeBarry and Donna Grant; *The Black Girl Next Door: A Memoir* by Jennifer Baszile; and *The Masks of Christ: Behind the Lies and Cover-Ups about the Life of Jesus* by Lynn Picknett and Clive Prince.

The Fireside imprint has traditionally published practical and inspirational books on subjects such as self-help, parenting and childcare, popular psychology, and health and medicine. The list includes how-to titles on just about any topic including games, sports, cooking, gardening, finding a job, and running a business. Among the Fireside bestselling authors are Sean Covey, Danny Dryer, Rick Lavoie, and Jay McGraw. Under its current mission, Fireside has also embraced popular culture with bestsellers from celebrities such as Fantasia, Allison DuBois, Carolyn Kepcher and Paris Hilton. Fireside publishes nonfiction titles in hardcover and trade paperback format, and reissues paperback books previously published in hardcover format.

Recent Fireside releases include 6 *Most Important Decisions You'll Ever Make Workbook* by Sean Covey; *All Pets Go To Heaven: The Spiritual Lives of the Animals We Love* by Sylvia Browne; *The Pitchfork 500: Our Guide to the Greatest Songs Since Punk* by Ryan Schreiber and Scott Plagenhoef; *Spent: The Proven Program to End Exhaustion and Feel Great Again* by Frank Lipman and Mollie Doyle; and *The Get 'Em Girls Guide to the Power of Cuisine: Perfect Recipes for Spicing Up Your Love Life* by Shakara Bridgers, Jeniece Isley, and Joan A. Davis.

Direct query letters and SASEs to:

Trish Todd, Editor-in-Chief—Humor, celebrity memoir, education, history, pop culture, fiction; she especially enjoys historical fiction and commercial women's fiction.

Michelle Howry, Senior Editor—Nonfiction, including health, relationships, self-help, food, memoir, investing; she's particularly interested in acquiring new books in all categories of practical nonfiction, bit is always looking for compelling narrative titles in these categories, as well.

Zachary Schisgal, Senior Editor—Nonfiction, including pop culture, sports, relationships, exercise, and fiction; acquisitions include a biography about Paul McCartney, a business book about the science of decision making.

Trish Lande Grader, Senior Editor—Fiction, especially mystery, suspense, crime, inspirational, and debut novels; she is the editor for authors J. A. Jance, Allison DuBois, Elizabeth Peters, Peter Robinson, Bruce Feiler, Mary Schiavo.

Amanda Patten, Senior Editor—Memoir and fiction, including debut novels; her interests include pop culture, memoir, humor, cultural studies, graphic novels. Her interests in fiction range from historical (especially anything that has to do with Jane Austen) to contemporary and edgy.

Sulay Hernandez, Editor—Fiction and nonfiction; she is looking for titles that are accessible, well-written, and engaging—commercial and literary fiction, narrative nonfiction, humor, pop culture, urban stories, women's fiction, and erotica. She loves dark novels, books that can't be easily categorized and have the potential for controversy, and is particularly interested in acquiring new voices in Latin and African American markets.

Meghan Stevenson, Editor—Nonfiction and fiction, especially smart and middlebrow commercial fiction, preferably multicultural or African-American in nature. She also loves fiction that ties in nonfiction hooks, especially music and history, and books for the audience searching for something to read after chick lit and before mid-life novels. In nonfiction, she is looking for prescriptive books, narrative nonfiction, biography/autobiography. She loves quirky nonfiction, especially relationship books, but her primary categories are music, pop culture, and memoir.

SIMON & SCHUSTER CHILDREN'S PUBLISHING

ALADDIN PAPERBACKS

ATHENEUM BOOKS FOR YOUNG READERS

LITTLE SIMON / LITTLE SIMON INSPIRATIONS

MARGARET K. MCELDERRY BOOKS

SIMON & SCHUSTER BOOKS FOR YOUNG READERS

SIMON PULSE

SIMON SCRIBBLES

1230 Avenue of the Americas, New York, NY 10020

212-698-7000

www.simonsays.com

Simon & Schuster Children's Publishing, one of the world's leading children's book publishers, is comprised of the following imprints: Aladdin Paperbacks, Atheneum Books for Young Readers, Libros Para Niños, Little Simon, Margaret K. McElderry Books, Simon & Schuster Books for Young Readers, Simon Pulse, and Simon Scribbles. Each imprint has a different focus and, as always, it behooves writers to thoroughly research prior to querying.

Simon & Schuster does not accept unsolicited manuscripts and recommends working with an agent.

Rubin Pfeffer, Publisher, Simon & Schuster Children's Publishing

ALADDIN PAPERBACKS

Aladdin Paperbacks publishes juvenile fiction and nonfiction early readers, chapter books, and middle grade books for ages 4–12. The imprint includes a line for beginning readers, Ready-to-Read books (including the *Henry & Mudge* series by Cynthia Rylant and Suçie Stevenson); and the Ready-for-Chapters line for newly independent readers (including *The Bears on Hemlock Mountain* by Alice Dalgliesh and *The Unicorn's Secret* series by Kathleen Duey).

The backbone of the Aladdin list is reprints from the hardcover imprints, including some of the most enduring children's books of the modern era, such as classic picture books like *Chicka Chicka Boom Boom* by Bill Martin Jr., John Archambault, and Lois Ehlert, and *Strega Nona* by Tomie DePaola; honored fiction like *From the Mixed-Up Files of Mrs. Basil E. Frankweiler* by E. L. Konigsburg; *Hatchet* by Gary Paulsen; *Frindle* by Andrew Clements; the *Shiloh* trilogy by Phyllis Reynolds Naylor; and the *Bunnicula* books by James Howe. Aladdin's strong reprint list also is supplemented by a limited number of original series and single titles.

Recent titles include *Maeve on the Red Carpet (Beacon Street Girls)* by Annie Bryant; *Identity Theft (Nancy Drew All New Girl Detective)* by Carolyn Keene; *Specter Rising (The Brimstone Network)* by Ton Sniegoski; *Take the Reins (Canterwood Crest)* by Jessica Burkhart; *Abraham Lincoln (10 Days)* by David Colbert; and *The Angel Files* by Karen Romano Young.

Send query letters with SASEs to:

Bethany Buck, Associate Publisher

Liesa Abrams, Senior Editor

Mark McVeigh, Editorial Director

Kate Angelella, Asst. Editor

ATHENEUM BOOKS FOR YOUNG READERS

Atheneum Books for Young Readers is a hardcover imprint with a focus on literary fiction and fine picture books for children and young adults. This imprint, founded in 1961 by legendary editor Jean Karl (1928-2000), has garnered awards and prizes for such books as *The View from Saturday* by E. L. Konigsburg; *Alexander and the Terrible, Horrible, No Good, Very Bad Day* by Judith Viorst and Ray Cruz; *Shiloh* by Phyllis Reynolds Naylor; *Bunnicula* by James Howe; *Abigail Adams* by Natalie Bober; *The Folk Keeper* by Franny Billingsley; and *True Believer* by Virginia Euwer Wolff.

Recent titles include *Anytime, Anywhere: A Child's Prayer* by Marcus Hummon, illustrated by Steven Johnson and Lou Fancher; *The Boy Who Moved a Mountain* by Mariflo Stephens; *Posy* by Linda Newbery, illustrated by Catherine Rayner; *DogFish* by Gillian Shields, illustrated by Dan Taylor; *The Ghosts of Luckless Gulch* by Anne Isaacs, illustrated by Dan Santat; and *Sleepsong* by George Ella Lyon, illustrated by Peter Catalanotto.

Direct query letters and SASEs to:

Justin Chanda, Associate Publisher

Susan Burke, Editor

Jordan Brown, Asst. Editor

LITTLE SIMON / LITTLE SIMON INSPIRATIONS

Little Simon creates novelty books for children, including pop-ups, lift-the-flaps, board books, and interactive books. Titles have included *Cinderella: A Pop-Up Fairy Tale* by Matthew Reinhart; the *Bugs in a Box* pop-up series by David Carter; and *Moo Baa La La La* by Sandra Boynton.

Little Simon Inspirations is a line of faith-based novelty-format books for children, under the Little Simon umbrella. This imprint has a focus on Christian nondenominational titles that explore a religious appreciation of everyday life.

Recent Little Simon titles include *A Busy Day at the Farm* by Doreen Cronin, illustrated by Betsy Lewin; *The Adventures of a Plastic Bottle: A Story About Recycling (Little Green Books)* by Alison Inches; *Shake It Up, Baby!* by Karen Katz; *Unexpected Treasures* by Victoria Osteen; and *Hug Hug!* by Lorie Ann Grover, illustrated by Rebecca Malone.

Direct query letters and SASEs to:

Alyson Grubard, Associate Publisher

Sonali Fry, Editorial Director

MARGARET K. MCELDERRY BOOKS

Founded by legendary editor Margaret K. McElderry in 1972, the imprint publishes in hardcover with an emphasis on picture books, poetry, middle grade and teen fiction.

Notable titles have included *Peter Pan in Scarlet* by Geraldine McCaughrean; *Ironside* by Holly Black; and *Skin* by Adrienne Maria Vrettos.

Other recent titles include *To Be Mona* by Kelly Easton; *Joseph* by Shelia P. Moses; *Bear Stays Up for Christmas* by Karma Wilson, illustrated by Jane Chapman; *The Blind Faith Hotel* by Pamela Todd; and *Captain Flinn and the Pirate Dinosaurs: Missing Treasure!* by Giles Andreae and Russell Ayto.

Send query letters with SASEs to:

Emma Dryden, Vice President and Editorial Director

Karen Wojtyla, Senior Editor

SIMON & SCHUSTER BOOKS FOR YOUNG READERS

PAULA WISEMAN BOOKS

Simon & Schuster Books for Young Readers publishes fiction and nonfiction titles for children of all ages, from preschool through teens, in hardcover format. Titles in this house spans the spectrum from social situations and self-esteem, to animals and pets, action and adventure, holidays and festivals, science fiction, fantasy, African American, and other ethnic stories. Paula Wiseman Books is the eponymous imprint helmed by treasured editor Paula Wiseman.

This list includes the classic *Eloise* books by Kay Thompson and Hilary Knight; *Sylvester and the Magic Pebble* by William Steig; *Frindle* by Andrew Clements; *Chicka Chicka Boom Boom* by Bill Martin, Jr., John Archambault, and Lois Ehlert; and *Click, Clack Moo: Cows That Type* by Doreen Cronin and Betsy Lewin. SSBFYR includes among its authors and illustrators Loren Long, John Lithgow, Derek Anderson, Kate Brian, Jon Scieszka and Rachel Cohn. Recent notable Simon & Schuster Books for Young Readers titles include *The Spiderwick Chronicles* by Tony DiTerlizzi and Holly Black; *Ellington Was Not a Street* by Ntzoke Shange, illustrated by Kadir Nelson; the *Pendragon* series by D. J. McHale; *Room One* by Andrew Clements; *Gideon the Cutpurse* by Linda Buckley-Archer; and the *Shadow Children* series by Margaret Petersen Haddix.

Other recent titles include *The Odd Egg* by Emily Gravett; *Wee Little Lamb* by Lauren Thompson, illustrated by John Butler; *Chicken Cheeks* by Michael Ian Black, illustrated by Kevin Hawkes; *My Brother Abe: Sally Lincoln's Story* by Harry Mazer; *Sweet Hereafter* by Angela Johnson; *The Sword of Waters (The Shield, Sword, and Crown)* by Hilari Bell, illustrated by Drew Willis; and *Melvin Might (Trucktown)* by Jon Scieszka, illustrated by David Shannon, David Gordon, and Loren Long.

And from Paula Wiseman Books: *The Teashop Girls* by Laura Schaefer and Sujean Rim; *Seabiscuit: The Wonder Horse* by Meghan McCarthy; and *Amelia's Science Fair Disaster* by Marissa Moss.

Send query letters with SASEs to:

David Gale, Editorial Director—Middle-grade and young adult novels; looks for sharp writing and fresh voices. Does not want to consider standard young adult problem novels or romances, but is interested in more unusual, hard-hitting, and literary young adult novels, also interested in fantasy.

Emily Meehan, Editor

Alexandra Cooper, Associate Editor

Paula Wiseman, Editorial Director, Paula Wiseman Books

Alexandra Penfold, Associate Editor, Paula Wiseman Books

SIMON PULSE

Simon Pulse produces juvenile fiction titles in mass market paperback and hardcover formats; many of this imprint's books have movie or television tie-ins. Categories include historical and medieval fiction, espionage, family, siblings, social situations, and self-esteem.

Included in Pulse are series like R. L. Stine's *Fear Street*; Cathy Hopkin's *Mates, Dates*; Scott Westerfield's *Specials*; *The Au Pairs* by Melissa de la Cruz; and contemporary classics like *Go Ask Alice*, National Book Award winners *The House of the Scorpion* by Nancy Farmer and *True Believer* by Virginia Euwer Wolff; and literary titles such as *The Dark Is Rising* sequence by Susan Cooper, and the *Tillerman Cycle* by Cynthia Voigt.

Recent titles include *Privilege* by Kate Brian; *Night World 2: Dark Angel* by L.J. Smith; *Wicked 2: Legacy & Spellbound* by Nancy Holder and Debbie Viguie; *What Would Alice Do?* by Eileen Cook; *Sea of Love* by Jamie Ponti; *What My Girlfriend Doesn't Know* by Sonya Sones; and *Belle: A Retelling of "Beauty and the Beast"* by Cameron Dokey and Mahlon F. Craft.

Direct query letters and SASEs to:

Bethany Buck, Associate Publisher

Jennifer Klonsky, Senior Editor

Anica Rissi, Editor

SIMON SCRIBBLES

Simon Scribbles was launched in 2006 to produce coloring and activity books. It releases 60 titles per year, including, most recently, *Easy to Be Green: Simple Activities You Can Do to Save the Earth (Little Green Books)* by Megan E. Bryant; *I Love to Color (Yo Gabba Gabba!)* by Lisa Rao; *Stuck on Dinosaurs: A Mega Sticker Book* by Siobhan Ciminera; *Going on a Road Trip (Playskool)* by Maggie Testa and Josie Yee; and *Wiggly Day (Wow! Wow! Wubbzy!)* by Tina Gallo.

Send queries with SASEs to:

Alyson Grubard, Associate Publisher

Siobhan Ciminera, Senior Editor

Lisa Rao, Editor

HACHETTE LIVRE

Hachette Livre, France's largest publishing company, is a wholly-owned subsidiary of Lagardère, a French company that is active in the global arenas of aerospace, defense, and media. In the United States, Hachette Livre publishes as Hachette Book Group, USA.

HACHETTE BOOK GROUP, USA

CENTER STREET

FAITHWORDS

GRAND CENTRAL PUBLISHING

LITTLE, BROWN AND COMPANY

LITTLE, BROWN BOOKS FOR YOUNG READERS

OCTOPUS BOOKS

ORBIT

YEN PRESS

237 Park Avenue, New York, NY 10017

212-364-1200

www.hachettebookgroupusa.com

In 2006, Hachette Livre acquired Time Warner Book Group from Time Warner, and renamed it Hachette Book Group USA. The terms of the sale stipulated that Warner Books must shed its name, and the publisher lost little time in rechristening as Grand Central Publishing. In April 2007, Hachette Book Group USA (HBG) moved to new offices on Park Avenue, just north of Grand Central Terminal. HBG is comprised of the following groups: Grand Central Publishing; Little, Brown and Company; Little, Brown Books for Young Readers; FaithWords; Center Street; Orbit; Octopus Books, and Yen Press.

Launching in 2009, Octopus Books is a division of Octopus Publishing Group, a leading publisher of illustrated nonfiction in the UK. The opening of a New York office allows Octopus greater reach, to "be a truly global publisher," in the words of CEO Alison Goff.

Publishers in the Hachette Book Group USA do not consider unsolicited manuscript submissions and unsolicited queries. The editors recommend working with a literary agent.

CENTER STREET

Two Creekside Crossing, Ten Cadillac Drive, Suite 220, Brentwood, TN 37027

615-221-0996   fax: 615-221-0962

Center Street is a general market imprint based near Nashville that was launched in 2005 to publish wholesome entertainment, helpful encouragement, and books of traditional values that appeal to readers in America's heartland. Unlike FaithWords, which publishes specifically for the Christian market, Center Street books are intended for a broad audience, and the list includes parenting and environmentalism titles, for instance.

Recent titles include *A is for Atticus: Baby Names from Great Books* by Lorilee Craker; *This Side of Heaven: A Novel* by Karen Kingsbury; *A Heart to Serve: The Passion to Bring Health, Hope, and Healing* by Bill Frist; *Try Darkness* by James Scott Bell; *Moving Forward: Taking the Lead in Your Life* by Dave Pelzer; *Trespassers Will Be Baptized: The Unordained Memoir of a Preacher's Daughter* by Elizabeth Emerson Hancock.

Rolf Zettersten, Publisher

Michelle Rapkin, Executive Editor—Especially high profile authors and notable, current event titles

Sarah Sper, Editor—Nonfiction including lifestyle, cooking, self-help

Christina Boys, Editor—Fiction and nonfiction, including lifestyle, business, and memoir

Meredith Pharaoh, Editor—Nonfiction especially lifestyle and advice

FAITHWORDS

Two Creekside Crossing, Ten Cadillac Drive, Suite 220, Brentwood, TN 37027

615-221-0996   fax: 615-221-0962

From its headquarters in Tennessee, FaithWords is an imprint that deals with Christian faith, spirituality, and religion, with fiction and nonfiction titles. The imprint publishes books for the broad Christian market reflecting a range of denominations and perspectives. Formerly known as Warner Faith, FaithWords titles include Christian chick-lit by Lisa Samson and inspirational fiction by T. D. Jakes, as well as traditional nonfiction religious titles.

FaithWords is the publisher of the best-selling books *Your Best Life Now* by Joel Osteen and *The Confident Woman: Start Today Living Boldly & Without Fear* by Joyce Meyer.

Recent titles include *The Fruit of My Lipstick: An All About Us Novel* by Shelly Adina; *Never Surrender: A Soldier's Journey to the Crossroads of Faith and Freedom* by Jerry Boykin; *How to Hear from God: Learn to Know His Voice and Make Right Decisions* by Joyce Meyer; *Greater Than You Think: A Theologian Answers Atheists About God* by Thomas D. Williams; and *Life Is a Gift: Inspiration from the Soon Departed* by Robert Fisher and Judy Fisher.

Rolf Zettersten, Publisher

Anne Goldsmith, Editor—All FaithWords titles, recent sales include YA fiction, memoir, inspirational self-help

GRAND CENTRAL PUBLISHING

5-SPOT

BUSINESS PLUS

FOREVER

SPRINGBOARD PRESS

TWELVE

WELLNESS CENTRAL

237 Park Avenue, New York, NY 10017

212-364-1200

www.hachettebookgroupusa.com

As Warner Books, Grand Central Publishing was esteemed for publishing mass market commercial fiction from authors like Nicholas Sparks and James Patterson. Known as Grand Central Publishing since April 2007, it still publishes a lot of commercial fiction, but has also started imprints that move in other directions and for which it expects to become equally well-known.

As for the name, Grand Central Publishing, publisher Jamie Raab dissects this way: Grand because they are big and impressive, Central because they embrace a larger audience of readers, and Publishing because emerging forms of publishing go beyond books and paper.

Grand Central produces hardcover, mass market, and trade paperback originals, as well as reprints. Nonfiction categories include biography, business, cooking, current affairs, history, house and home, humor, popular culture, psychology, self-help, sports, games books, and general reference; fiction titles include commercial novels and works in the categories of mystery and suspense, fantasy and science fiction, action thrillers, horror, and contemporary and historical romance.

The Grand Central imprints are 5-Spot, contemporary trade paperbacks for women with attitude; Business Plus, giving voice to innovative leaders and thinkers in the business world; Forever, publishing every kind of romance for every kind of romantic; Springboard Press, whose books offer a launch point for reinvention, renewal, and reflection for people in midlife; Twelve, a highly selective list of fiction and nonfiction focusing on only one new book per month; and Wellness Central, focusing on areas of health, fitness, and self-help. Altogether, Grand Central publishes about three hundred books per year.

Titles representative of the list include *I Am America (And So Can You)* by Stephen Colbert; *The Choice* by Nicholas Sparks; *The Vixen Diaries* by Karrine Steffans; *No Chance* by Janet Evanovich and Stephen J. Cannell; *Style A to Zoe* by Rachel Zoe; *Abraham's Children: Race, Identity, and the DNA of the Chosen People* by Jon Entine; *The Revolution: A Manifesto* by Ron Paul; and *Stone Cold* by David Baldacci.

Recent titles include *Up at the College* by Michele Andrea Bowen; *Keep the Faith* by Faith Evans; *The Little Giant of Aberdeen County* by Tiffany Baker; *Houston, We Have a Problema* by Gwendolyn Zepeda; *The Girl She Used to Be* by David Cristofano; and *Laura Rider's Masterpiece* by Jane Hamilton.

Jamie Raab, Senior Vice President and Publisher, oversees the publication of all Grand Central titles. She has a particular fondness for thrilling and emotional fiction, narrative nonfiction, and current affairs, and the authors she has acquired and/or edited include Stephen Colbert, Nicholas Delblanco, Nelson DeMille, Henry Louis Gates, Jr., Jane Goodall, Olivia Goldsmith, Billie Letts, Brad Meltzer, Michael Moore, Rosie O'Donnell, Nicholas Sparks, Jon Stewart, and Lalita Tademy.

Deb Futter, Editor-in-Chief, hardcovers; formerly Doubleday Deputy Editorial Director, she joined GCP in 2008. She has acquired and edited fiction (*A Map of the World* by Jane Hamilton, *Train* by Pete Dexter), kids' books (*The Alphabet from A to with Bonus Letter Z!* by Steve Martin and Roz Chast), and nonfiction (*The Argument Culture* by Deborah Tannen, *She's Not There* by Jennifer Finney Boylan), and particularly looks for books that are incredibly well-written and pull on the heartstrings.

Les Pockell, Associate Publisher, has held editorial positions at St. Martin's Press, Doubleday, Kodansha International, and the Book-of-the-Month Club in addition to Grand Central. He is generally involved in acquiring and editing backlist nonfiction titles, though he has been known to dabble in fiction, especially mysteries. In his spare time, he is an anthologist, having edited, among other titles, *The 100 Best Poems of All Time*.

Beth de Guzman, Editorial Director of Mass Market, has spent 20 years in publishing and has held positions at Berkley Books, Silhouette Books, and Bantam Books. She has edited over 30 *New York Times* best-sellers. At Grand Central, she oversees the mass market program and acquires commercial fiction and nonfiction. She is the editor of Faye Kellerman; *USA Today* best-selling romance author Sandra Hill; romantic suspense author Annie Solomon; the parenting book *When*

We're in Public, Pretend You Don't Know Me; the memoir *FBI Girl*; and chick-lit novel *Time Out for Good Behavior*.

Caryn Karmatz Rudy, Executive Editor, has been at Grand Central/Warner for 15 years. Her areas of interest are women's commercial fiction and women's interest nonfiction. Her nonfiction focus is on lifestyle, relationships, parenting, women's issues, and memoir, while in fiction she looks for a strong narrative voice and topical subjects. Some of the best-sellers she has worked on include *AmandaBright@Home* by Danielle Crittenden; *Swell: A Girl's Guide to the Good Life* by Ilene Rosenzweig and Cynthia Rowley; and *Jewtopia: The Chosen Book for the Chosen People* by Bryan Fogel and Sam Wolfson. She says her favorite novelists, like Joshilyn Jackson and Tiffany Baker, create characters who are real, flawed, witty, and utterly irresistible.

Jaime Levine, Executive Editor, works with such authors as David and Leigh Eddings, Walter Mosley, Nalo Hopkinson, and Gregory Benford. Her interests lie with science fiction, fantasy, thrillers and dark fiction. Past acquisitions include Thomas Monteleone's *Borderlands* trilogy and novels by Douglas Preston and Lincoln Child. She says, "I tend to gravitate toward big-budget thrillers, especially those with a fresh angle, perhaps a historical, archeological, supernatural, or scientific element."

Mitch Hoffman, Executive Editor, is acquiring books across a broad range of categories, including commercial fiction, politics, current events, narrative nonfiction, popular history, humor, and popular culture. He says, "What I look for above all else are great storytellers—writers who entertain us, who inform us, and inspire us."

Karen Kosztolnyik, Senior Editor, acquires fiction and nonfiction for all divisions including mass market, trade paperback, and hardcover. Her acquisition interests are romance, women's fiction, chick lit, suspense, and nonfiction concerning women's issues and pop culture. She is the editor of best-selling authors Carly Phillips and Wendy Corsi Straub writing as Wendy Markham, *How to Meet Cute Boys* novelist Deanne Kizis, romantic suspense author Karen Rose, historical romance author Claire Delacroix, and Megan Crane, author of the chick lit novel *English as a Second Language*. She also edited the personal biography *My Father, My President: A Personal Account of the Life of George H. W. Bush* by Doro Bush Koch.

Ben Greenberg, Editor, acquires in pop culture, humor, sex, politics, current events, narrative nonfiction, with some commercial fiction. Recent projects include *Boink: College Sex by the People Having It*.

Karen Thomas, Editor, formerly at Kensington and Dafina, she loves thrillers, mysteries, and books on popular culture, and is focused on growing a list of African American titles. She says, "As the black book market continues to grow, I know we will be among the leaders in quality works of fiction and nonfiction for these readers." She has been the editor for authors Teri Woods, Karrine Steffans, Felicia "Snoop" Pearson, Faith Evans, and Mary B. Morrison.

Selina McLemore, Editor, focuses on fiction for the Latino market, and romance and women's fiction; recent titles include *The Gifted Gabaldon Sisters* by Lorraine Lopez and *B as in Beauty* by Alberto Ferreras.

Leila Porteous, Associate Editor, acquires business, graphic novels, self-help, narrative nonfiction, pop culture, and personality driven titles.

Alex Logan, Assistant Editor, fiction and nonfiction; she hopes to acquire thrillers—she loves Daniel Silva, Harlan Coben, and Greg Iles—and commercial mysteries (think Kate White).

5-SPOT

5-Spot is said to be a list of books for women who want entertainment but refuse to leave their brains at the door. The imprint releases only about 15 new fiction and nonfiction titles per year, mostly in trade paper but also in hardcover. Recent acquisitions have been primarily in the women's fiction and romance categories, with a dash of nonfic-chick-lit.

Most recent titles include *The Smart One and the Pretty One* by Claire Scovell LaZebnik; *Live a Little* by Kim Green; *I'm with Stupid* by Eliane Szewczyk; *How the Other Half Hamptons* by Jasmin Rosemberg; *Live Alone and Like It: The Classic Guide for the Single Woman* by Marjorie Hills; and *Flirting with Forty* by Jane Porter.

Karen Kosztolnyik, Senior Editor—(See her description above)

Emily Griffin, Associate Editor—Projects for 5-Spot include *Knitting Under the Influence* by Claire LaZebnik; also acquires for narrative nonfiction GCP, including humor, politics, and memoir.

BUSINESS PLUS

Publisher of the bestselling personal finance book of all time, *Rich Dad, Poor Dad* by Robert T. Kiyosaki and Sharon L. Lechter, Business Plus (formerly Warner Business) seeks to give voice to innovative leaders and thinkers in the business world. This imprint focuses on titles in personal finance, marketing, management, CEO autobiographies, economic trends, careers, and leadership. The editors aim to be on the cutting-edge of business publishing. They release about twelve hardcover and twelve trade paperback books per year.

Recent titles include *Doing Business in 21st-Century India: How to Profit Today in Tomorrow's Most Exciting Market* by Gunjan Bagla; *Back on the Career Track: A Guide for Stay-at-Home Moms Who Want to Return to Work* by Carol Fishman Cohen and Vivian Steir Rabin; *Globality: Competing with Everyone fro Everywhere for Everything* by Hal Sirkin, Jim Hemerling, and Arindam Bhattacharya; *The No Asshole Rule: Building a Civilized Workplace and Surviving One That Isn't* by Robert I. Sutton; and *It's Our Ship: The No-Nonsense Guide to Leadership* by Captain D. Michael Abrashoff.

Rick Wolff, Vice President, Executive Editor, Business Plus, says, "To me, the very best part of book publishing is that initial spark of creativity that seemingly comes out of thin air when a new idea, concept, or story line is presented. Suddenly, the gears begin to turn, the light bulbs flash on, and that spring of pure enthusiasm begins to bubble up. I just love that sensation." Rick is also a sports fan and former professional baseball player and coach. Aside from business books, he acquires mostly nonfiction—autobiography, politics, humor, education, psychology, and parenting—with an occasional thriller, as well.

FOREVER

Forever publishes every kind of romance for every romantic reader, in mass market format. Recent titles include *Once Smitten, Twice Shy* by Lori Wilde; *Trouble in High Heels* by Leanne Banks; *Border Lass* by Amanda Scott; *Hungry for More* by Diana Holquist; *Insatiable Desire* by Rita Herron; and *My Wicked Enemy* by Carolyn Jewel.

Amy Pierpont, Editorial Director, Forever, and Senior Editor, GPC, works to publish a program chock-full of the best romantic suspense, paranormal, erotica, and contemporary and historical romance writers. She is also eager to acquire original projects across the genres and across all formats. She is a news and pop culture fan, and is delighted when a health titles, media-related book, or branded commercial lifestyle project crosses her desk.

Michelle Bidelspach, Associate Editor, fiction and nonfiction; she is looking for fiction with a strong voice, unforgettable characters, and a great hook, think Emily Griffin, Jodi Picoult, and Jane Green. In nonfiction, she is seeking pop culture, self-help in women's issues, and narrative nonfiction that is quirky and unique.

SPRINGBOARD PRESS

www.springboardpress.net

Springboard Press focuses on titles for and about baby boomers, with books to improve their lives, themselves, and their relationships. Topics range from memoir and popular culture to well-being, inspiration, relationships, career, life style, and, well, how to not look old.

Recent titles include *Nextville* by Barbara Corcoran and Warren Berger; *Getting Naked Again: Dating, Romance, Sex, and Love When You've Been Divorced, Widowed, Dumped, or Distracted* by Judith Sills; *Bobbi Brown's Makeup Manual: For Every Woman from Beginner to Pro* by Bobbi Brown; *Beyond the Mommy Years: How to Live Happily Ever After. . . After the Kids Leave Home* by Carin Rubenstein; *Measure of the Heart: A Father's Alzheimer's, A Daughter's Return* by Mary Ellen Geist; and *If Not Now, When?* by Esther Rantzen.

Karen Murgolo, Founding Editorial Director, Springboard Press, is looking for strong narrative nonfiction on subjects—from memoir to popular culture—that will resonate with readers, and prescriptive nonfiction books by authoritative experts in well-being, beauty, relationships, life-style, career, and self-help.

Natalie Kaire, Editor, Wellness and Springboard, acquires a wide range of projects in the diet, fitness, relationships, self-help, parenting, personal growth, and general health categories. She is looking for dynamic, personality-driven books; and high-concept, smart projects that offer a refreshing outlook and a new solution. She also acquires some general GPC nonfiction with a focus on pop culture and business.

TWELVE

www.twelvebooks.com

Because Twelve publishes only 12 new titles per year, this imprint looks for books that matter, books that enliven the national conversation, books that will sell at least 50,000 copies. The editors at Twelve look for meaningful stories, true and fictional, and singular books that will entertain and illuminate. The Twelve list includes mostly nonfiction with some fiction. A recent purchase was Senator Ted Kennedy's autobiography.

Each book receives marketing focus of the entire imprint for the month of its release, and is promoted well into its paperback life, therefore this imprint is known to put great marketing and editorial muscle behind each and every title.

Recent Twelve titles include *A Good Talk* by Daniel Menaker; *Apologize, Apologize!* by Elizabeth Kelly; *Douglass and Lincoln: The Lives of Self-Made Men* by John Stauffer; *The New Science of Parenting* by Po Bronson and Ashley Merryman; *Sex and Sensibility* by Liza Donnelly; and *How We Choose* by Sheena Iyengar.

Jonathan Karp, Publisher and Editor-in-Chief, says "Our minds are perennially open, so if you think your book is worthy of a month's worth of focus and zeal, we want to read it."

Cary Goldstein, Director of Publicity and Acquiring Editor, his editorial mandate is to discover and publish one work of literary fiction each year. He is looking for works that entertain and illuminate, books that are equal parts comedy and tragedy, that highlight the differences between how we see ourselves and how we actually are. Formerly with FSG, he has a passion for breaking out new voices in publishing.

WELLNESS CENTRAL

The Wellness Central list focuses on health, fitness, and self-help, or, as we like say, Mind/Body/Spirit. Recent titles include *50/50: Secrets I Learned Running 50 Marathons in 50 Days—and How You Too Can Achieve Super Endurance!* by Dean Karnazes and Matt Fitzgerald; *Juicing, Fasting, and Detoxing for Life: Unleash the Healing Power of Fresh Juices and Cleansing Diets* by John Calbom and Cherie Calbom; *The pH Miracle: Balance Your Diet, Reclaim Your Health* by Robert O. Young and Shelley Radford Young; and *Neris and India's Idiot-Proof Diet* by India Knight and Neris Thomas.

Diana Baroni, Editorial Director, Wellness Central, has been with Grand Central/Warner for 13 years. She acquires fiction and nonfiction titles for the hardcover and paperback lists, with a focus on health, self-help, diet, childcare, and women's issues. Her books include the *New York Times* best-sellers *Nice Girls Don't Get the Corner Office* by Lois Frankel, Ph.D.; *Satisfaction: The Art of the Female Orgasm* by Kim Cattrall and Mark Levinson; *The Wrinkle Cure* by Dr. Nicholas Perricone; *Live Now, Age Later* by Isadore Rosenfeld, MD; *Dr. Shapiro's Picture Per-*

fect Weight Loss by Dr. Howard Shapiro; and Kathy Smith's *Moving Through Menopause*. In general, she looks for projects that tackle a new subject matter, convey a unique approach or story, and/or have an author with a strong platform.

Natalie Kaire, Editor, Wellness and Springboard—Acquires a wide range of projects in the diet, fitness, relationships, self-help, parenting, personal growth, and general health categories. She is looking for dynamic, personality-driven books; and high-concept, smart projects that offer a refreshing outlook and a new solution. She also acquires some general GPC nonfiction with a focus on pop culture and business.

LITTLE, BROWN AND COMPANY

BACK BAY BOOKS

237 Park Avenue, New York, NY 10017

212-364-1100

www.hachettebookgroupusa.com

Little, Brown and Company is home to noted debut novelists like Eduardo Santiago and masters of the trade like Herman Wouk. The house publishes David Sedaris' essays and Holly Hobbie's pigs, Walter Mosley's mysteries and James Patterson's thrillers. Founded in 1837, Little, Brown originated as an independent house with a Boston home base, but joined Warner Books in Manhattan in 2002.

A former Little, Brown imprint, Bulfinch Press, was dissolved by parent HBG late in 2006. However, the imprimatur "a Bulfinch Press book" is added to traditional art books (photography, art, and museum-related titles) published as Little, Brown titles.

Recent titles from Little, Brown include *How to Profit from the Coming Rapture: Getting Ahead When You're Left Behind* by Ellis Weiner; *Girls in Trucks* by Katie Crouch; *Testimony* by Anita Shreeve; *Confetti Cakes for Kids* by Elisa Strauss; *Katie Brown Celebrates: Simple and Spectacular Parties All Year Round* by Katie Brown; and *Beat the Reaper* by Josh Bazell.

Geoff Shandler, Editor-in-Chief, primarily acquires histories, biographies, and journalism. Among the many authors he has worked with are James Bradley, John le Carré, Robert Dallek, Tom Shales, Ann Blackman, Robert Wright, William Least Heat-Moon, Gary Giddins, James Miller, Doug Stanton, Elaine Shannon, Elizabeth Royte, Eileen Welsome, and Luis Urrea. His numerous best-sellers and award winners include *An Unfinished Life, Flyboys, Blind Man's Bluff, Black Mass, Paris in the Fifties,* and *In Retrospect.*

Michael Pietsch, Senior Vice President and Publisher, has worked with the novelists Martin Amis, Peter Blauner, Michael Connelly, Martha Cooley, Tony Earley,

Janet Fitch, Mark Leyrier, Rick Moody, Walter Mosley, James Patterson, George Pelecanos, Alice Sebold, Anita Shreve, Nick Tosches, David Foster Wallace, and Stephen Wright; the nonfiction writers John Feinstein, Peter Guralnick, and David Sedaris; and the cartoonist R. Crumb. Prior to joining Little, Brown in 1991, Michael worked at Harmony Books and before that at Scribner, where he edited a posthumous memoir by Ernest Hemingway, *The Dangerous Summer*.

Terry Adams, Vice President and Director, Trade Paperbacks, began his career in book publishing as a floater at Farrar, Straus & Giroux. He then worked for many years as Editor and Advertising Manager at Alfred A. Knopf before joining Little, Brown in 1996. Among the writers he has worked with are Breena Clarke, Julian Barnes, Harold Brodkey, Craig Childs, Katherine Dunn, Denis Johnson, the Monks of New Skete, J.F. Powers, and Wendy Wasserstein.

Tracy Behar, Executive Editor, joined Little, Brown in 2004 after serving as Editorial Director at Atria and Washington Square Press. At Little, Brown she has edited authors Arianna Huffington and Dr. William Sears. Her editing interests include life-improvement categories such as psychology, parenting, health, creativity, and empowerment.

Reagan Arthur, Executive Editor, joined Little, Brown in May 2001. She was formerly a Senior Editor at Picador and St. Martin's Press. Her Little, Brown acquisitions include books by international best-sellers Ian Rankin and Kate Atkinson, story collections by Oscar Casares and Elizabeth Crane, and nonfiction from *McSweeneys* and *Forward* contributor Jennifer Traig and *Atlantic Monthly's* Caitlin Flanagan.

Pat Strachan, Senior Editor, joined Little, Brown in September 2002. She is acquiring literary fiction and general nonfiction. Most recently at Houghton Mifflin, she began her career at Farrar, Straus & Giroux, where she worked as an editor for 17 years. She was then a fiction editor at *The New Yorker*, returning to book publishing in 1991. She received the PEN/Roger Klein Award for Editing. Among the prose writers she has edited are Tom Wolfe, Elizabeth Benedict, Harold Bloom, Ian Frazier, James Kelman, Jamaica Kincaid, Wendy Lesser, Rosemary Mahoney, John McPhee, David Nasaw, Edna O'Brien, Peter Orner, Padgett Powell, Marilynne Robinson, Jim Shepard, and Tatyana Tolstaya. Her Little, Brown books include fiction by Christina Adam, Kathryn Davis, Michelle de Kretser, Lucia Nevai, and Michael Redhill.

Judy Clain, Senior Editor, joined Little Brown in 1998. She began her career as a film agent and was a Sony executive on *Deep End of the Ocean* and *Donnie Brasco*. She has edited novelists including Jody Shields (*The Fig Eater*), Simon Mawer (*The Fall*), Elisabeth Robinson (*The True and Outstanding Adventures of the Hunt Sisters*), and Robb Forman Dew (*The Evidence Against Her*). She has also edited narrative nonfiction by Kien Nguyen (*The Unwanted*) and Daphne de Marneffe (*Maternal Desire*), among others.

Asya Muchnick, Editor, joined Little, Brown in 2001, and has edited novelists

Alice Sebold (*The Lovely Bones*), Carolyn Parkhurst (*The Dogs of Babel*), and Elise Blackwell (*Hunger*), and nonfiction by Lisa Hilton (*Athénaïs: The Life of Louis XIV's Mistress*), William Poundstone (*How Would You Move Mount Fuji?*), and Asne Seierstad (*The Bookseller of Kabul*). Recent acquisitions include a look at how rulers through the ages have collected rare and exotic animals by art historian Marina Belozerskaya; a meditation on the meaning of suffering by *New Yorker* and *Harper's* contributor Peter Trachtenberg; and first novels by Jardine Libaire and Thomas O'Malley. Previously, she was at Knopf.

John Parsley, Senior Editor, joined Little, Brown in 2007. His acquisitions focus on serious and narrative nonfiction including popular and natural science, history, ideas books, music, sports, food and humor. A recent purchase: *The Man's Book* by Thomas Fink, PhD. He was previously at Thomas Dunne/St. Martin's.

BACK BAY BOOKS

Back Bay Books is the Little, Brown trade paperback imprint. It focuses on contemporary fiction, both reprints and originals. Recent titles from Back Bay include *By George: A Novel* by Wesley Stace; *Right Livelihoods: Three Novellas* by Rick Moody; *House of Rain: Tracking a Vanished Civilization Across the American Southwest* by Craig Childs; *Here If You Need Me: A True Story* by Kate Braestrup; *People Who Changed the World* by Rodney Castleden; and *Barefoot* by Elin Hilderhrand.

Terry Adams, Editor, Trade Paperbacks—Acquires in fiction and humor

---

LITTLE, BROWN BOOKS FOR YOUNG READERS

LB KIDS

POPPY

237 Park Avenue, New York, NY 10017

212-364-1100

www.hachettebookgroupusa.com

Little, Brown's children's books division produces picture books, board books, pop-up and lift-the-flap editions, chapter books, manga, and general fiction and nonfiction titles for middle and young adult readers. This division also issues resource guides and reference titles in careers, social issues, and intellectual topics for higher grade levels and the college-bound.

The house offers volumes in Spanish language and in dual Spanish/English editions and is on the lookout for multicultural titles. The LB Kids imprint features original novelty books as well as TV, brand, and licensed tie-in publishing programs.

Poppy, established in 2007, was created to release original paperbacks for teenage girls; the company's bestselling *Gossip Girl, Clique, Poseur, and A-List* series were placed under this new umbrella.

Representative Little, Brown Books for Young Readers titles include Caldecott winner *Saint George and the Dragon* illustrated by Trina Schart Hyman; Newbery winner *Maniac Magee* by Jerry Spinelli; *Toot & Puddle* by Holly Hobbie; *Daisy and the Egg* by Jane Simmons; *Kevin and His Dad* by Irene Smalls; *47* by Walter Mosley; *Maximum Ride: The Angel Experiment* by James Patterson; *The Jolly Pocket Postman* by Janet and Allen Ahlberg.

Recent releases include *ghostgirl* by Tonya Hurley; *The Dangerous Days of Daniel X* by James Patterson and Michael Ledwidge; *Ed Emberly's Rainbow Drawing Book* by Ed Emberley; *Billy Bones: A Tale from the Secrets Closet* by Christopher Lincoln, illustrated by Avi Ofer; *I Don't Want a Posh Dog* by Emma Dodd; *Fanny* by Holly Hobbie; *Sergio Makes a Splash* by Edel Rodriguez; and *Call Me Hope* by Gretchen Olson.

Megan Tingley, Publisher

Andrea Spooner, Editorial Director—Trade hardcover and paperback lists

Cindy Eagan, Editorial Director, Poppy—Teen paperbacks for girls

Liza Baker, Editorial Director, LB Kids—Novelty and media tie-ins

Jennifer Hunt, Executive Editor—Young adult, middle grade, picture books

Alvina Ling, Senior Editor—Picture books, early readers, middle grade

Nancy Conescu, Editor—Young adult, middle grade, thrillers

OCTOPUS BOOKS

www.octopusbooks.co.uk

Launching in 2009, this new-for-the-USA imprint is a leading publisher in the UK of illustrated adult nonfiction, with particular strengths in reference, art and design, cooking, mind/body/spirit, and popular culture.

Recent titles include *1001 Historic Sites You Must See Before You Die* edited by Richard Cavendish; *The Foodie Handbook* by Pim Techamuanvivit; *Superstretch* by Jacqueline Lysycia; *Unzipped* by Nicci Talbot; and *The Blissful Brain* by Dr. Shanida Nataraja.

Jonathan Stolper, Associate Publisher, Octopus Books

ORBIT

www.orbitbooks.net

Orbit publishes across the spectrum of Science Fiction and Fantasy writing, from action-packed urban fantasy to widescreen space opera, from sweeping epic adventures to near-future thrillers. Orbit editors look for genre fiction that is fresh and innovative to reach a very broad audience. They publish about 40 new titles each year. Orbit was launched in the fall of 2007.

Another imprint from across the pond, Orbit UK was established in 1974, and is the largest Science Fiction and Fantasy imprint in the UK. It is a separate entity from Orbit US, although obviously also owned by Hachette.

Recent Orbit titles include *Warrior* by Marie Brennan; *Ketos* by Philip Palmer; *Bitten to Death (Jaz Parks)* by Jennifer Rardin; *The Riven Kingdom (The Godspeaker Trilogy)* by Karen Miller; *Unmarked Graves* by Shaun Hutson; and *Hunter's Prayer (Jill Kismet)* by Lilith Saintcrow.

Orbit does not accept unsolicited manuscripts and recommends working with an agent.

Tim Holman, Publisher—Across the spectrum of Fantasy and Science Fiction

Devi Pillai, Editor—Science Fiction and paranormal

YEN PRESS

www.yenpress.us

Yen Press is the graphic novel and manga imprint from Hachette, publishing for kids and adults. They released their first list in 2007. Recent titles include *Y Square Plus* by Judith Park; *Alice on Deadlines* by Shiro Ihara; *Goong* by Son Hee Park; *Angel Diary* by Yun-Hee Lee; *The World of Quest* by Jason T. Kruse; and *Suzunari!* by Shoko Iwami.

The editors are looking to develop original American style graphic novels, as well as license manga from Asia.

Rich Johnson, Co-publishing Director—Yen Press

Kurt Hassler, Co-publishing Director—Yen Press

Tania Biswas, Asst. Editor

VERLAGSGRUPPE GEORG VON HOLTZBRINCK

Verlagsgruppe Georg von Holtzbrinck, Germany's second-largest publisher, owns more than 80 companies in 20 different countries; holdings include Macmillan in the UK and Die Zeit in Germany. The company is lately enjoying their greatest success in trade publishing based on best-seller lists and market share growth.

As of 2007, Macmillan is the name Holtzbrinck uses for all of its English-language divisions. The American division is known as Macmillan U.S. and is based in New York City.

HOLTZBRINCK PUBLISHERS

MACMILLAN U.S. GW

BEDFORD, FREEMAN & WORTH PUBLISHING GROUP

FARRAR, STRAUS & GIROUX

FEIWEL & FRIENDS

HENRY HOLT AND COMPANY

PALGRAVE MACMILLAN

PICADOR USA

ROARING BROOK PRESS

ST. MARTIN'S PRESS

TOM DOHERTY ASSOCIATES

175 Fifth Avenue, New York, NY 10010

646-307-5151

www.us.macmillan.com

In the USA, Macmillan is a group of publishing companies that includes renowned houses like Farrar, Straus & Giroux; St. Martin's; and Henry Holt; the companies include trade and educational imprints, and the Scientific American magazine. Formerly Holtzbrinck USA, the group changed its name to Macmillan in the USA in 2007, joining other English-language Holtzbrinck divisions in name.

Former Scholastic publisher Jean Feiwel joined Holtzbrinck in 2006 to start a broadly defined children's effort and to guide strategy within the group. As well as creating new children's imprints, like Feiwel & Friends and Square Fish, she is publishing into paperback and other formats.

John Sargent, CEO

John Sterling, EVP, Editor-at-Large

Jean Feiwel, Senior Vice President and Publisher of Children's Books

BEDFORD, FREEMAN & WORTH PUBLISHING GROUP

BEDFORD / ST. MARTIN'S

W.H. FREEMAN

WORTH PUBLISHERS

41 Madison Avenue, New York, NY 10010

212-576-9422   fax: 212-545-8318

www.bfwpub.com

Holtzbrinck merged their three college and university publishing houses Bedford / St. Martin's, W.H. Freeman, and Worth Publishers to become the Bedford, Freeman & and Worth Publishing Group. Each of the three publishers has its own separate subject area focus. Bedford / St. Martin's focuses on liberal arts and humanities; W.H. Freeman focuses on the sciences; Worth's areas of focus are Psychology, Economics, and Sociology.

BEDFORD / ST. MARTIN'S

33 Irving Place, New York, NY 10003

212-375-7000   fax: 212-614-1885

Boston office:

75 Arlington Street, Boston, MA 02116

617-399-4000   fax: 617-426-8582

www.bedfordstmartins.com

Bedford/St. Martin's creates textbooks that end up on college desks worldwide, titles that will seem familiar to anyone who has faced the first day of *Intro. to Public Speaking* or *English 101*. Bedford's titles include the best-selling textbook ever: *A Writer's Reference* by Diana Hacker. The list focuses on the disciplines of communication, English, history, music, philosophy, and religion.

Recent titles include *The Business Writer's Companion* by Gerald J. Alred, Charles T. Brusaw, and Walter E. Oliu; *The Winter's Tale: Texts and Contexts* by William Shakespeare, edited by Mario DiGangi; *The Essential Guide to Rhetoric* by William M. Keith and Christian O. Lundberg; *Listen* by Joseph Kerman and Gary Tomlinson; *World Religions: A Historical Approach* by Solomon A. Nigosian; and *The U.S. War with Mexico: A Brief History with Documents* by Ernesto Chavez.

This publisher's preferred method of receiving unagented and unsolicited submissions is via e-mail by subject:

Music: music@bedfordstmartins.com

Communication: communication@bedfordstmartins.com

History: history@bedfordstmartins.com

Business & Technical Writing: bus&tech@bedfordstmartins.com

Literature & Linguistics: lit&linguistics@bedfordstmartins.com

Developmental Reading and Writing: developmental@bedfordstmartins.com

Composition: composition@bedfordstmartins.com

W. H. FREEMAN

41 Madison Avenue, 37th floor, New York, NY 10010

212-576-9400   fax: 212-689-2383

www.whfreeman.com

Founded in 1948, W. H. Freeman publishes college and high school science textbooks written by scientists and teachers. Freeman's first book was *General Chemistry* by the late Nobel laureate Linus Pauling. That pioneering text revolutionized the chemistry curriculum and set the high standard of book production that established Freeman as a premier science publisher.

Recent titles include *Discovering the Universe* by Neil F. Comins and William J. Kaufman; *Earth's Climate: Past and Future* by William F. Ruddiman; *Calculus* by Jon Rogawski; *Reconceptualizing Mathematics* by Judy Sowder, Larry Sowder, and Susan Nickerson; *Introduction to the Practice of Statistics* by David S. Moore, George McCabe, and Bruce Craig; *World Regional Geography* by Lydia Mihelic Pulsipher and Alex Pulsipher; and *Lehninger Principles of Biochemistry* by David L. Nelson and Michael M. Cox.

This publisher's preferred method of receiving unagented and unsolicited submissions is via e-mail by subject:

Astronomy: Astronomymkt@whfreeman.com

Biology: Biology@whfreeman.com

Chemistry: Chemistrymktg@whfreeman.com

Geography: Geography@whfreeman.com

Mathematics: Mathmktg@whfreeman.com

Physics: Physics@whfreeman.com

WORTH PUBLISHERS

41 Madison Avenue, 35th floor, New York, NY 10010

212-576-9400   fax: 212-561-8281

www.worthpublishers.com

Since 1998, Worth has focused its efforts on publishing textbooks specifically in the social sciences of psychology, sociology, and economics. Among its global best sellers are David Myers' *Psychology* (the world's most popular introduction to psychology), Myers' *Exploring Psychology*, Kathleen Berger's *The Developing Person Through Childhood and Adolescence*, Elliot Aronson's *The Social Animal*, and N. Gregory Mankiw's *Macroeconomics*. In 2003, Worth expanded into the high school market with its new text, Blair-Broeker and Ernst's *Thinking About Psychology*.

Recent titles include *The Sociology of Health and Illness* by Peter Conrad; *States of Global Insecurity: Policy, Politics, and Society* by Daniel Béland; *Psychology: A Concise Introduction* by Richard A. Griggs; *Learning and Memory: From Brain to Behavior* by Mark A. Gluck, Eduardo Mercado, and Catherine E. Myers; *Core Economics* by Gerald Stone; and *International Economics* by Robert C. Feenstra and Alan M. Taylor.

This publisher's preferred method of receiving unagented and unsolicited submissions is via e-mail by subject:

Economics: Economics@worthpublishers.com

Psychology: Psychology@ worthpublishers.com

FARRAR, STRAUS & GIROUX

FABER AND FABER, INC.

FARRAR, STRAUS & GIROUX BOOKS FOR YOUNG READERS

HILL AND WANG

NORTH POINT PRESS

18 West 18th Street, New York, NY 10011

212-741-6900   fax: 212-633-9385

www.fsgbooks.com   e-mail: fsg.editorial@fsgbooks.com

blog: www.fsgpoetry.com

Farrar, Straus & Giroux (FSG) was founded in New York City in 1946 by Roger Straus and John Farrar; Robert Giroux joined the company in 1955. The firm is widely acclaimed for its international list of literary fiction, nonfiction, poetry, and children's books. FSG is also known for building authors over time through strong editorial relationships. This was the way Roger Straus built the company, and it continues so under current publisher Jonathan Galassi.

FSG authors have won extraordinary acclaim over the years, including numerous National Book Awards, Pulitzer Prizes, and 21 Nobel Prizes in literature. Nobel Prize winners include Knut Hamsun, Hermann Hesse, T. S. Eliot, Par Lagerkvist, Francois Mauriac, Juan Ramon Jimenez, Salvatore Quasimodo, Nelly Sachs, Czeslaw Milosz, Elias Canetti, William Golding, Wole Soyinka, Joseph Brodsky, Camilo Jose Cela, Nadine Gordimer, Derek Walcott, and Seamus Heaney.

Today's Farrar, Straus & Giroux list includes some of the most renowned names in poetry and fiction, including Richard Price, Denis Johnson, Elizabeth Bishop, Marilynne Robinson, Ted Hughes, Phillip Larkin, Michael Cunningham, Jonathan Franzen, Alice McDermott, and Scott Turow.

History, art history, natural history, current affairs, and science round out the list in nonfiction, represented by Thomas Friedman, Philip Gourevitch, Roy Jenkins, Gina Kolata, Ben Macintyre, Louis Menaud, Giles Milton, and John McPhee.

Sarah Crichton's imprint focuses on books with a more commercial bent than the rest of the FSG list, but retains the house commitment to quality and thoughtfulness.

Recent titles include *Fifty Miles from Tomorrow: A Memoir of Alaska and the Real People* by William L. Iggiagruk Hensley; *The End of My Addiction* by Olivier Ameisen; *Alpha Dogs: The Americans Who Turned Political Spin into a Global Business* by James Harding; *Exiles* by Ron Hansen; *Apples and Oranges: My Brother and Me, Lost and Found* by Marie Brenner; *Central Park in the Dark: More Mysteries of Urban Wildlife* by Marie Winn; *The Men's Club* by Leonard Michaels; *How Fiction Works* by James Woods; *A Better Angel* by Chris Adrian; and *The Private Lives of Pippa Lee* by Rebecca Miller.

All editorial inquiries should be e-mailed to the editorial department at fsg.editorial@fsgbooks.com. FSG does not accept manuscript submissions via e-mail. Queries may also be sent via mail with SASEs to:

Jonathan Galassi, Publisher—fiction, nonfiction, art history, belles lettres, business, and poetry

Eric Chinski, Editor-in-Chief—Science, history, business, general nonfiction

Courtney Hodell, Executive Editor—Fiction

Paul Elie, Senior Editor—Nonfiction, cooking, history

Mr. Lorin Stein, Editor—Fiction

Sarah Crichton, Publisher, Sarah Crichton Books

FABER AND FABER, INC.

Faber and Faber offers a unique list in popular culture, drama, music, and film, poetry. Among its authors are Courtney Love and Billy Corgan, as well as Pulitzer Prize-winning playwrights David Auburn, Margaret Edson, and Doug Wright; Pulitzer finalist Richard Greenberg; British dramatists Tom Stoppard and David Hare; and filmmaker and playwright Neil LaBute.

A 2008 initiative to grow this imprint is being led by new publisher Mitzi Angel, who was formerly editorial director at UK publisher Fourth Estate. FSG Publisher Jonathan Galassi said in the announcement, "The aim is to take the existing Faber, Inc., and expand and deepen it, working closely with our Faber colleagues in London to build the brand in a new way here. Under Mitzi's leadership, Faber, Inc., will be an innovative American imprint with a fresh approach to both fiction and nonfiction publishing. I'm excited that, at a time when some other publishers seem to be pulling back, the long-standing special relationship between Faber and FSG will enter a creative new phase under this talented publisher's guidance." The list will grow to 30 – 35 books per year.

Recent titles include *The Strangest Man* by Graham Farmelo; *Varieties of Weeping* by Sebastian Barry; *The Island at the End of the World* by Dam Taylor; *The Faber Pocket Guide to Haydn* by Richard Wigmore; *Chaplin* by Simon Louvish; *The Reel Truth: Everything You Didn't Know You Need to Know About Making an Independent Film* by Reed Martin; *Sing Me Back Home: Love, Death, and Country Music* by Dana Jennings; *I Have Fun Everywhere I Go: Savage Tales of Pot, Pom, Punk Rock, Pro Wrestling, Taking Apes, Evil Bosses, Dirty Blues, American Heroes, and the Most Notorious Magazines in the World* by Mike Edison; and *Reasons to Be Pretty: A Play* by Neil LaBute.

All editorial inquiries should be e-mailed to the editorial department at fsg.editorial@fsgbooks.com. FSG does not accept manuscript submissions via e-mail. Queries may be sent via mail with SASEs to:

Mitzi Angel, Publisher

Denise Oswald, Senior Editor—Pop culture, memoir, other nonfiction

FARRAR, STRAUS & GIROUX BOOKS FOR YOUNG READERS

www.fsgkidsbooks.com   e-mail: childrens.editorial@fsgbooks.com

The FSG juvenile program publishes fiction and nonfiction books for toddlers to young adults. This list includes many Caldecott, Newbery, and National Book Award winners. Award-winning authors include Jack Gantos, Madeleine L'Engle, Louis Sachar, Uri Shulevitz, Peter Sis, David Small, William Steig, and Sarah Stewart. Newer FSG authors include Kate Banks, Claudia Mills, Jack Gantos, Suzanne Fisher Staples, and Tim Wynne-Jones.

Recent titles include *Everything Beautiful in the World* by Lisa Levchuk; *Headlong* by Kathe Koja; *The Robot and the Bluebird* by David Lucas; *A Life in the Wild: George Schaller's Struggle to Save the Last Great Beasts* by Pamela S. Turner; *The House of Joyful Living* by Roni Schotter and Terry Widener; *Swiss Mist* by Randy Powell; *Addis Berner Bear Forgets* by Joel Stewart; *Last Night* by Hyewon Yum; *Manjiro: The Boy Who Risked His Life for Two Countries* by Emily Arnold McCully; and *Marveltown* by Bruce McCall.

All children's book editorial inquiries should be e-mailed to the editorial department at childrens.editorial@fsgbooks.com.

Direct all submissions with SASEs to the Children's Editorial Department.

Margaret Ferguson, Co-Publisher and Editorial Director

Michael Eisenberg, Associate Publisher

Wes Adams, Senior Editor

Janine O'Malley, Senior Editor

Beverly Reingold, Editor

Frances Foster, Publisher, Frances Foster Books

Melanie Kroupa, Publisher, Melanie Kroupa Books

HILL AND WANG

Hill and Wang focuses on books of academic interest for both the trade and college markets, in both hard and soft cover. The list is strong in American history, world history, and politics, and graphic nonfiction. Among its authors are Roland Barthes, Michael Burleigh, William Cronon, Langston Hughes, Robert Wiebe, and Eli Wiesel.

Recent titles include *To Tell the Truth Freely: The Life of Ida B. Wells* by Mia Bay; *Clash of Extremes: The Economic Origins of the Civil War* by Marc Egnal; *Isadora Duncan: A Graphic Biography* by Sabrina Jones and Paul Buhle; *Good Germs, Bad Germs: Health and Survival in a Bacterial World* by Jessica Snyder Sachs; *The H. L. Hunley: The Secret Hope of the Confederacy* by Tom Chaffin; *The Beautiful Soul* of John Woolman, *Apostle of Abolition* by Thomas P. Slaughter; and *The Great Delusion: A Mad Inventor, Death in the Tropics, and the Utopian Origins of Economic Growth* by Steven Stoll.

Query letters and SASEs may be directed to:

Thomas LeBien, Publisher

NORTH POINT PRESS

North Point Press specializes in hard and soft cover literary nonfiction, with an emphasis natural history, travel, ecology, music, food, and cultural criticism. Past and present authors include Peter Matthiessen, Evan Connell, Beryl Markham, A. J. Liebling, Margaret Visser, Wendell Berry, and M. F. K. Fisher.

Recent titles include *Mouth Wide Open: A Cook and His Appetite* by John Thorne and Matt Lewis Throne; *The Dirt on Clean: An Unsanitized History* by Katherine Ashenburg; *The Bhagavad Gita: A New Translation* by George Thompson; *The Body Toxic: How the Hazardous Chemistry of Everyday Things Threatens Our Health and Well-being* by Nena Baker; and *Trespass: Living at the Edge of the Promised Land* by Amy Irvine.

Eric Chinski, Editor-in-Chief

FEIWEL & FRIENDS

SQUARE FISH

175 Fifth Avenue, New York, NY 10010

646-307-5151

Feiwel & Friends is the new imprint developed by former Scholastic publisher Jean Feiwel, who joined Holtzbrinck in 2006. Feiwel commented, "My goals are to build a successful enterprise in a reinvented publishing model; to focus and ambitiously publish in paperback and other formats the outstanding children's backlists of Farrar Straus, Henry Holt, Roaring Brook Press and others, and to have a hand in directing Holtzbrinck's overall children's book publishing strategy — here and abroad."

Titles from Feiwel & Friends include *Fairy School Drop-Out* by Meredith Badger; *Wild Dancers #1: If Wishes Were Horses* by Sibley Miller, illustrated by Tara Larsen Chang and Jo Gershman; *Dangerous Times: The First Nathan Fox Mission* by Lynn Brittney; *Zac Power #1: Poison Island* by H. I. Larry and Ash Oswald; *Lincoln Shot: A President's Life Remembered* by Barry Denenberg and Christopher Bing; and *The Lost Island of Tamarind* by Nadia Aguiar.

Square Fish is a paperback imprint that reprints hardcover children's books from all of the Holtzbrinck publishers. The imprint launched in summer 2007 with Madeleine L'Engle's *Time Quintet*, which includes the classic *A Wrinkle in Time*.

More recent titles from Square Fish include *In the Name of God* by Paula Jolin; *Poison Ivy* by Amy Goldman Koss; *Wing Nut* by M. J. Auch; *A Houseful of Christmas* by Barbara Joosse, illustrated by Betsy Lewin; *A Room on Lorelei Street* by Mary E. Pearson; and *Space Pirate Sardine vs. the Brainwashing Machine* by Emmanuel Guibert, illustrated by Joann Sfar.

Direct queries and SASEs to:

Jean Feiwel, Publisher

Liz Szabla, Editor-in-Chief

SQUARE FISH

Square Fish is a paperback imprint that reprints hardcover children's books from all of the Holtzbrinck publishers. The imprint launched in summer 2007 with Madeleine L'Engle's *Time Quintet*, which includes the classic *A Wrinkle in Time*.

More recent titles from Square Fish include *The Velveteen Rabbit* by Margery Williams, illustrated by Michael Hague; *Circle Unbroken* by Margot Theis Raven, illustrated by E. B. Lewis; *George Washington's Teeth* by Deborah Chandra and Madeleine Comora, illustrated by Brock Cole; and *Rosa* by Nikki Giovanni, illustrated by Bryan Collier.

HENRY HOLT AND COMPANY

HENRY HOLT AND COMPANY BOOKS FOR YOUNG READERS

HENRY HOLT PAPERBACKS

METROPOLITAN BOOKS

TIMES BOOKS

175 Fifth Avenue, New York, NY 10010

646-307-5095   fax: 212-633-0748

www.henryholt.com

One of the oldest publishers in the U.S., Henry Holt is known for publishing high quality books, including those by authors such as Erich Fromm, Robert Frost, Hermann Hesse, Norman Mailer, Robert Louis Stevenson, Ivan Turgenev, and H. G. Wells. The publication program focuses on American and international fiction, biography, history, politics, science, psychology, health, and books for children.

Among its current authors are Siri Hustvedt, Rick Atkinson, Paul Auster, Robert Frost, Al and Tipper Gore, Tony Horwitz, David Levering Lewis, Thomas Pynchon, Salman Rushdie, and Gloria Steinem.

Recent titles include *The White Mary* by Kira Salak; *Volk's Shadow* by Brent Ghelfi; *Forecast: The Consequences of Climate Change, from the Amazon to the Arctic, from Darfur to Napa Valley* by Stephan Farris; *W.E.B. Du Bois: A Biography* by David Levering Lewis; *Lives of the Artists* by Calvin Tomkins; *In A Time of War: The Proud and Perilous Journey of West Point's Class of 2002* by Bill Murphy; *For the Love of Animals: The Rise of the Animal Protection Movement* by Kathryn Shevelow; and *The Man Who Ate the World: In Search of the Perfect Dinner* by Jay Rayner.

Holt and its adult imprints do not accept or read any unsolicited manuscripts or queries.

John Sterling, Publisher—Science, memoir, current events, thrillers

David Patterson, Senior Editor—Politics, religion, current events, narrative non-fiction, memoir

Sarah Knight, Editor—Fiction, including mysteries, thrillers, and gothics

Jack MacRae, Editor—Fiction and narrative nonfiction, especially art, pop culture, history, nature

Helen Atsma, Editor—Fiction, including debut

Supurna Banerjee, Associate Editor—Narrative nonfiction, pop culture, memoir

HENRY HOLT AND COMPANY BOOKS FOR YOUNG READERS

www.henryholtchildrensbooks.com

Henry Holt and Company Books for Young Readers publishes a wide range of children's books, from picture books for preschoolers to fiction for young adults.

Representative titles include *Panda Bear, Panda Bear, What Do You See?* by Bill Martin, Jr., illustrated by Eric Carle; *Tikki Tikki Tembo* by Arlene Mosel, illustrated by Blair Lent; *The Book of Three (The Chronicles of Prydain)* by Lloyd Alexander; *Whirligig* by Paul Fleischman; *My First Chinese New Year* by Karen Katz; and *Frog in Love* by Max Velthuijs.

Recent titles include *When I Grow Up: A Young Person's Guide to Interesting and Unusual Occupations* by Jessica Loy; *Charles and Emma: The Darwins' Leap of Faith* by Deborah Heiligman; *Masterpiece* by Elise Broach, illustrated by Kelly Murphy; *How Robin Saved Spring* by Debbie Ouellet; *Footprints in the Snow* by Mei Matsuoka; *Ice Bears* by Brenda Z. Guiberson, illustrated by Ilya Spirin; *Emmy and the Home for Troubled Girls* by Lynne Jonell, illustrated by Jonathan Bean; *Milagros: Girl from Away* by Meg Medina; and *Kings and Queens of the Bible* by Mary Hoffman and Christina Balit.

When submitting to Henry Holt and Company Books for Young Readers, send a manuscript and cover letter to: Submissions. Do not send a SASE; the editors will respond only to those manuscripts they wish to pursue. All other submissions will be recycled. No multiple submissions. Full guidelines are available at www.henryholtchildrensbooks.com.

Laura Godwin, Vice President and Associate Publisher

Sally Doherty, Executive Editor

Reka Simonsen, Editor—Picture books, middle grade, young adult

Robin Tordini, Editor—Young adult

Kate Farrell, Associate Editor—Young adult

Christy Ottaviano, Executive Editor, Christy Ottaviano Books—Literary and commercial picture books and fiction for all ages, books that encourage imagination and free-thinking, foster a sense of family and community, target the feelings of children and speak directly to children's interests

HENRY HOLT PAPERBACKS

Henry Holt Paperbacks, formerly Owl Books, reprints many of Henry Holt's titles in trade paperback format and publishes original paperback titles in the categories of health, self-help, parenting, and business/finance.

Titles representative of the Holt Paperbacks list include *Getting the Love You Want, 20th Anniversary Edition: A Guide for Couples* by Harville Hendrix; *Writing Your Dissertation in Fifteen Minutes a Day: A Guide to Starting, Revising, and Finishing Your Doctoral Thesis* by Joan Bolker; *The Autobiographer's Handbook: The 826 Valencia Guide to Writing Your Memoir* by Jennifer Traig; *Grammar Girl's Quick and Dirty Tips for Better Writing* by Mignon Fogarty; *The Ridiculous Race* by Steve Hely and Vali Changrasekaran; and *The Boys in the Trees: A Novel* by Mary Swan.

PUBLISHING CONGLOMERATES

METROPOLITAN BOOKS

This Henry Holt imprint is open to various genres, unconventional points of view, controversial opinions, and new voices. From short stories to social science, award-winning novels to American politics, foreign fiction to cutting-edge history and current affairs, Metropolitan is committed to diversity, distinction, and surprise.

Authors published by Metropolitan Books include Ann Crittenden, Mike Davis, Barbara Ehrenreich, Susan Faludi, Orlando Figes, Michael Frayn, Eduardo Galeano, Atul Gawande, Todd Gitlin, Arlie Russell Hochschild, Michael Ignatieff, Orville Schell, and Tom Segev.

Recent titles include *The Big Necessity: The Unmentionable World of Human Waste and Why It Matters* by Rose George; *The Pallbearers: Profiles of Four Who Brought Down America* by Roger Morris; *The Limits of Power: The End of American Exceptionalism* by Andrew Bacevich; *The Wrecking Crew: How Conservatives Rule* by Thomas Frank; *Hell's Cartel: IG Farben and the Making of Hitler's War Machine* by Diarmuid Jeffreys; *This Land is Their Land: Reports from a Divided Nation* by Barbara Ehrenreich; *House of Wits: An Intimate Portrait of the James Family* by Paul Fisher; and *The Book of Love: The Story of the Kamasutra* by James McConnachie.

Henry Holt and its adult imprints do not accept or read any unsolicited manuscripts or queries.

Sara Bershtel, Associate Publisher

Riva Hocherman, Senior Editor—History, current events, politics, fiction

TIMES BOOKS

Times Books, launched in 2001, is the result of a co-publishing agreement between Holt and the *New York Times*; its nonfiction list focuses on politics, current events, international relations, history, science, business, and American society and culture. About half of the imprint's books are written by *New York Times* reporters and the rest are written by other American intellectuals, journalists, and public figures.

Recent releases include *Brzezinski: A Life on the Grand Chessboard of Power* by Patrick Vaughan; *John Tyler: The American Presidents Series: The 10th President, 1841-1845* by Gary May; *The Jazz Ear: Conversations Over Music* by Ben Ratliff; *Emotional Awareness: Overcoming the Obstacles to Psychological Balance and Compassion* by Dalai Lama and Paul Ekman; *Loot: The Battle Over the Stolen Treasures of the Ancient World* by Sharon Waxman; and *Blue Dixie: Awakening the South's Democratic Majority* by Bob Moser.

Paul Golob, Editorial Director—History, current affairs, biography

Robin Dennis, Senior Editor—Health, science, sex, politics, current events

PALGRAVE MACMILLAN

175 Fifth Avenue, New York, NY 10010

212-982-3900

www.palgrave-usa.com

Formerly the Scholarly and Reference division of St. Martin's Press, Palgrave Macmillan is a global cross-market publisher with offices in the U.S. and the U.K. They publish monographs, upper-level and graduate-level texts, and sophisticated trade books for the general educated reader or scholar.

Palgrave publishes a wide range of nonfiction books in the humanities and social sciences. Books include specialized monographs that make original contributions to scholarship in their disciplines, upper-division supplemental texts and readers designed for classroom use, and trade titles written for a broad, educated, but nonacademic audience. Categories include history, politics, business, economics, literature and cultural studies, medieval studies, theater studies, education, religion, gender studies, anthropology, and Latino and Latin American studies.

Recent titles include *Lancaster Against York: The War of the Roses and the Foundation of Modern Britain* by Trevor Royle; *Demagogue: The Fight to Save Democracy from Its Worst Enemies* by Michael Signer; *The King of Madison Avenue: David Ogilvy and the Making of Modern Advertising* by Kenneth Roman; *The Campaign: Using Purpose to Fuel Big Business Goals* by Nikos Mourkogiannis; *The Dream: How a Young Entrepreneur Learned the Risks and Rewards of Internet Startups and Made Millions* by Gurbaksh Chahal and Pablo F. Fenjves; *Why Kids Kill: Inside the Minds of School Shooters* by Peter Langman; and *Taking Aim at the President: The Remarkable Story of a Housewife Assassin* by Geri Spieler.

Palgrave Macmillan welcomes book proposals and lists complete guidelines on their Web site. Send the proposal with SASE to the most relevant editor:

Airié Stuart, Publisher—Trade, current affairs, business

Farideh Koohi-Kamali, Executive Editor—Academic, literature, film, media, religion, anthropology, cultural studies, theatre, gender studies

Laurie Harting, Editor—Academic and professional, economics, business & management

Alessandra Bastagli, Senior Editor—Trade, history

Anthony Wahl, Editor—Academic, politics

Ms. Luba Ostashevsky, Editor—Trade & academic, Latin American studies, African studies, parenting, psychology, science

Chris Chappel, Editor—Academic, history

Julia Cohen, Editor—Academic, education

PICADOR USA

175 Fifth Avenue, 19th Floor, New York, NY 10010

212-674-5151   fax: 212-253-9627

www.picadorusa.com

Picador USA was founded by St. Martin's Press and is now the reprint house for Farrar, Straus & Giroux, Henry Holt, and other Holtzbrinck publishers. With an international list of world-class authors, Picador has rapidly established itself as one of the country's literary trade paperback imprints.

Recent titles include *The Housekeeper and the Professor* by Yoko Ogawa; *Bearing the Body* by Ehud Havazelet; *Gomorrah: A Personal Journey into the Violent International Empire of Naples' Organized Crime System* by Roberto Saviano; *A Wall in Palestine* by Rene Backmann; *The Painted Word* by Tom Wolfe; *The Bad Girl* by Mario Vargas Llosa; *Break and Enter* by Colin Harrison; *Cleopatra's Nose: 39 Varieties of Desire* by Judith Thurman; Coltrane: *The Story of a Sound* by Ben Ratliff; and *Moveable Feasts: From Ancient Rome to the 21st Century, the Incredible Journeys of the Food We Eat* by Sarah Murray.

Query letters and SASEs may be directed to:

Frances Coady, Publisher—Fiction, narrative nonfiction

David Rogers, Assistant Editor

ROARING BROOK PRESS

FIRST SECOND

175 Fifth Avenue, New York, NY 10010

212-674-5151

Roaring Brook Press published its debut list of children's books in Spring 2002 and less than a year later one of its picture books, Eric Rohmann's *My Friend Rabbit*, won the Caldecott Medal. Another Roaring Brook picture book, Mordicai Gerstein's *The Man Who Walked Between the Towers*, won the Caldecott medal in January 2004. This was the first time in 30 years that the Caldecott had been awarded to the same publisher two years in a row (in 1976 and 1977, Dial Press won for *Why Mosquitos Buzz in People's Ears* by Verna Aardema, illustrated by Leo and Diane Dillon, and *Ashanti to Zulu* by Margaret Musgrove, again illustrated by Leo and Diane Dillon).

Holtzbrinck acquired the Connecticut-based publisher in 2004, and it joined the Roaring Brook Press is an author-centered publisher with a small but eclectic list. They are seeking long-term relationships with their authors; they don't do series; they don't do merchandise. What they do is edgy teen fiction, middle grade fiction with humor, and high-quality picture books with an individual approach to art and format.

Holtzbrinck publishing group in New York. Roaring Brook publishes 40 books per year, half picture books and half novels for middle grade and young adult readers, and is in the midst of a growth pattern.

In 2006, Roaring Brook launched First Second, an imprint devoted to graphic novels. First Second editors seek to acquire titles that attract a diverse audience of readers by working on many different levels. First Second titles include *Alan's War: The Memories of G. I. Alan Cope* by Emmanuel Guibert; *Bourbon Island 1730* by Lewis Trondheim and Oliver Appollodorus; *Gus & His Gang* by Chris Blain; *The Lost Colony, Book Three: Last Rights* by Grady Klein; *The Amazing Remarkable Monsieur Leotard* by Eddie Campbell and Dan Best; and *Slow Storm* by Danica Novogorodoff.

Recent Roaring Brook titles include *Penina Levine Is a Potato Pancake* by Rebecca O'Connell, illustrated Majella Lue Sue; *What's Love?* by Deborah Carlin, photographs by Shelley Rotner; *The Cat's Tale: Why the Years Are Named for Animals* by Doris Orgel, illustrated Meilo So; *Hush Little Polar Bear* by Jeff Mack; *ABC3D* by Marion Bataille; *Let It Begin Here!: April 19, 1775: The Day the American Revolution Began* by Don Brown; *Just In Case: A Trickster Tale and Spanish Alphabet Book* by Yuyi Morales; and *KidChat Christmas: 200 Questions to Make You Think, Talk, and Giggle About Everyone's Favorite Holiday* by Bret Nicholaus and Paul Lowrie.

Direct queries and SASEs to:

Simon Boughton, Publisher

Nancy Mercado, Editor—Middle grade, picture books

Neal Porter, Editorial Director, Neal Porter Books

Mark Siegel, Editorial Director, First Second—Graphic novels

ST. MARTIN'S PRESS

GRIFFIN

MINOTAUR

THOMAS DUNNE BOOKS

TRUMAN TALLEY BOOKS

175 Fifth Avenue, New York, NY 10010

212-674-5151

www.stmartins.com

Founded in 1952 by Macmillan Publishers of England, St. Martin's Press is now one of the largest publishers in America. Together, their imprints produce over 700 books a year, and their editors are as equally committed to establishing new and innovative authors, as to maintaining a strong backlist of titles. Publishing in hardcover, trade paperback, and mass market formats enables St. Martin's Press to offer a diverse assortment of titles with wide-ranging appeal. St. Martin's is looking for new authors to discover, to build, and to support.

The house is particularly strong in a number of specialty areas, some with associated lines and imprints (including popular culture, international arts and letters, relationships, multicultural topics, science, business, and professional topics). St. Martin's publishes across the spectrum of trade nonfiction and hosts a wide range of popular and literary fiction.

After twenty-five years together, St. Martin's and Harvard's Let's Go Publications have parted ways, and their production/distribution contract expires in 2009. The Let's Go Web site continues at www.letsgo.com.

Representative titles from St. Martin's include *Last Call at Elaine's: A Journey from One Side of the Bar to the Other* by Brian McDonald; *The Disorganized Mind: Coaching your AD/HD Brain to Get Control of Your Tasks, Time, and Talents* by Nancy A. Ratey; *The Assassin: A Novel* by Stephen Coonts; *North Pakistan: Karakorum Conquered* by Nigel J. R. Allan; *The All-New Atkins Advantage: 12 Weeks to a New Body, a New You, a New Life* by Stuart L. Trager and Colette Heimowitz; and *Fish that Fake Orgasms: And Other Zoological Curiosities* by Matt Walker.

Recent titles include *Happy at Last: The Thinking Person's Guide to Finding Joy* by Richard O'Connor; *Peculiar Proverbs: Weird Words of Wisdom from Around the World* by Stephen Arnott; *A Promise to Ourselves: Fatherhood, Divorce, and Family Law* by Alec Baldwin; *Vincent Minnelli: Hollywood's Dark Dreamer* by Emanuel Levy; *Circumference: Erastosthenes and the Ancient Quest to Measure the Globe* by Nicholas Nicastro; *The Entity: Five Centuries of Secret Vatican Espionage* by Eric Frattini Alonso and Dick Cluster; *In Triumph's Wake: Three Royal Matriarchs, Three Tragic Daughters* by Julia P. Gelardi; and *The Inner Circle: A Mystery* by Mari Jungstedt.

Queries and SASEs may be directed to:

George Witte, Editor-in-Chief—Quality literary and commercial fiction, current affairs and issues, and narrative nonfiction; "During my twenty-two years here, I've taken particular pleasure in the number of first books we've published—many of those authors are now writing their fifth, tenth, fifteenth, or even twentieth book for us. Discovery, energy, and commitment to authors are the driving forces of our house."

Lisa Senz, Vice President, Associate Publisher, Reference Group—"We actively seek out titles that inform, educate, and amuse: both branded titles and titles that can become brands. Self-help, health, business, pop-culture, science/technology, and reference are all fair game."

Charles Spicer, Executive Editor—Commercial fiction: crime, suspense, mysteries, and historical fiction; nonfiction: true crime, biography and history; "I also oversee the True Crime Library Imprint, which has long been the most successful publisher of nonfiction crime, with many *New York Times* bestsellers and Edgar winners to its credit."

Elizabeth Beier, Executive Editor—"I couldn't be more enthusiastic about the kinds of books I work on—they span a generous variety of categories, from issues-oriented books to pop-culture, cookbooks to fiction, celebrity memoir to biography. Especially exciting is to work with first-time authors—I love introducing a writer to the process, trying to smooth the bumps along the way, and watching them take leaps as we pull the book together."

Hope Dellon, Executive Editor—Mysteries, serious contemporary and historical novels. "In nonfiction, my interests include biography, social history, and psychological memoirs. As the wife of a psychiatrist and mother of two daughters, I also find myself drawn to books on parenting, education, women's issues, and medicine."

Dori Weintraub, Editor-at-Large—Memoirs, biographies, literary fiction; "I'm a sucker for quirky subjects, the kind of things that don't immediately seem like an easy sell."

Jennifer Weis, Executive Editor and Manager, Concept Development—Commercial fiction: women's, thrillers, romance; commercial, YA; nonfiction: people books, narrative nonfiction, cookbooks, self-help, health and parenting, humor and popular culture; "The common theme of the novels I acquire is that they tell a story. From the most boldly commercial, to the quieter, what we call literary commercial crossover titles, they must make me keep turning the pages—usually, far into the night!" She is also looking, from a content/book perspective, to tie in with opportunities in areas of new media, branding, and Hollywood.

Philip Revzin, Senior Editor—Business, international subjects, reference, memoir; "Since I came to St. Martin's in 2005 after having worked for the *Wall Street Journal* for more than thirty years, I have a natural interest in business titles. Having lived in Europe and Asia, I also like international subjects. But most of all, as a journalist, I like well-reported books of general interest."

Keith Kahla, Executive Editor—Thrillers, crime fiction, historical, literary fiction, Asian fiction (domestic and translated), new age works, divination systems, biography and history; "What draws me to a particular book is the quality of the writing, and a distinct, compelling authorial voice. Editorially, I believe it isn't the topic, story, or 'hook' that is the determining factor for interesting and successful books—it's the execution of the work by a uniquely talented author."

B. J. Berti, Senior Editor—She started at St. Martin's in 2005 with a mandate to reinvigorate the line of craft, style, and home books and develop a range of new titles in this area. In addition to practical nonfiction titles like *Easy Knitted Socks*, she is also interested in considering books that are not specifically craft but have a strong practical "how-to" component, like *The Art of Friendship*. She writes, "An attractively designed books with unique projects of information and something new to teach is what appeals to me most."

Marc Resnick, Senior Editor—Outdoor adventure, sports, military, popular culture, memoirs, thrillers, commercial fiction; "I have been working at St. Martin's Press since 1996—my first job in publishing."

Michael Flamini, Executive Editor—He acquires in history, politics, currents affairs, memoirs, and cookbooks. He says, "It's an eclectic list, but why be boring? Life's too short and I hope my publishing reflects that philosophy."

Monique Patterson, Senior Editor—She joined St. Martin's in 2000 and acquires for all parts of the list and with wide variety; "The nonfiction that I like to do is mostly commercial and in fiction my tastes run from fun to suspenseful, from dark to breezy, from emotional to sexy—preferably a delicious combination of any of these."

Nichole Argyres, Editor—"The search for a good story drives me both as a reader and as an editor. I love discovering stories with strong voices, beautiful language, and mysterious secrets. In nonfiction, I acquire idea books, memoirs, and platform-driven nonfiction of all kinds. I have a special interest in women's issues, current events, mental health, and medicine, as well as popular science and anything Greek."

Regina Scarpa, Editor—Fiction, including debut novels, and nonfiction , especially relationships, advice, finance, and health

Rose Hilliard, Associate Editor—Women's fiction and romance; "I'm on the lookout for exciting new romance authors in every subgenre, from romantic suspense to romantic comedy." She looks for stories with a great hook, an appealing voice, and winning characters that have her rooting for them from page one—and bonus points is a story that makers her laugh aloud or tear up. She is also considering branching out in the direction of pop-culture books.

Michael Homler, Editor—Biographies, history, pop science, crime fiction, sophisticated thrillers, and literary novels. "I'm really fascinated by material that breaks convention. At the same time, I look for solid voice-driven writing—something that makes the book and the author stand out from the pack. A sense of humor doesn't hurt either. In addition, I'm looking for more sports books, with a particular interest in baseball, which I can never get enough of."

Daniela Rapp, Associate Editor—Humor, pets, biography, food/travel/wine, pop science, mysteries, thrillers, historical fiction, literary fiction; "I am actively looking for young Native American writers, as well as fiction in translation (I read German, French, and Italian) and am intrigued by literary references and anything to do with swordfights."

Ms. Hilary Rubin Teeman, Associate Editor—Social and cultural history, narrative nonfiction, popular sociology, playful self-help, memoirs, up-market women's fiction, romantic suspense, chick lit, literate commercial fiction, thrillers, and edgy YA novels; "I'm particularly interested in anything geared toward the twenty-to-thirty-something market."

David Moldawer, Associate Editor—Narrative nonfiction, humor, popular culture, science, technology, reference, and sports, also memoir and some fiction

GRIFFIN

Griffin, a St. Martin's imprint, publishes trade paperbacks, with a strong emphasis in "how to" nonfiction, contemporary fiction, travel, biography, and current culture.
The paperback originals program is dedicated to producing new and fresh voices in genres such as African American Street Fiction and Young Adult.
Recent releases include *Dancing through Life: Lessons Learned On and Off the Dance Floor* by Antoinette Benevento and Edwin Dobb; *Knee Surgery: The Essential Guide to Total Knee Recovery* by Daniel Fulham O'Neill; *The Promise: Making Your Life Rich by Harnessing the Power of Your Mind* by Victor Davich; *Second Time Around* by Marcia Willett; *Perfect Figures: The Lore of Numbers and How We Learned to Count* by Bunny Crumpacker; *Symphony* by Jude Morgan; *A Charmed Life: Growing Up in Macbeth's Castle* by Liza Campbell; *Felt Jewelry: 25 Pieces to Make Using a Variety of Simple Felting Techniques* by Teresa Searle; *The Lady Upstairs: Dorothy Schiff and the New York Post* by Marilyn Nissenson; and *Single with Benefits* by Relentless Aaron.

Jennifer Enderlin, Vice President and Associate Publisher, St. Martin's Paperbacks, Executive Editor—"I grew up reading commercial women's fiction—haunting, romantic novels; sexy, hilarious novels; and three-hankie reads." She also writes, "And commercial nonfiction is another pleasure of mine: popular psychology, self-help, relationships, and memoir. I also love collections of humorous observational essays."

MINOTAUR

www.minotaurbooks.com

Minotaur publishes mystery and all its sub-genres, but doesn't kill itself with gravity. A comic crime novel is not an oxymoron at this imprint. The position at Minotaur is that a good mystery is any good novel that has a crime as the foundation of the story. St. Martin's Press began releasing mystery novels in the 1950s—publishing classics like *Enter A Murderer* by Ngaio Marsh—and created Minotaur in 1999 to recognize the importance of the genre to the list.

Andy Martin, formerly of Crown and Sterling, became Minotaur publisher in 2006; he has said that the fun in his job is discovering, launching, and marketing major new talent, like John Hart, Marcus Sakey, Chelsea Cain, and Louise Penny. Minotaur publishes about 135 books per year.

Recent Minotaur titles include *A Deadly Silver Sea* by Bob Morris; *The Lost Witness (Lena Gamble Novels)* by Robert Ellis; *Quick Study: A Murder 1010 Mystery* by Maggie Barbieri; *Teaser (Hallie Ahern Mysteries)* by Jan Brogan; *Bamboo and Blood: An Inspector O Novel* by James Church; *Spider Season: A Benjamin Justice Novel* by John Morgan Wilson; and *Baring Arms: A Me and Mr. Jones Mystery* by Jo-Ann Power.

Titles also representative of Minotaur's list include *A Deeper Sleep: A Kate Shugak Novel* by Dana Stabenow; *The Highly Effective Detective* by Richard Yancey; *Hog Wild: A Tarot Card Mystery* by Cathy Pickens; *Afterimage* by Kathleen George; *Deadly Shoals* by Joan Druett; and *Luck Be a Lady, Don't Die: A Rat Pack Mystery* by Robert J. Randisi.

Andrew Martin, Vice President and Publisher, Minotaur—Mysteries and crime fiction; everything from cozies and international thrillers to police procedurals and amateur sleuths

Ms. Kelley Ragland, Executive Editor, Minotaur—Mystery, suspense fiction, crime; "My taste in crime runs the gamut from cozy to hardboiled but is becoming increasingly dark and more serious."

THOMAS DUNNE BOOKS

www.thomasdunnebooks.com

The Thomas Dunne imprint produces roughly 200 titles per year—about 50/50 fiction/nonfiction—and covers a wide array of interests that include commercial fiction, mysteries, military histories, biographies, divination, politics, philosophy, humor, literary fiction, and current events.

Thomas Dunne editors have a wide range of tastes, backgrounds, even ages—from mid-twenties to late eighties—they believe that almost any book of commercial or literary merit will find a good home in their house.

Representative titles include *Preferred Lies: A Journey into the Heart of Scottish Golf* by Andrew Greig; *Siege of Heaven* by Tom Harper; *The Sword of Venice: Book Two of the Venetians* by Thomas Quinn; *Artisan Bread in Five Minutes a Day: The Discovery That Revolutionizes Home Baking* by Jeff Hertsberg and Zoe Francois; *A Boy Named Shel: The Life and Times of Shel Silverstein* by Lisa Rogak; and *Classic Cocktails: A Modern Shake* by Mark Kingwell.

Recent releases include *Exposed: Confessions of a Wedding Photographer* by Claire Lewis; *State of Confusion: Political Manipulation and the Assault on the American Mind* by Dr. Bryant Welch; *The Writing Class* by Jincy Willett; *The Adventure of Arthur Conan Doyle: A Biography* by Russell Miller; *The Edge of Terror: The Heroic Story of American Families Trapped in Japanese-occupied Philippines* by Scott Walker; *Absolute Honor: A Novel* by C.C. Humphreys; *Beautiful Sheep: Portraits of Champion Breeds* by Kathryn Dun; *Courage* by Alan Littell; *Sinatra in Hollywood* by Tom Santopietro; *In Search of Time: The Science of a Curious Dimension* by Dan Falk; *Radioman: An Eyewitness Account of Pearl Harbor and World War II in the Pacific* by Carol Edgemon Hipperson; and *The Great Comeback: How Abraham Lincoln Beat the Odds to Win the 1860 Republican Nomination* by Gary Ecelbarger.

The Tony Hillerman Prize for first mysteries set in the Southwest was announced in 2007. For details on the competition guidelines see the Web site.

Queries and SASEs should be directed to:

Thomas L. Dunne, Vice President, Executive Editor, Publisher—Eclectic interests, commercial women's fiction, mysteries, military histories, biographies, divination systems, politics, philosophy, humor, literary fiction, and current events; he says that many of the biggest authors he has personally edited have been British—Rosamunde Pilcher, Frederick Forsyth, Wilbur Smith, Michael Palin— but also he has edited first books by Americans Dan Brown and Madeleine Wickham (aka Sophie Kinsella). In nonfiction, he has a particular interest in politics, history, biography, and current events.

Peter Wolverton, Senior Editor and Associate Publisher—Fiction: commercial and popular literature, genre mysteries; and a wide range of nonfiction consistent with the Thomas Dunne list; he says: "During my seventeen years in the business, I've published a wide variety of titles, but inevitably I find myself drawn to sports books (of all kinds), explosive thrillers and mysteries, outdoor literature (a particular passion—I'm always looking for the next Stegner or Mosher), the early years of NASA and the Apollo missions, and I occasionally journey into every genre."

Ruth Cavin, Senior Editor and Associate Publisher—crime fiction, contemporary fiction, anecdotal science and medicine, novelties (quotation books); "Although people in publishing who know me at all think I publish only mystery novels, they're wrong." Although she does love good mysteries, she is free to pick out anything she likes as long as it's well-written, interesting, and she thinks it will sell.

Rob Kirkpatrick, Senior Editor—Pop culture, sports, politics, current events; "I'm on the lookout for strong, platform-friendly nonfiction titles in sports, pop culture, history, and politics, as well as (on a very, very select basis) fiction."

Erin Brown, Editor—Acquires women's fiction, ranging from commercial women's fiction to more literary novels, all featuring strong female characters. She writes that she is partial to mysteries with smart and sassy female sleuths.

Marcia Markland, Editor—Fiction and nonfiction: "As a former editor of The Mystery Guild, my taste naturally leans toward suspense fiction. My favorite category right now is what I think of as the semi-literary thriller. I also like police procedurals and legal thrillers. International suspense writing fascinates me. I devour disaster novels of any stripe, so if any given topic will make me lose sleep, that's the project for me." In nonfiction, she likes issue books, nature, and animals. She likes reading manuscripts that are a bit offbeat, and is most likely to request a manuscript that reflects a passionate belief on the part of the author, regardless of subject matter.

Karyn Marcus, Editor—Nonfiction with a focus on science, music, food, and humor; "I'm looking to acquire fiction projects which combine quality prose with clever plotting, particularly those with strong female protagonists. I'm also interested in writers working on a series of thrillers or historicals who are prolific enough to do a book a year. In nonfiction, my interests range from layman's science, psychology, and sociology to memoir and contemporary biography. Books about dogs, and animals in general, always make the top of my list."

Peter Joseph, Editor—History, biography/autobiography, narrative nonfiction, travel, humor, pop-culture, film, music, social history, mysteries, thrillers, historical and literary fiction. He also manages the Tony Hillerman Prize for first mysteries set in the Southwest.

Joel Ariaratnam, Editor—History, memoir, literary nonfiction; "A few areas of special interest to me are: science (mathematics, physics, biology, and the history of science), politics, social and cultural studies, memoir, and international fiction."

Toni Plummer, Associate Editor—Fiction and nonfiction, including sassy relationship advice, humor, and mysteries; "My nonfiction interests include memoir, narrative, advice/relationships, and social issues. My taste in mysteries runs the gamut, from gritty police procedurals (*Bound by Blood* by Rick Nelson) to eloquent historicals (*City of Silver* by Annamaria Alfieri; set in Peru, 1650) to hilarious cozies (*Murder at Longbourn* by Tracy Kiely; think Jane Austen meets the classic English mystery)."

Diana Szu, Associate Editor—Chick lit, reference and lifestyle, mysteries, fiction with Asian hooks; "When I first arrived at Thomas Dunne Books, my reading list primarily consisted of literary and ethnic fiction--particularly anything Asian--as well as religious and sociological nonfiction on modern-day issues. While these genres continue to be my favorites, I also do enjoy well-crafted women's fiction, mysteries, and narrative nonfiction with a compelling voice, in addition to cookbooks, crafting guides, and memoirs/biographies.

Kathleen Gilligan, Associate Editor—Women's fiction and memoirs; "Whether it's a narrative of motherhood, or a quirky 24-year-old with an aversion to lipstick; I'm acquiring works with curious, genuine narrators—writing of a profound and well-crafted voice."

John Schoenfelder, Editorial Assistant—Fiction, science fiction, mysteries, crime; "I look for clarity of content that immediately grabs one's attention and simply, makes me want to turn to the next page."

TRUMAN TALLEY BOOKS

The Truman Talley imprint is run by Truman "Mac" Talley, who has been one of New York's most respected editors over the past 40 years. The list focuses on law, business, and leadership.

Recent titles include *The Time of Their Lives: The Golden Age of Great American Book Publishers, Their Editors, and Authors* by Al Silverman; *The Iranian Time Bomb: The Mullah Zealots' Quest for Destruction* by Michael A. Ledeen; *The Swordless Samurai: Leadership Wisdom of Japan's Sixteenth-Century Legend—Toyotomi Hideyoshi* by Kitami Masao and Tim Clark; *Taste: Acquiring What Money Can't Buy* by Letitia Baldrige; and *Panasonic: The Largest Corporate Restructuring in History* by Francis McInerney.

Direct queries and SASEs to:

Truman Talley, Publisher—"I seek out strong nonfiction titles that take on big topics."

TOM DOHERTY ASSOCIATES

FORGE

ORB

SEVEN SEAS

TOR

TOR TEEN / STARSCAPE BOOKS

175 Fifth Avenue, New York NY 10010

212-674-5151   fax: 212-420-9314

www.tor-forge.com

Tom Doherty Associates is a publishing company known for its science fiction and fantasy list, including the best-selling *Sword of Truth* series by Terry Goodkind. It has been part of the Holtzbrinck Group since 1995 and publishes under five imprints: Forge, Orb, Seven Seas, Tor, and Tor Teen / Starscape.

Tor Books is the world's most successful science fiction imprint and has won the Locus Award for Best Science Fiction publisher for the past fifteen years in a row. It publishes science fiction and fantasy in both paperback and hardcover formats. Forge Books publishes nonfiction, thrillers, suspense, mysteries, historicals, and Westerns, targeted to the mainstream audience. Orb publishes reprints of science fiction classics. Children's and middle grade titles are published under the Starscape imprint; young adult titles are published under Tor Teen. Seven Seas is manga.

Recent Tor titles include *The Breath of God* by Harry Turtledove; *Fathom* by Cherie Priest; *The Stars, Like Dust* by Isaac Asimov; *Busted Flush* by George R. R. Martin; *Bones of the Dragon* by Margaret Weis and Tracy Hickman;

Fools' Experiments by Edward M. Lerner; *Thirteen Orphans* by Jane Lindskold; and *The Lord-Protector's Daughter (Corean Chronicles)* by L. E. Modesitt.

Recent Forge titles include *Dreams Beneath Your Feet* by Win Blevins; *Harold and Me: My Life, Love, and Hard Times with Harold Robbins* by Jann Robbins; *By the Sword: A Repairman Jack Novel* by F. Paul Wilson; *An Irish Country Christmas* by Patrick Taylor; *Vulcan's Fire: Harold Coyle's Strategic Solutions, Inc.* by Harold Coyle and Barrett Tillman; and Rogue Warrior: *Dictator's Ransom* by Richard Marcinko and Jim DeFelice.

Recent Orb titles include *Fractions: The First Half of the Fall Revolution* by Ken MacLeod; *The Phoenix Guards* by Steven Brust; *Inferno* by Larry Niven and Jerry Pournelle; *The Vampire Tapestry* by Suzy McKee Charnas; and *The Voyage of the Space Beagle* by A. E. van Vogt.

Recent Starscape and Tor Teen titles include *They Came From Below* by Blake Nelson; *Little Brother* by Cory Doctorow; *The Night Children* by Kit Reed; *The Secret of Laurel Oaks* by Lois Ruby; and *Chance Fortune in the Shadow Zone* by Shane Berryhill.

Recent titles from Seven Seas include *Dragon Blade Warrior* by Rieko Koshimizu; *Hollow Fields* by Madeleine Rosca; *Destiny's Hand* by Nunzio DeFilippis, Christina Weir, and Mel Calingo; and *Avalon: Web of Magic* by Rachel Roberts.

Thomas Doherty has an open submission policy, which is explained in detail on their Web site. In short, send the first three chapters and a 3-10 page synopsis, with a cover letter, and a business-sized SASE for their response. Your manuscript will be recycled after it is reviewed by a member of their editorial staff and who will then send you a letter in response.

Patrick Nielsen Hayden, Senior Editor—Science fiction

David Hartwell, Editor—Science fiction

Bob Gleason, Editor—Thrillers, mysteries, crime, science fiction

Heather Osborne, Editor—Women's fiction, fantasy

Eric Raab, Editor—Thrillers, crime, mysteries, science fiction

Paul Stevens, Editor—Science fiction, fantasy, horror, global hooks

Claire Eddy, Editor—Mysteries, thrillers, fantasy

Susan Chang, Senior Editor—Children's and young adult

Anna Genoese, Editor—Paranormal romance

NEWS CORPORATION

News Corporation is a worldwide media and entertainment corporation with subsidiaries that include HarperCollins, one of the world's largest English-language publishers. News Corp. chairman and major shareholder Rupert Murdoch turned his family's business into a multinational media corporation, which now has 40,000 employees and annual revenues in excess of $28 billion.

News Corp.'s $69 billion in assets include MySpace.com, Fox Broadcasting, Twentieth Century Fox, Blue Sky Studios, Dow Jones, the *New York Post*, and many, many other newspapers, radio stations, and magazines.

HARPERCOLLINS PUBLISHERS

HARPERCOLLINS GENERAL BOOKS GROUP

HARPERCOLLINS CHILDREN'S BOOKS GROUP

ZONDERVAN

HarperCollins publishes a diverse list of commercial, trade, professional, academic, and mass market books in hardcover, paperback, and multimedia editions—fiction, nonfiction, poetry, history, reference, business, children's books, cookbooks, romance, mystery, art, and style. If the subject exists, there's likely a HarperCollins title representing it, or will be very soon.

Recent HarperCollins mega-hits include *The Daring Book for Girls* by Andrea J. Buchanan and Miriam Peskowitz, *The Dangerous Book for Boys* by Conn and Hal Iggulden, *Deceptively Delicious* by Jessica Seinfeld, and *Lemony Snicket's A Series of Unfortunate Events* books.

HarperCollins's most recent initiatives include digitizing their content to create a global digital warehouse. As well, the publisher is focusing on building itself into a truly global publishing company rather than simply a company with publishing operations around the world, with significant initiatives in China and India.

Harper and Row (founded in 1817) was an early publisher of Mark Twain, the Bronte sisters, and Charles Dickens. In the U.K., William Collins and Sons, founded in 1819, published H. G. Wells, C. S. Lewis, and Agatha Christie. HarperCollins formed when News Corp. acquired both of these publishers in 1987 and 1990. The publisher has continued to expand with subsequent acquisitions including Fourth Estate, Avon Books, William Morrow, and Amistad. The company has revenues that top $1 billion annually.

With more than thirty imprints, HarperCollins serves an enormous audience and provides a home for hundreds of authors, from debut novelists like Bryan Charles (*Grab On To Me Tightly As If I Knew the Way*) to former presidents like Ronald Reagan (*The Reagan Diaries*).

For submissions to all imprints, please note that HarperCollins Publishers prefers material submitted by literary agents and previously published authors.

HARPERCOLLINS GENERAL BOOKS GROUP

AMISTAD PRESS

AVON

COLLINS

COLLINS DESIGN

ECCO

EOS

HARPER PERENNIAL

HARPER PERENNIAL MODERN CLASSICS

HARPER STUDIO

HARPERAUDIO / CAEDMON

HARPERCOLLINS

HARPERENTERTAINMENT

HARPERONE

MORROW COOKBOOKS

WILLIAM MORROW

RAYO

10 East 53rd Street, New York, NY 10022-5299

212-207-7000

www.harpercollins.com

blogs: publishinginsider.typepad.com

www.olivereader.com

cruelestmonth.typepad.com

HarperCollins General Books Group is a broad-based publisher with strengths in literary and commercial fiction, business books, cookbooks, mystery, romance, reference, religious, and spiritual books. The company has revenues that top $1 billion annually.

Recent best-sellers from HarperCollins include *Lady Killer* by Lisa Scottoline, *My Grandfather's Son* by Clarence Thomas, *The Reagan Diaries* by Ronald Reagan, *At the Center of the Storm* by George Tenet, *The Measure of a Man* by Sidney Poitier, *The Pursuit of Happyness* by Chris Gardner, *The Volumetrics Eating Plan* by Barbara Rolls, *Bad Dog, Marley!* by John Grogan, and *Warriors: The New Prophecy* by Erin Hunter.

In 2008, HarperCollins co-founded a book-to-film unit, Sharp Independent HarperCollins, helmed by producer Jeff Sharp. They hope to get more movies made from HarperCollins books; one novel optioned for Sharp and acquired for HarperCollins in 2008 is *The Leisure Seeker*, by Michael Zadoorian.

The newest HarperCollins imprint, Harper Studio, founded in 2008 by former Hyperion founder and publisher Bob Miller, is defined as a publishing studio that challenges conventional trade standards, including royalties and returns.

A former imprint, Regan Books, was dissolved late in 2006 when founder Judith Regan was fired from HarperCollins after the company decide to not release *If I Did It*, O.J. Simpson's hypothetical murder confession. Regan, who was successful with best-sellers like *How to Make Love Like a Porn Star* by Jenna Jamison, filed a defamation suit that was settled out of court by HarperCollins in 2008.

Also in 2008, CEO Jane Friedman left the company and was replaced by company president Brian Murray.

A great and unique development at Harper is Author Tools, a group of Web based applications to support the development of author Web pages, with features like blogs, coming attractions, Q&As, photos, links to other articles and posts, and browse inside widgets.

HarperCollins has three blogs, which will be useful to check for insider tips and information. One of the blogs, called Publishing Insider, is from marketing guru Carl Lennertz and is at http://publishinginsider.typepad.com. The Harper Perennial blog, named after their oval-shaped logo, is The Olive Reader, at http://www.olivereader.com. The HarperCollins poetry blog, called Cruelest Month, is at http://cruelestmonth.typepad.com. Many of the imprints also have pages on MySpace.com.

AMISTAD PRESS

Amistad Press publishes works by and about people of African descent and on subjects and themes that have significant influence on the intellectual, cultural, and historical perspectives of a world audience. The house published Edward P. Jones' Pulitzer Prize-winning novel, *The Known World*.

This imprint is named for the 1839 slave rebellion on board a Spanish schooner, *Amistad*, and the resulting 1841 Supreme Court case that found the rebels to be free people. The Africans traveled home in 1842.

Newest releases from Amistad include *The Legs Are the Last to Go: Aging, Acting, Marrying, and Other Things I Learned the Hard Way* by Diahann Carroll; *Alek: My Life from Sudanese Refugee to International Supermodel* by Alek Wek; *Deconstructing Sammy: Music, Money Madness, and the Mob* by Matt Birkbeck; *The Naked Truth: Young, Beautiful, and (HIV) Positive* by Marvelyn Brown and Courtney Martin; *Start Where You Are* by Chris Gardner and Mim E. Rivas; and *Words of Wisdom: Daily Affirmations of Faith from Run's House to Yours* by Reverend Run.

Direct query letters and SASE's to:

Dawn Davis, Editorial Director—All categories, including memoir, business, fiction, and history

Christina Morgan, Editor—All categories including biography

AVON

e-mail: avonromance@harpercollins.com

Founded in 1941, Avon Books is the second-oldest paperback publishing house in the U.S. Acquired by HarperCollins in 1999, Avon publishes titles for adults and young adult readers. It is recognized for pioneering the historical romance category and continues to produce commercial literature for the broadest possible audience in mass market paperback format.

Avon includes several imprints. In trade paperback, Avon A focuses on contemporary romance and other chick lit titles. An imprint called Avon Red publishes steamy erotic romance. A new imprint, Avon Inspire, moves into Christian fiction for women, and is run from HarperOne in San Francisco. (You may read more about Avon Inspire in the HarperOne section, below).

Recent Avon mass market books include *Bedtime for Bonsai* by Elaine Fox; *Everlasting* by Kathleen Woodiwiss; *The Highland Groom* by Sarah Gabriel; *Never Dare a Duke* by Gayle Callen; *To Sin with a Stranger* by Kathryn Caskie *When the Duke Returns* by Eloisa James; *All I Want for Christmas Is a Vampire* by Kerrelyn Sparks; and *The Bride Price* by Anne Mallory.

Avon trade paper titles include *Confessions of a Beauty Addict* by Nadine Habosh; *Caesar's Women* by Colleen McCullogh; *Bedding Down* by Rachel Kramer Bussel; *With Violets* by Elizabeth Robards; and *Dangerous Heart* by Tracey Bateman.

Avon Books is actively seeking imaginative stories that can establish new voices in historical and contemporary romance, romantic suspense and paranormal, and African American romance. Detailed manuscript and submission guidelines are available online or by written request with SASE.

Send a brief e-mail query with no more than a two-page description of the book, with the word Query in the subject area. Do not send attachments and do not include the title of the manuscript in the subject area as this often leads to spam filtering. You will receive a response one way or another within approximately two weeks. The e-mail address is: avonromance@harpercollins.com.

Liate Stehlik, Senior Vice President, Publisher

Carrie Feron, Vice President and Executive Editor, Avon and William Morrow

Lucia Macro, Executive Editor—All categories including historical and contemporary romance

Lyssa Keusch, Executive Editor, Avon and William Morrow—Especially historical romances and thrillers

May **Chen**, Editor—All categories including historical, erotica, and paranormal

Erica **Tsang**, Executive Editor—All categories especially historical

COLLINS

Well-known in the U.K., nonfiction imprint Collins made its debut in the U.S. in late 2005. Collins is comprised of five groups: Collins Wellness, Collins Reference, Collins Lifestyle, Collins Design, and Collins Business. Also, Collins has formed a joint publishing program with Smithsonian Books, under the leadership of Bruce Nichols.

Current books include *Beyond Wall Street: The Rise of Private Equity and the Future of Investing* by David Rubenstein; *Campaigning for President* by Jordan M. Wright; *Do Cats Hear With Their Feet?: Where Cats Come From, What We Know About Them, and What They Think About Us* by Jake Page; *The Great Life Makeover: A Mid-Life Couples' Guide to Sex, Weight, and Mood for the Best Years of Your Life—and Your Relationship* by Daniel Monti and Anthony Bazzan; *The Natural History of America* by American Museum of Natural History; *Punching In: One Man's Undercover Adventures on the Front Lines of American's Best-Known Companies* by Alex Frankel; and *Who Gives: Candid Conversations with the World's Most Successful Philanthropists* by Lisa Endlich.

Direct query letters and SASEs to:

Steve **Ross**, President and Publisher—Pop culture, memoir, media

Bruce **Nichols**, VP, Publisher, Collins—Reference, Smithsonian, and books covering politics, current events, sports, and humor

Mary Ellen **O'Neill**, Publisher, Wellness/Lifestyle—Author-platform-driven advice, self-help, how-to, health (emotional, physical, and, occasionally, spiritual)

Hollis **Heimbouch**, Publisher, Collins Business—All business titles, women's leadership

Adam **Bellow**, VP, Executive Editor—Narrative nonfiction, including politics, history, current events

Nancy **Miller**, VP, Executive Editor—Narrative nonfiction including science, psychology, and memoir

Gillian **Blake**, Executive Editor—Narrative nonfiction, particularly memoir and history

Serena **Jones**, Editor—Narrative nonfiction including memoir and lifestyle

Bill **Strachan**, Editor—Narrative nonfiction, including music, politics

Toni **Sciarra**, Executive Editor, Wellness/Lifestyle/Reference—Practical nonfiction with special interest in health, medical, wellness, psychology, lifestyle issues, and parenting

Caroline **Sutton**, Executive Editor, Wellness/Lifestyle—Practical nonfiction, wellness and lifestyle, particularly health and medicine

Ben **Loehnen**, Senior Editor, Collins Business—All business areas especially marketing, psychology, and the Internet

Donna Sanzone, Executive Editor— Reference, Smithsonian, and books covering natural history, art, American history and culture, and sciences

Lisa Hacken, Editor— Illustrated reference in natural history, science, American history and culture and other topics suitable for Collins/Smithsonian

Stephanie Meyers, Asst. Editor— Reference, Smithsonian, and books covering politics, current events, sports, and humor

COLLINS DESIGN

Collins Design books focus on all areas of design including architecture, interior design, graphic design, animation, art, style, and popular culture. They seek to publish stunning, visual books that capture and illuminate trends.

Recent Collins Design books include *Sci-Fi Art: A Graphic History* by Alex Summersby; *Gothic Art Now* by Jasmine Becket-Griffith; *Hollywood Pinups* by Timothy White; *Project Fashion: Mix, Match, and Color Your Own Line* by Maite Lafuente; *Style File: The World's Most Elegantly Dressed* by Ik Ud; *Ultimate Illustration* by Eva Minguet; and *Vintage Shoes* by Caroline Cox.

Direct queries and SASEs to:

Marta Schooler, Vice President and Publisher, Collins Design

Elizabeth Sullivan, Senior Editor—Particularly pop culture, fashion, style

EOS

A science fiction and fantasy imprint, Eos has gained a positive reputation for its progressive editorial style, bold packaging, and innovative promotional campaigns. Named for the Greek goddess of the dawn, Eos looks for work that "transcends the ordinary in science fiction and fantasy." Best-selling Eos authors include Raymond E. Feist, Anne McCaffrey, and Gregory Benford.

Recent Eos books include *Queen of Oblivion (The Heartstone Trilogy)* by Gates Carwyn and Todd Fahnestock; *A Fistful of Charms* by Kim Harrison; *Avatars: Book Three: Kingdom of Twilight* by Tui T. Sutherland; *Daylight Runner* by Oisin McGann; *Rogue's Home: A Knight and Rogue Novel* by Hilari Bell; and *The Otherworldlies* by Jennifer Anne Kogler.

Direct query letters and SASEs to:

Lisa Gallagher, Publisher, William Morrow, HarperEntertainment, and Eos

Jennifer Brehl, Editorial Director, William Morrow, Eos

Diana Gill, Executive Editor, Eos—Especially fantasy

Emily Krump, Editor, Eos—Especially Science Fiction

HARPER PERENNIAL

Home of such esteemed and award-winning authors as Barbara Kingsolver, Ann Patchett, Howard Zinn, and Harper Lee, Harper Perennial has been publishing fiction, nonfiction and the classics for nearly 50 years. Perennial's broad range varies from Matt Groening's *The Simpsons* to Thomas Moore's *Care of the Soul*. A trade paperback format imprint, Harper Perennial publishes fiction and nonfiction originals and reprints.

Titles representative of Perennial's list include *A Broom of One's Own: Words on Writing, Housecleaning, and Life* by Nancy Peacock; *Sick: The Untold Story of America's Health Care Crisis—and the People Who Pay the Price* by Jonathan Cohn; *The Camel Bookmobile: A Novel* by Masha Hamilton; *Daughters of the North* by Sarah Hall; and *Dog Years: A Memoir* by Mark Doty.

Recent titles include *Savage Kingdom* by Benjamin Wooley; *Meeting Point* by Roisin McAuley; *Endangered Species* by Stephen M. Younger, PhD; *Dog Years* by Mark Doty; *Who by Fire* by Diana Spechler; and *The Unbearable Lightness of Being* by Milan Kundera.

Direct queries and SASEs to:

Carrie Kania, Publisher, Harper Perennial and Harper Paperbacks—Commercial and literary fiction

Cal Morgan, VP, Editorial Director, Harper Perennial and Harper Paperbacks

Jeanette Perez, Editor, Perennial—Fiction, including coming of age, debuts, and crime hooks

John Williams, Editor, Harper Perennial—Fiction, particularly humor

Michael Signorelli, Editor, Harper Perennial—Fiction, crime hooks

HARPER PERENNIAL MODERN CLASSICS

The Harper Perennial Modern Classics imprint is home to many great writers and their most significant works. Featuring classic books from writers as diverse as Richard Wright, Harper Lee, Thomas Pynchon, Aldous Huxley, Sylvia Plath, and Thornton Wilder, Harper Perennial Modern Classics is the foundation stone for Harper Perennial itself. The newly redesigned Harper Perennial Modern Classics line is being expanded to include more contemporary classics.

Recent titles include *Seraph on the Suwanee* by Zora Neale Hurston; *Basic Writings* by Martin Heidegger; *The Phenomenon of Man* by De Chardin Pier Teilhard; *The Female Eunuch* by Germaine Greer; *Zen and the Art of Motorcycle Maintenance: An Inquiry into Values* by Robert M. Pirsig; and *The Golden Notebook* by Doris Lessing.

HARPER STUDIO

Harper Studio is the newest HarperCollins imprint, founded in 2008 by former Hyperion founder and publisher Bob Miller, who seeks to set up a new business model. It is defined as a publishing studio that challenges conventional trade standards, including royalties and book store returns. Authors will be compensated through a profit-sharing model, rather than royalties, and books will be promoted utilizing online publicity, advertising, and marketing. Books for the new imprint will be "short" like Steve Martin's *Shopgirl*, and will cost around $20. This imprint will release 25 new titles per year.

Miller is looking for new authors and established authors looking to publish something less commercial. "Our goal will be effectively to publish books that might not otherwise emerge in an increasingly 'big book' environment, an environment in which established authors are under enormous pressure to top their previous successes, while new authors are finding it harder and harder to be published at all," he stated.

Other titles that Bob Miller acquired at Hyperion that give clues to his future acquisition interests include *The Five People You Meet in Heaven* by Mitch Albom and *The Best-Loved Poems of Jacqueline Kennedy Onassis*.

Query with SASE to:

Bob Miller, Publisher

Debbie Stier, SVP, Associate Publisher

Julia Cheiffetz, Senior Editor

HARPERAUDIO / CAEDMON

HarperAudio proudly traces its roots back to 1952, when Dylan Thomas first recorded for the Caedmon label. For more than five decades Harper Audio/Caedmon has been synonymous not only with distinguished poets reading their works, but also with equally distinguished authors and readers performing classic and contemporary texts.

HarperAudio is expanding its audio book publishing program for both children and adults, achieving strong sales and recognition for quality. Award-winning titles include *Charlie and the Chocolate Factory* by Roald Dahl performed by Eric Idle; *Winnie-the-Pooh* by A. A. Milne performed by Jim Broadbent; and *The John Cheever Audio Collection*, performed by Meryl Streep and George Plimpton.

HARPERCOLLINS

HarperCollins produces adult hardcover books, trade paperbacks, and mass market paperback editions that cover the breadth of trade publishing categories, including feature biographies (celebrities, sports, and historical), business, mysteries and thrillers, popular culture, humor, inspiration, and how-to (including cookbooks and health), in addition to works in most reference categories. The editors strive to find books that come from the heart of our literary, popular, and intellectual culture.

Best-selling authors include Milan Kundera, Michael Chabon, Barbara Kingsolver, Michael Crichton, Dr. Laura Schlessinger, Emeril Lagasse, Tony Hillerman, Barbara Taylor Bradford, Louise Erdrich, Anne Rivers Siddons, and Ursula K. Le Guin.

Recent fiction books include *Emma's Table* by Philip Galanes; *Goldengrove* by Francine Prose; *In the Dark* by Mark Billingham; *Everything Under the Sky* by Matilde Asensi; *City of Refuge* by Tom Piazza; *An Expert in Murder* by Nicola Upson; and *Bright Shiny Morning* by James Frey.

Recent nonfiction titles include *Guyland: The Perilous World Where Boys Become Men* by Michael Kimmel; *Going Dutch: How England Plundered Holland's Glory* by Lisa Jardine; *Epilogue: A Memoir* by Anne Roiphe; *The Closing of the American Border: Terrorism, Immi-*

gration, and Security Since 9/11 by Edward Alden; and *For the Thrill of It: Leopold, Loeb, and the Murder That Shocked Chicago* by Simon Baatz.

Direct queries and SASEs to:

Jonathan Burnham, Publisher—Celebrity and high profile memoir and fiction

David Hirshey, Executive Editor—Sports, pop culture, celebrity books, politics, current affairs

Tim Duggan, Executive Editor—Serious nonfiction, literary fiction

Carolyn Marino, Executive Editor, William Morrow— Commercial fiction and memoir including thrillers, mysteries, crime,

Claire Wachtel, Executive Editor—Fiction, memoirs, narrative nonfiction

Cal Morgan, VP, Executive Editor—Acquires hardcovers for Harper

Kate Hamill, Editor—Fiction, memoir, sports

Matthew Benjamin, Editor—Sports, pop culture, lifestyle, how-to, reference

Lisa Sharkey, Senior Vice President, Creative Development Team—Relationships, lifestyle, advice

Doug Grad, Senior Editor, Creative Development Team—Fiction (including debut) and nonfiction (including sports, crime, current events)

Matt Harper, Editor, Creative Development Team—Humor, crime, health

Stephanie Fraser, Associate Editor, Creative Development Team

HARPERENTERTAINMENT

HarperEntertainment editors look for cutting-edge entertainment books with edgy personalities. This imprint publishes high-profile memoirs, and television and movie tie-ins, releasing 12–15 new hardcover books per year.

Recent titles include *Here's the Story* by Maureen McCormick; *Pieces of My Heart: A Life* by Robert Wagner; *Coraline Movie Tie-In Edition* by Neil Gaiman and Dave McKean; *Got the Life* by Reggie Arvizu; and *Marley Movie Tie-in Edition* by John Grogan.

Direct queries and SASEs to:

Lisa Gallagher, Publisher, William Morrow, HarperEntertainment, and Eos

Mauro DiPreta, Editorial Director— Pop culture, humor, commercial nonfiction

Erin Stein, Executive Editor—Entertainment

HARPERONE

353 Sacramento Street, Suite 500, San Francisco, CA 94111

415-477-4400

In 2007, HarperSanFrancisco changed its name to HarperOne to completely dispel the idea that it is a regional publisher, not that we ever thought that it was. One look at the list tells you that this imprint publishes books important and subtle, large and small, titles that explore the full range of spiritual and religious literature. It releases about 85 titles annually, with a backlist of some 800 titles.

HarperOne strives to be the preeminent publisher of the most important books across the spectrum of religion, spirituality, and personal growth, with authors who are the world's leading voices of wisdom, learning, faith, change, hope and healing.

By respecting all spiritual traditions, the editors strive to offer their readers paths leading to personal growth and well-being. In addition to traditional religious titles, HarperOne publishes inspirational fiction. Classic titles include *The Alchemist* by Paulo Coehlo; *The Heart of Christianity: Rediscovering a Life of Faith* by Marcus J. Borg; *God's Politics: Why the Right Gets it Wrong and the Left Doesn't Get It* by Jim Wallis; *The Essential Rumi* by Coleman Banks; *The Right Questions: Ten Essential Questions to Guide You to an Extraordinary Life* by Debbie Ford; and *The World's Religions* by Huston Smith.

HarperOne started a new line of Christian romance fiction for women in 2007 under the Avon Inspire imprint; it is edited by Cindy DiTiberio. She said, "Avon Inspire is gentle reading, safe reading. They end with a kiss and a proposal. ...It's *Sex & the City* without the sex." This imprint publishes one historical and one contemporary romance per season. Avon Inspire titles include *Hidden (Sisters of the Heart)* by Shelley Shepard Gray; *Twice Loved (Belles of Timber Creek)* by Lori Copeland; and *For Pete's Sake (The Piper Love Chronicles)* by Linda Windsor.

In 2008, HarperOne initiated an annual award, the Huston Smith Publishing Prize, for previously unpublished writers who complete manuscripts that are effective in promoting religious understanding. Details are available from the editors and at www.hustonsmithprize.com.

Recent titles representative of HarperOne list include *The One Thing Holding You Back: Unleashing the Power of Emotional Connection* by Raphael Cushnir; *Discovering God: The Origins of the Great Religions and the Evolution of Belief* by Rodney Stark; *Born Country: My Life in Alabama—How Faith, Family, and Music Brought Me Home* by Randy Owen; *Christianity's Dangerous Idea: The Protestant Revolution—A History from the Sixteenth Century to the Twenty-First* by Alister McGrath; *Jesus: A Story of the Man Who Would Become Christ* by Deepak Chopra; and *The Nag Hammadi Scriptures: The Revised and Updated Translation of Sacred Gnostic Texts Complete in One Volume* by Marvin Meyer and James M. Robinson.

Query letters and SASEs should be directed to:

Mark Tauber, Senior VP, Publisher—Books on hybrid topics, such as the intersection of religion and politics, parenting and spirituality, and the Christian green movement

Michael Maudlin, VP, Editorial Director

Gideon Weil, Executive Editor—Buddhism, meditation, lifestyle

Eric Brandt, Senior Editor—Science, world religions, finance, lifestyle, narrative nonfiction

Roger Freet, Senior Editor—Memoir, music, history, Christianity, fiction

Cynthia DiTiberio, Associate Editor—Avon Inspire, nonfiction for HarperOne

Jan Weed, Asst. Editor—Lifestyle

MORROW COOKBOOKS

Morrow has a long standing history of publishing some of the finest cookbooks in the industry, including *The Cake Bible* by Rose Levy Beranbaum; *Cookwise: The Secrets of Cooking Revealed* by Shirley Corriher; *Authentic Mexican* by Rick Bayless and Deann Groen Bayless; and *Chez Panisse Vegetables* by Alice L. Waters.

Recent books include *Simple Italian Snacks: More Recipes from America's Favorite Panini Bar* by Jason Denton and Katheryn Kellinger; *Hometown Get-Togethers: Memorable Meals for Great Gatherings* by Candace Floyd and Jill Melton; *Impossible to Easy: 125 Delicious Recipes to Help You Put Great Meals on the Table Every Day* by Robert Irvine and Brian O'Reilly; *Autumn Gatherings: Casual Food to Enjoy with Family and Friends* by Rick Rodgers; and *Real Food for Healthy Kids: 200+ Easy, Wholesome Recipes* by Tanya Wenman Steel and Tracey Seaman.

Direct queries and SASEs to:

David Sweeney, Cookbook Director, Editor

WILLIAM MORROW

William Morrow, acquired in 1999 by HarperCollins Publishing, is one of the nation's leading publishers of general trade books, including best-selling fiction, nonfiction, and cookbooks.

William Morrow has an 80-year legacy of bringing fiction and nonfiction to the broadest possible audience, including works from best-selling authors Bruce Feiler, Neil Gaiman, Dennis Lehane, Neal Stephenson, John Grogan, Elmore Leonard, Ray Bradbury, Steven Levitt and Stephen J. Dubner, Susan Elizabeth Phillips, Christopher Moore, Sena Jeter Naslund, James Rollins, and Cokie Roberts.

Recent nonfiction titles include *Asian Dining Rules: Essential Strategies for Eating Out at Japanese, Chinese, Southeast Asian, Korean, and Indian Restaurants* by Steven A. Shaw; *Beef: The Untold Story of How Cattle Made the Modern World* by Andrew Rimas and Evan Fraser; *Drinking Problems at the Fountain of Youth* by Beth Teitell; *Tales from the Dad Side: Misadventures in Fatherhood* by Steve Doocy; *Happy Hour is for Amateurs: A Lost Decade in the World's Worst Profession* by Philadelphia Lawyer; *Six Six Six: The FBI Agent, the Mob Killer, and the Bloody Alliance the Feds Tried to Hide* by Peter Lance; *The Rise of the Fourth Reich: The Secret Societies That Threaten to Take Over America* by Jim Marr; and *It Word* by Jesse Sheidlower.

Recent fiction includes *Desperately Seeking Sushi: A Madeline Bean Culinary Mystery* by Jerrilyn Farmer; *The Dracula Dossier: A Novel of Suspense* by James Reese; *Ghost Radio* by Leopoldo Gout; *The Given Day* by Dennis Lehane; *Anathem* by Neal Stephenson; *The Black Tower* by Louis Bayard; *The Orphan in the Tower* by Louis Bayard; and *Goodbye and Amen: A Novel* by Beth Gutcheon.

Direct query letters and SASEs to:

Lisa Gallagher, Publisher, William Morrow, HarperEntertainment, and Eos

Jennifer Brehl, Editorial Director, William Morrow, Eos

Carolyn Marino, Executive Editor—Commercial fiction, mysteries, suspense, and women's fiction

Marjorie Braman, VP, Executive Editor, William Morrow—Fiction, thrillers, mysteries, religion and crime hooks, debut novels

Peter Hubbard, Editor, William Morrow—Science fiction, popular culture, science

Laurie Chittenden, Executive Editor—Commercial nonfiction and fiction

Lyssa Keusch, Executive Editor, Avon and William Morrow—Commercial fiction

Diana Gill, Executive Editor, Eos and William Morrow—Science Fiction, fantasy

Henry Ferris, Executive Editor—Commercial nonfiction and fiction, politics, humor

David Highfill, Executive Editor—Commercial nonfiction and fiction, sports, memoir

Cassie Jones, Executive Editor—Nonfiction, including fashion, lifestyle

David Sweeney, Cookbook Director, Editor—Food, lifestyle

Jennifer Pooley, Editor—Commercial nonfiction and fiction, humor, memoir, sports, paranormal, debut fiction

Sarah Durand, Editor—Commercial nonfiction and fiction, debut fiction, thrillers, science, lifestyle

Katherine Nintzel, Editor—Fiction, Science Fiction, fantasy

RAYO

Rayo publishes hardcover and paperback books that exemplify the diversity within Hispanic communities, in both English and Spanish-language editions. Rayo strives to connect culture with thought and to invigorate tradition with spirit. The imprint's eclectic publishing list has included titles in both nonfiction and fiction since it was founded in 2000. Because of the line's continual success, it has expanded to include more bilingual children's books, spiritual, self-help, and general reference titles. Rayo publishes 75 titles per year.

Recent award-winning titles include *The Holy Vote* by Ray Suarez; *The Money In You!* by Julie Stav; *The Love Diet* by Mabel Iam; *The World Cup* by Fernando Fiore; *Cautivado por la Alegria* by C. S. Lewis; *Celia* by Celia Cruz with Ana Cristina Reymundo; and *La Ola Latina* by Jorge Ramos.

Other recent Rayo titles include *A Vivir Bien!: Usa lo que Tienes para Conseguir lo que Quieres* by Marilu Henner; *Revela Tu Brillo: Los Cuatro Pasos para Transformar Tu Vida y Revelar lo Mejor de Ti* by Simon T. Bailey; *En los tiempos de guerra: La historia de un soldado* by Ricardo S. Sanchez and Donald T. Phillips; *El Libro de la Moda* by Nina Garcia; *Al Brode del Abismo: Novela* by Benjamin Alire Saenz; and *Que Hay Detras de tu Nombre* by Mabel Iam.

Direct queries and SASEs to:

Rene Alegria, Publisher

HARPERCOLLINS CHILDREN'S BOOKS GROUP

AMISTAD PRESS

COLLINS

JOANNA COTLER BOOKS

EOS

LAURA GERINGER BOOKS

GREENWILLOW BOOKS

HARPERCOLLINS CHILDREN'S BOOKS

HARPERFESTIVAL

HARPERTEEN

HARPERTROPHY

RAYO

KATHERINE TEGEN BOOKS

1350 Avenue of the Americas, New York, NY 10019

212-261-6500

www.harpercollinschildrens.com

www.harperteen.com

The broad range of imprints within HarperCollins Children's Group reflects the strength of house as it both embraces new markets and values traditional literature for children.

Bestsellers include *The End* by Lemony Snicket, *Fancy Nancy and the Posh Puppy* by Jane O'Connor, *Bridge to Terabithia* by Katherine Paterson, *The Night Before Christmas* by Clement Moore, *Is There Really a Human Race?* by Jamie Lee Curtis, *Charlotte's Web The Movie Storybook* by Kate Egan, and *Thanks to You* by Julie Andrews and Emma Hamilton,

AMISTAD PRESS

Amistad publishes works by and about people of African descent on subjects and themes that have significant influence on the intellectual, cultural, and historical perspectives of a world audience. Amistad for young readers is the home of Nina Crews, David Diaz, Julius Lester, Jerry Pinkney, Joyce Carol Thomas, and Donna L. Washington.

Recent titles include *Guardian* by Julius Lester; *Doo-Wop Pop* by Roni Schotter, illustrated by Bryan Collier; *Little Divas* by Philana Marie Boles; *Obama: A Promise of Change* by David Mendell; *Boycott Blues: How Rosa Parks Inspired a Nation* by Andrea Davis Pinkney, illustrated by Brian Pinkney; *The Blacker the Berry* by Joyce Carol Thomas, illustrated by Floyd Cooper; *Oh, Brother!* by Nikki Grimes, illustrated by Mike Benny; *Lift Every Voice and Shine* by James Weldon Johnson, illustrated by Bryan Collier; and *When Harriet Met Sojourner* by Catherine Clinton, illustrated by Shane W. Evans.

Direct queries and SASEs to:

Dawn Davis, Editorial Director

COLLINS

With the mega-bestseller *The Dangerous Book for Boys* by Conn and Hal Iggulden, Collins newest children's imprint includes nonfiction and reference titles. With books for toddlers to teens, the list includes Seymour Simon's award winning titles, Let's Read and Find Out Science series, and books co-published by the Smithsonian Institution, the Emily Post Institute, and TIME for Kids.

Recent titles include *Declare Yourself: Speak. Connect. Act. Vote. More Than 50 Celebrated Americans Tell You Why* by Declare Yourself; *The Human Body* by Seymour Simon; and *Extreme Space* by Tim Furniss.

Matthew Benjamin, Editor—*Daring Book for Girls* by Andrea Buchanan and Miriam Peskowitz

JOANNA COTLER BOOKS

Joanna Cotler Books publishes literary and commercial picture books and fiction for all ages. Authors and illustrators include award winners, best-sellers, and luminaries such as Clive Barker, Francesca Lia Block, Sharon Creech, Jamie Lee Curtis, Laura Cornell, Patricia MacLachlan, Barbara Robinson, Art Spiegelman, Jerry Spinelli, and William Steig.

Recent titles indicative of Joanna Cotler's list are *Hate That Cat* by Sharon Creech; *The Leanin' Dog* by K. A. Nuzum; *Louise, The Adventures of a Chicken* by Kate Dicamillo, illustrated by Harry Bliss; *Big Words for Little People* by Jamie Lee Curtis, illustrated by Laura Cornell; and *How to (Un)cage a Girl* by Francesca Lia Block.

Joanna Cotler, Senior Vice President and Publisher

EOS

Eos offers exciting and innovative titles for the young adult science fiction and fantasy reader. The books are intended to be engaging enough to appeal to adults, and include *Fire-us Trilogy* by Jennifer Armstrong and Nancy Butche; *The Books of Magic* by Hillari Bell; and *Sacred Sacrament* by Sherryl Jordan, author of several critically acclaimed and award-winning books including *The Raging Quiet*, a School Library Journal Best Book, and the ALA Best Books for Young Adults.

Recent Eos books for children include *Daylight Runner* by Oisin McGann; *Darkwing* by Kenneth Oppel; *Worldweavers: Spellspam* by Alma Alexander; *Troll Blood* by Katherine Langrish; and *The Princess and the Hound* by Mette Ivie Harrison.

Direct query letters and SASEs to:

Diana Gill, Executive Editor

Emily Krump, Editor

LAURA GERINGER BOOKS

Laura Geringer Books strives to provide children with books by award-winning, best-selling, and innovative authors and artists who continually set new standards of excellence. The list includes authors William Joyce, Laura Numeroff, Felicia Bond, Bruce Brooks, Richard Egielski, and Sarah Weeks.

Recent titles include *Into the Dark* by Peter Abrahams; *The Life and Crimes of Bernetta Wallflower* by Lisa Graff; *Schmuel and the Magic Clock* by Jason Robert Brown; *Mascot to the Resue!* by Peter David, illustrated by Colleen Doran; *RuneWarriors* by James Jennewein, illustrated by Tom S. Parker; and *Forbidden Tales: Sword* by Da Chen.

Direct query letters and SASEs to:

Laura Geringer, Senior Vice President and Publisher

Jill Santopolo, Editor—Young adult, middle grade

GREENWILLOW BOOKS

Greenwillow, founded in 1974, publishes books in hardcover and library bindings for children of all ages. They strive for books filled with emotion, honesty, and depth, books that have something to say to children and an artful way of saying it.

Recent titles that are representative of the Greenwillow list include *The Lucky Ones* by Stephanie Greene; *Bird Lake Moon* by Kevin Henkes; *The Gollywhopper Games* by Jody Feldman, illustrated by Victoria Jamieson; *Attack of the Fiend* by Joseph Delaney; and *The Entertainer and the Dybbuk* by Syd Fleishman.

Virginia Duncan, Vice-President, Publisher—Young adult, middle grade, picture books

Steve Geck, Executive Editor

HARPERCOLLINS CHILDREN'S BOOKS

HarperCollins Children's Books is known worldwide for its tradition of publishing quality books in hardcover, library binding, and paperback for children, from toddlers through teens. This imprint also releases several successful series, such as *I Can Read*, *Math Start*, and *Let's Read and Find Out*, plus seemingly non-stop titles from authors Meg Cabot and Lemony Snicket.

A new imprint at HarperCollins is Bowen Press, founded by publisher Brenda Bowen who had previously been editor-in-chief at Disney Books for Children. She has said she will focus on attracting new authors and artists and will look for graphic novels, books on cultural trends, and titles with global reach.

Recent releases for ages 4–8 include *At the Train Station* by Anne F. Rockwell; *Hug a Bug* by Eileen Spinelli, illustrated by Dan Andreasen; *Love Splat* by Rob Scotton; *If You Give a Bear a Brownie* by Laura Joffe Numeroff; *The Lump of Coal* by Lemony Snicket, illustrated by Brett Helquist; and *How to Drive Your Sister Crazy* by Diane Z. Shore, illustrated by Laura Rankin.

Recent releases for ages 9-12 include *Flyboy of Underwhere* by Bruce Hale, illustrated by Shane Hillman; *Going for Gold: Mission: Save Cleopatra!* by Annie Dalton; and *The Floods: Witch Friend* by Colin Thompson, illustrated by Crab Scrambly.

Recent releases for teens include *The Graveyard Book* by Neil Gaiman, illustrated by Dave McKean; *Nation* by Terry Pratchett; and *Dragon Road: Golden Mountain Chronicles* by Laurence Yep.

Send query letters and SASEs to:

Kate Jackson, Editor-in-Chief

Maria Modugno, Editorial Director

Rosemary Brosnan, Executive Editor

Susan Rich, Executive Editor—Young adult

Farrin Jacobs, Executive Editor—Teen fiction

Tara Weikum, Executive Editor—Young adult, middle grade fiction

Anne Hoppe, Executive Editor—Manga, fantasy, fiction

Melanie Donovan, Senior Editor

Barbara Lalicki, Editor

Clarissa Hutton, Editor

Kristin Daly, Editor—Young adult

Phoebe Yeh, Editor—Middle grade

Brenda Bowen, Publisher, Bowen Press—Graphic novels, international titles, and pop culture

HARPERFESTIVAL

HarperFestival is home to books, novelties, and merchandise for the very young: children up to six years of age. Classic board books, such as *Goodnight Moon* and *Runaway Bunny* established the list over ten years ago. Today, Festival produces a wide range of novelty and holiday titles as well as character-based programs such as Biscuit, Little Critter, and the Berenstain Bears.

Recent books include *The Berenstain Bears' Valentine Party* by Jan & Mike Berenstain; *Fisher-Price: I Love My Family!* by Alexis Barad, illustrated by Kristen Berger; and *Charming Ponies: A Pony in Need* by Lois K. Szymanski.

Jodi Harris, Editorial Director

HARPERTEEN

HarperTeen has a great track record with young adult titles like *Bad Kitty* by Michele Jaffe, *Monster* by Walter Dean Myers, *Big Mouth and Ugly Girl* by Joyce Carol Oates; *Bridge to Terabithia* by Katherine Paterson, illustrated by Donna Diamond; *Coraline* by Neil Gaiman, illustrated by Dave McKean, and many, many other successful and award-winning books.

This imprint produces original titles and previously published books in both hardcover and paperback formats. In addition to typical teen fare, HarperTeen imprint regularly publishes fiction that deals with difficult personal and social issues like the death of a parent or senseless violence.

The imprint recently began a MySpace site for fans, which may also have useful information for authors: www.myspace.com/harperteen.

Recent titles include *Stargazer* by Claudia Gray; *Wicked Dead: Skin* by Stefan Petrucha and Thomas Pendleton; *Love and Peaches* by Jodi Lynn Anderson; *Beastly* by Alex Flinn; *Dear Julia* by Amy Bronwen Zemser; and *Freeze Frame* by Heidi Ayarbe.

Farrin Jacobs, Executive Editor

HARPERTROPHY

HarperTrophy is a leading paperback imprint for children, producing original fiction and nonfiction, as well as paperback reprints of previously published titles. From picture books by Maurice Sendak to novels by Laura Ingalls Wilder, E. B. White, Katherine Paterson, and Beverly Cleary, Trophy continues its tradition of offering a broad list of the old and the new.

Recent titles include *Danny and the Dinosaur Anniversary Box Set* by Syd Hoff; *Phantom Stallion: Wild Horse Island #9: Snowfire* by Terri Farley; *Rotten School #4: Lose, Team, Lose* by R.I. Stine, illustrated by Trip Park; *Fancy Nancy Sees Stars* by Jane O'Connor, illustrated by Robin Preiss Glasser and Ted Enik; and *Magic Trixie Sleeps Over* by Jill Thompson.

RAYO

Rayo publishes books that embody the diversity within the Latino community, in both English and Spanish-language editions. This imprint strives to publish titles that connect culture with thought and invigorate tradition with spirit, and does so with a reliably award-winning flair.

Recent titles for children include *Tu si puedes, Gabriela!: Como puendo crecer fuerte y sana?* by Dra. Isabel and Eric Vasallo, illustrated by Priscilla Garcia Burris; *Ven, gatita, ven!* by Pat Mora, illustrated by Maribel Suarez; and *El capitan Cheech* by Cheech Marin, illustrated by Orlando L. Ramirez.

Direct queries and SASEs to:

Rene Alegria, Publisher

KATHERINE TEGEN BOOKS

This imprint is looking for books made from stories that entertain, inform, and capture the excitement and emotions of children's lives. Katherine Tegen is a publisher who believes that "narratives created through memorable characters and original voices are the most powerful way to connect the reader with the experience of growing up in our world." The editors buy fantasy, middle grade, and young adult, as well as picture books.

Recent titles include *Olu's Dream* by Shane Evans; *Geek Chic: The Zoey Zone* by Margie Palatini; *The Hunt for the Seventh* by Christine Morton-Shaw; *Mucumber McGee and the Lunch Lady's Liver* by Patrick Loehr; *Santa's Snow Kitten* by Sue Stainton, illustrated by Anne Mortimer; *Vampire Kisses: Blood Relatives* by Ellen Schreiber, illustrated by Rem; and *The Night Before Christmas* by Clement Clarke Moore, illustrations by Hilary Knight.

Direct queries and SASEs to:

Katherine Tegen, Publisher

ZONDERVAN

VIDA

ZONDERKIDZ

5300 Patterson Avenue SE, Grand Rapids, MI 49530

616-698-6900   fax: 616-698-3235

www.zondervan.com   e-mail: submissions@zondervan.com

Founded in 1931 in a Michigan farmhouse by brothers Pat and Bernie Zondervan, Zondervan Publishing House became a division of HarperCollins in 1988. Zondervan publishes both fiction and nonfiction Christian-oriented books and has held at least five (and as many as 10) out of the top 10 positions on the Christian Booksellers bestseller lists since 1995. It is considered by many to be the top Christian publisher.

Zondervan is publisher of the 20-million-copy best-seller, *The Purpose-Driven Life: What on Earth Am I Here For?* by Rick Warren, as well as other notable titles like *Ever After* by Karen Kingsbury; *The Myth of a Christian Nation: How the Quest for Political Power is Destroying the Church* by Gregory A. Boyd; *Boundaries* by Dr. Henry Cloud and Dr. John Townsend; and *The Case for Christ: A Journalist's Personal Investigation of Evidence for Jesus* by Lee Strobel.

Zondervan also publishes faith-based fiction for adults and children including *Faithgirlz* series for 9-12 year olds and the *Kanner Lake* series for adults.

Although Zondervan specializes in publishing Bibles and books, the house also produces a wide variety of resources, including audio books, eBooks, videos, CD ROMs, and inspirational gifts. Zondervan has two imprints; Zonderkidz, with children's books, and Vida, with Spanish language editions.

As the world's largest Bible publisher, Zondervan holds exclusive publishing rights to the New International Version of the Bible—the most popular translation of the Bible—and has distributed more than 150 million copies worldwide. Zondervan publishes approximately 50 Bible products, 150 books, 80 gifts, and 50 new media products each year. Zondervan acquires and develops about 100 new titles each year.

Recent titles include *The Faith: What Christians Believe, Why They Believe It, and Why It Matters* by Charles W. Colson and Harold Fickett; *The Blue Parakeet: Rethinking How You Read the Bible* by Scot McKnight; *Every Now and Then (9/11 Series)* by Karen Kingsbury; *Hear and Do: An Inductive Study in James* by Barry Shafer; *A Faith and Culture Devotional: Daily Readings on Art, Science, and Life* by Kelly Monrow Kullberg and Lael Arrington; and *Dark Pursuit* by Brandilyn Collins.

Recent releases from Zonderkidz include *Adventure Bible Storybook* by Catherine DeVries; *Church Summer Camp* by Mike Thaler; *Ali Cat is a Scaredy-Cat* by Dandi Daley Mackall, illustrated by Janet McDonnell; and *Jake Learns to Share* by Crystal Bowman.

Direct queries and SASEs to:

Dudley Delffs, Vice President and Publisher—Looking for fresh voices and new authors; formerly Editor-in-Chief at Waterbrook

Paul Engle, Executive Editor—Memoir, inspirationals

Jay Howver, Editor—Inspirationals, young adults

Andy Meisenheimer, Editor—Inspirationals, current events

Angela Scheff, Editor—Inspirationals, media tie-ins, current events, lifestyle

Sue Brower, Editor—Romance, mystery, religious fiction, inspirational books

Barbara Scott, Editor, Zonderkidz—Picture books, young adults, fantasies

PEARSON

Pearson is an international media company based in the United Kingdom with businesses in education, business information, and consumer publishing. Pearson's 30,000 employees are in 60 countries, connecting a family of businesses that draws on common assets and shares a common purpose: to help customers live and learn. In addition to the Penguin Group, Pearson divisions include Pearson Education and the Financial Times Group.

The Penguin Group, with primary operations in the U. K., Australia, the U. S., and Canada, and smaller operations in South Africa and India, is led by CEO and Chairman, John Makinson.

The Penguin Group is the world's second-largest English-language trade book publisher.

PENGUIN GROUP (USA) INC.

PENGUIN PUTNAM ADULT DIVISION

PENGUIN PUTNAM YOUNG READERS DIVISION

DORLING KINDERSLEY / DK PUBLISHING

Penguin Group (USA) Inc. is the U.S. affiliate of the Penguin Group. Formed in 1996 as a result of the merger between Penguin Books USA and the Putnam Berkley Group, Penguin Group (USA), under the stewardship of Chief Executive Officer David Shanks, is a leading U. S. adult and children's trade book publisher.

Penguin Group (USA) publishes under a wide range of prominent imprints and trademarks, among them Berkley Books, Dutton, Grosset & Dunlap, New American Library, Penguin, Philomel, G. P. Putnam's Sons, Riverhead, Viking, and Frederick Warne. The Penguin Group's roster of best-selling authors includes, among hundreds of others, Dorothy Allison, Nevada Barr, Saul Bellow, A. Scott Berg, Maeve Binchy, Harold Bloom, Sylvia Browne, Tom Clancy, Robin Cook, Patricia Cornwell, Catherine Coulter, Clive Cussler, Eric Jerome Dickey, Richard Paul Evans, Helen Fielding, Ken Follett, Sue Grafton, W. E. B. Griffin, Nick Hornby, Spencer Johnson, Jan Karon, Anne Lamott, James McBride, Terry McMillan, Arthur Miller, Jacqueline Mitchard, Toni Morrison, Kathleen Norris, Joyce Carol Oates, Robert B. Parker, Nora Roberts, John Sandford, Carol Shields, John Steinbeck, Amy Tan, Kurt Vonnegut, and the Dalai Lama.

The Penguin Group is renowned for its success with breakthrough paperbacks, like Elizabeth Gilbert's *Eat, Pray, Love*; Sue Monk Kidd's *The Mermaid Chair*, Khaled Hosseini's *A Thousand Splendid Suns*; Greg Mortenson and David Oliver Relin's *Three Cups of Tea*; and Kim Edwards' *The Memory Keeper's Daughter*. Paperback sales head Norman Lidofsky said of the success, "There's no magic, no crystal balls. The books grow organically and then we focus on it and never stop. We've coined a phrase, 'These books should be brought up during every sales call, every account, every time.'"

Penguin Group is also a global leader in children's publishing, through its Books for Young Readers, with preeminent imprints such as Dial Books, Dutton, Grosset & Dunlap, Philomel, Puffin, Speak, Firebird, G. P. Putnam's Sons, Viking, and Frederick Warne. These imprints are home to acclaimed authors Ludwig Bemelmans, Judy Blume, Jan Brett, Eric Carle, Roald Dahl, Tomie dePaola, Don Freeman, Hardie Gramatky, Eric Hill, Brian Jacques, Robert McCloskey, A. A. Milne, Richard Peck, Patricia Polacco, and dozens of other popular authors.

Illustrated nonfiction publisher Dorling Kindersley / DK Publishing has been a part of the Penguin Group since 2000. In 2007, DK in New York largely ceased acquiring books for U. S. readers, focusing instead on the international market.

PENGUIN PUTNAM ADULT DIVISION

ACE BOOKS

ALPHA BOOKS

AVERY

BERKLEY BOOKS

DUTTON

GOTHAM BOOKS

HPBOOKS

HUDSON STREET PRESS

JOVE BOOKS

NEW AMERICAN LIBRARY / NAL

PENGUIN PRAISE

PENGUIN PRESS

PERIGEE BOOKS

PLUME

PORTFOLIO

G.P. PUTNAM'S SONS

RIVERHEAD BOOKS

SENTINEL

JEREMY P. TARCHER

VIKING PRESS

375 Hudson Street, New York, NY 10014

212-366-2000   fax: 212-366-2666

www.us.penguingroup.com

blog: http://thepenguinblog.typepad.com

The Adult Division of Penguin Putnam had a been a strong performer for many years. Penguin USA President Susan Petersen Kennedy said recently, "It's very nice when both the economic side and the artistic side coincide."

Best-selling 2008 titles for Penguin Putnam included Pulitzer winner *The Brief Wondrous Life of Oscar Wao* by Junot Diaz; *A New Earth* by Eckhart Tolle; *Three Cups of Tea: One Man's Mission to Promote Peace . . . One School at a Time* by Greg Mortenson and David Oliver Relin; *In Defense of Food: An Eater's Manifesto* by Michael Pollan; *Eat, Pray, Love* by Elizabeth Gilbert; *Hold Tight* by Harlan Coben; *Creation in Death* by J.D. Robb; and *Small Favor* by Jim Butcher.

Kennedy says, "The mass market business as a whole seems to have steadied," adding, "it's not what it was five years ago but it's different. It's a fertile ground for new formats and for developing authors and finding audiences." This is an excellent opportunity for new authors to keep in mind as they build their careers.

Authors should definitely check out the Penguin blog, where editors post the latest news from the company: new acquisitions, sneak previews from works in progress, industry gossip, and advice on how to get published. Although it comes from the U.K. editorial office, the blog offers insight into the day-to-day running of the company and how books are made.

Penguin Putnam houses PenguinClassics.com, an online community devoted to classic titles. The company also launched Penguin Lives, a series of short biographies about well-known historical and cultural figures, written by some of today's most respected authors. In addition, Penguin Putnam resumed its Pelican Shakespeare series, which has remained one of the best-selling series of Shakespeare's plays since the line was introduced in the mid-1960s.

Kathryn Court, Publisher

Stephen Morrison, Editor-in-Chief and Associate Publisher

ACE BOOKS

Ace Books, founded in 1953 by A. A. Wyn, is the oldest continuously operating science fiction publisher in the U.S. Ace released some of the most outstanding science fiction writers of the 1950s and 1960s, including Samuel R. Delany, Philip K. Dick, Ursula K. Le Guin, and Robert Silverberg.

Ace produces original titles in hardcover and mass market paperback, as well as reprints previously published in hardcover and trade paperback fiction.

Recent titles include *The Knights of the Cornerstone* by James P. Blaylock; *Princeps' Fury* by Jim Butcher; *Unusual Suspects: Stories of Mystery & Fantasy* by Dana Stabenow; *The Crown* by Deborah Chester; *The Devil's Eye: An Alex Benedict Novel* by Jack McDevitt; *New Tricks* by John Levitt; *Fortune and Fate* by Sharon Shinn; and *The Flame and the Shadow* by Denise Rossetti.

Direct query letters and SASEs to:

Ginjer Buchanan, Editor-in-Chief, Ace and Roc—Science fiction, fantasy, true crime, thrillers

Anne Sowards, Editor—Science fiction, fantasy, thrillers

Jessica Wade, Associate Editor—Fantasy, paranormal, Science fiction

ALPHA BOOKS

800 E. 96th Street, Indianapolis, IN 46240

fax: 317-428-3504

375 Hudson Street, New York, NY 10014

212-366-2000

www.idiotsguides.com   e-mail: submissions@idiotsguides.com

With the slogan "knowledge for life," Alpha Books publishes original nonfiction and how-to titles for adults who seek to learn new skills or otherwise enrich their lives. Alpha publishes the very popular series, *The Complete Idiot's Guides*.

With more than 400 titles already in print, *The Complete Idiot's Guides* is one of the world's most easily recognizable title series. Despite the dizzying success of the series, ideas and manuscripts are continually welcomed.

Best-selling topics include personal finance, business, health/fitness, foreign language, New Age, and relationships. A random selection of recent titles is *The Complete Idiot's Guide to Pugs*, *The Complete Idiot's Guide to Drawing Manga*, *The Complete Idiot's Guide to Boosting Your Metabolism*, *The Complete Idiot's Guide to Green Building and Remodeling*, and *The Complete Idiot's Guide to Saltwater Aquariums*.

Send proposals via e-mail or regular mail (with SASEs). It is okay to send electronic submissions with proposals as an e-mail attachment. Submit to the attention of the Editorial Coordinator in the Indianapolis office or at submissions@ idiotsguides.com. Detailed submission guidelines are available on the Web site.

Mike Sanders, Editorial Director (IN office)—How-to, including real estate

Ms. Randy Ladenheim-Gil, Executive Editor (NY office)—Including parenting

Paul Dinas, Senior Acquisitions Editor (NY office)—Including sex, relationships

Michele Wells, Acquisitions Editor (NY office)—Including health

Tom Stevens, Acquisitions Editor (IN office)

Billy Fields, Senior Managing Editor (IN office)

AVERY

Avery's publishing program is dedicated primarily to complementary medicine, nutrition, and healthful cooking. It was established in 1976 as a college textbook publisher specializing in niche areas. Through a series of alliances, most notably with Hippocrates Health Institute, Avery began a program of health books by such authors as Ann Wigmore and Michio Kushi, whose work on macrobiotics helped propel the Avery list in the health food and alternative markets. The firm was acquired by the Penguin Group in 1999 and currently publishes 30 new titles per year.

In addition to producing original titles in hardcover and paperback formats, Avery has a backlist of several hundred titles in trade and mass market formats that include works by pioneers in alternative healing, scientists, and health care professionals involved in cutting-edge research.

Titles representative of the Avery list are *The Natural Superwoman: The Scientifically Backed Program for Feeling Great, Looking Younger, and Enjoying Amazing Energy at Any Age* by Uzzi Reiss and Yfat Reiss; *Knock Yourself Up: No Man? No Problem: A Tell-All Guide to Becoming a Single Mom* by Louise Sloan; *Shut Up and Live! (You Know How)* by Marion Downs; *The MS Recovery Diet* by Ann Sawyer and Judith Bachrach; and *From Fatigued to Fantastic: Overcome Chronic Fatigue and Fibromyalgia* by Jacob Teitelbaum.

Recent titles include *The World is Fat: The Fads, Trends, Policies, and Products That Are Fattening the Human Race* by Barry Popkin; *Built for Show: Four Body-Changing Workout Programs for Guys Who Want to Build Muscle, Lose Fat, and Look Good Enough to Hook Up* by Nate Green; *The Keeler Migraine Method: A Groundbreaking, Individualized Treatment Program from the Renowned Headache Clinic* by Robert Cowan; *Unexpected Blessings: Finding Hope and Healing in the Face of Illness* by Roxanne Black; and *Prescription for Nutritional Healing: The A-to-Z Guide to Supplements* by Phyllis A. Balch.

Direct your query letter and SASE to:

Megan Newman, Publisher, Avery Books and Viking Studio—High profile memoir, health, diet

Lucia Watson, Editor, Avery Books and Viking Studio—Parenting, cooking, relationships

BERKLEY BOOKS

Berkley Books, under the leadership of President and Publisher Leslie Gelbman, publishes more than 500 titles per year under the Berkley, Jove, Ace, Berkley Praise, Berkley Jam, Berkley Sensation, Berkley Boulevard, and Berkley Caliber imprints, in mass market paperback, trade paperback, hardcover, and multimedia formats.

Recent nonfiction titles include *God Said Yes* by Heather Hornback-Bland and Ninie Hammon; *Call of Duty: My Life Before, During and After the Band of Brothers* by Lt. Lynn "Buck" Compton with Marcus Brotherton; *Travels With Barley: The Quest for the Perfect Beer Joint* by Ken Wells; *The Nursing Home Guide: A Doctor Reveals What You Need to Know About Long-Term Care* by Joshua Schor; and *A Dance With the Devil: A True Story of Marriage to a Psychopath* by Barbara Bentley.

Recent fiction titles include *Blue Moon* by Laurell K. Hamilton; *Comstock Cross Fire: A Man of Honor Novel* by Gary Franklin; *Double the Pleasure* by Lori Foster; *The Eyes of Darkness* by Dean Koontz; *Into the Fire* by Bill Yenne; *The King's Daughter* by Sandra Worth; and *Trident Force* by Michael Howe.

Direct query letters and SASEs to:

Ms. Leslie Gelbman, President, Publisher, Editor-in-Chief—Wide range of projects in fiction and nonfiction

Susan Allison, Vice President and Editorial Director—Fiction including fantasy, women's fiction

Tom Colgan, Executive Editor—Wide range of commercial fiction and nonfiction, including history, business, inspiration, biography, military, thrillers, adventure, and suspense

Natalee Rosenstein, Vice President, Senior Executive Editor—General fiction and thrillers, history, politics

Cindy Hwang, Senior Editor—Women's fiction, popular culture, young adult, paranormal romance, historical romance, contemporary romance

Denise Silvestro, Executive Editor—Lifestyle, memoir, parenting, health, humor, business, leadership

Kate Seaver, Senior Editor—Fiction including paranormal romance, erotica, Berkley Heat titles

Wendy McCurdy, Editor—Romance, women's fiction, Berkley Heat

Jackie Cantor, Editor—Narrative nonfiction, memoir, fiction, historical fiction

Leis Pederson, Editor— Women's fiction, romance, Berkley Heat, Berkley Sensation

Andie Avila, Editor—Narrative nonfiction, memoir, parenting

Carolyn Morrisroe, Editor—Mystery, fiction

Emily Rapoport, Assistant Editor—Nonfiction including parenting, business, blogs

Katie Day, Assistant Editor—Fiction, mystery, thrillers, true crime

DUTTON

Dutton dates back to 1852, when Edward Payson Dutton founded a bookselling firm, E. P. Dutton, in Boston. Dutton currently publishes about 50 hardcover titles per year, fiction and nonfiction.

Dutton authors include Maeve Binchy (Scarlet Feather), John Jakes (On Secret Service), Sylvia Browne (Life on the Other Side and Past Lives, Future Healing), Eric Jerome Dickey (Between Lovers), John Lescroart (The Hearing), Jenny McCarthy (Baby Laughs), Wendy Northcutt (The Darwin Awards), Darin Strauss (Chang and Eng), Barbara Parker (Suspicion of Vengeance), Dave Pelzer (Help Yourself), Randall

Robinson (The Debt), and Tracy Chevalier (Girl with a Pearl Earring and Falling Angels).

Recent titles include The Darwin Awards Next Evolution by Wendy Northcutt; Getting Along Famously: Secrets of Classic Friendship by Melissa Hellstern; The Prodigal God: Christianity Through the Parable of the Prodigal Sons by Timothy Keller; More Information Than You Require by John Hodgman; The Way I Am by Eminem; Lulu in Marrakech by Diane Johnson; and Good People by Marcus Sakey.

Direct query letters and SASEs to:

Brian Tart, President and Publisher—Fiction

Trena Keating, Editor-in-Chief—Fiction, including debut, and high-profile memoir

Amy Hertz, Editor-at-large—Science, history, advice, parenting, memoir

Stephen Morrow, Executive Editor—Entertaining books on serious subjects, popular science

Julie Doughty, Editor—Fiction, memoir

Ben Sevier, Editor—Fiction, memoir

GOTHAM BOOKS

The Gotham Books imprint strives for both commercial and literary success in its titles. This nonfiction imprint publishes 35 books per year. Its emphasis is on self-help, spirituality, business, sports, travel writing, biography, food, current affairs, health, humor, and narrative nonfiction

Representative titles include Eats, Shoots & Leaves: The Zero Tolerance Approach to Punctuation by Lynne Truss; How Starbucks Saved My Life: A Son of Privilege Learns to Live Like Everyone Else by Michael Gates Gill; Inside the Helmet: My Life as a Sunday Afternoon Warrior by Michael Strahan with Jay Glazer; The Seventh at St. Andrews: How Scotsman David McLay Kidd and His Ragtag Band Built the First New Course on Golf's Holy Soil in Nearly a Century by Scott Gummer; Children of Jihad: A Young American's Travels Among the Youth of the Middle East by Jared Cohen; American Band: Music, Dreams, and Coming of Age in the Heartland by Kristen Laine; and Tastes Like Cuba: An Exile's Hunger for Home by Eduardo Machado and Michael Domitrovich.

Recent releases include The Hardest Working Man: How James Brown Saved the Soul of America by James Sullivan; American Therapy: The Rise of Psychotherapy in the United States by Jonathan Engel; Our Magnificent Bastard Tongue: The Untold Story of English by John McWhorter; The Lucky Guide to Mastering Any Style: Creating Iconic Looks and Making Them Your Own by Kim France; Tiki Barker's Pure Hard Workout: Stop Wasting Time and Start Building Real Strength and Muscle by Tiki Barber and Joe Carini; and Tomorrow You Go Home: One Man's Harrowing Imprisonment in a Modern-Day Russian Gulag by Tig Hague.

Direct query letters and SASEs to:

William Shinker, President and Publisher—Fiction and nonfiction, including investing, popular culture, and biography

Lauren Marino, Executive Editor—Nonfiction, lifestyle, advice, memoir

Erin Moore, Senior Editor—Narrative nonfiction, pop culture, advice, memoir, reference

Brett Valley, Editor—Pop culture, sports, memoir, current events

Patrick Mulligan, Associate Editor—Pop culture, narrative nonfiction, memoir, humor

Jessica Sindler, Associate Editor—Memoir, science

HP BOOKS

HOME

Acquired by the Putnam Berkley Group in 1993, HP Books originated in Tucson, Arizona, as publishers of nonfiction books in the categories of cooking, automotive, photography, gardening, health, and child care. An imprint, Home, was established in 2006 to specialize in cooking, crafts, and creative lifestyle.

HP Books releases about twenty books per year in trade paperback and a few in hardcover. Among the stars of the list, Mable Hoffman's *Crockery Cookery* recently celebrated its 20th year in print with more than 5 million copies sold.

Recent titles representative of this list include *This Crazy Vegan Life: A Prescription for an Endangered Species* by Christina Pirello; *How to Build Performance Nissan Sport Compacts* by Sarah Forst; *Casserole Crazy: Hot Stuff for Your Oven* by Emily Farris; *Happy Gloves: Charming Softy Friends Made from Colorful Gloves* by Miyako Kanamori; and *Extreme Pumpkins II: Take Back Halloween and Freak Out a Few More Neighbors* by Tom Nardone.

Direct query letters and SASEs to:

John Duff, Publisher, Perigee, HP Books, Home, Prentice Hall Press

Marian Lizzi, Editor-in-Chief—Humor, parenting, cooking, health

Michael Lufty, Editorial Director—Automotive

HUDSON STREET PRESS

Hudson Street Press's list was launched in the winter of 2005. Publishing as a Viking imprint, Hudson Street focuses on narrative and practical nonfiction: memoirs, biography, sex, self-help, relationships, money, women's issues, health/diet, science, and popular history.

Hudson Street Press looks for books exploring issues that keep people up at night and for voice-driven narratives with emotional resonance. Their mission is to publish authors who bring a new perspective or a unique voice to the traditionally successful nonfiction categories. They publish approximately 30 books per year.

Recent titles include *Body with Soul: Steady Your Sugar, Cut Your Cholesterol, and Get a Jump on Your Best Health* by Randy Jackson; *Winging It: Dispatches from an (Almost) Empty Nest* by Catherine Goldhammer; *Learning to Breathe: One Woman's Journey of Spirit and*

Survival by Alison Wright; *Kiss My Math* by Danica McKellar; and *Kick the Balls: An Offensive Suburban Odyssey* by Alan Black.

Claire Ferraro, Publisher, Viking

Luke Dempsey, Editor-in-Chief—Memoir, narrative nonfiction, sports, health

JOVE BOOKS

Jove is the mass market paperback imprint of the Berkley group. It originated as Pyramid Books, which was founded in 1949 by Alfred R. Plaine and Matthew Huttner, and was sold to the Walter Reade Organization in the late 1960s. In the early 1970s Pyramid published the first four titles in John Jakes' *Kent Family Chronicles*. These popular titles, among others, drew the attention of Harcourt Brace Jovanovich, which was looking for a paperback division, and in 1975 Pyramid was bought by HBJ and its name changed to Jove.

The Jove imprint is known for such significant best-selling authors such as Nora Roberts, Catherine Coulter, Steve Martini, Jayne Ann Krentz, Dick Francis, and W.E.B. Griffin.

Recent titles include *Fish Out of Water* by MaryJanice Davidson; *The Gunsmith 324: Ball and Chain* by J. R. Roberts; *The Pagan Stone: The Sign of Seven Trilogy* by Nora Roberts; *Tall, Dark, and Texan* by Jodi Thomas; *A Christmas To Remember: A Cape Light Novel* by Thomas Kinkade and Katherine Spencer; *Freezing Point* by Karen Dionne; *River Runs Red* by Jeffrey J. Mariotte; and *Servant: The Acceptance* by L. L. Foster.

Direct query letters and SASEs to:

Ms. Leslie Gelbman, President, Publisher, Editor-in-Chief—Wide range of projects in fiction and nonfiction

NEW AMERICAN LIBRARY/NAL

ONYX

ROC

SIGNET

New American Library—popularly known as NAL—publishes a diverse and exciting range of paperback books, including *New York Times* best-sellers by Maeve Binchy, Stuart Woods, John Lescroart, Ken Follett, Sylvia Browne, Catherine Coulter, Stuart Woods, Greg Iles, and John Jakes. Under the Signet, Onyx, and Roc imprints, NAL publishes both fiction and nonfiction and has recently expanded its trade paperback and hardcover programs in addition to the core mass market format. As part of NAL's ongoing efforts to initiate new developments in areas of commercial fiction and nonfiction, its editors are looking for strong, innovative authors who offer distinctive voices and original ideas.

ONYX

Onyx produces mass market and trade paperbacks, both reprints and originals. Titles representative of the list include *Lover Revealed: A Novel of the Black Dagger Brotherhood* by J.R. Ward; *Visibility* by Boris Starling; *Skinny-Dipping* by Connie Brockway; *Garden of Darkness* by Anne Frasier; *The Perfect Fake* by Barbara Parker; *Havoc* by Jack Du Brul; *The Man With a Load of Mischief* by Martha Grimes; *Snow Blind* by P. J. Tracy; and *Fear* by Jeff Abbott.

Recent titles include *Death Song* by Michael McGarrity; *An Innocent Client* by Scott Pratt; *Midnight's Daughter* by Karen Chance; *Tremor: A John Taft Novel* by Craig Dirgo; *Trashed* by Alison Gaylin; *Requiem For An Assassin* by Barry Eisler; *Twilight Fall: A Novel of the Darklyn* by Lynn Viehl; and *Wild & Hexy* by Vicki Lewis Thompson.

ROC

Roc publishes science fiction and fantasy, reprints and originals, in hardcover, trade paperback and mass market formats. Best-sellers include The Dresden Files series by Jim Butcher, the Cassandra Palmer series by Karen Chance, and the Black Jewels novels by Anne Bishop.

Recent releases include Dragon Strike by E. E. Knight; The United States of Atlantis by Harry Turtledove; Peacekeeper: A Major Ariane Kedros Novel by Laura E. Reeve; Seraphs: A Rogue Mage Novel by Faith Hunter; The Black Ship: A Novel of Crosspointe by Diana Pharaoh Francis; Heir to Sevenwaters by Juliet Marillier; and Magic to the Bone by Devon Monk.

Ginjer Buchanan, Editor-in-Chief, Ace and Roc—Science fiction, fantasy, true crime, thrillers

Anne Sowards, Editor—Science fiction, fantasy, thrillers

Jessica Wade, Associate Editor—Fantasy, paranormal, Science fiction

SIGNET

This imprint produces mass market paperback reprints, as well as some original titles in mass market paperback format.

Recent Signet Classic reissue titles include *Atlas Shrugged* by Ayn Rand; *Mansfield Park* by Jane Austen; *Gulliver's Travels* by Jonathan Swift; and *The Return of the Native* by Thomas Hardy.

Other recent titles include *Dark Nights Dark Dreams: Sisterhood of the Sight* by Savannah Russe; *Devil May Ride* by Wendy Roberts; *Mr. Monk Goes to Germany* by Lee Goldberg; *Mrs. Mallory and A Time To Die* by Hazel Holt; *The Woods* by Harlan Coben; and *Phantom Touch* by Julie Leto.

For all of NAL, direct query letters and SASEs to:

Kara Welsh, Publisher, NAL—Fiction, romance

Claire Zion, Editorial Director—Fiction, including Accent and Eclipse titles

Ellen Edwards, Executive Editor—Fiction, romance, mystery

Tracy Bernstein, Executive Editor—Mystery, romance, nonfiction

Kara Cesare, Executive Editor—Fiction, including debut, memoir, romance

Laura Cifelli, Senior Editor—Fiction, thrillers, romance, supernaturals

Mark Chait, Senior Editor—History, military, politics, humor, health, sports, nonfiction, memoir, Caliber (military) and Celebra (Hispanic and Latino) titles

Kristen Weber, Senior Editor—Crime memoir and novels—traditional, cozies, noir, thrillers, or private eye—and dark chick lit mysteries

Anne Bohner, Editor—Chick lit, young adult romance

Becky Vinter, Editor—Romance, including historical and contemporary

Kerry Donovan, Associate Editor—Romance

Brent Howard, Associate Editor—Mystery, thrillers, history, military

PENGUIN PRAISE

In 2006, Penguin announced the creation of Penguin Praise, a Christian publishing program. Rather than an entirely freestanding publishing program, Praise books are issued in conjunction with other Penguin Group imprints; the launch program includes existing Penguin Group authors such as T. D. Jakes and Rev. Don Piper. Penguin Praise has licensed exclusive trade rights to the Contemporary English Version (CEV) edition of the Bible from the American Bible Society.

Direct queries with SASEs to:

Joel Fotinos, Publisher

PENGUIN PRESS

Dedicated to publishing literary nonfiction and select fiction, this is an imprint that embraces new writers. Penguin Press publishes 40 titles a year, including those by authors Alan Greenspan, Al Gore, Thomas Pynchon, Ruth Reigl, and Nicholas Wade. In 2005, the Penguin Press introduced The Penguin History of American Life, a series of 50 books that range across all of American history.

Recent titles that are indicative of this list include *The Ascent of Money* by Niall Ferguson; *The Harney & Sons Guide to Tea* by Michael Harney; *The Unpossessed City: A Novel* by Jon Fasman; *Remix: Making Art and Commerce Thrive in the Hybrid Economy* by Lawrence Lessig; *Tried by War: Abraham Lincoln as Commander in Chief* by James McPherson; *The Partnership: A History of Goldman Sachs* by Charles D. Ellis; and *The China Lover* by Ian Buruma.

Direct query letters and SASEs to:

Ann Godoff, President and Publisher—Debut fiction, narrative nonfiction

Eamon Dolan, Editor-in-Chief—Narrative nonfiction, current affairs, politics, fiction

Vanessa Mobley, Editor—Narrative nonfiction, history, politics, current events

Laura Stickney, Associate Editor—Fiction and nonfiction

Jane Fleming, Associate Editor—Narrative nonfiction, pop culture, fiction

PERIGEE BOOKS

Perigee Books, originally created as the trade paperback imprint for G. P. Putnam's Sons, has expanded into hardcover as well as original paperback publishing. This imprint features an eclectic range of nonfiction titles including careers, decorating, cookbooks, parenting, health, fitness, relationships, self-help, humor, puzzles, and memoirs. Perigee also publishes the *52 Brilliant Ideas* how-to series with recent titles: *Discover Your Roots*, *Raising Pre-Teens*, *Land Your Dream Job*, *Defeat Depression*, and *Boost Your Heart Health*.

Other recent titles include *It's Not About Food: End Your Obsession with Food and Weight* by Carol Emery Normandi and Lauralee Roark; *Nonverbal Learning Disorder: Understanding and Coping with NLD and Asperger's—What Parents and Teachers Need to Know* by Rondalyn Varney Whitney; *The Complete Guide to Prescription and Nonprescription Drugs 2009* by H. Winter Griffith and Stephen Moore; *Nothing Rhymes with Orange: Perfect Words for Poets, Songwriters, and Rhymers* by Bessie G. Redfield and Hope Vestergaard; *Once Again to Zelda: The Stories Behind Literature's Most Intriguing Dedications* by Marlene Wagman-Geller; and *Smart Words: Vocabulary for the Erudite* by Mim Harrison.

Direct query letters and SASEs to:

John Duff, Publisher, Perigee, HP Books, Home, Prentice Hall Press

Marian Lizzi, Editor-in-Chief—Prescriptive nonfiction, health/fitness, humor, parenting, relationships and communication

Maria Gagliano, Associate Editor—Lifestyle, health, fashion, cooking, pop culture, craft, business, reference, communications

Meg Leder, Editor—Pop culture, lifestyle, communications, fashion, reference

Jeanette Shaw, Assistant Editor—Reference, pop culture

PLUME

Plume, founded in 1970 as the trade paperback imprint of New American Library, is now recognized as one of the preeminent trade paperback imprints. A recent mega-success is with the paperback edition of Eckhart Tolle's *A New Earth: Awakening to Your Life's Purpose*.

Other recent Plume titles include *Time Flies When You're in a Coma: The Wisdom of the Metal Gods* by Mike Daly, Michael Azzerad, and Mark Weiss; *What Every American Should Know About the Middle East* by Melissa Rossi; *The Natural Cat: The Comprehensive Guide to Optimum Care* by Anitra Frazier and Norma Eckroate; *Before Your Dog Can Eat Your Homework, First You Have to Do It: Life Lessons from a Wise Old Dog to a Young Boy* by John O'Hurley; *Innovate Like Edison: The Five-Step System for Breakthrough Business Success* by Michael J. Gelb and Sarah Miller Caldicott; *Red: Teenage Girls Write About What Fires*

Up Their Lives Today by Amy Goldwasser; and *The Lover's Knot: A Someday Quilts Mystery* by Clare O'Donohue.

Direct query letters and SASEs to:

Cherise Davis, Editor-in-Chief—Prescriptive nonfiction, investing, business

Ms. Signe Pike, Editor—Literary, historical, and commercial fiction; romance, narrative nonfiction, especially pop culture, food, and memoir

Emily Haynes, Editor—Prescriptive nonfiction, true crime, reference, current events, history, politics, finances, some fiction

PORTFOLIO

Portfolio is an imprint that publishes business and career books. Best-sellers indicative of the list include *Purple Cow: Transform Your Business by Being Remarkable* by Seth Godin; *The Starfish and the Spider: The Unstoppable Power of Leaderless Organization* by Ori Brafman and Rod Beckstrom; and *The Art of the Start: The Time-Tested, Battle-Hardened Guide for Anyone Starting Anything* by Guy Kawasaki.

Recent titles include *Financial Instruments: Equities, Debt, Derivatives, and Alternative Investments* by David M. Weiss; *The Forever Portfolio: How to Pick Stocks That You Can Hold for the Long Run* by James Altucher; *There's No Elevator to the Top: A Leading Headhunter Shares the Advancement Strategies of the World's Most Successful Executives* by Umesh Ramakrishnan; *Let's Get Real or Let's Not Play: Transforming the Buyer/Seller Relationship* by Mahan Khalso and Randy Illig; *Reality Check: The Irreverent Guide to Outsmarting, Outmanaging, and Outmarketing Your Competition* by Guy Kawasaki; and *How Toyota Became #1: Leadership Lessons from the World's Greatest Car Company* by David Magee.

Direct queries and SASEs to:

Adrian Zackheim, Publisher, Portfolio and Sentinel—Leadership, high profile memoirs, investing

Jeffrey Krames, Editorial Director—General business, leadership, financial advice, investing

Tim Sullivan, Senior Editor—Economics, business, sociology

G.P. PUTNAM'S SONS

AMY EINHORN BOOKS

Putnam produces a broad range of nonfiction and fiction titles. Formats for original titles include hardcover, trade paperback, and audio cassette. Putnam also publishes paperback reprints.

Former Grand Central hardcover editor-in-chief Amy Einhorn founded her eponymous imprint at Putman in 2007, with initial titles to be released late in 2009. Einhorn has said she is looking for intelligent writing with strong narrative and great story-telling. Her previous best-sellers at Grand Central include *I Like You* by Amy Sedaris, *The Red Hat Society* by Sue Ellen Cooper, and *Free Food for Millionaires* by Min Jin.

Titles representative of Putnam's list include *Who Moved My Cheese? An Amazing Way to Deal with Change in Your Work and in Your Life* by Spencer Johnson and Kenneth Blanchard; *The Cat Who Smelled Smoke* by Lilian Jackson Braun; *Orpheus Deception* by David Stone; *Guilty* by Karen Robards; *Wicked City* by Ace Atkins; *Falling Into Manholes* by Wendy Merrill; *The Man Who Made Lists* by Josh Kendall; *Sepulchre* by Kate Mosse; *The Ghost War* by Alex Berenson; *Strangers in Death* by J. D. Robb; and *The Pajama Girls of Lambert Square* by Rosina Lippi.

Recent titles include *Twenty-Odd Ducks: Why, Every Punctuation Mark Counts!* by Lynne Truss and Bonnie Timmons; *Black Ops* by W.E.B. Griffin; *Bone by Bone* by Carol O'Connell; *Running Hot* by Jayne Ann Krentz; *Scarpetta* by Patricia Cornwell; *Flight: New and Selected Poems* by Linda Bierds; *Salvation in Death* by J. D. Robb; *Bob Schieffer's America* by Bob Schieffer; *Rough Weather* by Robert B. Parker; *Devil's Brood* by Sharon Kay Penman; and *Confessions of a Contractor* by Richard Murphy.

Direct query letters with SASEs to:

Neil Nyren, Editor-in-Chief—Serious and commercial fiction and nonfiction

Peternelle van Arsdale, Executive Editor—Fiction and memoir

Christine Pepe, Senior Editor—Women's fiction, mysteries, thrillers, suspense, general nonfiction and parenting

Rachel Kahan, Senior Editor—Fiction, narrative nonfiction, memoir

Rachel Holtzman, Assistant Editor—Narrative nonfiction, memoir

Amy Einhorn, Publisher, Amy Einhorn Books—Fiction, narrative nonfiction, commercial nonfiction

RIVERHEAD BOOKS

Riverhead focuses on literary fiction; spiritual texts, including the books from the Dalai Lama; and memoirs and other narrative nonfiction. This is another good house for new authors of fiction and narrative nonfiction, including memoirists. Although, as the embarrassed publisher of 2008's fake-memoir *Love and Consequences* by Margaret B. Jones, be ready for rigorous fact finding by Riverhead editors.

Representative Riverhead titles include *The Braindead Megaphone* by George Saunders; *The Magical Life of Long Tack Sam: An Illustrated Memoir* by Ann Marie Fleming; *Wild Harmonies: A Life of Music and Wolves* by Helene Grimaud; *The New Kings of Nonfiction* edited by Ira Glass; *Home from the Vinyl Café: A Year of Stories* by Stuart McLean; *The Surrendered* by Chang-Rae Lee; *Please Excuse My Daughter* by Julie Klan; and *Draining the Sea* by Micheline Aharonian Marcom.

Recent titles include *Foreskin's Lament* by Shalom Auslunder; *College Girl* by Patricia Weitz; *The Invention of Air* by Steven Johnson; *Miles from Nowhere* by Nami Mun; *The Lost Art of Walking* by Geoff Nicholson; *The Jesuit and the Skull* by Amir Aczel; *The Bond* by Sampson David, George Jenkins, and Rameck Hunt; and *Slam* by Nick Hornby.

Direct query letters and SASEs to:

Geoffrey Kloske, Publisher—Narrative nonfiction, biography, fiction

Mr. Sean McDonald, Vice President & Executive Editor—Fiction and narrative nonfiction, memoir

Jake Morrissey, Executive Editor—Narrative nonfiction, science, history, culture, religion, spirituality, humor, historical fiction and thrillers

Sarah McGrath, Executive Editor—Literary fiction and narrative nonfiction, memoir, debut fiction

Megan Lynch, Senior Editor—Literary fiction and nonfiction, including debuts, historical fiction, short stories, and humor

Laura Perciasepe, Assistant Editor

SENTINEL

If you're wondering who bought Donald Rumsfeld's memoir last year, look no further. Sentinel is a politically conservative imprint of Penguin, established in 2003. It has a mandate to publish right-of-center books on politics, history, public policy, culture, and religion. The imprint publishes 10–15 new titles per year, in both hardcover and paperback.

Recent titles include *Common Sense: Inside the Grassroots Movement That's Changing America* by Mike Huckabee; *48 Liberal Lies About American History (That You Probably Learned in School)* by Larry Schweikart; *The New Case Against Immigration: Both Legal and Illegal* by Mark Krikorian; *The Dirty Dozen: How Twelve Supreme Court Cases Radically Expanded Government and Eroded Freedom* by Robert A. Levy and William Mellor.

Direct queries and SASEs to:

Adrian Zackheim, Publisher, Portfolio and Sentinel—Leadership, high profile memoirs, investing

Tim Sullivan, Senior Editor—Economics, business, sociology

JEREMY P. TARCHER

Jeremy P. Tarcher publishes some 50 titles annually in both hardcover and paperback, covering a broad spectrum of topics that range from current affairs, social commentary, literary nonfiction, and creativity to spirituality/religion, health, psychology, parenting, business, and other topics. It has had numerous national best-sellers including *Drawing on the Right Side of the Brain* and *Seven Years in Tibet*. Recent best-sellers include *Quarterlife Crisis; Trust Us, We're Experts; and The Hard Questions*. Tarcher also produces paperback reprints of previously published titles.

Recent titles include *The Joy of Appreciative Living: Your 28-Day Plan to Greater Happiness in 3 Incredibly Easy Steps* by Jacqueline Kelm; *Stuck* by Anneli Rufus; *Casanova: The World's Most Notorious Lover* by Ian Kelly; *Think and Grow Rich Deluxe Edition* by Napoleon Hill; *A Deeper Faith* by Jeff Golliher; *The Christmas Chronicles* by Jeff Gunn; *Homeschooling: A Family's Journey* by Martine Millman and Gregory Millman; and *The Power of Giving* by Azim Jamal and Harvey McKinnon.

Direct query letters and SASEs to:

Joel Fotinos, Publisher

Mitch Horowitz, Editor-in-Chief—Focuses on new trends in spirituality, science, social thought, and personal growth

Sara Carder, Editor—Practical nonfiction and narrative nonfiction, spirituality, reference, advice, relationships, memoir

VIKING PRESS

STUDIO

The Viking Press, founded in 1925, currently publishes 100 books per year in hardcover format, both fiction and nonfiction. This house issues a broad range of literary and commercial titles. Viking likes to be known for orchestrating the successful launch of new and relatively unknown writers. Viking also produces illustrated nonfiction titles through its imprint, Studio.

Titles representative of Viking's list include *Eat, Pray, Love: One Woman's Search for Everything Across Italy, India and Indonesia* by Elizabeth Gilbert; *Rumpole Misbehaves: A Novel* by John Mortimer; *A New America: Awakening the National Spirit* by Lou Dobbs; *Elizabeth & Leicester: Power, Passion, Politics* by Sarah Gristwood; *Last Night at the Lobster* by Stewart O'Nan; *Alice: Alice Roosevelt Longworth, from White House Princess to Washington Power Broker* by Stacy A. Cordery; and *The Sharper Your Knife, the Less You Cry: Love, Laughter, and Tears at the World's Most Famous Cooking School* by Kathleen Flinn.

Studio titles include *Indexed* by Jessica Hagy; *The Sweet Melissa Baking Book: Recipes From the Beloved Bakery for Everyone's Favorite Treats* by Melissa Murphy; and *All Is Forgiven, Move On: Our Lady of Weight Loss's 101 Fat-Burning Steps on Your Journey to Sveltsville* by Janice Taylor.

Recent Viking releases include *Making It All Work: Winning at the Game of Work and Business of Life* by David Allen; *Why We Suck: A Feel Good Guide to Staying Fat, Loud, Lazy and Stupid* by Dr. Denis Leary; *Gerard Manley Hopkins: A Life* by Paul Mariani; *Woof!: Writers on Dogs* by Lee Montgomery; *The Qur'an* by Tarif Khalidi; *Deaf Sentence: A Novel* by David Lodge; *Songs for the Missing: A Novel* by Stewart O'Nan; and *Sun in a Bottle: The Strange History of Fusion and the Science of Wishful Thinking* by Charles Seife.

Direct query letters and SASEs to:

Paul Slovak, Publisher, Viking—poetry, literary fiction, beat work (Kerouac and the like), intellectual nonfiction

Wendy Wolf, Executive Editor, Editorial Director for Nonfiction

Molly Stern, Executive Editor, Editorial Director for Fiction

Rick Kot, Executive Editor—Commercial works in nonfiction and current affairs

Carolyn Carlson, Executive Editor—Fiction, memoir

Joshua Kendall, Senior Editor—Fiction and nonfiction

Kendra Harpster, Editor—Fiction, including mysteries, women's fiction

Sabila Khan, Editor—Nonfiction

Alessandra Lusardi, Editor—Nonfiction, memoirs, journalism, social science, popular science, pop culture

Liz Van Hoose, Associate Editor—Commercial fiction, nonfiction, current affairs

Kevin Doughten, Associate Editor—Fiction, nonfiction, memoir

Megan Newman, Publisher, Avery Books and Viking Studio—High profile memoir, health, diet

Lucia Watson, Editor, Avery Books and Viking Studio—Parenting, cooking, relationships

Jeff Galas, Editor, Avery Books and Viking Studio—Spirituality, science, health

---

PENGUIN PUTNAM YOUNG READERS DIVISION

DIAL BOOKS FOR YOUNG READERS

DUTTON CHILDREN'S BOOKS

FIREBIRD

GROSSET & DUNLAP

PHILOMEL BOOKS

PRICE STERN SLOAN

PUFFIN BOOKS

G. P. PUTNAM'S SONS BOOKS FOR YOUNG READERS

RAZORBILL

VIKING CHILDREN'S BOOKS

FREDERICK WARNE

345 Hudson Street, New York, NY 10014

212-414-3600

www.us.penguingroup.com

Penguin Putnam Books for Young Readers produces titles for children of all ages. This house offers an array of distinctive divisions, imprints, and affiliates of Penguin Putnam's component houses, including Dial Books for Young Readers, Dutton, Firebird, Frederick Warne, Grosset & Dunlap, Philomel, Price Stern Sloan, Puffin Books, and Viking Children's Books, and their newest imprint, Speak. Together, these imprints produce a broad range of titles serving every market in children's book publishing.

DIAL BOOKS FOR YOUNG READERS

Dial Books for Young Readers is a hardcover trade children's book division publishing 50 titles per year for children from preschool age through young adult, fiction and non-fiction titles. This Penguin Group (USA) Inc. imprint traces its roots to 1880 and the founding of The Dial, a monthly literary magazine that published such literary giants as e. e. cummings, T. S. Eliot, D. H. Lawrence, and Gertrude Stein.

Since the children's list was launched in 1961, Dial has been known for books of high literary merit and fine design for readers of all ages. It has pioneered books for the young, including the first quality board books published in the U.S. Dial introduced its Easy-to-Read series in 1979 to publish full-color early readers with popular children's book authors and artists, including James Marshall, creator of the Fox series.

Representative titles include *River Between Us* by Richard Peck (a Book Award finalist and winner of the Scott O'Dell Award); *Bronx Masquerade* by Nikki Grimes; *Parts* by Todd Arnold; *The Rules of Survival* by Nancy Werlin; and *A Year Down Yonder* by Richard Peck.

Recent titles include *Blood and Goo and Boogers Too: A Heart-pounding Pop-up Guide to the Circulatory & Respiratory Systems* by Steve Alton and Nick Sharratt; *Doggone Dogs* by Karen Beaumont, illustrated by David Catrow; *Magical Kids II: The Smallest Girl Ever and The Boy Who Could Fly* by Sally Gardner; *The Moon Over Star* by Dianna Hutts Aston, illustrated by Jerry Pinkney; *The Signs of the Sinister Sorcerer: A John Bellairs Mystery Featuring Lewis Barnavelt* by Brad Strickland; and *Something Wicked* by Alan M. Gratz.

Dial Books for Young Readers accepts unsolicited manuscripts of entire picture books or the first ten pages of longer works, with cover letters. Do not include SASEs as they will only contact within four months those authors they want to publish. All other submissions will be recycled without comment. Send submissions through the mail only to:

Lauri Hornik, Vice President and Publisher

Kate Harrison, Senior Editor—Middle grade, young adult

Robyn Meshulam, Editor— Picture books, middle grade, young adult

Alisha Niehaus, Editor—Picture books, middle grade, young adult

Liz Waniewski, Editor— Picture books, middle grade, young adult

PUBLISHING CONGLOMERATES

DUTTON CHILDREN'S BOOKS

Dutton Children's Books is one of the oldest continually operating children's publishers in the U.S. Edward Payson Dutton opened the doors of his Boston bookshop in 1852 and shortly thereafter began to release "fresh and entertaining" books for young readers.

More than 150 years later, Dutton's tagline, "Every book a promise," reflects the imprint's mission to create high-quality books that will transport young readers. Today, the Dutton list looks very different, but its commitment to excellence, freshness, and entertainment has not changed.

The recent list includes *Gamer Girl* by Mari Mancusi; *A Cold Winter's Good Knight* by Shelley Moore Thomas, illustrated by Jennifer Plecas; *Can You Spell Revolution?* by Matt Beam; *Boy, Were We Wrong About the Solar System* by Kathleen V. Kudlinski, illustrated by John Rocco; *Small Fry* by Jamie Levi Adoff; *The Way of the Warrior* by Andrew Matthews; and *The Wild Swans* by Amy Erlich, illustrated by Susan Jeffers.

Direct query letters and SASEs to:

Stephanie Owens Lurie, President and Publisher

Julie Strauss-Gabel, Associate Editorial Director—Young adult, middle grade

Maureen Sullivan, Executive Editor—Young adult, middle grade, picture books

Sarah Shumway, Associate Editor—Young adult

FIREBIRD

www.firebirdbooks.com

Firebird is a paperback science fiction and fantasy imprint specifically designed to appeal to both teenagers and adults. Launched in January 2002, Firebird books are all reprints, drawn from a variety of sources: the children's imprints at PPI; adult genre imprints (Ace and Roc); outside hardcover houses; and the authors themselves. All have covers by adult genre artists, and feature a short essay or autobiography written by their authors. The imprint publishes between 12 and 18 books each year.

Titles include *Changeling* by Delia Sherman; *Spirits That Walk in Shadow* by Nina Hoffman; *Epic* by Conor Kostick; *Beyond the Gates* by Molly Gloss; *Snow White and Rose Red* by Patricia Wrede; *The Seven Towers* by Patricia C. Wrede; and *Voyage of the Slaves* by Brian Jacques.

Sharyn November, Editor

GROSSET & DUNLAP

Grosset & Dunlap produces about 125 mass market children's books each year in hardcover, paperback, library binding, and other formats. Since the 1940s, in addition to the original Nancy Drew and Hardy Boys series, Grosset has published the Illustrated Junior Library. This collection of hardcover editions of *Little Women*, *Tom Sawyer*, and more than 20 other classics is a mainstay of practically every bookstore selling children's books.

Other series include *Smart About Art* (all about art for kids 5-9); *Katie Kazoo; Strawberry Shortcake; Spot; Miss Spider; The Wiggles; The Weebles;* and *Who Was. . . ? (a biography series for kids 8-11).*

Recent titles include *A Tale of Two Tails (Hank Zipper)* by Henry Winkler, illustrated by Lin Oliver; *Who Was Abraham Lincoln! (Who Was. . . ?)* by Janet Pascal, illustrated by Nancy Harrison and John O'Brien; *Hand-Off #4 (Backyard Sports)* by Michael Teitelbaum, illustrated by Ron Zalme; *The Princess and the Pea (Super Why!)* by Angela Santomero; and *The Search for Autumn (Treetures)* by Megan E. Bryant.

Direct query letters and SASEs to:

Debra Dorfman, President and Publisher

PHILOMEL BOOKS

Philomel Books was created in the early 1980s from World Publishing Books for Young People by editor and publisher Ann Beneduce. Beneduce was a pioneer in choosing books that would sell to both trade and institutional markets, so for the new list she chose the name Philomel, a term for an English nightingale that also means "love of learning." Titles are published in hardcover, as well as with school and library binding.

Philomel editors are interested in publishing historical fiction, fantasy, popular fiction, and books with a social conscience. Publishing books and ideas that celebrate a child's potential in worlds past and present is Philomel's goal.

Titles indicative of this list include *Quantum Prophecy: Sakkara* by Michael Carroll; *Sally and the Purple Socks* by Lisze Bechtold; *Come Fly With Me* by Satomi Ichikawa; *Kaito's Cloth* by Glenda Milard, illustrated by Gaye Chapman; *Skylar* by Mary Cuffe-Perez, illustrated by Renata Liwska; and *There Was a Man Who Loved a Rat and Other Vile Little Poems* by Gerda Rovetch, illustrated by Lissa Rovetch.

Recent titles include *The Very Hungry Caterpillar Pop-Up Book* by Eric Carle; *Love is a Good Thing to Feel* by Barbara Joosse, illustrated by Jennifer Plecas; *Long Shot: A Comeback Kids Novel* by Mike Lupica; *Someone for Mr. Sussmann* by Patricia Polacco; *Ranger's Apprentice: The Sorcerer of the North* by John Flanagan; *The Deep Freeze of Bartholomew Tullock* by Alex Williams; and *Pete and Pickles* by Berkeley Breathed.

Direct query letters and SASEs to:

Michael Green, President and Publisher

Patricia Gauch, Editor

PRICE STERN SLOAN

Price Stern Sloan (PSS) was founded in Los Angeles in the 1960s to publish the Mad Libs series that Roger Price and Leonard Stern had concocted during their stint as writers for Steve Allen's *Tonight Show*. Along with their partner Larry Sloan, they expanded the company into a wide variety of publishing categories, especially children's books, novelty formats, and humor. The company's proprietary brands include Mad Libs, Wee Sing, Mr. Men & Little Miss, Serendipity, Crazy Games, and Doodle Art.

With about 75 new titles per year, PSS continues to publish successfully its proprietary brands, as well as titles that fall into the preschool children's mass merchandise categories. PSS also produces a successful annual list of desk calendars and occasional humor titles for the adult market. In addition to producing original titles, this imprint reissues previously published books.

Recent titles include *He Loves Me, He Loves Me Not (Mad Libs)* by Roger Price and Leonard Stern; *Puppy Love* by Salina Yoon; *Dinosaurs Mad Art* by Salina Yoon; *The 12 Dogs of Christmas* by Ed Heck; *Little Miss Christmas (Mr. Men and Little Miss)* by Roger Hargreaves; and *Miranda Mania: An Unauthorized Biography* by Lexi Ryals.

Direct query letters and SASEs to:

Debra Dorfman, President and Publisher

PUFFIN BOOKS

SPEAK

Puffin Books was founded on a strong literary tradition and a commitment to publishing a successful mix of classic children's fiction and brand new literature for children. Over the years, Puffin has transformed from a small, yet distinguished paperback house into one of the largest and most diverse children's publishers in the business, publishing everything from picture books to groundbreaking middle-grade and teen fiction. In addition to publishing new editions of literary fiction, Puffin has started several original series with broad commercial appeal.

Puffin produces titles for young readers in every age group: lift-the-flaps and picture books for young children, Puffin Easy-to-Reads for first-time readers, Puffin Chapters and historical and contemporary fiction for middle-graders, and critically acclaimed novels for older readers under the Speak imprint. The house has a backlist packed with award-winning children's literature, including Robert McCloskey's Caldecott Medal winner *Make Way For Ducklings*, Ludwig Bemelmans' Caldecott Honor book *Madeline*, and Don Freeman's classic *Corduroy*.

Speak is a Puffin imprint aimed at the teen market, bringing classic and cutting-edge fiction and nonfiction in a paperback format for older children. Award winning titles from Speak include *Speak* by Laurie Halse Anderson; *The Land* by Mildred Taylor, and *A Step from Heaven* by An Na. Original series *Missing Persons* and *Sweep* have also been very successful for Speak.

Other notable Speak titles include *LBD: It's A Girl Thing* by Grace Dent; *The Westing Game* by Ellen Raskin; *Fat Kid Rules the World* by K. L. Going; *Postcards from No Man's Land* by Aidan Chambers; and *Hush* by Jacqueline Woodson.

Classic Puffin picture book titles include *The Gingerbread Boy* by Ludwig Bemelmans, illustrated by Jan Brett; *The Very Hungry Caterpillar* by Eric Carle; *Strega Nona* by Tomie dePaola; *The Snowy Day* by Ezra Jack Keats; and *Max and Ruby* by Rosemary Wells.

Middle-graders and teen readers titles include *Time Cat and The Chronicles of Pyrdain* by Lloyd Alexander; *Charlie and the Chocolate Factory* by Roald Dahl; *Amber Brown* by Paula Danziger; *The Outsiders* by S. E. Hinton; *Pippi Longstocking* by Astrid Lindgren; *Roll of Thunder, Hear My Cry* by Mildred D. Taylor; and *Miracle's Boys* by Jacqueline Woodson.

Recent titles include *A Perfect Pair (The English Roses)* by Madonna, illustrated by Jeffrey Fulvimari; *A Song of Harlem* by Patricia McKissack; *Eclipse: Book Twelve (Sweep)* by Cate Tiernan; *The Rogues* by Jane Yolen and Richard G. Harrison; *Escape from Earth: New Adventures in Space* by Jack Dann and Gardner Dozois; and *Forever Amber Brown* by Paula Danziger.

Direct query letters and manuscripts with SASEs to:

Eileen Bishop Kreit, President and Publisher

Jennifer Bonnell, Editor

Angelle Pilkington, Editor

Karen Chaplin, Editor

G. P. PUTNAM'S SONS BOOKS FOR YOUNG READERS

G. P. Putnam's Sons Books for Young Readers publishes about 50 trade hardcover books for children per year. It publishes popular novels and picture books for toddlers to middle-readers, aged 9-12.

G. P. Putnam's Sons is the home of celebrated picture-book creators Tomie dePaola, Jan Brett, Eric Hill, Rachael Isadora, Maira Kalman, Keiko Kasza, and Peggy Rathmann. Award-winning authors for older readers include Joan Bauer, Paula Danziger, Jean Fritz, Vicki Grove, Suzy Kline, Robin McKinley, Jacqueline Woodson, and Laurence Yep.

Recent titles include *Rapunzel* by Rachel Isadora; *Spot Says Goodnight* by Eric Hill; *The Nice Book* by David Ezra Stein; *Humpty Dumpty Climbs Again* by Dave Horowitz; *Jackson's Blanket* by Nancy Cote; *Samuel Blink and the Runaway Troll* by Matt Haig; *Goblins!: An UnderEarth Adventure* by Royce Buckingham; *Chalice* by Robin McKinley; *The Youngest Templar: Keeper of the Grail* by Michael Spradin; and *Voss* by David Ives.

Direct queries and SASEs to:

Nancy Paulsen, President & Publisher

Susan Kochan, Editorial Director

Stacey Barney, Editor

RAZORBILL

Razorbill, which launched in Fall 2004, is dedicated to publishing teen and 'tween books for "kids who love to read, hate to read, want to read, need to read." A typical Razorbill book is contemporary commercial fiction, with a high-concept plot hook and a fresh, eye-catching package—a book that a young reader will pick up on his or her own. The imprint publishes between 30 and 40 new titles a year, both stand-alone titles and limited series (3-6 books.) Formats range from paperback to hardcover, with an emphasis on alternative formats and trim sizes.

Razorbill's launch list included the critically acclaimed *So Yesterday*, a novel from

Scott Westerfeld. Other authors who publish with Razorbill are Michael Simmons (*Finding Lubchenko*, Summer 2005), whose 2003 *Pool Boy* earned him a spot in PW's Flying Starts; Cate Tiernan (*Balefire*, Fall 2005), author of the hit Puffin series *Sweep*; Bill Rancic (*Beyond the Lemonade Stand*, Fall 2005), the very first winner of TV's *The Apprentice*; and debut author R. A. Nelson, whose *Teach Me* (Fall 2005) made the national news for its beautiful and unflinching portrayal of a love affair between a teacher and a student.

Recent titles include *Influence* by Mary Kate Olsen and Ashley Olsen; *Almost Famous, A Talent Novel* by Zoey Dean; *Shadow Kiss (Vampire Academy, Book 3)* by Richelle Mead; *Breathe My Name* by R. A. Nelson; *In Your Room* by Jordanna Frailberg; and *The Madness Continues, A Spud Novel* by John van de Ruit.

Ben Schrank, President and Publisher

Kristen Pettit, Editor—Young adult

Lexa Hillyer, Editor—Young adult

Jessica Rothenberg, Associate Editor—Middle grade, young adult

VIKING CHILDREN'S BOOKS

Viking Children's Books, founded in 1933, publishes approximately 60 titles per year, ranging from books for very young children, such as board and lift-the-flap books, to sophisticated fiction and nonfiction for teens. The current Viking list is known for classic characters such as Madeline, Corduroy, Pippi Longstocking, Roald Dahl's Matilda, Rosemary Wells' Max & Ruby, The Stinky Cheese Man, Cam Jansen, and Froggy.

Among the groundbreaking titles published by Viking are *The Outsiders* (1969), still the best-selling young adult book ever published; *The Snowy Day* (1963), which brought multicultural books mainstream recognition; and *The Stinky Cheese Man* (1992), widely hailed for its innovative design.

Recent titles include *Henry and the Valentine Surprise* by Nancy Carlson; *The Home-run King (Scraps of Time)* by Patricia McKissack and Gordon James; *Street Gang: The Complete History of Sesame Street* by Michael Davis; *W.E.B. Du Bois (Up Close)* by Tonya Bolden; *Happy New Year, Corduroy* by Don Freeman, illustrated by Lisa McCue; *All About Sleep From A to Zzzzz* by Elaine Scott, illustrated by John O'Brien; *Dishes* by Rich Wallace; *The Great Wide Sea* by Madaline Herlong; and *Iron Jaw and Hummingbird* by Chris Roberson.

Direct query letters and SASEs to:

Regina Hayes, Publisher

Joy Peskin, Editor

Tracy Gates, Editor

Catherine Frank, Associate Editor

FREDERICK WARNE

Frederick Warne was founded in 1865 by a bookseller turned publisher. The hallmarks of the publishing program are spin-offs of historic original works, such as books by authors Beatrix Potter and Cicely Mary Barker.

Recent titles include *Peter Rabbit and Friends Bedtime Stories* by Beatrix Potter; *Flower Fairies of the Autumn* by Cicely Mark Barker; *Flower Fairies Enchanted Parties* by Cicely Mary Barker; and *The Tale of Peter Rabbit and Benjamin Bunny: A Pop-up Adventure* by Beatrix Potter.

Sally Floyer, Managing Director

DORLING KINDERSLEY / DK PUBLISHING

375 Hudson Street, New York, NY 10014

212-213-4800

www.us.dk.com

DK Publishing releases an extensive range of both adult and children's reference titles, with their own distinctive illustration style. The adult list encompasses many subjects: gardening, conventional and holistic medicine, pregnancy, childcare, travel, cooking and wine, natural history, art, sports, popular culture, and languages. It includes manuals, encyclopedias, atlases, maps, and handbooks

DK's children's list covers a vast range of children's interests for every age group— dinosaurs, space, nature, history, religion, sport, and science. In addition, the publisher produces a number of richly illustrated and highly accessible encyclopedias for every age.

The U. S. group is focused primarily on global publishing and less on American acquisition; this was a 2007 shift in editorial structure.

Recent DK titles include *1001 Ways To Stay in Shape* by Susannah Marriot; *15-Minute Arabic* by DK Publishing; *Babycenter Mother and Baby Handbook* by Carol Cooper; *How to Photograph Absolutely Everything: Successful Pictures From Your Digital Camera* by Tom Ang; *In The Ocean* by DK Publishing; *Sushi: Taste & Technique* by Kimiko Barber and Hiroki Takemura; and *Secrets of a Sexpert* by Tracey Cox.

DK editors do not accept unsolicited manuscripts and require authors to be

Anja Schmidt, Executive Editor

PUBLISHING CONGLOMERATES

SECTION TWO

INDEPENDENT U.S. PRESSES

INDEPENDENT U.S. PRESSES

JEFF HERMAN

I get to see things a bit differently as an agent then I would as a writer. As discussed elsewhere, publishing houses have more or less fallen into two huge categories: the "globalized" conglomerates, and everyone else. The former can be counted on the fingers of one hand, yet they constitute at least half of all trade book revenues. The latter are countless in number and always expanding like an unseen universe.

Some of these players—the "micro-presses" not included here—have revenues that could be rivaled by a nine-year-old's lemonade stand. Whereas others are eight-figure operations.

Together the "independents" are the other half of the game. As a unified force, they are smaller than they were a decade ago, and are likely to keep getting smaller. But as their market-share shrinks, their indispensability only grows.

The choice of the word "independent" reflects the best word I could come up with, but it's not a perfect description. There are shades of gray, as in all things. Here you will find a few imprints of major houses that I felt operate in a particularly independent fashion. There are also cases where an independent house is distributed by one of the large mega-publishers, and it is listed here rather than with its large umbrella house.

In the end, it's quality that counts, not quantity. And the long-term consequences of the growing consolidation in the industry are not clear yet. Dominance leads to comfort, which leads to inertia. When the asteroids return, it's the ponderous dominators who will be the first to fall.

But it wasn't me who predicted that the meek will inherit the Earth.

So welcome to the world of the independent publisher. Rest assured, we have been very careful not to include any vanity publishers or "fly-by-nights" who will take your money and promise the world without any intention of delivering. The publishing houses we have included are established and reputable.

Independent publishers tend to be more open to direct queries and proposals from authors, rather than requiring that work be submitted through agents.

For some, an independent press might be a stepping-stone to a mega-press. For others, the right independent house is exactly the place to be. Often, a smaller press is able to offer more editorial attention, more authorial involvement throughout the process, and a more focused, long-term involvement with specialized audiences of readers and their communities.

It all depends—on you, your work, and on the methods of the publisher involved. So study each listing that seems of possible interest and look closely at their books.

In all cases, be sure to scrutinize their guidelines and prepare your material carefully. You want to put your best foot forward, and a clear query, followed by a well-written, well-organized proposal, is just as important for a small house as for a large one.

ABBEVILLE PUBLISHING GROUP

ABBEVILLE PRESS

ABBEVILLE KIDS

ARTABRAS

137 Varick Street, 5th Floor, New York, NY 10013

212-366-5585   fax: 212-366-6966

www.abbeville.com   e-mail: abbeville@abbeville.com

Since 1977, Abbeville has published a wide variety of distinctive art, photographic, and illustrated books. With an active backlist of over 700 titles, the Abbeville Publishing Group releases approximately 40 new titles annually in subjects ranging from the arts, gardening, fashion, and food and wine to travel and history. Titles are published in hardcover and trade paperback editions, with close attention given to production standards. Abbeville also produces printed gift items.

The Abbeville Press imprint publishes fine art and illustrated books for an international readership. Their Tiny Folio and miniSeries lines include palm-sized volumes popular in the gift shop sections of museums and bookstores. The Artabras imprint makes select Abbeville titles available at bargain prices. Abbeville Kids is an imprint for high-quality illustrated books geared to the youth market, especially designed to teach children about ways of seeing the world by interacting with art.

Recent favorites from Abbeville Press include *The Art Atlas* edited by John Onians; *Celestial Nights: Visions of an Ancient Land* by Neil Folberg; *Classic Wristwatches 2008/2009: The Price Guide for Vintage Watch Collectors* by Stefan Muser; *The Great Country Houses of Hungary* by Lord Michael Pratt, photographs by Gerhard Trumler; *The Green Bubble: Waste into Wealth, the New Energy Revolution* by Robert Bell; *The Japanese Alphabet: The 48 Essential Characters* by Gabriel Mandel; and *A World History of Photography: 4th Edition* by Naomi Rosenblum.

Longtime favorites from the Artabras imprint include *Ansel Adams: The National Park Service Photographs* and *Gardening for Pleasure: A Practical Guide to the Essential Skills*.

Abbeville Kids has *123 Caterpillar* and *ABC Snake* both illustrated by Calino; and *Family Favorites* by Molly Stevens, *The Brothers Grimm*, and *Hand Christian Andersen*.

Abbeville publications have received awards such as *Rum* by Dave Broom (Glenfiddich Food & Drink Awards 2004 Drink Book), *Curried Favors* (Winner of the Julia Child First Book Award, 1997), *The Vatican Frescoes of Michelangelo* (Carey-Thomas Award, 1982), *The Art of Florence* (Prix Vasari, 1988), *Botticelli* (Prix Vasari, 1990), *Piero della Francesca* (Prix Vasari, 1990), *Nothing But the Blues* (ASCAP, 1994), and *Empire* (Prix Foundation Napoleon, 1996).

Abbeville partners in the distribution of its books throughout the United States. Unsolicited manuscripts are not accepted, but query letters and SASEs may be directed to the editorial staff.

Cynthia Vance, Editor

ABC-CLIO

130 Cremona Drive, Santa Barbara, CA 93116-1911

805-968-1911   fax: 805-685-9685

www.abc-clio.com

Established in 1953, ABC-CLIO is a family-owned business specializing in history reference. It annually publishes approximately 80 encyclopedias, guides, and handbooks for teachers, students, and scholars. Its best-known reference works are the annotated *Historical Abstracts* and *America: History and Life*, both accessible online, which together represent the largest bibliographic history database in the world. Since 1961, ABC-CLIO has won over 80 best-reference awards from the American Library Association and Library Journal. They also have a large eBook program, with all reference book titles published in both print and electronic formats.

ABC-CLIO's publishing focus is on American and world history, politics, law, government, geography, popular and traditional culture, current issues, and history of religion, science, technology, and medicine. They generally accept single volume titles of approximately 80,000 to 150,000 words.

Recent ABC-CLIO titles include *The Encyclopedia of the Cold War: A Political, Social, and Military History* edited by Spencer C. Tucker and Priscilla Mary Roberts; *Treaties with American Indians: Encyclopedia of Rights, Conflicts, and Sovereignty* edited by Donald L. Fixico; *Women in the American Civil War* edited by Lisa Tendrich Frank; *The Encyclopedia of Love in World Religions* edited by Yudit Kornberg Greenberg; *The Ancient Indus Valley: New Perspectives* by Jane R. McIntosh; and *Women in the American West* by Laura E. Woodworth-Ney.

The company's corporate headquarters are in Santa Barbara, CA, with offices in Denver, CO, and Oxford, England. ABC-CLIO was founded by Eric Boehm and is headed today by Ron Boehm.

Query letters or proposals with CVs and SASEs should be addressed to the attention of the Editorial Director, Books.

ABINGDON PRESS

DIMENSIONS FOR LIVING

KINGSWOOD BOOKS

201 Eighth Avenue South, P.O. Box 801, Nashville, TN 37202-0801

615-749-6290

www.abingdonpress.com

Abingdon Press is one of the oldest houses in religious publishing. It has been in existence since 1789 and began as an imprint of the United Methodist Publishing House. Its efforts expanded in the 1920s with books in many different subject areas such as academics, inspirational and materials for church communities. In the early 1920s, Abingdon began publishing a wide array of academic, professional, inspirational, and life-affirming religious literature with the goal of enriching church communities across the globe.

Abingdon is open to a wide range of subject matter, which provides opportunity for writers who do not fit within the more narrow guidelines of other houses. Abingdon looks to include popular material as long as it has contemporary spiritual and ethical themes that influence the lives of its readership. For example, in *50 Ways to Pray: Practices from Many Traditions and Times*, Teresa A. Blythe considers a wide variety of prayer types, gleaned from centuries-old practices of Christian spiritual leaders, including the Christian mystics.

Abingdon publishes hardback and paperback editions, covering religious specialty, religious trade, and popular markets. They also publish professional reference and resources for the clergy, as well as academic and scholarly works in the fields of religious and Biblical history and theory. One new example of an adult Bible study book is *Hurry Less, Worry Less at Christmastime* by Judy Christie. This book helps busy people learn to celebrate more joyfully, peacefully, and deeply during the "holiday season" between Thanksgiving and New Year's Day.

Abingdon produced in-house the book *Super Simple Bible Lessons* for those people on the go who need a lift. On a more serious and scholarly note, Abingdon publishes such books as *The Organization of the United Methodist Church* by Jack Tuell as well as *1&2 Thessalonians (Abingdon New Testament Commentaries)* by Victor Paul Furnish, and *A Critical Introduction to the New Testament: Interpreting the Message and Meaning of Jesus Christ* by Carl R. Holladay. The latter book gives special emphasis to how the New Testament has helped shape the church's identity and theological outlook through the centuries as well as the role it has played in the broader cultures of both East and West.

Abingdon also issues several series of books for children and resources for Sunday school and general Christian education.

Dimensions for Living Books help Christian apply their faith to daily life. Recognizing that living faithfully in today's world isn't easy, Dimensions for Living offers daily mediations, inspiration, practical suggestions, faith-filled advice, and other helps for Christian living.

Kingswood Books is an academic imprint devoted the scholarly works in all periods and areas of Methodist and Wesleyan studies. This imprint honors John Wesley's lifelong commitment to an informed and reflective Christian life.

Recent Abingdon titles include *Too Many Irons in the Fire: And They're All Smoking* by Cynthia Bond Hopson; *Seeing Gray in a World of Black and White* by Adam Hamilton; *I Will Espouse You Forever* by Larry Lyke; *Seized by Truth* by Joel B. Green; *The Wide Open Spaces of God* by Beth Booram; *The Unshuttered Heart* by Ann Belford Ulanov; and *Studying the Old Testament* by Rhonda Burnette-Bletsch;

Dimensions for Living titles include *Goodbye, Murphy's Law: Whatever Can Go Wrong, God Can Make Right* by Pace Christie; *Celebrating the Gift of Marriage* by James W. Moor; *My Tummy Talked in Church Today* by Christy Colby Heno and James W. Moore; and *The Wide Open Spaces of God: A Journey with God Through the Landscapes of Life* by Beth Booram.

Recent Kingswood titles include *The Manuscript Journal of the Rev. Charles Wesley, M.A., Vols. 1 and 2* by Jr, S. T. Kimbrough and Kenneth G. C. Newport and *Early Methodist Spirituality* by Paul W. Chilcore.

In addition to distributing its own books, Abingdon Press handles the lists of several other smaller religious publishers. No multiple submissions. Query letters and SASEs should be directed to:

Robert Ratcliff, Editor, Academic Books—Books for Sunday and parochial schools and seminaries

Paul Franklin, Editor, Professional Books and Reference Books—Methodist doctrine and church practices for clergy and laity, dictionaries and general reference guides relevant to Methodist history and policy

Ron Kidd, Editor, Trade Books—Nonfiction books that help families and individuals live Christian lives; contemporary social themes of Christian relevance

Peg Augustine, Children's books

DIMENSIONS FOR LIVING

Dimensions for Living is an imprint of Abingdon devoted to general-interest religious trade books on practical Christian living. It publishes inspiration, devotion, self-help, home and family, as well as gift volumes. The editorial approach is to combine contemporary themes with mainstream Christian theology. "Quality books that celebrate life and affirm the Christian faith."

Examples of its recent titles include *A Match Made in Heaven: A Bible-Based Guide to Deepening Your Relationship with God* by Nancy C. Reeves, PhD; *My Tummy Talked in Church Today* by Christy Colby Heno; *Slay Your Giants* by Nell W. Mohney; *Celebrating the Gift of Marriage* and *Healing Where it Hurts* both by James W. Moore; *Hither and Yon: A Travel Guide for the Spiritual Journey* by Becca Stevens; *Lessons I Learned From My Grandchildren* by Delia Halverson; and *One More Miracle: Embracing God's Daily Blessings* by Marjorie L. Kimbrough.

Query letters and SASEs should be directed to:

Shirley Briese, Editor, Dimensions for Living

KINGSWOOD BOOKS

Kingswood books is an Abingdon imprint that publishes scholarly works in all areas of Methodist and Wesleyan studies. The imprint honors John Wesley's lifelong commitment to the Christian lifestyle. This commitment, which found expression in his extensive writing and publishing, took form in his establishment of the Kingswood School, near Bristol, England.

Most recent titles from Kingswood include *The Manuscript Journal of the Reverend Charles Wesley, M.A. Vol. 1 & 2* by S. T. Kimbrough Jr. and Kenneth G. C. Newport; *The Journals of Dr. Thomas Coke* edited by John Vickers; *Wesleyan Perspectives on the New Creation* by M. Douglas Meeks; *Early Methodist Spirituality: Selected Women's Writings* by Paul Chilcote; and *Early Methodist Life and Spirituality* by Lester Ruth.

HARRY N. ABRAMS, INC.

ABRAMS BOOKS

ABRAMS BOOKS FOR YOUNG READERS

ABRAMS IMAGE

AMULET BOOKS

STEWART, TABORI & CHANG

115 West 18th Street, New York, NY 10011

212-206-7715   fax: 212-519-1210

www.hnabooks.com

Harry N. Abrams, Inc. (HNA), is a prominent publisher of high-quality art and illustrated books. This house publishes and distributes approximately 250 titles annually and currently has more than 2,000 titles in print. HNA encompasses Abrams Books, Stewart, Tabori & Chang, Abrams Books for Young Readers, Amulet Books for Middle Grade and Young Adult, and Abrams Image.

Abrams is a specialist house and acquires nonfiction projects on a selective basis, giving particular weight to the national or international renown and credentials of artists, photographers, and writers. Their illustrated volumes (mainly in hardcover, with some trade paperback editions and series, as well as works in electronic formats) focus primarily on the fields of fine art, architecture, design, anthropology, archaeology, ethnology and culture, gardening and the home, crafts especially knitting, literary and art criticism, world history, travel, the natural sciences, and the creative use of technology and new media.

The Abrams Image imprint focuses on edgy pop culture books, but also had a best-seller with the 2007 book about philosophy, *Plato and a Platypus Walk into a Bar: Understanding Philosophy Through Jokes* by Thomas Cathcart and Daniel Klein. Stewart, Tabori & Chang editor Melanie Falick is one of the most respected publishing professionals focusing on crafts, especially knitting. This imprint also releases best-selling lifestyle, environmental, and food titles.

Amulet has a best-selling series, *The Sisters Grimm* by Michael Buckley, and Abrams Books For Young Readers should not be overlooked by authors of middle grade and young adult fiction.

HNA is a subsidiary of the prominent French publisher La Martinière Groupe. The house also serves as distributor for publications of the Vendome Press, the Whitney Museum of American Art, Booth-Clibborn Editions, the Royal Academy of Arts, Tate Publishing, and the Victoria and Albert Museum.

Abrams Books titles include *Great Houses of Texas* by Lisa Germany; *Architecture: A World History* by Jerzy Elzanowski, Joni Taylor, and Stephanie Tuerk; *Kirby: King of Comics* by Mark Evanier; *Beneath the Roses* by Gregory Crewdson and Russel Banks; *Making WAVES: Navy Women of World War II* by Evan Bachner; and *Worldchanging: A User's Guide for the 21st Century* by Alex Steffen.

Stewart, Tabori & Chang titles include *Alabama Stitch Book: Projects and Stories Celebrating Hand-Sewing, Quilting and Embroidery for Contemporary Sustainable Style* by Nathali Chanin, Stacie Stukin, and Robert Rausch; *Knitalong: Celebrating the Tradition of Knitting Together* by Larissa Brown and Martin John Brown; *Kim Parker Home* by Kim Parker and Albert Vecerka; and *Feasting on Asphalt: The River Run* by Alton Brown and Jean-Claude Dhien.

Abrams Books for Young Readers include *Because You Are My Baby* by Serry North and Marcellus Hall; *Hush, Little Dragon* by Boni Ashburn and Kelly Murphy; *A Horse's Tale: A Colonial Williamsburg Adventure* by Susan Lubner and Margi Moore; *Professor Bumble and the Monster of the Deep* by Daniel Napp; *Score! Fifty Poems to Motivate and Inspire* by Charles Ghigna and Julia Gorton; and *Sally Gets a Job* by Stephen Huneck.

Amulet Books for Middle Grade and Young Adult titles include *Anahita's Woven Riddle* by Meghan Nuttall Sayres; *Cicada Summer* by Andrea Beaty; *Diary of a Wimpy Kid* by Jeff Kinney; *l8r, g8r* by Lauren Myracle; *Something to Blog About* by Shana Norris; *Manga Shakespeare: The Tempest* by William Shakespeare, illustrated by Paul Duffield; and *Friends Forever? Why Your Friendships Are So Important* by Andree Pignet and Andrea Bussell.

Abrams Image titles include *No Wave: Post-Punk. Underground. New York. 1976-1980* by Thurston Moore and Byron Coley; *Pot Culture: The A-Z Guide to Stoner Language and Life* by Shirley Halperin and Steve Bloom; *The Facebook Book* by Greg Atwan and Evan Lushing; *How to Fly a Plane* by Nick Barnard and Lucy Pope; *The Art Doodle Book* by Lesley O'Mara; *Peeps Ahoy! A Candy-Coated Adventure on the High Seas* by Mark Masyga and Martin Ohlin; and *Tim Gunn: A Guide to Quality, Taste, and Style* by Tim Gunn and Kate Moloney.

Abrams distributes its own books in the U. S. and Canada.

Query letters and SASEs should be directed to the Editorial Department of the specific imprint to which you are submitting. If you are a nonfiction author, proposals may be sent directly to Abrams Books for Young Readers and Amulet Books and to Abrams Books only. Due to heavy volume, Stewart, Tabori, & Chang cannot accept unsolicited book proposals at this time, and Abrams Books for Young Readers and Amulet Books cannot accept unsolicited works of fiction (picture books, novels, or related formats).

Eric Himmel, Editor-in-Chief, Abrams

Susan Van Metre, Senior Editor, Amulet, Abrams Books for Young Readers

Deborah Aaronson, Editorial Director, Abrams

Leslie Stoker, Publisher, Stewart, Tabori, & Chang and Abrams Image

David Cashion, Editorial Director, Abrams Image

Melanie Falick, Senior Editor, Stewart, Tabori, & Chang—Knitting, crafts

Dervla Kelly, Editor, Stewart, Tabori, & Chang—Style, lifestyle

Luisa Weiss, Senior Editor, Stewart, Tabori, & Chang—Cookbooks, food narratives

ACADEMY CHICAGO PUBLISHERS

363 West Erie Street, 7E, Chicago, IL 60610

312-751-7300 / 800-248-READ   fax: 312/751-7306

www.academychicago.com   e-mail: info@academychicago.com

A small press with a noteworthy list, Academy Chicago publishes general nonfiction, art, history, and cultural studies, as well as fiction (including mysteries). The house also offers a line of classic reprints. Academy Chicago makes notable contributions to American letters.

Nonfiction from Academy Chicago includes popular works with an emphasis on contemporary culture, current events, and historical interpretation. The house does not publish science fiction, thrillers, cookbooks, self-help, books dealing with the supernatural, horror, books of photography, children's books, or books with explicit, gratuitous sex and violence.

Recent Academy Chicago titles include *In the House of My Bibi: Growing up in Revolutionary Iran* by Nastaran Kherad; *The Long Journey Home: A Novel* by Laurel Means; *Fever and Thirst: An American Doctor Among the Tribes of Kurdistan, 1835-1844* by Gordon Taylor; *The Man From Yesterday* by Seymour Shubin; *Avengers and Defenders: Glimpses of Chicago's Jewish Past* by Walter Roth; *Held at a Distance: My Rediscovery of Ethiopia* by Rebecca Haile; and *English History Made Brief, Irreverent, and Pleasurable* by Lacey Baldwin Smith.

Academy Chicago handles its own distribution. All submissions must be by regular mail, not by e-mail or by fax. Send the first three to four chapters, synopsis, cover letter and SASE to the Editorial Department.

Anita Miller, Editorial Director

ACCESS MED BOOKS [SEE THE MCGRAW-HILL COMPANIES]

ADAMS MEDIA

POLKA DOT PRESS

PLATINUM PRESS

PROVENANCE PRESS

57 Littlefield Street, Avon, MA 02322

508-427-7100   fax: 800-872-5628

www.adamsmedia.com

This midsize trade house has long been known for specific, high-quality content and impressive design. Primary areas of interest covered are business, leadership, parenting, pets, personal finance, motivational guidance, travel, weddings, and writing. Adams publishes both single-title breakouts and signature series, and releases under three imprints: Platinum Press, Polka Dot Press, and Provenance Press.

With their motto, "Value looks good," Adams Media particularly innovates in the fields of business, self-help, and New Age how-to books. Since being acquired by F + W Publications in 2003, Adams has been extending its reach and now has a list with over 300 books in 25 categories.

National bestsellers in the single-title category include *A Beginner's Guide to Day Trading Online* by Toni Turner; *Why Men Love Bitches* by Sherry Argov; *Please Stop Laughing at Me* by Jodee Blanco; *The Verbally Abusive Relationship* by Patricia Evans; and the teen hit, *Mean Chicks, Cliques and Dirty Tricks* by Erika V. Shearin Karres. Career and business bestsellers like Martin Yate's *Knock 'Em Dead* and Stephan Schiffman's *Closing Techniques* are also popular.

Perhaps the best known of Adams Media's output is the Everything series. This is the ubiquitous user-friendly how-to series with titles like *The Everything Father's First Year Book* and *The Everything Dog Book*. The Streetwise line is dedicated specifically to the small businessperson. The Cup of Comfort and Small Miracles series are meant to inspire readers with anthologies of true stories. Many of these anthologies have regular calls for submissions on the Adams Media Web site.

Recent Adams Media titles include *The Everything Kids' Fairies Puzzle and Activity Book* by Charles Timmerman and Caila Timmerman; *Why Does Santa Wear Red?* by Meera Lester; *The Divorced Girls' Society* by Vicki King and Jennifer O'Connell; *Forbidden Knowledge* by Michael Powell; *Stop Pissing Me Off* by Lynne Elsaguirre; *Knock 'em Dead, 2008* by Martin Yate, C.P.C.; *Let's Have a Dog Party* by Ingrid E. Newkirk; *The Little Black Apron* by Jodi Citrin, M.S., R.D., Melissa Gibson and Katie Nuanes; and the *Everything Green Living Book* by Diane Gow McDilda.

The Polka Dot Press imprint specializes in nonfiction for female readers ages 18-35. Polka Dot Press aims to bring the witty energy of 'chick lit' to the self-help shelf. Recent titles include *Have I Got a Guy for You: What Really Happens When Mom Fixes You Up* by Alix Strauss; *Date Decoder: Military Intelligence Techniques to Expose What He's Really Thinking* by Greg Hartley and Maryann Karinch; *The Fixer-Upper Man: Turn Mr. Maybe into Mr. Right in 5 Easy Steps* by Cooper Lawrence; and *The Divorced Girls' Society: Your Initiation into the Club You Never Thought You'd Join* by Vicki King and Jennifer O'Connell.

Platinum Press publishes prescriptive books on emerging trends in management, leadership, and investing for businesspeople. Platinum titles include *The Way of Innovation: Master the Five Elements of Change to Reinvent Your Products, Services, and Organization* by Kaihan Krippendorff; *Jump the Curve: 50 Essential Strategies to Help Your Company Stay Ahead of Emerging Technologies* by Jack Uldrich; and *The DNA of Leadership: Leverage Your Instincts to Communicate, Differentiate, Innovate* by Judith E. Glaser.

The Provenance Press imprint adds to the New Age shelf with "sophisticated books for the intermediate practitioner." Titles include *Passages Pagan Pregnancy: A Spiritual Journey from Maiden to Mother* by Arin Murphy-Hiscock; *Passages Handfasting: A Pagan Guide to Commitment Rituals* by Rev. Dr. Kendra Vaughn Hovey; and *Witch's Halloween: A Complete Guide to Magick, Incantations, Recipes, Spells, and Lore* by Gerina Dunwich.

Adams does its own distribution in the U.S., also operating through wholesales and jobbers. In the U.K. and elsewhere, Adams distributes via overseas distributors.

Adams Media welcomes book proposal submissions, including those from first-time authors. Mail your proposals with SASEs to "Book Proposals."

Paula Munier, Director of Acquisitions and Innovation—New brands, new series, inspiration, trends, self-help, women's interest, general trade

Meredith O'Hayre, Associate Project Manager—General interest

Peter Archer, Associate Editor—Business, personal finance, reference

Chelsea King, Associate Editor—Polka Dot Press, self-help, relationships, general trade

Andrea Norville, Assistant Editor—New Age/Provenance Press, general trade

Brendan O'Neill, Assistant Editor—Business, humor reference, general trade

Lisa Laing, Managing Editor—Everything Series

Katie McDonough, Project Editor—Everything Series Acquisitions

A. K. PETERS, LTD.

888 Worcester Street, Suite 230, Wellesley, MA 02482

781-416-2888   fax: 781-416-2889

www.akpeters.com   email: editorial@akpeters.com

A. K. Peters, founded in 1992 by Alice Peters and Klaus Peters, is a leading independent scientific technical publisher that specializes in computer science and mathematics. The list ranges from textbooks to advanced professional publications, a range of specialist trade titles, and scholarly monographs. A. K. Peters publishes around 20 new titles annually, and has over 200 titles in print. The guiding principle behind the company is its philosophy of working in service to the scientific community.

Recent titles from A. K. Peters include *Color Imaging: Fundamentals and Applications* by Erik Reinhard; *Erum Arif Khan*, et al; *Haptic Rendering: Foundations, Algorithms; and Applications* by Ming C. Lin and Miguel Otaduy; *Multiplayer Gaming and Engine Coding for the Torque Game Engine* by Edward F Maurina III; *Factorization: Unique and Otherwise* by Steven J. Weintraub; *Professional Techniques for Video Game Writing* by Wendy Despain; and *The Symmetries of Things* by John Horton Conway, Heidi Burgiel, and Chaim Goodman-Strauss.

Send queries and SASEs to:

Alice Peters, Publisher

Klaus Peters, Publisher

ALGONQUIN BOOKS OF CHAPEL HILL

SHANNON RAVENEL BOOKS

P.O. Box 2225, Chapel Hill, NC 27515

919-967-0108   fax: 919-933-0272

www.algonquin.com   e-mail: inquiry@algonquin.com

ARTISAN BOOKS

225 Varick St., New York, NY 10014-4381

212-254-5900   fax: 212-677-6692

www.artisanbooks.com   email: artisaninfo@workman.com

BLACK DOG AND LEVENTHAL

151 West 19th Street, New York, NY 10011

212-647-9336   fax: 212-871-9530

www.blackdogandleventhal.com   email: information@blackdogandleventhal.com

STOREY PUBLISHING

210 MASS MoCA Way, North Adams, Massachusetts 01247

413-346-2100   fax: 413-346-2199

http://storey.workman.com

TIMBER PRESS

113 SW 2nd Ave., Ste. 450, Portland, Oregon 97204

503-227-2878   fax: 503-227-3070

Algonquin Books was founded in 1982 with the mission statement, "Though we hope and expect that our books will gain their share of book club adoptions, mass paperback sales, and movie and television adaptations, it is their quality that will be our foremost consideration, for we believe that it is still possible to publish worthy fiction and nonfiction that will also be financially profitable for author, publisher, and bookseller."

This division of Workman Publishing Company maintains a literary orientation in commercial fiction and nonfiction. The house list represents the American tradition, ranging from the homespun to the progressive. Algonquin Books of Chapel Hill presents its titles in hardcover and trade paper editions with a look and feel befitting the publisher's emphasis on both the classical and contemporary—books designed to be comfortably handled when read. The Algonquin editorial organization operates from both the Chapel Hill and New York Workman offices. They publish 20–25 new books per year, of fiction, nonfiction, cookbooks, and lifestyle books.

Recent Algonquin titles include *Last Child in the Woods: Saving Our Children from Nature-Deficit Disorder* by Richard Louv; *The End of the World As We Know It: Scenes from a Life* by Robert Goolrick; *The Resurrectionist* by Jack O'Connell; *The Future of Love: A Novel* by Shirley Abbott; *Flower Confidential: The Good, the Bad, and the Beautiful* by Amy Stewart; *Mudbound* by Hillary Jordan; *Rock On: An Office Power Ballad* by Dan Kennedy; *The Sky Isn't Visible From Here: Scenes from a Life* by Felicia C. Sullivan; and *Every Last Cuckoo: A Novel* by Kate Maloy.

Algonquin founder Shannon Ravenel's imprint at Algonquin publishes both nonfiction and fiction with titles such as *Brave Enemies: A Novel of the American Revolution* by Robert Morgan; *The Ghost at the Table: A Novel* by Suzanne Berne; *On Agate Hill: A Novel* by Lee Smith; and *Saving the World* by Julia Alvarez.

Artisan Books, another division of Workman, is known for excellence of content, quality of illustration, and innovative printing. Their authors seek to contribute to the cultural life of a diverse and visually sophisticated readership. Recent tiles include *Beyond the Great Wall: Recipes and Travels in the Other China* by Jeffrey Alford and Naomi Duguid; *Flower* by Christopher Beane and Anthony F. Janson; *Dogs We Love* edited by

Michael J. Rosen; *This is Who I Am: Our Beauty in All Shapes and Sizes* by Rosanne Olson; and *Horses* by Yann Arthus-Bertrand and Jean-Louis Gouraud.

Black Dog and Leventhal seeks to publish strikingly original books of light reference, humor, cooking, sports, music, film, mysteries, entertainment, history, biography, and more. Many are unusual in format and rich with color and imagery. Titles include *Best Friend for Life: 75 Simple Ways to Make Me a Happy, Healthy, and Well-Behaved Dog* by Anne Bobby, photographs by Jim Dratfield; *Broadway Musicals: The 101 Greatest Shows of All Time* by Ken Bloom and Frank Vlastnik; *Take My Wife… 523 Jokes, Riddles, Quips, Quotes, and Wisecracks about Love Marriage, and the Battle of the Sexes* by Hugh Payne, Illustrated by Martha Gradisher; and *A Child's Introduction to the Environment* by Michael Drisolli and Denis Drisolli, illustrated by Meredith Hamilton.

Storey Publishing began on July 1st, 1983 with about 65 books and 100 bulletins on topics and carried as building your own log cabin, tanning leather yourself, and canning your garden's bumper crop of fruits and vegetables. Since then, Story gas maintained its independent streak while keeping a backlist of more than 450 titles. Storey wants books that offer fresh ideas, lend encouragement, and help the reader succeed at something specific.

Recent titles from Storey press include *Don't Throw it, Grow it! 68 Windowsill Plants from Kitchen Scraps* by Deborah Peterson; *Sew and Stow: 31 Fun Sewing Projects to Carry, Hold, and Organize Your Stuff, Your Home, and Yourself* by Betty Oppenheimer; *Dishing Up Vermont: 145 Authentic Recipes from the Green Mountain State* by Tracey Medeiros; *Let's Get Together* by DeeDee Stovel and Pamela Wakefield; and *The Veggie Gardener's Answer Book: Solutions to Every Problem You'll Ever Face* by Barabara W. Ellis.

Timber Press, located in Portland Oregon, has over four hundred titles in print and is considered the preeminent publisher of horticulture books. Timber Press began in 1980, publishing J.D. Vertee's Japanese Maples which is still in print. Besides horticulture, Timber Press also seeks to publish books about landscape design, food-related topics, fruit-growing titles, natural history, and the Pacific Northwest.

Timber Press titles include *A Garden Gallery: Inspiration from an Enchanted World of Plants and Artistry* by George Little and David Lewis; *Garden Your Way to Health and Fitness* by Bunny Guinness and Jacqueline Knox; *Planting Green Roofs and Living Walls* by Nigel Dunnett and Noel Kingsbury; *Portland Forest Hikes: Twenty Close-In Wilderness Walks* by James D. Thayer; and *The New Book of Salvias: Sages for Every Garden* by Betsy Clebsch.

Algonquin titles are distributed by its parent, Workman Publishing Company.

To submit your manuscript, send a 20-page sample of your work, a cover letter, a self-addressed envelope, and a check to cover return postage to the attention of the Editorial Department.

Ina Stern, Associate Publisher, Algonquin,

Chuck Adams, Executive Editor, Algonquin—Fiction

Amy Gash, Editor, Algonquin—Nonfiction

Shannon Ravenel, Director, Shannon Ravenel Books

Deborah Balmuth, Director of Editors, Storey Books—Building and mind/body/spirit

Deborah Burns, Acquiring Editor, Storey Books—Equine, animals, nature

Gwen Steege, Acquiring Editor, Storey Books—Gardening and Crafts

Margaret Sutherland, Acquiring Editor, Storey Books—Cooking, wine, and beer

Carline Perkins, Acquiring Editor, Storey books,

Lisa Hiley, Project Editor, Storey Books

Lizzie Stewart, Production Editor, Storey Books

Sarah Guare, Associate Editor, Storey Books

Liz Van Doren, Editor in Chief, Black Dog and Leventhal

Ann Bramson, Publisher, Artisan Books

Ingrid Bramozitch, Editor, Artisan Books—Home and style, general

Tom Fischer, Editor in Chief, Timber Press

Eve Goodman, Editorial Director, Timber Press

Juree Sondker, Acquisitions Editor, Timber Press

ALLWORTH PRESS

HELIOS PRESS

10 East 23rd Street, Suite 510, New York, NY, 10010

212-777-8395   fax: 212-777-8261

www.allworth.com

Allworth specializes in practical business and self-help books for creative professionals—artists, designers, photographers, writers, filmmakers, and performers, as well as books about business, law, and personal finance for the general public. Founded in 1989 by author, attorney, and artists' rights advocate Tad Crawford, the press first published a revised edition of *Crawford's Legal Guide for the Visual Artist*. Later titles offered helpful advice to both artists and to the general public on marketing, promotion, pricing, copyright, contracts, safety on the job, personal finance, and more. Today, Allworth Press publishes 40 titles annually and has a full-time staff of ten. The press has also published books of contemporary and classic critical writings on the visual arts.

Recent noteworthy titles from Allworth include *Challenge of Interior Design: Professional Values and Opportunities* by Mary V. Knackstedt; *Handbuilding Ceramic Forms* by Elisabeth S. Woody; *Acting the Song: Performance Skills for the Musical Theatre* by Tracey Moore and Allison Bergman; *Teaching Motion Design: Course Offerings and Class Projects from the Leading Undergraduate and Graduate Programs* by Steven Heller and Michael Dooley; and *Booking Performance Tours: Marketing and Acquiring Live Arts and Entertainment* by Tony Miocci.

In 1997 Allworth Press entered into a distribution agreement with Watson-Guptill Publications bringing books to shelves in the U.S. and Canada. Windsor Books International distributes Allworth publications in the U.K. and Europe. Allworth titles are also distributed in Australia, Southern Africa, the Philippines, Korea, Hong Kong, and Singapore.

Allworth Press enjoys excellent relationships with a number of publishing partners including the School of Visual Arts, the American Institute of Graphic Arts, the American Society of Media Photographers, the Authors Guild, Communication Arts magazine, the Direct Marketing Institute, and the Graphic Artists Guild.

Striking out in a new direction in 2001, Allworth initiated the Helios Press imprint with the aim of "helping us understand ourselves and the world around us." These titles focus on popular psychology and pressing sociological issues. Titles to date include *Unfolding Self: The Practice of Psychosynthesis* by Molly Young Brown; *The Inner Source: Exploring Hypnosis* by Donald S. Connery; *How to Escape Lifetime Security and Pursue your Impossible Dream: A Guide to Transforming Your Career* by Kenneth Atchity; *The World of the Paranormal: The Next Frontier* by Lawrence LeShan; and *Healing with Nature* by Susan Scott.

With over 250 titles in print, Allworth Press continues to publish practical guidance for creative people. Suggestions and insights are welcomed as an aid in determining the best projects and authors for the future.

Helios Press is currently not accepting submissions. Query letters and SASEs should be directed to:

Tad Crawford, Publisher

Bob Porter, Associate Publisher

ALPHA BOOKS [SEE PEARSON / PENGUIN GROUP]

ALYSON PUBLICATIONS

245 W 18th Street, Floor 12, New York, NY 10011

212-209-5175

www.alyson.com

Alyson Publications is the leading publisher of books by, for, and about lesbians, gay men, bisexuals, and transgender people from all economic and social segments of society and all ages. In fiction and nonfiction format, Alyson books explore the political, financial, medical, spiritual, social, and sexual aspects of gay, lesbian, bisexual, and transgender people and their contributions to and experiences of society.

Recent titles include *The 7-Day Dating and Relationship Plan for Gay Men: Practical Advice from the Gay Matchmaker* by Grant Wheaton and Dennis Courtney; *The Portable Queer: Out of the Mouths of Queers: A Compilation of Bon Mots, Words of Wisdom, and Sassy Sayings* by Erin McHugh; *Outsports Revolution: Truth and Myth in the World of Gay Sports* by Cyd Zeigler and Jim Buzinski; and *Paws and Effect: The Healing Power of Dogs* by Sharon Sakson.

Direct queries and SASEs to:

Richard Fumosa, Editor

AMACOM (AMERICAN MANAGEMENT ASSOCIATION)

1601 Broadway, New York, NY 10019-7420

212-586-8100   fax: 212-903-8168

www.amanet.org

AMACOM is the book publishing division of the American Management Association. AMACOM's titles focus on business and professional leadership issues. They explore the changing workplace, the old and new concerns of managers of all kinds, and the means of improving team performance.

AMACOM trade nonfiction lines include works that cover the fields of accounting and finance, customer service, human resources, international business, manufacturing, organization development, strategy, information and communication technology, personal finance, marketing, advertising and public relations, personal development, small business, supervision, sales, management, and training. AMACOM Books is now publishing books in health, parenting, emerging sciences, current events, and public policy.

AMACOM seeks world-class educators, successful executives, business owners, trainers, consultants, and journalists—all eager to share their insights and techniques with a broad audience. The primary audience is managers in large and small companies looking to improve their effectiveness, make their organizations more competitive, keep up with current trends and thinking, energize their staff, and inspire employees at all levels. AMACOM readers are definitely not mass market consumers. They want specialized materials and information on business issues that concern them most. AMACOM book buyers want more than a quick fix. They crave in-depth ideas and practical approaches they can try out on the job. They like to be on the leading edge and get a jump on the competition. They do not want secondhand information. They want to go straight to the source.

Noteworthy titles from AMACOM's list include *Outsourcing America: The True Cost of Shipping Jobs Overseas and What Can Be Done About It* by Ron Hira PhD, P.E. and Dr. Anil Hira; *Undercover: How I Went from Company Man to FBI Spy—and Exposed the Worst Healthcare Fraud in US History* by John W. Schilling; *Effective Executive Compensation* by Michael Dennis Graham, Thomas A. Roth, and Dawn Dugan; *Vulture Culture* by Eric D. Gerst; *In the Land of Difficult People* by Terrence L. Gargiulo and Gini G. Scott; *Managing Online Forums* by Patricia O'Keefe; *The Administrative Assistant's and Secretary's Handbook* by James Stroman, Kevin Wilson, and Jennifer Wauson; and *How to Negotiate Anything with Anyone Anywhere Around the World* by Frank L. Acuff.

AMACOM distributes its own products through multiple marketing channels, including retail trade, direct marketing, special sales, and international sales (through McGraw-Hill).

Proposals and SASEs should be directed to the appropriate editor:

Jacquelyn Flynn, Executive Editor—Training, Science and Technology, Self-Help, Parenting, Biography/Memoirs, Current Events, Pop Psychology; Jflynn@amanet.org

Ellen Kadin, Executive Editor—Marketing, Career, Communication Skills, Parenting, Biography/Memoirs, Current Events, Pop Psychology; Ekadin@amanet.org

Bob Nirkind, Senior Editor—Real Estate, Sales, Customer Service, Parenting, Biography/Memoirs, Current Events; Rnirkind@amanet.org

Robert Shuman, Senior Editor—Health, Project Management, Finance and Economics, Biography/Memoirs, Current Events; Rshuman@amanet.org

Christina M. Parisi, Executive Editor—Management, Human Resources, Leadership, Parenting, Biography/Memoirs, Current Events cparisi@amanet.org

---

AMERICAN PSYCHIATRIC PUBLISHING, INC.

1000 Wilson Boulevard, Suite 1825, Arlington, VA 22209-3901

703-907-7322   fax: 703-907-1091

www.appi.org   e-mail: appi@psych.org

American Psychiatric Publishing, Inc. (APPI) is one of the most respected publishers of books, journals, and multimedia on psychiatry, mental health, and behavioral science. The house releases professional, reference, and trade books, as well as college textbooks. APPI publishes a midsize booklist in hardcover and trade paper and also produces a number of professional journals. Selected reference works are issued in electronic formats.

APPI is a wholly owned subsidiary of the American Psychiatric Association. Its purpose is twofold: to serve as the distributor of publications of the Association and to publish books independent of the policies and procedures of the American Psychiatric Association. APPI has grown since its founding in 1981 into a full-service publishing house, including a staff of editorial, production, marketing, and business experts devoted to publishing for the field of psychiatry and mental health.

Under the direction of Robert E. Hales, M.D., and John McDuffie, editorial acquisition and development have the highest priority at APPI. APPI is unique in the extent to which it uses peer review in both the selection and final approval of publishing projects. Proposals are reviewed and developed at the earliest stages by an Editorial Board that brings psychiatric expertise from a diverse spectrum of the field. Full manuscripts are then peer-reviewed in their entirety, with final acceptance of the manuscript dependent on appropriate response to the peer reviews. Each year more than 200 projects are reviewed by as many as 750 specialist reviewers, and fewer than 30 are accepted in the typical year.

Although by far the major portion of the American Psychiatric list is geared toward the professional and academic markets, the house catalogs a small number of books in the areas of patient information and books for the general public, among which are selected titles marketed through trade channels.

Recent noteworthy titles from APPI include *Borderline Personality Disorder: A Clinical Guide, 2nd Edition* by John G. Gunderson, MD and Paul S. Links, M.D., F.R.C.P.C.; *Changing American Psychiatry: A Personal Perspective* by Melvin Sabshin, M.D.; *Recovering From Disability: Manual of Psychiatric Rehabilitation* by Robert P. Liberman, M.D.; *Textbooks of Violence Assessment and Management* edited by Robert I. Simon, M.D. and Kenneth Tardiff, M.D., M.P.H.; and *The American Psychiatric Publishing Textbook of Substance Abuse Treatment 4th Edition* edited by Marc Galanter, M.D. and Herbert D. Kleber, M.D.M.D., and Peter J. Buckley, M.D.

American Psychiatric Publishing is also the publisher of the profession's acknowledged clinical guidebook, *Diagnostic and Statistical Manual of Mental Disorders (4th edition, text revision)*, also known as *DSM-IVTR*.

American Psychiatric Publishing distributes through several regional distribution services.

Query letters and SASEs should be directed to:

Robert E. Hales, M.D., M.B.A., Editor-in-Chief

John McDuffie, Editorial Director

Pam Harley, ePublishing Development

Greg Kuney, Managing editor

AMERICAN PSYCHOLOGICAL ASSOCIATION, INC.

MAGINATION PRESS

750 First Street, NE, Washington, DC 20002-4242

800-374-2721 / 202-336-5792   fax: 202-336-5502

www.apa.org   e-mail: books@apa.org

Based in Washington, D.C., and founded in 1892, the American Psychological Association (APA) is a scientific and professional organization that represents psychology in the United States. With 148,000 members, APA is the largest association of psychologists worldwide. In their publications, the APA aims to promote psychological knowledge and the usefulness of psychologists through high standards of ethics, conduct, education, and achievement. They hope to advance scientific interests and inquiry, and the application of research findings to the promotion of health, education, and the public welfare.

Virtually all aspects of psychology are examined in APA publications: methodology, history, student aids, teaching, health, business strategies, violence, personality, and clinical issues. APA produces books, journals, publishing resources, continuing-education/home-study programs, audiocassettes, videotapes, and databases. Life Tools is a special series of APA books written to help the general public find the best advice that psychology can offer.

Recent entries in the APA list include *Studying Psychology in the United States: Expert Guidance for International Students* edited by Nadia T. Hasan, Nadya A. Fouad, and Carol Williams-Nickelson; *Psychology as a Major: Is It Right for Me and What Can I Do With My Degree* by Donna E. Palladino Schultheiss, PhD; *Surviving Graduate School in Psychology: A Pocket Memoir* by Tara L. Kuther, PhD; *Transcending Self-Interest: Psychological Explorations of the Quiet Ego* edited by Heidi A. Wayment, PhD and Jack J. Bauer, PhD; and *Undergraduate Writing in Psychology: Learning to Tell the Scientific Story* by R. Eric Landrum, PhD.

Magination Press is an APA children's imprint that publishes innovative books to help children ages 4-18 deal with the challenges and problems they face growing up. Topics include everyday situations, such as starting school and the growing family, as well as more serious psychological, clinical, or medical problems, such as divorce, depression, anxiety, asthma, attention disorders, bullying, death, and more. Formats include picture books, illustrated readers, interactive books, and nonfiction. Examples of recent Magination titles are *Harry Goes to the Hospital: A Story for Children About What It's Like to Be in the Hospital* by Howard Bennett, MD, illustrated by M.S. Weber and *What to Do When You Dread Your Bed: A Kid's Guide to Overcoming Problems with Sleep* by Dawn Huebner, PhD, illustrated by Bonnie Matthews.

A publication of the American Psychological Association that has wide influence in all areas of scholarly publishing, especially the social and behavioral sciences, is the

Publication Manual of the American Psychological Association (now in its 5th edition), a resource that guides writers and editors through manuscript preparation and production.

Query letters and SASEs should be directed to:

Julia Frank-McNeil, Senior Director, APA Books

Tyler Aune, Editorial Assistant, APA books

Becky Shaw, Project Editor, Magination Press

AMERICAN SOCIETY FOR TRAINING AND DEVELOPMENT (ASTD) BOOKS

1640 King Street, PO Box 1443, Alexandria, VA 22313-2043

703-683-8100   fax: 703-683-8103

www.astd.org   e-mail: customercare@astd.org

ASTD Books is a business-information specialist providing guides on workplace learning and performance, HR development, management, career-building, consulting, teamwork, IT issues, and creative problem solving. In addition to books, ASTD offers training kits, diagnostic tools, presentation materials, games and simulations, videos, audiocassettes, and computer software.

Founded in 1944, ASTD Books is the publishing wing of the American Society for Training and Development, a nonprofit membership organization. ASTD aims to address the most current workplace topics, the most innovative techniques, and the most experienced authors in the field. Books listed in the ASTD catalog are reviewed and selected by a distinguished and professional peer group.

Recent titles from ASTD include *The ASTD Handbook for Workplace Learning Professionals* edited by Elaine Beich; *Success for Hire: How to Find and Keep Outstanding Employees* by Alexandra Levit; *Put Emotional Intelligence to Work: EQuip Yourself for Success* by Jeff Feldman and Karl Mulle; *10 Steps to Successful Business Writing* by Jack E. Appleman; *Career Contentment: Don't Settle for Anything Less!* by Jeffrey Garton; and *Developing Great Managers: 20 "Power Hour" Conversations That Build Skills Fast* by Lisa Haneberg.

ASTD Books distributes its own list via a catalog, easy ordering and an online store. Some ASTD books are available through other publishing houses. ASTD also distributes and co-publishes books from a variety of other business-oriented publishers, including McGraw-Hill, Jossey-Bass, Berrett-Koheler, and others. ASTD also distributes through Amazon.com.

If you are writing on a book targeted to trainers that you think ASTD might like to publish, please contact ASTD at 703-683-9205. Guidelines for submitting a book proposal are available upon request. Query letters and SASEs should be directed to:

Mark Morrow, Senior Acquisitions Editor; mmorrow@astd.org

AMG PUBLISHERS

LIVING INK BOOKS

6915 Shallowford Road, Chattanooga, TN 37421

800-266-4977 / 423-894-6060   fax: 800-265-6690 / 423-894-9511

www.amgpublishers.com   e-mail: info@amgpublishers.com

AMG Publishers was created by AMG International in the 1960s with the sole purpose of teaching the Word of God as a beacon to a lost world. AMG has a broad interest in biblically oriented books including Biblical Reference, Applied Theology and Apologetics, Christian Ministry, Bible Study Books in the Following God series format, Christian Living, Women/Men/Family Issues, Single/Divorce Issues, Contemporary Issues, (unique) Devotionals, Inspirational, Prayer, Gift books, and young adult Fantasy fiction. AMG produces about 30 books per year.

AMG Publishers' focus is on books that help the reader get into the bible, facilitate interaction with Scripture, encourage and facilitate a reader's personal growth in areas such as personal devotion and skillful use of the bible, and encourage studying, understanding, and applying Scripture.

Recent examples include the *Hebrew-Greek Key Word Study Bible: New American Standard Bible 2008 Wide Margin Edition* edited by Spiros Zodhiates and Dr. Warren Baker; *Pastorals Commentary: 1,2 Timothy, Titus, & Philemon 21st Century Biblical Commentary Series* by Charles Ray; *How Do We Know the Bible Is True? and How is Christianity Different From Other Religions?* by John Ankerberg and Dillon Burroughs; and *Raising Responsive Children: A Bible Study for Moms* by Judi Rossi.

LIVING INK BOOKS

Living Ink Books is an imprint of AMG Publishers that focuses on subjects like Christian Living, Fiction, Inspirational and Devotional, and specialty Gift book products. This imprint also publishes several series, including Matterhon the Brave, Oracles of Fire, Angel Light, Dragons in Our Midst, Made Simple, and Twenty-third Psalm.

Recent Living Ink titles include Last of the Nephilim by Bryan Davis; The Believer's Guide to Legal Issues by Stephan Bloom; Not My Child: Contemporary Paganism and the New Spirituality by Linda Harvey; Angela's Answer by Pat Matuszak; and Prayer: The Timeless Secret of High-Impact Leaders by Dave Earley.

Query by e-mail or regular mail with SASE to:

Dan Penwell, Manager of Product Development / Acquisitions; danp@amginternational.org

Rick Steele, Bible Study, Christian living

Warren Baker, Bible Projects

AMULET BOOKS [SEE HARRY N. ABRAMS, INC.]

ANDREWS MCMEEL PUBLISHING

4520 Main Street, Ste. 700, Kansas City, MO 64111-7701

800-851-8923   fax: 816-932-6684

www.andrewsmcmeel.com

Andrews McMeel Publishing (AMP), a division of Andrews McMeel Universal, is a leading publisher of general nonfiction trade books, gift and humor books and calendars, publishing as many as 300 new works annually. Its titles—such as *The Complete Far Side* by Gary Larson and *The Blue Day Book* by Bradley Trevor—have enjoyed long stays on the *New York Times* Best Sellers Lists. In recent years, Andrews McMeel Publishing has expanded its scope and now offers books on a wide range of subjects (popular culture and lifestyles, popular psychology, self-help, and women's issues) appealing to readers of all ages and interests.

Recent titles are *Slurp: Drinks and Light Fare, All Day, All Night* by Nina Dreyer Hensley, Jim Hensley, and Paul Lowe; *Things Cooks Love: Implements. Ingredients. Recipes.* by Sur La Table and Marle Simmons; *Shoes, Chocs, Bags, and Frocks: The Wonderful World of Women* by Edward Monkton; *If These Boobs Could Talk: A Little Humor to Pump Up the Breastfeeding Mom* by Shannon Payette Seip and Adrienne Hedger; *Home Sweat Home: A For Better or For Worse Collection* by Lynn Johnston; *The Older I Get, the Less I Care* by Teresa Roberts Logan; and *The Grandmother Book: A Book About You for Your Grandchild* by Andy and Susan Hilford.

AMP publishes children's books under the Accord imprint. Recent titles include *Friends of a Dino2News and Firsts* by Arlen Cohn and Daniel Vasconsellos; *Max Makes Millions: The Adventures of Max Continue…* by William Boniface and Daniel Vasconsellos.

AMP is also the country's premier calendar publisher, annually publishing calendars based on many top-selling properties such as The Far Side®, Dilbert™, Disney, Mary Engelbreit, and Jeopardy! Gift books, such as those from the Tiny Tomes series, are also a specialty of this house.

Agents, please query. No unsolicited manuscripts are accepted. Query letters should be directed to:

Kirsty Melville, Publisher—Cooking

Christine Schillig, Editor-in-Chief—General nonfiction, all categories

Dorothy O'Brien, Vice President and Managing Director—Humor and general nonfiction

Patty Rice, Senior Editor, Book Division / Editorial Director, Gift Books—General nonfiction and gift books

Jean Lucas, Senior Editor—General nonfiction, illustrated books, humor, and New Age

Erin Friedrich, Editor—General nonfiction, gift books, humor

Ms. Lane Butler, Editor—Humor

THE APEX PRESS

THE BOOTSTRAP PRESS

Council on International and Public Affairs

777 United Nations Plaza, Suite 3C, New York, NY 10017

800-316-2739

Branch office:

P.O. Box 337, Croton-on-Hudson, NY 10520

www.cipa-apex.org   e-mail: cipany@igc.org

Introduced in 1990, the Apex Press is an imprint of the nonprofit research, education, and publishing group the Council on International and Public Affairs (CIPA). Apex publishes books to build a better world: hardcover and paperback titles offering critical analyses of and new approaches to economic, social, and political issues in the United States, other industrialized nations, and the Third World. Subjects include corporate accountability, grassroots and worker organization, and intercultural understanding. The primary focus is on justice, human rights, and the impact of technology on contemporary society.

The Council on International and Public Affairs was founded in 1954 and is a nonprofit research, education, and publishing group. The Council seeks to further the study and public understanding of problems and affairs of the peoples of the United States and other nations of the world through conferences, research, seminars and workshops, publications, and other means.

The Apex Press is the official publisher of books for POCLAD (the Program on Corporations, Law, and Democracy). POCLAD is a group dedicated to instigating conversations and actions to contest the authority of corporations to define culture, control governments, and to plunder the earth.

Titles from Apex Press include *Gaveling Down the Rabble: How "Free Trade" Is Stealing Our Democracy* by Jane Anne Morris; *Through Japanese Eyes, 4th Edition* by Richard

H. Minear; *The Rule of Property* by Karen Coulter; *Through Indian Eyes, 5th Edition* by Donald J. Johnson and Jean E. Johnson; and *Through Chinese Eyes, 3rd Edition: Tradition, Revolution, and Transformation* by Edward Vernoff and Peter J. Seybolt.

The Apex Press handles its own distribution. The house catalog includes books and additional resources (including videos) from a number of publishers worldwide.

THE BOOTSTRAP PRESS

The Bootstrap Press (inaugurated in 1988) is an imprint of the Intermediate Technology Development Group of North America (ITDG/North America) in cooperation with the Council on International and Public Affairs. Bootstrap's publishing interest focuses on social economics and community economic change; the house covers small-scale and intermediate-scale or appropriate technology in both industrialized and emerging countries, with an aim to promote more just and sustainable societies. Its books explore business and industry theory and how-to, gardening and agriculture, building and construction, and communications.

Representative titles from Bootstrap include *Chicken Little, Tomato Sauce, and Agriculture: Who Will Produce Tomorrow's Food?* by Joan Dye Gussow; *A World That Works: Building Blocks for a Just and Sustainable Society* edited by Trent Schroyer; and *Greening Cities: Building Just and Sustainable Communities* by Joan Roelofs.

Bootstrap publications are distributed with those of sibling operation the Apex Press.

For both Apex and Bootstrap, query letters and SASEs should be directed to:

Judi Rizzi, Publications Manager

Ward Morehouse, Publisher

APPLAUSE THEATRE & CINEMA BOOKS

19 West 21st Street, Suite 201, New York, NY 10010

212-575-9265   fax: 212-575-9270

AMADEUS PRESS

LIMELIGHT EDITIONS

19 West 21st Street, Suite 201, New York, NY 10010

212-575-9265   fax: 212-575-9270

www.applausepub.com   e-mail: info@applausepub.com

Now in its third decade, Applause is well established as one of the country's most important publishers of theatre and cinema books. The house is now owned and operated by Hal Leonard Corporation, the world's largest music print publisher.

The catalog covers everything from books on acting to biographies of theatre luminaries, reference books on music and film, screenplays, play scripts, anthologies, and many other topics all for seasoned pros, rookies, and aficionados of the entertainment arts. The Applause program covers hardback and paperback editions, among them a number of generously illustrated works. Applause issues stage plays and screenplays (many in translation and many in professional working-script format) that run the gamut from the classical repertory to contemporary works in drama, comedy, and musicals. Applause also offers audio works and a video library. The publisher's backlist is comprehensive. Special-production volumes encompass works that detail the background and history behind the creation of works for stage and screen, in addition to containing complete scripts.

Recent titles of interest are *Musical Scene Study: The Musicals of Rodgers and Hammerstein* edited by Tom Briggs; *Black Comedians on Black Comedy: How African-Americans Taught Us to Laugh* by Darryl J. Littleton; *The Alchemy of Theatre: The Divine Science: Essays on Theatre and the Art of Collaboration* by Robert Viagas; *Shirley Temple: A Pictorial History of the World's Greatest Child Star* by Rita Dubas; and *Rent: The Complete Book and Lyrics of the Broadway Musical* by Jonathan Larson.

Amadeus Press was founded by Richard Abel in 1987 as an imprint of Timber Press. A music lover, Abel recognized a gap between popular music titles of somewhat dubious quality issued by large commercial houses and the narrowly specialized scholarly publications of the university presses. Amadeus Press was started with the mission of publishing books that would appeal to a wide audience of discerning music lovers yet maintain their scholarly integrity. In 1990, the press received major attention with the publication of *Enrico Caruso: My Father and My Family* by Andrew Farkas and Enrico Caruso Jr. The company found new acclaim in the early 2000's with it's book/CD series called *Unlocking the Masters* which brings both experienced and new listeners to the world of classical music and opera. In 2006 the imprint was sold to the Hal Leonard Corporation. The mission of Amadeus is focused mainly on creating books that bring new listeners into the exciting world of classical music and opera.

Amadeus Press Books include *Choral Music in the Nineteenth Century* by Nick Strimple; *Franco Corelli: Prince of Tenors* by Rene Seghers; *So When Does the Fat Lady Sing? Questions and Answers About Life, Sex, Love, and—oh yes—Opera* by Michael Walsh; *The Infinite Variety of Music* by Leonard Bernstein; and *The Redeemer Reborn: Parsifal as the Fifth Opera of Wagner's Ring* by Paul Schofield.

Limelight Editions is one of the world's leading small presses of books on the performing arts, theater, cinema, music, and dance. It has recently become a part of the Hal Leonard Performing Arts Publishing Group. Titles from Limelight include *The Great American Book Musical: A Manifesto, Monograph, and Manual* by Denny Martin Flinn; *Spalding Gray's America* by William Demastes; *Voice for Performance: Training the Actor's Voice* by Linda Gates; *The Entertainment Sourcebook 2009* by The Association of Theatrical Artists and Craftspeople; *Pulitzer Prize Plays: The First Fifty Years 1917-1967, A Dramatic Reflection of American Life* by Dr. Paul Firestone; and *TheaterMania Presents Seats—New York: 160 Seating Plans to New York Metro Area Theatres, Concert Halls, and Sports Stadiums* by Jode Susan Millman.

Applause Theatre Books are distributed by Hal Leonard Corporation. Query letters and SASEs should be directed to:

Michael Messina, Managing Director

John Cerullo, Publisher—Amadeus Press/Limelight Editions; jcerullo@amadeuspress.com

Carol Flannery, Editorial Director—Amadeus Press;/Limelight Editions cflannery@amadeuspress.com

ARCADE PUBLISHING

116 John Street, #2810, New York, NY 10038

212-475-2633   fax: 212-353-8148

www.arcadepub.com   e-mail: info@arcadepub.com

Arcade Publishing (founded in 1988 by Jeannette and Richard Seaver) produces commercial and literary nonfiction, as well as selected poetry. Nonfiction standouts include issue-oriented titles, contemporary human-interest stories, and cultural historical works. Arcade's fiction list includes entrants in such categories as mystery, suspense, and thrillers. Arcade's program leans toward learned and enlightened reading. They have brought to the North American reading public works by 252 authors from 31 different countries.

Recent titles include *Cleaver: A Novel* by Tim Parks; *Life and Death are Wearing Me Out: A Novel* by Mo Yan; *The Juggling Pug* by Sean Bryan; *The Stem Cell Dilemma: Beacons of Hope or Harbingers of Doom* by Leo Furcht, M.D. and William Hoffman; *You Want Fries with That? A White-Collar Burnout Experiences Life at Minimum Wage* by Prioleau Alexander; *Africa Doesn't Matter: How the West Had Failed the Poorest Continent and What We Can Do About It* by Giles Bolton; *Golf: The Marvelous Mania* by Alistair Cooke; and *Starbucks Nation: A Novel* by Christ Ver Wiel.

Arcade Publishing is distributed by Hachette Book Group USA.

Arcade Publishing accepts submissions and queries only from agents. Query letters and SASEs should be directed to:

Richard Seaver, President and Editor-in-Chief

Jeannette Seaver, Publisher

Calvert Barksdale, Senior Vice President, General Manager, and Senior Editor

James Jayo, Associate Editor

JASON ARONSON, INC., PUBLISHERS [SEE ROWMAN & LITTLEFIELD PUBLISHING GROUP]

ATLANTIC BOOKS [SEE GROVE / ATLANTIC, INC.]

AUGSBERG FORTRESS BOOKS

Publishing House of the Evangelical Lutheran Church in America
FORTRESS PRESS

100 South Fifth Street, Suite 600, Minneapolis, MN 55402-1222

Mailing address:

P.O. Box 1209, Minneapolis, MN 55440-1209

612-330-3300 / 800-426-0115   fax: 612-330-3455

www.augsburgfortress.org   e-mail: booksub@augsburgfortress.org

Augsburg Fortress publishes titles in popular and professional religious categories. The publishing house produces about 100 books each year. The Augsburg Fortress list accents works of interest to general readers, in addition to books that appeal primarily to a mainstream religious readership and a solid selection of works geared to professional clergy and practitioners of pastoral counseling.

Categories include theology and pastoral care, Biblical and historical academic studies, the life and tradition of Martin Luther, self-improvement and recovery, and books for younger readers from nursery to young adults.

Recent titles include *Blessed to Follow: The Beatitudes as a Compass for Discipleship* by Martha Stortz; *1 & 2 Corintios: 1 & 2 Corinthians* by Efa'n Agosto; *The Augustana Story: Shaping Lutheran Identity in North America* by Dr. Maria Erling and Dr. Mark Granquist; *Being Well When We're Ill: Wholeness and Hope in Spite of Infirmity* by Marva J. Dawn; *Crazy Talk: A Not-So-Stuffy Dictionary of Theological Terms* by Rolf Jacobson; and *Opening the Book of Faith: Lutheran Insights for Bible Study* by Diane Jacobson, Mark Allan Powell, and Stan Olson.

Authors should note: Augsburg Fortress prefers to receive a proposal rather than a completed manuscript.

FORTRESS PRESS

The Fortress Press is the academic book imprint of Augsburg Fortress. Fortress Press focuses on the ever-changing religious worldview of the contemporary world. The Fortress list is keyed to issues of topical interest, tackled with vision and precision; these works address political and cultural issues and are often on the cusp of current religious debate, and the press is noted for significant publishing in the areas of Jewish-Christian studies, African American religion, religion and science, and feminist theology. The Fortress market orientation tilts toward both the general trade and the religious trade.

Titles from Fortress Press include *The Arrogance of Nations: Reading Romans in the Shadow of Empire* by Neil Elliot; *Faith and Fatherland: Parish Politics in Hitler's Germany* by Kyle Jantzen; *Social Ministry in the Lutheran Tradition* by Foster R. McCurley; *Creation: Law and Probability* by Fraser Watts; *Having Words with God: The Bible as Conversation* by Karl Allen Kuhn; and *A New Climate for Theology* by Sallie McFaque.

Query letters and SASEs should be directed to Book Submissions via regular mail or e-mail.

Beth Lewis, President & CEO; booksub@augsburgfortress.org

AVALON BOOKS

160 Madison Avenue, 5th Floor, New York, NY 10016

212-598-0222   fax: 212-979-1862

www.avalonbooks.com   e-mail: editorial@avalonbooks.com

Established as an imprint of Thomas Bouregy & Company, Inc. in 1950, the aim of the Avalon Books (not to be confused with the Avalon Publishing Group) is to provide readers with quality fiction in a variety of genres. The emphasis has always been on good and wholesome entertainment primarily for distribution to library and institutional markets on a subscriber basis. The specialties are mystery, mainstream romance, historical romance, and traditional genre Westerns. Avalon also produces a line of literary classics in reprint (on the Airmont Classics imprint).

The house emphasis on new original novels caters to the tastes and preferences of the all-important library readership. Stories should consist of those likely to be of high interest to the patrons of this wholesome core market. The house publishes 60 books per year.

Recent titles from Avalon Books include *To Commit* by Carolyn Brown; *The Golden Thread* by Amanda Harte; *The Crystal Skull Murders* by Glen Ebisch; *Sierra Skullduggery* by Jerry S. Drake; *Chocolate Secrets* by Zelda Benjamin; *Ada's Hear* by Sandra Wilkins; *Blood Redemption* by A.H. Holt; and *Adieu, My Love* by Lynn M. Turner.

Distribution is primarily through library sales. Submit a 2-3 page synopsis and the first three chapters of a manuscript, along with SASE to The Editors.

Face Black, Editor

Chelsea Gilmore, Assistant Editor

AVALON TRAVEL PUBLISHING [SEE PERSEUS]

B & H PUBLISHING GROUP

127 9th Avenue, North, MSN 114, Nashville, TN 37234-0115

615-251-2438

www.bhpublishinggroup.com

B&H is the trade publishing division of LifeWay Christian resources, owned by the Southern Baptist Convention. Formerly Broadman & Holman, this house began as a producer of bibles, textbooks and reference books. It is now a major publisher of Christian living, fiction, youth, and history for the Christian market. The B&N Espanol imprint focuses on Spanish-language titles.

B&H best-sellers include *Praying God's World* by Beth Moore, and *Experiencing God* by Dr. Henry Blackaby, as well as Oliver North's novels and Chuck Norris' autobiography.

In 2004, the company's Holman Bible division introduced the new *Holman Christian Standard Bible (HCSB)* translation and is also the largest publisher of Spanish language bibles in the United States.

Recent titles include *The Apologetics Study Bible* edited by Ted Cabal; *The Duchess and the Dragon* by Jamie Carie; *A Quick Word with Beth Moore: Scriptures and Quotations form Breaking Free* by Beth Moore; *American Heroes: In the Fight Against Radical Islam* by Oliver North; *Doctrine that Dances* by Robert Smith; and *The Promise: How God Works All Things Together for Good* by Robert Morgan.

Submit query with SASE to:

David Shepherd, Publisher

Thomas Walters, Senior Acquisitions Editor

BACKBEAT BOOKS

600 Harrison Street, San Francisco, CA 94107

415-947-6615   fax: 415-947-6015

www.backbeatbooks.com   e-mail: books@musicplayer.com

Backbeat Books specializes in music books in rock, jazz, blues, country, classical, and everything in between. Titles shed light on music and its makers. Since 1991, Backbeat Books (originally Miller Freeman Books) has published books for readers who are passionate about music, whether as performers or fans.

Backbeat Books is part of the Music Player Network, along with *Guitar Player*, *Bass Player*, *Keyboard*, and *EQ* magazines. The Music Player Network is a division of CMP Media, LLC, a leading integrated media company providing essential information and marketing services to the technology, healthcare, music, and entertainment technology industries.

Recent titles include *Frontman: Surviving the Rock Star Myth* by Richard Barone; *The Official Punk Rock Book of Lists* by Amy Wallace and Handsome Dick Manitoba; *The Guitar Player Book: The Ultimate Resource for Guitarists* by Vladmir Genin; *The Fender Electric Guitar Book 3rd Edition: A Complete History of Fender Instruments* by Tony Bacon; *The Greatest Music Never Sold* by Dan LeRoy; *The Folk Handbook: Working with Songs from the English Tradition* by David Atkinson et al; and *The Guitar Player Repair Guide 3rd Revised* Edition by Dan Erlewine.

Backbeat Books was recently acquired by the Hal Leonard Corporation.

Send proposals or queries to the Executive Editor at books@musicplayer.com or via regular mail.

Dorothy Cox, Publisher

BAEN PUBLISHING ENTERPRISES (BAEN BOOKS)

P.O. Box 1403, Riverdale, NY 10471

718-548-3100

www.baen.com   e-mail: info@baen.com

Baen publishes science fiction and fantasy writing. The house's new releases are generally published in mass market paperback format with targeted lead titles produced in trade paper and hardcover editions. Baen is also a prominent publisher of fiction series, collections, and anthologies geared to various subgenre traditions in science fiction and fantasy.

Founded in 1984, Baen concentrates its concise list on its proven categories of publishing strength. Baen's roster of writers includes John Ringo, Harry Turtledove, Martin Scott, Mercedes Lackey, Murray Leinster, Andre Norton, Lois McMaster Bujold, and Eric Flint.

Writers are encouraged to familiarize themselves with the house output. For science fiction, solid plot-work with scientific and philosophical undercurrents is a must. For fantasy, magical systems must be coherent and integral to the plot. For any Baen title, style need never call attention to itself.

Recent titles from the Baen catalog are *Time Spike* by Eric Flint and Marilyn Kosmatka; *The Tau Ceti Agenda* by Travis S. Taylor; *Farmer in the Sky* by Robert A. Heinlein; *Hell's Gate* by David Weber and Linda Evans; *Draw One in the Dark* by Sarah Hoyt; and *Blackcollar: The Judas Solution* by Timothy Zahn.

Electronic submissions are strongly preferred. Due to spam submissions are longer accepted by e-mail. Send manuscripts using the submission form at http://ftp.baen.com/Slush/submit.aspx. Only Rich Text Format (.rtf) files are accepted. Further details are available on the Web site. No multiple submissions. Query letters and SASEs may be directed to:

Toni Weisskopf, Executive Editor

BAKER PUBLISHING GROUP

BAKER ACADEMIC

BAKER BOOKS

BETHANY HOUSE

BRAZOS PRESS

CHOSEN BOOKS

REVELL

SPIRE BOOKS

Twin Brooks Industrial Park, 6030 East Fulton Road, Ada, MI 49301

Mailing address:

P.O. Box 6287, Grand Rapids, MI 49516-6287

616-676-9185   fax: 616-676-9573

www.bakerpublishinggroup.com

Baker Publishing Group is a major player in the Christian book market. Their mission is to publish writings that promote historic Christianity, irenically express the concerns of evangelism, and reflect the diversity of this movement. At the 2006 Christianity Today Book Awards, Baker Publishing Group won six, more than any other single publisher. Taking top honors in the Christian Living category was Ron Sider's *The Scandal of the Evangelical Conscience* (Baker Books). *Dictionary for the Interpretation of the Bible* by Kevin Vanhoozer (Baker Academic) took the top award in the Biblical Studies category. Awards of Merit went to *Real Sex: The Naked Truth About Chastity* (Brazos Press), *Startling Joy* (fiction, Revell), *The Changing Face of World Missions* (Baker Academic), and *Is the Reformation Over?* (Baker Academic).

BAKER ACADEMIC

As a Christian academic publisher, Baker Academic seeks thoughtful and scholarly works that enhance the pursuit of knowledge within the context of the Christian faith. Baker Academic publishes textbooks, reference books and scholarly works.

The main areas of specialty are biblical studies, theology (biblical, systematic, and historical), and church history. They also publish works in the areas of Christian education, Christian mission, and integrative works in a variety of liberal arts disciplines (e.g., literature, communication, ethics, psychology).

Recent Baker Academic titles include *Liberating Tradition: Women's Identity and Vocation in Christian Perspective* by Kristina LaCelle-Peterson; *Matthew: Exegetical Commentary on the New Testament* by David L. Turner; *Wealth and Poverty in Early Church and Society* by Susan R. Holman; *Archaeology and the New Testament* by John McRay; *God's Words in Human Words: An Evangelical Appropriation of Critical Biblical Scholarship* by Kenton L. Sparks; and *Is Reformation Over? An Evangelical Assessment of Contemporary Roman Catholicism* by Carolyn Nystrom and Mark A. Noll.

Baker Academic welcomes submissions from authors with academic credentials. Send a proposal by post or e-mail (submissions@bakeracademic.com)

BAKER BOOKS

The primary focus of the Baker trade division is the church. It publishes for pastors and church leaders, concentrating on topics such as preaching, worship, pastoral ministries, counseling, and leadership. Topics include the intersection of Christianity and culture, discipleship, spirituality, encouragement, relationships, marriage, and parenting. In addition, Baker trade publishes books that enable parents to pass their faith to their children.

Highlighting the Baker program: *Encountering God: 10 Ways to Experience His Presence* by David M. Edwards; *The Peacemaker Student Edition: Handling Conflict without Fighting Back or Running Away* by Ken Sande and Kevin Johnson; *Preaching to a Post-Everything World: Crafting Biblical Sermons That Connect with Our Culture* by Zach Eswine; *Prodigals and Those Who Love Them: Words of Encouragement for Those Who Wait* by Ruth Bell Graham; *Search and Rescue: Becoming a Disciple Who Makes a Difference* by Neil Cole; and *Ancient-Future Worship: Proclaiming and Enacting God's Narrative* by Robert E. Webber.

Baker Books accepts manuscripts only through literary agents. All unsolicited manuscripts received will be returned to the sender without review.

BETHANY HOUSE

www.bethanyhouse.com   fax: 952-996-1304

Recognized as a pioneer and leader in Christian fiction, Bethany House publishes nearly 120 titles annually in subjects including historical and contemporary fiction, Christian living, family, health, devotional, children's, classics, and theology. Bethany House titles are often found on the Christian best-seller lists.

Recent titles include *The Cure* by Athol Dickson; *Danny Gospel* by David Athley; *The Dead Whisper On* by T.L. Hines; *Fearless* by Robin Parrish; *The Forbidden* by Beverly Lewis; *In High Places* by Tom Morrissey; *Quiet Moments for a Mother's Heart: Time for You to Reflect and Reenergize* by Bethany House; *Road to Nowhere* by Paul Robertson; *The Warriors* by Mark Andrew Olsen; and *Between Heaven and Ground Zero: One Woman's Struggle for Survival and Faith in the Ashes of 9/11* by Leslie Haskin.

Bethany House only accepts one-page facsimile proposals directed to Adult Nonfiction, Adult Fiction, or YA/children editors. Detailed tips for writing a successful query are on the Bethany House Web site; in general, familiarize yourself with the Bethany House list and read their books, tell the editor why you chose to query them, and deliver a fantastic one-paragraph description of your manuscript. Fax to 952-996-1304.

BRAZOS PRESS

P.O. Box 4287, Wheaton, IL 60189

www.brazospress.com   e-mail: rclapp@brazospress.com

Brazos Press is a publisher of theology and theologically-based cultural criticism, grounded in and growing out of the Great Tradition common to Roman Catholic, Eastern Orthodox, Anabaptist, Protestant, and Protestant evangelical Christianity.

Recent titles include *Can Christianity Cure Obsessive-Compulsive Disorder? A Psychiatrist Explores the Role of Faith in Treatment* by Ian Osborn; *Getting into Character: The Art of First-Person Narrative Preaching* by Stephen Chapin Garner; *New Monasticism: What It Has to Say to Today's Church* by Jonathan Wilson-Hartgrove; *Reviving Evangelical Ethics: The Promises and Pitfalls of Classic Models of Morality* by Wyndy Worbin Reuschling; and *Vulnerable Communion: A Theology of Disability and Hospitality* by Thomas E. Reynolds.

Rodney Clapp, Editorial Director

CHOSEN BOOKS

Chosen is the division of Bethany that explores the ministry of the Holy Spirit in areas like intercessory prayer, spiritual warfare, evangelism, prophecy, healing, and general charismatic interest. Several hundred titles over more than 30 years, from Charles Colson's *Born Again* to Cindy Jacobs's *Possessing the Gates of the Enemy*, reflect the publishing mandate of Chosen Books to publish well-crafted books that recognize the gifts and ministry of the Holy Spirit and help readers live more empowered and effective lives for Jesus Christ.

Recent titles include *Intimate Friendship with God: Through Understanding the Fear of the Lord* by Joy Dawson; *Prophetic Fishing: Evangelism in the Power of the Spirit* by Jean Krisle Blasi; *The Mantle of Esther: Discovering the Power of Intercession* by Larry Christenson; *Breaking the Threefold Demonic Cord: How to Discern and Defeat the Lies of Jezebel, Athaliah, and Delilah* by Sandie Freed; *Storm Warrior: A Believer's Strategy for Victory* by Bonnie Chavda and Mahesh Chavda; and *Dominion! How Kingdom Action Can Change the World* by C. Peter Wagner.

Chosen Books accept manuscripts only through literary agents. All unsolicited manuscripts received will be returned to the sender without review.

FLEMING H. REVELL

Revell looks for practical books that help bring the Christian faith to everyday life. The list includes fiction, Christian living, self-help, marriage, family, and youth books.

Recent titles include *Mom, You Make It All Better: Encouraging Words from Real Moms* by Elisa Morgan; *Due to Rising Energy Costs, the Light at the End of the Tunnel Has Been Turned Off: How to Have a Happy, Fabulous Life Even When Your Circumstances Look Dim* by Karen Scalf Linamen; *Five Simple Ways to Grow a Great Family* by Carol Kuykendall; *Glimpses of Heaven: True Stories of Hope and Peace at the End of Life's Journey* by Trudy Harris; and *Kill Me If You Can: A Patricia Amble Mystery* by Nicole Young.

Revell accepts manuscripts only through literary agents. All unsolicited manuscripts received will be returned to the sender without review.

BARRICADE BOOKS INC.

185 Bridge Plaza North, Suite 308-A, Fort Lee, NJ 07024

201-944-7600   fax: 201-944-6363

www.barricadebooks.com   e-mail: customerservice@barricadebooks.com

Barricade publishes nonfiction and welcomes provocative material; its mission is to publish books that preserve, protect, and extend the First Amendment. House interests include arts and entertainment, pop culture, cultural studies, biography, history, politics and current events, true crime, Jewish interest, New Age, psychology, health and sexuality, and how-to/self-help.

Barricade Books was founded in 1991 by veteran publisher Lyle Stuart, who had previously founded Lyle Stuart Inc. (Lyle Stuart Inc. was sold and eventually became the Carol Publishing Group before Carol closed its doors in late 1999.) Barricade was launched in order to continue the tradition begun in 1956, when Lyle Stuart left his career as a newspaper reporter to become a publisher. That tradition is to specialize in books other publishers might hesitate to publish because the books are too controversial.

Recent titles from Barricade include *The Mafia and the Machine: The Story of the Kansas City Mob* by Frank Hayde; *Promises Kept: One Man's Journey Against Incredible Odds* by Ernest Michel; *Roosevelt and the Holocaust* by Robert Beir; *Frank Nitti: The True Story of Chicago's Notorious "Enforcer"* by Ronald Humble; and *Mark It With a Stone: A Moving Account of a Young Boy's Struggle to Survive the Nazi Death Camps* by Joseph Horn.

Complete proposals (including author bio, marketing plan, comparative titles and sample chapters) and SASEs should be directed to:

Carole Stuart, Publisher

Allan Wilson, Senior Editor

BARRON'S / BARRON'S EDUCATIONAL SERIES, INC.

250 Wireless Boulevard, Hauppauge, NY 11788

800-645-3476   fax: 631-434-3723

www.barronseduc.com   e-mail: barrons@barronseduc.com

Founded in 1941, Barron's Educational Series, Inc. rapidly became a leading publisher of test preparation manuals and school directories. Among the most widely recognized of Barron's many titles in these areas are its SAT I and ACT test prep books, Regents Exams books, and Profiles of American Colleges. In recent years, Barron's has expanded into many other publishing fields, introducing extensive lines of children's books, foreign language learning books and cassettes, pet care manuals, New Age books, cookbooks, business and financial advice books, parenting advice books, and art instruction books, as well as learning materials on audiocassette, VCR, Compact Disc, and CD-ROM. On average, Barron's publishes up to 300 new titles a year and maintains an extensive backlist of well over 2,000 titles. The focus remains educational.

The house offers a number of practical business series, retirement and parenting keys, programs on skills development in foreign languages (as well as in English), healthy cooking, arts and crafts techniques, biographies of well-known artists, and home and garden titles. Books on pets and pet care include numerous titles keyed to particular breeds and species of birds, fish, dogs, and cats.

Children's and young adult books and books of family interest include series on pets, nature and the environment, dinosaurs, sports, fantasy, adventure, and humor. Many of these are picture storybooks, illustrated works, and popular reference titles of general interest.

Barron's children's and young adult titles include *Patche's Easter Adventure* by Hans Wilhelm; *My Slide and See Books: Sounds* by Colin Petty; *Teddy Bear's Picnic* by Paulina

Malinen; *Little People Shape Book: Astronaut* by Giovanni Caviezel, illustrated by C. Mesturini; *Why Am I So Tired? "A First Look at..." Childhood Diabetes* by Pat Thomas, Illustrated by Lesley Harker; *Secret Agent File*, text by Moira Butterfield, design by Tony Potter; *Rembrandt and the Boy Who Drew Dogs* by Molly Blaisdell, illustrated by Nancy Lane; and *Mini Art: Cartoons* by Tony Potter.

Barron's offers an extensive general-interest series lineup of interest to students and educators: the Masters of Music series, the Megascope series, the Bravo series, the History series, the Natural World series, and the Literature Made Easy series.

Recent titles from Barron's are *1001 Historic Sites You Must See Before You Die* edited by Richard Cavendish; *Get Fit With Your Dog: A Companion Guide to Health* by Karen Sullivan; *Writing a Successful College Application Essay 4th Edition* by George Ehrenhaft; *Now You're Talking Arabic In No Time* by Hilary Wise PhD; *SAT Subject Test Math Level 2—2008* by Richard Ku, M.A. and Howard P. Dodge; *Modern Mandarin Chinese For Beginners* by Monika Mey; *Complete Guide to Materials and Techniques for Drawing and Painting* by David Sanmiguel; and *How to Write Better Resumes and Cover Letters 2nd Edition* by Pat Criscito, CPRW.

Barron's handles its own distribution. Send query letters with SASEs to the Acquisitions Manager.

Anna Damaskos, General Editor

Robert O'Sullivan, Managing Editor

BASIC BOOKS [SEE PERSEUS BOOK GROUP]

BASKERVILLE PUBLISHERS

7105 Golf Club Drive, Suite 1102, #112, Fort Worth, TX 76179

817-923-1064 / 866-526-2312   fax: 817-886-8713

www.baskervillepublishers.com   e-mail: authors@baskervillepublishers.com

Baskerville Publishers is a publisher of literary fiction and nonfiction, particularly books of interest to lovers of serious music and opera.

Baskerville titles include *Corelli: A Man, A Voice: 2nd Edition, Revised and Expanded* by Marina Boagno; *Domingo: My Operatic Roles* by Helena Matheopoulos; *Lauritz Melchior: The Golden Years of Bayreuth* by Ib Melchior; *Mario Lanza: An American Tragedy* by Armando Cesari; *Marilyn Horne: The Song Continues* by Marilyn Horne with Jane Scovell; *Just Doll: Book One in the Staten Bay Trilogy* by Janice Daugharty; *Joeseph Brodsky: A*

Personal Memoir by Ludmila Shtern; *The Fat Friend* by Julie Edelson; *The Sweet-Scented Manuscript* by Tito Perdue; and *Let Me See* by Kirsten Dodge.

Send queries and SASEs to:

F. Ann Whitaker, Controller

BEACON PRESS

25 Beacon Street, Boston, MA 02108

617-742-2110   fax: 617-742- 3097

www.beacon.org

Beacon Press celebrated its 150th anniversary in 2004. The Press has been a light of independent American publishing since 1854, when the house was established by the Unitarian Universalist Church. This is an independent publisher of serious nonfiction and fiction. The output is meant to change the way readers think about fundamental issues; they promote such values as freedom of speech and thought; diversity, religious pluralism, and anti-racism; and respect for diversity in all areas of life.

Beacon has published many groundbreaking classics, including James Baldwin's *Notes of a Native Son*, Herbert Marcuse's *One-Dimensional Man*, Jean Baker Miller's *Toward a New Psychology of Women*, and Mary Daly's *Gyn/Ecology*. In 1971, Beacon printed the Senator Gravel Edition of *The Pentagon Papers* in five volumes. This groundbreaking achievement marked the first time those papers had appeared in book form. Beacon is also the publisher of Marian Wright Edelman's best-selling book, *The Measure of Our Success: A Letter to My Children and Yours*, and Cornel West's acclaimed *Race Matters*.

Recent publications include *Acts of Faith: The Soul of an American Muslim: the Struggle for the Soul of a Generation* by Eboo Patel; *American Dreamers: What Dreams Tell Us about the Political Psychology of Conservatives, Liberals, and Everyone Else* by Kelly Bulkeley; *American Furies: Crime, Punishment, and Vengeance in the Age of Mass Imprisonment* by Sasha Abramsky; *In Defense of Childhood: Protecting Kids' Inner Wilderness* by Chris Mercogliano; *Love You to Pieces: Creative Writers on Raising a Child with Special Needs* edited by Suzanne Kamata; *Not Keeping Up with Our Parents: The Decline of the Professional Middle Class* by Nan Mooney; and *Surprised by God: How I Learned to Stop Worrying and Love Religion* by Danya Ruttenberg.

Beacon's current publishing program emphasizes African-American studies, anthropology, essays, gay/lesbian/gender studies, education, children and family issues, nature and the environment, religion, science and society, and women's studies. Beacon's continuing commitment to diversity is reflected in their Bluestreak books, which feature innovative literary writing by women. The series includes many acclaimed books, including the best sellers *Kindred* by Octavia Butler, *The Healing* by

Gayl Jones, and *A Thousand Pieces of Gold* by Ruthann Lum McCunn.

Beacon is an associate member of the Association of American University Presses and a department of the Unitarian Universalist Association.

Beacon Press is distributed to the trade by Houghton Mifflin.

Query letters, proposals, CVs, and SASEs should be sent by regular mail to the Editorial Department.

Amy Caldwell, Executive Editor

Gayatri Patnaik, Executive Editor

Brian Halley, Editor

Allison Trzop, Assistant Editor

BEAR AND COMPANY [SEE INNER TRADITIONS / BEAR AND COMPANY]

BENBELLA BOOKS

6440 N. Central Expressway, Suite 503, Dallas, TX 75206

214-750-3600

www.benbellabooks.com   email: feedback@benbellabooks.com

BenBella is an independent publishing house based in Dallas, Texas. Founded by Glenn Yeffeth in 2001, BenBella specializes in nonfiction books on popular culture, health, and nutrition, along with books on science, politics, psychology, and other topics.

BenBella publishes the acclaimed Smart Pop series, a series of anthologies on the best of pop culture. The Smart Pop series is where the world's smartest philosophers, scientists, psychologists, and religious scholars write—in clear English—about pop culture, and take television and movies seriously—but not too seriously.

Recent titles from BenBella Books include *Batman Unauthorized: Vigilantes, Jokers, and Heroes in Gotham City* edited by Dennis O'Neil; *The Psychology of Superheroes: An Unauthorized Exploration* edited by Robin Rosenberg, PhD; *History Revisited: The Great Battles: Eminent Historians Take On the Great Works of Alternative History* by J. David Markham and Mike Resnick; *The Science of Michael Crichton: An Unauthorized Exploration in the Real Science Behind the Fictional Worlds of Michael Crichton* by Kevin Grazier, PhD; and *The Miami Mediterranean Diet: Lose Weight and Lower Your Risk of Heart Disease* by Michael Ozner, MD.

BenBella is looking for nonfiction only. Address queries and SASEs to Editorial Submissions.

Glenn Yeffeth, Publisher

Adrienne Lang, Publishing Associate

Leah Wilson, Senior Editor

Yara Abuta, Production Manager

MATTHEW BENDER & COMPANY, INC.

744 Broad Street, Newark, NJ 07102

973-820-2000 / 800-833-9844   fax: 518-487-3584

www.bender.com

Founded in 1887, Matthew Bender is a member of the Reed Elsevier plc group and a leading provider of analytical legal research information (general references as well as state-specific works) in print, CD-ROM, and via the Internet. Their comprehensive legal information covers every major practice area and is authored by the leading experts in the legal community. Matthew Bender & Co, Inc. produces works in the fields of law, accounting, banking, insurance, and related professions. Areas of Bender concentration include general accounting, administrative law, admiralty, bankruptcy, civil rights law, computer law, elder law, employment/labor, environmental, estate and financial planning, federal practice and procedure, government, health care, immigration, insurance, intellectual property, law-office management, personal injury/medico-legal, products liability, real estate, securities, taxation, and worker's compensation.

Matthew Bender works in print include authoritative treatises and expert legal analysis such as *Collier on Bankruptcy, Moore's Federal Practice, Nimmer on Copyright*, and much more. Bender produces treatises, textbooks, manuals, and form books, as well as newsletters and periodicals. Many Matthew Bender publications are available in the CD-ROM format on the Internet and on LexisNexis.

Practicing attorneys often serve as contributing legal writers in their areas of expertise. Bender considers itself an essential partner with law professionals, providing integrated information, resources, and tools, and delivering that information in formats that help its customers reach solutions with confidence.

Representative titles from Bender include *Sanctions: The Federal Law of Litigation Abuse, 4th Edition* by Gregory P. Joseph; *Moore's Answerguide Federal Pretrial Civil Litigation* by the Law Firm of Jenner & Block, LLP; *The Lawyer's Guide to the AMA Guides and California Workers' Compensation, 2008 Edition* by Robert G. Rassp; and *Bender's Tax Return Manual 2008 Edition* by M. Kevin Bryant, JD, CPA.

Bender handles its own distribution. Query letters and SASEs should be directed to the Editorial Department.

BERRETT-KOEHLER PUBLISHERS

235 Montgomery Street, Suite 650, San Francisco, CA 94104-2916

415-288-0260   fax: 425-362-2512

www.bkconnection.com   e-mail: bkpub@bkpub.com

Founded in 1992, Berrett-Koehler Publishers is committed to supporting the movement toward a more enlightened work world. The house specializes in nonfiction titles that help integrate our values with our work and work lives in the hope of creating more humane and effective organizations. More specifically, the books focus on business, management, leadership, career development, entrepreneurship, human resources, and global sustainability.

The work world is going through tumultuous changes, from the decline of job security to the rise of new structures for organizing people and work. BK believes that change is needed at all levels—individual, organizational, community, and global. Their titles address each of these levels whether applying new scientific models to leadership, reclaiming spiritual values in the workplace, or using humor to cast light on the business world.

Just as BK publications are redefining the boundaries of business literature, the house is also "opening up new space" in the design and operation of their own business. Partnering with authors, suppliers, subcontractors, employees, customers, and societal and environmental communities, BK makes all involved in the creation of their books "stakeholders." They are striving to create a more equitable, open, and participative environment than is typically the case in the increasingly "lean and mean" world of corporate publishing.

Berrett-Koehler's current affairs line is called BK Currents. These titles explore the critical intersections between business and society with an eye on social and economic justice.

Recent titles include *Community: The Structure of Belonging* by Peter Block; *Framing the Future: How Progressive Values Can Win Elections and Influence People* by Bernie Horn; *Implementing the Four Levels: A Practical Guide for Effective Evaluation of Training Programs* by Donald L. Kirkpatrick and James D. Kirkpatrick; *Making Sustainability Work* by Marc J. Epstein; *Prisoners of Our Thoughts: Viktor Frankl's Principles for Discovering Meaning in Life and Work* by Alex Pattakos; and *Zenobia: The Curious Book of Business* by Matthew Emmens and Beth Kephart.

Berrett-Koehler tends its own multichanneled distribution, through bookstores, direct-mail brochures, catalogs, a toll-free telephone-order number, book clubs, association book services, e-books, and special sales to business, government, and nonprofit organizations. The house is distributed to the trade via Publishers Group West.

Query letters and SASEs should be directed to:

Steven Piersanti, Publisher

Johanna Vondeling, Editorial Director

Jeevan Sivasubramaniam, Senior Managing Editor

BETHANY HOUSE [SEE BAKER PUBLISHING GROUP]

BEYOND WORDS

20827 N.W. Cornell Road, Suite 500, Hillsboro, OR 97124-9808

503-531-8700   fax: 503-531-8773

www.beyondword.com   e-mail: info@beyondword.com

Founded in 1984 by Cynthia Black and Richard Cohen, Beyond Words is a boutique publisher that has sold over two million books and has over 200 titles in print, *The Secret* is their most famous book to date. In 2006, Beyond Words formed a co-publishing deal with Simon and Schuster's Atria imprint; while Beyond Words continues to publish 10 to 15 titles per year, Atria handles the marketing, publication design, and production for all Beyond Words titles.

Subjects include mind, body, & spirit, global native wisdom, spiritual lifestyles, spiritual parenting, holistic health, and science and spirituality. Beyond Words is the publisher of our own Deborah Herman's *Spiritual Writing from Inspiration to Publication*.

Other recent titles include *Sixty Seconds: One Moment Changes Everything* by Phil Bolsta; *Wishing: How to Fulfill Your Heart's Desires* by Elizabeth Harper; *The Circles* by Kerry Armstrong; and *Nurturing Spirituality in Children—Revised Edition* by Peggy Joy Jenkins.

Beyond Words looks for authors who have passion for their books and want to work in a collaborative way. Most of their titles are by first-time authors. The editors seek to discover new authors and develop best-selling book projects.

Beyond Words no longer publishes children's, cooking, or photography books. Due to high volume of submissions, they are unable to accept unsolicited manuscripts; however they are accepting submissions from literary agents or trusted advisers.

Cindy Black, President, Editor-in-Chief

Lindsay Brown, Managing Editor

BLOOMBERG PRESS

731 Lexington Avenue, New York, NY 10022

212-318-2000   fax: 917-369-5000

www.bloomberg.com/books   e-mail: press@bloomberg.com

Bloomberg Press publishes practical books for financial professionals as well as books of general interest on investing, economics, law, and current affairs. More than 130 titles have been released since 1996. The books are written by leading practitioners and specialists, including Bloomberg News reporters and columnists, and are published in more than 20 languages. The Press also publishes cartoon collections with *The New Yorker* and distributes the *Economist* line of books in the U.S.

Bloomberg Press is part of Bloomberg LP, the global, multimedia information service that provides news, data, and analysis to financial markets and businesses. The parent company's core product is the Bloomberg Professional service, the real-time financial-information network often referred to on Wall Street as "the Bloomberg." Bloomberg LP is the parent of Bloomberg News, which provides instantaneous electronic news to clients of the Bloomberg Professional service, to newspapers, and to other electronic media. Bloomberg News operates its own radio, Web, and television enterprises (Bloomberg Radio, Bloomberg.com, Bloomberg Television) in multiple languages 24/7 worldwide, and has been the source of a number of award-winning public-affairs books published by Bloomberg Press.

The goal at Bloomberg Press is to deliver a useful picture of how the capital markets work. Bloomberg Press books emphasize clear explanations and practical information. Authors are either prominent authorities or financial journalists. Target readers are brokers, traders, money managers, CEOs, CFOs, bankers, other professionals, and sophisticated investors. Subjects include investment intelligence, portfolio management, markets, financial instruments (equities, bonds, derivatives, real estate, alternative investments), financial analytics, risk management, financial planning, and economic analysis of use to traders, hedge fund managers, businesses and policymakers.

Bloomberg Press titles include *Option Strategies for Directionless Markets: Trading with Butterflies, Iron Butterflies, and Condors* by Anthony J. Salbia; Bonds: *The Unbeaten Path to Secure Investment Growth* by Hidley Richelson and Stan Richelson; *Breakthroughs in Technical Analysis: New Thinking from the World's Top Minds* edited by David Keller; and *Powerlines: Words That Sell Brands, Grip Fans, and Sometimes Change History* by Steve Cone.

Bloomberg Press is distributed by Ingram Publisher Services in North America and by Kogan Page outside the Americas. Bloomberg Press also markets its books and subsidiary rights to corporations and selling partners internationally through a variety of direct outlets, including traditional print venues and electronic distribution.

Bloomberg Press typically does not publish management, strategy, leadership, professional development, entrepreneurship, personal finance, or general consumer books.

Query first by email at press@bloomberg.com. Submissions and SASEs should be directed to the Editorial Acquisitions Department.

John Crutcher, Publisher

Stephen Isaacs, Editorial Director

BLOOMSBURY USA

BLOOMSBURY PRESS

BLOOMSBURY CHILDREN'S BOOKS USA

175 Fifth Avenue, 8th Floor, New York, NY 10010

212-674-5151   fax: 212-780-0015

www.bloomsburyusa.com   e-mail: info@bloomsburyusa.com

WALKER PUBLISHING COMPANY

646-307-5151   fax: 212-727-0984

www.walkerbooks.com

Bloomsbury USA, launched in 1998 by Bloomsbury Publishing plc, is an independent publisher of high-quality fiction and nonfiction for adults and children. Bloomsbury Publishing plc is a London-based publisher best known for literary novels and for being the original *Harry Potter* publisher. In 2004, Bloomsbury purchased U.S.-based Walker Publishing (see the separate entry). The acquisition and integration of Walker enabled Bloomsbury to broaden its presence in the U.S. market, especially in adult narrative nonfiction and children's nonfiction. In 2008, Bloomsbury debuts a new imprint, Bloomsbury Press, devoted to serious nonfiction and headed by Peter Ginna, former editorial director of Oxford University Press.

Bloomsbury USA adult titles include works in fiction, arts, memoir, science, travel, history, biography, food, humor, sports, gardening, relationships and self-help, crime, women's studies, reference, and current affairs.

Recent releases include *The Great Warming: Climate Change and the Rise and Fall of Civilizations* by Brian Fagan; *Schott's Almanac 2008* by Ben Schott; *The Gum Thief: Boxed Set* by Douglas Coupland; *The Book of Dave* by Will Self; *How to Talk About Books You Haven't Read* by Pierre Bayard; *An Ordinary Spy* by Joseph Weisberg; *Poster Child* by Emily Rapp; *How to Build a Robot Army* by Daniel H. Wilson; and *Zeus: A Journey Across Greece in the Footsteps of a God* by Tom Stone.

Titles from Bloomsbury Press include *The Art Instinct: Beauty, Pleasure, and Human Evolution* by Denis Dutton; *The Cuba Wars: Fidel Castro, The United States, and the Next Revolution* by Daniel P. Erikson; *The Irish Americans: A History* by Jay P. Dolan; *A Falling Off the Edge: Travels Through the Dark Heart of Globalization* by Alex Perry; and *Philan-*

throcapitalism: *How the Rich Are Trying to Save the World* by Matthew Bishop and Michael Green.

Recent children's titles from Bloomsbury USA include *Peiling and the Chicken-Fried Christmas* by Pauline Chen; *Big Fat Manifesto* by Susan Vaught; *Pandora Gets Jealous* by Carolyn Hennesy; *Trigger* by Susan Vaught; *Ophelia* by Lisa Klein; and *Merry Christmas, Cheeps!* by Julie Stiegmeyer.

Bloomsbury Children's Books welcomes picture book manuscripts and queries for longer works, whether fiction or nonfiction. They publish picture books, chapter books, easy readers, middle grade and YA novels, fantasy, and some nonfiction. With queries, please include a synopsis of the book and the first ten pages or first chapter to the Children's Book Acquisitions Department. Please do not send originals or only copies, because Bloomsbury Children's Books no longer respond to unsolicited submissions, and will only contact authors if they are interested in acquiring the work.

Bloomsbury USA does not accept unsolicited submissions, and does not assume responsibility for unsolicited manuscripts they receive. They consider manuscripts represented by established literary agents.

Because of new postal weight regulations, Bloomsbury cannot return any manuscripts, art, or other materials. Please only include recyclable materials with your submission, and send a letter-sized stamped envelope for their response only.

Karen Rinaldi, Publisher, Bloomsbury, USA

Melanie Cecka, Executive Editor, Bloomsbury Children's USA

Peter Ginna, Director, Bloomsbury Press

WALKER PUBLISHING COMPANY

Walker Publishing Company became an imprint of Bloomsbury USA when it was acquired by Bloomsbury in 2004. During the course of its 47-year history as an independent, Walker has published best sellers in its adult and children's lists; recently they have published Dava Sobel's best sellers, *Longitude* and *Galileo's Daughter*, Mark Kurlansky's *Cod and Salt*, Ross King's *Michelangelo and the Pope's Ceiling*, and Judith Finchler's children's classic, *Testing Miss Malarkey*, illustrated by Kevin O'Malley.

Walker has been credited in *Business Week* as "a pioneer of a now-ubiquitous book genre—stories about forgotten people or offbeat things that changed the world." Sometimes called microhistories, these books are biographies of inanimate objects—like salt or longitude. Walker publisher, George Gibson, said recently that he looks to acquire manuscripts with great storytelling and fine writing. He publishes books for "thoughtful folks."

The prolific Isaac Asimov published more books with Walker than with any other publisher, and now David Bodanis (*E=mc2*), Simon Singh (*Fermat's Enigma*), Chet Raymo (*Climbing Brandon and An Intimate Look at the Night Sky*) and, most recently, Harvard astronomer Owen Gingerich (*The Book Nobody Read*), have published with Walker.

Beth Walker started the children's division, which has now been a central part of the company for some 40 years, featuring authors such as Barbara Cooney, Tomie de

Paola, Michael McCurdy, and Pat and Fred McKissack, whose *Long Hard Journey* won the Coretta Scott King Award.

While mystery/thriller publishing is somewhat less the focus of the house, it has published John le Carré. Please note that Walker does not publish adult fiction outside of the mystery category. The house no longer publishes Westerns, thrillers, or Regency romance novels.

Recent Walker titles include *The Other Side of Silence: A Novel* by Bill Pronzini; *The Twilight Zone: The After Hours* created by Rod Sterling, adapted by Mark Kneece and illustrated by Rebekah Isaacs; *What Do Muslims Believe? The Roots and Realities of Modern Islam* by Ziauddin Sardar; and *Working IX to V: Orgy Planners, Funeral Clowns, and Other Prized Professions of the Ancient World* by Vicki Leon.

Recent Walker Young Readers titles include *Tigers in Red Weather: A Quest For The last Wild Tigers* by Ruth Padel; *Slang: The Topical Dictionary of Americanisms* by Paul Dickson; *28: Stories of AIDS in Africa* by Stephanie Nolen; *Silence of Songbirds* by Bridget Stutchbury; *Mahjong All Day Long* by Ginnie Lo; and *Look Closer: Art Masterpieces through the Ages* by Caroline Desnoettes.

Walker Young Readers is actively seeking middle-grade and YA novels and well-paced picture book manuscripts for the preschool and early elementary age levels. They do not publish folk tales, fairy tales, text books, myths, legends, series, novelties, science fiction, fantasy, or horror.

Submit your manuscript—or the first seventy-five pages of it—with SASE for a response only to (they recycle all submissions and return only their response):

George Gibson, Publisher, Walker

Emily Easton, Publisher, Walker Children's

Jacqueline Johnson, Editor, Walker—Adult non-fiction as per house interests.

BLUEBRIDGE BOOKS

240 West 35th Street, Suite 500, New York, NY 10001

212-244-4166   fax: 212-279-0927

www.bluebridgebooks.com   e-mail: janguerth@bluebridgebooks.com

BlueBridge is an independent publisher of international non-fiction based in New York City. BlueBridge subjects range from culture, history, biography, travel, and current affairs to spirituality, self-help, and inspiration, is a press focusing on books about spirituality. Publisher and founder, Jan-Erik Guerth, started BlueBridge after four years directing the Hidden Spring imprint of Paulist Press. Guerth left Hidden Spring in 2003 and spent a year preparing for the launch of BlueBridge, which he founded with his own money and investments from friends and family. BlueBridge is currently publishing six to eight books a year.

Recent titles from BlueBridge include *Horse: How the Horse has Shaped Civilizations* by J. Edward Chamberlin; *The Door of No Return: The History of Cape Coast Castle and the Atlantic Slave Trade* by William St. Clair; *The Friendship of Women: The Hidden Tradition of the Bible* by Joan Chittster; *A Mystic Garden: Working with Soil, Attending to Soul and Inviting Silence: Universal Principles of Meditation* by Gunilla Norris; and *The Book of Contemplation: 77 Words for Thought and Mediation* by H. Wyatt Rollins.

BlueBridge is distributed by IPG. Send queries and SASEs to

Jan-Erik Guerth, Publisher

THE BOOTSTRAP PRESS [SEE THE APEX PRESS]

BOYDS MILLS PRESS

A Subsidiary of Highlights for Children

815 Church Street, Honesdale, PA 18431

570-253-1164 / 800-490-5111

www.boydsmillspress.com e-mail: contact@boydsmillspress.com

CALKINS CREEK BOOKS

FRONT STREET

LEMINSCAAT

WORDSONG

Boyds Mills Press, the trade division of Highlights for Children, Inc., was launched in 1990. Publishing books was a logical step for Highlights, which has a long tradition of helping children develop a love of reading. Boyds Mills produces books for children, picture books, novels, nonfiction, and poetry—nonsensical verse, as well as more serious fare. The press promotes a solid seasonal list of new titles and hosts a hefty backlist of titles that challenge, inspire, and entertain.

Boyds Mills Press reaches children primarily through bookstores, libraries, and schools. The list runs about 50 books per year. Poetry, published under the Wordsong imprint, is the only imprint of its kind devoted exclusively to poetry for children.

Respect for children is among the highest priorities when Boyds Mills Press acquires a manuscript. They aim to publish good stories with lasting value, avoid the trendy, and never publish a book simply to fill a market need. Whether pure entertainment or more challenging subject matter, the story always comes first.

Recent Boyds Mills titles include *Imagine A Dragon* by Laurence Pringle, illustrated by Eujin Kim Neilan; *Turtle Girl* by Carol Crowe, illustrated by Jim Postier; *Everywhere the Cow Says "Moo"* by Ellen Slusky Winstein, illustrated by Kenneth Andersson; *Ookpik: The Travels of a Snowy Owl* by Bruce Hiscock; *The Puzzle of the Platypus and Other Explorations of Science in Action* by Jack Myers, illustrated by John Rice; *Wolfsnail: A Backyard Predator* by Sarah C. Campbell; and *The Best Eid Ever* by Asma Mobin-Uddin, illustrated by Laura Jacobsen.

The Calkins Creek Books imprint introduces children to the people, places, and events that shaped American history. Through picture books, chapter books, and novels for ages eight and up, combining original and extensive research with creative energetic writing, Calkins authors transport their readers back in time to recognizable places with living and breathing people. Recent books from Calkins Creek include *Farmer George Plants a Nation* by Peggy Thomas, illustrated by Larry Johnson; *Healing Water: A Hawaiian Story* by Joyce Moyer Hostetter; *Robert J. Jackson: New Deal Lawyer, Supreme Court Justice, Nuremberg Prosecutor* by Gail Jarrow; and *The Shakeress* by Kimberley Heuston.

Front Street publishes young adult fiction that deals with children in crisis or children at risk, and offers hope and comfort no matter how difficult the subject matter. Their picture books emphasize art and design. Recent titles from Front Street include *The Book of Jude* by Kimberley Heuston; *Child of Dandelions* by Shenaaz Nanji; *Dani Benonni: Long May He Live* by Bart Moeyaert; *Drive* by Nathan Clement; *Frontier Wolf* by Rosemary Sutcliff; and *Lizard Love* by Wendy Townsend.

Leminscaat is a highly esteemed publishing house located in Rotterdam, The Netherlands. Their list represents the broad traditions of European picture books and incorporates the best contemporary art, design, and story. Some titles from Leminscaat include *Like People* by Ingrid and Dieter Schubert; *The Sweetest Kiss* by Maranke Rinck, illustrated by Martijn van der Linden; *A Strange Day* by Iris can der Heide, illustrated by Marijke ten Cate; and *The Wish* by Erik van Os, illustrated by Paula Gerritsen.

Wordsong is the only imprint in children's publishing in America that is dedicated to poetry. Their books range from the silly to the serious and are infused with the wordplay and imagery that lets readers view the world in new and thoughtful ways. Latest from Wordsong include *Barefoot: Poems for Naked Feet* by Stefi Weisburd; *Black Stars in a White Night Sky* by JonArno Lawson, illustrated by Sherman Tjia; *A Crossing of Zebras: Animal Packs in Poetry* by Marjorie Maddox, illustrated by Philip Huber.

Boyds Mills Press handles its own distribution.

This publisher is actively seeking picture books, middle-grade and young adult novels, and nonfiction and poetry for all ages. Send manuscripts, query letters, and SASEs to:

Larry Rosler, Editorial Director

Carolyn P. Yoder, Editor—Calkins Creek

Andy Boyles, Editor—Science and Natural History

Joy Neaves, Editor—Front Street; jrneaves@frontstreetbooks.com

Joan Hyman, Editor—Wordsong

GEORGE BRAZILLER, INC.

171 Madison Avenue, New York, NY 10016

212-889-0909   fax: 212-689-5405

www.georgebraziller.com   e-mail: info@georgebraziller.com

Founded in 1955 and celebrating more than half a century in business, George Braziller, Inc., is a small, independent publishing house based in New York City. The house publishes international literature and beautiful books on art and design, architecture, and art movements and history. The house also publishes selected literary titles, as well as philosophy, science, history, criticism, and biographical works. Much of Braziller's fiction and poetry is foreign literature in translation, although the publisher does publish original literary novels (such as works by Janet Frame) and works in the English language that have received initial publication elsewhere. The house aims to be consistently discovering new writers and exploring new areas in the world of art.

Braziller also has a strong interest in literary criticism and writing relating to the arts, in addition to a small selection of contemporary and modern poetry. Essential Readings in Black Literature is a Braziller series that features world-class writers from around the globe. Other Braziller series include Library of Far Eastern Art and New Directions in Architecture.

Braziller recently introduced a Young Adult series with titles including *Figs and Fate: Stories about Growing Up in the Arab World Today* by Elsa Marston; and *changing, changing* by Aracelis Girmay.

Other recent titles include *The Sixty Nine Stations of the Kisokaido* by Hiroshige and Eisen; *Look Close, See Far: A Cultural Portrait of the Maya* with photographs by Bruce T. Martin; *Mountains of the Hear: Paintings of Kameda Bosai* with commentary by Stephen Addiss; *Convivencia: Jews, Muslims, and Christians in Medieval Spain* edited by Vivian Mann, Thomas Glick, and Jerrilynn Dodds; *To A Nightingale: Sonnets and Poems from Sappho to Borges* edited by Edward Hirsch.

Braziller titles are distributed by W.W. Norton & Co.

Submissions with manuscript and CV should be directed to:

George Braziller, Publisher

BRAZOS PRESS [SEE BAKER PUBLISHING GROUP]

BROADMAN & HOLMAN [SEE B & H PUBLISHING GROUP]

BROWN TROUT PUBLISHERS

P.O. Box 280070, San Francisco, CA 94128-0070

800-777-7812

www.browntrout.com   production@browntrout.com

Brown Trout is the leading publisher of calendars worldwide, producing and distributing over 900 titles per year in various formats. They also publish illustrated books in the following subjects: animals, architecture, astrology, humor, fantasy, photography, poetry, religions, science, self-help, and travel.

Recent titles include *The Floridas: The Sunshine State* by Clay Henderson, photography by Ian Adams; *Wild and Scenic Indiana* by Russell Sanders, photography by Rich Clark; *Within the Stone* with photography by Bill Atkinson; *For the Love of Dachshunds* by Robert Hutchinson, photography by Mark Raycroft, Isabelle Francais et al; *Dragon World* by Rob Brown; and *Images in Stone: Southwest Rock Art* by Polly Schaafsma, photographs by David Muench.

Brown Trout is interested in hearing from professional photographers. Tell them your subjects and format in a query letter via e-mail to production@browntrout.com.

BURNS & OATES [SEE CONTINUUM INTERNATIONAL PUBLISHING GROUP]

CANONGATE BOOKS [SEE GROVE / ATLANTIC, INC.]

CAREER PRESS

NEW PAGE BOOKS

3 Tice Road, P.O. Box 687, Franklin Lakes, NJ 07417

201-848-0310 / 800-227-3371

www.careerpress.com

www.newpagebooks.com

With their motto "Enriching Your Life One Book at a Time," Career Press publishes general nonfiction that addresses real, practical needs. Their useful, accessible "how-to" books reach a broad market of average Americans—people grappling with issues relating to job-hunting, career management, education, money management, and personal goals.

Career Press was launched in 1985 with a commitment to publish quality books on careers, business, reference, motivation, sales, personal finance, real estate, and more. Career Press publishes quality books on topics most needed in the marketplace, written by established, credentialed, media-savvy professionals, and then promotes and publicizes them full force. They are seeking books in the categories of business, career, job search, college preparation, small business, entrepreneurship, motivation, sales, negotiation, study aids, and reference. This list is not comprehensive, and other categories are published based on the project's tone, approach, and sales potential.

Recent titles from Career Press include *Fiscal Fitness: 8 Steps to Wealth and Health From America's Leaders of Fitness and Finance* by Jack LaLanne and Matthew J. Rettick; *How to Sell Yourself: Using Leadership, Likeability, and Luck to Succeed* by Arch Lustberg; *All Star Sales Teams: 8 Steps to Spectacular Success Using Goals, Values, Vision, and Rewards* by Dan Kleinmann; *100 Ways to Motivate Others: How Great Leaders Can Produce Insane Results Without Driving Other People Crazy* by Steve Chandler and Scott Richardson; and *Family, Inc.: How to Manage Parents, Siblings Spouses, Children, and In-Laws in the Family Business* by Larry and Laura Collin.

In 2000 Career Press created a new imprint, New Page Books, to expand the category list to include New Age, supernatural/paranormal, ancient mysteries, Wicca, mythology, alternative health, nutrition/wellness, pop history, and weddings.

Recent titles from New Page include *Flying Saucers and Science: A Scientist Investigates the Mysteries of UFOs, Interstellar Travel, Crashes, and Government Cover-Ups* by Stanton T. Friedman, MSc; *Dark Matters: Unifying Matter, Dark Matter, Dark Energy, and the Universal Grid* by Dr. Percy Seymour; *2013: The End of Days or a New Beginning? Envisioning the World After the Events of 2012* by Marie D. Jones; and *The United Symbolism of America: Deciphering Hidden Meanings in America's Most Familiar Art, Architecture, and Logos* by Robert Hieronimus, PhD with Laura Cartner.

Career Press/New Page Books distributes its own list.

Query letters, proposals, and SASEs should be directed to the Acquisitions Department.

Michael Pye, Acquisitions Editor; mpye@careerpress.com

CCC PUBLICATIONS

9725 Lurline Avenue, Chatsworth, CA 91311

818-718-0507   fax: 818-718-0655

Founded in 1983, CCC Publications accents nonfiction trade books in crisply targeted categories: relationships, self-help and how-to, humor, inspiration, humorous inspirational titles, age-related and over-the-hill titles, gift books, and a series catalogued as On the Edge. CCC has published a number of books by best-selling author Jan King.

Recent CCC titles include *The Poetry Oracle* by Amber Guetebier and Brenda Knight and *Sacred Places North America: 108 Destinations* by Brad Olsen.

Best-selling CCC titles have included *Hormones from Hell: The Ultimate Women's Humor Book* by Jan King; *Farting: Gas Past, Present, and Future* by Desmond Mullan; and *50 Ways to Hustle Your Friends* by Jim Karol.

From the On the Edge series: *Men are Pigs, Women are Bitches* by Jerry King; *The Very, Very Sexy Adult Dot to Dot Book* by Tony Goffe; and *The Complete Wimp's Guide to Sex* by Jed Pascoe.

CCC handles its own distribution.

Query and SASEs should be directed to the Editorial Staff.

CEDAR FORT, INC.

CFI BOOKS

BONNEVILLE BOOKS

COUNCIL PRESS

SWEETWATER BOOKS

2373 West 700 South, Springville, UT 84663

801-489-4084 / 800-SKYBOOK   fax: 801-489-1097 / 800-388-3727

www.cedarfort.com

HORIZON PUBLISHERS

191 N. 560 East, Bountiful, UT 84010-3628

801-295-9451 / 866-818-6277   fax: 801-298-1305

www.horizonpublishersbooks.com

e-mail: service@horizonpublishersbookstore.com

Cedar Fort was founded in May 1896 and initially produced LDS books for other publishers as an LDS book printer broker. Founder Lyle Mortimer began distributing LDS books and other items until in September 1987 the company released its first publication, *Beyond the Veil* by Lee Nelson, which became an immediate bestseller.

CFI searches for life-enriching, edifying, and enhancing LDS books geared to the Latter-day Saint marker in any form. In recent years the company has published several highly acclaimed novels and continues to branch out into the world beyond the LDS books market, both in the traditional manner and on the internet and alternative markets.

CFI Books publishes LDS doctrinal books, scriptural commentaries, self-help, cookbooks, and some fiction. Recent titles from CFI Books include *The End of Times* by Connie Joslin; *Evidences of the True Church* by Dennis K. Brown; *The Fun Never Stops: Games for Families, Groups, and Special Occasions* by MaryLou Bailey; *Jacob Hamblin* by Hartt Wixom; *The Pioneers: A Course in Miracles* by Shirley Bahlmann; *Starting Over Single: A Guide for Previously Married Latter-Day Saints* by Teena Read; and *Waiting for the Light to Change* by Annette Haws.

Bonneville Books mainly publishes LDS fiction. Titles from Bonneville Books include *Against the Giant* by Christy Hardman; *Spare Change* by Aubrey Mace; *Heaven Scent* by Rebecca Talley; *Make Me a Home* by Tamra Norton; *Caleb's Quest* by Chris Esseltine; *Fields in Sunshine Upon the Hill: An Anthology of Short Stories and Poetry* by Clay McConkie; *Makeover* by Shannon Guymon; *Reasonable Doubt* by Marcia Mickelson; and *Don't You Marry the Mormon Boys* by Janet Kay Jensen.

Council Press mostly publishes historical fiction and nonfiction. Titles include *The White Bedouin* by George Potter; *The Bearded White God of Ancient America: The Legend of Quetzalcoatl* by Donald Hemingway and W. David Hemmingway; *Jumping Off Places* by Laura Stratton Friel.

Sweetwater Books produces books intended primarily for the national market. Titles include *Trust in the Lord: Reflections of Jesus Christ* by Deen Kemsley and *The Shell Game* by Steve Alten.

Send a query letter and SASE to:

Kammi Rencher, Acquisitions Editor

Jeffrey Marsh, Acquisitions Editor

HORIZON PUBLISHERS

Horizon Publishers is a family-run corporation that publishes wholesome, informative books and tapes for a variety of marketplaces. In 2004, Horizon was acquired by Cedar

Fort, Inc. (CFI), a leading publisher of LDS (Latter-day Saints) fiction and nonfiction titles since its founding in 1986; CFI now publishes 100 titles per year, roughly 25% of the Utah book market. In a unique arrangement, CFI is slowly acquiring Horizon's assets; Horizon continues its editorial operations while CFI picks up production and distribution.

Established in 1971, Horizon Publishers has various product lines in which it has "distinctive competencies"—publishing areas in which it is noted for having a strong offering of products of noteworthy quality. In the general trade market, these areas include such topics as outdoor life, camping, Dutch-oven and outdoor cooking, cookbooks, outdoor survival skills, food storage, gardening, emergency preparedness, life-after-death and near-death experiences, marriage and family life, and counted cross-stitch designs.

Many of Horizon Publishers' books are written for readers in the general religious marketplace. Numerous books the firm produces are for the general Christian marketplace, including those on marriage, family life, raising and teaching children, Bible studies, and comparative religions.

Much of Horizon's religious publishing is directed to members of the Latter-day Saint faith, though the company is privately owned and a completely independent organization—it is not an "official outlet" or "spokesman" for The Church of Jesus Christ of Latter-day Saints, and the LDS Church does not exercise any control or supervision of what Horizon Publishers produces or publishes.

As in the general trade marketplace, Horizon Publishers has distinctive competencies in the LDS marketplace, including scriptural studies, books on doctrine, missionary items, defense-of-the-faith books and tapes, wholesome fiction, food storage and emergency readiness products, self-help books, near-death and life-after-death studies, angels, prophecy and the last days, inspirational counted cross-stitch (including designs of almost all of the Mormon temples), Latter-day Saint and Utah history, etc.

Recent titles include *9 New Mormon Temples: Learn How to Cross-Stitch Temples* by Jean D. Crowther; *The Godhead: New Scriptural Insights on the Father, the Son, and the Holy Ghost and How to Understand the Book of Isaiah* by Duane S. Crowther.

Horizon Publishers is distributed by Cedar Fort.

The editorial board of Horizon Publishers seeks products that will lift, inspire, inform, and entertain its readers. Horizon publishes 20–30 new titles per year, selecting its new releases from the 2,000-plus queries and manuscripts it receives annually. Direct queries, proposals, and SASEs to the Editorial Board.

Jean D. Crowther, Founder and CEO

Duane S. Crowther, Founder and CEO

CELESTIAL ARTS [SEE TEN SPEED PRESS]

CHELSEA GREEN PUBLISHING COMPANY

P.O. Box 428, 85 North Main Street, Suite 120, White River Junction, VT 05001

802-295-6300   fax: 802-295-6444

www.chelseagreen.com   e-mail: info@chelseagreen.com

Chelsea Green publishes trade nonfiction on sustainable living, organic gardening and food, renewable energy and green building, nature and the environment, and books on political and social issues. Founded in 1984, Chelsea Green Publishing is an independent and individualistic firm; the house continues to grow its list with about 20 new releases each year (in hardcover and trade paper formats) and a hardy backlist with well over 400 titles in print. Chelsea Green sees publishing as a tool for effecting cultural change. Their purpose is "to stop the destruction of the natural world by challenging the beliefs and practices that are enabling this destruction and by providing inspirational and practical alternatives that promote sustainable living."

Recent Chelsea Green titles are *The End of America: A Letter of Warning to a Young Patriot* by Naomi Wolf; *Exposed: The Toxic Chemistry of Everyday Products and What's At Stake for American Power* by Mark Schapiro; *Surviving America's Depression Epidemic: How to find Morale, Energy, and Community in a World Gone Crazy* by Bruce E. Levine; *The Man Who Hated Work and Loved Labor: The Life and Times of Tony Mazzocchi* by Les Leopold; *Javatrekker: Dispatches from the World of Fair Trade Coffee* by Dean Cycon; and *Sharing the Harvest: A Citizen's Guide to Community Supported Agriculture* by Elizabeth Henderson.

Chelsea Green handles its own distribution and distributes for a number of other small, innovative independent presses such as Green Books, Ltd.; Otto Graphics; Ecological Design Press; Harmonious Press; and Seed Savers Exchange.

An electronic query may be addressed to submissions@chelseagreen.com. Proposals with SASEs should be directed via regular mail to:

Margo Baldwin, President and Publisher; mbaldwin@chelseagreen.com

Shay Totten, Editorial Director; stotten@chelseagreen.com

Ben Watson, Senior Consulting Editor; bwatson@chelseagreen.com

CHOCKSTONE [SEE THE GLOBE PEQUOT PRESS]

CHOSEN BOOKS [SEE BAKER PUBLISHING GROUP]

CHRONICLE BOOKS

680 Second Street, San Francisco, CA 94107

415-537-4200 / 800-722-6657   fax: 415-537-4460

www.chroniclebooks.com   e-mail: frontdesk@chroniclebooks.com

Chronicle Books was founded in 1967 and over the years has developed a reputation for award-winning, innovative books. The company continues to challenge conventional publishing wisdom, setting trends in both subject and format. Chronicle titles include cookbooks, fine art, design, photography, architecture titles, nature books, poetry and literary fiction, travel guides, and gift items. Chronicle publishes about 175 books per year.

Titles of note include Martha Zamora's *Frida Kahlo: The Brush of Anguish* (1990), and Nick Bantock's *Griffin & Sabine* (1991). Originally slated for an edition of 10,000, this interactive book became the most talked-about title of the year and a *New York Times* best seller for 50 weeks. The two subsequent volumes in the trilogy, *Sabine's Notebook* and *The Golden Mean*, were also *Times* best sellers. A more recent monster hit was the *Worst-Case Scenario* franchise.

The company brought the same innovative philosophy to cookbooks with its four-color release of *Sushi* (1981), which sold 90,000 copies and is still in print. Chronicle Books also publishes James McNair's eye-catching cookbooks, all perennial bestsellers having sold over one million copies.

The Children's list was launched in 1988 and has published the best-selling *Mama, Do You Love Me?* (over one million copies in hardcover), *Ten Little Rabbits* (450,000 copies), and N.C. Wyeth's *Pilgrims* (100,000 copies). The list has grown to include not only traditional picture books but also affordable paperbacks, board books, plush toys, and novelty merchandise.

In 1992, Chronicle Books launched its gift division to develop ancillary products such as the Griffin & Sabine address book and writing box, the best-selling 52 Deck series, and a motorcycle journal and address book based on the Harley-Davidson image archives.

Recent Chronicle titles are *Eco Dog: Healthy Living for Your Pet* by Corbett Marshall and Jim Deskivich, photographs by Aimee Herring; *Modern Dog: 20 Years of Poster Art* by Mike Strassburger and Robynne Raye; *Every Day is Mothers Day* by Darrin Zeer, illustrated by Katy Dockrill; *Top Chef: The Cookbook* foreword by Tom Colicchio; *1,001 Pearls of Yoga Wisdom: Take Your Practice Beyond the Mat* by Liz Lark; and *How to Cheat in Sports: Professional Tricks Exposed!* by Scott Ostler.

Recent Chronicle Children's books include *Hide-and-Seek Big Trucks and Diggers* by Betty Ann Schwartz; *It's a Money Thing! A Girl's Guide to Managing Money* by Susan Estelle Kwas; *Paleo Bugs: Survival of the Creepiest* by Timothy J. Bradley; *T is for Tugboat: Navigating the Seas from A to Z* by Traci N. Todd and Sara Gillingham; *Wave* by Suzy Lee; *Grandma Calls Me Beautiful* by Barbara M. Joosse and Barbara Lavellee; and *How to Raise Your Parents: A Teen Girl's Survival Guide* by Sarah O. and Bella Phair.

For adult titles, query letters, proposals, and SASEs should be directed via regular mail only to the Editorial Staff. Fiction authors should submit the entire manuscript.

With children's titles, projects for older children should be submitted by a query letter, synopsis, and three sample chapters, with SASE. Projects for younger children may be sent in their entirety. Send via regular mail to the Children's Division.

Sarah Malarkey, Publishing Director

Jodi Warshaw, Senior Editor

Victoria Rock, Editor-at-Large—Children's

Jay C. Schaffer, Editorial Director

Bill LeBlond, Editorial Director—Cookbooks

CITADEL [SEE KENSINGTON PUBLISHING CORP.]

CITY LIGHTS PUBLISHERS

261 Columbus Avenue, San Francisco, CA 94133

415-362- 8193   fax: 415-362-4921

www.citylights.com   e-mail: staff@citylights.com

City Lights publishes literary essays and criticism, biography, philosophy, literary fiction (including first novels), poetry, books on political and social issues and ecumenical volumes featuring both words and visual images.

City Lights Booksellers and Publishers is a renowned American institution. Founded in 1953 by Beat poet Lawrence Ferlinghetti, its San Francisco bookstore is a North Beach landmark and, above all else, a resolute cultural tradition.

City Lights initially featured the Pocket Poets series, which introduced such writers as Gregory Corso, Allen Ginsberg, Jack Kerouac, and other Beats to a wider audience. Since then, as successive literary generations have commenced and terminated, City Lights continues to flourish. Today, it has nearly 200 titles in print and puts out a dozen new titles each year.

Recent City Lights titles include *Writing For A Democratic Society: The Tom Hayden Reader* by Tom Hayden; *Voices of the Chicago 8: A Generation on Trial* by Tom Hayden, Frank Condon, and Ron Sossi; *Crude Reflections/Cruda Realidad: Oil, Ruin, and Resistance in the Amazon Rainforest* by Lou Dematteis and Kayana Szymczak; *Portions From a Wine-Stained Notebook: Uncollected Stories and Essays, 1944-1990* by Charles Bukowski, edited by David Calonne; *Tau* by Philip Lamantia: *Journey to the End* by John Hoffman and Philip Lamantia; and *State of Exile: Pocket Poets Number 58* by Cristina Peri Rossi.

City Lights is distributed by Consortium Book Sales and Distribution and has its own in-house mail-order fulfillment department.

Query letters and SASEs should be directed to:

Elaine Katzenberger, Acquisitions Editor—Latin American literature, women's studies, fiction

James Brook, Acquisitions Editor—Nonfiction

Nancy J. Peters, Publisher and Executive Editor

Robert Sharrard, Acquisitions Editor—Poetry and literature

CLARION CHILDREN'S BOOKS [SEE HOUGHTON MIFFLIN]

CLEIS PRESS

P.O. Box 14697, San Francisco, CA 94114

415-575-4700 / 800-780-2279   fax: 415-575-4705

www.cleispress.com   e-mail: cleis@cleispress.com

Founded in 1980, Cleis Press publishes 34 new books a year on sexual politics and self-help, lesbian and gay studies and culture, sex guides, feminism, fiction, erotica, humor, and translations of world-class literature. Cleis titles cross markets from niches of gender and sexuality to reach the widest possible audiences.

Projects from Cleis Press garner numerous awards and reviews—and include many best-selling books. The house is committed to publishing the most original, creative, and provocative works by women and men in the U.S. and Canada.

Recent titles from the Cleis list include *My Miserable, Lonely, Lesbian Pregnancy* by Andrea Askowitz; *The Palace of Verities* by James Lear; *Hard Hats: Gay Erotic Stories* edited by Neil Plakcy; *Yes Sir: Erotic Stories of Female Submissions* edited by Rachel Kramer Bussel; *K is for Kinky*, edited by Alison Tyler; and *Healing Sex: A Mind-Body Approach to Healing Sexual Trauma* by Staci Haines.

Cleis Press is represented to the book trade by Publishers Group West.

Please do not send submissions via USPS or any other delivery service. Email queries only are accepted. Book proposals and sample chapters with SASEs should be directed to:

Frédérique Delacoste, Publisher and Acquisitions Editor; fdelacoste@cleispress.com

---

CLEVELAND STATE UNIVERSITY POETRY CENTER

2121 Euclid Avenue, RT 1841, Cleveland, Ohio 44115-2214

216-687-3986 / 888-278-6473   fax: 216-687-6943

www.csuohio.edu/poetrycenter   e-mail: poetrycenter@csuohio.edu

The Cleveland State University Poetry Center was founded in 1962 to offer encouragement to poets and writers and to further the public's knowledge of and appreciation for contemporary poetry. The Series Editor and Director is Michael Dumanis. The Poetry Center Manager is Rita Grabowski.

The Poetry Center began publishing in 1971 and since that time has developed a list of 145 nationally distributed titles. The press publishes poets of local, regional, and international reach, generally under the aegis of one or another of the center's ongoing series. Under its flying-unicorn logo, CSU Poetry Center most often publishes trade paper editions, but has also offered some titles in hardbound. Its publications include the national "CSU Poetry Series," the "Cleveland Poets Series" for Ohio writers, as well as other titles of interest, including the Imagination series. CSU Poetry Center presents a variety of styles and viewpoints—some with evident sociopolitical bent, others with broadly inspirational themes, and others notable for their strong individualistic inflections.

The current editorial board consists of David Evett, Bonnie Jacobson, Ted Lardner, Ruth Schwartz, and Leonard Trawick. The Cleveland State University Poetry Center

Prize of $1,000 is awarded for the best book-length manuscript in two categories sub-mitted annually from November 1st up through March 1st. There is a $25.00 readers fee The "Open" Competition is limited to poets who have published at least one book-length collection of their poems. The "First Book" Competition is for poets who have not previously published a full-length collection. Send a business-sized, self-addressed, stamped envelope for complete contest guidelines, or check the "Contest Guidelines" link on their website.

The Poetry Center also sponsors the Annual Ruthanne Wiley Novella Contest, offering a $1,000 prize and publication for a novella of 60 to 120 pages. There is a $25.00 readers fee, and the submission period runs from April 1st up to October 1st.

Some titles from the Cleveland State University Poetry Center are *To See the Earth* by Philip Metres; *A Martyr for Suzy Kosasovitch* by Patrick Michael Finn; *Sunflower Brother* by Sam Witt; *A Momentary Jokebook* by Jayson Iwen; *Piece Work* by Barbara Presnell; *Duo: Novellas, Isn't That Just Like You* by Eric Anderson and *Nothing and Two* by Ruthanne Wiley.

Poetry Center books are distributed through Partners Book Distributing, Ingram, and Spring Church Book Company.

The Poetry Center accepts manuscripts only from submitted between November 1 and February 1 ($25 entry fee; full manuscripts only). For complete guidelines on the Center's annual competitions, visit the Web site or send request plus SASE to:

Ted Lardner, Director

Rita Grabowski, Director

COFFEE HOUSE PRESS

27 North Fourth Street, Suite 400, Minneapolis, MN 55401

612-338-0125   fax: 612-338-4004

www.coffeehousepress.org

Coffee House Press was founded in 1984, and took its name from the long tradition of coffee houses as places for the free exchange of ideas, where each individual had equal time for expression, regardless of station or background. The press is an award-win-ning, nonprofit literary publisher dedicated to innovation in the craft of writing and preservation of the tradition of book arts. Coffee House produces books that present the dreams and ambitions of people who have been underrepresented in published lit-erature, books that shape our national consciousness while strengthening a larger sense of community. The house produces contemporary poetry, short fiction, and novels. Contemporary writing that is challenging, thought-provoking, daring, vibrant, funny or lyrical is the key.

Coffee House Press aims to enrich our literary heritage; and to contribute to the cultural life of our community. Coffee House Press publishes books that advance the craft of writing; the house colophon is a steaming book that lets the reader know (as the Coffee House motto runs) "where good books are brewing."

Recent titles from Coffee House include *The Latehomecomer: A Hmong Family Memoir* by Kao Kaila Yang; *Open Line: A Novel* by Ellen Hawley; *Night Train: Stories* by Lise Erdrich; *Rounding the Human Corners: Poems* by Linda Hogan; *Things I Must Have Known: Poems* by A.B. Spellman; *Isle of the Signatories: Poems* by Marjorie Welsh; *Saltwater Empire: Poems* by Raymond McDaniel; and *The Romance of Happy Workers: Poems* by Anne Boyer.

Coffee House Press oversees its own marketing and sales network with the assistance of regional representatives; trade distribution is handled by Consortium.

Coffee House is not accepting new poetry submissions now. For fiction, query letters with 20–30 page samples and SASEs should be directed to:

Christopher Fischbach, Senior Editor

COLLECTOR BOOKS

A Division of the Schroeder Publishing Company

5801 Kentucky Dam Road, Paducah, KY 42003-9323

Mailing address:

P.O. Box 3009, Paducah, KY 42003-9323.

270-898-6211   fax: 270-898-8890

www.collectorbooks.com   e-mail: editor@collectorbooks.com

Collector Books was founded in 1969 and is a division of Schroeder Publishing Company. The house is dedicated to bringing the most up-to-date information and values to collectors in an attractive high-quality format. Their books are designed to be practical, easy-to-use tools to assist collectors in their pursuit of antiques and collectibles. The range of collectibles covered is always growing and now includes fields such as Depression-era glass, pottery and porcelain, china and dinnerware, cookie jars and salt shakers, stoneware, paper collectibles, Barbie dolls, dolls, toys, quilts, tools and weapons, jewelry, and accessories, furniture, advertising memorabilia, bottles, Christmas collectibles, cigarette lighters, decoys, doorstops, and gas station memorabilia.

Collector's publications are liberally illustrated editions, generally filled with histories, production facts and lore, research sources, and identification information. Collector Books also produces inventory ledgers for professional dealers and avid collectors. The house produces a midsize list of new offerings each year and maintains a sizable backlist of nearly 400 titles.

Every August, Collector publishes *Schroeder's Antiques Price Guide*, which features more than 50,000 listings and hundreds of photographs for identification and current values, as well as background and historical information.

Recent Collector Book's titles are *The Encyclopedia of Collectible Children's Book* by Diane McClure Jones and Rosemary Jones; *A Pictorial Guide to Costume Jewelry* by Ariel Bloom; *The Antique and Collectible Dictionary* by Robert Reed and Claudette Reed; *English China Patterns and Pieces* by Mary Frank Gatson; *Ancient Indian Artifacts Vol. 1: Introduction to Collecting* by Jim Bennett; *Matchbox Toys 1947 to 2007 Fifth Edition* by Dana Johnson; *Rumrull Pottery the Ohio Years 1938-1942* by Francesca Fisher; and *The Encyclopedia of Universal Potteries* by David J. Chorey.

Collector Books looks for its authors to be knowledgeable people who are considered experts within their fields. Writers who feel there is a real need for a book on their collectible subject and have available a large comprehensive collection are invited to contact the publisher at the house's mailing address.

Collector Books distributes its own list, targeting particularly bookstore buyers and antiques-trade professionals. Collector Books operates an especially strong mail-order program and purveys selected works from other publishers, including out-of-print titles in the collectibles and antiques field. Query letters and SASEs should be directed to:

Bill Schroeder, Publisher

CONARI PRESS [SEE RED WHEEL / WEISER, LLC]

CONTINUUM INTERNATIONAL PUBLISHING GROUP

BURNS & OATES

T&T CLARK, USA

THOEMMES PRESS

15 East 26th Street, New York, NY 10010

212-953-5858   fax: 212-953-5944

www.continuumbooks.com   e-mail: info@continuum-books.com

Continuum is the trade and academic imprint of the Continuum International Publishing Group, a growing family of religious, trade and academic publishers headquartered in London, with offices in New York, Harrisburg, Denver, Bristol and Poole. Continuum publishes high-quality nonfiction in the humanities, including theology and religious studies, spirituality, philosophy, education, linguistics, literature, performing arts, the social sciences, women's studies, and popular culture. With a wide range of books from their popular music series, 33 1/3, to works by the great Jewish theologian Abraham Joshua Heschel, Jonathan Sacks, Chief Rabbi of Britain and the Commonwealth, and philosopher Roger Scruton, Continuum's books are read by academics, educators, librarians, students and the intellectually curious around the world. Its output consists of trade books, texts, scholarly monographs, and reference works. Continuum offers about 500 new publications a year, as well as nearly 6,000 established backlist titles.

From the Continuum list are *Disputed Truth: Memoirs* by Hans Kung; *Internationalizing the University* by Yvonne Turner and Sue Robson; *John Osborne's Look Back in Anger* by Aleks Sierz; *Truth, Meaning, and Realism: Essays in the Philosophy of Thought* by A. C. Grayling; *Culturally Speaking: Culture, Communication, and Politeness Theory* by Helen Spencer-Oately; and *Who's Afraid of Deleuze and Guattari? (Continuum Studies in Continental Philosophy)* by Gregg Lambert.

Burns & Oates is the premier Roman Catholic publishing imprint in Great Britain, and a leading imprint throughout the English-speaking world. Authors include Timothy Radcliffe OP, Joseph Ratzinger (now Pope Benedict XVI), Cardinal Daneels, Eamon Duffy, Cardinal Walter Kasper, and Anselm Grün. Recent titles include *Touched by God: Ten Monastic Journeys* by Laurenthia Johns; *The Origins of the Cult of the Virgin Mary* by Chris Maunder; and *Thought of Pope Benedict XVI: An Introduction to the Theology of Joeseph Ratzinger* by Aidan Nichol.

T&T Clark's tradition of publishing works by world-class scholars in both Europe and North America stretches back to 1821, when it was founded in Edinburgh by Thomas Clark (he was joined in 1846 by his nephew, also named Thomas). T&T Clark became part of Continuum in 2000. In 2003, the three religious academic imprints of Sheffield Academic Press, Trinity Press International and T&T Clark were united under one imprint.

The list includes past and present biblical scholars such as James D. G. Dunn, Richard Hays, Martin Hengel and Gerd Theissen, and theologians such as Karl Barth, Wolfhart Pannenberg, Karl Rahner and T.F. Torrance. Recent T&T Clark titles include *Divine and Human Agency in Paul and His Cultural Environment* by John M. G. Barclay and Simon J. Gathercole; *Who Do My Opponents Say That I Am? An Investigation of the Accusations Against Jesus* by Scot McKnight and Joeseph B. Modica; *Christianity and Scripture: Interdisciplinary Perspectives* by Andrew T. Lincoln and Angus Paddison; and *No Longer Male and Female: Interpreting Galatians 3:28 in Early Christianity* by Pauline Hogan.

Thoemmes Press began in 1989 as an adjunct to Thoemmes Antiquarian Books. Subsequently Thoemmes Press became independent. The press rapidly established an international reputation for scholarly reference publishing. In particular, it published primary source material (often in facsimile form, but sometimes re-set) and Biographical Dictionaries in Philosophy and allied areas of intellectual history. Recent Thoemmes Press titles include *The Biographical Dictionary of British Economists* by Donald Rutherford; *British Education: Or, The Source of the Disorders of Great Britain* by

Thomas Sheridan; *The Dictionary of Seventeenth-Century French Philosophers* by Luc Fois-neau.

Continuum is distributed through Books International. Continuum also distributes the publishing programs of Chiron Publications, Daimon Publications, Spring Publications, and Paragon House.

Query letters via e-mail are preferred, or send via regular mail with SASEs, to the appropriate editor:

David Barker, Ph.D., U.S. Editorial Director—Film, music & popular culture; david@continuum-books.com

Henry Carrigan, Publisher, T&T Clark US—Biblical studies, theology & religious studies; hcarriga@continuum-books.com

Frank Oveis, VP and Senior Editor (also acquiring projects for Burns & Oates)—Catholic studies, spirituality, Judaica, and current affairs; frank@continuum-books.com

Evander Lomke, VP and Senior Editor (also acquiring projects for Thoemmes Press)—Literary criticism, performing arts, social thought, and women's studies; evander@continuum-books.com

COOL SPRING PRESS [SEE THOMAS NELSON, INC.]

COPPER CANYON PRESS

P.O. Box 271, Port Townsend, WA 98368

360-385-4925 / 877-501-1393   fax: 360-385-4985

www.coppercanyonpress.org   e-mail: poetry@coppercanyonpress.org

Copper Canyon Press was founded in 1972 in the belief that good poetry is essential to the individual spirit and a necessary element in a thriving culture. The press publishes poetry exclusively and has established an international reputation for its commitment to its authors, editorial acumen, and dedication to expanding the audience of poetry. The Copper Canyon mission is to publish poetry distinguished in both content and design, within the context of belief that the publisher's art—like the poet's—is sacramental. The press publishes in hardcover and paperback.

Copper Canyon Press publishes new collections of poetry by both revered and emerging American poets, anthologies, prose books about poetry, translations of classical and contemporary work from many of the world's cultures, and re-issues of out-of-print poetry classics. Within its ambitious vision, there are limitations; Copper Canyon generally does not sign many new writers. The house assigns its resources to furthering its established roster. The publisher's success in its aim is proven through abundant and continuing recognition of its authors via honors, awards, grants, and fellowships.

Copper Canyon has published more than 300 books and CDs, including works by Nobel Laureates Pablo Neruda, Odysseas Elytis, Octavio Paz, Vincente Aleixandre, and Czeslaw Milosz; Pulitzer Prize-winners Carolyn Kizer, Maxine Kumin, and W.S. Merwin; and National Book Award winners Hayden Carruth and Lucille Clifton.

Recent titles from Copper Canyon are *Cuckoo's Blood: Versions of Zen Masters* by Stephen Berg; *Factory of Tears* by Valzhyna Mort; *Human Dark With Sugar* by Brenda Shaughnessy; and *Rising, Falling, Hovering* by C.D. Wright.

Copper Canyon distributes to the trade via Consortium.

Copper Canyon Press has suspended its annual Hayden Carruth Award while exploring other options for considering the work of new and emerging poets. For now, unsolicited manuscripts will not be accepted, however, queries will be read from poets who have previously published a book.

All queries must include an SASE, a one-page cover letter, and a biographical vitae. Query letters and SASEs should be directed to:

Michael Wiegers, Executive Editor

COUNCIL OAKS BOOKS

WILDCAT CANYON PRESS

2015 E. 15th Street, Suite B, Tulsa, OK 74104

918-743-BOOK / 800-247-8850   fax: 918-743-4288

www.counciloakbooks.com

Council Oaks Books, founded in 1984, is a publisher of nonfiction books based in personal, intimate history (memoirs, letters, diaries); nature, animals, and wildlife; Native American history and spiritual teachings; African American history and contemporary experience; small illustrated inspirational gift books; and unique vintage photo books and Americana. Best sellers include *The Four Agreements* by Don Miguel Ruiz and *Wise Talk, Wild Women* by Gwen Mazer.

Recent Council Oaks titles include *Thank God for Evolution* by Michael Dowd; *Chateau Beyond Time* by Michael Tobias; *James and the Lost Heirs of Jesus* by Kenneth Hanson; *Sanctuary* by Michael Tobias and Jane Morrison; *Sound, Peace, Power* by Joseph Rael; and *The Enzyme Factor: Diet For the Future That Will Prevent Heart Disease, Cure Cancer, and Stop Type 2 Diabetes* by Hiromi Shinya, MD.

Wildcat Canyon Press publishes books about relationships, women's issues, home and family, with a focus on personal growth. The editors at this imprint strive to create books that inspire reflection and improve the quality of life. Council Oaks and Wildcat Canyon Press categories include body/mind/spirit, cookbooks, environment/natural world, history, multicultural, and women's studies/feminist.

Wildcat Canyon titles include *Urban Etiquette* by Charles Purdy; *40 over 40* by Brenda Kinsel; *Hip Girls' Handbook for the Working World* by Jennifer Musselman and Patty Fletcher; and *Taming Your Inner Brat: A Guide for Transforming Self-Defeating Behavior* by Pauline Wallin.

Query and SASEs to:

Sally Dennison, Ph.D., Publisher

J. COUNTRYMAN [SEE THOMAS NELSON, INC.]

THE COUNTRYMAN PRESS [SEE W.W. NORTON & COMPANY]

COUNTRYSPORT PRESS [SEE DOWN EAST BOOKS]

CROSSING PRESS [SEE TEN SPEED PRESS]

CROSSROAD PUBLISHING COMPANY

HERDER & HERDER

16 Penn Plaza / 481 8th Ave., Suite 1550, New York NY 10001

212-868-1801   fax: 212-868-2171

www.crossroadpublishing.com   e-mail: ask@crossroadpublishing.com

Crossroad Publishing Company (founded in 1980) publishes general interest and scholarly titles in religion, Catholicism, spirituality, and personal improvement. Its books include spirituality, religion, mind/body/spirit, and counseling for general and popular religious markets. The Herder & Herder imprint publishes books in theology, Christian mysticism, religious studies, and religious education for professionals and active members of Catholic and mainstream Protestant churches.

Crossroad and sibling imprint Herder & Herder is a U.S.-based wing of the international firm Verlag Herder (founded in 1798). The programs of Crossroad and Herder & Herder offer books by some of the most distinguished authors in the U.S. and abroad in the fields of theology, spirituality, religious education, women's studies, world religions, psychology, and counseling.

Crossroad looks for authors who can form long-term and personal publishing relationships.

Titles from Crossroad include *The Practice of Communicative Theology: An Introduction to a New Theological Culture* by Bradford Hinze, Matthias Schrarer, and Bernd Hilberath; *The Soul of a Leader: Finding Your Path the Fulfillment and Success* by Margaret Benefiel; *What Your Money Means: And How to Use It Well* by Frank J. Henna; *The Grand Inquisitor* by John Zmirak and Carla Miller; *The Im-Possibility of Interreligious Dialogue* by Catherine Cornille; and *Against the Grain: Christianity and Democracy, War and Peace* by George Weigel.

Titles from Herder & Herder include *The Harvest of Mysticism in Medieval Germany* by Bernard McGinn; *Leadership in the Church* by Walter Cardinal Kasper; *The Church Women Want: Catholic Women in Dialogue* edited by Elizabeth A. Johnson; *The Local Church* by Christopher Ruddy; *The Systematic Thought of Hans Urs von Balthasar* by Kevin Mongrain; and *Anti-Catholicism in America* by Mark S. Massa.

E-mail submissions are preferred and should be sent to editor@crossroadpublishing.com with the word "submission" in the subject line. Query letters and SASE should be directed to:

John Jones, Editorial Director (Herder & Herder queries)

Nancy Neal, Pre-Press Manager

CROSSWAY BOOKS

1300 Crescent Street, Wheaton, IL 60187-5883

630-682-4300   fax: 630-682-4785

www.gnpcb.org

Crossway Books (founded in 1938) is a division of Good News Publishers. Crossway produces a small list of books with an evangelical Christian perspective aimed at both the religious and general audience, including issue-oriented nonfiction, evangelical works, inspiration, and fiction.

From the Crossway list: *Because He Loves Me: How Christ Transforms Our Daily Life* by Elyse M. Fitzpatrick; *Things That Cannot Be Shaken: Holding Fast To Your Faith in a Relativistic World* by K. Scott Oliphint and Rod Mays; *Engaging with the Holy Spirit: Real Questions, Practical Answers* by Graham A. Cole; *Mormonism Explained: What Latter-day Saints Teach and Practice* by Andrew Jackson; *12 Challenges Churches Face* by Mark Denver; and *Daniel: Resolute Faith in a Hostile World* by Woodrow Kroll.

Sample children's books: *The Toddler's 1-2-3 Bible Storybook* by Carolyn Larsen, illustrated by Caron Turk; *Keeping Holiday* by Starr Meade; *ESV Illustrated Family Bible: 270 Selection from the Holy Bible* by Zbigniew Freus; *Kindness Counts* by Debbie Anderson; *Tell Me About Heaven* by Randy Alcorn, illustrated by Ron DiCianni; and *The Big Picture Story Bible* by David Helm, illustrated by Gail Schoonmaker.

Crossway Books invites query letters regarding works written from an evangelical Christian perspective. No unsolicited manuscripts will be accepted. Send query letters and SASEs to:

Jill Carter, Editorial Administrator

Marvin Padgett, Vice President, Editorial

DA CAPO PRESS [SEE PERSEUS BOOK GROUP]

DALKEY ARCHIVE PRESS

University of Illinois, 1805 S. Wright Street, MC-011, Champaign IL 61820

217-244-5700   fax: 217-244-9142

www.dalkeyarchive.com   e-mail: contact@dalkeyarchive.com

The aim of Dalkey Archive, a division of the Center for Book Culture, is to bring under one roof the best of modern and contemporary literature and to create a space where this literature is protected from the whims of the marketplace. At the heart of the house's mission is a dedication to breakthrough artistic expression in fiction and an educational, interpretive function that goes beyond what most publishers are doing. Unlike many small presses, and certainly unlike commercial presses, Dalkey has always been rooted in critical inquiry, most evident in the *Review of Contemporary Fiction*, the periodical from which the book publisher is an offshoot and more recently in the new periodical, *CONTEXT*. When the press first started operations in 1984, the *Review* was providing criticism on overlooked writers, and the press was in many cases publishing those same writers, or writers who belonged to a similar subversive aesthetic tradition. Since its founding, the press has published over 250 works of world literature and criticism. Dalkey Archive Press is currently seeking book-length scholarly works.

Recent Dalkey Archive Press titles include *Knowledge of Hell* by Antonio Lobo Antunes; *The Temple of the Wild Geese and Bamboo Dolls of Echizen* by Tsutomu Mizukami; *Life Itself: Louis Paul Boon as Innovator of the Novel* by A.M.A. van der Oever; *Polynomials and Pollen: Parables, Proverbs, Paradigms, and Praise* by Lois by Jay Wright; *I'd Like* by Amanda Michalopoulous; *Hotel Crystal* by Olivier Rolin; *The Count of Concord* by Nicholas Delbanco; *Diary of a Blood Donor* by Mati Unt; and *Monsieur* by Jean-Philippe Toussaint.

Dalkey Archive handles its own distribution.

Query letters and SASEs should be directed to:

John O'Brien, Director

IVAN R. DEE, PUBLISHER [SEE ROWMAN & LITTLEFIELD PUBLISHING GROUP]

DEVORSS & COMPANY

P.O. Box 1389, Camarillo, CA 93011-1389

805-322-9010 / 800-843-5743   fax: 805-322-9011

www.devorss.com   e-mail: service@devorss.com

Devorss & Company has been publishing metaphysical and spiritual books since 1929. The house was founded in Los Angeles by Douglas Kimball DeVorss, who set up as a publisher of what today would be called Body/Mind/Spirit books. At that time, the term was New Thought, and Los Angeles was already home to many centers, institutes, and churches that taught a new, "metaphysical," brand of philosophy and spirituality.

Recent Devorss titles include *How to Use Your 12 Gifts from God* by William Warch; *The Heart of Mysticism: Infinite Way Letters 1955-1959* by Joel S. Goldsmith; *The Smile That Went Around the World* by Patrice Karst; *The Way Out* by Joseph Benner; *Attaining the Unattainable: The Will of God* by Jim Rosemergy; and *Toning: The Healing Power of the Voice* by Laurel E. Keyes and Don Campbell.

Devorss & Company distributes its own titles.

Submit queries, proposals, and SASEs via regular mail to Editorial Submissions. Queries only may be sent to editorial@devorss.com.

DIMENSIONS FOR LIVING [SEE ABINGDON PRESS]

DISCIPLESHIP RESOURCES

UPPER ROOM BOOKS

Delivery address:

1908 Grand Avenue, Nashville TN 37212

Mailing address:

P.O. Box 840, Nashville, TN 37202-0840

800-814-7833

www.discipleshipresources.org   e-mail: discipleshipresources@gbod.org

Discipleship Resources (founded in 1951) is the publishing component of the General Board of Discipleship, one of the major program boards of the United Methodist Church. Areas of publishing interest encompass United Methodist history, doctrine, and theology, as well as Bible study, Christian education, ethnic church concerns, evangelism, ministry of the laity, stewardship, United Methodist men, and worship.

The mission of Discipleship resources is "to provide quality resources that respond to the needs of United Methodist leaders and congregation members, as they seek to become and encourage others to become disciples of Jesus Christ."

A Discipleship Resources imprint, Upper Room Books is an ecumenical nonprofit religious publisher focused on books that help readers discover, develop, and enrich a life of devotion and attention to God. Books published by The Upper Room present to individuals and to groups the possibility and promise of an intimate, life-giving relationship with God. These books further assist readers along their spiritual path by offering guidance toward a disciplined life that includes prayer and action. The Upper Room publishes between 25 and 30 books each year.

Recent titles from Discipleship Resources include *Dirty Word: The Vulgar, Offensive Languages of the Kingdom of God* by Jim Walker; *In Love Again and Making It Work: Successful Remarriage* by Duck Dunn; *David's Harp: Returning Harmony to Conflicted Congregations* by Bill Kemp; and *7 Myths of the United Methodist Church* by Craig Kenneth Miller et al.

Recent titles from Upper Room Books include *Birthed in Prayer: Pregnancy as a Spiritual Journey* by Kim Barker, Linda De Mellion, and Leigh Harrison; *Living with Purpose in a Worn-Out Body: Spiritual Encouragement for Older Adults* by Missy Buchanan; *Living Into Answers: A Workbook for Personal Spiritual Discernment* by Valerie K. Isenhower and Judith A. Todd; and *A Life-Shaping Prayer: 52 Meditations in the Wesleyan Spirit* by Paul Wesley Chilcote.

Query letters with one sample chapter and SASEs should be directed to the Editor; e-mail submissions may be sent to kduncan@gbod.org.

DISNEY PRESS [SEE HYPERION]

DORCHESTER PUBLISHING COMPANY

HARD CASE CRIME

LOVE SPELL

LEISURE

SMOOCH

MAKING IT

200 Madison Avenue, Suite 2000, New York, NY 10016

800-481-9191

www.dorchesterpub.com

WILDSIDE PRESS

9710 Traville Gateway Dr., #234, Rockville, MD 20850

301-762-1305

www.wildsidepress.com   e-mail: editorial@wildsidepress.com

Dorchester is the oldest independent mass market publisher in America. From its founding in 1971, Dorchester editors have strived to bring the freshest authors to millions of fans. Although mostly known for romance, Dorchester also publishes horror, westerns, and thrillers under its Leisure Books imprint. Dorchester has recently added Science Fiction and Fantasy titles from the Wildside press imprint, and has begun distributing the bestselling Family Doctor series of health guides in the U.S. and Canada.

Dorchester has given a start to hundreds of first-time authors. Authors like Madeline Baker, Norah Hess, Cassie Edwards, Patricia Gaffney, Catherine Hart, Shirl Henke, Dara Joy, Jayne Ann Krentz, Christine Feehan, and Connie Mason all began their publishing careers with Dorchester.

Dorchester is the leader in consistently publishing romances in specialty genres like time-travel, paranormal, futuristic, faerie tale, and heartspell (which involves a little magic in the affairs of the heart).

Leisure is Dorchester's flagship imprint that publishes romances, fantasy, science fiction, horror, thrillers, and more. Recent titles from Leisure include *The Black Rider* by Max Brand; *Brides of the Impaler* by Edward Lee; *Café au Lait* by Liane Spicer; *Covenant* by Jon Everson; *The Dragon Earl* by Jade Lee; *The Engineer Reconditioned* by Neal Asher; *Science Fiction: The Best of the Year* by Rich Horton; *Shotgun Marshal* by Ward Everett; *Stand By Your Hitman* by Leslie Langtry; and *The Apocalypse Directive* by Douglas MacKinnon.

Hard Case Crime is an award-winning line of pulp-style mysteries. Recent titles from Hard Case Crime include *Zero Cool* by John Lange; *Money Shot* by Christa Faust; *Dead Street* by Mickey Spillane; *Slide* by Ken Bruen and Jason Starr; and *Blackmailer* by George Axelrod.

The Smooch imprint is for Young Adult readers. Recent titles from Smooch include *Finding the Forger* by Libby Sternberg; *I am So Jinxed!* by Naomi Marsh; and *Circus of the Darned* by Katie Maxwell.

In 1994 Dorchester created Love Spell imprint to react to the market for newer types of romance. Recent titles from Love Spell include *Weddings Can Be Murder* by Christie Craig; *Phantom* by Lindsay Randall; *A Curious Affair* by Melanie Jackson; *The Sisters Grimm* by Minda Webber; *Hidden (Shomi Action Romance)* by Eve Kenin; *Electra Galaxy's Mr. Interstellar Feller* by Candace Sams; and *Blood Sport* by Judith E. French.

Since its founding in 1989, Wildside Press has become one of the industry's leading publishers of science fiction and fantasy. Wildside also runs the Prime Books, Point Blank, and Juno Books imprints. Talent includes award-winner Robert Silverberg, bestseller Alan Dean Foster, and Robert E. Howard, creator of Conan the Barbarian. Wildside press has been nominated six times for the World Fantasy Award for Publishing Excellence.

Recent titles from Wildside include *H.P. Lovecraft's Cthulu Mythos: A Weird Tales Retrospective* by John Gregory Betancourt and Robert Weinberg; *Walking to the Moon* by Sean McMullen; *Tempting the Gods: The Selected Stories* by Tanith Lee by Tanith Lee; *Frank Merriwell's Son* by Burt L. Standish; *Phantom Detective: Fangs of Murder* by Robert Wallace; *Airship Progress and Airship Problems* by Commander Garland Fulton; and *The Cock Crows Murder and Other Tales from the Pulps* by Robert Leslie Bellem.

Making It Press was launched in 2004 for trade paperback chick-lit novels. Recent titles from Making It include *Alibi in High Heels and Killer in High Heels* by Gemma Halliday; *Guns Will Keep Us Together* by Leslie Langtry; *Method Man* by Naomi Neale; and *If the Shoe Fits* by Stephanie Rowe.

Dorchester is currently acquiring the following: romance, horror, Westerns, and thrillers. Wildside Press is not currently accepting submissions, however, they are seeking fantasy novels with female protagonists for their Juno Books imprint. Detailed guidelines are available on their Web site. Submit query with first three chapters and SASE to the editorial staff.

Alicia Condon, Editorial Director—Romance all genres

Don D'Auria, Editorial Director—Horrors, thrillers, New westerns

Chris Keeslar, Senior Editor—Romance all genres, fantasy

Leah Hultenschmidt, Editor—Romance all genres, westerns

John Gregory Betancourt, Publisher, Wildside

DOWN EAST BOOKS

COUNTRYSPORT PRESS

P.O. Box 679, Camden, ME 04843

Street Address: 680 Commercial Street (US Route 1), Rockport, ME 04856

207-594-9544   fax: 207-594-0147

www.downeastbooks.com   e-mail: info@downeastbooks.com

www.countrysportpress.com

Down East Enterprise began at a kitchen table in 1954 with the creation of Down East magazine. In 1967, *Leroy the Lobster* was published and Down East Books was born. Today, Down East Books is the largest book publisher in the state of Maine and has published over 750 books. With the Countrysport Press imprint, Down East has a backlist of many hundreds of titles that grows by dozens of new books every year.

Although Down East Books is the largest book publisher in Maine, it is still a relatively small, regional publisher specializing in books with a strong Maine or New England theme. Current subject areas include general interest nonfiction, art and photography, regional attractions and travel guides, biography and memoir, gardening, cooking, crafts, history, nature and ecology, nautical books, and fiction. A fully developed regional connection is critical in Down East fiction titles, too.

Down East also publishes children's books, and here also the regional subject and setting are highly desirable. Note that the New England setting must be integral to the work; a story that with little or no change could be set in another region would not meet their requirements.

Under the Countrysport Press imprint, Down East publishes sporting titles on hunting, fishing, target shooting, dog training, cooking, and fine guns and fishing tackle. These titles include both "how-to" books and memoir and sporting literature. Recent Countrysport Press titles include *More Shotguns and Shooting* by Michael McIntosh; *Dangerous Game Rifles* by Terry Wieland; *A Bird in the Hand* by Ted Nelson Lundrigan; and *A Hunter's Book of Days* by Charles Fergus.

Recent Down East titles include At Home by the Sea: *Houses Designed for Living at the Water's Edge* by Bruce Snider, photography by Brian Vanden Brink; *A Healing Touch: True Stories of Life, Death, and Hospice* by Richard Russo; *Our Point of View: Fourteen Years at a Maine Lighthouse* by Thomas Mark Szelog and Lee Ann Szelog; *At Home in Maine: Houses Designed to Fit the Land* by Christopher Glass; *The Story of Sugarloaf* by John Christie; and *Acadia Panorama: Images of Maine's National Park* by Alan Nyiri.

Mark your package "Book Proposal" and direct queries and SASEs to:

Karen Womer, Head Editor

Michael Steere, Associate Editor

WILLIAM B. EERDMANS PUBLISHING COMPANY

EERDMANS BOOKS FOR YOUNG READERS

2140 Oak Industrial Dr. NE, Grand Rapids, MI 49505

616-459-4591 / 800-253-7521   fax: 616-459-6540

www.eerdmans.com   e-mail: info@eerdmans.com

William B. Eerdmans Publishing Company (founded in 1911) is one of the largest independent nondenominational Christian religious publishers in the U.S. Founded in 1911 and still independently owned, Eerdmans Publishing Company has long been known for publishing a wide range of religious books, from academic works in theology, Biblical studies, religious history, and reference to popular titles in spirituality, social and cultural criticism, and literature.

Eerdmans publishes titles of general interest; religious, academic, and theological works; books for young readers; regional histories; and American religious history. The house offers a Christian handle on such areas as anthropology, Biblical studies, and religious approaches to biography, African American studies, church administration, music, philosophy, psychology, science, social issues, current and historical theology, and women's interests.

New on the Eerdmans list: *Wedding Rites: A Complete Guide to Traditional Vows, Music, Ceremonies, Blessings, and Interfaith Services* by Michael P. Foley; *Christ and Culture Revisited* by D.A. Carson; *Christ Plays in Ten Thousand Places* by Eugene H. Peterson; *Looking Before and After* by Alan Jacobs; and *The Consolations of Theology* edited by Brian S. Rosner.

Query letters, proposals, and SASEs should be directed to:

Jon Pott, Editor-in-Chief

EERDMANS BOOKS FOR YOUNG READERS

Eerdmans Books for Young Readers, founded in 1995 as an imprint of William B. Eerdmans Publishing Company, seeks to publish beautifully written and illustrated books that nurture children's faith in God and help young people to explore and understand the wonder, joy, and challenges of life.

Eerdmans Books for Young Readers publishes picture books and middle reader and young adult fiction and nonfiction. They seek manuscripts that are honest, wise, and hopeful, but also publish stories that simply delight the editors with their storyline, characters, or good humor. Stories that celebrate diversity, stories of historical significance, and stories that relate to current issues are of special interest to them at this time. The house considers manuscripts that address spiritual themes in authentic and imaginative ways without being didactic. They currently publish 12–18 books a year.

Some recent titles include *I, Vivaldi* by Janice Shefelman, illustrated by Tom Shefelman; *Garmann's Summer* by Stian Hole; *Always with You* by Ruth Vander Zee, illustrated by Ronald Himler; *Psalms for Young Children* by Marie-Hele Delval, illustrated by Arno; *Cottonball Colin* by Jeanne Willis, Illustrated by Tony Ross; *Attack of the Turtle* by Drew Carlson; and *Alice's Birthday Pig* by Tim Kennemore.

Eerdmans Books for Young Readers will only consider exclusive submissions that are clearly marked as such on the outside of the envelope. They do not accept simultaneous submissions and those sent will be discarded. Query letters with proposal or sample chapters and SASEs should be directed to:

Shannon White, Editor, Young Readers

ENTREPRENEUR PRESS

2445 McCabe Way, 4th Floor, Irvine, CA 92614

949-261-2325 / 800-864-6864   fax: 949-261-7729

www.smallbizbooks.com   e-mail: jcalmes@entrepreneur.com

Entrepreneur Press, a division of Entrepreneur Media, Inc. (publishers of *Entrepreneur*

Magazine), publishes trade books offering practical advice and inspirational success stories for business owners and aspiring entrepreneurs. The goal of the house is to provide essential business information to help plan, run, and grow small businesses. Areas of expertise include instructional business books, and motivational, management, marketing, new economy, e-commerce, and personal finance titles that appeal to a broad spectrum of the business book-buying audience.

Titles include *Asset Protection* by Robert F. Klueger; *The Home Office From Hell Cure* by Jeffrey A. Landers; *The Ultimate Guide to Search Engine Optimization* by Jon Rognerud; *Retail in Detail, 4th Edition* by Ronald L. Bond; *The Business Traveler Guide to Los Angeles* by Jason R. Rich; *The Operations Manual for LLC's* by Michael Spadaccni; *Mastering Online Marketing* by Mitch Meyerson and Mary Eule Scarborough; and *Moonlighting on the Internet* by Yanik Silver with Robert Olic.

Entrepreneur Press books are distributed to the trade by National Book Network. Query letters and SASEs should be directed to:

Jere L. Calmes, Editorial Director

ESPN BOOKS [SEE HYPERION]

M. EVANS AND COMPANY [SEE ROWMAN & LITTLEFIELD PUBLISHING GROUP]

FACTS ON FILE

132 West 31st Street, 17th Floor, New York, NY 10001

212-967-8800 / 800-322-8755   fax: 212-967-9196 / 800-678-3633

www.factsonfile.com   e-mail: editorial@factsonfile.com

Facts On File (founded in 1940) is a dynamic popular-reference publisher. The house has many award-winning titles to its credit, and many Facts On File publications feature an innovative production approach. The publisher is extremely well tuned to specific category markets, which it targets with marked commercial consistency.

Facts On File is one of the nation's top providers of resources for teaching and learning. They produce high-quality reproducible handouts, online databases, CD-ROMS, and print reference and information titles in a broad popular range, including literature, science, geography, nature, technology, world history, American history, business, popular culture, fashion, design, sports, health, current affairs and politics, and the environment. Facts on File is also the first place that many teachers, students, librarians and parents turn for general reference works. They offer a broad selection of historical and cultural atlases, dictionaries, and encyclopedias geared toward professional as well as popular interests, and are one of the pioneers of the electronic multimedia-publishing frontier.

Facts On File has made a renewed commitment to its goal of becoming the premier print and electronic reference publisher in the industry. It is striving to be the beacon and a guide for librarians, teachers, students, parents, and researchers to look to for award-winning materials, cutting-edge trends, and innovative products. This is the publisher to be sought when the requirements are nebulous and the transitions are turbulent.

The year 1998 brought the launch of the trade imprint Checkmark Books. It was created to provide booksellers and consumers with quality resources focused on topics such as business, careers, fitness, health and nutrition, history, nature, parenting, pop culture, and self-help.

Recent Facts On File books include *Earth Science: Decade by Decade* by Christina Reed; *The Encyclopedia of Phobias, Fears, and Anxieties, 3rd Edition* by Ronald M. Doctor Ph.D., Ada P. Kahn, Ph.D., and Christine Adamec; *Immigration and Migration* by Rayna Bailey; and *The Facts on File Companion to the World Novel, 1900 to Present, 2-Volume Set* by Michael D. Sollars.

Examples of Checkmark Books are *Career Opportunities in the Energy Industry* by James Robert Parish and Allen Taylor; *Food Alert!* by Morton Satin; *The Facts on File Dictionary of Foreign Words and Phrases* by Martin H. Manser; *Natural Disasters* by Lee Davis; *The Encyclopedia of American Religion and Politics* by Paul A. Djupe and Laura R. Olson; *Ferguson Career Coach: Managing Your Career in the Theater and Performing Arts* by Shelly Field; and *Airline Pilot: Virtual Apprentice* by Ron Rauf and Monique Vescia.

The On File program is an award-winning collection of reference materials. Spanning virtually every subject in the middle- and high-school curricula, each On File contains hundreds of images that visually depict complex subjects in a way that will both engage and inform young people. Even students at the elementary and college levels will find the material useful. Filled with hundreds of exciting hands-on activities, projects, exercises, and experiments, On File binders encourage critical thinking and allow students to actively participate in their educational process.

Facts On File utilizes individualized marketing and distribution programs that are particularly strong in the areas of corporate, institutional, and library sales.

Query letters, proposals, and SASEs should be directed to:

Laurie Likoff, Editorial Director

Frank Darmstadt, Editor—Science and Math

FAIRVIEW PRESS

2450 Riverside Avenue, Minneapolis, MN 55454

612-672- 4180 / 800-544-8207   fax: 612-672-4980

www.fairviewpress.org   e-mail: press@fairview.org

Fairview Press publishes books dedicated to the physical, emotional, and spiritual health of children, adults, and seniors—specializing in books on aging and eldercare, grief and bereavement, health and wellness, inspiration, and parenting and childcare.

The house is a division of Fairview Health Services, a regional health care provider affiliated with the University of Minnesota. This affiliation, combined with their award-winning books, has caused industry experts to name Fairview Press as one of the "Top 50 Dependent Publishers" in the U.S. Fairview authors have been featured on CNN, CBS, NBC's *Today* show, National Public Radio, and in hundreds of other local, national, and international media outlets.

At this time, Fairview is particularly interested in acquiring manuscripts that deal with the following topics: pregnancy and childbirth, health issues for young adults, complementary/holistic/integrative medicine, diet & exercise, and inspiration and mindfulness. The are de-emphasizing their previous focus on end-of-life issues, but will consider proposals on any topic pertaining to physical, emotional, or spiritual wellness.

Recent Fairview Press titles include *Great Feet For Life: Footcare and Footwear for the Healthy Aging* by Paula Langer, DPM; *Late-Life Love: Romance and New Relationships in Later Years* by Connie Goldman; *Adopted and Wondering: Drawing Out Feelings* by Marge Heegaard, MA, LCSW; *What Happy Couple do: Belly Button Fuzz and Bare-Chested Hugs—The Loving Little Rituals of Romance* by Carol J. Bruess, PhD and Anna D.H. Kudak, MA; *Fighting For My Life: Growing Up With Cancer* by Amy M. Mareck; and *Secrets of Becoming a Late Bloomer: Staying Creative, Aware, and Involved in Midlife and Beyond* by Connie Goldman and Richard Mahler.

Fairview Press operates through a variety of sales venues; the press is distributed to the trade through National Book Network.

Query letters, proposals, and SASEs should be addressed to:

Steve Deger, Manager

FAITH COMMUNICATIONS [SEE HEALTH COMMUNICATIONS, INC.]

FALCON GUIDES [SEE THE GLOBE PEQUOT PRESS]

FANTAGRAPHICS BOOKS

7563 Lake City Way NE, Seattle, WA 98115

206-524-1967 / 800-657-1100   fax: 206-524-2104

www.fantagraphics.com   e-mail: fbicomix@fantagraphics.com

blog: www.fantagraphics.com/blog

Fantagraphics publishes comics and comic art. The house features a list of mainstream, classic, and underground offerings and also purveys a strong line of erotic comics and comics-related books. Fantagraphics Books (inaugurated in 1976) produces trade paperbacks, hardbound editions, and quality fine-art album editions of graphic productions, in addition to comic books, comics-related magazines, and a line of gift items dedicated to this most accessible literary form.

Comics creators cataloged by Fantagraphics include Peter Bagge, Vaughn Bode, Daniel Clowes, Guido Crepax, Robert Crumb, Dame Darcy, Kim Deitch, Julie Doucet, Jules Feiffer, Frank Frazetta, Drew Friedman, Rick Geary, Los Bros. Hernandez, Peter Kuper, Terry LeBan, Douglas Michael, Joe Sacco, Gilbert Shelton, Art Spiegelman, Ralph Steadman, Basil Wolverton, and Wallace Wood.

Recent Fantagraphics titles include *Rebel Visions: The Underground Comix Revolution 1963-1975* by Patrick Rosenkranz; *Bottomless Belly Button* by Dash Shaw; *Explainers: The Complete Village Voice Strips 1956-1966* by Jules Feiffer; *Amor T Cohetes: A Love and Rockets Book* by Los Bros. Hernandez; *Castle Waiting: The "Hand Made" Special Edition* by Linda Medley; *Most Outrageous* by Bob Levin; *Safe Area Gorazde* by Joe Sacco; and *Hall of Best Knowledge* by Ray Fenwick.

Fantagraphics distributes its own list and catalogs selections from a number of other comics- and graphics-oriented publishers, in addition to audio CDs, computer CD-ROMs, videotapes, and books, posters, and calendars.

Take note of the originality and diversity of the themes and approaches to drawing in such Fantagraphics titles as *Love & Rockets* (stories of life in Latin America and Chicano L.A. which draw on influences as diverse as Luis Buñuel, Frida Kahlo, and Hank Ketcham); *Palestine* (journalistic autobiography in the Middle East); *Eightball* (surrealism mixed with kitsch culture in stories alternately humorous and painfully personal); and *Naughty Bits* (feminist humor and short stories which both attack and commiserate). Prior to submitting, try to develop your own, equally individual voice; originality, aesthetic maturity, and graphic storytelling skill are the signs by which Fantagraphics judges whether or not your submission is ripe for publication. Query letters should be accompanied by short, carefully selected samples and SASE.

FELDHEIM PUBLISHERS

208 Airport Executive Park, Nanuet, NY 10954

845-356-2282 / 800-237-7149   fax: 845-425-1908

www.feldheim.com

Feldheim Publishers (founded in 1954) is among the leading houses in areas of Jewish thought, translations from Hebrew of classical works, dictionaries and general reference works, textbooks, and guides for Sabbaths and festivals, as well as literature for readers ages 3 and up. The Feldheim publishing program is expanding and the house releases an increasing number of titles each season. Feldheim retains a comprehensive backlist.

Recent titles include *Hilchot Chagim: Laws and Customs of the Jewish Year* by Harav Mardechai Eliyahu; *Real Kids, Vol. 1* by Chaim Walder; *A Voice Shall Sing Forth: Commentary of the Dubner Maggid on the Song of Songs* translated by David M. Zucker; *Bar Mitzvah Mysteries #2: Stop, Thief!* by Aidel Stein; *Haggadah Shel Pesach Ki Yishalcha* by Chagai Wilowsky; and *In Their Shadow: Wisdom and Guidance of the Gedolim Vol. 1* by Rav Shlomo Lorincz.Bulman.

Feldheim handles its own distribution and offers the books of additional publishers such as American Yisroel Chai Press and Targum Press.

Query letters and SASEs should be directed to:

Yitzchak Feldheim, President

FLUX [SEE LLEWELLYN WORLDWIDE]

FOCUS ON THE FAMILY BOOK PUBLISHING

8605 Explorer Drive, Colorado Springs, CO 80920-1051

719-531-3400   fax: 719-268-4841

www.family.org

The Focus on the Family Book Publishing house is based on a ministry that is dedicated to the preservation of the family and of marriage. They produce many books in-house but often hire writers in a "work for hire" situation. They will look at new material from authors if it fits within their guidelines and standards and offers a fresh perspective on these subjects. They also publish fiction if it has a strong theme reflecting family values. Their list includes approximately 15–20 titles per year.

Focus on the Family Publishing was founded by author Dr. James Dobson, Ph.D. Its ministry is to spread the Gospel of Jesus Christ through a practical outreach to homes. The strong principles found in their books are summed up in the following statement: "The values and techniques taught to parents are drawn from the wisdom of the Bible and Judeo-Christian ethic, rather than from the humanistic notions of today's theorists. In short, Focus on the Family is a reflection of what we believe to be the recommendations of the Creator Himself, who ordained the family and gave it His blessing."

Recent titles include *The Most Important Year in a Woman's Life: What Every Bride Needs to Know* by Robert and Bobbie Wolgemuth; *The Most Important Year in a Man's Life: What Every Groom Needs to Know* by Mark and Susan Devries; *Countdown for Couples: Preparing for the Adventure of Marriage* by Dale and Susan Mathis; *Discovering God* by Phillip W. Rodgers; *God Loves Us, Little One* by Allia Zobel Nolan; and *Do Hard Things: A Teenage Rebellion Against Low Expectations* by Alex and Brett Harris.

Focus on the Family is currently accepting manuscripts and proposals for family advice and fiction. However, they will only accept submissions from an agent.

Mark Maddox, Senior Editor

Julie Kuss, Acquisitions Manager

FORTRESS PRESS [SEE AUGSBURG FORTRESS BOOKS]

FREE SPIRIT PUBLISHING

217 Fifth Avenue North, Suite 200, Minneapolis, MN 55401-1299

612-338-2068 / 800-735-7323   fax: 612-337-5050

www.freespirit.com   e-mail: help4kids@freespirit.com

For over 20 years, Free Spirit's mission has been to provide children and teens—and the adults who care for and about them—the tools they need to succeed in life and to make a positive difference in the world.

Based in Minneapolis, Minn., Free Spirit Publishing is known for its unique understanding of what kids want (and need) to know to navigate life successfully. The house built its reputation as the leading publisher of self-help books for teens and kids. Their books and other learning materials are practical, positive, pro-kid, and solution focused. Free Spirit is not afraid to tackle tough topics such as teen depression, kids and anxiety, grief and loss, juvenile justice, and conflict resolution. Free Spirit also offers sound advice with a sense of humor on relevant issues including stress management, character building, puberty, school success, self-esteem, and more. The house aims to meet all kids—toddlers, teens, and in-betweens—where they are (not where we wish they were), and support them to develop their talents, build resiliency, and foster a positive outlook on life so they can reach their goals.

Founded by Judy Galbraith, a former classroom teacher and education specialist, Free Spirit pushes boundaries on behalf of young people. For example, they pioneered use of the term "learning differences" to replace "learning disabilities" because they know that kids with LD are eager and able to learn—just in a different way. Free Spirit is also a recognized leader in meeting the needs of another special population—gifted and talented youth. Judy Galbraith's groundbreaking *The Gifted Kids' Survival Guides*, first published in 1984, have remained perennial best-sellers (300,000 copies in print) through several updates and revisions. One of Free Spirit's newest ventures is in expanding early childhood offerings, with titles such as *Hands Are Not for Hitting* (100,000 copies in print).

Recent titles include *Expert Approaches to Support Gifted Learners* by Margaret Wayne Gosfield; *On Those Runaway Days* by Alison Feigh illustrated by Laura Logan; *See You Later, Procrastinator!* by Pamela Espeland and Elizabeth Verdick; *Fighting Invisible Tigers: Stress Management for Teens* by Earl Hipp; *Mad: How to Deal with Your Anger and Get Respect* by James J. Crist, PhD, and *Psychology for Kids Vol. 1: 40 Fun Quizzes that Help You Learn About Yourself* by Jonni Kincher.

Free Spirit's distribution is through the trade market, as well as direct to schools and other youth-serving venues.

Query letters and SASEs should be directed to:

Judy Galbraith, Founder and President

Heidi Stier, Acquisitions Editor

FRIENDSHIP PRESS

475 Riverside Drive, Room 860, New York, NY 10115-0050

212-870-2496   fax: 212-870-2550

www.ncccusa.org/friend/fphome.html

The Friendship list encompasses religious books, as well as mainstream trade titles in the public-interest realm that address contemporary topics including cultural pluralism, the media, global awareness, health and wholeness, technology and the environment, human rights, and world peace. Friendship also produces ecumenical religious, spiritual, inspirational, and educational program materials intended for the use of adults, youths, and children. The house offers several lines of videos, maps, notecards, and informational posters.

Friendship Press was established in 1902 as a missionary education movement in the U.S. and Canada. Now part of the National Council of the Churches of Christ, USA, Friendship Press is a leading ecumenical publisher of educational materials for schools and parishes.

Noted Friendship authors include Margaret Mead, Pearl Buck, Joseph Diescho, Wole Soyinka, Rogoberta Menchu, John R. Mott, Phillip Potter, Leslie Newbigin, Masao Takenaka, and Emilio Castro. Friendship Press books have been reviewed by the *New York Times* and *Publishers Weekly* and are recommended for use in colleges, universities, and seminars.

General titles include Saint John's Bible: *Gospels and Acts* by Donald Jackson; *Illuminating the Word: The Making of Saint John's Bible* by Christopher Calderhead; *Witness to Genocide: The Children of Rwanda; Drawings by Child Survivors of the Rwandan Genocide of 1994*, edited by Richard A. Salem, forward by Hillary R. Clinton; *God is One: The Way of Islam* by R, Marston Speight; and *Families Valued: Parenting and Politics for the Good of All Children* by Jack Nelson-Pallmeyer.

Direct queries and SASEs to:

Mary Byrne Hoffman, Editor

FULCRUM PUBLISHING

SPEAKER'S CORNER

4960 Table Mountain Drive, Suite 100, Golden, CO 80403

303-277-1623 / 800-992-2908 fax: 303-279-7111 / 800-726-7112

www.fulcrum-books.com

SPECK PRESS

P.O. Box 102004, Denver, CO 80222

303-277-1623 / 800-992-2908 fax: 800-726-7112

www.speckpress.com email: books@speckpress.com

Fulcrum is a trade publisher focusing on books that inspire readers to live life to the fullest and learn something new each day. In fiction and nonfiction, subjects include health and wellness, Western culture, outdoor and travel, Native American, memoirs and literature, gardening, environment and nature, and children's titles.

Fulcrum has published books from prominent politicians (Gov. Richard Lamm, Sen. Gary Hart, Sen. Eugene McCarthy), leading Native Americans (Wilma Mankiller, Vine Deloria Jr., Joseph Bruchac), master gardeners (Lauren Springer, Tom Peace, Richard Hartlage), and important organizations in the environmental community (Campaign for America's Wilderness, World Wilderness Congress, Defenders of Wildlife).

Recent Fulcrum releases are *Cruisin' the Fossil Freeway: An Epoch Tale of a Scientist and an Artist on the 5,000-Mile Paleo Road Trip* by Kirk Johnson, illustrated by Ray Troll; *Dizzying Heights: The Aspen Novel* by Bruce Ducker; *Migrations Patterns: Stories* by Gary Schanbacher; *Power of the People: America's New Electricity Choices* by Carol Sue Tombari; *The Dark Intrigue: The True Story of a Civil War Conspiracy*; and *The Principled Politician: The Story of Ralph Carr*.

SPEAKER'S CORNER

Speaker's Corner is an imprint that publishes books on public policy. Some books from Speaker's Corner include *Daddy On Board: Parenting Roles for the 21st Century* by Dottie Lamm; *Power of the People: America's New Electricity Choices* by Carol Sue Tombari; *Under the Eagle's Wing: A National Security Strategy of the United States for 2009* by Gary Hart; *A Solitary War: A Diplomat's Chronicle of the Iraq War and Its Lessons* by Heraldo Muñoz; *No Higher Calling, No Greater Responsibility: A Prosecutor Makes His Case* by John Suthers; *Beyond Cowboy Politics: Colorado and the New West* edited by Adam Schrager, Samuel Scinta, and Shannon Hassan.

SPECK PRESS

Speck Press is an imprint that explores cultures and subcultures trough nonfiction and crime fiction books—revealing scenes that are typically invisible to the casual observer. They currently publish around 6 new titles a year, in the areas of subculture, music, environment issues, art, politics, travel, and gift books. New titles from Speck include *Generation What? Dispatches from the Quarter-Life Crisis* edited by Bess Vanrenen; *Roller Derby: The History and All-Girl Revival of the Greatest Sport on Wheels* by Catherine Mabe; and Dekok and *Variations on Murder* by Baantjer.

Fulcrum handles its own distribution. Query letters and SASEs should be directed to:

Bob Baron, President and Publisher, Fulcrum

Derek Lawrence, Publisher (Speck Press)

Susan Hill-Newton, Editor (Speck Press

GENEVA PRESS [SEE PRESBYTERIAN PUBLISHING CORPORATION]

THE GLOBE PEQUOT PRESS

INSIDERS' GUIDES

FALCON GUIDES

FOOTPRINT GUIDES

CHOCKSTONE

THE LYONS PRESS

246 Goose Lane #200, P.O. Box 480, Guilford, CT 06437-0833

203-458-4500 / 800-820-2329   fax: 800-508-8938

www.globepequot.com   e-mail: info@globepequot.com

The Pequot Press, whose name was adapted from a local Indian tribe, was founded in 1947 as an adjunct to the Stonington Printing Company in Stonington, Conn. The Boston Globe Newspaper Company purchased the press in Frebruary, 1981, formalizing an association that had begun in 1978. Today, more than 60 years after the publication of its first monograph, The Globe Pequot Press has established an international reputation for publication of regional guides to a myriad of travel destinations in this country and around the world and is among the top three sources for travel books in the U.S. Globe Pequot is owned by Georgia-based Morris Communications, a privately held media company with diversified holdings that include newspaper and magazine publishing, outdoor advertising, radio broadcasting, book publishing and distribution.

Globe Pequot publishes approximately 600 new books each year. In addition to publishing its own imprint, it offers marketing and fulfillment services to client publishers whose combined annual output currently exceeds 200 new titles. Its 75,000-square-foot warehouse holds well over one million units representing approximately 4,000 titles in print, comprising books on domestic and international travel, outdoor recreation, sports, how-to, history, fiction, health and fitness, cooking, and nature.

The Globe Pequot line primarily publishes travel guides, with some select nature titles, cookbooks, and home-based business books. Insider's Guides are travel and relocation guides written by local authors. Falcon Guides specialize in outdoor recreation, both how-to and where-to, with hiking, biking, climbing, and other specialized lines, including regional history. Footprint Guides publishes guides for experienced independent travelers looking to get off the beaten track. Chockstone books focus on the subject of rock climbing. The Lyons Press is primarily a publisher of practical and literary books, as well as being the most distinguished publisher of fishing books in the world (see below for Lyons Press).

In the travel arena, Globe Pequot is well regarded for several best-selling series and also distributes for a number of travel-specialist houses. Among Globe Pequot lines: Quick Escapes (weekend and day trips keyed to metropolitan areas or regions); Romantic Days and Nights; Recommended Bed & Breakfasts; Fun with the Family Guides; Cadogan Guides to destinations worldwide for the discriminating traveler; and the popular Off-the-Beaten-Path series. Globe Pequot also updates a variety of annuals, among them Europe by Eurorail. Globe Pequot's regionally keyed books also cover such interest areas as biking, hiking, mountaineering, skiing, and family activities in the wilderness and on the beach.

Globe Pequot titles include *Stud Muffins: Luscious, Delectable, Yummy (and Good Muffin Recipes, too!)* by Judi Guizado, Gilda Jimenez, Shari Hartz, and Tammy Aldag; *Authentik: Chic New York City* by Authentik; *Josh and Isadora: A True Tale of Loss and Love in the Holocaust* by Michael Benavav; *Invisible Chains: Shawn Hornbeck and the Kidnapping Case that Shook the Nation* by Kristina Sauerwein; and *Mom is Always Right: Words That Celebrate the World's Smartest Moms* edited by Patricia Harris.

Query letters and SASEs should be directed to the Submissions Editor with a note on the envelope as to the subject category.

Scott Watrous, President

Laura Strom, Executive Editor

LYONS PRESS

Now an imprint of Globe Pequot, Lyons Press was founded by Nick Lyons in 1984 and has established an international reputation for publishing outstanding titles in its core categories of fishing, hunting, horses, sports, pets, history, adventure, the outdoors, self-reliant living, and reference.

Recent Lyons purchases include a book of ghostly cat tales, the story of a puppy befriending U.S. soldiers in Iraq, a history of the U.S. Space Program, and an exploration of the world of modern-day shipping, indicating an expansion from their core editorial direction.

Titles include *The Man Who Swam the Amazon: 3,274 miles on the World's Deadliest River* by Martin Strel and Matthew Mohlke; *Murdered by Mumia: A Life Sentence of Loss, Pain, and Injustice* by Maureen Faulkner and Michael A. Smerconish; *Truth At Last: The Untold Story of James Earl Ray and the Assassination of Martin Luther King Jr.* by John Larry Ray and Lyndon Barsten; *How Can You Defend Those People* by Mickey Sherman; and *My Home, My Money Pit: Your Guide to Every Home Improvement Adventure* by Tom Kraeutler and Leslie Segrete.

Direct proposals with SASEs to the Submissions Editor.

Gene Brissie, Associate Publisher

Tom McCarthy, Executive Editor—Sports

Holly Rubino, Editor—Animals and pets, lifestyle, self help

Kaleena Cote, Editor

Keith Wallman, Editor

DAVID R. GODINE, PUBLISHER

BLACK SPARROW BOOKS

9 Hamilton Place, Boston, MA 02108-4715

617-451-9600   fax: 617-350-0250

www.godine.com   e-mail: info@godine.com

David R. Godine, Inc., founded in 1970, is a small publishing house located in Boston producing between 20 and 30 titles per year and maintaining an active reprint program. The company is independent and its list tends to reflect the individual tastes and interests of its president and founder, David Godine.

At Godine, quality has remained foremost. All of their hardcover and softcover books are printed on acid-free paper. Many hardcovers are still bound in full cloth. The list is deliberately eclectic and features works that many other publishers can't or won't support, books that won't necessarily become best-sellers but that still deserve publication. In a world of spinoffs and commercial product, Godine's list stands apart by offering original fiction and nonfiction of the highest rank, rediscovered masterworks, translations of outstanding world literature, poetry, art, photography, and beautifully designed books for children.

Recently, Godine launched two new series: Imago Mundi, a line of original books devoted to photography and the graphic arts; and Verba Mundi, featuring the most notable contemporary world literature in translation. Volumes in the Imago Mundi series, which has received praise from reviewers and booksellers alike, include *Jean Cocteau: The Mirror and the Mask* by Julie Saul and *Small Rooms & Hidden Places* by Ronald W. Wohlauer. Verba Mundi has so far published works by world- renowned authors Georges Perec, Jose Donoso, Isaac Babel, and Anna Seghers, and has introduced new voices such as Sylvie Germain (whose *Book of Nights* was named a Notable Book of the Year by the *New York Times*) and the acclaimed Swedish novelist Goran Tunstrom, author of *The Christmas Oratorio*.

Additionally, on July 1, 2002, John Martin, the founder and for 36 years the publisher of Black Sparrow Press, closed down his shop in Santa Rosa, Calif. After finding new homes for four of his authors—Charles Bukowski, Paul Bowles, John Fante, and Wyndham Lewis—he entrusted the rest of his backlist to a fellow publisher, David R. Godine. The agreement was simple: Godine would keep Black Sparrow's offerings available to the trade, keep the best-selling titles in print, and keep the house's spirit alive through judicious acquisitions. In short, Black Sparrow Press would be reborn— as Black Sparrow Books at David R. Godine, Publisher.

Recent titles from Godine include *Arctic Circle: Birth & Rebirth in the Land of Caribou* by Robert Reid; *The Book of Camp-Lore and Woodcraft* by Daniel C. Beard; *The Likes of Us: Photography and the Farm Security Administration* by Stu Cohen; *Fillets of Plaice* by Gerald Durrell; *Lucy's Summer* by Donald Hall and Michael McCurdy; *All Around the Block: An Alphabet* by Judy Pelikan; *The Immigrant's Contract* by Leland Kinsey; *Seimmer in the Secret Sea* by William Kotzwinkle; *Cider with Rosie* by Laurie Lee; and *Cat, What Is That?* by Tony Johnston and Wendell Minor.

Recent titles from Black Sparrow Books include *Metropolitan Tang* by Linda Bamber; *Jazz and Twelve O'Clock Tales* by Wanda Coleman; *Birds, Beasts, and Flowers!* D.H. Lawrence; *Holocaust* by Charles Reznikoff; *The Brooklyn Novels* by Daniel Fuchs; and *Jamie is My Heart's Desire* by Alfred Chester.

Godine distributes its own titles in the U.S. For sales in U.K. and Europe, please contact Airlift Book Company. For sales in Canada, please contact Hushion House Publishing. For sales in Australia, please contact Wakefield Press, Pty, Ltd.

Do not telephone the office or submit anything via e-mail. Query letters and SASEs should be directed to:

David R. Godine, Publisher

GOSPEL LIGHT PUBLICATIONS

REGAL BOOKS

1957 Eastmen Avenue, Ventura, CA 93003

805-644-9721 / 800-446-7735

www.gospellight.com

Founded in 1933 by Dr. Henrietta Mears, Gospel Light is committed to providing effective resources for evangelism, discipleship, and Christian education through Sunday school and Vacation Bible school curricula, videos, and children's music.

Gospel Light highlights include *Clergy Tax* by J. David Epstein; *A New Kind of Conservative* by Joel Hunter; *Fusion,* by Nelson Searcy with Jennifer Henson; *I Want to Believe* by Mel Lawrenz; *Raising Fit Kids in a Fat World* by Judy Halliday, RN and Joanie Jack, MD; *The Relief of Imperfection* by Joan C. Webb; *Yes, Lord* by Harold Bredesen with Pat King; and *The Big Book of Create-Your-Own Bible Lessons* by Sharon Short.

The Regal Book Division (founded in 1965) specializes in needs-oriented books and building efforts aimed at church leadership and families. Recent Regal titles include *Marriage on the Rock: God's Design for Your Dream Marriage* by Jimmy and Karen Evans; *Chasing the Dragon* by Jackie Pullinger; *When Necessary Use Words* by Mike

Pilavachi; *The Ultimate Survival Guide for Children's Ministry* by Ivy Beckwith; *Shaping Your Family's Faith* by Jack and Dona Eggar; and *Punk Monk* by Pete Grieg and Andy Freeman.

Queries, proposals, and SASEs should be directed to Acquisitions Editor.

GRAYWOLF PRESS

2402 University Avenue, Suite 203, Saint Paul, MN 55114

fax: 651-641-0036

www.graywolfpress.org

Since 1974, Graywolf has been an important outlet for American poetry and helped keep fine literature off the extinction list. Their list also includes novels, short stories, memoirs, and essays, and features such writers as Elizabeth Alexander, Charles Baxter, Sven Birkerts, Linda Gregg, Eamon Grennan, Tony Hoagland, Jane Kenyon, William Kittredge, Carl Phillips, William Stafford, David Treuer, and Brenda Ueland. A commitment to quality, and a willingness to embrace or invent new models, has kept Graywolf at the forefront of the small press movement. Today, Graywolf is considered one of the nation's leading nonprofit literary publishers. The house publishes about 25 new books per year.

Representative of the Graywolf list are *The End* by Salvatore Scibona; *Confessions of a Former Child: A Therapist's Memoir* by Daniel Tomasulo; *Stump* by Niall Griffiths; *Modern Life* by Matthew Harvey; *Lions Don't Eat Us* by Constance Quarterman Bridges; *Feeling as Foreign Language: The Good Strangeness of Poetry* by Alice Fulton; and *And Give You Peace* by Jessica Treadway.

In 2002, Graywolf moved its distribution to the prestigious New York publishers Farrar, Straus & Giroux, an alliance that confirms Graywolf's position as a significant American publisher and one that will offer many new opportunities for the press to increase its services to readers and writers.

Query letters and SASEs should be directed to:

Katie Dublinski, Editorial Director

Jeff Shotts, Senior Editor

GREAT SOURCE EDUCATION GROUP [SEE HOUGHTON MIFFLIN]

GREENWOOD PUBLISHING GROUP

A Division of Harcourt

GREENWOOD PRESS

PRAEGER PUBLISHERS

HEINEMANN USA

LIBRARIES UNLIMITED

88 Post Road West, Box 5007, Westport, CT 06881-5007

203-226-3571   fax: 203-222-1502

www.greenwood.com   e-mail: editorial@greenwood.com

Heinemann USA address:

361 Hanover Street, Portsmouth, NH 03801

603-431-7894

www.heinemann.com   e-mail: proposals@heinemann.com

The Greenwood Publishing Group is one of the world's leading publishers of reference titles, academic and general interest books, texts, books for librarians and other professionals, and electronic resources. With over 18,000 titles in print, GPG publishes some 1,000 books each year, many of which are recognized with annual awards from Choice, Library Journal, the American Library Association, and other scholarly and professional organizations. Greenwood is a division of Harcourt and a member of the Reed-Elsevier family of professional and educational publishers.

GPG imprint Greenwood Press publishes reference books in all subject areas taught in middle schools, high schools, and colleges, as well as on topics of general interest. Their many award-winning titles in the social sciences and humanities range from in-depth multivolume encyclopedias to more concise handbooks, guides, and even biographies.

Best-selling titles from Greenwood include *How to Write and Publish a Scientific Paper* by Robert A. Day and Barbara Gastel; *Proposal Planning and Writing* by Lynn E. Miner and Jeremy T. Miner; *Tiger Woods: A Biography (Greenwood Biographies)* by Lawrence J. Londino; *Culture and Customs of Uganda* by Kefa M. Otiso; and *Madonna: A Biography* by Mary Cross.

GPG Imprint Praeger Publishers has a distinguished history (since 1949) of producing scholarly and professional books in the social sciences and humanities, with special strengths in modern history, military studies, psychology, business, current events and social issues, international affairs, politics, visual and performing arts, and literature. Praeger books serve the needs of scholars and general readers alike by providing the best of contemporary scholarship to the widest possible audience.

Recent titles from Greenwood and Praeger include *Crash Course in Reference* by Charlotte Ford; *Military Transformation and Modern Warfare* by Elinor Sloan; *Culture and Customs of Senegal* by Eric S. Ross; *Retiring as a Career: Making the Most of Your Retirement* by Betsy Kyte Newman; *Going to School in Sub-Saharan Africa* by Jim and Bridget Omatseye; *A History of Multiple Sclerosis* by Colin. L. Talley; *Weary of War: Life on the Confederate Home Front* by Joe A. Mobley; and *The Words and Music of Prince* by James E. Perone.

Heinemann USA is a national leader in the publishing of professional books for teachers of language arts K-12, and has growing lists in math, science, social studies, and art education. In 1987, Boynton/Cook, the leading publisher of professional books for English teachers at the middle and high school levels and for college English teachers, joined Heinemann. The company also has an active presence in several niche markets, most notably in theatre and arts, and Third World writing, with literature lists in the Caribbean, Asia, Middle East, and Africa.

Recent Heinemann titles include *Bullying (Tough Topics)* by Elizabeth Raum; *Management by Process: A Practical Road-Map to Sustainable Business Process Management* by John Jeston and Johan Nelis; *The Anatomy Colouring and Workbook* by Stuart Porter; *All Around Texas: Regions and Resources* by Mark Stewart; and *Mapping the United States (First Guide to Maps)* by Marta Segal Block.

Libraries Unlimited serves the needs of the library profession through quality publications for library and information science students and faculty, practicing librarians, media specialists, and teachers. Titles include *African Legends, Myths, and Folktales for Readers Theatre* by Anthony D. Bongaman Fredericks; *Reading and Writing to Learn: Strategies Across the Curriculum* by Katherine W. Kuta; and *American Reference Books Annual 2008* by Shannon G. Hysell.

For Libraries Unlimited submissions, please query one of the editors listed below via e-mail prior to sending a proposal.

To submit to Heinemann, e-mail proposals@heinemann.com or send your proposal or query via regular mail with SASE to the Acquisitions Editor.

For submissions to Praeger and Greenwood, please classify your project as either reference (Greenwood Press) or non-reference (Praeger), and send your proposal to the appropriate editor. If you cannot identify the appropriate editor, or if you are writing on an interdisciplinary topic such as women's studies, send an e-mail outlining your proposal to editorial@greenwood.com or send via mail to the Acquisitions Department. Send proposals or queries via e-mail or regular mail with SASEs.

Jeff Olsen—Business and economics (Greenwood and Praeger); jeff.olsen@greenwood.com

Suzanne Staszak-Silva—Crime, literature, religion (Praeger); sstaszak@greenwood.com

Kristi Ward—Contemporary music, popular culture and media, sports (Greenwood); kristi.ward@greenwood.com

Daniel Harmon—Contemporary music, popular culture and media, sports, arts

(Praeger); daniel.harmon@greenwood.com

Sandy Towers—Current events, media literacy (Greenwood); sandy.towers@greenwood.com

Robert Hutchinson—Interdisciplinary (Praeger); robert.hutchinson@greenwood.com

Wendi Schnaufer—Food, social issues, world cultures, multicultural/African American/Latino American/Asian American/Native American Issues (Greenwood); wendi.schnaufer@greenwood.com

Debby Adams—Health & medicine, high school reference, young adult literature, arts (Greenwood); debra.adams@greenwood.com

Kevin Downing—Health & medicine (Greenwood); kevin.downing@greenwood.com

Debora Carvalko—Psychology, social work (Praeger); dcarvalk@greenwood.com

George Butler—Literature/college reference (Greenwood); gbutler@greenwood.com

Adam Kane—Military History (Praeger); adam.kane@greenwood.com

Barbara Ittner—Public library and high school reference books (Libraries Unlimited); barbara.ittner@lu.com

Sharon Coatney—School library books (Libraries Unlimited); sharon.coatney@lu.com

Sue Easun—Textbooks and reference books (Libraries Unlimited); sue.easun@lu.com

GROVE / ATLANTIC, INC.

GROVE PRESS

ATLANTIC MONTHLY PRESS

ATLANTIC BOOKS

CANONGATE BOOKS

841 Broadway, 4th Floor, New York, NY 10003

212-614-7850   fax: 212-614-7886

www.groveatlantic.com   e-mail: info@groveatlantic.com

Grove / Atlantic publishes trade nonfiction and fiction; these works often display a contemporary cultural bent or an issue-oriented edge. Grove Press and Atlantic

Monthly Press, two formerly independent houses, were united under the Grove / Atlantic corporate crest in 1993. Grove / Atlantic operates from the former Grove headquarters on Broadway (with Atlantic having relocated from its pervious digs at nearby Union Square West). The publisher operates essentially as one house, while maintaining the distinction of two major imprints.

Atlantic Monthly Press was founded in 1917 as an imprint of Little, Brown. During the next 16 years, the press's books won more than 16 Pulitzer Prizes and National Book Awards. Among the press's best-selling award-winning titles published during those years were *Mutiny on the Bounty*, *Goodbye Mr. Chips*, *Drums Along the Mohawk*, *Ship of Fools*, *Fire in the Lake*, *The Soul of the New Machine*, and *Blue Highways*. In 1985, the press was spun off from the magazine and became independent.

Grove Press was founded in 1951 by literary trailblazer Barney Rosset, who established a tradition of enterprising lists that featured some of the finest and most fearless writing from around the globe. This literary institution was purchased by Ann Getty in 1985, in league with the U.K.-based publisher Weidenfeld & Nicholson; the publisher operated briefly under the sobriquet Grove Weidenfeld. With the early retreat of the Weidenfeld interests, the fate of Grove was a popular topic of publishing tattle rumored to be perpetually on the block, both prior and subsequent to the house's merger with Atlantic Monthly.

In February 1993, Grove Press and Atlantic Monthly Press merged to form Grove / Atlantic, Inc. Publishing under these two imprints, Grove / Atlantic, Inc., continues to publish books that have been in the forefront of the American literary and publishing scene for more than 75 years. Imprints Canongate Books and Atlantic Books are based in the U.K. and may be reached via e-mail at enquireies@groveatlantic.co.uk.

Recent Grove / Atlantic titles include *A Splendid Exchange: How Trade Shaped the World* by William J. Bernstein; *So Brave, Young, and Handsome* by Leif Enger; *The Girl of His Dreams* by Donna Leon; *Leisureville* by Andrew D. Blechman; *House Rules* by Mike Lawson; *White Protestant Nation: The Rise of the American Conservative Movement* by Allan J. Lichtman; *The Sand Castle* by Rita Mae Brown; and *T.H.U.G. L.I.F.E.* by Sanyika Shakur; *The Yoga Teacher* by Alexandra Gray; *The Rebel's Hour* by Lieve Joris; *How the Soldier Repairs the Gramophone* by Sasa Stanisic; and *Tiger, Tiger* by Galaxy Craze.

Grove / Atlantic books are distributed by Perseus.

Grove / Atlantic accepts unsolicited manuscripts only from literary agents. Direct queries and SASEs to:

Morgan Entrekin, Publisher

Elisabeth Schmitz, Executive Editor—Fiction, narrative nonfiction

Joan Bingham, Editor—History

HAMPTON ROADS PUBLISHING

1125 Stoney Ridge Road, Charlottesville, VA 22902

434-296-2772

www.hamptonroadspub.com e-mail: submissions@hrpub.com

Hampton Roads is a nonfiction publisher that describes its titles as messages for the evolving human spirit. The catalog consists of spiritual self-help from the mystical to the practical; subjects include body/mind/spirit, astrology and divination, dreams and dreaming, past lives, reincarnation, the animal world, psychics, remote viewing, business and leadership, visionary fiction, natural solutions for health problems, self-care health advice, the political dimensions of medicine, new science, studies in consciousness, out-of-body experiences, near-death experiences, exploring the afterlife, earth energies, crop circles, and shamanism. Hampton Roads publishes best-selling authors such as Richard Bach, Neal Donald Walsch, and Mary Summer Rain. The Young Spirit line focuses on New Age titles for children.

Recent titles include *Conscious Health: The Complete owner's Manual for Healing Naturally* by Ron Garner; *Alchemy of the Heart: Transform Turmoil into Peace Through Emotional Integration* by Michael Brown; *Do You See What I See? Memoirs of a Blind Biker* by Russel Targ; *Midnights with the Mystic: A Little Guide to Freedom and Bliss* by Cheryl Simone and Sadhguru Jaggi Vasudev; and *A Mind for Murder: A Real-Life Files of a Psychic Investigator* by Noreen Renier.

Hampton Roads editors prefer electronic submissions sent as Word attachments via e-mail to submissions@hrpub.com. Send proposals via regular mail to the Acquisitions Editor, but be aware they will not be returned.

Jack Jennings, Chief Editor

HARCOURT TRADE PUBLISHERS

HARCOURT TRADE PUBLISHERS

HARCOURT

HARCOURT CHILDREN'S BOOKS

HARVEST BOOKS

525 B Street, Suite 1900, San Diego, CA 92101

619-231-6616

New York office:

15 East 26th Street, 15th Floor, New York, NY 10010

212-592-1000

www.harcourtbooks.com

Harcourt Trade Publishers, acquired by Houghton Mifflin Company in 2007, publishes fiction and nonfiction for readers of all ages using several imprints, including Harcourt for hardcover books, the Harvest Books imprint for adult paperbacks, and Harcourt Children's Books, which includes the imprints of Gulliver Books, Silver Whistle, Red Wagon Books, Harcourt Young Classics, Green Light Readers, Voyager Books/Libros Viajeros, Harcourt Paperbacks, Odyssey Classics, and Magic Carpet Books. Harcourt Trade Publishers has two locations in the U.S.: the company headquarters in San Diego and an editorial/sales/marketing/rights office in New York, which is where all submissions should go. Information about Harcourt Education may be found at www.harcourt.com.

Harcourt is dedicated to publishing general interest books in a variety of areas and genres, including fiction, literature, poetry, history, current events, sociology, science, autobiography, and language for adult readers, and quality board books and novelty items, illustrated picture books, easy readers, and novels for children of all ages.

Although the trade publishing program was trimmed markedly through the early 1990s, Harcourt remains particularly potent in the arena of educational materials and texts, as well as professional reference. The editors at Harcourt Trade are particularly proud of launching authors with debut novels.

Recent titles from Harcourt include *Streams of Babel* by Carol Plum-Ucci; *Twice Upon a Marigold* by Jean Ferris; *Uh-oh!* by Rachel Isadora; *A Voice in the Wind* by Kathryn Lasky; *Lavinia* by Ursuala K. Le Guin; *All Souls* by Christine Schutt; and *A Church of Her Own: What Happens When a Woman Takes the Pulpit* by Sarah Sentilles.

Harvest Books is the adult paperback imprint for Harcourt. In addition to publishing paperback versions of hardcovers, Harvest Books includes original paperback introductions of well-known and emerging authors. Recent Harvest releases include *Be Near Me* by Andrew O'Hagan; *Generation Loss* by Elizabeth Hand; *Untapped: The Scramble for Africa's Oil* by John Ghazvinian; *The Hot Topic: What WE Can Do About Global Warming* by Grabrielle Walker and David King; and *A Pig in Provence: Good Food and Simple Pleasures in the South of France* by Georgeanne Brennan.

Harcourt Children's Books is a leader in its field. The original publisher of such classics as *The Little Prince, Mary Poppins, The Borrowers, Half Magic, Ginger Pye*, and *The Moffats*, Harcourt Children's Books continues its literary tradition by publishing many diverse talents, including Janet Stevens, David Diaz, Gerald McDermott, Audrey and Don Wood, Han Nolan, Janell Cannon, Debra Frasier, Mem Fox, Julius Lester, Eve Bunting, Lois Ehlert, Douglas Florian, Stephen Gammel, Ann Rinaldi, Diane Duane, Jane Yolen, Cynthia Rylant, Marissa Moss, Bruce Coville, Steven Kellogg, Leo and Diane Dillon, Thomas Locker, and many others.

Recent Harcourt Children's Books titles include *The Letter Writer* by Ann Rinaldi; *Mystery Ride!* by Scott Magoon; *Snow* by Cynthia Rylant and Lauren Stringer; *Christ-*

mas Farm by Mary Lyn Ray and Barry Root; *The Faerie Door* by Bruce Maxwell; *Graceling* by Kristin Cashore; *Ten Little Fingers and Ten Little Toes* by Mem Fox and Helen Oxenbury; *The Unnameables* by Ellen Booraem; and *Wangari's Trees of Peace: A True Story from Africa*.

Harcourt does not accept unsolicited query letters, e-mails, or manuscripts, except from literary agents.

Andrea Schulz, Editor-in-Chief (NY)—General fiction and nonfiction

Tina Pohlman, Editorial Director, Trade Paperbacks/Harvest (NY)—General fiction and nonfiction, Harvest

Ann Patty, Executive Editor (NY)—General nonfiction and fiction

Jenna Johnson, Editor (NY)—General nonfiction, food

Adrienne Brodeur, Editor (NY)—Fiction

Andrea Welsh, Editor (NY)—Harcourt Children's

HARLEQUIN ENTERPRISES, LTD.

HARLEQUIN BOOKS

HQN BOOKS

KIMANI PRESS

LUNA BOOKS

RED DRESS INK

SILHOUETTE BOOKS

STEEPLE HILL BOOKS

233 Broadway, Suite 1001, New York, NY 10279

212-553-4200

www.EHarlequin.com

Harlequin Enterprises, Ltd., is the world's leading publisher of romance fiction and women's fiction. The Toronto-based company publishes some 115 titles a month in 25 languages in 95 international markets on six continents. Harlequin is unique in the publishing industry, developing more new authors than any other publisher, and currently publishes over 1,300 authors from around the world. Harlequin is a division of the Torstar Corporation, a Toronto-based media company that also owns over 100 newspapers, a TV station, and various online ventures.

The Harlequin Enterprises home base in Ontario, Canada, issues the greater portion of Harlequin Books series (please see listing for Harlequin Books in the directory of Canadian Presses), while the New York office issues several Harlequin series, as well as the HQN, LUNA, Kimani, Red Dress Ink, Silhouette, and Steeple Hill lists. The editorial acquisitions departments for Mills & Boon, Harlequin Romance, and Harlequin Presents are located at the operation's U.K. offices (listed with Canada).

Each of the various lines within the Harlequin series of romance novels stakes out particular market-niche segments of reader interest within the overall categories of romance fiction and women's fiction. The best way to learn which imprint is appropriate for your manuscript is to read books already in print. There are 33 lines altogether, and each has its own submission and editorial guidelines. These guidelines are explored in great detail on the Harlequin Web site or may be requested via regular mail (with SASE) from the editors.

HARLEQUIN BOOKS

Harlequin Books in New York is home to Harlequin Intrigue and Harlequin NEXT. Following are general guidelines to these New York lines:

Harlequin Intrigue features taut, edge-of-the-seat contemporary romantic suspense tales of intrigue and desire. Kidnappings, stalkings, and women in jeopardy coupled with best-selling romantic themes are examples of story lines the editors love most. Whether a murder mystery, psychological suspense or thriller, the love story must be inextricably bound to the mystery where all loose ends are tied up neatly and shared dangers lead right to shared passions. As long as they're in jeopardy and falling in love, the heroes and heroines may traverse a landscape as wide as the world itself.

Recent Harlequin Intrigue titles are *Second Chance Cowboy* by B. J. Daniels; *Cold Case Connection* by Kathleen Long; *Twin Targets* by Jessica Andersen; *With the Material Witness in the Safehouse* by Carla Cassidy; *In the Flesh* by Rita Herron; and *Stargazer's Woman* by Aimee Thurlo

Harlequin NEXT is looking for stories that are a natural extension of series fiction—stories that celebrate all the stages of a woman's life, not just marriage and new motherhood. These stories will be warm, entertaining and sometimes even inspiring and will feature women facing a wide variety of life stages: from that first baby at 45 to the first date after divorce or widowhood; from that first day of college to dealing with three generations living in the same house. The books are complex, diverse and reflect living and loving in today's complex, diverse world. These stories will end in a happy and satisfying manner, though not necessarily in a romantic resolution. These will be novels for which romance is a piece of the pie, rather than the whole one.

Some recent Harlequin NEXT titles are *Risky Business* by Merline Lovelace and *Who Creamed Peaches, Anyway?* by Stevi Mittman;

Harlequin invites submissions from both published and unpublished writers. They prefer a query with synopsis and 1-3 chapters. Make sure your query is clear as to which line it is intended for. See writing guidelines on Web site.

Margaret Marbury, Director of Harlequin Single Titles

HQN BOOKS

HQN Books publishes mainstream romance fiction for readers around the world. Because HQN Books is a mainstream imprint, there are no tip sheets, although manuscripts are expected to range between 100,000-150,000 words. Recent titles include *The Darkest Night* by Gena Showalter; *Express Male* by Elizabeth Bevarly; *Lawman* by Diana Palmer; *Dial M for Mischief* by Kasey Michaels; *The Loner* by Geralyn Dawson; and *The Sorceress of Belmair* by Beatrice Small.

Direct your query letter to:

Tracy Farrell, Executive Editor—HQN Books

LUNA BOOKS

LUNA titles deliver a compelling, female-focused fantasy with vivid characters, rich worlds, strong, sympathetic women and romantic subplots. LUNA Books editors want emotionally complex, sweeping stories that highlight the inner female power. Whether the heroine is on a quest to save the world—or someone or something important to her—discover her past or develop her own abilities, these stories are involving, gripping and sweep the reader away into a detailed, convincing world. They also contain romantic subplots that enhance the main story but don't become the focus of the novel.

Titles include *Free Fall* by Laura Anne Gilman; *Fortune's Fool* by Mercedes Lackey; *House of Cards* by C.E. Murphy; *Keepers of the Flame* by Robin D. Owens; *The Morcai Battalion* by Diana Palmer, and *Voice of Crow* by Jeri Smith-Ready.

Query with synopsis and 1–3 chapters:

Tracey Farrell, Executive Editor, LUNA

KIMANI PRESS

Kimani Press, a new division of Harlequin, is home to four of the industry's leading imprints targeting the African American reader including Arabesque, Sepia, New Spirit, TRU, and Kimani Romance, which is the industry's only African American series romance program. As with the other Harlequin divisions, Kimani has different lines, each with its own guidelines available online or by querying the editors via regular mail.

Arabesque Inspirational Romances offer uplifting, contemporary love stories featuring realistic African American characters that resolve relationship conflicts through the perspective of strong moral beliefs. Arabesque Inspirational Romances may include several points of view, and offer classic contemporary settings.

Arabesque Romances offer contemporary, sophisticated and entertaining love stories featuring realistic African American characters that resolve natural relationship conflicts such as issues of trust, compatibility and outlook on life, with satisfying endings. Arabesque Romances may reflect several points of view and can include a wide variety of story subgenres including classic romance, contemporary romance, romantic comedy and romantic suspense or romantic thriller.

Arabesque titles include *Controversy* by Adrianne Byrd; *Charade* by Donna Hill;

Sweet Like Honey by Kim Louise; *One Special Moment* by Brenda Jackson, *When Love Falls* by Celeste O. Norfleet; and *Three Wishes* by Janice Sims.

The New Spirit imprint publishes an inspirational line of fiction and nonfiction that predominately features African American characters. These novels are entertaining and thought-provoking, and the characters will work to overcome and resolve challenges through the power of prayer and faith. These novels will not feature any profanity or explicit sex, but cover a variety of genres from contemporary women's fiction to historicals. The focus of New Spirit nonfiction books is to encourage and motivate readers by offering material that advocates empowerment, spiritual and emotional growth, and guidance on building strong personal relationships. Some New Spirit titles are *Secrets of a Sinner* by Yolanda Tonette Sanders; *This Far by Faith* by Linda Hudson-Smith, Kendra Norman-Bellamy, and Stacy H. Adams; *He's Saved...But Is He For Real?* by Kimberly Brooks; *You Deserve More* by Jewel Diamond Taylor; *Joy Comes This Morning* by Norma Deshields Brown; and *Gems for the Journey* by Vikki Johnson.

The newly introduced Kimani TRU is a new fiction imprint targeted to a younger audience of African-American readers. This imprint is aimed at illustrating real-life situations young African-American readers encounter without being preachy or naïve. The stories will reflect current trends in pop culture as well as storylines taken straight from the headlines. Recent titles are *If I Were Your Boyfriend* by Earl Sewell; *She Said, She Said* by Celeste O. Norfleet and Jennifer Norfleet; *16 Isn't Always Sweet* by Cassandra Carter; and *A Matter of Attitude* by Hayden.

Kimani Romance offers sexy, dramatic, sophisticated and entertaining love stories featuring realistic African American characters that work through compelling emotional conflicts on their way to committed and satisfying relationships. Told primarily from the heroine's point of view, Kimani Romances will keep it real with true-to-life African American characters that turn up the heat and sizzle with passion. Recent titles are *Irresistible Forces* by Brenda Jackson; *This Time for Good* by Carmen Green; *Indiscriminate Attraction* by Linda Hudson-Smith; and *Her Kind of Man* by Pamela Yaye.

The Sepia imprint publishes mainstream fiction titles that predominately feature African American characters. Sepia releases a broad range of books that entertain, inform and enrich the lives of readers. Sepia editors will review both contemporary and historical novels with subgenre plots, such as suspense-driven thrillers, paranormal and mystery, and novels that focus on social and relationship issues, as well as those that offer a realistic display of urban life. Sepia titles include *The Knees of Gullah Island* by Dwight Fryer; *After Hours* by Rochelle Alers; *Hook, Line, and Single* by Marcia King-Gamble; *On the Line* by Donna Hill, and *Pleasure Seekers* by Rochelle Alers.

For all Kimani imprints and lines, send a detailed synopsis and three sample chapters (published authors) or a detailed synopsis and a complete manuscript (unpublished authors).

Evette Porter, Editor—Kimani TRU, Arabesque Inspirational Romance and Arabesque Romances

Glenda Howard, Senior Editor—Kimani Press, New Spirit, Sepia

Kelly Martin, Associate Senior Editor—Kimani Press, Kimani Romance

INDEPENDENT U.S. PRESSES

RED DRESS INK

Red Dress Ink continues to define, as well as offer books relevant to, the 21st-century woman. But they're not just about leading the chick lit revolution; they're about leading women's fiction with attitude. The Red Dress Ink editors are looking for novels that really set themselves apart from the average chick lit book, from young and crazy tales to contemplative and witty narratives and anything in between. RDI titles include *Welcome to the Real World* by Carole Matthews; *Something Good* by Fiona Gibson; *All Eyes on Her* by Poonam Sharma; *Notes from the Backseat* by Jody Gerhman; *The Hunt* by Jennifer Sturman; *Sorcery and the Single Girl* by Mindy Klasky; *Obsession, Deceit, and Really Dark Chocolate* by Kyra Davis; and *Wednesday Night Watches* by Lee Nichols.

RDI has its own Web site: www.RedDressInk.com.

Red Dress Ink does not accept unsolicited manuscripts or proposals.

SILHOUETTE

Silhouette Books are intense thrillers, mysteries, and even werewolf stories—but always also romances. Each imprint has its own guidelines for length, plot, and characters. We recommend writing to the appropriate editor for guidelines or reading them online prior to writing your manuscript.

Silhouette Desire books are filled to the brim with strong, intense storylines. These sensual love stories immediately involve the reader in the romantic conflict and the quest for a happily-ever-after resolution. The novels should be fast-paced reads, and present the hero and heroine's conflict by the end of chapter one in order for the reader to understand what obstacles will impact the characters for the remainder of the novel. Recent titles include *Boardrooms and a Billionaire Heir* by Paula Roe; *Falling for King's Fortune* by Maureen Child; *Mistress for a Month* by Ann Major; *Dante's Stolen Wife* by Day Leclaire; *Shattered by the CEO* by Emilie Rose; and *The Desert Lord's Baby* by Olivia Gates.

Silhouette Romantic Suspense books offer an escape read where true-to-life heroines find themselves in the throes of extraordinary circumstances, and in the arms of powerful heroes. These books combine all the elements of category novels with the excitement of romantic suspense, creating big, sweeping romances amid dangerous and suspenseful settings. Recent titles include *Secret Agent Affair* by Marie Ferrarella; *The Guardian* by Linda Winstead Jones; *The Black Sheep P.I.* by Karen Whiddon; and *Heart of a Thief* by Gail Barrett.

Launched at the end of 2006, Silhouette Nocturne is looking for stories that deliver a dark, very sexy read that will entertain readers and take them from everyday life to an atmospheric, complex, paranormal world filled with characters struggling with life and death issues. These stories will be fast-paced, action-packed and mission-oriented, with a strong level of sensuality. The hero is a key figure—powerful, mysterious and totally attractive to the heroine. In fact, both main characters are very powerful, and their conflict is based on this element. The author must be able to set up a unique existence for the characters, with its own set of rules and mythologies; these are stories of vampires, shape-shifters, werewolves, psychic powers, etc., set in contemporary times. Recent titles include *Dark Deceiver* by Pamela Palmer; *Wild Hunt* by Lori Devoti; *Scions: Insurrection* by Patrice Michelle; *Last Wolf Watching and Last Wolf Hunting* by Rhyannon Byrd; *Mind Games* by Merline Lovelace; *Beast of Desire* by Lisa Renee Jones; and *The Quest* by Lindsay McKenna.

Silhouette Special Edition books are sophisticated, substantial stories packed with emotion. Special Edition demands writers eager to probe characters deeply, to explore issues that heighten the drama of living and loving, to create compelling romantic plots. Whether the sensuality is sizzling or subtle, whether the plot is wildly innovative or satisfyingly traditional, the novel's emotional vividness, its depth and dimension, should clearly label it a very special contemporary romance. Subplots are welcome, but must further or parallel the developing romantic relationship in a meaningful way. Recent titles include *Her Mr. Right?* by Karen Rose Smith; *The Prince's Royal Dilemma* by Brenda Harlen; *The Millionaires Makeover* by Lillian Darcy; *The Baby Plan* by Kate Little; *Her Miracle Man* by Karen Sandler; and *Their Secret Child* by Mary J. Forbes.

Melissa Jeglinski, Senior Editor—Silhouette Desire

Patience Smith, Associate Senior Editor—Silhouette Romantic Suspense

Tara Gavin, Editorial Director—Silhouette Nocturne

Gail Chasan, Senior Editor—Silhouette Special Edition

STEEPLE HILL

Steeple Hill's fiction that inspires features wholesome Christian entertainment that will help women to better guide themselves, their families, and other women in their communities toward purposeful, faith-driven lives. All Steeple Hill editors are looking for authors writing from a Christian worldview and conveying their personal faith and ministry values in entertaining fiction that will touch the hearts of believers and seekers everywhere.

This Harlequin imprint is comprised of the following lines: Steeple Hill Café, Love Inspired, Love Inspired Historical, Love Inspired Suspense, and Steeple Hill Women's Fiction. Steeple Hill Café is for the hip, modern woman of faith.

The Love Inspired line is a series of contemporary, inspirational romances that feature Christian characters facing the many challenges of life and love in today's world. Recent titles include *Family Ever After* by Margaret Daley; *Lone Star Courtship* by Mae Nunn; *Time for Grace* by Kate Welsh; *Where Love Abides* by Irene Hannon.

Love Inspired Historical is a series of historical romances launched October 2007 featuring Christian characters facing the many challenges of life and love in a variety of historical time periods. Recent titles include *The Redemption of Jake Scully* by Elaine Barbieri; *Masked by Moonlight* by Allie Pleiter; *The Road to Love* by Linda Ford; *The Bounty Hunter's Bride* by Victoria Bylin; *Hearts in the Highlands* by Ruth Axtell Morren; and *Legacy of Secrets* by Sara Mitchell.

Steeple Hill Love Inspired Suspense is a series of edge-of-your-seat, contemporary romantic suspense tales of intrigue and romance featuring Christian characters facing challenges to their faith and to their lives. Recent titles include *Danger in a Small Town* by Ginny Aiken; *A Face in the Shadows* by Lenora Worth; *Bayou Judgment* by Robin Caroll; and *Deadly Exposure* by Cara Putman.

The Steeple Hill Women's Fiction program is dedicated to publishing inspirational Christian women's fiction that depicts the struggles the characters encounter as they learn important lessons about trust and the power of faith. Recent titles include *Thread of Deceit* by Catherine Palmer; *Over the Waters* by Deborah Raney; and *Million Dollar Dilemma* by Judy Baer.

As with many programs developed for the Christian market, the Steeple Hill books have very specific guidelines, which may be requested from the editors or read online at eHarlequin.com.

To submit your work, send a detailed synopsis, three sample chapters, and SASE to:

Joan Marlow Golan, Executive Editor—Steeple Hill Café and Steeple Hill Women's Fiction

Krista Stroever, Associate Senior Editor—Steeple Hill Love Inspired and Love Inspired Suspense

Melissa Endlich, Editor—Love Inspired Historical

THE HARVARD COMMON PRESS

535 Albany Street, Boston, MA 02118

617-423-5803   fax: 617-695-9794

www.harvardcommonpress.com   e-mail: editorial@harvardcommonpress.com

Founded in 1976, the Harvard Common Press publishes a wide variety of award-winning books on cooking, parenting, childbirth, and home gardening. The house is devoted to the home and home living. They have recently celebrated two new James Beard nominations for *Get Saucy* by Grace Parisi and for *Perfect Party Food* by Diane Phillips.

Best-sellers from Harvard Common include *The Nursing Mother's Companion* by Kathleen Huggins; *Vegan Planet: 400 Irresistible Recipes with Fantastic Flavors from Home and Around the World* by Robin Robertson; and *Not Your Mother's Slow Cooker Cookbook* by Beth Hensperger and Julie Kaufmann.

Titles include *Cheese The Joy of Pregnancy* by Toni Kropp RN; *Hors d'Oeurvres* by Hallie Harron; *BBQ Bash: The Be-All End-All Party Guide, From Barefoot to Black Tie* by Karen Adler and Judith Fertig; *New Vegetarian Grill: 250 Flame-Kissed Recipes for Fresh Inspired Meals; Parenting Your Internationally Adopted Child: From Your First Hours Together Through the Teen Years* by Patty Cogen; *After Miscarriage: Medical Facts and Emotional Support for Pregnancy Loss* by Krissi Danielsson.

Query letters and SASEs should be directed to:

Jane Dornbusch, Managing Editor

Valerie Cimino, Executive Editor

HARVEST BOOKS [SEE HARCOURT TRADE PUBLISHERS]

HARVEST HOUSE PUBLISHERS

990 Owen Loop North, Eugene, OR 97402

517-343-0123   fax: 541-302-0731

www.harvesthousepublishers.com

Harvest House is one of the largest American publishers of Christian literature with more than 160 new books per year and a backlist of more than 700 titles. The house was founded in 1974 by Bob Hawkins, Sr., and has been run for the past 15 years by current president Bob Hawkins, Jr. Harvest House publishes in three main subject areas: self-help (relationships, family, money, Christian living), Bible helps (Bibles, Bible studies, topical studies), and full-color gift books featuring name-brand artists. Recent releases include fiction and nonfiction for children and adults. Subjects include humor, Christian history, media, technology, politics, parenting, youth, relationships, family, Christian living, contemporary values, cults and the occult, personal awareness, inspiration, and spiritual growth.

Harvest House best-sellers include *Cassidy and Sabrina* by Lori Wick; *My Beautiful Broken Shell* by Carol Hamblet Adams and D. Morgan; *Grandma, Do You Remember When?* by Jim Daly; *The Power of a Praying Wife* by Stormie Omartian; and *30 Days to Taming Your Tongue* by Deborah Smith Pegues.

Recent titles include *Changing Your World One Diaper of at a Time: A Reflective Journey Through Your Baby's First Year* by Marla Taviano; *A New Leash on Life* by Rachael Hale; *Learning to Fly* by Roxanne Henke; *Good Manners for Every Occasion: How to Look Smart and Act Right* by Emilie Barnes; *How to Find Your Personal Path to Success: Keys to Living Out Your Purpose and Passion* by Robin Chaddock; *Knowing the Heart of the Father* by David Eckman; *Playing God* by Michelle McKinney Hammond; and *When Women Walk Alone: A 31-Day Devotional Companion* by Cindi McMenamin.

Harvest House does not accept unsolicited manuscripts or queries, except from agents.

Nick Harrison, Senior Editor
Steve Miller, Senior Editor
Rod Morris, Senior Editor

HAY HOUSE

PRINCESS BOOKS

SMILEY BOOKS

NEW BEGINNINGS PRESS

P.O. Box 5100, Carlsbad, CA 92018-5100

www.hayhouse.com   e-mail: editorial@hayhouse.com

Hay House was founded in 1984 by Louise L. Hay to self-publish her first two books, *Heal Your Body* and *You Can Heal Your Life*, both of which became best-sellers and established Ms. Hay as a leader in the New Age movement.

Now full-scale, Hay House publishes nonfiction only in the areas of self-help, New Age, sociology, philosophy, psychology, health, business, finance, men's/women's issues, inspirational memoirs, and celebrity biographies. Subjects include social issues, current events, ecology, business, food and nutrition, education, the environment, alternative health / medicine, money and finance, nature, recreation, religion, men's and women's issues, spiritual growth, and fitness. All titles have a positive self-help slant to them.

Hay House currently publishes approximately 300 books and 350 audio programs by more than 130 authors, and employs a full-time staff of 100-plus. They average 50 new titles per year. Imprints include Princess Books (titles from author John Edward of *Crossing Over* fame), Smiley Books (titles from Hay House author Tavis Smiley), and New Beginnings Press (financial titles).

Best-selling titles from Hay House are *Secrets and Mysteries of the World* by Sylvia Browne; *The Power of Intention* by Dr. Wayne W. Dyer; and *Yes, You Can Be a Successful Income Investor* by Ben Stein and Phil DeMuth.

Hay House titles include *Soul Lessons and Soul Purpose: A Channeled Guide to Why You Are Here* by Sonia Choquette; *Key to Yourself: Opening to Door to a Joyful Life from Within* by Venice J. Bloodworth, PhD and Debbie Ford; *The 12-Second Sequence Special Edition DVD Kit* by Jorge Cruise; *Relax: You May Only Have a Few Minutes Left: Using the Power of Humor to Overcome Stress in Your Life and Work* by Loretta LaRoche; *Russell Grant's Zodiac Baby Names* by Russell Grant; and *Love Has Forgotten No One: The Answer to Life* by Gary Renard.

Princess Books titles include *Final Beginnings: The Tunnel* by John Edward and Natasha Stoynoff; *Practical Praying* by John Edward; and *Cracking the Coconut Code* by Mary Jo McCabe.

Smiley Books' latest release is *The Covenant in Action* by Tavis Smiley with PolicyLink and The Jamestown Project.

Recent titles from New Beginnings Press include *How to Ruin the United States of America*, and *Yes, You Can Get A Financial Life! Your Lifetime Guide to Financial Planning* both by Ben Stein and Phil DeMuth.

Hay House only accepts submissions from agents. See the Web site for details or submit hard copy proposals by mail only to Editorial Department Submissions.

Patricia Gift, Editor

HAZELDEN PUBLISHING AND EDUCATIONAL SERVICES

15251 Pleasant Valley Road, P.O. Box 176, Center City, MN 55012-0176

800-328-9000   fax: 651-213-4590

www.hazelden.org/bookplace   e-mail: customersupport@hazelden.org

Hazelden Publishing and Educational Services (established 1954) specializes in trade books that address issues relevant to alcoholism, drug addiction, and closely related psychology issues. Related topics include eating disorders, family and relationship issues, spirituality, codependency, compulsive gambling, sex addiction, depression, grief, treatment, and recovery. On the non-trade side of the publishing operation, the house publishes curricula, videos, pamphlets, and other publications for treatment programs, hospitals, schools, churches, correctional facilities, government and military agencies, as well as mental health and counseling agencies. Hazelden Publishing and Educational Services is a division of the Hazelden Foundation, which also operates a network of addiction recovery centers. The publisher has a concentration in materials related to the Twelve-Step approach.

Hazelden publishes information that helps build recovery in the lives of individuals, families and communities affected by alcoholism, drug dependency, and related diseases. Hazelden publications and services are intended to meet a full range of issues for alcoholics, drug addicts, families, counselors, educators, doctors, and other professionals. Hazelden publications support Twelve-Step philosophy and a holistic approach that addresses the needs of the mind, body, and spirit.

Hazelden publishes content in several formats: print (books, pamphlets, workbooks, curricula), multi-media (video, audio, electronic), and live trainings. Their publications are sold to bookstores, treatment programs, hospitals, schools, churches, correctional facilities, government and military agencies, mental health and counseling agencies, and private corporations' employee-related programs.

Best-sellers from this house include *Out of the Shadows: Understanding Sexual Addiction* by Patrick Carnes PhD; *Twenty-Four Hours a Day* by Bill W.; *Codependent No More* by Melody Beattie; and *Accepting Ourselves and Others* by Sheppard Kominars.

Hazelden editors look for innovative materials that address issues relevant to substance abuse, prevention, treatment, and recovery. Topics include alcoholism, nicotine, and drug addictions; family and relationship issues; spirituality; eating disorders, gambling, other addictive and compulsive behaviors; mental health; and historical information on the Twelve Steps.

Recent titles include *Blackout Girl: Growing Up and Drying Out in America* by Jennifer Storm; *12 Stupid Things That Mess Up Recovery: Avoiding Relapse Through Self-Awareness and Right Action* by Allen Berger, PhD; *A Woman's Guide to Recovery* by Brenda Iliff; *In Our Own Words: Stories of Young AAs in Recovery from the pages of AA Grapevine*; and *The Sports Lover's Guide to Recovery* by Andrew L. Dieden.

Hazelden Books are distributed exclusively by Health Communications, Inc. Submit proposals with SASEs to the Editorial Department.

Nick Motu, Publisher and Vice President

Richard Solly, Senior Editor

Sid Farrar, Director of Content Development and Production

HEALTH COMMUNICATIONS, INC.

HCI TEENS

SIMCHA PRESS

3201 Southwest 15th Street, Deerfield Beach, FL 33442

954-360-0909 / 800-441-5569   fax: 954-360-0034

www.hcibooks.com

Health Communications, Inc. (HCI) has been publishing books that change lives since 1977. HCI: The Life Issues Publisher has the goal of creating personal abundance for readers and customers, one book at a time.

In 1994, HCI published the first *Chicken Soup for the Soul* book, which not only became a best-seller, but continues to be an international publishing phenomena. Books in the series have sold nearly 100 million copies.

Originally operating as a publisher of informational pamphlets for the recovery community, HCI moved into mainstream publishing in the 1980s with its first *New York Times* best-seller, the 1983 *Adult Children of Alcoholics* by Dr. Janet Woititz, a veritable "bible" of the ACOA movement. This first best-seller was followed by *Bradshaw On: The Family*, and *Healing the Shame That Binds You* both by John Bradshaw.

Aware of the significant shifts in the recovery movement, HCI actively expanded its book list to include a broader selection of titles. Now regarded as The Life Issues Publisher, HCI continues a tradition of providing readers with inspiring and motivating personal growth and self-help books.

Publisher of quality books on life issues, HCI's broad base of over 900 titles encompasses self-help, spirituality, addictions and recovery, psychology, parenting, relationships, religion, inspiration, health and wellness, and more.

Recent HCI titles include *Chicken Soup for the Father and Son Soul: Celebrating the Bond That Connects Generations* by Jack Canfield, Mark Victor Hansen, Dorothy Firman, and Ted Slawski; *Life Lessons for Mastering the Law of Attraction: 7 Ingredients for Living a Prosperous Life* by Jeanna Gabellini and Eva Gregory; *Purr More, Hiss Less: Heavenly Lessons I Learned from My Cat* by Allia Zobel Nolan and Erika Oller; and *Staging Your Comeback: A Complete Beauty Revival for Women over 45* by Christopher Hopkins.

HCI TEENS

HCI Teens delivers the facts and fiction teens are asking for. HCI's commitment to teens is firm, up front and to the point: Give teens what they want, what they need, and most important give teens a variety of quality content from which they can learn, grow and enjoy all life has to offer now and in the future. The backbone for the imprint include the best-selling titles from Chicken Soup for the Teenage Soul series, Taste Berries for Teens series by Bettie and Jennifer Youngs, and the Teen Love series by Kimberly Kirberger. Recent titles include *The Success Principles for Teens: How to Get From Where You Are to Where You Want to Be* by Jack Canfield and Kent Healy; *Chicken Soup for the American Idol Soul* by Debra Poneman, Jack Canfield, and Mark Victor Hansen; *Chicken Soup For the Soul Presents Teens Talkin' Faith* by Michelle L. Trujillo, Jack Canfield, and Mark Victor Hansen; *Jon and Jayne's Guide to Making Friends and "Getting" the Guy (Or Girl)* by Gary and Carol Rosenberg.

SIMCHA PRESS

In the spirit of simcha, the symbol of celebration and joy, Simcha Press offers titles for those on the path of Jewish enrichment. The imprint's mission is to publish books in the realm of Jewish spirituality that will uplift and enrich the lives of its readers. Its first books were released in 2000.

New titles from Simcha Press include *Genesis—The Book With Seventy Faces: A Guide for the Family* by Esther Takac; *The Remarkable Invention that Saves Zion* by Yehudit Stupeniker; *Tales from the Talmud* by Rachel Trugman; *Purr-im Cat* by Wendy Ruth Gottlieb; *Mr. Mentch (Meet the Yids)* by Mamas; and *Hear Her Voice: Twelve Jewish Women Who Changed the World* by Miriam P. Feinberg and Miriam Klein Shapiro.

Health Communications distributes its own list. In addition, HCI is the exclusive trade distributor for Hazelden Publishing.

Due to new postal regulations, HCI can no longer use a SASE to return parcels weighing 16 ounces or more. Therefore, they no longer return any submissions weighing 16 ounces or more even if a SASE is included. See their Web site for more detailed submission guidelines. Query letters, proposals, and SASEs should be directed to the editorial staff.

Michele Matrisciani, Editorial Director

HEBREW PUBLISHING COMPANY

P.O. Box 222, Spencertown, NY 12165

518-392-3322   fax: 518-392-4280

Hebrew Publishing Company (established in 1901) offers a wide range of titles in such categories as reference materials and dictionaries; religions, law, and thought; Rabbinic literature; literature, history, and biography, children's books, Hebrew-language texts and Hebrew culture; Yiddish; the Bible in English and in Hebrew/English; prayers and liturgy, including daily (Hebrew only and Hebrew/English), Sabbath, high holidays, festivals, memorials, and Purim; Hanukkah; educational materials; sermons and aids of the rabbi; and calendars. The house publishes a limited number of new titles and maintains an established backlist.

On the HPC list: *Yom Kippur* by Philip Birnbaum; *Judaism as a Civilization* by Mordecai Kaplan; *Acharon Hamohikanim (The Last of the Mohicans)* by James Fenimore Cooper; *Business Ethics in Jewish Law* by Leo Jung; *Encyclopedia of Jewish Concepts* by Philip Birnbaum; and *Jewish Tales and Legends* by Menachem Glen.

Hebrew Publishing Company oversees its own distribution, utilizing the services of independent fulfillment and distribution firms.

Query letters and SASEs should be directed to:

Charles Lieber, President

HEBREW UNION COLLEGE PRESS

A Division of the Hebrew Union College-Jewish Institute of Religion

3101 Clifton Avenue, Cincinnati, OH 45220-2488

513-221-1875, extension 3292

www.huc.edu/newspubs/press   e-mail: hucpress@huc.edu

As part of the Hebrew Union College-Jewish Institute of Religion, the Hebrew Union College Press (founded 1921) publishes scholarly Judaica for an international academic readership.

Always concerned with quality of scholarship rather than sales potential, the Hebrew Union College Press has from its inception devoted its resources and efforts to the publication of works of the highest caliber for its niche audience. HUCP has co-publishing projects with other institutions, including Harvard University Press, KTAV Publishing House, University of Alabama Press, Yale University Press, Klau Library, Skirball Museum, and Kunstresim.

Titles include *Let Me Continue to Speak the Truth: Bertha Pappenheim as Author and Activist* by Elizabeth Loentz; *My Dear Daughter: Rabbi Benjamin Slonik and the Education of Jewish Women in Sixteenth-Century Poland* by Edward Fram; *The New Tradition: Essays on Modern Hebrew Literature* by Gershon Shaked; and *Nelson Glueck: Biblical Archaeologist and President of the Hebrew Union College Jewish Institute of Religion* by Jonathan M. Brown and Laurence Kutler.

Hebrew Union College Press is distributed by Wayne State University Press.

HUCP welcomes the submission of scholarly manuscripts in all areas of Judaica. Address all editorial inquiries to:

Professor Michael A. Meyer, Chair, Publications Committee

Barbara Selya, Managing Editor

HEINEMANN USA [SEE GREENWOOD PUBLISHING GROUP]

HELIOS PRESS [SEE ALLWORTH PRESS]

HERDER & HERDER [SEE CROSSROAD PUBLISHING COMPANY]

HILL STREET PRESS

191 East Broad Street, Suite 214, Athens, GA 30601

706-613-7200   fax: 706-613-7204

www.hillstreetpress.com   e-mail: editorial@hillstreetpress.com

Hill Street Press (founded 1998) publishes approximately 20 titles annually in, current events, history, politics, fiction, memoir, African American studies, gender/women's studies, gay/lesbian interest, nature/gardening, music, business, and sports. They also publish a line of 100% thematic crossword puzzle books under the Hot Cross Books imprint. Although many of Hill Street's books spring from the American South, the house seeks to publish books that transcend regionalism and appeal to the reader of any region.

HSP seeks to serve as incubator and archive for both the most promising and the most established writers, to offer an extraordinary range of perspectives on a multitude of subjects, while always avoiding the hackneyed notions of the South as the exclusive province of the gothic or the sentimental dominion of moonlight and magnolias.

Recent Hill Street Press titles include *Stone Age Santa* by Kevin O'Donnell, illustrated by Boo Young Kim and David Heo; *Tim and Sally's Vegetable Garden* by H. Grady Thrasher and Elaine Rabon; *Cooking with Jack: The New Jack Daniel's Cookbook* by Lynne Tolley and Mindy Merrell; and *The Presidents and First Ladies Crossword* compiled by Andrew Smith.

HSP titles are distributed exclusively by Independent Publishers Group and other representatives internationally.

HSP is accepting nonfiction submissions; they are not accepting unsolicited fiction queries or manuscripts. All puzzles and games are developed in-house; they do not accept submissions for these games. See Web site for detailed submission guidelines. All query letters, proposals, and SASEs should be directed to:

Tom Payton, President and Publisher, payton@hillstreetpress.com

Judy Long, Vice President and Editor-in-Chief, long@hillstreetpress.com

---

HIPPOCRENE BOOKS

171 Madison Avenue, New York, NY 10016

212-685-4371   fax: 212-779-9338

www.hippocrenebooks.com   e-mail: info@hippocrenebooks.com

Over more than 35 years, Hippocrene Books has become one of America's foremost publishers of foreign-language reference books and ethnic cookbooks. As a small publishing house in a marketplace dominated by conglomerates, Hippocrene has succeeded by continually reinventing its list while maintaining a strong international and ethnic orientation. In addition to cookbooks and foreign-language reference books, Hippocrene publishes on the subjects of history, Judaica, leisure, love poetry, militaria, Polish interest, proverbs, travel, and weddings.

George Blagowidow founded the company in 1970. The name Hippocrene comes from Greek mythology and refers to the sacred fountain of the Muses that was the source of their inspiration. Hippocrene's international focus derives from Blagowidow's passion for travel and his personal history.

Currently, Hippocrene features over 64 cuisines in its cookbook program. In addition to its conventional history list, the company launched a series of Illustrated Histories in 1998. Each book features the political and cultural history of a region, accompanied by black-and-white pictures. Leading titles include *Spain: An Illustrated History* and *The Celtic World: An Illustrated History*. New publishing areas also comprise international editions of poetry, short stories, proverbs, and folk tales. *Classic French Love Poems* edited by Lisa Neal and *Pakistani Folk Tales: Toontoony Pie and Other Stories* by Ashraf Siddiqui and Marilyn Lerch are representative titles.

Recent titles include *Regional Greek Cooking* by Dean and Catherine Karayanis; *Flavorful India: Treasured Recipes from a Gujarati Family* by Priti Chitnis Gress; *Aprovecho: A Mexican-American Border Cookbook* by Teresa Cordero-Cordell and Robert Cordell; *Aramaic, Modern Dictionary and Phrasebook* by Nicholas Awdem Nineb Lamassu and Nicholas Al-Jeloo; *Beginner's Danish with 2 audio CD's* by Nete Schmidt; *Norse Warfare: Unconventional Battle Strategies of the Ancient Vikings* by Martina Sprague; and *Ancient Rome in So Many Words* by Christopher Francese.

Query letters and SASEs should be directed to the editorial staff.

Anne McBride, Editor-in-Chief

HORIZON PUBLISHERS [SEE CEDAR FORT INC.]

HOUGHTON MIFFLIN COMPANY

HARCOURT (SEE SEPARATE ENTRY)

HOUGHTON MIFFLIN TRADE AND REFERENCE

HOUGHTON MIFFLIN BOOKS FOR CHILDREN

   KINGFISHER

   CLARION BOOKS

HOUGHTON MIFFLIN SCHOOL DIVISION

HOUGHTON MIFFLIN COLLEGE DIVISION

Boston office:

222 Berkeley Street, Boston, MA 02116-3764

617-351-5000

New York office:

215 Park Avenue South, New York, NY 10003

212-420-5800

www.hmco.com

www.eduplace.com

GREAT SOURCE EDUCATION GROUP

Wilmington, MA office:

181 Ballardvale Street, Wilmington, MA 01887

800-289-4490   fax: 800-289-3994

www.greatsource.com

MCDOUGAL-LITTELL

Illinois office:

1900 S. Batavia, Geneva, IL 60134

800-442-2043   fax: 630-208-5886 / 888-872-8380

www.mcdougallittell.com

Boston-based Houghton Mifflin Company is one of the leading educational publishers in the U.S., publishing textbooks, instructional technology, assessments, and other educational materials for teachers and students of every age. The company also publishes an extensive line of reference works and award-winning trade fiction and nonfiction for adults and young readers. With more than $1.4 billion in sales per year, Houghton Mifflin is comprised of six divisions: Trade and Reference Division, Great Source Education Group, College Division, McDougal Littell, School Division, and Riverside Publishing (standardized tests).

In December 2006, Houghton Mifflin was acquired by HM Rivergroup, an Irish holding company led by Riverdeep Chief Executive Barry O'Callaghan; the combined group was renamed Houghton Mifflin Riverdeep Group. In 2007, Houghton Mifflin Company acquired Harcourt Education, Harcourt Trade, and Greenwood-Heinemann divisions of Reed Elsevier, and became the largest educational publisher in the world.

With its origins dating back to 1832, Houghton Mifflin Company combines its tradition of excellence with a commitment to innovation in order to satisfy the lifelong need to learn and be entertained.

Today, the Trade and Reference Division of Houghton Mifflin publishes about 400 books a year, including adult trade books, Mariner trade paperbacks, the American Heritage dictionaries, Peterson Field Guides, Taylor Guides, Kingfisher Books, the Best American Series, Houghton Mifflin Children's Books, Walter Lorraine Books, and Clarion Books.

HOUGHTON MIFFLIN ADULT TRADE GROUP

The Adult Trade Group publishes fiction and nonfiction of the highest quality, intended for a general audience. As part of a major educational publisher, HM is dedicated to publishing works that will become a part of the canon taught in schools and colleges in the future. In nonfiction, the roster includes fine writers in such categories as history, natural history, biography and memoir, science, and economics, including such preeminent figures as Winston Churchill, Arthur M. Schlesinger, Jr., and John Kenneth Galbraith. They also have a proud tradition of publishing works of social criticism that have spoken with great power through the generations, including Rachel Carson's *Silent Spring*, James Agee and Walker Evans's *Let Us Now Praise Famous Men*, the works of Jane Goodall and, recently, the best-selling *Constantine's Sword* by James Carroll, and *Fast Food Nation* by Eric Schlosser.

On the literary side, Houghton Mifflin launched the careers of such writers as Willa Cather, A. B. Guthrie, Jr., Robert Penn Warren, Ann Petry, Elizabeth Bishop, Philip Roth, Willie Morris, and Robert Stone. Their fiction list today also includes such distinguished names as Tim O'Brien, John Edgar Wideman, and Edna O'Brien.

Houghton Mifflin's commitment to poetry also spans well over 100 years. The current roster of poets includes Donald Hall, the current poet laureate, Natasha Trethewey, the 2007 Winner of the Pulitzer Prize in Poetry, Galway Kinnell, Grace Schulman, Alan Shapiro, Michael Collier, and Glyn Maxwell, among others.

Recently the adult trade group has rededicated itself to publishing veteran writers of the greatest stature and discovering the most promising emerging voices. The Pulitzer Prize in fiction has been awarded to Houghton Mifflin authors twice in the past few years: in 1998 to Philip Roth, for *American Pastoral*, and in 2000 to Jhumpa Lahiri, for her first book, *Interpreter of Maladies*. In 1996 the National Book Award was given to James Carroll for his memoir, *An American Requiem*. In 1997 the National Book Critics Circle Award went to Penelope Fitzgerald's acclaimed novel *The Blue Flower*.

Recent titles include *Madness: A Bipolar Life* by Marya Hornbacher; *Dear American Airlines: A Novel* by Jonathan Miles; *Native Guard* by Natasha Trethewy; *God Particles: Poems* by Thomas Lux; *The Perfect Recipe for Losing Weight and Eating Great* by Pam Anderson; *Old War: Poems* by Alan Shapiro; *Flights Against the Sunset: Stories that Reunited a Mother and Son* by Kenn Kaufman; and *Arnie and Jack: Palmer, Nicklaus, and Golf's Greatest Rivalry* by Ian O'Connor.

The adult trade group does not accept unsolicited manuscript submissions for fiction, nonfiction, or poetry, except through a literary agent. Send lexical submissions to the Dictionary Department at the Boston address.

Ken Carpenter, Director of Trade Paperbacks (Boston)—Fiction, nonfiction

Amanda Cook, Senior Editor (Boston)—Serious nonfiction, current issues, business/finance

Anton Mueller, Senior Editor (Boston)—General nonfiction, fiction, narrative nonfiction, political and cultural issues

INDEPENDENT U.S. PRESSES

Ms. Rux Martin, Senior Editor (Boston)—Cooking

Susan Canavan, Editor (Boston)—Nonfiction, culture

Jane Rosenman, Executive Editor (NY)—Fiction

Deanne Urmy, Executive Editor (NY)—General nonfiction

Anjali Singh, Senior Editor (NY)—Fiction, including debut novels

Webster Younce, Senior Editor (NY)—Fiction, humor

HOUGHTON MIFFLIN CHILDREN'S BOOKS

Houghton Mifflin Company began publishing books for young readers in 1937 with a list of four titles, including *Choo Choo* by Virginia Lee Burton. Houghton Mifflin Children's Books now publishes more than 100 titles each year, and they are proud to encourage and cultivate new talent.

Their list consists of some of the most recognized creators in the field of children's literature, including H. A. and Margret Rey, Caldecott medalist Virginia Lee Burton, Bill Peet, Holling C. Holling, Newbery medalist Elizabeth George Speare, Newbery medalist Scott O'Dell, James Marshall, Caldecott medalist Chris Van Allsburg, and many other award-winning authors and illustrators. Houghton Mifflin authors and illustrators have created some of the best-loved characters in children's literature, including the incorrigible Curious George, Lyle the Crocodile, George and Martha, Mike Mulligan and his trusty steam shovel, MaryAnne, and Tacky the Penguin. Over the years, Houghton Mifflin Children's Books authors have been awarded eight Caldecott Medals, eleven Caldecott Honors, seven Newbery Medals, and eleven Newbery Honors, among many other accolades.

Walter Lorraine Books, an imprint of Houghton Mifflin Company, was formed in 1995. In addition to developing new talent, Walter Lorraine Books publishes such award-winning authors and illustrators as Caldecott medalist David Macaulay, Caldecott medalist Allen Say, Newbery medalist Lois Lowry, Helen Lester, Lynn Munsinger, Arthur Geisert, Bernard Waber, Susan Meddaugh, and many others.

Recent titles from Houghton Mifflin Children's Books include *Tracking Trash: Flotsam, Jetsam, and the Science of Ocean Motion* by Loree Griffin Burns; *Girlwood* by Claire Dean; *Keeping Score* by Linda Sue Park; *Trouble* by Gary D. Schmidt; *When I Crossed No-Bob* by Margaret McMullan; *A Certain Slant of Light* by Laura Whitcomb; and *Stay With Me* by Garret Freymann-Weyr.

Houghton Mifflin Children's Books no longer responds to any unsolicited submission unless they are interested in publishing it. Please do not include a self-addressed stamped envelope. Submissions will be recycled, and you will not hear from them regarding the status of your submission unless they are interested, in which case you can expect to hear back within 12 weeks. Send to Submissions at the Boston address.

Betsy Groban, Publisher (Boston), Houghton Mifflin Children's Book Group

Margaret Raymo, Editorial Director, Houghton Mifflin Children's Book Group (Boston)

KINGFISHER

Kingfisher is an award-winning publisher of nonfiction and fiction for children of all ages. Known around the world for its informative and engaging reference books, activity books, and early learning books, Kingfisher also receives widespread acclaim for its classic anthologies for 5–14 year-olds and original picture books for very young children. The house was acquired by HM in 2002.

Recent Kingfisher titles include *Tooth Fairy in Trouble (I Am reading)* by Julia Jarman and Miriam Latimer; *Wild at Heart: Animal Stories* by Michael Morpurgo; *Ask Dr. K. Fisher About Creepy-Crawlies* by Claire Llewellyn and Kate Sheppard; *I Wonder Why There's a Hole in the Sky: and Other Questions About the Environment* by Sean Callery; and *Champion Crackups* by Gary Swift.

Houghton Mifflin Children's Books no longer responds to any unsolicited submission unless they are interested in publishing it. Please do not include a self-addressed stamped envelope. Submissions will be recycled, and you will not hear from them regarding the status of your submission unless they are interested, in which case you can expect to hear back within 12 weeks. Send to Submissions at the Boston address.

CLARION BOOKS

Clarion Books began publishing children's fiction and picture books in 1965 with a list of six titles. In 1979 it was bought by and became an imprint of Houghton Mifflin. The list has expanded to nearly 60 titles a year and includes nonfiction as well as fiction and picture books. In 1987 Clarion received its first Newbery Honor Medal, for *On My Honor* by Marion Dane Bauer, and in 1988 it had its first Newbery Medal winner, *Lincoln: A Photobiography* by Russell Freedman. Since then Clarion books have received children's book honors and awards nearly every year. Clarion's award-winning titles include *The Three Pigs* (2002 Caldecott Medal), *Tuesday* (Caldecott Medal), and *Sector 7* (Caldecott Honor), all written and illustrated by David Wiesner; *A Single Shard* (2002 Newbery Medal) by Linda Sue Park; *The Midwife's Apprentice* (Newbery Medal) and *Catherine Called Birdy* (Newbery Honor), both by Karen Cushman; *Sir Walter Raleigh and The Quest for El Dorado* (the inaugural Sibert Medal) by Marc Aronson; and *My Rows and Piles of Coins* (Coretta Scott King Honor for illustration) by Tololwa M. Mollel, illustrated by E. B. Lewis.

Recent titles include *The Dove Dove: Funny Homograph Riddles* by Marvin Terban; *Mary Wore Her Red Dress and Henry Wore His Green Sneakers* by Merle Peek; *Our Library* by Even Bunting and Maggie Smith; *Painting the Wild Frontier: The Art and Adventures of George Catlin* by Susanna Reich; *Storyteller* by Edward Myers; and *This is Your Life Cycle* by Heather Lynn Miller and Michael Chesworth.

In the picture books area, the editors are looking for active picture book stories with a beginning, middle, and end—stories that deal fully and honestly with children's emotions. You do not need to provide illustrations or find an illustrator; if your manuscript is accepted, the publisher will handle this. No query letter is necessary for picture book manuscripts and/or dummies.

In the nonfiction area, the editors are interested in hearing about social studies, science, concept, wordplay, holiday, historical, and biography ideas for all age levels. Send a query letter or proposal with a sample chapter(s) on all nonfiction projects.

In the fiction area, the editors are seeking lively stories for ages 8–12 and ages 10–14. They are also looking for transitional chapter books (12–20 manuscript pages) for ages 6–9 and for short novels of 40–80 manuscript pages suitable for ages 7–10. Clarion is highly selective in the areas of historical fiction, fantasy, and science fiction. A novel must be superlatively written in order to find a place on the list. The editors prefer to see complete manuscripts.

Address all submissions to with SASEs to the attention of the Editorial Department in NY.

Dinah Stevenson, Publisher, Clarion (NY)

Jennifer Wingertzahn, Editor, Clarion (NY)

HOUGHTON MIFFLIN SCHOOL DIVISION

Houghton Mifflin School Division publishes resources for teachers, students, and parents for pre-K through grade 8. The School Division's renowned author teams rely on extensive market and independent research to inform the pedagogical structure of each program. Ancillary products such as workbooks, teacher guides, audio-visual guides, and computer software provide additional support for students and teachers at each grade level. The school division is headquartered in Boston. Authors may learn more at www.eduplace.com.

HOUGHTON MIFFLIN COLLEGE DIVISION

Houghton Mifflin College Division makes knowledge accessible and meaningful to learners at four-year, community, and career colleges. With an inclusive approach to content and pedagogy, the division publishes textbooks, study guides, technology tools, and other materials primarily for introductory-level college courses. The house is headquartered in Boston. Authors may learn more at www.college.hmco.com.

GREAT SOURCE EDUCATION GROUP

Great Source Education Group publishes standards-based, proven solutions for reading, language arts, math, and science for pre-K through grade 12. Great Source also produces effective materials for summer school, after school, and intervention programs, quality test preparation, and resources to meet the needs of a wide variety of learning styles, including those of English learners. Outstanding research-based professional development offerings solidify Great Source's commitment to helping educators make a difference in classrooms every day.

Great Source welcomes submission of supplementary materials for students in grades pre-K through grade 12 and their teachers. Send submissions to the Editorial Department. Further details are available by request or on the Web site, which is www.greatsource.com.

MCDOUGAL-LITTELL

McDougal-Littell publishes an extensive offering of print and technology materials for language arts, mathematics, social studies, world languages, and science for grades 6–12.

McDougal-Littell, which is based in Illinois, was acquired by Houghton Mifflin in 1994. More information is available at www.mcdougallittell.com.

HQN BOOKS [SEE HARLEQUIN ENTERPRISES, LTD.]

HUMAN KINETICS

P.O. Box 5076, Champaign, IL 61825-5076

800-747-4457   fax: 217-351-1549

www.humankinetics.com   e-mail: webmaster@hkusa.com

Human Kinetics aims to convert all information about physical activity into knowledge—information that people can use to make a positive difference in their lives. In today's world, survival of the fittest means survival of the best informed. Building that knowledge is the role of Human Kinetics (HK).

Human Kinetics published its first book in 1974. Today, HK produces textbooks and their ancillaries, consumer books, software, videos, audiocassettes, journals, and distance education courses. The world headquarters are located in Champaign, Illinois, with offices in the U.K., Canada, Australia, and New Zealand to bolster their international efforts. Their annual sales, including international operations, surpass $37 million.

A privately held company, Human Kinetics publishes more than 120 books and 20 journals annually. They have expanded operations to that of an "information packager," utilizing whatever media source can best deliver the information to the consumer. Their objective is to make a positive difference in the quality of life of all people by promoting physical activity, by seeking out the foremost experts in a particular field and assisting them in delivering the most current information in the best format.

HK's two academic book divisions—the Scientific, Technical, and Medical (STM) Division; and the Health, Physical Education, Recreation and Dance (HPERD) Division—publish textbooks and reference books for students, scholars, and professionals in the company's fields of interest.

HK's Trade Book Division (formerly called Leisure Press) publishes expertly written books for the general public and for such groups as coaches, athletes, and fitness enthusiasts.

Recent titles include *Playing Tennis After 50: Your Guide to Strategy, Technique, Equipment, and the Tennis Lifestyle* by Kathy Woods and Ron Woods; *Fitness Swimming, 2nd Edition* by Emmet Hines; *Essentials of Strength Training and Conditioning* by Thomas R. Baechle and Roger W. Earle; *Field Hockey Steps to Success* by Elizabeth Anders and Sue Myers; and *Football's Eagle and Stack Defenses* by Ron Vanderlinden and Joe Paterno.

HK handles its own distribution.

Query letters, proposals, and SASEs should be directed to the Editorial Department of the division to which you are submitting. Detailed guidelines are available on the Web site.

Rainer Martens, President and Publisher

Julie Marx Goodreau, Director, Trade Division

HYPERION

ABC DAYTIME PRESS

DISNEY PRESS

HYPERION BOOKS FOR CHILDREN

ESPN BOOKS

MIRAMAX BOOKS

WENNER BOOKS

77 W. 66th Street, New York, NY 10023-6298

212-456-0100

www.hyperionbooks.com

Hyperion Books for Children offices:

114 Fifth Avenue, New York, NY 10011-5690

212-633-4400

www.hyperionbooksforchildren.com

ESPN Books:

19 E. 34th Street, New York, NY 10016

212-515-1000

www.espnbooks.com

Wenner Books:

1290 Avenue of the Americas, 2nd Floor, New York, NY 10104

212-484-4254

www.wennerbooks.com e-mail: corey.seymour@wennermedia.com

Hyperion, which was founded by The Walt Disney Company in 1991, publishes general-interest fiction, literary works, and nonfiction in the areas of popular culture, health and wellness, business, current topical interest, popular psychology, self-help, and humor. The house publishes books in hardcover, trade paperback, and mass-market paperback formats. Hyperion also operates a very strong children's program. Imprints ESPN focuses on sports titles, and Wenner publishes music titles. The Miramax imprint remained with Hyperion after the Disney-Weinstein brothers split in 2005, with the Weinsteins developing their own at-print-time-still-unnamed publishing division run by Rob Weisbach.

Recent adult titles include *Just Who Will You Be? Big Question, Little Book, Answer Within* by Maria Shriver; *For One More Day: A Novel* by Mitch Albom; *O, The Oprah Magazine Cookbook recipes selected from O, the Oprah Magazine; Home: A Memoir of My Early Years* by Julie Andrews; *Standing Up to the Madness: Ordinary Heroes in Extraordinary Times* by Amy Goodman and Dave Goodman; *Everything They Had: Sportswriting From David Halberstam; Jo Frost's Confident Baby Care* by Jo Frost; and *New South Grilling: Fresh and Exciting Recipes from the Third Coast* by Robert St. John.

Hyperion Books for Children published its first book in August 1991: *See Squares,* a paperback counting book by Joy N. Hulme, illustrated by Carol Schwartz. Since then, Hyperion Books for Children and its imprints have published books by Julie Andrews, Rosemary Wells, Louise Erdrich, William Nicholson, Michael Dorris, Jules Feiffer, Toni Morrison, Jon Agee, Paul Zindel, and William Wegman, among others. Hyperion Books for Children's imprints include *Jump at the Sun,* the first children's book imprint to celebrate black culture for all children, and *Volo,* a paperback original series.

Recent children's titles include *We Are the Ship: The Story of Negro League Baseball* by Kadir Nelson; *WOW Mealtime* by Kathy Robinson and Sam Williams; *Big Plans* by Bob Shea, illustrated by Lane Smith; *Airman* by Eoin Colfer; *There is a Bird On Your Head!* by Mo Willems; and *The Market* by J.M. Steele.

ESPN Books titles include *Steroid Nation: The Secret History of America's True Drug Addiction* by Shaun Assael; *Fairway to Hell: Around the World in 18 Holes* by Frank Lidz; *Game On: The All American Race to Make Champions of Our Children* by Tom Farrey; *Fathers & Sons & Sports: Great Sports Writing* by Mike Lupica; *ESPN Sports Almanac 2008* by Mike Morrison and Gerry Brown; *ESPN Guide to Psycho Fan Behavior* by Warren St. John; and *Breaker Boys: The NFL's Greatest Team and the Stolen 1925 Championship* by David Fleming.

Titles from Wenner include *Bob Dylan: The Essential Interviews* by Jonathan Cott; *The 500 Greatest Albums of All Time* by Joe Levy; *I'm Coming to Take You To Lunch: A Fantastic Tale of Boys, Booze, and How Wham! Were Sold to China* by Niman Napier-Bell; and

Stairway to Heaven: The Final Resting Places of Rock's Legends by J.D. Reed and Maddy Miller.

Hyperion accepts unsolicited manuscripts only from literary agents. Query letters and SASEs should be directed to the editorial staff.

Gretchen Young, Executive Editor, Hyperion

Ms. Leslie Wells, Executive Editor, Hyperion

Donna Bray, Editorial Director, Hyperion Books for Children

Jennifer Besser, Editor, Hyperion Books for Teens and Children

Linda Ng, Editor, ESPN Books

Robert Wallace, Editor-in-Chief, Wenner Media

Arianne Lewin, Editor--Books for Teens

Sarah Mandell, Editor--General nonfiction

Brenda Copeland, Editor

Kristen Kiser, Executive Editor

INDUSTRIAL PRESS

989 Avenue of the Americas, New York, NY 10018

212-889-6330 / 888-528-7852   fax: 212-545-8327

www.industrialpress.com   e-mail: info@industrialpress.com

Founded in 1883, Industrial Press is the leading technical and reference publisher for engineering, technology, manufacturing and education.

The house's flagship title, *Machinery's Handbook*, now in its 90th year, remains unchallenged as "The Bible" in its field, the most popular engineering title of all time. The new 28th edition remains true to the Handbook's original design as an extraordinary comprehensive yet practical and easy-to-use reference for mechanical and manufacturing engineers, designers, draftsmen, toolmakers, and machinists.

Recent titles include *A Millwright's Guide to Motor Pump Alignment, 2nd Edition* by Tom Harlon; *Countersinking Handbook* by LaRoux Gillespie; *The Journey to Improved Business Performance; Grinding Technology: Theory and Applications of Machining with Abrasives, 2nd Edition* by Stephen Malkin and Chansheng Guo; and *The Little Black Book of Maintenance Excellence* by Daniel T. Dailey.

Industrial Press handles its own distribution.

Industrial Press is expanding its list of professional and educational titles in addition to starting a new program in electronic publishing. Additional information is available in the Authors section of the Web site. Contact with proposals or queries:

John F. Carleo, Editorial Director; jcarleo@industrialpress.com

INNER TRADITIONS / BEAR AND COMPANY

PO Box 388, One Park Street, Rochester, VT 05767-0388

802-767-3174/800-246-8648   fax: 802-767-3726

www.innertraditions.com   e-mail: submissions@innertraditions.com

Inner Traditions, Bear & Company is one of the largest publishers of books on spiritual and healing traditions of the world. Their titles focus on ancient mysteries, alternative health, indigenous cultures, religion, sexuality, tarot, and divination. With over 1,000 books in print, Inner Traditions has eleven imprints: Inner Traditions, Bear & Co., Bear Cub Books, Bindu Books, Destiny Books, Destiny Recordings, Destiny Audio Editions, Inner Traditions en Español, Healing Arts Press, Park Street Press, and Inner Traditions India.

Inner Traditions books represent the spiritual, cultural, and mythic traditions of the world, focusing on inner wisdom and the perennial philosophies.

Bear & Company's focus is on ancient wisdom, new science, visionary fiction, Western thought, indigenous traditions, Maya studies, extraterrestrial consciousness, and complementary medicine.

Bear Cub Books are for kids and Bindu books are for teens. Healing Arts Press focuses on alternative medicine and holistic health; Destiny Books are New Age and metaphysical titles with special emphasis on self-transformation, the occult, and psychological well-being; Destiny Audio Editions are books on tape and CD from a variety of Inner Traditions imprints, plus original spoken word titles. Park Street Press releases books on travel, psychology, consumer and environmental issues, archeology, women's and men's studies, and fine art. Inner Traditions en Español is the Spanish-language publishing program.

Recent titles include *William Blake's Sexual Path to Spiritual Vision* by Marsha Keith Schuchard; *The Ancient Celtic Festivals: How We Celebrate Them Today* by Clare Walker Leslie and Frank E. Gerace; *Traditional Thai Yoga: The Posture and Healing Practices of Ruesri Dat Ton* by Enrico Corsu and Elena Fanfani; *Creating the Soul Body: The Sacred Science of Immortality* by Robert E. Cox; *The Last Pagan: Julian the Apostate and the Death of the Ancient World* by Adrian Murdoch; *The Neanderthal Legacy: Reawakening Our Genetic and Cultural Origins* by Stan Gooch; and *Past Life Dreamwork: Healing the Soul through Understanding Karmic Patterns* by Sabine Lucas, PhD.

Recent titles for children and teens include *Animals in the Sates: Chinese Astrology for Children* by Gregory Crawford; *Ganga: The River that Flows from Heaven to Earth* by Vatsala Sperling, illustrated by Harish Johari and Pieter Weltevrede; *How Would It Feel* by Mary Beth Goddard, illustrated by Anna Mycek-Wodecki; *The Journey of Tunuri and the Blue Deer: A Huichol Indian Story* by James Endredy, illustrated by Maria Hernandez de la Cruz and Casimiro de la Cruz Lopez.

Query via e-mail or regular mail with SASE. Send cover letter with manuscript or proposal by regular mail with SASE to the acquisitions editor:

Jeanie Levitan, Vice President of Editorial
Jon Graham, Acquisitions Editor

INSIDERS' GUIDES [SEE GLOBE PEQUOT PRESS]

INSPIRIO [SEE ZONDERVAN PUBLISHING HOUSE]

INTERNATIONAL MARINE [SEE MCGRAW-HILL]

INTERVARSITY PRESS

A Division of InterVarsity Christian Fellowship / USA

Letters: P.O. Box 1400, Downers Grove, IL 60515

Packages: 430 Plaza Dr., Westmont IL 60559

630-734-4000   fax: 630-734-4200

www.ivpress.com   e-mail: submissions@ivpress.com

InterVarsity Press is the publishing arm of InterVarsity Christian Fellowship campus ministry and has been publishing Christian books for more than 50 years. Their program is comprised of three imprints: IVP Books (general interest), IVP Academic (research and classroom use), and IVP Connect (study guides for churches and small groups). A new imprint, Formation, was launched in 2006.

As an extension of InterVarsity Christian Fellowship, InterVarsity Press serves those in the university, the church and the world by publishing resources that equip and encourage people to follow Jesus as Savior and Lord in all of Life.

Andy Le Peau, IVP's editorial director, appealed to tradition to describe their new Formatio imprint: "People are looking for a spirituality that is rooted in the history of the church and in Scripture."

Recent titles include *The Attentive Life: Discerning God's Presence in All Things* by Leighton Ford; *Deuteronomy* by J.A. Thompson; *Jesus Made in America: A Cultural History from the Puritans to "The Passion"* by Stephen J. Nichols; *Love, The Ultimate Apologetic* by Art Lindsay; *Salvation Belongs to Our God: Celebrating the Bibles Central Story* by Christopher Wright; *There's a Teenager in My House: 101 Questions Parents Ask* edited by Wayne Rice; and *Who Gets to Narrate the World? Contending for the Christian Story in an Age of Rivals* by Robert E. Webber.

Current interests are listed on the Web site. IVP is particularly interested in authors with diverse backgrounds and experiences, especially non-Anglos, women, and "knowledgeable and experienced people more than writers." If you are associated with a college or seminary and have an academic manuscript, you may submit it to the attention of the Academic Editor. If you are a pastor or a previously published author, you may submit it to the attention of the General Books Editor. Their preference is to receive a chapter-by-chapter summary, two complete sample chapters and your résumé.

Address queries with SASEs to:

Andrew Le Peau, Editorial Director

ISLAND PRESS

1718 Connecticut Avenue, NW, Suite 300, Washington, DC 20009

202-232-7933 / 800-828-1302   fax: 202-234-1328

www.islandpress.org   e-mail: editors@islandpress.org

Island Press was established in 1984 to meet the need for reliable, peer-reviewed information to help solve environmental problems. The house identifies innovative thinkers and emerging trends in the environmental field. They work with world-renowned experts and aspiring authors to develop cross-disciplinary solutions to environmental challenges, making sure this information is communicated effectively to the widest possible audience.

Island Press publishes approximately 40 new titles per year on topics ranging from biodiversity and land use to forest management, agriculture, marine science, climate change, and energy. In addition, Island Press is engaged in several collaborative partnerships designed to help facilitate the stimulation of new ideas, new information products, and targeted outreach to specific audiences. Their Communication Partnership for Science and the Sea (COMPASS) is one such example.

The Shearwater Books imprint publishes trade titles in environmental history, environmental literature, scientific memoirs, and general interest.

Throughout its 19-year history, Island Press has led the way in shaping and advancing acceptance of several new, interdisciplinary fields of endeavor. The house has 30 employees and a 16-member board of directors.

Recent titles include *Revolution on the Range The Rise of a New Ranch in the American West* by Courtney White; *More: Population, Nature, and What Women Want* by Robert Engelman; *A Guide to Impact Fees and Housing Affordability* by Arthur Chris Nelson, Liza K. Bowles, et al.; *Water War in the Klamath Basin: Macho Law, Combat Biology, and Dirty Politics* by Holly D. Doremus and A. Dan Tarlock; *Sudden Moves* by Charlottes Vale Allen; and *State of the Wild 2008-2009: A Global Portrait of Wildlife, Wildlands, and Oceans* by Ward Woods.

Query letters and SASEs should be directed to:

Todd Baldwin, Vice President and Associate Publisher

Barbara Dean, Executive Editor

Jonathan Cobb, Executive Editor

Heather Boyer, Senior Editor

Barbara Youngblood, Developmental Editor

JEWISH LIGHTS PUBLISHING

Sunset Farm Offices, Route 4, P.O. Box 237, Woodstock, VT 05091

802-457-4000   fax: 802-457-4004

www.jewishlights.com   e-mail: editorial@jewishlights.com

Jewish Lights publishes books that reflect the Jewish wisdom tradition for people of all faiths and backgrounds. Stuart Matlins, founder and publisher of Jewish Lights Publishing, was presented with the 2006 American Jewish Distinguished Service Award for engaging people of all faiths and backgrounds to help them learn about who Jewish people are, where they come from, and what the future can be made to hold.

Jewish Lights' authors draw on the Jewish wisdom tradition to deal with the quest for the self and for finding meaning in life. Jewish Lights books are nonfiction almost exclusively, covering topics including religion, Jewish life cycle, theology, philosophy, history, and spirituality. They also publish two books for children annually.

Recent titles include *Spiritual Activism: A Jewish Guide to Leadership and Repairing the World* by Rabbi Avraham Weiss; *Disaster Spiritual Care: Practical Clergy Responses to Community, Regional, and National Tragedy* edited by Stephen B. Robert, BCJC and Re. Willard W. C. Ashley, SR, Dmin, DH; *Rabbi Harvey Rides Again: A Graphic Novel of Jewish Folktales Let Lose in the Wild West* by Steve Sheinkin; and *Moses & the Journey to Leadership: Timeless Lessons of Effective Management from the Bible to Today* by Dr. Norman J. Cohen.

Direct proposals and SASEs via regular mail to the Submissions Editor. No digital or e-mail submissions. Jewish Lights does not publish biography, haggadot, or poetry.

Stuart Matlins, Publisher

THE JEWISH PUBLICATION SOCIETY

2100 Arch Street, 2nd Floor, Philadelphia, PA 19103

215-832-0608 / 800-234-3151   fax: 215-568-2017

www.jewishpub.org   e-mail: jewishbook@jewishpub.org

The Jewish Publication Society (JPS) specializes in books of Jewish interest, especially traditional religious works (including the Torah), folktales, and commentaries and resources for Jewish life. JPS is over a century old, and is a nonprofit publisher.

The JPS collection *Legends of the Jews* first appeared in 1909. Lately, JPS has undertaken documenting Jewish tales and legends from the around the world in a series of six massive volumes. The first, *Folktales of the Jews: Tales from the Sephardic Dispersion*, released late in 2006, also contains a detailed commentary by University of Pennsylvania folklorist Dan Ben-Amos.

Recent titles include *From Krakow to Krypton: Jews and Comic Books* by Arie Kaplan; *Rashi's Daughter, Secret Scholar* by Maggie Anton; *Introduction to Islam for Jews* by Reuven Firestone; *Waiting for Rain: Reflections at the Turning of the Year* by Bryna Jocheved Levy; *Jewish Choices, Jewish Voices: Body* by Elliot Dorff and Louis Newman; *Stringing the Pearls: How to Read the Weekly Torah Portion* by James S. Diamond; and *The Brothers Schlemiel* by Mark Binder and Zevi Blum.

For children's titles, JPS is most interested in manuscripts for short story and folktale collections and for young adult novels—all with strong Jewish themes—and for new titles in their Kids' Catalog series. They generally do not acquire stories on immigrant themes or the Holocaust. For adult titles, they are not seeking fiction, poetry, memoirs, spirituality, inspiration, monographs, or books about the Holocaust. Please see the Web site for further details.

Direct queries with resumes and SASEs to Acquisitions.

Rena Potok, Senior Acquisitions Editor

Janet L. Liss, Managing Editor

JOSSEY-BASS [SEE JOHN WILEY & SONS]

JUDSON PRESS

A Division of the American Baptist Churches, USA

P.O. Box 851, Valley Forge, PA 19482-0851

via UPS/FedEx: 558 N Gulph Rd., King of Prussia, PA 19406

800-458-3766   fax: 610-768-2107

www.judsonpress.com   e-mail: acquisitions@judsonpress.com

Judson Press is the publishing arm of the American Baptist Churches, USA, a Protestant denomination that includes 1.5 million members. Judson Press is a religious book publisher specializing in books on African American and multicultural issues, practical resources for churches, Baptist history, self-help, and inspirational titles for adults and children. It puts out 12-14 books a year, with more than 300 titles in print, ranging from the classic best-seller for pastors, *The Star Book for Ministers*, to the latest inspirational volume, *Before the Thunder Rolls: Devotions for NASCAR Fans*.

Jusdon Press's primary niches are the following: Baptist history and identity, pastoral and sermon helps, small-group studies, discipleship, Christian education (not curriculum), seasonal program resources, and African American resources, sermons, inspiration, and self-help.

Their most wanted projects currently include new titles for their "Work of the Church" series, new titles from their "Star Book for Pastors" series, seasonal programs for Lent/Easter and Advent/Christmas, Baptist identity resources for new church members and for older children, devotional books for sports fans and hobbyists, titles for the "African American Christian's Guide" series, and multicultural preaching and ministry resources.

Titles include *Letters of Light for First Ladies* by Rev. Dr. Cecilia Williams Bryant; *7 Leadership Imperatives from a Wild Man* by Joeseph Robinson Jr., *Morning Meetings With Jesus: 180 Devotions for Teachers* by Susan O'Carrol Drake; *Playbook for Christian Manhood: 12 Key Plays for Black Teen Boys* by James C. Perking; *Christian Educator's Guide to Evaluating and Developing Curriculum* by Nancy Ferguson; *Steal Away: Devotions for Baseball Fans* by Hugh Poland; and *Tempted to Leave the Cross: Renewing the Call to Discipleship* by Rev. Ernest Flores.

Query with SASE to:

Laura Alden, Publisher

Rebecca Irwin-Diehl, Editor

KAR-BEN PUBLISHING [SEE LERNER PUBLISHING GROUP]

KAPLAN PUBLISHING

(Formerly Dearborn Trade)

New York Offices:

1 Liberty Plaza, 24th Floor, New York, NY 10006

800-527-8378

www.kaplanpublishing.com   jennifer.farthing@kaplan.com

Kaplan Publishing is one of the nation's leading education, career and business publishers, with offices in New York. Kaplan produces more than 150 books a year on test preparation, admissions, academic and professional development, general business, management, sales, marketing, real estate, finance, and investing. Kaplan has recently started focusing on publishing medical and legal books. Imprints include Dearborn Home Inspection Education, Dearborn Real Estate Education, Kaplan AEC Education, Kaplan Business, Kaplan CPA Education, Kaplan Financial, Kaplan Education. The press is in the process of reorganizing the Chicago-based Dearborn imprints.

Kaplan titles are *Find Your Inner Ugly Betty: 25 Career Lessons for the Young Professional* by Tanner Stransky; *Financial Armageddon: Protect Your Future from Economic Collapse* by Michael J. Panzer; *All About Mortgages: Insider Tips to Find the Right Mortgage and Refinance Your Home* by Julie Garton-Good; *For Sale By Owner* by Robert Irwin; *The Homeowner's Guide to Foreclosure* by James I. Wiedemer; *KAPLAN SAT 2009 Comprehensive Program*; *Direct Your Own Life: How to Be a Star in Any Field You Choose* by Efren Ramirez and Chris Barrett.

There are two divisions of Kaplan: test-prep and trade. Currently, acquisitions for both divisions are being handled out of the New York office. Query letters, proposals, and SASEs should be directed to:

Shannon Berning, Acquisitions Editor; shannon.berning@kaplan.com

KENSINGTON PUBLISHING

KENSINGTON BOOKS

PINNACLE BOOKS

ZEBRA BOOKS

APHRODISIA

BRAVA

DAFINA

CITADEL

850 Third Avenue, New York, NY 10022

877-422-3665

www.kensingtonbooks.com

Kensington Publishing (founded 1974) is an independent U.S. publisher of hardcover, trade and mass market paperback books. From the time their first book became a best-seller (*Appointment in Dallas* by Hugh McDonald), Kensington has been known as a David-vs.-Goliath publisher of titles in the full spectrum of categories, from fiction and romance to health and nonfiction. Kensington now accounts for about 7% of all mass market paperback sales in the U.S. Through the Kensington, Zebra, Pinnacle and Citadel press imprints, the company releases close to 600 new books per year and has a backlist of more than 3,000 titles.

Specializing in areas such as African American (Dafina), gay and lesbian, erotic romance (Brava), Wicca, and alternative health (Twin Streams) and romance, Kensington launched Aphrodisia, a new erotica line in trade paper and e-book, in 2006.

Kensington continues to be a full-range publisher large enough to command respect in the market, yet small enough to maintain author, reader and retailer loyalty. The company is able to respond quickly to trends, put books into the hands of readers faster than larger publishers can, and support them with targeted promotional and marketing programs to generate reader excitement.

Kensington Books is the imprint for the hardcover and trade paper line. The line is currently made up of 5–8 titles each month. The typical genres are alternative health, mysteries (Partners In Crime), romance, erotica, and self-help. Kensington Mass Market features paperback titles with an emphasis on mysteries and fiction. Tradition-ally these titles are first published in hardcover. Alternative health titles also are pub-lished in this format for sale in the mass retailers.

Recent Kensington titles include *Hotter Than Hell* by Jackie Kessler; *Hounded to Death* by Laurien Berensson; *Project Jennifer* by Jill Amy Rosenblatt; *The Queen's Lady* by Barbara Kyle; *Sisters of Misery* by Megan Kelley Hall; *Sweet and Sinful* by Jodu Lynn

Copeland; *Closer to Fine* by Meri Weiss; *Handbags and Homicide* by Dorothy Howell; and *Hungry For It* by Fiona Zedde.

From the Brava line: *Hardcore Hardboiled* by Todd Robinson; *Hot Date* by Amy Garvey; *Superb and Sexy* by Jill Shalvis; *Temperatures Rising* by Karen Kelley; *When He Was Bad* by Cynthia Eden and Shelly Laurenston; *Ask For It* by Sylvia Day; *Baddest Bad Boys* by Shannon McKenna, E.C. Sheedy, and Cate Noble; *Hotter After Midnight* by Cynthia Eden; *The One I Want* by Nancy Warren; and *The Beast In Him* by Shelly Laurenston.

Erotic Romance from the Aphrodisia line includes *Nights in Black Leather* by Noelle Mack; *Trio* by P.F. Kozack, Devyn Quinn and Jane Ledger; *Dark Master* by Tawny Taylor; *Only With a Cowboy* by P.J. Mellor, Melissa MacNeal, and Vonna Harper; *Promiscuous* by R. Moreen Clarke; *Black Silk* by Sharon Page; *Exposing Casey* by Deanna Lee; and *She's On Top* by Susan Lyons.

From Dafina: *Deliver Me From Evil* by Mary Monroe; *The Jump Off* by Doug Dixon; *Let's Get It On* by Cheris Hodges; *No More Good* by Angela Winters; *Shortie Like Mine* by Ni-Ni Simone; *Sleeping With The Enemy* by Wahida Clark and Kiki Swinson; *Who's Loving You* by Mary B. Morrison; *Bodyslick* by Sibley H. John; and *A Rare Groove* by Sophia Shaw.

From the Urban Soul line: *I Was Your Fool* by Jacqueline M. Smith; *Twenty-eight Days* by Nina Tracy; *Different Is All the Same* by Kamryn Donavan; *Cajun Moon* by Gigi Gunn; *Before I Let Go* by Kimberly T. Matthews; *Double Platinum* by Sheila M. Goss; *A Box of White Chocolate* by Daamon Speller; and *Love is Simple: Forever is Tricky* by Casondra Siegers.

Pinnacle Books is the imprint that features best-selling commercial fiction, including thrillers and true crime. Recent titles include *Alone in the Ashes* by William W. Johnstone; *Bad Moon Rising* by Jonathan Maberry; *Blood Bond: Texas Gundown* by William W. Johnstone and J. A. Johnstone; *Die Smiling* by Linda Ladd; *First We'll Kill My Husband* by Lyn Riddle; *Broken Trail* by Alan Geoffrion; *Don't Ever Tell* by Brandon Massey; and *I'll Be Watching You* by M. William Phelps.

Zebra Books, the company's flagship imprint, is primarily made up of a large number of historical romance titles, but the list also generally includes one or two lead contemporary romances, westerns, horror and humor. The Zebra imprint consists of some 20 titles per month. Recent Zebra titles include *Lost In You* by Alix Rickloff; *A Rake's Guide to Pleasure* by Victoria Dahl; *Storm Born* by Rochelle Mead; *Wild Roses* by Hannah Howell; *Beloved Embrace* by Cassie Edwards; *Crazy In Love* by Janet Daily; and *Her One Desire* by Kimberly Killion.

Citadel features nonfiction and is currently undergoing an expansion and repositioning of the list, as evidenced by recent purchases in women's nonfiction and cultural trend nonfiction. Recent Citadel titles include *Mother Gooseberg's Book of Jewish Nursery Rhymes* by Jeff Dubinsky and Lila Dubinsky; *Underrated* by Josh Abraham, Nick Jezarian, and Geoff Wolinetz; *King of the Godfathers* by Anthony DeStefano; *Pursuit* by Clint Johnson; *Every Hand Revealed* by Gus Hansen; *Grandmothers Against the War: How We Got Off Our Fannies and Stood Up for Peace* by Joan Wile, *A Million Words and Counting* by Paul J.J. Payack; and *Miss Becky's Break-Up Boot Camp* by Becky Rutledge.

Kensington is open to submissions. Submit completed work or synopsis with the first three chapters to whichever editor you feel is the best person to review your work. No e-mail submissions, only regular mail with SASE.

John Scognamiglio, Editor-in-Chief, Kensington—Fiction including chick lit, historical romance, women's contemporary fiction, gay fiction and nonfiction, mysteries, suspense, horror, mainstream fiction, memoirs, erotica, jscognamiglio@kensingtonbooks.com

Michaela Hamilton, Editor-in-Chief, Citadel—Nonfiction including popular culture, current events, narrative nonfiction, true crime, business, biography, law enforcement, military; selected fiction including thrillers, mainstream novels, mhamilton@kensingtonbooks.com

Kate Duffy, Editorial Director—Romance, historical romance, contemporary romance, Brava erotic romance, fiction, mysteries, thrillers, kduffy@kensingtonbooks.com

Audrey LaFehr, Editorial Director—Women's fiction, romance, romantic suspense, thrillers, erotica, multicultural fiction), alafehr@kensingtonbooks.com

Selena James, Executive Editor, Dafina—General fiction, nonfiction, African-American fiction, pop culture, inspirational, young adult, and romance; sjames@kensingtonbooks.com

Gary Goldstein, Senior Editor—True crime, westerns, thrillers, military fiction and nonfiction, sports, how-to, science, world and American history, narrative nonfiction, ggolstein@kensingtonbooks.com

Danielle Chiotti, Senior Editor, Citadel—Women's interest nonfiction including dating and relationships, weddings, memoirs, narrative nonfiction, general self-help, cooking, dchiotti@kensingtonbooks.com

Richard Ember, Editor, Citadel Press—general nonfiction, biography, history, narrative nonfiction, memoirs, gambling, sports, popular culture, and fratire; rember@kensingtonbooks.com

Mike Shohl, Editor, Citadel--Pop culture, entertainment, music, male interest, fratire, sports, popular science/popular psychology, humor, martial arts, mshohl@kensingtonbooks.com

Hilary Sares, Editor—Contemporary romance, historical romance, romantic suspense and thrillers, women's fiction, erotic romance and erotica, hsares@kensingtonbooks.com

Rakia A. Clark, Editor, Dafina--literary and contemporary mulicultural fiction, especially African American; nonfiction interest, including memoir, history, pop culture, and entertainment, rclark@kensingtonbooks.com

KIMANI PRESS [SEE HARLEQUIN ENTERPRISES, LTD.]

KINGFISHER BOOKS [SEE HOUGHTON MIFFLIN]

KINGSWOOD BOOKS [SEE ABINGDON PRESS]

KLUTZ [SEE SCHOLASTIC]

H. J. KRAMER [SEE NEW WORLD LIBRARY]

KRAUSE PUBLICATIONS

700 East State Street, Iola, WI 54990-0001

888-457-2873 / 715-445-2214   fax: 715-445-4087

www.krause.com

Krause Publications, a division of F+W Publications, is the world's largest publisher of leisure-time periodicals and books on collectibles, arts and crafts, hunting, and fishing. A special interest publisher targeting hobbyists and enthusiasts, Krause imprints cover writing; crafts; scrapbooking; graphic design; fine art; comics, fantasy art and manga; antiques and collectibles; coins; and the outdoors. The book division publishes over

125 titles annually and currently has 750 titles available.

Recent titles include *Old Gunsights and Rifle Scopes: Identification an Price Guide* by Nick Stroebel; *Polymer Clay Mixed Media Jewelry: Fresh Techniques, Projects, and Inspiration* by Shirley Rufener; *Stander Catalog of World coins 1601-1700* by Colin R. Bruce and Thomas Michael; *Standard Catalog of Mercedes-Benz* by Jim Luikens and Mary Hedberg; *100 Appliqué Motifs* by Deborah Green; *Petretti's Coca-Cola Collectibles Price Guide* by Allan Petretti; *Collectible Fishing Lures* by Russel E. Lewis; and *Warman's Lunch Boxes Field Guide* by Karen Obrien and Joe Soucy.

Query letters and SASEs should be directed to the editorial staff.

Dianne Wheeler, Publishing Director

Joe Kertzman, Editor, Antiques and Collectibles

Derrek Sigler, Editor, Firearms and Outdoors

Randy Thern, Editor, Coin Collecting

Candy Wiza, Editor, Sewing and Quilting

KTAV PUBLISHING HOUSE

930 Newark Avenue, 4th Floor, Jersey City, NJ 07306

201-963-9524   fax: 201-963-0102

www.ktav.com   e-mail: questions@ktav.com

KTAV Publishing House (founded 1924) features books of Jewish interest, including scholarly Judaica, sermonica, textbooks, and books for younger readers. KTAV also markets religious educational materials, gifts, and decorative items. Many KTAV titles in the scholarly vein relate the history of Jewish thought and culture within the context of broader issues and thus are appealing to the interested general reader. KTAV subjects include Judaica, Torah study, Jewish law, contemporary Halachic thought, sermonica, Jewish history, Jewish thought, contemporary Jewry, and Torah and science.

Recent titles include *Bubbe Meisis: Jewish Myths, Jewish Realities* by Rabbi Ronald H. Isaacs; *Day by Day in Jewish Sports History* by Bob Weschler; *Japanese Kosher Cooking: Sushi and More* by Kinue Weinstein; *Manischewitz: The Matzo Family* by Laura Manischewitz Alpern; *Shaarei Simchah: Gates of Joy* by Aden Berkowitz and Rivka Haut; and *Why Hebrew Goes From Right to Left: 201 Things You Never Knew About Judaism* by Rabbi Ronald H. Isaacs.

Queries and SASEs should be directed to:

Bernard Scharfstein, Vice President; bernie@ktav.com

Adam Bengal, Managing Editor, adam@ktav.com

LARK BOOKS

67 Broadway, Asheville, NC 28801

828-253-0467

www.larkbooks.com   e-mail: info@larkbooks.com

Lark Books published their first book 20 years ago, and since then their list has grown to more than 300 books, with 60 to 70 new titles now appearing every year. President and publisher Carol Taylor calls Lark Books "a destination for do-it-yourselfers looking for information, inspiration, source materials, and a lively exchange of ideas." The Lark Books list is composed primarily of reference and how-to books with step-by-step instructions of practical subjects including ceramics; crafts, pets; and other lifestyle topics. Lark Books has published how-to books teaching basketry, weaving, woodworking, ceramics, knitting, jewelry, paper, needlework, sewing, and general crafts from wreath making to rug hooking. They do not publish fiction, and only rarely publish non-illustrated books. The children's list focuses on nonfiction, including crafts and hobbies, games, science experiments, sports, and illustrated board books. Lark Books also publishes a variety of camera manuals and how-to reference books on photography and digital imaging techniques.

Recent titles from Lark Books include *Masters: Art Quilts: Major Works by Leading Artists* by Martha Sielman; *The Complete Guide to High Dynamic Range Digital Photography* by Ferrell McCollough; *Wrap, Stitch, Fold, and Rivet: Making Designer Metal Jewelry* by Mary Hettmansperger; *Doodle Stitching: Fresh and Fun Embroidery for Beginners* by Aimee Ray; *500 Pendants and Lockets: Contemporary Interpretations of Classic Adornments* by Lark Books; and *Magic Lantern Guides: Nikon D80* by Simon Stafford.

Send queries to the attention of the category editor, e.g. material on a ceramics books should be addressed to the Ceramics Editor, a craft book proposal should be addressed to the Craft Acquisitions Editor, and so on. All children's book submissions should be sent to the attention of the Children's Acquisitions Editor.

LATIN AMERICAN LITERARY REVIEW PRESS

P.O. Box 17660, Pittsburgh, PA 15235

412-824-7903   fax: 412-351-0770

www.lalrp.org   e-mail: editor@lalrp.org

Latin American Literary Review Press was established in 1980 with the principal objective of familiarizing readers outside the field with Latin American literature. LALRP's emphasis has been on publishing translations of creative writing (Discovery series) and literary criticism (Exploration series). These initial titles were followed by bilingual Spanish/English editions of poetry, books of Spanish music, and young adult titles. Currently, LALRP publishes fewer than five new books per year.

The house has always aimed for excellence in publishing, and has relied on a prestigious body of academic editors and distinguished and accomplished translators. The press receives financial support from the National Endowment for the Arts, the Pennsylvania Council on the Arts, and from various other institutions and private foundations.

Titles include *Of My Real Life I Know Nothing* by Ana Maria Moix; *The Imposter* by Rodolfo Usigli; *The Sharpener and Other Stories* by Andres Berger-Kiss; *Chola* by Mi-Chille L. Rios; *Chronicle of San Gabriel* by Julio Ramon Ribeyro, translated by John Penuel; *Memories of Underdevelopment* by Edmundo Desnores, translated by Al Schaller; and *Beer Cans in the Rio de la Plata* by Jorge Stamadianos, translated by Leland Chambers.

Query letters and SASEs should be directed to the editorial staff.

Yvette Miller, President

LEARNINGEXPRESS, LLC

55 Broadway, 8th Floor, New York, NY 10006

212-995-2566   fax: 212-995-5512

www.learningexpressllc.com   e-mail: customerservice@learningexpressllc.com

LearningExpress is a leading publisher of print and online study guides, test preparation, career guidance, and practical skills materials. LearnATest.com/Library, its online interactive resource, offers practice tests and exercises for academic and career exams. Founded in 1995 in affiliation with Random House, LearningExpress emerged as an industry leader in customized test-preparation publishing and as an expert source for information on targeted careers, vocational professions, and academic exams. In August 1999, Allen & Company, Inc., and a select group of private investors purchased a significant equity interest in the company.

LearningExpress offers more than 300 online, interactive practice exams and course series, as well as over 200 titles in print and more than 150 eBooks. All LearningExpress materials are developed by leading educators and industry experts. LearningExpress was named the finalist for two 2008 Codie Awards.

Titles include *Corrections Officer Exam; Express Review Guides: Math Word Problems; Praxis I, 3rd Edition: PPST: Pre Professional Skills Test; CLEP (The College-Level Examination Program); English to the Max: 1,200 Questions That Will Maximize Your English Power; Becoming a Caseworker;* and *Pass the U.S. Citizenship Exam, 2008 Edition.*

Query letters and SASEs should be directed to the editorial staff.

Karen Wolny, Editorial Director

LERNER PUBLISHING GROUP

KAR-BEN PUBLISHING

241 1st Avenue N., Minneapolis, MN 55401

800-328-4929   fax: 800-332-1132

www.lernerbooks.com   e-mail: info@lernerbooks.com

Kar-Ben editorial offices:

800-328-4929 x229   fax: 612-332-7615

www.karben.com   e-mail: editorial@karben.com

Founded in 1959, Lerner Publishing Group is a large independent children's book publisher. With more than 3,500 titles in print, Lerner Publishing Group creates high-quality children's books for schools, libraries, and bookstores on a variety of subjects including biographies, social studies, science, language-arts curriculum, geography, sports, vehicles, picture books, activity books, multicultural issues, and fiction.

Lerner is proud to have published the 2006 Robert F. Silbert Informational Book Medal winner *Secrets of a Civil War Submarine: Solving the Mysteries of the H. L. Hunley* by Sally M. Walker. This important award, established by the Association for Library Service to Children, honors the most distinguished informational book published in English during the preceding Year

Lerner Publishing Group publishes distinctive books for children of all ages including picture books, fiction, and nonfiction. Imprints include Twenty-First Century Books, Carolrhoda Books, Millbrook Press, First Avenue Editions, ediciones Lerner, LernerClassroom, Graphic Universe, and Kar-Ben Publishing.

Lerner titles include *Barry Bonds (Amazing Athletes)* by Jeff Savage; *Armoured Dinosaurs (Meet the Dinosaurs)* by Don Lessem; *Atlanta (Graphic Universe)* by Justine Korman Fontes, Ron Fontes and Thomas Yeates; *China in Pictures (Visual Geography)* by Alison Behnke; *Zebras (Nature Watch)* by Lynn M. Stone; and *Argentina (Country Explorers)* by Suzanne Paul Dell'Oro.

Lerner Publishing Group no longer accepts unsolicited submissions as of 2007.

KAR-BEN PUBLISHING

Kar-Ben Publishing offers an expansive Jewish library for children, families, and teachers. The Kar-Ben list encompasses presentations keyed to high holidays, the Sabbath, culture and tradition, and general interest concepts. Founded in 1975 by two friends to publish the children's Passover haggadah they had created. *My Very Own Haggadah*, now in its 30th anniversary printing, went on to sell over 2 million copies.

In 2001, Kar-Ben was purchased by Lerner Publishing Group in Minneapolis, although editorial operations have remained in Maryland. Under Lerner's leadership, Kar-Ben Publishing now publishes over a dozen new titles of Jewish content each year, developing a growing Jewish library for children and branching out from pre-school and young children's works into pre-teen and young adult fiction and nonfiction. Kar-Ben has created many award-winning children's titles on such subjects as Jewish holidays, crafts, folktales, and contemporary stories. Best-sellers include *The Mouse in the Matzah Factory* by Francine Medoff, illustrated by Nicole in Den Bosch; the *Sammy Spider* series by Sylvia A. Rouss and Katherine Janus Kahn; and *Six Million Paper Clips: The Making of a Children's Holocaust Memorial* by Peter W. Schroeder and Dagmar Schroeder-Hildebrand.

Recent titles include *It's Israel's Birthday!* by Ellen Dietrick, photographs by Tod Cohen; *Keeping Israel Safe* by Barbara Sofer; *Let My People Go!* by Tilda Balsley, illustrated by Ilene Richard; *Private Joel and the Sewell Mountain Seder* by Byrna J. Fireside, illustrated by Shawn Costello; and *Sammy Spider's First Shavuot* by Sylvia A. Rouss, illustrated by Katherine Janus Kahn.

Kar-Ben considers fiction and nonfiction for preschool through high school, including holiday books, life-cycle stories, Bible tales, folktales, board books, and activity books. In particular, they look for stories that reflect the ethnic and cultural diversity of today's Jewish family. They do not publish games, textbooks, or books in Hebrew. To submit, send to the attention of the Editorial Office.

Joanna Sussman, Director

LIBRARIES UNLIMITED [SEE GREENWOOD PUBLISHING GROUP]

LIFT EVERY VOICE [SEE MOODY PUBLISHERS]

LIGUORI PUBLICATIONS

One Liguori Drive, Liguori, MO 63057-9999

800-325-9521   fax: 636-464-8449

www.liguori.org

Located near St. Louis, Liguori Publications is a midsize Catholic publishing house that produces books, pamphlets, educational materials, *Liguorian* magazine, and software.

The purpose of Liguori Publications is to effectively communicate the word of God in the Catholic tradition by growing and expanding their outreach to Catholics of all ages through print and electronic media. They provide English- and Spanish-language (Libros Liguori) products. Imprint Liguori Triumph Books emphasizes an ecumenical perspective in the religious trade market.

Titles include *Called to Be Sent: Co-Missioned as Disciples Today* by Anthony J. Gittins; *Give Them What You Have: Interpreting the New Testament for Today* by John J. Denniston; *Joseph Elmer Cardinal Ritter: His Life and times* by Nicholas Schneider; *We Hold These Truths: Catholicism and American Political Life* by Richard W. Miller; *Church History 101: A Concise Overview* by Christopher M. Bellitto; and *Our Lady of Guadalupe: A New Interpretation of the Story, Apparitions and Image* by Jose Luis Guerrero.

Submit proposals with SASEs to the Editorial Department.

LIVING INK BOOKS [SEE AMG PUBLISHERS]

LLEWELLYN WORLDWIDE

FLUX

MIDNIGHT INK

2143 Wooddale Drive, Woodbury, MN 55125

651-291-1970/800-THE-MOON   fax: 651-291-1908

www.llewellyn.com   e-mail: billk@llewelyn.com

Llewellyn Worldwide is one of the oldest and largest independent New Age publishers in the U.S., with over a century of leadership in the industry on such subjects as self-help, metaphysical studies, mysticism, alternative health, divination, astrology, tarot, the paranormal, witchcraft, paganism, Wicca, magick, goddess lore, and garden witchery. They are seeking new authors.

In the past few years, Llewellyn has expanded into fiction for adults and young adults. Midnight Ink, a new imprint of Llewellyn, offers paperback mystery novels. Llewellyn's new imprint of young adult fiction, Flux, debuted in 2006. Llewellyn Espanol, their Spanish-language imprint, boasts over 50 titles.

The Llewellyn emphasis is on the practical: how it works, how it is done and self-help material. The book should appeal to readers with basic skills and knowledge and the information presented should be well within the reach of the average reader.

Recent publications from Llewellyn include *Faith and Magick in the Armed Forces: A Handbook for Pagans in the Military* by Stefani E. Barner; *Goddess Afoot! Practicing Magic with Celtic and Norse Goddesses* by Michelle Syke; *Mother Nature's Herbal: A Complete Guide for Experiencing the Beauty, Knowledge, and Synergy of Everything that Grows* by Judith Griffin; and *The Real Witches' Craft: The Definitive Handbook of Advanced Magical Techniques* by Kate West.

Recent releases from Midnight Ink include *August Moon* by Jess Lourey; *Murder at Hotel Cinema* by Daniel Edward Craig; *TKO* by Tom Schreck; *Murder Talks Turkey: A Yooper Mystery* by Deb Baker; *Whiskey and Water: A Whiskey Mattimoe Mystery* by Nina Wright; and *Shadow Waltz: A Marjorie McClelland Mystery* by Amy Patricia Meade.

Recent releases from Flux include *The Way He Lived* by Emily Wing Smith; *At Face Value* by Emily Franklin; *Busted: Confessions of an Accidental Player* by John Antony; *Lament: The Faerie Queen's Deception* by Maggie Stiefvater; *Dead Girl Walking* by Linda Joy Singleston; *Remember This* by S.T. Underdahl; and *Swimming with Sharks* by Debbie Fischer.

Llewellyn accepts submissions directly from authors (including first-time authors) and from literary agents. Submit proposals or complete manuscripts through regular mail only with SASE to:

Elysia Gallo, Acquisitions Editor

Andrew Karre, Acquisitions Editor—Flux

Barbara Moore, Editor—Midnight Ink

LONELY PLANET PUBLICATIONS

150 Linden Street, Oakland, CA 94607

800-275-8555/510-893-8555 fax: 510-893-8572

www.lonelyplanet.com e-mail: info@lonelyplanet.com

blog: www.lonelyplanet.com/tonywheeler

Lonely Planet began in the early 1970s after founders Tony and Maureen Wheeler completed an overland journey from London through Asia and on to Australia. That trip resulted in the first Lonely Planet guidebook—*Across Asia on the Cheap*—and laid the foundations of the world's leading independent travel publisher. Tony and Maureen are still the proud owners, still on the road, and still finding the time to continually push the boundaries of travel publishing.

Lonely Planet's head office is in Australia; the crew in Oakland publishes books for the Americas.

Lonely Planet creates and delivers the world's most compelling and comprehensive travel content, giving travelers trustworthy information, engaging opinions, powerful images and informed perspectives on destinations around the globe. They have over 600 guidebooks and products in print.

The house's titles cover every corner of the planet with guidebooks published in languages including French, Italian, Spanish, Korean and Japanese.

Recent titles include *Banff, Jasper, and Glacier National Parks Guide* by Oliver Berry and Brendan Sainsbury; *Greek Islands Travel Guide* by Paul Hellander et al.; *Los Angeles and Southern California Travel Guide* by Andrea Schulte-Peevers et al.; *Southeast Asia on a Shoestring* by China Williams et al.; *USA Travel Guide* by Jeff Campbell et al.; and *Yosemite, Sequoia and Kings Canyon National Parks Guide* by Danny Palmerlee and Beth Kohn.

They have a pool of 200 authors from over 20 countries. No matter how obscure the query or specialized the topic, Lonely Planet can usually find an in-house expert. In the U.S., Lonely Planet distributes its own publications. See their Web site for detailed submission guidelines and tips.

Query letters and SASEs should be directed to:

Tony Wheeler, Co-owner

Maureen Wheeler, Co-owner

LOTUS PRESS

P.O. Box 325/Twin Lakes, WI 53181

Shipping address:

1100 Lotus Drive, Building 3, Silver Lake, WI 53170

262-889-8561   fax: 262-889-2461

www.lotuspress.com   e-mail: lotuspress@lotuspress.com

Lotus Press is one of the leading publishers in its field of alternative health and wellness. Of particular interest is the Lotus Press list of titles in the field of Ayurveda, which are considered to be the standard works in the field and have been reprinted in many different languages worldwide. Lotus Press titles appear in more than 23 languages thanks to an active foreign rights translation program.

In addition to Ayurveda, Lotus Press has actively sought out titles on traditional healing modalities as well as energetic healing. This includes herbalism, Native American health, Chinese traditional herbal medicine, aromatherapy, Reiki and much more.

Lotus Press was founded in 1981 by Santosh and Karuna Krinsky. Since that time, the house has grown its list of publications to more than 300 titles, and is currently publishing about 20–25 new titles per year.

On the Lotus Press list: *Ayurvedic Healing for Women, 2nd Edition: Herbal Gynecology* by Atreya; *Ayurvedic Spa: Treatments for Large and Small Spas As Well as Home Care* by

Robert Sachs; *Light on the Origins of Reiki: A Handbook for Practicing the Original Reiki of Usui and Hayashi*; *Om the Eternal Witness: Secrets of the Mandukya Upanishad* by Swami Rama; and *Journey to Enlightenment* by Ross Bishop.

Direct query letters, proposals, and SASEs to:

Cathy Hoselton, Assistant to the President

LUNA BOOKS [SEE HARLEQUIN ENTERPRISES, LTD.]

LYONS PRESS [SEE GLOBE PEQUOT PRESS]

MACADAM/CAGE PUBLISHING

155 Sansome Street, Suite 550, San Francisco, CA 94104

415-986-7502   fax: 415-968-7414

www.macadamcage.com

MacAdam/Cage Publishing was founded as an independent trade publisher in 1998 by David Poindexter with the aim of publishing books of quality fiction and nonfiction. Publishers of *The Time Traveler's Wife* by Audrey Niffenegger, a debut novel that became a publishing phenomenon in Fall 2003, this house is committed to bringing new and talented voices to the literary marketplace.

In 1999 MacAdam/Cage Publishing acquired the independent press MacMurray & Beck, well known in the industry for launching authors such as Patricia Henley (*Hummingbird House*), William Gay (*The Long Home*), and Susan Vreeland (*Girl in Hyacinth Blue*) and heavily supported by the bookselling trade with many BookSense 76 picks as well as appearances in chain store fiction programs that highlight new authors. MacAdam/Cage Publishing represents independent publishing at its best.

Recent titles include *Salvage* by Jane F. Kotapish; *The Lost Highway* by David Adams Richards; *AK-47: The Story of a Gun* by Michael Hodges; *Machine* by Peter Adolphsen; *Pelican Road* by Howard Bahr; *The Wait* by Frank Turner Hollon; *No One Tells Everything* by Rae Meadows; *Commonwealth* by Joey Goebel; and *Awesome* by Jack Pendarvis.

MacAdam Cage will not accept submission in these categories: romance, science fiction, fantasy, supernatural, self-help, poetry, thrillers, religion, spirituality, children's, young adult, cookbooks, parenting, family, military science, or medical. They also do not accept one-page proposals, complete manuscripts, submissions on disk, or e-mail submissions. Send a cover letter, brief synopsis, author biography, 30-page sample and SASE to Manuscript Submission.

Kate Nitze, Editor

Dave Adams, Editor

Khristina Wenzinger, Editor

Soumeya Bendimerad, Associate Editor

MAGINATION PRESS [SEE AMERICAN PSYCHOLOGICAL ASSOCIATION, INC.]

MANIC D PRESS

P.O. Box 410804, San Francisco, CA 94141

415-648-8288

www.manicdpress.com   e-mail: info@manicdpress.com

Manic D Press was founded by Jennifer Joseph in 1984 as an alternative outlet for young writers seeking to bring their work into print. Manic D Press publishes unusual fiction, narrative poetry, contemporary art, rock photography, comix, cultural studies, GLBT, and alternative travel trade paperbacks and hardcovers by new and established authors.

Recent titles include *Imaginationally: Michael's Lovable Fun of Dictionaries* by Michael Bernard Loggins; *Juicy Mother 2: How they Met* edited by Jennifer Camper; *The Rise and Fall of the Third Leg* by John Longhi; and *Dahlia Season: Stories and a Novella* by Myriam Gurba.

Distribution in the U.S. is through Consortium, in Canada through PGC, and in the U.K. through Turnaround Publishers Services LP.

Before submitting your work to Manic D, the publisher requests that you read at least one book they have already published to familiarize yourself with their line. In your cover letter, tell them which book you have read and what you thought about it. Be specific.

E-mail submission are preferred. Send submissions to subs@manicdpress.com. Manuscripts are read twice a year, during the months of January and July only. Send 5–10 poems, 3–5 short stories, or a synopsis and first chapter of a novel with your cover letter and SASE to the attention of the editors.

Jennifer Joseph, Publisher

MARLOWE & COMPANY [SEE PERSEUS]

MCDOUGAL-LITTELL [SEE HOUGHTON MIFFLIN]

MCFARLAND & COMPANY

960 NC Highway 88 West, Jefferson, NC 28640

Mailing address:

Box 611, Jefferson, NC 28640

336-246-4460   fax: 336-246-5018

www.mcfarlandpub.com   e-mail: info@mcfarlandpub.com

McFarland & Company, Inc., Publishers, founded in 1979, is located in Jefferson, North Carolina, a small town nestled in the northwestern corner of the state. The company is now one of the leading publishers of scholarly and reference books in the U.S., with 3,200 titles published to date, including nearly 2,100 still in print. McFarland publishes 290 new titles each year for a worldwide market; many of them have received awards as outstanding reference or academic titles. McFarland is recognized for its serious works in a variety of fields, including performing arts (especially film), sport and leisure (especially baseball and chess), military history, popular culture, and automotive history, among other topics.

Recent titles include *Florida Paper Money: An Illustrated History, 1817-1934; The Influence of Imagination: Essays on Science fiction and Fantasy as Agents of Social Change* by Lee Easton and Randy Schroeder; *Eddie Collins: A Baseball Biography* by Rick Huhn; *The Dakota People: A History of the Dakota, Lakota and Nakota through 1863* by Jessica Dawn

Palmer; *African Americans in the United Sates Army in World War II* by Bryan D. Booker; and *Drummer Boy Willie McGee: Civil War Hero and Fraud* by Thomas Fox.

Authors may contact the house with a query letter, a full proposal, or a finished manuscript with cover letter. See the Web site for more details.

Queries may be directed to:

Steve Wilson, Editor Director; swilson@mcfarlandpub.com

Gary Mitchem, Acquisitions Editor; gmitchem@mcfarlandpub.com

David Alff, Editor; dalff@mcfarlandpub.com

THE MCGRAW-HILL COMPANIES, INC.

MCGRAW-HILL PROFESSIONAL

ACCESS MED BOOKS

SCHAUM'S MCGRAW-HILL

Two Penn Plaza, New York, NY 10121-2298

212-512-2000   fax: 212-904-6096

Burr Ridge address:

1333 Burr Ridge Parkway, Burr Ridge, IL 60527

www.mhprofessional.com

INTERNATIONAL MARINE

P.O. Box 235, Thomaston, Maine, 04861

www.internationalmarine.com

OSBORNE MEDIA / MCGRAW-HILL

160 Spear Street, Suite 700, San Francisco, CA 94105

www.osborne.com

WRIGHT GROUP / MCGRAW-HILL

220 East Danieldale Road, DeSoto, TX 75115

800-648-2970   fax: 800-593-4418

www.wrightgroup.com

The McGraw-Hill Companies, Inc., is a publicly traded corporation headquartered in New York City, focused on education, publishing, and financial services for a global market. It publishes numerous textbooks and magazines, including Business Week and Aviation Week, and is the parent company of Standard & Poor's and J.D. Power and Associates.

The myriad of McGraw-Hill book publishing divisions and imprints may be explored in depth at www.mhprofessional.com and www.mcgraw-hill.com.

MCGRAW-HILL PROFESSIONAL

The McGraw-Hill Professional division focuses on professional, reference, and trade publishing. The division produces general interest books, study guides, software, multimedia, and online products for its five core publishing programs Business, Medical, Education, Technical, and Consumer.

This broad list includes titles in business, economics, computers, education, family and relationships, foreign language study, health and fitness, history, language arts and disciplines, mathematics, medical, nature, psychology and psychiatry, science, self-help, social science, sports and recreation, technology, engineering, transportation, travel, hobbies, gardening, house and home, humor, music, performing arts, and photography. Partnerships include Harvard Medical School, Investor's Business Daily, and Standard & Poor's. McGraw-Hill is also the distributor of books from American Diabetes Association, American Pharmacists Association, Entrepreneur Press, and Teach Yourself.

Aviation titles include *Planning and Design of Airports, 5th edition* by Robert M. Horonjeff et al.; *Airplane Ownership* by Ron Wanttaja; *Illustrated Buyer's Guide to Used Airplanes* by Bill Clarke; *Kit Airplane Construction* by Ron Wanttaja; *101 Things To Do After You Get Your Private Pilot's License* by LeRoy Cook; *Aviation Maintenance Management* by Harry A. Kinniaon; and *AIM/FAR 2006* by Charles F. Spence.

Engineering and architecture titles include *Bridge and Highway Structure Rehabilitation and Repair* by Mohiuddin A. Khan; *Industrial Energy Efficiency Handbook* by Kenneth E. Bannister and Jane Alexander; *Thermodynamics Demystified* by James Pohl; *Design of Reinforced Masonry Structure* by Narenda Taly; *Moving The Earth* by Herbert L. Nichols and David Day; and *Steel Water Storage Tanks* by Steve Meier.

Direct queries and SASEs to:

Steve Chapman, Publisher (NY)—Aviation, electrical engineering; steve_chapman@mcgraw-hill.com

Joy Bramble, Senior Editor (NY)—Architecture, construction; joy_bramble@mcgraw-hill.com

Taisuke Soda, Senior Editor—Engineering; taisuke_soda@mcgraw-hill.com

Larry Hager, Senior Editor (NY)—Civil engineering, construction, technical trades; larry_hager@mcgraw-hill.com

Judy Bass, Senior Editor (NY)—TAB Electronics; judy_bass@mcgraw-hill.com

MCGRAW-HILL PROFESSIONAL (GENERAL TRADE AND BUSINESS)

McGraw-Hill Professional titles in self-help and health include *Happier: Learn the Secrets to Daily Joy and Lasting Fulfillment* by Tal Ben-Shahar; *Why Hasn't He Called: How Guys Really Think and How to Get the Right One Interested in You* by Matt Titus and Tamsen Fadal; *Your Perfect Fit* by Paige Adam-Geller and Ashley Borden; *Put Passion First: Why Sexual Chemistry is the Key to Finding and Keeping Lasting Love* by Carol Cassell, PhD; and *Broccoli for the Brain: 75 Puzzles and Exercises to Boost Your Brain Power* by Michel Noir, PhD.

Business McGraw-Hill subjects include accounting; marketing and sales; careers; communication; e-business; economics; finance and investing; general business; human resources and training; international business; management and leadership; personal finance; quality; real estate; and small business and entrepreneurship.

Titles include *Jacked Up: The Inside Story of How Jack Welch Talked GE into Becoming the World's Greatest Company* by Bill Lane; *One Nation Under debt: Hamilton, Jefferson, and the History of What We Owe* by Robert E. Wright; *Personality Not Included: Why Companies Lose Their Authenticity and How Great Brands Get It Back* by Rohit Bhargava; *Where's Your WOW? 16 Ways to Make Your Competitors With They Were You!* by Robyn Freedman-Spizman and Rick Frishman; and *Silicon Dragon: How China is Winning the Tech Race* by Rebecca Fannin.

Direct query and SASE to:

Philip Ruppel, Vice President and Group Publisher (NY)—Trade

Herb Schaffner, Publisher (NY)—General business

Mary Glenn, Editorial Director, Business (NY)—Management and management theory, self-help with a business focus, marketing and sales, topical books with global appeal that can cross over into serious nonfiction; mary_glenn@mcgraw-hill.com

Jeanne Glasser, Senior Editor (NY)—Business and management; jeanne_glasser@mcgraw-hill.com

Leah Spiro, Senior Editor (NY)—Business and management; leah_spiro@mcgraw-hill.com

Emily Carleton, Editor (NY)—General self-help/how-to

Donya Dickerson, Editor (NY)—Business and management; donya_dickerson@mcgraw-hill.com

Judith McCarthy, Publisher (NY)—Health, self-help, parenting; judith_mccarthy@mcgraw-hill.com

Deb Brody, Executive Editor (NY)— Health, self-help, parenting; deborah_brody@mcgraw-hill.com

John Aherne, Senior Editor (NY)—Health, self-help; john_aherne@mcgraw-hill.com

Johanna Bowman, Editor (NY)—Self-help; johanna_bowman@mcgraw-hill.com

Ron Martirano, Editor (NY)—Sports; ron_martirano@mcgraw-hill.com

Sarah Pelz, Associate Editor (NY)—Self help, parenting, health; sarah_pelz@mcgraw-hill.com

Emily Carleson, Editor—Business and popular self-help

MCGRAW HILL MEDICAL / ACCESS MED

Part of McGraw-Hill Professional Division, Access Med provides books for medical professionals on subjects including basic science, clinical medicine, nursing, pharmacy, allied health, and test prep and review.

Titles include *Williams' Gynecology* by John O Schorge et al.; *Fishman's Pulmonary Diseases and Disorders* by Alfred P. Fishman et al.; *First Aid for Family Medicine Boards* by Tao Le; and *Pharmacy Law: Textbook and Review* by Debra B. Feinberg.

If you are a medical, nursing, or health-related professional or instructor with a book project or a well-established course syllabus, McGraw-Hill Medical / Access Med would like to hear from you.

Direct query with SASE to:

Joe Rusko, Editor-in-Chief, Medical Book Group (NY); joe_rusko@mcgraw-hill.com

Michael Brown, Senior Editor (NY)—Clinical laboratory science, imaging sciences, mortuary science, pharmacy, all allied health occupations; michael_brown@mcgraw-hill.com

Quincy McDonald, Senior Editor (NY)—Nursing; quincy_mcdonald@mcgraw-hill.com

Anne Sydor, Senior Editor (NY)—Dermatology, OB/GYN, neurology, neuroscience, psychiatry; anne_sydor@mcgraw-hill.com

James F. Shanahan, Executive Editor (Burr Ridge, IL)—Harrison's, internal medicine, clinical pharmacology, family; james_shanahan@mcgraw-hill.com

Jason Malley, Editor (Burr Ridge, IL)—Basic sciences, clerkship books; jason_malley@mcgraw-hill.com

SCHAUM'S MCGRAW-HILL

Schaum's McGraw-Hill publishes series of home study guides for adults and young adults, some of which manage to get the words easy and quantum mechanics into the same title.

Titles include *Schaum's Quick Guide to Writing Great Research Papers* by Laurie Rozakis *Bob Miller's Algebra for the Clueless, 2nd Edition* by Bob Miller; *Schaum's Easy Outline of Quantum Mechanics* by Eliahu Zaarur and Phinik Peuven; *Schaum's Outline of Italian Grammar* by Joseph Germano; and *5 Steps to a 5 on the Advanced Placement Exams*.

Direct queries and SASEs to:

Ellen Mendlow, Publisher, Schaum's, Test-Prep, and Study Guides; ellen_mendlow@mcgraw-hill.com

Chuck Wall, Senior Editor, Test-Prep, Study Guides; charles_wall@mcgraw-hill.com

INTERNATIONAL MARINE

Part of the McGraw-Hill Trade Division, International Marine has been publishing books about boats since 1970. Located near the Rockport and Camden harbors of mid-coast Maine, IM has published more than 200 titles covering everything from knots to sailboat racing, plus an impressive lineup of nautical adventure books. International Marine is always seeking new authors and has extensive guidelines online at www.internationalmarine.com or by request from the editors.

Titles representative of the list include *The Intracoastal Waterway Chartbook: Norfolk, Virginia to Miami, Florida* by John J. Kettlewell; *World Cruising Routes* by Jimmy Cornell; *Confident Powerboating* by Stu Reininger; *Emergency Navigation, 2nd Edition* by David Burch; *Practical Boat Mechanics* by Ben L. Evridge; *George Washington's Secret Navy* by James L. Nelson; *Adlard Coles' Heavy Weather Sailing 6th edition* by Peter Bruce; *On-Board Medical Emergency Hanbook* by Spike Briggs and Campbell MacKenzie; and *The On-Board Weather Handbook* by Chris Tibbs.

Direct query letters and SASEs to:

Jonathon Eaton, Editorial Director—Boating, outdoors; jonathan_eaton@mcgraw-hill.com

Molly Mulhern, Director of Editing, Design, and Production; molly_mulhern@mcgraw-hill.com

MCGRAW-HILL / OSBORNE

McGraw-Hill/Osborne Media, a unit of McGraw-Hill Education, is a leading publisher of self-paced computer training materials, including user and reference guides, best-selling series on computer certification, titles on business and technology, and high-level but practical titles on networking, programming, and Web development tools. McGraw-Hill/Osborne Media is the official press of Oracle, Corel, and Intuit. From its home base across the east bay from San Francisco, McGraw-Hill/Osborne Media is seeking proposals from computer-savvy authors.

Titles include *SAP Project System Handbook* by Kieron Dowling; *IBM Cognos 8 Business Intelligence: The Official Guide* by Dan Colitich; *Nintendo Wii Flash Game Creator's Guide* by Todd Perkins; *Secret of the Rock Star Programmers: Riding the IT Crest* by Ed Burns; *OCA Oracle Database 11g: Administration I Exam Guide* by John Watson; and *Herb Schildt's C++ Programming Cookbook* by Herbert Schildt.

Direct proposals with SASEs to Manuscript Proposal. See the Web site for detailed proposal tips and guidelines.

Roger Stewart, Editorial Director, Consumer Computing; roger_stewart@mcgraw-hill.com

Wendy Rinaldi, Editorial Director, Programming and Web Development; wendy_rinaldi@mcgraw-hill.com

Jane Brownlow, Executive Editor, Networking and Communications; jane_brownlow@mcgraw-hill.com

Timothy Green, Senior Acquisitions Editor, Certification & Career; timothy_green@mcgraw-hill.com

Elizabeth McClain, Acquisitions Editor, Databases & ERP, Oracle Press; Elizabeth_mcclain@mcgraw-hill.com

Margaret Morin, Acquisitions Editor, Consumer Computing; margaret_morin@mcgraw-hill.com

WRIGHT GROUP / MCGRAW-HILL

Wright Group/McGraw-Hill is a division of McGraw-Hill Education and is a leading provider of successful, creative, and flexible solutions for teachers and students in grades pre-K through adult. Their books provide innovative literacy, professional development, early childhood, world language, adult basic education, and mathematics resources to energize the classroom. For more than 25 years, Wright Group/McGraw-Hill has provided educators with captivating materials, research-based strategies, and proven ideas to make teaching better, more effective, and more engaging for all students.

The editors believes that no single teaching method works with every learner, so Wright Group/McGraw-Hill provides various approaches that allow educators to "Enjoy Success, Achieve Results." Products include Music, Movement, and More; Gear Up!; X-Zone; and Weekday Workouts for Vocabulary.

Please send your queries and SASEs to the attention of the Editorial Department.

MCSWEENEY'S

McSweeney's West:

849 Valencia Street, San Francisco, CA 94110

McSweeney's East:

826 NYC, 372 Fifth Ave., Brooklyn, NY 11215

Founded by author Dave Eggers, McSweeney's is a small, independent press based in San Francisco that is committed to helping find new voices—Neal Pollack, Amy Fusselman, and Paul Collins—to publishing works of gifted but under-appreciated writers, such as Lydia Davis and Stephen Dixon—and to always push the literary form forward. One also finds here best-selling authors like Dave Eggers and Nick Hornby.

McSweeney's has a very active Web site and an amazing quarterly; it is a place to find and share interesting, quirky, and/or brilliant fiction, essays, memoirs, children's titles, and humor.

Recent titles include *Maps and Legends* by Michael Chabon; *The Berliner Ensemble Thanks You All* by Marcel Dzama; *Underground America: Narratives of Undocumented Lives* edited by Peter Orner; and *Where to Invade Next* edited by Stephen Elliott.

Send complete manuscript or sample chapters via e-mail or regular mail.

Barb Bersche, Publisher

MEADOWBROOK PRESS

5451 Smetana Drive, Minnetonka, MN 55343

800-338-2232   fax: 952-930-1940

www.meadowbrookpress.com   e-mail: editorial@meadowbrookpress.com

Meadowbrook Press (founded 1975) specializes in books about parenting, pregnancy, baby care, child care, humorous poetry for children, party planning, and children's activities. Meadowbrook is also the country's No. 1 publisher of baby name books, with eight baby-naming books in print and total sales of over 6 million copies.

Recent titles include *I'm Allergic to School: Funny Poems and Songs about School* by Robert Pottle, illustrated by Mike and Carl Gordon; *Baby Bites* by Bridget Swinney; *The Breastfeeding Diaries: Laugh-out-Loud Stories Written by Real Moms* edited by Kate Davis, illustrated by B.K. Taylor; *The New Baby Name Survey* by Bruce Lanksy; *I Hope I Don't Strike Out* by Bruce Lansky, edited by Angela Wiechmann; illustrated by Stephen Carpenter; and *5-Star Baby Name Advisor* by Bruce Lansky, edited by Megan McGinnis, Angela Wiechmann, and Alicia Ester, Illustrated by Tamara Peterson.

The Meadowbrook editorial staff develops and writes books as well as acquires and edits titles written by outside authors. The house is not currently accepting unsolicited manuscripts or queries for the following genres: adult fiction, adult poetry, humor, and children's fiction. Also, they do not currently publish picture books for children, travel titles, scholarly, or literary works.

See the Web site for submission guidelines and send all appropriate queries and SASEs to "Submissions Editor."

Bruce Lansky, Publisher

MESORAH PUBLICATIONS

4401 Second Avenue, Brooklyn, NY 11232

718-921-9000/800-637-6724   fax: 718-680-1875

www.artscroll.com   e-mail: info@artscroll.com

Mesorah Publications produces books of contemporary Jewish interest written by authors with sophisticated firsthand knowledge of Orthodox religious practices, history, and culture. It is also noted for its works in traditional Judaica, Bible study, Talmud, liturgical materials, Jewish history, and juvenile literature. Founded in 1976, Mesorah Publications remains true to tradition in all of its publications, as expressed in the motto: Mesorah Publications . . .helping to preserve the heritage, one book at a time.

Recent titles include *The Fortune Seeker* by Libby Lazewnik; *Living and Parenting: A Down-to-Earth Guide* by Rabbi Yakov Horowitz; *Rav Asher Weiss On the Haggadah* by Rabbi Asher Weiss; *Miggid Stories for Children: Holidays and Around the Year* by Chaviva Pfeiffer; *A Touch of Warmth: Heartwarming Stories Glowing with Inspiration* by Rabbi Yechiel Spero; *The Simchah Handbook* by Rabbi David Weinberger; and *In Black and White: and Other Stories About Overcoming Life's Struggles* by Dov Haller.

Address queries and SASEs to Acquisitions Editor.

MIDNIGHT INK [SEE LLEWELLYN WORLDWIDE]

MILKWEED EDITIONS

1011 Washington Avenue South, Suite 300, Minneapolis, MN 55415-1246

612-332-3192 / 800-520-6455   fax: 612-215-2550

www.milkweed.org   e-mail: editor@milkweed.org

Milkweed Editions is a nonprofit literary press, publishing 15–20 books a year. Founded in 1979, the house publishes literary fiction, nonfiction about the natural world, poetry, and novels for young readers. They have published over 200 titles. The editors at Milkweed Editions believe that literature is a transformative art, and that each book bears a responsibility to convey the essential experiences of the human heart and spirit.

Although a small press, Milkweed also offers prizes for adult fiction and children's literature in their prestigious literary awards. Guidelines for the prizes are available online or by request through regular mail. The World As Home is a Milkweed Web site that fosters ecological literacy and renewal by linking literary writing about the natural world to specific ecoregions and to organizations active in preserving natural landscapes or focused on the art of writing.

Milkweed authors include Ken Kalfus, Susan Straight, Marilyn Chin, Larry Watson, Bill Holm, Paul Gruchow, Janisse Ray, Pattiann Rogers, and many others, including emerging and mid-career authors.

Titles include *Discovering Pig Magic* by Julie Crabtree; *Fiction on a Stick: New Stories by Minnesota Writers* by Daniel Slager; *Slant* by Laura Williams; *The Windows of Brimnes: An American in Iceland* by Bill Holm; *The Farther Shore* by Matthew Eck; *A Whaler's Dictionary* by Dan Beachy-Quick; *Driftless* by David Rhodes; *The Love of Impermanent Things: A Threshold Ecology* by Mary Rose O'Reilly; and *Shopping for Porcupine: A Life in Arctic Alaska* by Seth Katner.

Milkweed does not accept submissions on disc or via e-mail. Send the complete manuscript or a proposal with sample chapters, outline, and cover letter. Direct submissions to the Fiction Reader (or Nonfiction, Poetry, or Children's, as appropriate); include a SASE.

Daniel Slager, Editor-in-Chief

Jim Cihlar, Managing Editor

MIRA BOOKS [SEE HARLEQUIN ENTERPRISES, LTD., CANADA]

MIRAMAX BOOKS [SEE HYPERION]

MOODY PUBLISHERS

LIFT EVERY VOICE

A Division of the Moody Bible Institute

820 North LaSalle Boulevard, Chicago, IL 60610-3284

312-329-2101

www.moodypublishers.org   e-mail: acquisitions@moody.edu

Moody Publishers was founded in 1894 by D.L. Moody eight years after he had founded the Moody Bible Institute, which continues to be a well-known evangelical institution. The house publishes fiction, nonfiction, and children's titles for the Christian markets.

The Moody Publishers' mission is to educate and edify the Christian and to evangelize the non-Christian by ethically publishing conservative, evangelical Christian literature and other media for all ages around the world; and to help provide resources for Moody Bible Institute in its training of future Christian leaders.

Moody Publishers partners with the Institute for Black Family Development in the creation of a joint imprint, Lift Every Voice. The vision for this endeavor is to see African American Christians encouraged in their faith in Jesus Christ through quality books written by African Americans. While Moody Publishers had already published several African American authors, such as Tony Evans, Clarence Schuler, Lois Evans, and Crawford Loritts, Lift Every Voice products will be targeted almost exclusively to African Americans.

Moody titles include *Christ in the Feast of Pentecost* by David Brickner; *Get Married: What Women Can Do to Help it Happen* by Candice Watters; *Good Intentions: Nine Dicey Social and Economic Issues Viewed through the Eyes of Faith* by Charles M. North and Bob Smietana; *The Heart of the Five Love Languages* by Gary Chapman; *Lies Young Women Believe: And the Truth That Sets Them Free* by Nancy Leigh DeMoss and Dannah Gresh; *Living for Jesus Beyond the Spiritual High* by Greg Speck; and *Meet Me at the Well: Take a Month and Water Your Soul* by Virelle Kidder.

Lift Every Voice titles include *Sisters in Faith* by Stephanie Perry-Moor and Michelle Clark Jenkins; *A Promise and a Rainbow* by Mabel Elizabeth Singletary; *Secret Sex Wars: A Battle Cry For Purity* by Robert S. Scott; *The Truth About Love* by Tia McCollors; *Yet with a Steady Beat: The Black Church Through a Psychological and Biblical Lens* by Lee June; and *When Love's in View: Finding Focus in Dating and Relationships* by Conway Edwards and Jada Edwards.

Moody Publishers reviews unsolicited fiction manuscripts, but does not review unsolicited nonfiction manuscripts except from literary agents. Query letters and SASEs should be directed to:

Dave deWit, Director of Acquisitions

THE MOUNTAINEERS BOOKS

SKIPSTONE

A Division of The Mountaineers Club

1001 SW Klickitat Way, Suite 201, Seattle, WA 98134

206-223-6303   fax: 206-223-6306

www.mountaineersbooks.org   e-mail: mbooks@mountaineersbooks.org

The Mountaineers Books specializes in outdoor titles by experts. Born from the hand-scribbled trail maps and wilderness passion of its members, Washington's nearly 100-year-old Mountaineers Club established the nonprofit Mountaineers Books in 1960 to express and share its love of the natural outdoors. The house produces guidebooks, instructional texts, historical works, adventure narratives, natural history guides, and works on environmental conservation.

Today, with more than 500 titles in print, The Mountaineers Books is a leading publisher of quality outdoor books, including many award winners. For those hiking with the family, cycling over a country road, clinging to a big wall or dreaming of a trek in Nepal, The Mountaineers Books has the guidance for creating the next journey in confidence and safety. The house focuses on non-competitive, non-motorized, self-propelled sports such as mountain climbing, hiking, walking, skiing, snowshoeing, and adventure travel. They also publish works on environmental and conservation subjects, narratives of mountaineering expeditions and adventure travel, outdoor guidebooks to specific areas, mountaineering history, safety/first aid, and books on skills and techniques for the above sports. The house does not publish fiction, general tourist guides, or guides dealing with hunting, fishing, snowmobiling, RV travel, horseback riding, or team sports.

The Skipstone imprint, launched in 2007, publishes nonfiction books on eco-conscious lifestyle topics, including sustainable home care, food/cooking, pet care, gardening, crafts, humor, and entertaining with a green focus.

Mountaineers Press titles include *Forget Me Not: A Memoir* by Jennifer Lowe; *How to Knit In the Woods: 20 Project for the Great Outdoors* by Shannon Okey; *Paddling Washington: Flatwater and Whitewater Routes in Washington State and the Inland Northwest* by Rich Landers et al.; *Day Hiking: Mount Rainer* by Dan Nelson, photography by Alan Bauer; and *The Best Fort Collins Hikes: The Colorado Mountain Club Pack Guide* by John Gascoyne.

Skipstone titles include *Dog Park Wisdom: Real World Advice for Choosing, Caring For, and Understanding Your Canine Companion* by Lisa Wogan, photography by Bev Sparks; *Chefs on the Farm: Recipes and Inspiration from the Quillisascut Farm School of the Domestic Arts* by Shannon Borg; *Blue Tarp: Best Uses, Worst Abuses of the (Unsightly) Fabric that Binds America* by Ron Judd; *Eat Where You Live: How to Find and Enjoy Fantastic Local and Sustainable Produce No Matter Where You Live* by Lou Bendrick; and *The Salvage Studio: Sustainable Home Comforts to Organize, Entertain, and Inspire* by Amy Duncan.

If you plan to submit an adventure narrative, please request information about the Barbara Savage Miles From Nowhere Memorial Award. The Mountaineers Books does not publish fiction, general tourist guides, or guides dealing with hunting, fishing, snowmobiling, RV travel, horseback riding, or team sports.

Submit query letters, manuscripts, and/or proposals by regular mail only to Acquisitions.

Kate Rogers, Editor-in-Chief

MULTNOMAH PUBLISHERS, INC. [SEE BERTELSMANN AG / RANDOM HOUSE / WATERBROOK MULTNOMAH]

MUSEUM OF NEW MEXICO PRESS

725 Camino Lejo, Santa Fe, NM 87505

Mailing address:

P.O. Box 2087, Santa Fe, NM 87504

505-476-1155   fax: 505-476-1156

www.mnmpress.org

Founded in 1951, the Museum of New Mexico Press is an award-winning publisher of finely designed and crafted books that reflect the collections of the Museum of New Mexico and explore the culture of the Southwest. Specializations include fine art and folk art, photography, Native Americana, the Hispanic Southwest, nature and gardening, and architecture and style.

Recent titles include *Changing Dreams: A Generation of Oaxaca's Woodcarvers* by Shepard Bush, photographs by Vicki Ragan; *In New Mexico Light: Photographs* by Douglas Kent Hall; *Mexican Modern* by Luis-Martin Lozano and David Craven; *Stone: A Substantial Witness* photographs by David Scheinbaum with an essay by Jo Anne Van Tilburg; and *Village of Painters* by Frank J. Korom, photography by Paul Smutko.

The house requests that authors submit book proposals rather than full manuscripts for review. For proposal guidelines, see the Web site. Send proposals with cover letters, CVs, and SASEs to: and Gail Bird by Diana F. Pardue.

Mary Wachs, Editorial Director, mary.wachs@state.nm.us

NAKED INK [SEE THOMAS NELSON PUBLISHERS]

NATARAJ PUBLISHING [SEE NEW WORLD LIBRARY]

NATION BOOKS [SEE PERSEUS]

NATIONAL GEOGRAPHIC SOCIETY

National Geographic Books (General Audience):

P.O. Box 10543, Des Moines, IA 50340

888-647-6733 / 515-362-3345

National Geographic Children's Books

P.O. Box 4002864, Des Moines, IA 50340

877-873-6846

www.nationalgeographic.com   e-mail: askngs@nationalgeographic.com

Founded in 1888, the National Geographic Society is one of the world's largest non-profit scientific and educational organizations. Their mission is to increase and diffuse geographic knowledge while promoting the conservation of the world's cultural, historical and natural resources. National Geographic has funded over 7,000 scientific research projects, supports an education program combating geography illiteracy and reflects the world through magazines, television programs, books, videos, maps, interactive media and merchandise.

The Press publishes quality, illustrated nonfiction books, including reference books, photography books and travel guides. Subjects of focus are adventure and exploration, animals and nature, culture and history, geography and reference, photography, science and space, and educational materials for kids.

Recent titles include Planetology: *How Earth is Unlocking the Secrets of the Solar System* by Tom Jones and Ellen Stofan; *Warriors in Uniform: The Legacy of American Indian Heroism* by Herman J. Viola; *Undersea Animals: A Dramatic Dimensional Visit to Strange Underwater Realms* by Jane H. Buxton, illustrated by Jerry Pinkney; *1000 Events That Shaped the World* introduction by Jared Diamond; *Organize Your Digital Life: How to Store Your Photographs, Music, Videos, and Personal Documents in a Digital World* by

Aimee Balridge; and *Freedom in My Heart: Voices From the United States National Slavery Museum* by Cynthia Jacobs Carter.

Query letters and SASEs should be directed to the editorial staff of the Book Division.

Stephen Mico, Senior Vice President, Publisher, Children's and Educational titles

Kevin Mulroy, Senior Vice President, Publisher, Books

Virginia Koeth, Editor—Children's Books

Lisa Thomas, Senior Editor

NAVAL INSTITUTE PRESS

An imprint of the United States Naval Institute

291 Wood Road, Annapolis, MD 21402

410-224-3378   fax: 410-269-7940

www.usni.org/navalinstitutepress/index.asp

Naval Institute Press, situated on the grounds of the U.S. Naval Academy, is the book-publishing imprint of the U.S. Naval Institute, a private, independent, nonprofit professional society for members of the military services and civilians who share an interest in naval and maritime affairs. USNI was established in 1873 at the Naval Academy in Annapolis; the press inaugurated its publishing program in 1898 with a series of basic guides to U.S. naval practice.

Naval Institute Press features trade books, in addition to the house's targeted professional and reference titles. Areas of NIP interest include how-to books on boating, navigation, battle histories, and biographies, as well as occasional selected titles in fiction (typically with a nautical adventure orientation). Specific categories encompass such fields as seamanship, naval history and literature, the Age of Sail, aviation, aircraft, World War II naval history, ships and aircraft, current naval affairs, naval science, and general naval resources and guidebooks.

The Press produces more than 70 titles each year. With its long-established tradition of publishing excellence in the fields of naval, military, and maritime history, the NIP provides the serious reader with an invaluable resource. Categories include history and reference.

Recent titles include *The Lost Battalion of Tet: Breakout of the 2/12th Cavalry at Hue* by Charles A. Krohn; *Tip of the Spear: U.S. Marine Light Armor in the Gulf War* by G.J. Michaels; *Slaughter at Goliad: The Mexican Massacre of 400 Texas Volunteers* by Jay A. Stout; *Nimitz* by E. B. Porter; *Contrails Over the Mojave: The Golden Age of Jet Flight Testing at the Edwards Air Force Base* by George J. Marrett; *The Terrorist Perspectives Project: Strategic and Operational Views of Al Qaida and Associated Movements* by Mark E. Stout et al.; and *The Canons of Jihad: Terrorists' Strategy for Defeating America* edited by Jim Lacey.

Submit a proposal or the entire manuscript (paper copy) via regular mail. Send all queries and SASEs to the Acquisitions Editors.

Thomas Cutler, Director of Professional Publishing

Susan Todd Brook, Acquisitions Editor

Elizabeth Bauman, Assistant Editor

THOMAS NELSON PUBLISHERS

J. COUNTRYMAN

TOMMY NELSON

NELSON BOOKS

WESTBOW

NELSON CURRENT

W PUBLISHING GROUP

COOL SPRINGS PRESS

NELSON IMPACT

RUTLEDGE HILL

NAKED INK

501 Nelson Place, P.O. Box 141000, Nashville, TN 37214-1000

800-251-4000

www.thomasnelson.com

Blog: www.michaelhyatt.com/fromwhereisit

Thomas Nelson Publishers is the world's largest Christian publishing company and the ninth-largest publishing company of any kind. Recently purchased by InterMedia Partners, Thomas Nelson continues with Michael Hyatt as president of this religious publishing company. The company was founded in 1798 by Scotsman Thomas Nelson, who sought to make Christian works and classic literature affordable for the common folk. Today, categories include business books, children/young adult trade, reference, religious, Spanish language, and general trade.

Thomas Nelson works through a number of imprints, including J. Countryman, Nelson Books, Nelson Business, Tommy Nelson, Grupo Nelson, WestBow Press, W Publishing Group, Rutledge Hill Press, Nelson Current, Nelson Reference & Electronic, Nelson Impact, Nelson Bibles, Naked Ink, and Cool Springs Press.

J. Countryman focuses on God-centered gift books. W focuses on books written by religious leaders who show how written words will impact people forever. Nelson Current publishes fiercely independent ideas from a variety of political and social positions. Cool Springs Press publishes books for gardeners. WestBow Press publishes fiction. Tommy Nelson publishes for children. Nelson Impact provides study tools and church curriculum. Grupo Nelson is the Spanish-language imprint for Thomas Nelson.

In 1999, Rutledge Hill Press was acquired by Thomas Nelson Publishers. It creates books that inspire, educate, and entertain—and make it to best-seller lists.

Thomas Nelson's willingness to publish trade books for the general market is perhaps best exemplified by the 2006 launch of imprint Naked Ink, which targets 18–35 year-olds and is meant to "inspire a generation of readers who seek imaginative, honest and relevant information through entertainment and pop-culture driven products."

Recent Thomas Nelson fiction titles include *Adam* by Ted Dekker; *The Perfect Life* by Robin Lee Hatcher; *The Convenient Groom* by Denise Hunter; *Illuminated* by Matt Bronleewe; *Full Circle* by Davis Bunn; *Flywheel* by Eric Wilson; *Abomination* by Colleen Coble; and *White Lightning* by Minton Sparks.

Recent nonfiction titles include *Walking with God: Talk to Him. Hear From Him. Really.* by John Elderege; *A Tale of Two Sons: The Inside Story of a Father, His Sons and a Shocking Murder* by John MacArthur; *Leadership Gold: Lessons I've Learned from a Lifetime of Leading* by John C. Maxwell; *Following Prince Caspian: Further Adventures with the Lion of Narnia* by Thomas Williams; *The Way We Will Be 50 Years from Today: 60 Of the World's Greatest Minds Share Their Visions of the Next Half-Century* by Mike Wallace; and *Couples Who Pray: The Most Intimate Act Between A Man and a Woman* by Squire Rushnell and Louise DuArt.

Recent children's titles include *Believing in Narnia: A Kids Guide to Unlocking the Secret Symbols of Faith in C.S. Lewis' The Chronicles of Narnia* by Natalie Nichols Gillespie; *The Purple Ponies: Gigi, God's Little Princess* by Sheila Walsh; *The Really Woolly Holy Bible; and God's Great Big Love For Me* by Max Lucado, illustrated by Laura Logan.

David Moberg, Group Publisher—Practical living, spiritual growth and Christian thought; dmoberg@thomasnelson.com

Joey Paul, Publisher—Practical living; jpaul@thomasnelson.com

Matt Baugher, Publisher—Spiritual growth and Christian thought; mbaugher@thomasnelson.com

Debbie Wickwire, Acquisitions Editor—Practical living; dwickwire@thomasnelson.com

John Mason, Vice President of Acquisitions—Spiritual growth and Christian thought; jmason@thomasnelson.com

Allen Arnold, Publisher—Fiction; aarnold@thomasnelson.com

Ami McConnell, Senior Acquisitions Editor—Fiction; amcconnell@thomasnelson.com

Amanda Bostic, Associate Acquisitions Editor—Fiction; abostic@thomasnelson.com

Wayne Hastings, Group Publisher—Bible reference and curriculum; whastings@thomasnelson.com

Karen Artl, Sr. Acquisitions Editor—Bible reference and curriculum; kartl@thomasnelson.com

Bob Sanford, Publisher—Bible Study; bsanford@thomasnelson.com

Frank Couch, Publisher—Curriculum and translation development; fcouch@thomasnelson.com

Todd Shuttleworth, Group Publisher—Specialty and global publishing; tshuttleworth@thomasnelson.com

Larry Downs, Publisher—Spanish; ldowns@thomasnelson.com

Laura Minchew, Publisher—Children's Books and Education; lminchew@thomasnelson.com

Dan Lynch, Publisher—Family Entertainment; dlynch@thomasnelson.com

Mark Gilroy, Publisher—Gift Books; mgilroy@thomasnelson.com

David Dunham, Group Publisher—General interest and lifestyle, business, and culture; ddunham@thomasnelson.com

Joel Miller, Publisher—Business and culture; joel.miller@thomasnelson.com

Pamela Clements, Publisher—General interest and lifestyle; pclements@thomasnelson.com

Geoff Stone, Editor-in-Chief—General interest and lifestyle; gstone@thomasnelson.com

Victor Oliver, Senior Acquisitions Editor—General interest and lifestyle, business and culture; voliver@thomasnelson.com

NEW HORIZON PRESS

SMALL HORIZONS

Mailing address:

P.O. Box 669, Far Hills, NJ 07931

908-604-6311 / 800-533-7978 fax: 908-604-6330

P.O. Box 669, Far Hills, NJ 07931

www.newhorizonpressbooks.com   e-mail: nhp@newhorizonpressbooks.com

New Horizon Press (established 1982) publishes 12–14 books a year examining the everyday hero among us, and social concerns. The company focuses on true crime, battles for justice, current events with a journalistic stance as well as psychological and social problems, women's and men's issues, and parenting advice written by experts with credentials in their fields. The house develops three primary lines of titles: hardcover, trade paper and children's books.

Introduced in 1992, Small Horizons, an illustrated children's Let's Talk series teaches crisis, coping, tolerance and service skills. Expanding the scope and success of NHP's books are targeted promotions and publicity via local and national print, TV shows and strong subsidiary rights.

Titles include *Permanent Adolescence: Why Boys Don't Grow Up* by Joe Carmichael; *Courageous Journey: Walking the Lost Boys Path from the Sudan to America* by Barbara Youree, Ayuel Leek, and Beny Ngor; *Catch My Mother's Killer: A Brutal Sex Slayer, A Loving Daughter's Plea* by Paula Mints; *Overcoming Your Parents' Divorce: 5 Steps to a Happy Relationship* by Elisabeth Joy LaMotte; and *So Why Have You Never Been Married? 10 Insights Into Why He Hasn't Wed* by Carl Weisman.

Small Horizons titles include *The Boy Who Sat by the Window* by Chris Loftis, illustrated by Catharine Gallagher; *The Empty Place: A Child's Guide Through Grief* by Dr. Roberta Temes, illustrated by Kim Carlisle; *I Am So Angry, I Could Scream* by Laura Fox, M.A., illustrated by Chris Sabatino; and *I Don't Want to Go to School: Helping Children Cope with Separation Anxiety* by Nancy J. Pando, L.I.S.C., illustrated by Kathy Voerg.

See the Web site for submission guidelines. Query letters and SASEs should be directed to Ms. P. Patty. To send an e-mail inquiry, put "Attn: Ms. P. Patty" in the subject line and send to nhp@newhorizonpressbooks.com.

NEW LEAF PUBLISHING GROUP

3142 Highway 103 North, Green Forest, AR 72638

Mailing address:

P.O. Box 726, Green Forest, AR 72638

870-438-5288   fax: 870-438-5120

www.newleafpublishinggroup.com   e-mail: nlp@newleafpress.com

New Leaf Publishing (established 1975) is a non-denominational Christian publishing house located in Arkansas. Subjects covered include Christian living, prophecy and eschatology, theology, applied Christianity, Bible study, family/home/marriage, friendship, love, education, evangelism, devotional works and humor.

In 1996, New Leaf Press bought Master Books, the only publishing house in the world that publishes creation-based material exclusively, including evolution-free homeschool products. In 2003, a third imprint, Balfour Books, was launched to publish books on the importance of Israel and the Middle East, as well their relevance to America.

Recent titles include *Darwin's Plantation: Evolution's Racist Roots* by Ken Ham; *Evolution: The Grand Experiment* by Dr. Carl Werner, photographs by Debbie Werner; *Common Bond: Real Stories of Struggles and Successes Inspired by the Album* by Todd Braschler and Jill Laffoon; and *An Uninvited Guest: On Woman's Journey from Cancer to Hope* by Jeana Floyd.

Recent titles from Master Books include *The New Answers Book: Volume II* by Ken Ham; *The Cave Book (Wonders of Creation)* by Emil Silverstru; *Flood By Design (Design Series)* by Mike Oard; *Your Guide to the Grand Canyon* by Tom Vail et al.; *Dinosaur Fun with Letters* by Bryan Miller; and *The Answer Book for Kids: 25 Questions on Dinosaurs and the Flood of Noah* by Cindy Malott.

Recent titles from Balfour include *Nations United: How the United Nations Undermines Israel and the West* by Alex Grobman; *The Case for Democracy: The Power of Freedom to Overcome Tyranny and Terror* by Natan Sharansky, Ron Dermer, and Anatoly Shchatansky; *God's Covenant With Israel* by Bunyamin Elon; and *Dateline Jerusalem* by Zola Levitt.

See the Web site or write the house to request a proposal guideline document. Send proposal with SASE to:

Tim Dudley, President and Publisher

NEWMARKET PRESS

A Division of Newmarket Publishing and Communications Company

18 East 48th Street, New York, NY 10017

212-832-3575   fax: 212-832-3629

www.newmarketpress.com   e-mail: mailbox@newmarketpress.com

Newmarket Publishing and Communications Company, and its publishing arm Newmarket Press, were founded in 1981 by President and Publisher Esther Margolis. Now in its 25th year with more than 300 books published, Newmarket Press is one of the few mainstream trade publishing houses in New York City under independent, entrepreneurial ownership. With W.W. Norton contracted as its distributor, Newmarket now publishes about 20-30 mainly nonfiction books a year, primarily in the areas of childcare and parenting, film and performing arts, psychology, health and nutrition, biography, history, business and personal finance, and popular self-help and reference.

Newmarket's list includes such popular and acclaimed books as the million-copy best-selling What's Happening To My Body? series by Lynda Madaras, Suze Orman's *You've Earned It, Don't Lose It*; Biographies of Condoleeze Rice and Buster Keaton; Dr. Georgia Witkin's *The Female Stress Syndrome* and *The Male Stress Syndrome*, Gene Hackman and Daniel Lenihan's first novel *Wake of the Perdido Star*, and *Shalom, Friend: The Life and Legacy Of Yitzhak Rabin*, winner of the 1996 National Jewish Book Award in nonfiction. In addition, Newmarket has created a successful niche in publishing books in film, theater and performing arts, and is especially noted for the illustrated moviebooks published on such films as *The Matrix; Dreamgirls; Planet of the Apes; Moulin Rouge; Crouching Tiger, Hidden Dragon; Magnolia; Cradle Will Rock; Sense and Sensibility; Saving Private Ryan; Dances With Wolves;* and *The Age Of Innocence*, and for its acclaimed Newmarket Shooting Script® Series, featuring books on the films *Little Miss Sunshines; Eternal Sunshine of the Spotless Mind; Traffic; Erin Brockovich; Cast Away; American Beauty; Man on the Moon; The Truman Show; The Shawshank Redemption; Dead Man Walking* and *The People vs. Larry Flynt*, among others, and the "Newmarket Words Of" Series on Gandhi, King, Tutu, Truman, and Schweitzer, and inspirational selections from the writings of the Nobel Peace Prize winners, The Words of Peace.

Recent titles include *The Words of Peace: Selections from the Speeches of the Winners of the Nobel Peace Prize* edited by Irwin Abrams; *What Every 21st Century Parent Needs to Know* by Rev. Debra W. Haffner, MPH, M. Div; *Atonement: The Shooting Script* by Ian McEwan and Christopher Hampton; *Juno: The Shooting Script* by Diablo Cody; *On Your Mark, Get Set, Grow! A "What's Happening to My Body?" Book for Younger Boys* by Lynda Madaras; and *Outliving Heart Disease: The 10 New Rules for Prevention and Treatment* by Dr. Richard A. Stein.

See the Web site for submissions suggestions. Queries, proposals, and SASEs may be directed to the editorial department.

Esther Margolis, President and Publisher

Keith Hollaman, Executive Editor

NEW PAGE BOOKS [SEE CAREER PRESS]

NEW WORLD LIBRARY

H. J. KRAMER

STARSEED PRESS

NATARAJ PUBLISHING

14 Pamaron Way, Novato, CA 94949

415-884-2100   fax: 415-884-2199

www.newworldlibrary.com

New World Library is a 31-year-old independent publisher of mind-body-spirit and related titles, located just north of San Francisco. Some of their best-sellers include *The Power of Now* by Eckhart Tolle, *The Seven Spiritual Laws of Success* by Deepak Chopra, and *Creative Visualization* by Shakti Gawain. New World Library publishes about 35–40 new titles annually, with a backlist of 250 books.

In 2000, New World Library entered into a joint venture with H.J. Kramer, the publisher of such authors as Dan Millman, Sanaya Roman, and John Robbins. New World Library assumed responsibility for many functional areas of H.J. Kramer, including sales, marketing, subsidiary rights, fulfillment, production, and accounting. H.J. Kramer has continued to focus on author relationships and acquiring and developing new books, particularly new children's titles from Holly Bea. Starseed Press focuses on titles for younger readers (ages 4–8). The Nataraj imprint primarily publishes titles by New World founder, Shakti Gawain.

New World seeks manuscripts in the following subject areas: spirituality, personal growth, women's interest, religion, sustainable business, the human-animal relationship, Native American interest, and the environment. Their works appeal to a large, general audience.

Recent titles include *The Hero with a Thousand Faces* by Joeseph Campbell; *How to Think Like a Millionaire* by Mark Fisher and Marc Allen; *Saying Goodbye to Your Angel Animals: Finding Comfort after Losing Your Pet* by Allen Anderson and Linda Anderson; *Do It Anyway: Finding Personal Meaning and Deep Happiness by Living the Paradoxical Commandments* by Kent M. Keith; *The Emotional Lives of Animals: A Leading Scientist Explores Animal Joy, Sorrow, Empathy, and Why They Matter* by Marc Bekoff and Jane Goodall.

Direct submissions with SASEs to Submissions Editor.

Georgia Hughes, Editorial Director

Munro Magruder, Associate Publisher

Jason Gardner, Senior Editor

Vanessa Brown, Acquisitions Editor

Linda Kramer, H. J. Kramer President

NOLO

950 Parker Street, Berkeley, CA 94710-2524

800-728-3555   fax: 800-645-0895

www.nolo.com   e-mail: cs@nolo.com

Nolo is one of the nation's leading providers of do-it-yourself legal solutions for consumers and small businesses. The house goal is to help people handle their own everyday legal matters—or learn enough about them to make working with a lawyer a more satisfying experience. According to Nolo, "Americans who are armed with solid legal knowledge are confident, active participants in their legal system—and slowly but inevitably, their participation makes that system more open and democratic. Nolo is proud to be part of that process."

Since 1971, Nolo has offered affordable, plain-English books, forms and software on a wide range of legal issues, including wills, estate planning, retirement, elder care, personal finance, taxes, housing, real estate, divorce and child custody. They also offer materials on human resources, employment, intellectual property, and starting and running a small business.

With a staff of lawyer-editors, the house pays attention not only to changes in the law, but to feedback from customers, lawyers, judges and court staffers. Nolo publishes legal self-help books and software for consumers, small businesses and nonprofit organizations. They specialize in helping people handle their own legal tasks—for example, write a will, file a small claims court lawsuit, start a small business or non-profit, or apply for a patent. Nolo does not publish fiction, first-person accounts, biographies or any other material that strays too far from its step-by-step approach to helping individuals, businesses and nonprofits solve specific legal problems.

Titles include *The Foreclosure Survival Guide: Keep Your House or Walk Away with Money in Your Pocket* by Stephen Elias; *Consultant and Independent Contractor Agreements* by Stephen Fishman; *Wow! I'm in Business: A Crash Course in Business Basics* by Richard Stim and Lisa Guerin; *Finance and Marriage Visas: A Couple's Guide to U.S. Immigration* by Ilona Bray; *Quick and Legal Will Book* by Denis Clifford; *Marketing Without Advertising: Easy Ways to Build a Business Your Customers Will Love and Recommend* by Michael Phillips and Salli Raspberry.

Queries and SASEs should be directed to the Acquisitions Editors.

Marcia Stewart, Acquisitions Editor

Tamara Traeder, Acquisitions Editor

W. W. NORTON & COMPANY

THE COUNTRYMAN PRESS

500 Fifth Avenue, New York, NY 10110

212-354-5500   fax 212-869-0856

www.wwnorton.com   e-mail: manuscripts@wwnorton.com

The Countryman Press:

802-457-4826   fax: 802-457-1678

P.O. Box 748, Woodstock, VT 05091

www.countrymanpress.com   e-mail: countrymanpress@wwnorton.com

Publishers of adult trade fiction, nonfiction, professional psychology, and architecture books, W.W. Norton & Company is the oldest and largest publishing house owned wholly by its employees. Norton strives to carry out the imperative of its founder to publish books not for a single season, but for the years—in fiction, nonfiction, poetry, college textbooks, cookbooks, art books and professional books. W.W. Norton & Company now publishes about 400 books annually in hardcover and paperback.

The roots of the company date back to 1923, when William Warder Norton and his wife, Mary D. Herter Norton, began publishing lectures delivered at the People's Institute, the adult education division of New York City's Cooper Union. The Nortons soon expanded their program beyond the Institute, acquiring manuscripts by celebrated academics from America and abroad.

For years, Norton has been known for its distinguished publishing programs in both the trade and the college textbook areas. Early in its history Norton entered the fields of philosophy, music, and psychology, publishing acclaimed works by Bertrand Russell, Paul Henry Lang, and Sigmund Freud (as his principal American publisher).

In the past few decades, the firm has published best-selling books by such authors as economists Paul Krugman and Joseph Stiglitz, paleontologist Stephen Jay Gould, physicist Richard Feynman, and historians Peter Gay, Jonathan Spence, Christopher Lasch, and George F. Kennan. Norton has also developed a more eclectic list, with prominent titles including *Helter Skelter* by Vincent Bugliosi and Curt Gentry; Jared Diamond's Pulitzer Prize-winning best-seller *Guns, Germs, and Steel*; Judy Rogers's *The Zuni Café Cookbook*; Patrick O'Brian's critically acclaimed naval adventures; the works of National Book Award-winning fiction author Andrea Barrett; *Liar's Poker* and *Moneyball* by Michael Lewis; Fareed Zakaria's *The Future of Freedom*; and Sebastian Junger's *The Perfect Storm*.

At the same time, the college department has strengthened its offerings with leading titles in economics, psychology, political science, and sociology. In 1985, Norton expanded its publishing program with Norton Professional Books, specializing in books on psychotherapy and, more recently, neuroscience. The Professional Books program has also moved into the fields of architecture and design.

In 1996, Norton acquired the distinguished Vermont firm The Countryman Press and added well-respected nature, history, and outdoor recreation titles to the Norton list. In 2003, Berkshire House Press joined Norton, becoming part of the Vermont operation.

Recent titles include *Bonk: The Curious Coupling of Science and Sex* by Mary Roach; *Wrack and Ruin* by Don Lee; *Earth: The Sequel, The Race to Reinvent Energy and Stop Global Warming* by Fred Krupp and Miriam Horn; and *The Post-American World* by Fareed Zakaria.

Recent titles from Norton Professional Books includes *Corrugated Iron: Building on the Frontier* by Adam Mornement and Simon Holloway; *Sourcebook of Scandinavian Furniture: Designs for the 21st Century* by Judith Gura; *Magical Moments of Change: How Psychotherapy Turns Kids Around* by Lenore Terr; and *The Mindful Brain: Reflection and Attunement in the Cultivation of Well-Being* by Daniel J. Siegel.

W.W. Norton does consider books from the following categories: juvenile or young adult, religious, occult or paranormal, genre fiction such as formula romances, sci-fi or westerns, arts and crafts, and inspirational poetry.

W.W. Norton accepts unsolicited submissions by e-mail only. To submit your proposal by e-mail, paste the text of your query letter and/or sample chapter into the body of the e-mail message. Do not send attachments. Keep your proposal under six pages. If you are submitting poetry, again, try to send fewer than six poems. All submissions should be sent to manuscripts@@wwnorton.com.

Alane Mason, Senior Editor—Cultural and intellectual history, literary fiction

Amy Cherry, Senior Editor—African American issues, contemporary biographies, social issues

Jill Bialosky, Vice President—Literary fiction and nonfiction, biographies

Robert Weil, Executive Editor—Translations, intellectual history, social sciences, German and Jewish subjects

Drake McFeely, President—Science, social sciences

Maria Guarnaschelli, Senior Editor—Science, food, fiction

THE COUNTRYMAN PRESS

As Vermont's oldest name in publishing, The Countryman Press maintains a tradition of producing books of substance and quality. The company began in Taftsville, Vermont, in 1973 in Peter and Jane Jennison's farmhouse kitchen. In 1996 the press became a division of W.W. Norton & Company, Inc. Countryman retains its own identity, however, with editorial and production offices in Woodstock, Vermont.

Countryman publishes about 50 books per year with more than 250 books in print. Subjects include travel, food, gardening, country living, nature, New England history, and crafts. The Explorer's Guide travel series has sold over half a million copies.

The Backcountry Guides imprint features where-to books on outdoor sports activities, including fishing, cycling, walking and paddling. The best-selling 50 Hikes series has sold more than one million copies.

Countryman titles include *New Orleans and Cajun Country: Great Destinations Including Natchitoches, Natchez, and Vicksburg* by Carol Gelderman; *Austin, San Antonio and the Texas Hill Country: Great Destinations: A Complete Guide* by Amy K. Brown; *EatingWell's Comfort Foods Made Healthy: The Classic Makeovers Cookbook* by Jessie Price; *Cider, Hard and Sweet: History, Traditions, and Making Your Own* by Ben Watson; and *Covered Bridges of New England* by Jeffery Blackman.

Direct query letter or proposal with SASE to:

Kermit Hummel, Editorial Director

O'REILLY MEDIA

1005 Gravenstein Highway North, Sebastapol, CA 95472

707-827-7000 / 800-998-9938   fax: 707-829-0104

www.oreilly.com

O'Reilly Media is a premier information source for leading-edge computer technologies. Smart books written for smart people—with animals sketched on the front covers—O'Reilly titles are not for dummies. However, geekdom is translated into down-to-earth text for recent titles like *Secure Programming with Static Analysis* by Brian Chess and Jacob West; *Fuzzing: Brute Force Vulnerability Discovery* by Michael Sutton, Adam Greene, and Pedram Amini; *Getting Started with Silverlight* by Shawn Wildermuth; *Rails on Windows* by Curt Hibbs and Brian Hogan; and *The Rails Way* by Obie Fernandez.

This house is vastly interested in the newest technologies, thus it's best to check the Author section of their Web site for the evolving list of what they're looking for right now; you'll find it here: oreilly.com/oreilly/author/intro.csp.

Recent titles from O'Reilly include *Flex 3 Cookbook: Code-Recipes, Tips, and Tricks for RIA Developers* by Joshua Noble and Todd Anderson; *JavaScript: The Good Parts* by Douglas Crockford; *Illustrated Guide to Home Chemistry Experiments: All Lab, No Lecture* by Robert Bruce Thompson; *Wikipedia Reader's Guide: The Missing Manual* by John Broughton; *Painting the Web* by Shelley Powers; *Essential Silverlight 2 Up-to-Date* by Christian Wenz; and *Make Projects: Small Form Factor PCs* by Duane Wessels and Matthew J. Weaver.

Send your proposal to proposals@oreilly.com with a descriptive subject line.

Mike Hendrickson, Associate Publisher

Robert Luhn, Executive Editor, Consumer Books Division

Brett Johnson, Associate Editor, Consumer Books

Simon St. Laurent, Associate Editor—Systems, programming

Brian Sawyer, Editor—Hacks

Michele Filshie, Editor

OSBORNE MEDIA [SEE MCGRAW-HILL]

INDEPENDENT U.S. PRESS

...OOK PRESS

...ISHING

...reet, New York, NY 10012

...fax: 845-679-8571

www.overlookpress.com

blog: theoverlookpress.blogspot.com

The Overlook Press (founded 1971) is an independent general interest publisher. The publishing program consists of some 100 new books per year, evenly divided between hardcovers and trade paperbacks. The list is eclectic, but areas of strength include interesting fiction, history, biography, drama, and design.

The house was launched by owner Peter Mayer as a home for distinguished books that had been "overlooked" by larger houses. The publishing formula proved reliable, and now Overlook has nearly 1,000 titles in print. Their fiction includes novels by solidly commercial authors including espionage novelist Robert Littell (*The Company*, 90,000 sold) and international phenomenon Penny Vincenzi, whose Edwardian era family saga *No Angel* is widely acclaimed as stunning entertainment. More success came in April 2004 with *Dragon's Eye* by Andy Oakes, a thriller set in modern Shanghai. In a more literary vein, there is *Hash* by top Swedish novelist Torgny Lindgren and Michele Slung's anthology of garden writing, *The Garden of Reading*.

History is the mainstay of the house's nonfiction list and notable books include Paul Cartledge's *The Spartans*, basis of a PBS documentary on this civilization, and Adrienne Mayor's *Greek Fire, Poison Arrows and Scorpion Bombs: Biochemical Warfare in the Ancient World*.

In 2002 Overlook acquired Ardis, the premier publisher of Russian literature in English. They have given that program new presence with handsome new paperback editions of titles long unavailable. More recently Overlook acquired the 106-year-old U.K. publisher Duckworth.

Recent titles from Overlook include *Enlightenment* by Maureen Freely; *The Darkroom of Damocles* by Willem Frederick Hermans; *The Lolita Effect* by M. Gigi Durham; *By Hook or By Crook* by David Crystal; *An Appeal to Reason* by Nigel Lawson; *The Collected Plays of Edward Albee 1966-1977* by Edwards Albee; *R.F.K. Must Die* by Robert Blair Kaiser; *Genesis Machines* by Martyn Amos; *The Week-End Book: A Sociable Anthology*; *David and Winston* by Robert Llyod George; *How to Fish* by Chris Yates; and *The 4th of July* by Peter de Bolla.

Overlook Press titles distributed to the trade by Penguin Putnam.

The house recommends working with an agent. However, queries and SASEs may be directed to the editors.

Peter Mayer, President and Publisher

David Shoemaker, Senior Editor

Aaron Schlechter, Editor

Juliet Grames, Editor

PALADIN PRESS

Gunbarrel Tech Center

7077 Winchester Circle, Boulder, CO 80301

303-443-7250   fax: 303-442-8741

www.paladin-press.com   e-mail: editorial@paladin-press.com

Controversial even before a 1999 multimillion dollar settlement related to the use of a murder how-to manual *Hit Man*—no longer available—Paladin Press publishes books and videotapes on personal and financial freedom, survival and preparedness, firearms and shooting, martial arts and self-defense, military and police tactics, knives and knife fighting, and more.

The company came into existence in September 1970 when Peder Lund joined Robert K. Brown as a partner in a book publishing venture previously known as Panther Publications. As former military men and adventurers, Lund and Brown were convinced there was a market for books on specialized military and action/adventure topics. Both men also firmly believed that the First Amendment guaranteed Americans the right to read about whatever subjects they desired, and this became the cornerstone of Paladin's publishing philosophy.

Recent titles include *Congo Warriors* by Mike Hoare; *Critter Control* by Larry Grupp; *Gang Investigator's Handbook: A Law-Enforcement Guide to Identifying and Combating Violent Street Gangs* by Matthew David O'Deane, PhD; *History of Sniping and Sharpshooting* by Maj. John L. Plaster, USAR; *How to Become a Master Handgunner: The Mechanics of X-Count Shooting* by Charles Stephens; *Jim Cirillo's Tales of the Stakeout Squad* by Paul Kirchner; *Last Safari* by Basi Maartens.

Submit a proposal and SASE to the Editorial Department.

Donna Duvall, Editor Director

Cathy Wirtes, Senior Editor

PATHFINDER PRESS

4794 Clark Howell Highway, Suite B-5, College Park, GA 30349

Mailing address:

P.O. Box 162767, Atlanta, GA 30321-2767

404-669-0600   fax: 707-667-1141

www.pathfinderpress.com   e-mail: pathfinder@pathfinderpress.com

Since 1940, Pathfinder Press has published books, booklets, pamphlets, posters, and postcards focusing on issues affecting working people worldwide. The house produces titles in English, Spanish, French, Swedish, Farsi, Greek, Icelandic, and Russian. Pathfinder also distributes the journal New International.

Subjects include black and African studies; women's rights; the Cuban revolution in world politics; revolutionaries and working-class fighters; fascism, big business, and the labor movement; Russia, Eastern Europe, and the Balkans; scientific views of politics and economics; trade unions: past present, and future; U.S. history and politics; Latin America and the Caribbean; the Middle East and China; and art, culture, and politics. Pathfinder is usually associated with schools of thought such as populism, internationalism, utopianism, socialism, and communism.

The Pathfinder mural that once adorned the company's original editorial digs in Manhattan's far West Village featured a depiction of a gargantuan printing press in action, as well as portraits of revolutionary leaders whose writings and speeches were published by Pathfinder; this community cultural icon represented the work of more than 80 artists from 20 countries.

Pathfinder titles include *Is Socialist Revolution in the U.S. Possible?* by Mary-Alice Water, Olympia Newton, and Norton Sandler; *Our History is Still Being Written: The Story of Three Chinese-Cuban Generals in the Cuban Revolution* by Armando Choy, Gustavo Chui, Moises Sio Wong, and Mary-Alice Waters; *Cuba and the Coming American Revolution* by Jack Barnes; and *Teamster Power* by Farrell Dobbs.

Direct queries and SASEs to:

Mary-Alice Waters, President

Elizabeth Stone, Managing Editor

PAULIST PRESS

997 Macarthur Boulevard, Mahwah, NJ 07430-9990

201-825-7300 / 800-218-1903   fax: 800-836-3161

Founded in 1866 by the Paulist Fathers as the Catholic Publication Society, Paulist Press publishes hardcover and trade originals for general readers, and distinguished scholarly books, in the areas of religion, spirituality, and theology. Paulist Press publishes ecumenical theology, Roman Catholic studies and books on scripture, liturgy, spirituality, church history, and philosophy as well as works on faith and culture. Their list is oriented toward adult-level nonfiction, although they do offer a growing selection of children's stories and activity books. Children's categories include picture books, prayer books, chapter books, young adult biographies, Catholic guidebooks, and gift books.

Titles from Paulist Press include *Finding the Monk Within: Great Monastic Values for Today* by Edward C. Sellner; *Doing Time: Finding Hope and San Quentin* by Dennis J. Burke; *Our Daily Bread: Glimpsing the Eurachrist through the Centuries* by Ralph Wright, OS; *The Interpretation of Scripture: In Defense of the Historical-Critical Method* by Joeseph A. Fitzmyer, SJ; and *Seeking God's Face: Faith in an Age of Perplexity* by Notto R. Thelle.

Children's titles include *Beyond the Clouds* by David R. Collins; *Prove It, God!* by Amy Wellborn; *Francis of Assisi: Coloring and Activity Fun for Children*; *My First Book of Prayers* by Daniel J. Porter and Rev. Victor Hoagland, CP; *Angel! Angel!* by Cherie Pless Dittmer; *Write On!* by Patricia L. Fry; *Balloons by Trevor* by Anne Good Cave; and *I Know Things Now* by Carl Koch.

Query letters and SASEs should be directed to:

Rev. Lawrence Boadt, C.S.P., Publisher and President

Susan O'Keefe, Children's Book Editor

PEACHPIT PRESS

ADOBE PRESS

APPLE CERTIFIED

LYNDA.COM

NEW RIDERS

NEW RIDERS GAMES

1249 Eighth Street, Berkeley, CA 94710

510-524-2178

www.peachpit.com   e-mail: proposals@peachpit.com

Peachpit Press has been publishing top-notch books on the latest in graphic design, desktop publishing, multimedia, Web publishing, and general computing since 1986.

Their titles feature step-by-step explanations, timesaving techniques, savvy insider tips, and expert advice for computer users of all sorts. Peachpit is a part of Pearson Education, the world's largest integrated educational publisher.

Imprints include Peachpit Press, New Riders Press, New Riders Games, Adobe Press, Apple Certified, Lynda.com, and other imprints and series for creative computer users.

Recent titles from Peachpit include *Breaking Out of the Web Browser with Adobe AIR, Rough Cuts* by Michael Labriola and Jeff Tapper; *ActionScript 3.0: Visual Quickstart Guide* by Derrick Ypenburg; *Digital Foundations: A Basic Course in Media Design* by Michael Mandiberg and Xtine Burrough; *Creating a Web Video in Silverlight: Visual QuickProject Guide* by Bruce Hyslop; *Now You Know Palm Centro* by Patrick Amers; and *Photoshop CS3: Visual QuickPro Guide* by Elaine Weinmann and Peter Lourekas.

Adobe Press is the official source of training materials for Adobe software and inspiration for digital communicators. Titles from Adobe Press include *Adobe Flash ActionScript 3 Classroom in a Book* by the Adobe Creative Team; *The ActionScript 3.0 Migration Guide: Making the Move from ActionScript 2* by Kris Hadlock; *Adobe Flex 3: Training from the Source* by Jeff Tapper, Michael Labriola, Matthew Boles, and James Talbot; and *Adobe ColdFusion 8 Web Application Construction Kit* by Ben Forta et al; and *Adobe Photoshop CS3 How-Tos: 100 Essential Techniques* by Chris Orwig.

Books from Apple Certified come with Apple's seal of approval and contain complete courses designed to help users master Mac apps. New titles include *Apple Training Series: Mac OS X Server Essentials, 2nd Edition* by Schoun Regan and David Pugh; *Apple Pro Training Series: Color* by Michael Wohl and David Gross; *Logic Pro 8: Beyond the Basics*; and *Apple Pro Training Series: Final Cut Express 4* by Diana Weynand.

Lynda.com is an award-wining education provider of Hands-On Training instructional books, video training on CD and DVD, self-paced online learning, and events for creative designers, developers, instructors, students, hobbyists, and anyone who wants to learn. Titles from Lynda include *Photoshop CS3 for Designers* by Ted LoCascio; *Photoshop CS3 Portrait Retouching Essentials* by Chris Orwig; *Photoshop CS3: Sharpening Images* by Deke McClelland; *Logic Pro 8 Essential Training* by Joe Godfrey; *QuickBooks Pro 2008 Essential Training* by Suzanne Robertson; and *Keynote '08 Essential Training* by David Rivers.

New Riders produces beautiful instruction books that provide a forum for the leading voices in creative and information technologies. New Riders includes the Voices That Matter series and the AIGA Design Press. New titles include *The Open Brand: When Push Comes to Pull in a Web-Made World* by Kelly Mooney and Nita Rollins; *Building Findable Websites: Web Standards, SEO, and Beyond* by Aarron Walter; *The Moment It Clicks: Photography Secrets From One of the World's Top Shooters* by Joe McNally; and *I, Avatar: The Culture and Consequences of Having a Second Life* by Mark Stephen Meadows.

New Riders Games takes game books where they've never gone before. As the game resource, NRG touches every category: programming, design, art, and celebrity savvy. Titles include *Level Design for Games: Creating Compelling Game Experiences* by Phil Co; *3ds max 7 Fundamentals* by Ted Boardman; *Game Character Development with Maya* by Anthony Ward; *Audio for Games: Planning, Process, and Production* by Alexander Brandon; *Chris Crawford on Interactive Storytelling* by Chris Crawford; and *Creating the Art of the Game* by Matthew Omernick.

Peachpit is always looking for new authors and innovative book ideas. Mail your completed proposal to "Book Proposals" or e-mail it to proposals@peachpit.com.

Marjorie Baer, Executive Editor

Keasley Jones, Associate Publisher

PEACHTREE PUBLISHERS

1700 Chattahoochee Avenue, Atlanta, GA 30318

404-876-8761 / 800-241-0113   fax: 404-875-2578 / 800-875-8909

www.peachtree-online.com   e-mail: hello@peachtree-online.com

Peachtree is an award-winning trade publisher featuring children's picture books and chapter books for the very young child through young adult. Other categories include health and parenting, and the best of the South, including fiction, high quality gift, and regional guides. They publish about 20 books per year.

Recent titles include *The Wheat Doll* by Alison Randall and Bill Farnsworth; *Trick or Treat on Monster Street* by Danny Schnitzlein and Matt Faulkner; *The Story Blanket* by Ferida Wolff, Harriet May Savitz, and Elena Odriozola; *Monsoon Afternoon* by Kashmira Sheth and Yoshiko Jaeggi; *Kiss! Kiss! Yuck! Yuck!* by Kyle Mewburn, Ali Teo, and John O'Reilly; *Jack's 100th Day of School* by Lester L. Laminack and Judy Love, and *First Dog Fala* by Elizabeth Van Steenwyk and Michael Montgomery.

Direct submissions and SASEs to:

Margaret Quinlin, Publisher

Kathy Landwehr, Associate Publisher

PELICAN PUBLISHING COMPANY

1000 Burmaster Street, Gretna, LA 70053-2246

504-368-1175 / 800-843-1724   fax: 504-368-1195

www.epelican.com   e-mail: editorial@pelicanpub.com

Called "innovative" by the *New York Times*, Pelican Publishing is the largest independent trade book publisher in the South. Once the publisher of William Faulkner, Pelican is now owned by the Calhouns, a family of self-professed bibliophiles.

The house publishes an average of 70 titles a year and has about 1,500 currently in print. Specialties are art/architecture books, cooking/cookbooks, motivational, travel guides, history (especially Louisiana/regional), nonfiction, children's books (illustrated and otherwise), social commentary, folklore, and textbooks. For fiction, only historical works are considered for publication.

Recent titles include *Freedom of Religion, The First Amendment, and the Supreme Court: How the Court Flunked History* by Barry Adamson; *Best Editorial Cartoons of the Year 2008* edited by Charles Brooks; *Frank Davis Makes Good Groceries! A New Orleans Cookbook* by Frank Davis; *Savannah Classic Desserts* by Janice Shay, photography by Whitlaw Llewellyn; and *200 Texan Outlaws and Lawmen 1835-1935* by Laurence J. Yadon.

The editors seek writers on the cutting edge of ideas.

To submit, send a query letter with SASE to the editors. Short children's manuscripts may be sent in their entirety at the initial contact. Direct queries and SASEs to:

Milburn Calhoun, Publisher

Nina Kooij, Editor-in-Chief

PERMANENT PRESS

SECOND CHANCE PRESS

4170 Noyac Road, Sag Harbor, NY 11963

631-725-1101

www.thepermanentpress.com   e-mail: info@thepermanentpress.com

The Permanent Press (founded 1978 by Martin and Judith Shepard) committed itself to publishing works of social and literary merit and has, over the years, gained a reputation as one of the finest small independent presses in America. The Permanent Press is a publisher of literary fiction—and occasionally nonfiction. They publish books that are artfully written, about 12 per year.

The imprint Second Chance Press reprints books of merit that had been out-of-print for at least 20 years. The Second Chance mission is to find literary fiction gems worth republishing; they have published Berry Fleming, Halldor Laxness, Richard Lortz, William Herrick, and Joseph Stanley Pennell.

Unlike most publishers, The Permanent Press keeps (nearly all) their titles in print indefinitely.

Recent titles include *The Night Battles* by M. F. Bloxam; *Baby Jesus Pawnshop* by Lucia Orth; *Three Minutes on Love* by Roccie Hill; *Revelation of Fire* by Alla Avilova; *Walking the Dog* by Charles Davis; *In the Name of Sarah Pogford* by Jon Edward Jordan; *Grandma Gets Laid* by Ken Shakin; *Head Wounds* by Chris Knopf; *Serpent in the Garden of Dreams* by Robin Messing; *To Enter Jerusalem* by Craig Eisendrath; *A Richer Dust* by Amy Boaz, and *Planet of the Dates* by Paul McComas.

Send the first 20 pages or so with query letter and SASE. Direct submissions to:

Judith Shepard, Publisher

PERSEA BOOKS

853 Broadway, Suite 604, New York, NY 10003

fax: 212-260-1902

www.perseabooks.com

Founded in 1975 by Karen and Michael Braziller, Persea is a small literary press of books for adults and young adults. Their titles cover a wide range of themes, styles, and genres. They have published poetry, fiction, essays, memoir, biography, titles of Jewish and Middle Eastern interest, women's studies, American Indian folklore, and revived classics, as well as a notable selection of works in translation.

They have been expanding their Young Adult list, with intelligent books by authors such as Anne Mazer, Gary Soto, and Marie Raphael. These works complement their acclaimed series of literary anthologies for youths, which include *America Street: A Multicultural Anthology of Stories, Imagining America: Stories from the Promised Land, A Walk in My World: International Short Stories About Youth, Starting With "I": Personal Essays by Teenagers*, and many more.

Recent Persea titles include *A Boy From Ireland* by Marie Raphael; *The Logan Topographies* by Alena Hairston; *The Music Lover's Poetry Anthology* edited by Helen Handley Houghton and Maureen McCarthy Draper; *My American Kundiman* by Patrick Rosal; *Outside Rules: Short Stories About Non-Conformist Youth* edited by Claire Robson; and *Things are Disappearing Here* by Kate Northrop.

Direct queries and SASEs to the attention of the Fiction Editor (or nonfiction or poetry, as appropriate).

Michael Braziller, Publisher

Karen Braziller, Editorial Director

PERSEUS

BASIC BOOKS

BASIC CIVITAS

VANGUARD PRESS

387 Park Avenue South, New York, NY 10016

212-340-8100

www.basicbooks.com   e-mail: perseus-promos@perseusbooks.com

www.basiccivitasbooks.com

www.vanguardpressbooks.com

AVALON TRAVEL PUBLISHING

SEAL PRESS

1700 4th Street, Berkeley, CA 94710

510-528-1444

www.travelmatters.com   e-mail: acquisitions@avalonpub.com

www.sealpress.com

DA CAPO

Eleven Cambridge Center, Cambridge, MA 02142

617-252-5200

www.dacapopress.com

NATION BOOKS

PUBLICAFFAIRS

250 West 57th Street, Suite 1321, New York, NY 10107

212-397-6666   fax: 212-397-4277

www.nationbooks.com

www.publicaffairsbooks.com   e-mail: publicaffairs@perseusbooks.com

RUNNING PRESS

125 South 22 Street, Philadelphia, PA 19103

215-567-5080

www.perseusbooksgroup.com/runningpress   e-mail: perseus-promos@perseus-books.com

WESTVIEW PRESS

2465 Central Avenue, Boulder, CO 80301

303-444-3541   fax: 720-406-7336

www.westviewpress.com

The Perseus Books Group was founded with the belief that insightful books of quality are both necessary and desirable, that an innovative model is possible, that authors, readers, booksellers—and books—matter. That innovative model includes Perseus' mission to empower independent publishers to reach their potential whether those publishers are owned by Perseus Books, joint venture partnerships, or clients for whom they provide services. Perseus very recently acquired both distributor Consortium and publisher Avalon Publishing Group, and in doing so has greatly expanded its depth and breadth in the publishing world.

In the process of combining Avalon Publishing Group with Perseus operations, several imprints were closed or sold; these include Counterpoint, Shoemaker & Hoard, Thunder's Mouth Press, and Carrol & Graf.

Each of the remaining Perseus and former Avalon imprints is editorially independent and individually focused, with offices from California to Massachusetts. As a whole, Perseus' publishing spans the breakthroughs in science to the great public issues, from military history to modern maternity, from African American scholars to novelists just breaking out, from choosing a great wine or a great president, from gift giving to required reading.

David Steinberger, President, Perseus Books Group

BASIC BOOKS

Since its founding in 1952, Basic Books has helped shape public debate by publishing award-winning books in psychology, science, politics, sociology, current affairs, and history. Basic seeks to publish serious nonfiction by leading intellectuals, scholars, and journalists; to create books that change the way people think, as exemplified by recent best-sellers, *Second Chance* by Zbigniew Brzezinski and *I Am a Strange Look* by Douglas Hofstadter.

Recent titles include *Gross National Happiness* by Arthur C. Brooks; *Who's Your City? How the Creative Economy is Making Where to Live the Most Important Decision of Your Life* by Richard Florida; *Lifting Depression: A Neuroscientist's Hands-On Approach to Activating Your Brain's Healing Power* by Kelly Lambert; *Reinventing the Sacred: A New View of Science, Reason, and Religion* by Stuart Kauffman; *Yeltsin: A Life* by Timothy J. Colton; *A History of Iran: Empire of the Mind* by Michael Axworthy; and *If By Sea: The Forging of the American Navy* by Geroge Daughan.

Basic does not accept unsolicited proposals or manuscripts. Direct queries with SASEs to:

John Sherer, Publisher

Lara Heimert, Executive Editor—Religion, history

William Frucht, Senior Editor—Science, economics, technology, and social change

Jo Ann Miller, Editor—Psychology, law, women's studies, current affairs

BASIC CIVITAS

Basic Civitas Books is devoted to publishing the best new work in African and African American studies. With authors that include Michael Eric Dyson, Cornel West, Stanley Crouch, Vernon Jordan, and Henry Louis Gates, Jr., Basic Civitas has greatly advanced the influence and presence of African American works in the marketplace.

Titles include *Racial Paranoia: The Unintended Consequences of Political Correctness* by John. L. Jackson, Jr.; *Party Crashing: How the Hip-Hop Generation Declared Political Independence* by Keli Goff; *April 4th, 1968: Martin Luther King Jr.'s Death and How It Changed America* by Michael Eric Dyson; *Introducing Bert Williams: Burnt Cork, Broadway, and the Story of America's First Black Star* by Camille Forbes; *An Unbroken Agony: Haiti, from Revolution to the Kidnapping of a President* by Randall Robinson; *Debating Race* by Michael Eric Dyson; and *Being Sugar Ray: Sugar Ray Robinson, America's Greatest Boxer and First Celebrity Athlete* by Kenneth Shropshire.

Basic Civitas does not accept unsolicited proposals or manuscripts. Direct queries with SASEs to:

John Sherer, Publisher

Chris Greenberg, Associate Editor

VANGUARD PRESS

When Perseus acquired CDS Distribution in 2005, part of that acquisition was a small publishing program that CDS had started called CDS Books. Based in New York and now called Vanguard Press, this publisher provides its authors innovative financial and creative partnerships. The Vanguard mission is to have a selective publishing list, and to look at every book as an event. The editors strive to craft substantial, focused, and energetic marketing campaigns that will reach the widest possible audience. This publisher reportedly offers substantial marketing budgets and higher than standard royalties, but does not offer advances.

In just a short time, Vanguard has built a striking list including *Scavenger* by *New York Times* bestselling author David Morrell, *Quantico* by Hugo and Nebula Award-winning author Greg Bear and the soon-to-be-published 30th anniversary edition of *Roots* by Alex Haley, winner of the Pulitzer Prize.

New titles from Vanguard Press include *At First Sight: A Novel of Obsession* by Stephen J. Cannell; *The Abduction Mass Market* by Mark Gimenez; *The Dark of Day* by Barbara Parker; *To the Death* by Patrick Robinson; *Domestic Affairs* by Eileen Goudge; and *The Prosecution of George W. Bush for Murder* by Vincent Bugliosi.

Vanguard Press does not accept unsolicited manuscripts or book proposals. Direct queries with SASEs to:

Roger Cooper, Vice President, Publisher

AVALON TRAVEL PUBLISHING

Avalon Travel Publishing is the largest independent travel publisher based in the U.S. Avalon Travel Publishing guides feature a combination of practicality and spirit, offering a unique traveler-to-traveler perspective perfect for an afternoon hike, around-the-world journey, or anything in between. America's best-selling travel writer, Rick Steves, is published by Avalon with 29 annually updated guidebooks to Europe selling over 800,000 copies every year. *Rick Steves' Best of Europe 2007* and *Rick Steves' European Christmas* are recent successes. The celebrated Moon Handbooks and Moon Metro series, including titles like *Moon Handbooks Rhode Island* and *Moon Metro Las Angeles*, are known for travel guidance that is encyclopedic, meticulously detailed, and conveniently aimed at those with a standard-sized travel budget. The Foghorn Outdoors series is aimed at campers, hikers, boaters, anglers, bikers, and golfers. These guides, like *Foghorn Outdoors 250 Great Hikes in California's National Parks* by Ann Marie Brown and *Foghorn Outdoors Montana, Wyoming, & Idaho Camping* by Judy Kinnaman, cover local outdoor recreation in the U.S. Other Avalon Travel series are The Dog Lover's Companion, Moon Living Abroad, and Road Trip USA.

Recent titles include *Moon San Diego* by Ericka Chickowski; *Rick Steves' Istanbul* by Lale Surmen Aran and Tankut Aran; *Queens in the Kingdom* by Jeffrey Epstein and Eddie Shapiro; *Road Trip USA* by Jamie Jensen; *The Practical Nomad* by Edward Hasbrouck; and *The Dog Lover's Companion to New England* by JoAnna Downey and Christian J. Lau.

Send proposal by e-mail with attachment or by regular mail with SASE to the Acquisitions Editor, acquisitions@avalonpub.com.

Bill Newlin, Publisher, Avalon Travel

Sabrina Young, Editor

SEAL PRESS

Press was founded in 1976 to provide a forum for women writers and feminist issues. Since then, Seal has published groundbreaking books that represent the diverse voices and interests of women—their lives, literature, and concerns. Seal's list includes books on women's health, parenting, outdoor adventure and travel, popular culture, gender and women's studies, and current affairs.

Seal publishes books by and for women, with an emphasis on original, lively, radical, empowering, and culturally diverse nonfiction that addresses contemporary issues from a women's perspective.

Recent Seal titles include *Bento Box in the Heartland: My Japanese Girlhood in Whitebread America* by Linda Furiya; *He's a Stud, She's a Slut, and 49 Other Double Standards Every Woman Should Know* by Jessica Valenti; *Half-Assed: A Weight-Loss Memoir* by Jeannette Fulda; *Sex and Bacon: Why I Love Things That Are Very, Very Bad for Me* by Sarah Katherine Lewis; *Choosing You: Deciding to Have a Baby on My Own* by Alexandra Soiseth; *The Boss of You: Everything a Woman Needs to Know to Start, Run, and Maintain Her Own Business* by Emira Mears and Lauren Bacon; and *Transgender History* by Susan Stryker.

Send proposal with SASE to the Acquisitions Editor.

Krista Lyons-Gould, Publisher

Jill Rothenberg, Senior Editor

Brooke Warner, Acquisitions Editor

DA CAPO PRESS

Da Capo is an Italian musical term meaning from the beginning and Da Capo Press was once known primarily as a publisher of music and culture titles. Da Capo is an imprint of Perseus, where a reorganization in 2004 expanded Da Capo when it absorbed the Perseus health, parenting, and reference/how-to program. This means titles such as *Third Coast: OutKast, Timbaland and the Rise of Dirty South Hip Hop*, by Roni Sarig, and *Muscle Your Way Through Menopause*, by Judith Sherman-Wolin, all find a home at Da Capo.

With editorial offices in both New York and Massachusetts, Da Capo Press publishes hardcover and paperback editions in American and world history, biography, music, film, art, photography, sports, humor, and popular culture.

A Da Capo imprint launched in 2004, Lifelong Books, consolidated Da Capo titles on pregnancy, parenting, health, fitness, and relationships. New titles from Lifelong include the Staying Sane series edited by Pam Brodowsky and Evelyn Fazio, Mari Winsor's *Pilates* bestsellers, and Dr. Mike Riera's *Field Guide to the American Teenager*. The Marlowe & Company brand from Da Capo also focuses on health and wellness titles.

Da Capo best-sellers include H. G. Bissinger's *Friday Night Lights*, Alex Kershaw's *The Bedford Boys: One American Town's Ultimate D-Day Sacrifice*, Toby Young's *How to Lose Friends and Alienate People*, Pier Paul Read's *The Templars*, Michael Flocker's *The Metrosexual Guide to Style*, and *Kind of Blue: The Making of the Miles Davis Masterpiece* by Ashley Kahn.

Most recent Da Capo titles include *Escape from the Deep* by Alex Kershaw; *Baseball Field Guide: An In-Depth Illustrated Guide to the Complete Rules of Baseball* by Paul Hamburger and Dan Formosa; *The Terra Cotta Army: China's First Emperor and the Birth of a Nation* by John Man; *Man Killed by Pheasant: And Other Kinships* by John Price; *If I'd Known Then: Women In Their 20's and 30's Write Letters to Their Younger Selves* by Ellyn Spragins; and *Too Soon Old, Too Late Smart: Thirty True Things You Need to Know Now* by Gordon Livingston.

Da Capo Press does not accept unsolicited manuscripts or proposals.

Ben Schafer, Editor (NY)

Robert Pigeon, Senior Editor (Philadelphia)

Matthew Lore, Vice President and Executive Editor, Lifelong (NY)

Katie McHugh, Senior Editor, Lifelong (NY)

Renee Sedliar, Senior Editor, Lifelong (Emeryville)

Wendy Holt Francis, Senior Editor, Lifelong (NY)

NATION BOOKS

Nation Books, a co-publishing venture with The Nation Institute, publishes works from a progressive perspective.

Recent titles include *Blackwater: The Rise of the World's Most Powerful Mercenary Army* by Jeremy Scahill; *Lords of the Land: The War for Israel's Settlements in the Occupied Territories, 1967-2007* by Idith Zertal, PhD and Ekiva Eldar; *I See Black People: The Rise and Fall of African American-Owned Television and Radio* by Kristal Brent Zook; *How to Rule the World: The Coming Battle Over the Global Economy* by Mark Engler; *Eight O'Clock Ferry to the Windward Side: Seeking Justice in Guantanamo Bay* by Clive Stafford Smith; *Sovereign Bones: New Native American Writing* by Eric Gansworth; and *Antiwar Soldier: How to Dissent Within the Ranks of the Military* by Jonathan W. Hutto.

No unsolicited manuscripts or proposals. Direct queries with SASEs to:

Carl Bromley, Editorial Director

Ruth Baldwin, Associate Editor

PUBLICAFFAIRS

PublicAffairs is one of the nation's primary providers of good books about things that matter. The house specializes in current events, recent history, and other pressing issues affecting contemporary society. PublicAffairs publishes original nonfiction works by field experts from journalists to politicians, from political dissidents to leaders in the arts.

PublicAffairs specializes in journalism, history, biography, and memoir. Recent titles include *Welcome to Shirley: A Memoir from an Atomic Town* by Kelly McMasters; *The New Paradigm for Financial Markets: The Credit Crisis of 2008 and What It Means* by George Soros; *The Trillion Dollar Meltdown: Easy Money, High Rollers, and the Great Credit Crash* by Charles R. Morris; *This Moment on Earth: Today's New Environmentalists and Their Vision for the Future* by John Kerry and Teresa Heinz Kerry; *A Choice of Enemies* by Lawrence Freedman; and *Defending Identity* by Natan Sharansky.

No e-mail submissions. Direct proposals and SASEs to PublicAffairs Submissions.

Susan Weinberg, Publisher

Peter Osnos, Editor-at-Large

Clive Priddle, Editorial Director

Lindsay Jones, Editor

RUNNING PRESS

One of the country's largest independent trade publishers, Running Press Publishers has been providing consumers with an innovative list of quality books and book-related kits since 1972.

Running Press creates more than 200 new titles a year under four imprints: Running Press, Running Press Miniature Editions, Running Press Kids, and Courage

Books. Titles cover a broad range of categories, including general nonfiction, science, history, children's fiction and nonfiction, food and wine, pop culture, lifestyle, photo-essay, and illustrated gift books.

Running Press has had extraordinary success with its minibooks and kits. It is the publisher of innovative multimedia books.

Running Press is headquartered in two historic brownstones in Philadelphia, with additional offices in New York City and London.

Recent titles include *Cathy's Book: If Found Call (650) 266-8263* by Sean Stewart and Jordan Weisman; *Skinny Bitch in the Kitch: Kick-Ass Solutions for Hungry Gals Who Want to Stop Cooking Crap (and Start Looking Hot!)* by Rory Freedman and Kim Barnouin; *Change the Way You See Yourself: Through Asset-Based Thinking* by Hank Wasiak and Kathryn D. Cramer, PhD; *Motherhood to Otherhood: Using the Lessons Learned as a Mom to Create a New Life* by Julia Roberts; *The Sneaky Chef: How to Cheat on Your Man (In the Kitchen!): Hiding Healthy Foods in Hearty Meals Any Guy Will Love* by Missy Chase Lapine; and *America at Home* by Rick Smolan.

For children's titles, to submit a proposal for interactive nonfiction, basic concepts books (such as letters, numbers, opposites, or shapes), or beginning reading projects, send a query letter accompanied by a brief outline or table of contents. When submitting a picture-book proposal, send the entire manuscript. Note that at this time Running Press Kids is not publishing novels or any fiction longer than picture-book length.

For their general interest lists (Running Press and Courage Books), they specialize in publishing illustrated nonfiction. They very rarely publish any new fiction or poetry and are not seeking submissions in those categories at this time. They also do not accept proposals for Miniature Editions of any kind. To submit a proposal for an appropriate work of nonfiction, please send a query letter accompanied by a brief outline or table of contents.

Direct all Running Press submissions to the Philadelphia office, to the attention of the Submissions Editor at Running Press Kids, or the Assistant of the Editorial Director at Running Press Book Publishers for adult titles.

Lisa Clancy, Associate Editorial Director

Jennifer Kasius, Senior Editor

Greg Jones, Editorial Director

Kelli Chipponeri, Editor—Running Press Kids

Diana von Glahn, Editor—Cookbooks

WESTVIEW PRESS

For over 30 years, Westview Press has been a leading publisher of best-selling under-graduate and graduate textbooks, including classics like Jay MacLeod's *Ain't No Makin' It*; Arthur Goldschmidt's *A Concise History of the Middle East*; *Social Theory* by Charles Lemert; Rosemarie Putnam Tong's *Feminist Thought*; William Cleveland's *A History of the Modern Middle East*; Leland Roth's *Understanding Architecture*; and *Philosophy of Mind* by Jaeg-won Kim.

The house was founded in Boulder, Colorado, as a scholarly press of social science textbooks, monographs, and general interest books. Today, Westview focuses on textbooks in core disciplines such as American politics, anthropology, area studies, art history, history, international relations, philosophy, and sociology.

Recent titles include *Mightier than the Sword: How the News Media Have Shaped American History* by Rodger Streitmatter; *The Holocaust: Roots, History, and Aftermath* by David M. Crowe; *Dictionary of Subjects and Symbols in Art* by James A. Hall; *Rigoberta Menchu and the Story of All Poor Guatemalans* by David Stoll; *The Lesbian and Gay Movements: Assimilation or Liberation?* by Craig A. Rimmerman; *Social Stratification: Class, Race and Gender in Sociological Perspective* by David B. Grusky; and *Human Adaptability: an Introduction to Ecological Anthropology, 3rd edition* by Emilio Moran.

Westview Press does not accept unsolicited manuscripts or book proposals. Direct queries with SASEs to:

Cathleen Tetro, Associate Publisher

Karl Yambert, Senior Editor—Anthropology, archaeology, area studies

Steve Catalano, Senior Editor—History, politics

PETERSON'S

A Division of the Thomson Corporation

Princeton Pike Corporate Center

2000 Lenox Drive, P.O. Box 67005, Lawrenceville, NJ 08648

609-896-1800

www.petersons.com

Peterson's is one of the nation's most comprehensive education resources. Since 1966 Peterson's has helped to connect individuals, educational institutions, and corporations through critically acclaimed books. The house reaches an estimated 105 million consumers annually with information about colleges and universities, career schools, graduate programs, distance learning, executive training, private secondary schools, summer opportunities, study abroad, financial aid, test preparation, and career exploration.

Peterson's is part of the Thomson Corporation, a global leader in providing integrated information solutions to business and professional customers.

Titles from Peterson's include *Paying for College: Answers to All Your Questions About Financial Aid, Scholarships, Tuition Payment Plans, and Everything Else You Need to Know; Scholarships, Grants, & Prizes 2009* by Fern Oram; *Peterson's MBA Programs 2009; College Guide for Visual Arts Majors 2009: Real World Admission Guide for All Fine Arts, Design, and Media Majors; Culinary Schools 12th Edition;* and *Summer Programs for Kids and Teenagers 2009.*

Query letters and SASEs should be directed to:

Fern Oram, Editorial Director

THE PILGRIM PRESS

UNITED CHURCH PRESS

700 Prospect Avenue, East Cleveland, OH 44115-1100

216-736-3764   fax: 216-736- 2207

www.pilgrimpress.com e-mail: pilgrim@ucc.org

The Pilgrim Press (founded in 1645 and established in the U.S. in 1895) is the book publishing banner of the publishing wing of the United Church of Christ. The house has a tradition of publishing books and other resources that challenge, encourage, and inspire, and are crafted in accordance with fine standards of content, design, and production.

Comprised of two imprints—Pilgrim Press and United Church—Pilgrim's trade motto is: Books at the Nexus of Religion and Culture. The Pilgrim Press is a Christian-related imprint that focuses on three areas: theological ethics (including science, technology, and medicine); human identity, relationships, and sexuality (including feminist and gay/lesbian issues); and activist spirituality (having a social dimension). United Church Press is a Pilgrim imprint geared primarily toward readers of inspirational materials. They publish 50–60 new titles each year.

Titles indicative of the Pilgrim list include *God Comes Out: A Queer Homiletic* by Olive Elaine Hinnant; *Jesus and Those Bodacious Women* by Linda H. Hollies; *Limited Liberty: The Legacy of Four Pentecostal Women Pioneers* by Estrelda Alexander; *Sage Sisters: Essential Lessons of African American Women in Ministry* by Linda H. Hollies.

Titles from United Church include *Affirming Faith: A Confirmand's Journal* by Thomas E. Dipko; *Theology and Identity: Traditions, Movements, and Polity in the United Church of Christ* by Daniel L. Johnson and Charles E. Hambrick-Stowe; *Christ, Creeds, and Life: Conversations About the Center of Our Faith* by Anne T. Thayer and Douglas Jacobsen; and *The Hidelberg Catechism: A New Translation for the Twenty-First Century* by Lee C., III Barrett.

The Pilgrim Press oversees its own distribution.

See the Web site for an e-mail submission form. As well, queries may be sent via regular mail with SASE to:

Timothy Staveteig, Publisher

Kim Sadler; Editorial Director

PINNACLE BOOKS [SEE KENSINGTON PUBLISHING]

PLATINUM PRESS [SEE ADAMS MEDIA]

POLKA DOT PRESS [SEE ADAMS MEDIA]

POMEGRANATE COMMUNICATIONS, INC.

775A Southpoint Boulevard, Petaluma, CA 94954-1495

Mailing address:

P.O. Box 808022, Petaluma, CA 94975-8022

707-782-9000 / 800-227-1428   fax: 707-782-9810

www.pomegranatecommunications.com   e-mail: info@pomegranate.com

Pomegranate publishes an attractive array of lavish graphic titles and specialty items around subjects such as fine art, architecture, travel, ethnic culture, and crafts. Pomegranate is also among the premier publishers of calendars, posters and poster art, note cards, games, puzzles, specialty sets, and popular topical card decks. The house is located in Northern California.

Pomegranate has its roots in San Francisco's 1960s psychedelic art explosion, when founder Thomas F. Burke distributed posters from the Avalon Ballroom and the Fillmore Auditorium. He worked with seminal poster companies such as East Totem West—two of whose iconic posters, White Rabbit and Cheshire Cat, are still in Pomegranate's line.

Recent titles include *The New Jewish Family Kitchen: 40 Kosher Recipes for Jewish Hol-*

idays + Everyday! by Devorah Rosen Goldman; *Fairies 2009* by Michael Hague; *The Hapless Child* by Edward Gorey; *Edwin Deakin: California Painter of the Picturesque* by Scott A. Shields and Alfred C. Jr. Harrison; *Timothy J. Clark* by Jean Stern and Lisa Farrington; *Cape Dorset Prints: A Retrospective: Fifty Years of Printmaking at the Kinngait Studios* by Leslie Boyd Ryan; *Evolution: Five Decades of Printmaking by David C. Driskell*, by Adrienne L. Childs et al and *Gustave Baumann's Southwest* by Joeseph Traugott.

Query letters and SASEs should be directed to the Submissions Department.

Thomas F. Burke, President

Zoe Katherine (Katie) Burke, Publisher

POTOMAC BOOKS, INC.

22841 Quicksilver Drive, Dulles, VA 20166

703-661-1548 fax: 703-661-1547

www.potomacbooksinc.com email: pbimail@presswarehouse.com

Founded in 1983 as part of Brassey's Ltd., a distinguished British publishing house dating back to the 19th century, Potomac Books was acquired by American book distributor Books International in 1999. With strong roots in military history, Potomac Books has expanded its editorial focus to include general history, world and national affairs, foreign policy, defense and national security, intelligence, memoirs, biographies, and sports. The house publishes 85 new titles per year.

Recent titles include *Etched in Purple: One Soldier's War in Europe* by Frank Irgang; *The Flying Greek: An Immigrant Fighter Ace's WWII Odyssey with the RAF, USAAF, and French Resistance* by Col. Steve N. Pisanos; *Gatekeeper: Memoirs of a CIA Polygraph Examiner* by John F. Sullivan; *Genghis Khan: History's Greatest Empire Builder* by Paul Lococo, Jr.; *Home Run: The Definitive History of Baseball's Ultimate Weapon* by David Vincent; *Sock It To 'Em Tigers: The Incredible Story of the 1968 Detroit Tigers* edited by Mark Pattison and David Raglin; and *Tennis Confidential II* by Paul Fein.

No e-mail submissions. See Web site for further details. Query letters and proposals with SASEs may be directed to:

Elizabeth Demers, Editor—History: military and naval, diplomatic, political, and other, current events, international relations, intelligence, security studies, terrorism, and military life; Elizabeth.Demers@booksintl.com

Hilary Claggett, Editor—Politics, international relations, terrorism, public policy, social issues, veterans affairs, current events, global issues, and security studies; Hilary.Claggett@booksintl.com

Kevin Cuddihy, Editor—Sports, general interest, and Most Wanted series; Kevin@booksintl.com

PRAEGER [SEE GREENWOOD PUBLISHING GROUP]

PRESBYTERIAN PUBLISHING CORPORATION

GENEVA PRESS

WESTMINSTER/JOHN KNOX

100 Witherspoon Street, Room 2047, Louisville, KY 40202-1396

502-569-5052 / 800-227-2872   fax: 502-569-5113 / 800-541-5113

www.ppcbooks.com   e-mail: customer_service@presbypub.com

The Presbyterian Publishing Corporation (PPC) is the denominational publisher for the Presbyterian Church (USA), but the materials it issues under its Westminster John Knox Press imprint cover the spectrum of modern religious thought and represent the work of scholarly and popular authors of many different religious affiliations. PPC's Geneva Press imprint is for a specifically Presbyterian audience. The house publishes 95 new books each year and manages a backlist of over 1,600 titles.

For 160 years, PPC and its predecessors have served clergy, scholars, students, and lay people. Most of its publications are used in the spiritual formation of clergy and laity, the training of seminarians, the dissemination of religious scholars' work, and the preparation for ministry of lay church leaders. One of PPC's principal aims is to help readers of its publications achieve biblical and theological literacy. It is a nonprofit corporation, sustained by its sales.

Westminster/John Knox (WJK) represents the publications unit of the Presbyterian Church (USA). The house unites the former independents Westminster Press and John Knox Press, which were originally founded as one entity in 1838, then separated into distinct enterprises, and again merged as WJK following the reunion of the Northern and Southern Presbyterian Churches in 1983.

WJK publishes general-interest religious trade books, as well as academic and professional works in Biblical studies, theology, philosophy, ethics, history, archaeology, personal growth, and pastoral counseling. Among its series are Literary Currents in Biblical Interpretation, Family Living in Pastoral Perspective, Gender and the Biblical Tradition, and the Presbyterian Presence: The Twentieth-Century Experience. It has also gained popularity for its unofficial series of "Gospel According to..." books that explore religion and pop culture.

WJK's recent titles include *To Do Justice: A Guide for Progressive Christians* by Rebecca Todd Peters and Elizabeth Hinson Hasty; *A Guide to Preaching and Leading Worship* by William H. Willimon; *The God of Second Chances* by Erik Kolbell; *A Short*

World History of Christianity by Robert Bruce Mullin; *The Suburban Church: Practical Advice for Authentic Ministry* by Arthur H. Dekruyter, Quentin Schultze, and Leith Anderson; and *Cross Talk: Preaching Redemption Here and Now* by Sally A. Brown.

Geneva Press titles include *A History of Presbyterian Missions: 1944-2007* by Scott W. Sunquist; *Theology in Service of the Church: Essays in Honor of Joseph D. Small 3rd* by Charles A. Wiley; *A New Church for a New World* by John M. Buchanan; *The Rhythm of Discipleship* by Luther D. Ivory; *The Presbyterian Handbook for Pastors* by Paul J. Blom; and *Theology for Liberal Presbyterians and Other Endangered Species* by Douglas Ottati.

WJK distributes its list through Spring Arbor. The house also represents titles from other publishers, including Orbis Books, Pilgrim Press, Saint Andrew Press of Scotland, and Presbyterian Publishing Corporation.

Query letters and SASEs should be directed to:

Julie Tonini, Managing Editor for Editorial

Philip Law, UK Publishing Director; plaw@wjkbooks.com

Stephanie Egnotovich, Executive Editor; segnotovich@wjkbooks.com

Don McKim, Academic and Reference Editor; dmckim@wjkbooks.com

Jon Berquist, Senior Academic Editor; jberquist@wjkbooks.com

David Maxwell, Acquisitions Editor; dmaxwell@wjkbooks.com

PROFESSIONAL PUBLICATIONS

1250 Fifth Avenue, Belmont, CA 94002

650-593-9119 / 800-426-1178   fax: 650-592-4519

www.ppi2pass.com   e-mail: acquisitions@ppi2pass.com

Professional Publications, located in Belmont, California, was established as an independent publisher of professional licensing exam review materials since 1975. The house maintains a reputation as a leader in engineering, architecture, and interior design exam review. More than 800,000 exam candidates have used these publications. The mission is simple: to help readers pass their exams.

PPI is developing a series of practical, real-world advice books for new managers and is looking for authors and manuscripts about negotiation, finance for non-financial managers, and intellectual property law. In addition, PPI is looking for LEED-certified engineers and architects to work on another new series of books, now in development.

PPI titles include *Engineering Your Start-Up* by James A. Swanson and Michael L. Baird; *Concrete Design for the Civil and Structural PE Exams* by C. Dale Buckner; *Industrial Discipline-Specific Review for the FE/EIT Exam* by the UN Department of Industrial Engineering; *LEED CI Sample Exam: Commercial Interiors* by Holly Williams Leppo and Michael Crowe; and *Surveying Solved Problems for the Fs and PS Exams* by Jan Van Sickle.

Queries may be directed to acquisitions@ppi2pass.com or to the Acquisitions Editor at the mailing address above.

PROMETHEUS BOOKS

HUMANITY BOOKS

PYR

59 John Glenn Drive, Amherst, NY 14228-2197

716-691-0133 / 800-421-0351   fax: 716-564-2711

www.prometheusbooks.com   e-mail: editorial@prometheusbooks.com

www.pyrsf.com   Pyr blog: pyrsf.blogspot.com

One of the leading publishers in philosophy, popular science, and critical thinking, Prometheus Books has more than 1,500 books in print and produces an average of 100 new titles each year. Founded in 1969, this house took its name from the courageous Greek god who gave fire to humans, lighting the way to reason, intelligence, and independence, among other things. The house is located near Buffalo, NY.

Among the categories of books published are popular science, science and the paranormal, contemporary issues, social science and current events, children's fiction and nonfiction, history, religion and politics, philosophy, humanism, Islamic studies, Jewish studies, biblical criticism, psychology, women's issues, health, self-help, sexuality, reference, and more. Prometheus also maintains a strong backlist that includes hundreds of established classics in literature, philosophy, and the sciences.

In addition, Prometheus has developed two imprints: Humanity Books for academic works across the humanities, and Pyr (the Greek word for fire) for science fiction and speculative fiction.

Recent titles from Prometheus include *Ad Women: How They Impact What We Need, Want, and Buy* by Juliann Sivulka; *ChemoBrain: How Cancer Therapies Can Affect Your Mind* by Ellen Clegg; *Cosmic Connection: How Astronomical Events Impact Life on Earth* by Jeff Kanipe; *Creating Space for Happiness: The Secret of Giving Room* by Anthony J. Castro; *Forbidden Fruit: The Ethics of Secularism* by Paul Kurtz; *Intelligence Wars: Lessons from Baghdad* by Steven K. Oaehern; *Carl Sagan: A Biography* by Ray Spangenburg and Kit Moser; and *Deadly Decisions: How False Knowledge Sank the Titanic, Blew Up the Shuttle, and Led America into War* by Christopher Burns.

Recent Humanity Books titles include *Gender Identities in a Globalized World* by Ana Marta Gonzales and Victor Seidler; *F.C.S. Schiller on Pragmatism and Humanism: Selected Writings, 1891-1939* by John R. Shook and Hugh McDonald; *The Ontological Argument from Descartes to Hegel* by Kevin J. Harrelson; *The Remarkable Existentialists* by Michael Allen Fox; *People Unlike Us* by Jeremy J. Millet; *The Reaches of Democracy: From Eastern*

Europe to the Western Balkans by Nenad Kecmanovic; and *Culture and Conflict in the Middle East* by Philip Carl Salzman.

Recent titles from Pyr include *MultiReal (The Jump 225 Trilogy)* by David Louis Edelman; *Son of Man* by Robert Silverberg; *Sagramanda: A Novel of Near-Future India* by Alan Dean Foster; *The Crooked Letter: Books of the Cataclysm: One* by Sean Williams; *The Martian General's Daughter* by Theodore Judson; *Before They Are Hanged* by Joe Abercrombie; and *Bright of the Sky* by Kay Kenyon.

Query via regular mail or e-mail (do not send attachments with e-mails).

Steven L. Mitchell, Editor-in-Chief; editorial@prometheusbooks.com

Lou Anders, Editorial Director, Pyr; landers@prometheusbooks.com

---

PROVENANCE PRESS [SEE ADAMS MEDIA]

PYR [SEE PROMETHEUS BOOKS]

QUARRY BOOKS [SEE ROCKPORT PUBLISHERS]

QUIRK BOOKS

215 Church Street, Philadelphia, PA 19106

215-627-3581   fax: 215-627-5220

www.quirkbooks.com   e-mail: general@quirkbooks.com

Founded by the folks who authored the Worst-Case Scenario franchise, Quirk Books editors seek to be publishers of high-quality irreverence. The mission of this house is to originate, develop, and publish nontraditional and innovative nonfiction books that are objects of desire editorially, graphically, and physically. Quirk also functions as a book packager, developing and selling recent titles to St. Martin's and Potter, among others.

Quirk's recent titles include *The Anti-War Quote Book* edited by Eric Groves, Sr.; *Casino Confidential: A Pit Boss's Guide to Beating the House* by Anonymous; *Creepy Cute Crochet: Zombies, Ninjas, Robots, and More!* by Christen Haden; *The Groom's Instruction Manual: How to Survive and Possible Even Enjoy the Most Bewildering Ceremony Known to Man* by Shandon Fowler; *Field Guide to Luck: How to Use and Interpret Charms, Signs, and Superstitions* by Alys R. Yablon; *The Indiana Jones Handbook: and The Complete Adventurers Guide* by Denise Kiernan and Joseph D'Agnese.

Direct brief queries to Editorial Submissions via fax, e-mail (submissions@quirkbooks.com), or regular mail with SASE.

Jason Rekulak, Editorial Director; jason@quirkbooks.com

Melissa Wagner, Editor; melissa@quirkbooks.com

Sharyn Rosart, Editor/Publisher; srosart@earthlink.net

QUIVER [SEE ROCKPORT PUBLISHERS]

RAGGED MOUNTAIN PRESS [SEE MCGRAW-HILL]

RED DRESS INK [SEE HARLEQUIN ENTERPRISES, LTD.]

RED WHEEL / WEISER

RED WHEEL

CONARI BOOKS

WEISER BOOKS

500 Third Street, Suite 230, San Francisco, CA 94107

www.redwheelweiser.com

www.conari.com

Red Wheel/Weiser, LLC, is the publisher of Red Wheel, Weiser, and Conari Books. The house primarily publishes in the category of body/mind/spirit, about 60 books per year among the three imprints.

In 2006, the entire Red Wheel/Weiser Conari editorial department relocated from Boston to San Francisco. At the same time, Red Wheel/Weiser Conari consolidated its Maine operations department and the Boston sales and marketing department moved to a new office in Newburyport, Mass.

Red Wheel, the newest of the three imprints, founded in 2000, publishes practical, helpful books, most with a spiritual element. The Red Wheel editors look for spunky self-help, inspirational self-help, and spiritual self-help titles. Recent titles include *Reaching In, Reaching Out: Second Acts that Change Lives* by Mary Beth Sammon; *Get Up* by Bucky Sinister; *Healer of Souls* by Dawn Paul; *God for President: A Parable About the Power of Love* by Lisa Venable; *Codependence and the Power of Detachment: How to Set Boundaries and Make Your Life Your Own* by Karen Casey; and *Chakra Foods* by Deanna Minich.

Conari Books, founded in 1989 in Berkeley, California, was acquired by Red Wheel/Weiser in 2002. Conari topics include spirituality, personal growth, parenting, and social issues. Recent titles include *Stoking the Fires: 9 Ways to Rekindle Passion and Imagination* by Phil Cousineau; *This is Not the Life I ordered: 50 ways to Keep Your Head Above Water When Life Keeps Dragging You Down* by Deborah Collins Stephens, Michealene Cristini Risley, Jackie Speier, and Jan Yanehiro; *Serenity: Simple Steps for Recovering Peace of Mind, Real Happiness, and Great Relationships* by Jane Nelson; *Urgent Message from Mother: Gather the Women and Save the World* by Jean Shinoda Bolen; *Lean Forward Into Your Life: Begin Each Day as if It Were on Purpose* by Mary Anne Radmacher; *The Food Intolerance Bible: A Nutritionist's Plan to Beat Food Cravings, Fatigue, Mood Swings, Bloating, Headaches, and IBS (with over 70 recipes)* by Antoinette Savill and Antony Haynes.

Weiser Books has a long history as one of American's preeminent publishers of esoteric and occult teachings from traditions around the world and throughout time. Areas of Weiser publishing interest include self-transformation, alternative healing methods, meditation, metaphysics, consciousness, magic, astrology, tarot, astral projection, Kabbalah, earth religions, Eastern philosophy and religions, Buddhism, t'ai chi, healing, and Tibetan studies. The publisher specializes in books relating to all facets of the secret and hidden teachings worldwide.

Recent titles from Weiser include *The Weiser Concise Guide to Aleister Crowley* by Rochars Kaczinski; *The Essential Laws of Fearless Living: Find the Power to Never Feel Powerless Again* by Guy Finley; *The Code: Use the Laws of Manifestation to Achieve Your Highest Good* by Tony Burroughs; *The God Theory: Universes, Zero Point Fields and What's Behind it All* by Bernard Haisch; *Friends on a Rotten Day: The Astrology of Friendships* by Hazel Dixon-Cooper; *Serpent of Light: and Beyond 2012* by Drunvalo Melchizedek.

Submissions are accepted via regular mail only. For all three imprints, query letters, proposals, or manuscripts with SASEs should be directed to Pat Bryce.

Ms. Pat Bryce, Acquisitions Editor

REGAL BOOKS [SEE GOSPEL LIGHT PUBLICATIONS]

REGNERY

A Division of Eagle Publishing

One Massachusetts Avenue, North West, Washington, DC 20001

202-216-0600 / 888-219-4747   fax: 202-216-0612

www.regnery.com   e-mail: submissions@regnery.com

Founded in 1947, Regnery has become the country's most popular publisher of books for conservatives. Regnery publishes books in the fields of current affairs, politics, history, culture, and biography. Regnery was the publisher of 2004's *Unfit for Command: Swift Boast Veterans Speak Out Against John Kerry*, among other new conservative best-sellers.

In 1993 Regnery became part of the newly founded Eagle Publishing, which also includes Human Events, the national conservative weekly; the Conservative Book Club; and the Evans & Novak Political Report.

Recent titles include *Sacred Ground* by Tim Ruck; *The Wit and Wisdom of Ronald Reagan* by James C. Humes; *The Politically Incorrect Guide to the Bible* by Robert J. Hutchison; *Originalism: A Quarter-Century of Debate* by Steven G. Calabresi; and *Power to the People* by Laura Ingraham.

Queries and SASEs may be directed via regular mail or e-mail:

Marji Ross, Publisher

REVELL [SEE BAKER PUBLISHING GROUP]

RIZZOLI, USA

UNIVERSE INTERNATIONAL PUBLICATIONS

A Division of RCS Media Group, Italy

300 Park Avenue South, 3rd Floor, New York, NY 10010

212-387-3400   fax: 212-387-3535

www.rizzoliusa.com

Rizzoli began its New York operations in 1974 as an integral part of its parent company, the Italian communications giant, RCS Media Group. The house is a leader in illustrated books in the fields of art, architecture, interior design, photography, haute couture, and gastronomy. In 1990, Rizzoli added the Universe imprint, marking Rizzoli's entrée into the pop-culture worlds of humor, fashion, beauty, sports, performing arts, and gay and alternative lifestyles. It also contributed a successful calendar program and published economical versions of Rizzoli books.

Under the direction of Senior Editor Robb Pearlman, who joined the company in 2006, the company plans to expand its children's book and calendar lines.

Recent Rizzoli titles include *100 Classis Golf Tips from Leading Ladies' Teaching and Touring Pros* edited by Christopher Obetz, illustrated by Anthony Ravielli; *Epic Spots: The Places You Must Skate Before You Die* by the Editors of *Thrasher Magazine*; *Ancient Italy from Above* by Antonio Attini and Marcello Bertinetti; *Beyond the Bread Basket* by Jean Francois Piege and Patrick Mikanowski; *Animals of Africa* by Thomas B. Allen; and *Marie-Antoinette and the Last Garden at Versailles* by Christian Duvernois.

Rizzoli titles are distributed thorough St. Martin's Press.

Rizzoli does accept unsolicited proposals. All queries with SASEs should be directed to Editorial Submissions.

Charles Miers, Publisher

Robb Pearlman, Senior Editor—Children's books, calendars, and licensing

ROCKPORT PUBLISHERS

FAIR WINDS PRESS

QUARRY BOOKS

QUIVER

A Member of the Quayside Publishing Group

100 Cummings Center. Suit 406-L. Beverly, MA 01915

978-282-9590   fax: 978-283-2742

www.rockpub.com   e-mail: e-info@rockpub.com

Rockport Publishers creates beautiful illustrated source books for professional designers and artisans of all types. Their books present the best design work from around the world, showing how work gets done, and the inspiration behind the art.

Subjects include graphic design, architecture, and interior design. In 2001 Rockport Publishers launched Fair Winds Press to focus on a wide range of mind, body and spirit topics that excite readers and help them answer life's fundamental questions. The Quarry Books imprint, launched in 2003, provides practical general reference in categories such as crafts, home style, pet care, and personal improvement. Quiver, launched in 2006, offers titles about sex.

Recent Quiver titles include *The Orgasm Bible: The Latest Research and Techniques for Reaching More Powerful Climaxes More Often* by Susan Crain Bakos; *Getting the Sex You Want: Shed Your Inhibitions and Reach New Heights of Passion Together* by Tammy Nelson; *Position Sex Card Deck: 50 Wild Sex Positions You Probably Haven't Tried* by Lola Rawlins; *The Position Sex Bible: More Positions Than You Could Possible Imagine Trying* by Randi Foxx.

Recent Quarry titles include *Universal Design for the Home: Great Looking, Great Living Design for All Ages, Abilities, and Circumstances* by Wendy A. Jordan; *Outdoor Stonework: The Timeless, Practical, and Aesthetic Value of Stone* by Laurel Saville; *Art Journals and Creative Healing: Restoring the Spirit Through Self-Expression* by Sharon Soneff; *Vintage Collage-Works: Artful Ideas with Antique Ephemera* by Sunny Koch and Mary Jo Koch; *Jean Therapy: Denim Deconstruction for the Conscientious Crafter* by Scatha G. Allison with Marla Stefanelli; *The Art of Decorative Paper Stencils: Fold, Cut, and Open* by Kanako Yaguchi; *The Cardmaker's Workbook: The Complete Guide to Design, Color, and Construction Techniques for Beautiful Cards* by Jenn Mason; *Sweater Surgery: How to Make New Things from Old Sweaters* by Stefanie Girard.

Recent Fair Winds titles include *Six Week Bikini Countdown: Tone Your Butt, Abs, Thighs Fast Combining Pilates with Select Strength and Cardio Internal Training Workouts* by Karon Karter; *Organizing Solutions for People with Attention Deficit Disorder: Tips and Tools to Help You Take Charge of Your Life and Get Organized* by Susan C. Pinsky; *Voyager Tarot: Intuition Cards for the 21st Century* by James Wanless; *Borderline Personality Disorder in*

Adolescents: A Complete Guide to Understanding and Coping When Your Adolescent Has BPD by Blaise A. Aguirre; *Turning the Knights Templar Key: The Secret Legacy of the Knights Templar and the Origins of Freemasonry* by Robert Lomas; *The Addicts Guide to Everything Sodoku* by Fiorella Grossi; *Supercharge Your Immune System: 100 Ways to Fight Autoimmune Illnesses—One Glass at a Time* by Ellen Brown.

Recent Rockport titles include *The Best of Business Card Design 8* by Rex Peteet; *Cutting-Edge Patterns and Textures* by Estel Vilaseca; *Building Design Portfolios: Innovative Concepts for Presenting Your Work* by Sara Eisenman; *Salons and Spas: The Architecture of Beauty* by Julie Sinclair Eakin; *Color, Space, and Style: All the Details Interior Designers Need to Know But Can Never Find* by Chris Gimley and Mimi Love; *Color Design Workbook: A Real World Guide to Using Color in Graphic Design* by Adams Morioka; *Design for Special Events: 500 of the Best Logos, Invitations, and Graphics* by Peleg Top.

Direct queries and SASEs to:

Winnie Prentiss, Publisher

Emily Potts, Acquisitions Editor

William Kiester, Publisher, Fair Winds / Quiver

Rochelle Bourgault, Acquisitions Editor, Quarry

RODALE, INC.

33 East Minor Street, Emmaus, PA 18098-0099

610-967-5171   fax: 610-967-8963

New York address:

733 Third Avenue, 15th Floor, New York, NY 10017-3204

212-697-2040   fax: 212-682-2237

www.rodale.com   e-mail: reader_service@rodale.com

Rodale publishes acclaimed nonfiction books on health, fitness, cooking, gardening, spirituality, self-help, nature and more. Recent *New York Times* best-sellers include Al Gore's *An Inconvenient Truth*; *The Abs Diet for Women* by David Zinczenko; *LL Cool J's Platinum Workout* by LL Cool J; *The South Beach Heart Program* by Arthur Agaston; and *Joy Bauer's Food Cures* by Joy Bauer.

Rodale Books has also been developing titles in new genres including memoirs, biographies, narrative nonfiction, self-help, science and nature, psychology, current events and personal finance.

Recent titles include *The Live Earth Global Warming Survival Handbook* by David de Rothschild; *Twice as Good: Condoleezza Rice and Her Path to Power* by Marcus Mabry; *Everyday Miracles* by Ardath Rodale; *Harvey Walden's No Excuses! Fitness Workout* by Harvey Walden IV; *The Dynamic Path* by James M. Citrin; and *The Complete Travel*

Detective Bible by Peter Greenberg.

Please send proposals and SASEs to the editors via regular mail or e-mail at book proposals@rodale.com.

Susan Berg, Editor (PA)—Women's health

Nancy Hancock, Editor (NY)—Health and Lifestyles

Pam Krauss, Editor —Women's health, popular psychology

ROUTLEDGE

An Imprint of Taylor and Francis Books

2 Park Square, Milton Park, Abingdon, Oxford OX14 4RN

+44 (0) 20 7017 6000   fax: +44 (0) 20 7017 6699

www.routledge-ny.com

Routledge produces adult nonfiction for the trade and academic markets. The house produces titles in the humanities and social sciences with more specific focus on current events, communications, media, cultural studies, education, self-improvement, world political studies, philosophy, economics, feminist theory, gender studies, history, and literary criticism. Routledge is an imprint of Taylor and Francis Books.

Recent titles include *Museums and Community: Ideas, Issues, and Challenges* by Elizabeth Crooke; *Towards the Virtuous University: The Moral Bases of Academic Practice* by Jon Nixon; *Identity of the Constitutional Subject: Self hood, Citizenship, Culture, and Community* by Michael Rosenfeld; *Children, Structure, and Agency: Realities Across the Developing World* by G.K. Lieten; *Global Trafficking in Women and Children* edited by Obi N.I. Ebbe and Dilip K. Das; and *The State of Sex: Nevada's Brothel Industry* by Kathryn Hausbeck and Barbara G. Brents.

See the Web site for submission guidelines. Send your proposal with SASE via regular mail to the Editorial Department; your proposal will be forwarded to the appropriate editor.

Michael Kerns—Politics

Catherine Bernard—Education

Nancy Hale—Business

Matthew Byrnie—Media studies, communications, literature, cultural studies

Kimberly Guinta—History

Constance Ditzel—Music

Kate Ahl—Philosophy

George Zimmar—Psychiatry, clinical psychology, psychotherapy, family therapy

Dana Bliss—Counseling, grief and trauma studies, social work

ROWMAN & LITTLEFIELD

JASON ARONSON, INC., PUBLISHERS

4501 Forbes Boulevard, Suite 200, Lanham, MD 20706

301-459-3366   fax: 301-429-5748

www.rowmanlittlefield.com

www.rlpgbooks.com

www.aronson.com

New York office:

200 Park Avenue South, Suite 1109, New York, NY 10003

212-529-3888   fax: 212-529-4223

M. EVANS

TAYLOR TRADE

5360 Manhattan Circle #100, Boulder, CO 80303

www.rlpgtrade.com   e-mail: tradeeditorial@rowman.com

IVAN R. DEE, PUBLISHER

NEW AMSTERDAM BOOKS

J. S. SANDERS

1332 North Halsted Street, Chicago, IL, 60622-2694

312-787-6262   fax: 312-787-6269

www.ivanrdee.com   e-mail: elephant@ivanrdee.com

The Rowman & Littlefield Publishing Group is one of the largest and fastest-growing independent publishers and distributors in North America. The company publishes more than 20 imprints in virtually all fields in the humanities and social sciences for the academic and trade markets. Rowman & Littlefield also owns National Book Network, which is North America's second-largest distributor of independent trade book publishers. NBN recently created two new divisions: Biblio Distribution for small trade publishers and FaithWorks for CBA publishers.

RLPG built its list quickly by acquiring small companies and niche publishers, especially over the past five years. These have been either merged into existing imprints or have continued to exist as stand-alone RLPG imprints.

Rowman & Littlefield is an independent press devoted to publishing scholarly books in the best tradition of university presses; innovative, thought-provoking texts for college courses; and crossover trade books intended to convey scholarly trends to an educated readership.

Recent titles include *China's Tibet?: Autonomy or Assimilation* by Warren W. Smith Jr.; *The Keys to the White House: A Surefire Guide to Predicting the Next President (2008 edition)* by Allan J. Lichtman; *Greeks and Romans Bearing Gifts: How the Ancients Inspired the Founding Fathers* by Carl J. Richard; *Founding Father: How C-SPAN's Brian Lamb Changed Politics in America* by Stephen E. Frantzich; *Immigration and the American Dream: Battling the Political Hype and Hysteria* by Margaret Sands Orchowski; *The Patient Will See You Now: How Advances in Science, Medicine, and Technology Will Lead To a Personalized Health Care System* by Carey James Kriz; *Beneath a Northern Sky: A Short History of the Gettysburg Campaign (2nd ed.)* by Steven E. Woodworth; *Beijing's Games: What the Olympics Mean to China* by Susan Brownell; *China Ink: The Changing Face of Chinese Journalism* by Judy Polembaum; *Education Myths: What Special Interest Groups Want You to Believe About Our Schools—And Why It Isn't So* by Jay P. Greene.

An academic or scholarly author would do well to explore online the various RLPG imprints, or to query this publisher for guidelines. To submit to Rowman & Littlefield, direct your query to the appropriate editor:

Ross Miller, Ph.D., Acquisitions Editor for Religious Studies (NY); rmiller@rowman.com

Alan McClare, VP and Executive Editor for Sociology and Education (NY); amcclare@rowman.com

Niels Aaboe, Executive Editor for Political Science and American History (NY); naaboe@rowman.com

Susan McEachern, Vice President and Editorial Director (CO)—International studies, geography, history; smceachern@rowman.com

Jessica Gribble, Acquisitions Editor (CO)—Women's studies, Asian American studies, history, area studies, geography; jgribble@rowman.com

Janice Braunstein, Assistant Managing Editor (CO); jbraunstein@rowman.com

Jack Meinhardt, Acquisitions Editor (MD)—All other areas; jmeinhardt@rowman.com

JASON ARONSON, INC., PUBLISHERS

Jason Aronson is the publisher of highly regarded psychotherapy and Judaica books. Dedicated to publishing professional, scholarly works, their list of Judaica authors spans the entire spectrum of approaches to Jewish tradition: Orthodox, Hasidic, Reconstructionalist, Reform, Conservative, Renewal, unaffiliated, and secular. Topics include anti-Semitism, Baal Shem Tov, classics in translation, family, folklore and storytelling, Gematria, Hasidism, history, holidays, Holocaust, Israel, Jewish law, kabbalah, Maimonides, marriage, meditation, prayer, Talmud, theology, Torah, travel, women's studies, and more.

In the subject of psychotherapy, Jason Aronson Inc. offers more titles from a broader range of psychotherapists than any other publisher. Topics include child therapy, family therapy, eating disorders, substance abuse, short-term therapy, bereavement, stress, trauma, object relations therapy, personality disorder, depression, couple therapy,

sexual abuse, play therapy, psychoanalysis, psychology, transference, and more.
Send proposal with CV and SASE to:

Arthur T. Pomponio, Editorial Director for Jason Aronson (NY); apomponio@rowman.com

Mary Catherine La Mar, Acquisitions Editor for Jason Aronson (NY); mlamae@rowman.com

TAYLOR TRADE

M. EVANS

The Taylor Trade Publishing program consists of an award-winning list of books on gardening, health, history, family issues, sports, entertainment, nature, field guides, house and home, and children's titles. Taylor Trade operates out of Boulder, CO.

Recent Taylor titles include *Indoor Gardening the Organic Way: How to Create a Natural and Sustaining Environment for Your Houseplants* by Julie Bawdin Davis; *Blood Feud: Detroit Red Wings v. Colorado Avalanche: The Inside Story of Pro Sports' Nastiest and Best Rivalry of Its Era* by Adrian Dater; and *The Book of Caddyshack: Everything You Ever Wanted to Know About the Greatest Movie Ever Made* by Scott Martin.

Recently acquired by Rowman & Littlefield, M. Evans and Company, Inc. has been publishing thought-provoking titles with a clear, constantly honed commercial focus in its favored market niches for over 40 years. M. Evans has become an imprint of Taylor Trade, with editorial operations in Colorado, as well.

The M. Evans front list features high-profile offerings in topical issues, investigative stories in politics, business, and entertainment, and popular biography. The core Evans program accents popular nonfiction books, primarily self-help related, in the areas of health and fitness, human relationships, business and finance, and lifestyle and cuisine.

Recent M. Evans titles include *Las Vegas Babylon: True Tales of Glitter, Glamour, and Greed* by Jeff Burbank; *Labor of the Heart: A Parent's Guide to the Decisions and Emotions in Adoption* by Kathleen L. Whitten; *The Left Stuff: How the Left-Handed Have Survived and Thrived in a Right-Handed World* by Melissa Roth; *Syndrome W: A Women's Guide to Reversing Mid-Life Weight Gain* by Harriet R. Mogul.

Taylor Trade Publishing is especially interested in regional gardening, nature, field guides, cooking, sports, self-help, Texana/Western history, general history and entertainment. They do not publish fiction or poetry. However, proposals from institutions such as museums or galleries pertaining to their collections are strongly encouraged.

Query letters and SASEs should be directed to the Editorial Department; e-mail generates the quickest response. If querying by e-mail, note "Book Proposal" in the subject line.

Rick Rinehart, Editorial Director; rrinehart@rowman.com

Dulcie Wilcox, Acquisitions Editor; dwilcox@rowman.com

IVAN R. DEE

NEW AMSTERDAM BOOKS

J. S. SANDERS

Ivan R. Dee publishes serious nonfiction trade books in history, politics, biography, literature, philosophy, and theater. Similar to Basic Books and the Free Press in their heyday, Ivan R. Dee produces books that are provocative, controversial, and aimed at the intelligent layperson. They are routinely reviewed in the *New York Times*, the *Washington Post*, the *New York Review of Books*, and other influential publications. Ivan R. Dee paperbacks are also used extensively in college courses as supplementary reading.

Founded in 1988 by Ivan Dee, the house was acquired in 1998 by the Rowman & Littlefield Publishing Group. Ivan Dee continues as publisher in the company's Chicago headquarters.

New Amsterdam Books, an imprint of Ivan R. Dee, Publisher, publishes distinguished books for the serious general reader. Highlights include art and art history, fiction in translation, theatre, Scottish studies, Victorian studies, religion, and history. New Amsterdam Books is not currently accepting submissions.

J.S. Sanders & Company, an imprint of Ivan R. Dee, Publisher, was founded by John Sanders of Nashville, Tenn., to publish and republish general trade books on Southern culture, history, and literature, including the Southern Classics series, which "restores to our awareness some of the South's most important writers of the nineteenth and twentieth centuries" (*Hudson Review*). Many classic novels about the South, as well as histories and biographies of the region and its leaders, are still in print today thanks to J.S. Sanders. J.S. Sanders is not currently accepting submissions.

Among Ivan R. Dee's authors are Brooke Allen, Ira Berkow, Isaiah Berlin, Jeremy Bernstein, Robert Brustein, Ivan Bunin, Theodore Dalrymple, Roger Daniels, Joseph Epstein, Renee Fox, John Gross, Raul Hilberg, Gertrude Himmelfarb, Aldous Huxley, Ismail Kadare, Roger Kimball, Adam Kirsch, Hilton Kramer, David Kyvig, Primo Levi, Heather MacDonald, William O'Neill, Joseph Parisi, John Prados, Carl Sandburg, Richard Schickel, Arthur Schnitzler, Budd Schulberg, Red Smith, B. Traven, and Ben Wattenberg.

Recent Ivan R. Dee titles include *A Secular Faith: Why Christianity Favors the Separation of Church and State* by Darryl Hart; *Safe for Democracy: The Secret Wars of the CIA* by John Prados; *100 Essential Modern Poems by Women* edited by Joseph Parisi and Kathleen Welton; *The End of Baseball: A Novel* by Peter Schilling Jr.; *Worst Enemy: The Reluctant Transformation of the American Military* by John Arguilla; *Do No Harm: How a Magic Bullet for Prostate Cancer Became a Medical Quandary* by Stewart Justman; *The Quest For Absolute Security: The Failed Relations Among U.S. Intelligence Agencies* by Athan Theoharis.

Query letters with sample chapters or proposal and SASEs should be directed to the attention of the Editorial Department.

Ivan Dee, President

J. S. SANDERS [SEE ROWMAN & LITTLEFIELD]

SASQUATCH BOOKS

119 South Main, Suite 400, Seattle, WA 98104

206-467-4300 / 800-775-0817   fax: 206-467-4301

www.sasquatchbooks.com

Sasquatch Books is one of the nation's premier regional presses, with titles for and about the Pacific Northwest, Alaska, and California. Founded in 1986, Sasquatch's publishing program celebrates regionally written works. Their top-selling Best Places travel guides serve the most popular destinations and locations of the West. Sasquatch also publishes widely in the subjects of food, wine, gardening, nature, photography, children's books, and regional history. With more than 200 books on the West, this house offers an exploration of the lifestyle, landscape, and worldview of its region.

Submit a query, proposal, or complete manuscript to the editors:

Terence Maikels, Acquisitions Editor

SCHAUM'S MCGRAW-HILL [SEE MCGRAW-HILL]

SCHOLASTIC, INC.

KLUTZ

557 Broadway, New York, NY 10012

212-343-6100

www.scholastic.com

Klutz address:

450 Lambert Avenue, Palo Alto, CA 94306

650-857-0888 / 800-737-4123

www.klutz.com e-mail: thefolks@klutz.com

Scholastic is a global children's publishing and media company and is the USA's largest publisher and distributor of children's books. Recognizing that literacy is the cornerstone of a child's intellectual, personal, and cultural growth, Scholastic creates quality products and services that educate, entertain, and motivate children, and are designed to help enlarge their understanding of the world around them.

Scholastic publishes over 750 new books each year. The list includes *Harry Potter, Captain Underpants, Clifford the Big Red Dog, I Spy*, and *The Magic Schoolbus*. Best-selling titles include *How Do Dinosaurs Say Goodnight?, No, David!, Inkheart, Charlie Bone, Chasing Vermeer*, and *The Day My Butt Went Psycho*.

Scholastic imprints include Scholastic Press, Arthur A. Levine Books, Cartwheel Books, The Blue Sky Press, and Orchard Books. As well, Scholastic acquired Klutz (see below) five years ago.

Scholastic Library Publishing is a leading provider of print and online reference products for school and public libraries, with a broad array of products through its well-known Grolier, Children's Press, Franklin Watts, and Grolier Online imprints.

Recent titles include *The Calder Game* by Blue Balliett, illustrated by Brett Helquist; *LaRue for Mayor: Letters From the Campaign Trail* by Mark Teague; *Saving Mr. Nibbles* by Patrick Carman; and *Everything But the Kitchen Sink: Weird Stuff You Didn't Know About Food* by Frieda Wishinsky and Elizabeth MacLeod; and *Once Upon a Prom Date* by Jeanie LeNy.

Scholastic considers submissions from agents or previously published authors. Arthur A. Levine considers queries from everyone. Submissions and SASEs should be directed to:

Andrea Davis Pinkney, Vice President—Publisher, Hardcover, and Early Childhood

David Levithan, Executive Editor—Trade

Kara LaReau, Executive Editor

Arthur A. Levine, Vice President and Editorial Director—Arthur A. Levine Books

KLUTZ

Based in Palo Alto, California, Klutz is the creator of kid's activity products including books, kits, toys, and other kids' stuff that stimulate their growth through creativity. Klutz' products combine clear instructions with everything you need to give kids a hands-on learning experience that ranges from the artistic to the scientific, and beyond. Founded in 1977 by three Stanford students, Klutz was purchased by Scholastic in 2002, but maintains editorial offices in California's silicon valley. Klutz makes cool stuff; their credo is: Create wonderful things, be good, have fun.

Imprints include Klutz Latino (Spanish language) and Chicken Socks (for readers ages 4-8).

Recent titles include *The 15 Greatest Board Games in the World* by the Editors of Klutz; *My All-Time Top 5: A Book of Lists for You and Your Friends* by Karen Phillips; *Draw it Again and Again, and Again, and Again* by the Editors of Klutz; *Quick Draw Flip Books* by Michael Sherman; *Mother Nature Goes Nuts!: Amazing Natural Disasters* by the Editors of Klutz.

Query with SASE to:

John Cassidy, Founder and Chief Creative Officer

SEAL PRESS [SEE PERSEUS]

SECOND CHANCE PRESS [SEE PERMANENT PRESS]

SELF-COUNSEL PRESS

A Division of Entrepreneur Press

1704 North State Street, Bellingham, WA 98225

360-676-4530 / 877-877-6490   fax: 360-676-4549

www.self-counsel.com   e-mail: orderdesk@self-counsel.com

Vancouver editorial office:

1481 Charlotte Road, North Vancouver, BC V7J 1H1 Canada

604-986-3366

A pioneer in the self-help law titles in North America, Self-Counsel Press published its first Divorce Guide in 1971. Self-Counsel produces business how-to, legal reference, self-help, and practical psychology books. Topical areas include entrepreneurship, the legal system, business training, the family, and human resources development and management. The house also produces titles geared to lifestyles and business and legal issues in Florida, Oregon, and Washington.

The house tries to anticipate a need for basic, understandable information and fill that need by publishing an informative, clearly written and reasonably priced how-to book for the layperson. They publish as many as 30 new titles each year, as well as revising more than 50 of their backlist titles to ensure that their books are always up to date regarding changes in legislation or current procedures and practices. All legal titles are authored by lawyers.

Direct proposals and SASEs to the Acquisitions Editor in either Canada or the U.S., depending on the market for which you are writing.

Diana Douglas, President, drdouglas@self-counsel.com

SEVEN STORIES

SIETE CUENTOS

140 Watts Street, New York, NY 10013

212-226-8760   fax: 212-226-1411

www.sevenstories.com   e-mail: info@sevenstories.com

Seven Stories Press is an independent book publisher based in New York City, with distribution throughout the U.S., Canada, England, Australia, and New Zealand. Under the direction of publisher Dan Simon, perhaps no other small independent house in America has consistently attracted so many important voices away from the corporate publishing sector.

Authors include Nelson Algren, Kate Braverman, Octavia Butler, Harriet Scott Chessman, Assia Djebar, Ariel Dorfman, Martin Duberman, Alan Dugan, Annie Ernaux, Barry Gifford, Stanley Moss, Peter Plate, Charley Rosen, Ted Solotaroff, Lee Stringer, Alice Walker, Martin Winckler and Kurt Vonnegut, together with political titles by voices of conscience, including Daw Aung San Suu Kyi, Tom Athanasiou, the Boston Women's Health Book Collective, the Center for Constitutional Rights, Fairness & Accuracy in Reporting, Noam Chomsky, Angela Davis, Shere Hite, Robert McChesney, Phil Jackson, Ralph Nader, Gary Null, Benjamin Pogrund, Project Censored, Luis J. Rodriguez, Barbara Seaman, Vandana Shiva, Leora Tanenbaum, Koigi wa Wamwere, Gary Webb and Howard Zinn.

On several notable occasions, Seven Stories has stepped in to publish—on First Amendment grounds—important books that were being refused the right to publish for political reasons, including Pulitzer Prize-winning journalist Gary Webb's *Dark Alliance*, about the CIA-Contra-crack cocaine connection; Carol Felsenthal's biography of the Newhouse family, *Citizen Newhouse*; and distinguished journalist and death row inmate Mumia Abu-Jamal's censored essays in *All Things Censored*.

Siete Cuentos, Seven Stories's Spanish-language imprint, launched in 2000 and now edited by Sara Villa, represents a major ongoing effort on the part of Seven Stories to introduce important English-language texts to Spanish-language readers on the one hand, for example the Spanish-language editions of *Our Bodies, Ourselves, Nuestros cuerpos, nuestras vidas*, a project of the Boston Women's Health Book Collective; and Howard Zinn's *A People's History of the United States, La otra historia de los Estados Unidos*; and on the other hand to provide Spanish-language readers in the U.S. with the best in fiction and literature written in Spanish. The literary side of Siete Cuentos has published new and classic texts by Ariel Dorfman, including *Death and the Maiden, La muerte y la doncella* and *Heading South, Looking North, Rumbo al sur, deseando el norte*, and new fiction by Ángela Vallvey and Sonia Rivera-Valdés.

Recent Seven Stories titles include *A Political Odyssey: The Rise of American Militarism and One Man's Fight to Stop It* by Mike Gravel and Joe Lauria; *Everybody Talks About the Weather...We Don't: The Writings of Ulrike Meinhof* edited by Karin Bauer; *No Blood, No Foul* by Charley Rosen; *Live Through This: On Creativity and Self-Destruction* by Sabrina Chapadjiev; *The Hidden History of 9-11* edited by Paul Zarembka; *The Voice of Hope: Conversations with Alan Clements* by Aung San Suu Kyi; *Rogue Economics: Capitalism's New Reality* by Loretta Napoleoni; and *Goodbye Mr. Socialism* by Antonio Negri and Raf Scelsi.

Seven Stories is accepting submissions of query letters with one or two sample chapters only. Direct your submission to:

Dan Simon, Publisher

SHAMBHALA

300 Massachusetts Avenue, Boston, MA 02115

617-424-0030   fax: 617-236-1563

www.shambhala.com   e-mail: editors@shambhala.com

With classic titles like *Meditation in Action* by Chögyam Trungpa, *Writing Down the Bones* by Natalie Goldberg, and *The Tao of Physics* by Fritjof Capra, Shambhala is a foremost representative of the wave of publishers specializing in the arena of contemporary globalized spiritual and cultural interest. Since Shambhala's inception (the house was founded in 1969), the field has blossomed into a still-burgeoning readership, as underscored by the many smaller independent presses and large corporate houses that tend this market. Yet Shambhala quietly continues to publish "what's real and not the glitz."

Shambhala publishes hardcover and paperback titles on creativity, philosophy, psychology, medical arts and healing, mythology, folklore, religion, art, literature, cooking, martial arts, and cultural studies. Shambhala generally issues a modest list of new titles each year and tends a flourishing backlist; the house periodically updates some of its perennial sellers in revised editions.

Shambhala produces a number of distinct lines, including gift editions and special interest imprints. Shambhala Dragon Editions accents the sacred teachings of Asian masters. Shambhala Centaur Editions offers classics of world literature in small-sized gift editions. The New Science Library concentrates on titles relating to science, technology, and the environment. Shambhala co-publishes C.G. Jung Foundation Books with the C.G. Jung Foundation for Analytical Psychology. Shambhala Redstone Editions are fine-boxed sets composed of books, postcards, games, art objects, and foldouts. Shambhala Lion Editions are spoken-word audiotape cassette presentations. New Seeds publishes such Christian mystics as Thomas Merton; Trumpeter Books publishes humanistic titles with mainstream marketability. Integral Books, an imprint with author Ken Wilber as editorial director, was launched in 2007. Shambhala purchased Weatherhill in 2004, giving it the classic *Zen Mind, Beginner's Mind* by Japanese Zen master Shunryu Suzuki.

Recent titles from Shambhala include *The Happiness Trap: How to Stop Struggling and Start Living* by Russ Harris; *I Love Dirt!: 52 Activities to Help You and Your Kids Discover the Wonders of Nature* by Jennifer Ward, illustrated by Richard Louv; *Training the Samurai Mind: A Bushido Sourcebook* translated by Thomas Cleary; *The Wisdom of Maimonides: The Life and Writings of the Jewish Sage* by Edward Hoffman; *Dragon Thunder: My Life with Chog yam Trung pa* by Carolyn Rose Gumian and Diana J. Mukpo; *Bringing the Sacred to Life: The Daily Practice of Zen Ritual* by John Daido Loori; *Comfortable with Uncertainty: 108 Techniques on Cultivating Fearlessness and Compassion* by Joanna Rotte; *The Creative Family: How to Encourage Imagination and Nurture Family Connections* by Amanda Soule.

Shambhala distributes to the trade via Random House and also services individual and special orders through its own house fulfillment department.

Proposals and SASEs should be directed to the Editorial Assistant. No e-mail submissions.

Jonathan Green, Associate Publisher

David O'Neal, Senior Editor

Peter Turner, Executive Editor

Emily Bower, Editor

Eden Steinberg, Editor, Trumpeter Books

M. E. SHARPE

EAST GATE BOOKS

SHARPE REFERENCE

80 Business Park Drive, Armonk, NY 10504

914-273-1800 / 800-541-6563   fax: 914-273-2106

www.mesharpe.com

Founded in 1958, M.E. Sharpe is a privately held publisher of books and journals in the social sciences and humanities, including economics, political science, management, public administration, and history. They also publish both original works and translations in Asian and East European studies. Several Nobel Prize winners, including e Kenzaburo and Wasily Leontief, are among the M.E. Sharpe authors.

The East Gate imprint publishes in Asian studies. M.E. Sharpe also publishes single and multivolume reference works designed to meet the needs of students and researchers from high school through college under the Sharpe Reference imprint.

Recent titles include *Public Management in Global Perspective* by Salvatore Schiavo-Campo and Hazel M. McFerson; *Currents in American History: A Brief History of the U.S.* by Terry D. Bilhartz and Alan C. Elliott; *Go Figure!: New Directions in Advertising Rhetoric* by Edward F. McQuarrie and Barbara J. Phillips; *Chronologies of Modern Terrorism* by Barry Rubin and Judith Colp Rubin; *America's Social Health: Putting Social Issues Back on the Public Agenda* by Marque-Luisa Miringoff and Sandra Opdycke; *Biographical Dictionary of Central and Eastern Europe in the Twentieth Century* edited by Wojcieck Roszkowski and Jan Kofman.

Queries with SASEs may be directed to:

Patricia Kolb, Vice President and Editorial Director—All areas, all disciplines; pkolb@mesharpe.com

Lynn Taylor, Executive Editor—Economics, business, media studies; ltaylor@mesharpe.com

Steven Drummond, Executive Editor—History, political science; sdrummond@kc.rr.com

Harry Briggs, Executive Editor—Management, marketing, public administration; hbriggs@mesharpe.com

Todd Hallman, Executive Editor—Sharpe Reference; thallman@mesharpe.com

Peter Mavrikis, Acquisitions Editor—Sharpe Reference; pmavrikis@mesharpe.com

SIERRA CLUB BOOKS

SIERRA CLUB BOOKS FOR KIDS

85 Second Street, San Francisco, CA 94105

415-977-5500   fax: 415-977-5799

www.sierraclub.org/books   e-mail: books.publishing@sierraclub.org

The Sierra Club, founded in 1892 by John Muir, has for more than a century stood in the forefront of the study and protection of the earth's scenic, environmental, and ecological resources; Sierra Club Books is part of the nonprofit effort the club carries on as a public trust.

Sierra Club publishes works in the categories of nature, technology, outdoor activities, mountaineering, health, gardening, natural history, travel, and environmental issues. Sierra Club series include the Adventure Travel Guides, Sierra Club Totebooks, Naturalists Guides, Natural Traveler, the John Muir Library, and Guides to the Natural Area of the United States. Sierra Club Books has a strong division that publishes works dedicated to children and young adults.

The books represent the following areas: the finest in outdoor photographic artistry; thought-provoking discussions of ecological issues; literary masterworks by naturalist authors; and authoritative handbooks to the best recreational activities the natural world offers. Today, the need to protect and expand John Muir's legacy is greater than ever—to help stop the relentless abuse of irreplaceable wilderness land, save endangered species, and protect the global environment.

Recent titles include *The Grandest of Live: Eye to Eye with Whales* by Douglas Chadwick; *Hey Mr. Green: Sierra Magazine's Answer Guy Tackles Your Toughest Green Living Questions* by Bob Schildgren; *Into Thick Air: Biking to the Bellybutton of Six Continents* by Jom Malusa; *Seven Wonders for a Cool Planet: Everyday Things to Help Solve Global Warming* by Eric Sorensen and the staff of Sightline Institute.

Sierra Club Books are distributed by the University of California Press.

Direct queries and SASEs to:

Helen Sweetland, Publisher

Ellen Landau, Acting Editorial Director

SIETE CUENTOS [SEE SEVEN STORIES]

SIGNATURE BOOKS

564 West 400 North Street, Salt Lake City, UT 84116-3411

801-531-1483   fax: 801-531-1488

www.signaturebooks.com   e-mail: people@signaturebooks.com

Signature Books was founded in 1980 to promote the study of Mormonism and related issues pertaining to the Rocky Mountain area. The Signature list emphasizes contemporary literature, as well as scholarly works relevant to the Intermountain West. Signature Books publishes subjects that range from outlaw biographies and Mormonism to speculative theology, from demographics to humor. In addition, Signature publishes novels and collections of poetry of local interest. They publish 12 new titles per year.

Recent titles include *The Skeleton in Grandpa's Barn: And Other Stories of Growing Up in Utah* edited by Stanford J. Layton; *The William E. McLellin Papers, 1854-1880* edited by Stan Larson and Samuel J. Passey; *The Mormon Church on Trial: Transcripts of the Reed Smoot Hearings* edited by Michael Harold Paulos; *Breathe Life into Your Life Story: How to Write a Story People Will Want to Read* by Dawn Thurston and Morris Thurston, illustrated by Amy Reeder Hadley; and *Making the Ghost Dance* by David Kranes.

Signature Publications oversees distribution of its titles via in-house ordering services and a national network of wholesalers. Signature Books does not accept unsolicited manuscripts. Query letters and SASEs should be directed to:

Gary James Bergera, Acquisitions Editor

Ron Priddis, Managing Director

SILHOUETTE [SEE HARLEQUIN ENTERPRISES, LTD.]

SIMCHA PRESS [SEE HEALTH COMMUNICATIONS, INC.]

GIBBS SMITH, PUBLISHER

P.O. Box 667, Layton, UT 84041

801-544-9800   fax: 801-546-8852

www.gibbs-smith.com

Founded in 1969, Gibbs Smith, Publisher, specializes in beautifully illustrated lifestyle books, with topics including design and architecture, cooking, business, holiday, sports, and children's books. From their farm in Utah, the editors produce books with a mission to enrich and inspire humankind the world over.

Recent titles include *Fine Texas Cuisine* by Jon Bonnell; *Pottery and Plants: Unique Garden Pairings* by James Fraioli; *Pink Princess Spa Cookbook* by Barbara Beery; *Code Name: Polar Ice* by Jean-Michel Cousteau and James Fraioli, illustrated by Joe St. Pierre;

and *An Outline of European Architecture* by Nicholaus Pevsner.

Submit proposals or manuscripts via e-mail to mbarlow@gibbs-smith.com or via regular mail to the editors:

Suzanne Taylor, Vice President and Editorial Director

Linda Nimori, Editor

Melissa Barlow, Associate Editor

Jennifer Grillone, Senior Editor

SOHO PRESS, INC.

SOHO CRIME

853 Broadway, New York, NY 10003

212-260-1900   fax: 212-260-1902

www.sohopress.com   e-mail: soho@sohopress.com

Soho Press, Inc., an independent press established in 1986, publishes literary fiction and nonfiction.

Soho Press primarily publishes fiction, with the occasional autobiography or cultural historical account. They are eager to find work from new writers and place a high priority on publishing quality unsolicited materials. The Soho Crime imprint focuses on procedurals set in exotic locales.

Recent titles include *Anthem of a Reluctant Prophet* by Joanne Proulx; *The Secret Hangman* by Peter Lovesy; *The Glass Devil* by Helene Tursten; *Chain of Evidence* by Garry Disher; *The Night Birds* by Thomas Maltman; *Death on the Holy Mountain* by David Dickinson; *Reconstruction* by Mick Herron; *The Elfish Gene: Dungeons, Dragons, and Growing Up Strange* by Mark Barrowcliffe; *The Samatarian's Secret* by Matt Beyon.

No submissions via e-mail. The editors prefer a query letter with three chapters of a completed work (preferably the first three chapters), with a brief outline and CV. Direct submissions with SASEs to:

Laura Hruska, Publisher and Editor-in-Chief

Katie Herman, Editor

SOURCEBOOKS, INC.

CASABLANCA PRESS

JABBERWOCKY

LANDMARK

HYSTERIA PUBLICATIONS

MEDIAFUSION

SPHINX PUBLISHING

1935 Brookdale Road, Suite 139, Naperville, IL 60563

630-961-3900 / 800-43-BRIGHT   fax: 630-961-2168

www.sourcebooks.com   e-mail: info@sourcebooks.com

Chicago's leading independent book publisher, Sourcebooks is exceptionally strong in business, romance, parenting, self-help, and fiction titles. Under the MediaFusion imprint, Sourcebooks also publishes mixed media titles including Poetry Speaks to Children and the Sourcebooks Shakespeare series. The house was founded in 1987 by Dominique Raccah, and has been one of the fastest-growing companies in America, with many best-sellers.

In 2007, Sourcebooks launched the Jabberwocky imprint for children's titles including *The Fairy Chronicles* by J. H. Sweet and *I Love You More* by Laura Duksta, illustrated by Karen Keesler. In the Landmark fiction imprint, the house has done very well with books that continue famous stories from Jane Austen including *Mr. Darcy's Diary* and *More Letters from Pemberley: Mrs. Darcy's Story Unfolds* by Jane Dawkins.

Other Sourcebooks imprints include Hysteria Publications, a publisher of humor and women's interest books; Casablanca Press with romance and horror genre fiction and nonfiction titles; and Sphinx Publishing, which focuses on self-help law titles.

Recent Sourcebooks titles include *1001 Healthy Baby Answers: Pediatricians' Answers to All the Questions You Didn't Know to Ask* by Gary C. Morchower; *1858: Abraham Lincoln, Jefferson Davis, Robert E. Lee, Ulysses S. Grant, and the War They Failed to See* by Bruce Chadwick; *50 Ways to Hex Your Lover* by Linda Wisdom; *75 Biggest Myths About College Admissions* by Jerry Israel; *Bankruptcy for Small Business* by Wendell Schollander and Wes Schollander; *The Change Your Life Challenge* by Brook Noel; *The Adventure Book of Outdoor Games* by Scott Strother.

Sourcebooks is actively seeking romance fiction and authors of romance may submit a word document including their first four chapters via e-mail to deb.werksman@sourcebooks.com. For all genres other than romance, the house is only accepting fiction from agents. Nonfiction authors should direct book proposals by mail to "Editorial Submissions." No e-mail submissions or phone calls (with the exception of romance fiction, as above). Please see the Sourcebooks Web site for additional information.

Agents may direct submissions to:

Todd Stocke, Editorial Director—General nonfiction, reference, multimedia formats; todd.stocke@sourcebooks.com

Peter Lynch, Editorial Manager, Trade—Business, general nonfiction, fiction; peter.lynch@sourcebooks.com

Erin Shanahan, Editorial Manager, Sphinx Publishing—Legal; erin.shanahan@sourcebooks.com

Shana Drehs, Senior Editor—Adult trade; shana.drehs@sourcebooks.com

Todd Green, Editor, MediaFusion—todd.green@sourcebooks.com

Hillel Black, Executive Editor—Fiction, history, science, business, biography, medicine, relationships; (390 5th Avenue, Suite 910, New York, NY 10018; 212-414-1701 fax: 212-594-2289); hillwen@aol.com

Deborah Werksman, Editorial Manager, Gift Books—Gift books, humor, women's interests, relationships, dating, parenting, romance fiction; (955 Connecticut Avenue, Suite 5310, Bridgeport, CT 06607; 203-333-9399) deb.werksman@sourcebooks.com

Lyron Bennett, Editor, Jabberwocky—Children's books; lyron.bennett@sourcebooks.com; (390 5th Avenue, Suite 910, New York, NY 10018; 212-414-1701 fax: 212-594-2289)

SPIRE BOOKS [SEE BAKER PUBLISHING GROUP]

SPRINGER

233 Spring Street, New York, NY 10013

212-460-1500 / 800-SPRINGER   fax: 212-460-1575

www.springer.com   e-mail: service-ny@spring.com

Springer is one of the world's most renowned scientific publishing companies. Its publications cover subjects ranging from the natural sciences, mathematics, engineering, and computer science to medicine and psychology. In the fields of economics and law, Springer offers an increasing number of books in management science. Since the 2004 merger with Dutch scientific house Kluwer Academic Publishing, the range of products has increased; it now includes publications on the arts and social science.

Springer's authors are highly qualified experts. More than 150 Nobel Prize winners, plus scientists, doctors, and engineers such as Robert Koch, Fredinand Sauerbruch, Albert Einstein, Werner von Siemens, and Otto Hahn have published their works at Springer.

Recent titles include *Children and the Dark Side of Human Experience: Confronting Global Realities and Rethinking Child Development* by James Garbarino; *Why Popcorn Costs So Much at the Movies and Other Pricing Puzzles* by Richard B. McKenzie; *The Buzz About Bees: Biology of a Superorganism* by Jüngen Tautz; *Faith Is: Looking for Faith and Religion* edited by Lukas Neiderberger and Lars Miller; *African Americans and AIDS: A Community in Crisis* edited by Donna H. McCree, Kenneth T. Jones, and Ann O'Leary.

Submit proposals and SASEs to:

William Curtis, Editorial Director—Life sciences and medicine, william.curtis@springer.com

Hans Koelsch, Directorial Editor—Mathematics, physics, engineering, hans.koelsch@springer.com

John Kimmel, Executive Editor—Statistics, computer science, john.kimmel@springer.com

---

SQUARE ONE PUBLISHERS

115 Herricks Road, Garden City Park, NY 11040

516-535-2010 / 877-900-BOOK   fax: 516-535-2014

www.squareonepublishers.com

Square One publishing sees itself as recapturing the spirit of the 1920's, 30's, and 40's: the Golden Age of independent publishing. They feel that advances in print technology have given birth to a revival of the original sense of entrepreneurial spirit and excitement that characterized the early pioneers. Supporting this conviction, *Publishers Weekly* has named Square One Publishers one of the fastest-growing indie publishers in the U.S. for the third year in a row. Square One is interested in manuscripts on alternative health, collectibles, cooking, gambling, health, how-to, parenting, personal finance, postcards, self-help, and writing.

Recent titles from Square One include *The Irlen Revolution: A Guide to Overcoming Learning Disabilities* by Helen Irlen and Larry Trivieri Jr.; *Natural Alternative to Nexium, Maalox, Tagament, Prilosec, and Other Acid Blockers* by Martie Whittekin; *Mobile Home Wealth: How to Turn and Empty Lot into a Moneymaking Asset* by Zalman Velvel; *Pea in a Pod: Your Complete Guide to Pregnancy, Childbirth, and Beyond* by Linda Goldberg; and *Desktop Handicapping by Thoroughbred Racing: Gaining the Winning Edge with Your PC* by Howard Berenbon.

Address queries and SASEs to:

Rudy Shur, Publisher

ST. ANTHONY MESSENGER PRESS

Franciscan Communications

28 West Liberty Street, Cincinnati, OH 45202

513-241-5615 / 800-488-0488   fax: 513-241-0399

www.americancatholic.org   e-mail: samadmin@americancatholic.org

St. Anthony Messenger Press (founded in 1970) and Franciscan Communications publishes Catholic religious works and resources for parishes, schools, and individuals. The house also owns the video/print imprints Ikonographics and Fischer Productions.

Areas of St. Anthony Messenger's publishing interest include Franciscan topics, Catholic identity, family life, morality and ethics, parish ministry, pastoral ministry, prayer helps, sacraments, saints and Christian heroes, Scripture, seasonal favorites, small-group resources, spirituality for every day, children's books, and youth ministry. The house produces books (hardcover and paperback, many in economically priced editions), magazines, audiotapes and videocassettes, as well as educational programs and an award-winning Website.

Recent titles include *Together But Alone: When God Means Something Different to Your Spouse* by Donna Erickson Couch; *Saints Off the Pedestal: Real Saints for Real People* by Amanda Roberts; *Mary and Me: Catholic Women Reflect on the Mother of God* by Ginny Kubitz Moyer; *The Miracle of Lourdes: A Message of Healing and Hope* by John Lochran; *Song of the Sparrow: New Poems and Meditations* by Murray Bodo; *Bridges of Faith: and Building a Relationship with a Sister Parish* by Dennis P. O'Connor.

St. Anthony Messenger Press also offers music CDs, computer software, videos, and audiocassettes.

St. Anthony Messenger Press distributes books through Ingram, Spring Arbor, Riverside Distributors, Appalachian Inc., Baker & Taylor, and ABS/Guardian.

Query letters and SASEs should be directed to:

Lisa Biedenbach, Editorial Director, Books, LisaB@AmericanCatholic.org

STEEPLE HILL [SEE HARLEQUIN ENTERPRISES, LTD.]

STERLING PUBLISHING CO., INC.

A division of Barnes and Noble

387 Park Avenue South, 10th Floor, New York, NY 10016-8810

212-532-7160

www.sterlingpub.com   e-mail: online@sterlingpub.com

Sterling Publishing (founded 1949 and acquired by Barnes and Noble in 2003) is one of the world's leading publishers of nonfiction titles with more than 5,000 books in print. Among its best-selling titles are *The Big Book of Knitting*, *The Good Housekeeping Cookbook*, and *Windows on the World Complete Wine Course*. Subject categories in which the company excels include puzzles and games, crafts, gardening, woodworking, health, and children's books.

With an unusual title and packaging, *Yoga for Wimps* became a best seller in 2001 and marked the launch of an ongoing series that includes *Orchids for Wimps* and *Meditation for Wimps*. Another success is the novelty-packaged Sit and Solve series. Many of Sterling's children's books, such as *Sometimes I Like to Curl Up in a Ball* and *I Know a Rhino*, are critically acclaimed best-sellers.

Recent titles include *Kim Lyons' Your Body, Your Life: The 12-Week Program to Optimum Physical, Mental, and Emotional Fitness* by Kim Lyons and Lara McGlashan; *Doo Wop: The Music, the Era* by "Cousin Brucie" Morrow with Rich Maloof; *Tony Bennett in the Studio: A Life of Art and Music* by Tony Bennett with Robert Sullivan; *Lacy Little Knits: Clingy, Soft, and a Little Risqué* by Iris Schreier; *The Boy's Body Book* by Kelli Dunham, illustrated by Steven Bjorkman.

To submit to Sterling, send a proposal with CV and SASE via regular mail. Submissions should be sent to the attention of the category editor, e.g., the material on a woodworking book should be addressed to the "Woodworking Editor"; a craft book proposal should be addressed to the "Craft Editor"; and so on. All children's book submissions should be sent to the attention of the "Children's Book Editor."

Frances Gilbert, Editor-in-Chief, Children's Publishing

David Nelson, Editor—Adult Books

STEWART, TABORI, CHANG [SEE HARRY N. ABRAMS, INC.]

SYBEX, INC. [SEE JOHN WILEY & SONS]

TAYLOR TRADE [SEE ROWMAN & LITTLEFIELD]

TEN SPEED PRESS

CELESTIAL ARTS

CROSSING PRESS

TEN SPEED PRESS

TRICYCLE PRESS

P.O. Box 7123, Berkeley, CA 94707

510-559-1600   fax: 510-559-1629

www.tenspeed.com

Founder Philip Wood began the Ten Speed Press in 1971 with *Anybody's Bike Book*, still in print with more than a million copies sold. Ten Speed went on to build its reputation with titles including *What Color is Your Parachute?*, *Moosewood Cookbook*, *White Trash Cooking*, *Why Cats Paint*, and *Flattened Fauna*. Ten Speed Press publishes 150 books per year under its four imprints: Ten Speed Press, Celestial Arts, Crossing Press, and Tricycle Press.

Julie Bennett, an acquiring editor at Ten Speed, said recently that the press is in the process of expanding its list in the area of "quirky" or "alternative" crafts. "We're hoping it's where the cookbook world was ten to 15 years ago," she said. As the design elements of the books are improved, consumers will buy crafts books as they do cookbooks, for inspiration, whether they make the crafts in them or not, Bennett predicted. Other Ten Speed categories include how-to, cooking, business/career, relationships, gardening, gift, humor, and pop culture.

Recent titles from Ten Speed include *The River Cottage Family Cookbook* by High Fearnley-Whittingstall and Fizz Carr; *So You Want to Score?: The SAT Secrets the College Board Doesn't Want You to Know* by Elizabeth S. King; *Takashi's Japanese Noodle Book* by Takashi Yagihashi; *The Little Black Book for the Entrepreneur* by Fernando Trias de Bes;

DIY Kitchen: 25 Edible Crafts for the Weekend Warrior by Karen Solomon.

Tricycle Press is the children's imprint for Ten Speed. They focus on board books, picture books, young adult novels, and real-life books to help kids understand themselves and the world. Recent titles from Tricycle include *A Curious Collection of Cats* by Betsy Franco; *Eco Babies Wear Green* by Michelle Coleman; *Where in the Wild?: Camouflaged Creatures Concealed and Revealed* by David W. Schwartz and Yael Schy; *Winter Babies Wear Layers* by Michelle Sinclair Coleman and Nathalie Dion.

CELESTIAL ARTS

Celestial Arts was founded by poster printer Hal Kramer in San Francisco in 1963. During the Human Potential Movement of the seventies, Celestial Arts blossomed into a book publisher and made a name for itself with best-sellers like *Loving Someone Gay* and Virginia Satir's inspirational poem-book *Self-Esteem*.

The Celestial Arts imprint was acquired by Ten Speed Press in 1983 and continues to publish a diverse list of alternative medicine, health, nutrition, parenting, inspiration, self-help, and spirituality titles.

Recent titles include *Alternative Medicine Definitive Guide: Arthritis* by Ellen Kamhi and Eugene Zampieron; *Stumbling Toward Enlightenment (new ed.)* by Geri Larken; *The Enlightened Diet: Seven Weight-loss Solutions That Nourish Body, Mind, and Soul* by Deborah Kesten and Larry Scherwitz; *Calm and Compassionate Children* by Susan Usha Dermond.

CROSSING PRESS

Crossing Press (originally called New Books) began as a small poetry publisher founded by poet John Gill in the village of Trumansburg, New York, just outside of Ithaca, in 1963. He changed the press's name to the Crossing Press in 1969 (after consulting the I Ching, as legend has it) and began branching out into literature, feminist and political works, and cookbooks. Early landmarks include *The Male Muse* (1974), a pioneering collection of gay poetry, and unique cookbooks like *Moog's Musical Eatery* (1978). In 1986, the company relocated to northern California and, in 2002, it was acquired by Ten Speed Press.

The Crossing Press publishes a wide range of hardcover and trade paperback editions of books, videos, and audios on natural healing, spirituality, alternative healing practices, and, occasionally, cooking. Dedicated to social and spiritual change, Crossing Press focuses on metaphysics, alternative therapies, mysticism, feminism, herbal medicine, and chakra and color healing.

Recent titles include *Cards of Destiny: A Birthday Book and Daily Divination Guide* by Sharon Jeffers; *Aromatherapy: A Complete Guide to the Healing Art* by Kathi Melville and Mindy Green; *Sister Outsider: Essays and Speeches (commemorative ed.)* by Audre Lorde; *Attracting Your Perfect Body Through the Chakras* by Cyndi Dale.

For all Ten Speed imprints, direct queries, proposals, and SASEs to the attention of "Acquisition Editors" for the specific imprint. No unsolicited e-mail submissions.

Lorena Jones, Publisher

Aaron Wehner, Editorial Director, Ten Speed

Nicole Geiger, Publisher, Tricycle Press—Children's books

Jo Ann Deck, Publisher, Celestial Arts and Crossing Press

THAMES & HUDSON, INC.

500 Fifth Avenue, New York, NY 10110

212-354-3763   fax: 212-398-1252

www.thamesandhudsonusa.com   e-mail: BookInfo@thames.wwnorton.com

Thames & Hudson is one of the world's most eminent publishers of illustrated books. The house releases high-quality, well-printed books on art, architecture, design, photography, decorative arts, archaeology, history, religion, and spirituality, as well as a number of titles for children.

Recent titles include The Advertising Concept Book by Pete Barry; Ancient Bodies, Ancient Lives: Sex, Gender, and Archaeology by Rosemary A. Joyce; People and the Sky: Our Ancestors and the Cosmos by Anthony Aveni; Light, Air, and Openness: Modern Architecture Between the Wars by Paul Overy; Face: The New Photographic Portrait by William A. Ewing; Icons of Graphic Design by Stephen Heller and Mirko Ilic; The Ancient World at War edited by Philip de Souza; Adventures in Tornado Alley: The Storm Chasers by Mike Hollingshead and Eric Nguyen; and Motionless Journey: From a Heritage in the Himalayas by Matthieu Ricard.

Thames & Hudson is distributed in the U.S. by W.W. Norton & Company, Inc., and in Canada by Penguin.

Authors should query by postcard or e-mail at BookInfo@thames.wwnorton.com.

Peter Warner, President

Susan Dwyer, Vice President

THEATRE COMMUNICATIONS GROUP

520 Eighth Avenue, 24th Floor, New York, NY 10018-4156

212-609-5900   fax: 212-609-5901

www.tcg.org   e-mail: tcg@tcg.org

The mission of the Theatre Communications Group is to strengthen, nurture and promote the not-for-profit professional American theater by celebrating differences in aesthetics, culture, organizational structure and geography. The house produces American

Theatre magazine and the ArtSEARCH employment bulletin. They also publish plays, translations and theater reference books. TCG awards grants to individuals and institutions; interested authors should peruse the house Web site for a myriad of opportunities to connect to the professional theater world.

Recent titles include *August: Osage County* by Tracy Letts; *Drunk Enough to Say I Love You* by Caryl Churchill; *The Seafarer* by Conor McPherson; *Exits and Entrances* by Athol Fugard.

Direct queries with SASEs to:

Terence Nemeth, Publisher

Kathy Sova, Editorial Director; ksova@tcg.org

Molly Metzler, Associate Editor

TIN HOUSE BOOKS

2601 N.W. Thurman Street, Portland, OR 97210

503-219-0622

www.tinhouse.com/books

After three years working with Bloomsbury USA on a joint publishing venture known as Tin House Books/Bloomsbury, Tin House Books is now an independent company with offices in Portland, Oregon. Tin House continues to publish new literary voices as well as reprints of contemporary and classic works of fiction and nonfiction. The mission of Tin House Books remains constant: to publish compelling and authentic narratives of our time. Tin House salutes the artistic edge but remains rooted in the tenets of the classic storytelling tradition.

Tin House Books' first focus is the launch of the New Voice Series: story cycles, collections, novels, and memoir by first-time authors. The house also publishes the Tin House literary journal.

Recent titles include *Girl Factory* by Jim Kruso; *Salvation* by Lucia Nevai; *You Don't Know Me: A Citizen's Guide to Republican Family Values* by Win McCormack; *Do Me: Tales of Sex and Love from Tim House*; *Ovenman* by Jeff Parker.

Distribution is through Publisher's Group West.

Tin House Books no longer reads unsolicited submissions by authors without representation, but this may change. Check the Tin House Books website for more information.

Lee Montgomery, Editorial Director

Meg Storey, Assistant Editor

TRAFALGAR SQUARE BOOKS

PO Box 257, 288 Howe Hill Road, North Pomfret, Vermont, 05053

802-457-1911 / 800-423-4525

www.horseandriderbooks.com   e-mail: info@horseandriderbooks.com

Trafalgar Square published its first horse book, *Centered Riding* by Sally Swift, in 1985 and the book remains one of the bestselling horse books of all time. This book was the spark that led Ted and Caroline Robbins, Trafalgar Square's owners, to start up a horse book publishing business. Previously, Trafalgar Square was a book distribution outlet for British publishers. Since it's beginnings in 1985, Trafalgar Square has published over 85 horse books, and has a growing list of titles on dressage, jumping, training, western riding, horse care, driving, and more. Trafalgar Square has also ventured into video, DVD, and audio publishing.

Trafalgar Square has published such authors as Jane Savoi, Linda Tellington-Jones, William Steinkraus, Mary Wanless, Clinton Anderson, Charles de Kunffy, Sylvia Loch, Richard Shrake, Betsy Steiner, Kyra Kyrklund, Alois Podhajsky, Paul Belasik, Jessica Jahiel, and more.

Recent titles from Trafalgar Square include *Human to Horseman: A Journey of Discovery, Growth, and Celebration* by Rick Lamb; *Reining Essentials* by Sandy Collier with Jennifer Forsberg Meyer; *Western Horse's Pain-Free Back and Saddle-Fit Book* by Joyce Harman; and *Tug of War: Classical Versus "Modern" Dressage* by Gerd Heuschmann.

Send queries and SASEs to by email to info@horseandriderbooks.com.

TRICYCLE PRESS [SEE TEN SPEED PRESS]

TUTTLE PUBLISHING

A Member of the Periplus Publishing Group

364 Innovation Drive, North Clarendon, VT 05759

802-773-8930 / 800-526-2778   fax: 802-773-6993 / 800-329-8885

www.tuttlepublishing.com   e-mail: info@tuttlepublishing.com

Tuttle Publishing was founded by Charles Tuttle in Tokyo in 1948. The publisher's mission was to publish "books to span the East and West." In the early 1950s the company began publishing a large number of titles on Japanese language, arts and culture. In 1983, Charles Tuttle was awarded the Order of the Sacred Treasure by the Emperor of Japan for his services to Japanese-American understanding. Tuttle is now the USA arm of the Periplus Publishing Group, the world's leading publisher of books on Asia.

Eric Oey, a cousin of Charles E. Tuttle, founded Periplus Editions in 1988 in Berkeley, California, and merged the two companies in 1996. With offices in Vermont, Singapore, Tokyo, Hong Kong, and Jakarta, Tuttle Publishing has become the largest English-language book publishing and distribution company in Asia.

Recent titles include *The X-Guard* by Marcelo Garcia, Glen Cardoza, and Erich Krauss; *The Shaolin Grandmasters' Text: History, Philosophy, and Gung Fu of Shaolin Ch'an* by Order of Shaolin Ch'an; *China Style* by Sharon Leece and Michael Freeman; *Ninjutsu: The Art of Invisibility* by Donn F. Draeger; and *Rosalind Creasy's Recipes From the Garden* by Rosalind Creasy.

To submit, send a complete book proposal and SASE to Editorial Acquisitions.

Ed Walters, Editorial Director

TYNDALE HOUSE PUBLISHERS

HEARTQUEST

351 Executive Drive, Carol Stream, IL 60188

800-323-9400   fax: 800-684-0247

www.tyndale.com   e-mail: customer@tyndale.com

Tyndale House Publishers (founded in 1962) offers a comprehensive program in Christian living: devotional, inspirational, and general nonfiction, from a nondenominational evangelical perspective. Tyndale's publishing interest also encompasses religious fiction and children's books. The house publishes the best-selling Living Bible and the Left Behind series. Tyndale produces hardcover, trade paperback, and mass-market paperback originals, as well as reprints.

Recent nonfiction titles include *Fixing Family Fiction* by Claudia Arp, David Arp, John Bell, and Margaret Bell; *On the Anvil* by Max Lucdo; *The Savvy Bride's Guide Answer Book* edited by Wilford Wooton and Phillip J. Swihart; *Looking For God* by Nancy Ortberg; *Life Savors* compiled by Jeanette Gardner Littleton and James Stuart Bell; *Choosing Your Faith* by Mark Mittleberg.

Tyndale fiction includes mainstream novels, as well as a number of inspirational romance series, including works set in Revolutionary War and Civil War milieus. The house is interested in evangelical Christian-theme romance in other historical periods (including Regency), as well as those with a humorous twist. HeartQuest is the romance fiction line of Tyndale.

Recent fiction titles include *Summer Snow* by Nicole Baart; *Torrent Falls* by Jan Watson; *She Always Wore Red* by Angela Hunt; *A Kiss of Adventure* by Catherine Palmer; *On Sparrow Hill* by Maureen Lang; *By Reason of Insanity* by Randy Singer.

Tyndale Children's books target all ages from birth through high school. Most are on topics of specific interest to children in Christian families (i.e., the Bible or prayer). The others are on themes that interest all children (i.e., friends or fears), but these themes are presented from a clearly Christian perspective.

In a publishing partnership with the American Association of Christian Counselors, Tyndale offers books written by leading Christian counselors that integrate counseling principles and Biblical theology as they offer authoritative analysis and research for the Professional Counseling Library. Titles include *Counseling Children Through the World of Play* by Daniel Sweeney, Ph.D.; *Psychology, Theology, and Spirituality in Christian Counseling* by Mark R. McMinn; *Counseling Through the Maze of Divorce* by George Ohlschlager; *Treating Sex Offenders* by Daniel Henderson; *Brief Counseling* by Gary J. Oliver; and *Treating Victims of Sexual Abuse* by Diane Langberg.

Tyndale House oversees its own distribution. Tyndale also distributes books from Focus on the Family.

Tyndale is not accepting manuscript proposals from anyone except literary agents or writers whose work has already been published.

Jonathan Farrar, Acquisitions Director

Carol Traver, Acquisitions Editor

UNIVERSE INTERNATIONAL PUBLICATIONS [SEE RIZZOLI, USA]

UNITED CHURCH PRESS [SEE THE PILGRIM PRESS]

URJ PRESS

633 Third Avenue, New York, NY 10017

888-489-8242 / 212-650-4120   fax: 212-650-4119

www.urjpress.com   e-mail: press@urj.org

Formerly UAHC Press, URJ Press publishes in the areas of religion (Jewish), Reform Judaism, textbooks, audiovisual materials, social action, biography, and life cycles and holidays. In its trade categories, URJ Press accents juvenile fiction and adult nonfiction books, as well as titles in basic Judaism and inspirational works. The house catalogs books, audiocassettes, videotapes, and multimedia products, suitable for use in both the classroom and the home.

URJ Press provides the highest quality in religious educational materials and has done so for well over 100 years. The publishers are committed to providing their readers with the foremost in materials and service, to be a continuing resource for books, publications, audiocassettes, videotapes, and multimedia.

Indicative of URJ Press interests are *Jonah: A Modern Commentary* translation and commentary by Leonard S. Kravitz and Kerry M. Olitzky; *A Taste of Torah: An Introduction to the Thirteen Challenging Bible Stories* by Ronald H. Isaacs; *The Torah: A Women's Commentary* edited by Tamara Cohn Eskenazi and Andrea Weiss; *A Taste of Hebrew* by Rabbi Aaron Starr; *Swords and Plowshares: Jewish Views of War and Peace* by Edwin C. Goldberg; *Inside Intermarriage: A Christian Partner's Perspective on Raising a Jewish Family* by James Keen.

Children's titles from URJ include *My Cousin Tamar Lives in Israel* by Michelle Shapiro Abraham; *America: The Jewish Experience* by Sondra Leiman; *At Camp Kee Tov: Ethics for Jewish Juniors* by Helen Fine, illustrated by Seymour Fleishman; *Book of Miracles: A Young Person's Guide to Jewish Spirituality* by Lawrence Kushner, illustrated by Devis Grebu; *Drugs, Sex, and Integrity: What Judaism Say?* by Daniel F. Polish, Daniel B. Syme, and Bernard M. Zlotowitz, illustrated by Jos D'az.

URJ Press handles its own distribution.

Query letters, proposals, and SASEs should be directed to:

Rabbi Hara Person, Editor-in-Chief

VEDANTA PRESS

Vedanta Society of Southern California
1946 Vedanta Place, Hollywood, CA 90068
323-960-1727

www.vedanta.com   e-mail: info@vedanta.com

Vedanta's publishing interests include meditation, religions and philosophies, and women's studies. In addition to its list of titles imported from the East (primarily from Indian publishers), Vedanta's program embraces works of Western origin. The publisher catalogs titles from other publishers and also sells audiotapes and videotapes.

The house publishes books on the philosophy of Vedanta, with an aim to engage a wide variety of temperaments, using a broad spectrum of methods, in order to attain the realization of each individual personality's divinity within. Vedanta Press (founded in 1947) is a subsidiary of the Vedanta Society of Southern California.

Recent titles include *Consciousness: A Deeper Scientific Search (Papers read at a seminar at the Ramakrishna Institute of Culture)*; *Days in an Indian Monastery* by Sister Devamata; *Four Yogas: A Guide to the Spiritual Paths* by Swami Adiswarananda; *Hindu Rites, Rituals, Customs, and Traditions: A-Z on the Hindu Way of Life* by Prem P. Bhalla.

Backlist from the press includes *The Compassionate Mother* translated by Swami Tanamayananda; *The Essential Rumi* by Rumi; *Mahabharata for Children* by Swami Raghaveshananda; *Myths and Legends of the Hindus and Buddhists* by Sister Nivedita and Ananda and K. Coomaraswamy; *Principles of Tantra* by Sir John Woodroffe; *Ramakrishna and Christ: The Supermystics* by Paul Hourihan; *Ramakrishna and His Gospel* by Swami Bhuteshananda; *The World Sri Ramakrishna Knew* by Dr. Jaladhi Kumar Sarkar; *Yoga for Beginners* by Swami Gnaneswarananda; *How to Know God: The Yoga Aphorisms of Patanjali* (translated by Swami Prabhavananda and Christopher Isherwood); *The Upanishads: Breath of the Eternal* (translated by Swami Prabhavananda and Frederick Manchester); *Women Saints: East and West* (edited by Swami Ghanananda and Sir John Stewart-Wallace); *The Sermon on the Mount According to Vedanta* by Swami Prabhavananda; *Seeing God Everywhere: A Practical Guide to Spiritual Living* by Swami Shraddhananda; and *Six Lighted Windows: Memories of Swamis in the West* by Swami Yogeshananda.

Vedanta publishes many classic Vedic works in a variety of editions and translations. Among them is *Bhagavad Gita: The Song of God* (translated by Swami Prabhavananda and Christopher Isherwood; introduction by Aldous Huxley).

Vedanta Press handles its own distribution, with many titles available from Baker and Taylor, DeVross and Company, and New Leaf Distributors.

Vedanta's books originate in-house, though the publisher is open to considering additional projects that may fall within its program. Vedanta does not wish to receive unsolicited manuscripts.

Query letters and SASEs should be directed to:

Bob Adjemian, General Manager

VERSO

20 Jay Street, 10th Floor, Brooklyn, NY 11201-8346

781-246-8160   fax: 781-246-8165

www.versobooks.com   e-mail: versony@versobooks.com

With global sales approaching $3 million per year and over 350 titles in print, Verso can justifiably claim to be the largest radical publisher in the English-language world. The house publishes critical nonfiction in social science, humanities, history, and current affairs, such as Tariq Ali's *The Clash of Fundamentalism* and Laura Flanders' *Bushwomen: How They Won the White House for Their Man*; and trade titles such as Karen Finley's *George and Martha*.

Verso (meaning in printers' parlance 'the lefthand page') was founded in 1970 by the London-based New Left Review, a journal of left-wing theory with a worldwide readership of 40,000. The company remains independent to this day. The company's head office is located in London, where a staff of 12 produces a program of 60 new titles each year.

Originally trading as New Left Books, the company developed an early reputation as a translator of classic works of European literature and politics by authors such as Jean-Paul Sartre, Walter Benjamin, Louis Althusser, Theodor Adorno, Herbert Marcuse, Ernest Mandel and Max Weber. More recent translations include the work of Giovanni Arrighi, Norberto Bobbio, Guy Debord, Giles Deleuze, Che Guevara, Carlo Ginzburg, Andre Gorz, Jürgen Habermas, Gabriel García Marquez and Paul Virilio.

Commissioning intelligent, critical works located at the intersection of the academic and trade markets, Verso has many key authors in English in the social sciences and humanities, with particular strength in politics, cultural studies, history, philosophy, sociology and literary criticism. Such writers include Tariq Ali, Benedict Anderson, Perry Anderson, Michèle Barrett, Robin Blackburn, Terry Eagleton, Paul Gilroy, Stuart Hall, Eric Hobsbawm, Victor Kiernan, Steven Lukes, E.P. Thompson and Raymond Williams.

From early on in its life, the company retained US rights and has added to its imports a range of distinguished North American-based writers. Editors located on both East and West coasts have signed authors including Noam Chomsky, Alexander Cockburn, Marc Cooper, Mike Davis, Juan Gonzalez, Christopher Hitchens, Frederic Jameson, Andrew Kopkind, Lewis Lapham, Manning Marable, David Roediger, Andrew Ross, Edward Said and Michele Wallace.

North America today comprises 65% of the company's worldwide sales. In the spring of 1995 Verso opened an office in New York. Primarily handling marketing and publicity work, the American office now has a staff of four.

Verso stands today as a publisher combining editorial intelligence, elegant production and marketing flair. Having quadrupled in size over the past decade, the company will continue its progress towards the mainstream of the industry without compromising its radical commitment.

Recent titles include *If I Am Not Myself: Confessions of an Anti-Zionist Jew* by Mike Marqusee; *Commie Girl in the O.C.* by Rebecca Schoenkopf; *A People's History of the World* by Chris Harman; *In Defense of Lost Causes* by Slavoj Zizek; *Politics Noir: Dark Tales From the Corridors of Power* edited by Gary Phillips; *Casualty Figures: How Five Men Survived the First World War* by Michele Barrett.

Send proposals (lengths of ten pages or fewer) and SASEs to the Editorial Department.

Amy Scholder, US General Manager

VISIBLE INK PRESS

43311 Joy Road, #414, Canton, MI 48187-2075

734-667-3211   fax: 734-667-4311

www.visibleink.com

A Detroit phenomena since 1990 and a continuing surprise to everyone involved, Visible Ink Press publishes mega-works of popular reference that inform and entertain in the areas of culture, science, history, religion, and government. All of their titles could be classified as popular reference.

Recent titles include *The Handy Supreme Court Answer Book* by David L. Hudson, Jr.; *Real Ghosts, Restless Spirits, and Haunted Places* by Brad Steiger; *American Murder: Criminals, Crime, and the Media* by Mike Mayol; *Black Firsts: 4,000 Ground-Breaking and Pioneering Events (2nd ed.)* by Jessie Carney Smith.

Visible Ink is not currently accepting unsolicited manuscripts, but the editors encourage authors to check the Web site as this policy may soon change. Direct queries and SASEs to:

Roger Janecke, President

Megan Hiller, Editorial Director

WALKER PUBLISHING [SEE BLOOMSBURY]

WATERBROOK [SEE RANDOM HOUSE]

WATSON-GUPTILL PUBLICATIONS

AMPHOTO BOOKS

BACK STAGE BOOKS

BILLBOARD BOOKS

WATSON-GUPTILL

LONE EAGLE

A Division of Random House

1745 Broadway, New York, NY 10019

212-751-2000

www.watsonguptill.com   e-mail: info@watsonguptill.com

Due to the recent sale of the firm to Random House, it was not certain at press time what, if any, front-list acquisitions activity there might be.

WEISER [SEE RED WHEEL / WEISER]

WESTVIEW [SEE PERSEUS]

JOHN WILEY & SONS

FISHER INVESTMENTS PRESS

JOSSEY-BASS

WILEY CHILDREN'S BOOKS

SYBEX

WILEY-BLACKWELL

111 River Street, Hoboken, NJ 07030-5774

201-748-6000   fax: 201-748-6088

www.wiley.com   e-mail: info@wiley.com

Indianapolis address:

10475 Crosspoint Boulevard, Indianapolis, IN 46256

317-572-3000

www.dummies.com

Jossey-Bass and Sybex address:

989 Market Street, San Francisco, CA 94103-1741

415-433-1740   fax: 415-433-0499

www.josseybass.com

www.sybex.com   e-mail: sybexproposals@wiley.com

Wiley-Blackwell address:

Commerce Place, 350 Main Street, Malden, MA 02148

781-388-8200   fax: 781-388-8210

www.blackwellpublishing.com

Wiley-Blackwell Publishing Professional address:

2121 State Avenue, Ames, IA 50014-8300

www.blackwellprofessional.com

Wiley was founded in 1807, during the Jefferson presidency. In the early years, Wiley was best known for the works of Washington Irving, Edgar Allan Poe, Herman Melville, and other 19th century American literary giants. By the turn of the century, Wiley was established as a leading publisher of scientific and technical information. The company went public in 1962 and was listed on the NYSE in 1995.

In 2007, Wiley acquired academic and professional publisher Blackwell Publishing for over $1 billion. Blackwell was merged it into Wiley's global scientific, technical, and medical business. Also in 2007, its bicentennial year, Wiley announced record revenue.

Wiley is a global publisher of print and electronic products, specializing in scientific, technical, and medical books and journals; professional and consumer books and subscription services; and textbooks and other educational materials for undergraduate and graduate students as well as lifelong learners. Wiley publishes in a variety of formats.

The Scientific, Technical, and Medical Division produces books, journals, and electronic products for academic and professional markets. Wiley STMD's primary fields of interest are chemistry, the life sciences, medicine, and mathematical and physical sciences. This is the largest of Wiley's divisions and now includes Wiley-Blackwell (see below).

The Professional and Trade Division produces nonfiction book and electronic products for the professional, business, and general interest consumer markets. Its primary fields of interest are accounting, architecture, engineering, business, finance and investment, children, computers, society (including current affairs, health, parenting, self-help, reference, history, biography, science, and nature), hospitality, law, psychology, and real estate. Also included are the following Wiley brands: Betty Crocker, Bible, CliffsNotes, Cracking the Code, Dummies, Frommer's, Howell, Novell Press, Secrets, 3D Visual, Webster's New World Dictionary, Weekend Crash Course, and Weight Watchers. Wiley content travels well. Approximately 40% of the company's revenue is generated outside the United States.

The company provides "must-have" content to targeted communities of interest. Wiley's deep reservoir of quality content, constantly replenished, offers a tremendous source of competitive advantage. Technology is making this content more accessible to customers worldwide and is adding value for them by delivering it in interactive and/or fully searchable formats. Approximately 25% of global revenue is currently Web-enabled.

With about 3,500 employees worldwide, Wiley has operations in the United States, Europe (England, Germany and Russia), Canada, Asia, and Australia. The Company has U.S. publishing, marketing, and distribution centers in New Jersey, California, Virginia, Illinois, Indiana, and Ohio. Wiley's worldwide headquarters are located in Hoboken, New Jersey, just across the river from Manhattan.

Recent titles include *What's the Secret?: To Providing a World-Class Customer Experience* by John DiJulius III; *The Little Book of Bull Moves in Bear Markets: How to Keep Your Portfolio Up When the Market is Down* by Peter D. Schiff; *No Sudden Moves: The Hangover Cure in Legend, Lore, and Recipes* by Elissa Altman; *Confessions of a Sub-prime Lender: How Greed, Fraud, and Ignorance Caused the Greatest Business Debacle in US History* by Richard Betner; *Splintered States: The End of the American Empire and What Investors Need To Do Now* by Michael Panzner; *Have Your Cake and Eat It Too: 75 Gluten, Dairy, Nut, Soy, and Egg-Free Delicious Desserts* by Elizabeth Gorden.

Wiley's proposal submission guidelines are rather specific. Please see the page "Submission Guidelines" on the Web site. It is Wiley's policy not to accept unsolicited proposals for books in the For Dummies series. For everything else, send a proposal with

SASE to the attention of the appropriate editor or division (Professional and Trade Division or Scientific, Technical, and Medical Division).

David Pugh, Senior Editor—Finance, investing, e-commerce, corporate tie-ins (NJ)

Shannon Vargo, Associate Editor—Business Subjects (NJ)

Stephen Power, Senior Editor—Popular science, current events (NJ)

Tom Miller, Executive Editor—General interest, health (NJ)

Debra Englander, Executive Editor—Investing, finance, money (NJ)

Hana Lane, Executive Editor—History/biography (NJ)

Sheck Cho, Executive Editor—Technology, business, politics (NJ)

Richard Narramore, Senior Editor—General business (NJ)

Matthew Holt, Senior Editor—General business, marketing, careers (NJ)

Kathleen Cox, Acquisitions Editor—For Dummies series (IN)

Mike Lewis, Editor, Dummies series (NJ)

Kate Bradford, Editor, Jossey Bass, books for teachers and about educational subjects (NJ)

Linda Ingroia, Editor, Cooking and restaurant management (NJ)

Crystel Winkler, Editor, Health, popular psychology, relationships

FISHER INVESTMENTS PRESS

Fisher Investments Press draws upon the expertise of bestselling author and investor Ken Fisher to offer investing advice and education for a wide audience. Says Ken Fisher: "Our goal in partnering with Wiley to create Fisher Investments Press was to reach a wide and diverse investment audience. Working together, we've developed an investment series that can offer insight to the full spectrum of investors, from novices to professionals." The first Fisher Investments title, *10 Roads to Riches* by Ken Fisher, focuses on various methods of wealth accumulation, from old-fashioned saving to inheritance and business enterprise.

More titles from Fisher Investments Press include *Globalize Your Portfolio for the 21st Century; Bear Hunting: How to Spot and Slay the Next Bear Market;* and *Investment Spinach: Financial Advice You Don't Want, but Need,* all by Ken Fisher and Fisher Investments staff.

David Pugh, Senior Editor

JOSSEY-BASS

Jossey-Bass publishes books, periodicals, and other media to inform and inspire those interested in developing themselves, their organizations and their communities. Jossey-Bass' publications feature the work of some of the world's best-known authors in leadership, business, education, religion and spirituality, parenting, nonprofit, public health and health administration, conflict resolution and relationships. Publishing nearly 250 new titles each year, Jossey-Bass was acquired by Wiley in 1999, but maintains largely independent operations in San Francisco.

In religion and spirituality, Jossey-Bass publishes a broad range of trade books that support readers in their spiritual journeys, including some that combine general spirituality and self-improvement. Most of their books have been drawn from Christian and Jewish traditions, but they are looking to expand in a thoughtful way into other traditions. They are also looking for books on the intersection of faith/spirituality, culture, and history.

Recent titles include *Teaching the Whole Game: Seven Principles for Meaningful and Lasting Learning* by David Perkins; *Raising Baby Green Guide to Healthy Nutrition* by Alan Greene; *The Deciding Factor: The Power of Analytics to Make Every Decision a Winner* by Larry Rosenberger and John Nash; *Leadership in Times of Crisis: Six Lessons* by Joseph Grano with Mark Levine; *The Myth of Multitasking: How "Doing It All" Gets Nothing Done* by Dave Crenshaw.

Submit proposals, queries, and SASEs to the Editorial Assistant for the relevant series (Business, Education, Health, Higher Education, Nonprofit and Social Leadership, General Interest, Psychology, or Religion).

Alan Rinzler, Executive Editor—Popular psychology, Jewish religion and spirituality

Susan Williams, Senior Editor—Business and management

Sheryl Fullerton, Executive Editor—Spirituality and religion

Rebecca Browning, Editor

Karen Murphy, Editor—Business, nonprofit corporations

SYBEX

Sybex pioneered computer book publishing in 1976 and has as its mission to bring practical skills to computer users through comprehensive, high-quality education and reference materials. Their series range from the reputable Mastering best-sellers, used by millions to gain in-depth understanding of the latest computer topics, to certification Study Guides that help students prepare for challenging exams, to Maya Press books that service the needs of highly specialized 3D imaging and design markets. Sybex was acquired by John Wiley & Sons in 2005 and publishes about 100 new books per year.

Recent titles include *Introducing Revit Architecture 2009* by Greg Demchale, Tatyana Dzambazova, and Eddy Krygiel; *Mastering VBA for Microsoft Office 2007* by Richard Mansfield; *Advanced Painter Techniques* by Don Seegmiller; *Search Engine Optimization: An Hour a Day (2nd ed.)* by Jennifer Grappone and Gradiva Couzin; *Introducing Auto-CAD Civil 3D 2009* by James Wedding and Dana Probert; *Mastering SQL Server 2005 Reporting Services Infrastructure Design* by Joseph L. Jorden.

Direct queries and proposals to sybexproposals@wiley.com and include the word Proposal at the beginning of the subject line.

WILEY-BLACKWELL

Commerce Place, 350 Main Street, Malden, MA 02148

781-388-8200   fax: 781-388-8210

www.blackwellpublishing.com

Wiley-Blackwell Publishing Professional address:

2121 State Avenue, Ames, IA 50014-8300

www.blackwellprofessional.com

e-mail: acquisitions@ames.blackwellpublishing.com

Wiley-Blackwell was formed in February 2007 as a result of the merger between Blackwell Publishing Ltd. and John Wiley & Sons, Inc.'s Scientific, Technical, and Medical business. Wiley-Blackwell is organized into five broad divisions: Life Science, Physical Sciences, Professional, Medical, Social Sciences and Humanities. Blackwell-Wiley is run by Senior Vice President for Scientific, Technical, and Medical Publishing, Eric Swanson. By June of 2008, Wiley-Blackwell will have integrated the two business by combining many infrastructure and distribution processes as well as launching a single Web platform.

Recent titles from Wiley-Blackwell include *(Re)Thinking "Art": A Guide for Beginners* by Steve Shipps; *10 Moral Paradoxes* by Saul Smilansky; *24 and Philosophy* by Jennifer Hart Weed, Richard Brian Davis, and Ronald Weed; *A Practical Manual of Diabetic Foot Care (2nd ed.)* by Michael Edmons, Althea V.M. Foster, and Lee Sanders; *Better Living Through Reality TV* by Laurie Ouelette and James Hay; *Early Human Kinship* by Nicholas J. Allen, Hilary Callan, Robin Dunbar, and Wendy James.

Recent titles from Wiley-Blackwell Professional include *Carbon Capture and Sequestration: Integrating Technology, Monitoring, Regulation* by Elizabeth Wilson and David Gerard; *Physics at a Glance* by Tim Mills; *Structure and Reactivity in Organic Chemistry* by Mark Moloney; *Trans Fatty Acids* by Alberst Dijkstra, Richard J. Hamilton, and Wolf Hamm.

Wiley-Blackwell welcomes inquiries form prospective authors. Note that e-mail addresses will likely change as the Wiley-Blackwell Web presence launches mid-2008. Submit proposals via e-mail or postal mail with SASEs to the appropriate acquiring editor.

Steve Smith, International Editorial Director (Boston)—Academic and Science Books; ssmith@bos.blackwellpublishing.com

Jayne M. Fargnoli, Executive Editor (Boston)—Cultural Studies; jfargnoli@bos.blackwellpublishing.com

George Lobell, Executive Editor (Boston)—Economics and Finance; globell@bos.blackwellpublishing.com

Christine M. Cardone, Executive Editor (Boston)—Psychology; ccardone@bos.blackwellpublishing.com

Sarah Coleman, Project Editor (Boston)—Psychology; scoleman@bos.blackwellpublishing.com

Peter Coveney, Executive Editor (Boston)—History; peter.coveney@bos.blackwellpublishing.com

Ken Provencher, Senior Project Editor (Boston)—Sociology and History; kprovencher@bos.blackwellpublishing.com

Rosalie Robertson, Senior Aquisitions Editor (Boston)—Anthropology and Archaeology; RRobertson@bos.blackwellpublishing.com

Jeffrey T. Dean, Senior Acquisitions Editor (Boston)—Philosophy; jdean@bos.blackwellpublishing.com

Danielle Descoteaux, Acquisitions Editor (Boston)—Linguistics; ddescoteaux@bos.blackwellpublishing.com

Elizabeth Swayze, Acquisitions Editor (Boston)—Communication and Media Studies, Journalism; elizabeth.swayze@bos.blackwellpublishing.com

Deirdre Ilkson, Editorial Assistant (Boston)—Anthropology, Archaeology and US History; dilkson@bos.blackwellpublishing.com

Jamie Harlan, Assistant Editor (Boston)—Philosophy; jharlan@bos.blackwellpublishing.com

Haze Humbert, Assistant Acquisitions Editor (Boston)—Classics and Ancient History; hhumbert@bos.blackwellpublishing.com

Antonia Seymour, Vice President, Professional Publishing (Ames); antonia.seymour@ames.blackwellpublishing.com

Susan Farmer, Commissioning Editor (Ames)—Chemistry; susan.farmer@ames.blackwellpublishing.com

Mark Barrett, Commissioning Editor (Ames)—Food Science; mark.barrett@ames.blackwellpublishing.com

Erin Gardner, Associate Commissioning Editor (Ames)—Veterinary; erin.gardner@ames.blackwellpublishing.com

Justin Jeffryes, Associate Commissioning Editor (Ames)—Agriculture, Aquaculture and Plant Science; justin.jeffryes@ames.blackwellpublishing.com

WENNER BOOKS [SEE HYPERION]

WESTMINSTER JOHN KNOX PRESS [SEE PPC]

WILLIAMSON PUBLISHING COMPANY

An Imprint of Ideals Publications and Guideposts

535 Metroplex Drive, Nashville, TN 37211

800-586-2572

www.idealspublications.com   e-mail: atyourservice@guideposts.org

A partner with Ideals Publications, a division of Guideposts, Williamson publishes nonfiction books that encourage children to succeed by helping them to discover their creative capacity. Kids Can!, Little Hands, Kaleidoscope Kids, Quick Starts for Kids, and Good Times books encourage curiosity and exploration with irresistible graphics and open-ended instruction. The house publishes hands-on learning books in science and nature, arts and crafts, math and history, cooking, social studies and more, featuring new Kaleidoscope Kids and Kids Can! titles. Its publishing program is committed to maintaining excellent quality while providing good value for parents, teachers, and children.

Williamson Publishing Company (founded in 1983) is known for a wide variety of works and viewpoints, united through an enthusiastic, upbeat, purposeful how-to approach. Williamson typically produces 16 new titles each year and commands a comprehensive backlist.

Ideals Publications, based in Nashville, Tennessee, is the retail book sales and distribution outlet of Guideposts; including Guideposts Books, Candy Cane Press, Williamson Books, and Ideals Press.

Recent titles from Williamson include *And God Said Let There Be Laughter* by Mary Hollingworth; *China* by Debbi Michiko Florence; *Easter in the Garden* by Pamela Kennedy; *Ella the Baby Elephant: An Elephant Family Story* by Kathleen Duey; *The Kids' Multicultural Cookbook* by Deanne F. Cook; *Leap into Space* by Nancy Castaldo; *The Little Hands Art Book* by Judy Press.

Ideals Publications does not accept submissions by e-mail or fax. Send a SASE to "Guidelines" to receive writers' guidelines. Please address queries and SASEs to the editors.

WILLOW CREEK PRESS, INC.

P.O. Box 147, Minocqua, WI 54548

715-358-7010 / 800-850-9453

www.willowcreekpress.com   e-mail: info@willowcreekpress.com

Willow Creek Press is a publisher whose primary commitment is to publish books specializing in nature, outdoor and sporting topics, gardening, wildlife and animal books, and cookbooks. They also publish nature, wildlife, fishing, and sporting calendars.

Its location in the Wisconsin Northwoods helps keep Willow Creek Press off the publishing world's radar. But, a few years ago, the house did get noticed with the release of *Just Labs*, a unique and colorful tribute to Labrador retrievers. The book quickly became a bestseller (with over 250,000 copies in print). Now an entire line of popular Willow Creek Press titles evokes the myriad joys of dog and cat ownership. Today they are known for these high-quality, light-hearted books and feature over 40 such titles in a continually expanding line.

Recent titles include *The Baby Bonding Book for Dads* by James di Properzio; *Chi-WOWhua!* by Melissa Sovey; *Mewsings: Exploring the Feline Mystique* by Fona Green; *Call of the Northwoods* by David C. Evers and Kate Taylor; *How to Make Love and Dinner at the Same Time* by Rebecca Field Jager; *Garden Voices: Stories of Women and Their Gardens* by Carolyn Freas Rapp.

Please provide SASE with all correspondence if you want your materials returned. Address all inquiries or proposals to:

Andrea Donner, Managing Editor

WISDOM PUBLICATIONS

199 Elm Street, Somerville, MA 02144

617-776-7416   fax: 617-776-7841

www.wisdompubs.org   e-mail: editors@wisdompubs.org

Wisdom Publications, a not-for-profit publisher, is dedicated to making available authentic Buddhist works for the benefit of all. The house publishes translations of the sutras and tantras, commentaries and teachings of past and contemporary Buddhist masters, and original works by the world's leading Buddhist scholars. Wisdom Publications was named one of the top 10 fastest-growing small publishers in the country (the company has been in the United States since 1989) by Publishers Weekly in 1996.

Wisdom titles are published in appreciation of Buddhism as a living philosophy and with the commitment to preserve and transmit important works from all the major Buddhist traditions. Wisdom products are distributed worldwide and have been translated into a dozen foreign languages.

Wisdom publishes the celebrated Tibetan Art Calendar, containing 13 full-color reproductions of the world's finest Indo-Tibetan thangka paintings, accompanied by detailed iconographical descriptions.

Wisdom Publications has made a commitment to producing books with environmental mindfulness.

Recent Wisdom titles include *The Buddha's Teachings on Prosperity: At Home, at Work, in the World* by Bhikku Rahula Basnagoda; *Focused and Fearless: A Meditator's Guide to States of Deep Joy, Calm, and Clarity* by Shaila Catherine; *Real Meditation in Minutes a Day: Enhancing Your Performance, Relationships, Spirituality, and Health* by Joseph Arpaia and Lobsang Rapgay; *Ending the Pursuit of Happiness: A Zen Guide* by Barry Magid; *Money, Sex, War, Karma: Notes for a Buddhist Revolution* by David R. Loy; *One Hundred Days of Solitude: Losing My Self and Finding Grace on a Zen Retreat* by Jane Dobisz; *The Essence of Zen: The Teaching of Sekkei Harada* by Sekkei Harada and Daigahu Rumme; *Warrior-King of Shambala: Remembering Chogyam Trungpa* by Jeremy Hayward and Sakyong Mipham Rinpoche.

Wisdom Publications is distributed to the trade in the United States and Canada by National Book Network (NBN). Query letters and SASEs should be directed to Acquisitions Editor via regular mail or e-mail. Complete proposal specifications are available on the Web site.

Tim McNeill, Publisher

WORKMAN PUBLISHING COMPANY

ALGONQUIN BOOKS OF CHAPEL HILL (SEE SEPARATE ENTRY)

225 Varick St., New York, NY 10014-4381

212-254-5900   fax: 212-254-8098

www.workman.com   e-mail: info@workman.com

Books, calendars, trends. Workman is a publisher that's always around big ideas. *B. Kliban's Cat, 1,000 Places to See Before You Die, The Silver Palate Cookbook, Bad Cat* the original *Page-A-Day Calendars,* the *What to Expect* books, *BRAIN QUEST*—landmark bestsellers such as these reflect a knack for publishing books and calendars that lead.

Workman's first book, 1968's *Yoga 28-Day Exercise Plan* is currently in its twenty-eighth printing. Their books are known for having an appealing trade-paperback format with high standards of design and production. Authors who are authorities, who tour extensively and are spokespeople for their subjects, work with Workman. Workman also sometimes goes with unexpected formats such as the packaging of books with objects. And above all, the house prides itself on value through conscientious, aggressive pricing.

Once a book is published, Workman stays after it through promotion and publicity. Take, for example, the case of *The Official Preppy Handbook*, and how an idiosyncratic bestseller was transformed into a phenomenon, complete with posters and stationery—even pins and nightshirts. Or *What to Expect When You're Expecting*, which started with a modest 6,700-copy advance in 1984 and has grown into America's pregnancy bible, currently with 10 million copies in print.

Perhaps more telling is the fact that over two-thirds of all the books the house has published in the last twenty-eight years are still in print, with a fair share of titles that have over one million copies in print, including *BRAIN QUEST*, *The Silver Palate Cookbook*, *The New Basics Cookbook*, *All I Need to Know I Learned from My Cat*, *The Magic Locket*, and *The Bones Book & Skeleton*.

Recent titles from Workman include *The Hollywood Assistants Handbook: 86 Rules for Aspiring Power Players* by Hilary Stamm and Peter Norwalk; *The Wedding Book: The Big Book for Your Big Day* by Mindy Weiss and Lisbeth Levine; *Best of Stuntology* by Sam Bartlett; *The Garden Primer (2nd ed.)* by Barbara Damrosch; *Bag the Elephant: How to Win and Keep BIG Customers* by Steve Kaplan.

Please send your queries and SASEs to the attention of the Editorial Department.

Peter Workman, Publisher

Susan Bolotin, Editor-in-Chief

Suzanne Rafer, Executive Editor

Janet Harris, Editor—Non-book products (calendars)

Raquel Jaramillo, Director of Children's Publishing

WRIGHT GROUP/MCGRAW-HILL [SEE MCGRAW-HILL]

WRITER'S DIGEST

4700 E. Galbraith Road, Cincinnati, OH 45236

513-531-2690

www.writersdigest.com   e-mail: writersdig@fwpubs.com

Writer's Digest is the world's leading magazine for writers, founded in 1920. Today this house provides a variety of books, magazines, special interest publications, educational courses, conferences, Web sites and more.

Publications include: *Writer's Yearbook*, published annually, *Scriptwriting Secrets*, *Getting Started in Writing*, *Start Writing Now* and a variety of other special interest publications for writers.

Book imprints include Writer's Digest Books, Walking Stick Press and the only club exclusively for writers, Writer's Digest Book Club.

All are part of F&W Publications, a leading publisher of books and magazines for creative people. F&W Publications is headquartered in Cincinnati, Ohio, with additional offices in New York, Denver and Devon, England.

Recent titles include *Glimmer Train Guide to Writing Fiction, Vol. 2* by Susan Burmeister-Brown and Linda Swanson Davies; *The Pirate Primer* by George Choundas; *The Writing the Life Poetic* by Sage Cohen; *Get Known Before the Book Deal: Use Your Personal Strengths to Grow an Author Platform* by Christina Katz; *Howdunit: Weapons, Technology, and Surveillance* by Sheila Stephens; and *Take Ten* by Bonnie Neubauer.

Send a query and SASE to:

Jane Friedman, Editorial Director, jane.friedman@fwpubs.com

ZEBRA BOOKS [SEE KENSINGTON PUBLISHING]

SECTION THREE

UNIVERSITY PRESSES

THE UNIVERSITY AS PUBLISHER

FROM ACADEMIC PRESS
TO COMMERCIAL PRESENCE

WILLIAM HAMILTON
Director, University of Hawaii Press
2840 Kolowalu Street, Honolulu, HI 96822

You nod as you glance at the ads in the book reviews, you are aware of the spots you heard or saw on radio and late-night television, and you recognize the authors from television interviews and radio call-in shows. So you know that today's university presses publish much more than scholarly monographs and academic tomes.

Although the monograph is—and will always be—the bread and butter of the university press, several factors over the past quarter century have compelled university presses to look beyond their primary publishing mission of disseminating scholarship. The reductions in financial support from parent institutions, library-budget cutbacks by federal and local governments, and the increasing scarcity of grants to underwrite the costs of publishing monographs have put these presses under severe financial pressure. The watchword for university presses, even in the 1970s, was survival.

While university presses were fighting for their lives, their commercial counterparts also experienced difficult changes. The commercial sector responded by selling off unprofitable and incompatible lists or merging with other publishers; many houses were bought out by larger concerns. Publishers began to concentrate their editorial and marketing resources on a few new titles that would generate larger revenues. Books that commercial publishers now categorized as financial risks, the university presses saw as means of entry into new markets and opportunities to revive sagging publishing programs.

Take a look through one of the really good bookstores in your area. You'll find university press imprints on regional cookbooks, popular fiction, serious nonfiction, calendars, literature in translation, reference works, finely produced art books, and a considerable number of upper-division textbooks. Books and other items normally associated with commercial publishers are now a regular and important part of university press publishing.

There are approximately 100 university presses in North America, including U.S. branches of the venerable Oxford University Press and Cambridge University Press. Of the largest American university presses—California, Chicago, Columbia, Harvard, MIT, Princeton, Texas, and Yale—each publishes well over 100 books per year. Many of these titles are trade books that are sold in retail outlets throughout the world.

The medium-sized university presses—approximately 20 fit this category—publish between 50 and 100 books a year. Presses such as Washington, Indiana, Cornell, North Carolina, Johns Hopkins, and Stanford are well established as publishers of important works worthy of broad circulation.

All but the smallest university presses have developed extensive channels of distribution, which ensure that their books will be widely available in bookstores and wherever serious books are sold. Small university presses usually retain larger university presses or commissioned sales firms to represent them.

University Press Trade Publishing

The two most common trade areas in which university presses publish are (1) regional titles and (2) nonfiction titles that reflect the research interests of their parent universities.

For example, University of Hawaii Press publishes approximately 30 new books a year with Asian or Pacific Rim themes. Typically, 8 to 10 of these books are trade titles. Recent titles have included Japanese literature in translation, a lavishly illustrated book on Thai textiles, books on forms of Chinese architecture, and a historical guide to ancient Burmese temples. This is a typical university press trade list—a diverse, intellectually stimulating selection of books that will be read by a variety of well-informed, responsive general readers.

For projects with special trade potential, some of the major university presses enter into copublishing arrangements with commercial publishers—notably in the fields of art books and serious nonfiction with a current-issues slant—and there seems to be more of these high-profile projects lately.

Certain of the larger and medium-sized university presses have in the past few years hired editors with experience in commercial publishing to add extra dimensions and impact to the portion of their program with a trade orientation.

It's too early to know whether these observations represent trends. Even if so, the repercussions remain to be seen. Obviously, with the publishing community as a whole going through a period of change, it pays to stay tuned to events.

University Press Authors

Where do university press authors come from? The majority of them are involved in one way or another with a university, research center, or public agency, or are experts in a particular academic field. Very few would list their primary occupation as author. Most of the books they write are the result of years of research or reflect years of experience in their fields.

The university press is not overly concerned about the number of academic degrees following its trade book authors' names. What matters is the author's thoroughness in addressing the topic, regardless of his or her residence, age, or amount of formal education. A rigorous evaluation of content and style determines whether the manuscript meets the university press's standards.

University Press Acquisition Process

Several of the other essays in this volume provide specific strategies for you to follow to ensure that your book idea receives consideration from your publisher of choice—but let me interject a cautionary note: The major commercial publishers are extremely difficult to approach unless you have an agent, and obtaining an agent can be more difficult than finding a publisher!

The commercial publishers are so overwhelmed by unsolicited manuscripts that you would be among the fortunate few if your proposal or manuscript even received a thorough reading. Your unagented proposal or manuscript will most likely be read by an editorial assistant, returned unread, or thrown on the slush pile unread and unreturned.

An alternative to the commercial publisher is the university press. Not only will the university press respond; but the response will also generally come from the decision maker—the acquisitions editor.

Before approaching any publisher, however, you must perform a personal assessment of your expectations for your book. If you are writing because you want your book to be on the bestseller list, go to a medium to large commercial press. If you are writing to make a financial killing, go to a large commercial publisher. If you are writing in the hope that your book will be a literary success, contribute to knowledge, be widely distributed, provide a modest royalty, and be in print for several years, you should consider a university press.

Should a University Press Be Your First Choice?

That depends on the subject matter. It is very difficult to sell a commercial publisher on what appears on the surface to be a book with a limited market. For example, Tom Clancy was unable to sell *The Hunt for Red October* to a commercial publisher because the content was considered too technical for the average reader of action-adventure books. Clancy sent the manuscript to a university press that specialized in military-related topics. Naval Institute Press had the foresight to see the literary and commercial value of Clancy's work. As they say, the rest is history. Tom Clancy created the present-day technothriller genre and has accumulated royalties well into the millions of dollars. Once Clancy became a known commodity, the commercial publishers began courting him. All of his subsequent books have been published by commercial houses.

How do you find the university press that is suitable for you? You must research the university press industry. Start by finding out something about university presses. In addition to the listings in the directory of publishers and editors appearing in this book, most university presses are listed in *Literary Market Place*.

A far better and more complete source is *The Association of American University Presses Directory*. The AAUP directory offers a detailed description of each AAUP member press, with a summary of its publishing program. The directory lists the names and responsibilities of each press's key staff, including the acquisitions editors. Each press states its editorial program—what it will consider for publication. A section on submitting manuscripts provides a detailed description of what the university press expects a proposal to contain. Another useful feature is the comprehensive subject grid, which identifies more than 125 subject areas and lists the university presses that publish in each of them.

An updated edition of *The Association of American University Presses Directory* is published every fall and is available for a nominal charge from the AAUP central offices in New York City or through its distributor, University of Chicago Press.

Most university presses are also regional publishers. They publish titles that reflect local interests and tastes and are intended for sale primarily in the university press's local region. For example, University of Hawaii Press has more than 250 titles on Hawaii. The books—both trade and scholarly—cover practically every topic one can think of. Books on native birds, trees, marine life, local history, native culture, and an endless variety of other topics can be found in local stores, including chain bookstores.

This regional pattern is repeated by university presses throughout the country. University of Washington Press publishes several titles each year on the Pacific Northwest and Alaska. Rutgers University Press publishes regional fiction. University of New Mexico Press publishes books on art and photography, most dealing with the desert Southwest. Louisiana State University Press publishes Southern history and literature. Nebraska publishes on the American West.

Almost all university presses publish important regional nonfiction. If your book naturally fits a particular region, you should do everything possible to get a university press located in that region to evaluate your manuscript.

Do not mistake the regional nature of the university press for an inability to sell books nationally—or globally. As mentioned earlier, most university presses have established channels of distribution and use the same resources that commercial publishers use for book distribution. The major difference is that the primary retail outlets for university press books tend to be bookstores associated with universities, smaller academic bookstores, specialized literary bookstores, and independent bookstores that carry a large number of titles.

Matching books to buyers is not as difficult as you might think. Most patrons of university press bookstores know these stores are likely to carry the books they want.

Traditionally, very few university press titles are sold through major chain bookstores outside their local region. Even so, this truism is subject to change. Some of the biggest bookstore chains are experimenting with university press sections in their large superstores.

What to Expect at a University Press
You should expect a personal reply from the acquisitions editor. If the acquisitions editor expresses interest, you can expect the evaluation process to take as long as 6 to 8

months. For reasons known only to editorial staffs—commercial, as well as those of university presses—manuscripts sit and sit and sit. Then they go out for review, come back, and go out for review again!

Once a favorable evaluation is received, the editor must submit the book to the press's editorial board. It is not until the editorial board approves the manuscript for publication that a university press is authorized to publish the book under its imprint.

A word about editorial boards: The imprint of a university press is typically controlled by an editorial board appointed from the faculty. Each project presented to the editorial board is accompanied by a set of peer reviews, the acquisitions editor's summary of the reviews, and the author's replies to the reviews. The project is discussed with the press's management and voted upon.

Decisions from the editorial board range from approval, through conditional approval, to flat rejection. Most university presses present to the editorial board only those projects they feel stand a strong chance of acceptance—approximately 10 to 15 percent of the projects submitted annually. So if you have been told that your book is being submitted to the editorial board, there's a good chance that the book will be accepted.

Once a book has been accepted by the editorial board, the acquisitions editor is authorized to offer the author a publishing contract. The publishing contract of a university press is quite similar to a commercial publisher's contract. The majority of the paragraphs read the same. The difference is most apparent in two areas—submission of the manuscript and financial terms.

University presses view publishing schedules as very flexible. If the author needs an extra 6 to 12 months to polish the manuscript, the market is not going to be affected too much. If the author needs additional time to proofread the galleys or page proofs, the press is willing to go along. Why? Because a university press is publishing for the long term. The book is going to be in print for several years. It is not unusual for a first printing of a university press title to be available for 10 or more years. Under normal circumstances the topic will be timeless, enduring, and therefore of lasting interest.

University presses go to great lengths to ensure that a book is as close to error-free as possible. The academic and stylistic integrity of the work is foremost in the editor's mind. Not only the content, but the notes, references, bibliography, and index should be flawless—and all charts, graphs, maps, and other illustrations perfectly keyed.

It does not matter whether the book is a limited-market monograph or serious nonfiction for a popular trade. The university press devotes the same amount of care to the editorial and production processes to ensure that the book is as accurate and complete as possible. Which leads us to the second difference—the financial terms.

Commercial publishers follow the maxim that time is money. The goal of the organization is to maximize shareholder wealth. Often the decision to publish a book is based solely on financial considerations. If a book must be available for a specific season in order to meet its financial goals, pressure may be applied to editorial by marketing, and editorial in turn puts pressure on the author to meet the agreed-upon schedule. This pressure may result in mistakes, typos, and inaccuracies—but will also assure timely publication and provide the publisher with the opportunity to earn its expected profit. At the commercial publishing house, senior management is measured by its ability to meet annual financial goals.

University presses are not-for-profit organizations. Their basic mission is to publish books of high merit that contribute to universal knowledge. Financial considerations are secondary to what the author has to say. A thoroughly researched, meticulously documented, and clearly written book is more important than meeting a specific publication date. The university press market will accept the book when it appears.

Do not get the impression that university presses are entirely insensitive to schedules or market conditions. University presses are aware that certain books—primarily textbooks and topical trade titles—must be published at specific times of the year if sales are to be maximized. But less than 20 percent of any year's list would fall into such a category.

University Presses and Author Remuneration

What about advances? Royalties? Surely, university presses offer these amenities —which is not to suggest they must be commensurate with the rates paid by commercial houses.

No and yes. No royalties are paid on a predetermined number of copies of scholarly monographs—usually 1,000 to 2,000.

A royalty is usually paid on textbooks and trade books. The royalty will be based on the title's sales revenue (net sales) and will usually be a sliding-scale royalty, ranging from as low as 5 percent to as high as 15 percent.

As with commercial publishers, royalties are entirely negotiable. Do not be afraid or embarrassed to discuss them with your publisher. Just remember that university presses rarely have surplus funds to apply to generous advances or high royalty rates. However, the larger the university press, the more likely you are to get an advance for a trade book.

Never expect an advance for a monograph or supplemental textbook.

When Considering a University Press

When you're deciding where to submit your manuscript, keep the following in mind. University presses produce approximately 10 percent of the books published in the United States each year. University presses win approximately 20 percent of the annual major book awards. Yet university presses generate just 2 percent of the annual sales revenue.

So if you want to write a book that is taken seriously and will be carefully reviewed and edited; if you want to be treated as an important part of the publishing process and want your book to have a good chance to win an award; and if you are not too concerned about the financial rewards—then a university press may very well be the publisher for you.

CAMBRIDGE UNIVERSITY PRESS

32 Avenue of the Americas, New York, NY 10013-2473

212-924-3900 fax: 212-691-3239

www.cambridge.org/us

Cambridge University Press is the world's oldest printing and publishing house, and is dedicated to the advancement and dissemination of knowledge. Internationally, Cambridge publishes over 1,200 titles and 200 journals every year.

The Manhattan office acquires and publishes books in many areas of the humanities and social sciences, with particular focus on subjects including law, history, political science and economics; it is also active across a broad spectrum of science and medicine publishing. It administers some of the prestigious journals issued by the press and it also publishes an extremely successful list of books aimed at those learning American English as a foreign or second language.

The press is now in a real sense a "world publisher." English is the dominant world language of scholarship and science, and the press seeks to attract the best authors and publish the best work in the English language worldwide; it currently has over 24,000 authors in 108 countries, including well over 8,000 in the USA, over 1,300 in Australia, and over 100 each (and rising fast) in countries as various as Japan, Russia, South Africa, Spain and Israel. The press publishes and distributes the whole of this varied output through its own network around the world: There are branches in North America, Australia, Africa, Brazil and Spain, all representing the whole list, supported by sales offices in every major center; there are editorial offices in New York, Melbourne, Cape Town, Madrid, Singapore and Tokyo, each contributing to it their own related publishing programs; and the press's websites are visited by over 2.5 million people worldwide.

Recent Cambridge University titles include *Changing White Attitudes toward Black Political Leadership* by Zoltan L. Hajnal; *Evaluating Campaign Quality: Can the Electoral Process be Improved?* by L. Sandy Maisel, Darrell M. West, and Brett M. Clifton; *What Is Intelligence* by James R. Flynn; *Continuous and Discrete Time Signals and Systems* by Mrinal Mandal and Amir Asif; *The Research Imagination* by Paul S. Gray, John B Williamson, David A. Karp, and John Dalphin; *A Literary History of Women's Writing in Britain, 1660-1789* by Susan Staves; and *The Image of St. Francis* by Rosalind B. Brooke.

Submit queries (with SASEs if by regular mail) to the appropriate editor:

Andrew Beck—Anthropology, Jewish studies, religion; abeck@cambridge.org

Frank Smith—American history, business history, economic history, history of science, Latin American studies, African studies; fsmith@cambridge.org

Beatrice Rehl—Philosophy, classical art and archaeology; brehl@cambridge.org

Eric Crahan—History and political science; ecrahan@cambridge.org

Scott Parris—Economics and finance; sparris@cambridge.org

John Berger—Law; jberger@cambridge.org

Andrew Winnard—Language and Linguistics; awinnard@cambridge.org

Ed Parsons—Textbooks in political science, sociology, and criminology; eparsons@cambridge.org

Lewis Bateman—Political science, history; lbateman@cambridge.org

Eric Schwartz—Psychology; eschwartz@cambridge.org

Lauren Cowles—Academic computer science, statistics; lcowles@cambridge.org

Mark Strauss—Anesthesia, Emergency Medicine, Psychiatry, Pathology, OB/GYN/Repro Medicine; mstrauss@cambridge.org

Allan Ross—Biotechnology, pharmacology, molecular biology, genetics, and neuroscience; aross@cambridge.org

Beth Barry—Dermatology, gastroenterology, hematology/oncology, neurology; bbarry@cambridge.org

Peter Gordon—Mechanical, chemical and aerospace engineering; pgordon@cambridge.org

Aidan Gill—Education: assessment, history and music, and all areas not otherwise listed; agill@cambridge.org

Fiona Kelly—Education: classics (Latin, Greek); fkelly@cambridge.org

Sandra Eldridge—Education: primary literacy/English; seldridge@cambridge.org

Natasha Marsh—Education: primary mathematics/numeracy and cross-curricular; nmarsh@cambridge.org

Matthew Winson—Education: secondary English and languages; mwinson@cambridge.org

Claire Fensome—Education: secondary geography, environment, and information/communications technology; cfensome@cambridge.org

Jean Carnall—Education: secondary mathematics; jcarnall@cambridge.org

Peter Canning—Education: secondary sciences and design/technology; pcanning@cambridge.org

Debbie Goldblatt—English for language teaching: adult courses; dgoldblatt@cambridge.org

Sally Searby—English for language teaching: Adult Education; ssearby@cambridge.org

Kathleen Corley—English for language teaching: Applied linguistics and professional books for teachers; kcorley@cambridge.org

Bernard Seal—English for academic purposes and pre-academic ESL reading and writing; bseal@cambridge.org

Jane Mairs— Grammar, pronunciation and exams; jmairs@cambridge.org

Lesley Koustaff—Primary and secondary courses; lkoustaff@cambridge.org

Paul Heacock—Reference and vocabulary; pheacock@cambridge.org

Karen Brock—Short courses and general EFL listening, speaking, reading and writing; kbrock@cambridge.org

COLUMBIA UNIVERSITY PRESS

61 W. 62nd Street, New York, NY 10023

212-459-0600 fax: 212-459-3678

www.columbia.edu/cu/cup

Columbia University Press was founded in 1893 as a nonprofit corporation, separate from Columbia University although bearing its name and associated closely with it. The purpose of the press expressed in the Certificate of Incorporation was to "promote the study of economic, historical, literary, scientific and other subjects; and to promote and encourage the publication of literary works embodying original research in such subjects."

In its first quarter century the list focused on politics with books by two U.S. presidents, Woodrow Wilson and William Howard Taft. In 1927, the press began publishing major multivolume works. By 1931 the press had grown to such an extent that it published an annual list of 83 new titles—more than any other American university press and 25th among all U.S. publishers.

With the publication of *The Columbia Encyclopedia* in 1935, the press began to develop a list of general reference works in print (several are now in electronic form) that has set it apart from all other American university presses. King's Crown Press was established in 1940 as an imprint for Columbia dissertations: publication was a requirement for a Columbia Ph.D. until the 1950s. In addition, Columbia University's professional program in social work stimulated a strong list of books in that field.

In the 1960s the press became the first—and it is still the only—American university press to publish music. The imprints Columbia University Music Press (for BMI composers) and Kings Crown Music Press (for ASCAP composers) were created to publish new music written by Americans. Twentieth-Century Continental Fiction, the press's first fiction series, was launched in the 1980s with novels by Juan Benet (*Return to Region*, translated by Gregory Rabassa) and other leading Iberian Spanish writers not before published in English. In 2007 the Press launched Columbia Business School Publishing, an imprint that will publish practical works of importance by academic and financial professionals.

Columbia now publishes around 160 titles a year in the areas of Asian studies, literature, biology, business, culinary history, current affairs, economics, environmental sciences, film and media studies, finance, history, international affairs, literary studies,

Middle Eastern studies, New York City history, philosophy neuroscience, paleontology, political theory, religion, and social work.

Recent titles include *When Principles Pay: Corporate Social Responsibility and the Bottom Line* by Geoffrey Heal; *The Politics of Chaos in the Middle East* by Olivier Roy; *Memories of Life in Lhasa Under Chinese Rule* by Tubeten Khetsun; *Enchantment: The Seductress in Opera* by Jean Starobinski; *Art's Claim to Truth* by Gianni Vattimo; *The Song of Everlasting Sorrow: A Novel of Shanghai* by Wang Anyi, translated by Michael Berry and Susan Chan Egan; *Keeping Out the Other: A Critical Introduction to Immigration Enforcement Today* edited by David C. Brotherton and Philip Kretsedemas; and *Humanity's Footprint: Momentum, Impact, and Out Global Environment* by Walter Dodds.

Columbia University Press accepts proposals by e-mail or regular mail. However, do not send large files by e-mail. Direct proposals (with SASEs if by regular mail) to the appropriate editor:

Jennifer Crewe, Associate Director and Editorial Director—Literary and cultural studies, film, Asian humanities, food history, New York City; jc373@columbia.edu

Peter Dimock, Senior Executive Editor—American history and American studies, Middle East history, political philosophy; contact via Kabir Dandona at kd2047@columbia.edu

Lauren Dockett, Executive Editor—Gerontology, Psychology, social work; ld2237@columbia.edu

Patrick Fitzgerald, Publisher for the Life Sciences—Conservation biology, environmental sciences, ecology, neuroscience, paleobiology, public health, biomedical sciences; pf2134@columbia.edu

Philip Leventhal, Associate Editor—Literary studies, cultural studies, journalism, media; pl2164@columbia.edu

Wendy Lochner, Senior Executive Editor—Animal studies, religion, philosophy; wl2003@columbia.edu

Anne Routon, Associate Editor—Asian history, international relations, anthropology; akr36@columbia.edu

Myles Thompson, Publisher, Finance and Economics—Finance, economics; mt2312@columbia.edu

CORNELL UNIVERSITY PRESS

Sage House, 512 East State Street, Ithaca, NY 14850

607-277-2338   fax: 607-277-2374

www.cornellpress.cornell.edu

Cornell University Press was established in 1869, giving it the distinction of being the first university press to be established in the United States, although it was inactive for several decades between 1890 and 1930. The house offers 150 new titles a year in many disciplines, including anthropology, classics, cultural studies, history, literary criticism and theory, medieval studies, philosophy, politics and international relations, psychology and psychiatry, and women's studies. Their many books in the life sciences and natural history are published under the Comstock Publishing Associates imprint, and a list of books in industrial and labor relations is offered under the ILR Press imprint.

Recent titles include *Cars for Comrades: The Life of the Soviet Automobile* by Lewis H. Siegelbaum; *The Caregiver: A Life with Alzheimer's* by Aaron Alterra; *The End of the West? Crisis and Change in the Atlantic Order* edited by Jeffrey Anderson, G. John Ikenberry, and Thomas Risse; *A Bird-Finding Guide to Panama* by George R. Angehr, Dodge Engleman, and Lorna Engleman; *Humanitarianism in Question: Politics, Power, Ethics* edited by Michael Barnett and Thomas G. Weiss; *Base Politics: Democratic Change and the U.S. Military Overseas* by Alexander Cooley; and *Occupational Hazards: Success and Failure in Military Occupation* by David M. Edelstein.

The house distributes its own titles. Queries and SASEs may be directed to:

Peter J. Potter, Editor in Chief—Literature, medieval studies, classics and ancient history

John G. Ackerman, Director—European history, intellectual history, Russian/East European studies, music

Frances Benson, Editorial Director—Business, labor, workplace issues, health care

Roger Haydon, Executive Editor—Political science, international relations, Asian studies, philosophy

Michael J. McGandy, Acquisitions Editor—American history, American politics, law, New York State, regional books

Heidi Steinmetz Lovette, Science Acquisitions Editor, Comstock Publishing Associates—Biology and natural history, ornithology, herpetology, ichthyology, mammology, entomology, botany, plant sciences

Peter Wissoker, Acquisitions Editor—Anthropology, geography, sociology, urban studies

DUKE UNIVERSITY PRESS

905 West Main Street, Suite 18B, Durham, NC 27701

919-687-3600 / 888-651-0122   fax: 919-688-3524 / 888-651-0124

www.dukeupress.edu   e-mail: dukepress@duke.edu

Duke University Press publishes approximately 120 books annually and more than 30 journals. This places the press's books publishing program among the 20 largest at American university presses, and the journals publishing program among the five largest. The relative magnitude of the journals program within the press is unique among American university presses: There is no other publisher of more than 15 journals that also publishes fewer than 175 books per year.

The press publishes primarily in the humanities and social sciences and issues a few publications for primarily professional audiences (e.g., in law or medicine). It is best known for its publications in the broad and interdisciplinary area of theory and history of cultural production, and it is known in general as a publisher willing to take chances with nontraditional and interdisciplinary publications, both books and journals.

Like many other university presses, in addition to scholarly titles, Duke looks for books with crossover appeal for general audiences. For example, *Good Bread Is Back: A Contemporary History of French Bread, the Way It Is Made, and the People Who Make It* by Steven Kaplan appeals to "foodies" as well as scholars.

Other recent titles include *Mondo Exotica: Sounds, Visions, Obsessions of the Cocktail Generation* by Francesco Adinolfi; *In an Abusive State: How Neoliberalism Appropriated the Feminist Movement against Sexual Violence* by Kristin Bumiller; *Ruling Oneself Out: A theory of Collective Abdications* by Ivan Ermakoff; *History, the Human, and the World Between* by R. Radhakirshnan; *Visible Histories, Disappearing Women: Producing Muslim Womanhood in Late Colonial Bengal* by Mahua Sarkar; and *Postsocialism and Cultural Politics: China in the Last Decade of the Twentieth Century* by Xudong Zhang.

Duke University Press requests that you submit a printed copy of your proposal by mail. If you'd like to inquire about potential interest in your project, you may submit a short query by e-mail. Do not submit full proposals electronically unless specifically asked to do so. Direct queries and submissions to:

Ken Wissoker, Editorial Director—Anthropology, cultural studies, postcolonial theory, lesbian and gay studies, construction of race, gender and national identity, literary criticism, film and television, popular music, visual studies; kwiss@duke.edu

J. Reynolds Smith, Executive Editor—Literary theory and history, cultural theory and practice, religion, American studies, Latin American studies, Asian studies, race and ethnicity, science and technology studies, sociology, contemporary music; j.smith@duke.edu

Valerie Millholland, Senior Editor— Latin American history and politics, European history and politics, American history, women's history, environmental studies, labor history, political science; vmill@duke.edu

Miriam Angress, Assistant Editor— Religion, women's studies, history, humanities, cultural studies; mangress@dukepress.edu

Courtney Berger, Assistant Editor—Political theory, feminist theory, film and television, American studies, cultural studies of food; cberger@dukeupress.edu

THE FEMINIST PRESS AT THE CITY UNIVERSITY OF NEW YORK

The Graduate Center, 365 Fifth Avenue, Suite 5406, New York, NY 10016

212-817-7925   fax: 212-817-1593

www.feministpress.org

The mission of the Feminist Press is to publish and promote the most potent voices of women from all eras and all regions of the globe. Now in its 38th year, the press has brought more than 300 critically acclaimed works by and about women into print, enriching the literary canon, expanding the historical record, and influencing public discourse about issues fundamental to women.

In addition to publishing new works, this renowned house recovers precious out-of-print and never-in-print documents, establishing the history of women around the globe. The press develops core curriculum materials for all classroom levels, providing young women with strong role models. In recognition of its special role in bringing awareness to international women's issues, the Feminist Press was granted NGO status with the Economic and Social Council of the United Nations in 2000.

The Feminist Press is interested in acquiring primary texts that will have broad, long-term sales in bookstores, as well as the possibility of consistent adoption for college classrooms or use in secondary school classrooms. Through publications and projects, The Feminist Press attempts to contribute to the rediscovery of the history of women in the United States and internationally and to the emergence of a more humane society.

Recent titles from the Feminist Press include *From Eve to Dawn: A History of Women in the World Vol. 1* and *Vol. 2* by Marilyn French; *Arguing with the Storm: Stories by Yiddish Women Writers* edited by Rhea Tregebov; *Mistress of Herself: Speeches and Letters of Ernestine Rose, Early Women's Rights Leader* edited by Paula Doress-Worters; *The Amputated Memory: A Novel* by Werewere Liking; and *The Circle of Empowerment: Twenty-five Yeas of the UN Committee on the Elimination of Discrimination Against Women* edited by Hanna Beate Schopp-Schilling.

Please note that this house does not publish original fiction, original poetry, drama, doctoral dissertations, or original literary criticism. For the time being, the house has also ceased publishing books for children.

To submit, send an e-mail of no more than 200 words describing your book project with the word "submission" in the subject line. Your e-mail should very briefly explain the type of book you are proposing and who you are. Do not send a proposal unless the editors request it, as they will discard all submission materials that arrive without an invitation. Send e-mail query to:

Anjoli Roy, Associate Editor; aroy@gc.cuny.edu

FORDHAM UNIVERSITY PRESS

University Box L, 2546 Belmont Avenue, Bronx, NY 10458

718-817-4795   fax 718-817-4785

www.fordhampress.com

Fordham University Press was established in 1907 not only to represent and uphold the values and traditions of the University itself, but also to further those values and traditions through the dissemination of scholarly research and ideas.

The press publishes primarily in the humanities and the social sciences, with an emphasis on the fields of philosophy, theology, history, classics, communications, economics, sociology, business, political science and law, as well as literature and the fine arts. Additionally, the press publishes books focusing on the metropolitan New York region and books of interest to the general public.

Recent titles include *Summers with Lincoln: Looking for the Man in the Monuments* by James A. Percoco; *Derrida Vis-à-vis Lacan: Interweaving Deconstruction and Psychoanalysis* by Andrea Hurst; *Lost Waterfront: The Decline and Rebirth of Manhattan's Western Shore* with photographs by Shelley Seccombe; *Unbecoming Subjects*: Judith Butler, *Moral Responsibility, and Critical Responsibility* by Annika Thiem; *Victor Herbert: A Theatrical Life* by Neil Gould; *Noli Me Tangere: On the Raising of the Body* by Jean-Luc Nancy, Translated by Sarah Clift; and *Catholics in New York: Society, Culture, and Politics, 1808-1946* edited by Terry Golway.

Direct proposals and SASEs to:

Mary-Lou Elias Pena, Assistant to the Director—History, especially World War II, the Civil War and Reconstruction, politics, urban and ethnic studies, media, and New York and the region

Helen Tartar, Editorial Director—Philosophy, religion, theology, literary studies, anthropology, law, or any other fields in the humanities or social sciences

GEORGETOWN UNIVERSITY PRESS

3240 Prospect Street, NW, Washington, DC 20007

202-687-5889   fax: 202-687-6340

press.georgetown.edu   e-mail: gupress@georgetown.edu

Georgetown University Press supports the academic mission of Georgetown University by publishing scholarly books and journals for a diverse, worldwide readership. These publications, written by an international group of authors representing a broad range of intellectual perspectives, reflect the academic and institutional strengths of the university. They publish peer-reviewed works in five subjects: bioethics; international affairs and human rights; languages and linguistics; political science, public policy and public management; and religion and ethics.

The beginnings of Georgetown University Press can be traced to 1964; they currently publish approximately 40 new books a year, as well as two journals, with an active list of close to 500 titles. These publications primarily service the scholarly community, and many also reach into the general reading public. Many help to unite people speaking different languages, literally and figuratively, and all attempt to illuminate, clarify and respond to the world's most difficult questions.

Recent titles include *Politics in the Parish: The Political Influence of Catholic Priests* by Gregory Allen Smith; *Careers in International Affairs, Eighth Edition* edited by Maria Minto Carland and Candace Faber; *Brussels Versus the Beltway: Advocacy in the United States and the European Union; The Dynamics of Performance Management: Constructing Information and Reform* by Donald P. Moynihan; *Governance in Dark Time: Practical Philosophy for Public Service* by Camilla Stivers; and *Sustaining Linguistics Diversity: Endangered and Minority Languages and Language Varieties.*

Georgetown University Press does not publish poetry, fiction, memoirs, children's books, *Festschriften*, symposium proceedings, or unrevised dissertations. Send cover letter, prospectus, and SASE via regular mail:

Richard Brown, Ph.D., Director—Bioethics, international affairs and human rights, religion and politics, and religion and ethics; reb7@georgetown.edu

Gail Grella, Associate Director and Acquisitions Editor—languages, linguistics; grellag1@georgetown.edu

Donald Jacobs, Acquisitions Editor—International affairs, human rights, public policy, and public management; dpj5@georgetown.edu

HARVARD BUSINESS SCHOOL PRESS

60 Harvard Way, Boston, MA 02163

617-783-7400   fax: 617-783-7555

New York office:

75 Rockefeller Plaza, 15th Floor, New York, NY 10019-6926

www.hbsp.harvard.edu   e-mail: asandoval@hbsp.harvard.edu

Harvard Business School Press seeks to influence real-world change by maximizing the reach and impact of its essential offering—ideas. The editors accept proposals for books that take a harder, broader look at the questions that business people face every day. The press is a business unit of Harvard Business School Publishing (HBSP).

HBSP was founded in 1994 as a not-for-profit, wholly-owned subsidiary of Harvard University. Its mission is to improve the practice of management in a changing world. HBSP does this by serving as a bridge between academia and enterprises around the globe through its publications and reach into three markets: academic, enterprise, and individual managers.

HBSP has about 250 employees, primarily based in Boston, with an office in New York City. Its business units are Harvard Business Review magazine and article reprints, Harvard Business School Press, Harvard Business School Publishing Newsletters, Harvard Business School Publishing Conferences, Harvard Business School Publishing Higher Education, and Harvard Business School Publishing eLearning.

Recent titles include *Creative Capital: Georges Doriot and the Birth of Venture Capital* by Spencer E. Ante; *Groundswell* by Charlene Li and Josh Bernoff; *Authenticity: What Consumers Really Want* by B. Joeseph Pine II and James Gilmore; *Innovation to the Core: A Blueprint for Transforming the Way Your Company Innovates* by Peter Skarzynski and Rowan Gibson; *Power of Unreasonable People: How Social Entrepreneurs Create Markets that Change the World* by John Elkington and Pamela Hartigan; *Retire Retirement: Career Strategies for the Bookmer Generation* by Tamara Erickson; *Five Future Strategies You Need Right Now* by George Stalk Jr.; and *Talent on Demand: Managing Talent in the Age of Uncertainty.*

Harvard Business School Press distributes through Perseus.

Send proposals and SASEs via regular mail or e-mail to Sarah Green, Editorial Coordinator (Boston); sgreen@hbsp.harvard.edu.

Jacqueline Murphy, Senior Editor (Boston)

Jeff Kehoe, Senior Editor (Boston)

Melinda Adams Merino, Editor (Boston)

Kirsten D. Sandberg, Executive Editor (NY)

HARVARD UNIVERSITY PRESS

BELKNAP PRESS

79 Garden Street, Cambridge, MA 02138

800-405-1619 / 401-531-2800   fax: 401-531-2801

www.hup.harvard.edu   e-mail: contact_HUP@harvard.edu

blog: harvardpress.typepad.com

podcast: www.hup.harvard.edu/audio/index.html

Publisher of enduring tomes such as *Lovejoy's Great Chain of Being*; *Giedion's Space, Time, and Architecture*; *Langer's Philosophy in a New Key*; and Kelly's *Eleanor of Aquitaine and the Four Kings*; Harvard University Press (HUP) holds an exalted position within the university press world. Still, its editors look to attract an audience of general readers as well as scholars, and the press welcomes considered nonfiction proposals.

HUP publishes scholarly books and thoughtful books for the educated general reader in history, philosophy, American literature, law, economics, public policy, natural science, history of science, psychology, and education, and reference books in all the above fields. The Belknap Press imprint, established in 1949, strives to publish books of long-lasting importance, superior scholarship and production, chosen whether or not they might be profitable, thanks to the bequest of Waldron Phoenix Belknap, Jr.

Recent Belknap titles include *The Collected Prose of Robert Frost* edited by Mark Richardson; *Lamentations of Youth: The Diaries of Gershom Scholem, 1912-1919* edited by Anthony David Skinner; and *A Reef in Time: The Great Barrier Reef from Beginning to End* by J.E.N. Veron.

Recent HUP titles include The Betrayal of Faith: The Tragic Journey of a Colonial Native Convert by Emma Anderson; *Experiments in Ethics* by Kwame Anthony Appiah; *Icons* by Robin Cormack; *Pain and Its Transformation: The Interface of Biology and Culture* by Sarah Coakley; *Sexual Fluidity: Understanding Women's Love and Desire* by Lisa M. Diamond; *Oil Empire: Visions of Prosperity in Australian Dalicia* by Alison Fleig Frank; *On Nuclear Terrorism* by Michael Levi; *The Evolving World: Evolution in Everyday Life* by David P. Mindell; and *The Fire Spreads: Holiness and Pentecostalism in the American South* by Randall J. Stephens.

All HUP books are published in English, with translation rights bought by publishers in other countries. The house does not publish original fiction, original poetry, religious inspiration or revelation, cookbooks, guidebooks, children's books, art and photography books, Festschriften, conference volumes, unrevised dissertations, or autobiographies.

The HUP Web site offers photographs of the editors that you may or may not wish to peruse prior to submitting, as well as detailed submission guidelines that you will not want to miss. No electronic submissions. Submit proposals and SASEs to:

Michael Fisher, Editor-in-Chief—Evolutionary theory, evolutionary developmental biology, biological and evolutionary anthropology, neuroscience, systems biology and bioinformatives, human genetics, science and society, history of technology; also books for general readers in physics, astronomy, earth science, chemistry, engineering, and mathematics

Joyce Seltzer, Senior Executive Editor for History and Contemporary Affairs—Serious and scholarly nonfiction that appeals to a general intellectual audience as well as to students and scholars in a variety of disciplines

Lindsay Waters, Executive Editor for the Humanities—Philosophy, literary studies, cultural studies, film, Asian cultural studies, pop culture, conflicting relations among the races in the United States and around the world

Michael Aronson, Senior Editor for Social Sciences—Economics, business, law, political science, sociology

Ann Downer-Hazell, Editor for Life Sciences and Health—Life sciences including natural history, non-primate animal behavior, and evolutionary and organismic biology; consumer and public health medicine, history of medicine, history of life sciences; marine biology, botany/ethnobotany, paleontology, microbiology

Elizabeth Knoll, Senior Editor for Behavioral Sciences and Law—Education, psychology, law

Shamila Sen, Editor for the Humanities—World religions, classics

Kathleen McDermott, Editor for History and Social Sciences—American history, Atlantic history, European history from late medieval to modern, Russian and Central European history, Asian history, international relations, global history, military history, U. S. Western history, Native American history, legal history

Jennifer Snodgrass, Editor for Reference and Special Projects—Reference books and related projects, electronic or multimedia proposals, Loeb Classical Library, The I Tatti Renaissance Library

John Kulka, Executive Editor-At-Large—American, English, and world literature, modernism, history of criticism, theory, the American publishing industry, political journalism, globalization, democracy, and human dignity

HOWARD UNIVERSITY PRESS

2225 Georgia Avenue, NW, Suite 718, Washington, DC 20059

202-238-2570 fax: 202-588-9849

www.hupress.howard.edu e-mail: howardupress@howard.edu

Howard University Press is dedicated to publishing noteworthy new scholarship that addresses the contributions, conditions, and concerns of African Americans, other people of African descent, and people of color around the globe.

Recent titles include *No Boundaries: A Cancer Surgeon's Odyssey* by LaSalle D. Leffall, Jr. M.D.; *Horace T. Ward: Desegregation of the University of Georgia, Civil Rights Advocacy* by Maurice C. Daniels; *And Then We Heard the Thunder* by John Oliver Killens; *First Freed: Washington D.C. in the Emancipation Era* edited by Elizabeth Clark-Lewis; *One-Third of a Nation: African American Perspectives* edited by Lorenzo Morris and Ura Jean Oyemade Bailey; *The American Paradox: Politics and Justice* by Patrick J. Gallo; *The Black Seminole Legacy and North American Politics, 1693-1845* by Bruce Edward Tyman; *Genocide in Rwanda: A Collective Memory* edited by John A. Berry and Carol Pott Berry; *Manichean Psychology: Racism and the Minds of People of African Descent* by Camera Jules P. Harrell;

Please submit proposals, resumes, and SASEs by regular mail to the attention of the Editorial Department.

D. Kamali Anderson, Director

INDIANA UNIVERSITY PRESS

601 N. Morton Street, Bloomington, IN 47404

(812) 855-8817 / 800-842-6796

www.iupress.indiana.edu e-mail: iupress@indiana.edu

Currently the second-largest public university press, Indiana University Press (IU Press) wants to publish books that will matter 20 or even a 100 years from now—books that make a difference today and will live on into the future through their reverberations in the minds of teachers and writers.

As an academic press, their mandate is to serve the world of scholarship and culture as a professional, not-for-profit publisher. Founded in 1950, IU Press is recognized internationally as a leading academic publisher specializing in the humanities and social sciences. They produce more than 140 new books annually, in addition to 30 journals, and maintain a backlist of some 2,000 titles. The press emphasizes scholarship but also publishes text, trade and reference titles. Their program is financed primarily by income from sales, supplemented, to a minor extent, by gifts and grants from a variety of outside sources.

IU Press books have won many awards for scholarly merit and design, including two National Book Awards, three Herskovits Awards in African studies, and several National Jewish Book Awards. Numerous IU Press titles are selected every year by Choice as outstanding academic books.

Recent titles include *Images of a Journey: India in Diaspora* by Steve Raymer; *Human Rights at the U.N.: The Political History of Universal Justice* by Roger Normand and Sarah Zaidi; *The Bolsheviks in Power: The First Year of Soviet Rule in Petrograd* by Alexander Rabinowitch; *Miles Smiles: Miles Davis and the Invention of Post-Bop; Taliaferro: Breaking*

Barriers from the NFL Draft to the Ivory Tower by Dawn Knight; *The Grand Luxe Express: Traveling in High Style* by Karl Zimmerman; *Masterworks for the Indiana University Art Museum* edited by Linda Baden with photographs by Michael Cavanagh and Kevin Montague; and *Mammals of Indiana* by John O. Whitaker Jr. and Russel E. Mumford.

IU Press welcomes submissions in their fields of publication, which are: African American studies; Africa; anthropology; Asia and South Asia; bioethics; Civil War; classical and ancient studies; cultural studies; dinosaurs; film and media; folklore; general interest; history; Holocaust; international studies; Jewish studies; Latin America and the Caribbean; Medieval and Renaissance Studies; Middle East and Central Asia; Midwest, Indiana, and regional; military history; music, paleontology; philanthropy and nonprofit studies; philosophy; railroads and transportation; religion; Russia and Eastern Europe; and women's and gender studies.

Please submit your inquiry to one editor only. Preliminary inquiries without attachments may be posted by e-mail, but it is recommended that submissions be sent by mail. Direct submissions to:

Janet Rabinowitch, Director—Russian and East European studies, Jewish and Holocaust studies, and international studies; jrabinow@indiana.edu

Robert Sloan, Editorial Director—U.S. history, African-American studies, bioethics, philanthropy, military history, paleontology, and natural history; rjsloan@indiana.edu

Dee Mortensen, Sponsoring Editor—African studies, religion, and philosophy; mortense@indiana.edu

Jane Behnken, Sponsoring Editor—Music, cinema, and media studies; jbehnken@indiana.edu

Rebecca Tolen, Sponsoring Editor—Anthropology, Asian studies, political science/international relations, folklore; retolen@indiana.edu

Linda Oblack, Assistant Sponsoring Editor—Regional trade, regional natural history, railroads past and present; loblack@indiana.edu

---

JOHNS HOPKINS UNIVERSITY PRESS

2715 North Charles Street, Baltimore, MD 21218-4363
410- 516-6900   fax: 410-516-6968
www.press.jhu.edu

Daniel Coit Gilman, the first president of the Johns Hopkins University, inaugurated the press in 1878. For Gilman, publishing, along with teaching and research, was a primary obligation of a great university. Since that time, the Johns Hopkins University Press has carried the name and mission of the university to every corner of the world.

The press has published more than 6,000 titles, of which almost half remain in print today.

The press began as the University's Publication Agency, publishing the *American Journal of Mathematics* in its first year and the *American Chemical Journal* in its second. The agency published its first book, *Sidney Lanier: A Memorial Tribute*, in 1881 to honor the poet who was one of the university's first writers in residence. In 1891, the Publication Agency became the Johns Hopkins Press; since 1972, it has been known as the Johns Hopkins University Press (JHU Press).

Today JHU Press is one of the world's largest university presses, publishing 58 scholarly periodicals and more than 200 new books each year.

Recent JHU Press titles include *Bang! The Complete History of the Universe* by Brian May, Patrick Moore, and Chris Lintott; *Gilles Deleuze: Cinema and Philosophy* by Paola Marrati, translated by Alisa Hartz; *The State of Disunion: Regional Sources of Modern American Partisanship* by Nicole Mellow; *Adam's Ancestors: Race, Religion, and the Politics of Human Origins* by David N. Livingstone; and *Public Expenditures, Growth, and Poverty: Lessons from Developing Countries* edited by Shenggen Fan.

Direct queries with SASEs to the appropriate acquiring editor:

Trevor C. Lipscombe, Editor-in-Chief—Mathematics, physics, and astronomy; tcl@press.jhu.edu

Jacqueline C. Wehmueller, Executive Editor—Consumer health, history of medicine, education; jwehmueller@press.jhu.edu

Henry Y.K. Tom, Executive Editor —Social sciences; htom@press.jhu.edu

Wendy Harris, Senior Acquisitions Editor—Clinical medicine, public health, health policy; wharris@press.jhu.edu

Robert J. Brugger, Senior Acquisitions Editor—American history, history of science and technology, regional books; rbrugger@press.jhu.edu

Vincent J. Burke, Senior Acquisitions Editor—Biology and life sciences; vjb@press.jhu.edu

Michael Lonegro, Acquisitions Editor—Humanities, ancient studies; mlonegro@press.jhu.edu

Ashleigh Elliot McKown, Assistant Editor—Higher education; aem@press.jhu.edu

KENT STATE UNIVERSITY PRESS

307 Lowry Hall, P.O. Box 5190, Kent OH 44242

330-672-7913   fax: 330-672-3104

upress.kent.edu   e-mail: ksupress@kent.edu

The Kent State University Press began in 1965 under the direction of Howard Allen and published in the university faculty strengths in literary criticism. In 1972 Paul Rohmann became the press's second director and expanded the press's publishing program to include regional studies and ethnomusicology. In 1985 historian John Hubbell assumed the directorship and for 15 years saw the staff and publishing program grow to include widely regarded lists in Civil War history and Ohio history. Today, under director Will Underwood, the press publishes 30–35 titles a year and reaches a large and appreciative audience.

Recent titles include *More Than a Contest Between Armies: Essays on the Civil War Era* edited by James Marten and A. Kristen Foster; *Columbia and the United States: The Making of an Inter-American Alliance 1939-1960* by Bradley Lynn Coleman; *Spotlit Girl* by Kevin Oberlin; *Tornado* by Ted Lardner; *Murder on Several Occasions* by Jonathan Goodman; *From Broadway to Cleveland: A History of Hanna Theatre* by John Vacha; *Dreaming Baseball: A Novel* by James T. Farrell; *The Chicago White Sox* by Warren Brown; and *Meade's Army: The Private Notebooks of Lt. Col. Theodore Lyman* edited by David W. Lowe.

The Kent State University Press is especially interested in acquiring scholarly works in history, including military, Civil War, U.S. diplomatic, American cultural, women's and art history; literary studies; titles of regional interest for Ohio; scholarly biographies; archaeological research; the arts; and general nonfiction. Direct query letters with SASEs to:

Joanna H. Craig, Acquiring Editor

LOUISIANA STATE UNIVERSITY PRESS

P.O. Box 25053, Baton Rouge, LA 70894-5053

800-861-3477   fax: 225-576-6461

www.lsu.edu/lsupress

Founded in 1935, the Louisiana State University Press is a nonprofit book publisher dedicated to the publication of scholarly, general interest, and regional books. As an integral part of LSU, the press shares the university's goal of the dissemination of knowledge and culture. LSU Press is one of the oldest and largest university presses in the South and only university press to have won a Pulitzer Prize in both fiction and poetry.

The press is perhaps most widely recognized as the original publisher of John Kennedy Toole's Pulitzer Prize-winning novel *A Confederacy of Dunces*. The winner of the 2006 Pulitzer Prize for poetry, *Late Wife* by Claudia Emerson, was also published by the press. Through the years, its books have earned many prestigious honors, including a total of three Pulitzer Prizes, the National Book Award, the National Book Critics Circle Award, the Booker Prize, the American Book Award, the Los Angeles Times Book Prize, the Bancroft Prize, the Lincoln Prize, the Lamont Poetry Selection by the Academy of American Poets, and numerous others.

LSU Press publishes approximately 80 new books each year as well as a backlist of some 1,000 titles. Their primary areas of focus include Southern history, biography, and literature; the Civil War and World War II; poetry; political philosophy and political communications; music studies, particularly jazz; geography and environmental studies; and illustrated books about the Gulf South region. In the mid-1990s the press launched the acclaimed paperback fiction reprint series Voices of the South and in 2005, after a hiatus of about a decade, resumed publishing original fiction under the new series Yellow Shoe Fiction, edited by Michael Griffith.

This is a press that cares whether people outside a narrow theory specialty will understand a text. "We want work that is as accessible as possible," said executive editor John Easterly.

Recent titles *Slantwise: Poems* by Betty Adcock; *Blind Rain; Poems* by Bruce Bond; *Encyclopedia of Civil War Shipwrecks* by W. Craig Gaines; *Molly the Pony: A True Story* by Pam Kaster; *Black Americans and Organized Labor: A New History* by Paul D. Moreno; *Selected Letters of Robert Penn Warren* edited by Randy Hendricks and James A. Perkins; *White Masculinity in the Recent South* edited by Trent Watts; and *Carnival of Fury: Robert Charles and the New Orleans Race Riot of 1900* by William Ivy Hair.

Proposals for everything except fiction should include a cover letter, table of contents, sample chapters, information about competitive titles, and a resume or curriculum vitae. Fiction proposals should include a cover letter, a one-page summary of the work, a brief sample from the work, and a resume. The press is not currently accepting poetry manuscripts. Submit to the appropriate acquisitions editor by regular mail:

John Easterly, Executive Editor—Poetry, fiction, literary studies, regional interest

Rand Dotson, U.S. History and Southern Studies Editor—Slavery, Civil War, Reconstruction, 19th- and 20th-century South, Louisiana roots music

Margaret Hart, Trade Editor—general interest

Alisa Plant, European/Atlantic World History, and Media Studies Editor

Joseph Powell, Environmental Studies and Geography Editor

MASSACHUSETTS INSTITUTE OF TECHNOLOGY / THE MIT PRESS

55 Hayward Street, Cambridge, MA 02142-1493

617-253-5646 fax: 617-258-6779

www.mitpress.mit.edu blog: mitpress.typepad.com

The MIT Press is the only university press in the United States whose list is based in science and technology. This does not mean that science and engineering are all they publish; rather, they are committed to the edges and frontiers of the world—to exploring new fields and new modes of inquiry.

The press publishes about 200 new books a year and are a major publishing presence in fields as diverse as architecture, social theory, economics, cognitive science, and computational science. The MIT Press has a long-term commitment to both design excellence and the efficient and creative use of new technologies. Their goal is to create books that are challenging, creative, attractive, and yet affordable to individual readers. The MIT Press history starts in 1926 when the physicist Max Born visited MIT to deliver a set of lectures on Problems of Atomic Dynamics. The institute published the lectures under its own imprint, and that book is numbered 1 in the archives of The MIT Press. In 1932, James R. Killian Jr.—editor of MIT's alumni magazine and future scientific advisor to President Kennedy and tenth president of MIT—engineered the creation of an institute-sponsored imprint called Technology Press, which published eight titles over the next five years. In 1937, John Wiley & Sons took on editorial and marketing functions for the young imprint, which during the next 25 years published 125 titles. In 1962, MIT amicably severed the Wiley connection and upgraded its imprint to an independent publishing house, naming it The MIT Press. The creative burst and explosive growth of the 1960s slackened with the library cutbacks of the early 1970s, and by the end of that decade the press knew that it had to rethink what it was doing. They developed a strategy of focusing the list on a few key areas and publishing in depth in those areas. The initial core consisted of architecture, computer science and artificial intelligence, economics, and the emerging interdiscipline of cognitive science. The plan worked wonderfully, and by the mid-1980s the press was again thriving. As the list developed, occasional offshoots sprouted (neuroscience, for example, was spun off from cognitive science in 1987), while a few smaller areas in which they continued to publish—technology studies, aesthetic theory, design, and social theory—have remained viable and interesting components of what has become a unique mix. Their latest addition was an environmental science list, started in the early 1990s.

Recent titles include the *Handbook of Antitrust Economics* by Paolo Buccirossi; *3D Shape: Its Unique Place in Visual Perception* by Zygmunt Pizlo; *The Road to Democracy in Iran* by Akbar Ganji; *From Betamax to Blockbuster: Video Stores and the Invention of Movies on Video* by Joshua M. Greenberg; *Access Denied: The Practice* and Policy of Global Internet Filtering by Roland J. Delbert, John G. Palfrey and Rafal Rohozinski, and Jonathan Zittrain; and Affinity, That Elusive Dream: A Genealogy of the Chemical Revolution by Mi. Gyung Kim.

The MIT Press accepts proposals via e-mail or regular mail with SASE. Submit your proposal to the appropriate editor:

Roger Conover, Executive Editor—Art, architecture: visual and cultural studies; conover@mit.edu

Tom Stone, Editor—Cognitive science, linguistics, philosophy, Bradford Books, Zone Books; tstone@mit.ecu

Robert Prior, Executive Editor—Computer science, quantitative biology; prior@mit.edu

Doug Sery, Editor—Design, new media, game studies; dsery@mit.edu

John S. Covell, Editor—Economics, finance, business; jcovell@mit.edu

Clay Morgan, Editor—Environmental and political science, bioethics; claym@mit.edu

Adam Brunstein, Acquisitions Editor—Computer science, linguistics; adam@mit.edu

Jane Macdonald, Acquisitions Editor—Economics, finance, business; janem@mit.edu

Marguerite Avery, Acquisitions Editor—Science, technology, and society; mavery@mit.edu

---

NEW YORK UNIVERSITY PRESS

838 Broadway, 3rd Floor, New York, NY 10003-4812

212-998-2575 fax: 212-995-3833

www.nyupress.org e-mail: information@nyupress.org

The NYU Press believes in the idea that academic research and opinion can and should have a prominent place at the table of public debate. At a time of continued upheaval in publishing, some presses, NYU Press among them, detect profound opportunities in this unstable landscape. Rather than bemoaning a lost age, when libraries more or less financed university press operations, these presses are emphasizing their strengths. Convinced that intellectual heft and a user-friendly efficiency need not be mutually exclusive, the staff at NYU Press has sought, in recent years, to redefine what it means to be a university press.

Most importantly, they do not believe that the sole purpose of a university press is to publish works of objective social science, though to be sure this remains an important role of the house mandate. Rather, NYU Press also eagerly embraces the role of a gadfly. They oftentimes publish books on the same issue from different poles of the political spectrum in the same catalog, to generate dialogue, engender debate, and resist pat categorization of the publishing program. Rather than praise diversity as an abstract goal, they embrace ideological diversity as a crucial, defining ingredient for a healthy program.

On a logistical level, NYU Press believes that, in the world of nonfiction publishing, the scales have far too long been tipped in favor of the publishers. The house therefore rejects exclusive review, encouraging authors to submit their manuscripts widely, should they wish to do so, to ensure their decision, if they publish with this house, is an educated one, not the result of artificial restrictions. NYU Press believes that any long-term relationship between an author and publisher must be predicated on mutual respect. Thus, they place enormous emphasis on a close working relationship with authors. Further, they provide high-quality production and decades of craft experience. Importantly, they can provide all these advantages alongside one crucial guarantee: No one will ever take this house over.

NYU Press is interested in titles that explore issues of race and ethnicity. They are also highly interested in media studies and American studies.

Recent titles include *The Political Thought of Elizabeth Cady Stanton: Women's Rights and the American Political Traditions* by Sue Davis; *Raising Freedom's Child: Black Children and Visions of the Future after Slavery* by Mary Niall Mitchell; *City of Disorder: How the Quality of Life Campaign Transformed New York Politics* by Alex S. Vitale; *John Devoy's Catalpa Expeditions* edited by Philip Fennel and Marie King; *Abandoned: Foundlings in Nineteenth-Century New York* by Julie Miller; and *American Catholic History: A documentary Reader* edited by Mark Massa and Catherine Osborne.

NYU Press is the exclusive North American distributor for Berg Publishers, Monthly Review Press, Lawrence & Wishart, and Rivers Oram (Pandora).

New York University Press handles distribution through its own sales office, as well as a network of regional sales and marketing representatives.

Query letters and SASEs should be directed to:

Eric Zinner, Editor-in-Chief—Literary criticism and cultural studies, media studies, American history

Ilene Kalish, Executive Editor—Sociology, politics and anthropology

Jennifer Hammer, Editor—Religion and psychology

Deborah Gershenowitz, Senior Editor—American history to 1900, American military history, law

NORTHWESTERN UNIVERSITY PRESS

629 Noyes Street, Evanston, IL 60208-4210

847-491-2046   fax: 847-491-8150

www.nupress.northwestern.edu   e-mail: nupress@northwestern.edu

From its inception Northwestern University Press has striven to be at the forefront in publishing not only scholarly works in different disciplines, but also quality works of fiction, nonfiction, and literary criticism.

Founded in 1893, the early years of the press were dedicated to the publication of legal periodicals and scholarly books dealing with the law. In 1957 the press was established as a separate university publishing company and began expanding its offerings with new series in various fields, including African studies, phenomenology and existential philosophy, literature, and literary criticism.

In the late 1960s, the press published Viola Spolin's landmark volume, *Improvisation for the Theater: A Handbook of Teaching and Directing Techniques*. This "bible" of improvisational theater has sold more than 100,000 copies since its publication and, with several other Spolin titles, forms a cornerstone of the press's publishing program. The press continues its commitment to theater and performance studies, most recently with the publication of Mary Zimmerman's *Metamorphoses*, the script of her Broadway show that was nominated for the 2002 Tony award for Best Play and Best Scenic Design, and won the 2002 Tony award for Best Director.

The 1960s also saw the beginnings of the Northwestern University Press-Newberry Library alliance in publishing the definitive edition of the writings of Herman Melville in conjunction with the Modern Language Association.

The press won major translation awards in the early 1990s for Fyodor Dostoevsky's *Writer's Diary: Volume I, 1873-1876* (translated by Kenneth Lantz) and Ignacy Krasicki's *Adventures of Mr. Nicholas Wisdom* (translated by Thomas H. Hoisington). In 1997 the press won a National Book Award for Poetry for William Meredith's *Effort at Speech*. In 2001 *The Jardin des Plantes* by Claude Simon, translated by Jordan Stump, was awarded the French-American Foundation Translation Prize. Meena Alexander, author of the poetry book entitled *Illiterate Heart* (TriQuarterly Books), won the 2002 PEN Open Book award.

Since 1992 Northwestern University Press has doubled its publishing output. In addition to the works of contemporary European writers, the press has also begun to reissue lost or previously untranslated works of important European authors, including Nobel Prize winners Heinrich Böll and Grazia Deledda. Scholarly series include Rethinking Theory, Studies in Russian Literature and Theory, Writings from an Unbound Europe, Avant-Garde and Modernism Studies, and Studies in Phenomenology and Existential Philosophy In 1992 the press joined forces with *TriQuarterly* magazine—Northwestern University's innovative literary journal aimed at a sophisticated and diverse readership—to establish the TriQuarterly Books imprint, which is devoted primarily to contemporary American fiction and poetry. In addition, the press has a second trade imprint, Hydra Books, which features contemporary fiction, poetry, and nonfiction in translation. In 1997 *TriQuarterly* magazine itself became a publication of the press. In 2002 the press began publishing Chicago regional titles, such as *A Court That Shaped America: Chicago's Federal Court from Abe Lincoln to Abbie Hoffman* by Richard Cahan.

Recent titles include *Effort at Speech: New and Selected Poems* by William Meredith; *Bentley on Brecht* by Eric Bentley; *Fuchsia in Cambodia: Poems* by Roy Jacobstein; *Bridges of Memory Vol. 2: Chicago's Second Generation of Black Migration* by Timuel D. Black; *Harold! Photographs from the Harold Washington Years* by Antonio Dickey, Marc PoKempner, and Salim Muwakkil; *The People Are the News: Grant Pick's Chicago Stories* by John Pick; *Chief O'Neill's Sketchy Recollections of an Eventful Life in Chicago* by Francis O'Neill; and *True Stories: A Century of Literary Journalism* by Norman Sims and Ted Conover.

To submit fiction, poetry, or general nonfiction, please send the complete manuscript or several sample chapters along with biographical information on the author, including a list of previously published books. Because of the high volume of submissions, allow at least 16 weeks for the review of your manuscript.

To submit a scholarly manuscript, please send a proposal, cover letter, and CV. Allow approximately 12 weeks for the review of your manuscript.

Please do not call. Send queries and SASEs to: Acquisitions Department.

Henry L. Carrigan Jr., Senior Editor; h-carrigan@northwestern.edu

Mike Levine, Acquisitions Editor; mike-levine@northwestern.edu

Jenny Gavacs, Assistant Acquisitions Editor; j-gavacs@northwestern.edu

Anne Gendler, Managing Editor; a-gendler@northwestern.edu

Serena Brommel, Senior Project Editor; s-brommel@northwestern.edu

Jessica Paumier, Senior Project Editor; j-paumier@northwestern.edu

---

OHIO STATE UNIVERSITY PRESS

180 Pressey Hall, 1070 Carmack Road, Columbus, OH 43210-1002

614-292-6930 fax: 614-292-2065

www.ohiostatepress.org

The Ohio State University Press was established in 1957 and currently publishes 30 new books a year. Areas of specialization include literary studies, including narrative theory; history, including business history, medieval history and history of crime; political science, including legislative studies; and Victorian studies, urban studies, and women's health. They also publish annual winners of short fiction and poetry prizes, the details of which are available at www.ohiostatepress.org.

Recent titles include *Everything Lost: The Latin American Notebooks of William S. Burroughs* edited by Geoffrey D. Smith, John M. Bennet, and Oliver Harris; *Joeseph Conrad: Voice, Sequence, History, Genre* edited by Jakob Lothe, Jeremy Hathorn, and Hames Phelan; *The Chekhovian Intertext: Dialogue with a Classic* by Lyudmila Parts; *The Black Aesthetic Unbound: Theorizing the Dilemma of Eighteenth-Century African American Literature* by April C. E. Langley; *Victorian Freaks: the Social Context of Freakery in Britain* edited by Marlene Tromp; and *Home Economics: Domestic Fraud in Victorian England* by Rebecca Stern.

Ohio State University Press oversees its own sales and distribution. Scholars proposing manuscripts for publication should submit whatever materials they feel are necessary for the acquisitions department at Ohio State University Press to make informed decisions about the project. Query letters and SASEs should be directed to:

Sandy Crooms, Senior Editor—Literary studies, Victorian studies, narrative, American studies, women's studies, women and health; sandy.crooms@osupress.org

Malcolm Litchfield, Acquisitions Editor—Medieval studies, literary theory other than narrative; ml@osupress.org

Eugene O'Connor, Ph.D., Acquisitions Editor—Classics; Eugene@osupress.org

---

OXFORD UNIVERSITY PRESS

198 Madison Avenue, New York, NY 10016

212-726-6000

www.oup-usa.org blog: blog.oup.com

Oxford University Press, Inc. (OUP USA), is by far the largest American university press and perhaps the most diverse publisher of its type. It publishes works that further Oxford University's objective of excellence in research, scholarship, and education. The press had its origins in the information technology revolution of the late 15th century, which began with the invention of printing from movable type. The first book was printed in Oxford in 1478. In 1586, the university itself obtained a decree confirming its privilege to print books. This was further enhanced in the Great Charter secured by Archbishop Laud from King Charles I, which entitled the university to print "all manner of books." The university first appointed delegates to oversee this privilege in 1633. Minutes recording their deliberations date back to 1668, and OUP as it exists today began to develop in a recognizable way from that time.

OUP's international expansion began with the opening of a U.S. office in 1896. The office was established initially simply to sell bibles published in Oxford, but by the

1920s, the office began to produce books on its own. The first nonfiction work published by OUP USA, *The Life of Sir William Osler*, won the Pulitzer Prize in 1926. Six more Pulitzers, several National Book Awards, and over a dozen Bancroft Prizes in American history have followed since.

Oxford's New York office is editorially independent of the British home office and handles distribution of its own list, as well as titles originating from Oxford's branches worldwide. OUP USA publishes at a variety of levels, for a wide range of audiences in almost every academic discipline. The main criteria in evaluating new titles are quality and contribution to the furtherance of scholarship and education. OUP USA produces approximately 500 titles each year, of which 250 are scholarly research monographs, and imports close to 800 such works from their U.K. and branch offices. OUP USA has 3,300 scholarly books in print and stocks another 8,700 imports from other OUP offices around the world. All publications are first vetted by OUP's delegates, who are leading scholars at Oxford University and from other top U.S. institutions.

OUP editor Shannon McLachlan said recently that the press is especially interested in acquiring titles that explore "material based studies," and such topics as print culture, environmentalism, and literature and the law.

Recent titles include *What Hath God Wrought: The Transformation of America, 1815-1848* by Daniel Walker Howe; *Safire's Political Dictionary* by William Safire; *Doubt is their Product: How Industry's Assault on Science Threatens Your Health* by David Michaels; *Murder of a Medici Princess* by Caroline P. Murphy; *Flower Hunters* by Mary Grabbing; *Baseball's Great Experiment: Jackie Robinson and His Legacy* by Jules Tiger

OUP USA welcomes submissions. Potential authors should include a cover letter, a copy of their CV, a prospectus, and sample chapters from the work (if available). In general all material should be unbound and double-spaced on single-sided paper. Material may be sent in care of the appropriate editor:

Niko Pfund, Academic Publisher

Joan Bossert, Associate Publisher—Neuroscience, consumer health, psychological and behavioral sciences; joan.bossert@oup.com

Catharine Carlin, Associate Publisher—Cognitive neuroscience, cognitive psychology; Catharine.carlin@oup.com

Susan Ferber, Editor—American and world history, art history, academic art and architecture; susan.ferber@oup.com

Peter Prescott, Editor—Life sciences, earth science, environmental science; peter.prescott@oup.com

Jeremy Lewis, Editor—Chemistry; jeremy.lewis@oup.com

Peter Ohlin, Editor—Bioethics, linguistics, philosophy; peter.ohlin@oup.com

Cynthia Read, Senior Editor—Religion; cynthia.read@oup.com

Nancy Toff, Editorial Director—Children's and young adult books, history; nancy.toff@oup.com

Donald Kraus, Executive Editor—Bibles; donald.kraus@oup.com

Shannon McLachlan, Editor—American studies, classical studies, English language and literature, literary studies, film; shannon.mclachlan@oup.com

Terry Vaughn, Editor—Business management, economics, finance and financial economics; terry.vaugh@oup.com

Mariclaire Cloutier, Editor—Forensic psychology, clinical psychology; mariclaire.cloutier@oup.com

Peter Prescott, Editor—Life sciences; peter.prescott@oup.com

Theo Calderera, Editor—Religion (academic); theo.calderera@oup.com

Michael Penn, Editor—Mathematics, statistics; michael.penn@oup.com

William Lamsback, Editor—Medicine, neurology; william.lamsback@oup.com

Carrie Pedersen, Editor—Medicine, public health; carrie.pedersen@oup.com

Suzanne Ryan, Editor—Music; suzanne.ryan@oup.com

Sonke Adlung, Editor—Physics; songke.adlung@oup.com

Marion Osmun, Editor—Psychiatry (medical); marion.osmun@oup.com

Jennifer Rappaport, Editor—Developmental psychology; Jennifer.rappaport@oup.com

PENN STATE UNIVERSITY PRESS

820 North University Drive, University Support Building 1, Suite C, University Park, PA 16802-1003

814-865-1327 fax: 814-863-1408

www.psupress.psu.edu e-mail: info@psupress.org

The Penn State University Press is dedicated to serving the university community, the citizens of Pennsylvania, and the worldwide network of scholars by publishing books and journals of the highest quality. In fulfilling its role as part of the University's division of research and graduate education, the press promotes the advance of scholarship by disseminating knowledge—new information, interpretations, methods of analysis—and strives to reflect academic strengths of the university. As an integral part of the university community, the press collaborates with alumni, friends, faculty, and staff in producing books about aspects of university life and history. As the publishing arm of a land-grant and state-supported institution, the press recognizes its special responsibility to develop books about Pennsylvania, both scholarly and popular, that enhance interest in the region and spread awareness of the state's history, culture, and environment.

The origins of the press go back to 1945, when a committee at the university was appointed "to study the advisability and practicability of establishing a Pennsylvania

State College Press." No immediate action was taken, but in 1953, as a first experiment in university press publishing, the Department of Public Information (then directed by Louis H. Bell) issued a book entitled *Penn State Yankee: The Autobiography of Fred Lewis Pattee*, which Mr. Bell himself edited and designed. The experiment evidently proved successful enough to persuade the trustees board in 1956 to establish the Pennsylvania State University Press "on an experimental basis."

The press's strengths include core areas such as art history and literary criticism as well as fields such as philosophy, religion, history (mainly U.S. and European), and some of the social sciences (especially political science and sociology).

Recent titles include *Cezanne's Bathers: Biography and the Erotics of Paint* by Aruna D'Souza; *Counterfeit Amateurs: An Athlete's Journey Through the Sixties to the Age of Academic Capitalism* by Allen L. Sack; *Inside the Soviet Alternate Universe: The Cold War's End and the Soviet Union's Fall Reappraised; An Entrenched Legacy: How the New Deal Constitutional Revolution Continues to Shape the Role of the Supreme Court* by Patrick M. Garry.

If you have questions about submissions, Penn State Press invites you to call or e-mail with Manuscript Submissions in the subject line. Direct queries and SASEs to:

Patrick H. Alexander, Editor-in-Chief—American Studies, European history and culture, history, medieval and early modern studies, philosophy, regional studies, religion, religious studies, romance studies, and Slavic studies; pha3@psu.edu

Eleanor Goodman PhD, Executive Editor for the Arts & Humanities—Art and art History, architectural history, European history and Culture (Spanish, French), literature, medieval and early modern studies, visual culture; ehg11@psu.edu

Sanford G. Thatcher, Director—Latin American studies, law, philosophy (feminist, legal, political), political science, and sociology; sgt3@psu.edu

---

PRINCETON UNIVERSITY PRESS

41 William Street, Princeton, NJ 08540-5237

609-258-4900   fax: 609-258-6305

www.pup.princeton.edu

U.K. office:

3 Market Place, Woodstock, Oxfordshire OX20 1SY, U.K.

011-44-1993-814500

Princeton University Press, which celebrated its 100th anniversary in 2005, is one of the country's largest and oldest university presses. The press publishes some 200 new books in hardcover each year and another 90 paperback reprints. With a goal to disseminate scholarship both within academia and to society at large, the press produces publications that range across more than 40 disciplines, from art history to ornithology and political science to philosophy.

The press is an independent publisher with close connections, both formal and informal, to Princeton University. Its five-member editorial board, which makes controlling decisions about which books will bear the press's imprint, is appointed from the faculty by the president of the university, and nine of the 15 members of the press's board must have a Princeton University connection.

Recent titles include *On Bullshit* by Harry G. Frankfurt; *Cop in the Hood* by Peter Moskos; *Souled Out: Reclaiming Faith and Politics After the Religious Right* by E.J. Dionne, Jr., *Life in Cold Blood* by David Attenborough; *The Rise And Fall of The Islamic State; Torture and Democracy* by Darius Rejall; *Beyond UFOs: The Search for Extraterrestrial Life and its Astonishing Implications for Our Future* by Jeffrey Bennet; *Unequal Democracy: The Political Economy of the New Gilded Age* by Larry M. Bartels; *Macroeconomic Theory: A Dynamic General Equilibrium Approach* by Michael Wickens.

The Bollingen Series, established in 1941, is sponsored by the Bollingen Foundation and has been published by Princeton since 1967. Bollingen titles are works of original scholarship, translations, or new editions of classics. An ongoing Bollingen project is Mythos: The Princeton/Bollingen series in world mythology. Titles representative of the list include *The Collected Works of Samuel Taylor Coleridge, Volume 15: Opus Maximum*, edited by Thomas McFarland; *The I Ching or Book of Changes* edited by Hellmut Wilhelm, translated by Cary F. Baynes; and *Essays on a Science of Mythology: The Myth of the Divine Child and the Mysteries of Eleusis* by C.G. Jung and C. Kerényi.

Books from the Princeton Science Library include *Fearful Symmetry: The Search for Beauty in Modern Physics* by A. Zee; *Eye and Brain: The Psychology of Seeing* by Richard L. Gregory; *Flatland: A Romance of Many Dimensions* by Edwin Abbott Abbott; and *Why Big Fierce Animals Are Rare: An Ecologist's Perspective* by Paul A. Colinvaux.

Princeton University Press handles distribution through the offices of California/Princeton Fulfillment Services, as well as regional sales representation worldwide. Princeton University Press does not accept unsolicited proposals or manuscripts via e-mail. Queries or brief proposals along with a copy of your CV and SASEs should be mailed via regular mail to the Editor-in-Chief or other appropriate editor:

Peter Dougherty, Director

Brigitta van Rheinberg, Editor-in-Chief—History (American, European, Middle Eastern, Jewish, Asian, Medieval, Ancient, and World)

Robert Kirk, Executive Editor—Natural history, biology, ornithology, field guides

Chuck Myers, Executive Editor—Political science, law

Richard Baggaley (**U.K. office**), European Publishing Director—Finance and economics

Fred Appel, Associate Editor—Music, anthropology, and literature

Vickie Kearn, Executive Editor—Mathematics

Ingrid Gnerlich, Senior Editor—Physical sciences, earth sciences

Hanne Winarsky, Editor—Literature, art

Seth Ditchik, Senior Editor—Economics, finance, behavioral & cognitive sciences

Alison Kalett, Editor—Biology, earth sciences

Clara Platter, Assistant Editor—American history

Anna Savarese, Senior Editor—Reference

Robert Tempio, Editor—Philosophy, classics, ancient world

RUTGERS UNIVERSITY PRESS

100 Joyce Kilmer Avenue, Piscataway, NJ 08854-8099

732-445-7762 ext. 605   fax: 732-445-7039

www.rutgerspress.rutgers.edu

Since its founding in 1936 as a nonprofit publisher, Rutgers University Press has been dedicated to the advancement and dissemination of knowledge to scholars, students, and the general reading public. An integral part of one of the leading public research and teaching universities in the U.S., the press reflects and is essential to the university's missions of research, instruction, and service. To carry out these goals, the house publishes books in print and electronic format in a broad array of disciplines across the humanities, social sciences, and sciences. Fulfilling a mandate to serve the people of New Jersey, it also publishes books of scholarly and popular interest on the state and surrounding region.

Working with authors throughout the world, the house seeks books that meet high editorial standards, facilitate the exchange of ideas, enhance teaching, and make scholarship accessible to a wide range of readers. The press's overriding ambition is nothing less than to help make the world better, one book at a time, through a publication program of superior scholarship and popular appeal. The press celebrates and affirms its role as a major cultural institution that contributes significantly to the ideas that shape the critical issues of our time.

In 2007, the press expects to publish 100 new titles in the humanities, social sciences, and sciences. The press's strengths include history, sociology, anthropology, religion, media, film studies, women's studies, African American studies, Asian American studies, public health, the history of medicine, evolutionary biology, the environment, and books about the Mid-Atlantic region.

The press publishes several book series that represent innovative scholarship in the fields of art studies, evolutionary studies, literary studies, and communications and media studies. Leslie Mitchner, associate director and editor-in-chief at Rutgers University Press, recently noted two new series: one on multi-ethnic literatures of the

Americas and one on "subterranean lives," defined as "first-person accounts from the 19th and 20th centuries by members of oppositional and stigmatized subcultures," as being subject matters about which the press is particularly excited.

Recent titles published by Rutgers University Press include *Entering Cultural Communities: Diversity and Change on the Nonprofit Arts; Youth, Crime and Justice: A Global Inquiry* by Clayton A. Hartjen; *Making Room in the Clinic: Nurse Practitioners and the Evolution of Modern Health Care* by Julie Fairman; *Biofeedback for the Brain: How Neurotherapy Effectively Treat Depression, ADHD, Autism, and More* by Paul G. Swingle, PhD; *Saving Sickly Children: The Tuberculosis Preventorium in American Life, 1909-1970* by Cynthia A. Connolly; *The Contested Boundaries of American Public Health* edited by James Colgrove, Gerald E. Markowitz, and David Rosner; and *The Horse Who Drank the Sky: Film Experience Beyond Narrative and Theory* by Murray Pomerance.

Rutgers is proud to announce Rivergate Books, an imprint devoted to New Jersey and surrounding states. New titles from Rivergate include *New Jersey Politics and Government: The Suburbs Come of Age* by Barbara G. Salmore and Stephen A. Salmore; *Rutgers Football: A Gridiron Tradition in Scarlet* by Michael J. Pellowski; *No Minor Accomplishment: The Revival of New Jersey Professional Baseball* by Bob Golon; *Local Heroes: The Asbury Park Music Scene* by Anders Martensson; and *Waste Is a Terrible Thing to Mind: Risk, Radiation, and Distrust of Government* by John Weingart.

Rutgers University Press handles its own distribution.

Query letters and SASEs should be directed to:

Leslie Mitchner, Associate Director and Editor-in-Chief—Humanities, literature, film, communications; lmitch@rutgers.edu

Doreen Valentine, Science, Health and Medicine Editor; dvalen@rutgers.edu

Adi Hovav, Social Sciences and Religion Editor; adih@rutgers.edu

Beth Kressel, Associate Editor—Jewish Studies; bkres@rutgers.edu

---

STANFORD UNIVERSITY PRESS

1450 Page Mill Road, Palo Alto, CA 94304-1124

650-723-9434   fax: 650-725-3457

www.sup.org   e-mail: info@www.sup.org

Stanford University Press maintains specific publishing strategies that mirror not only Stanford's commitment to the unfettered creation and communication of new knowledge, but also its commitment to offering an undergraduate education that is unrivaled among research universities, and its commitment to training tomorrow's leaders in a range of graduate professional disciplines.

They do this by making available a range of highly specialized and peer-reviewed research that otherwise might not be published; making major foreign-language works available in translation here, and making books available in foreign-language editions abroad; keeping books in print and debate alive, often for decades; publishing the work of new scholars, thereby adding their voices and views to ongoing debates—and often precipitating new ones; publishing textbooks for upper-level undergraduate courses and graduate courses; publishing reference works for professional practitioners; making all works for which the house has electronic rights available through the main electronic aggregators, including ebrary, netLibrary, Questia, Google, and Books 24x7.

In pursuit of these strategies, the press publishes about 130 books per year. About two-thirds of these books are scholarly monographs and textbooks in the humanities and the social sciences, with a strong concentration in history, literature, philosophy, and Asian studies, and growing lists in politics, sociology, anthropology, and religion. The remaining one-third are textbooks, professional reference works, and monographs in law, business, economics, public policy, and education. Tenure monographs account for about 20% of their scholarly output, and translations account for about 12%.

In keeping with the high intellectual quality of the works the house publishes, the press ensures that every title it releases benefits from exacting professional standards for editing, design, and manufacturing. It also ensures that each book is carefully positioned in the market channel most appropriate for reaching its primary audience—that is, libraries, bookstores, online vendors, electronic collections, and searchable databases. Working hard to maintain this commitment to intellectual quality and high production values is a creative, energetic, and enthusiastic staff who work closely together to make the whole process from manuscript creation to publication both seamless for the author and timely for the buyer. Their efforts are augmented by a global sales, marketing, and distribution network that gives access to wholesale and retail buyers in all the key markets of the Americas, Europe, Asia, and Australia.

Recent titles include *Mimesis and Theory: essays on Literature and Criticism 1953-2005* by Rene Girad; *The Time of the Crime: Phenomenology, Psychoanalysis, Italian Film* by Domietta Torlasco; *Murmured Conversations: A Treatise on Poetry and Buddhism by the Poet Monk Shinkei* by Esperanza Ramirez-Christensen; *Revolution within the Revolution: Cotton Textile Workers and the Mexican Labor Regime, 1910-1923* by Jeffrey Bortz; *Cinematic Thinking: Philosophical Approaches to the New Cinema* edited by James Phillips; and *Uneasy Reunions: Immigration, Citizenship, and Family Life in Post-1997 Hong Kong* by Nicole Newendorp.Stanford University Press books are distributed by Cambridge University Press Distribution Center.

Initial inquiries about publication should be made directly to the appropriate sponsoring editor at the press. Do not send complete manuscripts until invited to do so by the editor. Query letters and SASEs should be directed to:

Geoffrey Burn, Director and Acquisitions Editor—Business strategy and security studies; grhburn@stanford.edu

Norris Pope, Director of Scholarly Publishing—History, Latin American Studies, and Jewish Studies; npope@Stanford.edu

Kate Wahl, Senior Editor—Sociology, law and Middle East studies

Margo Beth Crouppen, Acquisitions Editor—Economics and organizational studies; mbcrouppen@stanford.edu

Stacy Wagner, Acquisitions Editor—Asian studies, Asian American studies, and political science; swagner@stanford.edu

Emily-Jane Cohen, Acquisitions Editor—Literature, philosophy, and religion; Beatrice@stanford.edu

STATE UNIVERSITY OF NEW YORK PRESS

194 Washington Avenue, Suite 305, Albany, NY 12210-2384

518-472-5000   fax: 518-472-5038

www.sunypress.edu   e-mail: info@sunypress.edu

State University of New York Press (SUNY Press) publishes scholarly and trade books in support of the university's commitments to teaching, research, and public service. With an editorial board made up of SUNY faculty from throughout the state, SUNY Press has a large catalog, featuring authors from around the world.

From a modest beginning in 1966, SUNY Press has become one of the largest public university presses in the U.S., with an annual output of some 170 books and a backlist of more than 3,400 titles. The press publishes chiefly in the humanities and social sciences, and has attained national recognition in the areas of education, philosophy, religion, Jewish studies, Asian studies, political science, and sociology, with increasing growth in the areas of literature, film studies, communication, women's studies, and environmental studies.

Recent titles include *The Future of Invention: Rhetoric, Postmodernism, and the Problem Of Change* by John Mucklebaur; *Sin, Sex, and Democracy: Antigay Rhetoric and the Christian Right* by Cynthia Burack; *Soundings on Cinema: Speaking to Film and Film Artists* by Bert Cardullo; *Now Playing: Early Moviegoing and the Regulation of Fun* by Paul S. Moore; and *Always at Odds? Creating Alignment between Faculty and Administrative Values* by Mary C. Wright.

SUNY Press accepts simultaneous submissions of proposals; however, at the manuscript review stage they prefer an exclusive review. To submit, send a proposal with SASE to:

Jane Bunker, Editor-in-Chief

SYRACUSE UNIVERSITY PRESS

621 Skytop Road, Suite 110, Syracuse, NY 13244-5290

315-443-5534 fax: 315-443-5545

syracuseuniversitypress.syr.edu e-mail: supress@syr.edu

Syracuse University Press was founded in 1943 by Chancellor William Pearson Tolley, with the intent to enhance the school's academic standing. With more than 1,200 titles in print today, the press consistently earns international critical acclaim and attracts award-winning authors of note.

Each year Syracuse University Press publishes new books in specialized areas including New York State, Middle East Studies, Judaica, geography, Irish studies, Native American studies, religion, television and popular culture.

Recent titles include *One Family's Response to Terrorism: A Daughter's Memoir* by Susan Kerr van de Ven; *Child in Jerusalem* by Felicity Ashbee; *Contemporary Iraqi Fiction: An Anthology* edited and translated by Shakir Mustafa; *Two Grandmothers from Baghdad: And Other Memoirs of Monkith Saaid* by Rebecca Joubin; and *Providence Has Freed Our Hands: Women's Missions and the American Encounter with Japan* by Karen K. Seat.

Syracuse University Press distributes its list via its own in-house offices and utilizes a variety of distribution services worldwide.

Please send a proposal with SASE to:

Mary Shelden Evans, Executive Editor; msevans@syr.edu

Glenn Wright, Acquisitions Editor; glwright@syr.edu

TEXAS A&M UNIVERSITY PRESS

John H. Lindsey Building, Lewis Street, 4354 TAMU, College Station, TX, 77843-4354

979-845-1436 fax: 949-847-8752

www.tamu.edu/upress e-mail: dlv@tampress.tamu.edu

Founded in 1974, Texas A&M University Press is the principal publishing arm of one of this nation's leading research institutions. The press's primary mission is to select, produce, market, and disseminate scholarly publications of outstanding quality and originality and thereby help the university achieve its paramount purposes of teaching, research, public service, and dissemination of the results of scholarly inquiry. In conjunction with the long-term development of its editorial program, the press draws on and supports the intellectual activities of the university and reflects the standards and stature of scholarship that are fostered by this institution.

The press falls under the administrative aegis of the provost, the chief academic officer of the University, and is an integral part of its parent institution. The press imprint is controlled by an advisory committee composed of senior members of the university's faculty, who are chosen for their own scholarly acumen and publishing experience. Manuscripts, whether by outside authors or by members of the Texas A&M faculty (currently around 15% of the total author list), must have been reviewed favorably by both the press's director and editorial staff and at least two experts in that field before being submitted to the faculty advisory committee for approval. Of the hundreds of manuscripts and proposals that come to the press each year, most do not survive this rigorous selection process.

The press's editorial interests span a range of significant fields, including agriculture, anthropology, nautical archaeology, architecture, borderland studies, Eastern Europe, economics, military history, natural history, presidential studies, veterinary medicine, and works on the history and culture of Texas and the surrounding region. Many of these fields of interest reflect outstanding departmental and programmatic strengths at Texas A&M University. Overall, the press seeks to maintain high standards in traditional areas of academic inquiry while also exploring innovative fields of research and new forms of scholarly communication.

The press currently publishes more than 70 new titles a year in these fields. Of the total of nearly 930 books published by the press in its 34-year history, the great majority remains in print or are available in on-demand and electronic editions.

Recent titles include *Capturing Nature: The Cement Sculpture of Dionicio Rodriguez* by Patsy Pittman Light; *The Birth of a Texas Ghost Town* by Mary Jane Gentry; *As it Was* by Douglas John Cater; *Inside the VC and the NVA* by Michael Lee Lanning; *Black Women in Texas History* edited by Bruce A. Glasrud and Merline Pitre; *A Dragon Lives Forever* by Thomas R. Hargrove; *North of the Port* by Anthony Bukoski; *Building the Borderlands* by Casey Walsh; and *Flash Floods in Texas* by Jonathan Burnett.

Texas A&M University Press manages its own distribution network and handles distribution for several other regional, academically oriented presses.

Query letters and SASEs should be directed to Diana L. Vance:

Diana L. Vance, Editorial Assistant, Acquisitions; dlv@tampress.tamu.edu

Mary Lenn Dixon, Editor-in-Chief; mld@tampress.tamu.edu

Shannon Davies, Senior Editor, Natural Sciences; shannondavies@autin.rr.edu

Thom Lemmons, Managing Editor; tl@tampress.tamu.edu

Jennifer Ann Hobson, Project Editor; jah@tampress.tamu.edu

UNIVERSITY OF ALABAMA PRESS

USPS Address: Box 870380, Tuscaloosa, AL 35487-0380

Physical/Shipping Address: 200 Hackberry Lane, 2nd Floor McMillan Bldg., Tuscaloosa, AL 35401

205-348-5180 fax: 205-348-9201

www.uapress.ua.edu

As the university's primary scholarly publishing arm, the University of Alabama Press seeks to be an agent in the advancement of learning and the dissemination of scholarship. The press applies the highest standards to all phases of publishing, including acquisitions, editorial, production and marketing. An editorial board comprised of representatives from all doctoral degree-granting state universities within Alabama oversees the publishing program. Projects are selected that support, extend, and preserve academic research. The press also publishes books that foster an understanding of history of cultures of this state and region.

The University of Alabama Press publishes in the following areas: American history; Southern history and culture; American religious history; Latin American history; American archaeology; Southeastern archaeology; Caribbean archaeology; historical archaeology; ethnohistory; anthropology; American literature and criticism; rhetoric and communication; creative nonfiction; linguistics, esp. dialectology; African American studies; Native American studies; Judaic studies; public administration; theater; natural history and environmental studies; American social and cultural history; sports history; military history; regional studies of Alabama and the southern U.S., including trade titles. Submissions are not invited in poetry, fiction, or drama.

Special series from Alabama include Classics in Southeastern Archaeology; Contemporary American Indian Studies; Deep South Books; Alabama: The Forge of History; Judaic Studies; Library of Alabama Classics; Modern and Contemporary Poetics; The Modern South; Religion and American Culture; Rhetoric, Culture, and Social Critique; and Studies in American Literary Realism and Naturalism.

Choice magazine awarded the University of Alabama Press 2005 Outstanding Academic Titles for these four books: *Dialect and Dichotomy: Literary Representations of African American Speech* by Lisa Cohen Minnick; *Faulkner the Storyteller* by Blair Labatt; *Game Work: Language, Power, and Computer Game Culture* by Ken S. McAllister; and *The Rock Art of Eastern North America: Capturing images and Insight* by Carol Diaz-Granados and James R. Duncan.

Other recent Alabama titles include *Full Fathom Five: A Daughter's Search* by Mary Lee Coe Fowler; *Unknown Waters: A First-Hand Account of the Historic Under-Ice Survey of the Siberian Continental Shelf* by Alfred S. McLaren; *The Metal Life Car: The Inventor, the Imposter, and the Business of Lifesaving* by George E. Buker; *If It Takes All Summer: Martine Luther King, the KKK and State's Rights in St. Augustine, 1964* by Dan R. Warren;

The Bird is Gone: A Manifesto by Stephen Graham Jones; and *Freshwater Mussels of Alabama and the Mobile Basin in Georgia, Mississippi, and Tennessee* by James D. Williams, Arthur E. Bogan, and Jeffrey T. Garner

Submit your proposal with cover letter and CV by regular mail to the appropriate acquisitions editor (for questions, feel free to contact the appropriate editor by e-mail):

Daniel J.J. Ross, Director—American history, Southern history and culture, American military history, American religious history, Latin American history, Jewish studies, regional studies of Alabama and the southern U.S., including regional trade titles; danross@uapress.ua.edu

Judith Knight, Senior Acquisitions Editor—American archaeology, Southeastern archaeology, Caribbean archaeology, historical archaeology, Native American studies, ethnohistory, anthropology; jknight@uapress.ua.edu

Daniel Waterman, Acquisitions Editor for Humanities—American literature and criticism, rhetoric and communication, creative nonfiction, linguistics, African American studies, public administration, theater, natural history and environmental studies; waterman@uapress.ua.edu

Elizabeth Motherwell, Acquisitions Editor for Natural History and the Environment—Natural history and environmental trade titles; emother@uapress.ua.edu

Claire Lewis Evans, Associate Editor for Digital and Electronic Publishing—Digital projects; cevans@uapress.ua.edu

UNIVERSITY OF ARIZONA PRESS

355 S. Euclid Avenue, Suite 103, Tucson, AZ 85719

520-621-1441   fax: 520-621-8899

www.uapress.arizona.edu   e-mail: uapress@uapress.arizona.edu

The University of Arizona Press, founded in 1959 as a department of the University of Arizona, is a nonprofit publisher of scholarly and regional books. As a delegate of the University of Arizona to the larger world, the press publishes the work of scholars wherever they may be, concentrating upon scholarship that reflects the special strengths of the University of Arizona, Arizona State University, and Northern Arizona University.

The University of Arizona Press publishes about 55 books annually and has some 783 books in print. These include scholarly titles in American Indian studies, anthropology, archaeology, environmental studies, geography, Chicano studies, history, Latin American studies, and the space sciences.

The UA Press also publishes general interest books on Arizona and the Southwest borderlands. In addition, the press publishes books of personal essays, such as Nancy Mairs's Plaintext and two series in literature: Sun Tracks: An American Indian Literary Series and Camino del Sol: A Chicana/o Literary Series.

Recent titles include *Arab/American: Landscape, Culture, and Cuisine in Two Great Deserts* by Gary Paul Nabhan; *The Oldest We've Ever Been: Seven True Stories of Midlife Transitions* edited by Maud Lavin; *If I Die in Juarez* by Stella Pope Duarte; *Jim Burns' Arizona Birds: From the Backyard to the Backwoods* by Jim Burns; *Global Health: Why Cultural Perceptions, Social Representations, and Biopolitics Matter* by Mark Nichter; and *The Borders Within: Encounters Between Mexico and the U.S.* by Douglas Monroy.

University of Arizona Press handles its own distribution and also distributes titles originating from the publishing programs of such enterprises and institutions as Oregon State University Press, the Arizona State Museum, and archaeological and environmental consulting firms.

Query letters and SASEs should be directed to:

Patti Hartmann, Acquiring Editor, Humanities—Native American literature and studies, Latina/o literature and studies, environmental writing, Western and environmental history, Latin American studies; hartmann@uapress.arizona.edu

Allyson Carter, Acquiring Editor, Social Sciences and Sciences—Anthropology, archaeology, ethnohistory, Southwest studies, environmental studies, conservation biology, natural history, popular astronomy, space sciences, geography; acarter@uapress@arizona.edu

UNIVERSITY OF ARKANSAS PRESS

McIlroy House, 201 Ozark Avenue, Fayetteville, AR 72701

479-575-3246 / 800-626-0090 fax: 479-575-6044

www.uapress.com e-mail: uapress@uark.edu

The University of Arkansas Press was founded in 1980 as the book publishing division of the University of Arkansas. A member of the Association of American University Presses, it publishes approximately 20 titles a year in the following subjects: history, Southern history, African American history, Civil War studies, poetics and literary criticism, Middle East studies, Arkansas and regional studies, music, and cultural studies. About a third of its titles fall under the general heading of Arkansas and Regional Studies. The press also publishes books of poetry and the winners of the Arabic Translation Award.

The press is charged by the university's trustees with the publication of books in service to the academic community and for the enrichment of the broader culture, especially works of value that are likely to be turned aside by commercial houses. This press, like all university presses, has as its central and continuing mission the dissemination of the fruits of research and creative activity.

Recent titles include *Inclined to Speak: An Anthology of Contemporary Arab-American Poetry* edited by Hayan Charara; *Rift: Poems* by Barbara Heifgott Hyett; *Now You're the Enemy: Poems* by James Allen Hall; *During Wind and Rain: the Jones Family Farm in the Arkansas Delta 1848-2006* by Margaret Jones Bolsterli; *Guide to Missouri Confederate Unites, 1861-1865* by James E. Mcghee; *Adventures in the Wild: Tales from Biologists of the Natural State* edited by Joy Trauth and Aldemaro Romero; *With All Deliberate Speed: Implementing Brown v. Board of Education* edited by Brian J. Daughterity and Charles C. Bolton; and *Epitaph for Little Rock: an Fiftieth Anniversary Retrospective on the Central High Crisis* edited by John A. Kirk.

Query letters and SASEs should be directed to:

Lawrence J. Malley, Director and Acquisitions Editor; lmalley@uark.edu

Julie Watkins, Acquisitions Assistant; jewatki@uark.edu

UNIVERSITY OF CALIFORNIA PRESS

2120 Berkeley Way, Berkeley, CA 94720-1012

510-642-4247 fax: 510-643-7127

www.ucpress.edu e-mail: askucp@ucpress.edu

Founded in 1893, University of California Press is one of the nation's largest and most adventurous scholarly publishers. Each year they publish approximately 200 new books and 50 multi-issue journals in the humanities, social sciences, and natural sciences and keep about 4,000 book titles in print.

The nonprofit publishing arm of the University of California system, UC Press attracts manuscripts from the world's foremost scholars, writers, artists, and public intellectuals. About one-fourth of its authors are affiliated with the University of California.

UC Press publishes in the areas of art, music, cinema and media studies, classics, literature, anthropology, sociology, archaeology, history, religious studies, Asian studies, biological sciences, food studies, natural history, and public health.

The UC Press, which publishes the food studies journal *Gastronomica*, has had considerable crossover success with books about wines, and continues to acquire titles on food and drink. For instance, it recently published *Meals to Come: A History of the Future of Food* by Warren Belasco.

Other recent titles include *Stat-Spotting: A Field Guide to Identifying Dubious Data* by Joel Best; *Pet Food Politics: The Chihuahua in the Coal Mine* by Marion Nestle; *One Thousand Languages: Living Endangered and Lost* edited by Peter K. Austin; *Sand: the Never-ending Story* by Michael Welland; *The Arts of China* edited by Michael Sullivan; *Guantanamo: A Working-Class History between Empire and Revolution* by Jana K. Lipman;

Cracks in the Pavement: Social Change and Resilience in Poor Neighborhoods by Martin Sanchez-Jankowsi; and *Promising Genomics: Iceland and decode Genetics in a World of Speculation* by Mike Fortun.

University of California Press distributes its own list.

Query letters and SASEs should be directed to:

Rachel Berchten, Editor—Poetry, poetics

Blake Edgar, Editor—Enology, biology, archaeology, viticulture

Laura Cerruti, Editor—Online references

Chuck Crumly, Editor—Organismal biology, ecology, evolution, environment

Stephanie Fay, Editor—Art history, classical studies

Mary Francis, Editor—Music, cinema

Stanley Holwitz, Assistant Director—Anthropology, Jewish studies, public health

Niels Hooper, Editor—History (except Asia), American studies

Deborah Kirshman, Editor—Museum co-publications

Sheila Levine, Editorial Director—Food studies, regional studies

Reed Malcolm, Editor—Religion (sociology/history/anthropology), politics, Asian studies

Naomi Schneider, Executive Editor—Sociology, politics, anthropology, Latin American studies

Jenny Wapner, Editor—Natural history, organismal biology

Lynne Withey, Editor—Public health

UNIVERSITY OF CHICAGO PRESS

1427 East 60th Street, Chicago, IL 60637

773-702-7700   fax: 773-702-9756

www.press.uchicago.edu   blog: http://pressblog.uchicago.edu

Since its founding in 1891 as one of the three original divisions of the University of Chicago, the press has embraced as its mission the obligation to disseminate scholarship of the highest standard and to publish serious works that promote education, foster public understanding, and enrich cultural life. Through their books and journals programs, they seek not only to advance scholarly conversation within and across traditional disciplines but, in keeping with the University of Chicago's experimental tradition, to help define new areas of knowledge and intellectual endeavor.

In addition to publishing the results of research for communities of scholars, the press presents innovative scholarship in ways that inform and engage general readers. The editors develop reference works and educational texts that draw upon and support the emphases of the university's scholarly programs and that extend the intellectual reach of the press. The house publishes significant nonscholarly work by writers, artists, and intellectuals from within and beyond the academy; translations of important foreign-language texts, both historical and contemporary; and books that contribute to the public's understanding of Chicago and its region. In all of this, the press is guided by the judgment of individual editors who work to build a broad but coherent publishing program engaged with authors and readers worldwide.

As many university presses search for books that will have crossover appeal to general audience readers, the University of Chicago Press takes a more highbrow approach than some. The press recently spent heavily to promote a book that appeals to serious music lovers: *Divas and Scholars: Performing Italian Opera*, by Philip Gossett.

Other recent titles include *Maps: Finding Our Place in the World* edited by James R. Ackerman and Robert W. Karrow Jr.; *Telling About Society* by Howard S. Becker; *Madame Proust: A Biography* by Evelyne Bloch-Dano; *The Chicago Guide to Your Career in Science: A Toolkit for Students and Postdocs* by Victor A. Bloomfield and Esam E. El-Fakahany; *The Gold Leaf Lady and Other Parapsychological Investigations* by Stephen E. Braude; *Castles, Battles, and Bombs: How Economics Explains Military History* by Jurgen Brauer and Hubert van Tuyll; *Vietnam Zippos: American Soldier's engravings and Stories (1965-1973)* by Sherry Buchanan; and *Global Fever: How to Treat Climate Change* by William H. Calvin.

University of Chicago Press distributes its own list.

Query letters and SASEs should be directed to:

Alan G. Thomas, Editorial Director, Humanities and Sciences—Literary criticism and theory, religious studies; athomas@press.uchicago.edu

Paul Schellinger, Editorial Director, Reference—Dictionaries, encyclopedias, guides, atlases, and other general reference; pschellinger@press.uchicago.edu

John Tryneski, Editorial Director, Social Sciences and Paperback Publishing—Political science, law and society; jtryneski@press.uchicago.edu

Christie Henry, Executive Editor—Biological science, behavior, conservation, ecology, environment, evolution, natural history, paleobiology, geography, earth sciences; chenry@press.uchicago.edu

Susan Bielstein, Executive Editor—Art, architecture, ancient archeology, classics, film studies; sbielstein@press.uchicago.edu

T. David Brent, Executive Editor—Anthropology, paleoanthropology, philosophy, psychology; dbrent@press.uchicago.edu

Karen Merikangas Darling, Editor—Science studies (history, philosophy, and social studies of science, medicine, and technology); kdarling@press.uchicago.edu

Robert P. Devens, Editor—American history, Chicago, and other regional publishing; redevens@press.uchicago.edu

Elizabeth Branch Dryson, Associate Editor—Ethnomusicology, interdisciplinary philosophy, and education; ebranchdyson@press.uchicago.edu

Kathleen K. Hansell, Editor—Music; khansell@press.uchicago.edu

Margaret Hivnor, Paperback Editor; mhivnor@press.uchicago.edu

Jennifer S. Howard, Associate Editor—Physical sciences (astrophysics, general physics, and mathematics); jhoward@press.uchicago.edu

Douglas Mitchell, Executive Editor—Sociology, history, sexuality studies, rhetoric; dmitchell@press.uchicago.edu

David Morrow, Senior Editor—Reference works, including regional reference; dmorrow@press.uchicago.edu

David Pervin, Senior Editor—Economics, economic history, business, law; dpervin@press.uchicago.edu

Randolph Petilos, Assistant Editor—Medieval studies, poetry in translation; rpetilos@press.uchicago.edu

---

UNIVERSITY OF GEORGIA PRESS

330 Research Drive, Athens, GA 30602-4901

706-369-6130   fax: 706-369-6131

www.ugapress.uga.edu   e-mail: books@ugapress.uga.edu

The University of Georgia Press is the oldest and largest publishing house in the state and one of the largest publishing houses in the South. The press publishes 70–80 titles each year, in a range of academic disciplines as well as books of interest to the general reader, and has nearly a thousand titles in print.

Since its founding in 1938, the University of Georgia Press has as its primary mission to support and enhance the university's place as a major research institution by publishing outstanding works of scholarship and literature by scholars and writers throughout the world as well as the university's own faculty.

As the publishing program of the press has evolved, this mission has taken on three distinct dimensions:

Works of scholarship. The press is committed to publishing important new scholarship in the following subject areas: American and Southern history and literature, African American studies, civil rights history, legal history, Civil War studies, Native American studies, folklore and material culture, women's studies, and environmental studies.

Regional books. The press has a long history of publishing books about the state and region for general readers. Their regional publishing program includes architectural guides, state histories, field guides to the region's flora and fauna, biographies, editions of diaries and letters, outdoor guides, and the work of some of the state's most accomplished artists, photographers, poets, and fiction writers.

Creative and literary works. This area of the list includes books published in conjunction with the Flannery O'Connor Award for Short Fiction, the Associated Writing Programs Award for Creative Nonfiction, and the Cave Canem Poetry Prize. Please write to the press for entry requirements and submission guidelines for these awards.

Recent titles include *Winners Have Yet to be Announced: A Song for Donny Hathaway* by Ed Pavlic; *Motoring: The Highway Experience in America* by John A. Jakle and Keith A. Sculle; *Margaret Fuller, Wandering Pilgrim* by Meg McGavran Murray; *Cornbread Nation 4: The Best of Southern Food Writing* edited by John T. Edge, Dale Reed, and John Reed; *Savage Barbecue: Race, culture, and the Invention of America's First Food* by Andrew Warnes; *Stirring the Mud: On Swamps, Bogs, and Human Imagination* by Barbara Hurd; and *Silent Retreats: Stories* by Philip F. Deaver.

The University of Georgia Press oversees its own distribution.

Query letters and SASEs should be directed to:

Nancy Grayson, Associate Director and Editor-in-Chief—American and Southern history, American literature, Southern studies, African American studies, legal history, women's studies, and international affairs; ngrayson@ugapress.uga.edu

Derek Krissoff, Senior Acquisitions Editor—American and Southern history, urban studies, African American studies, civil rights, and popular music; dkrissoff@ugapress.uga.edu

Judy Purdy, Acquisitions Editor—Natural history, environmental studies, nature writing, nature photography, horticulture and botany; jpurdy@ugapress.uga.edu

Erika Stevens, Acquisitions Editor—American studies, environmental history, popular culture and cultural studies, cinema/media studies, current events, Appalachian studies; estevens@ugapress.uga.edu

Nicole Mitchell, Director—General interest books about Georgia and the South; mitchell@ugapress.uga.edu

UNIVERSITY OF HAWAI'I PRESS

2840 Kolowalu Street, Honolulu, HI 96822-1888

1-808-956-8255   fax: 808-988-6052

www.uhpress.hawaii.edu   e-mail: uhpbooks@hawaii.edu

Areas of University of Hawai'i Press (UHP) publishing interest include cultural history, economics, social history, travel, arts and crafts, costume, marine biology, natural history, botany, ecology, religion, law, political science, anthropology, and general reference; particular UHP emphasis is on regional topics relating to Hawaii, and scholarly and academic books on East Asia, South and Southeast Asia, and Hawai'i and the Pacific.

University of Hawai`i Press (started in 1947) publishes books for the general trade, as well as titles keyed to the academic market. UHP also issues a series of special-interest journals. The house maintains an established backlist.

Recent titles include *Studies in Islam and Society in Southeast Asia* by William R. Roff; *Interpreting Southeast Asia's Past: Monument, Image, and Text* edited by Elisabeth Bacus, Ian Glover, and Peter Sharrock; *Malaysian Foreign Policy in the Matahir Era (1981-2003): Dilemmas of Development* by Karaminder Singh Dhillon; *The Agricultural Market Economy in Myanmar: Economic Transition and rural Disparities* by Ikuko Okamoto; *Singapore: The Perpetual Territorial Revolution* by Rodolphe de Konick; Jule Drolet; Marc Girard; *Impressions of the Goh Chok Tong Years in Singapore* edited by Bridget Welsh, James Chin, Arun Mahizhan, and Tan Tarn; and *Bandung Revisited* by Tan See Sung.

The University of Hawai`i Press handles its own distribution via a network that includes in-house fulfillment services, as well as independent sales representatives.

Query letters and SASEs should be directed to:

Keith Leber, Acquisitions Editor—Natural history and science, scholarly and popular guide books, reference books; kleber@hawaii.edu

Pamela Kelley, Acquisitions Editor—Southeast Asian studies—all disciplines, and East Asian literature; pkelley@hawaii.edu

Patricia Crosby, Executive Editor—East Asian Studies—all disciplines except literature, Buddhist studies; pcrosby@hawaii.edu

Masako Ikeda, Acquisitions Editor— Hawai`ian and Pacific Studies—all disciplines, Asian American studies—all disciplines, general interest books on Hawai`i and the Pacific; masakoi@hawaii.edu

UNIVERSITY OF ILLINOIS PRESS

1325 South Oak Street, Champaign, IL 61820-6903

217-333-0950 fax: 217-244-8082

www.press.uillinois.edu e-mail: uipress@uillinois.edu

The University of Illinois Press was established in 1918 as a not-for-profit scholarly publisher at the university. It became one of the founding members of the Association of American University Presses in 1937 and now ranks as one of the country's larger and most distinguished university presses. The house publishes works of high quality for scholars, students, and the citizens of the state and beyond. Its local staff of 46 brings out about 120 books each year, as well as 26 journals.

The University of Illinois Press publishes scholarly books and serious nonfiction, with special interests in Abraham Lincoln studies; African American studies; American history; anthropology; Appalachian studies; archaeology; architecture; Asian American studies; communications; folklore; food studies; immigration and ethnic history; Judaic studies; labor history; literature; military history; Mormon history; music; Native American studies; philosophy; poetry; political science; religious studies; sociology; southern history; sport history; translations; transnational cultural studies; western history; women's studies. Note that this press does not publish original fiction, and only considers poetry submissions in February.

The University of Illinois Press has high hopes for the crossover appeal of books like *The Turkey: An American Story*, by Andrew F. Smith. The book mixes the history of the turkey, discussion of its role in American history, and its preparation. Editor-in-chief Joan Catapano said recently that editors at UI Press are primarily looking for works on American authors. She said that there is a strong interest in studies of African American literature, but she also noted that two recent books by the press that have sold quite well fall in the category of scholarship on dead white men, in these cases Zane Grey and Frank Norris. Catapano said that she was looking for books that were "informed with theory," but "not the heavy theory of a decade ago."

Recent titles include *Lonesome Cowgirls and Honky-Tonk Angels: the Women of Barn Dance Radio* by Kristine McCusker; *Voting the Gender Gap* edited by Lois Duke Whitaker; *America on the World Stage: A Global Approach to U.S. History* edited by Gary W. Richard and Ted Dickson; *Raymond Queneau, Letters, Numbers, Forms: Essays, 1928-70* translated by Jordan Stump; *Women for President: Media Bias in Eight Campaigns* by Erika Falk; and *Follow Your Heart: Moving with the Giants of Jazz, Swing, and Rhythm and Blues* by Joe Evans.

The University of Illinois Press distributes its own list, as well as books from other university publishers, including Vanderbilt University Press.

Proposals and SASEs should be directed to the appropriate editor:

Willis G. Regier, Director—Lincoln studies, Nietzsche studies, classics, translations, sports history, Classical music, military history, ancient religion, literature; wregier@uillinois.edu

Joan Catapano, Associate Director and Editor-in-Chief—Women's studies, African American studies, film, dance, anthropology, cultural studies, history, philosophy; jcatapan@uillinois.edu

Laurie Matheson, Senior Acquisitions Editor—American history, Appalachian studies, labor history, music, sociology; lmatheso@uillinois.edu

Kendra Boileau, Senior Acquisitions Editor—Asian American Studies, Communications Studies, Food Studies, History, Religion, Asian Studies; kboileau@uillinois.edu

UNIVERSITY OF IOWA PRESS

119 West Park Road, 100 Kuhl House, Iowa City, IA 52242-1000

319-335-2000 fax: 319-335-2055

www.uiowapress.org e-mail: uipress@uiowa.edu

Established in 1938, the University of Iowa Press operated for many years as an irregular imprint of the university. In 1969, John Simmons was named the first director of the press and the imprint was officially organized under a board of faculty advisors. Since 1985, the press has published 30–35 new titles a year. As always, it seeks good manuscripts from campus authors, but its efforts have expanded significantly, and press authors and customers now come from countries around the world. As Daniel Coit Gilman, founder of the first university press at Johns Hopkins University, said, it is a university's task to "advance knowledge, and to diffuse it not merely among those who can attend the daily lectures—but far and wide." The University of Iowa Press considers this to be its main trust.

As one of the few book publishers in the state of Iowa, the press considers it a mission to publish excellent books on Iowa and the Midwest. But since the press's role is much broader than that of a regional press, the bulk of its list appeals to a wider audience. The University of Iowa Press books receive national attention in a great variety of scholarly journals, newspapers, magazines, and other major book-reviewing media.

Awards won by the University of Iowa Press include a 2006 Outstanding Academic Title by *Choice* magazine for *Walt Whitman and the Earth: A Study in Ecopoetics* by M. Jimmie Killingsworth. The book is part of the Iowa Whitman Series edited by Ed Folsom, Roy J. and Lucille A. Carver.

The University of Iowa Press seeks proposals to add to its list in the following areas: literary studies, including Whitman studies and poetics; letters and diaries; American studies, literary nonfiction and thematic edited anthologies, particularly poetry anthologies; the craft of writing; literature and medicine; theatre studies; archaeology; the natural history of the Upper Midwest; and regional history and culture. Single Author short fiction and poetry are published through series only.

Moreover, the press is actively looking for literary works dealing with the intersection of the humanities and medicine, works of narrative medicine, fiction, poetry, and memoir by health care professionals and patients, and conceptual works that illuminate health and illness from the perspective of the humanities. They have recently published titles on Midwestern archeology and the Andean region.

Recent titles include *Family Bible* by Melissa J. Delbridge; *Lady's-slippers in Your Pocket: A Guide to the Native Lady's-slipper Orchids, Cypripedium, of the United States and Canada* by Paul Martin Brown; *Return to Warden's Grove: Science, Desire, and the Lives of Sparrows* by Christopher Norment; *Truth in Nonfiction: Essays* edited by David Lazar; *Teaching Life: Letters from a Life in Literature* by Dale Salwak; *Mushrooms and other Fungi of the Midcontinental United States* by D.M. Huffman, L.H. Tiffany, G. Knaphaus, and R.A.

Healy; *The Emerald Horizon: The History of Nature in Iowa* by Cornelia F. Mutel; and *Patient Listening: A Doctor's Guide* edited by Loreen Herwaldt.

University of Iowa Press books are distributed by the University of Chicago Distribution Center.

Query letters and SASEs should be directed to:

Holly Carver, Director and Editor; holly-carver@uiowa.edu

Joseph Parsons, Acquiring Editor; joeseph-parsons@uiowa.edu

Charlotte Wright, Managing Editor; charlotte-wright@uiowa.edu

UNIVERSITY OF MASSACHUSETTS PRESS

P.O. Box 429, Amherst, MA 01004

413-545-2217 fax: 413-545-1226

www.umass.edu/umpress e-mail: info@umpress.umass.edu

Founded in 1963, the University of Massachusetts Press is the book publishing arm of the University of Massachusetts. Its mission is to publish first-rate books, edit them carefully, design them well, and market them vigorously. In so doing, it supports and enhances the university's role as a major research institution.

The editors at UMass Press think of book publishing as a collaborative venture— a partnership between author and press staff—and they work hard to see that their authors are happy with every phase of the process.

Since its inception, the press has sold more than 2,000,000 volumes. Today it has over 900 titles in print. Seven employees, along with student assistants and outside sales representatives, produce and distribute some 30–40 new titles annually.

The press imprint is overseen by a faculty committee, whose members represent a broad spectrum of university departments. In addition to publishing works of scholarship, the press produces books of more general interest for a wider readership. With the annual Juniper Prizes, the press also publishes fiction and poetry. For the rules of the contests, please refer to the website or request guidelines via regular mail.

Recent titles include *Political Waters: The Long, Dirty, Contentious, Incredibly Expensive but Eventually Triumphant History of Boston Harbor* by Eric Jay Dolin; *Corner of the Dead* by Lynn Lurie; *Murder and the Death Penalty in Massachusetts* by Alan Rogers; *Heavier Than Air* by Nona Caspers; *Letters of Transit* by Theodore Worozbyt; *Moving Encounters: Sympathy and the Indian Question in Antebellum Literature* by Laura L. Mielke; *Abolitionist Politics and the Coming of the Civil War* by James Brewer Stewart; *From the Civil War to the Apocalypse: Postmodern History and American Fiction* by Timothy Parrish; and *Religious Liberty in America: the First Amendment in Historical and Contemporary Perspective* by Bruce T. Murray.

The University of Massachusetts Press publishes scholarly books and serious nonfiction. Please note that they consider fiction and poetry only through their annual Juniper Prize contests. Also, they do not normally publish *Festschriften*, conference proceedings, or unrevised doctoral dissertations.

Submit proposals with SASEs or e-mail queries to:

Clark Dougan, Acquisitions Editor; cdougan@umpress.umass.edu

UNIVERSITY OF MICHIGAN PRESS

839 Greene Street, Ann Arbor, MI 48104-3209

734-764-4388 fax: 734-615-1540

www.press.umich.edu

University of Michigan Press publishes trade nonfiction and works of scholarly and academic interest. Topic areas and categories include African American studies, anthropology, archaeology, Asian studies, classical studies, literary criticism and theory, economics, education, German studies, history, linguistics, law, literary biography, literature, Michigan and the Great Lakes region, music, physical sciences, philosophy and religion, poetry, political science, psychology, sociology, theater and drama, women's studies, disability studies, and gay and lesbian studies.

University of Michigan Press executes a major program to publish an abundant list of textbooks, monographs, academic literature, undergraduate texts, and a wide variety of books for general readers. Subject areas here encompass disciplines within the behavioral sciences, as well as the humanities. University of Michigan Press publishes in hardcover and paperback editions. Ann Arbor Paperbacks is an imprint geared toward the general trade market.

Recent titles include *Above West Michigan: Aerial Photography of West Michigan* by Marge Beaver; *The Accent of Success: A Practical Guide for International Students in U.S. Colleges* by Eric B. Shiraev and Gerald L. Boyd; *Anarchy Alive! Anti-Authoritarian Politics from Practice to Theory* by Uri Gordon; *Ancient India in Its Wider World* by Grant Parker and Carla Sinopoli; *Israel and the Clash of Civilizations: Iraq, Iran, and the Plan to Remake the Middle East* by Jonathan Cook; *Melville Unfolding, Sexuality, Politics, and Versions of Typee* by John Bryant; and *Pluralizing Pasts: Heritage, Identity, and Place in Multicultural Societies* by Gregory Ashworth, Brian Graham, and John Tunbridge.

The University of Michigan Press handles distribution through a worldwide network of independent sales representatives.

Query letters and SASEs should be directed to:

LeAnn Fields, Senior Executive Editor—Class studies, theater, performance studies; lfields@umich.edu

Mary Erwin, Acquiring Editor—Michigan and Great Lakes; merwin@umich.edu

Christopher J. Hebert, Senior Acquiring Editor—Music, fiction, classics and archaeology, early modern history, German studies; hebertc@umich.edu

Alison MacKeen, Acquiring Editor—New media, literary, cultural studies; amackeen@umich.edu

Kelly Sippell, English as a Second Language Manager and Executive Editor— ESL, applied linguistics; ksippell@umich.edu

Ellen McCarthy, Senior Acquiring Editor—Michigan and Great Lakes titles; emcc@umich.edu

Phil Pochoda, Acquiring Editor—American History; pochoda@umich.edu

Melody Herr, Acquiring Editor—Politics, Law, Economics; mrherr@umich.edu

UNIVERSITY OF MINNESOTA PRESS

111 Third Avenue South, Suite 290, Minneapolis, MN 55401

612-627-1970 fax: 612-627-1980

www.upress.umn.edu e-mail: ump@umn.edu

The University of Minnesota Press (founded in 1925) is a not-for-profit publisher of academic books for scholars and selected general interest titles. Areas of emphasis include American studies, anthropology, art and aesthetics, cultural theory, film and media studies, gay and lesbian studies, geography, literary theory, political and social theory, race and ethnic studies, sociology, and urban studies. The Press is among the most active publishers of translations of significant works of European and Latin American thought and scholarship. The press also maintains a long-standing commitment to publish books that focus on Minnesota and the Upper Midwest, including regional nonfiction, history, and natural science. They do not publish original fiction or poetry.

Douglas Armato, director of the University of Minnesota Press, said recently that he is especially looking for interdisciplinary work including titles on media studies, research on video games, and analysis of graphic novels.

Recent titles include *Open Your Eyes: Deaf Studies Talking* edited by H-Dirksen L. Bauman; *Robot Ghosts and Wired Dreams: Japanese Science Fiction From Origins to Anime* edited by Christopher Bolton, Istvan Csicsery-Ronay Jr., and Takayuki Tatsumi; *Morgan Park: Duluth, U.S. Steel, and the Forging of a Company Town* by Arnold R. Alanen; *French Theory: How Foucault, Derrida, Deleuze and Co. Transformed the Intellectual Life of the United States* by Francois Cusset and translated by Jeff Fort; *Literary Theory: An Introduction* by Terry Eagleton; and *Bios: Biopolitics and Philosophy* by Roberto Esposito, translated by Timothy Campbell.

University of Minnesota Press order fulfillment is handled by the Chicago Distribution Center and in the U.K. and Europe through Plymbridge Distributors, Ltd.

Proposals in areas not listed below should be addressed to the Executive Editor. Query letters, proposals, and SASEs should be directed to:

Richard Morrison, Executive Editor—American studies, art and visual culture, literary and cultural studies

Todd Orjala, Senior Editor for Regional Studies and Contemporary Affairs—Regional history and culture, regional natural history

Pieter Martin, Editor—Architecture, legal studies, politics and international studies, Scandinavian studies, urban studies

Jason Weidemann, Editor—Anthropology, Asian culture, cinema and media studies, geography, native studies, sociology

Douglas Armato, Director—Digital culture, philosophy, social theory

Beverly Kaemmer, Associate director/test division manager—MMPI, psychology

UNIVERSITY OF MISSOURI PRESS

2910 LeMone Boulevard, Columbia, MO 65201

573-882-7641   fax: 573-884-4498

www.umsystem.edu/upress   e-mail: upress@umsystem.edu

The University of Missouri Press was founded in 1958 by William Peden, writer and dedicated member of Missouri's English Department faculty. The press has now grown to publish more than 70 titles per year in the areas of American and world history, including intellectual history and biography; African American studies; women's studies; American, British, and Latin American literary criticism; journalism; political science, particularly philosophy and ethics; regional studies of the American heartland; short fiction; and creative nonfiction.

Premier scholars and writers published by the University of Missouri Press include Rowland Berthoff, Cleanth Brooks, Bruce Clayton, Noble Cunningham, Henry Steele Commager, Eugene Davidson, Drew Gilpin Faust, Eugene D. Genovese, George Garrett, Mary Lago, Naomi Lebowitz, John Lukacs, Andrew Lytle, George F. Kennan, Louis Martz, and Heather Ross Miller. But the press is also home to numerous previously unpublished young scholars who will be contributing to the scholarly debates and discoveries of the future. In addition, they look for titles with crossover appeal for general readers like 2006's *The St. Louis Baseball Reader* by Richard Peterson, which was heavily promoted by the press.

Other recent titles include *Recognizing and Surviving Heart Attacks and Strokes: Lifesaving Advice You need Now* by Glenn O. Turner; *Of Spies and Spokesmen: My Life as a Cold War Correspondent* by Nicholas Daniloff; *The Eighteen-Year-Old Replacement: Facing Combat in Patton's Third Army* by R. Richard Kingsbury; *A Red Boyhood: Growing Up*

Under Stalin by Anatole Konstantin; *A President, a Church, and Trails West: Competing Histories in Independence, Missouri* by John E. Taylor; *A Journalism of Humanity: A Candid History of the World's First Journalism School* by Steve Weinberg; *The Philosopher and the Storyteller: Eric Voegelin and Twentieth-Century Literature* by Charles R. Embry.

The University of Missouri Press handles its own distributional services.

The University of Missouri Press's chief areas of publishing emphasis are American history, political philosophy, journalism, and literary criticism with a primary focus on American and British literature. However, they are glad to receive inquiries from almost any area of work in the humanities. They do publish creative nonfiction and an occasional short-story collection, but no poetry or original novels.

Query letters and SASEs should be directed to:

Beverly Jarrett, Director and Editor-in-Chief

Clair Willcox, Acquisitions Editor

Gary Kass, Acquisitions Editor

UNIVERSITY OF NEBRASKA PRESS

1111 Lincoln Mall, Lincoln, NE 68588- 0630

402-472-3581   fax: 402-472-3584

www.nebraskapress.unl.edu   e-mail: pressmail@unl.edu

As a publisher of scholarly and popular books for more than 60 years, the University of Nebraska Press is a distinctive member of the University of Nebraska-Lincoln community. Through the work of its staff and resulting publications, the press fulfills the three primary missions of its host university: research, teaching, and service. Reporting to the vice chancellor for research and in cooperation with a faculty advisory board, the press actively encourages, develops, publishes, and disseminates first-rate, creative literary work, memoirs, and the results of national and international scholarly research in several fields. The press facilitates teaching through its publications and develops projects particularly suited for undergraduate and graduate university classrooms. The press serves the university community directly by publishing the work of many UNL faculty authors, maintaining long-term publishing associations with prominent university organizations, sponsoring campuswide events, hosting publishing workshops, and enhancing the international visibility of the university through its publicity efforts and reviews of its books. The press's sustained commitment to publications on the peoples, culture, and heritage of Nebraska reflect decades of service to its home state.

Bison Books is the quality trade paperback imprint of the University of Nebraska Press. Launched in 1960, priced inexpensively, and sold in drugstores and highway tourist gift shops as well as bookstores, the Bison Books line appeared as an affordable means of publishing "original works and reissues of books of permanent value in all fields of knowledge." The idea of the Bison Books imprint was a particularly bold and far-sighted move for a smallish university press in 1960—publishing scholarship in paperback, rather than the more "dignified" cloth, was a rather radical notion, as was selling books in drugstores and gift shops. Today Bison Books publishes in a wide variety of subject areas, including Western Americana; Native American history and culture; military history; sports; Bison Frontiers of Imagination, a science fiction line; classic Nebraska authors, including Willa Cather, Mari Sandoz, John G. Neihardt, Wright Morris, Weldon Kees, and Loren Eiseley; and philosophy and religion.

Recent University of Nebraska Press titles include *A Sacred Feast: Reflections on Sacred Harp Singing and Dinner on the Ground* by Kathryn Eastburn; *Hard Air: Adventures from the Edge of Flying* by W. Scott Olsen; *To a Distant Day: The Rocket Pioneers* by Chris Gainor; *Ed Barrow: The Bulldog Who Built the Yankee's First Dynasty* by Daniel R. Levitt; *Chief Bender's Burden: The Silent Struggle of a Baseball Star* by Tom Swift; *Venezuelan Bust, Baseball Boom: Andres Reiner and Scouting on the New Frontier* by Milton H. Jamail; *What Becomes You* by Aaron Raz Link and Hilda Raz; and *Pieces From Life's Crazy Quilt* by Marvin V. Arnett.

Queries and SASEs should be directed to:

Ladette Randolf, Associate Director—Humanities

Rob Taylor, Acquiring Editor—Sports

Heather Lundine, Editor-in-Chief—History

Matt Bokovoy, Acquiring Editor—Native Studies

UNIVERSITY OF NEW MEXICO PRESS

1312 Basehart SE, Albuquerque, NM 87106-4363

800-249-7737   fax: 505-272-7778

www.unmpress.com   e-mail: **unmpress@unm.edu**

University of New Mexico Press (UNM Press) is a publisher of general, scholarly, and regional trade books in hardcover and paperback editions. Among areas of strong New Mexico interest are anthropology, archaeology, cultures of the American West, folkways, Latin American studies, literature, art and architecture, photography, crafts, biography, women's studies, travel, and the outdoors. UNM Press offers a robust list of books in subject areas pertinent to the American Southwest, including native Anasazi, Navajo, Hopi, Zuni, and Apache cultures; Nuevomexicano (New Mexican) culture; the pre-Columbian Americas; and Latin American affairs. UNM Press also publishes works of regional fiction and belles lettres, both contemporary and classical.

The press is home to the literary journal *Blue Mesa Review*. The Pasó por Aquí series makes available texts from the Nuevomexicano literary heritage (many editions in bilingual format). Diálogos is a series in Latin American studies, specializing in books with crossover potential in both academic and general markets.

Recent titles include *Spring's Edge: A Ranch Wife's Chronicles* by Laurie Wagner *Buyer*; *Mountain Time: A Yellowstone Memoir* by Paul Schullery; *Hiking Alone: Trails Out, Trails Home* by Mary Beath; *The Migrant Project: Contemporary California Farm Workers* by Rick Nahmias; *G-Dog and the Homeboys: Father: Greg Boyle and the Gangs of East Los Angeles* by Celeste Fremon; *The Black Panther Party: Service to the People Programs* edited by David Hilliard; *Ghosts of El Grullo* by Patricia Santana; and *Taste of Tombstone: A Hearty Helping of History* by Sherry Monahan.

University of New Mexico Press handles distribution for its own list and also works through regional sales representatives.

Query letters and SASEs should be directed to:

W. Clark Whitehorn

University of New Mexico Press

MSC04 2820, 1 University of New Mexico, Albuquerque, NM 87131-0001

Letters regarding anthropology, archaeology, and religious studies should be sent to:

Lisa Pacheco

University of New Mexico Press

MSC04 2820, 1 University of New Mexico, Albuquerque, NM 87131-0001

UNIVERSITY OF NORTH CAROLINA PRESS

116 South Boundary Street, Chapel Hill, NC 27514-3808

919-966-3561 / 800-848-6224   fax: 919-966-3829

www.uncpress.unc.edu   e-mail: uncpress@unc.edu

For more than 80 years, the University of North Carolina Press (UNC Press) has earned national and international recognition for quality books and the thoughtful way they are published. A fundamental commitment to publishing excellence defines UNC Press, made possible by the generous support of individual and institutional donors who created its endowment.

Reflecting the mission of its parent institution, the 16-campus UNC system, the press exists both to advance scholarship by supporting teaching and research and to serve the people of the state and beyond. Since 1922, the first university press in the South and one of the first in the nation, UNC Press has published outstanding work in pursuit of its dual aims.

UNC Press books explore important questions, spark lively debates, generate ideas, and move fields of inquiry forward. They illuminate the life of the mind. With more than 4,000 titles published and almost 1,500 titles still in print, UNC Press produces books that endure.

Over the years, UNC Press books have amassed hundreds of prestigious awards, including the National Book Award, the Pulitzer Prize in History, and the top prizes given by leading scholarly societies and respected organizations sch as the American Bar Association, the American Institute of Architects, and the Royal Society of Canada.

When the press was founded in 1922, university presses published work strictly for scholars and by scholars, primarily those from the home faculty. Today, press authors come from all across the nation and around the world. UNC Press's readers come from inside and outside academia, as the press reaches a crossover audience of general readers with titles like *Pets in America: A History* by Kathleen C. Grier and *Gardening With Heirloom Seeds* by Lynn Coulter.

Other recent titles include *Counter-revolution of the Word: The Conservative Attack on Modern Poetry, 1945-1960* by Alan Filreis; *Havana and the Atlantic in the Sixteenth Century* by Alejandro de la Fuente; *The Warrior Image: Soldiers in American Culture from the Second World War to the Vietnam Era* by Andre J. Huebner; *Victims and Villains in Vasari's Lives* by Andre Ladis; *The Book of Salsa: A Chronicle of Urban Music from the Caribbean to New York City*; *Burying the Dead but Not the Past: Ladies' Memorial Associations and the Lost Cause* by Caroline E. Janney; *Men of Letters in the Early Republic: Cultivating Forums of Citizenship* by Catherine O'Donnell Kaplan; and *African Cherokees in Indian Territory: From Chattel to Citizens* by Celia E. Naylor.

University of North Carolina Press handles its own distribution with the assistance of regional sales representatives.

Query letters and SASEs should be directed to:

David Perry, Assistant Director and Editor-in-Chief—History, regional trade, Civil War; david_perry@unc.edu

Charles Grench, Assistant Director and Senior Editor—History, classics, economics and business history, law and legal studies, political science, African American history, Cold War; charles_grench@unc.edu

Elaine Maisner, Senior Editor—Religious studies, Latin American, regional trade, folklore; elaine_maisner@unc.edu

Mark Simpson-Vos, Editor for Special Projects—Native American studies, electronic publishing; mark_simpson-vas@unc.edu

Sian Hunter, Senior Editor—African American studies, American studies, gender studies, literary studies, media studies, cultural studies, social medicine, Appalachian studies; sian_hunter@unc.edu

Mark Simpson-Vos, Editor—Native American studies, ethnohistory, regional trade, and special projects

UNIVERSITY OF OKLAHOMA PRESS

1005 Asp Avenue, Norman, OK 73019-6051

405-325- 2000

www.oupress.com e-mail: acquisitions@ou.edu

During its more than 75 years of continuous operation, the University of Oklahoma Press (OU Press) has gained international recognition as an outstanding publisher of scholarly literature. It was the first university press established in the Southwest, and the fourth in the western half of the country.

The press began as the idea of William Bennett Bizzell, fifth president of the University of Oklahoma and a wide-ranging humanist and book collector. Over the years, the press has grown from a staff of one—the first director, Joseph A. Brandt—to an active and capable team of some 40 members.

Building on the foundation laid by their four previous directors, OU Press continues its dedication to the publication of outstanding scholarly works. Under the guidance of the present director, John Drayton, the major goal of the press is to strengthen its position as a preeminent publisher of books about the American West and American Indians, while expanding its program in other scholarly disciplines, including classical studies, military history, political science, and natural science.

Recent titles include *A Texas Journey: The Centennial Photographs of Polly Smith* by Evelyn Barker; *Cultural Contact and Linguistic Relativity among the Indians of Northwestern California* by Sean O'Neill; *Does People Do It? A Memoir* by Fred Harris; *Napoleon's Enfant Terrible: General Dominique Vandamme* by John G. Gallaher; *Borrowed Soldiers: Americans Under British Command, 1918* by John S. D. Eisenhower and Mitchell A. Yockelson; and William Clark: *Indian Diplomat* by Jay H. Buckley

Query letters with SASEs should be directed to:

Charles E. Rankin, Associate Director, Editor-in-Chief—American West, military history; cerankin@ou.edu

Matt Bokovoy, Editor—Western history (20th century and urban), Chicana/o literature, natural history, political science; mbokovoy@ou.edu

Allessandra Jacobi, Editor—American Indian, Mesoamerican, and Latin American studies; jacobi@ou.edu

Kirk Bjornsgaard, Editor—Regional studies; kirkb@ou.edu

John Drayton, Senior Associate Director and Publisher—Classical studies; jdrayton@ou.edu

UNIVERSITY PRESSES

UNIVERSITY OF SOUTH CAROLINA PRESS

1600 Hampton Street, 5th Floor, Columbia, SC 29208

803-777-5243 / 800-768-2500 fax: 800-868-0740

www.sc.edu/uscpress

The University of South Carolina Press shares the central mission of its university: to advance knowledge and enrich the state's cultural heritage. Established in 1944, it is one of the oldest publishing houses in the South and among the largest in the Southeast. With more than 1,500 published books to its credit, 800 in print, and 50 new books published each year, the press is important in enhancing the scholarly reputation and worldwide visibility of the University of South Carolina.

The University of South Carolina Press publishes works of original scholarship in the fields of history (American, African American, Southern, Civil War, culinary, maritime, and women's), regional studies, literature, religious studies, rhetoric, and social work.

Recent titles include *The Seven Deadly Virtues and Other Lively Essays: Coming of Age as a Writer, Teacher, Risk Taker* by Lynn Z. Bloom; *Women of Conscience: Social Reform in Danville Illinois, 1890-1930* by Janet D. Cornelius and Martha LaFrenz Kay; *Fighting for Honor: The History of African Martial Arts Traditions in the Atlantic World* by T.J. Desch Obi; *Guardian of Savannah: Fort McAllister, Georgia; in the Civil War and Beyond* by Roger S. Durham; *Understanding Tony Kushner* by James Fisher; and *Jazz and Blues Musicians of South Carolina: Interviews with Jabbo, Dizzy, Drink, and Others* by Benjamin V. Franklin.

University of South Carolina Press oversees its own distribution.

Queries with SASEs should be directed to:

Linda Haines Fogle, Assistant Director for Operations—Trade titles, literature, religious studies, rhetoric, social work, general inquiries; lfogle@gwm.sc.ude

Alexander Moore, Acquisitions Editor—History, regional studies; alexm@gwm.sc.edu

UNIVERSITY OF TENNESSEE PRESS

110 Conference Center, 600 Henley Street, Knoxville, TN 37996-4108

865-974-3321   fax: 865-974-3724

www.utpress.org

The University of Tennessee Press is dedicated to playing a significant role in the intellectual life of the University of Tennessee system, the academic community in general, and the citizens of the state of Tennessee by publishing high-quality works of original scholarship in selected fields as well as highly accurate and informative regional studies and literary fiction. By utilizing current technology to provide the best possible vehicles for the publication of scholarly and regional works, the press preserves and disseminates information for scholars, students, and general readers.

The University of Tennessee Press was established as a scholarly publisher in 1940 by the university trustees. Its mandate was threefold: to stimulate scholarly research in many fields; to channel such studies to a large readership; and to extend the university's regional leadership by publishing worthy projects about the South, including those by non-university authors.

The press has earned a national reputation for excellence with its lists in African American studies, Southern history, Appalachian studies, material culture, and literary studies, as well as many regional books written for general readers. Over the years, its important publications have included Richard Beale Davis's *Intellectual Life in the Colonial South*, which won the 1978 National Book Award in history; Charles Hudson's *The Southeastern Indians* (1976), still the standard work on the subject; Jo Ann Gibson Robinson's *The Montgomery Bus Boycott and the Women Who Started It* (1978); Durwood Dunn's *Cades Cove: The Life and Death of a Southern Appalachian Community* (1988); and James Lee McDonough's *Shiloh—In Hell Before Night* (1977).

Recent titles include *To Lift Up My Race: The Essential Writing of Samuel Robert Cassius* edited by Edward J. Robinson; *Rugby, Tennessee: Some Account of the Settlement Founded on the Cumberland Plateau* by Thomas Hughes; *Flannery O'Connor: A Life* by Jean W. Cash; *Inventing Black Women: African American Women Poets and Self-Representation, 1877-2000* by Ajuan Maria Mance; and *On Harper Lee: Essays and Reflections* edited by Alice Hall Perty.

Books from the University of Tennessee Press are distributed by the Chicago Distribution Center.

Query letters and SASEs should be directed to:

Scot Danforth, Acquisitions Editor

UNIVERSITY OF TEXAS PRESS

P.O. Box 7819, Austin, TX 78713-7819

512-471-7233 fax: 512-232-7178

www.utexas.edu/utpress e-mail: utpress@uts.cc.utexas.edu

By launching a scholarly press in 1950, the University of Texas made several important statements: books matter; books educate; and publishing good books is a public responsibility and a valuable component of the state's system of higher education.

As part of its mission to serve the people of Texas, the press also produces books of general interest for a wider audience, covering, in particular, the history, culture, arts, and natural history of the state. To these, the press has recently added accounts of the contributions of African and Native Americans, Latinos, and women. Major areas of concentration are anthropology, Old and New World archaeology, architecture, art history, botany, classics and the Ancient World, conservation and the environment, Egyptology, film and media studies, geography, sandscape, Latin American and Latino studies, literary modernism, Mexican American studies, marine science, Middle Eastern studies, ornithology, pre-Columbian studies, Texas and Western studies, and women's studies.

The University of Texas Press has published more than 2,000 books over five decades. Currently a staff of 50, under the direction of Joanna Hitchcock, brings out some 90 books and 11 journals annually.

Recent titles include *Why the Humanities Matter: A Commonsense Approach* by Frederick Luis Aldama; *Drugs, Thugs, and Divas: Telenovelas and Narco-Dramas in Latin America* by O. Hugo Benavides; *The Journey Home* by Dermont Bolger; *Diva: Defiance and Passion in Early Italian Cinema* by Angela Dalle Vacche; *The Year She Disappeared* by Ann Harleman; *One Ranger Returns* by H. Joaquin Jackson; and *Creating Outdoor Classroom: Schoolyard Habitats and Gardens for the Southwest* by Lauri Johnson

University of Texas Press handles its own distribution.

Query letters and SASEs should be directed to:

Jim Burr, Sponsoring Editor—Classics and ancient world, film and media studies, Middle East Studies, Jewish studies, Old World archaeology, architecture, applied languages

William Bishel, Sponsoring Editor—Texana, ornithology, botany, natural history, environmental studies

Theresa May, Editor-in-Chief—Latin American studies, Latino/a studies, Native American studies, anthropology, New World archaeology, photography

Allison Faust, Sponsoring Editor—Music, geography, art, Texas art, culture; Alison@utpress.ppb.utexas.edu

Casey Kittrell, Assistant Editor—Fiction; casey@utpress.ppb.utexas.edu

UNIVERSITY OF VIRGINIA PRESS

Box 400318, Charlottesville, VA 22904

Phone: 434-924-3468

www.upress.virginia.edu   e-mail: upressva@virginia.edu

The University of Virginia Press (UVaP) was founded in 1963 to advance the intellectual interests not only of the University of Virginia, but of institutions of higher learning throughout the state. UVaP currently publishes 50–60 new titles annually.

The UVaP editorial program focuses primarily on the humanities and social sciences with special concentrations in American history, African American studies, Southern studies, literature, ecocriticism, and regional books. While it continuously pursues new titles, UVaP also maintains a backlist of over 1,000 titles in print.

Active series include the Papers of George Washington; the Papers of James Madison; the Victorian Literature and Culture Series; CARAF Books (translations of Francophone literature); New World Studies; the Carter G. Woodson Institute Series in Black Studies; Under the Sign of Nature: Explorations in Ecocriticism; The American South Series; A Nation Divided: New Studies in the Civil War; Constitutionalism and Democracy; Race, Ethnicity, and Politics; Reconsiderations in Southern African History; Studies in Early Modern German History; Studies in Religion and Culture; Southern Texts Society; and the Virginia Bookshelf series of regional reprints.

UVaP's list has always been strong in early American history, reflected in books it released last fall about such figures as Jefferson and Washington (see below). 2007 marks the 400th anniversary of the Jamestown settlement and UVaP also just released *Jamestown: The Buried Truth*, by William M. Kelso, the head archaeologist of the Jamestown Rediscovery Project.

Other recent titles include *Darwin's Fox and My Coyote* by Holly Menino; *Legacy: Walter Chrysler Jr. and the Untold Story of Norfolk's Chrysler Museum of Art* by Peggy Earle; *Opportunity Time: A Memoir* by Governor Linwood Holton; *Sacred Order/Social Order, Vol. 3: The Jew of Culture: Freud, Moses and Modernity* by Phillip Rieff; *All That Mighty Heart: London Poems* edited by Lisa Russ Spaar; and *Buildings of Delaware* by W. Barksdale Maynard.

The Electronic Imprint of the UVaP publishes digital scholarship in the humanities and social sciences issued under the ROTUNDA imprint. (rotunda.upress.virginia.edu). Rotunda was created for the publication of original digital scholarship along with newly digitized critical and documentary editions in the humanities and social sciences. For further information, contact Rotunda via e-mail at rotunda-upress@virginia.edu.

Submit UVaP queries and SASEs to:

Cathie Brettschneider, Humanities Editor; cib8b@virginia.edu

Richard K. Holway, History and Social Sciences Editor; rkh2a@virginia,.edu

Boyd Zenner, Architecture and Environmental Editor; bz2v@virginia.edu

UNIVERSITY OF WASHINGTON PRESS

P.O. Box 50096, Seattle, WA 98145-5096

206-543-4050 fax: 206-543-3932

www.washington.edu/uwpress e-mail: uwpress@u.washington.edu

The University of Washington Press (UW Press) publishes titles that cover a wide variety of academic fields, with especially distinguished lists in Asian studies, Middle Eastern studies, environmental history, biography, anthropology, Western history, natural history, marine studies, architectural history, and art. The Press has published approximately 3,800 books, of which about 1,400 are still in print. UW Press publishes about sixty new titles a year.

The press is recognized as the world's foremost publisher on the art and culture of the Northwest Coast Indians and Alaskan Eskimos, and as the leader in the publication of materials dealing with the Asian American experience. Such series as A History of East Central Europe, Studies in Modernity and National Identity, American Ethnic and Cultural Studies, Asian Law Series, Korean Studies of the Henry M. Jackson School of International Studies, Studies on Ethnic Groups in China, Literary Conjugations, In Vivo, and the Pacific Northwest Poetry Series, have brought distinction to the press and the university.

As a nonprofit cultural organization, the house has the sole function of finding, developing, selecting, and publishing scholarship of high quality and enduring value. UW Press has published books by several Nobel laureates, as well as many other internationally known figures in the humanities, arts, and sciences.

The imprint of the University of Washington Press is under the control of a faculty committee appointed by the university's president. The approval of the University Press Committee is required before any book may be published. The press's editors work closely with the faculty committee to select those books that will carry the University of Washington imprint. About one-third of the books published by the press originate within the University of Washington. Of the manuscripts and proposals that are submitted annually from all over the world, less than 5% are accepted for publication.

Recent titles include *Bits of Life: Feminism at the Intersections of Media, Bioscience, and Technology* edited by Anneke Smelik and Nina Lykke; *Black Womanhood: Images, Icons and Ideologies of the African Body* edited by Barbara Thompson; *The Country in the City: The Greening of the San Francisco Bay Area* by Richard A. Walker; *How Many Machine Guns Does It Take to Cook One Meal? The Seattle and San Francisco General Strikes* by Victoria Johnson; *The Interweaving of Rituals: Funerals in the Cultural Exchange between China and Europe;* and *The Lost Wolves of Japan* by Brett L. Walker.

UW Press handles its own distribution via its home office and a number of regional sales representatives, and also distributes for a number of other specialist publishers and arts institutions, including the Tate Gallery, Asian Art Museum of San

Francisco, Reaktion Books, Columbus Museum of Art, National Portrait Gallery of the Smithsonian Institution, Exhibitions International, and Idaho State Historical Society.

Query letters and SASEs should be directed to:

Lorri Hagman, Executive Editor—Asian studies, cultural and environmental anthropology; lhagman@u.washingon.edu

Marianne Keddington-Lang, Acquisitions Editor—Western history, environmental studies, Native American studies; mkedlang@u.washington.edu

UNIVERSITY OF WISCONSIN PRESS

1930 Monroe Street, 3rd Floor, Madison, WI 53711-2059

608-263-1110   fax: 608-263-1120

www.wisc.edu/wisconsinpress   e-mail: uwiscpress@uwpress.wisc.edu

Located in Madison, Wisconsin, the University of Wisconsin Press was founded in 1936, and publishes both books and journals. Since its first book appeared in 1937, the press has published and distributed more than 3,000 titles. They have more than 1,400 titles currently in print, including books of general interest (biography, fiction, natural history, poetry, photography, fishing, food, travel, etc.), scholarly books (American studies, anthropology, art, classics, environmental studies, ethnic studies, film, gay and lesbian studies, history, Jewish studies, literary criticism, Slavic studies, etc.), and regional books about Wisconsin and the Upper Midwest. They publish and distribute new books each year in these fields.

Among their book series are the Brittingham Prize in Poetry, the Felix Pollak Prize in Poetry, Wisconsin Studies in Autobiography, Wisconsin Studies in Classics, Living Out: Gay and Lesbian Autobiography, Studies in Dance History, George L. Mosse Series in Modern European Cultural and Intellectual History, The History of American Thought and Culture, and Publications of the Wisconsin Center for Pushkin Studies.

The press is a division of the Graduate School of the University of Wisconsin–Madison. Residing within the university's graduate school, UW Press draws on and supports the intellectual activities of the graduate school and its faculty and enhances the university's overall missions of research and instruction. Although they publish many books and journals produced by faculty from the University of Wisconsin campuses, they also publish books and journals from scholars around the U.S. and the world. The house has authors residing in many different countries, from Australia to Zimbabwe. They have co-published English-language books with publishers in England, Ireland, Turkey, Italy, and Japan. The University of Wisconsin Press books have been translated into dozens of foreign languages.

The press also distributes and/or publishes books for other institutions, including Chazen Museum of Art, Center for Upper Midwest Culture, Dryad Press, Ginkgo Press, International Brecht Society, Max Kade Institute for German American Studies, Milwaukee Art Museum, Popular Press, Society of Dance History Scholars, University of Wisconsin–Madison, University of Wisconsin–Milwaukee, Wisconsin Arts Board, and Wisconsin Historical Society.

Recent titles include *Human Goodness* by Yi-Fu Tuan; *Field Guide to Wisconsin Sedges: an Introduction to the Genus Carex (Cyperaceae)* by Andrew L. Hipp; *I Thought We Were Making Movies, Not History* by Walter Mirisch; *With Honor: Melvin Laird in War, Peace, and Politics* by Dale Van Atta; *I Hear Voices: A Memoir of Love, Death, and the Radio* by Jean Feraca; *Meditations on Rising and Falling* by Philip Pardi; and *The Royal Baker's Daughter* by Barbara Goldberg.

Distribution for University of Wisconsin Press publications is through the Chicago Distribution Center; trade sales are garnered nationwide by the press's formidable lineup of regional field representatives.

Query letters and SASEs should be directed to:

Raphael Kadushin, Senior Acquisitions Editor—autobiography/memoir, biography, classical studies, dance, performance, film, food, gender studies, GLBT studies, Jewish studies, Latino/a memoirs, travel; kadushin@wisc.edu

Gwen Walker, Ph.D., Acquisitions Editor—African studies, anthropology, environmental studies, Irish studies, Latin American studies, Slavic studies, Southeast Asian studies, U.S. history; gcwalker@wisc.edu

---

UNIVERSITY PRESS OF COLORADO

5589 Arapahoe Avenue, Suite 206C, Boulder, CO 80303

720-406-8849   fax: 720-406-3443

www.upcolorado.com

Founded in 1965, the University Press of Colorado is a nonprofit cooperative publishing enterprise supported, in part, by Adams State College, Colorado State University, Fort Lewis College, Mesa State College, Metropolitan State College of Denver, University of Colorado, University of Northern Colorado, and Western State College of Colorado. The press publishes 30–35 new titles each year, with the goal of facilitating communication among scholars and providing the peoples of the state and region with a fair assessment of their histories, cultures, and resources. The press has extended the reach and reputation of supporting institutions and has made scholarship of the highest level in many diverse fields widely available.

Recent titles include *Antonio Buero-Vellejo: Four Tragedies of Conscience* by Antonio Buero-Vallejo and Patricia O'Connor; *Rabinal Achi: A fifteenth-Century Maya Dynastic*

Drama by Alain Breton and Teresa L. Fagan; *Embracing Watershed Politics* by William Blomquist and Edella Schlager; *Mockeries and Metamorphoses of an Aztec God* by Besson, translated by Michel Olivier; and *The Arapaho Language* by Andrew Cowell and Alonzo Moss Sr.

The University Press of Colorado is currently accepting manuscript proposals in anthropology, archaeology, environmental studies, history, law, Native American studies, and the natural sciences as well as projects about the state of Colorado and the Rocky Mountain region. They are also accepting submissions for the following series: Atomic History & Culture, Mesoamerican Worlds, Mining the American West, Timberline Books, and The Women's West (nonfiction only). The University Press of Colorado is not currently accepting proposals in fiction or poetry.

Scholars proposing manuscripts for publication should submit a prospectus to the acquisitions department before submitting a complete manuscript. Submissions are accepted via mail and e-mail. No phone calls. Address manuscript submission inquiries to:

Darrin Pratt, Director and Acquiring Editor; darrin@upcolorado.com

UNIVERSITY PRESS OF FLORIDA

15 NW 15th Street, Gainesville, FL 32611

352-392-1351 / 800-226-3822 fax: (352) 392-7302

www.upf.com

The University Press of Florida, the scholarly publishing arm of the State University System, representing all ten universities, is charged by the Board of Regents with publishing books of intellectual distinction and significance, books that will contribute to improving the quality of higher education in the state, and books of general and regional interest and usefulness to the people of Florida, reflecting its rich historical, cultural, and intellectual heritage and resources. The press may publish original works by State University System faculty members, meritorious works originating elsewhere, important out-of-print books, and other projects related to its backlist that will contribute to a coherent and effective publishing program—one that will supplement and extend programs of instruction and research offered by the universities.

UPF has published over 2,500 volumes since its inception and currently releases nearly 100 new titles each year.

Subjects include African studies, anthropology and archaeology, art, dance, music, law, literature, Middle East studies, natural history, Russian studies, history, Florida, Latin America studies, political science, science and technology, and sociology.

Recent titles include *Pilgrims in the Land of Alligators* by Jeff Kilnkenberg; *Silver Springs* by Gary Monroe; *Remembering Nureyev* by Rudi van Dantzig; *The Fosse Style* by

Debra McWaters; *Swimming Up the Tigris: Real Life Encounters with Iraq* by Barbara Nimri Aziz; and *The Rise and Fall of Dodgertown: 60 Years of Baseball in Vero Beach* by Rody Johnson.

To submit a manuscript, send a one-page letter of inquiry to Editor-in-Chief John Byram, to determine the University Press of Florida's interest in your project. Please include your full postal address.

John Byram, Associate Director and Editor-in-Chief

Amy Gorelick, Senior Acquisitions Editor

Derek Krissoff, Senior Acquisitions Editor

UNIVERSITY PRESS OF KANSAS

2502 Westbrooke Circle, Lawrence, KS 66045-4444

785-864-4154   fax 785-864-4586

www.kansaspress.ku.edu   e-mail upress@ku.edu

The University Press of Kansas publishes scholarly books that advance knowledge and regional books that contribute to the understanding of Kansas, the Great Plains, and the Midwest. Founded in 1946, it represents the six state universities: Emporia State University, Fort Hays State University, Kansas State University, Pittsburg State University, the University of Kansas, and Wichita State University.

University Press of Kansas, known for its studies of presidents and politics, regularly produces crossover books that appeal to a general audience of readers, like 2006's *Hillary Rodham Clinton: Polarizing First Lady* by Gil Troy, a professor of history at McGill University.

Profiled by *The Chronicle of Higher Education* (3 July 1998) as "a distinctive model of success in turbulent times," the press focuses generally on history, political science, and philosophy. More specifically, it concentrates on presidential studies, military studies, American history (especially political, cultural, intellectual, and western), U.S. government and public policy, legal studies, and social and political philosophy.

Other recent titles include *The Liberals' Moment: The McGovern Insurgency and the Identity Crisis of the Democratic Party* by Bruce Miroff; *American Angels: Useful Spirits in the Material World* by Peter Gardella; *Counterculture Green: The Whole Earth Catalog and American Environmentalism* by Andrew G. Kirk; *The Supreme Court: An Essential History* by Peter C. Hoffer, William H. Hoffer, and N. E. H. Hull; *Hip-Hop Revolution: The Culture and Politics of Rap* by Jeffrey O.G. Ogbar; and *Death of the Wehrmacht: The German Campaigns of 1942* by Robert M. Citino.

Direct queries, proposals, and SASEs to:

Fred M. Woodward, Director—American government and public policy, presidential studies, American political thought, urban politics, Kansas and regional studies; fwoodward@ku.edu

Michael Briggs, Editor-in-Chief—Military history and intelligence studies, law and legal history, political science; mbrigss@ku.edu

Kalyani Fernando, Acquisitions Editor—Western history and Native American studies, environmental studies, American studies, women's studies; kfernando@ku.edu

UNIVERSITY PRESS OF MISSISSIPPI

3825 Ridgewood Road, Jackson, MS 39211-6492

601-432-6205 / 800-737-7788 fax: 601-432-6217

www.upress.state.ms.us e-mail: press@ihl.state.ms.us

The University Press of Mississippi was founded in 1970 and is supported by Mississippi's eight state universities. UPM publishes scholarly books and books that interpret the South and its culture to the nation and the world. From its offices in Jackson, the University Press of Mississippi acquires, edits, distributes, and promotes more than 60 new books every year. Over the years, the press has published more than 900 titles and distributed more than 2,500,000 copies worldwide, each with the Mississippi imprint. Out of the approximately 600 submissions they receive, the UPM publishes an average of 60 manuscripts a year.

The University Press of Mississippi is a nonprofit publisher that serves an academic and general audience. The editorial program focuses on the following areas: scholarly and trade titles in African American studies; American studies, literature, history, and culture; art and architecture; biography and memoir; ethnic studies; film studies; folklore and folk art; health; memoir and biography; military history; music; natural sciences; performance; photography; popular culture; reference; Southern studies; sports; women's studies; other liberal arts. Special series include American Made Music; Chancellor Porter L. Fortune Symposium in Southern History, Conversations with Comic Artists, Conversations with Filmmakers, Faulkner and Yoknapatawpha, Hollywood Legends, Literary Conversations, Margaret Walker Alexander Series in African American Studies, Southern Icons, Studies in Popular Culture, Understanding Health and Sickness, Willie Morris Books in Memoir and Biography, and Writers and Their Works.

In 1996, University Press of Mississippi published *The Light in the Piazza and Other Italian Tales* by Elizabeth Spencer, which provided the inspiration for the 2006 Tony Award-winning musical The Light in the Piazza.

Recent titles include *What Moves at the Margin: Selected Nonfiction* by Toni Morrison, edited by Carolyn C. Denard; *Southern Shade: A Plant Selection Guide* by Jo Kellum; *The Guitar in America: Victorian Era to Jazz Age* by Jeffrey J. Noonan; *Working with Walt:*

Interviews with Disney Artists; Confronting Modernity: Art and Society in Louisiana by Richard Megraw; and *Garry Trudeau: Doonesbury and the Aesthetics of Satire* by Kerry D. Soper.

Submit proposal, CV, and SASE to the appropriate editor:

Seetha Srinivasan, Director—African American studies, American studies, ethnic studies, health, fiction, popular culture, women's studies; ssrinivasan@ihl.state.ms.us

Craig Gill, Assistant Director and Editor-in-Chief—Art, architecture, folklore and folk art, history, music, natural sciences, photography, Southern studies; cgill@ihl.state.ms.us

Anne Stascavage, Managing Editor—Performance studies; astascavage@ihl.state.ms.us

Walter Biggins, Editor—wbiggins@ihl.state.ms.us

UNIVERSITY PRESS OF NEW ENGLAND (TUFTS, NORTHEASTERN, DARTMOUTH, BRANDEIS, VERMONT, NEW HAMPSHIRE)

1 Court Street, Suite 250, Lebanon, NH 03766

603-448-1533   fax: 603-448-7006

www.upne.com

University Press of New England (UPNE) is an award-winning university press supported by a consortium of schools—Brandeis University, Dartmouth College, the University of New Hampshire, Northeastern University, Tufts University and University of Vermont—and based at Dartmouth College since 1970. UPNE has earned a reputation for excellence in scholarly, instructional, reference, literary and artistic, and general-interest books. Many of these are published cooperatively with one of the member institutions and carry a joint imprint. Others are published under the University Press of New England imprint.

The publishing program reflects strengths in the humanities, liberal arts, fine, decorative, and performing arts, literature, New England culture, and interdisciplinary studies. The press publishes and distributes more than 80 titles annually, with sales of more than $2.5 million. A professional staff of 24 maintains high standards in editorial, design and production, marketing, order fulfillment, and business operations.

University Press of New England publishes books for scholars, teachers, students, and the general public. The press concentrates in American studies, literature, history, and cultural studies; art, architecture, and material culture; ethnic studies (including African American, Jewish, Native American, and Shaker studies); international studies; nature and the environment; and New England history and culture. The Hardscrabble Books imprint publishes fiction of New England.

Recent titles include *Memoirs by Hans Jonas; Just Seconds from the Ocean: Costal Living in the Wake of Katrina* by William Sargent; *Writing on a Stone: Scenes from a Maine Island Life* by Christina Mardsen Gillis; *Early Modern Civilization and Its Political and Cultural Dynamism* by Heinz Schilling; *Ethics through Literature: Ascetic and Aesthetic Reading in Western Culture* by Brian Stock; and *Out in the Storm: Drug-Addicted Women Living as Shoplifters and Sex Workers* by Gail A. Caputo.

It is best to contact this press early in one's development process, even at the proposal stage. Send a proposal with SASE to:

Phyllis Deutsch, Editor-in-Chief; Phyllis.D.Deutsch@dartmouth.edu

Ellen Wicklum, Senior Acquisitions Editor; M.Ellen.Wicklum@dartmouth.edu

Richard Pult, Acquisitions Editor; Richard.Pult@dartmouth.edu

UTAH STATE UNIVERSITY PRESS

7800 Old Main Hill, Logan, UT 84322

435-797-1362

www.usu.edu/usupress

Utah State University Press is a refereed scholarly publisher and division of Utah State University. Established in 1972, the press's mandate is to acquire and publish books of superior quality that win the esteem of readers and that appropriately represent the university to the community of scholars. Vital also to their mission is publication for a broader community, including students, who use the books in their studies, and general readers, who find in them enjoyment as well as enlightenment.

Utah State University Press is an established publisher in the fields of composition studies, creative writing, folklore, Native American studies, nature and environment, and Western history, including Mormon history and Western women's history. They also sponsor the annual May Swenson Poetry Award.

Recent titles include *The Activist WPA: Changing Stories about Writing and Writers* by Linda Adler-Kassner; *Writing-Intensive: Becoming W-Faculty in a New Writing Curriculum* by Wendy Strachan; *Literacy, Sexuality, Pedagogy: Theory and Practice for Composition Studies* by Jonathan Alexander; *Out of Style: Reanimating Stylistic Study in Rhetoric and Composition* by Paul Butler; *Always a Cowboy: Judge Wilson McCarthy and the Rescue of the Denver & Rio Grande Western Railroad* by Will Bagley.

Utah State University Press is a refereed scholarly press, publishing principally folklore studies, Western history, composition studies, and regional studies and works, including a small number of literary works.

Direct proposals with SASEs to:

Michael Spooner, Director; michael.spooner@usu.edu

John Alley, Executive Editor; john.alley@usu.edu

VANDERBILT UNIVERSITY PRESS

VU Station B 351813, Nashville, TN 37235-1813

615-322-3585 fax: 615-343-8823

www.vanderbilt.edu/vupress e-mail: vupress@vanderbilt.edu

Established in 1940, Vanderbilt University Press is the principal publishing arm of one of the nation's leading research universities. The press's primary mission is to select, produce, market, and disseminate scholarly publications of outstanding quality and originality. In conjunction with the long-term development of its editorial program, the press draws on and supports the intellectual activities of the university and its faculty. Although its main emphasis falls in the area of scholarly publishing, the press also publishes books of substance and significance that are of interest to the general public, including regional books. In this regard, the press also supports Vanderbilt's service and outreach to the larger local and national community.

The editorial interests of Vanderbilt University Press include most areas of the humanities and social sciences, as well as health care and education. The press seeks intellectually provocative and socially significant works in these areas, as well as works that are interdisciplinary or that blend scholarly and practical concerns. In addition the press maintains an active co-publishing program with Nashville-based Country Music Foundation Press. At present, Vanderbilt publishes some 20 new titles each year. Of the total of some 300 works published by the press in its five-decade history, more than 125 remain in print.

Vanderbilt publications are marketed aggressively through catalogs, direct mail, exhibits, reviews, advertising, and sales representation to the book trade throughout this country and abroad. Warehousing and worldwide order fulfillment services are provided by the University of Oklahoma Press in Norman, Oklahoma.

Recent titles include *The Moon in the Water* by Kathy J. Phillips; *With Music and Justice for All: Some Southerners and Their Passions* by Frye Gaillard; *Old Age in a New Age: The Promise of Transformative Nursing Homes* by Beth Baker; *Playing the Changes: Milt Hinton's Life in Stories and Photographs* by Milt Hinton, David Berger, and Holly Maxson; and *Japan 1945: A U.S. Marine's Photographs from Ground Zero.*

Direct query letters and SASEs to:

Michael Ames, Director

WAYNE STATE UNIVERSITY PRESS

The Leonard N. Simons Building, 4809 Woodward Avenue, Detroit, MI 48201-1309

313-577-6120 fax: 313-577-6131

wsupress.wayne.edu

Wayne State University Press is a distinctive urban publisher committed to supporting its parent institution's core research, teaching, and service mission by generating high quality scholarly and general interest works of global importance. Through its publishing program, the press disseminates research, advances education, and serves the local community while expanding the international reputation of the press and the university.

Wayne State University Press is an established midsize university press that publishes approximately 40 new books and six journals per year. Subject areas featured in the current publishing program include Africana studies, Armenian Studies, children's studies, classical studies, fairy-tale and folklore studies, film and television studies, German Studies, Great Lakes and Michigan, humor studies, Jewish studies, labor and urban studies, literature, and speech and language pathology.

Recent titles include *Summer Dreams: The Story of Bob-lo Island* by Patrick Livingston; *Trespassing: Dirt Stories & Field Notes* by Janet Kauffman; *It Was All Right: Mitch Ryder's Life in Music* by James A. Mitchell; *Back to School: Jewish Day School in the Lives of Adult Jews* by Alex Pomson and Randal F. Schnoor; *Dear Chester, Dear John: Letters between Chester Himes and John A. Williams* edited by John A. Williams and Lori Williams; *Wide Awake in Someone Else's Dream* by M.L. Lieber; and *After-Music* by Conrad Hilberry.

To submit, send a letter of inquiry or proposal with SASE to:

Kathryn Wildfong, Acquisitions Manager—Africana studies, Jewish studies, Great Lakes and Michigan; k.wildfong@wayne.edu

Annie Martin, Acquisitions Editor—Film and TV studies, fairy-tale studies, children's studies; annie.martin@wayne.edu

Jane Hoehner, Acquisitions Editor—Speech and language pathology; jane.hoehner@wayne.edu

UNIVERSITY PRESSES

WESLEYAN UNIVERSITY PRESS

215 Long Lane, Middletown, CT 06459

860.685.7711   fax: 860.685.7712

www.wesleyan.edu/wespress

The mission of Wesleyan University Press is to develop and maintain a sound and vigorous publishing program that serves the academic ends and intellectual life of the university. In addition, the press formulated three broad goals meant to insure that the press would fulfill its mission:

"To acquire and publish scholarly and broadly intellectual works that make significant contributions to knowledge in traditional fields of inquiry or expression, and to new and cross-disciplinary fields of inquiry or expression; to enhance the intellectual life of the Wesleyan community through the involvement of faculty and students in the publishing programs and activities of the press; and to project the name and image of the university and to enhance its reputation as an academic institution of the highest quality."

Publishing in its current form since 1959, Wesleyan University Press has lived through many transitions while continuing to thrive. It has published an internationally renowned poetry series since its inception, releasing more than 250 titles and collecting four Pulitzer Prizes, a Bollingen, and two National Book Awards in that one series alone.

Recent titles include *The Dancer Within: Intimate Conversations with Great Dancers* by Rose Eichenbaum and Aron Hirt-Manheimer; *The Films of Samuel Fuller: If You Die, I'll Kill You* by Lisa Dombrowski; *The Collected Poems of Barbara Guest* by Barbara Guest, edited by Hadley Guest; *Solkattu Manual: An Introduction to the Language of Rhythm in South Indian Music* by David P. Nelson; *Coming to You Wherever You Are: Much Music, MTV and Youth Identities*; and *Colonialism and the Emergence of Science Fiction* by John Rieder.

The Wesleyan Poetry Program accepts manuscripts by invitation only until further notice. Their publications in nonfiction concentrate in the areas of dance, music/culture, film/TV and media studies, and science fiction studies. They will accept proposals for books in these areas only. The equivalent of a cover letter may be submitted by e-mail/attachment, but do not submit full proposals electronically unless asked to do so.

Direct queries, proposals with CVs, and SASEs to:

Suzanna Tamminen, Director and Editor-in-Chief; stamminen@wesleyan.edu

Send music/culture, film/TV & media studies, science fiction studies, and Connecticut history submissions to:

Parker Smathers, Editor; psmather@wesleyan.edu

YALE UNIVERSITY PRESS

302 Temple Street, New Haven, CT 06511

P.O. Box 209040, New Haven, CT 06520-9040

203-432-0960   fax: 203-432-0948

www.yale.edu/yup   e-mail: yupmkt@yalevm.cis.yale.edu

London office:

47 Bedford Square, London WC1B3DP

020 7079 4900   fax: 020 7029 4901

www.yalebooks.co.uk

blog: yalepress.typepad.com/yalepresslog

By publishing serious works that contribute to a global understanding of human affairs, Yale University Press aids in the discovery and dissemination of light and truth, lux et veritas, which is a central purpose of Yale University. The press's publications are books and other materials that further scholarly investigation, advance interdisciplinary inquiry, stimulate public debate, educate both within and outside the classroom, and enhance cultural life. Through the distribution of works that combine excellence in scholarship with skillful editing, design, production, and marketing, the press demonstrates its commitment to increasing the range and vigor of intellectual pursuits within the university and elsewhere. With an innovative and entrepreneurial spirit, Yale University Press continually extends its horizons to embody university press publishing at its best.

One hundred years and over 7,000 titles ago Yale University Press was founded by a young graduate and his wife. In its first few years, owned entirely by the founders and guided by a committee of the Yale Corporation, whimsy played a part in the publishing of dozens of books of poetry, many from the literary renaissance then at Yale—MacLeish, Farrar, Luce, and the Benéts, for example—and soon the Yale Shakespeare, and the Yale Series of Younger Poets, which are going strong today. Then there were the many books for children, another surprise from a university press. These were in addition to such works of solid scholarship as Farrand's 1911 Records of the 1787 Constitutional Convention, also still in print, and the Chronicles of America, the Yale Review from time to time, and the many long Yale series of studies in history and literature and economics and language. Beyond their content, these books were distinguished by their looks, for Carl Purington Rollins designed them over three decades, gathering praise all the while. Among its series then and now are the many shelves of volumes of the papers of Walpole and Franklin and Edwards, and today's new and ambitious series on the Culture & Civilization of China and the Annals of Communism. The Yale Pelican History of Art recently joined a long list of art books that was already perhaps the best in the world.

The London office of the Yale Press was first established in 1961 as a marketing base, and in 1973 commenced publishing its own list. It now has a unique position as the only American university press with a full-scale publishing operation and publishing program in Europe. Working closely with the Paul Mellon Centre for Studies in British Art, it swiftly built a preeminent reputation for its art history and architecture titles. Its range now extends to trade history and biography, politics, music, religion, literature and contemporary affairs, and its books have won many of the leading British literary prizes and awards, as well as receiving notable attention in reviews, journals and broadcasting.

The Bancroft Prize for 2006, among the most prestigious in the field of history, was awarded to Yale University Press title *Dwelling Place: A Plantation Epic* by Erskine Clarke.

Other recent titles include *Hubbub: Filth, Noise, and Stench in England, 1600-1770* by Emily Cockayne; *Grand Scale: Monumental Prints in the Age of Dürer and Titian* edited by Larry Silver and Elizabeth Wyckoff; *National Gallery Catalogues: The Sixteenth-Century Italian Paintings Volume II: Venice 1540-1600* by Nicholas Penny; *The Working Woman's Pregnancy Book* by Marjorie Greenfield MD; *Andrew Bush: Drive* by Andrew Bush; and *The Art of Natural History: Illustrated Treatises and Botanical Paintings, 1400-1850.*

Yale University Press handles its own distribution.

Query letters, proposals, and SASEs should be directed to:

New Haven Office:

Jean E. Thomson Black, Senior Editor—Life sciences, physical sciences, environmental sciences, medicine

Jennifer Banks, Editor—Literature, literary studies, religion, philosophy

Jonathan Brent, Editorial Director—Literature, literary studies, theater, Slavic studies

Keith Condon, Editor—Politics, political science, music

Laura Davulis, Assistant Editor—history, current events

Patricia Fidler, Publisher—Art and architecture

Michelle Komie, Associate Editor—Art and architecture

Michael O'Malley, Editor—Business, economics, and law

Mary Jane Peluso, Publisher—Foreign languages and ESL (contact for special instructions on how to submit a proposal for languages and ESL)

Christopher Rogers, Executive Editor—History, current events

Time Shea, Development Editor—Foreign languages and ESL

Vadim Staklo, Associate Editor—Reference

London Office:

Robert Baldock, Managing Director, London, and Editorial Director (Humanities)—History, biography, politics, music, history of religion, contemporary affairs

Gillian Malpass, Publisher (Art & Architecture)—History of art, history of architecture, history of fashion

Heather McCallum, Publisher, Trade Books, London—history, politics, current affairs, international affairs, biography, history of science

Sally Salvesen, Senior Editor (Pevsner, Pelican History of Art, Decorative Arts & Design)

SECTION FOUR

CANADIAN BOOK PUBLISHERS

CANADIAN BOOK PUBLISHING

AND THE CANADIAN MARKET

GREG IOANNOU
President
Colborne Communications, Toronto
www.colcomm.ca   e-mail: greg@colcomm.ca
tel: 416-214-0183

Colborne Communications provides a full range of services to the book publishing industry, taking books from initial conception through writing, editing, design, layout, and print production.

There's good and bad news about the Canadian publishing industry for writers. First, the bad: Breaking in isn't easy. The good news: Most Canadian publishers are interested in new writers. They have to be, because small- to mid-sized Canadian houses operate mainly on government grant money. In order to get that grant money, houses must publish Canadian authors. They also can't afford bidding wars. Instead, they often find new authors, develop them, and hope they stay—or that their fame will add value to the house's backlist.

The key to getting published is to make sure that you're sending the right manuscript to the right publisher, using an appropriate style for submissions. Publishers are less frustrated by poor writing than they are by poorly executed submissions.

If you've written a non-fiction book about rural Nova Scotia, don't send your manuscript to a children's publisher in Vancouver. Research the publishers first instead of spamming busy editors with manuscripts that don't fit their house's list.

The Internet is a fantastic tool for writers. It's easier to research potential publishers online than it is to sit at the library and search through Quill & Quire's Canadian

Publishers Directory—though that is still a valuable resource.

Do an online search for Canadian publishers. A few places to start are the Association of Canadian Publishers—who provide a search form by genre and province—and the Canadian Publishers' Council. The Canadian Children's Book Centre is particularly focused and has an annual publication that lists publishers who accept unsolicited manuscripts and artwork. If you see a publisher whose mandate seems to match your book idea, visit their website and locate their submission requirements, or contact a Canadian agent.

Rather than sending your manuscript everywhere, write custom proposals that show the publisher that you know what they publish, you've read their submission guidelines thoroughly, and your manuscript adheres to those requirements. It is okay to show enthusiasm for the press, or to suggest where you think your manuscript fits on their list. But don't act as though the publisher would be lucky to get your book. Do not threaten publishers with deadlines; you may bully yourself into an automatic rejection. Take the time to write a brief but informative proposal, including a chapter-by-chapter outline if appropriate, and send a sample of your work. Include the approximate word count, genre, and reading level in the cover letter. Consider contacting the Canadian Authors Association or The Writers' Union of Canada for more information on writing for the Canadian market.

If you're a foreign writer hoping to be published in Canada, offer some form of subject-matter expertise. It's like immigrating to another country: You need to have a skill that a Canadian doesn't have.

American writers should remember that Canada is not part of the United States; Canadian publishers cannot use U.S. stamps to return manuscripts. Use International Reply Coupons (available at any post office) instead.

ANNICK PRESS LIMITED

15 Patricia Avenue, Toronto, ON M2M 1H9, Canada

416-221-4802   fax: 416-221-8400

www.annickpress.com

Annick Press publishes children's literature, specifically picture books, nonfiction, and juvenile and young adult novels. The company has won many prestigious design and publishing awards. Annick Press was the first children's publisher to receive the Canadian Booksellers Association's Publisher of the Year award. Annick publishes books for children ages six months to 12 years and for young adults, approximately 30 titles annually. A select number of books are published in French and Spanish editions.

Recent titles include *The Curse of Akkad: Climate Upheavals That Rocked Human History* by Peter Christie; *Royal Murder: The Deadly Intrigue of Ten Sovereigns* by Elizabeth MacLeod; *Super Crocs and Monster Wings: Modern Animals' Ancient Past* by Claire Eamer; *Wonder Kids: The Remarkable Lives of Nine Child Prodigies* by Charis Cotter; *Apprentice's Masterpiece: The Story Medieval Spain* by Melanie Little; and *The Pact of the Wolves* by Nina Blazon.

Annick Press is committed to publishing only Canadian authors. Further, they are not currently accepting manuscripts for picture books. However, they are interested in receiving manuscripts featuring teen fiction, middle reader (ages 8–11) fiction, and middle reader and teen nonfiction. Address all submissions to "The Editors," so that they may properly register your manuscript.

Rick Wilks, Director

Colleen MacMillan, Associate Publisher

ANVIL PRESS

278 East First Avenue, Vancouver, BC V5T 1A6, Canada

604-876-8710   fax: 604-879-2667

www.anvilpress.com

Anvil Press is a literary publisher interested in contemporary, progressive literature in all genres. It was created in 1988 to publish *sub-TERRAIN* magazine, which explores alternative literature and art; three years later the press moved into publishing books as well. The Anvil Press mission is to discover, nurture, and promote new and established Canadian literary talent. They publish 8–10 titles per year and sponsor the International 3-Day Novel Contest, which involves writing an entire novel over the Labour

Day Weekend and is explained in detail at www.3daynovel.com. They are not interested in publishing genre novels (Sci-Fi, Horror, Romance, etc).

Recent Anvil titles include *Black Rabbit and Other Stories* by Salvatore Difalco; *Rental Van* by Clint Burnham; *I Cut My Finger* by Stuart Ross; *Transitions of a Still Life: The Ceramic Works of Tam Irving* with text by Carol E. Mayer; and *At Home with History: The Untold Secrets of Heritage Homes* by Eve Lazarus.

Direct query letters and SASEs to:

Brian Kaufman, Publisher

ARSENAL PULP PRESS

341 Water Street, Suite 200, Vancouver, BC V6B 1B8, Canada

604-687-4233 / 888-600-PULP   fax: 604-687-4283

www.arsenalpulp.com

Arsenal Pulp Press is a publisher of provocative and stimulating books that challenge the status quo in the following genres: cultural studies, political/sociological studies, regional studies and guides (particularly for British Columbia), cookbooks, gay and lesbian literature, visual art, multicultural literature, literary fiction (no genre fiction, such as sci-fi, thrillers, or romance), youth culture, and health. They have had particular success with cookbooks.

Recent Arsenal titles include *Eat, Drink, and Be Vegan* by Dreena Burton; *The Carnivorous Lamb* by Agustin Gomez-Arcos; *Soucouyant* by David Chariandy; *New World Provence: Modern French Cooking for Friends and Family* by Alessandra Quaglia and Jean-Francis Quaglia; *Ottawa: The Unknown City* by Rob McLennan; and *First-Person Queer: Who We Are (So Far)* edited by Richard Labonte and Lawrence Schimel.

Submissions should include a marketing analysis, synopsis, and a 50- to 60-page sample. Direct your query and SASE to the Editorial Board.

BEACH HOLME PUBLISHING

409 Granville Street, Suite 1010, Vancouver, BC V6C 1T2, Canada

604-733-4868   fax: 604-733-4860

www.beachholme.bc.ca

Beach Holme Publishing specializes in Canadian literary fiction, plays, poetry, literary nonfiction, and young adult fiction. They bring indigenous creative writing to a wider

Canadian audience and have published award-winning authors including Evelyn Lau, Joe Rosenblatt, and Dorothy Park.

Beach Holme's line of young adult fiction is geared to children ages 8–13, and often features historical Canadian settings and situations.

Recent titles include *White Jade Tiger* by Julie Lawson; *False Shuffles* by Jane Urquhart; *Last Days in Africville* by Dorothy Perk; *Little Emperors: A Year with the Future of China* by JoAnn Dionne; *Natural Disasters* by Andrea MacPherson; and *Hesitation Before Birth* by Bert Almon.

Direct queries and SASEs to:

Michael Carroll, Publisher

BRICK BOOKS

431 Boler Road, Box 20081, London, ON N6K 4G6, Canada

519-657-8579

www.brickbooks.ca

Brick Books is a small literary press based in London, Ontario, which seeks to foster interesting, ambitious, and compelling work by Canadian poets. Brick Books was nominated for the prestigious Canadian Booksellers Association Libris award for Best Small Press Publisher of the Year 2006. They publish 7 new books and 5-10 reprints every year.

Recent titles include *Night Work: The Sawchuck Poems* by Randall Maggs; *Spirit Engine* by John Donlan; *The Luskville Reductions* by Monty Reid; *Daughters of Men* by Brenda Leifso; *Thin Moon Psalm* by Sheri Benning; *Woodshedding* by S.E. Venart; and *Two Hemispheres* by Nadine McInnis.

Brick Books can publish only authors who are Canadian citizens or landed immigrants. To submit, you may send the fully completed manuscript or a sample of 8–10 poems. Please note that they will only accept submissions between January 1 and April 30. Submissions received outside of the reading period will be returned. Please allow 3–4 months for a response.

CORMORANT BOOKS

215 Spadina Avenue, Studio 230, Toronto, ON M5T 2C7, Canada

416-929-4957   fax: 416-929-3596

www.cormorantbooks.com

Cormorant Books seeks to publish the best new work in the area of literary fiction and creative nonfiction for the adult market. This award-winning house publishes a select list of literary fiction, trade nonfiction, and works of fiction in translation.

The press recently launched a Cormorant monograph series, which brings unique perspectives to Canadian literary works from the country's leading academics, writers, and critical thinkers. The first work in the series is *The Cadence of Civil Elegies* by Robert Lecker.

Recent titles from Cormorant include *The Only Snow in Havana* by Elizabeth Hay; *No Beautiful Shore* by Beverly Stone; *The Frankenstein Murders* by Kathyln Bradshaw; *Oongah* by Mary Tilberg; *Walking on Water* by Jancis M. Andrews; *Silver Salts* by Mark Blagrave; and *The Collected Stage Drama of Marie-Claire Blais* by Marie-Claire Blais.

Cormorant Books is not currently accepting unsolicited manuscripts, and unsolicited manuscripts will be recycled. Check their Web site to see if this policy is changed.

Query letters and SASEs should be directed to:

J. Marc Côté, President and Publisher

COTEAU BOOKS

2517 Victoria Avenue, Regina, SK S4P 0T2, Canada

306-777-0170   fax: 306-522-5152

www.coteaubooks.com

Based in Regina, Coteau publishes novels, juvenile fiction, creative nonfiction (including the *Herstory* calendar), drama, and authors from all parts of Canada. The press seeks to give literary voice to its community, and places a special emphasis on Saskatchewan and prairie writers. It also has an active program of presenting and developing new writers.

Recent Coteau titles include *The Cult of Quick Repair* by Dede Crane; *Ghost Voyages IV: Champlain & Cartier* by Cora Taylor; *Katie Be Quiet* by Darcy Tamayose; *Love of Mirrors* by Gary Hyland; *My Human Comedy* by Gerald Hill; *Red Dust, Red Sky* by Paul S. Sunga; and *Run Like Jäger* by Karen Bass.

Coteau publishes only authors who are Canadian citizens. No simultaneous submissions, and only hard copy submissions are considered. You may send the full manuscript or a sample (3–4 stories or chapters; 20–25 poems) accompanied by a self-addressed envelope of appropriate size to:

Nik Burton, Managing Editor

CUMULUS PRESS

PO Box 5205, Station B, Montréal, QB H3B 4B5, Canada

514-523-1975

www.cumuluspress.com

Cumulus Press is an emerging publisher seeking fiction and poetry from new and established writers. They have a particular interest in social justice, human rights, and dissenting approaches to capitalist structures. The press supports independent, creative expression and is a founding organizer of Expozine, Montréal's annual small press, comic, and zine fair, which is celebrating its 7th anniversary in Fall 2008.

The Trendil Anthology Series places the apprenticeship of young Canadian writers 24 years and under as a priority of the Cumulus Press program. The series' books design features a chapbook by established and respected authors set aside in the French flaps of each edition's front cover. So far the series has published *Book 1: Poetry: Running with Scissors*; *Book 2: Short Fiction: Rising to a Tension*; and *Book 3: Travel Writing: Navigating Customs*. Submissions should be sent to the Cumulus Press physical address.

Other recent titles include *The Freedom I Stole* by Jason 'Blackbird' Selman; *EXTRACTION!: Comic Reportage* edited by Frédéric Dubois, Marc Tessier & David Widgington; *Picture This!: Posters of Social Movements in Quebec* edited by Jean-Pierre Boyer, Jean Desjardins & David Widgington; *Talking Book* edited by Kaie Kellough & Jason Selman; *The Hero Book* by Scott Waters; *North of 9/11* by David Bermans; and *Maps of Our Bodies: & The Borders We Have Agreed Upon* by Taien Ng-Chan.

Cumulus Press does not accept unsolicited manuscripts. However, if you really think that Cumulus will be interested in your work, send a maximum 3-page proposal including biography, synopsis, writing credits, email, etc. You may query electronically at info@cumuluspress.com. Direct all other queries with SASEs to:

David Widgington, Publisher

DOUGLAS & MCINTYRE PUBLISHING GROUP

GREYSTONE BOOKS

Suite 201, 2323 Quebec Street, Vancouver, BC V5T 4S7, Canada

604-254-7191 fax: 604-254-9099

Toronto office:

Suite 500 720, Bathurst Street, Toronto, ON M5S 2R4, Canada

416-537-2501 fax: 416-537-4647

www.douglas-mcintyre.com

Douglas & McIntyre Publishing Group is an independent publishing house with two distinct imprints: Douglas & McIntyre and Greystone Books. The group publishes popular Canadian trade books for a global market, with many international successes, particularly in the areas of natural science and the environment.

Douglas & McIntyre publishes a broad general program of adult fiction and non-fiction, with an emphasis on art and architecture, Native studies, Canadian history, biography and social issues, aviation, popular memoir, and food and wine. Greystone Books titles focus on natural history and science, the environment, popular culture, and health and sports. Together, the two imprints release 75 new titles per year.

Recent titles from Douglas & McIntyre include *Abstract Painting in Canada* by Roald Nasgaard; *Arc of the Medicine Line* by Tony Rees; *Carl Von Clausewitz's On War* by Hew Strachan; *Ciopinno's Mediterranean Grill* by Pino Posteraro and Gérard Boyer; *Empty Casing* by Fred Doucette and Roméo Dallaire; and *A Guidebook to Contemporary Architecture in Montreal* by Nancy Dunton and Helen Malkin.

Titles indicative of the Greystone list include *An Ecology of Enchantment* by Des Kennedy; *Food, Sex, and Salmonella* by David Waltnet-Toews; *The Great Lakes* by Wayne Grady and Emily Damstra; *It Ain't Easy* by Paul Myers; *Jumbo* by Paul Chambers; and *Reflections on a Hockey Season* produced by The National Hockey League.

Query letters and SASEs should be directed to the Editorial Panel.

Scott McIntyre, President and Publisher

DRAWN AND QUARTERLY

P.O. BOX 48056, Montréal, QB H2V 4S8, Canada

514-279-0691

www.drawnandquarterly.com

Drawn and Quarterly is an award-winning publisher of graphic novels, comic books, and comic book series with over 20 new titles per year. The publisher acquires new comic books, art books, and graphic novels by renowned cartoonists and newcomers from around the globe.

Drawn & Quarterly welcomes submissions for consideration in a number of their publishing venues, including a new talent forum (Drawn & Quarterly Showcase), a regular anthology (Drawn & Quarterly), and a seasonal selection of general graphic novels, comic books, and comic book series.

Recent titles include *Paul Goes Fishing* by Michel Rabagliati; *Haunted* by Philippe Dupuy; *Shortcomings* by Adrian Tomine; *365 Days: A Diary* by Julie Doucet; *White Rapids* by Pascal Blanchet; *Moomin: The Complete Tove Jansson Comic Strip, Book Two* by Tove Jansson; and *ACME Novelty Datevook: Volume Two* by Chris Ware;

Drawn & Quarterly prefers to receive electronic submissions. E-mail Web site URLs or JPEG samples of your work to: chris@drawnandquarterly.com.

If you are unable to submit via e-mail, mail b&w photocopies of your work, no more than 8 pages. Do not include SASE as Drawn and Quarterly will not return work and will contact you only if they're interested in publishing your art.

Chris Oliveros, Publisher

THE DUNDURN GROUP

500 – 3 Church Street, Toronto, ON M5E 1M2, Canada

416-214-5544   fax: 416-214-5556

www.dundurn.com

Dundurn Press Limited was established in 1972 to bring Canadian history and biography to a general readership. Politics, history, and biography were the original mandate, which quickly expanded to include literary and art criticism, and large illustrated art books.

In the 1990s, Dundurn acquired three other Canadian publishing houses: Hounslow Press, Simon & Pierre, and Boardwalk Books. These companies further broadened Dundurn's editorial mandate to include popular nonfiction, literary fiction, and young adult books. Dundurn also publishes mysteries.

Recent titles include *Toronto: The Way We Were* by Mike Filey; *The Big Book of Canadian Ghost Stories* by John Robert Colombo; *Canada in Sudan: War Without Borders* by Peter Pigott; *Eight Decades: The Selected Writings of W. Gunther Plaut* by W. Gunther Plaut and Jonathan V. Plaut; *John Arpin: Keyboard Virtuoso* by Robert Popple; *Now You Know Hockey: The Book of Answers* by Doug Lennox; and *Glenn Gould: A Musical Force* by Vladimir Konieczny.

To submit, please send the complete proposal or manuscript or three sample chapters to the attention of the "Acquisitions Editor." Fiction submissions will be reviewed twice annually, in the spring and in the fall. E-mail submissions are not considered. While authors outside Canada are considered, be sure to include an international reply coupon with the SASE.

Kirk Howard, President and Publisher

Barry Jowett, Editorial Director—Fiction

Tony Hawke, Editorial Director—Nonfiction

Michael R. Carroll, Editorial Director

ECW PRESS

200 - 2120 Queen Street East, Toronto, ON M4E 1E2, Canada

416-694-3348   fax: 416-698-9906

www.ecwpress.com

ECW Press publishes nonfiction and fiction for the adult market. Now in its 25th year, ECW has published close to 1,000 books that are distributed throughout the English-speaking world and translated into dozens of languages. Their list includes poetry and fiction, pop culture and political analysis, sports books, biography, and travel guides. ECW releases 60–70 new titles per year.

Recent titles include *Benoit: Wrestling with the Horror that Destroyed a Family and Crippled a Sport* by Steven Johnson, Heath McCoy, and Irvin Muchnik; *Ghost Rider: Travels on the Healing Road* by Neil Peart; *Pain and Passion: The History of Stampede Wrestling* by Heath McCoy; *From the Flight Deck: Plane Talk and Sky Science* by Doug Morris; *Judas Priest: Heavy Metal Painkillers—An Illustrated History* by Martin Popoff; and *Rifke: An Improbable Life* by Rosalie Wise Sharp.

ECW publishes only Canadian-authored poetry and fiction. For nonfiction (literary and commercial) they consider proposals from anywhere. Instead of a SASE, you may include an e-mail address in your cover letter where they could e-mail a reply to your query. Please send a proposal and SASE to the appropriate editor:

Jack David, Publisher—Business, sports, mystery fiction, true crime, biographies

David Caron, Co-Publisher—Sci-fi, graphic novels, history

Jennifer Hale, Senior Editor—Pop culture, music, celebrity biographies, television, film, fiction, and creative nonfiction

Michael Holmes, Senior Editor—Literary fiction, poetry, wrestling

Adrienne Guthrie, Projects Developer—Corporate books

FIREFLY BOOKS LTD

66 Leek Crescent, Richmond Hill, ON L4B 1H1, Canada

416-499-8412   fax: 416-499-8313

www.fireflybooks.com

Firefly Books, established in 1977, is a North American publisher and distributor of nonfiction and children's books. Firefly's admirable goal is to bring readers beautifully produced books written by experts at reasonable prices.

Firefly Books has particular strengths in cookbooks, gardening, astronomy, health, natural history, pictorial books, reference books (especially for children), and sports. Firefly has published books as diverse as Robert Munsch and Sheila McGraw's *Love You Forever* (over 17 million copies in print) and Terence Dickinson's *Nightwatch: A Practical Guide to Viewing the Universe (Third Edition: Revised and Expanded for Use Through 2010)*.

Recent titles include *Landscape Planning: Practical Techniques for the Home Gardener* by Judith Adam; *Hostas* by Rosemary Barrett and photography by Derek Hughes; *The Complete Herb Book* by Jekka McVicar; *The English Roses* by David Austin; *Encyclopedia of Planting Combinations: Over 4000 Color and Planting Schemes* by Tony Lord and photography by Andrew Lawson; *Sucessful Bonsai: Raising Exotic Miniature Trees* by David Squire; *Time-Saving Gardener* by Carolyn Hutchinson; and *Build Your Own Birdhouses and Feeders* by John Perkins.

Firefly Books does not accept unsolicited manuscripts. However, it does accept proposals for illustrated non-fiction. Firefly does not publish children's books. Direct queries and SASEs to:

Lionel Koffler, President and Publisher

Michael Warrick, Associate Publisher

FITZHENRY & WHITESIDE LTD.

FIFTH HOUSE PUBLISHERS

195 Allstate Parkway, Markham, ON L3R 4T8, Canada

905-477-9700 / 800-387-9776   fax: 905-477-9179 / 800-260-9777

www.fitzhenry.ca

Fitzhenry & Whiteside Ltd. specializes in trade nonfiction and children's books. The firm also offers a textbook list and a small list of literary fiction. They publish or reprint 60–80 titles per year. The house specializes in history, natural sciences, forestry, ecology, biography, psychology, reference, Canadiana, antiques, art, photography, children's and young adult fiction and nonfiction.

Fitzhenry & Whiteside nonfiction titles range throughout Canadian history, biography, Native studies, nature, and antiques and collectibles. The children's book list includes early readers, picture books, and middle-grade and young adult novels. Markets include trade, school, library, professional and reference, college, mail order, and specialty.

Recent Fitzhenry & Whiteside titles include *A Time in the Arctic* by Bern Will Brown; *Anne of Green Gables Journal* illustrated by Muriel Wood; *Baby Mountain Sheep* by Aubrey Lang and with photography by Wayne Lynch; *Behind the Scenes: The Racehorse* by Nikki Tate; *Big Big Sky* by Kristyn Dunnion; *Broken Arrow: America's First Lost Nucelar Weapon*; and *Honouring Tradition: Reframing Native Art* produced by the Glenbow Museum.

Query letters and SASEs should be directed to:

Sharon Fitzhenry, President

Gail Winskill, Publisher—Children's Books

Luana Lindorfer, Rights Manager

FIFTH HOUSE PUBLISHERS

1511-1800 4 Street SW, Calgary, AB T2S 2S5, Canada

403-571-5230

In 1998, Fitzhenry & Whiteside purchased the Calgary-based publisher Fifth House, which remains an entirely separate corporation. Fifth House is committed to "bringing the West to the rest" by publishing fifteen books a year about the land and people who make Western Canada unique. Fifth House also organizes The Great West Collection.

Fifth House is known for best-selling books including *The Rez Sisters* by Tomson Highway; *Inside Out: A Hiker's Guide to Art of the Canadian Rockies* by Lisa Christensen; *Park Prisoners: The Untold Story of Western Canada's National Parks 1915-1946* by Bill Waiser; and *Amazing Animal Adventures Around the World* by Brian Keating.

Other recent Fifth House titles include *Quiet Revolution West* by John Weinstein; *Pumped* by David Finch; *Smart Curling* by Vera Pezer; *The Intrepid Explorer* by Ernie Lakusta; *The Great Klondike Gold Rush* by Pierre Berton; *Alberta Art and Artists* by Patricia Ainslie and Mary-Beth Laviolette; *Breaking Trail* by Tom Morimoto; and *Everett Baker's Saskatchewan* by Bill Waiser.

Query letters and SASEs should be directed to:

Charlene Dobmeier, Publisher, Fifth House

GASPEREAU PRESS

47 Church Avenue, Kentville, NS B4N 2M7, Canada

877-230-8232   fax: 902-678-7845

www.gaspereau.com

Gaspereau Press is a Nova Scotia-owned and operated trade publisher specializing in short-run editions of both literary and regional interest for the Canadian market. Their list includes poetry, local history books, literary essays, novels, and short story collections. Gaspereau was nominated for the prestigious Canadian Booksellers Association's Libris award for Best Small Press Publisher of the Year 2006.

Gaspereau is one of a handful of Canadian trade publishers that prints and binds books in-house. With only 16 paces between the editor's desk and the printing press, Gaspereau Press practices a form of 'craft' publishing that is influenced more by William Morris and the private press movement of the 19th century than by the contemporary publishing culture.

Recent titles include *I Got It From an Elder: Conversations in Healing Language* by Marilyn Iwam; *Late Nights With Wild Cowboys* by Johanna Skibsrud; *During* by Karen Houle; *The Man Who Said No: Reading Jacob Bailey, Loyalist* by Kent Thompson; *Wisdom & Metaphor* by Jan Zwicky; and *Ursa Major* by Robert Bringhurst.

When submitting, please include a cover letter, a list of previous publications, and a SASE. It typically takes 6–10 months to hear back from this publisher.

Gary Dunfield, Publisher

Andrew Steeves, Publisher

GOOSE LANE EDITIONS

500 Beaverbrook Court, Suite 330, Fredericton, NB E3B 5X4, Canada

888-926-8377   fax: 506-459-4991

www.gooselane.com

Goose Lane Editions is a small publishing house that specializes in literary fiction, poetry, and a select list of nonfiction titles including history, biography, Canadiana, and fine art books. It does not publish commercial fiction, genre fiction, or confessional works of any kind. Nor does it publish for the children's market.

Recent titles include *Back in 6 Years: A Journey round the Planet Without Leaving the Surface* by Tony Robinson-Smith; *Cricket in a Fist* by Naomi K. Lewis; *Building New Brunswick: An Architectural History* by John Leroux; *The Darren Effect* by Libby Creelman; *No Such Thing as a Free Ride? A Collection of Hitchhiker's Tales* by Simon and Tom Sykes; and *The Push and the Pull* by Carryl Whetter.

Goose Lane considers submissions from outside Canada only rarely, and only when both the author and the material have significant Canadian connections and the material is of extraordinarily high interest and literary merit. Writers should submit a synopsis, outline, and sample (30–50 pages) with a SASE if in Canada; international authors should include SASEs and international reply coupons with submissions.

Please query by mail or phone before submitting; direct queries and SASEs to:

Angela Williams, Editor—nonfiction

Ross Leckie, Editor—Poetry

Sharon McCartney, Editor—Poetry

Bethany Gibson, Editor—Nonfiction

GREAT PLAINS PUBLICATIONS

70 Arthur Street, Suite 420, Winnipeg, MB R3B 1G7, Canada

204-475-6799   fax: 204-475-0138

www.greatplains.mb.ca

Great Plains Publications is an award-winning prairie-based, general trade publisher specializing in regional history and biography. In recent years they have expanded their publishing program to include Canadian literary and young adult novels.

Great Plains Publications' mandate is to publish books that are written by Canadian prairie authors. They also publish books by Canadian authors not living on the prairies, but of specific interest to people living in this region (content, setting).

Recent titles include *The Encyclopedia of Manitoba; We Watch the Waves: Unravelling the Mystery of a Father's Death* by Susan Riley; *A Place Out of Time* by Alfred Silver; *Luck: A Bill Shmata Mystery* by Dave Carpenter; *The Expedition* by Clayton Bailey; *The Gem Lakes* by Rob Keough; and *Blue and Gold: 75 Years of Blue Bomber Glory* edited by Bob Irving.

Currently, Great Plains is not accepting proposals or manuscripts for poetry or children's picture books, how-to books, cookbooks, or self-help books. Address queries with sample chapters and SASEs to the attention of the Fiction Editor, Nonfiction Editor; or Young Adult Editor, depending on the genre of your work.

Gregg Shilliday, Publisher

HARLEQUIN ENTERPRISES LIMITED

HARLEQUIN BOOKS (CANADA)

MILLS & BOON/HARLEQUIN ENTERPRISES LTD.

WORLDWIDE LIBRARY

225 Duncan Mill Road, Don Mills, ON M3B 3K9, Canada

416-445-5860

www.eHarlequin.com

Harlequin Enterprises Limited is the world's leading publisher of romance fiction and women's fiction. The Toronto-based company publishes over 115 titles a month in 25 languages in 94 international markets on six continents. These books are written by more than 1,300 authors. With 131 million books sold in 2005—50% overseas and 96% outside Canada—it is both the country's most successful publisher and one of its most international businesses.

The Harlequin Enterprises home base in Ontario, Canada, issues the greater portion of the Harlequin Books series, while the New York office issues several Harlequin series, as well as the HQN, Kimani, Red Dress, Steeple Hill, and Silhouette lists (please see listing for Harlequin Books in the directory of Independent United States Presses). The editorial acquisitions departments for Mills & Boon, Harlequin Romance, and Harlequin Presents are located at the operation's United Kingdom offices (listed below). Harlequin Enterprises Limited in Canada also publishes the Worldwide Library, which features titles in the mystery, suspense, and thriller genres.

Each of the various lines within the Harlequin series of romance novels published in Canada, like their American counterparts, stakes out particular market-niche segments of reader interest within the overall categories of romance fiction and women's fiction. There are 33 lines altogether, and each has its own submission and editorial guidelines. These guidelines are explored in great detail on the Harlequin Web site.

HARLEQUIN BOOKS (CANADA)

Harlequin Books (Canada) is home to Harlequin Everlasting, American Romance, Blaze, Supperromance, MIRA, and Spice. The best way to learn which imprint is appropriate for your manuscript is to read books already in print. Harlequin offers detailed tip sheets on their website, eHarlequin.com, or by written request. Following are general quidelines to the imprints handled in Canada:

Harlequin Everlasting, brand-new in 2007, is a contemporary romance series. The novels in this series follow the life and relationship/s of one couple. These emotionally intense stories span considerably more time than the typical series romance—years or even an entire lifetime—and at 75,000 words, the books are longer than usual as well. Recent titles include *This Side of Heaven* by Anna Schmidt; *The Vow* by Rebecca Winters; *Christmas Presents and Past* by Janice Kay Johnson; and *The Soldier and the Rose* by Linda Barret.

American Romance features fast-paced, heartwarming stories about the pursuit of love, marriage, and family in America today. They're set in small towns and big cities, on ranches and in the wilderness, from Texas to Alaska—everywhere people live and love. For this series, Harlequin is looking for energetic writing and well-constructed plots based on contemporary characters. Titles indicative of the list include *Runaway Cowboy* by Judy Christenberry; *Marrying the Boss* by Megan Kelly; *The Marriage Recipe* by Michele Dunaway; and *Down Home Dixie* by Pamela Browning.

The Blaze series features sensuous, highly romantic, innovative stories that are sexy in premise and execution. The tone of the books can run from fun and flirtatious to dark and sensual. Writers can push the boundaries in terms of characterization, plot, and sexual explicitness. Recent titles include *One For the Road* by Crystal Green; *Sex, Straight Up* by Kathleen O'reilly' *French Kissing* by Nancy Warren; *Drop Dead Gorgeous* by Kimberly Raye; and *No Stopping Now* by Dawn Atkins.

The aim of a Harlequin Superromance novel is to produce a contemporary, involving read with a mainstream tone in its situations and characters, using romance as the major theme. To achieve this, emphasis should be placed on individual writing styles and unique and topical ideas. Titles include *Return of the Wild Son* by Cynthia Thomason; *Baby Be Mine* by Eve Gaddy; *A Kiss to Remember* by Kimberly Van Meter; *A Man Worth Keeping* by Molly O'Keefe; and *Heart of My Heart* by Stella MacLean.

MIRA Books is dedicated to mainstream single-title women's fiction in hardcover and paperback editions. Of interest to a primarily women's readership, MIRA titles span all genres, including thrillers, historical romances, relationship novels, and suspense. Recent titles include *The Hunted* by Rachel Lee; *The Healer* by Sharon Sala; *Rogue* by Rachel Vincent; *Last Known Victim* by Erica Spindler; and *The Death Dealer* by Heather Graham.

New in 2006, SPICE is Harlequin's single-title imprint for erotic fiction for the modern woman who also wants a great read. Titles include *Spies, Lies, & Naked Thighs* by Jina Bacarr; *Tempted* by Megan Hart; *Caine's Reckoning* by Sarah McCarty; *The Twelve Dancing Princesses* by Nancy Madore; and *Getting Some* by Kayla Perrin.

Harlequin will send prospective authors full editorial guidelines with suggested heroine and hero profiles, as well as information pertaining to manuscript length, setting, and sexual approach and content. This information is available upon written request from the publisher and online at eHarlequin.com.

Harlequin invites submissions from both published and unpublished writers. They prefer a query with synopsis and 1–3 chapters. Make sure your query is clear as to which line it is intended for: Harlequin Everlasting, American Romance, Blaze, Harlequin Supperromance, MIRA, or Spice. Direct your submission to:

Valerie Grey, Senior Editor—MIRA Books

Wanda Ottewell, Senior Editor—Harlequin Superromance

Paula Eykelhof, Executive Editor—Single titles

Kathleen Scheibling, Associate Senior Editor—American Romance

Susan Pezzack Swinwood, Editor—Spice

Brenda Chin, Associate Senior Editor—Blaze

MILLS & BOON/HARLEQUIN ENTERPRISES LTD.

HARLEQUIN PRESENTS

HARLEQUIN ROMANCE

Eton House, 18-24 Paradise Road, Richmond, Surrey TW9 1SR, United Kingdom

Acquisitions for Mills & Boon, Harlequin Romance, and Harlequin Presents are through the United Kingdom offices. You may query the offices to request a set of editorial guidelines supplied to prospective authors or read them online at eHarlequin.com.

A new line, Mills & Boon Modern books explore cosmopolitan, city romances between upscale men and women. Young characters in affluent urban settings—either North American or international—meet, flirt, share experiences, have great, passionate sex and fall in love, finally making a commitment that will bind them together, forever. Titles include *The Italian's Passionate Revenge* by Lucy Gordon; *The Greek Tycoon's Baby Bargain* by Sharon Kendrick; *Di Cesare's Pregnant Mistriss* by Chantelle Shaw; *The Billionaire's Virgin Mistress* by Sandra Field; *At the Sicilian's Count's Command* by Carole Mortimer; and *Blackmailed for Her Baby* by Elizabeth Power.

The Mills & Boon Medical Romance line involves intense emotional romances and medical drama set in a modern medical community. Recent titles include *Nurse Bride, Bayside Wedding* by Gill Sanderson; *Billionaire Doctor, Ordinary Nurse* by Carol Marinelli; *The Sheikh Surgeon's Baby* by Meredith Webber; and *The Outback Doctor's Surprise Bride* by Amy Andrews.

Mills & Boon Historical Romance novels cover a wide range of British and European historical civilizations up to and including the Second World War. Titles include

The Last Rake in London by Nicola Cornick; *The Outrageous Lady Feisham* by Louise Allen; *An Unconventional Miss* by Dorothy Elbury; and *The Warrior's Touch* by Michelle Willingham.

Harlequin Romance is the original line of romance fiction, the series that started it all—more than 35 years ago. These are warm, contemporary novels, filled with compassion and sensitivity, written by world-famous authors and by newcomers. Titles include *His Pregnant Housekeeper* by Caroline Anderson; *The Italian Playboy's Secret Son* by Rebecca Winters; *Her Sheikh Boss* by Carol Grace; and *Wanted: White Wedding* by Natasha Oakley.

Harlequin Presents is overall the bestselling Harlequin line, published in 16 different languages and sold in almost every country of the world. This line features heart-warming romance novels about spirited, independent women and strong, wealthy men. Although grounded in reality and reflective of contemporary, relevant trends, these fast-paced stories are essentially escapist romantic fantasies that take the reader on an emotional roller-coaster ride. Written in the third person, they can be from the male or female point of view, or seen through the eyes of both protagonists. Recent titles include *The Martinez Marriage Revenge* by Helen Bianchin; *Bought for the Frenchman's Pleasure* by Abby Green; *The Greek Tycoon's Convenient Bride* by Kate Hewitt; *Accidentally Pregnant, Conveniently Wed* by Sharon Kendrick; and *Innocent Wife, Baby of Shame* by Melanie Milburne.

Please submit the first three chapters along with a 1–2 page synopsis of your novel, with appropriate SASE to:

Tessa Shapcott, Senior Editor—Harlequin Presents (Mills & Boon Modern Romance), Modern Xtra Sensual

Bryony Green, Senior Editor—Harlequin Romance (Mills & Boon Tender Romance)

Linda Fildew, Senior Editor—Historical Romance

Sheila Hodgson, Senior Editor—Medical

WORLDWIDE LIBRARY

WORLDWIDE MYSTERY

GOLD EAGLE BOOKS

The Worldwide Library division of Harlequin Enterprises hosts two major imprints, Worldwide Mystery and Gold Eagle Books. Worldwide Library emphasizes genre fiction in the categories of mystery and suspense, action-adventure, futuristic fiction, war drama, and post-Holocaust thrillers. The house gives its titles (primarily mass-market paperbacks) solid marketing and promotional support.

The Worldwide Mystery imprint specializes in mainstream commercial mystery and detective fiction in reprint. This imprint has not been issuing previously unpublished, original fiction; however, Worldwide is not to be overlooked as a resource regarding potential reprint-rights sales in this field. The house generally keeps lines of popular writers' ongoing series in print for a number of seasons, sometimes indefinitely.

Titles in reprint at Worldwide include *Death Climbs a Tree* by Sara Frommer; *Pier Pressure* by Dorothy Francis; *Died in the Wool* by Rett MacPherson; *Dahlia's Gone* by Katie Estill; and *Big Black Hole* by Wilma Kahn.

Gold Eagle Books is known for a fast-and-furious slate of men's action and adventure series with paramilitary and future-world themes. Series include Deathlands, the Destroyer, the Executioner, and Stony Man. Gold Eagle also publishes Super Books keyed to the various series—longer novels with more fully developed plots. Prospective authors should be familiar with the guidelines and regular characters associated with each series.

Query letters and SASEs should be directed to:

Feroze Mohammed, Senior Editor

Heather Locker, Executive Editor

HOUSE OF ANANSI PRESS

GROUNDWOOD BOOKS

110 Spadina Avenue, Suite 801, Toronto, ON M5V 2K4, Canada

416-363-4343   fax: 416-363-1017

www.anansi.ca

House of Anansi Press specializes in finding and developing Canada's new writers of literary fiction, poetry, and nonfiction and in maintaining a culturally significant backlist that has accumulated since the house was founded 40 years ago.

Anansi started as a small press with a mandate to publish only Canadian writers, and quickly gained attention for publishing significant authors such as Margaret Atwood, Matt Cohen, Michael Ondaatje, and Erin Mouré, as well as George Grant and Northrop Frye. French-Canadian works in translation have also been an important part of the list, and prominent Anansi authors in translation include Roch Carrier, Anne Hébert, Lise Bissonnette, and Marie-Claire Blais.

Today, Anansi publishes Canadian and international writers of literary fiction, poetry, and serious nonfiction. They do not publish genre fiction (mysteries, thrillers, science fiction, or romance novels), nor do they publish self-help nonfiction.

Recent titles include *The Jesus Sayings* by Rex Weyler; *The City of Words* by Alberto Manguel; *The Lost Massey Lectures* produced by the CBC Massey Lectures Series; *The Anansi Reader* by Lynn Coady; *Die With Me* by Elena Forbes; *Portrait in Light and Shadow* by Maria Tippett; and *Long Story Short* by Elyse Friedman.

In lieu of sending complete unsolicited manuscripts, House of Anansi prefers to receive proposals in hard copy along with a detailed literary curriculum vitae and a 10–15-page sample from the manuscript. These materials should be sent to Manuscript Submissions.

Lynn Henry, Publisher

Janey Yoon, Managing Editor

GROUNDWOOD BOOKS

110 Spadina Avenue, Suite 801, Toronto, ON M5V 2K4, Canada

416-363-4343   fax: 416-363-1017

www.groundwoodbooks.com

Groundwood Books, an independent imprint of House of Anansi Press, is based in Toronto and publishes children's books for all ages, including fiction, picture books and nonfiction.

Their primary focus has been on works by Canadians, though they sometimes also buy manuscripts from authors in other countries. Many of their books tell the stories of people whose voices are not always heard. Books by the First Peoples of this hemisphere have always been a special interest, as have those of others who through circumstance have been marginalized and whose contribution to society is not always visible. Since 1998, Groundwood has been publishing works by people of Latin American origin living in the Americas both in English and in Spanish under the Libros Tigrillo imprint.

New titles include *The Betrayal of Africa* by Gerald Caplan; *The Black Book of Colors* by Menena Cottin; *Brave Deeds* by Ann Alma; *Circle + Square / Circulo + Cuadro: A Board Book for Babies* by Jill Hartley; *Dear Sylvia* by Alan Cumyn; *Girl From Mars* by Tamara Bach; *Mr. Karp's Last Glass* by Cary Fagan; and *Niwechihaw / I Help* by Caitlin Dale Nicholson.

Groundwood Books is always looking for new authors of novel-length fiction for children in all age areas, but does not accept unsolicited manuscripts for picture books. They like character-driven literary fiction and note that they do not publish high-interest/low-vocabulary fiction or stories with anthropomorphic animals or elves/fairies as their main characters.

Patsy Aldana, Vice President and Publisher—Groundwood

Nan Froman, Managing Editor—Groundwood

INSOMNIAC PRESS

192 Spadina Avenue, Suite 403, Toronto, ON M5T 2C2, Canada
416-504-6270   fax: 416-504-9313

www.insomniacpress.com

Insomniac Press is a midsize independent press that publishes nonfiction, fiction, and poetry for the adult markets. Insomniac always strives to publish the most exciting new writers it can find. Celebrated authors like Natalee Caple, Lynn Crosbie, Stephen Finucan, and A.F. Moritz either got their start at Insomniac, or have published important books with the house.

While it publishes a broad range of titles, Insomniac has also developed special niche areas, including black studies books, gay and lesbian books, celebrity musician-authored books (including titles by Matthew Good, Jann Arden, and Terri Clark), and noir mysteries.

Recent titles include *Tax Tips and Tax Shelters for Canadians* by Vlad Trkulja; *Juggling Dynamite* by Danielle Park; *The New Investment Frontier III* by Howard J. Atkinson; *At Last There is Nothing Left to Say* by Matthew Good; and *Breaking the Ice* by Cecil Harris.

Insomniac is actively seeking commercial and creative nonfiction on a wide range of subjects, including business, personal finance, gay and lesbian studies, and black Canadian studies. The house does not publish science fiction, cookbooks, romance, or children's books. The poetry list is also full for the foreseeable future. Insomniac does accept unsolicited manuscripts, but suggests that you query first with a short letter or e-mail describing the project. E-mail to mike@insomniacpress.com

Queries and SASEs can be directed to:

Mike O'Connor, Publisher

Dan Varrette, Managing Editor

JAMES LORIMER & COMPANY LIMITED

317 Adelaide Street West, Suite 1002, Toronto, ON M5V 1P9, Canada
416-362-4762 / 800-565-1975   fax: 416-362-3939

www.lorimer.ca

James Lorimer is a publisher of nonfiction, children's young adult novels, and illustrated guide books. They publish Canadian authors for a Canadian audience.

Recent titles include *Alison's Ghosts* by Mary Alice Downie and John Downie; *Birding at Point Pelee* by Henrietta O'Neill; *Car Nation: An Illustrated History of Canada's*

Transformation Behind the Wheel by Dmitry Anastakis; *Choice of Colors: How African American Quarterbacks Became Canadian Stars* by John Danakas; *Dundurn Castle* by Edward Smith; and *Fashioning Fabric: The Arts of Spinning and Weaving in Early Canada* by Adrienne D. Hood.

James Lorimer & Company is currently seeking manuscripts in the following Canadian genres: biography, history, cookbooks (with a Canadian or regional focus), education, public issues, and travel. Do not send entire manuscripts, just a proposal. Queries and SASEs should be mailed to the attention of the Senior Trade Editor.

Chris Keen, Publisher

Faye Smailes, Children's Book Editor

Lynn Schellenberg, Acquisitions Editor

KEY PORTER BOOKS LTD.

6 Adelaide Street East, 10th Floor, Toronto, ON M5C 1H6, Canada

416-862-7777   fax: 416-862-2304

www.keyporter.com

Key Porter Books Limited is one of Canada's most prominent independent publishers, launching more than 100 new books per year. The company is known internationally for its high-quality illustrated books and in Canada for its mainstream books of national interest. Key Porter publishes trade nonfiction, fiction, and children's books. Their areas of specialization include Canadian politics, fiction, history biography, environmental and social issues, children's literature, health, wildlife, conservation, sports, business, cookbooks, and photography.

Recent titles include *Frank Moores: The Time of His Life* by Janice Wells; *So Cool* by Dennis Lee; *Some Things I've Learned: Lessons on Motivation, Passion, Excellence, and More* by Cassie Campbell; *Full Circle: Death and Resurrection in Canadian Conservative Politics* by Bob Plamondon; *Diabetes: CMA Your Personal Health Series* by Sara Meltzer MD and Anne Belton RN; *Canada In 2020: Twenty Leading Voices Imagine Canada's Future* edited by Rudyard Griffiths.

Key Porter Books does not accept unsolicited manuscript submissions, but will review queries and proposals. Send queries and SASEs Attention: Submissions.

Jordan Fenn, Vice President and Publisher

LOBSTER PRESS LTD.

1620 Sherbrooke Street West, Suites C & D, Montreal, QC H3H 1C9, Canada

514-904-1100   fax: 514-904-1101

www.lobsterpress.com

Lobster Press publishes fiction and nonfiction books for children, tweens, teens, and their families. They are actively seeking new authors and manuscripts.

Recent titles published *I Don't Want to Go* by Addie Meyer Sanders, illustrated by Andrew Rowland; *The Months: Fun with Friends All Year 'Round!* by Sara Coleridge, illustrated by Kathy Weller; *Zibby Payne & the Party Problem* by Alison Bell; *Dear Jo: The Story of Losing Leah…and Searching For Hope* by Christina Kilbourne; *Tin Angel* by Shannon Cowan; *Come on, Mom: 75 Things for Mothers and Daughters to Do Together* by Cynthia MacGregor; and *YUM: Your Ultimate Manual for Good Nutrition* by Daina Kalnis, MSc RD, illustrated by Paula Becker.

Lobster Press also publishes a best-selling series of family guidebooks, *The Lobster Kids' Guides* to cities in the USA and Canada.

Lobster Press is seeking fresh, edgy fiction for young adults, high interest fiction for reluctant readers, and nonfiction for preteens and teens. They particularly seek titles that appeal to boys. Please send a complete manuscript, accompanied by a cover letter, resume, and synopsis of the story. Specify the genre of your work clearly on the envelope. Do not include a SASE as Lobster Press will recycle unwanted manuscripts and contact only those authors they wish to publish.

Alison Fripp, President and Publisher

Meghan Nolan, Editor

MAPLE TREE PRESS

51 Front Street East, Suite 200, Toronto, ON M5E 1B3, Canada

416-304-0702   fax: 416-304-0525

www.mapletreepress.com

Based in Toronto, Maple Tree Press has been publishing children's books for more than 30 years. They specialize in science and nature titles, but also look for nonfiction in a wide range of subjects, including Canadian culture, sports, crafts, activities, history, humor, and picture books. In addition, Maple Tree publishes under the Owl Books and Popular Mechanics for Kids imprints.

Recent titles indicative of the list include *A Whale Tale* by Frieda Wishinky; *Amaz-*

ing Things Animals Do by Marilyn Baillie; *Dino-WHY? The Dinosaur Question + Answer Book; Ha! Ha! Ha! and Much More! The Ultimate Round-up of Jokes, Riddles, Facts, and Puzzles* by Lyn Thomas; and *How Baseball Works* by Keltie Thomas.

Maple Tree Press publishes Canadian authors almost exclusively. They especially welcome submissions for children's books targeted to ages 3–12. Please send to the attention of the Submissions Editor.

Sheba Meland, President and Publisher

MCCLELLAND & STEWART

TUNDRA BOOKS

900 - 481 University Avenue, Toronto, ON M5G 2E9, Canada

416-598-1114   fax: 416-598-7764

www.mcclelland.com

Celebrating its 102nd anniversary this year, McClelland & Stewart (M&S) is something of a Canadian institution and was an early publisher of Lucy Maud Montgomery's *Anne of Green Gables* and Winston Churchill's *History of the English Speaking Peoples*. Today, they publish a wide range of poetry, fiction, and nonfiction.

M&S authors include Margaret Atwood, Sandra Birdsell, Mavis Gallant, Jack Hodgins, Alistair MacLeod, Rohinton Mistry, Alice Munro, Michael Ondaatje, and Jane Urquhart, but they also publish debut authors like Madeleine Thien.

Recent titles include *The Calling* by Inger Ash Wolfe; *Salvage* by Jane Kotapish; *The Dream World* by Alison Pick; *Orphic Politics* by Lim Liburn; *The Alchemy of Loss* by Abigail Carter; *The Volunteer* by Michael Ross and Jonathan Kay; *The Making of a Nurse* by Tilda Shalof; and *Leonard Woolf* by Victoria Glendinning.

Direct queries and SASEs to:

Douglas Pepper, President and Publisher.

Ellen Seligman, Vice President and Publisher (Fiction)

Susan Renouf, Vice President and Associate Publisher (Nonfiction)

TUNDRA BOOKS

75 Sherbourne Street, 5th floor, Toronto, ON M5A 2P9, Canada

www.tundrabooks.com

In 1995, M&S bought Tundra, a children's book publisher known for combining art and story in innovative ways. The previous publisher of Tundra, Douglas Gibson, is now the publisher of his own imprint within Tundra Books.

Tundra's newest venture is the re-introduction of a storybook format, which had been popular before World War II, to combine the beauty of picture books with more complex and longer stories.

Recent titles include *The Ancient Ocean Blues* by Jack Mitchell; *Call Me Mimi* by Francis Chalifour; *Dear Toni* by Cyndi Sand-Eveland; *Don't Eat That!* by Veronika Martenova Charles, illustrated by David Parkins; *Dr. Jekyll and Mr. Hyde* adapted by Alan Grant, illustrated by Cam Kennedy; *The Little Toy Shop* written and illustrated by Frances Wolfe; *One Hundred Shining Candles* by Janet Lunn, illustrated by Lindsay Grater; and *Wolf Man* by Edo Van Belkom.

Douglas Gibson was the first editorial imprint in Canada when it was established in 1986. The list is kept small at 5-10 titles a year, and represents Gibson's eclectic tastes in politics, history, biography, high adventure, and fine fiction.

Recent titles from Douglas Gibson include *The Years of Fire* by Yves Beauchemin; *Magna Cum Laude: How Frank Stronach Became Canada's Best Paid Man* by Wayne Lilley; *The Truth about Canada* by Hel Hurtig; and *Raisin Wine* by James K. Bartleman;

Tundra does not accept unsolicited manuscripts for picture books. Direct queries and SASEs to:

Kathy Lowinger, Publisher—Tundra Books
Douglas Gibson, Publisher—Douglas Gibson Books

MCGILL-QUEEN'S UNIVERSITY PRESS

Montreal office:

McGill University, 3430 McTavish Street, Montreal, QC H3A 1X9, Canada

514-398-3750   fax: 514-398-4333

Kingston office:

Queen's University, Kingston, ON K7L 3N6, Canada

613-533-2155   fax: 613-533-6822

www.mqup.mcgill.ca

McGill-Queen's University Press (MQUP) publishes original scholarly books and well-researched general interest books in all areas of the social sciences and humanities. While their emphasis is on providing an outlet for Canadian authors and scholarship, some of their authors are from outside Canada. More than half of their sales are international.

A joint venture of McGill University in Montreal, Quebec, and Queen's University in Kingston, Ontario, MQUP is both a specialist in the Canadian perspective and a publisher of international themes. A Canadian press with a global reach, the house aims to advance scholarship and contribute to culture by selling books.

Recent titles include *A Woman's Way Through Unknown Labrador* by Mina Benson

Hubbard; *Innovation, Science, Environment: Canadian Policies and Performance, 2008-2009* edited by Glen Toner; *Images of Justice* by Dorothy Harley Eber; *The Art and Science of Stanislaw Lem* edited by Peter Swirski; *The Sum of the Satisfaction: Canada in the Age of National Accounting*; and *Rocke Robertson: surgeon and Shepard of Change* by Richard W. Pound.

Extensive submitting details are on their Web site. In general, they welcome proposals quite early in the development process. Query letters and SASEs should be directed to:

Donald H. Akenson, Senior Editor (Kingston)

Joan Harcourt, Editor (Kingston)

Roger Martin, Editor (Kingston)

Kyle Madden, Deputy Senior Editor (Kingston)

Philip J. Cercone, Executive Director and Senior Editor (Montreal)

John Zucchi, Deputy Senior Editor (Montreal)

Joan McGilvray, Coordinating Editor (Montreal)

Jonathon Crago, Editor (Montreal)

Joanne Pisano, Permissions & Rights Coordinator (Montreal)

MCGRAW-HILL RYERSON LTD.

300 Water Street, Whitby, ON L1N 9B6, Canada

905-430-5116

www.mcgrawhill.ca

One of the 111 McGraw-Hill Companies around the globe, McGraw-Hill Ryerson is staffed and managed by Canadians but reports to its parent company in New York. Though primarily an educational division, McGraw-Hill Ryerson also has a thriving trade arm.

McGraw-Hill Ryerson's trade division publishes and distributes reference books on a wide array of subjects, including business, computing, engineering, science, reference, travel, and self-study foreign language programs. Other areas include outdoor recreation, child care and parenting, health, sports and fitness, and cooking and crafts.

Recent titles include *A Thousand Barrels a Second: The Coming Oil Break Point and the Challenges Facing an Energy Dependent World* by Peter Tertzakian; *My View From the Corner* by Angelo Dundee; *It's Not a Glass Ceiling, It's a Sticky Floor: Free Yourself From the Hidden Behaviors Sabotaging Your Career Success* by Rebecca Shambaugh; and *Influencer: The Power to Change Anything* by Kerry Patterson.

Query letters and SASEs should be directed to:

Lynda Walthert, Assistant to the Publisher

THE MERCURY PRESS

P.O. Box 672, Station P, Toronto, ON M5S 2Y4, Canada

416-531-4338   fax: 416-531-0765

www.themercurypress.ca

The Mercury Press, shortlisted for 1997 Publisher of the Year by the Canadian Booksellers Association, specializes in cutting-edge fiction and poetry, as well as nonfiction and murder mysteries. All titles are Canadian-authored.

The Mercury Press also publishes *Word: Canada's Magazine for Readers + Writers.* *Word* features literary event listings, columns, and reviews, and is a good starting place for learning about this publisher.

Recent Mercury Press titles include *The Closets of Time* edited by Beverly Daurio and Richard Truhlar; *High Hat, Trumpet, and Rhythm: the Life and Music of Valaida Snow* by Mark Miller; *The Humbugs Diet* by Robert Majzels; *Imagination in Action* edited by Carol Malyon; *The Prison Tangram* by Claire Huot; and *Snow Candy* by Terry Carroll.

Direct queries via regular mail with SASEs to:

Beverley A. Daurio, Editor

NEW SOCIETY PUBLISHERS

P.O. Box 189, Gabriola Island, BC V0R 1X0, Canada

250-247-9737   fax: 250-247-7471

www.newsociety.com

New Society Publishers' mission is to publish books that contribute in fundamental ways to building an ecologically sustainable and just society, and to do so with the least possible impact on the environment. Now more than 20 years old, New Society Publishers is an activist publisher focusing mostly on positive, solutions-oriented nonfiction books. New Society is the first North American publisher to announce it has gone carbon-neutral. In recognition of it's environmental program, New Society received the Jim Douglas British Columbia Publisher of the Year Award, 2003.

Recent titles include *Reinventing Collapse* by Dmitry Orlov; *Plan C: Community Survival Strategies for Peak Oil and Climate Change* by Pat Murphy; *Small is Possible: Life in a Local Economy* by Lyle Estill; *Choosing Green: The Home Buyer's Guide to Good Green Homes* by Jerry Yudelson; *How to Build With Grid Beam: A Fast, Easy, and Affordable System for Constructing Almost Anything* by Phil Jergenson, Richard Jergenson, and Wilma Keppel; and *Life, Money and Illusion: Living On Earth As If We Want To Stay* by Mike Nickerson.

New Society has extensive submission tips and guidelines on their Web site. Please send a proposal with SASE to:

Christopher Plant, Co-publisher and Acquisitions Editor

NOVALIS

St. Paul University, 223 Main Street, Ottawa, ON K1S 1C4, Canada

613-236-1393   fax: 613-782-3004

www.novalis.ca

Novalis is a religious publishing house in the Catholic tradition and is a part of Saint Paul University. Novalis publishes and distributes periodicals, books, brochures, and audio-visual resources touching on all aspects of spiritual life, especially from the Christian and Jewish traditions. While the greater part of its production is for the general public, Novalis also publishes more specialized works in the area of theology and religious studies.

Subjects include personal growth, self-help, spirituality and prayer, children's books, gardening, meditation, Church history, and Celtic spirituality, among others. Novalis has equally strong publishing programs in both of Canada's official languages.

Recent titles include *A Cry for Religious Diversity* by Richard Renshaw; *Bioethics Matters: A Guide for Concerned Catholics* by Moria McQueen; *Catholics and Slavery: A Compromising History* by John Perry; *Emerging From the Dark Age Ahead: The Future of the North American Church* by Charles Fensham; and *Feminist Theology With a Canadian Accent* edited by Mary Ann Beavis.

Direct queries and SASEs to:

Michael O'Hearn, Publisher

OOLICHAN BOOKS

P.O. Box 10, Lantzville, BC V0R 2H0, Canada

250-390-4839 / 877-390-4839   fax: 866-299-0026

www.oolichan.com

Oolichan Books is a literary press, publishing poetry, fiction, and nonfiction titles including literary criticism, memoirs, and books on regional history, First Nations, and policy issues. Their name is taken from the small fish, once plentiful in West Coast waters and a staple in the diet of First Nations people to whom it was sacred. The oolichan, often referred to as the candlefish, is believed to possess healing powers and guarantee longevity.

Recent Oolichan titles include *A Song For My Daughter* by Patricia Jean Smith; *A Crack In The Wall* by Betty Jane Hegerat; *Jake, The Baker, Makes A Cake* by P.K. Page, illustrated by Ruth Campbell; *Shirin and Salt Man* by Nilofar Chidmehr; *The House of the Easily Amused* by Shelley A. Leedahl; and *Elf the Eagle* by Ron Smith, Illustrated by Ruth Campbell.

Oolichan Books publishes only Canadian authors. Please send up to ten poems and three chapters of a manuscript along with a cover letter and CV. Note that they will not read a submission that arrives without a proper SASE for its return. You may direct submissions to:

Hiro Boga, Managing Editor

Pat Smith, Consulting Editor

ORCA BOOK PUBLISHERS

P.O. Box 5626, Station B, Victoria, BC V8R 6S4, Canada

800-210-5277 fax: 877-408-1551

www.orcabook.com

Orca Book Publishers focuses on children's books: picture books, and juvenile and young adult fiction. Their limited adult list focuses on general trade nonfiction, including travel and recreational guides, regional history, and biography.

Recent titles include *Art's Supplies* by Chris Tougas; *Emily Carr's Attic* by Diane Leger, illustrated by Michael Leger; *Alphabetter* by Dan Bar-el, illustrated by Graham Ross; *Buttercup's Lovely Day* by Carolyn Beck, illustrated by Andrea Beck; *Jeffrey and Sloth* by Kari-Lynn Winters, illustrated by Ben Hodson; *Feral* by Bev Cooke; and *Gotcha* by Shelley Hrdlitschka.

Their Orca Sports line features sports action combined with mystery/suspense. For ages 10+, Orca Sports seeks strong plots, credible character, simple language, and high-interest chapters. Some Orca Sports books include *Chief Honor* by Sigmund Brouwer; *Crossover* by Jeff Rud; *Dead in the Water* by Robin Stevenson; and *Two Foot Punch* by Anita Daher.

The Orca Currents line seeks intermediate novels with middle-school appropriate story lines for reluctant readers. Titles include *121 Express* by Monique Polak and *Crossboy* by Dayle Campbell Gaetz.

Orca is presently seeking manuscripts written by Canadian authors in the following genres: children's picture books, early chapter books, juvenile fiction, young adult fiction, and graphic novels. They are not seeking seasonal stories, board books, or "I Can Read" books.

While picture books submissions may be sent in their entirety, all other authors should query with sample chapters prior to sending complete manuscript. Please send to the appropriate editor, or check the Web site for further information.

Bob Tyrrell, Publisher and Senior Editor, Teen fiction

Christi Howes, Editor—Children's and picture books

Sarah Harvey, Editor—Young readers and juvenile novels

Melanie Jeffs, Editor—Intermediate novels aimed at reluctant readers

Andrew Woolridge, Associate Publisher and Editor—Teen novels aimed at reluctant readers

PENGUIN GROUP (CANADA)

90 Eglinton Avenue East, Suite 700, Toronto, ON M4P 2Y3, Canada

416-925-2249   fax: 416-925-0068

www.penguin.ca

Penguin Group (Canada)—then called Penguin Books—was founded in 1974. Initially a distribution arm for Penguin International, Penguin Books began publishing indigenous Canadian work in 1982 with such notable titles as Peter C. Newman's landmark history of the Hudson's Bay Company, *Company of Adventurers*, and fiction by Robertson Davies, Timothy Findley, Alice Munro, and Mordecai Richler.

Penguin Group (Canada) is determined to publish books that speak to the broadest reading public and address leading issues of social importance. Penguin's books cover subjects as diverse as Canadian nationalism, homelessness and mental illness, and health care and education.

Recent titles include *Clothes on Their Backs* by Linda Grant; *Counting the Stars* by Helen Dunmore; *My Revolutions* by Hari Kunzru; *Ten Year Nap* by Meg Wolitzer; *A Person of Interest* by Susan Choi; *Invisible Prey* by John Sanford; *Fallen Founder: Life of Aaron Burr* by Nancy Isenberg; and *Pocket Idiot's Guide to Ebay Motors* by Lissa McGrath.

As of November 1, 2005, Penguin Group (Canada) no longer accepts unsolicited manuscripts, and will not enter into correspondence about unpublished work, except with literary agents.

David Davidar, Publisher/President

Diane Turbide, Editorial director

Laura Shin, Editor—Crimes, thrillers, romance

Helen Rees, Senior Editor—General nonfiction

Nicole Winstanley, Executive editor—Children's literature

PLAYWRIGHTS CANADA PRESS

215 Spadina Avenue, Suite 230, Toronto, ON M5T 2C7, Canada

416-703-0013   fax: 416-408-3402

www.playwrightscanada.com

Playwrights Canada Press publishes Canadian plays, theatre criticism, history, biographies, and memoirs, and is the largest exclusive publisher of Canadian drama. It publishes roughly 32 books of plays, theatre history, and criticism every year. This publisher exists to raise the profile of Canadian playwrights and Canadian theatre and theatre practitioners. French plays by Canadian authors are published in translation, and the Press's mandate includes printing plays for young audiences.

Recent titles include *African-Canadian Theatre, Volume Two* edited by Maureen Moynagh; *An Anglophone is Coming to Dinner* by George Rideout; *Bella Donna* by David Copelin; *Birthright* by Constance Lindsay Skinner, adapted by Joan Bryans; *Cold Meat Party* by Brad Fraser; and *The Innocent Eye Test* by Michael Healey.

Query letters and SASEs should be directed to:

Annie Gibson, Publisher

Angela Reberio, Project Coordinator

THE PORCUPINE'S QUILL

68 Main Street, Erin, ON N0B 1T0, Canada

519-833-9158   fax: 519-833-9845

www.sentex.net/~pql/

Since 1974, The Porcupine's Quill has been publishing literary titles, especially novels, short stories, and poetry. Today they publish some 12 books per year.

The Porcupine's Quill is a small publisher with a tradition of publishing first books of poetry; they are proud that many of their writers graduated to large trade houses to publish best sellers.

Recent titles include *Always Now* by Margaret Avison; *The Dodecahedron* by Paul Glennon; and *Zero Gravity* by Sharon English.

The Porcupine's Quill does not accept unsolicited work. Instead, they seek out writers whose work has appeared in literary magazines such as *The New Quarterly*. Direct your query and SASE to:

John Metcalf, Senior Editor

Tim Inkster, Publisher

RAINCOAST BOOKS

9050 Shaughnessy Street, Vancouver, BC V6P 6E5, Canada

604-323-7100   fax: 604-323-2600

www.raincoast.com

Raincoast Books produces a wide range of fiction and nonfiction titles for adults and children; they also publish illustrated lifestyle books aimed at the gift market under the name Blue Heron Books. In total, they publish about 16 books per year and, with rare exceptions, only the work of Canadian authors.

The majority of their books are nonfiction, in the areas of travel writing, popular culture, sports, natural history, current events, biography and memoir, social issues, and history.

Recent titles include *Hit Me With Your Best Shot: The Ultimate Guide to Karaoke Domination* by Raina Lee; *Hall of Best Knowledge* by Ray Fenwick; *Lavinia* by Usula K. Le Gui; *The Suspicions of Mr. WHicher* by Kate Summerscale; *The Aviary Gate* by Katie Hickman; *The Invisible Nation* by Quil Lawerence; *The Hebrew Republic* by Bernard Avishai; and *Blood Matters* by Masha Gessen.

To submit, please send a query letter with a SASE via regular mail to the attention of the Editorial Department. Please allow up a minimum of nine months for a reply.

Allan MacDougall, President

Lynn Henry, Executive Editor

Joy Gugeler, Editorial Director—Fiction

Michelle Benjamin, Associate Publisher

RANDOM HOUSE CANADA

One Toronto Street, Suite 300, Toronto, ON M5C 2V6, Canada

416-364-4449   fax: 416-364-6863

www.randomhouse.ca

Random House of Canada was established in 1944 and in 1986 established its own indigenous Canadian publishing program. As a separate company, Doubleday Canada has been one of Canada's most prominent publishers for more than 40 years. Following the international merger of Random House and Bantam Doubleday in 1998, the two companies officially became one in Canada in 1999, representing sister companies' titles in this country and maintaining thriving Canadian publishing programs.

Under the Doubleday Canada imprint, the company publishes hardcover and trade paperback fiction and nonfiction books by leading Canadian authors, including Pierre Berton, Joy Fielding, Sheree Fitch, Evelyn Lau, Kevin Major, David Adams Richards, Russell Smith, Michael Turner, Jan Wong, and L.R. Wright, as well international authors including Kate Atkinson, Bill Bryson, Diana Gabaldon, and Ruth Rendell.

Under the imprint Seal Books the company is also Canada's preeminent mass market publisher, producing paperbacks by Margaret Atwood, Farley Mowat, Stevie Cameron, William Deverell, and the beloved Lucy Maud Montgomery. Under the imprints Random House Canada, Knopf Canada, Vintage Canada, the company publishes such internationally prominent Canadian writers as Carol Shields, Mordecai Richler, Ann-Marie MacDonald, Wayne Johnston, Alberto Manguel, and Michael Ondaatje as well as distinguished international authors.

Nonfiction areas include popular topical interest and current events, cooking, lifestyle and the arts, history and politics, biography and memoir, travel narrative, popular science, and business and economics. Recent nonfiction titles include *Who's Your City?* by Richard Florida; *A Brief History of Anxiety (Yours and Mine)* by Patricia Pearson; *In the Realm of Hungry Ghosts* by Gabor Mate; *The Sexual Paradox* by Susan Pinker; and *The Automatic Millionaire Homeowner, Canadian Edition* by David Bach.

Recent fiction titles include *Charley's Web* by Joy Fielding; *The Outcast* by Sadie Jones; *The Ravine* by Paul Quarrington; *A Partisan's Daughter* by Louis De Berniere's; and *Barnacle Love* by Anthony De Sa.

The list includes Canadian authors such as Douglas Coupland, Katherine Govier, Paul Quarrington, John MacLachlan Gray, Elyse Friedman, Billie Livingston, and Pulitzer Prize-winner Carol Shields.

Random House Canada does not accept unsolicited manuscripts. Query letters and SASEs should be directed to:

Louise Dennys, Publisher

Stacy Cameron, Editor

Suzanne Brandreth, Editor—Doubleday Canada

Kendall Anderson, Associate Editor

RED DEER PRESS

#1512, 1800 4th Street SW, Calgary, AB T2S 2S5 Canada

403-509-0800   fax: 403.228.6503

www.reddeerpress.com

Red Deer Press is an award-winning publisher of literary fiction, nonfiction, children's illustrated books, juvenile fiction, teen fiction, drama, and poetry. Red Deer Press's mandate is to publish books by, about, or of interest to Canadians, with special emphasis upon the Prairie West.

Red Deer Press publishes 18–20 new books per year, all written or illustrated by Canadians. Approximately 20% of their program is comprised of first–time authors and illustrators.

Recent titles indicative of the list include *Valley of Day-Glo* by Nick DiChario; *Identity Theft and Other Stories* by Robert J. Sawyer; *How To Make A Wave* by Lisa Hurst-Archer; *An Aboriginal Carol* by David Bouchard; *Fireside Al* by Alan Maitland, illustrated by Alan Daniel; *Egghead* by Caroline Pignat; *Dooley Takes the Fall* by Nora McClintock.

Send queries and SASEs to:

Richard Dionne, Publisher

Val Burke-Harland, Associate Publisher

Peter Carver, Children's Editor

RONSDALE PRESS

3350 West 21st Avenue, Vancouver, BC V6S 1G7, Canada

604-738-4688   fax: 604-731-4548

www.ronsdalepress.com

A literary publishing house, Ronsdale Press is dedicated to publishing books from across Canada and books that give Canadians new insights into themselves and their country. Ronsdale publishes fiction, poetry, regional history, biography and autobiography, plays, books of ideas about Canada, and children's books. Ronsdale accepts submissions only from Canadian authors.

Recent titles include *Cascadia: The Elusive Utopia* edited by Douglas Todd; *The Daughter's Path* by Barbara Ruth Bluman; *Hollyburn* by Francis Mansbridge; *The Anachronicles* by George McWhirter; *The Girl in the Backseat* by Norma Charles; *The Old Brown Suitcase* by Lillian Boraks-Nemetz; and *Writing the West Coast: In Love with Place* edited by Christine Lowther and Anita Sinner.

The press looks for thoughtful works that reveal the author has read deeply in contemporary and earlier literature and is working to create a text with innovative combinations of form and content that can bring genuinely new insights. Authors are welcome to send finished manuscripts or queries with samples, along with SASEs.

Peter Carver, Children's Editor

Aritha van Herk, Fiction Editor

Clem Martini, Drama Editor

Norman Ravvin, Jewish Fiction and Nonfiction Editor

SECOND STORY PRESS

20 Maud Street, Suite 401, Toronto, ON M5V 2M5, Canada

416-537-7850   fax: 416-537-0588

www.secondstorypress.ca

The Second Story Press list spans adult fiction and nonfiction, children's fiction, non-fiction and picture books, and young adult fiction and nonfiction. As a feminist press, they look for manuscripts dealing with the many diverse and varied aspects of the lives of girls and women. Some of their special interest areas include Judaica, Ability Issues, Coping with Cancer, and Queer Rights. They publish about 16 new books per year, primarily from Canadian authors.

Recent titles include *Men of Courage from our First Nations* by Vincent Schilling; *The Diary of Laura's Twin* by Kathy Kacer; *Headline: Murder* by April Lindgren; *Fantastic Female Filmmakers* by Suzanne Simoni; *The Songweavers* by Kathleen McDonnell; *Reconcilable Differences* by Cate Cochran; and *Zoe's Extraordinary Holiday Adventures* by Christina Minaki.

Second Story accepts unsolicited manuscripts with SASEs. Direct submissions to:

Margie Wolfe, Publisher

TALON BOOKS LTD.

P.O. Box 2076, Vancouver BC V6B 3S3, Canada

604-444-4889   fax: 604-485-5802

www.talonbooks.com

Talon Books publishes poetry, drama, fiction and nonfiction of the political, social, critical, and ethnographic variety.

Recent titles include *Adrift* by Marcus Youssef; *Benevolence* by Morris Panych; *The Berlin Blues* by Drew Hayden Taylor; *Charles Olson at the Harbor: A Biography* by Ralph Maud; *The Commons* by Stephern Collis; *Homechild* by Joan MacLeaod; *The Invisibility Exhibit* by Sachiko Murakami; *Making Theatre: A Life of Sharon Pollock* by Sherrill Grace; *Noise from the Laundry* by Weyman Chan; and *Sentenced to Light* by Fred Wah.

Submissions of drama, Fiction, ciritcism, history, and cultural studies are welcomed. Poetry, self-help, how-to, children's books, and genre books are not considered. Send submission and SASE to:

Kevin Williams, President

Karl Siegler, Publisher

UNIVERSITY OF ALBERTA PRESS

Ring House 2, University of Alberta, Edmonton, AB T6G 2E1, Canada

780-492-3662   fax: 780-492-0719

www.uap.ualberta.ca

A scholarly house, the University of Alberta Press publishes in the areas of biography, history, language, literature, natural history, regional interest, travel narratives, and reference books. The press seeks to contribute to the intellectual and cultural life of Alberta and Canada by publishing well-edited, research-based knowledge and creative thought that has undergone rigorous peer-review, is of real value to natural constituencies, adheres to quality publication standards, and is supported by diligent marketing efforts.

The University of Alberta Press is looking for original works of significant scholarship that are written for a reasonably wide readership. Canadian works that are analytical in nature are especially welcome, as are works by scholars who wish to interpret Canada, both past and present.

Recent titles include *Illuminating The Alberta Order of Excellence* by Jim Edwards, PC; *The Importance of Being Monogamous—Marriage and Nation Building in Western Canada to 1915* by Sarah Carter; *Lois Hole Speaks: Words That Matter* by Lois Hole; *The Trouble with Lions: A Glasgow Vet in Africa* by Jerry Haigh; *One Step Over the Line: Toward a History of Women in the North American West* edited by Sheila McManus; *Under the Holy Lake: A Memoir of Eastern Bhutan* by Ken Haigh; and *The Algal Bowl: Overfertilization of the World's Freshwaters and Estuaries* by John R. Vallentyne.

Submit queries and SASEs to:

Linda Cameron, Director

Michael Luski, Acquisitions Editor

Peter Midgley, Managing Editor

UNIVERSITY OF BRITISH COLUMBIA PRESS

2029 West Mall, Vancouver, BC V6T 1Z2, Canada

604-822-5959   fax: 604-822-6083

www.ubcpress.ubc.ca

University of British Columbia Press (UBC Press) is the publishing branch of the University of British Columbia. Established in 1971, it is among the largest university presses in Canada. It publishes more than 40 new books annually and have an active backlist of more than 700 titles.

UBC Press is widely acknowledged as one of the foremost publishers of political science, Native studies, and forestry books. Other areas of particular strength are Asian studies, Canadian history, environmental studies, planning, and urban studies. The Press publishes several series: Legal Dimensions, Law and Society, Canada and International Relations, Studies in Canadian Military History, Sexuality Studies, Sustainability and the Environment, Urbanization in Asia, First Nations Languages, Contemporary Chinese Studies, Pioneers of British Columbia, Pacific Rim Archaeology, and the Brenda and David McLean Canadian Studies series.

Recent titles include *Awful Splendor: A Fire History of Canada* by Stephen J. Pyne; *Taking the Air: Ideas and Change in Canada's National Parks* by Paul Kopas; *Nunavut: Rethinking Political Culture* by Ailsa Henderson; *From World Order to Global Disorder: States, Markets, and Dissent* by Dorval Brunelle, translated by Richard Howard; *Indigenous Storywork: Educating the Heart, Mind, Body, and Soul;* and *Negotiating Respsonsiblity: Law Murder, and States of Mind* by Kimberly White.

Query letters and SASEs should be directed to:

Peter Milroy, Director—Special projects, international rights

Jean Wilson, Associate Director, Editorial—BC and Western history, Native studies, Northern studies, sexuality, health, education

Emily Andrew, Senior Editor—Political science, military studies, Canadian history, sociology, film studies, education, women's studies

Randy Schmidt, Editor—Environmental studies, law and society, forestry, geography, planning and urban studies, natural history, sustainability

Melissa Pitts, Acquisitions Editor—Canadian history, sociology, urban studies and planning

UNIVERSITY OF MANITOBA PRESS

301 St. John's College, University of Manitoba, Winnipeg, MB R3T 2M5 Canada
204-474-9495   fax: 204-474-7566

www.umanitoba.ca/uofmpress

Founded in 1967, the University of Manitoba Press publishes innovative and exceptional books of scholarship and serious Canadian nonfiction. Their list includes books on Native studies, Canadian history, women's studies, Icelandic studies, aboriginal languages, film studies, biography, geography, nature, and Canadian literature and culture. They publish five to eight books a year, meaning each book receives the concentrated focus and attention that is often not possible in a larger press.

Recent titles include *The North End: Photographs* by John Paskievich with an introduction by Stephen Osborne; *Magic Weapons: Aboriginal Writers Remaking Community after Residential School* by Sam McKegney; *Imagined Homes: Soviet German Immigrants in Two Cities* by Hans Werner; *Constructing Tomorrow's Federalism: New Perspectives on Canadian Governance* edited by Ian Peach; and *My Parents: Memoirs of New World Icelanders* edited by Birna Bjarnadottir & Finnbogi Gudmundsson.

Queries and SASEs may be submitted to:

David Carr, Director and Editor

UNIVERSITY OF OTTAWA PRESS / LES PRESSES DE L'UNIVERSITÉ D'OTTAWA

542 King Edward, Ottawa, ON K1N 6N5, Canada

613-562-5246   fax: 613-562-5247

www.uopress.uottawa.ca

As Canada's only officially bilingual press, the University of Ottawa Press (UOP) is both uniquely Canadian and unique in Canada. Since 1936, UOP has supported cultural development through the publication of books in both French and English aimed at a general public interested in serious nonfiction.

UOP's editorial team works closely with its authors. Writers are supported in the preparation of their manuscript through peer reviews that help tighten the focus of the work before its final submission. By the time a manuscript is submitted to the Editorial Board to decide if it will be published, it has received a good deal of editorial development and revision.

Recent titles include *Waste Heritage: A Novel* by Irene Baird, edited by Colin Hill; *Hera, or Empathy: a Work of Utopian Fiction* by William Leiss; *Translating Canada* by Luise von Flotow & Reingard M. Nischik; *Rephrasing Heidegger: A Companion to Being and Time* by Reichard Sembera; and *Les Belles Ètrangères: Canadians in Paris* by Jane Koustas

Please direct query and SASE to:

Marie Clausén, Managing Editor

Heather Ritchie, Managing Editor—French titles

Marie-France Watson, Assistant Editor

UNIVERSITY OF TORONTO PRESS

10 Saint Mary Street, Suite 700, Toronto, ON M4Y 2W8, Canada
416-978-2239   fax: 416-978-4738

www.utpress.utoronto.ca

University of Toronto Press is Canada's oldest and largest scholarly publisher, and is among the top 15 university presses in North America in size. It is always on the lookout for strong, innovative, and interesting works of scholarship.

Established in 1901, University of Toronto Press publishes scholarly, reference, and general interest books on Canadian history and literature, medieval studies, and social sciences among other subjects, as well as scholarly journals. Approximately 130 new titles are released each year, and a backlist of more than 1,000 titles is maintained in print.

The house publishes in a range of fields, including history and politics; women's studies; health, family, and society; law and crime; economics; workplace communication; theory/culture; language, literature, semiotics, and drama; medieval studies; Renaissance studies; Erasmus; Italian-language studies; East European studies; classics; and nature. The list includes topical titles in Canadian studies, Native studies, sociology, anthropology, urban studies, modern languages, and music. A complete list of subjects as well as details on creating and submitting a manuscript are available on the University of Toronto Press Web site.

Recent titles include *Queer Inclusions, Continental Divisions: Public Recognition of Sexual Diversity in Canada and the United States* by David Rayside; *Canada's Jews: A People's Journey* by Gerald Tulchinsky; *Culinary Landmarks: A Bibliography of Canadian Cookbooks, 1825-1949* edited by Elizabeth Driver; *Court Government and the Collapse of Accountability in Canada and the United Kingdom* by Donald J. Savole; *Klaeber's Beowulf: Fourth Edition* edited by R.D. Fulk, Robert E. Bjork, and Johnn D. Niles; and *Canadian Content: Culture and the Quest for Nationhood* by Ryan Edwarson.

Query letters and SASEs should be directed to:

Virgil Duff, Executive Editor—Social sciences, scholarly medical books, law and criminology, women's studies

Len Husband, Editor—Canadian history, natural science, philosophy

Stephen Kotowych, Editor—Social Sciences

Richard Ratzoff, Editor—Book history, English literature, modern languages, Victorian studies

Siobhan McMenemy, Editor—Cultural studies, digital futures, film studies

Suzanne Rancourt, Editor—Humanities, rights and translations, classics, medieval and renaissance studies, music, religion, and theology

Ron Schoeffel, Editor—Erasmus studies, Italian studies, literary criticism, religion and theology

VÉHICULE PRESS

P.O.B. 125, Place du Parc Station, Montreal, QC H2X 4A3, Canada

514-844-6073   fax: 514-844-7543

www.vehiculepress.com

For more than 30 years, Véhicule Press has been publishing prize-winning poetry, fiction, social history, Quebec Studies, Jewish studies, jazz history, and restaurant guides.

Signal Editions is the poetry imprint of Véhicule Press. Since 1981, 65 poetry titles have been published, one-third of those by first-time authors. Esplanade Books is the fiction imprint of Véhicule Press. Esplanade publishes novels, novellas, and short story collections—books that fall between the cracks, works of unusual structure and form, and short sharp monologues.

Recent Véhicule Press titles include *The Empire's Missing Links* by Walid Bitar; *In Other Words: New English Writing from Quebec* edited by Claude Lalumiére; *Exploring Old Quebec* by Maude Bonenfant; *36 Cornelian Avenue* by Christopher Wiseman; *Sacred Ground on de la Savane: Montreal's Bron de Hirsch cemetery* by Danny Kucharsky; *Stuart Robertson's Tips on Container Gardening* by Stuart Robertson; and *Chef* by Jaspreet Singh.

For poetry and nonfiction submissions, please query first. For fiction submissions, please include a 25–30-page excerpt. Véhicule mostly publishes Canadian authors.

Simon Dardick, Publisher

Nancy Marrelli, Publisher

Andrew Steinmetz, Editor—Esplanade Books

Carmine Starnino, Editor—Signal Editions

WHITECAP BOOKS

351 Lynn Avenue, North Vancouver, BC V7J 2C4, Canada

604-980-9852   fax: 604-980-8197

www.whitecap.ca

Whitecap Books is one of Canada's largest independent publishers. In addition to the cookbooks, gift books, and coffee table books that it is primarily known for, Whitecap publishes gardening and crafts, photo-scenic, history, arts and entertainment, children's fiction and nonfiction, travel, sports and transportation books.

With a head office in Vancouver, British Columbia, and warehouse operations in Markham, Ontario, the house generates sales across Canada, from coast to coast to coast. In addition to traditional bookstores, Whitecap books can be found in many retail outlets, ranging from museums and clothing stores to gardening centers and cookware suppliers, thus special sales manuscripts might be successfully placed here.

Recent titles include *Cooking with Booze* by Ryan Jennings and David Steele; *Shellfish: The Cookbook* edited by Karen Barnaby; *The Canadian Hiker's & Backpackers Handbook* by Ben Gadd; *Start Fresh! Your Complete Guide to Midlifestyle Food and Fitness* by Diane and Dr. Doug Clement; and *Travel Best Bets* by Claire Newell.

Whitecap is delighted to receive submissions of queries with proposals and sample chapters. Be sure to include SASEs (and international reply coupons) and direct to "Rights and Acquisitions."

Robert McCullough, Publisher

XYZ ÉDITEUR / XYZ PUBLISHING

1781 rue Saint-Hubert, Montréal, QC H2L 3Z1, Canada

514-525-2170   fax: 514-525-7537

www.xyzedit.qc.ca

XYZ éditeur publishes novels, short stories, essays, and books for young adults in French. As XYZ Publishing, XYZ éditeur has also published books in English, including The Quest Library, a series of Canadian biographies for young adults. XYZ was recently acquired by The Dundurn Group.

Considered one of the most distinguished literary publishing houses in Quebec, XYZ éditeur publishes about 40 books per year, eight of them in English. Authors published by XYZ have won the most prestigious literary prizes of Quebec and Canada. More than 30 XYZ titles have been translated into English and other languages, including German, Spanish, Portuguese, Romanian, and Czech.

Recent titles in English include *The Master of Jalna: A Novel* by Mazo de la Boce; *Louis Riel* by Sharon Stewart; titles in French include *L'éte Funambule* by Louise Dupré; *Voyage au Viet Nam avec un Voyou* by Alain Olivier; *La Peau des Doigts* by Katia Belkhodja; *et Ravaler* by Martyne Rondeau.

XYZ Publishing does not publish genre literature (detective stories, science fiction, horror, fantasy, etc.). Please send a query with sample chapters and SASE to:

André Vanasse, Vice President and Publisher (French)

Rhonda Bailey, Publisher (English)

SECTION FIVE

LITERARY AGENTS

WHAT MAKES THIS AGENT DIRECTORY SPECIAL?

JEFF HERMAN

There are many books and Web sites that include lists of literary agents, but this directory is truly extraordinary because we go way beyond providing names, addresses and basic statistics. We have offered the agents included here the chance to "talk" about themselves, both professionally and personally, and to share their insights about all aspects of the publishing business. You will not only know who represents what and how to solicit them, but you will also get a sense about many of them as human beings and as potential business partners.

I am frequently asked why certain agents are not listed. I wish to be clear that literally dozens of excellent agents are not listed here, though I would like them to be. Each year I invite the 200-plus members of the Association of Author Representatives (AAR), as well as many excellent nonmember agents, to be in this book. However, just because an agent is not here does not mean that that agent is not qualified to be. The truth is that many agents are already saturated with as many clients as they can handle, or want to handle. They are not eager to invite unsolicited submissions from the general public, because their existing rosters and a few trusted referrals are more than they want to handle. Most agencies are small "mom and pop" businesses that are not inclined to take on a lot of staff and overhead. Their business model is to maximize revenues by limiting expenses and administrative tasks. Yet many qualified agents happily accept my invitation to be listed because they want to hear from as many fresh prospects as possible. If an agent does not explicitly confirm that he or she wants to be in this book, then that agent is not included here.

Each year many "false agents" endeavor to be included, and we do our best to keep them out. A false agent is anyone who masquerades as an agent for the sole purpose of stealing money from writers through various acts of clever deception. Letting such people into this book would be tantamount to inviting Col. Sanders into a hen house. With regret, I must concede instances in the past where I have been deceived by some of these deceivers. The consequences for these errors were predictable; I would receive numerous complaints from writers who came close to getting snagged by these hoodlums. Fortunately, most of the writers smelled the odor before it was too late; but sometimes I would hear from writers who didn't know what hit them until they were already pinched for a few bucks.

The bottom line is that my staff and I exercise due diligence about who gets listed. Nevertheless, some charlatans may manage to slip through our filters. Like hybrid software viruses, some of these serial grifters have the chutzpah to simply change their names and addresses as soon as word gets out about their scams. I am largely dependent upon you, the writers, to immediately let me know about any wrongful experiences you might have with any of the agencies in this book. That is how I can keep them out of future editions and help sound the alarm elsewhere, as can you. Please see the essay section for more information about this issue. Of course, do no shoot venom only because someone has rejected or disrespected you.

I am not trying to spread fear and paranoia. These unfortunate situations are very much the exception, not the rule. Any agent who has a bona fide list of sales to recognized publishers is legitimate.

AEI/ATCHITY ENTERTAINMENT INTERNATIONAL, INC (BOOK/FILM)

518 S. Fairfax Ave., Los Angeles CA 90036

Agent's name: Dr. Kenneth Atchity

Born: Eunice, Louisiana.

Education: B.A., Georgetown; M.Phil., Theater History—Ph.D., Comparative Literature, Yale.

Career history: Professor of comparative literature (classics, medieval, Renaissance creative writing), Occidental College (1970-1987); Instructor, UCLA Writer's Program (1970-1987). Author of 14 books, including *How to Escape Lifetime Security to Pursue Your Impossible Dream: A Guide to Transforming Your Career* (Helios); *How to Publish Your Novel* (SquareOne Books); *A Writer's Time: A Guide to the Creative Process, from Vision Through Revision* (Norton); and *Writing Treatments That Sell* (with Chi-Li Wong; Owl Books). Producer of 22 films, including *The Madam's Family: The Truth about Canal Street Brothel* (Ellen Burstyn, Annabella Sciorra, Dominique Swain) for CBS; *Life or Something Like It* (Angelina Jolie, Ed Burns) for 20th Century Fox, *Joe Somebody* (Tim Allen, Jim Belushi, Julie Bowen) for 20th Century Fox, *Champagne for Two* (Cinemax-HBO), *Amityville: The Evil Escapes* (NBC) *Shadow of Obsession* (NBC), and *Falling Over Backwards*. Sold *Ripley's Believe-It-Or-Not!* franchise to Paramount Pictures, AEI to produce with Alphaville (*The Mummy*) and Richard Zanuck (*Jaws*), script by Scott Alexander and Larry Karazewski (*The People vs. Larry Flynt*), Tim Burton directing, Jim Carrey starring; Steve Alten's *Meg* to New Line, script by Shane Salerno (*Shaft, Armaggedon*), directing Jan de Bont, AEI producing with Larry Gordon Productions (*Lara Croft*), Guillermo del Toro (*Hellboy*) and Nick Nunziata; John Scott Shepherd's *Henry's List of Wrongs* to New Line, script by Harley Peyton (*Less Than Zero, Moon Over Miami*), Marc Waters to direct, AEI producing with Zide-Perry Films (*American Pie, Final Destination*); Royce Buckingham's *Demon Keeper* to Fox 2000, etc.

Hobbies/personal interests: Collecting autographed editions, pitchers; tennis; travel.

Categories/subjects that you are most enthusiastic about agenting: We are focused on storytellers with bestselling potential in both New York publishing and Hollywood films. Basically don't send us material that doesn't have potential both as a book and as a television or film project. We love comedy; male action; Young adult—with strong narrative line, and not Harry Potter lookalike celebrity or "branded" books biography or otherwise; comic books, and films that can be franchises; personal achievement by nationally-known names. Nonfiction with national impact and national platform; business nonfiction by distinguished business leaders with built-in corporate tie-ins potential; female novel authors with fresh contemporary voice and/or film potential; visionary; heroic and true stories of every kind, including true crime; general interest and/or narrative nonfiction, especially true stories with TV or film potential;

celebrity biographies. Aside from that, we're dying to discover (a) the next Michael Chabon and/or (b) the next mainstream Hispanic American, Asian American, or African American novelist. The key is combining a major platform with a major message for the general public. Screenplays: All motion picture, as well as specific television movie, categories. Especially comedy (both broad comedy and romantic comedy); action franchise; adaptations of classics to modern times; new-angle horror; heroic true stories (past or present); families in crisis; serious drama for top stars, female-driven heroic stories.

What you don't want to agent: Drug-related, religious, category romance, small niche subjects, category mystery or Western, poetry, "interior" confessional fiction; novelty books.

If you were not an agent, what might you be doing instead: If I weren't a literary manager, writer, and producer, I'd be doing the same thing and calling it something else. A story merchant: finding, perfecting, selling and producing stories by serious storytellers determined to become globally known for their art and craft.

What's the best way for writers to solicit your interest: Query letter, including synopsis (with SASE). Please Note: All submissions to Jennifer Pope.

Do you charge reading or management fees: NO.

Can you provide an approximation by % of what you tend to represent by category: Fiction: 30%, nonfiction 40%, screenplays 30%.

How would you describe the client from Hell: He or she is so self-impressed it's impossible to provide constructive criticism; makes his package impossible to open, provides return envelope too small to be used, and tells us how to run our business.

How would you describe the perfect client: He or she comes in with an outstanding action or high-concept fiction or nonfiction book, plus an outline for two more, is delighted to take commercial direction on the writing and the career, markets his or her book relentlessly. The higher the concept the better.

How and why did you ever become an agent: Nearly two decades of teaching comparative literature and creative writing at Occidental College and the UCLA Writers Program, reviewing for the Los Angeles Times Book Review, and working with the dreams of creative people through DreamWorks (which I co-founded with Marsha Kinder) provided a natural foundation for this career. I made the transition from academic life through producing, but continued my publishing-consulting business by connecting my authors with agents. As I spent more and more time developing individuals' writing careers, as well as working directly with publishers in my search for film properties, it became obvious that literary management was the next step. True or fiction, what has always turned me on is a good story.

What do you think the future holds for writers, publishers, and agents: Nothing but continued growth and excitement as the distribution channels continue to evolve rapidly: all that remains the same is the insatiable need for stories and information.

MIRIAM ALTSHULER LITERARY AGENCY

53 Old Post Road North, Red Hook, NY 12571

845-758-9408   fax: 845-758-3118

www.miriamaltshulerliteraryagency.com   e-mail: miriam@maliterary.com

Agent's name: Miriam Altshuler
Born: New York, New York.
Education: Middlebury College.
Career history: Agent for 12 years at Russell and Volkening, Inc.; Started my own agency in 1994.
Hobbies/personal interests: Reading, skiing, horseback riding, the outdoors, my children.
Categories/subjects that you are most enthusiastic about agenting: Literary/commercial fiction and non-fiction, narrative non-fiction, memoirs, young adult novels. See my Web site: www.miriamaltshulerliteraryagency.com for further guidelines.
What you don't want to agent: Genre fiction, how-to, romance. See my Web site: www.miriamaltshulerliteraryagency.com for further guidelines.
Do you charge reading or management fees: No reading fees.
How and why did you ever become an agent: I love reading books and love working with people.

ARCADIA

31 Lake Place North, Danbury, CT 06810

203-797-0993

Web site under construction

Agent's name: Victoria Gould Pryor, pryor@arcadialit.com
Born: New York City.
Education: B.A. Pembroke College/Brown University (Modern Literature/History); M.A. NYU (Modern Literature).
Career story: My first job after college was at the John Cushman Agency. Moved to the Sterling Lord Agency and became hooked on agenting. At the Harold Matson Agency I began representing authors and then helped found Literistic, Ltd. Arcadia was launched in 1986.
Hobbies and special personal interests: Science, medicine, classical music and choral singing, gardening, current/foreign affairs, reading, art, woodworking.

Subjects and categories you like to agent: Nonfiction: Science/medicine, current affairs/popular culture, history, psychology, true crime, true business, investigative journalism, women's issues, biography, classical music, memoir, literary fiction.

Subjects and categories writers shouldn't bother pitching to you: Children's/YA, science fiction/fantasy, horror, humor, chick lit, technothrillers, picture books, memoirs about overcoming addiction or abuse.

What might you be doing if you weren't agenting: I'd be an unhappy and reasonably solvent doctor or lawyer, a content and struggling woodworker or landscape architect, or if I had a much better voice, an ecstatic and prosperous Wagnerian opera singer.

What's the most effective ways for writers to grab your attention: For fiction: a concise query letter with brief sample material (the novel's opening paragraphs, pages or chapters) and a SASE. In a query letter, I'm more drawn to a novel's description and themes, as opposed to a detailed plot synopsis. For non-fiction: a detailed query letter and SASE. It's fine to send a proposal with the letter, but please take the time to analyze what comparable books are already on the market and how your proposed book fills a niche. It's disheartening when a non-fiction author says "my book is totally unique" and then a quick check of Amazon reveals hundreds of books in that area. It's understood that each book is unique, but authors need to research the market and have a basic understanding of the book business (which you can get by reading some of the articles in this book) before approaching agents. E-mail queries without attachments are fine. If your subject and query letter are enticing, I'll ask you to send the file—either proposal or manuscript—as an attachment.

Do you charge fees separate from your commission, or offer non-agenting fee based services: No.

What are representative titles you have sold to publishers: *Listening Now* by Anjana Appachana (Random House); *State of the Unions: How Labor Can Revitalize Itself, Seize the National Debate on Values and Help Win Elections* by Philip Dine (McGraw-Hill); *Every Living Thing: Man's Obsessive Quest to Catalog Life, From Nanobacteria to New Monkeys* by Rob Dunn (Smithsonian Books); *When Sex Goes to School: Warring Views on Sex Since the Sixties* by Kristin Luker (Norton); *Salsa Dancing into the Social Sciences* by Kristin Luker (Harvard University Press); *Talking to the Enemy* by Avner Mandelman (Seven Stories Press); *Sleuth Investor* by Avner Mandelman (Mcgraw-Hill); *The ESP Enigma: The Scientific Case for Psychic Phenomena* by Diane Powell (Walker); *Love, Medicine and Miracles; Peace, Love and Healing; How to Live Between Office Visits* and *Prescriptions for Living* by Dr. Bernie Siegel (HarperCollins); *Help Me to Heal* by Dr. Bernie Siegel (Hay House); *Unstuck: A Supportive and Practical Guide to Working Through Writer's Block* by Jane Anne Staw (St. Martin's); *When the Air Hits Your Brain: Tales Of Neurosurgery* by Frank T. Vertosick, Jr. (Norton); *Why We Hurt: The Natural History of Pain*, and *The Genius Within: Discovering the Intelligence of Every Living Thing* by Frank T. Vertosick, Jr. (Harcourt); *Planet Earth* and *The Next One Hundred Years* by Jonathan Weiner (Bantam); *The Beak of the Finch* and *Time, Love, Memory* by Jonathan Weiner (Knopf).

Why did you become an agent, and how did you become one: The luck of the draw; I stumbled into the perfect (for me) field, combining a love of reading, people and business with a smattering of law and social work thrown in on the side.

How do you feel about writers: They're the most fascinating, delightful, talented, hard-working people I know, and life would be very dull without them.

What do you tell entities from other planets and dimensions about your job: It's a combination of industrial-strength reader, talent scout, business manager/career planner/ matchmaker, developmental editor, midwife to creativity and supporter of **professional dreams.**

What are your favorite books, movies, TV shows, and why: There are far too many favorites, even not including my own clients' work, to list. I admire nonfiction that helps us understand and/or changes the way we look at the world past and present (*History of the Jews, Embracing Defeat, And the Band Played On, What's the Matter with Kansas, Temperament*), illuminates areas of science (*Our Kind, How We Die, Love's Executioner, The Man Who Mistook His Wife for a Hat, Anatomy of Love*), introduces us to people who lived fascinating lives (*Nora*), quirky and compelling narratives (*Year of Reading Proust, A Heartbreaking Work of Staggering Genius*). Novels by Melville, Faulkner, Greene, Roth, Le Carre and Turow. *The Tin Drum, Love in The Time of Cholera, Ragtime, Life of Pi, Atonement,* etc., and I'm a sucker for literate, character-driven thrillers. This summer's vacation reading is fiction by Joe Kanon and non-fiction by Thomas Cahill. Movies and TV: That's for another year…

How would you describe "the writer from hell": The writer from hell delivers late or not at all, is not respectful of an agent's or editor's time, telephones to deliver complex information that should be put in writing. He/she is unable to hear or apply whatever information or advice is offered, and assumes that business ground rules be set aside for his/her work. Fortunately I don't represent anyone who resembles this.

How would you describe the publisher and/or editor from hell: Non-responsive (or very slow to respond); less than flexible and supportive.

What do you like best about your clients, and the editors and publishers you work with: At its best, the book business is about being part of a team with talented, dedicated and valiant professionals. We start with the strongest book possible and then add the publisher's expertise and support; the outcome is gratifying and sometimes even magical.

Will our business exist as we know it in 10 years or so from now: The trappings will be different but the core will still be the development and spreading of ideas. Creativity and the imagination will not have changed, and will still need nurturing.

ARTISTS AND ARTISANS, INC.

244 Madison Avenue, Suite 334, New York, NY 10016

212-924-9619   fax: 212-931-8377

www.artistsandartisans.com

Agents' names: Adam Chromy; Michelle Wolfson; Jamie Brenner, Jamie@artistsandartisans.com.

The following information pertains to Jamie Brenner.

Born: Philadelphia, Pennsylvania, 1974.

Education: The George Washington University, B.A. English.

Career story: Started in publishing as a publicity assistant at HarperCollins. I worked on books by super talented writers like Barbara Kingsolver, Louise Erdrich, and Erica Jong. Then a former colleague lured me over to Barnes & Noble—the company was just launching their online store to compete with Amazon. I worked there as an editor/buyer for a few years. During this time, a film industry connection got me a freelance job reading manuscripts for Miramax films, and I eventually became a book scout for a film production company. In 2007 I started at Artists and Artisans as a literary agent.

Hobbies and special personal interests: I'm very into pop culture, music, film. I'm fascinated by ballet. I'm interested in politics though I try not to be because there's so much disappointment.

Subjects and categories you like to agent: Women's fiction, especially novels straddling the line between commercial and literary fiction. I like horror novels that have a strong psychological element. I am always looking for memoir. I like political thrillers and literary mysteries.

Subjects and categories writers shouldn't bother pitching to you: Children's books, fantasy, science fiction, sports, spirituality.

What might you be doing if you weren't agenting: I don't know—but it would be something with books.

What's the most effective ways for writers to grab your attention: A simple email query that gives me a clear pitch for the book and an idea who the writer is.

Do you charge fees separate from your commission, or offer non-agenting fee based services: I never charge separate fees, nor do I offer fee-based services.

What are representative titles you have sold to publishers: *Insatiable, A Memoir* by Erica Rivera (Berkeley); *Liver Let Die* by Annelise Ryan (Kensington).

Why did you become an agent, and how did you become one: When I was scouting books for a film company, I routinely met with agents to hear about the books they had coming down the pike. One of these was my current colleague, Adam Chromy. It was his idea that I try agenting. Needless to say, he was very persuasive. And it was one of the best decisions I ever made.

How do you feel about writers: Writers are the people who helped shaped me. It is their words, stories, pain, insight, that have influenced the way I see the world and even brought the world to me when I was just a suburban girl. To me, they are the most important artists.

What do you tell entities from other planets and dimensions about your job: I never talk to entities from other planets about my job. Like Europeans, they think we discuss work too much.

What are your favorite books, movies, TV shows, and why: Favorite books—I could go on forever. I've read almost every Nelson DeMille book. I loved Cathi Hanauer's *Sweet Ruin*. I'm a big fan of Dani Shapiro's *Black and White* and *Slow Motion*. For family sagas, I love Susan Howatch's *The Wheel of Fortune*. Favorite in horror is Bentley Little's *The Mailman*. I have to stop now! Favorite films: *25th Hour*, *Pulp Fiction*, *Roger Dodger*, *A Walk on the Moon*, *About Last Night*, *High Art*.

How would you describe "the writer from hell": One who doesn't take the time to understand that this is a business.

How would you describe the publisher and/or editor from hell: One who could just as easily be buying/selling widgets.

What do you like best about your clients, and the editors and publishers you work with: At the end of the day, we share a passion.

The following information pertains to Adam Chomry.

Education: New York University Stern School of Business, B.S., 1992.

Career history: After a brief stint at a renowned literary agency, Adam Chomry went out on his own to represent a novel written by a close friend. The gamble paid off and the book was sold on a preemptive offer. Since that auspicious start in 2002, Adam's fresh, rule-breaking approach has led to dozens of book deals at major publishing houses, a national and New York Times Bestseller, and a number of film deals for his clients' projects.

Categories/subjects that you are most enthusiastic about agenting: I am still signing authors of fiction and narrative nonfiction as long as the writing is exceptional and the authors have something truly unique to say. He is also interested in practical nonfiction from authors with strong platforms and/or a point of view that challenges the status quo.

What you don't want to agent: Screenplays, photo or children's books.

What's the best way for writers to solicit your interest: Read and follow the submission guidelines on my Web site—www.artistsandartisans.com.

What are the most common mistakes writers make when pitching you: Pitching halfbaked ideas or projects is a turnoff.

Do you charge reading or management fees: No.

Can you provide an approximation by % of what you tend to represent by category: I spend half my time on fiction and non-fiction but because fiction is a tougher sell we end up with a list comprised of slightly more nonfiction.

How would you describe the client from Hell: I do not have any (at least not for long).

How would you describe the perfect client: They understand that being a professional author is 50% writing and 50% marketing and they energetically and enthusiastically pursue both.

What, if anything, can a writer do to increase the odds that you will become his or her agent: The author should do everything possible to make sure their book is of the highest quality AND make sure they understand their book's market and how to reach it. If they make this clear in a query, then it is hard to pass up.

How would you describe to someone (or thing) from another planet what it is that you do as an agent: I wouldn't waste time telling someone from another planet what I do, I would be trying to sign them for their memoir.

What do you think the future holds for writers, publishers, and agents: I like to remind my authors about the railroad companies of the last century and how they went out of business because they thought of themselves as "railroad companies" and not "transportation companies." So we don't just focus on author's books, we focus on the value of their stories and messages as intellectual property and plan ahead for delivering that IP through books, websites, TV, film or anything else that comes along.

On a personal level, what do you think people like about you and dislike about you: I think I get both reactions because I am a straight shooter.

Please list representative titles you have sold: *The Hookup Handbook*, (Simon Spotlight; film setup at Weinstein Bros.); *Pomegranate Soup* (Random House, international bestseller); *Jewtopia* (Warner, based on the hit off-broadway play); *World Made by Hand* and the sequel to the bestseller *The Long Emergency*, (Grove/Atlantic); additional titles on my Web site.

This information pertains to Michelle Wolfson.

Education: Dartmouth College, B.A. 1995; NYU Stern School of Business M.B.A. 2001.

Career history: After working outside of publishing for several years, first in non-profit and then finance, I made a switch to agenting. I worked for two years at Ralph M. Vicinanza, Ltd. and then joined Artists and Artisans Inc. in March 2006.

Categories/subjects that you are most enthusiastic about agenting: Mainstream and women's fiction, mysteries and thrillers; practical and narrative non-fiction, particularly of interest to women; humorous non-fiction.

What you don't want to agent: Screenplays, children's, science fiction, or horror.

What's the best way for writers to solicit your interest: e-mail query

Do you charge reading or management fees: No.

What are the most common mistakes writers make when pitching you: Apologizing for their ideas/presentation. If you don't love it, why would I?

How would you describe the perfect client: They understand that I want the same things for them that they want for themselves and we work together as a team to achieve success.

How and why did you ever become an agent: It's never the same on any two days but it's all directed towards books and reading, which I love.

What, if anything, can a writer do to increase the odds of you becoming his or

her agent: Make your project as good as you possibly can without me, then work hard on your query letter so that it grabs my attention.

On a personal level, what do you think people like about you and dislike about you: I'm straightforward and honest, yet tactful.

Please list representative titles you have sold: *Embracing Your Big Fat Ass* by Laura Banks and Janette Barber, the bestselling authors of *Breaking The Rules*, (Atria); *Who's Your Birth Order Love Match* (Marlowe And Company); *A Guide to Compatibility in Relationships from a Birth Order Perspective* by William Cane (The bestselling author of *The Art Of Kissing*); *Love Lessons from Arranged Marriages: Seven Surprising Secrets that Will Improve Your Relationship* by Reva Seth (Touchstone Fireside).

THE AUGUST AGENCY, LLC

www.augustagency.com

Agents' names: Cricket Freeman, Jeffery McGraw

Career story: Cricket Freeman, co-founder and agent: After years as a business owner engaged in sales and marketing, Cricket redirected her creativity toward the writing business, freelancing for magazines (more adventure than money) and business clients (more money than adventure). For a time she even slaved daily as the editor-in-chief of a national full-color glossy. In 1991, Cricket intertwined her art education, business experience, and writing skills to establish Possibilities Press to support small book publishers with writing, editing, design, and production services. Ever the entrepreneur, a decade later she shifted her focus exclusively to literary representation and founded The Christina Pechstein Agency. In 2004 she saw another fine opportunity to expand her business and her horizons and joined forces with Jeffery McGraw to launch The August Agency, where she operates from its headquarters in Florida.

Jeffery McGraw, co-founder and agent: Jeffery directs the New York operations of The August Agency LLC. He brings to the company a wide range of experience in publishing and television, with a concentrated background in editorial, legal, publicity, and content sales. He has worked for magazine and book publishers large and small, including *Soap Opera Weekly* as contributing reporter, HarperCollins as editor, Harry N. Abrams as publicity manager, and Leisure Publishing as magazine columnist. Throughout his career he has had the privilege to work with many different types of books—from exquisite art and illustrated coffee table tomes to *New York Times* bestselling fiction and nonfiction—and an equally diverse roster of remarkable authors and artists—among them Nancy Bartholomew, Elizabeth Berg, Cathy East Dubowski, Patricia Gaffney, Olivia Goldsmith, Andy Goldsworthy, Al Hirschfeld, Mary-Kate and Ashley Olsen, Bill O'Reilly, Joanne Pence, Betty Rollin, Ben Schonzeit, and Hunt Slonem.

Our company mind-set: Of any national literature, "the Augustan age" is considered the period of its highest state of excellence and refinement. The expression originated with the reign of the emperor Augustus, who fostered the golden age of Roman literature. Since then, the name has been ascribed to subsequent eras of great prosperity in artistic writing. The August Agency is founded on many of the same principles Augustus set in place to facilitate a stimulating venue where distinguished writers could flourish. More than just another literary and media management company in the business of selling creative projects, we approach the industry with a fresh point of view and innovative strategies that set us apart from other agencies. We firmly believe an agent is, among other things, an author's ultimate advocate, anchor, arbitrator, and advisor. At the August Agency, we not only embrace our authors' works but also the writers themselves and their careers.

What writers can expect from the August Agency: With our rich background of experience, we have developed a unique approach to the publishing industry that seems to work well for us and for our authors. Our fundamental belief is that we are all in this together. Neither of us is the employer, nor the employee, and we don't treat each other that way. Instead, we prefer to think of both parties as business partners in a mutually thrilling venture. The August Agency is a nurturing place where we all learn from each other, sell a lot of books, and have fun along the way. Our primary commitment as agents is taking care of our authors, helping to get their proposals in the best shape possible, and effectively marketing their work to publishing houses and beyond. We encourage our authors to follow our lead: Be a team player, meet deadlines, honor contracts, and, no matter how anxious they are about their work, try to have reasonable expectations. While we cannot promise publication for every writer's project, we can guarantee that their work will be put in front of the right people at the right time with the right degree of passion and enthusiasm behind it.

Subjects and categories you like to agent: The August Agency accepts electronic queries exclusively. We actively pursue a diverse array of writers to represent, with an emphasis in the following areas: Media/current events (seasoned journalists receive special favor here), popular culture, arts, and entertainment, political science, self-help, health, and spirituality, lifestyle, family, and home (including cookbooks, diet, and fitness), science, social sciences, criminology and investigation, history, economics, business and technology, biographies and memoirs, creative narrative nonfiction. In particular, we favor persuasive and prescriptive works, each with a full-bodied narrative command and an undeniable contemporary relevance.

Subjects and categories writers shouldn't bother pitching to you: At this time, we are not accepting submissions in the following areas: Self-published works, screen plays, children's books, cozy mysteries, genre romance, horror, poetry, science fiction, fantasy, short story collections, westerns, projects by blowhards, bigots, braggarts, bitches, and bastards!

What's the most effective ways for writers to grab your attention: To submit, please visit www.augustagency.com for complete details of and any updates to our submission guidelines, which currently include sending an email to submissions@augustagency.com containing the following: 1) The word "query" in the subject line, 2) A detailed summary of your book (one to two paragraphs only), 3) A chapter outline (for nonfiction only), 4) A brief paragraph explaining who you are and why you have chosen to write this particular book, 5) MOST IMPORTANT: The first 1,000 words or first chapter (note: this must be pasted within the body of your email; all emails with unsolicited attachments or lack of this writing sample within the body of the email may be deleted without being read), 6) The total page or word count of your completed manuscript, 7) Your full contact information (including telephone and email address).

If you want to be an ordinary writer, write an ordinary book. But if you want to be an extraordinary author, be prepared to go the extra mile. Our staff is made up of highly selective, seasoned publishing professionals who will give serious consideration to original, creative, and quality manuscripts from extraordinary authors.

Due to the volume of submissions we receive, we are unable to respond to all incoming e-mail. However, please note that every query is read and thoroughly reviewed by our staff. If we are interested in your project, you should receive a response to your e-mail within two to three weeks. At that time you will receive further instructions on how to submit a full-length copy of your proposal. We appreciate the opportunity to review your work and look forward to hearing from you.

Do you charge fees separate from your commission, or offer non-agenting fee based services: We do not charge a reading fee. The August Agency retains a commission of fifteen percent (15%) of all domestic sales and twenty percent (20%) of all foreign, film, dramatic, merchandising, and other sales.

BARER LITERARY, LLC

270 Lafayette Street, Suite 1504, New York, NY 10023

212-6913513   fax: 212-691-3540

Agent's name: Julie Barer
Born: New York, New York.
Education: Vassar College.
Career story: After working for six years at the prestigious New York literary agency Sanford J. Greenburger Associates, I left to start my own agency, Barer Literary, in December 2004. I represent a wide range of fiction writers who publish across the literary spectrum, and I am especially attracted to voice-driven projects that feel original and fresh. My list is extremely selective and I am interested in developing long term relationships with my clients. I attended the Jerusalem Book Fair as an Agent Fellow in 2003 and I am a member of the Association of Authors' Representatives. Before becoming an agent, I worked at Shakespeare & Co. Booksellers in New York City.

Subjects and categories you like to agent: Literary fiction, historical fiction, women's fiction, international fiction and nonfiction, narrative nonfiction, history, biography, memoir, travel.

Subjects and categories writers shouldn't bother pitching to you: Barer Literary does NOT handle the following: Health and fitness; business, investing, or finance; sports; mind, body, and spirit; reference; thrillers or suspense; military; romance; children's books, picture books, or young adult book; screenplays.

What might you be doing if you weren't agenting: As old fashioned as it sounds, if I wasn't an agent, I'd love to own a bookstore.

What's the most effective ways for writers to grab your attention: Do your research and make sure that our agency represents the kind of book you've written. Then send a well written and professional query letter with a self addressed stamped envelope.

Do you charge fees separate from your commission, or offer non-agenting fee based services: No.

What are representative titles you have sold to publishers: *Then We Came to the End* by Joshua Ferris (Little, Brown & Co.); *Still Life With Husband* by Lauren Fox

(Alfred A. Knopf); *What You Have Left* by Will Allison (Free Press); *Finding Nouf* by Zoe Ferraris (Houghton Mifflin); *People I Wanted to Be: Stories* by Gina Ochsner (Houghton Mifflin).

Why did you become an agent, and how did you become one: I became an agent first and foremost because I love to read, and I love the moment of discovering a wonderful novel or story that no one else has read yet, and being the person who helps bring that book out into the world. I also love being able to work closely with writers, and help shape their work, as well as their careers. Being an agent allows me to be involved with so many aspects of a book's life—from editing and placing a book with the right publisher to helping conceptualize cover art and promotion and beyond.

MEREDITH BERNSTEIN LITERARY AGENCY

2095 Broadway, Suite 505, New York, NY 10023

212-799-1007   fax: 212-799-1145

Agent's name: Meredith Bernstein
Born: Hartford, Connecticut.
Education: B.A., University of Rochester.
Career history: Story editor to film producers; literary agent.
Hobbies/personal interests: Reading, of course; travel; film; art; theater; ballet; fashion; contemporary art/craft; jewelry; meeting new people.
Categories/subjects that you are most enthusiastic about agenting: Almost anything wherein I can learn something new.
What you don't want to agent: Military history.
If you were not an agent, what might you be doing instead: Curating a craft museum; owning a store like Julie on Madison Avenue.

DANIEL BIAL AGENCY

41 W. 83rd St., Suite 5C, New York, NY 10024

212-721-1786

e-mail: dbialagency@msn.com

Agent's name: Daniel Bial
Education: B.A., Trinity College, English.
Career history: Editor for 15 years, including 10 years at HarperCollins. Founded agency in 1992.

Hobbies/personal interests: Travel, cooking, music, parenting.

Categories/subjects that you are most enthusiastic about agenting: Non-Fiction: Biography, business, cooking, current events, history, how-to, humor, Judaica, language, narrative nonfiction, popular culture, popular reference, popular science, psychology, sports, travel. Fiction: Quality fiction.

What you don't want to agent: Non-Fiction: Academic treatises, crafts, gift books. Fiction: Children's books, genre fiction, poetry, novels by first-time authors with no publishing credits.

If you were not an agent, what might you be doing instead: Writer, book doctor, or maybe a freelance celebrity advisor.

What's the best way for writers to solicit your interest: E-mail (about one page long with no attachments) or query letter with SASE.

What are the most common mistakes writers make when pitching you: A surprising number of writers devote time in their query letter to telling me about their shortcomings or previous failures. They essentially reject themselves.

Do you charge reading or management fees: No.

Can you provide an approximation by % of what you tend to represent by category: Non-Fiction: 95%, Fiction: 5%.

How would you describe the perfect client: Perfect clients produce trim, tight, ready-to-sell material. They know the business and how to get ahead. They recognize the importance of marketing and know that good intentions don't sell books, hard work does. They take pride in their work and their relationships.

How and why did you ever become an agent: I love books, good writing, interesting ideas, and love being part of the fascinating industry that makes it all happen.

What do you think the future holds for writers, publishers, and agents: Ever since the advent of the computer age, publishers have gotten smarter, and so have most agents and many writers. The old belief that quality sells itself has been proved wrong, and replaced with a more practical knowledge of what sells. As a result, publishers are selling more copies, and there are more blockbuster authors than ever before. Publishing has long been threatened by many other entertainment options (movies, games, etc.), and illiteracy remains a problem for the nation as a whole. But despite the occasional doom and gloom prediction, the overall business is chugging along quite well.

BLEECKER STREET ASSOCIATES, INC.

532 LaGuardia Place, #617, New York, NY 10012

212-677-4492   fax: 212-388-0001

Agent's name: Agnes Birnbaum
Born: Budapest, Hungary.
Career history: 16 years as editor before starting agency in 1984; senior editor at

Pocket, NAL; editor-in-chief of Award Books, later a division of Berkley.

Categories/subjects that you are most enthusiastic about agenting: History, biography, science, investigative reporting, true crime, health, psychology, true adventure, women's issues, also mystery/suspense, women's fiction.

What you don't want to agent: Poetry, science fiction, western, children's, film/TV scripts, plays, professional/academic books.

What's the best way for writers to solicit your interest: Short letter with SASE. No fax or e-mail.

Do you charge reading or management fees: No.

Can you provide an approximation by % of what you tend to represent by category: Fiction: 10%, Non-Fiction: 90%.

How and why did you ever become an agent: Love to read.

What, if anything, can a writer do to increase the odds of you becoming his or her agent: Send a great short letter about the book and themselves. We don't response without an SASE.

Do you have any particular opinions or impressions of editors and publishers in general: I like them; having been an editor I can understand their problems.

What are your favorite books, movies, TV shows, and why: The movie *The Big Lebowski*—wonderfully funny.

Please list representative titles you have sold: *Ophelia Speaks* (HarperCollins); *How the South Could Have Won the Civil War* (Crown); *Sex, Lies, and Handwriting* (S & S); *What I Know Is Me* (Doubleday/Harlem Moon); *Puppy Miracles* (Adams); *Big, Beautiful, and Pregnant* (Marlowe & Co.); *Buddha Baby* (Avon); *Muslim Women in America* (Kensington); *Impressario: Life and Times of Ed Sullivan* (Billboard Books); *Phantom Warrior* (Berkley); *The Flag, the Poet, and the Song* (Dutton); *Bloodstained Seas* (McGraw-Hill).

THE BLUMER LITERARY AGENCY, INC.

350 Seventh Avenue, Suite 2003, New York, NY 10001

212-947-3040   fax: 212-947-0460

Agent's name: Olivia B. Blumer
Born: Long Island, New York.
Education: B.A., English from Goucher College.
Career history: Worked for three publishers (Doubleday, Atheneum and Warner Books before becoming an agent ten years ago.
Hobbies/personal interests: Gardening, food and cooking, travel, tennis, reading (believe it or not).
Categories/subjects that you are most enthusiastic about agenting: Memoirs with a larger purpose, expository books on social and cultural phenomena, books that

spark interest in both ordinary and extraordinary things, groundbreaking guides/how to books, novel that explore the unexplored (in literature and in life).

What you don't want to agent: Victim lit, Ph.D. theses turned "intellectual" exposés, opportunistic books with no larger picture.

If you were not an agent, what might you be doing instead: Animal rescue.

What's the best way for writers to solicit your interest: A well-crafted, short, unambiguous letter with neither hype nor typos. Just the facts, please.

Do you charge reading or management fees: No.

Can you provide an approximation by % of what you tend to represent by category: Non-Fiction: 60%, Fiction: 40%.

What are the most common mistakes writers make when pitching you: Too much author bio and not enough information about the actual book (or vice versa); self-congratulatory author bio; don't tell me that all your friends love your book; non standardized, small (less that 12 point) type that is not double-spaced drives us crazy!

How would you describe the client from Hell: Those deaf to suggestions and those eager to please; whiners.

How would you describe the perfect client: Thick-skinned, talented, patient, hard working, long term vs. short term thinker who is not looking to get rich quick, attentive to suggestions and thorough in their execution.

How and why did you ever become an agent: A chance to invest in my own taste.

What, if anything, can a writer do to increase the odds of you becoming his or her agent: Don't nag, let your writing speak for itself.

How would you describe to someone (or thing) from another planet what it is that you do as an agent: Matchmaker, shoulder to cry on, banker, career counselor.

Do you have any particular opinions or impressions of editors and publishers in general: Majority is overworked and risk averse.

On a personal level, what do you think people like about you and dislike about you: Dislike: Direct, impatient; Like: Passionate, organized, eclectic taste, lots of varied experience in the book biz from retail to rights to publicity to editorial.

BOOKS & SUCH LITERARY AGENCY

52 Mission Circle, Suite 122, PMB 170, Santa Rosa, CA 94505

www.booksandsuch.biz   e-mail: representation@booksandsuch.biz

Agents' names: Janet Kobobel Grant, Wendy Lawton, Etta Wilson, Rachel Zurakowski

Subjects & categories you are interested in agenting, including fiction & non-fiction: Adult fiction and nonfiction, teen, middle readers.

Subjects & categories writers shouldn't even bother pitching to you: Fantasy, sci-fi, paranormal, gift books, poetry, plays.

What would you do if you weren't agenting: Edit fiction.

What's the best way for fiction writers to solicit your interest: Have a short, snappy hook that piques my interest. A great title also helps.

What's the best way for non-fiction writers to solicit your interest: Focus the idea on a specific but significantly populated group of potential readers, and a unique approach to a perenially popular topic.

Do you charge reading or any upfront fees: No.

In your experience, what are the most common pitching mistakes writers make: Not being able to talk about an idea succinctly. I don't want to hear an entire plotline nor an entire history of why someone wrote a manuscript.

Describe the client from Hell, even if you don't have any: E-mails several times a day; suffers from a huge insecurity and needs to be assured several times a week that, yes, publishing is insane but he/she is not; unrealistic expectations in terms of the financial reward of writing; unwilling to take criticism of work; doesn't meet deadlines; isn't willing to do the hard work of actually writing a great book—and a great proposal.

What's your definition of a great client: An innate sense of where the market is and how to write accordingly; capable of putting togeter a dazzling title and concept; works hard at improving the craft; has strong ideas on how to publicize him/herself as well as his/her writing; has the smarts to know when we need to talk and when we don't; relates well with everyone.

How can writers increase the odds that you will offer representation: Study our Web site to learn what type of writing really interests us and query us in the way we ask to be queried. An author who think his/her work is worthy of making an exception to the query process is just asking to be turned down.

Why did you become an agent, and how did you become one: As an editor, I found what I loved most about the publishing process was discovering authors and introducing them to the reading world. Eventually it occurred to me that agents to that a much higher percentage of the time than editors.

In your opinion, what do editors think of you: I've often been told that I'm tough but fair, that I have good instincts about what each publishing house is looking for.

What are some representative titles that you have sold: *Hideaway Series* by Robin Jones Gunn (Simon & Schuster); *Fishes and Loves* by Debbie Macomber (Simon & Schuster); *A Woman Named Sage* by DiAnn Mills (Zondervan); *Awaken My Heart* by DiAnn Mills (Avon Inspire); *Smotherly Love* by Debi Stack (Thomas Nelson); *Married, But Not Engaged* (Bethany House); *Snap 2 It* by Sondra Clark (Sourcebooks); *Getting Old Ain't for Wimps* by Karen O'Connor (Harvest House); *Having a Mary Heart in a Martha World* by Joanna Weaver (WaterBrook); *Summer of Light* by Dale Cramer (Bethany House).

RICK BROADHEAD & ASSOCIATES

47 St. Clair Avenue West, Suite #501, Toronto, Ontario, Canada M4V 3A5

416-929-0516

www.rbaliterary.com   e-mail: rba@rbaliterary.com

Don't be scared off by my address! I represent many American authors and I have made dozens of sales to major American publishers (see below). I welcome queries by e-mail.

Agent's name: Rick Broadhead

Education: B.B.A., York University; M.B.A., Schulich School of Business, York University.

Career history or story: I opened my literary agency in 2002 and quickly established myself as one of the leading agencies in the business. In addition to being one of the few literary agents who has a business background and MBA, I have the rare distinction of being a bestselling author. I wrote and co-wrote over 30 books prior to establishing my literary agency and this affords me a unique perspective on the industry that few agents possess. I have secured dozens and dozens of deals for my authors with large publishing houses across the United States, including Random House, HarperCollins, Hyperion, Penguin, St. Martin's Press, Running Press, Ten Speed Press, Wiley, Simon and Schuster, Harlequin, Jossey-Bass, Da Capo Press, Rodale, Thomas Nelson, Chronicle Books, Adams Media, Abrams, Warner Books/Hachette Book Group, and more. I work with co-agents in Los Angeles when a book project has potential on the big (or small) screen. One of my first book sales was quickly optioned by Paramount/CBS for development as a television sitcom.

My marketing and business expertise were acknowledged by my alma mater, York University, which awarded me their prestigious marketing medal for demonstrated excellence in marketing. My vast knowledge of the publishing industry, both as an author and an agent, and my strong relationships with editors have allowed me to consistently negotiate excellent deals for my clients. I'm a meticulous negotiator and I have secured many six-figure deals for my clients.

Subjects & categories you are interested in agenting, including fiction & non-fiction: I love history, politics, natural history (birding/nature), current affairs, biography, science, pop culture, relationships, self-help, health, medicine (I represent many doctors), military history, national security/intelligence, business, and humor. I especially love working with journalists and I have found many of my best clients after seeing their work in magazines or newspapers. I've also sold many books based on popular Web sites.

Subjects & categories writers shouldn't even bother pitching to you: Fiction, children's books, poetry, screenplays.

What's the best way for non-fiction writers to solicit your interest: A short query letter is best. Describe the book project and your credentials/platform.

Do you charge reading or any upfront fees: There are no reading or upfront fees.

In your experience, what are the most common pitching mistakes writers make: Overly long query letters; sending me a proposal that has clearly not been vetted for grammar and spelling mistakes; not having confidence in your work; pasting chapters into the body of an e-mail; sending attachments without asking first; cc'ing the same query letter to multiple literary agents simultaneously; not personalizing a query letter; sending a manuscript (electronically or in hard-copy) before an agent has requested it; pitching multiple book projects simultaneously. It can be overwhelming when an author pitches 4-5 ideas or projects at once. It implies that you're scattered and unfocused. Make sure you have a solid proposal ready before you contact a literary agent. It's quite demotivating when an author pitches an idea, gets me excited, then tells me the proposal is still in progress and weeks away from completion.

What's your definition of a great client: The best clients, not surprisingly, are those who make my job easier. They're professional, patient, prepared, flexible, open to my input, prompt to respond to my questions and needs, and their proposals are outstanding. Incessant phone calls and e-mails make my job very difficult since they take time away from selling. I really enjoy working with journalists and historians.

How can writers increase the odds that you will offer representation: First of all, you should know what types of books I'm most interested in, as I'm most likely to be receptive to a pitch if the book fits my interests and the subject categories I'm looking for. There are three major criteria I look for when evaluating book proposals (and query letters): (1) a talented writer; (2) a great concept (ideally, a book that is different from other books currently on the market); (3) an author with a platform, credentials, and the relevant expertise.

Books rarely sell themselves these days, so I look for authors who have a "platform." If you're a leading expert in your field or you have experience writing for major newspapers or magazines, I'm more likely to have success selling you to a major publisher. Similarly, if you have a popular blog or Web site or you're affiliated with a major organization or university/college, publishers are more likely to be interested in you. Remember that I have to sell your project to an editor, and then the editor has to sell your project internally to his/her colleagues (including the marketing and sales staff), and then the publisher has to sell your book to the book buyers at the chains and bookstores. You're most likely to get my attention if you write a succinct query letter that demonstrates your platform, the market potential of your book, and why your book is different. In short—get me excited! I'm particularly interested in experts and journalists who have had their work published in major newspapers and magazines. In the marketing section of your proposal, do not put together a full-blown marketing plan that includes a laundry list of ideas for book signings, press releases, a Web site, etc. This is one of the biggest mistakes authors make when crafting a book proposal. Publishers are most interested in the existing connections and relationships you have (with newspapers, television shows, Web sites, etc.) that will help the publisher sell your book when it's published.

Why did you become an agent, and how did you become one: I'm an entrepreneur at heart and I love the business side of publishing—finding great authors, pitching book ideas, negotiating deals, and being a part of an exciting and dynamic industry. I became a bestselling author early in my career and eight years later, after several successive bestsellers, I decided to put my business savvy and passion for publishing to work for other authors. I love what I do, and I love getting excited about a new book project that I can pitch to the editors I work with. There's something special about holding a book in your hand and realizing you played a part in its creation.

Describe to someone from another planet what you do as an agent: I help make dreams come true! A lot of writers question the value of an agent but my involvement will always result in a better deal for the author, whether it's in the advance/royalties, the selection of the publisher/editor, or better contract terms.

What are some representative titles that you have sold: *The Curse of the Labrador Duck* by Dr. Glen Chilton (Simon and Schuster); *Northern Armageddon: The Battle of the Plains of Abraham* by Peter MacLeod (Knopf/Random House USA); *Survive: Essential Skills and Tactics to Get You Out of Anywhere—Alive* by Les Stroud, host of "Survivorman" on the Discovery Channel (Collins/HarperCollins); *The Secret Sentry: The Top-Secret History of the National Security Agency* by Matthew Aid (Bloomsbury Press/Bloomsbury USA); *The Flavor Point Diet* by David Katz M.D. (Rodale); *Do Gentlemen Really Prefer Blondes?* by Jena Pincott (Bantam Dell/Random House USA); *Insultingly Stupid Movie Physics* by Tom Rogers (Sourcebooks); *The Quantum Ten: A Story of Passion, Tragedy, Ambition and Science* by Sheilla Jones (Oxford University Press USA); *101 Foods That Could Save Your Life* by David Grotto (Bantam Dell/Random House USA); *Bad Bridesmaid: Bachelorette Brawls and Taffeta Tantrums—What We Go Through For Her Big Day* by Siri Agrell (Henry Holt); *Ten Years Thinner: The Ultimate Lifestyle Program for Winding Back Your Physiological Clock—and Your Bathroom Scale* by Christine Lydon M.D. (Da Capo Press/Perseus Books Group); *It's a Dog's Life...and It's a Cat's World* by Justine Lee (Three Rivers Press/Random House USA); *Zero to a Million: How I Built a Company to $1 Million in Sales and How You Can, Too* by Ryan Allis (McGraw-Hill USA); *The Trouble With Africa: Why Foreign Aid Isn't Working* by Robert Calderisi (Palgrave USA/St. Martin's Press); *Twisted Triangle* by Caitlin Rother (Jossey Bass); *The Love Pirate: Murder, Sin, and Scandal in the Shadow* of Jesse James by Laura James (Sterling).

ANDREA BROWN LITERARY AGENCY

650-853-1976

www.andreabrownlit.com   e-mail: laura@andreabrownlit.com

As of January 07, we accept e-mail queries only. Please see our agency Web site for submission guidelines.

Agents' names: Andrea Brown, President. Laura Rennert, Senior Agent. Other agents also at the agency are Caryn Wiseman, Jennifer Jaeger, and Michelle Andelman.

The following information pertains to Andrea Brown.

What are representative titles you have sold to publishers: *Unwind* by Neal Shusterman (Simon & Schuster); *Circle Unbroken* by Margot Theis Raven (Farrar, Straus & Giroux).

How do you feel about writers: I got into publishing because I loved books, but I realized after becoming an agent, that I really loved writers even more than books. I am still, after 26 years as an agent, in awe of writers who can finish a book and keep a reader hooked.

What do you tell entities from other planets and dimensions about your job: I tell everyone who will listen that I have the best career: I get to work with intelligent, creative, wonderful people every day (that includes all my associates at the agency, not just our fabulous clients).

You're welcome to share your thoughts and sentiments about the business of writing and publishing: It is a wonderful time for children's book authors—the best in the 30 years I am in the business. It is also imperative that writers think about their audience more than ever. They must write the best book possible and also make certain that it is commercial. Ask, "would you pay $25 for this book?"

Will our business exist as we know it in 10 years or so from now: I think book publishing will always exist, but I think big changes are on the horizon, and the authors that can adapt will continue to be published. I don't think it will exist as it is.

The following information pertains to Laura Rennert.

Education: Ph.D in English Literature, University of Virginia, B.A., magna cum laude, Cornell University

Career history: Literary Agent, 10 years. Professor, 8 years of teaching English Literature at Santa Clara University, the University of Virginia, and Visiting Professor at Osaka University of Foreign Studies in Japan.

Hobbies/personal interests: Travel, movies, theatre, good food and wine, reading and writing, of course.

Categories/subjects that you are most enthusiastic about agenting: Ambitious voice-driven fiction, whether children's books or adult; literary mysteries and thrillers, compelling story-based narrative nonfiction; literary-commercial middle-grade and young adult fiction; crossover fiction; fiction. Regardless of genre, I look for works that are emotionally powerful and resonant.

What you don't want to agent: Westerns, adult fantasy, adult science fiction, prescriptive nonfiction, screenplays, new age fiction and non-fiction.

What's the best way for fiction writers to solicit your interest: Follow the guidelines on our Web site (www.andreabrownlit.com), and choose one agent to e-query. Target the agent for whom you feel your work is the best fit and take the time to do a little research. A strong query that demonstrates you've done your homework makes a good first impression. When someone tells me why they're approaching me, particularly, and demonstrates some knowledge of the market, I look closely at their work. Professionalism, passion, and confidence (not hubris) are attractive. A strong voice is one of my main criteria in work I choose to take on, and I'm already on the look out for it as I read query letters.

What's the best way for non-fiction writers to solicit your interest: I'm looking for a strong proposal and sample chapters – and pretty much look for the same criteria I mention above for fiction.

If you were not an agent, what might you be doing instead: If I weren't agenting, I'd probably be an editor, a professor of English Literature, or a writer ... pretty predictable, I'm afraid, although I do also have a secret fascination with dinosaurs – so maybe also paleontologist.

Do you charge reading or management fees: No.

Can you provide an approximation by % of what you tend to represent by category: Children's books: 70%, Adult fiction and Non-Fiction: 30%.

How would you describe the client from Hell: The client from hell wants constant updates, handholding, and attention all the time.

What are your favorite books, movies, TV shows, and why: Some of my favorite books are Jonathan Lethem's *Motherless Brooklyn*, A.S. Byatt's *Possession*, Barry Eisler's *The Last Assassin*, JK Rowling's *Harry Potter* novels, Terry Pratchett's *Wee Free Men* trilogy, all of Jane Austen's novels, and Madeleine L'Engle's *A Wrinkle in Time*. Although they are very different, what all of these works have in common is a marvelous, individualistic voice; characters that get under your skin; emotional power and resonance; masterful story-telling; a unique perspective; and vivid, evocative, visceral writing.

Please list representative titles you have sold: *The Five Ancestors Series* (Random House); *Becoming Chloe* (Knopf); *Storky: How I Won The Girl and Lost My Nickname* (Putnam); *Monsoon Summer* (Random House); *The Squishiness of Things* (Knopf); *The Strongbow Saga: Viking Warrior Book 1* (Harpercollins); *First Daughter: Extreme American Make-Over* (Dutton); *Revolution Is Not A Dinner Party* (Holt); *Evolution, Me, And Other Freaks of Nature* (Knopf); *Glass* (Margaret Mcelderry/Simon & Schuster); *Love In The Present Tense* (Doubleday); *Thirteen Reasons Why* (Razorbill/Penguin Group); *The Day I Killed James* (Knopf); *Chasing Windmills* (Doubleday) and *Madapple* (Knopf).

The following information pertains to Jennifer Jaeger.

Born: Los Angeles, California

Education: B.A. in English from UC Davis; minor in Social and Ethnic Relations with a focus on multicultural literature. Spent one year at the University of East Anglia in England. Studied education at Dominican University.

Career history or story: I worked in journalism and education before becoming a literary agent.

Hobbies, interests: Reading (of course), cooking, martial arts, stock market, travel, spa-days, theatre, early U.S. history.

Subjects & categories you are interested in agenting, including fiction & non-fiction: Picture books through YA, with a special interest in middle grade. I like humorous, literary, multicultural, edgy and offbeat material. I enjoy some paranormal, fantasy and historical manuscripts. Though I do not represent adult fiction, I am interested in crossover fiction.

Subjects & categories writers shouldn't even bother pitching to you: Please, no adult works.

What would you do if you weren't agenting: I would be teaching, learning languages in foreign countries, or working the counter at a bakery.

What's the best way for fiction writers to solicit your interest: Please e-mail your query along with the first 10 pages of your manuscript in the body of an e-mail. For picture books, include the entire manuscript. No attachments, please.

Do you charge reading or any upfront fees: No.

In your experience, what are the most common pitching mistakes writers make: No personalized greeting, no knowledge about my interests or the Andrea Brown Literary Agency, and unprofessional and unpolished query letters.

Describe the client from Hell, even if you don't have any: Such a client would be inflexible, greedy, and unnecessarily dramatic.

What's your definition of a great client: Great clients know their market and the business, they work tirelessly on their craft, they're open to revising and are willing to promote their work. They're also very patient.

Why did you become an agent, and how did you become one: Agenting is the perfect combination of my skills and interests: writing and editing, communication, and business. It is thrilling to know that I play a role in helping great and important books get published.

How do you feel about writers: I think authors are brave souls and the true celebrities.

What are your favorite books/TV shows/movies, and why: Books: *Even Cowgirls Get the Blues; Catherine Called Birdy; The Schwa Was Here; Passage to India;* and books by Jonathan Safran Foer and Toni Morrison. TV Shows: *The Office.* Movies: *Dirty Dancing, Rushmore, Sweet Home Alabama, and Little Miss Sunshine*

What are some representative titles that you have sold: (Please note that titles are subject to change). *The Down to Earth Guide to Global Warming* (Orchard/Scholastic); *Las Mantas de Milagros* (Holt); *Farwalker* (Bloomsbury); *Before You Were Here* and *The Cazuela that the Farm Maiden Stirred* (Viking and Charlesbridge, respectively); *Paris Pan Takes the Dare* (Puffin and Putnam/Penguin).

The following information pertains to Caryn Wiseman.

Education: M.B.A., Anderson School, UCLA; B.S., University of Virginia.

Career history or story: Caryn's fifteen years of business experience prior to joining the Agency emphasized editing and writing as well as sales, negotiation and client management.

Subjects & categories you are interested in agenting, including fiction & non-fiction: I handle children's books only: young adult and middle-grade fiction and non-fiction, chapter books, and picture books. I am particularly interested in sports; humorous chapter books and middle-grade fiction; "boy" books; YA that falls at the intersection of commercial and literary; YA that is edgy without being gratuitous; magical realism and reality-based fantasy; biography for kids of all ages; unique nonfiction; and African-American and Latino-themed literature in all age groups. I am always open to terrific children's work that doesn't fit these categories, however. For fiction, a fresh, unique voice is paramount, but the story must have great characterization and plot as well. I loves nonfiction that reads like fiction; that has a great "story behind the story". I do not represent adult projects. Please do not query her regarding adult work.

Subjects & categories writers shouldn't even bother pitching to you: Any adult projects.

What are some representative titles that you have sold: Some recent and forthcoming titles include: *The Qwikpick Adventure Society* by Sam Riddleburger (Dial); *Beneath My Mother's Feet* by Amjed Qamar (Mcelderry); *Flying Beneath the Radar* by Lisa Kline (Delacorte); *Beanball* by Gene Fehler (Clarion); *The Great Walloper Series* by Kevin Markey (Harpercollins); *Life In The Wild: The George Schaller Story* by Pamela S. Turner (FSG); *The Man Who Flies with Birds* by Carole G. Vogel (Millbrook).

CURTIS BROWN LTD.

10 Astor Place, New York, NY 10003

212-473-5400

Agents' names: Elizabeth Harding, Ginger Knowlton, Laura Blake Peterson,
The following information pertains to Elizabeth Harding.
Education: B.A. in English, University of Michigan (Ann Arbor)
Categories/subjects that you are most enthuiastic about agenting: Children's literature.

What's the best way for writers to solicit your interest: Query letter or sample chapters.

Can you provide an approximation by % of what you tend to represent by category: Children's: 100%.
The following information pertains to Ginger Knowlton.
Born: Before the 1960s in Princeton, New Jersey.
Education: Questionable, navy brat quality.
Career history: I worked in a factory assembling display cases in Mystic, Connecticut, for a time. Gained numerous pounds one summer working in a bakery in Mendocino, California. I've taught preschool and I directed an infant and toddler child-care center. That means I organized a lot of fundraisers. I started working at Curtis Brown in 1986.

Categories/subjects that you are most enthusiastic about agenting: Middle grade and teenage novels.

What you don't want to agent: I prefer to remain open to all ideas.

What's the best way for writers to solicit your interest: A simple, straightforward letter with a return envelope works well.

If you were not an agent, what might you be doing instead: I love my job, but if I had the luxury of not having to work, I would play tennis even more than I already do; I would tend my gardens more fastidiously; and I would spend more time playing with others.

Can you provide an approximation by % of what you tend to represent by category: Nonfiction, 5%; Fiction, 5%; Children's, 90%.

What are the most common mistakes writers make when pitching you: Expecting an answer within a week, but mostly poor quality writing.

How would you describe the client from Hell: Happy to report that I still don't have firsthand experience with a "client from Hell," so once again I will refrain from describing one (for fear of a self-fulfilling prophecy).

How would you describe the perfect client: Professional authors who respect my job as I respect theirs, who will maintain an open dialogue so we may learn from each other and continue to grow, who are optimistic and enthusiastic, and who continue to write books worthy of publication.

How and why did you ever become an agent: I asked Dad for money for graduate school. He offered me a job at Curtis Brown instead.

Do you have any particular opinions or impressions of editors or publishers in general: I have a lot of respect for editors and I think they have an incredibly difficult job. As in all professions, some are more gifted than others.

The following information pertains to Laura Blake Peterson.

Education: B.A., Vassar College.

Career history: 1986–present, Curtis Brown, Ltd.

Hobbies/personal interests: Gardening, pets, regional equestrian competitions.

Areas most interested in agenting: Exceptional fiction, narrative non-fiction, young adult fiction, anything outstanding.

What you don't want to agent: Fantasy, science fiction, poetry.

If you were not an agent, what might you be doing instead: Teaching, gardening, who knows?

What's the best way for writers to solicit your interest: The best way is through a referral from either a client of mine or an editor with whom I work.

Can you provide an approximation by % of what you tend to represent by category: Fiction: 40%; Non-fiction: 40%; Children's: 20%.

What are the most common mistakes writers make when pitching you: Calling, rather than sending a query letter.

How would you describe the client from Hell: Authors who call incessantly, preventing me from accomplishing anything on their behalf.

How would you describe the perfect client: A talented writer who knows the idiosyncrasies of the publishing business yet nonetheless remains determined to be a part of it; a writer with the skills and patience to participate in an often frustrating and quirky industry.

How and why did you ever become an agent: I love language. I can't imagine a better job than helping to bring a skilled writer to the attention of the book-buying public.

What, if anything, can a writer do to increase the odds that you will become his or her agent: Do their homework. Find out what I (or whoever they're contacting) like to read and represent, what books I've sold in the past, etc. Read this survey!

TRACY BROWN LITERARY AGENCY

P.O. Box 88, Scarsdale, New York 10583

914-400-4147   e-mail: tracy@brownlit.com

Agent's name: Tracy Brown
Born: Omaha, Nebraska.
Education: Williams College; Columbia University.
Career story: I worked my way up (and down) the book publishing editorial ladder for 25 years before becoming an agent in 2004. I came into the business at the age of 28 as an assistant in the publicity department at E.P. Dutton and then moved to junior editorial positions at Holt and Penguin. In 1988 I was offered the job of Editorial Director of Quality Paperback Book Club. Returning briefly to trade publishing in 1992 I initiated a new trade paperback list at Little, Brown called Back Bay and served as its first Editorial Director. In 1993 I returned to the book clubs when I was offered the position of Editor-in-Chief of Book-of-the-Month Club, a position I held until 1996 when I returned to the trade as an acquiring editor at Holt and then at Ballantine. In 2004 I decided to become an agent. My first three years were spent in association with Wendy Sherman Associates. I opened my own agency in 2007.

Hobbies and special personal interests: Travel, cooking, farmer's markets, Bob Dylan's music.

Subjects and categories you like to agent: 80% non-fiction: Current affairs, memoir, psychology, travel, nature, health; 20% literary fiction.

Subjects and categories writers shouldn't bother pitching to you: Science fiction, romance, YA.

What might you be doing if you weren't agenting: That's a scary thought.

What's the most effective ways for writers to grab your attention: Write a succinct and informative query letter that clearly states who you are and what you want to write about.

Do you charge fees separate from your commission, or offer non-agenting fee based services: No fees.

What are representative titles you have sold to publishers: *Mating in Captivity: Unlocking Erotic Intelligence* by Esther Perel (Harpercollins); *Perfect Girls, Starving Daughters* by Courtney E. Martin (Free Press); *The Man in The White Sharkskin Suit* by Lucette Lagnado (Ecco); *Why We're Losing the War on Cancer* by Clifton Leaf (Knopf); *Full Frontal Feminism* by Jessica Valenti (Seal Press); *Super in the City: A Novel* by Daphne Uviller (Bantam).

Why did you become an agent, and how did you become one: I'm amazed that I survived in corporate publishing for 25 consecutive years. Then there came a time when I wanted more freedom to select the authors I want to work with. The transition from editor to agent was relatively easy for me; acquiring books and selling them involve essentially the same skills.

How do you feel about writers: Their words have impacted by life more than any other art form.

What do you tell entities from other planets and dimensions about your job: Don't even try to make sense of the book business. Nobody knows why some books sell and others don't. This irrationality can be frustrating at times but is also a large part of why so many of us are attracted to the challenge of bringing worthy books to the public's attention.

What are your favorite books, movies, TV shows, and why: A client needs to trust that an agent knows how to do his/her job. Trying to micro-manage the process is going to make everyone miserable.

How would you describe "the writer from hell": A client needs to trust that an agent knows how to do his/her job. Trying to micro-manage the process is going to make everyone miserable.

How would you describe the publisher and/or editor from hell: I've known a few (luckily very few) editors and publishers who seem to feel that the agent is nothing but a troublemaker who must be thwarted at every turn.

What do you like best about your clients, and the editors and publishers you work with: I enjoy these relationships most when the topic of conversation is not always about work.

Do you wish to describe who you are: I receive a lot of queries addressed to "Ms" Tracy Brown. I'm used to this and don't mind, but it's probably best for potential clients to know that I'm one of the rare males with the name Tracy.

Will our business exist as we know it in 10 years or so from now: Definitely not as we know it today. But there will always be people who want to tell stories and other people will want to hear them. So most likely there will be a need for somebody to facilitate the process. I'm not worried—yet.

PEMA BROWNE, LTD.

11 Tena Place, Valley Cottage, NY 10989

845-268-0026

www.pemabrowneltd.com

Agent's name: Pema Browne

What are some representative titles that you have sold: *The Champion* (Zebra Historical Romance); *Highlander's Bride* (Zebra Historical Romance); *Kisses Don't Lie* (Zebra Contemporary Romance); *The House on Crystal Lake* (Cora Verlag German Rights).

SHEREE BYKOFSKY ASSOCIATES, INC.

P.O. Box 706, Brigantine, NJ 08203

Agent's name: Sheree Bykofsky

Born: September 1956, Queens, New York.

Education: B.A., State University of New York, Binghamton; M.A., in English and Comparative Literature, Columbia University.

Career history or story: Executive Editor/Book Producer, the Stonesong Press (1984–1996); Freelance Editor/Writer (1984); General Manager/Managing Editor, Chiron Press (1979–1984); Author and co-author of a dozen books, incuding three poker books with co-author Lou Krieger.

Hobbies, interests: Poker, Scrabble.

Subjects and categories that you are interested in agenting, including fiction and nonfiction: Popular reference, adult non-fiction (hardcovers and trade paperbacks), quality literary and commercial fiction (highly selective).

Subjects and categories writers shouldn't even bother pitching to you: Children's, young adult, genre romance, science fiction, horror, Westerns, occult and supernatural, fantasy.

What's the best way for fiction writers to solicit your interest: Send anequery le-tter, pasted into the body of your e-mail, to submitbee@aol.com. No attachments will be opened.

What's the best way for nonfiction writers to solicit your interest: See above.

Do you charge reading or any upfront fees: No.

In your experience, what are the most common pitching mistakes writers make: Excessive hubris; not explaining what the book is about; comparing book to bestsellers rather than showing how it is unique; paranoia (we're not going to steal your idea); sloppy grammar, punctuation, and spelling.

What's your definition of a great client: One who is not only a talented writer but also who is professional in every sense.

How can writers increase the odds that you will offer representation: I love a query letter that is as well written as the proposed book or a polished, perfect, professional proposal.

Please list representative titles you have sold: *Boyfriend University* (Wiley); *1001 Ways to Live Green* (Berkley); *Consiracy Nation* (Chicago Review); *Junk Jewelry* (Clarkson Potter); *The Thrill of the Chaste* (W); *When the Ghost Screams* (Andrews McMeel); *Death Waits for You* (Pocket).

CARNICELLI LITERARY MANAGEMENT

30 Bond Street, New York, NY 10012

www.carnicellilit.com e-mail: queries@carnicellilit.com

Agent's name: Matthew Carnicelli

Education: M.A. in English Literature, University of Toronto; B.A. in English Literature and Political Science, Washington University.

Career history: Editorial positions at the Penguin Group, Contemporary Books, and McGraw-Hill, 1991-2004. Started CLM in 2004.

Categories/subjects that you are most enthusiastic about agenting: Popular and serious nonfiction, from current events, history, biography/memoir, science, and business to sports, health, spirituality, and psychology. I handle very little fiction.

What you don't want to agent: Young adult, romance, westerns, fantasy, science fiction, screenplays.

If you were not an agent, what might you be doing instead: Editor, writer, or college professor.

What's the best way for writers to solicit your interest: Have a very clear and focused idea, and tell me why you are the writer best and most uniquely qualified to write about your subject.

Do you charge reading or management fees: No.

Please list representative titles you have sold: *The Comfort of Our Kind* by Tom Stoner (Thomas Dunne Books); *Fanatic: Ten Things All Sports Fans Must Do Before They Die* by Jim Gorant (Houghton-Mifflin); *Free to Hit and Fight: Charles Hamilton Houston, Thurgood Marshall, and the Struggle to End Segregation* by Rawn James, Jr. (Bloomsbury Press); *Goldrush in the Jungle: The Race to Find—and Possibly Save—the Rarest Animals of Vietnam's 'Lost World'* by Daniel Drollette, Jr. (Harmony); *Higher Sound: Awakening to the Sacred through Music* by Renee Cox Lorraine (Morning Light Press); *Life Disrupted: Getting Real about Chronic Illness in Your Twenties and Thirties* by Laurie Edwards (Walker); *Logo: The Life and Legend of Jerry West* by Roland Lazenby (Random House); *Lonely Courage: Behind Enemy Lines in France, 1940-44* by Samuel Southworth (Berkley Caliber); *Move Into Life: The Nine Essentials for Lifelong Vitality* by Anat Baniel (Harmony); *The Sky Isn't Visible from Here: Scenes from a Life* by Felicia C. Sullivan (Algonquin).

CASTIGLIA LITERARY AGENCY

1155 Camino del mar, Del Mar, CA 92014

Agents' names: Julie Castiglia, Winifred Golden, Sally Van Haitsma, Deborah Ritchken

Subjects & categories writers shouldn't even bother pitching to you: Horror, fantasy, poetry.

What would you do if you weren't agenting: Reading, lying on the beach, traveling.

What's the best way for fiction writers to solicit your interest: Query letter and two pages sample writing from project.

What's the best way for non-fiction writers to solicit your interest: Query letter.

Do you charge reading or any upfront fees: No.

In your experience, what are the most common pitching mistakes writers make: Unprofessional presentation, spelling errors, lack of knowledge about the publishing industry. Calling instead of writing. Lack of brevity. Submitting more than one project at a time.

Describe the client from Hell, even if you don't have any: Not listening to our advice, not trusting our judgment. Telling us what to do and how to do it.

What's your definition of a great client: Appreciate, loyal, trusting, trustworthy, knowing when we have information we will call them immediately. Sense of humor, sends us chocolates.

How can writers increase the odds that you will offer representation: Write a query that will knock our socks off. Be referred by editors, clients or other professionals or simply be brilliant writer.

Why did you become an agent, and how did you become one: Lost in the mists of time (Castiglia). I thought it was the CIA (Golden). I was seduced by the ghost of Thomas Hardy (Van Haitsma).

Describe to someone from another planet what you do as an agent: We sell manuscripts from writers unknown and known to publishers who magically turn them into books.

How do you feel about editors and publishers: Thank God for all of them.

How do you feel about writers: It depends if they can write.

What do you see in the near future for book publishing: I don't want to think about it.

What are your favorite books/TV shows/movies, and why: So many favorite books: *Middlesex, The Glass Castle, Nature of Airwater, Motherless Brooklyn, The Tender Bar.* TV shows: *House, The Starter Wife, Top Chef, Project Runway,* design and architecture shows. Movies: *The Empire of the Sun, Notes on a Scandal, The Devil Wears Prada, King Arthur.*

In your opinion, what do editors think of you: They respect and like us.

On a personal non-professional level, what do you think people think of you: Everyone loves me!!--Julie. Everyone loves Sally!! Everyone loves Winifred!! Why wouldn't they?

What are some representative titles that you have sold: *The Leisure Seeker* by Michael Zadoorian (Morrow/Harper); *Waiting for the Apocalypse* by Veronica Chater (Norton); *From Splendor to Revolution* by Julia Gelardi (St. Martin's); *Beautiful: The Life of Hedy Lamar* by Stephen Shearer (St. Martin's); *Forever L.A.* by Doug Keister (Gibbs Smith); *Barry Dixon Interiors* by Brian Coleman (Gibbs Smith); *Wesley the Owl* by Stacey O'Brien (Free Press/S & S).

CREATIVE CONVERGENCE

11040 Santa Monica Blvd., Suite 200, Los Angeles, CA 90025

310-954-8480   fax: 310-954-8481

www.creativecvg.com

Agent's name: Philippa Burgess
Born: October, 1974 in Trenton, New Jersey.
Education: Grew up in Upper Montclair, New Jersey and New York City. Graduated from USC: studied International Relations and Cinema-Television.
Career history or story: Started at ICM and went on to found boutique literary management company that evolved into Creative Convergence.
Subjects & categories you are interested in agenting, including fiction & non-fiction: We represent and co-represent published literary properties to bring to film and television, as well as work with branded clients to develop literary properties that are part of a larger media brand.
What would you do if you weren't agenting: We love entertainment, media and entrepreneurship. When we are not representing clients or packaging projects, we are writing, teaching, and speaking to writers and content creators.
What's the best way for fiction writers to solicit your interest: Referrals, published, credited or branded.
What's the best way for non-fiction writers to solicit your interest: Referrals, published, credited or branded.
Do you charge reading or any upfront fees: Our literary management department represents screenwriters and directors on commission only. Our production department is paid for fee for services and is paid by the studio. Our entertainment consulting services provides brand development and brand management for business endeavors that can be a combination of fees, commissions, or profit participation depending on the nature of the services rendered, that often include PR, media and business development. We also offer a brand development course entitled "Your Signature Story: From Content Creator to Media Brand" for a nominal fee.
In your experience, what are the most common pitching mistakes writers make: Lack clarity about: What the author brings to the story from their own experience; what they bring to the table in terms of knowledge about the industry; who their

audience is and how this story is relevant to them; what type of platform they are building to reach and remain engaged with their audience.

Describe the client from Hell, even if you don't have any: A general lack of respect for our time and the realities of the business is a turn off. Not to mention a gross sense of entitlement that often tied to a lack of ability or interest in doing their work to deliver a quality product.

What's your definition of a great client: Someone who takes responsibility for doing their work well, and continues to grow in their craft, relationships, and understanding of the business. We want a client to see our relationship as a team effort.

How can writers increase the odds that you will offer representation: Give us something amazing. Get it to us through a referral. Otherwise keep growing and learning, and it will come back around if it really is the right match.

Why did you become an agent, and how did you become one: Started at ICM and really liked it but saw their was a knowledge gap so I moved into management. The business kept changing and I found the knowledge gap was widening and a lot more people needed the information and coaching, specifically media brands. We retained our literary management while expanding into film and television production and entertainment consulting.

Describe to someone from another planet what you do as an agent: We take books and package them for film and television. Specifically in television we are looking for properties that we can package for network and cable series. We also look to work with content creators that are media brands that we can work to move their content across media platforms.

How do you feel about editors and publishers: We can only manage so many relationships so we don't actually deal very often with editors and publishers. Rather we work through literary agents when it comes to the publishing side of things. Being an entertainment company in Los Angeles we work closely with the equivalent in film and television.

How do you feel about writers: We love the smart ones! No really, we are passionate about writers and content creators. Beyond representing clients, packaging literary properties, or managing media brands we look to be a resource to writers are frequently found at writers conferences or teaching classes about the business.

What do you see in the near future for book publishing: Film, television, media, and publishing all need each other more than ever before. There is going to be a lot more cooperation between these different arenas of entertainment and media. However, the author needs to recognize that these professionals don't all speak the same language and thus needs to take a greater responsibility for moving their message across media platforms (and in doing so well, will stand to gain a lot more attention and regard from all parties).

In your opinion, what do editors think of you: We'd like to think that industry professionals see us as professional, resourceful, and forthright.

On a personal non-professional level, what do you think people think of you: We'd like to think that people see us as professional, resourceful, and forthright.

What are some representative titles that you have sold: 52 *Fights by Jennifer Jeanne*

Patterson (Penguin/Putnam), sold and produced as a TV pilot for ABC/Touchstone; *Men's Guide to the Women's Bathroom* (HarperCollins), sold as a TV pilot to CBS/Paramount (slated for production). *Thieves of Baghdad* (Bloomsbury) sold as a feature film to Warner Brothers with our client Jonathan Hunt co-producing. *They Come Back*, an original script written by Gary Boulton-Brown sold and produced for Lifetime. *Queen-size*, an original script written by Rod Johnson sold to Lifetime (slated for production).

CROSSMAN LITERARY AGENCY

65 East Scott Street, Suite 12E, Chicago, IL 60610

312-664-6470   fax: 312-664-7137

e-mail: crossmanla@aol.com

Agent's name: Nancy Crossman

Born: Chicago, Illinois.

Education: B.A. with honors, English Literature, DePaw University, Northwestern University School of Education.

Career history: Vice president, editorial director, associate publisher: Contemporary Books, Inc. 1979–1997.

Hobbies/personal interests: Golf, travel, classical music.

Categories/subjects that you are most enthusiastic about agenting: General non-fiction, self improvement, health, medicine, nutrition, fitness, cooking, sports, women's issues, pop culture, travel, business, parenting.

What you don't want to agent: Children's, young adults titles, poetry.

If you were not an agent, what might you be doing instead: Teaching, coaching girl's sports.

What's the best way for writers to solicit your interest: Query with synopsis and SASE.

Do you charge reading or management fees: No reading fees.

How would you describe the perfect client: Dream clients are professional and talented, work as team players and are passionate about their work.

How and why did you ever become an agent: After 18 years as the director of a publishing house, I left so that I could work on a variety of projects that personally interested me, as well as have more time to spend with my children.

What, if anything, can a writer do to increase the odds of you becoming his or her agent: Generate solid, convincing proposals. Be patient and have a good sense of humor.

Please list representative titles you have sold: The Cake Mix Doctor Cookbook Series (Workman); *Rules Brittania* (St. Martin's); *The Pocket Parent* (Workman); *The Petit Appetit* (Perigee Penguin); *What Your Doctor May Not Tell You About Fibrosis* (Warner).

CS INTERNATIONAL LITERARY AGENY

43 West 39th St., New York, NY 10018

212-921-1610

www.csliterary.com   e-mail: csliterary@aol.com

Agent's name: Cynthia Neeseman
Education: Columbia University.
Subjects & categories you are interested in agenting, including fiction & non-fiction: Fiction, non-fiction, screenplays.
Subjects & categories writers shouldn't even bother pitching to you: Pornography.
What would you do if you weren't agenting: Real estate and writing.
What's the best way for fiction writers to solicit your interest: Send short query letters that grab one's attention. Include telephone numbers, if available, as well as email and snail mail addresses. I like to talk to potential clients over the phone as a fast and efficient way to determine whether we will connect and be able to work together.
What's the best way for non-fiction writers to solicit your interest: See above.
Do you charge reading or any upfront fees: I charge reading fees if I believe a writer might need revision and/or I have doubts about marketability of subject matter and/or interest in submitted subject. I expect a writer to pay for expenses as they occur. My fees are very fair and moderate. I analyze manuscripts and screenplays as well as agenting because many writers benefit from revision. I like to help writers produce material that will sell and therefore I discuss all aspects of their efforts including marketability up front. It saves time and effort. I also read partial manuscripts. Sometimes a smaller first submission can be beneficial.
In your experience, what are the most common pitching mistakes writers make: They have not mastered the art of being succinct but pithy. In short, they ramble.
Why did you become an agent, and how did you become one: I have always been interested in writing and obtaining interesting information. I was a foreign correspondent and worked for a literary agent.
How do you feel about writers: Writers are wonderful.
What do you see in the near future for book publishing: More and more self-publishing. Marketing is often the secret to becoming a successful writer.

D4EO LITERARY AGENCY

7 Indian Valley Road, Weston, CT 06883

203-544-7180   fax: 203-544-7160

e-mail: d4eo@optonline.net

Agent's name: Robert G. (Bob) Diforio

Born: March 19, 1940; Mamaroneck, New York.

Education: Williams College 1964, Advanced Management Program (AMP) at Harvard Business School 1978.

Career history: Kable News Company 1964–1972, Book and Magazine Sales Rep 1964–1966, Manager Paperback Books Division 1966, VP Book Sales 1969, New American Library 1972–1989, VP General Sales Manager 1972–1974, Senior VP Marketing Director 1975–1978, Executive VP 1979, President, Publisher 1980, Chairman and CEO 1981–1989, Founded D4EO Literary Agency 1989.

Hobbies/personal interests: Golf.

Categories/subjects that you are most enthusiastic about agenting: Commercial fiction and non-fiction.

What you don't want to agent: Anything I don't like.

If you were not an agent, what might you be doing instead: Publisher.

What's the best way for writers to solicit your interest: Recommendation from a publisher or client.

Do you charge reading or management fees: No.

How and why did you ever become an agent: As a publisher I loved launching new writers, now I do it as an agent.

What, if anything, can a writer do to increase the odds that you will become his or her agent: Send me a ms. that I absolutely love.

How would you describe to someone (or thing) from another planet what it is that you do as an agent: I find the right editor/publisher for my client's work.

Please list representative titles you have sold: *A Treasure's Trove* (Treasure Trove Inc.); *Official Solutions Book To A Treasure Trove* (Treasure Trove, Inc.); *Secrets of the Alchemist Dar* (Treasure Trove Inc.); *Escape, Malice, Counterplay, Hoax, Fury* (all of the Butch Karp legal thrillers; Vanguard/Atria Books/Pocket Books); *Havoc, Deep Fire Rising, River of Ruin, Medusa Stone, Pandora's Curse, Charon's Landing, Vulcan's Forge* (Dutton/NAL); *Felony Murder, Shoot The Moon, Flat Lake In Winter, Irreparable Damage, Fog* (St. Martin's Press); *My Name is Jillian Gray* (Albin Michel); *The Mermaid's Song* (Delacort); *The 10th Case, Bronx Justice* and *Depraved Indifference* (Mira); *Anxiety Free* and *Here Comes the Sun* (Hay House); *Putting My Way* [Jack Nicklaus, Ken Bowden] (John Wiley & Sons); *Teeing Off* (Triumph Books); *Everything I Needed to Know I Learned at McDonald's* (McGraw Hill); *Accidental Landlord* and *Accidental Tycoon* (Alpha Books); *Skirts in the Boardroom* (John Wiley & Sons); *The Faraway Fairies* (Hatchette Australia); *Reindeer Christmas* (Paula Wiseman/Simon 7 Schuster); *The History of Medicine* and

Controversies in Science and *Ocean Sciences*, multi-book series (Facts on File); *Crazy Love, Cruising* (Pocket Books); *Expired, Criss Cross, Out A Order* (Kensington); *The Tiger's Mistress, Kiss of Spice* (Pocket Books); *Hellions* (Warner); *Take Me Out of the Bathtub, I'm Still Here in the Bathtub* (Margaret McElderry); *McKeag's Mountain, Wolf Mountain, Stranahan, Gavagan, O'Rourke's Revenge* (Kensington); *House of Pain, Behold A Pale Horse* (Tor); *The Last Pope* (Sourcebooks), *Via Magna*—Spain, *DiFel*—Portugal, *Eddie's World, Jimmy Bench Press, Charlie Opera, Cheapskates* (Carroll & Graf + UK and Russia sales); *Shakedown* (Pegasus); *Rift Zone* (Tor); *4th & Fixed* (Sourcebooks); *Dangerous Deceptions* (NAL); *Red Meat Cures Cancer* (Vintage); *Heretic, The Templar Chronicles* (Pocket Books), *Droemer-Knaur*—Germany, *Alfaret*—Russia, *Pleasure Control Trilogy* (Avon Red); Allure Author's Anthology (Avon Red); *Sexy Beast, Hell Kat, Inferno* (Aphrodesia); *Wild Wild Women of the West* (Aphrodesia); *Vampire Erotica 1 and 2* (Avon Red); *Solomon's Code, The Voynich Code* (sales in Russia, Bulgaria, Brazil). Nonfiction: *The Worry Cure* (Harmony Books); *Application Suicide* (Gotham); *Madscam* (Entrepreneur Press); *Commissions at Risk*—Dearborn (Kaplan); *How to Earn a Living Teaching On Line* (John Wiley); *The Secret of Hogan's Swing* (John Wiley); *The Blog Book* (Nelson Business); *The Expert's Guide to Poker Tells* (Triumph); *Collaborative Divorce* (Nolo); *The Trans Fat Free Kitchen* (HCI); *Feeding Your Kids Right* (Career Press); *Harriet Roth's Fat Counter* (NAL); *You Lost Them At Hello* (AMACOM); *Interactive Selling* (Career Press); *American Geisha* (Hunter House); *Presentation SOS* (Warner Books); *Their Last Words—A Tribute to Soldiers Who Lost Their Lives in Iraq* (Berkley Books); *Bringing The Thunder* (Stackpole); *Thunderhorse Six* (Citadel); *Cashing In on the Coming Real Estate Crash* (John Wiley); *Operation Black Biscuit* (Lyons Press); *Living Longer, Learning Later* (Sentient); *The S Factor: Sheila Kelley's Strip Workouts For Every Woman* (Workman Publishing); *Heart of the Storm* (John Wiley); *Leadership Secrets Of The Worlds Best CEOs* (Dearborn); *That's Not in my Science Book* (Taylor Trade Publishing); *Divorce Guide for Fathers: Nurturing The Extended Family* (Nolo); *Stop the Show!* (Thunder Mouth); *My Year in the Blogosphere* (Nelson Business Books); *The Cosmic Laws of Golf* (Berkley); *Seeing Lessons* (John Wiley); *The Gal's Got Bite* (St. Martin's Press); *Start Small Finish Big* (Warner); *Morgan Freeman Bio* (Barricade Books); *Living Well with Endometriosis* (Collins Reference); *Sex Secrets of Escorts Monet* (Alpha Books); *Ellen Degeneres updated edition* (Citadel/Kensington); *Living Well with Anxiety* (HarperResource); *Living Well with Menopause* (Collins Reference); *Business Lunchatations* (Chamberlain Bros.); *Sell Your Own Home* (Career Press); *The Science Teacher's Almanac* (John Wiley & Sons); *Fire Someone Today* (Nelson Books); *Out of the Pens of Kids* (Sasquatch Books); *The Golden State of Golf* (Sports Media); *Odyssey of an Eavesdropper* (Carroll & Graf); *The Future of Golf* (Sasquatch); *Major Memories Minor Moments* (Lyons Press); *ABLE!: One Company's Loyal, Disabled Workers Show That Love and Compassion Makes Good Business Sense* (BenBella Books); *Don't Chew Jesus* (BenBella Books); *Magnetic Selling* (AMACOM); *Winning The Interview Game—Everything You Need To Know To Land The Job* (AMACOM); *Rosie O'Donnell* (Carroll & Graf); *Eating With Your Anorexic* (McGraw Hill/Contemporary); *The Mojo Triangle: A Cultural History Of American Music* (Schirmer); *Life Isn't Fair* (Sourcebooks); *Profitable Candlestick Trading* (John Wiley); *Getting Started as a Freelance Writer* (Filbert); *From Science Fiction to Science Fantasy* (Ben Bella); *Real World Software Testing* (Charles River Media); *Howard*

Dean: In His Own Words (Rogak St. Martin's Press instant book); *Getting Entrepreneurial* (John Wiley); *I'm Right You're Wrong, Now What?* (Sourcebooks); *Diana Riggs Biography* (BenBella Books); *People Performance and Pay, The Hay Compensation Guide* (The Free Press); *Google Earth for Dummies, The PIG to Texas Hold'em, The PIG to Interviews, The PIG to Potty Training The Reluctant Child; The Pig to Stock Picking; The CIG to Real Estate Basics, The CIG to Designing Your Own Home, The CIG to Faith, The CIG to Party Plan Selling, The CIG to Success as a Mortgage Broker, The CIG To Successful Interviews, The CIG To Successful Business Plans, The CIG to Portrait Photography.*

DANIEL LITERARY GROUP

1701 Kingsbury Dr., Ste 100, Nashville TN 37215

615-730-8207

www.danielliterarygroup.com   e-mail: submissions@danielliterarygroup.com

Agent's name: Greg Daniel

Born: Lubbock, Texas.

Education: B.A., Wheaton College (Communications); M.A., summa cum laude, Trinity Divinity School (Theology).

Career story: I founded Daniel Literary Group in April 2007 after more than ten years in publishing, six of which were at the executive level at Thomas Nelson Publishers, the largest Christian publisher in the world. Most recently I was Vice President and Associate Publisher for W Publishing Group (formerly Word Publishing), a trade book division of Thomas Nelson.

Hobbies and special personal interests: Ultra endurance cycling, golf, motorcycling, crosswords, taxi driver for my kids.

Subjects and categories you like to agent: Nonfiction: areas: Biography/autobiography; business/economics; child guidance/parenting; current affairs; health/medicine; history; how-to; humor/satire; memoirs; nature/environment; popular culture; religious/inspirational; self-help/personal improvement; sports; theater/film; women's issues. Fiction areas: Action/adventure; contemporary issues; detective/police/crime; family saga; historical; humor/satire; literary; mainstream/contemporary; mystery/suspense; religious/inspirational; thriller, young adult.

Subjects and categories writers shouldn't bother pitching to you: Poetry, romance, science fiction, children's, screenplays, short stories, erotica.

What might you be doing if you weren't agenting: Nuclear physicist or gangster rapper.

What's the most effective ways for writers to grab your attention: Do your homework on what I represent and don't represent, and follow my submission guidelines. Sounds basic, but amazingly, 90% of the queries I receive ignore this advice. And please don't tell me that your Aunt Ethel or your pet cat read your manuscript and told you it was the most brilliant thing they'd ever read.

Do you charge fees separate from your commission, or offer non-agenting fee based services: No.

What are representative titles you have sold to publishers: *Green Gospel* (Harper-One); *Peaches and Daddy* (Overlook Press); *The Collapse of Distinction* (Thomas Nelson); *My Life as a Holy Roller* (WaterBrook/Multnomah Press); *Finding God in the Other* (Jossey-Bass/Wiley); *Wild Things* (Tyndale House); *The Sacredness of Questioning Everything* (Zondervan); *Reimagining Church* (Cook); *Holy Stability* (Paraclete); *Saints in Limbo* (WaterBrook/Multnomah Press); *Making the World Human Again* (Zondervan).

Why did you become an agent, and how did you become one: I loved being an editor and publisher, but I always envied the diversity of writers that an agent could choose to work with and the ability to concentrate on a smaller group of authors, building their careers and brands. So I finally took the plunge and left life as an editor/publisher to launch my own agency. It's been everything I hoped it would be.

What are your favorite books, movies, TV shows, and why: I love books, TV shows, and movies that are entertaining on one level but with a deeper level of meaning that keep me pondering them for days afterward. Movies such as *Seven Samurai*, *Babette's Feast*, *The Godfather*, and *Lars and the Real Girl*. And books such as *Peace Like a River*, *The Road*, *Brother to a Dragonfly*, and anything by Frederick Buechner.

How would you describe "the writer from hell": One with horns, a tail, and a pitchfork.

What do you like best about your clients, and the editors and publishers you work with: Book people, whether they're authors or editors, are absolutely the greatest group of people in the world to hang out with. Smart, witty, interesting, and fresh minty breath.

LIZA DAWSON ASSOCIATES

350 7th Avenue, Suite 2003, New York, NY 10001

212-465-9071   fax: 212-947-0460

www.lizadawsonassociates.com

Agents' names: Liza Dawson, queryLiza@lizadawsonassociates.com; Caitlin Blasdell, queryCaitlin@lizadawsonassociates.com; Anna Olswanger, queryAnna@lizadawsonassociates.com; Karen E. Quinones Miller, queryKaren@lizadawsonassociates.com; Havis Dawson, queryHavis@lizadawsonassociates.com; Victoria Horn, queryVictoria@lizadawsonassociates.com

The following information pertains to Liza Dawson.

Education: B.A. in History, Duke University; graduate of Radcliffe's Publishing Procedure Course.

Career history or story: Founded Liza Dawson Associates in 1998 after 20 years as Executive Editor and Vice President at William Morrow and Putnam.

Hobbies, interests: Local and national politics, archaeology, gardening, nagging spacey teenagers.

Subjects & categories you are interested in agenting, including fiction & non-fiction: Plot-driven literary fiction; upscale historicals and mysteries; pacey, well-textured thrillers; multi-cultural fiction written in a distinctive, memorable voice; parenting books by authors with platforms; history (especially ancient) written by excellent writers; psychology that says something fresh; politics with a point of view; narrative nonfiction, travel and memoirs written in a lively, moving tone which take you someplace unexpected.

Subjects & categories writers shouldn't even bother pitching to you: Poetry, Westerns, science fiction.

What would you do if you weren't agenting: Digging for ancient treasure in Italy.

What's the best way for writers to solicit your interest: Query via snail mail or e-mail.

Do you charge reading or any upfront fees: No reading fee.

What's your definition of a great client: A brilliant, funny, focused, fearless workaholic with lots of friends in the media.

What are some representative titles that you have sold: Sister Mine by Tawni O'Dell (Crown); The Genius by Jesse Kellerman (Putnam); Mozart And The Whale: An Asperger's Love Story by Jerry and Mary Newport; Zeus: Traveling through Greece with the God of Gods by Tom Stone (Bloomsbury); The Darker Side by Cody Mcfadyen (Bantam); The Guernsey Literary and Potato Peel Pie Society by Mary Ann Shaffer (Dial); Passin' by Karen E. Quinones Miller (Grand Central).

The following information pertains to Caitlin Blasdell.

Education: B.A., Williams College.

Career history or story: Senior Editor at Harper and Avon. With the agency since 2002.

Hobbies, interests: In the dim past, before being the mother of 3 small boys, I remember liking cross-country skiing, perennial gardening, baking, and art history.

Subjects & categories you are interested in agenting, including fiction & non-fiction: Science fiction, fantasy (for both adults and young adults), parenting, business, thrillers, and women's fiction.

Subjects & categories writers shouldn't even bother pitching to you: Horror, especially any books where small children die brutally, westerns, poetry, cookbooks, business.

What would you do if you weren't agenting: Organizing quality flexible childcare for working mothers.

What's the best way for writers to solicit your interest: Query via snail mail or e-mail.

Do you charge reading or any upfront fees: No reading fee.

What are some representative titles that you have sold: *Saturn's Children* by Charles Stross (Berkeley); *A Writer's Coach: An Editor's Guide to Words that Work* by Jack Hart (Pantheon).

The following information pertains to **Anna Olswanger.**

Education: B.A., Phi Beta Kappa, Rhodes College; M.A., University of Memphis; Certificate in Book Publishing, NYU.

Career history or story: With the agency since 2005. Coordinates the Jewish Children's Book Writers' Conference every fall at the 92nd Street Y. Teaches business writing at the Center for Training and Education at Johns Hopkins University and writing for physicians at Stony Brook University Hospital. Author of a children's book. She recently launched www.Host-a-Jewish-Book-Author.com.

Hobbies, interests: Birds, fine art, Israel.

Subjects & categories you are interested in agenting, including fiction & nonfiction: Gift books for adults, young adult fiction and nonfiction, children's illustrated books, and Judaica.

Subjects & categories writers shouldn't even bother pitching to you: Horror, occult, military/war, poetry, short story collections, government/politics, technical, textbooks.

What would you do if you weren't agenting: Building tree houses, traveling, photographing and painting, writing.

What's the best way for writers to solicit your interest: Query via snail mail or e-mail.

Do you charge reading or any upfront fees: No reading fee.

What are some representative titles that you have sold: *The Jewish Woman's Weekly Planner 2010* (Pomegranate); *Ant & Grasshopper* (McElderry/Simon & Schuster), *Sylvie* (Random House Children's Books).

The following information pertains to **Karen E. Quinones Miller.**

Education: B.A. in Journalism, Temple University.

Career history or story: With the agency since 2006; author of five Essence best selling novels; a client since 2002.

Hobbies, interests: National politics, Harlem Renaissance.

Subjects & categories you are interested in agenting, including fiction & nonfiction: Science fiction, fantasy (for both adults and young adults), parenting, business, thrillers, and women's fiction.

Subjects & categories writers shouldn't even bother pitching to you: Poetry.

What would you do if you weren't agenting: Running a luxury Bed & Breakfast in Harlem.

What's the best way for writers to solicit your interest: Query via snail mail or e-mail

Do you charge reading or any upfront fees: No reading fee.

What are some representative titles that you have sold: *A Rich Man's Baby* by Daaimah Poole; *All I Want Is Everything* (Kensington); *Hiding In Hip-Hop* (Atria); *We Take This Man* (Grand Central) co-agented with Audra Barrett of Audra Barrett Books; *Diamond Playgirls* (Kensington).

The following information pertains to Havis Dawson.

Education: B.A., Duke University.

Career history or story: Joined Liza Dawson Associates after 20 years of editing business-trade magazines.

Hobbies, interests: Smoking cigars and driving cheap, clapped-out sports cars (preferably doing both simultaneously).

Subjects & categories you are interested in agenting, including fiction & non-fiction: Military memoirs, southern fiction, fantasy, science fiction, thrillers, business and practical books as wells as spiritual books.

Subjects & categories writers shouldn't even bother pitching to you: Photo books, poetry, sports.

What would you do if you weren't agenting: The pleasantly sinew-taxing chores of gardening: digging holes, chopping tree roots, rolling big stones…

What's the best way for writers to solicit your interest: Query via snail mail or e-mail.

Do you charge reading or any upfront fees: No reading fee.

What are some representative titles that you have sold: *Flying Through Midnight: A Pilot's Dramatic Story of His Secret Missions Over Laos During the Vietnam War* by John T. Halliday (Scribner); *Law of Attraction: The Science of Attracting More of What You Want and Less of What You Don't* by Michael J. Losier (Grand Central)—co-agented with L. Dawson.

The following information pertains to Victoria Horn.

Education: B.A. in English, Grinnell College.

Career history or story: Victoria came to Liza Dawson Associates in April, 2008 after two years with Trident Media Group as an assistant.

Subjects & categories you are interested in agenting, including fiction & non-fiction: YA fiction, adult women's fiction, romance and literary fiction. She can't get enough truly well done magical realism and is a sucker for great historical novels. Victoria is open to narrative nonfiction, travel, memoir, pop culture or social science takes on current debates. She looks for sharp humor in unexpected places, a story that places her firmly in another world, and characters she can't leave behind. She loves strong voices and high concept hooks, or really well written stories about timeless subjects.

What's the best way for writers to solicit your interest: Query via snail mail or e-mail.

Do you charge reading or any upfront fees: No reading fee.

THE JENNIFER DECHIARA LITERARY AGENCY

31 East 32nd Street, Suite 300, New York, NY 10016

212-481-8484 fax: 212-481-9582

www.jdlit.com   e-mail: jenndec@aol.com

Agents' names: Jennifer DeChiara, Stephen Fraser
Born: New York, New York.
Career history: Freelance book editor for Simon & Schuster, and Random House; writing consultant for several major New York City corporations; literary agent with Perkins, Rubie Literary Agency and the Peter Rubie Literary Agency; founded the Jennifer DeChiara Literary Agency in 2001.

Hobbies/personal interests: Reading, movies, music, ballet, photography, sports, travel.

Categories/subjects that you are most enthusiastic about agenting: Children's books (picture books, middle grade, young adult), literary fiction, commercial fiction, chick lit., celebrity bios, mysteries/thrillers, self-help, parenting, humor, popculture; in general almost any well-written book, either fiction or non-fiction.

What you don't want to agent: Romance, erotica/porm, horror, science fiction, fantasy, poetry.

What's the best way for writers to solicit your interest: E-mail or snail mail a query letter.

Do you charge reading or management fees: No.

Can you provide an approximation by % of what you tend to represent by category: Children's Books: 50%, Adult Fiction: 25%, Adult Non-Fiction: 25%.

What are the most common mistakes writers make when pitching you: Phoning or faxing queries; calling to check that we received query letter or manuscript; expecting to meet me or showing up uninvited before I've agreed to represent them; interviewing me instead of the other way around; someone who raves about their material when the work has to speak for itself; someone who is more concerned about possible movie deals and marketing angles and the prestige of being an author rather than the actual writing; queries and manuscripts that are poorly written or that have typos; not sending an SASE.

How would you describe the client from Hell: Someone who calls or e-mails constantly for news; expects a phone call when there's nothing to discuss; expects me to perform according to their timetable; has no knowledge of the publishing business and doesn't think it's their job to learn; doesn't want to work on next book until the first one is sold; can't accept rejection or criticism; needs a lot of hand-holding; has a negative attitude; fails to work as part of a team. Every once in a while a Client from Hell slips into the agency, but once they show us their horns, we send them back to the inferno.

How would you describe the perfect client: Someone who is passionate about writing; thoroughly professional; appreciative and understanding of my efforts; and who works as part of a team.

How would you describe to someone (or thing) from another planet what it is that you do as an agent: I help make dreams come true.

Please list representative titles you have sold: *Geography Club* (HarperCollins); *Hazing Meri Sugarman* (Simon & Schuster); *His Cold Feet* (St. Martin's); *The Creative Write-Brain Workbook* (Writer's Digest); *Virgin Sex* (Hatherleigh Press); *The Book of Life Goes On: The Loyal Companion to TV's First True Family Show of Challenge* (Bear Manor Media).

DEFIORE AND COMPANY

72 Spring Street, Suite 304, New York, NY 10012

Agent's name: Brian DeFiore
Born: August 1956, Brooklyn, New York.
Education: B.A., S.U.N.Y. at New Paltz and Queens College;
Career history: 1999-Present: President, DeFiore and Co.; 1997-1998: SVP and Publisher, Villard Books, Random House; 1992-1997: VP aqnd Editor-in-Chief, Hyperion; 1988-1992: Senior Editor/VP and Editorial Director, Dell/Delacourte Press; 1983-1988: Editor, St. Martin's Press.

Hobbies/personal interests: Movies, theater, cycling, cooking, being a good dad to my daughters.

Categories/subjects that you are most enthusiastic about agenting: Intelligent commercial fiction, suspense fiction, narrative non-fiction, psychology/self-help, business, humor, virtually anything that is written beautifully.

What you don't want to agent: Category romance, poetry, computer books, anything written pedantically.

If you were not an agent, what might you be doing instead: Psychotherapy.

What's the best way for writers to solicit your interest: A drop-dead brilliant letter (sent by mail or e-mail). Publishing is a medium about the written word; a persuasively written letter indicates the right sort of talent. A sloppy or trite letter indicates the opposite.

Do you charge reading or management fees: No.

Can you provide an approximation by % of what you tend to represent by category: Fiction: 35%, Children's: 10%, Non-Fiction: 55%.

What are the most common mistakes writers make when pitching you: Pitching several books at once. Telling me how many other agents and/or publishers loved their work, but simply aren't taking new clients (yes, people really do this!)

How would you describe the client from Hell: Someone who hears but doesn't listen. Someone who thinks an agent's job is solely to bully publishers. Someone who has a cynical "I'll write whatever sells" attitude about their work.

How would you describe the perfect client: Someone whose work inspires me, and who respects and appreciates my role in the process.

How and why did you ever become an agent: After 18 years on the publishing and editorial side of the business, I was ready for a more entrepreneurial challenge. I love the publishing process, but I felt that too much of my time was spent on corporate posturing and not enough on books and authors., Now I can have it both ways.

What, if anything, can a writer do to increase the odds of you becoming his or her agent: Write brilliantly. There's not much else. Don't send me something until it's absolutely as good as it possibly can be.

How would you describe tosomeone (or thing) from another planet what it is that you do as an agent: I search for talented authors. Using my experience as a publisher, I work with my clients to get their submission material (manuscript or proposal) into the best possible shape to elicit a positive response from publishers. I orchestrate the sale to get the best combination of deal points and publishing house for the project. I negotiate the contract. I sell the subsidiary rights to those projects, often in concert with co-agents in Los Angeles and cities around the world. I oversee the publication effort and make sure the publisher is doing what needs to be done. I interpret the publisher's business needs for the author and vice versa. I strategize with my clients to develop their careers.

Do you have any particular opinions or impressions of editors and publishers: I admire the work they do; indeed I did it myself for several years. I think most editors and publishers have their hearts firmly planted in the right place. I wish that their corporate masters gave them more time and support to do their jobs well. They are under such pressure these last few years that editorial nurturing of authors has evolved into an obsessive quest for "the next big thing." It's always lovely to have "the next big thing," but I've yet to meet the publishing team who always knew that that was eighteen months in advance. I firmly believe that those publishers who focus on editorial quality and integrity over high concept and "platform" are the ones who will win in the end.

What are your favorite books, movies, TV shows, and why: TV: *The Sopranos, The Daily Show, Curb Your Enthusiasm*. Movies: *The Philadelphia Story, Network, Star Wars*.

Please list representative titles that you have sold: *The Extraordinary Adventures of Alfred Kropp* (Bloomsbury); *Post Secret: Extraordinary Confessions from Ordinary Lives* (Regan Books); *Target Underwear and a Vera Wang Gown* (Gotham); *Kick Up Your Heels (Before You're Too Old to Wear Them)* (Hay House); *All the Fishes Come Home to Roost* (Rodale); *All for a Few Perfect Waves* (William Morrow); *Dead Cat Bounce* (Harper Collins); *Lions in the Street* (Faber/FSG).

JOELLE DELBOURGO ASSOCIATES, INC.

516 Bloomfield Ave., Suite 5, Montclair, NJ 07042

fax: 973-783-6802

www.delbourgo.com   e-mail: info@delbourgo.com

Agents' names: Joelle Delbourgo, Molly Lyons
The following information pertains to Joelle Delbourgo
Education: B.A., magna cum laude, Phi Beta Kappa, Williams College (double-major in History and English Literature); M.A. with honors in English Literature from Columbia University.

Career history or story: Fall 1999 to present, President and Founder of Joelle Delbourgo Associates, Inc. 1996-1999, HarperCollins (1996-1997, Vice President, Editorial Diector; 1997-1999, Senior Vice President, Editor-in-Chief and Associate Publisher; 1980-1996 held various positions from Senior Editor to Vice President, Editor-in-Chief of Hardcover and Trade Paperback; 1976-1980, various editorial positions at Bantam Books).

Hobbies, interests: Cooking, travel.

Subjects & categories you are interested in agenting, including fiction & non-fiction: Serious non-fiction, including narrative non-fiction, history, psychology, women's issues, medicine and health, business, science, biography, memoir, sports, popular culture, lifestyle, thesis-based books and interdisciplinary approaches to non-fiction subjects, literary fiction, some commercial fiction, some historical fiction, and young adult books both fiction and nonfiction. I'm interested in serious thinkers, original ideas, and in a story well told.

Subjects & categories writers shouldn't even bother pitching to you: No category fiction (including romance, westerns, science fiction, and fantasy). No children's books or technical books.

What would you do if you weren't agenting: I would be a college professor or dean, perhaps, or a writer myself. Anything that involved life as learning. Publishing has been a continuous graduate school for me and has allowed me to hone my skills and knowledge, while pushing the envelope in those areas I'm curious about. My authors are often pioneers in their fields, and I get a firsthand education working with them. It really works both ways.

Do you charge reading or any upfront fees: We do not charge to read submissions, but by the same token, we are not obligated to analyze your work for you unless you become a client.

Can you provide an approximation by % of what you tend to represent by category: Fiction: 25%, Nonfiction: 75%.

In your experience, what are the most common pitching mistakes writers make: Pretending they know me when they don't; not sending an SASE, writing letters telling me how many other agents have rejected them already, or how little they know about the process. Goodbye!

Describe the client from Hell, even if you don't have any: Someone who approaches me by phone, send materials in miniscule type without an SASE or by disk; calls to find out if the package has arrived; won't take no for an answer; clients with a smattering of publishing knowledge that makes them second-guess the agent's every step.

What's your definition of a great client: A naturally gifted writer and thinker. The client who has been thinking about the idea or book for a long time and perhaps has tested the idea through research, or presentations such as lectures and workshops; who is passionate, committed, serious, respectful, and works hard over the long term to do right by the book. The client who understand that this is a partnership, between agent and client at first, and then with the editor and publisher. The client who is willing to market a book and is open to being guided in the process. My role is to guide, advise, cheer, facilitate, boost egos, solve problems, and be there when the going gets rough.

How can writers increase the odds that you will offer representation: Write me a fabulous and respectful query and follow the guidelines on my Web site.

Why did you become an agent, and how did you become one: I had put in 25 years on the corporate side, climbing the ladder from Editorial Assistant to many years as a top executive. I loved the publishing process, but it also grinds you down. I wanted to get back to what got me into publishing in the first place: working with writers and editors again. I also wanted to work for a company in which I could set the tone, one that is professional and generous and respectful, and the best way to do it seemed to be to create it myself!

Describe to someone from another planet what you do as an agent: I see myself as helping to shape the culture, by choosing to support and develop ideas I find exciting, bodies of information that need to be shared, and literary experiences that will touch readers' hearts and minds. I like being a catalyst in people's lives, occasionally helping them to live their dreams. I am a muse, mother, therapist, advocate, CEO, and friend. Sometimes I wish I had someone like that in my life!

How do you feel about editors and publishers: I'm nuts about them. Occasionally you meet those who aren't smart or good at their job, but most are exceptional. They love what they do and live every day in the hope that they'll discover something that can sell. I love the older, wiser, experienced ones who have perfected their craft, but I'm also very impressed with the taste and talents of the many young editors in the business who have the ear of their management and take their responsibilities very seriously.

How do you feel about writers: I have a great deal of respect for good writers. It is really challenging for any talented person to envision a work and bring it into being. It involves vision, dedication, hard work and the ability to sustain these qualities on a solitary basis.

What do you see in the near future for book publishing: I get really irritated by all of the gloom and doom about publishing. It's true that the traditional world of book publishing is shrinking, but it's equally true that there are marvelous new opportunities if you keep your eyes open. I'm fascinated with the opportunity that university presses have, for example, to develop what the "big" firms call "mid-list," or by the new trade lists being developed by McGraw-Hill, which was formally thought of primarily as a business publisher, and Rodale Books, which is rapidly expanding beyond direct mail. More and more, we need to think about new formats, novel ways to market content and creative new business models. While I am a realist, my philosophy is to think positively and go where the opportunity is. I hate it when people don't agree with me, but, hopefully, I'm right about books more often than I'm wrong; no one "owes" you anything. You want to sell books because they are good and because someone at the publishing house has a vision for how to bring them to market. When it works correctly, it's a beautiful thing.

What are your favorite books/TV shows/movies, and why: I am a fierce admirer of *Friday Night Lights*, which is one of the smartest new series on TV, and *Mad Men*, as well as anything on HBO. I devour anything by Philip Roth, who is probably my favorite American writer, but also read lighter fare such as Elinor Lipman's novels. This year's great reads included Kormac McCarthy's *The Road*, one of the bleakest and most haunting novel ever written; Sue Miller's *The Senator's Wife* and Jhumpa Lahiri's *Unaccustomed Earn*. I also read a lot of history, current affairs, and narrative nonfiction.

In your opinion, what do editors think of you: You should ask them! Once an editor, always an editor. Given my editorial background, they recognize me as a member of the tribe, as opposed to an adversary. I believe most respect my judgment, my sense of fairness and my professional integrity.

One a personal non-professional level, what do you think people think of you: Warm, intense, focused, occasionally intimidating but most people who are drawn to me like my ability to listen and connect with them.

What are some representative titles that you have sold: *The Gift of Neurodiversity: The Hidden Strengths of Autism, ADHD, Dyslexia and Other Brain Differences* by Thomas Armstrong (Da Capo/Perseus); *Retirement Heist: How Corporations are Plundering Pensions and Profiting from the Nest-Eggs of American Workers* by Ellen E. Schultz (of the *Wall Street Journal*) (Penguin Portfolio); *The New Frugality* by Chris Farrell (Bloomsbury USA); *Leadership in the Time of Crisis: Six Lessons* by Joseph J. Grano (Jossey-Bass/John Wiley); *Sneaky Chef to the Rescue* by Missy Chase Lapine (Running Press/Perseus); *Escape from Cubicle Nation* by Pamela Slim (Penguin Portfolio/Berkley); Untitled on the Roosevelts by Julie M. Fenster (Palgrave MacMillan); *Alexander the Great* by Philip Mitchell Freeman (Simon & Schuster); *Slouching Toward Adulthood: Why Young People Are Taking So Long to Grow up and What It Means for Society* by Richard Settersten and Barbara Ray (Bantam Books/Random House); *A Talent for Murder* by R. T. Jordan (Kensington); *Standing By: The Making of an Unlikely Military Family* by Alison Bukholtz (Tarcher/Penguin); *Mothers and Adult Daughters* by Linda Gordon and Susan Shaffer (Berkley/Penguin).

SANDRA DIJKSTRA

1155 Camino del Mar, PMB 515, Del Mar, CA 92014

Agent's name: Sandra Dijkstra

Born: New York, New York.

Education: B.A. in English, Adelphi; M.A. in Comparative Literature, UC Berkeley; Ph.D. in French Literature, UC San Diego.

Career history or story: University professor, literary agent.

Hobbies, interests: Reading, films.

Subjects & categories you are interested in agenting, including fiction & nonfiction: Specialize in literary and commercial fiction and nonfiction, especially biography, business, current affairs, health, history, psychology, popular culture, science, self-help, narrative non-fiction, and children's literature.

Subjects & categories writers shouldn't even bother pitching to you: Westerns, science-fiction, poetry collections, screenplays.

What would you do if you weren't agenting: I would be an editor and/or college professor.

What's the best way for fiction writers to solicit your interest: Please send a query letter by regular mail (e-mail submissions are NOT accepted) with 50 sample pages of your manuscript (double-spaced, single-sided), a 1-2 page synopsis, and SASE to our mailing address.

What's the best way for non-fiction writers to solicit your interest: Send 1-2 sample chapters, profile of competition, intended audience and market, author bio, and brief chapter outline.

Do you charge reading or any upfront fees: No.

In your experience, what are the most common pitching mistakes writers make: Incessant phone calls to check on the status of their submissions, or demanding reading notes on an unsolicited submission. Writers should also be careful not to over-hype their projects, and to remember to let us know about your platform or previous writing credentials.

Describe the client from Hell, even if you don't have any: The client from Hell is never satisfied and has expectations that exceed all possibilities of realization.

What's your definition of a great client: Dream clients ask the right questions, offer useful support material, and trust their agents. They do not email and/or call daily. These clients keep us apprised of progress and are professionals who understand that we are their partners and advocates. They help us to represent their best interests, trust us, and work like Hell to make his/her book happen after writing the best book possible.

How can writers increase the odds that you will offer representation: They should try to find a publisher, bookseller, librarian, or established author to recommend them to us. They should also try to publish their work in magazines, newspapers, or online—leading us to chase them!

Why did you become an agent, and how did you become one: I became an agent to publish books that help writers realize their dreams and make a difference in the world.

Describe to someone from another planet what you do as an agent: I read manuscripts and hope to fall in love. Then, when I do, I talk on the phone with editors and prepare them to fall in love. When I discover talent, I support it with all my heart, brain, and soul.

How do you feel about editors and publishers: Editors are overworked and underpaid. They are (most of them) dedicated and passionate about authors and books. In a perfect world, publishers would have more support, more money, and more time! Publishers would be "making public the book, in the fullest sense," which they try to do, often.

How do you feel about writers: Writers are our inspiration! Their work drives our work. There's nothing better than nurturing and campaigning for their books in the world.

What do you see in the near future for book publishing: Lots of joy when the publishing process works as it should. Lots of sorrow when it doesn't.

What are your favorite books/TV shows/movies, and why: Bill Maher, Jon Stewart, Keith Olbermann.

In your opinion, what do editors think of you: That I'm pushy—on the front and back end of the publishing process, which is my job.

What are some representative titles that you have sold: Non-fiction: *Devil's Highway* by Luis Urrea (Back Bay Books); *Religious Literacy* by Stephen Prothero (Harper San Francisco); *Winter World* by Bernd Heinrich (Harper Perennial); *God on Trial* by Peter Irons (Viking); *The Little Book that Beat the Market* by Joel Greenblatt (Wiley). Fiction: *Saving Fish From Drowning* by Amy Tan (Ballantine Books); *Snow Flower and the Secret Fan* by Lisa See (Random House); *Empress Orchid* by Anchee Min (Houghton Mifflin); *Lethally Blond* by Kate White (Warner); *Sweet Revenge* by Diane Mott Davidson (William Morrow).

JIM DONOVAN LITERARY

4515 Prentice, Suite 109, Dallas, TX 75206

e-mail queries: jdliterary@sbc.global.net

Agents' names: Jim Donovan, Melissa Shultz
Born: Brooklyn, New York.
Education: B.S., University of Texas.
Career history: In books since 1981 as a bookstore manager, chain-store buyer, published writer (*The Dallas Cowboys Encyclopedia*, 1996, Carol Publishing; *Custer and the Little Bighorn*, 2001, Voyager Press; *A Terrible Glory*, 2008, Little, Brown), freelance

editor, senior editor: Taylor Publishing, six years. Literary agent since 1993.

Categories/subjects that you are most enthusiastic about agenting: American history, biography, sports, popular culture, health, business, fiction, popular reference. Also, chicklit and parenting (address to Melissa Shultz).

What you don't want to agent: Children's, poetry, short stories, romance, religious/spiritual, technical, computer, fantasy/science fiction.

What's the best way for writers to solicit your interest: Non-fiction: An intelligent query letter that gets to the point and demonstrates that the writer knows the subject and has something to contribute—and it's not just a magazine article stretched to book length. Fiction: Solid writing and some publishing credentials at shorter length. Snail mail with query and SASE or email: jdlqueries@sbcglobal.net. No attachments please. We will respond to email queries only if we are interested.

Do you charge reading or management fees: No.

What are the most common mistakes writers make when pitching you: The top 10 query letter turnoffs: 1.) Don't use a form letter that begins with "To Whom It May Concern" or "Dear Editor." 2.) Don't say your writing is better than bestselling writers'. 3.) Don't mention your self-published books unless they've sold several thousand copies. 4.) Don't refer to your "fiction novel." 5.) Don't brag about how great or how funny your book is. 6.) Don't quote rave reviews from your relatives, friends, or editors whom you've paid. 7.) Don't tell the agent how you're positive your book will make both if you rich. 8.) Don't say it's one of five novels you've finished. 9.) Don't tell the editor that he'll be interested because it will make a great movie. 10.) Don't ask for advice or suggestions (if you don't think it's ready, why should they?).

What, if anything, can a writer do to increase the odds of you becoming his or her agent: Become published in reputable magazines, reviews, etc. before attempting a book. Most writers simply have no idea how hard it is to garner a contract for an unpublished writer.

Do you have any particular opinions or impressions of editors and publishers: Editors are the miners of the publishing world—they spend days and nights digging through endless layers of worthless material for the occasional golden nugget. Anything the agent or the writer can do to make their job easier is greatly appreciate, so I stress that to potential writers.

What do you think the future holds for writers, publishers, and agents: Most people—and that means most unpublished writers—do not appreciate the importance of good editing and publishing, which is why there will always be a need for editors and publishers—and agents.

Please list representative titles that you have sold: *Born to Be Hurt* by Sam Staggs (St. Martin's Press); *Go Down Together* by Jeff Guinn (Simon and Schuster); *The Last Real Season* by Mike Shropshire (Grand Central); *To Hell on a Fast Horse* by Mark Gardner (Morrow); *Twelve Mighty Orphans* by Jim Dent (St. Martin's Press).

DOYEN LITERARY SERVICES, INC.

1931 660th St., Newell, IA 50568

712-272-3300

www.barbaradoyen.com

Agent's name: Barbara Doyen, Pres.

Career story: We own perhaps the only literary agency in the world located on a rural acreage. The Editor-in-Chief of a national magazine once called from her NYC headquarters to ask us to look out the office windows and describe what we saw. She intended to send a photographer out to take some pictures for an article about virtual businesses, but couldn't fathom our answer: vast fields of corn and soybeans. Even stranger to her was that our office commute had nothing to do with subways, busses or trains. But this was years ago before the world had caught up to us; now many people dream of having successful businesses while living a country lifestyle and modern technology makes it doable from any location. Over 20 years ago, our agency began representing books of all kinds: children's board and picture books, teen and young adult fiction and nonfiction, and most adult categories. But as the business has grown, we've narrowed our focus to adult nonfiction—the kind of books you find in bookstores for the ordinary reader, plus a few that cross over into the textbook and library markets.

Subjects and categories you like to agent: We offer exceptional service that starts with extensive advice about preparing a winning book proposal and continues beyond the publisher's contract—we're there to assist through the whole process to ensure a positive outcome: successful books. We are known for our outstanding nonfiction authors who write knowledgeably and well and who deliver to deadline. We are primarily interested in acquiring excellent writers for all kinds of adult nonfiction books and a few textbooks. (Can you guess the reason for this repetition?) Can't Write? If you are an expert with a book idea but writing is not your strength, we may be able to help. We frequently pair authors and experts for successful book projects. Nonfiction topics: Advice/relationships, business/investing/finance, health/diet/fitness, history/politics/current affairs, how-to/DIY, lifestyle, psychology, self-improvement, cookbooks, pop culture, reference, narrative nonfiction, inspirational, biography, memoir and more.

Subjects and categories writers shouldn't bother pitching to you: We are not accepting fiction, poetry, or children's projects; however, we cover most adult nonfiction categories. (See the Third Simple Rule, below.)

What's the most effective ways for writers to grab your attention: While we have an existing full stable of wonderful authors, we are open to new talent—after all, we started the agency due to our passion for authors and publishing and we love fresh nonfiction voices and ideas. In order to consider new clients, however, we must have a Few Simple Rules: Please make your first contact to us be a query letter only—do not send your material until we request it. You may send your query letter via snail mail or email—the latter can be done through our website, above. Query us about adult nonfiction only. There now, that wasn't so bad, was it? Tip: Include your background and interests when querying us—you just never know what could come of it. We might have a book idea for you.

Do you charge fees separate from your commission, or offer non-agenting fee based services: Doyen Literary Services, Inc., operates on a commission basis only; we do not charge fees of any kind.

What are representative titles you have sold to publishers: *Healthy Aging for Dummies* by Brent Agin, M.D. and Sharon Perkins, R.N.; *The Complete Idiot's Guide to Playing the Fiddle* by Ellery Klein ; *Presidents' Most Wanted* by Nick Ragone.

DUNHAM LITERARY, INC.

156 Fifth Avenue, Suite 625, New York, NY 10010

212-929-0994

www.dunhamlit@yahoo.com

Agent's name: Jennie Dunham, Owner; Chris Morehouse, cm@dunhamlit.com
The following information pertains to Chris Morehouse.

Career story: Attorney admitted to New York State Bar for 25 years. Member of the Entertainment, Arts and Sports Law Section of the NYSBA. Member of AAR.

Subjects and categories you like to agent: I like to represent writers of adult nonfiction books in the categories of memoir, health, parenting, relationships and current affairs. I also represent authors of middle grade and young adult fiction and non-fiction. Topics of particular interest to me are sports (especially baseball), psychology, and women's issues (motherhood, work, self-help). I am not interested in the paranormal or religious topics.

What's the most effective ways for writers to grab your attention: No email queries please! Send Chris Morehouse query letters to 9 Normandy Lane, Manhasset, NY 11030.

How do you feel about writers: Like motherhood, writing is the hardest and loneliest profession, but the rewards are great when you do it well. I love my writers because they handle criticism and rejection with a sense of humor and as a learning experience.

EBELING & ASSOCIATES

www.ebelingagency.com

Agent's name: Michael Ebeling, ebothat@yahoo.com; Kristina Holmes, kristina@ebelingagency.com

The following information pertains to Michael Ebeling.

Born: June 13, 1963; Escondido, California.

Education: B.S. Business, Colorado University; M.A. Holistic Health and Wellness, Naropa University.

Career story: Michael Ebeling brings more than 15 years of publications, consulting, sales and applied management experience to Ebeling & Associates. Michael's experience with leading authors and publishing companies enables him to effectively advise and support clients in the execution of their goals. Michael spent seven years as the CEO of Alan Cohen Publications (ACP), managing the business and developing Alan's platform and branding from the ground up. During his tenure at ACP, Michael sold several Cohen titles to U.S. publishers and a number of foreign rights to more than 10 countries. In addition to increasing overall sales by 30%, Michael managed worldwide book tours and retreats, and branded the company message through mediums such as corporate DVDs, Web site, promotional materials and press kits. Michael also booked shows for the author on CNN, Fox News with Neil Cavuto, CNBC, WGN, and had article placements on MSN, CNET and in *Psychology Today's* Blues Buster, First for Women, and Body and Soul. Previously, Michael was the marketing director for Art After Five, a publishing house and gift line based in Colorado. During this time, he more than doubled sales and increased the client base by 50%. Combining a business degree from the University of Colorado and an M.A. in Health and Wellness from the Naropa Institute in Boulder, Colorado, along with his travels to India experiencing and studying the teachings of Indian masters, Michael has a unique background that enables him to merge the worlds of business and spirituality. He enjoys developing long-term relationships built with a deep sense of caring and integrity, and enjoys consulting with authors to create platforms and marketing strategies that drive and sell their books.

Hobbies and special personal interests: Surfing, yoga, Ultimate Frisbee, travel and reading.

Subjects and categories you like to agent: Prescriptive nonfiction including health, diet, nutrition, sports, self-help/personal growth, mind/body/spirit, humor, business, finance, and career books.

Subjects and categories writers shouldn't bother pitching to you: Fiction.

What might you be doing if you weren't agenting: I would be a professional traveler.

What's the most effective ways for writers to grab your attention: By adhering to the submission guidelines outlined on our Web site. We are looking for professional authors with strong platforms that want to get their message out to the world.

Do you charge fees separate from your commission, or offer non-agenting fee based services: Our agency offers consulting services for non-agented clients—usually involves sales/marketing/platform development coaching.

What are representative titles you have sold to publishers: *Counterintuitive: How Neuroscience is Revolutionizing Management* by Charles Jacobs, Ph.D. (Portfolio/Penguin); *The Loyalty Cure* by Timothy Keiningham and Lerzan Askoy (Benbella Books); *The Soul Truth: A Guide to Inner Peace* by Sheila and Marcus Gillette with Theo (Tarcher/Penguin); *Defenders of the Heart: 12 Strategies to a Richer, Fuller and More Satisfying Life* by Dr. Marilyn Kagan and Neil Einbund (Hay House); *Connecting to the Infinite: A 10-Step Approach to the Psychology of Yoga Poses* by Robert Butera (Llewellyn).

Why did you become an agent, and how did you become one: Because I love the book business and I love to sell. Put those two together and there you are—an agent.

What are your favorite books, movies, TV shows, and why: TV: *The Daily Show, Boston Legal, Grey's Anatomy, The Sopranos.* Movies: *Ray* and *What The Bleep! Do We Know.*

How would you describe "the writer from hell": 1) They call all the time. 2) They don't listen to what you tell them. 3) They think they should be on Oprah.

You're welcome to share your thoughts and sentiments about the business of writing and publishing: The publishing industry is going to become more and more competitive. It seems that everyone wants to write a book these days and there is only so much shelf space in the bookstores. Writers are going to have a more challenging time finding agents; agents will find it harder to place their clients; and the publishers' margins are shrinking because of this competition.

The following information pertains to Kristina Holmes.

Education: B.A. Anthropology, University of Hawaii, Manoa 2002.

Career story: After working in a number of editorial and freelance writing capacities, I began my career as a literary agent in 2005 at Ebeling & Associates. With over 15 years in the industry, Michael Ebeling provides much of the sales and marketing expertise with a big eye towards platform, while I have more of the literary eye. I have personally acquired and placed a variety of authors including investigative journalists, professional writers, bloggers, speakers, consultants, celebrities, entrepreneurs, memoirists, mediums, self-help leaders, psychologists and more. I'm very passionate about the type of books we represent—books that makes a positive impact on the world.

Hobbies and special personal interests: Do I dare say reading?! Beyond my love affair with books, I enjoy physical activities like hiking, biking, surfing, swimming, and going to the gym; nutrition, continuing education, astrology, metaphysics, photography, art, yoga, meditation, friends and nature.

Subjects and categories you like to agent: I love prescriptive, narrative, and literary projects (including memoir) in a variety of subjects. Genres I'm actively looking for in the prescriptive realm are health & wellness, mind/body/spirit, spirituality, women's issues, psychology, business, environment/green books, parenting and pop culture. Prescriptive books must have an established platform and a truly unique premise. Narrative/literary projects vary greatly—the ones that interest me the most have a very strong & polished voice with a great story behind it. In general, our agency is looking for a wide range of intelligent authors, whether they are serious, comic, edgy or eloquent.

Subjects and categories writers shouldn't bother pitching to you: Books that are negatively bent or overly dry; fiction.

What might you be doing if you weren't agenting: Traveling…

What's the most effective ways for writers to grab your attention: Write a succinct and savvy query including a brief statement about your book, why readers will love it and why you're the person to write it. Have solid credentials to write your book and demonstrate that you're a great writer by creating a clever query, proposal and sample material.

What are representative titles you have sold to publishers: See Michael's listing above.

How do you feel about writers: I LOVE WRITERS!! Writers are amazing individuals. True writers are artists, activists, mediators, educators, therapists, and much more. They may bring to light things we all know but in a way most of us can't express. Or perhaps they illuminate aspects of life that we've never considered and need to. I particularly love writers because they can make magic happen. How? By literally changing the way that we think, and as a result, who we are in the world. This is why I'm so passionate about positive change authors, those individuals that promote widespread and immeasurable compassion and integrity among readers through the written word.

How would you describe "the writer from hell": Unappreciative with an lack of willingness to do their part (write a great manuscript & book proposal, create and implement a successful promotion plan for the book), unable to accept constructive feedback, overly demanding, doesn't follow through with deadliness.

How would you describe the publisher and/or editor from hell: I haven't yet encountered a truly hellish editor, thankfully! Editors work hard and long hours, and tend to be very appreciative of the authors we bring their way. A few editors are unprofessional or nonresponsive, but the great majority are amazing people. Thank you, gracious colleagues…

What do you like best about your clients, and the editors and publishers you work with: Michael and I meet incredible people through our work and have the honor of guiding authors in their careers. It is a phenomenal business to be in for a variety of reasons. Through our authors and their networks, we are in the middle of a matrix of cutting edge leaders and thinkers—we become an integral part of exposing their ideas and knowledge to many readers around the world. It is a way for us to advocate certain issues, educate people or just make them laugh! And on a personal level, we love our clients. They are all very cool, fun and savvy individuals!

Do you wish to describe who you are: On a professional level, I'm encouraging, enthusiastic, savvy, determined, focused, motivated and relevant. I represent the younger sector of Americans who have had a lot of freedom to decide what they want in life and less of the societal constrictions that influenced older generations to follow a formulaic approach to life (education, marriage, kids, retirement). This environment has allowed us to consider alternative ways of being and living, which is very necessary for the health of our relationships, environment, economy and personal satisfaction in life. So, a big thanks to the older generations for helping to shape our history here in the U.S., while still so obviously fraught with political and social challenges, we have the opportunity to create our own reality; a freedom that so many others around the world lack. I get a lot of enjoyment out of being a literary agent, but I also look way beyond this to what I'm getting out of and giving to the world. I'm looking forward to being part of the positive growth and evolution occurring globally. Life is a deep mystery and something that I am profoundly grateful to be part of.

THE LISA EKUS GROUP, LLC

57 North Street, Hatfield, MA 01038

413-247-9325   fax: 413-247-9873

www.LisaEkus.com   e-mail: jfalla@LisaEkus.com

Agent's name: Lisa Ekus

Categories/subjects that you are most enthusiastic about agenting: Our primary interest is culinary titles, although we do consider some other non-fiction topics that are complementary, such as books on nutrition, health and wellness, and wine and beverages

What you don't want to agent: Fiction or poetry

What's the best way for writers to solicit your interest: We have proposal guidelines and other information about our agency on our Web site.

What, if anything, can a writer do to increase the odds of you becoming his or her agent: The best way for authors to approach us is with a formal query and/or proposal, and we appreciate if people do not call us. We follow up on all formal queries and submissions. We are a full member of the Association of Authors Representatives.

What do you think the future holds for book publishing: Despite an increasingly competitive marketplace, we continue to believe in a vibrant cookbook industry full of opportunity.

Please list representative titles that you have sold: Our Web site offers a comprehensive listing of our authors, book projects, and the many publishers with whom we have worked over the years. The agency celebrated its 25th anniversary this year. We began literary agenting services in 2000 and have negotiated book deals for more than 160 books since then. The business has four primary service areas: public relations, literary agenting, media training, and spokesperson opportunities.

THE ETHAN ELLENBERG LITERARY AGENCY

548 Broadway, New York, NY 10012

Agent's name: Ethan Ellenberg

Career history: Contracts Manager Berkley, associates Contracts Manager Bantam 1979-1984.

Categories/subjects that you are most enthusiastic about agenting: All commercial fiction: Romance, SF, Fantasy, Thriller, Mystery. All children's fiction: Picture book, middle grade YA. Narrative fiction: History, Health, Science, etc.

What you don't want to agent: Poetry

What's the best way for fiction writers to solicit your interest: By mail – see Web site. Synopsis / 1st 3 chapters / SASE.

What's the best way for non-fiction writers to solicit your interest: By mail – see Web site. Proposal / SASE.

Do you charge reading or managementfees: No.

What are the most common mistakes writers make when pitching you: Confusing lettrs. Too much personal information.

What, if anything, can a writer do to increase the odds of you becoming his or her agent: Write a great book.

Why did you become an agent, and how did you become one: Love books, felt it was the best job.

Describe to someone from another planet what you do as an agent: Represent authors, support them, handle their business.

What do you think the future holds for book publishing: continued impact of internet will affect us a lot.

Please list representative titles that you have sold: Christine Warren, six-book deal with St. Martin's; Susan Sizemore, three new paranormal romance titles to Pocket; MaryJanice Davidson, three new titles in the Undead series for Berkley; John Scalzi, another title in the OLD MAN'S WAR series to Tor; Karen Miller, three new fantasies to HarperCollins Australia; Ellora's Cave Publishing, thirteen new anthologies to Pocket; Bertrice Small, three new fantasy title to HON; Jim Tabor, *Forever on the Mountain*, coming from Norton in July, 2007; Susan Reinhardt, two new anthologies to Kensington; Eric Rohmann, *A Kitten Tale*, lead title from Knopf, January 2008; Ben Hillman, four non-fiction titles to Scholastic; and Martha Jocelyn, two new titles to Wendy Lamb.

ELAINE P. ENGLISH, PLLC

4710 41st Street, NW Suite D, Washington, DC 20016

202-362-5190   fax: 202-362-5192

www.elaineenglish.com   e-mail: Elaine@elaineenglish.com

Agent's name: Elaine P. English

Born: October 8, 1949; Asheville, North Carolina.

Education: Undergraduate in Latin (Magna Cum Laude) at Randolph Macon Woman's College; M.Ed. (Counseling & Personnel Services) University of Maryland; JD National Law Center at George Washington University.

Career history or story: After pursuing careers in teaching, social services, and personnel management, I completed law school and began working as an attorney for a public interest organization representing reporters and journalists on open government and media issues. I then joined a small firm with a publishing law/agenting practice. After that I had my own firm and managed a small literary agency. For more than 20 years in private practice, I have concentrated on Media and publishing issues. About six years ago, I decided to expand my practice to include agenting of commercial fiction. Now, on my own, I continue to pursue a practice of both legal and agenting services.

Hobbies, interests: Reading, hiking, natural photography.

Subjects & categories you are interested in agenting, including fiction & non-fiction: Women's Fiction, romance of all subgenres (both contemporary and historical, but primarily single titles), mysteries and thrillers.

Subjects & categories writers shouldn't even bother pitching to you: All Non-fiction (including memoirs), children's books, and inspirational projects.

What would you do if you weren't agenting: Simply practicing law.

What's the best way for fiction writers to solicit your interest: I accept (prefer) e-mail queries sent to queries@elaineenglish.com. I do not accept attachments to e-mails. Generally I will not make final decision without reading the entire manuscript.

What's the best way for non-fiction writers to solicit your interest: N/A.

Do you charge reading or any upfront fees: I charge no reading fees or any upfront costs. I may ask for reimbursement for copying and postage expenses only.

In your experience, what are the most common pitching mistakes writers make: I hate to see pitches that get bogged down in too much detail, while not giving a complete overview of the project. Also, I find that too many authors rush into submitting their manuscripts before they have actually completed editing, critiquing, and proofreading it.

Describe the client from Hell, even if you don't have any: The client who is not open to comments and criticism, and who refuses to learn anything about the realities of the publishing business.

What's your definition of a great client: A great client is one who sees his/her relationship with their agent as a partnership and is willing to work hard as a professional in this business. Of course, they are first and foremost an exceptionally talented writer.

How can writers increase the odds that you will offer representation: Know their target market and have a well-written, solid manuscript with an inventive plot, good pacing, strong dialogue and realistic, strong characters.

Why did you become an agent, and how did you become one: Because I love books, enjoy working with authors, and wanted to contribute, even in a small way, to the creative process by which the reading public is entertained.

What do you see in the near future for book publishing: The book publishing industry is clearly in a period of transition at the moment, and the precise parameters of the future are not that clear. I'm confident, though, that books, in some form, will be with us forever.

What are your favorite books/TV shows/movies, and why: *Jane Eyre* is my all time favorite books, in part, because it was my introduction into the wonderful world of women's fiction and romance. My taste in TV shows and movies is varied, but I tend to like character driven series. Frankly, with all the reading I do, there's not much TV time.

In your opinion, what do editors think of you: I hope that they think of me as a fair and reasonable professional who brings them quality projects.

What are some representative titles that you have sold: *Bond of Fire* and *The Northern Devil* by Diane Whiteside (Berkley; Kensington); *Pushing Pause* by Celeste Norfleet (Kimani TRU); *Trudy's Promise* Marcia Preston (Mira).

THE EPSTEIN LITERARY AGENCY

P.O. Box 356, Avon, MA 02322

www.epsteinliterary.com

Agent's name: Kate Epstein, kate@epsteinliterary.com
Born: New York City.
Education: B.A. with Highest Honors in English, University of Michigan.
Career story: I'm a publishing brat, then I spent a year at the University of Michigan Press. When I moved to Boston, I thought for sure I'd get back into the business. But the jobs paid so little and my husband was in school. So I did other stuff for three years. Then I started reading manuscripts for an agent and fell in love with publishing again and got a job in editorial. Then I decided on a change and became an agent. There's so much about publishing that's crazy and tough and not as great as it should be, but still, I love love love working with books and authors.

Hobbies and special personal interests: Raising my two kids. Reading—I've always resisted calling it a "hobby" because I don't consider eating or breathing to be hobbies, and I'm almost that dependent on it. I actually don't know how to go to sleep without reading. Feminism. I also have a vegetable garden and work out everyday, but I'm not necessarily proficient at either.

Subjects and categories you like to agent: 100% nonfiction for adults. Particularly interested in (in alpha order): Crafts, fashion, humor, inspiration, journalism, lifestyles, memoir, nonfiction narrative, parenting, pets, popular culture, reference, relationships, self-help, travel/adventure, women's interest.

Subjects and categories writers shouldn't bother pitching to you: Fiction, children's, poetry, screenplays.

What might you be doing if you weren't agenting: The longer I do it the harder it is to contemplate not agenting, but I loved being an acquisitions editor and could probably love it again. If I didn't work in publishing, I could imagine being a doula.

What's the most effective ways for writers to grab your attention: Make it clear you've read my website. I'm a sucker for compliments, like anyone else—especially if you've read something I agented.

Do you charge fees separate from your commission, or offer non-agenting fee based services: Nope.

What are representative titles you have sold to publishers: *A TV Guide to Life* by Jeff Alexander of *Television Without Pity* (Berkley Books); *Whatever You Do, Don't Run* by Peter Allison, (Globe Pequot-North America), (Nicholas Brealey-UK, South Africa), (Allen & Unwin-Australia), (Mouria-Dutch); *Don't Look Behind You* by Peter Allison (Globe Pequot-North America), (Allen & Unwin-Australia); *The Horses We Love, the Lessons We Learn* by Tena Bastian (Howell Book House); *You're Not the Worst Parent in the World* by Dr. Timothy Cavell (Fair Winds); *Your 401(canine) Plan* by Mary Jane Checchi (T.F.H. Publications); *The Green Horse* by Heather Cook (Howell Book House, a division of John Wiley & Sons, Inc.); *Rock Star Mommy* by Judy Davids (of the Mydols, Citadel); *Crochet for Men* by Drew Emborsky, The Crochet Dude, (Lark Books of Sterling); *The Everything Natural Health Book for Dogs* by Elaine Gewirtz and Shawn Messonier, D.V.M. (Adams Media); *Pets and the Planet* by Carol Frischmann (Howell Book House, a division of John Wiley & Sons, Inc.); *My Teen Has Had Sex, Now What Do I Do?* by Maureen Lyon, Ph.D., and Christina Antoniades (Rockport Publishing, a book for parents); *The New Holistic Way for Pets* by Paul McCutcheon, D.V.M. and Susan Weinstein (Ten Speed); *Knitting the Threads of Time* by Nora Murphy (New World Library); *Nail Your Law Job Interview* by Natalie Prescott and Oleg Cross (Career Press); *The Day After He Left for Iraq* by Melissa Seligman (Skyhorse); *Christmas Traditions* edited by Helen Szymanski (Adams Media, an F + W Publications Company); *Christmas Through a Child's Eyes* edited by Helen Szymanski (Adams Media, an F + W Publications Company); *The Secret Language of Knitters* by Mary Beth Temple (Andrews McMeel); *Hooked for Life: Adventures of a Crochet Zealot* by Mary Beth Temple (Andrews McMeel).

Why did you become an agent, and how did you become one: For four years I was an acquisitions editor, and I loved it. But then I stopped loving it—the corporate politics, the limitations on what kind of books I could do, feeling like my sympathies were with the writers but my job was to represent the publisher's interest (in the rare spaces where that is in conflict). I basically became an agent by putting out my shingle. I also took a number of more experienced agents to lunch and picked their brains—a number continue to provide support and advice, and I likewise share my knowledge when it's helpful. I've just joined the AAR, so in some ways I've arrived.

How do you feel about writers: Being a solo agent means that writers are my closest colleagues in many ways. I've always loved working with them and have enjoyed nurturing their varied processes—it keeps things interesting.

What are your favorite books, movies, TV shows, and why: I'm bad at picking favorite books, and I've become someone that rarely re-reads, so in a way my relationship with a book is always temporary. Though when it changes me that may be permanent. Some I've read recently that knocked me out are *Everything Conceivable* by Liza Mundy, *Here if You Need Me* by Kate Braestrup, and *Unaccustomed Earth* by Jhumpa Lahiri. All are wonderfully written, not fancily written (I don't like prose that calls attention to itself), and I really learned something. I read for pleasure, not to better myself particularly, but learning is a joy to me. Favorite TV shows is easy as I only watch two regularly now: *Battlestar Galactica* and *The Daily Show with Jon Stewart*. BSG inspires in me a deep love that comes from intriguing plot lines, great characters, cute actors. As to Jon, he makes the news interesting, which is a feat. I watch while lifting weights.

How would you describe "the writer from hell": Someone who is abusive to me or to editors. Life is too short to work with some people.

What do you like best about your clients, and the editors and publishers you work with: That they're all in the business of making books!

You're welcome to share your thoughts and sentiments about the business of writing and publishing: I think what inspires me most is how intimate the act of reading is, how books enter people's homes and lives. Whatever their subject.

Do you wish to describe who you are: In some ways I identify with the Little Engine that Could.

Will our business exist as we know it in 10 years or so from now: Yes, I believe it will, though certainly it will change.

FINE PRINT LITERARY MANAGEMENT

240 W. 35th Street, Ste. 500, New York, NY 10001

212-279-1282

www.fineprintlit.com

Agents' names: Amy Tipton; Colleen Lindsay, colleen@fineprintlit.com; Diane Freed, diane@fineprintlit.com; Gary Heidt, gary@fineprintlit.com; Janet Reid, janet@fineprintlit.com, June Clark, june@fineprintlit.com, Meredith Hays, Peter Rubie, peter@fineprintlit.com; Stephany Evans

The following information pertains to Amy Tipton.

Born: Jan. 27, Arlington, Texas.

Education: B.A. from Naropa University, M.A. and M.F.A. from New College of California.

Career story: I became an agent after working as a literary assistant and office manager at several literary agencies including JCA Literary Agency, Diana Finch Literary Agency, Gina Maccoby Literary Agency, and Liza Dawson Associates. I also worked as a book scout for Aram Fox, Inc. dealing with foreign rights and also worked as a freelance editor to Lauren Weisberger, author of The Devil Wears Prada.

Subjects and categories you like to agent: YA, commercial women's fiction.

Subjects and categories writers shouldn't bother pitching to you: Science fiction/fantasy.

What might you be doing if you weren't agenting: Writing or teaching.

Do you charge fees separate from your commission, or offer non-agenting fee based services: No.

What are representative titles you have sold to publishers: *Cracked Up To Be* by Courtney Summers (St. Martin's Press); Untitled by Amy Reed (Simon Pulse).

Why did you become an agent, and how did you become one: I just fell into it. I was Peter Rubie's assistant and he encouraged me to start taking on projects, to see if I could do it.

How do you feel about writers: I love writers. Of course.

What are your favorite books, movies, TV shows, and why: I probably have too many favorites to name… Books, recently? A lot of YA: *13 Reasons Why, Such A Pretty Girl, Looking for Alaska, The Fat Girl, Speak, Cracked Up To Be*, etc. All time? *The Abortion: An Historical Romance 1966, Breakfast at Tiffany's, To Kill a Mockingbird, Catcher in the Rye, The Stranger*. Authors I love: Richard Brautigan, Michelle Tea, Eileen Myles, Dorothy Allison, Tawni O'Dell, E. Lockheart, Patrick Carman, Courtney Summers, Daisy Whitney, Lauren Weisberger… As for movies, I love *Breakfast at Tiffany's, Surviving Desire, Secretary, Eternal Sunshine of the Spotless Mind, Down By Law, Ghost World, Serial Mom, Hedwig and the Angry Inch, Muriel's Wedding, Heathers*… I love these books/authors and movies because each one tells a great story.

How would you describe "the writer from hell": A writer who is (emotionally) high maintenance is hard to work with; someone who has ego and/or is constantly demanding attention—in the form of email or phone conversations—and second guessing you as an agent is difficult to work with.

The following information pertains to Colleen Lindsay.

Born: Burlingame, California; April 13.

Education: Life!

Career story: I spent most of my formative years hiding beneath the blankets with a flashlight and a book. My first job in publishing was in Northern California as a mass merchandise sales rep for Ballantine Books. For five years I served as Director of Publicity for Del Rey Books, a division of the Random House Publishing Group, where I specialized in the creative publicity and marketing of science fiction, fantasy, pop culture, YA fantasy, graphic novels and third-party licensed media. I've also worked as a freelance publicist and copywriter for several major trade publishers and as a book reviewer for the San Francisco Chronicle under the inimitable Pat Holt. My background in independent book publishing goes even further back to my first job as a bookstore manager in 1984 at the now-defunct San Francisco Bay Area bookstore Central Park Books. I also worked at Printers, Inc. Books in Palo Alto and spent six years as the marketing and events manager at Stacey's Bookstore in San Francisco.

Hobbies and special personal interests: Being faster than a speeding bullet. Gratuitous lifting of heavy objects in front of a mirror. Nerd-herding. Extracting cat claws from sofa. Occasionally getting Monopoly and Risk confused, thus resulting in the occasional unfortunate placement of hotels in the Ural Mountains while my army unwittingly invades Park Place. (Tragic!) Photography. Writing. Blogging. Sleeping whenever possible. And, of course, reading.

Subjects and categories you like to agent: Fiction of all types, both literary and commercial. I love writers who can engage me with amazing characters and a strong voice. Above all, I'm looking for writers who understand the importance of storytelling. I have a particular soft spot for and specialize in genre fiction: science fiction, fantasy, urban fantasy, paranormal romance, slipstream, new weird, horror, steampunk, space opera, military SF, cyberpunk and surrealism. I love YA and YA fantasy, too. In non-fiction, I'm looking for eloquent narrative non-fiction, works of LGBT interest and pop culture. I'd also like to see business or career books geared toward young women. And I'm very interested in graphic novels!

Subjects and categories writers shouldn't bother pitching to you: I don't represent any Christian fiction or nonfiction, inspirational, category romance, children's books, poetry or short stories.

What might you be doing if you weren't agenting: When I was a kid, I wanted to be (in the following order): A small Mexican boy named Pedro (in my head I had a sombrero and a burro), an astronaut, a veterinarian, a writer and an archaeologist. When I grown up, I still hope to become Indiana Jones. But for now, agenting fits nicely.

What's the most effective ways for writers to grab your attention: Shout? Wave? Throw an angry Pomeranian at me? Oh, wait, you mean as a writer? The most effective way to make me sit up and take notice is to write a damned good query letter with a strong hook. Let me know that you've actually read my submissions guidelines. This shows me that you're a professional, that you take your own career as seriously as I do.

Do you charge fees separate from your commission, or offer non-agenting fee based services: I'm freelance copywriter for several large publishers. I specialize in press materials and author Q&As.

What are representative titles you have sold to publishers: Well, since I am a brand-new agent (at the time of this writing, I've been working at Fineprint for about three months) I've only sold one book so far: *Total Oblivion, More or Less* by Alan Deniro (Bantam).

Why did you become an agent, and how did you become one: I'd been working in publishing for a number of years in marketing and publicity. While I really enjoyed the work, I also longed to be able to only work on those titles I really felt passionate about. After a layoff in 2007, several of my author and editor friends encouraged me to try to become an agent. The idea appealed to me but I didn't want to simply hang up my shingle and call myself an agent; too many people try this and they do a terrible disservice to their clients. I decided the best way to go about it was to do set up some information interviews with agents to learn more about it. I'd done close to twenty informational interviews by the time I met with Peter Rubie and Stephany Evans at FinePrint. We had a great conversation, talked for a couple of hours and by the time I got home later than evening, there was a job offer on my voicemail. It was kismet, I guess.

How do you feel about writers: I love writers. They make what I do possible.

What do you tell entities from other planets and dimensions about your job: If I met an entity from another planet, I'd be too busy buying him/her a beer and listening to his/her story so I could sell it!

What are your favorite books, movies, TV shows, and why: TV Shows: The new *Battlestar Galactica*: hands-down the strongest writing, ensemble cast and cinematography on television. Why this show hasn't won any Emmys for writing is seriously beyond me. Books: Oh, don't ask me that! I've worked in publishing or bookselling for more than twenty-three years. It would take all day to list all of my favorite books. Here's a random sampling: *Les Miserables* by Victor Hugo, *Always* by Nicola Griffith, *Dark Water's Embrace* by Stephen Leigh, *Perdido Street Station* by China Mieville, *Fall On Your Knees* by Anne Marie McDonald and *Operation Wandering Soul* by Richard Powers. I love good science fiction, fantasy, mystery, literary fiction, and queer stuff, with the occasional baffling foray into history. (Go figure.) Movies: Movies where things explode and pretty people disrobe. *The Lord of the Rings, Serenity, Wings of Desire, Children of Paradise*, Myazaki things.

How would you describe "the writer from hell": High maintenance. Life is too short for divas, and there are plenty of other writers out there who won't make an agents or editor's life miserable.

How would you describe the publisher and/or editor from hell: Editors who are non-responsive: they sit on manuscripts for months, sometimes years! They don't answer emails or return phone calls.

What do you like best about your clients, and the editors and publishers you work with: I love pretty much everything about what I do, honestly. I just wish I had more hours in the day to do it.

Do you wish to describe who you are: Professional nerd. Also, an amateur nerd of epic proportions. It's all good. I've recently overcome my terror of dancing in public. This mustn't be confused with an actual ability to dance, however.

Will our business exist as we know it in 10 years or so from now: Absolutely! And with the growing acceptance of e-book readers, books will become more accessible than ever before.

The following information pertains to Diane Freed.

Born: Sandwich, Illinois.

Education: B.S. in journalism, University of Illinois.

Career story: I've worked in the field of book publishing my entire career. I began at Prentice Hall as an editor/production coordinator, then on to *U.S. News & World Report* as a book editor and production supervisor. At Time-Life Books I produced direct mail promotional materials, and at Addison-Wesley/Pearson I was a book production supervisor. As owner and manager of my own publishing services company I worked as a book packager, producing titles for publishers from raw manuscript through electronic files to the printer. I became an agent when I joined the Peter Rubie Literary Agency, which later became FinePrint Literary Management in September 2007. Initially I focused on selling nonfiction, but now I'm representing fiction writers as well and enjoying it tremendously.

In each capacity, I've worked closely with authors in one way or another, so one of my strengths is the ability to collaborate well with them when producing proposals and working on manuscripts. I consider myself a sculptor of sorts: I like putting all the book parts together to make a product that readers can sit with and enjoy, and that they can learn from as well.

Hobbies and special personal interests: Swimming, boating, cooking, travel, movies, theatre.

Subjects and categories you like to agent: Nonfiction: Primarily relationship/advice, self-help, spirituality, health/fitness, memoir, current affairs, popular culture, women's issues, environment, humor. Fiction: commercial and literary fiction, partial to women's fiction. Generally, I can't resist a theme, fiction or nonfiction, in which the characters demonstrate real compassion for others in the lives they lead.

Subjects and categories writers shouldn't bother pitching to you: Poetry, science fiction.

What might you be doing if you weren't agenting: I'd be a book editor full time or seriously take up a favorite sport.

What's the most effective ways for writers to grab your attention: Write an honest, well-written query letter that tells me why your book is important, why it should be published now, and why you are the person to write it.

Do you charge fees separate from your commission, or offer non-agenting fee based services: As an agent, I do not charge fees separate from my commission. However, I do take on occasional, completely separate, editing and proofreading projects.

What are representative titles you have sold to publishers: *Natural Flexibility* by Charles Kenny (Hatherleigh); *Bufflehead Sisters* by Patricia DeLois (Berkley/Penguin); *Penguins in Amsterdam* by Patricia DeLois (Berkley/Penguin); *The Language of Comforting* by Val Walker (Jeremy Tarcher/Penguin); *Getting Past Your Breakup* by Susan Elliot (Da Capo/Perseus).

Why did you become an agent, and how did you become one: I became an agent because I like discovering new writers and being tuned in to what's on everyone's minds. I took Peter Rubie's course on the role of the literary agent, through New York University, which launched my agenting career.

How do you feel about writers: I can't help but like them a lot given what I do for a living! Most of all, I admire and respect them incredibly for their patience and perseverance.

What do you tell entities from other planets and dimensions about your job: I match up aspiring writers with editors at publishing houses that sell the type of books they have written.

What are your favorite books, movies, TV shows, and why: Tops on my book list would be any and all that had an impact on me when I was growing up, enabled me to see the bigger world, to walk in someone else's shoes: *Black Like Me, All Quiet on the Western Front, To Kill a Mockingbird,* Pearl Buck's stories. Favorite authors today include Lara Vapnyar, Geraldine Brooks, Larry McMurtry, Colm Toibin, Frank McCourt, John Irving, Anne Tyler, Alice Hoffman. Sedaris, Burroughs, and Keillor. Memoir: *Reading Lolita in Tehran* by Azar Nafisi, *The Glass Castle* by Jeannette Walls. Movies: *Thelma and Louise, Send Me No Flowers, Matchstick Men, The Sound of Music, Pulp Fiction, West Side Story.* TV: *Boston Legal, Sopranos, The Office, Charlie Rose Show.* Why? Not sure, but common threads might be that they feature inspirational characters that somehow touch me emotionally, or they just make me laugh. Or best of all, do both.

How would you describe "the writer from hell": Someone looking for an agent who calls out of the blue or e-mails me a chapter asking if I'll give it a quick critique. Then there is the client who calls at least once a day just to check up on how things are going.

How would you describe the publisher and/or editor from hell: Someone with poor communication skills and/or who doesn't follow up on things, but fortunately most editors aren't like this.

What do you like best about your clients, and the editors and publishers you work with: With clients, I like the collaboration process, discussing how to present the material—both the proposal and the text—in the best way possible so that it will catch an editor's eye. With editors, what I like best is the good feeling we each have upon discovering a new author/book, knowing that we both can appreciate and are excited about promoting what this person has written.

You're welcome to share your thoughts and sentiments about the business of writing and publishing: As an author, you should write from your heart, but be real about what's ahead if you want to be published. It's all about matchmaking from the moment you begin your search for a publisher: finding the right agent who believes in you and what you've written, who'll then find an editor/publisher who feels the same way, who'll in turn find—match you up with—that bigger audience who'll want to read and buy your book. And, as if you haven't heard this before: The best strategy you can have is to build your platform, especially for nonfiction, as editors always want a strong platform to show that you're getting yourself out there and have real credibility. Blogging regularly shows you have an audience; it's instant, free publicity for the publisher, so consider having your own blog if you don't already.

Do you wish to describe who you are: (See above.)

Will our business exist as we know it in 10 years or so from now: I hope so, but I think there will be much more niche stuff given how we can personalize our tastes more now with web sites, blogging, and so forth. Perhaps agents will focus on fewer types of books. And I do think that e-books will survive, although I'd predict that they will be more popular as reference books, texts, and the like rather than as mainstream fiction and nonfiction.

The following information pertains to Gary Heidt.

Born: Houston, Texas, 1970.

Education: Columbia University.

Subjects and categories you like to agent: Nonfiction: History, science, biography, reference, current affairs. Fiction: YA, very infrequently literary fiction.

Subjects and categories writers shouldn't bother pitching to you: Historical fiction, romance.

What might you be doing if you weren't agenting: Writing.

What's the most effective ways for writers to grab your attention: Good writing, evidence of hard work.

Do you charge fees separate from your commission, or offer non-agenting fee based services: No.

What are representative titles you have sold to publishers: *Third Class Superhero* by Charles Yu (Harcourt); *100 Girls* by Adam Gallardo and Todd Demong (Simon Pulse!); *The Uncensored Bible* by John Kaltner, Steve Mackenzie and Joel Kilpatrick (Harperone); *Beam Me Up Jesus* by Jim Gerard (Nation Books).

Why did you become an agent, and how did you become one: I love to read, and figured I'd get a job where I got to do it all the time. I was endowed with the sacred mantle by the great Stephany Evans.

How do you feel about writers: In general, the better a writer is, the more wonderful the personality. There are some exceptions, but the best writers are often deep, humble, compassionate, and dedicated to their work.

What do you tell entities from other planets and dimensions about your job: I sell long strings of letters.

What are your favorite books, movies, TV shows, and why: Some of my favorite books haven't been published yet. I know it doesn't make me seem very intellectual or mature, but I absolutely love big-budget special effects movies, particularly those concerning superheroes. I don't watch TV—I think many of my generation have been turned off by the tube.

How would you describe "the writer from hell": Often, the very worst writers are the ones with the biggest egos. Also, non-writers who want a big book deal but who don't want to share very much of the money with the co- or ghost-writer. Just because they don't really understand writing, they don't understand how important it is and how difficult.

How would you describe the publisher and/or editor from hell: The publisher from hell, through no fault of their own, goes bankrupt on the day your book is released. The editor from hell takes your submission but never reads it. Ever.

What do you like best about your clients, and the editors and publishers you work with: My clients are the smartest and most interesting people I've ever met. Editors and publishers are, in general, also extremely smart people, and a lot of fun to have lunch with.

You're welcome to share your thoughts and sentiments about the business of writing and publishing: The business is going through a lot of changes right now. People in marketing and sales have a much bigger say in acquisitions than ever before, and they are very risk-averse. I think they should find a way to categorize some of the riskier projects as R&D.

Do you wish to describe who you are: No.

Will our business exist as we know it in 10 years or so from now: Didn't you hear? The world ends December 21st, 2012, at 11 pm.

The following information pertains to Janet Reid.

Born: Seattle, Washington.

Hobbies and special personal interests: Contemporary art, contemporary music, justice and death penalty issues.

Subjects and categories you like to agent: Crime fiction, literary fiction tied to the west, cowgirl noir, how-to books, interesting and provocative books that everyone else sneers at.

Subjects and categories writers shouldn't bother pitching to you: Domestic, sexual, pastoral abuse. Poetry (although I represent poets for their narrative work), screenplays.

What might you be doing if you weren't agenting: Stalking Jack Reacher.

What's the most effective ways for writers to grab your attention: Write a compelling query letter on a twenty dollar bill.

Do you charge fees separate from your commission, or offer non-agenting fee based services: No.

What are representative titles you have sold to publishers: *Even* by Andrew Grant (Thomas Dunne Books); *The Breach* by Patrick Lee (Harper); *Standfast* by Kennedy Foster (Pocket); *The Little Book of Curses and Maledictions for Everyday Use* by DawnRae Downton (Skyhorse); *Chasing Smoke* by Bill Cameron (Bleak House Books); *Eternal Prison* by Jeff Somers (Orbit); *Flight of the Hornbill* by Eric Stone (Bleak House Books).

How do you feel about writers: Their work and their confidence in me allows me to earn a living doing what I love.

What do you tell entities from other planets and dimensions about your job: I try not to discuss my work when on vacation.

What are your favorite books, movies, TV shows, and why: The Wire. No further explanation needed.

How would you describe "the writer from hell": Well, I am Satan's literary agent, so I describe him as "mine."

How would you describe the publisher and/or editor from hell: There are no publishers or editors in hell. They rejected it as "not quite right for them."

What do you like best about your clients, and the editors and publishers you work with: Their brilliant writing and creativity. And they are hilarious. I'm so, so fortunate to have them on my list. As for editors: They work magic.

Do you wish to describe who you are: No. I don't want to scare anyone…yet.

Will our business exist as we know it in 10 years or so from now: Yes.

The following information pertains to June Clark.

Education: B.A. in Creative Writing/Mass Media, Queens College, NY; MA in Writing & Publishing, Emerson College, Boston, MA.

Career story: Marketing and promotion in cable TV, professional copywriter, published author, and playwright.

Hobbies and special personal interests: Writing, reading, traveling, music, food and wine, pets.

Subjects and categories you like to agent: Accepting limited submissions exclusively in commercial nonfiction areas of film/TV/ theater/film; entertainment biographies; health and beauty; reference and how-to; women's issues; relationships; self-help and pop psychology; food, cocktails and wine.

Subjects and categories writers shouldn't bother pitching to you: Sci-fi, horror, fantasy; military history; politics; Westerns; poetry; children's books; memoirs; short stories/novellas.

What might you be doing if you weren't agenting: Writing full time or working in theater.

What's the most effective ways for writers to grab your attention: Learn about the types of books I represent and tell me why you think I'm the right agent for your work. Then, show a strong platform or experience in the topic being written about and presenting a compelling query about your book.

Do you charge fees separate from your commission, or offer non-agenting fee based services: I have provided freelance writing/editing services but this work is always separate from our agency.

What are representative titles you have sold to publishers: *Black Comedians on Black Comedy: How African Americans Taught Us How to Laugh* by Darryl Littleton (Applause); *Eve's Bible: A Woman's Guide to the Old Testament* by Sarah Forth (St. Martin's Press); *The Vampress Girls* series by Jacy and Nik Nova (Kensington); *Beatleology: Embracing Your Inner Beatle* by Adam Jaquette and Roger Jaquette (Adams Media); *Simply Elegant Flowers* by Michael George (North Light); *Friends on a Rotten Day* by Hazel Dixon-Cooper (Weiser Books); *Bad Bosses, Crazy Coworkers & Other Office Idiots: 201 Smart Solutions to Every Problem at Work* by Vicky Oliver (Sourcebooks); *Obscene, Indecent, Immoral and Offensive: 100+ Years of Censored, Banned, and Controversial Films* by Stephen Tropiano (Limelight).

Why did you become an agent, and how did you become one: Was helping my agent, Peter Rubie, read query letters and found several projects I liked and was encouraged to pursue them. I continued agenting because it's a sociable job with exposure to interesting ideas and people. And as a writer myself, I can offer a well-rounded perspective to my clients.

How do you feel about writers: Sadly, I feel that being a talented writer is not enough in today's market. It is now necessary to have a great outreach and a reputation in your field or genre in order to get noticed by publishers. That means writers always need to be cultivating an audience for themselves and that's a tall order for many.

What do you tell entities from other planets and dimensions about your job: Not much, since they've never asked!

What are your favorite books, movies, TV shows, and why: In books, I enjoy edgy or witty writers that entertain like Dave Barry, David Sedaris, and Nora Ephron. On TV, I enjoy *In Treatment, Dexter, Real Time with Bill Maher, 30 Rock,* and a few guilty pleasures like *Top Chef* and *American Idol.* Movies... I rarely, if ever, go to the movies, I prefer live theater.

How would you describe "the writer from hell": Writers from hell are close-minded and resistant to suggestions on how to improve their work. They have difficulty meeting deadlines or effectively communicating with their editors and treat their agent like a secretary.

How would you describe the publisher and/or editor from hell: Publishers/editors from hell are those who don't return e-mails or phone calls from agents (and their authors), ask to see material but never respond to it, and expect the author to jump through unreasonable hoops or unrealistic delivery of material and then sit on the author's final manuscript for months without reading or honoring their end of the deal.

What do you like best about your clients, and the editors and publishers you work with: Open communication, positive attitude, respect for an author's work and editor's time, taking initiative, being proactive in their job or career, and acting professionally.

You're welcome to share your thoughts and sentiments about the business of writing and publishing: Publishing is going to have to reinvent itself, especially in our rapidly changing technology age. I think there will be a rise in eBooks and print on demand, both of which will make more sense, economically, in the long term. The challenge for all of us, particularly agents, will be in making sure that authors' rights and royalties will be protected. Publishers also need to put more efforts into promotion and place some focus on great concepts and great writing in balance with the whole "platform" issue.

Will our business exist as we know it in 10 years or so from now: I think publishing may go the way of the music business. Writers will become more creative in getting their work seen by the masses and possibly bypass publishers, due to the Internet. I also think the readers of tomorrow will become more comfortable with eBooks and there may be less printed books (saves paper and trees!).

The following information pertains to Meredith Hays.

Born: July 28, 1969 in Lynn, Massachusetts.

Education: B.A. from Skidmore College.

Career story: After attending the Radcliffe Publishing Program, I worked at Houghton Mifflin Co. in Boston in the now defunct Trade/Reference division, specializing in dictionaries. Moved to NYC and switched gears and worked at agencies, first Writers House, then Linda Chester & Associates, then Judith Ehrlich Literary Management and now FinePrint.

Hobbies and special personal interests: My family (husband, Reed, and son, Henry); animals (especially my cats).

Subjects and categories you like to agent: Fiction: Exceptional novels only; must be surprising, refreshing, and deeply satisfying no matter the subject. Nonfiction: Lifestyle; pop culture; animals; memoir (but no depressing or tragic stories!); crafts.

Subjects and categories writers shouldn't bother pitching to you: Fiction: No romance, westerns, sci-fi, fantasy, historical fiction, young adult, children's. Nonfiction: Cookbooks, diet, fitness, politics, finance.

What might you be doing if you weren't agenting: Dog trainer.

What's the most effective ways for writers to grab your attention: A short, well crafted, spell-checked query letter.

Do you charge fees separate from your commission, or offer non-agenting fee based services: No.

What are representative titles you have sold to publishers: *Rollergirl: Totally True Tales from the Track* by Melissa "Melicious" Joulwan (Touchstone); *Lonesome For Bears: A Woman's Journey in the Tracks of the Wilderness* by Linda Jo Hunter (The Lyons Press); *The Felt Bible* by Nikola Davidson (PotterCraft); *The Good Cat Spell Book* by Gillian Kemp (Celestial Arts/Ten Speed Press).

Why did you become an agent, and how did you become one: I went into publishing when I was right out of college and convinced that books were better company than people. When I moved to NYC the first job I was offered was at an agency and I liked how hands-on agenting is—how satisfying it is to follow a book from an idea to a manuscript to a finished published book.

How do you feel about writers: I admire their ability to stick with a subject long enough to create a book-length work.

What do you tell entities from other planets and dimensions about your job: Lots of work, little money.

What are your favorite books, movies, TV shows, and why: Books: *The Giant's House* by Elizabeth McCracken (because it's a lovely twisted love story); *The Time Traveler's Wife* by Audrey Niffenegger (because it's one of the only truly brave, unique and memorable stories I've come across); all of Jane Austen (because it's Jane Austen); all of Hemingway (because his dialogue cracks me up); *The End of the Affair* (because it's heart-wrenching). Movies: *Rebecca* (because it's pure gothic charm); BBC's *Pride & Prejudice* (because Colin Firth); *Bridget Jones' Diary* (because it's a guilty pleasure); *The Wedding Singer* (because of the music). TV: *Buffy the Vampire Slayer* (because it's brilliant); original *Mission Impossible* (because it's so stylized).

How would you describe "the writer from hell": One who is clueless about the industry. Oh, and impatient and unkind and contacts me all the time.

How would you describe the publisher and/or editor from hell: One who is mean and not willing to take risks or collaborate.

What do you like best about your clients, and the editors and publishers you work with: I like to work in tandem with clients & editors to create the best project possible. I'm open to new ideas and suggestions and am all for tweaking a manuscript if it will make it better.

Will our business exist as we know it in 10 years or so from now: Can't say because as a new mom I don't even know what's on my schedule for tomorrow!

The following information pertains to Peter Rubie.

Date and location of birth: Taplow, England, 1950.

Education: UK education system, NTCJ (Journalism Degree equivalent).

Career story: After college I worked in local and regional newspapers before moving to London to work in Fleet Street and then BBC Radio News. In 1981 I moved to the US and worked a variety of jobs including editor-in-chief of a local Manhattan, NY newspaper and freelance editor in publishing before becoming the fiction editor at Walker & Co., for six years or so. I left to become a partner in a small two-person literary agency, and started my own agency in 2000. In 2007 I merged my company with Imprint to form FinePrint (a company with nine agents as of this writing) of which I am the CEO.

Hobbies and special personal interests: Music, movies, Go, chess, reading, woodworking, computing, parenting, writing.

Subjects and categories you like to agent: Narrative nonfiction, parenting, pop science, history, current events, business; crime fiction, thrillers, offbeat literary, history, young adult and middle grade, literate SF and fantasy, things that excite and interest me.

Subjects and categories writers shouldn't bother pitching to you: Romance, women's fiction, scripts, poetry, poorly written material of any genre.

What might you be doing if you weren't agenting: Being a professional writer and jazz musician and earning a living as a carpenter (I'd have to be to do the other two things).

What's the most effective ways for writers to grab your attention: Write really well. Not gimmicky but just with a love of, and grasp of graceful English. Writing is about THINKING, so I'm looking for that VOICE that will engage me from word one.

Do you charge fees separate from your commission, or offer non-agenting fee based services: No.

What are representative titles you have sold to publishers: Atherton series (Little Brown), Land of Elyon series (Scholastic), and *Skeleton Creek* (Scholastic)—a cutting edge multimedia book internet project—by Patrick Carman; *First Copernican* by Dennis Danielson (Walker); *Enemy of the State* by Michael Scharf and Michael Newton (St Martin's Press); *On Night's Shore* by Randall Silvis (St Martin's); *Coyote's Wife* by Aimee and David Thurlo (TOR); *Soul Patch* by Reed Farrell Coleman (Bleak House).

Why did you become an agent, and how did you become one: I decided I spent so much time as an editor arguing on behalf of an author in-house it made sense to actually cross over and become an author's representative. I was one of several people let go by the house I was working for after my boss had the bad taste to accidentally drown, and so it made sense to make the move at that point.

How do you feel about writers: I spend every day talking with writers. The best are smart, funny, imaginative just who you would want to spend time with at work or at leisure. I have many friends who are writers, artists, and musicians. The worst are whinny, feel entitled for no good reason, feel aggrieved they're not getting their "due" and are unprofessional in their behaviour, acting worse than my 5 yr old. Guess who I prefer to be around.

What do you tell entities from other planets and dimensions about your job: Me, human. Do you know what a book is? It's where human beings do their best thinking and express their best ideas sometimes in the most beautiful language you can imagine.

What are your favorite books, movies, TV shows, and why: Too many to mention. All are what I would consider imaginative and well crafted pieces that throw a light on our world and how we deal with the people in it and our relationships to them.

How would you describe "the writer from hell": Unprofessional, demanding, doesn't get the industry and is only concerned with their ill informed opinion of what life should be, not dealing with what life actually is and making the most of that.

How would you describe the publisher and/or editor from hell: Don't communicate, lie to you, fail to keep promises, fail to follow up and look after your author in-house, are rude and dismissive, too lazy and too ignorant to edit properly.

What do you like best about your clients, and the editors and publishers you work with: They are smart, funny, imaginative, stimulating people who are a blast to hang out with and work with.

You're welcome to share your thoughts and sentiments about the business of writing and publishing: Publishing at present is struggling to come to terms with the speed that technology is changing the way we do things. The issue is not technology though, but how technology is changing how things have always been done and what model or models are going to replace the old ways. It's one reason senior publishing executives are leaving their institutions and starting up their own businesses based on their perception of how the industry is moving forward. Writers need to be writing about and coming to terms with these profound changes in the way we view and live our lives for better or worse, but too few are. Save me from another book about a dysfunctional childhood or relationship that is totally engrossed in its own misery and can't or won't relate to the lives of others.

Do you wish to describe who you are: Still figuring this one out.

Will our business exist as we know it in 10 years or so from now: Yes, but in 25 years—ah, that's a completely different question. People always want to read, and always want stories so publishing and books will still be around and valid. But in what form? Your guess is as good as mine.

The following information pertains to Stephany Evans.

Born: October 11, 1957; West Chester, Pennsylvania.

Education: Elizabethtown College, Elizabethtown, PA.

Hobbies and special personal interests: Running, mosaics, gallery-hopping, movies, reading, travel.

Subjects and categories you like to agent: Health, wellness, spirituality, food & wine, green/sustainability; narrative nonfiction; literary fiction, mysteries, women's fiction—both literary and commercial (romance, lite suspense, paranormal, historical).

Subjects and categories writers shouldn't bother pitching to you: Poetry, screenplays, children's books, parenting, true crime, fantasy, sci-fi, overtly moralistic tales; no abused women, no abused children.

What might you be doing if you weren't agenting: Reading, painting, home renovation, operate an art gallery.

What's the most effective ways for writers to grab your attention: Fine wine, flowers… but seriously: write well!

Do you charge fees separate from your commission, or offer non-agenting fee based services: No.

What are representative titles you have sold to publishers: *A Geography of Oysters* and *Fruitless Fall* by Rowan Jacobsen (Bloomsbury USA); *Do Dead People Watch You Shower?* By Concetta Bertoldi (HarperCollins); *Ina May's Guide to Childbirth* by Ina May Gaskin (BantamDell); *Fully Present: The Art & Science of Mindfulness* by Susan Smalley, Ph.D. and Diana Winston (DaCapo); *Soul Currency* by Ernest Chu (New World Library); *The Wisdom to Know the Difference* by Eileen Flanagan (Tarcher); *The Extra Mile* by Pam Reed (Rodale); *Something Borrowed* and *Love the One You're With* by Emily Giffin (St. Martins Press); *The Rose Variations* by Marisha Chamberlain (Soho Press); *Lee* and *Fields of Asphodel* by Tito Perdue (Overlook Press); *SEALed With A Kiss* by Mary Margret Daughtridge (Sourcebooks/Casablanca); *Nice Girls Don't Have Fangs* by Molly Harper (Pocket Books).

Why did you become an agent, and how did you become one: I never had any idea of being an agent. I feel extremely lucky to have met someone who offered me the opportunity, I loved it, and couldn't think of anything I'd like to do more.

How do you feel about writers: Lovely creatures! Many are my best friends.

What do you tell entities from other planets and dimensions about your job: I so rarely get to talk to such folk at all. We're usually catching up on other subjects.

What are your favorite books, movies, TV shows, and why: Too many too many too many too many! In books and movies, I tend to gravitate in two directions, either toward something lite and funny, or something dark and beautiful. In either case, the heart is most important, not the spectacle. TV is where I slum. Aside from PBS' *News Hour* and *Washington Week*, I most often will watch all the reality shows (except the ones where contestants eat gross things). In the little box, spectacle rules.

What do you like best about your clients, and the editors and publishers you work with: Their creativity, intelligence, heart, responsiveness, and their willingness to extend themselves, both to further their own careers and to make the world a better, more interesting place.

THE FIRM

9465 Wilshire Blvd., 6th floor, Beverly Hills, CA 90212

310-860-8000   fax: 310-860-8132

Agent's name: Alan Nevins

Education: Dual Major: B.S., Economics, UCLA; B.A., Motion Picture/Television Studies, UCLA.

Career history: Created in August 2002, and comprised of department head Alan Nevins and a team of literary associates, The Firm book division rose from the ashes of Renaissance, a successful literary agency of nine years standing, founded by Alan Nevins and two partners in 1993. Renaissance acquired the Irving Paul Lazar agency in 1993 after the death of famed super agent Irving "Swifty" Lazar. Alan Nevins had been Lazar's final and sole associate prior to forming Renaissance and the estate approached

Nevins about acquiring the Lazar enterprise. This acquisition, and that of the H.N. Swanson Agency, gave the infant Renaissance the enviable legacy of two of Hollywood's most colorful literary agents and solidified its place as a powerhouse literary firm supplying material to the New York publishers as well as the film/television community.

When Renaissance dissolved in 2002, Nevins joined music and film mogul The Firm as head of the book division. With longstanding and impressive relationships in Hollywood, London and New York, the agency currently represents more than 125 writers, boasts an extensive estate list and partners with more than thirty agencies worldwide for their film and ancillary rights. The Firm book division has major properties in development at the Hollywood studios and with the leading networks, a substantial backlist, and continues to attract some of the world's most sought after writers for both publishing and film representation.

Awards: Emmy Nomination, Executive Producer, *Homeless to Harvard: The Liz Murray Story*; Christopher Award, Executive Producer, *Homeless to Harvard: The Liz Murray Story*.

Categories/subjects that you are most enthusiastic about agenting: Commercial Fiction, Literary Fiction, Historical Fiction, Narrative Nonfiction, Current Affairs, Lifestyle, Women's fiction/Chick-Lit (original voices and storylines), Business, Children's: unique illustrations and creative storylines that truly stand out, YA fiction: focus on strong storytelling, prose and characters.

What you don't want to agent: Poetry, Short Stories.

What's the best way for writers to solicit your interest: Email query letter and synopsis to query@thefirmbooks.com.

What are the most common mistakes writers make when pitching you: Sending a proposal or manuscript without first contacting us. Sending single-spaced or otherwise improperly formatted manuscripts.

Please list representative titles you have sold: What to Expect When You're Expecting Series (Workman); *A Lotus Grows in the Mud* (Putnam); *Memories are Made of This* (Harmony); *By Myself and Then Some* by Lauren Bacall (HarperCollins); *Learning to Sing* (Random House); *Lost Laysen* (Scribner); *Tickled Pink* (Time Warner); *Deaf Child Crossing* (Simon & Schuster); *Less Is More* (Portfolio); *The Doors* (Hyperion); Larry Collins and Dominique Lapierre (All Titles); *The Black Dahlia Files* (HarperCollins); *Real Life Entertaining* (William Morrow); *Warren Beatty: A Private Man* (Harmony); *Audrey Hepburn: An Elegant Spirit* (Atria); Hank Zipzer YA Series (Penguin); Baggage Claim Simon & Schuster); *Love on the Dotted Line* by David E. Talbert (Simon & Schuster); *Emily's Reasons Why Not* (HarperCollins); *Tonight, Somewhere in New York* (Carroll & Graf); *Sins of the Seventh Sister* (Harmony); Roman Sub Rosa Series (St. Martin's); *The Sword of Attila* (St. Martin's); *Tomorrow to Be Brave* (Free Press).

FOLIO LITERARY MANAGEMENT, LLC

New York: 505 8th Avenue, Suite 603, New York, NY 10018

Washington, DC: 627 K St. NW, Suite 1200, Washington, DC 20006

212-400-1494   fax: 212-967-0977

www.foliolit.com   e-mail: See individual agent listings on Website

Agents' names: Jeff Kleinman, Paige Wheeler, Scott Hoffman, Erin Cartwright Niumata, Rachel Vater, Laney Katz Becker

The following information pertains to Jeff Kleinman.

Born: Cleveland, Ohio.

Education: B.A. with High Distinction, University of Virginia (English/Modern Studies) M.A., University of Chicago (Italian Language/Literature) J.D., Case Western Reserve University.

Career history or story: After graduating from the University of Virginia, I studied Renaissance history in Italy for several years, went to law school, and then joined a art & literary law firm. A few years later, I joined the Graybill & English Literary Agency before becoming one of the founders of Folio in 2006.

Hobbies, interests: Art, history, animals, esp horses (train dressage and event horses).

Subjects and categories you are intersted in agenting, including fiction and non-fiction: very well-written, character driven novels; some suspense, thrillers, historicals; otherwise mainstream commercial and literary fiction. Prescriptive Nonfiction: health, parenting, aging, nature, pets, how-to, etc. Narrative Nonfiction: especially books with an historical bent, but also art, nature, ecology, politics, military, espionage, cooking, equestrian, pets, memoir, biography.

Subjects and categories writers shouldn't even bother pitching to you: No mysteries, romance, Westerns, SF&F, children's or young adult, poetry, plays, screenplays.

What would you do if you weren't agenting: Practicing intellectual property law or training horses, or both.

What's the best way for fiction writers to solicit your interest: E-mail preferred (no attachments, please); include a cover letter and the first few pages of the novel.

What's the best way for non-fiction writers to solicit your interest: E-mail preferred (no attachments, please); otherwise snail-mail. Include a cover letter and perhaps a few pages of a sample chapter, and/or an outline.

Do you charge reading or any upfront fees: No charges. AAR members.

In your experience, wht are the most common pitching mistakes writers make: Groveling–just pretend this is a job application, and act like a professional; providing too much information–telling too much about the project, rather than being able to succinctly summarize it; sending a poorly formatted, difficult to read manuscript.

Describe the client from Hell, even if you don't have any: Someone who doesn't listen, doesn't incorporate suggestions, and believes that the world "owes" him (or her) a bestseller.

What's your definition of a great client: Someone who writes beautifully, who has marketing savvy and ability, who is friendly, accessible, easy to work with, fun to talk to, can follow directions and guidance without taking offense.

How can writers increase the odds that you will offer representation: For fiction, write a fabulous book with a fresh voice and compelling, unique perspective, and be able to sum up that book in a single, smart, intriguing sentence or two. For nonfiction, ENHANCE YOUR CREDENTIALS. Get published, or have some kind of platform or fresh perspective that really stands out above the crowd. Show me (so I can show a publisher) that you're a good risk for publication.

Why did you become an agent, and how did you become one: My law firm shared offices with an agency, and I did several book contracts. Gradually, I started reading manuscripts, talking to writers, and before long, there I was—a literary agent.

How do you feel about editors and publishers: I think that too often they're overworked and underpaid, and often don't have the time to really "connect the dots" in a manuscript or a proposal—so it's crucial that we (the writer and I) connect the dots for them.

How do you feel about writers: It depends on the writer.

What do you see in the near future for book publishing: something utterly new, that we haven't seen before. Maybe Microsoft will design it; maybe Pixar; but it's coming, and it'll revolutionize the industry.

In your opinion, what do editors think of you: That I'm honest, ethical, and have a solid list of clients.

What are some representative titles that you have sold: *The Widow of The South* by Robert Hicks (Warner); *Mockingbird and So It Goes* by Charles Shields' (Both To Holt); *Freezing Point* by Karen Dionne (Berkley); *I Was Only Trying to Help* by Quinn Cummings (Hyperion); *Finn* by Jon Clinch (Random House).

The following information pertains to Scott Hoffman.

Born: Holmdel, New Jersey.

Education: BA in Government from the College of William and Mary; MBA in Finance from New York University's Leonard N. Stern School of Business.

Career history or story: Publishing is a second career for me; before becoming a literary agent I ran a lobbying firm in Washington, DC. After a brief flirtation with finance, I realized my two favorite things in life were books and deals—so I figure out a way to do book deals for a living. In 2006, I was fortunate enough to find Jeff and Paige and start Folio with them.

Hobbies, interests: Chess, poker, opera, Bridge, golf, wine.

Subjects & categories you are interested in agenting, including fiction & nonfiction: Novels that fit perfectly in that sweet spot between really well written commercial fiction and accessible literary fiction (book-club type books); literary science fiction and fantasy; thrillers of all types; all kinds of narrative nonfiction, journalistic or academic nonfiction; edgy, cool pop-culture nonfiction.

Subjects & categories writers shouldn't even bother pitching to you: No kids' books, category romance, westerns, cozy mysteries, poetry, short stories, stage plays or screenplays.

What would you do if you weren't agenting: In venture capital or running for office.

What's the best way for fiction writers to solicit your interest: Check out our guidelines at www.foliolit.com

What's the best way for non-fiction writers to solicit your interest: Check out our guidelines at www.foliolit.com

Do you charge reading or any upfront fees: No charges. AAR members.

How do you feel about editors and publishers: I think there are many, many things traditional publishers do very well, and some other things they don't. One of the reasons we started Folio was to help authors market their own works—figure out ways to get individuals into bookstores to pick up their specific title.

How do you feel about writers: It takes a special kind of personality to be able to spend a year in a closet writing a book. I like special personalities.

What do you see in the near future for book publishing: Authors and their agents will begin to take a much more active approach in marketing their titles.

In your opinion, what do editors think of you: that I'm a fair and kind agent with a great eye for talent who's tough enough to always look out for his clients' best interests

What are some representative titles that you have sold: *Lessons From The CEO's Boss* by Anne Marie Fink (Crown Business); *The Fug Awards* by Heather Cocks and Jessica Morgan (Simon Spotlight Entertainment; *Volk's Game* by Brent Ghelfi (Holt); *The Kommandant's Girl* by Pam Jenoff (Mira); *The Preservationist* by David Maine (St. Martin's Press); *The Superman Wish* by John Hideyo Hamamura (Doubleday).

The following information pertains to: Erin Cartwright Niumata.

Born: Scranton, Pennsylvania.

Education: B.A. University of Delaware.

Career history or story: Erin has been in publishing for over fifteen years. She started as an editorial assistant at Simon and Schuster in the Touchstone/Fireside paperback division for several years; then moved over to Harper Collins as an editor, and then she went to Avalon Books as the Editorial Director, working on Romance, Mysteries and Westerns. Erin has edited many authors including Leon Uris, Stuart Woods, Phyllis Richman, Senator Fred Harris, Dean Ornish, Michael Lee West, Debbie Fields, Erica Jong, Brenda Maddox, Lawrence Otis Graham, and Joan Rivers.

Hobbies, interests: Dogs, reading, cycling, running, knitting, sewing.

Subjects & categories you are interested in agenting, including fiction & nonfiction: Fiction: commercial women's fiction, historical fiction, psychological thrillers, suspense, humor. I love sassy Southern and/or British heroines. Nonfiction: cookbooks, biographies, petcare/pets, parenting, self-help, pop-culture, humor, women's issues, fashion, decorating.

Subjects & categories writers shouldn't even bother pitching to you: Absolutely no romance, westerns, cozy mysteries, poetry, short story collections, business, travel memoirs, young adult, or picture books.

What would you do if you weren't agenting: I would be an editor or a teacher.

What's the best way for fiction writers to solicit your interest: I prefer a proposal (non-fiction) or a brief synopsis with the first 50 pages (fiction) with SASE. I receive too many e-mails to handle.

What's the best way for non-fiction writers to solicit your interest: Cover letter pitch explaining the book and the author's platform along with sample chapters and an outline.

Do you charge reading or any upfront fees: No charges. AAR members.

In your experience, what are the most common pitching mistakes writers make: Not following the submission guidelines and sending me something I don't represent. Or telling me that random people have read the book and think it's fantastic.

Describe the client from Hell, even if you don't have any: Someone who fights every piece of advice and calls/emails incessantly wanting updates or just to 'chat'.

What's your definition of a great client: Someone who is talented, has a great project, an open-minded attitude, eager to learn, ready to promote the book, and is happy to hear suggestions.

Why did you become an agent, and how did you become one: I was an editor for 16 years and decided to try my hand at agenting. So far, so good.

How do you feel about editors and publishers: Editors are overworked, attend entirely too many meetings, have piles of manuscripts that are all urgent, have very little time for anything - which is why agents are crucial for authors.

How do you feel about writers: Most are fantastic.

What are some representative titles that you have sold: *The House on Briar Hill* by Holly Jacobs (Harlequin); *Things That Make Us (Sic)* by Martha Brockenbrough (St. Martins); *Fabulous Felines* by Sandie Robins (TFH); *Sleeping With Ward Cleaver* by Jenny Gardiner (Dorchester).

The following information pertains to Rachel Vater.

Born: Covington, Kentucky.

Education: B.A. Northern Kentucky University.

Career history or story: Worked as an editor at Writers Digest Books before moving to New York City to be an assistant agent at the Donald Maass Literary Agency and then a literary agent with Lowenstein-Yost Associates. She joined Folio in 2007.

Hobbies, interests: Art, piano, theater.

Subjects & categories you are interested in agenting, including fiction & non-fiction: Fiction: fantasy, urban fantasy or anything with a paranormal element, YA novels (especially fantasy but also historical or anything dealing with contemporary teen issues), MG novels with a fun hip voice young teens can relate to. Nonfiction: pop culture, business, self-help or humor appealing to professional women.

Subjects & categories writers shouldn't even bother pitching to you: No category romance, westerns, poetry, short stories, screenplays, nor anything graphically violent.

What would you do if you weren't agenting: I would be an editor, designer, or musician.

What's the best way for fiction writers to solicit your interest: E-mail or postal mail. Query letter with first few pages. No attachments.

What's the best way for non-fiction writers to solicit your interest: Query via e-mail or postal mail, including credentials, platform, and outline.

Do you charge reading or any upfront fees: No charges. AAR members.

In your experience, what are the most common pitching mistakes writers make: Not knowing what their hook is—what makes the book stand out from the rest out there like it, and failing to emphasize that in the query.

Describe the client from Hell, even if you don't have any: A writer who won't gracefully accept editorial notes, and if he/she disagrees with any points, argues angrily instead of working with me/the editor to make the manuscript stronger or more clear.

What's your definition of a great client: A writer who mulls over edit notes carefully and implements them well and quickly, keeps a positive attitude, expresses gratitude to his/her agent and editor, is willing to promote his/her books with tireless enthusiasm.

How can writers increase the odds that you will offer representation: Know the market. Read a lot in your chosen genre and know what makes your book / series different and special.

Why did you become an agent, and how did you become one: I was an editor with Writers Digest Books, where I edited The Guide to Literary Agents. I had a chance to meet and interview a lot of agents. It sounded like a dream job to me, and it is.

How do you feel about editors and publishers: It's crucial for agents to know the preferences and quirks of each publishing house and the editors there. Several editors at the same imprint may all have different tastes, so it's important to keep up on who's looking for exactly what.

How do you feel about writers: Without them, I wouldn't have a job.

What do you see in the near future for book publishing: The ways in which an author can promote his/her book will keep expanding. New technology makes it easier, faster and cheaper to find and reach your target readership.

In your opinion, what do editors think of you: I'm a young ambitious agent building a great list.

What are some representative titles that you have sold: *Wicked Lovely* by Melissa Marr (Harpercollins Children's Books); *Halfway To The Grave* by Jeaniene Frost (Avon/Harpercollins); *Night Life* by Caitlin Kittredge (St. Martin's Press); *I So Don't Do Mysteries* by Barrie Summy (Delacorte Press); *Unpredictable* by Eileen Cook (Berkley).

The following information pertains to Laney Katz Becker.

Born: Toledo, Ohio.

Education: B.S., School of Communication, Northwestern University.

Career history or story: My background is as a writer. I started as a copywriter at the ad agency J. Walter Thompson. Over the next two decades I also worked as a freelance journalist; my articles have appeared in more than 50 magazines, including *Self, Seventeen, Health, First for Women.* I'm also an author (*Dear Stranger, Dearest Friend; Three Times Chai*). The process of having my first novel published introduced me to the agenting world and that was it—I was smitten.

Hobbies, interests: Tennis, sewing, reading, writing, theatre, spending time with my family, snuggling with my dog.

Subjects & categories you are interested in agenting, including fiction & non-fiction: Fiction: Anything well-suited to book club discussion, commercial/women's/mainstream/literary fiction that's got a fresh voice. Smart thrillers. Non-fiction: Memoirs, narratives about fascinating subjects that teach me something new, stories about people who've made a difference in the world. Also: pets, family, kids, women's issues, the environment and everything else that relates to my world.

Subjects & categories writers shouldn't even bother pitching to you: No romance, genre mysteries, children's, fantasy, science fiction, horror, Westerns.

What would you do if you weren't agenting: Something where I could continue to use my skills as a writer and voracious reader.

What's the best way for fiction writers to solicit your interest: I prefer an e-mail query with the first few pages embedded (no attachments). I also accept submissions by snail mail.

What's the best way for non-fiction writers to solicit your interest: Query via e-mail (preferred) or snail mail. Convince me there's a need for this book and why you're uniquely qualified to write and promote it.

Do you charge reading or any upfront fees: No charges. AAR members.

In your experience, what are the most common pitching mistakes writers make: Long, rambling query letters that leave me bored or confused. Being addressed as "Dear Agent," or "Dear Sir/Madam," or anything else that shows the author didn't bother to do his/her homework about me.

Describe the client from Hell, even if you don't have any: Defensive writers who don't listen and fail to say thank you. Writers who think they are (and should be) my top priority.

What's your definition of a great client: A talented writer who is also a wonderful person. Someone who is appreciative of suggestions, meets deadlines and is a pleasure to work with/talk to.

How can writers increase the odds that you will offer representation: If your work is compelling, thought-provoking and well-written, you'll get my attention. If your work is fresh and I don't feel like I've seen the idea/theme a million times before you'll stand an even better chance of winning me over.

Why did you become an agent, and how did you become one: Being an agent allows me to use all the skills I've developed as a writer/reader. Plus, I get to work with lots of interesting people—on all sides of the business.

Describe to someone from another planet what you do as an agent: Read, edit, find talented writers, help authors improve their projects, spend time with editors getting to know their tastes/preferences, sell wonderful manuscripts, help authors understand the publishing process, negotiate contracts, come up with fresh ideas about how to promote authors' works, pitch ideas, and finally…practice conflict resolution and hold an occasional hand or two.

How do you feel about editors and publishers: I think that agents and editors are more alike than different. We've all got piles of manuscripts on our desks and we're all trying to make the right connections. We love to read and are busy trying to shepherd projects we're passionate about through the process. We're all overworked/underpaid but we're doing what we do because we love it.

What are your favorite books/TV shows/movies, and why: Although it's no longer on the air, my favorite TV show of all time is *The West Wing*. My favorite movie is *Apollo 13*. My favorite book? I can't decide on just one.

In your opinion, what do editors think of you: They like the fact that I've already done the writing thing and bring that knowledge with me into the publishing world.

On a personal non-professional level, what do you think people think of you: I'm strong and I don't give up. I've faced many challenges – and keep battling back; I'm a mom whose kids have always been a priority; I'm Type-A, but I know it, which makes it sort of okay.

What are some representative titles that you have sold: *Obedience* by Will Lavender (Crown Books/Shaye Areheart); *Take Me Home: The Search for Meaning—and a Decent Restroom—in the Third World* by Eve Brown (Doubleday/Broadway).

The following information pertains to Paige Wheeler.

Born: Richmond, Virginia.

Education: B.A, magna cum laude, Boston University.

Career history or story: After working in bookstores in college, I moved to London and worked for a financial publisher. My first publishing job in the US was working in editorial for Harlequin/Silhouette. I then worked as an editor for an investment bank before switching over to agenting. My first agenting job was at Artists Agency, where I repped writers for TV, producers, celebrities as well as book authors. I started my own agency, Creative Media Agency Inc, and ran that for nine years before I met Jeff and Scott. Together we decided to form FOLIO in 2006 to meet the changing needs of authors.

Hobbies, interests: My puppy, reading (!), wine, antiques, interior design/reno.

Subjects & categories you are interested in agenting, including fiction & non-fiction: Fiction: I'm looking for very well written commercial and upscale fiction—it should have a fresh and fabulous voice; women's fiction, mysteries and thrillers (the smarter the better). Nonfiction: narrative and prescriptive—self help, how to, women's issues, business books (all types), pop culture, soft science, politics, travel, design.

Subjects & categories writers shouldn't even bother pitching to you: No Westerns, SF&F, children's, poetry, plays, screenplays.

What would you do if you weren't agenting: There's another option???

What's the best way for fiction writers to solicit your interest: I prefer an e-mail query with a synopsis, the first few pages embedded (no attachments). I also accept submissions by snail mail.

What's the best way for non-fiction writers to solicit your interest: E-mail query preferred but snail mail is fine, with a lot of information about the author and his/her platform. What is unique about this project and why is the author the perfect person to write it?

Do you charge reading or any upfront fees: No charges. AAR members.

In your experience, what are the most common pitching mistakes writers make: Oooh, I love groveling! Seriously, forgetting to include specifics (what the project is about), and not understanding the market for the book.

Describe the client from Hell, even if you don't have any: Writers who fail to realize that they are not my only client and aren't appreciative of all the things that I do behind the scenes.

What's your definition of a great client: A fabulous writer who understands the process of publishing, is a go-getter but is also patient and understanding of time constraints, and is appreciative of my hard work.

How can writers increase the odds that you will offer representation: If you're an outstanding writer with fresh ideas and an engaging voice, you'll get my attention. For nonfiction, it's about platform, platform, platform—and a unique slant on a concept or idea.

Why did you become an agent, and how did you become one: Again, there's another option????

Describe to someone from another planet what you do as an agent: Um, I don't handle SF& F so I wouldn't be able to communicate with them.

How do you feel about editors and publishers: I think pairing an author with the perfect editor for a project is the difference between merely getting published and building a very successful career. It's our job to find the perfect editor for a particular project.

How do you feel about writers: One of the things I love about this business is that I work with smart and talented people. In general, most writers are super informed and passionate people who are eager to share their ideas with a larger audience. I like people who possess a viewpoint or don't shy away from an idea and have the information to back it up.

What do you see in the near future for book publishing: Faster adaptation to emerging technologies—as long as it's financially beneficial to the publisher.

In your opinion, what do editors think of you: I'm both intrigued and horrified to find out, but I do hope it's that I'm tenacious, ambitious, and have the drive to succeed.

On a personal non-professional level, what do you think people think of you: Friends and family think that I should probably work less and enjoy life more.

What are some representative titles that you have sold: *On The Edge of the Woods* by Diane Tyrrel (Berkley Sensation); *Targeting the Job You Want* by Kate Wendleton (Career); *Once Upon a Time in Great Britian* by Melanie Wentz (Travel) (St. Martin's); *On Strike for Christmas* by Sheila Roberts (St. Martin's); *An Affair Most Wicked* by Julianne Maclean (Avon); *Don of the Dead* by Casey Daniels (Avon); *Sit Stay Slay* by Linda O. Johnston (Berkley Prime Crime).

The following information pertains to Celeste Fine.

Born: Redlands, California.

Education: BA in Government, magna cum laude, Harvard University.

Career history or story: After working as an assistant, foreign rights agent, foreign rights manager, and literary agent at Vigliano Associates and Trident Media Group, I joined Folio Literary Management in 2006.

Hobbies, interests: Pool, music, games, tequila.

Subjects & categories you are interested in agenting, including fiction & non-fiction: Nonfiction: 90% of my list is nonfiction—mostly platform-driven projects. Fiction: I do a select list of fiction—mostly projects with memorable characters.

Subjects & categories writers shouldn't even bother pitching to you: Women's fiction, romance, graphic novels.

What would you do if you weren't agenting: Rockstar.

What's the best way for fiction writers to solicit your interest: E-mail.

What's the best way for non-fiction writers to solicit your interest: E-mail

Do you charge reading or any upfront fees: No charges. AAR members.

In your experience, what are the most common pitching mistakes writers make: Not being able to provide a compelling sound bite of the project and not knowing their competition.

What's your definition of a great client: A client who is talented, expects to work as hard as I am on their project, and understands the business of publishing.

How can writers increase the odds that you will offer representation: Be an expert on your subject.

Why did you become an agent, and how did you become one: I fell in love with partnering with authors to make the most of their careers.

How do you feel about writers: A talented writer can change you. That is extraordinary.

What do you see in the near future for book publishing: I imagine there will be a lot of differences. Very exciting.

What are your favorite books/TV shows/movies, and why: *Tale of Two Cities* and *The Apologist*; *Arrested Development* and *The Closer*; *Confessions of a Dangerous Mind* and *The Departed*.

What are some representative titles that you have sold: *The Alchemy Of Aging Well* by Randy Raugh (Rodale); *The LCA's The 30-Day Diabetes Miracle And Cookbook* (Perigee); *The 99¢ Only Store Cookbook* by Christiane Jory (Adams Media); *Eat, Drink, And Be Gorgeous* by Esther Blum (Chronicle); *Unusually Stupid Celebrities* and *Unusually Stupid Politicians* by Kathy And Ross Petras (Villard); *It's Not News, It's Fark* by Drew Curtis (Gotham); *Good Granny, Bad Granny* by Mary Mchugh (Chronicle); *Confessions Of A Gambler* by Rayda Jacobs (Overlook); *Rightsizing* by Ciji Ware (Springboard Press).

JEANNE FREDERICKS LITERARY AGENCY, INC.

221 Benedict Hill Road, New Canaan, CT 06840

203-972-3011

www.jeannefredericks.com   e-mail: jeanne.fredericks@gmail.com

Agent's name: Jeanne Fredericks

Born: April 19, 1050, Mineola, New York.

Education: B.A. Mount Holyoke College, 1972, major in English; Radcliffe Publishing Procedures Course, 1972. M.B.A., New York University Graduate School of Business (now called Stern), major in marketing, 1972.

Career history: Established own agency in 1977 after being an agent and acting director of Susan P. Urstadt (1990-1996). Prior to that, I was an editorial director of Ziff-Davis Books (1980-1981), acquiring editor and the first female managing editor of Macmillan's Trade Division (1974-1980), and assistant to the editorial director and foreign/subsidiary rights director of Basic Books (1972-1974). Member of AAR and Authors Guild.

Hobbies/personal interests: Crew, swimming, yoga, reading, traveling, casual entertaining, gardening, photography, family activities, volunteering at church.

Categories/subjects that you are most enthusiastic about agenting: Practical, popular reference by authorities, especially in health, science, fitness, gardening, and women's issues. Also interested in business, cooking, elite sports, parenting, travel, and antiques/decorative arts.

What you don't want to agent: Horror, occult fiction, true crime, juvenile, textbooks, poetry, essays, plays, short stories, science fiction, pop culture, guides to computers and software, politics, pornography, overly depressing or violent topics, memoirs that are more suitable for one's family or that are not compelling enough for the trade market, romance, manuals for teachers.

If you were not an agent, what might you be doing instead: Reading and traveling more for pleasure, volunteering more, learning to play piano, writing or perhaps running a publishing company.

What's the best way for writers to solicit your interest: Please query with a SASE (or by e-mail without attachments to jeanne.fredericks@gmail.com). No phone calls, faxes, or deliveries that require signatures.

Do you charge reading or management fees: No.

Can you provide an approximation by % of what you tend to represent by category: 1% fiction (so far just from existing non-fiction clients); 0% children's; 99% non-fiction.

What are the most common mistakes writers make when pitching you: Calling me to describe their proposed books and giving me far too much detail. I'd much rather see that potential clients can write well before I spend valuable phone time with them. Also, claiming to have the only book on a subject when a quick check on the Internet reveals that there are competitive titles.

How would you describe the client from Hell: An arrogant, pushy, self-centered, unreliable writer who doesn't understand publishing or respect my time, and who vents anger in an unprofessional way.

How would you describe the perfect client: A creative, cooperative, media-savvy professional who is an expert in his or her field and who can offer information and guidance that is new and needed by a sizeable audience.

How and why did you ever become an agent: I reentered publishing as an agent because the flexible hours and home-based office was compatible with raising children. I enjoy working with creative authors who need my talents to find the right publishers for their worthy manuscripts and to negotiate fair contracts on their behalf. I'm still thrilled when I open a box of newly published books by one of my authors, knowing that I had a small role in making it happen. I'm also ever hopeful that the books I represent will make a positive difference in the lives of many people.

What, if anything, can a writer do to increase the odds that you will become his or her agent: Show me that they have thoroughly researched the competition and can convincingly explain why their proposed books are different, better, and needed by large, defined audiences. Be polite, patient, and willing to work hard to make their proposals ready for submission. Build their media experience and become in demand for regular workshops/presentations.

How would you describe to someone (or thing) from another planet what it is that you do as an agent: I select authors, find them the right publishers, negotiate the best deal for them, act as their advocate and diplomat through the publishing process, and handle the money side of the business for them so that they can concentrate on what they do best.

Do you have any particular opinions or impressions of editors and publishers in general: Having been on the editorial side of publishing for about 10 years, I have great respect for the demands on the time of a busy editor. I therefore try to be targeted and to the point when I telephone or email them and provide them with a one-page pitch letter that gives them the essence of what they need to make a proposal to management. I also make sure that the proposals I represent are focused, complete, and professional to make it easy for an editor to grasp the concept quickly and have a good sense of what the book will be like and why it will sell well. With few exceptions, editors value the creativity and hard work of authors and are intelligent and well meaning. Since they are often overwhelmed with manuscripts, paperwork, and meetings, though, they sometimes neglect some of their authors and need an agent's nudging and reminders. I think that some editors are frustrated by the emphasis on celebrity and platform in the selection process and wish there were more publishers willing to build the careers of authors who have writing talent and authority in their fields of expertise. I share that frustration with them.

Please list representative titles you have sold: *Your New Green Home* and *Beautiful Solar Homes* by Stephen Snyder and Dave Bonte (Gibbs Smith); *Lilias' Yoga Gets Better with Age* by Lilias! Folan (Rodale); *Waking the Warrior Goddess: Dr. Christine Horner's Program to Protect Against and Fight Breast Cancer* by Christine Horner, M.D. (Basic

Health); *Stealing with Style* and *The Big Steal* (novels) by Emyl Jenkins (Algonquin); *Raising an Optimistic Child* by Bob Murray, Ph.D. and Alicia Fortinberry (McGraw Hill); *Palm Springs Gardening* by Maureen Gilmer (Contemporary/McGraw Hill); *Sentinel of the Seas: Life and Death at the Most Dangerous Lighthouse Ever Built* by Dennis Powers (Kensington); *Melanoma* by Catherine M. Poole and Dupont Guerry, M.D. (Yale University Press); *Heal Your Heart with EECP* by Debra Braveman, M.D. (Celestial Arts); *Homescaping* by Anne Halpin (Rodale); *The Monopoly Guide to the Real Estate Marketplace* by Carolyn Janik (Sterling); *Cowboys and Dragons: Shattering Cultural Myths to Advance Chinese-American Business* by Charles Lee, Ph.D. (Dearborn); *The American Quilt* by Robert Shaw (Sterling); *No Limit: From the Cardroom to the Boardroom* by Donald Krause and Jeff Carter (AMACOM); *Rough Weather Seamanship for Sail and Power* by Roger Marshall (International Marine/McGraw Hill); *Building Within Nature* by Andy and Sally Wasowski (University of Minnesota Press); *The Green Market Baking Book* by Laura Martin (Sterling); *I Ching for Executives* by Donald Krause (AMACOM); *Whitelaw's World: The Adventures and Dangerous Times of Master Wreckers* by Dennis Powers (AMACOM); *Techniques of Graphite Pencil Drawing* by Katie Lee (Sterling); *Artful Watercolor* by Carolyn Janik and Lou Bonamarte (Sterling).

SARAH JANE FREYMANN LITERARY AGENCY

59 West 71st Street, # 9b, New York, NY 10023

212-362-9277   Steve Schwartz: 212-362-1998

www.sarahjanefreymann.com   e-mail: sarah@sarahjanefreymann.com, steve@sarahjanefreymann.com

Please send submissions to submissions@sarahjanefreymann.com

Agents' names: Sarah Jane Freymann, Steve Schwartz (Associate)
The following information pertains to Sarah Jane Freymann.
Born: Sarah Jane was born in London, England.
Education: Although I spent most of my childhood in New York City, I went to a French school—the Lycee Francais de New York. I also studied ballet with Balanchine. The environment at home was interestingly 19th century European.

Career history or story: My first real job was with the United Nations. I also worked as a model … in real estate … and as an editor in a publishing company.

Hobbies, interests: I am interested in spiritual journeys; adventures of all kinds that generate insight, growth, and a greater appreciation of the world, an inquisitive mind, and a gentle heart. But as they should, my personal interests and hobbies keep changing. Right now I am also into ballroom dancing...yoga...and knitting.

Subjects & categories you are interested in agenting, including fiction & non-fiction: Sarah Jane: Nonfiction: Spiritual, psychology, self-help; women's issues, health/medicine (conventional and alternative); cookbooks; narrative non-fiction; natural science, nature; memoirs; cutting-edge journalism; multi-cultural issues; parenting; lifestyle; Fiction: sophisticated mainstream and literary fiction with a distinctive voice. I would especially like to find literary, contemporary fiction and literary historical fiction.

Steve Schwartz: Nonfiction: Business; sports; humor; men's issues; politics; new technology; Fiction: Mystery/crime; thrillers, fantasy; historical sagas; adventure; sports—popular fiction in almost any genre as long as it grabs me from the first paragraph and doesn't let go.

Subjects & categories writers shouldn't even bother pitching to you: Westerns, screenplays, and almost anything channeled.

What would you do if you weren't agenting: Working with "doctors without borders;" working with children and adolescents; a star athlete; a competitive ballroom dancer; an opera singer (while at the same time, cultivating a quiet haven in a garden by the sea.)

What's the best way for fiction writers to solicit your interest: Via a well-written and interesting query letter with SASE, or via an e-mail query (with no attachments).

What's the best way for non-fiction writers to solicit your interest: Via a well-written and interesting query letter with SASE, or via an e-mail query (with no attachments).

Do you charge reading or any upfront fees: There are no reading or upfront fees.

In your experience, what are the most common pitching mistakes writers make: Calling and attempting to describe projects over the phone; characterizing a project as "The best…" "Startling…" "Never before in publishing history…" and so on; and telling us what they're going to say in an interview on the Oprah Winfrey show.

Describe the client from Hell, even if you don't have any: I honestly wouldn't know because I've never had any, but if there were such clients it would be people who aren't honest with us about themselves, the work, or who has seen it in the past or is reviewing it now.

What's your definition of a great client: Someone who is not only a natural storyteller and writes beautifully and with passion and intelligence, but who is also a nice human being—a "mensch." Someone with a sense of humor, who also has the patience, the willingness and the humility to rewrite and rework their material when necessary. And someone who appreciates the hard work and the passion that their agent brings to the job. I am fortunate to have several such clients.

How can writers increase the odds that you will offer representation: Submit a strong, clear, well-written query that sells both the book and its author, with the promise of substance rather than hype.

Why did you become an agent, and how did you become one: I became an agent by rushing in where angels feared to tread, and if I knew then what I know now … I'd do the same thing all over again.

Describe to someone from another planet what you do as an agent: That I am a treasure hunter in search of new universes and galaxies, and of new ways of looking at our old, familiar universe. That I assist writers in getting published by helping them edit and shape their proposals, and then by being a deal-maker, a matchmaker, and a negotiator once the work is ready to be launched.

How do you feel about editors and publishers: I love editors. They are intelligent, idealistic, well-informed, incredibly hardworking, and absolutely devoted to their books and to their authors.

How do you feel about writers: I have great respect for writers. They have the capacity to reveal the truth and create a new vision for the world.

What do you see in the near future for book publishing: Thanks in large measure to the Internet, the publishing universe (like the rest of the world) is becoming increasingly more global. This is a challenge—but it's a good one I think we should welcome.

In your opinion, what do editors think of you: I would imagine editors think I'm a straight shooter and a tough negotiator—but someone who is always fair, invariably gracious, and has terrific projects.

On a personal, nonprofessional level, what do you think people think of you: People say that I am charming, generous, elegant, warm, intuitive and passionate about my work. As to what people dislike, I suppose I can be opionated at times, but that is balanced by one of my favorite clients who said she was sorry that there "weren't more of me."

What are some representative titles that you have sold: *Souls of the Air: Invoking the Essence of Birds* by Sy Montgomery (Simon and Schuster); *The Perfect Recipe for Losing Weight and Eating Great: How to Change Your Life for Good* (NY Times Bestseller—Houghton Mifflin); *Mediterranean Hot & Spicy* by Aglaia Kremezi (Random House/Broadway); *Birth Day: A Pediatrician Explores the Science, the History, and the Wonder of Childbirth* by Dr. Mark Sloan (Random House/Ballantine); *How to Say It: Marketing with New Media* by Lena Claxton and Alison Woo (Penguin Group); *Wisdom 2.0: Ancient Secrets for the Creative and Constantly Connected* by Soren Gordhamer (Harper One); *Princely Palaces of India* by Melba Levick, Ameeta Nanji, and Mitchell Crites (Rizzoli); *100 Places Every Woman Should Go* by Stephanie Elizando Griest (Traveler's Tales) and *Mexican Enough: My Life Along the Border Lines* (Simon & Schuster/Atria); *I Want to be Left Behind: My Rapture Here on Earth* by Brenda Peterson (a Merloyd Lawrence book); *That Bird Has My Wings: The Autobiography of an Innocent Man* by Jarvis Jay Masters with an introduction by Pema Chödrön (Harper One); *Don't Start the Revolution Without Me* by Jesse Ventura (Skyhorse); *Bulletproof Faith: A Spiritual Survival Guide for Gay & Lesbian Christians* by Candace Chellow-Hodge (Jossey-Bass); *Stylish Sheds and Elegant Hideaways* by Debra Prinzing and William Wright (Clarkson Potter); *Tossed & Found: Customization, Reclamation, & Personalization for Your Home* by John and Linda Meyers (Steward, Tabori & Chang); *People of the Whale* by Linda Hogan (Fiction—Norton); and *Language for a New Century: Contemporary Poetry from the Middle East, Asia, and Beyond* compiled by Tina Chang, Ravi, Shankar, and Natalie Handal (Norton).

FULL CIRCLE LITERARY, LLC.

7676 Hazard Center Drive, Suite 500, San Diego, CA 92180

858-824-9269 (No phone queries, please!)

www.fullcircleliterary.com   www.fullcirclelit.blogspot.com

Agents' names: Lilly Ghahremani, Stefani Von Borstel. For adult fiction and non-fiction, please e-mail query to query@fullcircleliterary.com. For children's and teen fiction and nonfiction, please e-mail query to kidsquery@fullcircleliterary.com.

Born: Lilly: November 8, Chicago. Stefanie: Libra born in San Antonio, Texas.

Education: Lilly: J.D. from UCLA School of Law; B.A. in English from University of Michigan; M.B.A. from San Diego State University (expected 2009). Stefanie: B.A. in English and Professional Marketing Program, University of California, San Diego.

Career history: Lilly: Following law school, I decided to "use my powers for good." With some editing experience under my belt, I formally began my publishing career with a small firm that specialized in authors' affairs. Although I loved helping authors finalize the paperwork, addressing copyright affairs and doing some pitching to publishers, I wanted to really dig in and be involved in the creative process more, finding and growing talent and carrying it through to completion, so we launched Full Circle in 2004 to allow us to do just that. Stefanie: As an undergrad English Lit student, I started my first internship in the editorial department of Penguin/PSS where my first duties included reading submissions and testing copy for *Mad Libs!* I thought, wow, what a fun industry, this is for me! I moved on to working in the marketing department at Harcourt where I worked over the course of seven years in various publicity, advertising, and promotions positions. After experiencing both the editorial and marketing/sales side of trade publishing, I decided to combine my experience to help writers navigate the publishing world as an agent.

Hobbies and special personal interests: Lilly: Traveling, reading (of course!), dancing, collecting random pop trivia, Bikram yoga. Stefanie: Cooking and entertaining, flamenco and salsa dancing, tennis, travel, and foreign films.

Categories/subjects that you are most enthusiastic about agenting: Lilly: Green living, crafting books/Do-It-Yourself, pop culture, nonfiction how-to books written by an expert with a funny writing voice, and young adult. Stefanie: Multicultural fiction for adults, teens, and children (especially Latino), nonfiction how-to including parenting, green living, women's interest, quirky reference or pop culture.

What might you be doing if you weren't agenting: Lilly: Realistically I'd be doing the lawyer grind. Blech. Stefanie: I think I'd like to own a chocolate shop-children's boutique-bookstore—a combination of a few of my favorite things!

What's the most effective ways for writers to grab your attention: Lilly: Professionalism is underrated! Authors who do their research and are clear about why they're pitching to me (correctly!) will have my attention. Stefanie: I am always impressed when a writer is familiar with books and authors we've represented.

Do you charge fees separate from your commission, or offer non-agenting fee based services: Absolutely not. Full Circle does not charge any additional fees for its services, nor do we charge a reading fee.

Why did you become an agent, and how did you become one: Stefani: After working in both the editorial and marketing/sales side of trade publishing, I found that agenting is a great way to be involved in a book from the beginning. So I put my publishing experience to work and I became an agent to connect books with readers!

How do you feel about writers: Lilly: Writers are often the most unappreciated artists out there. Writing a book is no small feat, and writers are some of the most articulate clients you could possibly dream to work with. Plus they are fellow readers, which automatically brings them close to my heart! Stefanie: I am always amazed at the creative ideas and imagination that seem to fill writers from head to toe. Writing is a true craft!

What do you tell entities from other planets and dimensions about your job: Lilly: I tell them no, I didn't agent *The Da Vinci Code*! Stefanie: Many times people think that since I work with books that I must be a writer OR that I can print their book. I have to explain that I am fortunate to work with both writers and publishers, but I don't write or publish!

How would you describe "the writer from Hell": The problem writer wouldn't take the time to learn about the industry and what are (or aren't) realistic expectations of an agent or, more importantly, a publisher! On the flipside, a dream author is a self-starter, a self-promoter who realizes they are the foundation of a successful book, and that never changes, even with the biggest publisher or marketing budget.

How would you describe the publisher and/or editor from Hell: Lack of communication. Sending a manuscript and not hearing back is purgatory for agents, whether it's in the submission stage or delivery of a final manuscript.

What do you like best about your clients, and the editors and publishers you work with: Lilly: In general, I try to work with editors I feel a personal connection with—it's important to me that I leave my books in capable, caring hands. I am proud to work with publishers who bring enthusiasm and incredible insight into the projects we share. Stefanie: I have a passion for the books I represent that I truly share with my authors and the editors I work with. I love the spark of a new idea and seeing it transformed (after lots of work, of course) into a beautiful, printed page!

You're welcome to share your thoughts and sentiments about the business of writing and publishing: Stefanie: Everyone in our industry is in it because they love what they do. I think we're at a time when it's important to support each other and produce the best books that we all can so that readers will continue to read! And more often and at even the earliest age—we all win when there are more lifelong readers!

What are representative titles you have sold to publishers: Lilly's recent titles: *Sewing Green* by Betz White (Stewart, Tabori, & Chang); *Patternmaking* by Cal Patch (Potter Craft/Random House); *Hit Me With Your Best Shot* by Raina Lee (Chronicle Books); *Rockabye Baby* by Penny Warner (Chronicle Books). Stefanie's recent titles: *The Bilingual Edge: Why, When and How to Teach Your Child a Second Language* by Kendall King and Alison Mackey (HarperCollins); *I Love Dirt!: 52 Activities to Help You and Your*

Kids Discover the Wonders of Nature by Jennifer Ward (Shambhala); *Confetti Girl* by Diana Lopez (Little, Brown); *Pele: King of Soccer (Pelé: El Rey del Fútbol)* by Monica Brown and illustrated by Rudy Guiterrez (Rayo/HarperCollins); *What Can You Do with a Paleta?* By Carmen Tafolla and illustrated by Magaly Morales (Tricycle Press).

MAX GARTENBERG LITERARY AGENCY, LLC.

912 N. Pennsylvania Ave., Yardley, PA 19067

215-295-9230   fax: 215-295-9240

www.maxgartenberg.com   e-mail: agdevlin@aol.com

Agents' names: Max Gartenberg, Anne G. Devlin, Will Devlin

Career history: The Max Gartenberg Literary Agency has long been recognized as a source for fine fiction and non-fiction. Established in 1954 in New York City, the agency has migrated to the Philadelphia area, growing by two agents in the latest move.

Categories/subjects that you are most enthusiastic about agenting: Special interests: Non-Fiction, current events, women's issues, celebrity, health, literary fiction, true crime, commercial fiction, sports, politics, popular culture, biography, environment, narrative non-fiction, adolescent fiction and multicultural nonfiction.

What you don't want to agent: Poetry, New age, Fantasy.

What's the best way for writers to solicit your interest: Writers desirous of having their work handled by this agency should first send a one- or two-page query letter directed to an agent on staff. Simply put, the letter should describe the material being offered as well as relevant background information about the writer, and include an SASE for the agent's reply. If the material is of interest, the agent may request a sample or the entire manuscript. Unsolicited material will be returned unread if accompanied by sufficient postage for its return.

Do you charge reading or management fees: No.

Can you provide an approximation by % of what you tend to represent by category: Fiction: 30%, Non-Fiction: 70%.

What are the most common mistakes writers make when pitching you: Rather than describing his material and summarizing his qualifications, the writer's query letter asks for information about the agency, information readily available in such directories as *Jeff Herman's Guide and Literary Market Place* or on the Web. This tells that the writer is too lazy to do his homework and is probably a poor researcher, to boot.

How would you describe the client from Hell: Client who demands unceasing attention and is never satisfied with the deal the agent brings him (he always has friends whose agents got twice as much), who delivers his manuscript late and in such disrepair that it is unacceptable at first glance. And blames the agent for his mess. This is not an imaginary character.

How would you describe the perfect client: A writing professional who can be counted on to produce a well-made, literate, enlightening, and enjoyable book with a minimum of Sturm and Drang. Fortunately, this is not an imaginary character, either.

What, if anything, can a writer do to increase the odds that you will become his or her agent: Write a brilliant query letter and, when asked, follow it up with a manuscript or proposal that is even better. Remember that the waiting is the hardest part.

Please list representative titles that you have sold: *Charles Addams: A Cartoonist's Life* (Random House); *Ogallala Blue* (W.W. Norton); *Encyclopedia of Pollution* and *Encyclopedia of Earthquakes and Volcanoes* (Facts On File); *Jack and Lem* (DaCapo Press Press); *Passing Gas and Other Towns Along the American Highway* (Ten Speed Press); *What Patients Taught Me* and *Country Hospital* (Sasquatch Books); *Winning the Disability Challenge* (New Horizon Press); *How to Talk to Your Child's Doctor* (Prometheus Press).

FRANCES GOLDIN LITERARY AGENCY, INC.

57 E. 11th St. Suite 5B, New York, NY 10003

212-777-0047   fax: 212-228-1660

www.goldinlit.com

Agents' names: Ellen Geiger, eg@goldinlit.com; Sam Stoloff, ss@goldinlit.com; Matt McGowan

The following information pertains to Ellen Geiger.

Born: New York, New York.

Education: B.A., Barnard; M.A., University of California.

Career history or story: I started agenting while working as an executive at a PBS station almost 20 years ago and have been at it ever since.

Hobbies, interests: Shockingly enough, I still love to read. I'm also a politics and history fan, and play a mean game of Scrabble.

Subjects & categories you are interested in agenting, including fiction & nonfiction: Serious nonfiction of all sorts, history, science, current affairs, business, progressive politics, arts and culture, film, interesting memoirs, cutting-edge issues. In fiction, literary fiction, women's fiction, thrillers, mysteries, historical.

Subjects & categories writers shouldn't even bother pitching to you: No new age or flaky science, romance novels or science fiction.

What would you do if you weren't agenting: Travel and do more volunteer work; although these days I could work from anywhere if I had my Blackberry along.

What's the best way for fiction writers to solicit your interest: Be able to write well and have an original idea, which is surprisingly hard to find. Understand the genre you're writing in. Have a track record, ideally, or some writing classes under your belt so you have a good sense of the form. Have done several drafts of your novel: there's nothing that makes my heart sink faster than to read that I'm the first one to read your first draft.

What's the best way for non-fiction writers to solicit your interest: Have a good grasp of your idea and some credentials to back it up. Have researched the market and the competition. Have good writing skills or be willing to team up with a writer to make the book the best it can be.

Do you charge reading or any upfront fees: Absolutely not. No real agent who is a member of the AAR (Association of Author's Representatives) does.

In your experience, what are the most common pitching mistakes writers make: To tell me what a great FILM their book will make. To not be able to summarize the plot briefly or create an interesting hook to get me eager to read more. To submit a query letter filled with typos and grammatical errors.

Describe the client from Hell, even if you don't have any: Worst is the writer who doesn't trust the agent and second-guesses your decisions, typically someone who solicits advice from everyone in their family including the dog. Another no-no is a bitter, pessimistic person who can't be pleased no matter what happens: If the review of their book is on page 3 of the *NY Times*, they're angry it's not on page 1. Usually I can screen these people out early on, but occasionally I am surprised, as they often masquerade as nice people until publication time.

What's your definition of a great client: Easy. Someone who can write well, and deliver on time! And it's great if that person is also someone who is emotionally mature enough to withstand the natural ups and downs of the publishing process.

How can writers increase the odds that you will offer representation: A referral is guaranteed to get immediate attention. Having a track record and/or good credentials. Having a promotional platform for your book or a good plan for one. Having studied the craft of writing at reputable schools and workshops. Being educated and realistic about the realities of the publishing world.

Why did you become an agent, and how did you become one: It's my calling; I've always worked in arts representation. When I was 25 I owned part of a nightclub, and in a sense, I've been doing that kind of work ever since. I was mentored into the business by a top agent.

Describe to someone from another planet what you do as an agent: In the most general way, do everything possible to get the writer a great deal and help them achieve the best possible publication and promotion of their work. Then make sure they get paid.

How do you feel about editors and publishers: I realize they are under enormous pressure to perform to today's bottom-line oriented standards. Still, I wish they would take more chances and back up their books with real promotion.

How do you feel about writers: By nature, I am predisposed to like creative people and admire those who have the courage of their convictions and believe in their talent.

What do you see in the near future for book publishing: I hope publishers will understand that they must promote the books they buy better. Promotion is the weak link in the chain. We're now in a period of wild experimentation with web-based content, and I think that will shake out in the next few years. And, no matter how sexy they make those e-book readers, people will always prefer holding a real book in their hands.

What are your favorite books/TV shows/movies, and why: Among our clients, our author Barbara Kingsolver's *Poisonwood Bible* for its sweep, narrative brilliance and social relevance, our author Ann Jones' *Kabul in Winter: Life Without Peace in Afghanistan*, for it's brilliant depiction of the forgotten lives of women and men in wartime, our author Dorothy Allison's *Bastard out of Carolina* because it's just one of the best memoirs ever written. *Suite Francaise* for it's historical impact and moving origins, *Fieldwork* by Mischa Berlinski for its scope and ideas, Jeffrey Eugenidies' *Middlesex* because it's a tour de force of writing and history, *Then we Came to the End* for it's shrewd, ironic and ultimately moving insights into contemporary culture. In TV: *Mad Men* for it's genius depicting the 1960's era, *The Closer* for Kyra Sedgwick's fab character, *Six Feet Under* and *The Sopranos* for their high water marks in narrative storytelling. In theater: I love all kinds of theater but recently saw the superb revival of *Sunday in the Park with George* and love it for it's tribute to the glory, persistence and purity of art – surely a theme anyone in our profession can embrace.

In your opinion, what do editors think of you: Smart, fair, dedicated, experienced, a good negotiator, tough on contracts.

On a personal non-professional level, what do you think people think of you: Together, organized, friendly, a bit of an egghead, good sense of humor.

What are some representative titles that you have sold: Fiction: *Monkeewrench* by PJ Tracy (Putnam); *The Sunday List of Dreams* by Kris Radish (Bantam); *The Penguin Who Knew Too Much* by Donna Andrews (St.Martin's); *The Saddlemaker's Wife* by Earlene Fowler (Berkley). Non-fiction: *Kabul in Winter: Life Without Peace in Afghanistan* by Ann Jones (Holt/Metropolitan); *The American Plague: The Untold Story of Yellow Fever, the Epidemic that Shaped our History* by Molly Crosby (Berkley); *If the Creek Don't Rise: My Life Out West with the Last Black Widow of the Civil War* by Rita Williams (Harcourt); *How to Read the Bible* by James L. Kugel (Free Press); *Gringos in Paradise* by Barry Golson (Scribner); *Free Exercise, Expensive Gas: A Church-State Road Trip* by Jay Wexler (Beacon).

The following information pertains to Sam Stoloff.

Born: Nov. 14, 1960, New York City.

Education: B.A., Columbia University, 1984; M.F.A., Cornell University, 1988; M.A., Cornell University, 1991; Ph.D., Cornell University (defended dissertation but have not yet received degree, and I may never, just out of laziness).

Career history or story: I taught college courses in English literature, creative writing, American history, and film studies for a number of years, at Cornell, Ithaca College, and the State University of New York. I've been with the Frances Goldin Agency since 1997. Being an agent is better.

Hobbies, interests: I spend most of my non-working time these days with my kids, so you could call that my main hobby. I love to cook and I'm a bit of a foodie and small-time gardener, I sort-of-collect wine, I'm a big fan of the New York Mets, I play tennis, I'm a bit of a political junkie and obsess to an unhealthy degree about the outrages of the Bush administration, and I read books (novels, journalism, history) for pleasure when I can. I like a good game of Scrabble or poker. I love movies, but haven't seen many since my first kid was born.

Subjects & categories you are interested in agenting, including fiction & non-fiction: Smart journalism, history, books on current events and public affairs, books about food, sports, popular culture, economics, psychology, original graphic works, wonderfully written novels, stories and memoirs.

Subjects & categories writers shouldn't even bother pitching to you: Most genre fiction (unless literary), self-help, diet books, practical nonfiction, pet books, celebrity bios, screenplays.

What would you do if you weren't agenting: I'd probably either be a professor of American studies (literature, history, film), or a writer. Possibly a Washington think-tank type.

What's the best way for fiction writers to solicit your interest: Write a smart, succinct query letter describing the book (only one book, not every available manuscript), and previous publications, if any. I still prefer paper to email, although I can see the writing on the wall.

What's the best way for nonfiction writers to solicit your interest: Write a smart, succinct query letter describing a fabulous project, and previous publications or other credentials, if any.

Do you charge reading or any upfront fees: No.

In your experience, what are the most common pitching mistakes writers make: Failure to actually describe the project. Pitching more than one thing at a time. Telling me my business (e.g. "Knopf would be the ideal publisher for this book"). Assuming an unearned familiarity.

Describe the client from Hell, even if you don't have any: Thin-skinned, with an aversion to editorial feedback, and an inflated sense of literary importance and wildly unrealistic expectations about what publishing a book means; unable to acknowledge the work of others on their behalf.

What's your definition of a great client: Thick-skinned, welcoming of editorial feedback, and with a becoming sense of modesty about themselves; freely expressive of gratitude for the work others do on their behalf. And wonderfully talented, of course.

How can writers increase the odds that you will offer representation: Be professional and courteous.

Why did you become an agent, and how did you become one: Frances Goldin is an old family friend, and I have long admired her integrity, her dedication, her loyalty to her clients, and the quality of the writers she has worked with. It looked pretty good to me!

What do you see in the near future for book publishing: The transition to electronic books will be a gradual one. Reading on paper and on screen will co-exist for some time, although I think that when there's a knockout ebook reader with a great screen and a decent price, the migration to ebooks will begin in earnest. Book publishers will struggle to adapt, as the means for distributing and consuming words continue to change. Writers will still write, agents will still represent them, but publishers and booksellers face big institutional upheavals.

What are your favorite books/TV shows/movies, and why: My favorite movie is *Vertigo*. My favorite book is probably *The Great Gatsby*, or maybe *House of Mirth*. My favorite TV show is *The Wire*.

What are some representative titles that you have sold: *A Brief History of the Flood* by Jean Harfenist (Knopf); *Jesus Land* by Julia Scheeres (Counterpoint); *Too Late to Die Young* by Harriet McBryde Johnson (Holt); *Blocking the Courthouse Door* by Stephanie Mencimer (Free Press); *Lullabies for Little Criminals* by Heather O'Neill (Harper-Collins); *A People's History of Science* by Clifford Conner (Nation Books); *The Daring Book for Girls* by Miriam Peskowitz and Andrea Buchanan (HarperCollins); *Dirty Diplomacy* by Craig Murray (Scribner); *New York at War* by Steven Jaffe (Basic Books).

The following information pertains to Matt McGowan.

Born: June 19, 1972; Antwerp, Belgium.

Education: B.A., Colby College.

Career history: I started in 1994 as an assistant at St. Martin's Press. After a year I moved on to assist retired Pantheon publisher Fred Jordan revive a small press called Fromm International. Fred was very generous, encouraging me to try just about anything from designing jackets to acquiring books. He was also inspiring in that he had published these icons like Jack Kerouac and Allen Ginsberg during the heyday of Grove Press/Evergreen Review, where he worked for over 30 years, and had these absurd stories about going to a Mets game with Samuel Beckett, drinking in Paris with William Burroughs, and being chased around the Grove offices by Valerie Solanas and her ice pick. I've always looked up to the Grove legacy and Grove founder Barney Rosset and think landing at Frances Goldin, after a short stint at another agency, was really fortunate as Frances has similar convictions about books and writers.

Categories/subjects that you are most enthusiastic about agenting: Narrative nonfiction; literary, unusual, and/or humorous essays; travel; sports narratives (particularly soccer); smart commercial fiction; distinctive literary fiction; pop culture; music; peculiar histories; quirky and accessible food, business, science, or sociology.

What you don't want to agent: Romance, religion, diet, reference; I see a lot of "edgy" first novels that romanticize drug use or depravity which I quickly pass on.

What's the best way for writers to solicit your interest: Query letter or brief e-mail.

Do you charge reading or management fees: No.

What are the most common mistakes writers make when pitching you: Making letters too "pitchy", I like a straight-forward, informational query letter.

How and why did you ever become an agent: I read a novel in college which I learned had a really difficult time getting published and that bred these idealistic notions about publishing and recognizing talented writers and helping them break through. That led to me doing an internship in New York my senior year and I was actually attracted to the business of it all as much as anything.

What do you think the future holds for writers, publishers, and agents: I doubt books as we think of them today will survive, technology seems to be developing too fast, as well as consumer expectations, but authors and ideas will always be around and there should always be a market for them.

What are your favorite books, movies, TV shows, and why: TV: *Entourage, Scrubs, Flip This House,* Anthony Bourdain's show, *No Reservations.* Books: *I am not Jackson Pollock* by John Haskell; *Natasha* by David Bezmogzis; *The Miracle of Castel di Sangro* by Joe McGinniss; *Where I Was From* by Joan Didion.

On a personal level, what do you think people like about you and dislike about you: I think my some of my more difficult and literary clients are appreciative that I work hard for them when their work is not clearly commercial. One of them sends me a fruit basket every Christmas at least. I'm sure there are some things people don't like but let's not go there.

Please list representative titles you have sold: *The Lifespan of a Fact: An Essay* (FSG); *The Open Curtain: A Novel* (Coffee House); *To Air is Human: One Man's Quest to Become the World's Greatest Air Guitarist* (Riverhead); *Kicking Out, Kicking On: On the Road with the Fans, Freaks, and Fiends at the World's Biggest Sporting Event, World Cup 2006* (Harcourt); *Neck Deep: Odd Essays* (Graywolf); *The Perfect Baby Handbook: A Guide for the Excessively Motivated New Parent* (HarperCollins); *Bank: A Novel* (Little Brown).

IRENE GOODMAN

80 Fifth Avenue, Suite 1101, New York, NY 10011

www.irenegoodman.com

Agent's name: Irene Goodman

Education: B.A. and M.A. from the University of Michigan.

Career history or story: I've been an agent for 29 years and counting. I've had my share of major bestsellers, discoveries in the slush, and wonderful long-term relationships.

Subjects & categories you are interested in agenting, including fiction & non-fiction: Quality fiction, including genre fiction; narrative and prescriptive non-fiction.

What would you do if you weren't agenting: I don't know how to do anything else. Fortunately, I'm very good at this.

What's the best way for fiction writers to solicit your interest: Briefly.

What's the best way for non-fiction writers to solicit your interest: With a solid, clever idea and a strong platform.

Do you charge reading or any upfront fees: No.

In your experience, what are the most common pitching mistakes writers make: They are boring.

Describe the client from Hell, even if you don't have any: I'm too polite to say.

What's your definition of a great client: That would be someone who is talented, ambitious, and smart but who has a healthy sense of humor about his or her work and doesn't take it all too seriously.

How can writers increase the odds that you will offer representation: By being that good.

Why did you become an agent, and how did you become one: I started as an editorial assistant to a publisher and then worked for an agent. I quickly saw that I was suited to it.

How do you feel about editors and publishers: I love them.

How do you feel about writers: I love them too.

What are your favorite books/TV shows/movies, and why: *Jane Eyre, The Godfather, Of Human Bondage, Boston Legal, The Sopranos.*

In your opinion, what do editors think of you: They respect me. They like me, but know I will kill for my authors.

ASHLEY GRAYSON LITERARY AGENCY

1342 W. 18th Street, San Pedro, CA 90732

310-514-0267 or 310-548-4672   fax: 310-831-0036

www.graysonagency.com

Agents' names: Ashley Grayson, graysonagent@earthlink.net; Carolyn Grayson, carolyngraysonagent@earthlink.net; Denise Dumars, denise.graysonagent@earthlink.net; Lois Winston, lois.graysonagent@earthlink.net

Education: A Grayson: B.S. in Physics. C. Grayson: B.A., English, Wellesley College; M.B.A., U.C.L.A. Dumars: B.A. in English/Creative Writing, Cal State Univ. Long Beach; M.A. in English/Creative Writing, Cal State Univ. Dominguez Hills. Winston: B.F.A. graphic design/illustration, Tyler School of Art/Temple University.

Career story: A. Grayson: Computer sales, Management Consultant, founded Ashley Grayson Literary Agency in 1976. C. Grayson: Market Research Analyst; Marketing Consultant; Agent since 1994. Dumars: Library Professional, College English Instructor, Journalist, Literary Agent, published author of three books, five chapbooks and numerous articles, reviews, poems, and short stories. Winston: Art director, designer and editor in consumer crafts industry; published author of two novels, contributor to three fiction and one non-fiction anthologies; author of numerous magazine articles; agent since 2005.

Hobbies and special personal interests: A. Grayson: languages, opera, gardening. C. Grayson: reading, gardening, roses, beach, investing, wine, cooking. Dumars: travel, horror films, metaphysics, attending poetry readings, experimental theatre and punk rock concerts. Winston: Broadway theater, reading, travel, wandering around art museums.

Subjects and categories you like to agent: We love to agent books that make us want to run out and tell the world about the book and the author. We love novels that are exceedingly well-written, with characters we want to spend time with; clever, high-concept ideas often with a good dose of humor; wonderful, fresh stories that draw us in, keep us turning the pages, and are just so darn fun to read. In non-fiction, we look for books that are fresh, commercial, high-concept and promotable, from an author with a national platform. We're especially looking for narrative-driven non-fiction books about health and science topics and cultural history. In children's books: we seek authors and books with unique voice and the right sensibilities for the market, whether quirky and fun or more serious. We are extremely selective about children's non-fiction.

A. Grayson: Strong, well-written literary and commercial fiction, historical fiction, dark fantasy, mysteries, thrillers, young adult, humorous or edgy children's fiction. C. Grayson: Women's fiction (including romance and multi-cultural); historical fiction; mysteries; suspense; women-oriented fantasy; horror; children's books, from chapter books to YA. Non-fiction: contemporary self-help, business, pop culture, science, true crime, and a very few gift or highly illustrated books, narrative non-fiction. Dumars: Horror and dark fantasy fiction, offbeat literary and women's fiction, ethnic fiction; and non-fiction that is related to pop-culture topics, especially Goth and Noir, and metaphysical writings, especially related to Wicca, paganism, magick, goddess religion and general New Age topics-as long as it is positive in tone. Winston: women's fiction, romance (all sub-genres except inspiration romance), romantic suspense, thrillers, and traditional mysteries. Humor is always a plus but not slapstick.

Subjects and categories writers shouldn't bother pitching to you: The Agency does not represent screenplays, poetry, short stories, novellas, most novelty books, textbooks, most memoirs, especially stories of abuse or addiction recovery. In fiction: Dark fiction is fine; gore solely for the sake of shocking the reader is not for us. C. Grayson: I'm not inclined to read and represent women's fiction in which the life of the heroine is full of depression and angst; I do like a happy ending. Winston: I'm not partial to dark paranormals (light and/or humorous paranormals are okay), and I prefer historical novels over historical romances.

What might you be doing if you weren't agenting: Dumars: Writing, teaching, and traveling, which I pretty much do already. Winston: Working on my own novels.

What's the most effective ways for writers to grab your attention: Send us something smart, fresh, captivatingly written and beautifully crafted.

Dumars: Write a book that is truly new and fills a need, not just a version of something that's currently popular. My interests are very specific, so research them carefully before sending your work to me. List publications you've published in, and organizations you belong to that demonstrate your interest in the field.

For fiction: We are still accepting clients who are previously published by a known publisher. The agency is temporarily closed to queries from writers who are not published at book length, with the following exceptions: (1) Authors recommended by a client, published author, or editor who has read the work in question; (2) Authors we have met at conferences and from whom we have requested submissions; (3) Authors who have been published in quality small presses or magazines. We have had excellent success selling first-time novelists, but at this time we must concentrate on the needs of professional authors who need our intellectual property management skills and financial skills. If you meet these criteria, please query us, listing publishing credits with titles, publishers, and dates published. Query Ashley Grayson, Carolyn Grayson, and Lois Winston by email only. Include the first three pages of the manuscript in the body of your email; do not send attachments unless requested. Denise Dumars prefers queries sent by ordinary post; include first three pages and SASE. Do not send queries by overnight service and never ever by certified mail. Do not query more than one agent in our agency, whether by email or post; we will make sure that your query reaches the right person.

For nonfiction: query with proposal. Note: We cannot review self-published works to evaluate moving them to mainstream publishers. Please send query letter by email, including brief bio or C.V., and the Market and Competition sections of your proposal.

Do you charge fees separate from your commission, or offer non-agenting fee based services: We do not offer non-agenting fee-based services. We do charge for some extraordinary expenses such as bank wires, overnight mail delivery, or posting books to foreign lands.

What are representative titles you have sold to publishers: *Tales of the Madman Underground* by John Barnes (Viking Children's Books); *Move Your Stuff, Change Your Life* by Karen Rauch Carter (Simon & Schuster); *The Middle of Somewhere* by J.B. Cheaney (Knopf Books for Young Readers); *Moongobble and Me* (series) by Bruce Coville (Simon & Schuster Children's Books); *Ball Don't Lie* by Matt de la Peña (Delacorte); *Be Blesséd* by Denise Dumars (New Page); *Grease Monkey* by Tim Eldred (Tor); *Bride of the Fat White Vampire* by Andrew Fox (Ballantine); *Child of a Dead God* by Barb and J. C. Hendee (ROC/Penguin); *Mars Crossing* by Geoffrey A. Landis (Tor); *Tiny Little Troubles* by Marc Lecard (St. Martin's); *Sleeping Freshmen Never Lie* by David Lubar (Dutton); *Théâtre Illuminata: Eyes Like Stars* by Lisa Mantchev (Feiwel and Friends); *The Healing Power of Faery* by Edain McCoy (Provenance/Adams Media); *Sex Starved and Sex Drive* by Jill Myles (Pocket Books); *But I Don't Feel Too Old to Be a Mommy* by Doreen Nagle (Health Communications); *Phoenix Unrisen* by Kathleen Nance (Dorchester); *Alosha* by Christopher Pike (Tor/Forge); *Cave Paintings to Picasso* by Henry Sayre (Chronicle Books); *Wiley and Grampa's Creature Features* (series) by Kirk Scroggs (Little Brown Books for Young Readers); *Cat Yoga* by Rick Tillotson (Clarkson Potter); *The Boy with the Lampshade on His Head* by Bruce Wetter (Atheneum); *Raven* by Allison van Diepen (Simon Pulse); *Kitty and the Silver Bullet* by Carrie Vaughn (Warner); *I Wish I Never Met You* by Denise Wheatley (Simon & Schuster/Touchstone); *Love, Lies and a Double Shot of Deception* by Lois Winston (Dorchester).

Why did you become an agent, and how did you become one: A. Grayson: I love to read books and sell new ideas. The real reason I became an agent is that Judy-Lynn Del Rey (the late founder of the Del Rey imprint at Random House) told me in 1976 that I should. She had great insight-I'm still having a great time. C. Grayson: I love to read, including contracts, and I love to help authors move up in their careers. Dumars: Because I was tired of seeing people signing book contracts without understanding them. I wanted to help authors, especially those I knew in the genre fiction and New Age arenas. On suggestion from Dan Hooker, Ashley Grayson took me on as a manuscript evaluator, reading the slush pile, and gradually I worked my way up to Agent. Winston: Ashley thought I'd be an asset to the agency, and like Denise, I've worked my way up to agenting.

How do you feel about writers: Dumars: I think I'm quoting Ben Franklin here when I say we have to hang together or they'll hang us all separately. Winston: Ditto what Denise said.

What do you tell entities from other planets and dimensions about your job: Many people think we get paid to read for a living, but that's only the beginning of what we do. We use our judgment to select and market wonderful manuscripts to the most appropriate editors at the most appropriate houses; we read contracts with a thorough-going understanding of terms and negotiate the best terms we can in every deal; read royalty statements with an eagle eye; work with publishers and authors to promote the books; sell subrights, including negotiating contracts for foreign editions, film and TV; and are the authors' advocates in all publishing matters.

What are your favorite books, movies, TV shows, and why: C. Grayson: My favorite books are my clients' of course; I like movies with clever screenwriting: many of the Coen Brothers movies, especially *Barton Fink* and *The Man Who Wasn't There*; TV Shows: *Law & Order*; *CSI: Las Vegas*; *Mystery!* Winston: Books: Ditto what Carolyn said about my clients' books; TV: *House, Lost, Bones, The Shield, Burn Notice, Law & Order*; Movies: *Chicago, Casablanca, Singing in the Rain, Same Time Next Year, Shakespeare in Love.* Dumars: Favorite TV shows: currently, *Lost* and *Heroes.* Movies: My all-time favorite movies are *Repo Man, Casablanca,* and *Interview With the Vampire.* My favorite movie this year so far has been *Pan's Labyrinth.*

How would you describe "the writer from hell": A. Grayson: Of course, we don't represent any writers from Hell, but such a person is more interested in the celebrity of being an author than in actually writing books. Anyone who doesn't work on the next book until the present one sells. Any clients who want to second-guess their agent. Dumars: A person who is unprofessional--doesn't return calls or make deadlines. Someone who is not interested in being a professional writer but instead sees writing only as advancing an agenda or as a charity project; clients who listen to gossip and believe it instead of believing their agent. Not that I've ever heard of such a writer, of course. Winston: An author who believes every word he/she has written is etched in platinum and refuses to even consider revising.

How would you describe the publisher and/or editor from hell: We love our clients—they always have great ideas simmering for the next book or two, their works are continually fresh and exciting, they continue to charm and delight us with their innovative and creative ideas and work, are genuinely enthusiastic about the business, and they understand publishing is a business. They are relentlessly surprising, and never bewildering—their work is stunning. We love editors for their enthusiasm for books and authors. We look forward to continuing to work with editors and publishers to find ways to publish and sell creative works as technology, industry business models, and even the form of the book, change.

Will our business exist as we know it in 10 years or so from now: No, it will not. Readers have changed in their style of reading and reasons to read, as well as in what they read, and where and how they read. The new Generation Y population neither lives like, nor thinks like, nor reads like the Boomers and Gen X readers. New bestsellers must address these changes and authors must adapt to sell big now and continue to win loyal readers in the next fifteen years. Publishers, distributors and retailers have demonstrated repeatedly that they do not want to continue performing the activities associated with their traditional businesses and desire to move to a model in which no book is manufactured or stocked until the customer buys it. This works well for downloadable games and software and it is inevitable that books will be next. As an agency, we are prepared to operate in such a future and to protect and grow our client's intellectual property investments. We are paying attention, but are not worried.

Dumars: Niche marketing, which is what I see already on MySpace and similar areas. When my students started wearing t-shirts of death metal bands from Outer Mongolia that I had never heard of, and they in turn had never heard of the MTV and VH1 rock bands I listen to, I realized that there had been a quantum shift in how people relate to entertainment in general. Maybe it will signal a return to the independent bookstore that caters to a particular clientele. We can only hope.

SANFORD J. GREENBURGER ASSOCIATES

55 Fifth Ave., New York, NY 10003

Agent's name: Matt Bialer

Born: December 20, 1962

Education: B.A., Vassar College.

Career history or story: Spent 14 years in the book department at the William Morris Agency. Have been in the business since 1985.

Hobbies, interests: Painting, photography, outdoors, music (rock, jazz, classical).

Subjects & categories you are interested in agenting, including fiction & non-fiction: Thrillers, urban fantasy, epic fantasy, cross-over science fiction, some romance, pop music books, narrative non-fiction, literary fiction, women's fiction, sports.

Subjects & categories writers shouldn't even bother pitching to you: Self-help, diet books.

What would you do if you weren't agenting: Paint (watercolor) and take black and white street photographs.

What's the best way for fiction writers to solicit your interest: Be aware of what I represent (At least some of it) and see if what you wrote jives with my taste.

What's the best way for non-fiction writers to solicit your interest: Letter.

Do you charge reading or any upfront fees: No.

In your experience, what are the most common pitching mistakes writers make: They just shotgun it out there without any thought as to who the agent is and what they do.

Describe the client from Hell, even if you don't have any: That's a tough one. Generally speaking it is a client who does no t listen, who does not get how things are properly done in the business.

What's your definition of a great client: Listens. Trusts. And has a good rapport. A great relationship with the client is me not telling the writer what to do buy an ongoing dialogue. I like clients who can teach me a thing or two.

How can writers increase the odds that you will offer representation: Do the homework on what is out there and successful that is like your project. And be realistic about it. And find out about the agent you are pitching.

Why did you become an agent, and how did you become one: I love books and publishing. I like creativity. I like to help make a project come to fruition. I became one because I started at an agency and just never looked back.

Describe to someone from another planet what you do as an agent: I manage book careers. I help a writer sell their book to a publisher. I am a matchmaker between project and editor/publisher and then I help manage the publishing of the book in both the U.S. and throughout the world.

How do you feel about editors and publishers: In a perfect world, I love them both but of course I have my preferences. Some editors and pubishers are more effective than others or better at a certain kind of book.

How do you feel about writers: Love them.

What do you see in the near future for book publishing: Still trying to find itself in a world full of competing media whether a million TV channels, computers, ipods, etc.

What are your favorite books/TV shows/movies, and why: Books: Cormac McCarthy, Tolkien, Stephen King, Hemingway, Dennis Lehane, Tad Williams, Pynchon, Phil Dick. TV: *Heroes*, *Without a Trace*. Movies: Too many to name.

In your opinion, what do editors think of you: I think I am well respected and am well known in the industry.

On a personal non-professional level, what do you think people think of you: They love me!

What are some representative titles that you have sold: *Otherland* and *Shadowmarch* series by Tad Williams; *The Name of the Wind* by Patrick Rothfuss; *The Ice-Man: Confessions of a Mafia Contract Killer* by Philip Carlo; *The People Series* by Michael Gear and Kathleen O'Neal Gear; *Truancy: Some Kids Were Rebellious* by Isamu Fukui; *Zanesville* by Kris Saknussemm; *The Bone Thief* by Thomas O'Callaghan.

THE CHARLOTTE GUSAY LITERARY AGENCY

10532 Blythe Avenue, Los Angeles, CA 90064

310-559-0831   fax: 310-559-2639

www.gusay.com   e-mail: gusay1@ca.rr.com (For Queries Only)

Agent's name: Charlotte Gusay

Education: B.A. in English Literature/Theater; General Secondary Life Teaching Credential.

Career history: Taught in secondary schools for several years. Interest in filmmaking developed. Founded (with partners) a documentary film company in the early

1970s. Soon became interested in the fledgling audio-publishing business. Became the Managing Editor for the Center for Cassette Studies/Scanfax, producing audio programs, interviews, and documentaries. In 1976 founded George Sand, Books, in West Hollywood, one of the most prestigious and popular bookshops in Los Angeles. It specialized in fiction and poetry, sponsored readings and events. Patronized by the Hollywood community's glitterati and literati, George Sand, Books, was the place to go when looking for the "best" literature and quality books. It was here that the marketing of books was preeminent. It closed in 1987. Two years later the Charlotte Gusay Literary Agency was opened.

Hobbies/personal interests: Gardens and gardening, architecture, magazines (a magazine junkie), good fiction (especially juicy novels), reading, anything French, anything Greek.

Categories/subjects that you are most enthusiastic about agenting: I enjoy both fiction and nonfiction. Prefer commercial, mainstream but quality material. Especially like books that can be marketed as film material. Also, like material that is innovative, unusual, eclectic, nonsexist. Will consider literary fiction with crossover potential. TCGLA is a signatory to the Writers' Guild and so represents screenplays and screenwriters selectively. I enjoy unusual children's books and illustrators, but have begun to limit children's projects to young adult novels especially if they have film possibilities.

What you don't want to agent: Prefer not consider science fiction or horror, poetry or short stories (with few exceptions), or the romance genres per se.

If you were not an agent, what might you be doing instead: I would travel to Istanbul and become a foreign agent. I would re-read all of Marcel Proust. I would re-read Jane Austen. Work on my French. Study Greek (Actually I do now.) Play the piano. Tap dance.

What's the best way for writers to solicit your interest: First: Send one-page query letter with SASE. Then: After we've read your query and if we request your material (book, proposal, whatever it is), note the following guidelines: For fiction: Send approximately the first 50 pages and a synopsis, along with your credentials (i.e., list of previous publications, and/or list of magazine articles, and/or any pertinent information, education, and background.) For nonfiction: Send a proposal consisting of an overview, chapter outline, author biography, sample chapters, marketing and audience research, and survey of the competition. Important note: Material will not be returned without an SASE. Second important note: Seduce me with humor and intelligence. Always be polite and professional.

Do you charge reading or management fees: No reading fee. No editorial fees. When a client is signed, the client and I share 50/50% out-of-pocket expenses. In certain cases, I charge a nominal processing fee especially when considering unsolicited submissions decided upon as and when queries arrive in my office. (Note: Charlotte – ever the teacher - sponsors a mentoring internship program for young college graduates interested in entering and training in the publishing/book business. Any such Processing Fees help fund this program.)

Can you provide an approximation by % of what you tend to represent by category: Non-fiction, 40%; fiction, 15%; children's, 10%; books to film/screenplays, 35%.

What are the most common mistakes writers make when pitching you: Clients must understand the role of agents and that agents represent only the material they feel they can best handle or—more importantly—material they are completely enthusiastic about and feel they can sell. Potential clients must understand that any given agent may or may not be an editor, a sounding board, a proposal writer, or a guidance counselor. Because of the enormous amount of submissions, queries, and proposals, we most often have only time to say yes or no to your project. Above all, when clients don't understand why in the world we can't respond to a multiple submission with regard to their "900-page novel" within a few days, all we can do is shake our heads and wonder if that potential client realizes we are human.

How would you describe the client from Hell: The client from hell is the one who does not understand the hard work we do for our clients. Or the one who refuses to build a career in a cumulative manner, but rather goes from one agent to the next and so on. Or clients who circulate their manuscripts without cooperating with their agents. Or those who think it all happens by magic. Or those who have not done their homework and who do not understand the nuts and bolts of the business.

How would you describe the perfect client: The perfect client is the one who cooperates. The one who appreciates how hard we work for our clients. The one who submits everything on time, in lean, edited, proofed, professional copies of manuscripts and professionally prepared proposals. Clients who understand the crucial necessity of promoting their own books until the last one in the publisher's warehouse is gone. Those who work hard on their book selling in tandem with the agent. The author/agent relationship, like a marriage, is a cooperative affair built on mutual trust, and it is cumulative. The dream client will happily do absolutely whatever is necessary to reach the goal.

How and why did you ever become an agent: With a great entrepreneurial spirit, cold calls, seat-of the pants daring, 12 years in the retail book business (as founder and owner of a prestigious book shop in Los Angeles called George Sand, Books), and 25 years of business experience, including producing films and editing spoken-word audio programs; Agenting is the most challenging and rewarding experience I've ever had.

What, if anything, can a writer do to increase the odds of you becoming his or her agent: A writer must be professional. Be courteous. Be patient. Understand that we are human. Pay careful attention to the kinds of projects we represent. Query us only if your project fits with our agency profile. Know what we are overworked, always swamped with hundreds of queries. Know that we love and understand writers.

How would you describe to someone (or thing) from another planet what it is that you do as an agent: My job is essentially that of a bookseller. I sell books. To publishers, producers, and ultimately to the retail book trade. Sometimes, I develop a book idea. Sometimes, I develop someone's story, help the writer get a proposal written. I've even written proposals myself because I believed strongly in the book, or the person's story, or the salability of an idea. For fiction writers with potential, I sometimes make cursory suggestions. However, I must be clear—I am not an editor. Most often I help writers find a professional editor to work on their novel before it is submitted to a publishing house. That is key. The manuscript must be pristine. I repeat: A manuscript must be complete, polished, and professional.

Do you have any particular opinions or impressions of editors and publishers in general: Publishers continue to be in great flux and continue to have a difficult time these days. The "conglomeratizing" and "electrifying" aspects of the publishing business are taking over the publishing / book businesses. It's going to be very interesting to see where especially the electronics of the book business ends up. However, still and all, publishers are still and always looking for the next great writer, the next great book, and a way to make both successful. (That means making money.)

Editors are still overworked and underpaid. Therefore, if you wish to have the best chance of having your work accepted, you must do their work for them and don't complain. That is the reality of the editor's milieu. Editors are usually very smart. Most always, if they're any good, they are temperamental, and they know their particular publisher's market. If interested, they know how to make your work fit into their list. Do what your editor (and agent) tells you. No argument.

The publishing business continues to be overpublished. I read somewhere that 240,000 books were pubished within the last year. Be reminded that only one percent (1%) of manuscripts submitted to publishing houses were actually accepted for publication (according to Dee Power, co-author with Brian Hill, in their book The Making of a Bestseller.)

What do you think the future holds for writers, publishers, and agents: As long as there is intelligent life on earth, there will be writers who must express themselves in whatever way or medium they will. As to whether that work will be published—in book form by a major, established publisher paying actual money for it—is doubtful. I repeat my note above, only one percent (1%) of manuscripts submitted to publishing houses will actually be accepted for publication. If you have an agent who is enthusiastic about your work, or your book, you will certainly increase that percentage. Remember that most major publishing houses will accept manuscripts only from agents.

What are your favorite books, movies, TV shows, and why:: Recent films and not-so-recent films I liked: *Shakespeare in Love, Slam, Chasing Amy*, Bas Luhrman's *Romeo and Juliet*, the Marx Brothers films. A few of my all-time favorite films are *Runaway Train, The English Patient, Dr. Zhivago, Cabaret, Rebel Without a Cause, Woman in the Dunes*. A few favorite television shows; Any masterpiece theatre; *American Idol, Entourage, Weeds*. And many, many books—A few all time favorites: Austen's *Pride and Prejudice*, Hemingway's *The Sun Also Rises, The English Patient, Dr. Zhivago, Housekeeping* and many more. The one thing these have in common for me: They held my attention and I was moved in some important way, and the writing is superb.

On a personal level, what do you think people like about you and dislike about you: People like my intelligence and enthusiasm. In my agent mode, people don't like my selectivity or they don't understand it. If I reject a project, often the writer feels bleak and…well…rejected. Hopefully, writers will come to understand that I accept projects, very selectively. That is important for writers to understand.

Please list representative titles you have sold: *Mother Ash* (Forthcoming from Red Hen Press) and *American Fugue* (Forthcoming from Etruscan Press) both by National Endowment of the Arts International Award Recipient Alexis Stamatis;

Honesty Sells: The Art and Practice of Telling the Truth—for Profit—in Business, in Sales, in Life (three pending offers as of this writing); *Forty-One Seconds: From Terror to Freedom* (Presidio Press/Ballantine); *Richard Landry Estates* (Oro Editions); *Beachglass* (St. Martin's Press); *The Dead Emcee Scrolls: The Lost Teachings of Hip Hop* (MTV/Simon & Schuster); *Said the Shotgun to the Head* (MTV/Simon & Schuster); *Meeting Across the River: Stories Inspired by the Haunting Bruce Springsteen Song* (story contributed by Randy Michael Signor) (Bloomsbury Publishing); *Other Sorrows, Other Joys: The Marriage of Catherine Sophia Boucher and William Blake: A Novel* (St. Martin's Press); *Imperial Mongolian Cooking: Recipes from the Kingdoms of Genghis Khan* by Marc Cramer (Hippocrene Publishers); *Somebody's Child: Stories from the Private Files of an Adoption Attorney* by Randi Barrow (Perigee/Penguin Putnam, Inc.); *Retro Chic: A Guide to Fabulous Vintage and Designer Resale Shopping in North America & Online* by Diana Eden & Gloria Lintermans (Really Great Books); *The Spoken Word Revolution: An Essay, Poem and an Audio Contribution* by Saul Williams (SourceBooks); *Rio L.A.: Tales from the Los Angeles River* by Patt Morrison, with photographs by Mark Lamonica (Angel City Press). Films: *What Angels Know: The Story of Elizabeth Barrett and Robert Browning* (screenplay optioned by producer Marta Anderson); *Somebody's Child: Stories from the Private Files of an Adoption Attorney* by Randi Barrow (Perigee/Penguin Putnam, Inc.), optioned by Green/Epstein/Bacino Productions for a television series; *A Place Called Waco: A Survivor's Story* by David Thibodeau and Leon Whiteson (Public Affairs/ Perseus Book Group), optioned to Showtime for a television movie; *Love Groucho: Letters from Groucho Marx to His Daughter Miriam*, edited by Miriam Marx Allen (Faber & Faber, Straus & Giroux U.S., and Faber & Faber U.K.), sold to CBS. We have many books in submission and development at this writing and at any given time.

REECE HALSEY NORTH/REECE HALSEY PARIS

98 Main Street, #704, Tiburon, CA 94920

415-789-9191

www.reecehalseynorth.com

Agents' names: Kimberley Cameron, Elizabeth Evans, April Eberhardt, april@ reecehalseynorth.com.
The following information pertains to Elizabeth Evans.
Born: Milwaukee, Wisconsin.
Education: B.A. Hamilton College, English; M.F.A. in Writing, University of San Francisco.
Career story: I interned at Zyzzyva Magazine before beginning my M.F.A. at the University of San Francisco in 2004. While at USF, I joined Reece Halsey North as a reader and editor. I completed my M.F.A. in 2006 and have been an associate agent since that time.

Hobbies and special personal interests: Hobbies: Hiking in the mountains, anything to do with boats. I like fresh air. When the weather keeps me indoors, I'll cozy up with a good book and a cup of tea. Personal interests: Appetizers, bright colors, travels abroad, flowers, aquariums, angel food cake.

Subjects and categories you like to agent: I represent a wide range of nonfiction and fiction, including biography, history, memoir, pop culture, literary fiction, upmarket commercial fiction, historical fiction and mysteries. I'm especially drawn to voice-driven fiction and narrative nonfiction in unfamiliar or exotic settings. I'm looking for excellent writing that strikes at the heart of the human condition. And I always enjoy a good love story.

Subjects and categories writers shouldn't bother pitching to you: I do not handle children's or young adult books, poetry or screenplays.

What might you be doing if you weren't agenting: If not agenting, I would run an organic artisanal cheesery in Wisconsin. Or I'd be a professional organizer.

What's the most effective ways for writers to grab your attention: I prefer a polite, well-written query letter accompanied by the appropriate submission materials (please see our website). Please do not call the office to pitch your project over the phone. Some ideas might stand out, but great writing is what captures my attention.

Do you charge fees separate from your commission, or offer non-agenting fee based services: No.

What are representative titles you have sold to publishers: *The Geography of Love* by Glenda Burgess (Broadway/Doubleday); *Courage to Surrender* by Tommy Hellsten (Ten Speed Press); *A Trace of Smoke* by Rebecca Cantrell (Tor/Forge Books); *Lonely Heart: The Life and Times of Nathanael West* by Joe Woodward (Atlas & Co.).

Why did you become an agent, and how did you become one: I didn't know about agenting until a writing professor suggested I contact Kimberley Cameron about a reading internship. I knew immediately this was the perfect job for me. Agenting is very business oriented but also appeals to my creative side. I've always enjoyed reading and editing, and I find working with my clients very satisfying. Each day is unique and filled with possibilities.

How do you feel about writers: I have an enormous amount of respect for writers. It takes such determination and discipline to write. And confidence. I admire that. I appreciate the opportunity to read another person's work.

What do you tell entities from other planets and dimensions about your job: Shhh, don't bother me. I'm reading!

What are your favorite books, movies, TV shows, and why: *Don't Lets Go to the Dogs Tonight* by Alexandra Fuller, *Housekeeping* by Marilynn Robinson, *Life and Death in Shanghai* by Nien Cheng, *The Power of One* by Bryce Courtenay, *Reading Lolita in Tehran* by Azar Nafisi, *Child of My Heart* by Alice McDermott, *Woman Hollering Creek* by Sandra Cisneros, *The Virgin Suicides* by Jeffrey Eugenides, *Beloved* and *Jazz* by Toni Morrison, *Prep* by Curtis Sittenfeld, *Howards End* by E.M. Forster, anything by Kazuo Ishiguro. All these books give me shivers when I read them. I tend to like films with a sense of whimsy. Favorite movies are *Big Fish*, *The Neverending Story*, *Moulin Rouge*, *Rushmore*. I don't watch much TV, but I got sucked into *The Tudors* on Showtime. My guilty pleasure is *Gossip Girl*.

How would you describe "the writer from hell": The writer from hell shows an unhealthy desperation and forgets his/her manners. I enjoy working with writers who are serious and professional and recognize that publishing is a business.

How would you describe the publisher and/or editor from hell: The publisher/editor from hell? No such thing, they're all angels!

Will our business exist as we know it in 10 years or so from now: I'm curious and interested in the new technology that's changing publishing, but I hope books will be around forever. My favorite books are dog-earred, underlined, highlighted, spines cracked, pages warped from falling into the bathtub, stained with finger prints of chocolate or berry juice...and there's something wonderfully real and intimate about that. In my moves across the country, I've never been able to part with my books. I might be sentimental, but I think there are many people out there who feel the way I do.

The following information pertains to Kimberley Cameron.

Born: Los Angeles, California.

Education: Marlborough School For Girls, Humboldt State University, Mount St. Mary's College.

Career history: Former publisher, Knightsbridge Publishing Company. She has been a partner with Dorris Halsey since 1993.

Hobbies/personal interests: France, reading for the sheer pleasure of it.

Categories/subjects that you are most enthusiastic about agenting: Writing that touches the heart.

What you don't want to agent: Children's books, poetry.

If you were not an agent, what might you be doing instead: Reading.

What's the best way for writers to solicit your interest: Please send all query letters by email to Amy Burkhardt at info@reecehalseynorth.com. For nonfiction, please attach a complete proposal with sample chapters. For fiction, please attach the first three chapters and a brief synopsis.

Do you charge reading or management fees: No.

Can you provide an approximation by % of what you tend to represent by category: Fiction: 50%, nonfiction: 50%.

What are the most common mistakes writers make when pitching you: We are always impressed by politeness, in a well-written letter or otherwise. Their most common mistake is using too many rhetorical adjectives to describe their own work.

How would you describe the client from Hell: One who doesn't know that publishing is a business, and should be conducted in a businesslike manner.

How would you describe the perfect client: A writer who understands the publishing business and is respectful of an agent's time.

How and why did you ever become an agent: We both love books and what they have to teach us. We both understand how important and powerful the written word is and appreciate what it takes to be a good writer.

What, if anything, can a writer do to increase the odds of you becoming his or her agent: Be polite and do your homework—know what we represent and market your work only when it's ready.

How would you describe to someone (or thing) from another planet what it is that you do as an agent: READ. Guide writer's through the writing and publishing process...

Do you have any particular opinions or impressions of editors and publishers in general: Editors and publishers are in this business for the love of books—they are all overworked but do the best they can.

What do you think the future holds for writers, publishers, and agents: There will always be readers—what form books will take we cannot imagine. There are searchers for knowledge, spiritual and otherwise that will always be looking for enlightenment.

On a personal level, what do you think people like about you and dislike about you: They like that I'm serious about helping writers—they might dislike that I must be extremely selective about the material I represent...

Please list representative titles you have sold: Please visit my Web site: www.kimberleycameron.com.

The following information pertains to April Eberhardt.

Date and place of birth: Small-town New Jersey, during a kinder, gentler era.

Education: B.A. Hamilton College, Anthropology and French; CPLF, University of Paris; M.B.A., Finance and Marketing, Boston University.

Career history or story: Twenty years as strategist in corporate America; seven years as head of my own women's clothing design company; three years with Zoetrope: All-Story; three years as agent.

Hobbies, interests: Hobbies: Designing new ways to do familiar things, introducing people with similar interests, figuring out families. Spending the whole weekend reading and hiking. Personal interests: Smart design. Anything orange or chartreuse. Travel to Paris, Sweden, and Switzerland (or any lush, cool location where I can walk or hike.) Rocks, volcanoes and owls. Fifties food, especially offbeat meat loaf recipes, mashed potatoes and butterscotch pudding.

Subjects & categories you are interested in agenting, including fiction & non-fiction: I favor interlinked collections of short stories, as well as contemporary women's fiction featuring smart protagonists. Family fiction always catches my eye, as does the good American novel, albeit nothing too serious, romantic or historical. Extra credit if it's set in a city or New Jersey. I'm a fan of first-time authors, the here and now, a fast pace, irony and bite.

Subjects & categories writers shouldn't even bother pitching to you: I don't represent children's or young adult works, thrillers, murders or mysteries, Westerns or war themes, history, romance or poetry. No space porn, please. (Yes, it's a genre.)

What would you do if you weren't agenting: If not agenting, I would found a literary magazine dedicated to new writers, or else figure out a way for first-time authors to self-publish and garner worldwide distribution and acclaim quickly, and make money at it too. (I know, I know—that's what the Internet is for.) Or maybe I'd be an inventor, a design and color consultant, or an Alpine hiking guide.

What's the best way for fiction writers to solicit your interest: I prefer a short, concise emailed query accompanied by the first couple of chapters. No snail mail or phone calls. No lengthy synopses. To me the truth is in the writing.

Do you charge reading or any upfront fees: No.

Describe the client from Hell, even if you don't have any: The author who calls or emails too often to see what I've done for her today, suggesting she doesn't trust or believe that I'm working really hard to find a good home for her work.

Why did you become an agent, and how did you become one: I became an agent because I take great satisfaction in introducing literary talent to the world, and because it's gratifying to find the right house and editor for an author. You could say I'm a professional cheerleader and matchmaker of sorts.

How do you feel about editors and publishers: The clients and editors I work with are gleamingly five-star. Otherwise why would I keep working with them?

How do you feel about writers: I am in awe of writers and their ability to create stirring, imaginative fiction out of thin air. Nothing thrills or transports me like seeing the world through another person's brain.

What do you see in the near future for book publishing: Back to inventing: I'd love to design a gel-pack type of floppy reader, thin so that it rolls/folds up for travel, but opens out to a big, light, bright screen for day or nighttime reading. You could download your favorite books (and manuscripts) to it wirelessly. Maybe I'd make it microwaveable and freezable, too, so you could put it on your neck when you're tired.

What are your favorite books/TV shows/movies, and why: Best books: *The Girls' Guide to Hunting and Fishing* by Melissa Bank, *Nice Big American Baby* by Judith Budnitz, *The Dive From Clausen's Pier* by Ann Packer. Anything by Laurie Colwin. Favorite films: *Swimming Pool* or *Under the Sand* with Charlotte Rampling; Terrence Malick's *Days of Heaven*; Kathleen Turner in *Body Heat*; *American Gigolo* starring a young Richard Gere and Lauren Hutton.

HARTLINE LITERARY AGENCY

123 Queenston Dr., Pittsburgh, PA 15235

412-829-2483

www.hartlineliterary.com

Agents' names: Joyce Hart, joyce@hartlineliterary.com; Tamela Hancock Murray, tamela@hartlineliterary.com, Terry Burns, terry@hartlineliterary.com; Diana Flegal, diana@hartlineliterary.com; Erik Schmidgal, erikws@hartlineliterary.com

The following information pertains to Joyce Hart.

Born: August 7. Place: Iowa City, Iowa.

Education: Open Bible College, Des Moines, Iowa (now in Eugene, Oregon).

Career story: Started as a secretary to the vice president and editorial staff at Whitaker House, Springdale, Pennsylvania in 1978, until 1989. The last three years I was the vice president of marketing. Worked in all aspects of the publishing house.

Hobbies and special personal interests: Reading, traveling, dogs.

Subjects and categories you like to agent: Most adult novels, most genres except fantasy, sci fi, nonfiction adult books—self-help, spirituality, prayer, family.

Subjects and categories writers shouldn't bother pitching to you: Sci fi, fantasy, poetry, gay and lesbian, paranormal, memoirs.

What might you be doing if you weren't agenting: Teaching, working in a bookstore, speaking to women's groups.

What's the most effective ways for writers to grab your attention: A well-written, well-researched proposal. Following our guidelines on our Web site.

Do you charge fees separate from your commission, or offer non-agenting fee based services: Once in a while we'll charge for postage if it's overnight or very high. Most of the time we don't bother. No fees for non-agenting services. We don't do any editing, etc.

What are representative titles you have sold to publishers: *A Mending at the Edge*—a Christy Finalist—the latest of 14 books by Jane Kirkpatrick; *Kiss Me Like You Mean It*, the latest of 8 books by David E. Clarke; *Family of the Heart* by Dorothy Clark (Steeple Hill); *Amish Peace in an English Word* by Suzanne Fisher (Revell); *Final Deposit* by Lisa Harris (Steeple Hill); *Paper Bag Christmas* by Kevin Milne (Center Street); *Happy Tails* by Linda Winn (Thomas Nelson).

Why did you become an agent, and how did you become one: I became an agent because I quit my corporate job and wanted to stay in this industry. I found my niche. I started Hartline Marketing in 1990 and Hartline Literary in 1992. I was a publisher's rep for 11 or more years and did the literary agency part-time. Eventually, the agency became my full time job.

How do you feel about writers: I like working with authors for the most part. If they are prima donnas, then it's not so much fun. Most are great and my good friends.

What do you tell entities from other planets and dimensions about your job: I don't know how to answer this one...

What are your favorite books, movies, TV shows, and why: Favorite books: *Yada Yada* series by Neta Jackson; mystery/suspense books. I have many favorite authors. Movies: two most favorite are *Sound of Music*, because of the music and the story. *Steel Magnolias*—I love the characters and their relationships with one another. TV Shows: *Murder, She Wrote*; *Diagnosis Murder, Jane Doe*—all mysteries and I like the characters.

How would you describe "the writer from hell": One who rewrites and rewrites, not flexible, calls me all hours of the day and night, hard to work with those.

How would you describe the publisher and/or editor from hell: An editor who never responds to e-mails or phone calls. Snobbish editors. Most editors and publishers I work with are good friends.

What do you like best about your clients, and the editors and publishers you work with: I like seeing good writing and compelling stories, good non-fiction. I like my clients who are loyal to our agency. Most are willing to work hard and give us a good proposal to present to the editors. Most of the editors are great to work with. I love it when they call me and ask me if I have a client who could write specific book or on a specific subject. I like to help the author and editor develop a good product.

You're welcome to share your thoughts and sentiments about the business of writing and publishing: I love the publishing world. It is not an easy profession, getting harder all the time. Publishers are asking for "household names" more than ever. Sometimes the "market driven" part of the business gets discouraging. Especially when sales turns down a really good book.

Do you wish to describe who you are: A pretty ordinary, hard working woman. The wife of a minister, a mother and a grandmother. Someone who counts her blessings and is grateful for a job that has brought great satisfaction in her life.

Will our business exist as we know it in 10 years or so from now: I think our business will exist in the next 10 years or so. It has changed a lot in the past 5 years and will continue to change. More and more people are buying online, we're seeing more e-books, but the growth is not huge. However, I think we will always have print books, books that people can hold in their hands.

The following information pertains to Tamela Hancock Murray, www.tamela-hancockmurray.com, tamelaagents@juno.com.

Born: Petersburg, Virginia; September 6.

Education: Lynchburg College, Honors in Journalism.

Career story: Tamela has been with Hartline Literary Agency since 2001. She has many happy and successful clients. A professional writer since 1994, she is also an award-winning, bestselling author in her own right.

Hobbies and special personal interests: Reading is Tamela's favorite hobby, a great convenience since her job as an agent requires so much reading! She especially enjoys time spent with her family and friends. Travel fascinates her.

Subjects and categories you like to agent: Tamela's focus is on inspirational titles. She enjoys fiction and nonfiction. Novelists with stories geared to a mainstream audience stand the best chance of gaining her representation. Writers with an outstanding platform have the best chance of success when submitting nonfiction.

Subjects and categories writers shouldn't bother pitching to you: Erotica, science fiction, experimental, stream of consciousness, horror. I don't mind seeing Christianity explored in a thoughtful manner, but I will not represent any work that is obviously offensive to Christians.

What might you be doing if you weren't agenting: Writing for newspapers and magazines.

What's the most effective ways for writers to grab your attention: Client referrals are the number one way to get my attention. Barring a referral, a top notch proposal showing me how you will partner with your publisher to make your book a success is the best way to gain my attention. I do review each submission so if you don't hear from me in three months, feel free to resubmit and let me know it's your second try. If you are accepted for representation by another agent before hearing back from me, I would greatly appreciate it if you could let me know so I can disregard your submission and wish you the best.

Do you charge fees separate from your commission, or offer non-agenting fee

based services: I charge no fees. No reading fees, no critique fees, nothing but industry standard commission.

What are representative titles you have sold to publishers: *Heart of the West* series by Maggie Brendan (Revell Books); *Stupid About Men* by Deborah Dunn (Howard Books); *My Heart Remembers* by Kim Vogel Sawyer (Bethany House).

Why did you become an agent, and how did you become one: I believe in the books I present to editors and I love making authors' dreams come true. I became an agent because my agent, Joyce Hart, wanted to expand her business and she was willing to take a chance on me. I'm so glad she did!

How do you feel about writers: I love writers! Since I'm a writer myself, I understand what they go through to get published and to keep their career momentum going. I understand the frustration of the near-miss and the pain of multiple rejections. I also celebrate with them when that all-important contract comes through. Gaining new book contracts never gets old for me. The twentieth book is just as exciting as the first.

What do you tell entities from other planets and dimensions about your job: I spend a lot of time reading, advising, answering questions, hand-holding, and making friends.

What are your favorite books, movies, TV shows, and why: My tastes are eclectic. I like to read books on Western Mysticism from the Middle Ages. I also enjoy romantic books and suspense. Silent films are a treat. The other night my husband and I stayed up much too late watching *Lorna Doone*. As for TV, *Clean House* is fun to watch. My tastes are often dominated by my mood at the time, whether I want entertainment or wish to be challenged.

How would you describe "the writer from hell": This writer would refuse to cooperate with editors, send me lots of chain-letter emails, and be flighty and unpredictable, with a poor work ethic. Thankfully I have wonderful writers who are just super!

How would you describe the publisher and/or editor from hell: I really hate having to act as a bill collector. I like when a publisher pays on time. The hellish editor is one who refuses to answer legitimate calls and/or e-mails.

What do you like best about your clients, and the editors and publishers you work with: I love how dedicated my clients are to the writing craft, and their wonderful attitudes about complying with editors' requests. I love how my editors don't make irrational, unreasonable requests and how they treat my authors with respect. I love publishers who do a top notch job of marketing.

You're welcome to share your thoughts and sentiments about the business of writing and publishing: A talented, persistent writer willing to be flexible and sensitive to the market has the best chance of success.

Do you wish to describe who you are: My goal is to be a benefit and a blessing to all who work with me.

Will our business exist as we know it in 10 years or so from now: Yes, and the quality of our books will only get better. Electronic formats may gain in popularity, but I think we'll always have leather-bound, hardback, and paperback books.

The following information pertains to Terry Burns.

Born: August 21, 1942.

Education: B.B.A. West Texas State; advanced studies at Southern Methodist University.

Career story: Chamber of commerce executive for 27 years, professional writer of inspirational fiction 10 years, agent at Hartline for over two years. As a writer have 24 books in print, and as an agent have a diverse and growing client list.

Hobbies and special personal interests: Camping and RV.

Subjects and categories you like to agent: Historical fiction and romance, mysteries, thriller/suspense, inspirationals, non-fiction, a good well written book I can see the market for and feel I have the right contacts to address that market.

Subjects and categories writers shouldn't bother pitching to you: Fantasy and sci-fi, erotica or anything of that nature.

What might you be doing if you weren't agenting: Writing more.

What's the most effective ways for writers to grab your attention: Read the submission guidelines and send me just exactly what I want to see in the exact manner I ask to see it.

Do you charge fees separate from your commission, or offer non-agenting fee based services: No, our agency does have a provision to charge for copies and postage if appropriate.

What are representative titles you have sold to publishers: *Rhapsody in Red* (Moody); *The Birth to Five Book* (Revell); *Beyond the Smoke* (BJU Press); *Tribute* (Kregel); Two separate 5 book youth series to Capstone Press; *Rekindle Your Dreams* (Bridge Logos).

Why did you become an agent, and how did you become one: The owner of this agency, Joyce Hart, was my agent for a number of years and still is. She recruited me to work with her. I decided I could do more good by helping a number of people get their work out than doing a book or two a year myself, although I do still write.

How do you feel about writers: Most agents come from a publishing background. I came from a writing background. Whether that is an advantage or a disadvantage it does give me an unusually good report with writers.

What do you tell entities from other planets and dimensions about your job: To go home because I don't rep sci-fi.

What are your favorite books, movies, TV shows, and why: I grew up on *Bonanza* and *Gunsmoke* and Gene and Roy at the movies. I love westerns. I'd write and rep a bunch of them if there was a market for them right now. As to shows today it takes something pretty interesting to get me away from whatever I'm doing.

How would you describe "the writer from hell": Let me put it this way, I don't take orders very well.

How would you describe the publisher and/or editor from hell: The only ones that really bother me are the ones whose idea of a response to a submission is just to never respond. Fortunately there aren't many of those.

What do you like best about your clients, and the editors and publishers you work with: The love of the words, the desire to get a good story out there that will entertain, that will impact emotions, that will cause someone to stop and think, possible even bring some change into their lives. I love to work with people on both ends that are trying to make something happen with the written word.

You're welcome to share your thoughts and sentiments about the business of writing and publishing: See above.

Do you wish to describe who you are: Just a good old boy that likes to try and help people get their words out into the marketplace.

Will our business exist as we know it in 10 years or so from now: Yes. There have been changes over the years, but they have tended to be additional sources of publishing, not replacing previous forms. We will see digital and audio and some of the other changes taking place now continue to grow, but we'll still see publishing as we know it continue to exist.

The following information pertains to Diana L. Flegal.

Born: July 24; Johnstown, Pennsylvania.

Education: Certified dental assistant; certified X-ray technologist; 13 credits shy of a degree in anthropology and missions from Maryland Bible College and Seminary.

Career story: Served as a third world health care giver in Haiti one year. Chairside dental assistant 23 years; Apologetics teacher at Grace Bible Academy Sioux Falls South Dakota; Women's Bible study leader; youth leader; Sunday School leader; pastor's wife; editorial assistant to Joyce Hart CEO and founder of Hartline literary Agency; literary agent.

Hobbies and special personal interests: Crafting, decorating my home, reading, gardening, traveling.

Subjects and categories you like to agent: Inspirational nonfiction, inspirational literary fiction, inspirational gift books, animal books (moving stories about animals and the people that love them).

Subjects and categories writers shouldn't bother pitching to you: Gay/lesbian, paranormal, New Age or anything that is not from a Christian Worldview . I'll take a look at most anything else if it is well written.

What might you be doing if you weren't agenting: Life coaching.

What's the most effective ways for writers to grab your attention: Good story line with a fast pace. Do not bog me down with minute details of your personal life story. Readers do not want to know these things.

Do you charge fees separate from your commission, or offer non-agenting fee based services: I charge for copies that I must print for submission and the postage for same. That is all. Honest!

What are representative titles you have sold to publishers: I am a relatively new agent and have not made my first sale. A lot of good stuff out there now being read by editors.

Why did you become an agent, and how did you become one: A voracious reader from little on, I have always wanted to be paid to read. As Joyce Hart's first reader, I learned what good writing was, what editors were looking for and what did not sell. I began to realize that I could be an agent.

How do you feel about writers: I love writers because before I was an agent, I was a reader. I love the printed word, newspapers, magazines, digests, and novels, how to's etc. so without writers I wouldn't have those precious stolen moments in time when I am swept away to another place and time, country or planet. My life would not be at all as joyful and varied as it is.

What do you tell entities from other planets and dimensions about your job: It is the best reason to relocate to Planet Earth. We have free libraries and they can get their own card. You don't need an extension cord and any battery packs. Just daylight and a comfy chair. It is so worth learning English for!

What are your favorite books, movies, TV shows, and why: The Bible has the top slot to be sure. As to fiction, I love mysteries best, Elizabeth Peters and her pen name Anne Perry is my absolute favorite author. I have read most everything she has written and that is a lot of books. Google her sometime. Christy Barritt, Ron and Janet Benrey too. Mauve Binchey is my favorite secular author, read everything she has written, then non fiction how to, John Ortberg, Erwin McManus, T.D. Jakes, Philip Yantzy, Max Lucado, John Maxwell, Donald Miller. Writing Books: Anne Lamott's *Bird by Bird* is one of the best, then Terry Whalin's *How to Write a Non Fiction Book Proposal*, along with Julia Cameron and William Zinsser.

How would you describe "the writer from hell": I try to steer clear of them. But I guess they are the ones that write their life story with every small detail included expecting it to be a bestseller and it is only interesting to them…

How would you describe the publisher and/or editor from hell: Don't know too many, but I would say they are the ones who clear their desk and send out the form rejection letters and never give your proposal a glance. Or at the least fail to tell me what exactly they ARE looking for.

What do you like best about your clients, and the editors and publishers you work with: The creative comments and critiques that editors give help my writers become better writers. You can tell the ones (editors) that truly love what they do and that they care about representing good writing. They take that extra minute to say a nice thing that keeps you trying all the more to make a match for the writer and the editor. As for my clients, they have become my extended family. We support one another with words and deeds. In my case we encourage one another to go beyond our limitations to attempt excellence. I care so much for each one and their stories that I lay awake at night trying to strategize a plan to enable their success.

You're welcome to share your thoughts and sentiments about the business of writing and publishing: It is a tough business, getting tougher every year, but I believe this means that the really well turned phrase and good story will shine forth and find its place. And we will be all the better for having known one another and shared the time it takes to read a book together. My life will be enriched as well as the others that just happen to come across that good read, or received a gift or had nothing better to do so out of boredom picked up a book to fill the time. Their lives will be changed, the world will be a better place to live in and more aliens will desire to visit. They will begin savings accounts and place a poster on the wall of their bedrooms and dream of the day they come to Planet Earth and get their very own Library card with their name on it.

Do you wish to describe who you are: I am a lover of books, a dreamer of dreams, an armchair traveler and a visionary and a missionary. I'm also a blond by birth.

Will our business exist as we know it in 10 years or so from now: I plan on being a literary agent until I pass from this life on to the next. It is something that I can do from anyplace in the world. I plan to be so successful that I will travel extensively, representing my authors anywhere I go. I appreciate the technology that allows this and hope I can enjoy the health to follow my dreams of helping dig wells in Africa, build orphanages in third world countries and help a school in Tanzania where a friend of mine teaches.

JOHN HAWKINS & ASSOCIATES, INC.

71 West 23rd Street, Suite 1600, New York, NY 10019

212-807-7040   fax: 212-807-9555

www.jhalit.com

Agents' names: Anne Hawkins, ahawkins@jhalit.com; Moses Cardona, moses@jhalit.com; William Reiss, reiss@jhalit.com

The following information pertains to Anne Hawkins.

Education: B.A., Bryn Mawr College.

Career history: I have been a literary agent for over ten years. Prior to that, I worked in various businesses and in English education. I also played the bassoon professionally.

Hobbies/personal interests: I love classical music, ballet, opera, and theater. Cooking is one of my favorite forms of weekend relaxation. I also collect African tribal art.

Categories/subjects that you are most enthusiastic about agenting: Adult mainstream literary and commercial fiction, including mystery/suspense/thriller. A small number of upper middle grade and young adult projects. Adult nonfiction projects concerning history, public policy, science, medicine, nature/outdoors, and women's issues

What you don't want to agent: Adult fiction: romance, westerns, horror, science fiction, fantasy Adult non-fiction: advice/relationships, business, self-help, spirituality, most how-to. Juvenile: picture books or books for very young readers

If you were not an agent, what might you be doing instead: I might work as a museum curator or in a nursery that specializes in exotic trees and shrubs.

What's the best way for writers to solicit your interest: Write a brief, engaging query letter and include a few sample pages.

Do you charge reading or management fees: No.

Can you provide an approximation by % of what you tend to represent by category: Adult Fiction: 45%, adult nonfiction: 45%, upper middle grade or young adult fiction: 10%.

What are the most common mistakes writers make when pitching you: Pitching multiple, unrelated projects at the same time is a big mistake, since it's hard enough to find the right agent for even one book. Pitching projects of a type that I don't handle is foolish and a waste of everyone's time. (Readers of this book won't have that problem.)

How would you describe the client from Hell: Authors can be a quirky bunch, and "quirky" is fine. But arrogant, unreasonably demanding, inflexible, mean spirited behavior sours an agent-client relationship every time.

How would you describe the perfect client: Glorious talent aside, the perfect client is distinguished by good sense, good humor, and good manners.

How and why did you ever become an agent: My brother-in-law, John Hawkins, encouraged me to join the agency.

What, if anything, can a writer do to increase the odds of you becoming his or her agent: A referral from some I know (author, other publishing professional, or personal friend) will get my immediate attention. Over 50% of my clients have come to me through some kind of referral.

How would you describe to someone (or thing) from another planet what it is that you do as an agent: I represent the business interests of authors to publishing houses, provide advocacy, act as a sounding board for editorial issues, and help authors make wise career choices.

Do you have any particular opinions or impressions of editors and publishers in general: Most people in this industry are smart, interesting, and fun to work with.

On a personal level, what do you think people like about you and dislike about you: I always try to be forthright and honest. Most people like that, but a few find it daunting.

Please list representative titles you have sold: *Tears of Pearl* (St. Martins); *Beauty Pearls for Chemo Girls* (Kensington); *Off the Menu* (NAL); *Matters of Faith* (Berkley).

The following information pertains to Moses Cardona.

Born: October 1966, New York, New York.

Education: B.S., New York University.

Career history: All with John Hawkins & Associates: Began as Bookkeeper, promoted to Rights Director, and currently: General Manager/Literary Agent of the agency.

Hobbies/personal interests: Comics, basketball, jigsaw puzzles.

Categories/subjects that you are most enthusiastic about agenting: Multi-cultural, gay fiction, literary fiction.

What you don't want to agent: Poetry, Children's, military, mafia fiction.

If you were not an agent, what might you be doing instead: Running a bed and breakfast.

What's the best way for writers to solicit your interest: Query Letter, with sample chapters, or e-mail query.

Do you charge reading or management fees: No.

Can you provide an approximation by % of what you tend to represent by category: Multicultural: 50%, Fiction—mysteries, literary, science fiction/horror: 30%,

Science/business: 10%, Other: 10%.

What are the most common mistakes writers make when pitching you: Pitching more than one project. Misspelling agent's name, information.

How would you describe the client from Hell: Having unrealistic ideas about publishing industry.

How would you describe the perfect client: Good manners, patience, a bit of attitude and a great sense of humor.

How and why did you ever become an agent: I fell into the business through a client of the agency.

What, if anything, can a writer do to increase the odds of you becoming his or her agent: Patience and be a great storyteller.

How would you describe to someone (or thing) from another planet what it is that you do as an agent: I help place ideas onto various formats, film, books, magazines for mass distribution around the planet.

What are your favorite books, movies, TV shows, and why: *Mary Tyler Moore Show*, great cast, writing—timeless; *All About Eve*, best movie about art, theater, and people; *The Stand*, probably one of the best epic books about humanity.

On a personal level, what do you think people like about you and dislike about you: I'm brutally honest.

Please list representative titles you have sold: *Tarnished Beauty* (Atria Books); *White Nights* (St Martins/Minotaur); *Red Bones* (St. Martins/Minotaur).

The following information pertains to William Reiss.

Born: 1942, New York, New York.

Education: B.A., Kenyon College.

Career history: Freelance Researcher; Editorial Assistant to Lombard Jones (a graphic designer and editor), encyclopedia editor, Funk & Wagnalls Standard Reference Library.

Categories/subjects that you are most enthusiastic about agenting: Biographies, nonfiction historical narratives, archaeology, science fiction and fantasy, mysteries and suspense, true-crime narratives, natural history, children's fiction, adult fiction (literary and commercial).

What you don't want to agent: Romance novels, poetry, plays.

What's the best way for writers to solicit your interest: Telephone or send a letter describing the project, with a few sample pages to provide a sense of writing style.

Do you charge reading or management fees: No.

Please list representative titles you have sold: *Shiloh* (S&S/Atheneum Children's Books); *The Madman's Tale* (Ballantine); *White Oleander* (Little, Brown); *Allegiance: Fort Sumter, Charleston, and the Beginning of the Civil War* (Harcourt); *Exit Strategy* (Jove); *Ghosts in the Snow* (Bantam); *Son of a Witch* (Regan Books/HarperCollins).

HEACOCK LITERARY AGENCY, INC.

Catt LeBaigue, AAR; Tom Dark

Author's Representatives

1020 Hollywood Way, #439, Burbank, CA 91505

www.heacockliteraryagency.com

e-mail: catt@heacockliteraryagency.com; tom@heacockliteraryagency.com

Headquarters:

Rosalie Grace Heacock Thompson, AAR

507 Grand Blvd., P.O. Box 226, Cloudcroft, NM 88317-0226

Agent's name: Catt LeBaigue
Born: 12/30, California
Education: B.A., Music, California State University, San Bernardino; plus a Certificate in Writing in upper division and graduate level courses, CSUSB

Career history: Eighteen years in the television and film industry for Columbia, Lorimar, Sony, Fox, Paramount, and Warner Bros. studios. Catt LeBaigue joined the Heacock Literary Agency, working full time as an agent, in 2005. Tom Dark is our newest agent, joining in 2008.

Hobbies/personal interests: I grew up as an American living abroad in the diplomatic community. A highlight in my life was in 2005, when a full-blooded traditional aboriginal tribe in Australia adopted me, gave me a new name and invited me to dance in their sacred dances. I raise horses and live close to nature. My interests are meditation, dreams, Jung, reading, travel, drawing, sculpting, and animals.

Categories/subjects that you are most enthusiastic about agenting: The Heacock Literary Agency was founded in 1978 with a vision to get significant books into the marketplace, books with the potential to empower and fortify consciousness. Books can change the individual from the inside out and individual consciousness can transform the world. Trade Non-fiction: Art, architecture, animal communication, diplomacy, ecology, indigenous cultures, invention, the mind and learning processes, formal science and the connection to inner knowing, social sciences, travel, wilderness awareness, body, mind and spirit. We seek innovative books which present solutions to problems. Trade Fiction: Children's, especially middle-grade and YA. Adult fiction: literary, no short stories.

What you don't want to agent: True crime, abuse accounts and books that do not contribute to the reader's well-being and peace of mind.

If you were not an agent, what might you be doing instead: I see my work as an author's representative, not just as my job, but as the best way that I can contribute to humanity and the health of the planet. If I wasn't agenting, I'd be seeking another way that is just as powerful to make a difference.

What's the most effective ways for writers to grab your attention: E-mail without attachments, unless requested. Not accepting postal mail queries.

Do you charge reading or any upfront fees: No.

Can you provide an approximation by % of what you tend to represent by category: 30% Adult Non-fiction; 40% Children's, 30% Fiction.

What are the most common mistakes writers make when pitching you: The writer should take care in composing the inquiry since this is the first impression the agent receives of the writer's ability to convey his or her ideas. Any background information will enhance the writer's chance of attracting interest. Non-fiction books should be presented with a book proposal. Including the word count of the final manuscript is helpful.

How would you describe "the writer from hell": The client from hell seeks only monetary gain or fame and cannot see beyond themselves.

How would you describe the perfect client: The perfect client delights me with fine writing, is considerate, and expresses appreciation for our efforts.

How and why did you ever become an agent: Since the founding of the agency by my uncle James B. Heacock and my aunt Rosalie Grace Heacock Thompson, in 1978, I knew that one day, after a career in Hollywood, I would turn to agenting books. I focused my education with that in mind and followed the publishing business closely through the years, occasionally working for the agency. After spending eighteen years in the entertainment industry working in film and television, I felt it was time to switch careers. I joined the agency in 2005, as full time agent, representing trade fiction and non-fiction. We do not handle screenplays at this time.

What, if anything, can a writer do to increase the odds of you becoming his or her agent: Timing is the critical element here. If the author is presenting a simply wonderful book about a very crowded subject which already has wonderful books out, the representative cannot spend his or her time trying to place it. The author should be familiar with what is "out there" and concentrate efforts on what needs to be out there.

How would you describe to someone (or thing) from another planet what it is that you do as an agent: The literary agent reads and evaluates book proposals and manuscripts, presents those which are accepted to appropriate publishers, negotiates the very best contract possible and carefully reviews all royalty statements after publication. The literary agent is basically a business manager for the author's writing efforts, serves also as a sounding board when the author wants to test new ideas and distributes the authors' monies promptly.

Do you have any particular opinions or impressions of editors and publishers in general: Editors and publishers impress me as dedicated, book-loving individuals who behave with integrity and honor.

What do you think the future holds for writers, publishers and agents: The future is bright for all three. Books continue to be the thought processes of humanity and to make vast contributions to society.

On a personal level, what do you think people like about you and dislike about you: As Robbie Burns once wrote: "Oh would someone giftie give me, to see myself as others see me..."

Please list representative titles you have sold: The Heacock Literary Agency has sold over 1,100 books to over 100 publishers.

DAVID HENDIN

PO Box 805, Nyack, NY 10960

Agent's name: David Hendin
Born: December 16, 1945, St. Louis, Missouri.
Education: B.S. in Biology, Education University of Missouri, Columbia 1967. M.A. in Journalism, University of Missouri, Columbia, 1970.
Career history: Columnist, feature writer, executive (including senior vice president, newspaper syndication, and president, publishing division) United Feature Syndicate, Inc. 1970-1993.
What's the best way for writers to solicit your interest: We are not accepting any new clients.
Do you charge reading or management fees: No.
Can you provide an approximation by % of what you tend to represent by category: Fiction: 40%, Non-Fiction: 60%.
How would you describe to someone (or thing) from another planet what it is that you do as an agent: I have fun with writers.
Please list representative titles you have sold: *Miss Manners Guide to Weddings (For Better, Not Worse)* by Judith and Jacobina Martin (W.W. Norton); *Clubbed to Death* by Elaine Viets (Signet/Penguin).

THE JEFF HERMAN AGENCY

PO Box 1522 or 3 Elm Street, Stockbridge, MA 01262

413-298-0077   fax: 413-298-8188

www.jeffherman.com

The following information pertains to **Jeff Herman**
Agent's name: Jeff Herman, jeff@jeffherman.com
Born: 12/17/58. North Shore Hospital, Manhasset, NY
Education: Bachelors, Syracuse University
Career history: I started to genuinely work for a living in 1981 as an in-house publicist at a small publishing house, Schocken Books, now a tiny fragment of Random House. I learned how to call reporters and producers to get them to interview authors.

It really wasn't too hard to do. To make more money I started working for public relation agencies that had high paying corporate clients. I had to come up with story ideas about filing cabinets, mineral water, chocolate chip cookies, and many other consumer products and services. I actually liked the work; it could be fun. But I also had to deal with a lot of bosses who I thought were stupid and emotionally challenged, and I was expected to attend and stay awake at meetings at which people kept talking. I was good at the work but failed at playing office. In my late twenties I said I was a literary agent and then I became one and stayed that way, even as other things changed.

Hobbies/personal interests: I haven't had any hobbies since I was a child, when I had a few. Adults said it was good to have hobbies and they bought me hobby stuff like old coins, stamps, baseball cards and a chess set. And I think I actually liked it. But when I got older my hobbies felt like my GI Joe dolls, something to hide and be covert about. And then it all just seemed to fade away. I still don't know what happened to the cards and the GI Joes; my mother denies discarding them. I think I sold the coins and stamps for beer money when I was a freshman. That was a long answer. Nothing interests me until it does, but it might never happen twice.

Categories/subjects that you are most enthusiastic about agenting: Let's cut to the chase: If I feel like I can sell it then I'll "like it", even if I would never actually read it on my own time. I don't like selling fiction, but I like reading some of it on my own time. Give me your non-fiction for agenting.

Subjects & categories writers shouldn't even bother pitching to you: Fiction is a long shot for me.

If you were not an agent, what might you be doing instead: I'd like to be walking around a lot where there's good air, a lot of round hills and tall trees, meadows and dirt paths, a few clusters of goofy humans and animals, and places to buy decent coffee. But if that's all I would do then what would I be?

What's the most effective ways for writers to grab your attention: Act like you like me.

Do you charge reading or any upfront fees: NO.

What are representative titles you have sold to publishers : I've sold many hundreds. See a partial list at www.jeffherman.com.

How and why did you ever become an agent: My career story above explains some of the trajectory. The way I became a bona fide literary agent was by succeeding at what we are essentially supposed to do, which is discover decent written product and sell it to publishers. I taught myself how to negotiate the deals by reading books on the subject. It's easy to get people to show you what they have written. It takes a certain skill or intuition to know whether or not something can be sold to a publisher, but if you really want to succeed at something, then you can learn how to do it, and figure out who you need to know.

How do you feel about writers: I don't think I'll ever understand where hard core writers get the discipline and fire to spend so much time writing. To me it always felt like "homework". And then there's something else about them I can't identify. It's like they sometimes have an extra pulse, or a mind that's separate from the one you think you know.

How would you describe to someone (or thing) from another planet what it is that you do as an agent: They have never asked. Actually, they already seem to know more than I could tell them about anything. If you ever really want a dose of confusion, ask them what they do.

What are your favorite books, movies, TV shows, and why: The various *Law and Order* serials, because they are usually good. I liked the first season of *Mad Men*, and now I'm thinking that maybe they shouldn't have made a second season.

How would you describe "the writer from hell": I've become both more and less tolerant over the years, and have learned to re-direct or preempt certain characteristics that I don't like, and to be less annoyed in general. In truth, anything that makes us uncomfortable can feel like hell. But sometimes it's better to deal with it and learn why it feels hellish. So in that sense, writers from hell can be a transient or transforming experience. Sometimes, they get good advances and royalties.

How would you describe the publisher and/or editor from hell: Irredeemably burned out but not yet gone.

What do you like best about your clients, and the editors and publishers you work with: Cooperation. Respect. Patience. Appreciation. Fairness. Humility.

You're welcome to share your thoughts and sentiments about the business of writing and publishing: It will always be a very interesting and happening place to be. If you want a thought, feeling or fact to last for a long time, you'll write it down. If you want to revisit who you were, or understand someone else, it's best to read what may have been written down. Written words are like mountains.

Do you wish to describe who you are : I don't know how to answer this question.

Finally, will our business exist as we know it in 10 years or so from now: Probably not. People will of course still write and read, but the production and distribution of written products will be very different than anyone is currently predicting.

The following information pertains to Deborah Levine Herman.

Born: Long Island, New York, Oct. 4- old enough

Education: Undergrad BA with Honors in Liberal Arts, Ohio State University; Juris Doctorate from the Ohio State University College of Law in a dual degree with the Graduate School of Journalism (MA); Certified Child custody mediator.

Career history: An Assistant Attorney General State of Ohio, Litigator , Freelance writer, Mediator, Author, Jeff Herman Literary Agency, LLC, author's manager.

Hobbies/personal interest: I am an avid collector of yard sale and flea market treasure. Beading is my passion as is spending time spoiling my horse. I am not a great rider so I mostly like to treat him as a pet. I love my dogs and cats, enjoy reading and have morbid fascination with true crime. I am also addicted to popping bubble wrap. I like the type with the little bubbles the best. Oh, I guess I also enjoy my three kids, who, thank God, seem to be moving toward adulthood. Oh, one last thing, I enjoy spending time with my special someone who is never boring.

Categories/subjects that you are most enthusiastic about agenting: My tastes are eclectic. I focus on non-fiction, especially self-help because I need so much of it. I have been exploring many new avenues over the past year and like trends that can make a difference. I love celebrity books. I am interested in spiritual material, but it has to be well executed. In other words, do your homework. Watch for my new book: *Deborah Herman's Guide to Spiritual Writing and Publishing* for more info.

What you don't want to agent: Fiction, Children's, or poetry. I don't like things that are arrogant. But you wouldn't be able to determine that, would you?

If you were not an agent, what would you be doing: I love agenting and always try to be writing as well. On my off hours I like beading, playing with my horse, napping with my dogs….oh, I get to do that too. Isn't it great?

What's the best way for fiction writers to solicit your interest: Please don't try. I love to read a good book, but I don't have time to consider materials we simply don't represent.

What's the best way for non-fiction writers to solicit your interest: Query first. Then have a good proposal ready. I am pretty immediate if I like something so I won't want to hear that you were just testing out an idea.

Do you charge reading fees or try to sell non-agent services: Heavens no. Some people contact me directly to consult with them on proposals since we did "write the book." However, this is never a part of the agency. Any of my clients would have to go through the submission process with my partner like anyone else. I can say that they would have a pretty good proposal to submit, but the rest is up to them. My consultation business is called "Crystal Clear Writing Consultants."

Do you require any kind of upfront payments from your clients: No!!!

Can you provide an approximation by % of what you tend to represent by category: All the same. We represent books at a 15% rate.

What are the most common mistakes writers make when pitching you: Being unclear. We represent almost entirely non-fiction. Therefore the hook needs to be strong. Presentation is important, but the most important thing is that I can visualize the book and who you are by the query or proposal.

How would you describe the client from Hell: Someone who is arrogant, demanding and unappreciative. I do not like people who call the office and try to bully the support staff. What people don't know is that I often answer the phone with my "receptionist voice," so they are definitely shooting themselves in the foot.

How would you describe your dream client: Each client relationship is different. Someone who can hear constructive suggestions without responding defensively. We only have your best interests at heart and may see ways to improve your chances for a sale. I like interesting people who care about what they are doing for the greater good.

How and why did you become an agent: I began as a writer and wrote so many horrible book proposals that Jeff felt sorry for me. He had me screen proposals for him and I learned what I was doing wrong. I wrote some of my own books and saw the business from both sides.

What, if anything, can a writer do to increase the odds of you becoming his or her agent: Bribery. Nah. Have a good book in the categories I like. Be confident but polite and appreciate that writing comes from a universal source.

How would you describe to someone (or thing) from another planet what it is that you do as an agent: Do they have books on other planets or simply know all through mental telepathy? I will have to add that question to the tape loop I have playing to try to get an answer from deep space.

Do you have any particular opinions or impressions of editors and publishers in general: They are people like you and me except they are power hungry megalomaniacs with the authority to make us weep. Just kidding!!! I find that editors and publishers are typically creative people who love books. It helps if they have good business sense because it is the only way they are able to succeed and build a prosperous publishing house. Many of their decisions are a gamble. They have to have vision.

What do you think the future holds for writers, publishers, and agents: The differences we are facing are in delivery, not product. Technology changes daily, but curiosity and the need for mental stimulation continues. Then, again, who knows about the next generation. As a parent of teenagers, I can only hope they continue to read.

What are your favorite books, movies, TV shows, and why: As for television, my tastes are leaning more toward entertainment with low intensity. I am overwhelmed with all the violence. Sometimes I watch the reality shows on VH1 to keep up with my teen and to be in the same room with her. I prefer shows with spookiness like *Ghost Whisperer* but my guilty pleasure is reruns of shows like *Frazier* and *Will and Grace*.

In your opinion, what do editors think of you: They think I am tenacious and passionate about the books I represent.

Representative titles: See under Jeff Herman. Oh, I take credit for everything.

HIDDEN VALUE GROUP

1240 E. Ontario Ave; STE #102-148, Corona, CA 92881

951-549-8891

www.hiddenvaluegroup.com

Agent's name: Nancy Jernigan

Career history or story: Christianity Today, Inc.: Marketing Manager; Focus on the Family: Director of Marketing; Nest Entertainment: Director of Marketing; Buy.com: Head of Customer Relationship Management.

Hobbies, interests: Rock Climbing, reading.

Subjects & categories you are interested in agenting, including fiction & nonfiction: Family, marriage, parenting, fiction, women's issues, inspirational, self-help, etc.

JULIE A. HILL AND ASSOC., LLC

1155 Camino Del Mar #530, Del Mar, CA 92014

www.publishersmarketplace.com/members/hillagent   e-mail: hillagent@aol.com
(no esubmissions please)

Agents' names: Julie Hill, hillagent@aol.com

Born: Pasadena, California; May 13.

Education: Education: BA, University of Arizona; UC Berkeley Publishing Course. I am also a guest lecturer at San Diego State University in the graduate level Thesis Writing Course.

Career story: Writer then agent...see below.

Hobbies and special personal interests: Gardening, cooking, TRAVEL

Subjects and categories you like to agent: Psychology, memoir, Jewish memoir, especially anything Holocaust related, self help and advice are favorites too and travel, lots of travel. New spins on new age too.

Subjects and categories writers shouldn't bother pitching to you: Fantasy, horror, children's, business.

What might you be doing if you weren't agenting: Gardening, traveling, eating!

What's the most effective ways for writers to grab your attention: Perfect book proposal! Thorough (please, please) market survey and developed platform, including Internet presence.

Do you charge fees separate from your commission, or offer non-agenting fee based services: I offer contract consultation at an hourly fee. Often writers sell something themselves and need help with the contract, thus I am here to help! I enjoy contract negotiation.

What are representative titles you have sold to publishers: A few: *Return to Naples: My Italian Bar Mitzvah and Other Discoveries* by Robert Zweig, Ph.D (Barricade); Frommers and Dummies titles for Walt Disney World and Orlando by Laura Lea Miller (4 different titles, revised yearly; Barnes and Noble Travel Bestseller List); *Café Life: Venice, Cafe Life: San Francisco*, and *Cafe Life: Seattle* by Joe Wolff and Roger Paperno, photographer (Interlink Books)—Their *Café Life: Florence* won a Travel Book of the Year Award for 2006; *A Blessing in Disguise* by Andrea Joy Cohen, M.D. (Berkely/Penguin)—made the *LA Times* (and others) bestseller list.

Why did you become an agent, and how did you become one: I was writing for periodicals (and online horoscopes) and I watched my friends who were also writers struggling to find good representation, and felt I could help writers get what they deserve. I also wanted to be a career developer and manager, which I do for my authors. Most agents only sell books, which is fine, but there is so much more to making a career out of writing and I want to help my authors prosper.

How do you feel about writers: I love them, of course.

What do you tell entities from other planets and dimensions about your job: That they don't want it. Space travel has many more benefits, including long distance travel without airport hassles.

What are your favorite books, movies, TV shows, and why: *Boston Legal.* So smart, so socially responsible.

How would you describe "the writer from hell": Cannot/will not take direction. Calls to chat. May not know the term "platform." Say they are "going to develop a Website."

How would you describe the publisher and/or editor from hell: Suggests one of your writers formulate a proposal for something they have conceived, then turns the proposal down. Oh God, I could go on, but mostly I want to go on the record here as appreciating the good ones, and there are far more good ones that bad. Many are even great.

What do you like best about your clients, and the editors and publishers you work with: Smart, smart, smart. Efficient. Don't need a lot of reminding to get the job done.

You're welcome to share your thoughts and sentiments about the business of writing and publishing: Writers conferences tend to focus on the theme that unknown writers get huge advances, get discovered by Hollywood, and their lives are forever transformed with one book. You may as well bet on Big Brown to win the Triple Crown. Fun to talk about, but unlikely. Someone, somewhere, said "publishing isn't a business, it's a casino." More true than not, but one can improve one's odds by doing the work, doing it well, and doing it because "it calls you."

Do you wish to describe who you are: A pretty nice but short tempered woman.

Will our business exist as we know it in 10 years or so from now: A Great Question…wish I knew…being an astrologer. I forecast more electronic media, but not as much as the electronic people would have you think. I do feel pubs will do more with agents online, in fact, one of my last deals was done totally by email. The book has been released and is very successful, and I've never heard this editor's voice. I know it seems strange, but we are both happy with the efficiency, and happy with having a record of every word that was said and every term every negotiated, and how it went down. Believe me, this can be very useful going forward, both for me, my author and the publisher. Further forecast: Despite hundreds of cable channels to keep us entertained, books will thrive because there is nothing more satisfying than a quiet read provided by a great author…nothing.

HORNFISCHER LITERARY MANAGEMENT, L.P.

P.O. Box 50544, Austin, TX 78763

5050 Laguna Blvd Ste 112-330, Elk Grove, CA 95758

e-mail: jim@hornfischerlit.com

Agent's name: Jim Hornfischer, President.

Born: 1965, Massachusetts.

Education: B.A., Colgate University; J.D., University of Texas at Austin.

Career history: President, Hornfischer Literary Management, Austin, 2001-present; Agent, Literary Group International, New York, 1993-2001; Editorial positions, McGraw-Hill, HarperCollins, New York, 1987-92.

Categories/subjects that you are most enthusiastic about agenting: All types of high-quality narrative nonfiction, including current events, biography, memoir, U.S. and world history, military history, popular science, medicine/health, business, law and culture.

What you don't want to agent: Fiction and poetry, and most self-help/inspirational.

What's the best way for writers to solicit your interest: A smartly tailored personal letter that suggests professionalism and/or accomplishment, together with 30-50 pages of good material that supports your optimism. Please include an overview of the book and its market, author bio (and reviews and other media if available), chapter summaries, and one to three sample chapters.

Do you charge reading or management fees: No reading fees. Commission structure is 15% domestic, 25% foreign. Sold approximately 16 titles last year. The approximate percentage of all submissions (from queries through manuscripts) that I rejected?: The same parade-drenching number as the rest of them.

What are the most common mistakes writers make when pitching you: Failing to identify the unique space in the universe (or at least in the bookstore) that their proposed book will occupy. Everything follows from that simple act.

How would you describe the perfect client: Thinks big, drinks from glasses that are half full, writes even grocery lists with narrative momentum, keeps an open ear for useful advice and runs with it in brilliant and surprising ways.

How and why did you ever become an agent: Getting a good book published, especially one that might not otherwise have been, can be rewarding in a life-affirming sort of way.

What, if anything, can a writer do to increase the odds that you will become his or her agent: Grasp the rudiments of the business (even if as an artist you'd prefer not to bother), temper your ambition with patience and a long view, and refine and improve your craft continuously. It's all in the writing.

How would you describe to someone (or thing) from another planet what it is that you do as an agent: My wife always tells me that I shatter dreams for a living, because I send back so many rejections. I prefer to think that, for those writers for whom I do useful work, I help make them. I do a little writing, too: www.jameshornfischer.com.

Do you have any particular opinions or impressions of editors and publishers in general: Editors: The good ones are the heart and soul of their companies, and management should listen to them more closely. Publishers: I am in awe of the process by which a talented group of people can rally collectively to insert a new voice into the national conversation. It happens all too rarely, but when it does you look back and marvel at the peculiar alchemy of it all.

Please list representative titles you have sold: *Flags of Our Fathers* by James Bradley with Ron Powers (Bantam); *Traitor to His Class: The Privileged Life and Radical Presidency of Franklin Delano Roosevelt* by H. W. Brands (Doubleday); *The Scent of the Missing: A Handler's Journey Beside a Search-and-Rescue Dog* by Susannah Charleson (Houghton Mifflin); *The Next 100 Years: A Forecast for the 21st Century* by George Friedman (Doubleday); *Ghost: Confessions of a Counterterrorism Agent* by Fred Burton (Random House); *American Pests: The Losing War on Insects, from Colonial Times to DDT* by James E. McWilliams (Columbia); *Rose Bowl Dreams: A Memoir of Faith, Family and Football* by Adam Jones (Thomas Dunne Books); *How to Break a Terrorist: The U.S. Interrogators Who Used Brains, Not Brutality, to Take Down the Deadliest Man in Iraq* by Matthew Alexander with John Bruning (Free Press); *Mark Twain: A Life* by Ron Powers (Free Press); *Obama: From Promise to Power* by David Mendell (Harper/Amistad); *House to House: A Soldier's Memoir* by David Bellavia with John Bruning (Free Press).

ANDREA HURST LITERARY MANAGEMENT

P.O. Box 19010, Sacramento, CA 95819

5050 Laguna Blvd Ste 112-330, Elk Grove, CA 95758

www.andreahurst.com   e-mail: andrea@andreahurst.com, judy@andreahurst.com

Agents' names: Andrea Hurst, Judy Mikalonis.
The following information pertains to Andrea Hurst.
Born: Los Angeles, California.
Education: Bachelor's degree in Expressive Arts.
Career history or story: President of Andrea Hurst Literary Management, works with both major and regional publishing houses, and her client list includes emerging new voices and *NY Times* best selling authors such as Dr. Bernie Siegel. With over 20 years in the publishing industry, Andrea is a published author, (*Lazy Dog's Guide to Enlightenment*) skilled acquisition and development editor, speaker, and literary judge. Her areas of expertise include sales, promotion, and production in the publishing and entertainment fields. She is an instructor for the Whidbey Island MA program in Creative Writing.

Hobbies, interests: Animal welfare, reading fine novels, writing fiction, Gourmet Natural Food.

Subjects & categories you are interested in agenting, including fiction & non-fiction: Prescriptive and narrative nonfiction: Parenting, relationships, women's issues, personal growth, health & wellness, science, business, true crime, animals, pop culture, humor, cookbooks, gift books, spirituality, metaphysical, psychology, and self-help. Fiction: Adult commercial fiction, women's fiction.

Subjects & categories writers shouldn't even bother pitching to you: Science fiction/fantasy, western, horror.

What would you do if you weren't agenting: I would be a best-selling fiction author living on Whidbey Island, although I would still probably keep some of my best clients.

What's the best way for fiction writers to solicit your interest: Take the time to learn the craft of writing and have your work professionally edited before sending it out. Be sure your query letter is compelling and shows off your writing style.

What's the best way for non-fiction writers to solicit your interest: Write a knock-out book proposal with a long and detailed marketing section. Send a query letter first by e-mail.

Do you charge reading or any upfront fees: No.

In your experience, what are the most common pitching mistakes writers make: Not researching to find the appropriate agency match for their work. It is very easy to locate an agent's website and figure out what they are looking for, how they want it submitted, and what their name is! Not following directions and not having a strong query letter.

Describe the client from Hell, even if you don't have any: A writer who is not familiar with the publishing business and has unrealistic expectations can turn quickly into a client from Hell. Particularly someone who is not willing to edit their work, can't make deadlines, and has an attitude that everyone else should accommodate.

What's your definition of a great client: Luckily, I have many of those. A great client follows directions willingly, meets and exceeds deadlines and expectations, and has a can-do attitude. We have a mutual trust and they let me do my job.

How can writers increase the odds that you will offer representation: Write exceptionally well, have a unique, well-researched idea that is pitched through a complete book proposal for nonfiction, or a synopsis and sample chapters for fiction. Have a strong platform that you are building on a daily basis and be committed to a long-term writing career. Be willing to work hard to promote your writing and continue to improve your craft through classes, critique groups, conferences, etc.

Why did you become an agent, and how did you become one: The publishing business has been in my blood from a very early age. As a writer myself, I understand the business from both sides. My first book published was *Everybody's Natural Food's Cookbook* through New World Library. Marc Allen, the publisher, taught me the business from the ground up. After that, I was hooked. I worked as a freelance editor, ghostwriter, and instructor for many years, including a position as an acquisition and development editor for a children's publisher in Seattle. My extensive list of editorial contacts, coupled with my strong marketing background acquired through working at Columbia Records, led me on a natural course to becoming an agent.

Describe to someone from another planet what you do as an agent: Just about everything from editing to selling, and networking to acting as a coach and mentor. The job is never done.

How do you feel about editors and publishers: They are the gatekeepers that provide the opportunity for wonderful books to reach the world.

How do you feel about writers: I am always looking for the exceptional ones that have a great story to tell or wonderful information to share. Every query I receive is another opportunity to discover a great writer.

In your opinion, what do editors think of you: That I am professional, accessible, genuine, and represent talented and reliable clients.

What are some representative titles that you have sold: *Love, Magic & Mudpies* by Dr. Bernie Siegel (Rodale); *Dare to Wear Your Soul on the Outside* by Dr. Gloria Burgess (Jossey-Bass/Wiley); *A Course in Happiness* by Dr. Mardi Horowitz (Tarcher/Penguin); *True Self, True Wealth* by Peter Cole (Daisy Reese); *Beyond Words* (Atria); *Best Recipes From Italy's Food Festivals* by James Fraioli/Leonardo Curti Gibbs (Smith Publishers).

The following information pertains to Judy Mikalonis.

Subjects & categories you are interested in agenting, including fiction & non-fiction: Christian nonfiction, Christian fiction, adult nonfiction, YA fiction.

Subjects & categories writers shouldn't even bother pitching to you: No science fiction, no historical fiction, no supernatural thrillers.

What's the best way for fiction writers to solicit your interest: Write amazingly well and tell a transformative story.

What's the best way for non-fiction writers to solicit your interest: Write a damn good proposal and have an amazing platform.

Do you charge reading or any upfront fees: No.

In your experience, what are the most common pitching mistakes writers make: Not being prepared to sell their story. No immediate relevance to the reader apparent in their pitch. Can't tell me what their protagonist wants (fiction).

How can writers increase the odds that you will offer representation: Write really well. Write a good proposal. Follow directions and e-mail queries only. Do not mail a query.

KELLER MEDIA, INC.

23852 West Pacific Coast Highway, Suite 701, Malibu, CA 90265

310-457-3490

e-mail: Query@KellerMedia.com

Agent's name: Wendy Keller

Born: Chicago, Illinois, 20th Century.

Education: Arizona State University, B.A., Journalism with minors in History and French.

Career history: 1980-1985 Print Journalist; 1988–1989 Agency Aide; 1989–present Literary Agent/Agency Owner.

Hobbies/personal interests: Fighting snails in my garden, managing my teenager's hectic social schedule, part-time taxi service for aforementioned teenager, reading very large stacks of books for fun and profit.

Categories/subjects that you are most enthusiastic about agenting: Any nonfiction book intended for adults, including: Business (sales, management, marketing and finance); spirituality/inspiration (esp. Divine Feminine/Goddess related); women's issues (any from health to family to relationships to other); self-help (parenting, relationships, mental wellness, health, education, etc.); science/physics (esp. quantum physics); history (any—World, American, esp. European); biography (celebrity or known names only); sports; popular psychology; current affairs; Chick Lit; how-to (do anything); cookbooks (only by authors with their own show on TV or radio, well-known restaurant or big web presence); consumer reference; gift books (illustrated or not).

What you don't want to agent: NO to juvenile, fiction, Christian, scripts, erotica, poetry or true crime. No illustrated books. NO to first person accounts of overcoming some medical, mental or addiction trauma. NO to first person accounts of sexual abuse or crime. NO books written from inside penitentiaries. NO books channeled by dead spirits or dead celebrities, e.g., Mother Theresa (she seems to be popular), Princess Di, Curt Cobain, John Lennon, Einstein, etc. (PS—all these names are from queries received in the last six months or so!) NO books written by your dog or cat, goldfish, hamster, etc. That's probably pretty clear. You get the idea, right?

If you were not an agent, what might you be doing instead: Oh, I don't know. I think I'd be running a small, extremely organized, profitable, tidy country somewhere. Or practicing improving my French, Italian or Spanish language skills. Or finally taking that trip to Morocco…

What's the best way for writers to solicit your interest: It's even easier than that! There's only ONE way to really get my interest: SEND AN E-MAIL. I prefer it so much to paper queries! Query@KellerMedia.com I promise whoever reads it will really look at it before they decide what to do with it.

Do you charge reading or management fees: Absolutely not! Agents who do should be immediately burned at the stake! Same with agents who ask for exclusive time periods to consider your work. Heck, if it's good, we will be fighting one another for it. Of course, in a genteel way. Send it to all who ask for it, and then if someone actually offers representation, call the slow ones and give them X days to respond. May the best woman win!

Can you provide an approximation by % of what you tend to represent by category: Non-Fiction book rights, English language: 60%, Speaking fees for clients: 20%, Foreign rights/audio/ancillary: 20%.

What are the most common mistakes writers make when pitching you: They send me stuff that is absolutely NOT what I handle. (See "What you don't want to agent" above) OR they have little to no qualifications for their topic. E.g., male authors who want to write a guide to menopause and aren't even doctors, how to be a millionaire books by paupers, business books by people who know little more than middle management, science books that have so been done a thousand times before.

How would you describe the client from Hell: Clients from Hell are those who are so convinced they will be on Oprah, make the best seller list, get a major six figure advance but their book is on something like "start your own home-based fertilizer business" or "The Ten Best Potato Salad Recipes in America Today." Geez! Get real! And, of course, unilaterally I get annoyed with people who won't accept editing well, or who lie about their qualifications.

How would you describe the perfect client: Read my sold list! I have so many wonderful clients. Of course, the perfect ones I do not yet represent are people who have their own TV or radio show (or infomercial) broadcasting nationwide, and/or a national speaking platform in the USA, or who work for a company that is or they themselves are a household name. Pulitzer and Nobel prize winners always welcome!

How and why did you ever become an agent: I was training to be an Olympic typist and I crushed my fingers trying to get spare change out of a public payphone.

What, if anything, can a writer do to increase the odds of you becoming his or her agent: Have a massive, impressive, powerful media or speaking platform already in place, or the finances, drive, team and/or contacts to erect it. Everything else can be arranged.

How would you describe to someone (or thing) from another planet what it is that you do as an agent: I make hundreds of phone calls; I fly to New York; I smile at a lot of people, even incoherent cab drivers; I make more phone calls; I cash very, very large checks, skim them for 15% (sometimes 20%); and I make smart people really, really happy (and sometimes famous).

Do you have any particular opinions or impressions of editors and publishers in general: I worship at the feet of publishers and editors. I am grateful for their wisdom and ability to write very large checks. I honor their ability to motivate their curmudgeonly publicity departments to work hard for my clients' best interests. In summary, they are the blessed souls about to pay for my kid's college education.

What do you think the future holds for writers, publishers, and agents: A lot, lot, lot of books. In many forms and formats, now known or which may be developed at some time in the future.

Do you have any favorite (current) TV shows, films, or books that you especially like and how come: "How come"? Jeff Herman, are you from Texas now?

On a personal level, what do you think people like about you and dislike about you: Authors like two things about me: One, I absolutely get the job done, always. I'm extremely focused, efficient, organized and productive. Two, my mother was a pit bull, my father a Harvard English professor, so I'm a great person to have on your side, unless I skip my distemper shot.

Please list representative titles you have sold: *Our Own Worst Enemy* (Warner Books); *Inner Wisdom* (Simon and Schuster); *Questions from Earth, Answers from Heaven* (St. Martin's Press); *Who's Afraid to be a Millionaire?* (Wiley); *The Ultimate Smoothie Book* (Warner Books); *Raising a Secure Child* (Viking/Penguin); *101 Ways to Promote Yourself* (HarperCollins); *Hiring Smart* (Crown Books); *The Encouraging Parent* (Random House); *Bringing Home The Business* (Penguin/Perigee); *The Power Path* (New World Library); *Secrets of Successful Negotiation For Women* (Career Press); *Ethics and Etiquette* (Entrepreneur Press); *Heart at Work* (McGraw Hill); *Seven Secrets to Raising a Secure Child* (Penguin); *Never Make Another Cold Call* (Kaplan/Dearborn); *I Closed My Eyes* (Hazelden); *The Acorn Principle* (St. Martin's Press); *Be the Person YOU Want to Be Using NLP* (Random House); *The Jesus Path* (Red Wheel/Weiser).

NATASHA KERN LITERARY AGENCY

P.O. Box 1069, White Salmon, WA 98672

www.natashakern.com   e-mail you queries to: queries@natashakern.com

Education: University of North Carolina, Chapel Hill; Columbia University, New York; New York University

Career history: Publicist and editor for New York publishers and acquisitions editor for New York agents prior to founding her own agency in 1986. Natasha Kern has personally sold over 700 books and has worked on close to 1,000 during her career in publishing.

Hobbies/personal interests: Gardening, travel, animals and birds, yoga, performing arts, history, geology and, of course, family and reading.

Categories/subject that you are most enthusiastic about agenting: Fiction: I am actively looking for big historical novels; inspirational fiction; romantic suspense; romantic comedies; mainstream women's fiction; young adult fiction. Nonfiction: narrative nonfiction, health, science, women's issues, parenting, spirituality, self-help, social issues—especially topics that inspire positive thought, action or change, and books by authorities in their field.

What you don't want to agent: Fiction: horror and fantasy, short stories, children's. Nonfiction: true crime, sports, cookbooks, poetry, gift books, coffee table books, computers, technical, scholarly or reference, stage plays, scripts or screenplays

If you were not an agent, what might you be doing instead: I have been an agent for 20 years because I love doing it. This is a calling for me and I can't imagine doing anything else. I love my clients. I love books. I like assisting writers to earn a living at what they do best.

What's the best way for writers to solicit your interest: Send a query letter with a chapter of your novel and a 2-4 page synopsis. Include the genre, submission history (publishers/agents), estimated word count, a brief bio with your writing credits, information about how complete the project is, name of previous agent (if any). Everything is read and we respond within a few weeks. Do NOT send an SASE. We will contact you within two weeks of receipt of your query if we are interested. We will not contact you if we are not interested. If we like your submission, we will call you or e-mail so include your phone number and e-mail address! For nonfiction include a description of your subject and why your book is newer, better or different than others on the subject; your credentials for writing your book; the targeted audience and your plans for publicizing your book; and whether a proposal is available. Do NOT send sample chapters or a proposal unless requested. We do not accept queries by phone, e-mail, or online

Do you charge reading fees or management fees: We do not charge to read queries or any kind of reading fee. However, if a query does fit the genres we represent, and the writer would like more explicit information about the reasons the query has not been accepted, we offer a consulting service for writers similar to the personal attention you would receive in a meeting with an agent at a writers' conference. This service is described in detail on our Web site at www.natashakern.com. For a fee of $75.00, you can resend the query material with an SASE, and we will provide a one-page, written assessment of your submission so you can understand why you are receiving rejections and hopefully improve your chances of submitting successfully to an agent. The idea here is if you are never told what you are doing wrong, it is hard to learn and improve. Several writers have told us that they followed our guidance and obtained representation.

Percentage (%) of representation by category: Fiction: 60%, Non-Fiction: 40%.

Approximate number of titles sold during the past year: June 2006–May 2006: 72 titles.

Approximately what percentage of all the submissions you receive do you reject: 99% of unsolicited; 85% solicited partials, proposals and manuscripts; and 30% of referrals. From 6,000 queries every year, approximately 10 writers are accepted for representation. Write a good query! We are selective but we do want to find successful writers of the future and have launched the careers of many successful writers.

What are some of the most common mistakes writers make when pitching to you: Not researching what we represent! Not describing the material or project adequately. Not knowing the standards and conventions of the genres we represent. Querying by fax, phone, or e-mail. Sending unrequested material. Exaggerated claims or credentials. Comparing themselves favorably to current best-selling authors. Lack of professionalism. Not knowing the craft of writing. Not having an original concept. Omitting the ending from a synopsis. Not following directions. The majority of queries are rejected because the writer has simply not taken the time to learn, study and practice to produce something salable, basically the equivalent of taking a week of music lessons and hoping to play Carnegie Hall.

How would you describe your client from Hell: I do not have any clients like this. All of my clients are people I respect and admire as individuals as well as writers. They are committed to their own success and know that I am committed to helping them to achieve it. They understand the complex tasks involved in agenting, including sales, negotiations, editorial, arbitration, foreign and film rights, etc. and we work as a team to ensure the best outcome for their work. Usually problem clients who are difficult to work with are identified before a contract is signed.

How would you describe the perfect client: One who participates in a mutually respectful business relationship, is clear about needs and goals and communicates about career planning. If we know what you need and want, we can help you to achieve it. A dream client has a gift for language and storytelling, a commitment to a writing career, a desire to learn and grow, and a passion for excellence. This client understands that many people have to work together for a book to succeed and that everything in publishing takes far longer than one imagines. Trust and communication are truly essential. How wonderful that all of my clients are dream clients.

How and why did you become an agent: When I left New York, I knew that I wanted to stay in publishing. However, editorial work was not sufficiently satisfying by itself. I knew I could acquire and develop salable properties and that my background gave me expertise in sales and running a company. I wanted to work with people long term and not just on a single project or phase of one. Plus, I had an entrepreneurial temperament and experience negotiating big money deals from raising venture capital for high tech firms. When I developed literary projects for other agents that did not sell, I knew I could sell them myself, so I did. I've never regretted that decision. Agenting combined my love of books, my affinity for deal-making, and my preference for trusting my own intuition. I sold 28 books the first year the agency was in business.

What can writers do to increase the odds that they will get you to be their agent: A client who is willing to listen, learn, and work hard to succeed. If there are writing problems I will get this author help to produce a salable proposal. I have worked with some writers six months or more before their novel or proposal was in top notch shape to sell it. I am looking for talent and commitment and if I feel it is a good match, I make a commitment to that writer in return. In nonfiction, the author's passionate belief in the subject as well as expertise and a defined audience are appealing. In fiction, a wonderful, fresh authorial voice, a page-turning plot that really does keep me up at night after a long day, well-structured chapters and imaginative prose. A writer who can pull me into another point of view and another world I don't want to leave. In fiction, the writing is everything. We are glad to encourage promising writers who still need to master some aspects of craft if they are willing to work with me or an editor.

How would you actually describe to someone from another planet what you do for a living: Unpublished writers often think an agent's job is only sales and negotiations. Of course, every writer wants a sale and to see the book in print. However, an agent's job goes far beyond just deal-making because building a career and helping a writer to earn a living from writing requires a long-term strategy and often a complex chess game of moving from one house or genre to another. I am often involved in a book's development from the initial concept through preparation of a proposal, editorial advice, selection of appropriate editors, submissions, negotiations and contract changes to final signature. Then troubleshooting publication problems begins from editorial issues to cover problems, title changes, reviewing jacket blurbs and the myriad of things that arise in the course of publication; troubleshooting marketing problems including reviewing publicity planning, press kits and releases, working on cross-promotions and product placement, distribution concerns, suggestions about creating a website and working with private publicists. Since I represent writers who, for the most part, want a writing career and not just a one-book deal after the first book has been turned in work begins on a follow-up, fulfilling option clauses (and making sure they do not restrict an authors ability to write whatever she wishes), long-term career planning and strategies and often multi-book deals. Of course, handling an author's financial affairs is paramount, including auditing royalty statements, collecting unpaid monies, providing tax documents like 1099s and foreign tax forms, etc. In addition, I handle legal issues of many kinds from reversion of rights to their allocation; subsidiary sales including foreign rights, film rights, audio, video and other rights; handling career crises or conflicts with publishers; assisting writers with career transitions or when problems arise like their book being "orphaned"; providing expertise at writers conferences; educating clients about the publishing industry and its vicissitudes; keeping in touch with editors and their acquisitions interest or concerns about clients; attending industry events like Book Expo; Consulting with writing groups—I am currently on the Board of the Faith, Hope and Love Chapter of RWA; meeting personally with clients, editors and others in the industry; traveling to New York and Hollywood several times each year; answering hundreds of e-mails each week; reviewing queries and partials; talking on the phone a lot; reading the work of clients and prospective clients and keeping up with trends; working with office staff and upgrading corporate procedures and technical support; supervising bookkeeper and accountant; articles and interviews for trade publications, etc. It's a long day.

What do you think about editors and publishers: Editors are indispensable and every writer should be blessed with a good one. It is one of my primary goals to match each client with the editor who is perfect for him or her. I often succeed and the result is magical like all great collaborations: Fred Astaire and Ginger Rogers; Maxwell Perkins and Thomas Wolfe; Gilbert & Sullivan. Writers are more successful in great partnerships. No one can be objective about their own work or realistically expect to recognize all flaws. Most artistic endeavors require a coach--a voice coach, a dance teacher, a master painter. Writing is no exception. There are gifted editors, both private editors and those at publishing houses, who can turn a strong manuscript into a great one, a gifted author into a best-selling one. I want all my clients to have that opportunity. Publishers are going to have some interesting times ahead in the volatile new world of publishing, with challenges at every turn. Developing new talent and valuing the writers who are creating their long-term success would seem to be prerequisites for meeting these challenges. We keep up wit changes in the industry like ebooks and POD and also work with new emerging presses and imprints as well as major publishers. We can help authors to understand the publisher's point of view (and vice versa) in all situations so a win-win deal will result.

On a personal level, what do you think people like about you and dislike about you: I think I am liked for my authenticity and honesty even when I have to tell a writer her material needs more work or a concept isn't salable. It is entirely possible I may be disliked for my bluntness as well. However, I feel it is a disservice to writers to fail to be clear with them. My passion for the books I represent and the fact that I deeply care about my clients and their success is an asset as well as my industry knowledge and professionalism. My clients appreciate it that I go the extra mile for them to ensure their success. I hate to give up on anything I undertake so I usually do succeed in achieving my goals and can help my clients to do the same. Even though I have strong opinions, I am also interested in learning new things from the experts—one of the joys of my job.

You're welcome to share your thoughts and sentiments about the business of writing and publishing: Believe in yourself and your own gifts. Keep in mind that the challenge for every writer is twofold—to have something to say and to have the mastery of the craft to say it well. Study and practice plotting, pacing, point of view, etc. so you can express exactly what you want to say. Nothing is more important than being true to your own artistic vision and understanding the requirements of the medium you have chosen to express it, whether you are writing a symphony a haiku or a novel. Keep in mind that in imitating other writers you can only be second rate at being them. Expressing your own inner thoughts, feelings, and stories in your own way is the only path to real success. Your world, your history, your experiences, your insights cannot be duplicated by anyone else. Bring us in to share your vision, your imagination. No one can do it better than you can because the truth of your uniqueness is what you are here to offer everyone else. It is what moves us and takes us outside of our own lives when we read what you have written.

Please list representative titles you have sold: *The Winds of Sonoma* by Nikka Arana (Baker); *The Secret Life of God* by David Aaron (Shambhala); *Wicked Fantasy* by Nina Bangs (Berkley); *Bastard Tongues* by Derek Bickerton (Farrar, Straus); *Up Pops the Devil* by Angela Benson (Harper Collins); *Mai Tai to Murder* by Candy Calvert (Midnight Ink); *Unlawful Contact* by Pamela Clare (Berkley); *Hope is the Thing with Feathers* by Christopher Cokinos (Warner); *Cutting Loose* by Nadine Dajani (Forge); *Precious Cargo* by Clyde Ford (Vanguard); *Betrayed* by Jamie Leigh Hansen (TOR); *Sexiest Man Alive* by Diana Holquist (Warner); *The Quiet Game* by Greg Iles (Putnam-Penguin); *Elvis Takes a Backseat* by Leanna Ellis (B & H); *The Perfect Life* by Robin Hatcher (Thomas Nelson); *The Ecological Garden* by Toby Hemenway (Chelsea Green); *Perfect* by Harry Kraus (Zondervan); *Scent of Sake* by Joyce Lebra (Morrow); *A Passion Most Pure* by Julie Lessman (Revell); *A Texan's Honor* by Harold Lowry (Leisure); *Love Like Hallelujah* by Lutishia Lovely (Dafina); *Highland Warrior* by Connie Mason (Leisure); *A Reason To Believe* by Maureen McKade (Berkley); *Skull Mantra* by Eliot Pattison (St. Martin's); *Bone Rattler* by Eliot Pattison (Counterpoint); *Just One Bite* by Kimberly Raye (Ballantine); *Seaside Cinderella* by Anna Schmidt (Steeple Hill); *Painless Childbirth* by Giuditta Tornetta (Cumberland House); *The Secret Lives of the Sushi Club* by Christy Yorke (Berkley).

THE KNIGHT AGENCY

www.KnightAgency.net   e-mail: submissions@knightagency.net

Agents' names: Deidre Knight, Pamela Harty, Lucienne Diver, Elaine Spencer, Nephele Tempest

The following information pertains to Deidre Knight.

Born: July 12.

Hobbies and special personal interests: My first true passion is the written word: Beyond reading I have also always been an avid writer, penning my first story when I was 7 years old for the *Atlanta Journal-Constitution*. This humble beginning was the start of many great writing adventures, leading me to a love of fan-fiction and consequently, my ultimate dream come true, my own publishing contract with Penguin Putnam. I am also passionate about spending time with my family, photography, kayaking, international travel, science-fiction television, the spa and great music.

Subjects and categories you like to agent: I am probably most known for my clients within the romance and women's fiction genre (all spectrums) but my tastes are much more broad. I also have a love for great literary fiction, young adult material, all things paranormal, anything with a southern-flair and great special interest non-fiction titles.

Subjects and categories writers shouldn't bother pitching to you: Our agency is very diverse and between our five agents, if you have a great story there is a chance we can find the right agent for your novel. However, despite this diversity we aren't interested in children's or picture books, poetry, screenplays, short story collections, biographies, military titles, or anything with gratuitous violence.

What might you be doing if you weren't agenting: I am an entrepreneur at heart so if I hadn't started the Knight Agency I'm not sure specifically what I would be doing, but I have little doubt I would be running some other business. I'm a natural visionary and a free spirit, so really the possibilities are endless.

What's the most effective ways for writers to grab your attention: I am easily swayed by enthusiasm and passion. I myself am a very "excitable" person and so if I can feel your energy in your story I'm instantly hooked.

Do you charge fees separate from your commission, or offer non-agenting fee based services: The Knight Agency doesn't charge any fees for anything related to the publishing process beyond the 15% commission we take off of a completed sale.

What do you like best about your clients, and the editors and publishers you work with: I think that this industry is one of the greatest businesses out there, hence the reason I have tied myself into it in so many different capacities. It's exciting, dynamic, and it keeps us each on our toes since every day is a new journey. I can think of few other professions where you are blessed enough to meet as many fascinating individuals and cross paths with so many brilliant minds. I'm proud to not only be a associated with the publishing business but a strong contributing force, we are lucky at the end of the day to look at the shelf, see a book and say "I did that."

The following information pertains to Pamela Harty.

Born: July; Atlanta, Georgia.

Career story: I started at The Knight Agency after the birth of my second child. I was eager to work with my sister Deidre Knight after leaving a successful sales career. That was almost 9 years ago!

Hobbies and special personal interests: I am a runner and cyclist. I love to paint and of course…read.

Subjects and categories you like to agent: I am interested in romance, of course, including historical, suspense and paranormal, as well as young adult and women's commercial fiction. I'm also interested in some nonfiction, including health, narrative nonfiction, relationships and pop culture.

What might you be doing if you weren't agenting: Painting and cycling in France.

The following information pertains to Lucienne Diver.

Born: April 27, 1971; Baltimore, Maryland.

Education: Graduated summa cum laude from The State University of New York at Potsdam.

Career story: I spent 15 years at Spectrum Literary Agency before moving in 2008 to The Knight Agency.

Hobbies and special personal interests: Writing, forensics, theatre, beading, scrapbooking, yoga, photography.

Subjects and categories you like to agent: Fantasy, romance, romantica, thrillers, mystery/suspense, young adult.

Subjects and categories writers shouldn't bother pitching to you: Nonfiction, children's books.

What might you be doing if you weren't agenting: I can't imagine doing anything else.

What's the most effective ways for writers to grab your attention: Be brilliant. Come up with wonderful ideas in an original voice and keep the pace pounding.

What are representative titles you have sold to publishers: *The Iron Hunt* by Marjorie M. Liu (Ace/Berkley); *Strange Brew* (anthology) edited by P.N. Elrod (St. Martins); *Come the Night* by Susan Krinard (HQN).

What are your favorite books, movies, TV shows, and why: I love anything by Joss Whedon. He's got a talent for perfectly melding dark and light, a well developed sense of the absurd, an amazing flare for dialogue and wonderful characters. That's what I look for in the books I represent as well.

Will our business exist as we know it in 10 years or so from now: Absolutely! Books—good stories that challenge our minds and imaginations—are eternal.

The following informaiton pertains to Elaine Spencer.

Born: January 7; Toledo, Ohio.

Hobbies and special personal interests: When I'm not reading I love spending time outdoors and in the water, working out, cooking, shopping, traveling, dining out and cheering on my beloved Georgia Bulldogs.

Subjects and categories you like to agent: My tastes really run the gamut; I love most anything that has a strong distinctive voice and vivid heartfelt emotional stakes. I am looking for diverse women's fiction and romance, original young adult and middle grade stories, edge of the seat suspense, interesting and high-platform non-fiction and straight commercial and literary fiction.

Subjects and categories writers shouldn't bother pitching to you: I am wide open to most genres but obviously don't handle those that aren't represented by the agency as a whole. I'm also not the sci-fi gal at the agency, nor am I typically into any boundary-pushing erotica.

What might you be doing if you weren't agenting: I would be a personal shopper. I love to shop, whether it's for me or for someone else—tell me what you need and I'm your gal.

What's the most effective ways for writers to grab your attention: One of the sure-fire ways to impress me is to wow me with your knowledge of the market and your craft right off the bat. I am always inclined to continue reading when I can tell the author is treating their writing life as a career and are proceeding as a professional.

What do you like best about your clients, and the editors and publishers you work with: I have a very personal and unique relationship with each of my clients. I love that I can relate to each of them on a professional yet individual level. I truly believe that one of the bedrocks of a strong relationship is communication, and I adore the one-on-one tie I have to each of my authors.

The following information pertains to **Nephele Tempest.**

Education: The University of Chicago, B.A. in English Language and Literature.

Hobbies and special personal interests: Reading (naturally), film, theater, music, traveling, photography and cooking.

Subjects and categories you like to agent: Fiction only; commercial literary, women's fiction, urban fantasy, romantic suspense, historical fiction, science-fiction/fantasy and young adult.

Subjects and categories writers shouldn't bother pitching to you: No mysteries, inspirational or nonfiction, please.

What's the most effective ways for writers to grab your attention: Please follow our submissions guidelines. Nothing turns me off faster than someone trying to be "clever and original" by ignoring our requests regarding how to submit materials. Beyond that, polish your book to the very best of your abilities, and then give it one more edit before submitting. The extra effort will definitely show.

What are representative titles you have sold to publishers: *No Regrets* by Shannon K. Butcher (Grand Central Publishing); *Slave to Sensation* by Nalini Singh (Berkley); *Angels' Blood* by Nalini Singh (Berkley); *Mayhem in High Heels* by Gemma Halliday (Dorchester); *According to Jane: A Novel About Pride, Prejudice and the Pursuit of the Perfect Guy* by Marilyn Brant (Kensington); *Burning Alive* by Shannon K. Butcher (NAL); *Major Crush* by Jennifer Echols (Simon Pulse).

What do you like best about your clients, and the editors and publishers you work with: I love that I work with a wide range of very different and interesting people, all of whom share my love of books. It makes for a wonderful workday, knowing that at any moment someone might call me with a great new book idea or a recommendation for something fabulous they think I should read. It's a business of kindred spirits.

KRAAS LITERARY AGENCY

281-870-9770

e-mail: irenekraas@sbcglobal.net

Agent's name: Irene W. Kraas, Principal

Born: Are you kidding??? New York, New York.

Education: M.Ed. University of Rochester.

Career history: Too long to enumerate: A sample: Beltway Bandit (DC consultant); Career Counselor; Agent.

Hobbies/personal interests: Reading, walking, eating and enjoying life.

Subjects & categories you are interested in agenting, including fiction & non-fiction: I am looking for psychological thrillers. NO mysteries, please. Think James Patterson, less Patricia Cornwell. In terms of young adult/juvenile fiction, I am only acquiring those works that show a unique situation (preferably in history) through the eyes of a child/or young adult. I am also, especially looking for innovative middle grade material. I am stilling looking for quality adult historical fiction such as *The Courtier's Secret*, *The Red Tent* and *The Girl with the Pearl Earring*.

What you don't want to agent: Please see above.

If you were not an agent, what might you be doing instead: I've done what I've wanted all along and this is the ultimate. However, if I had to choose, I would be a rich publisher and publish all those great books that I've had rejected.

What's the best way for fiction writers to solicit your interest: Please send an e-mail query to me at irenekraas@sbcglobal.net. After that initial correspondence, I will let you know if we wish to see additional material.

What's the best way for non-fiction writers to solicit your interest: Same as above.

Do you charge reading or any upfront fees: Under no circumstances do we require an upfront reading fee! We never charge a reading fee. With pdf documents there are no other fees except those described in my contract that pertain to normal commissions.

What are the most common mistakes writers make when pitching you: Not following my submission guidelines.

How would you describe the client from Hell: I'll take the fifth, thanks.

How would you describe the perfect client: Great writers who trust me to do the very best for them.

How and why did you ever become an agent: I went from 20 years in business consulting to being the great American writer to agenting. I love using my business acumen in helping first-time authors get a break and helping established authors break out.

What, if anything, can a writer do to increase the odds of you becoming his or her agent: Be extremely talented—it's a tight market, so understand that it's very competitive and make sure that you're manuscript is ready to go when you submit it to me.

Also, make sure that what you send me is a genre that I'm actually interested in representing.

How would you describe to someone (or thing) from another planet what it is that you do as an agent: I read, read, read. Then I sell, sell, sell.

How do you feel about editors and publishers: Mostly editors are top-notch people interested in good writing. Regarding publishers, well, let's just say that they don't always see the big picture as clearly as we'd like and they don't necessarily have the author's best interests in mind. But, that's why there are agents!

How do you feel about writers: Would I be in this business if I didn't like them? Of course one has to sort between those who have talent and those that don't.

What do see in the near future for book publishing: I think it will remain pretty much as is. People who read still want to hold a book. Of course there will be a few changes regarding electronic editions and print on demand.

What are your favorite books, movies, TV shows, and why: *24*, *The Sopranos*, you get the idea. I now have to add *Deadwood*. I absolutely love it. I love great ensemble work and high quality acting and innovative story lines. I don't like comedy.

In your opinion, what do editors think of you: I'm pretty sure they think well of me. After all you don't stay in this business for 18 years as a very small agency (just me these days), if you don't try to match editors with submissions. When I send something out, they are always ready to read.

On a personal non-professional level, what do you think people think of you: Wow that's a toughie. I assume some like me and some don't. Is there more to be said?

Please list representative titles you have sold: Authors include Hilari Bell, Janet Lee Carey, Mark Terry, Chelsea Quinn Yarbro and Richard Uhlig. We have sold far too many books to list here, but please feel free to look at our Web site (www.kraasliteraryagency.com) or e-mail me.

KT PUBLIC RELATIONS & LITERARY SERVICES

1905 Cricklewood Cove, Fogelsville, PA 18051

610-395-6298

www.ktpublicrelations.com

Visit our new Blog: www.newliteraryagents.blogspot.com

Agents' names: Kae Tienstra, kae@ktpublicrelations.com, Jon Tienstra, jon@ktpublicrelations.com

The following information pertains to Kae Tienstra.
Born: Denver, Colorado on June 3.
Education: B.A. in Speech/Drama, minor in English.
Career story: I stayed at home for 13 years to raise our three children, letting my

husband Jon do the hunting and gathering in the corporate world. To save my sanity and bring in a bit of my own money I began a freelance writing career. I wrote articles for publications like The Mother Earth News, Organic Gardening, and our local newspaper and magazines. I also "ghost-wrote" a local history and photography book and penned a one-act play. When Jon quit his job to go back to school I was hired by Rodale, Inc. as publicity assistant. I moved up quickly to director of publicity for the book division and stayed at Rodale in that capacity for 13 years. I left Rodale to launch my own publicity firm, KT Public Relations, in 1993. (Jon joined the firm a few years after that.) Over the years we've represented large publishers such as Random House, Putnam, Harper Collins, and John Wiley and Sons, as well as smaller publishers and authors. We launched our literary agency in 2006 and changed the name of our company to reflect our two businesses—KT Public Relations and Literary Services.

Hobbies and special personal interests: I'm an avid reader, which is no surprise. Gardening is a passion, especially perennials and herbs. Jon and I spend much of our down time cooking and love to sample great wines. We walk two miles every morning, travel when we can, and try to spend as much time as possible with our grandsons Rob and Max.

Subjects and categories you like to agent: Women's fiction, quirky, contemporary fantasy, mysteries, YA; Nonfiction: Gardening, health, cookbooks, narrative nonfiction, animals, nature, parenting, psychology, relationships.

Subjects and categories writers shouldn't bother pitching to you: Christian, "swords and dragons" fantasy, erotica, children's, poetry, political, inspirational/new age.

What might you be doing if you weren't agenting: I'd be writing my own books.

What's the most effective ways for writers to grab your attention: In your query letter by describing in the first sentence the essence of your book. In the next sentence, tell me its genre and word count. Then give me the best written paragraph you can craft about why this book is the cat's pajamas. Then, wind things up by giving me a few sentences about you as a writer. (Don't bother to tell me where you live or who you married.) Then, stop already! If you have done your job, I should want to see some chapters.

Do you charge fees separate from your commission, or offer non-agenting fee based services: We don't charge any up-front fees. Our commission is the standard 15% and, if the book is sold, we subtract postage and copy fees from the advance. We are publicists as well as agents, but we don't publicize our agenting clients' books. We provide publicity / marketing counsel and guidance to our authors as part of our agenting job.

What are representative titles you have sold to publishers: *100 Recipes You Can't Eat* by Alexa Lett (Putnam); *Are You Ready for Lasting Love?* by Patty S. Welles (Marlowe & Company); *Gordath Wood* by Patrice Sarath (Putnam/Ace).

Why did you become an agent, and how did you become one: I brought two books to the attention of an agent friend who encouraged me (and Jon) to consider becoming agents ourselves. It seemed the right time to use our knowledge of publishing and publicity to create an agency grounded by this foundation.

How do you feel about writers: I really love writers who know their business. I love writers who are talented, but understand that talent will only get them so far. I love writers who study the publishing business, go to writer's conferences, ask questions, and READ, READ, READ. I love writers who read their favorite authors, read out of their comfort zone, and read books, blogs, magazines, websites and newsletters about book publishing. I love writers who have a sense of humor and who don't take themselves too seriously.

What do you tell entities from other planets and dimensions about your job: I tell them I am a detective searching for the next great book.

What are your favorite books, movies, TV shows, and why: Anything by John Steinbeck because of his compassion; *Babbitt* by Sinclair Lewis, because of its setting and sense of satire; *The Jump Off Creek* by Molly Gloss because it reminds me what toughness and will can accomplish; *The Naked and the Dead* by Norman Mailer which I just began reading recently—amazing; *Madame Bovary* by Flaubert—I don't really know why. I don't like *Emma Bovary*, but this book is perfect. *The Great Gatsby* because no one writes like F. Scott Fitzgerald. Favorite movies: Anything done by Christopher Guest, particularly *Best in Show* because the humor is just my style. Guilty pleasures: Old movies on TBS, especially Fred Astaire when I'm in a bad mood. TV shows: HBO only, especially *Six Feet Under*. (OK, I'll admit to watching *What Not to Wear* on TLC.)

How would you describe "the writer from hell": Knows nothing about the industry, does not intend to learn and is sure she/he has the next big book that editors will "buy in a heartbeat." AND, this author cannot write her way out of a paper bag.

How would you describe the publisher and/or editor from hell: My "editor/publisher from hell" does not exist—yet. So far they have all been helpful, kind and generous to us. It's true! I just remembered one exception, the subsidiary publisher who did not come clean about how he works. (But we should have done our homework earlier!)

What do you like best about your clients, and the editors and publishers you work with: I like clients who become partners in the process of finding a publisher for their books. These clients don't call, they email. They don't demand, they request. They have good ideas which they share and they also share our enthusiasm for the process. We like the editors and publishers who are open and friendly and who look to us as resources. Some editors tell us where we've gone wrong and we really appreciate it, being new to this side of the business. Other editors give us hints and tips which are so useful.

Will our business exist as we know it in 10 years or so from now: Everything changes. That's the one true thing. The book business is changing under our feet. In ten years? Who knows? All we can do is hold on for the ride and try to innovate, not duplicate.

The following information pertains to Jon Tienstra.

Born: Born in Harvey, Illinois, January 5.

Education: B.A. in English Literature; Masters in Library Science.

Career story: After graduating college I worked at Alpo Pet Foods as director of product quality control, then for 10 years as director of environmental control. I spent another decade at a competing pet food company because the kids needed shoes. Finally, I was able to leave pet food behind and go back to school where I took a Masters degree in library science. I spent two years at the Rodale Experimental Farm as the organic vegetable gardener before I joined KT Public Relations as an unpaid intern.

Hobbies and special personal interests: I'm an avid reader of most everything. I collect old vegetable gardening books and love car racing of almost all types. You'll find me in the kitchen cooking / creating during off-hours. I wish I had more time to paint, but stacks of chapters are always the priority.

Subjects and categories you like to agent: Fiction: Science fiction/fantasy, mysteries, YA, literary fiction, police/detective; Nonfiction: Gardening, military.

Subjects and categories writers shouldn't bother pitching to you: Christian, "swords and dragons" fantasy, erotica, children's, poetry, political, inspirational/new age, short stories, novellas.

What might you be doing if you weren't agenting: My whole life has led me to this point.

What's the most effective ways for writers to grab your attention: Do your homework and make your query pitch-perfect.

Do you charge fees separate from your commission, or offer non-agenting fee based services: We don't charge any up-front fees. Our commission is the standard 15% and, if the book is sold, we subtract postage and copy fees from the advance. We are publicists as well as agents, but we don't publicize our agenting clients' books. We provide publicity / marketing counsel and guidance to our authors as part of our agenting job.

What are representative titles you have sold to publishers: See Kae's listing above.

Why did you become an agent, and how did you become one: All the interesting and fun parts of my life have come together at this focal point.

How do you feel about writers: I really love writers but don't love lazy writers.

What do you tell entities from other planets and dimensions about your job: I tell them I am on a treasure hunt for an explanation of what it all means.

What are your favorite books, movies, TV shows, and why: Books: I can't list them all. Movies: *Blade Runner, The Fifth Element, Constantine, Matrix, Apocalypse Now, Das Boat.* TV: HBO and the Speed Channel.

Will our business exist as we know it in 10 years or so from now: Of course not. Change is inevitable. We embrace it as much as possible.

MICHAEL LARSEN/ELIZABETH POMADA LITERARY AGENTS

1029 Jones Street, San Francisco, CA 94109

415-673-0939

www.larsenpomada.com

Agents' names: Elizabeth Pomada. Larsenpoma@aol.com. Michael Larsen, Larsen poma@aol.com

Born: Pomada: June 12; New York, New York. Larsen: January 8; New York, New York.

Education: Pomada: Cornell '62. Larsen: CCNY '63.

Career story: Pomada: Worked at Holt, Rinehart & Winston; David McKay; and the Dial Press. Began the agency in 1972. Larsen: Worked at William Morrow, Bantam, and Pyramid (now merged with Berkley). Co-founded the agency in 1972. Member: AAR. The agency has sold hundred of books, mostly by new writers, to more than a hundred publishers. Wrote *How to Write a Book Proposal*, and *How to Get a Literary Agent*, both of which are now in their third edition. Co-authored *How to Write with a Collaborator*, with Hal Zina Bennett and *Guerilla Marketing for Writers: 100 Weapons for Selling Your Work* with client Jay Conrad Levinson, author of the 25+ Guerilla Marketing series; and Rick Frishman, president of Planned Television Arts.

Hobbies and special personal interests: Pomada: France, architectural color, reading, travel. Larsen: Going to the movies, listening to jazz (mostly 40s-60s) and classical music (mostly 1685-1791), seeing plays, visiting France, reading a book without the phone ringing, bringing people together.

Subjects and categories you like to agent: Pomada: I like positive narrative nonfiction—something that will make me feel good when I've read it. I like travel narrative that makes me hunt for my passport. And I like fiction of all kinds, from very literary to very commercial, romance, mystery, thriller, etc. Something that will keep me reading past my bedtime. Larsen: I'm looking books that will change the world, that will mean something 10 years from now. Books that will add to my knowledge. Nonfiction. Something new & different. Something that will help us face the future.

Subjects and categories writers shouldn't bother pitching to you: Pomada: Please do not send poetry, children's books, fantasy, sci-fi, westerns, misery memoirs or disease-of-the-month stories. No abuse of any kind. Larsen. Please do not send books I've already read or sold, diet books, religious tomes, yesterday's news.

What might you be doing if you weren't agenting: Pomada: If I weren't agenting, I'd be reading good books. Maybe writing a few. Larsen: If I weren't agenting, I'd be publishing, or helping to publish, books that should be published.

What's the most effective ways for writers to grab your attention: The most effective way to grab our attention? Write beautifully. Craft does leap off the page. Follow the submission guidelines on our Website.

Do you charge fees separate from your commission, or offer non-agenting fee based services: We do not charge fees separate from our commission or offer non-agenting fee based services.

What are representative titles you have sold to publishers: *The Scalpel & The Soul* by Allan Hamilton (Tarcher); *The Solemn Lantern Maker* by Merlinda Bobis (Delta); *Shadow Isle* by Katharine Kerr (DAW); *Guerrilla Marketing* by Jay Conrad Levinson (Houghton).

Why did you become an agent, and how did you become one: Pomada: I became an agent when I moved to San Francisco and was told there were no publishing jobs for me in the city. The employment agent represented writers and artists and she said, pointing to a wall of manuscripts, "meanwhile, people send me these things and I don't know what do to with them." I went in every Tuesday afternoon and actually found two books that were salable—so started then. Larsen: I became an agent when Patty Hearst was captured. I knew there was a book in it and ended up selling it in four phone calls. I figured being an agent was easy! And joined Elizabeth.

How do you feel about writers: It depends on when you ask. Most mean well. But too many think the world owes them a living and don't understand that they have to do their homework and be responsible for their success.

What do you tell entities from other planets and dimensions about your job: We tell them that we're the middlemen, the matchmakers between publishers and authors.

What are your favorite books, movies, TV shows, and why: Pomada: Favorite books: *Desiree* by Annemarie Selinko because it's romance that's basically true and historical and *Gone With The Wind* by Margaret Mitchell because in the different readings from when I was a child to know, I've seen different things and learned about life. Favorite movie: *An American in Paris*. Larsen: Favorite book: *The Leopard* by G. Lampedusa: history and life and philosophy all in one. Favorite movie: *Lawrence Of Arabia*—best writing, best direction, best acting, best relevance, best music, as true today as it was then.

How would you describe "the writer from hell": Pomada: A nudge who thinks he knows more than I do about the business. Larsen: I wrote about that in my book, How to Get a Literary Agent: someone who thinks that he is my only client and only reason for living.

How would you describe the publisher and/or editor from hell: The publisher cheats on royalties and holds back an impossible reserve against returns just so the author won't get any money. The editor simply disappears and doesn't answer phone calls, emails, etc. I won't name names but I could.

What do you like best about your clients, and the editors and publishers you work with: I like clients who are genuinely interested in their writing, their careers, the business. It's also special if they are human and interested in me as a human being, too. Friends are nice. I like publishers and editors who are still interested in writers and good writing—even though commerce is important. And all should see publishing/writing as part of life, not the only reason for living.

Will our business exist as we know it in 10 years or so from now: Our business will exist 10 years or so from now, but not as we know it. Writers will still need to have people on their side, but publishing and selling will change dramatically and machines are sure to take over much of the world—including publishing and bookselling. Do we really have ten years left?

LAUNCHBOOKS LITERARY AGENCY

566 Sweet Pea Place, Encinitas, CA 92024

760-944-9909

www.launchbooks.com   e-mail: david@launchbooks.com

Agent's name: David Fugate

Born: June 11, 1969 in Richmond, Kentucky. Moved to Springfield, Ohio when I was 2, and then to San Diego, California when I was 8 and have been here ever since.

Education: Bachelor of Arts with honors in English/American Literature from the University of California, San Diego.

Career history or story: In 1992 I began as an intern at the Margret McBride Literary Agency while still a student at UC San Diego. Upon graduation I was hired by the McBride Agency to handle submissions and focus on project development. In 1994 I moved to Waterside Productions, Inc., and over the next 11+ years represented more than 700 book projects that generated over $10,000,000 for authors. In August of 2005 I went out on my own to form LaunchBooks Literary Agency so that I could focus more exclusively on working with authors and projects that I'm truly passionate about.

Hobbies, interests: Reading, a variety of sports (especially basketball, soccer and skiing), video games, online culture (things like Second Life, blogs, virtual communities, etc.), renewable energy, China, world affairs, new music and film (especially foreign films, drama, and the few really good sci-fi and comedies that come out each year).

Subjects & categories you are interested in agenting, including fiction & non-fiction: 95% of the projects I represent are non-fiction and within that category I have a broad range of interests including history, politics, current affairs, narrative non-fiction, health, business, biography, true crime, memoir, parenting, sports, pop culture, how-to, computers and technology, reference, diet and humor. In the fiction space I'm interested in humor science fiction, thrillers, mysteries, and mainstream/topical titles.

Subjects & categories writers shouldn't even bother pitching to you: Religion, spirituality, children's, romance, horror, short stories, poetry.

What's the best way for fiction writers to solicit your interest: An e-mail query and a synopsis. However, if an author also wants to attach the first 25-30 pages of their novel as a Word attachment, I'm often happy to read that, as well.

What's the best way for non-fiction writers to solicit your interest: An e-mail query and a proposal.

Do you charge reading or any upfront fees: No, I don't charge any upfront or reading fees.

How can writers increase the odds that you will offer representation: It's critical these days that authors have a clear sense of where their book fits into the market and the ability to communicate why their book will sell. It has also become more and more important for an author to have a strong marketing platform. Fortunately, there are now more ways than ever for authors do develop a platform for both themselves and their books, and having one will increase both the odds that I'll offer representation and that a publisher will pick up the book.

What are some representative titles that you have sold: *The Ghost Train* by Jon Jeter (W.W. Norton); *The Making of Second Life* by Wagner James Au (HarperCollins); *Everyday Edisons* by Louis Foreman and Jill Gilbert Welytok (Workman); *Branding Only Works on Cows* by Jonathan Baskin (Grand Central); *The Art of Deception* by Kevin Mitnick and William L. Simon (John Wiley & Sons); *Lifehacker* by Gina Trapani (John Wiley & Sons); *Transcending CSS* by Andy Clarke (Peachpit); *The Zen of CSS* by Molly Holzschlag and Jeff Zeldman (Peachpit); *U.S. Military History for Dummies* by John McManus (John Wiley & Sons).

PAUL S. LEVINE LITERARY AGENCY

1054 Superba Avenue, Venice, CA 90291

310-450-6711, 800-883-0490   fax: 310-450-0181

e-mail: pslevine@ix.netcom.com

Carrier Pigeon: Use street address; train pigeon well.

Strippergram: Must be gorgeous and have a great routine.

Agent's name: Paul S. Levine
Born: March 16, 1954; New York, NY
Education: B. Comm., Concordia University, Montreal (1977); MBA, York University, Toronto (1978); JD, University of Southern California, Los Angeles (1981).
Career history: Attorney for more than 24 years.
Categories/subjects that you are most enthusiastic about agenting: Commercial fiction and non-fiction for adults, children and young adults.
What you don't want to agent: Science fiction, fantasy, and horror.
If you were not an agent, what might you be doing instead: Practicing entertainment law; reading good books.
What's the best way for writers to solicit your interst: Query letter ONLY by snail mail, e-mail, fax, carrier pigeon, or strippergram.
Do you charge reading or management fees: No.
Can you provide an approximation by % of what you tend to represent by category: Fiction: 35%, Children's: 15%, Non-Fiction: 50%.

What are some of the most common mistakes writers make when pitching you: Telling me that they're writing to me because they're looking for a literary agent. Duh!

How would you describe the client from Hell: One who calls, faxes, e-mails, or sends carrier pigeons or strippergrams every day. One who constantly needs reassurance that each rejection letter does not mean that the client's project lacks merit and that the client is an awful person.

How would you describe the perfect client: The opposite of the above.

How and why did you ever become an agent: I have loved the book business ever since I started practicing law in 1980. My first client was a major book publisher in Los Angeles.

What, if anything, can writers do to increase the odds that you will become his or her agent: Be referred by an existing client or colleague.

How would you describe to someone (or thing) from another planet what it is you do as an agent: I represent writers—book authors, screenwriters, and writer-producers.

Do you have any particular opinions or impressions of editors and publishers in general: I love them.

LEVINE GREENBERG LITERARY AGENCY

307 Seventh Avenue, Suite 2407, New York, NY 10001

212-337-0934   Fax: 212-337-0948

www.levinegreenberg.com   e-mail: James Levine: jlevine@levinegreenberg.com; Daniel Greenberg: dgreenberg@levinegreenberg.com; Stephanie Kip Rostan: srostan@levinegreenberg.com; Jenoyne Adams: jadams@levinegreenberg.com; Victoria Skurnick: vskurnick@levinegreenberg.com; Danielle Svetcov: dsvetcov@levinegreenberg.com; Elizabeth Fisher: efisher@levinegreenberg.com; Lindsay Edgecombe: ledgecombe@levinegreenberg.com; Monika Verma: mverma@levinegreenberg.com

Agents' names: James Levine, Daniel Greenberg, Stephanie Kip Rostan, Jenoyne Adams, Victoria Skurnick, Danielle Svetcov, Elizabeth Fisher, Lindsay Edgecombe, Monika Verma.

Career history or story: Founded in 1989 by author and academic entrepreneur James Levine, we have grown into a firm of 13 people with offices in New York, San Francisco and Los Angeles. We represent fiction and non-fiction in virtually every category.

Most of our titles are published by imprints of the major houses, but we have also worked with almost fifty independent and/or university presses.

Our strong foreign rights department works internationally with a respected network of co-agents to place our titles with leading foreign publishers, and we are regular participants at the Frankfurt Book Fair and Book Expo America. Our co-agents in Hollywood handle movie and television rights with major studios and production companies.

Subjects & categories you are interested in agenting, including fiction & non-fiction: Our agents have such wide and varied preferences that our list excludes few genres. As far as fiction is concerned: commercial women's literature, literary fiction, ethnic fiction, young-adult literature, romance, and suspense have been successfully represented by a number of our agents. Additionally, LGLA is no stranger to business, self-help, humor, food, child development, pet, science, narrative non-fiction, and political titles, all of which are of interest to our agents. Our full list can be found at our website.

What's the best way for fiction writers to solicit your interest: The thorough online submission form located at our website (http://www.levinegreenberg.com), which allows for attaching proposals and sample chapters, is the best way to submit work.

Do you charge reading or any upfront fees: No.

What are some representative titles that you have sold: *Sex, Drugs, and Cocoa Puffs* by Chuck Klosterman (Scribner); *Love is a Mix Tape* by Rob Sheffield (Crown); *Fifty Places to Play Golf Before You Die* by Chris Santella; *Green Eggs and Ham Cookbook* by Georgeanne Brennan (Random House); *The Five Dysfunctions of a Team: A Leadership Fable* by Patrick Lencioni (Jossey-Bass); *Queen Bees & Wannabes: Helping Your Daughter Survive Cliques, Gossip, Boyfriends & Other Realities of Adolescence* by Rosalind Wiseman (Crown); *Why Good Things Happen to Good People: The Exciting New Research that Proves the Link Between Doing Good and Living a Longer, Healthier, Happier Life* by Stephen Post, Ph.D., and Jill Neimark (Broadway); *Extraordinary Knowing: Science, Skepticism, and the Inexplicable Powers of the Human Mind* by Elizabeth Lloyd Mayer, Ph.D. (Bantam); *The Spellman Files* by Lisa Lutz (Simon & Schuster); *The Insufficiency of Maps* by Nora Pierce (Atria); *Getting Warmer* by Carol Snow (Berkley).

LITERARY SERVICES INC.

P.O. Box 888, Barnegat, NJ 08005

609-698-7162

www.LiteraryServicesInc.com

Cynthia Zigmund: 2228 North Lakewood, Chicago, IL 60614

e-mail: cunthia.zigmund@SBCGLOBAL.net

> **Agent's name:** John Willig
> **Born:** 1954, New York, NY
> **Education:** Brown University, 1976.

Career history or story: 30 years of publishing experience. Started working as a college "traveler" in academic publishing; became an executive editor for business books with Prentice Hall before starting the agency. I was fortunate to grow up surrounded by books and the great Irish love of authors and writing.

Hobbies, interests: Primary interest has been to be actively involved with raising my two sons (now ages 21 and 18). I enjoy athletics—tennis, swimming, and baseball—and the arts. Hoping to begin piano lessons soon and classes in the martial arts. Any day at the beach is a slice of heaven.

Subjects & categories you are interested in agenting, including fiction & non-fiction: We work exclusively in nonfiction. We do not accept memoirs! Per our Web-site, our core topic areas are in business, investing, careers, self-help, history, science, current events and global issues. That being said, we've recently sold a faith-based prayer book, a body image improvement book and a new work on intuition. Religion and spirituality are topic areas of increasing interest with us.

Subjects & categories writers shouldn't even bother pitching to you: Children's books, science fiction.

What would you do if you weren't agenting: History teacher and baseball or basketball coach. There are days though that the allure of the sea and becoming a tuna boat captain sound just right.

What's the best way for fiction writers to solicit your interest: Right now they shouldn't. While I'm very interested in narrative non-fiction, we're not yet ready to agent fiction.

What's the best way for non-fiction writers to solicit your interest: Per our company Web site and submission segment, an email answering a few key questions before sending proposals and chapters. I value sample chapters with a well thought out proposal.

Do you charge reading or any upfront fees: No reading fees. In addition to our author representation, we offer coaching services for authors who are determined (and have decided) to self-publish. This service is based on our extensive editorial, development and marketing experience working for publishers. It is not intended to be a pre-requisite for representation. It is not a fee we charge to prospective clients. It is intended to help writers venturing into unchartered waters but have decided that for them the best route is to self-publish. Again, the service is offered to help writers!

In your experience, what are the most common pitching mistakes writers make: Exaggerating the market size/potential; spending too much time criticizing the competition/bestsellers and not enough on their platform; arrogant tone leading to unreasonable expectations.

Describe the client from Hell, even if you don't have any: Per the above, I place a high premium on the quality of the author's attitude and learning about what type of person they are and what it will be like to work with them. Publishers do not need me to bring them 'jerks' to work with so I have my own set of little tests before I'm willing to take on a prospect.

What's your definition of a great client: Someone with a great learning attitude, a sense of humor and some humility. Organized, responsive, flexible.

How can writers increase the odds that you will offer representation: Passion is a given. I worry when there is not enough or too much. I'm more impressed with someone who has done their homework, researching the market, investing time and resources into the writing, and/or has been actively developing their 'community' of potential interested buyers of their book.

Why did you become an agent, and how did you become one: To work closely with writers in developing their ideas and sharing successes (making dreams a reality). I decided to become an agent in the midst of a corporate reorganization (that did not have the best inerest of authors on the radar screen).

Describe to someone from another planet what you do as an agent: I work as a writer's advocate. In doing so, this involves many 'hats' such as financial consultant, writing coach, legal counsel, personal advisor/cheerleader/therapist.

How do you feel about editors and publishers: Without them I'm on the tuna boat! Having been one, I know how challenging it is to prodiuce succesful books, and it is very challenging today. They deserve my respect and admiration—this does not compromise my ability to aggressively represent my clients and their best interests.

What do you see in the near future for book publishing: Our business will exist as we know it 10 years from now (thankfully) but not without significant and ongoing changes to formats and presentation styles.

What are your favorite books/TV shows/movies, and why: TV: *The Sopranos*; Books: I love historical/thriller fiction (in the tradition of the *Alienist*, C. Carr). I collect Jazz age authors Fitzgerald, Hemingway, Wolfe, Stein. Movies: So many!

In your opinion, what do editors think of you: Professional, knowledgeable about publishing; represents high quality authors and projects; can be a good working partner.

On a personal non-professional level, what do you think people think of you: I hope as a 'good man.'

What are some representative titles that you have sold: *The Pursuit of Elegance* by Matt May (Doubleday/Currency); *The 2020 Workplace* by Jeanne Meister (HarperCollins); *The CompleteLandlord.com Series* by William Lederer (John Wiley & Sons); *Investing in the Sustainable World* by Matthew Kiernan (AMACOM); *Carve Your Own Road* by Jennifer Remling (Career Press); *Love Your Body, Live Your Dreams* by Sarah Maira Dreisbach (AdamsMedia); *Restoring Who We Are* by Martin Melaver (Chelsea Green Publishers); *The Global Talent Showdown* by Edward Gordon (Berret Koehler); *The Recycling Robot* by Robert Malone (Workman Publishers).

TONI LOPOPOLO LITERARY MANAGEMENT

8837 School House Lane, Coopersburg, PA 18036

215-679-0560 fax: 215-679-0561

e-mail: Lopopolobooks@aol.com   Susan's e-mail: Donnsett@verizon.net

Agents' names: Toni Lopopolo, Susan Setteducato
Born: Toni: July 18, Los Angeles, California; Susan: September 11, 1953, Newark, New Jersey.
Education: Toni: Graduate work at State University at San Francisco and UC Berkeley; Susan: Moore College of Art, Philadelphia.
Career history: 1990-Present: Literary Agent; 1981-1990: Executive Editor, St. Martin's Press; 1975-1981: Executive Editor, MacMillan; 1973-1975: Paperback Marketing Manager, Houghton-Mifflin; 1970-1973: Publicity Associate, Bantam Books.
Hobbies/personal interests: Toni: A Jack Russell Terrier named Babbitt; my five Italian Greyhounds, Sophie Jean, Harley, Kiss, Cabrini Girl, and Santini; some are rescues; starting book reading groups that really discuss the books read, and my fiction writing workshops. Susan: painting in acrylics, sign painting, gardening, raising sheep, growing apples.
Categories/subjects that you are most enthusiastic about agenting: Toni: Mystery series set in other countries; mysteries set in USA with ethnic protagonists. Illustrated children's books; business, parenting, women's and family health, personal growth, psychology, paranormal, anything about dogs.
What you don't want to agent: Toni: Poetry, movie scripts.
If you were not an agent, what might you be doing instead: Buying, restoring, and flipping older houses. Also I'd have more dogs.
What's the best way for writers to solicit your interest: With a great query letter and a personal greeting. Also, when it's obvious to me that the writer has done his/her homework re: writing, and publishing.
Do you charge reading or management fees: No.
Can you provide an approximation by % of what you tend to represent by category: Non-Fiction: 90%; Fiction: 10%.
What are the most common mistakes writers make when pitching you: Toni: Sending mail that has to be signed for; why not include a stamped, self-addressed postcard if they are that insecure. Telling me they've written a sure-fire bestseller before I've had a chance to read their pages.
How would you describe the client from Hell: The terminally insecure.
How would you describe the perfect client: The secure professional writer who trusts and believes in him or herself, and the agent they hired.
How and why did you ever become an agent: Opening a literary agency seemed a natural segue after all those years in book publishing. I also enjoy the process of working with a talented writer and managing that writer's career.

What, if anything, can a writer do to increase the odds of you becoming his or her agent: For non-fiction, submitting an excellently crafted book proposal. For fiction, mastering the skills that make up their craft plus talent as a unique storyteller. Also, have their manuscripts edited by a professional editor before submitting the novel to this agency. Writers who have done their homework and who show strong self-confidence are welcome.

How would you describe to someone (or thing) from another planet what it is that you do as an agent: I trade black dots on something white called paper for $$$$.

Do you have any particular opinions or impressions of editors and publishers in general: Because I worked as an editor for many years, I am very empathetic to their workloads and plight in the machinery of a publishing house. Publishers fight to make a profit; it must be daunting.

What do you think the future holds for writers, publishers, and agents: Despite all the electronic gadgets and ways to publish electronically, people of the future will still want to read, own, and collect bound books that they can hold in their hands. The next ten years will stay essentially the same. Worthy books will be published. And many unworthy books will be published as well. Writers have to master their skills, especially novelists, and keep up with the trends and the shorter and shorter attention spans of their readers. And now that most publishers are owned by conglomerates, maybe smaller publishers will flourish and take a chance on books that might have smaller readerships. Some agents will become paperless, sell lots of electronic rights, and still worry about the next big sale.

What are your favorite books, movies, TV shows, and why: Films: *Capote*, *Walk The Line*, *40 Year Old Virgin*, *Wedding Crashers*. The first two because of the excellence of the writing, the actors, and the directors. The other two because I haven't laughed that much in a long time. I'll watch anything Vince Vaughn does, and Philip Seymour Hoffman amazes me. T.V.: *The Sopranos*, though they ran out of gas this season, *Rescue Me* which keeps getting better and better. Almost anything on HGTV because I learned all the techniques and contracting skills, which helped when I began restoring my house. *Curb Appeal* is a favorite. All the dog shows on Animal Planet, especially the ones with the cops who rescue abused and abandoned dogs. Helen Mirren and Jeremy Irons in *Elizabeth I*, on HBO.

On a personal level, what do you think people like about you and dislike about you: They are impressed with my experience and the fact that I will help them with editing. I've been in publishing since 1970 and an agent since 1991. There is a blog written by a man who called me a stupid bitch; he comes up on Google along with my other credits. I think some people are not happy with a laid back style of working; and some people really love it. I don't mince words and some people appreciate that and some are offended.

Please list representative titles you have sold: *Do Not Go Gently* (HarperCollins); *Hoodoo Man*, *Green Money* (Ballantine); *Lifebank*, *Remote Intrusion* (Dell); *Tuesday's Child*, *The Reckoning* (Pocketbooks); *Legacy*, *Catriona* (Kensington). Nonfiction: *Organizing From The Right Side of the Brain* (St. Martin's Press); *Stein On Writing* (St. Martin's Press); *Real-Life Homseschooling* (Fireside); *Leader of the Pack* (HarperPaperbacks);

Choosing a Dog (Berkley); *Five Simple Steps To Emotional Healing* (Simon and Schuster); *Time Management for Creative People, Career Management for Creative People, Money Management for Creative People, Self-Promotion for Creatice People* (ThreeRivers Press); *The Wild Idea Club: An Innovative and Effective Way to Encourage Your Employees to Quit Complaining and Start Solving Problems* (Career Press).

JULIA LORD LITERARY MANAGEMENT

38 West 9th Street, New York, NY 10011

212-995-2333   fax: 212-995-2332

Agent's name: Julia Lord
Born: 1962.
Education: Kenyon College.
Career history or story: Actor, actor's agent, opening the literary department of Monty Silver Agency in the late 80s. Had twins. Freelance editing, opened JLLM in 1999.
Hobbies, interests: Marathons, triathlons, politics, history, music, travel.
Subjects & categories you are interested in agenting, including fiction & non-fiction: Fiction: 40%, non-fiction: 60%. History that comes alive, anything smart with a good sense of humor.
Subjects & categories writers shouldn't even bother pitching to you: NO romance, science fiction or children's.
Why did you become an agent, and how did you become one: I became an agent because I've always loved books and wanted to be an advocate for writers. I even married one!
What are some representative titles that you have sold: *Plato and a Platypus Walk Into a Bar...Understanding Philosophy Through Jokes* by Cathcart/Klein (Abrams); *Aaronsohn's Maps* by Patricia Goldstone (Harcourt); *NYPD Confidential* by Leonard Levitt (Thomas Dunne/St. Martin's); *How NOT to Write a Novel* by Howard Mittelmark and Sandra Newman (Collins); *A Common Ordinary Murder* by Donald Pfarrer (Random House).

NANCY LOVE LITERARY AGENCY

250 E. 65th St., Suite 4A, New York, NY 10065

e-mail: nloveag@aol.com

To contact: Do not send a proposal. Query first by mail or e-mail. Be sure to include response information.

Agent's name: Nancy Love

Born: Philadelphia.

Education: Attended Bryn Mawr College; graduated Phi Beta Kappa, cum laude, University of Pennsylvania.

Career story: Worked as an editor and writer for city magazines (managing editor *Philadelphia Magazine*, editor-in-chief *Boston Magazine*) editor *American Home Magazine*, and *CUE*. Editor of Washingtonian Books, a joint venture with *Washingtonian Magazine*. Freelance book and magazine writer and magazine consultant. I started agenting when friends suggested I stop giving away writing advice and start getting paid for it.

Subjects and categories you like to agent: What I am looking for: Nonfiction only. Please do not send fiction. I want narrative nonfiction, memoir, health, parenting, foreign affairs, expose, women's issues, biography, history, politics, crime, pop science.

What might you be doing if you weren't agenting: I love to travel, and if I weren't a literary agent, I would spend all of my time traveling and writing about it. Otherwise, if I had more time, I'd spend it reading and hanging out with friends.

What's the most effective ways for writers to grab your attention: To get my attention, have an introduction from a writer I know or write a wonderful pitch letter.

Do you charge fees separate from your commission, or offer non-agenting fee based services: No fees.

What are representative titles you have sold to publishers: *Building Better Brains* by Judy Willis, M.D., Ed.D. (Sourcebooks); *Addiction-Proof Your Child* by Stanton Peele, Ph.D., J.D. (Three Rivers Press); *All the Shah's Men* (John Wiley); *Overthrow* by Stephen Kinzer (Times Books); *Forgotten Ellis Island* by Lorie Conway (Smithsonian Books) (PBS Special); *What You Should Know About Vaccines* by Paul Offit, M.D. (John Wiley); *Overkill* by James Alan Fox and Jack Levin (Perseus).

What do you tell entities from other planets and dimensions about your job: My job involves being a shrink, lawyer, editor, friend, mother, and guru—and it's the best job I've ever had.

What do you like best about your clients, and the editors and publishers you work with: I guess the most important thing I get from my clients and the people I work with in publishing is a window into other worlds that they are writing about and the books they are publishing.

You're welcome to share your thoughts and sentiments about the business of writing and publishing: If I could share one piece of advice with people trying to establish themselves in the book world, it would be this: Do your research before you start trying to find an agent. You spend years writing a book, so spend a few weeks finding out as much as you can about publishing and how it works. You will be astonished at how much easier it makes everything for you.

Will our business exist as we know it in 10 years or so from now: The book business is in a state of flux. How it will sort out, no one knows now. But publishing has always changed over the years, maybe just not this fast.

LOWENSTEIN-YOST ASSOCIATES, INC.

121 West 27th Street, Suite 601, NY, NY 10001-6262

212-206-1630

Agent's name: Nancy Yost

Education: B.A. Comparative Lit./UNLV.

Career history or story: In the publishing industry: Contracts, Random House; editor, Avon Books; now agent.

Hobbies, interests: Reading (still!), diving, opera, antiquing, theatre/dance, eating.

Subjects & categories you are interested in agenting, including fiction & non-fiction: Crime/suspense/thrillers (contemporary and historical); women's fiction—upmarket and commercial, narrative non-fiction about history, natural science, culture, the arts.

Subjects & categories writers shouldn't even bother pitching to you: No textbooks, screenplays, sci-fi, poetry, political non-fiction, westerns, children's books.

What would you do if you weren't agenting: A different answer daily, but it consistently involves diving, shopping and playing with animals…

What's the best way for fiction writers to solicit your interest: By query letter and first chapter, but not electronically! My e-mail a) 'blocker' kicks things out, b) if I don't recognize sender, I delete the message—sorry!

What's the best way for non-fiction writers to solicit your interest: See above.

Do you charge reading or any upfront fees: No.

In your experience, what are the most common pitching mistakes writers make: Sending material that I don't represent, sending material that is in need of extensive revision/polish, saying that 'this material will make a great movie' means it will make a great book.

Describe the client from Hell, even if you don't have any: Bad attitude, bad manners, incomplete communication of goals and opinions, unrealistic or unvoiced expectations, unreliable work habits, phone calls at home on weekends or after hours…

What's your definition of a great client: Curious, creative, reliable, honest, dedicated to their craft and the adventure of the career. Oh, and they could currently be on the *NYT* Bestseller list, and have family members in high positions at Ingrams, B&N, etc.

How can writers increase the odds that you will offer representation: Write a really good book.

Why did you become an agent, and how did you become one: I love books, and I can't write them, I like the challenge, complexity and variety of the industry, and I like the kind of people who care about books and human issues.

How do you feel about editors and publishers: Hardworking (and overworked), dedicated and smart.

What are your favorite books/TV shows/movies, and why: Couldn't possibly list them all, but movies would have to include *The Philadelphia Story* and *Silence of the Lambs*; TV this season: *The Closer, The Shield, Project Runway, Scrubs, BBC Mystery Mondays, 30 Rock, Ugly Betty*.

What are some representative titles that you have sold: *Case of Lies* by Perri O'Shaughnessy (Delacorte); *In a Dark House* by Deborah Crombie (Morrow); *Seize the Night* by Sherrilyn Kenyon (St. Martins); *What Price Love* by Stephanie Laurens (Morrow); *Flirting with Danger* by Suzanne Enoch (Avon); *Beneath a Silent Moon* by Tracy Grant (Morrow); *Assault and Pepper* by Tamar Myers (Dutton); *The Accidental Virgin* by Valerie Frankel (Harper); *Overkill* by Linda Castillo (Berkley); *Black Lace* by Beverly Jenkins (Avon); *Chosen Prey* and *Seduced* by Magic by Cheyenne McCray (St. Martins); *House of Dark Delights* by Louisa Burton (Bantam); *A Piece of Normal* by Sandy Kahn Shelton (Crown).

LYONS LITERARY LLC

116 West 23rd St., Suite 500, New York, NY 10011

212-851-8428

www.lyonsliterary.com   e-mail: info@lyonsliterary.com

Agent's name: Jonathan Lyons

Born: San Antonio, Texas.

Education: B.A., Washington University in St. Louis; J.D., Benjamin N. Cardozo School of Law.

Career history or story: After working briefly as a litigation attorney, Jonathan joined Curtis Brown, Ltd. Four years later Jonathan joined McIntosh & Otis, Inc., where he served as agent and rights manager. In January of 2007 Jonathan founded Lyons Literary LLC. He is a member of the Association of Authors' Representatives, The Authors Guild, American Bar Association, New York State Bar Association, and the New York State Intellectual Property Law Section.

Subjects & categories you are interested in agenting, including fiction & non-fiction: Narrative nonfiction, history, cooking/food writing, pop culture, sports, women's issues, biographies, military, science/pop science, entertainment, politics, true crime, thrillers, mysteries, women's fiction, literary fiction.

Subjects & categories writers shouldn't even bother pitching to you: Romance, picture books, short story collections.

What's the best way for fiction writers to solicit your interest: Submission via the agency Web site.

What's the best way for non-fiction writers to solicit your interest: Submission via the agency Web site.

Do you charge reading or any upfront fees: NO.

DONALD MAASS LITERARY AGENCY

121 W. 27th Street, Suite 801, New York, NY 10001

212-727-8383 ext. 11

e-mail: sbarbara@maassagency.com

Agents' names: Stephen Barbara, Cameron McClure; cmcclure@maassagency.com
The following information pertains to Stephen Barbara.
Born: August 17, 1980; New Haven, Connecticut.
Education: BA '02 in English Literature (with a focus on literary criticism), University of Chicago.

Career history or story: I worked briefly on the editorial side at HarperCollins, before joining the Fifi Oscard Agency as an assistant in late 2004. Then in January of 2006 I became agent and contracts director at the Donald Maass Literary Agency.

Hobbies, interests: I follow Italian soccer, enjoy traveling, and am an avid reader of business and narrative non-fiction books.

Subjects & categories you are interested in agenting, including fiction & non-fiction: YA and middle-grade novels, picture books, SFF, literary fiction, mystery/suspense, memoir, business, narrative nonfiction, health and fitness.

Subjects & categories writers shouldn't even bother pitching to you: Romance novels and screenplays.

What would you do if you weren't agenting: Cry, gnash my teeth, pull my hair out. I love my job.

What's the best way for fiction writers to solicit your interest: Send me a 1-page query letter via e-mail with the first 5 pages pasted into the body of the e-mail. Please mention any writing credits and/or endorsements from other writers.

What's the best way for non-fiction writers to solicit your interest: Send me a 1-page query letter via e-mail. Please mention relevant credentials and any info. on your platform.

Do you charge reading or any upfront fees: No.

In your experience, what are the most common pitching mistakes writers make: It's best to avoid baseless hype ('my writing has been compared to Tolstoy's') and masses of description. They smack of a lack of confidence. Be clear, succinct, and to-the-point.

Describe the client from Hell, even if you don't have any: The client from Hell is someone who's badly in need of career help, but who won't listen to advice and blames others for problems he himself has created.

What's your definition of a great client: Hardworking, ambitious, optimistic, reasonable, but most of all trusting.

How can writers increase the odds that you will offer representation: Write a smart query letter and terrific manuscript and the odds go up. Extra kudos for flattering me—if you know something about who I represent and my track record that's generally a good sign.

Why did you become an agent, and how did you become one: Edmund Wilson was probably the writer who most filled me with awe of the New York publishing world when I was growing up, and I knew even in college I wanted to enter into that world and become an editor or agent. But agenting best suited my independent, entrepreneurial instincts.

What do you see in the near future for book publishing: I think we'll see publishers pushing fewer titles with more sales potential each season. Fewer chances for authors to break out, less tolerance for mid-list sales, more and more of an emphasis on the blockbuster or runaway hit. I'm not complaining of course, publishing is a business.

What are your favorite books/TV shows/movies, and why: Some of my favorite books include *Feed* by M.T. Anderson, *Liar's Poker* by Michael Lewis, *The Russian Debutante's Handbook* by Gary Shteyngart, *Small is the New Big* by Seth Godin, and the Artemis Fowl series. I'm a big fan of *Curb Your Enthusiasm* and *Entourage*, for TV series.

In your opinion, what do editors think of you: They think well of me well enough to read my projects quickly, make offers on them, invite me to lunches and drink dates. And that's all very pleasing, naturally.

What are some representative titles that you have sold: *If I Should Fall* by Lauren Oliver (Bowen Press, HarperCollins); *Wish U Wr Dead* by Todd Strasser (Egmont US); *The Pillow Book of Lotus Lowenstein* by Libby Schmais (Delacorte Press); *Kindred* by Tammar Stein (Alfred Knopf); *The Little Sleep* by Paul Tremblay (Henry Holt); *The Secret of Zoom* by Lynne Jonell (Henry Holt); *The Dead Family Diaz* and a second picture book by P.J. Bracegirdle (Dial Books); *The Body Fat Solution* by Tom Venuto (Avery, division of Penguin); *The Big Splash* by Jack D. Ferraiolo (Amulet Books); *Dead is the New Black* by Marlene Perez (Houghton Mifflin Harcourt); *Freeze Frame* by Heidi Ayarbe (Laura Geringer Books).

The following information pertains to Cameron McClure.

Born: January 5, California.

Education: B. A. from University of California, Santa Barbara; Major: English and Spanish; Minor: History.

Career story: I've been with the Donald Maass Literary Agency since 2004; previously I worked as an assistant agent for Curtis Brown, New York.

Hobbies and special personal interests: Bicycling, listening to music, Karaoke, soccer, yoga, reading.

Subjects and categories you like to agent: Fiction: Literary mysteries and crime ficstion, urban fantasy and light science fiction, speculative fiction, women's fiction, suspense, strongly plotted literary fiction, novels with a strong sense of mystery or atmosphere. Nonfiction: Narrative nonfiction, true crime, memoir, projects on emerging subcultures.

Subjects and categories writers shouldn't bother pitching to you: Picture books, poetry, and prescriptive nonfiction.

What's the most effective ways for writers to grab your attention: E-mail me a query letter with a short pitch of your book, any publishing credits, and your openingfi ve pages. For nonfiction, send me the overview from your proposal. Please don't send attachments. I respond to all e-queries that are addressed to me and follow these guidelines. If sending a query by post, please include an SASE for my reply.

Do you charge fees separate from your commission, or offer non-agenting fee based services: No, but I respond favorably to chocolate.

What are representative titles you have sold to publishers: *Liberation* by Brian Francis Slattery (Tor Books); *The Whole World* by Emily Winsolow (Bantam Dell); *The Actress* by Elizabeth Sims (St. Martin's Press); *The Best of 2600: A Hacker Odyssey* by Emmanuel Goldstein (Wiley).

Why did you become an agent, and how did you become one: I moved to New York because I wanted o work in publishing, and I was drawn to agenting in particular because of the freedom agents have—I can sign up any type of book I fall for, as long as I believe I can sell it. I also love the diversity of the job—we are readers, editors, negotiators, peace-makers, and spend a lot of time socializing. I get a lot of satisfaction out of contributing to book culture.

What are your favorite books, movies, TV shows, and why: Some recent great reads for me have been *Sharp Objects* by Gillian Flynn, *The Spellman Files* by Lisa Lutz, *The Intuitionist* by Colson Whitehead, and some of my favorite authors are Jonathan Lethem, Dennis Lehane, Jodi Picoult, Elizabeth George, and Jeffrey Ford.

MACGREGOR LITERARY

2373 NW 185th Ave., Suite 165, Hillsboro, OR 97124

www.macgregorliterary.com

Agents' names: Chip MacGregor, Sandra Bishop

Education: Chip graduated from Portland State University in 1979, earned an MA from Biola University in 1984, did his doctoral work at the University of Oregon, and spent time at a post-doc at Regent's Park College, Oxford University. Sandra graduated from university after Chip—she's much younger. And smarter.

Career story: Chip started a long career in publishing in 1977, when he took a job as a copy editor with Clearing Magazine. He made his living as a freelance writer, worked as an editor and Senior Editor with publishers, and served as Associate Publisher with Time-Warner. He began representing authors eleven years ago. Sandra has made her living as a writer and editor for years, after working as an editor with a publishing house in Oregon. She began working with authors as an agent in 2007.

Hobbies and special personal interests: Chip has authored numerous books, loves watching Shakespeare, and has served as an editor for the International Brotherhood of Magicians for several years. Sandra has strong background in marketing, and enjoys being out of doors with her husband and son.

Subjects and categories you like to agent: Commercial fiction and non-fiction. We have significant experience working with the CBA (religious) market, with both fiction and nonfiction titles—particularly self-help, Christian Living, and Emergent projects.

Subjects and categories writers shouldn't bother pitching to you: Sci-fi, fantasy, poetry, children's books, general market YA, sexually explicit romance novels.

What might you be doing if you weren't agenting: Chip would be working as a card magician; Sandra would be running the government. Both wish they could be Speedo models.

What's the most effective ways for writers to grab your attention: Every agent is looking for a combination of three things: a GREAT IDEA, expressed through GREAT WRITING, by someone with a GREAT PLATFORM. But nothing trumps great writing. Much of what we see isn't bad, it's just not special. The ideas are average, the writing pedestrian. If you really want to grab out attention, come to us with a fabulous, out-of-the-box story, presented with writing that is stunning.

Do you charge fees separate from your commission, or offer non-agenting fee based services: No.

What are representative titles you have sold to publishers: *Quaker Summer*, a novel by Lisa Samson that was named by PW as one of their "top 100 books of the year;" *Never Say Diet*, a health book by Chantel Hobbs, who appeared on *Oprah* and on the cover of *People Magazine* (Random House); *Murder, Mayhem, and a Fine Man*, by Claudia Mair Burney, which has received rave reviews (Simon & Schuster).

Why did you become an agent, and how did you become one: On a macro level, we became agents because we both love books and words and believe they can help make the world a better place. But on a real-world level, both of us became agents because it fit our skill sets. We both began our careers as writers and editors, started working with authors, and naturally moved toward helping writers create strong proposals and sell them.

How do you feel about writers: Both of us love the creative side of writers, and enjoy the process of helping focus an idea, sharpen the words, and organize the content. We've spent our lives working with writers, love hanging around with them, and particularly enjoy helping them succeed in the very difficult process of establishing careers as artists.

What do you tell entities from other planets and dimensions about your job: If you were to study the last thousand years of life on earth, you'd discover the most significant invention was the creation of movable type. It allowed mankind to move from an oral tradition to a written one, raised the level of education in the world, and helped the common person see how he or she could live a transcendent life. Writing changed the world like nothing else. As an agent, I believe I get to play a part in that world-changing process known as publishing. I meet with writers, help them focus their ideas, insist they create the best book possible, and work to help make their book succeed in the market.

What are your favorite books, movies, TV shows, and why: Favorite books include *Huckleberry Finn, The Ragamuffin Gospel, A Distant Mirror, Treasure Island, Nostromo, The Education of Henry Adams, One Hundred Years Of Solitude.* Favorite movies would be *Citizen Kane, Casablanca, The Third Man, Schindler's List, The Thin Man, The Wizard of Oz, Gone With the Wind, Vertigo, The Godfather.* All of them cause us to think about the choices we make, and how that affects us over time.

How would you describe "the writer from hell": Sends me 27 emails per day, doesn't listen to advice, needs to know daily that I love him, and has mistaken me for his mother.

How would you describe the publisher and/or editor from hell: He insists on my showing him a proposal on an exclusive, then takes six months to get back to me... except he doesn't get back to me, I get back to him and he says, "Oh...did you send that?" And yes... this has happened to me. Deciphering publisher happy-talk is one of the roles of a good agent.

What do you like best about your clients, and the editors and publishers you work with: They understand books and publishing. They listen. I like them. They're easy to get along with.

You're welcome to share your thoughts and sentiments about the business of writing and publishing: We love the industry. Frankly, helping get books published in just about the most fun thing on the planet, and both of us appreciate the opportunity we have to participate in the process. I can think of books I've read that have changed me—James Agee's *A Death in the Family*, Henri Nouwen's *In the Name of Jesus*, Dostoyevsky's *Brothers Karamazov*. I was never the same after reading Pascal's *Pensees*. It's why I continue to work with books and words—in hopes of occasionally finding that book that will change me. I'm not sure I believe I'm ever going to help publish a book that will change the world, but I MUST believe I can help publish a book that can change a life. And, in seeing that happen, continue to have hope that the world can be a better place.

Do you wish to describe who you are: Chip is a 50-year-old literary agent who is a lifelong words guy. He's been working in the industry for three decades, is well known in the industry, and understands what makes a book work. He's also been married for more than a quarter century to a very forgiving woman, and has three grown children who also love books and words. Sandra is an experienced writer and editor who knows what makes books sing. Both of them have made their living as authors, so they know how to balance the "art" of writing with the "real-world" aspect of making a living.

Will our business exist as we know it in 10 years or so from now: Absolutely. The written word has been around since the dawn of time, and publishing has worked nicely for the last 500 years. The delivery systems may change a bit, but people still have stories to tell, and people are still looking for wisdom and the story that will change them, and books have a long-term history in the world and in our culture. In ten years, we'll still be in the book business, and still hoping to see that great book that can change our lives.

MANUS & ASSOCIATES LITERARY AGENCY

425 Sherman Avenue, Suite 200, Palo Alto, CA 94306

650-470-5151   fax: 650-470-5159

www.ManusLit.com   e-mail: SLEE@ManusLit.com

Agents' name: Jillian Manus, Stephanie Lee, Dena Fischer, Jandy Nelson, Penny Nelson

The following information pertains to Jillian Manus.

Born: April 26, New York.

Education: B.A. from New York University.

Career history: Ms. Manus has been a television agent at International Creative Management, director of development at Warner Brothers and Universal Studios, vice president of media acquisitions at Trender AG, and an associate publisher of two national magazines covering entertainment and technology. Because of this remarkably comprehensive background, she is a much sought after speaker on writing, women in business and motherhood, politics, and the media industry.

Hobbies/personal interests: Ms. Manus lends her time to professional, artistic, and political endeavors. She serves on several local and national boards including the Board of Trustees for New York University, the Dean's Council for the Tisch School of the Arts, the board for the W.I.S.H. List (Women in the Senate and House), the board of College Track, and the Advisory Board for Stanford Hospital's Cancer Center. She is also the Chair for the Governor and First Lady's Conference for Women and Families and serves on the board of the California Museum for History, Women and the Arts. In addition Ms. Manus has served on Governor Schwarzenegger's transition team and is presently involved in his economic recovery team Ms. Manus also remains very active in the development efforts of numerous literacy and mentoring programs across the country including serving on the Leadership Advisory Council for Save the Children.

Categories/subjects that you are most enthusiastic about agenting: Ms. Manus is known for paying special attention to books that empower people physically, psychologically and spiritually. She brings to her work extensive knowledge of the marketplace and editorial sensitivity that has been acquired in the course of a distinguished and multi-faceted career. Literary Fiction, Multi-Cultural Fiction, Women's Fiction, Southern Fiction, Narrative Nonfiction, Memoir, Health, Popular Science, Politics, Popular Culture, Women's Issues, History, Sophisticated Self Help

What you don't want to agent: Poetry, children's, science fiction, fantasy, westerns, romance, cookbooks.

If you were not an agent, what might you be doing instead: Teaching, climbing Everest, being a rock star!

What's the best way for writers to solicit your interest: Write a captivating pitch letter and send with: for fiction: the first 30 pages of a novel, for nonfiction: send a proposal. Always include an SASE for response.

Do you charge reading or management fees: No.

Can you provide an approximation by % of what you tend to represent by category: Non-Fiction: 60%, Fiction: 40%.

What are the most common mistakes writers make when pitching you: Call instead of writing, submitting work before it's ready.

What, if anything, can a writer do to increase the odds of you becoming his or her agent: Write a STRONG book or proposal!

Please list representative titles you have sold: *One Minute Millionaire; Cracking the Millionaire Code; Unbreakable Laws of Success; GO LONG; Be Inspired, Be Humble, and Make a Total Commitment to Life; Words of Wisdom; God, Can You Hear Me?; The Secret Language of Girlfriends; Space Between the Stars; Yoga Journal Magazine; Yoga as Medicine; Yoga Escapes; Red Cross*. Some of her *New York Times* best-sellers have been: *Cane River, Gettysburg, One Minute Millionaire, All the President's Children*, and *Missed Fortune*.

This information pertains to Stephanie Lee.

Born: August 6, 1976, Palo Alto, California.

Education: B.A. in English/Creative Writing (Fiction) from Stanford University.

Career history: I started interning here at Manus & Associates in college and never left!

Hobbies/personal interests: Crafting, crocheting, kitsch, obsessive blog-reading, eBay, pop-culture in general.

Categories/subjects that you are most enthusiastic about agenting: I like prescriptive nonfiction including women's issues, GenX/GenY issues, dating/relationships, and smart self-help served with humor, and narrative non-fiction, intriguing memoirs, popular science, popular culture, and young adult. Fiction interests include commercial literary fiction, women's fiction, chick-lit, multicultural fiction, edgy thrillers, young adult, and new voices.

What you don't want to agent: Poetry, science fiction, fantasy, romance, children's books.

If you were not an agent, what might you be doing instead: Running a magazine, or designing knitwear.

What's the best way for writers to solicit your interest: Write a killer query letter and sample/proposal that I just can't say no to. Also, do your research and make sure the agent you are submitting to accepts the type of book you are pitching.

Do you charge reading or management fees: No.

Can you provide an approximation by % of what you tend to represent by category: Non-Fiction: 70%, Fiction: 30%.

What are the most common mistakes writers make when pitching you: They forget to include their contact information and SASE, forget to include the title of their book, send me material that I don't represent, send full un-solicited manuscripts, provide too much or too little information in a query letter (you don't want to just give us a long, drawn-out, boring plot re-hash or a page with just one sentence on it, but you want to give us a concise and compelling pitch or teaser for your book).

How would you describe the client from Hell: Someone who can't respect/accept the fact that we have more than just one client :), someone who isn't a hard worker and just hopes that their book will magically succeed, someone who constantly fights the system instead of trying to work with it.

How would you describe the perfect client: Creative, professional, prolific, flexible, deadline-oriented, and NICE! Sending chocolate on Valentine's Day is also a plus.

How and why did you ever become an agent: Because I am completely and utterly addicted to books, and because I got lucky and found myself working for an awesome company.

What, if anything, can a writer do to increase the odds of you becoming his or her agent: Fiction: write the best book you can, hone your craft, really polish those opening pages, and create an mind-blowing query letter. If short-stories are in your blood, get published in journals! Do what you can to get your name out there. Non-fiction: do your research and make sure there is a market for your book, that your book fills a need, and that you are the best person in the world to write this book. Also do what you can to develop your platform and get your name out there, as an expert, a speaker, a columnist, anything.

How would you describe to someone (or thing) from another planet what it is that you do as an agent: I used to say that agenting was like treasure-hunting, but now it seems a little more like gardening. You set out to find a remarkable seedling, water it, prune it, talk to it, find the most ideal location for its kind and plant it there, and hopefully see it grow into something beautiful. Sometimes you find a fabulous tree that needs a nudge or a new sunny spot, sometimes you fall in love with a tiny seed and nurture it from the very beginning. This extended metaphor is getting a little crazy.

Do you have any particular opinions or impressions of editors and publishers in general: Publishing is a very business-minded arena, so more creative people can sometimes be surprised by this. A good agent will help guide you through.

What do you think the future holds for writers, publishers, and agents: Robots writing e-books about robots. I'm not sure. I would love to see more support for first fiction and short stories.

What are your favorite books, movies, TV shows, and why: I've only recently gotten cable TV. I'm a low-brow junky, apparently. I'm often watching/listening to Bravo, E!, and the Food Network. I know. Nobody will respect me now! I am very entertained and intrigued by the humor of human nature. I love films by Charlie Kauffman and Wes Anderson. They are about very quirky people and very quirky circumstances, yet so well-done and so engaging.

Please list representative titles you have sold: *Why You're Still Single* (Plume); *Tales from the Scale: Real Women Weigh in on Thunder Thighs, Cheese Fries, and Feeling Good…At Any Size* (Adams Media); *Avoiding Prison and Other Noble Vacation Goals: Adventures in Love and Danger* (Three Rivers Press); *I Can't Believe I'm Buying This Book: A Commonsense Guide to Successful Internet Dating* (Ten Speed Press); *Love Like That* (Red Dress

Ink); *Want Some Get Some* plus untitled second novel (Kensington); *Guerilla War for Extra Credit* (Dutton Children's).

This information pertains to Dena Fischer.

Born: 4/24/??; New York, NY.

Education: B.A., English Lit., UCLA, 1987.

Career history: Formerly a development/production executive in the film business in Los Angeles.

Categories/subjects that you are most enthusiastic about agenting: Literary fiction, mainstream fiction, narrative nonfiction, selected practical nonfiction in areas such as health, parenting, pop culture, social commentary, current events.

What you don't want to agent: Genre fiction, science fiction, romance, westerns, techno-thrillers, horror, fantasy, young adult.

What's the best way for writers to solicit your interest: An irresistible cover letter.

Do you charge reading or management fees: No.

Can you provide an approximation by % of what you tend to represent by category: Fiction: 50%, Non-Fiction: 50%.

Please list representative titles you have sold: *Lifeguarding: A Memoir of Secrets, Swimming and the South* (Harmony Books); *Baby Lists* (Adams Media); *ScreamFree Parenting: The Revolutionary Approach to Raising Your Kids by Keeping Your Cool* (Broadway Books); *Beauty & the Brain: The Doctors' Prescription for Inner & Outer Beauty* (Contemporary Books).

This information pertains to Jandy Nelson.

Born: November 25, 1965, New York.

Education: Cornell University B.A.; Brown University M.F.A.

Career history: I worked in the theater and academia before becoming a literary agent.

Hobbies/personal interests: Poetry, film, theater, travel, cooking, running, hiking, festivity.

Categories/subjects that you are most enthusiastic about agenting: Literary fiction, multi-cultural fiction, women's fiction, southern fiction, narrative nonfiction, memoir, health, popular science, politics, popular culture, women's issues, history, sophisticated self help.

What you don't want to agent: Children's, genre fiction, cookbooks.

If you were not an agent, what might you be doing instead: Teaching, climbing Everest, being a rock star!

What's the best way for writers to solicit your interest: Write a captivating pitch letter and send with: for fiction: the first 30 pages of a novel, for nonfiction: send a proposal. Always include an SASE for response.

Do you charge reading or management fees: No.

Can you provide an approximation by % of what you tend to represent by category: Non-Fiction: 60%, Fiction: 40%.

What are the most common mistakes writers make when pitching you: Call instead of writing, submitting work before it's ready.

How and why did you ever become an agent: I badgered Jillian Manus until she hired me. I became an agent to work with writers and to help bring books into the world that will move, enrich, inspire and delight.

What, if anything, can a writer do to increase the odds of you becoming his or her agent: Write a kickass book or proposal!

Do you have any particular opinions or impressions of editors and publishers in general: They are the wizards behind the curtains.

Please list representative titles you have sold: *Catfish & Mandala* (FSG); *The Mercy of Thin Air* (Atria); *Anything You Say Can and Will Be Used Against You* (Harper-Collins); *Lily Dale* (HarperSF); *The New Menopause Book* (Avery); *Geisha: A Life* (Atria); *The Territory of Men* (Random House); *The World of Normal Boys* (Kensington).

This information pertains to Penny Nelson.

Career history: I have had a varied career that has included science research and years in public radio as a producer and host. Now I have combined my interests and experience to become an literary agent representing non-fiction work.

Hobbies/personal interests: Martial arts, pop culture, and following socio-political trends.

Categories/subjects that you are most enthusiastic about agenting: I represent only non-fiction at this time, with a strong interest in current affairs/politics, social trends, and lifestyle/self help topics. It is very helpful if the author has strong professional credentials related to the material being presented. And, for self-help material, it is important that the author has an established platform.

What's the best way for writers to solicit your interest: Send a well-written query letter that clearly expresses the topic and the author's credentials.

Do you charge reading or management fees: No.

Please list representative titles you have sold: *The Jesus Machine* (St. Martin's Press); *The Fine Art of Small Talk* (Hyperion); *Where War Lives* (McClelland and Stewart); *The Best New York Sports Arguments* (Sourcebooks, Inc); *Confusing Love with Obsession* (Hazelden); *Se Habla Dinero: The Everyday Guide to Financial Success* (Wiley).

MARCH TENTH, INC.

4 Myrtle Street, Haworth, NJ 07641

201-387-6551 fax: 201-387-6552

e-mail: schoron@aol.com

Agent's name: Sandra Choron

Education: B.A., Lehman College.

Career history: Editor, Hawthorn Books, 1971–1979; Editor, Dell Publishing, 1979–1981; Founded March Tenth, Inc. in 1981.

Hobbies/personal interests: Reading, needlework, traveling.

Categories/subjects that you are most enthusiastic about agenting: Pop culture, especially music and leisure subjects; general non-fiction; literary fiction.

What you don't want to agent: Genre fiction, cookbooks, children's books, science.

If you were not an agent, what might you be doing instead: I would be a writer, of course.

What's the best way for writers to solicit your interest: Send me a nuts-and-bolts description of your work via e-mail or snail-mail.

Do you charge reading or management fees: No.

Can you provide an approximation by % of what you tend to represent by category: Non-Fiction: 90%, Fiction: 10%.

What are the most common mistakes writers make when pitching you: They hype their books by making unrealistic claims.

How would you describe the client from Hell: One who simply isn't ready for the realities of book publishing.

How would you describe the perfect client: Tall, dark . . .

How and why did you ever become an agent: As an editor, I felt limited by the tastes of the one publisher for whom I worked. Agenting allows me to pursue a wide range of subjects and books. I am a kid in a candy store!

What, if anything, can a writer do to increase the odds of you becoming his or her agent: Nothing, really; the work must speak for itself. But being responsive to guidance always helps.

How would you describe to someone (or thing) from another planet what it is that you do as an agent: To quote a famous predecessor:"I dash hopes."

Do you have any particular opinions or impressions of editors and publishers in general: Editors? Put four of 'em in a room and you'll get five opinions. Happily, no two are alike.

What do you think the future holds for writers, publishers, and agents: Technological advances have made publishing a far more democratic industry in recent years. It will become more and more difficult to separate the wheat from the chaff, which makes agenting all the more interesting and challenging. I look forward to it.

What are your favorite books, movies, TV shows, and why: I like reality TV, mostly for the live angst.

On a personal level, what do you think people like about you and dislike about you: People respond to my enthusiasm and to the fact that I believe that books should be fun to assemble. I'm sure there are people out there who don't like me; I have no idea what their problem is.

Please list representative titles you have sold: *Bruce Springsteen on Tour* (Bloomsbury); *The Art of Woody Guthrie* (Rizzoli); *The Annotated Grateful Dead Lyrics* (Dodd, Trist); *The 100 Simple Secrets* (series) (Harper San Francisco); *The Appalachians* (Random House).

DENISE MARCIL LITERARY AGENCY, INC.

156 Fifth Ave, Suite 625, New York, NY 10010

www.denisemarcilagency.com

Agents' names: Denise Marcil; Anne Marie O'Farrell, amof86@aol.com
The following information pertains to Denise Marcil.
Born: February 14–Valentine's Day, Troy, New York
Education: Skidmore College, B.A. English, with Honors
Career history: Avon Books, editorial assistant, Simon & Schuster, Inc., assistant editor, Denise Marcil Literary Agency, Inc., president.
Hobbies/personal interests: Ballroom dancing, theater, attending dance performances from contemporary to classic ballet, art history, travel, outdoor adventures, fly fishing.
Categories/subjects that you are most enthusiastic about agenting: Fiction: Women's fiction, thrillers, suspense. Nonfiction: Self-help, popular reference, business.
What you don't want to agent: Memoirs, sci-fi, children's books, political fiction or nonfiction, science.
If you were not an agent, what might you be doing instead: I can't imagine I'd ever find anything else I could feel so passionately about, but if I had to choose another career, I'd be a dancer or art history teacher.
What's the best way for writers to solicit your interest: With a well-written and compelling one-page query letter and SASE.
Do you charge reading or management fees: No.
Do you require any kind of upfront payments from your clients: No.
Can you provide an approximation by % of what you tend to represent by category: Fiction: 50%, Women's Fiction: 40%, Suspense: 10%, Children's: 0%, Non-Fiction: 50%, Self-Help: 35%, Business: 15%.
What are the most common mistakes writers make when pitching you: Never make a cold call, demand to speak with me, and pester my assistant long after she's

informed you on proper procedure. Never assume you are an exception to the rule.

How would you describe the client from Hell: This person is unprofessional, unwilling to learn, unable to take constructive criticism and refuses to adjust unrealistic expectations of the industry.

How would you describe the perfect client: He or she is appreciative of the work my staff and I do on his or her behalf. A dream client is professional, enthusiastic (but not overbearing) constantly at work refining his or her craft, and, most importantly, a talented and creative writer.

How and why did you ever become an agent: A book-lover and avid reader since childhood, I majored in English in college and pursued a publishing career. Following a few years working for publishers, a job offer by an agent opened that side of the business to me. I discovered I enjoyed selling which coincided with my talent for persuasion. Combined with my editorial skills, I discovered a career that became a passion and successful business.

What, if anything, can a writer do to increase the odds of you becoming his or her agent: We want to represent strong writers with fresh ideas. People who are professional, well-mannered, and polite always have a better chance of getting my attention. Do your homework to assure that I represent your type of book. Following-up is one thing, but no one likes a nagger.

How would you actually describe what you do for a living: I'm the author's business partner who guides, develops, and manages his/her writing career. I'm the advocate and cheerleader for the author and the liaison between the author and the publisher. I balance the author's expectations with the realities of the publishing industry.

What are your favorite books, movies, TV shows, and why: Books: *The Secret Life of Bees* by Sue Monk Kidd, Films: *March of the Penguins*

What do you think the future holds for writers, publishers, and agents: Like most businesses, publishing constantly changes as new technologies and new means of distribution evolve. The changes offer all stakeholders both opportunities and challenges. Authors will have more ways to self-publish their work; publishers will have to address how to protect authors' copyrights with the availability of books on the Internet, including Google's plan to scan 18 million books. Agents, authors, and publishers should work together to ensure the longevity of book publishing.

Do you have any particular opinions or impressions of editors and publishers in general: They market and distribute the author's work and play an invaluable role in an author's success. They're on the author's team.

On a personal level, what do you think people like about you and dislike about you: I think people like my generosity of spirit and my direct, honest, straight-forward manner. Perhaps some don't like my direct, straight-forward manner!

Please list representative titles you have sold: *Seaview Inn* by Sherryl Woods (Mira); *Trigger City* and *Big City, Bad Blood* by Sean Chercover (Morrow); *Red Cat* by Peter Spiegelman (Knopf); *The Baby Book* by Dr. William Sears, Martha Sears, R.N., Dr. Robert Sears, and Dr. James Sears (Little, Brown); The Vaccine Book by Dr. Robert Sears (Little, Brown); *The 10 Minute Body Makeover* by Sean Foy (Workman).

The following information pertains to Anne Marie O'Farrell.

Education: B.A. Queens College.

Career history: Director, Westwinds Learning Center; executive producer, New York Dinner Theater; agent, Denise Marcil Literary Agency, Inc. since 1986.

Hobbies/personal interests: Biking, traveling, reading, tennis, personal growth.

Categories/subjects that you are most enthusiastic about agenting: Business, personal growth, spirituality/New Age and theater.

What's the best way for writers to solicit your interest: One page query letter and SASE with any other relevant credentials sent directly to my office at Anne Marie O'Farrell, 86 Dennis Street, Manhasset, NY 11030.

Do you charge reading or management fees: No.

How and why did you ever become an agent: I find it extremely fulfilling to help bring new ideas, information and creativity into the world that helps improve and expans humanity's understanding and quality of life.

Do you have any particular opinions or impressions of editors and publishers in general: I love to work with people who are passionate about their ideas, who love to think outside the box and are open to brainstorming.

Please list representative titles you have sold: *Seth Speaks, the Nature of Personal Reality* (New World Library); *Hell Yes: The Secrets to a life of Joy and Ease* (Andrews McMeel); *Without a Doubt: A Cogniive Therapy Program for Eliminating Doubt and Building Confidence* (Perigee); *Twinkle, Twinkle Little Star* (Charlesbridge); *Out of Body Adventures* (McGraw Hill); *Parental Alienation and Intervention* (Rowman and Littlefield).

MARTIN LITERARY MANAGEMENT

321 High School Road NE, Suite D-3, #316, Bainbridge, WA 98110

206-201-3504   206-201-3506 (fax on request only, please—save a tree)

17328 Ventura Blvd., Suite 138, Encino, CA 91316

818-595-1130   fax: on request only

www.MartinLiteraryManagement.com

Agent's name: Sharlene L. Martin, Sharlene@MartinLiteraryManagement.com; Ginny Weissman

Born: Feb 8th—I'm an Aquarius; New Haven, Connecticut.

Education: B.A., University of Bridgeport, UCLA School of Entertainment.

Career history or story: I've always been highly eclectic and entrepreneurial. And although I began working for American Airlines right out of college (I had wanderlust), I became one of 12 nationwide recruiters for flight attendants and was pleased to hire the first males there. I had a great office in the Chrysler Building in NYC and enjoyed giving people a chance to change their lives at 35,000 feet.

I left AAL to start the nation's first American Nanny Agency—Helping Hands, Inc. The universe seemed to pat that endeavor on the back; I won "Entrepreneur of the Year" from *Entrepreneur Magazine*, and Small Businessperson of the Year from the Chamber of Commerce.

In 1989 I sold the company to a competitor, and moved to California. I started a production company with a former network journalist/broadcaster, and was an independent producer for a number of years, in addition to doing freelance Casting for independent and feature films. Because of that experience, I was invited to join a reality television production company and spent time doing acquisitions and talent management. It was there that I realized my love of the "business" wasn't about show business—it was about working with passionate and skilled writers. I soon left to start Martin Literary Management. The lovely success that has followed seems a natural result of the fact that I've never been happier in any line of work.

Hobbies, interests: Reading novels on weekends (I read nonfiction all day for work), hiking, visiting my grown kids in Seattle (8 miles across Puget Sound by ferry), great food and occasional travel, provided that it's First Class and Four Stars! Yes, I am a material girl. You will catch me camping out on the same day that you… oh, forget it. It's not going to happen.

Subjects & categories you are interested in agenting, including fiction & non-fiction: Non-Fiction ONLY. I love great, narrative non-fiction that is adaptable to film. Within that category, I do meaningful Memoirs, fun Pop Culture subjects, True Crime books, Business books, How-To books along with Self-Help (Prescriptive) books provided that they are original in tone and do not re-hash familiar material. And of course, I love doing celebrity bios. My New York agent, Ronnie Gramazio, handles all of our fiction work, and Ginny Weissman is our Mind, Body, and Spirit agent.

Subjects & categories writers shouldn't even bother pitching to you: NO Fiction for me—only nonfiction. Also, for similar reasons: NO art books, poetry, essays, or short stories. I regret having to say this, and know that it is discouraging to some writers. You must not give up your work, or your search for representation, if you work in the long forms. However, if you do articles, essays or short stories, I strongly advise you to represent yourself. Just use a clear and concise query letter to editors whom you address by name after learning something of their past work. Impeccable manners help you, even when you are not aware of it. Trust them. People who convince writers to "stand out" by being confrontational or self-pitying in their presentation are giving terrible advice.

MOST OF ALL: I don't want anything to do with a neurotic author. If you are crazy, that's not necessarily a problem, just try to hide it. You don't need to fix your problems before I will represent your work, but you do have to keep them away from me. I run a considerate agency with a mandate to treat people as we would wish to be treated, but I draw the line at tolerating any author who tries to put me in a position of fixing his or her life. There are a disappointing number of such people. Professionalism, like the use of good manners, helps you in ways you may never even see, but which are real.

What would you do if you weren't agenting: Sorry, no time to think about it!

What's the best way for non-fiction writers to solicit your interest: Send me an email (no hard copy letters) with a great query letter. You must learn HOW TO WRITE a query letter if you want to be taken seriously. There are plenty of good books on the market that will tell you how. Put all of your query into the BODY of the email (no attachments due to virus risk). If your query is compelling, we will quickly respond with a request for the manuscript or book proposal. Please, no hard copies. We're only dealing electronically these days. If you don't have a computer, you can't be a writer in the 21st century. Electronic writing is essential—especially when editing your book with a publisher.

Do you charge reading or any upfront fees: No.

In your experience, what are the most common pitching mistakes writers make: BIGGEST MISTAKE: Calling to pitch over the phone. No! "Just wanted to see if you have any interest first…" No! I can't tell how well you write by the sound of your voice. When you take the time to do it right, that sends the signal that you can read and follow directions, which will be of utmost importance to your publishing editor if you're lucky enough to land one. HATE IT when authors send unsolicited attachments that take forever to download. Failure to address me personally in your query: what, I'm supposed to respect your SPAM? And finally: If you have not run spell check, then you have just told me to turn and run away from you, no matter what words you use in your letter.

Describe the client from Hell, even if you don't have any: I really don't have any (anymore), which the testimonials on my website will support. But I suppose it could manifest in any form wherein a writer becomes an energy vortex and attempts to suck time and energy from you when you are already working at capacity. I don't know what can be done with such clueless and self-absorbed people except to cut and run, because in my experience it makes no difference how many times you explain it to them, they always think that their concerns and their problems are exceptions to the rule.

What's your definition of a great client: The writer who understands that my time is valuable and does not waste it. The writer is willing to spend money on a professional editor if needed, or a publicist to ensure the best outcome of our team effort. This person knows that I won't send anything out for submission until it is absolutely ready, and this writer understands that the policy is in THEIR own best interest, whether or not it pleases their desire for instant gratification. That ideal writer has a reasonable sense of gratitude to their editor and publisher for giving them the chance to shine in a highly competitive arena, and hopefully to me, after I secure them a book deal.

How can writers increase the odds that you will offer representation: DO YOUR RESEARCH. Invest the time in checking the sites of any agent who will receive your query. Spamming is for idiots. If you have checked it out and know that your work is within the parameters of the things I represent, just write that great query letter I keep mentioning. It WILL be received, it WILL be read, and my agency WILL respond to you. If we are interested, we respond right away. If the work is wrong for us, you will know within a few weeks, at the worst, and usually much less. And finally, DO NOT CALL me on the phone to pitch me—I'm busy selling my clients' work!

Why did you become an agent, and how did you become one: The "why" is simple: I love the written word. Although I was editor of my high school literary magazine, I never realized my passion for books until later in my career. My mate, Anthony Flacco, was already a published author when we met. I fell in love with him—sight unseen—over his written words. We met 15 years ago when I optioned one of his screenplays during my time as an independent producer. After learning a few of his past horror stories with slippery agents, I vowed to be the agent he never had, and to be the same for all my other clients as well. And by the way, I've sold three books for him in the past three years! I want to make a difference in writers' lives by helping them realize their dreams. It's how I realize my own, and this is the path that gets me to that place.

Describe to someone from another planet what you do as an agent: I represent wonderful writers and help to make their literary dreams come true. I do lots of reading, plenty of persuasive selling, and creative career counseling.

How do you feel about editors and publishers: I have always believed that if you cannot love and admire them, then you should please get out of the publishing game. I cannot imagine how they keep up with their work loads, and most of the ones that I've worked with are really smart, curious and interesting people.

How do you feel about writers: I stand in awe of the abilities of the finest among them, people who conjure wonderful phrases and weave imaginative tapestries that most of us would be baffled in attempting to do. The lengths to which they are will to go in order to advance their work can be astonishing. With those writers who deserve the title "author," I take inspiration from their love of the written word when they will pour countless hours and sometimes many years in the quest to perfect their craft. I find it easy to work long and hard for such people.

What do you see in the near future for book publishing: The great unanswered question revolves around self-publishing for the internet, and the truth is that nobody knows. So far, what we can confirm is that self-publishing is certainly not the albatross around a book's neck that it once was. The term "vanity press" is going out of style. I myself have taken on clients who have self-published, met with moderate success and online, and wanted to "go mainstream." One got a book contract for six figures. Now, I do not believe that self-publishing can ever take the place of a mainstream publishing industry, because SOMEBODY has to slog through the avalanche of self-serving nonsense that many people put out in hopes of gaining a lucrative contract with minimal effort. The mainstream publishing business has industry readers to do that. Believe me, you don't want that task dumped on an unsuspecting public.

What are your favorite books/TV shows/movies, and why: TV: *Grey's Anatomy*, *Entourage*, *Medium*, THE RICHES, and almost anything on the Discovery Channel. BOOKS: *The Glass Castle*, by Jeanette Walls, *The Devil Wears Prada*, by Lauren Weisberger, *The Devil in the White City*, by Erik Larson, *The Kite Runner*, by Khaled Hosseini, and *The Last Nightingale*, by Anthony Flacco.

In your opinion, what do editors think of you: I KNOW that they consider me someone who respects their commitment and their boundaries, and who will not approach them with a manuscript or proposal unless I have carefully determined that they would be a good publishing house for that particular piece of work! And, they know when they get a proposal from me, it's a polished, well crafted piece of writing.

On a personal non-professional level, what do you think people think of you: If they like supportive people who make their own dreams come true by making the dreams of others their concern, then I think that they generally like me just fine. Most say my middle name is "Tenacious."

What are some representative titles that you have sold: *Tiny Dancer* by Anthony Flacco (St. Martin's); *But You Knew That Already* by Dougall Fraser (Rodale); *Front of the Class* by Brad Cohen (VanderWyck& Burnham); *Success Within* by Felicia Wysocky (Champion Press); *You'll Never Nanny in This Town Again* by Suzanne Hansen (Crown, Random House); *Secrets of Voice-Over Success* by Joan Baker (Sentient); *Take Command* by Kelly Perdew (Regnery); *Shopportunity* by Kate Newlin (Collins Business); *Everybody Wants Your Money* by David Latko (Collins Business); *A Place to Go, A Place to Grow* by Lou Dantzler (Rodale); *The Tabloid Prodigy* by Marlise Kast (Running Press); *The Last Nightingale* by Anthony Flacco (Ballantine); *Seven Myths of Modern Judaism* by Rabbi Art Blecher (Palgrave); *Making the Connection* by Leslie Sanchez (Palgrave); *Winning Nice* by Dawna Stone (Center Street); *Getting Sober* by Kelly Madigan (McGraw Hill); *My Horse, My Partner* by Lisa Wysocky (Lyons Press); *Secret Cyber Lives* by Candice Kelsey (Marlowe); *An Unfinished Canvas* by Phyllis Gobbell and Mike Glasgow (Berkley Publishing); *Stop the Misery* by Dr. Stan Kapuchinski (HCI); *Smotherhood* by Amanda Lamb (Globe Pequot/SKIRT); *Low Carb Reading* by John Heath and Lisa Adams (Sourcebooks); *Hot Flashes with a Cool Beat* by Janet Horn and Robin Miller (New Harbinger); *Humble Little Condom* by Anne Morriss (Prometheus); *Prince of Darkness* by Alan Weisman (Sterling); *Truth at Last* by Lyndon Barsten and John Larry Ray (Lyons Press); *Fur Shui* by Paula Brown (Lyons Press); *Deadly Dose* by Amanda Lamb (Berkley/Penguin); *Street Guide to Scholarships* by Kimberly Ann Stezala (Amacom); *Metaphysics of Fat* by Catherine Poole (Llewellyn); *Face It* by Babak Azizzadeh and Doug Hamilton (Wiley); *River of No Return* by Jeffrey Ford (Cumberland); *The Bridge* by Michael Glasgow (Thomas Nelson); *If I Did It* by Goldman Family (Beaufort); *Passion Brands* by Kate Newlin (Prometheus); *Smart Mama's Green Guide* by Jennifer Taggert (Center Street); *Crossroads* by Martin Cheek (Amacom); *I'm Sorry I Missed, Mr. President* by Geri Spieler (Palgrave); *Happily Ever After* by Jessica Bram (HCI); *The BreakUp Chronicles* by Lisa Steadman (Adams Media); *Changing the Odds* by Susan Neuman (Praeger); *Of Wicked Intention* by Kevin Flynn (New Horizon); *The Hidden Man* by Anthony Flacco (Ballantine).

The following information pertains to Ginny Weissman: Mind, Body, Spirit Division.

Born: Nov. 17th—I'm a Scorpio. Chicago, Ilinois.

Education: Northeastern Illinois University.

Career history or story: Ginny Weissman began her career as a journalist at *The Chicago Tribune*. During her eleven-year tenure at the *Tribune*, she held a variety of management positions including editor of the *TV Week* magazine (circulation 1.2 million). She interviewed hundreds of celebrities and wrote personality profiles and articles about the importance of family programming. She is the author of two critically acclaimed, best-selling books, *The Dick Van Dyke Show, Anatomy of a Classic* (St. Martin's Press) and *Champagne Music, The Lawrence Welk Show* (St. Martin's Press). As an adjunct professor at Northwestern University, Ginny taught writing for film and television. She believed that the future of the entertainment industry would be determined by the work of today's students and taught ethics and responsibility along with technique. Her numerous television credits include *Investigative Reports, American Justice*, and *The Unexplained* for A&E, *Wrath of God* for The History Channel, *Chicago's Lifeline* for The Discovery Health Channel and *Highway to Heaven* starring Michael Landon for NBC. Ginny was the Supervising Producer and Director for two Emmy Award-winning children's PBS specials and music videos featuring Gaia who sings while performing American Sign Language. She also wrote and produced an Emmy-nominated documentary, *Magic by the Lake: The Edgewater Beach Hotel*, for the PBS series, *Chicago Stories*. In addition, she was a producer for the PBS magazine series, *Chicago Tomorrow*.

Humanitarian work plays a large part in Ginny's life. After the terrorist attacks on September 11th, Ginny organized fundraisers for the ASPCA Disaster Fund and Canine Rescue effort. After a trip to Peru, she organized a Christmas toy drive for the children living in poverty near the mountains of Machu Picchu. She is known for her valued, long-time commitment to nonprofit organizations such as the Easter Seal Society and served as co host for their annual telethons for fifteen years. The Easter Seal Society honored her with the "Communications Award" for outstanding public service supporting the needs and rights of persons with disabilities. She was honored again by The Easter Seal Society with the "Outstanding Service Award" for fifteen years of dedication and service. Ginny also was the recipient of the Mother Theodore Guerin High School McManus Alumna Award which honors an outstanding graduate who has "distinguished herself in service to the community and achievement in her career." Ginny served for eight years on the Board of Governors for the Chicago/Midwest Chapter of the National Academy of Television Arts & Sciences and was elected second vice-president. She has served as a judge for the Emmy Awards, the Humanitas Prize, a prestigious national award for television writing and Script, a film writing competition held by the Illinois and Chicago Film Offices. She co-founded Windy City West and hosted ten annual parties for transplanted Chicagoans working in the Hollywood entertainment industry, and produced a television special about Windy City West for NBC 5 in Chicago.

Hobbies, interests: I am an animal advocate. I rescue cats and find them good homes. I like to watch movies, mostly romantic comedies, especially about time travel. I exercise everyday. My work leaves me very little time for anything but catching up on my reading.

Subjects & categories you are interested in agenting, including fiction & non-fiction: Non-Fiction ONLY. I head up the Mind, Body, Spirit Division which is my favorite genre to read. I am looking for authors who have had life-changing experiences, have a strong platform and want to make a difference in the world.

Subjects & categories writers shouldn't even bother pitching to you: NO Fiction. I don't represent novels or children's books even if they are spiritually based. MOST OF ALL: I am not looking for authors who are trying to publish their journals after years of therapy.

What would you do if you weren't agenting: Producing documentaries (my previous career), volunteering at an animal shelter or sitting under a palm tree in Maui.

What's the best way for fiction writers to solicit your interest: Ronnie Gramazio in our NYC office handles fiction for MLM.

What's the best way for non-fiction writers to solicit your interest: Send me an e-mail with a great query letter. You must learn HOW TO WRITE a query letter if you want to be taken seriously. There are plenty of good books on the market that will tell you how. Put all of your query into the BODY of the e-mail—no attachments (virus risk). If your query is compelling, we will quickly respond with a request for the book proposal.

Do you charge reading or any upfront fees: No.

In your experience, what are the most common pitching mistakes writers make: Calling to pitch over the phone. No! "Just wanted to see if you have any interest first…" No! Please take the time to do it right. That sends the signal that you can read and follow directions, which will be of utmost importance to your publishing editor, if you're lucky enough to land one. HATE IT when authors send unsolicited attachments. I will not download them. Failure to address me personally in your query or include me in a mass mailing. And finally: If you have not run spell check, you have told me to turn and run, no matter what words you use in your letter.

Describe the client from Hell, even if you don't have any: I have fired two clients who have lied to me and misrepresented themselves. I will NOT tolerate anything but full disclosure and complete honesty in a working relationship.

What's your definition of a great client: That writer understands that my time is valuable and does not waste it. The writer is willing to spend money on a professional editor if needed, or a publicist to ensure the best outcome of our team effort. This person knows that I won't send anything out for submission until it is absolutely ready, and this writer understands that the policy is in THEIR own best interest, whether or not it pleases their desire for instant gratification. That ideal writer has a reasonable sense of gratitude to their editor and publisher for giving them the chance to shine in a highly competitive arena, and hopefully to me, after I secure them a book deal. Also, the writer must be willing to work as hard at writing and promoting the book as I do to sell it.

How can writers increase the odds that you will offer representation: DO YOUR RESEARCH. Invest the time in checking out our website before you send your query letter (by e-mail only) and be sure that you know what genre I represent. I am not going to read your query for your novel or children's book or an "idea you are thinking of writing about." And finally, DO NOT call me on the phone to pitch me—I'm busy selling my clients' work! We will respond to your query letter by e-mail.

Why did you become an agent, and how did you become one: Sharlene Martin and I have known each other for over 15 years. We have similar backgrounds as TV producers. In November, 2007, she asked me to join Martin Literary Management as the Head of the new Mind, Body, Spirit Division. I had been managing an author and thought it was a perfect fit to take on additional clients. I also like that we are a management company as well, which means we don't stop after selling our client's book. We help our clients continue to build their platform for promoting their book and look for opportunities for film and TV, speaking engagements and future books.

Describe to someone from another planet what you do as an agent: I take someone who has a compelling life experience or a professional background that makes them an expert in a certain field and help them translate that information into a book and platform that will be of interest to a publisher.

How do you feel about editors and publishers: I have found them to be accessible and courteous and willing to give feedback about what the like and don't like in our client's proposal, and also what subjects they are interested in for their own "lists."

How do you feel about writers: I started my career as a writer and editor for the Chicago Tribune and have written throughout my career including for television. I also have two published books with St. Martin's Press, *The Dick Van Dyke Show* and *Champagne Music* so they are "my people."

What do you see in the near future for book publishing: I think at this time on the planet when information travels around the world in seconds, traditional publishing seems behind the times. It is difficult to keep a nonfiction book timely when it will not get published for 12-18 months after it is written. I hope that print on demand technology and innovative marketing can speed up that process.

What are your favorite books/TV shows/movies, and why: TV: My guilty pleasures are: *Desperate Housewives, Dancing with the Stars, Ugly Betty* and *Deal or No Deal*. Books: *Eat, Pray, Love* by Elizabeth Gilbert, *Living an Uncommon Life* by John St. Augustine and anything by Shirley MacLaine or Julia Cameron or Wayne Dyer. Movies: *It's a Wonderful Life, The Way We Were, Hairspray* and most romantic comedies and time travel movies. I love to cry and fall in love with the characters. I have no interest in today's silly comedies or high-tech movies.

In your opinion, what do editors think of you: I am fortunate that I have Sharlene Martin's reputation preceding me since she is so well liked and respected, so I am fortunate that some of that spills over on to me.

On a personal non-professional level, what do you think people think of you: I have always made friends easily and have many life-long friendships. I also still keep in touch with colleagues who I have worked with decades ago so I think I can safely say I am easy to get along with and well-liked.

E. J. MCCARTHY AGENCY

1104 Shelter Bay Ave., Mill Valley, CA 94941

212-832-3428   fax: 212-829-9610

Agent's name: Mr. E. J. McCarthy

Education: Fairfield College Preparatory School, Fairfield, CT; Fordham University, New York, NY, Bachelor of Arts degree in English.

Career history: Started as editorial assistant in 1988 at Doubleday Book Clubs, editor at Dell Publishing; former executive editor, Presidio Press (Ballantine/Random House). Currently owner of E. J. McCarthy Agency.

Hobbies/personal interests: Media matters, politics and public policy, books, newspapers, magazines, talk radio and sports radio, music of all kinds, television, movies (mostly documentaries), travel, hiking, running, tennis, golf, baseball fan (Giants, A's, and Mets).

Categories/subjects that you are most enthusiastic about agenting: Literary fiction and nonfiction, politics, history, biography, memoir, media, sports, military history.

What you don't want to agent: Science fiction, horror, romance, young adult.

If you were not an agent, what might you be doing instead: I would like to own and operate a publishing house.

What's the best way for writers to solicit your interest: Send an e-mail query to ejmagency@gmail.com.

Do you charge reading or management fees: No, I do not charge reading fees or try to sell non-agent services, nor do I require any kind of upfront payments.

Can you provide an approximation by % of what you tend to represent by category: Fiction: 5%; Nonfiction: 95%. Twelve titles weres sold last year. 99.9% rejection rate.

What are the most common mistakes writers make when pitching you: Not getting right to the point having to do with what their book is about. Sending material single-spaced, double sided. Using paper clips, staples, and those big black clips to separate chapters. Forget to number the pages consecutively—or worse, sending a double-sided manuscript without page numbers. Those who don't know the audience or market for their book ("anyone who reads" doesn't cut it). Neglect to tell me that the project has already been submitted to other agents or to publishers. Expect a response within a day or two. Forget to tell me about author's unique credentials.

How would you describe the client from Hell: An author who expects miracles as far as publisher promotion, one who has an unrealistic sense of what an agent can do to get a publisher to promote and market their book. An author with an overblown ego. One who sends angry e-mails, or too many e-mails (sometimes a friendly phone call will work wonders). An author who asks "is it my job or your job" questions, for example: "why should I solicit author blurbs, isn't that the agent's job?"

How would you describe the perfect client: Someone responsible, hard working, patient, grateful for how well things are going (and if they're not, gentle suggestions on how to improve things), polite, responsive, friendly, willing to do whatever it takes to help the book project in any way. A sense of humor is good. And one who refers other promising authors to me—probably the best compliment of all.

How and why did you ever become an agent: I wanted to be an agent for many years, essentially when I began my career in book publishing. I believed that I would be a good agent because I loved working with authors, and was a passionate advocate for them as an editor. I knew I would enjoy the independence of being an agent. I was confident in my ability to reach a variety of editorial boards at many different publishing houses. In June 2003 the time had come: I felt that I was knowledgeable about the book publishing business, and I couldn't imagine doing anything else. I was lucky that I knew many excellent agents and book publishing people—I met and consulted with several of them before I officially opened shop.

What, if anything, can a writer do to increase the odds that you will become his or her agent: Follow up the initial submission in about a week or ten days with a phone call. If you don't hear from me quickly, please don't worry—I get several thousand queries each year. An occasional nudge is most welcomed. Please consult books and websites dedicated to writing book proposals (such as Jeff Herman's *Write the Perfect Book Proposal*) before you send anything out. Know your audience, the market, know other successful titles in your subject area. Make sure you communicate to me what your credentials are, and if you know any famous or noted authors, respected public figures, or other experts in your field who might provide you with a prepublication endorsement. Have realistic expectations.

How would you describe to someone (or thing) from another planet what it is that you do as an agent: I work with prospective authors to find the right editor and publisher for their books. I endeavor to ensure that all goes well regarding contracts, payments, royalties, and any important issues regarding the author and publisher. I also spend a lot of time reading and rejecting material.

Do you have any particular opinions or impressions of editors and publishers in general: I respect and admire them. I was an editor for many years; I know it is a demanding job with modest financial compensation. But it has great rewards: i.e., playing an integral role in the editing and publishing of a great book is a wonderful feeling, one you won't forget for the rest of your life. We wouldn't have great books without great editors and great publishers.

Please list representative titles you have sold: *The Sling and the Stone* by Thomas X. Hammes (Motorbooks); *One Bullet Away* by Nathaniel Fick (Houghton Mifflin); *Playing the Enemy's Game* by Keith Nolan (Motorbooks); *Blood Stripes* by David J. Danelo (Stackpole), *The Border* by David J. Danelo (Stackpole); *Slaughter at Goliad* by Jay Stout (Naval Institute Press); *Rage Company* by Thomas Daly (John Wiley & Sons); *The Unforgiving Minute* by Craig Mullaney (Penguin Press).

MENDEL MEDIA GROUP LLC

115 West 30th Street, Suite 800, New York, NY 10001

646-239-9896 fax: 212-695-4717

www.mendelmedia.com e-mail: scott@mendelmedia.com

Agent's name: Scott Mendel, Managing Partner

Born: New York

Education: A.B., Bowdoin College (Brunswick, Maine), M.A., University of Chicago, Ph.D. (ABD), University of Chicago

Career history: With a background in academia, Scott Mendel has worked in publishing since the early 1990s, first as a magazine editor and freelance technical writer and then as an Associate and, ultimately, the Vice President and Director of the late Jane Jordan Browne's Chicago-based literary agency. In November 2002, he opened the Mendel Media Group in New York. Scott holds a bachelor's degree, Summa cum laude, from Bowdoin College in Brunswick, Maine. He earned a master's degree in English language and literature from the University of Chicago, and is completing his Ph.D. at that institution, with a doctoral dissertation on American Yiddish literature and the meaning of the category, "American literature." Scott has taught literature, English, and Yiddish at a number of institutions, including the Choate-Rosemary Hall Preparatory School in Connecticut, the Hyde Park Cluster of Theological Seminaries in Chicago, Bowdoin College, the University of Chicago, and the University of Illinois at Chicago, where he most recently held an appointment as Lecturer in Jewish Studies. He wrote the book *A Prosecutor's Guide to Hate Crime*, which was published through a grant from the U.S. Department of Justice, and which has been in print in new editions for several years. He has been the Managing Editor of a monthly and quarterly health care magazine, *Positively Aware*, and editor of the Maine literary journal, *The Quill*, which began publishing in 1897. Scott has written a produced play, several works of fiction, and many book columns, news articles, and opinion pieces. He is a member of the Association of Authors' Representatives, the Author's Guild, the Mystery Writers of America, the Romance Writers of America, the Society of Children's Book Writers & Illustrators, the Modern Language Association, and the American Association of University Professors.

Categories/subjects that you are most enthusiastic about agenting: History, narrative non-fiction, current affairs, biography, politics, popular culture. Smart literary and commercial fiction.

If you were not an agent, what might you be doing instead: I was a college instructor for a number of years before becoming an agent. I'd still be doing that.

What's the best way for writers to solicit your interest: Please follow the procedure below. If we want to read more, we'll ask for it by email or phone. If you would like a response, in the event we can't take on your project or don't want to read more, you should include a pre-addressed return mailer with sufficient return postage already affixed for the return of your materials—or just include a standard self-addressed stamped envelope, in which case we'll respond with a note but discard the submitted materials. Please do not send inquiries by e-mail or fax. Fiction queries: If you have a novel you would like to submit, please send the first twenty pages and a synopsis by regular post to the address above, along with a detailed letter about your publication history and the history of the project, if it has been submitted previously to publishers or other agents. Non-fiction queries: If you have a completed nonfiction book proposal and sample chapters, you should mail those by regular post to the address above, along with a detailed letter about your publication history and the history of the project, if it has been submitted previously to publishers or other agents.

Do you charge reading or management fees: No.

Can you provide an approximation by % of what you tend to represent by category: My literary agency's clientele includes both fiction writers and nonfiction writers, the latter group comprised mainly of professional journalists and very senior academics writing for the broadest possible trade readership and author-experts writing prescriptive books. On the nonfiction side, I am usually interested in compelling works on history, current events, Jewish topics, personal finance and economics, show business, health, mass culture, sports, politics, science and biography that I believe will find both a wide readership and critical admiration. I represent a number of people who work in the media, generally in the news business.

What are the most common mistakes writers make when pitching you: Instead of going to www.mendelmedia.com/FAQ, they call to ask questions about how to send a query. A surprising number of aspiring writers pitch projects that have been unsuccessfully shopped to numerous houses already, so I always ask if a project has already been submitted to and rejected by publishers. Also, we are pitched projects every day by authors who have work we can't help them with: the agency does not represent children's picture books, cozy mystery novels, poetry, drama, screenplays, or any prescriptive nonfiction projects for which the author does not have established professional expertise and/or media credentials.

How would you describe the perfect client: There are as many "dream" clients as there are writers, I think. I like working for clients who are focused on practical career-related matters. Nothing is less impressive to me than a lack of clear focus on goals and expectations, so my dream clients are clear with me and with themselves about what they want to accomplish. I want to be challenged by my clients work, by their writing, and not by the drama of everyday life.

Please list representative titles you have sold: first-time novelist Wade Rubenstein, *Gullboy* (Counterpoint Press/Perseus); comedian/screenwriter/novelist Adam Felber, *Schrödinger's Ball* (Villard/Random House); World Trade Center and Jewish Museum Berlin master architect Daniel Libeskind, *Breaking Ground: Adventures in Life and Architecture* (Riverhead/Penguin and numerous publishers around the world); Hoover Institution Senior Fellow and Stanford University professor Larry Diamond, *Squandered Victory: The Story of the Bungled U.S. Attempt to Build Democracy in Iraq* (Times Books/Henry Holt) and Universal Democracy (Times Books/Henry Holt); University of Chicago Professor Robert A. Pape, *Dying to Win: The Strategic Logic of Suicide Ter-*

rorism (Random House); Dovid Katz, Ph.D., *Words on Fire: The Unfinished Story of Yiddish* (Basic Books); Behzad Yaghmaian, Ph.D., *Embracing the Infidel: Stories of Muslim Migrants on the Journey West* (Delacorte/Bantam Dell); National Public Radio national news anchor Nora Raum, *Surviving Personal Bankruptcy* (Gotham/Penguin); Annie Sprinkle, Ph.D., *Dr. Sprinkle's Spectacular Sex: Make Over Your Love Life with One of the World's Great Experts on Sex* (Tarcher/Penguin; Goldmann/Random House); Active Parenting founder Michael Popkin, Ph.D., *Parenting the Spirited Child* (Touchstone Fireside/Simon & Schuster); Anne-Marie Cusac, the George Polk and Project Censored Award-winning longtime investigative journalist at The Progressive magazine, *Cruel & Unusual: Punishment in America* (Yale University Press); June Skinner Sawyers, *The Beatles: Alone and Together* (Penguin); Best-selling celebrity biographer Mark Bego, *Piano Man: The Life and Times of Billy Joel,* (Chamberlain Bros../Penguin); Lisa Rogak, *The Man Behind the DaVinci Code: An Unauthorized Biography of Dan Brown* (Andrews McMeel in the US, and many other publishers around the world); Dr. Robert Atkins: *The True Story of the Man Behind the War on Carbohydrates* (Chamberlain Bros./Penguin; UK, Robson Books; Spanish, Random House Mondadori Mexico); and *No Happy Endings: The Life of Shel Silverstein* (St. Martin's Press); Dave DeWitt, the bestselling cookbook author, *The Spicy Food Lover's Bible* (Stewart Tabori & Chang); Ray "Dr. BBQ" Lampe, *Dr. BBQ's Big Time Barbeque: Recipes, Secrets and Tall Tales of a BBQ Champion* (St. Martin's Press); Long-time Kiplinger's Personal Finance real estate writer Elizabeth Razzi, *The Fearless Home Buyer and The Fearless Home Seller* (Stewart Tabori & Chang); Novelty and gift book packager Ray Strobel of Strobooks LLC, *The Panda Principles: A Black Eye isn't the End of the World* (Andrews McMeel); Paulette Wolf & Jodi Wolf, proprietors of the top-shelf event planning firm PWE-E, *Event Planning Made Easy: 7 Simple Steps to Making Your Business or Private Event a Huge Success* (McGraw Hill); Joanne Jacobs, longtime education writer at the *San Jose Mercury News*, *Our School* (Palgrave Macmillan).

THE MENZA-BARRON AGENCY

511 Avenue of the Americas, New York, NY 10001

212-889-6850

Agents' names: Claudia Menza, Manie Barron

Categories/subjects that you are most enthusiastic about agenting: Menza: African American fiction (literary or commercial), and African American non-fiction. Barron: African American fiction, especially thrillers and paranormal fiction, and African American narrative non-fiction.

What's the best way for writers to solicit your interest: Menza: Query letter with SASE, by snail mail. Barron: Query letter with SASE and a 2-chapter sample by snail mail.

Do you charge reading or management fees: No.

MEWS BOOKS, LTD.

20 Bluewater Hill, Westport, CT 06880

203-227-1836   fax: 203-227-1144

Agents' names: Sidney B. Kramer; Fran Pollack, Assoc.

Education: New York University, Brooklyn Law School, St. Lawrence University, JD.

Career history: (One of three) founders of Bantam Books; senior vice president (22 years), founder and managing director of Bantam's London subsidiary, Corgi Books; president, New American Library (formerly Penguin Books); consultant and manager, Cassell and Collier MacMillan, London; president and owner of Remarkable Bookshop, Westport, CT; president of Mews Books Ltd.; literary agent and attorney (NY and CT Bar specializing in literary matters).

Categories/subjects that you are most enthusiastic about agenting: Children's books, all ages that are creative, charming, self-sufficient prose suited to a stated age group. We want professional work even from first timers; medical and scientific non-fiction, technical and for the layman; cookery; parenting; college text and reference works; non-fiction all subjects; fiction all categories but must be outstanding in their genre for plot and writing.

What you don't want to agent: All subjects badly written.

What's the best way for writers to solicit your interest: Must have an outline of the work in a page or two in enough detail (but not too much) so that an editor can pick up the story at any point in the manuscript. No cliff hangers like "The reader ill be delighted with the new turn of events, everything turns out well." Don't ask us for editorial advice. We want professional work. Give your background and accreditation and market estimate in a separate statement. Send all material by snail mail, not e-mail. Do not send manuscript unless requested. SASE. We want to know if the work has been submitted elsewhere and with what results. We ask for an exclusive while reading so that we don't spin our wheels and duplicate efforts by others (occasional exceptions for established authors). Tell us if you have been published. (Priority) pending contracts will be reviewed and negotiated.

Do you charge reading or management fees: No reading fees. If we accept your work we do charge for duplication and some direct office overhead incurred in processing, usually less than $100.

Can you provide an approximation by % of what you tend to represent by category: Fiction: 20%, Children's: 40%, Non-Fiction: 20%, Other: 20%.

What are the most common mistakes writers make when pitching you: Unclear presentations; misspellings; poor grammar in letter.

How would you describe the client from Hell: We have none. A disruptive client is invited elsewhere.

How would you describe the perfect client: All our clients are patient and understanding of the publishing process and understand that editors take their time.

How and why did you ever become an agent: A perfect fit for a person with my background: A former publisher and an experienced attorney.

Do you have any particular opinions or impressions of editors and publishers in general: Nice people who are overwhelmed by the flood of unpublishable material.

Please list representative titles you have sold: Richard Scarry's children's books (some bilingual); Susan Love's breast books; *Hotter than Hell* and other cookery titles, Jane Butel; *Overcoming Impotence*, Dr. J. Stephen Jones; Tom Wolsky technical computer books; Math Series, Debra Ross; *When Bad Grammar Happens*, Ann Batko; Dr. Gilbert Rose's psychiatry books; Len Rosen's various college texts; journalism anthologies; titles on offer; novels; biography; young adult (all major publishers).

NELSON LITERARY AGENCY, LLC

1732 Wazee Street, Suite 207, Denver, CO 80202

www.nelsonagency.com

Visit our Web site before submitting. E-mail queries and electronic submissions only. Member: Association of Authors' Representatives, Romance Writers of America, Science Fiction & Fantasy Writers of America.

Agent's name: Kristin Nelson

Education: BA University of Missouri—Columbia; MA Purdue University.

Career history or story: The Nelson Agency was established in 2002. Before that, founding literary agent Kristin Nelson worked for Jody Rein Books. She went on her own to represent all types of fiction—including genre fiction like SF&F and romance.

Subjects & categories you are interested in agenting, including fiction & non-fiction: Right now our list is strong in Women's fiction and romance but we are continuing to look for new, strong voices. We are actively building our lists in Science Fiction & Fantasy, young adult (all kinds), and we love to have more literary commercial (such as *The Kiterunner* and *Joy Luck Club*). We look for a strong commercial bent—even for literary fiction. We'd love to take on more memoir and narrative nonfiction.

Subjects & categories writers shouldn't even bother pitching to you: We don't represent horror, thrillers, nonfiction (except for memoir or narrative). Definitely no cookbooks, gift books etc. Also, we don't handle children's picture books or middle-grade chapter books.

What's the best way for fiction writers to solicit your interest: We are a paper-free office. Please visit our Web site first and then send us an e-mail query letter. If we are interested in your material, we'll email detailed instructions on how to upload your sample pages or proposal to our secure electronic submissions database. We do not accept any queries or materials by snail mail. All materials sent by snail mail will be returned unread.

What's the best way for non-fiction writers to solicit your interest: See above.

Do you charge reading or any upfront fees: No. Any reimbursed expenses are after a work has sold and deducted from a publisher payment.

In your experience, what are the most common pitching mistakes writers make: Mistakes: 1. Not nailing the pitch blurb in the query letter (or not having a clear story hook); 2. Describing a work as every genre under the sun. What that signals is that you don't have an understanding of your work's place in the market; 3. Antagonistic or whining queries.

Describe the client from Hell, even if you don't have any: We've been lucky. We truly enjoy all our clients. However, a client from Hell would be one who is not internet or tech savvy (and refuses to work at becoming so).

What's your definition of a great client: Someone who is serious about the business of writing and publishing, who is tech savvy, and is willing to go the distance to promote his or her work. And, he or she writes like a dream and is fast—at least a book a year.

How can writers increase the odds that you will offer representation: Write a terrific novel.

Describe to someone from another planet what you do as an agent: We represent and advocate for authors by placing their materials in front of publishers, negotiating the deal (and watching out for the author's interests), trouble-shooting during the publishing process, and then guiding that author's career.

What are your favorite books/TV shows/movies, and why: A&E's *Pride and Prejudice, Almost Famous, Casablanca, Clueless, Age of Innocence, Enchanted April, Undercover Brother, Star Wars, Lord of the Rings,* any Doris Day movie.

In your opinion, what do editors think of you: Nice but one tough negotiator.

What are some representative titles that you have sold: *I'd Tell You I Love You But Then I'd Have to Kill You* and *Cross My Heart and Hope to Spy* by Ally Carter (Hyperion Books For Children); *Bachelorette #1* by Jennifer O'Connell (New American Library); *Plan B,* by Jennifer O'Connell (MTV/Pocket Books); *Everything I Needed to Know About Being a Girl I Learned from Judy Blume* Edited by Jennifer O'Connell (Simon & Schuster); *Enchanted Inc., Once Upon Stilettos* and *Damsel Under Stress* by Shanna Swendson (Ballantine); *Code of Love* and *The Winter Prince* by Cheryl Sawyer (New American Library); *Finders Keepers, Gabriel's Ghost, An Accidental Goddess, Games of Command* by Linnea Sinclair (Bantam Spectra); *No Place Safe* by Kim Reid (Kensington); *Prime Time* by Hank Phillippi Ryan (Harlequin); *Magic Lost, Trouble Found* by Lisa Shearin (Ace, Berkley); *Rumble on the Bayou* by Jana Deleon.

NORTHERN LIGHTS LITERARY SERVICES LLC

306 North Center Valley Rd. Sandpoint, ID 83864

888-558-4354

www.northernlightsls.com

Agent's name: Sammie Justesen, sammie@northernlightsls.com

Born: Born in Bedford, Indiana. Let's forget the year!

Education: Purdue University, Indiana University, Harvard (one great year).

Career story: I worked as a registered nurse for over twenty years, but couldn't stay away from writing. I became a clinical editor for Mosby, then worked as a freelance editor and writer for other medical publishers. I edited fiction for several years until several clients asked me to represent them with publishers. I opened Northern Lights Literary Services in 2004 and began selling books. Though we left the east coast and moved to northern Idaho, the Internet allows us to compete with New York agencies.

Hobbies and special personal interests: Reading (of course), watercolor painting, photography, swimming, and watching wildlife from our office in northern Idaho (moose, bear, elk, turkey, and eagles).

Subjects and categories you like to agent: We accept fiction and nonfiction in almost any category, as long as it's well written and marketable.

Subjects and categories writers shouldn't bother pitching to you: We don't accept erotica, fantasy, poetry, horror, or children and young adult books.

What might you be doing if you weren't agenting: I'd try and make a living with my artwork, which is even harder than succeeding as a writer. I must be a masochist.

What's the most effective ways for writers to grab your attention: I prefer email queries, well written and to the point. Write your query with a confident voice; don't run yourself down, but don't oversell your book either. Let the writing speak for itself.

Do you charge fees separate from your commission, or offer non-agenting fee based services: I still accept editing jobs from time to time.

What are representative titles you have sold to publishers: *Rutbusters* by Myra Daniels (Benbella Press); *The Road to Fruition: Recipes From the Smokey Mountains* by Joan Aller (Andrews McMeel); *Change Your Mindset, Not Your Man* by Sally Watkins, M.S.W (Adams Media); *Sea Fare: A Chef's Journey Across the Ocean* by Victoria Allman (Interpublicity); *Act With Love* by Russ Harris (New Harbinger); *You Can Live More Simply* by Patrice Lewis (Thomas Nelson); *The Mouth Trap* by Gary Siegel, Ph.D. (Career Press); *Creating a Million-Dollar-a-Year Sales Income Through Client Referrals* by Paul Mccord (Wiley); *The Happiness Trap* by Russ Harris (Shambhala); *The Power of Purrs* and *The Power of Paws* by Gary Shiebler (Lyons Press); *Unraveling the Mystery Of Fibromyalgia and Chronic Fatigue Syndrome* by Daniel Dantini, M.D. (Addicus Books).

Why did you become an agent, and how did you become one: I became an agent because I love discovering new projects and bringing authors and editors together. I crave those moments when I call an author and say, "I have an offer for your book!"

How do you feel about writers: My best friends are writers! I'm a writer! I love writers!

What do you tell entities from other planets and dimensions about your job: On this planet, millions of beings torture themselves by creating books they hope other humans will read. I try and sell those books to harried editors who hope the public will open their wallets. Beam me up, Scottie!

What are your favorite books, movies, TV shows, and why: I'm a junkie for self-help books and also love mysteries, memoirs, and biographies. I probably own every how-to-paint watercolor book ever written. I don't watch much television, but I like movies that are cerebral enough to hold my interest. No comic book derivatives, please! My favorite media provides entertainment, teaches me something, and inspires me.

How would you describe "the writer from hell": Writers from hell go ballistic when I respond to a query with helpful suggestions. Their friends love the book, so it's perfect. Clients from hell expect to hear from me every other day and don't trust me to do my job. Luckily I don't encounter many of these folks. Most writers are great.

How would you describe the publisher and/or editor from hell: Editors and publishers are wonderful; often overworked and underpaid. I mutter and complain when they hold manuscripts for months without responding, but I understand why that happens.

What do you like best about your clients, and the editors and publishers you work with: The camaraderie of working together to create books people fall in love with.

Will our business exist as we know it in 10 years or so from now: The Internet will continue changing the world, but I hope people will never stop reading.

ALLEN O'SHEA LITERARY AGENCY

615 Westover Road, Stamford, CT 06902

203-359-9965 fax: 203-357-9909

www.publishersmarketplace.com/members/AllenOShea

e-mail: MA615@aol.com

Agent's name: Marilyn Allen

Education: Trained as an English teacher.

Career history: I worked for many years on the publishing side in senior sales and marketing positions for Warner, Penguin, Simon and Schuster, and Harper Collins.

Hobbies/personal interests: Travel, reading, tennis.

Categories/subjects that you are most enthusiastic about agenting: Non-fiction; health, parenting, business, cooking, memoir, lifestyle, sports, narrative non-fiction.

Subjects & categories writers shouldn't even bother pitching to you: Poetry, children's, genre fiction.

If you were not an agent, what might you be doing instead: Running marketing department for a publisher or teaching literature.

What's the best way for fiction writers to solicit your interest: Not my area of interest.

What's the best way for non-fiction writers to solicit your interest: E-mail me.

Do you charge reading or any upfront fees: Never.

What are the most common mistakes writers make when pitching you: Failure to research competition and no marketing plans.

Describe the client from Hell, even if you don't have any: A client who has unreasonable expectations about the industry; expects things like a quick sale to a publisher, a large advance, extensive marketing and book reviews.

What's your definition of a great client: A great client is a writer who creates a smart proposal, understands his audience and the marketplace and works collaboratively with me. Love writers who are experts in their field and have cutting edge research.

How and why did you ever become an agent: I became an agent because I like to work with writers. I started my agency after a long publishing career.

What, if anything, can a writer do to increase the odds of you becoming his or her agent: Send me a good proposal with a fresh new idea. I love submissions that are complete and well thought out.

How would you describe to someone (or thing) from another planet what it is that you do as an agent: I help writers shape their book projects, then find them a publishing home and do everything in between.

How do you feel about editors and publishers: Really love working with most of them.

How do you feel about writers: Really love working with most of them.

What do you see in the near future for book publishing: Fewer books being published.

What are your favorite books, movies, TV shows, and why: I have so many favorite books. I just finished *A Year of Magical Thinking* by Joan Didion and loved it. I look forward to vacation so that I can select books I want to read for pleasure. I love the history channel and travel channel.

In your opinion, what do editors think of you: They trust me and like to work with me. I have a marketing background and they often look to me for ideas. I solve problems for them.

On a personal non-professional level, what do you think people think of you: They think I'm fun and collegial.

Please list representative titles you have sold: Many books sold. Please check our Web page.

THE PARK LITERARY GROUP, LLC

270 Lafayette Street, Suite 1504, New York, NY 10012

212-691-3500   fax: 212-691-3540

www.parkliterary.com

The Park Literary Group was founded in January 2005, when Theresa Park and several colleagues left the venerable literary agency, Sanford J. Greenburger Associates. Theresa had been an agent at Greenburger for more than 10 years, but at the age of 37 was eager to try building a new venture. A full-service literary agency, The Park Literary Group represents fiction and nonfiction with a boutique approach: an emphasis on servicing a relatively small number of clients, with the highest professional standards and focused personal attention. With a full-time foreign rights director and excellent relationships with film and television co-agents in Los Angeles, the agency brings to bear excellent resources and a wealth of experience in exploiting all rights associated with an author's work.

Agents' names: Theresa Park, Shannon O'Keefe, Abigail Koons

Education: Theresa: B.A., University of California, Santa Cruz; J.D., Harvard Law School. Shannon: B.A., University of Notre Dame; M.F.A., University of Notre Dame. Abigail: B.A., Boston University.

Career history:

The following information pertains to Theresa Park:

Theresa began her career as a literary agent at Sanford J. Greenburger Associates in 1994. (Prior to that, she was an attorney at Cooley Godward, a Silicon Valley law firm). She represents a mixture of plot-driven fiction and serious nonfiction. Some of her clients include Nicholas Sparks, Debbie Macomber, Emily Giffin, Laura Zigman, Linda Nichols, Robert Whitaker, Lee Silver, B.R. Myers, and Thomas Levenson. A graduate of U.C. Santa Cruz and Harvard Law School, she is married to Greg Irikura, a photographer, and has two children.

The following information pertains to Abagail Koons:

Eager to work with emerging and established talent, Abigail is currently looking to add to her list of diverse and engaging authors. Her passion for travel makes her a natural fit for adventure and travel narrative non-fiction, and she is also seeking projects about popular science, history, politics, current events and art. She is also interested in working with commercial fiction, especially superb thrillers and mysteries. As the Foreign Rights Director, she continues to build on her prior experience with agent Nicholas Ellison, as well as her time with EF Education, a multinational corporation based in Sweden. Abigail is a graduate of Boston University.

Categories/subjects that you are most enthusiastic about agenting: Theresa: Commercial fiction (thrillers, love stories, historical novels, etc.) and serious nonfiction (including narrative history, science, memoir, serious psychology, history and biography). Shannon: Commercial and literary fiction (modern love stories, social comedies, graphic novels, and young adult novels) and nonfiction (including cookbooks, sports, music, education, travel, and popular culture). Abigail: Commercial fiction (thrillers and quirky comedies) and nonfiction (adventure and travel narratives, memoirs, political science, art and art history, business, and science).

What you don't want to agent: Theresa: Cookbooks, diet books, fitness, children's books, humor. Shannon: Religious or spiritual books, science fiction, fitness. Abigail: Young adult, psychology, romance, westerns, genre science fiction and fantasy.

If you were not an agent, what might you be doing instead: Theresa: I can't imagine doing anything else—I really love being an agent, and feel privileged to be able to follow my passion. Shannon: This is my career of choice and I'm thrilled to be doing it. Abigail: In that fantasy world where no one has a full-time job, I would spend my days traveling and reading. This is the next best thing.

What's the best way for writers to solicit your interest: A one-page letter, brief synopsis, and one to three chapters, snail-mailed (NOT emailed), with an SASE.

Do you charge reading or management fees: No—never.

Can you provide an approximation by % of what you tend to represent by category: Fiction: 50%, Non-Fiction: 50%.

What are the most common mistakes writers make when pitching you: Poor grammar and spelling in written materials. Gimmicky attempts to attract attention through means other than a professional query. Overly aggressive or unprofessional behavior.

How would you describe the perfect client: Professional, disciplined, hardworking, emotionally stable, great people skills and social judgment, down-to-earth, direct.

How and why did you ever become an agent: Theresa: I love books, I love to work with people, and I love to do deals! Also, given my background as a transactional lawyer, it seemed like the right area of publishing for me. One of the best things about being a lawyer was having clients—I enjoy getting to know people and working closely with them on their manuscripts and proposals; the personal rewards of watching a client's career blossom are the best part of my job. Shannon: As an agent, I have the opportunity not only to do all of the things I would gladly do for free (reading, writing, editing) but also work with extremely talented and creative people—authors, editors, publishers. The idea of finding something relatively raw and working with the author and the project through publication remains both a thrill and a great privilege. Abigail: After dabbling in law and international economics, I decided that my career needed a healthy dose of creativity to balance out the business aspects. Being an agent allows me to utilize my business and organizational skills while working with truly wonderful clients and fascinating projects everyday.

What, if anything, can a writer do to increase the odds of you becoming his or her agent: Be professional; send concise, effective query letters.

How would you describe to someone (or thing) from another planet what it is that you do as an agent: We are advocates for and advisors to writers—in addition to each acting as a salesperson, negotiator and long-term strategist.

Do you have any particular opinions or impressions of editors and publishers in general: Their quality and commitment to authors varies widely—it is impossible to generalize.

Please list representative titles you have sold: Theresa: *The Notebook, Message In A Bottle, A Walk To Remember, The Rescue, A Bend In The Road, Nights In Rodanthe, The Guardian, The Wedding, Three Weeks With My Brother, True Believer, At First Sight, Dear John, The Choice* (Warner Books); *Piece Of Work* (Warner Books); *Inamorata* (Viking); *Handyman* (Delacorte), *Not A Sparrow Falls, If I Gained The World, At The Scent Of Water, In Search of Eden* (Bethany House); *Doomed Queens* (Broadway); *Challenging Nature: The Clash Of Science And Spirituality At The New Frontiers Of Life* (Ecco); *The Lost Men: The Harrowing Saga Of Shackleton's Ross Sea Party* (Viking); *A Reader's Manifesto* (Melville House); *Remember Me: A Lively Tour Of The New American Way Of Death* (Collins). Shannon: *I Like Food, Food Tastes Good: In The Kitchen With Your Favorite Bands* (Hyperion). Abagail: *Shop Naked: The History of Catalogs* (Princeton Architectural Press).

PMA LITERARY AND FILM MANAGEMENT, INC.

45 W. 21st St., 4th Floor, New York, NY 10010

212-929-1222   fax: 212-206-0238

Agent's name: Peter Miller
Born: Atlantic City, New Jersey.
Education: B.A., Monmouth University.
Career story: Known as the "Literary Lion," Peter Miller has been an extraordinarily active literary and film manager for more than thirty years. He is President of PMA Literary and Film Management, Inc. and Millenium Lion, Inc.; he and his company have successfully managed over 1,000 books worldwide as well as dozens of motion picture and television properties. These works include fifteen *New York Times* bestsellers, and fourteen produced films that Miller has managed or executive produced. Three of those films have been nominated for a total of seven Emmy Awards: *Goodbye, Miss Fourth of July* (The Disney Channel, four nominations); *A Gift of Love* (Showtime, two nominations); and *Helter Skelter* (CBS, one nomination). In addition, Miller has a number of film and television projects currently in active development, with some nearing production, in association with Warner Bros. Features, Sony Pictures Television, Warner Bros. Television, DreamWorks and many other producers and production companies.

Hobbies and special personal interests: I collect statues and images of lions, which have been celebrated by man since the beginning of time. I also enjoy traveling, films, wine and adventure.

Subjects and categories you like to agent: Quality fiction and narrative non-fiction with global marketing and motion picture and television production potential.

Subjects and categories writers shouldn't bother pitching to you: Poetry, pornography or anything low or mid-list.

What might you be doing if you weren't agenting: I would probably be an antique dealer.

What's the most effective ways for writers to grab your attention: By writing a powerful, succinct, and perfect e-mail or pitch letter.

Do you charge fees separate from your commission, or offer non-agenting fee based services: No.

What are representative titles you have sold to publishers: Non-Fiction: *The Element* by Sir Ken Robinson and Lou Aronica (Viking); *Strategic Acceleration* by Tony Jeary (Vanguard Press/Perseus Books Group); *The Culture Code* by Clotaire Rapaille (Broadway/Doubleday/Random House); *Ten Prayers God Always Says Yes To* by Anthony DeStefano (Doubleday Religion); *Nathan Hale* by M. William Phelps (Thomas Dunne Books/St. Martin's Press). Fiction: *Offspring* by Liam Jackson (Thomas Dunne Books/St. Martin's Press); *No More Good* by Angela Winters (Dafina/Kensington); *A Twisted Ladder* by Rhodi Hawk (TOR); *Perfect Victim* by Jay Bonansinga (Kensington); *No Rest for the Wiccan* by Madelyn Alt (Berkeley/Penguin).

Why did you become an agent, and how did you become one: When I moved to New York many moons ago, I was producing an off-off-Broadway production. I then met a Broadway producer and we decided to start a literary agency. I never looked back.

How do you feel about writers: I have the utmost respect for writers, as they are the true geniuses in society.

What do you tell entities from other planets and dimensions about your job: I would tell them to write something special so I could be the literary manager of the first alien to get published in America.

What are your favorite books, movies, TV shows, and why: *Being There* by Jerzy Kosinsk and *Steppenwolf* by Herman Hesse; Movies: *Dr. Zhivago*, *The Godfather* and *Austin Powers*; TV shows: *Boston Legal*, *Entourage* and *The Sopranos*.

How would you describe "the writer from hell": One that doesn't know how to communicate but doesn't stop trying to communicate with us.

How would you describe the publisher and/or editor from hell: One that makes an offer during an auction and then disappears.

What do you like best about your clients, and the editors and publishers you work with: I like the truly talented authors that we manage that just allow me to do my job and the publishers that do everything they say they're going to do.

You're welcome to share your thoughts and sentiments about the business of writing and publishing: Fortunately, having spent 30 years in the industry, I've learned how to grow with ever-constant sea changes like the one we are presently experiencing in the digital delivery of content.

Do you wish to describe who you are: I'm a passionate, intellectual property developer who loves to get 6 figure advances for his clients. My favorite two words are "Bidding War".

Will our business exist as we know it in 10 years or so from now: Absolutely.

THE AARON PRIEST AGENCY

708 3rd Avenue, 23rd Floor, New York, NY 10017

212-818-0344   fax: 212-573-9417

Agents' names: Aaron Priest, Lisa Erbach Vance, Lucy Childs
Career history: The Aaron Priest Literary Agency was established in 1974.
Categories/subjects that you are most enthusiastic about agenting: Vance: General fiction, mystery, thrillers, upmarket women's fiction, historical fiction, narrative non-fiction, memoir; Childs: Literary and commercial fiction, memoir, edgy women's fiction; Priest: Thrillers, commercial and literary fiction; For all three agents: No science fiction, no poetry, no screenplays, no horror, no fantasy.
What's the best way for writers to solicit your interest: Please submit a query letter via e-mail to querypriest@aaronpriest.com for Aaron Priest, querychilds@aaronpriest.com for Lucy Childs, queryvance@aaronpriest.com, for Lisa Erbach Vance. The query should be about one page long describing your work as well as your background. No attachments, however a first chapter pasted into the body of an e-mail query is acceptable. Please do not submit to more than one agent at this agency. (We urge you to consider each agent's emphasis before submitting.) We will get back to you within three weeks, but only if interested.
Do you charge reading or management fees: No.
Can you provide an approximation by % of what you tend to represent by category: Fiction: 90%, Non-Fiction: 10%.

SUSAN ANN PROTTER, LITERARY AGENT

110 West 40th Street, Suite 1408, New York, NY 10018

212-840-0480

Agent's name: Susan Ann Protter
Career history: Associate director, Subsidiary Right Department, Harper & Row Publishers, Inc.; founded Susan Ann Protter Agency in 1971.
Hobbies/personal interests: Sailing, opera, travel, languages, dogs and pets, tennis.
Categories/subjects that you are most enthusiastic about agenting: Fiction: suspense including mysteries and thrillers; women's fiction; commercial science fiction and fantasy; Non-fiction by recognized experts only in the following areas: general and women's health; parenting; how-to; popular science and medicine; memoir; biography; history; middle eastern subjects; books by established journalists.

What you don't want to agent: Romance, westerns, children's books, high fantasy, horror, and textbooks.

What's the best way for writers to solicit your interest: One-page query letter with SASE (no e-mail), which gives overview, brief synopsis, author's background. If interested, we will request first 30 pages and outline with SASE. No reply without SASE.

Do you charge reading or management fees: No reading fee.

Can you provide an approximation by % of what you tend to represent by category: Non-Fiction: 45%, Fiction: 55%.

What are the most common mistakes writers make when pitching you: They do not do their homework.

What, if anything, can a writer do to increase the odds of you becoming his or her agent: As an agent, I am looking for writers who genuinely care about their craft but understand current commercial trends as well. It is important that we share the same visions and goals regarding their work.

Please list representative titles you have sold: *20 Teachable Virtues* (Perigree); *Einstein for Dummies* (Wiley); *Understanding Islam* (Plume/Penguin); *Flowers: How They Changed the World* (Prometheus Books); *Getting Organized* and *The Organized Executive* (Warner Books); *Growing and Changing* (Perigree); *House of Storms* (Ace); *The House of God* (St. Martin's/Delta); *The Last Secret* (Midnight Ink/Llewellyn); *Mass Hate* (Perseus); *Mad Professor* (Thunders Mouth Press); *Night Falls on Damascus* (Thomas Dunne Books); *Operation Solomon: The Evacuation of the Ethiopian Jews to Israel* (Oxford); *The Real Vitamin and Mineral Book* (Avery/Penguin); *The Space Opera Renaissance* (TOR).

THE QUADRIVIUM GROUP

7512 Dr. Phillips Boulevard, Suite #50-229, Orlando, FL 32819

407-516-1857

www.TheQuadriviumGroup.com

Agent's name: Steve Blount, SteveBlount@TheQuadriviumGroup.com
Born: Waycross, GA
Education: B.B.A., The University of Georgia; M.B.A., Thunderbird School of Global Management
Career history: After ten years in banking (profitability analyst, strategic planner, mergers & acquisitions), I made the jump into Christian publishing and retail (Life-Way), starting out on the corporate side doing strategic planning, but soon getting into product development, marketing, and sales for the core publishing business. After a successful decade there, I became COO of a faith-based marketing firm that represented major ministry clients such as Billy Graham, Joyce Meyer, Joel Osteen, T. D.

Jakes, and more. I've always enjoyed helping those with a compelling message to reach their audiences, whether as their publisher, book marketer, media consultant, or agent.

Categories/subjects that you are most enthusiastic about agenting: Christian non-fiction, Christian/inspirational fiction, crossover books

What you don't want to agent: Poetry

If you were not an agent, what might you be doing instead: I'd find some other way to help people with compelling life stories or other great messages to reach their audiences

What, if anything, can a writer do to increase the odds that you will become his or her agent: A great proposal, including a powerful hook

Do you charge fees separate from your commission, or offer non-agenting fee based services : Only extraordinary costs with client's permission; no reading fees.

How and why did you ever become an agent: After leaving publishing, a number of my authors and publishing colleagues encouraged me to become an agent. There seemed to be a need for someone who understood the inner workings of the business to help authors with compelling life stories and ideas to navigate through the often difficult publishing process.

QUICKSILVER BOOKS LITERARY AGENTS

508 Central Park Avenue, #5101, Scarsdale, NY 10583

tel/fax: 914-722-4664

www.quicksilver.com   e-mail: quickbooks@optonline.net

Agent's name: Bob Silverstein, President
Born: October 3, 1936; New York, New York.
Education: B.A., City College of New York.
Career history: Bob Silverstein is president of Quicksilver Books, a literary agency and former book packaging and publishing firm established in 1973. QB is responsible for the creation of many national and international bestsellers, including novelized versions of such highly-acclaimed films as *The Last Tango in Paris, Shampoo,* and *Chariots of Fire.* All of these titles were published in the U.S. and Canada as Dell/Quicksilver paperbacks. For more than 35 years, Mr. Silverman has successfully divided his career between books and movies. After graduation from the City College of New York and post-graduate work in comparative literature at the City University of New York (Hunter College), he entered publishing as an associate editor with Gold Medal Books and later became an editor of the Crest and Premier divisions of Fawcett Publications. Between 1962 and 1965, Mr. Silverstein served as managing editor of Dell Books and as senior editor of the newly-formed Delacorte Press. In 1965 he joined Anthony Quinn Productions as associate producer and story editor, assisting the actor in preparing his autobiography as well as shaping screenplays for production in the U.S.

and Europe. From 1967 to 1970, Mr. Silverstein was senior unit publicist for United Artists and MGM on major motion pictures filmed on location throughout Europe. In this capacity he worked closely with producers Carlo Ponti, David Wolper, Harry Belafonte, and others. Mr. Silverstein has also co-produced several independent documentary and feature films, as well as a number of television commercials for the Ogilvy & Mather ad agency. In 1971 he returned to publishing as senior projects editor for Bantam Books. Among his acquisitions were such cutting-edge titles as *Gestalt Therapy, Verbatim*, and *In and Out of the Garbage Pail* by Frits Perls.

After several years he left to start his own company, Quicksilver Books, Inc. and since then has collaborated with writers in producing many popular works of fiction and non-fiction, including the previously mentioned movie tie-ins. Other Quicksilver projects, many still in print, include books inspired by new therapies and holistic healing techniques such as Gestalt, Transactional Analysis, Rolfing, etc. Among them are *The Body Reveals* (HarperCollins, 4 editions, 12 printings); *Own Your Own Life* (McKay/Bantam), *Psychology Today* Book Club (main section); *Chalk Talks on Alcohol* (HarperSanFrancisco, 15 printings); the international bestseller *Children Learn What They Live* (Workman); and recent bestsellers by Dr. Lois P. Frankel *Nice Girls Don't Get the Corner Office* and *Nice Girls Don't Get Rich* (Warner Books). As a literary agency (founded in 1987), Quicksilver Books is primarily interested in mainstreaming adult fiction, with special emphasis on commercial and literary novels. Non-fiction categories include: narrative adventure, self-help, psychology, environmental issues, nutrition, health, cooking, healing, alternative therapies, music, New Age, science, medicine, reference, biography, and inspirational memoirs.

Hobbies/personal interests: Painting, tennis, international travel, spending time with my wife and children.

Categories/subjects that you are most enthusiastic about agenting: Inspirational classics, blockbuster literary novels, best-selling narrative non-fiction, great memoirs and biographies, outstanding cookbooks, meaningful self-help. Books that uplift the spirit and that can make a positive difference in people's lives.

What you don't want to agent: Fantasy, science-fiction.

If you were not an agent, what might you be doing instead: Painting, traveling, meditating, writing/collaborating on books and movies.

What's the best way for writers to solicit your interest: By query letter or e-mail.

Do you charge reading or management fees: No.

Can you provide an approximation by % of what you tend to represent by category: Fiction (literary fiction, women's novels, suspense thrillers): 15%, Nonfiction: 85%.

What are the most common mistakes writers make when pitching you: They say nothing about themselves. Their letters are full of spelling mistakes. They tell but they don't sell.

How would you describe the client from Hell: Full of ego, demanding, unaware of their part in the marketing process.

How would you describe the perfect client: Objective, intelligent, sympathetic, humble, emotionally and spiritually attuned.

How and why did you ever become an agent: Initially I was an editor, then a packager/publisher. When the markets changed in the 80s I went with the flow and became an agent.

What, if anything, can a writer do to increase the odds that you will become his or her agent: 1.) Have something original to offer; 2.) Be aware of market needs and categories; 3.) Present it professionally; 4.) Have a platform to help market the book.

How would you describe to someone (or thing) from another planet what it is that you do as an agent: I consider myself an alchemist/healer-helper to turn lead into gold.

Do you have any particular opinions or impressions of editors and publishers in general: I come from their ranks. Some stand taller than others. All have a job to do and, for the most part, I respect their efforts. Occasionally, I'm even impressed.

Do you have any favorite (current) TV shows, films, or books that you especially like and how come: I like cooking shows, *This Old House, The Sopranos, 24*, Discovery and History channels, an occasional movie—no sitcoms.

Please list representative titles you have sold: *Jefferson's Great Gamble and Young Patriots* (Sourcebooks); *Look Great Naked* (Penguin); *Sculpting Her Body Perfect* (Human Kinetics); *The Inextinguishable Symphony* (Wiley); *Nice Girls Don't Get the Corner Office* and *Nice Girls Don't Get Rich* (Warner); *The National Public Radio Guide to Building a Classical CD Library* (Workman); *Children Learn What They Live* (Workman); *The Complete Books of Vinyasa Yoga* (Marlowe & Co.); *The Pump Energy Food* (Hyperion); *Real Food Daily Cookbook* (Ten Speed Press); *Help Me to Heal* (Hay House); *The National Public Radio Listener's Encyclopedia of Classical Music* (Workman); *The Complete Book of Ayurvedic Home Remedies* (Harmony); *Dinner at Mr. Jefferson's* (Wiley); *Indian Vegan Cooking* (Perigee); *Macrobiotics for Dummies* (Wiley); *Simply Mexican* (Ten Speed Press).

RAINES & RAINES

103 Kenyon Road, Medusa, NY 12120

518-239-8311   fax: 518-239-6029

Agents' names: Theron Raines, Joan Raines, Keith Korman
Education: T. Raines: Columbia, Oxford.
What's the best way for writers to solicit your interest: One-page letter.
Please list representative titles you have sold: *Deliverance* by James Dickey; *Forrest Gump* by Winston Groom; *Die Hard* by Roderick Thorpe; *Ball Four* by Bouton and Shecter; *The Destruction of the European Jews* by Raul Hilberg; *The Man Who Walked Between the Towers* by Mordicai Gerstein (Caldecott winner); *My Dog Skip* by Willie Morris; *Brain Quest* by Chris Welles Feder; *Legacy* by Rich Lowry; *The Contender* by Robert Lipsyte; *Active Faith* by Ralph Reed; *The Glory of Their Times* by Lawrence Ritter; *How to Eat Fried Worms* by Thomas Rockwell; *The Uses of Enchantment* by Bruce

Bettelheim; *Silhousette Against the Sky: A Daughter Remembers Orson Welles* (tentative title) by Chris Welles Feder (Algonquin).

RED SOFA LITERARY

2163 Grand Avenue Suite 2, Saint Paul, MN 55105

651-224-6670

www.redsofaliterary.com   e-mail: dawn@redsofaliterary.com

Agent's name: Dawn Frederick, Owner & Literary Agent.

Born: March 2nd, Atlanta, Georgia.

Education: I attended the University of Tennessee, earning a Bachelor's Degree in Human Ecology, and Master's Degree in Information Sciences from the School of Information Sciences (an ALA accredited institution).

Career story: I bring experience from the bookstore frontlines, independent publishing, and the library field, over 15 years of experience to be precise. It was pure coincidence (and part fate) my path crossed with Laurie Harper (of Sebastian Literary Agency) in 2002. Over the next 5 years, I learned the ins & outs of being a Literary Agent, with marked success. In 2008, I decided to branch out, launching Red Sofa Literary. And yes, I do own a big, red couch.

Hobbies and special personal interests: Where do we start? I am a natural risk-taker, and it's very much reflected in my personal life. There are the sports I avidly participate in: Roller Derby (Rolling Ref for the Minnesota Rollergirls, known as Mani-Ax), Broomball (on three teams now), currently Women's Lacrosse (taking MN by storm it seems), and Bicycling (a much calmer outlet for the energy). Plus, I am a fan of all things quirky, which is a foundation for Red Sofa Literary. So, you should never be surprised if I attend an eclectic event/show/movie, as those are things that always appealing.

Subjects and categories you like to agent: Biography—historical, media-related, political—NO PERSONAL MEMOIRS; creative nonfiction—it needs to be smart, with noticeable platform, and highly commercial; history; humor; popular culture, especially Americana, and anything quirky; social issues/current affairs—women's studies; sports—less mainstream, more extreme sport, ex: Roller Derby; women's narratives—chicklit nonfiction, Latina, African-American, and more; young adult—nonfiction.

Subjects and categories writers shouldn't bother pitching to you: I cannot emphasize enough that I will NOT represent any personal memoirs, romances, science fiction, westerns, parenting, and/or religious books. I sadly get multiple queries in this category daily, and end up rejecting all of them.

What might you be doing if you weren't agenting: Going to law school, more than likely.

What's the most effective ways for writers to grab your attention: I love a smart, narrative voice from a writer, and even more so when he/she has done her figurative homework on Red Sofa Literary. That kind of work stands out significantly.

Do you charge fees separate from your commission, or offer non-agenting fee based services: I would only in the event the accepted publisher deal is for an advance of less than $15,000. Red Sofa Literary may charge back a one-time US $100 fee for partial reimbursement for the postage and phone expenses incurred prior to securing the publishing deal. The majority of the time, I never have to worry about this.

What are representative titles you have sold to publishers: *The Secrets of Skinny Chicks* (McGraw-Hill); *Finding Betty Crocker: The Secret Life of America's First Lady of Food* by Susan Marks (HarperCollins); *Stuck on You: The Indispensable History of Band-Aid Brand Bandages* by Susan Marks (Collector's Press).

What are your favorite books, movies, TV shows, and why: I have lots of favorite things, however if you cornered me and I had to list my Top 10 TV shows, they would be (in no particular order): *Buffy the Vampire Slayer, Six Feet Under, Sopranos, Alias, 24, Melrose Place, Queer as Folk, Sex in the City, L Word, and Freaks & Geeks*. Books, that's a hard question, it all depends on my mood and what I'm currently reading. Just know I have lots of favorites, that I'm well-read, and I'm always up for recommendations.

How would you describe "the writer from hell": Anyone who doesn't promote him/herself, thereby making it difficult to sell the person's platform, which makes the agent's job more difficult. In addition, too many emails/phone calls in a short period of time. I always try to answer them quickly, but if an author has contacted me without giving me time to respond, and does this consistently, it tries my patience.

What do you like best about your clients, and the editors and publishers you work with: I absolutely love that we all carry a passion for books, good ideas, and our constant desire to find forums to discuss these topics.

HELEN REES LITERARY AGENCY

376 North Street, Boston, MA 02113

617-227-9014

WE DO NOT ACCEPT ELECTRONIC SUBMISSIONS.
Agent's name: Lorin Rees, lorin@reesagency.com
Education: B.A., Bard College; M.B.A., Boston University
Career story: After many years trying to change the world by working in non profit organizations and with socially responsible enterprises, I became a literary agent. My journey has exposed me to incredibly diverse and wonderful experiences that inspire me everyday. In no particular order, I've worked with underprivileged children, been a park ranger at a national park, advocated for the homeless, consulted small businesses, led the marketing efforts for an innovative food service company and worked at as line

cook. Now, I am dedicated to making an impact through books. I cherish my work and feel extremely fortunate and blessed be a literary agent.

Subjects and categories you like to agent: Business, history, self-help, literary fiction, popular culture, narrative nonfiction, mystery.

Subjects and categories writers shouldn't bother pitching to you: Romance, fantasy, sci-fi, poetry.

What might you be doing if you weren't agenting: That's hard to imagine.

What's the most effective ways for writers to grab your attention: Just present your work. There're no gimmicks or tricks here.

Do you charge fees separate from your commission, or offer non-agenting fee based services: None.

What are representative titles you have sold to publishers: *Words That Work*, and *What American's Really Want...Really* by Frank Luntz (Hyperion); *Blood Makes the Grass Grow Green* and *The Border Crosser* by Johnny Rico (Random House); *Travel Writing* by Pete Ferry (Harcourt); Primal Health: Stone Age Secrets to *Health and Happiness* by Dr. William Meller (Perigee); *It Pays to be Civil* by Christine Pearson and Christine Porath (Portfolio); *Brandsimple* by Allen Adamson (Palgrave Macmillan); *Who: Solve Your #1 Problem* by Geoff Smart and Randy Street (Random House).

Why did you become an agent, and how did you become one: It was destiny. The clouds parted, the stars aligned, and the moon shone brightly. (I'm not kidding.)

What do you tell entities from other planets and dimensions about your job: I read a lot.

What are your favorite books, movies, TV shows, and why: I love too many wonderful books and movies to list.

How would you describe "the writer from hell": That's a difficult question to answer because I wouldn't work with a "writer from hell." I not only admire the people I work with, I like them on a personal level and consider many my friends.

How would you describe the publisher and/or editor from hell: Are you trying to get me in trouble?

What do you like best about your clients, and the editors and publishers you work with: There is nothing more satisfying than being part of a successful creative collaboration.

You're welcome to share your thoughts and sentiments about the business of writing and publishing: This is a fair business that requires patience and perseverance. While some terrible books are successful, in the end, truly great books and authors stand the test of time and get, in most cases, the recognition they deserve.

Do you wish to describe who you are: I'm about 6', 190lbs with a shaved head.

Will our business exist as we know it in 10 years or so from now: Mostly. There will be many differences due to technology and changing demographics, but the elements of publishing will remain the same. Writers will always need a publisher, and publishers will always need writers. And somewhere in the middle there is a literary agent.

JODI RHODES LITERARY AGENCY

8840 Villa La Jolla Drive, Suite 315 , La Jolla, CA 92037

www.jodierhodesliterary.com

Agents' names: Jodie Rhodes, President; Clark McCutcheon, fiction editor at large; Bob McCarter, nonfiction editor at large; Jill Hughes foreign rights; Contact for all queries, Jodie Rhodes.

Born: Montreal, Canada.

Education: B.A. Ohio Wesleyan University. Pursued M.A. at Ohio State concurrently with my husband pursuing his Ph.D. at Ohio State but ended up doing his research and writing his papers instead of my own.

Career history or story: A year out of college, I worked as an editor at McGraw-Hill for their school division based in Columbus, Ohio. Left that for a job as a copywriter at a small agency, also in Columbus, Ohio. Then moved to W.B. Doner in Detroit where I was told no woman could be a copywriter because either directly or indirectly every account was connected to the auto industry and "everyone knew women didn't understand anything about cars," so I became a media buyer. I grew up in Detroit and was eager to leave and see the world, so I took off for San Francisco (what a magical city!) and started my own business there, an upscale employment agency titled simply Rhodes Personnel Agency. At that time, the city was flooded with young women emigrating from Britain. I shall always remember the one who wrote, in the space listing work experience, "general dogsbody." When Hoeffer, Dietrich and Brown in San Francisco called my agency, looking for a media buyer, I placed myself with them and sold the business.

A large regional agency in LA, that handled Mattel Toys among other big accounts, recruited me for twice the money and I moved down there. Had a brief stint as Marketing Director for Whamo Toys. They invented the Hula Hoop. Then joined N.W. Ayer and was promoted to VP Media Director a few years later. Quit to pursue a writing career and sold two novels: one to Bantam and one to Putnam—the latter made the *LA Times* bestseller list its first week in print. Could not sell a third novel and grudgingly went back to advertising but only as a consultant. Here's a story to pop your eyes. The agency I consulted for was supposed to be the new Mary Wells. It had Suzuki when Suzuki was hot It also had a technology company. I only met the president of it once but was blown away by him. Then I heard the agency dropped the account because they felt this president was too dense to understand their creative strategy. "Are you nuts?" I cried. "This is one of the most brilliant, creative human beings I've ever met." They just sneered at me—after all I was just a media person. Well, the president's name was Bill Gates and the tech company Microsoft.

Hobbies, interests: A hobby that grew into a vice was option trading. I was an active trader in the market for many years, concurrent with my positions in advertising. The day I realized I was in trouble was when I had so much money rolling in from option trades that I began regarding my salary as chump change. I now only hold stocks that pay strong dividends. Love bridge and am a Life Master. Am a passionate but rather inept tennis player. Have always loved horses and riding. Bike regularly. If you'd asked about passions, I would include my deep personal concern with the "throwaway children" in both this country and worldwide. Before I became an agent, I served as a guardian ad litem for the San Diego Juvenile Court Systems and worked (freely, as a volunteer) for Voices for Children. A recent sale, *Chloe Doe* by Suzanne Phillips, is the story of a 17 year old girl who fled from a brutalizing home at age 12 and has been supporting herself by selling her body on the streets of LA since she was 12. I was determined to get this book published and contacted 29 editors simultaneously in the U.S. and UK. Targeted to the YA market, it scared many publishers but I am happy to say we made a big sale and it's created a worldwide buzz.

Subjects and categories you are interested in agenting, including fiction and nonfiction: What's really hot today are edgy, literary YA/Teen novels and if you're a truly gifted writer who has a strong story idea for one, I'd love to see it. These books are outselling adult fiction 3 to 1. Editors who used to handle only adult trade novels are now acquiring these books. To give you an idea of just how hot they are, editors tend to disappear before major holidays and it's normally impossible to reach them. But the Friday before Thanksgiving I fell madly in love with a YA/Teen novel I read nonstop from the moment I opened it to the last page, immediately offered the author representation and was so excited I spent the weekend writing the pitch letter, mailed it to 14 editors on Monday, on Tuesday 12 of them asked to see the complete manuscript (many emailing from their home or their family's home), on Wednesday, Editorial Director Phoebe Yeh at HarperCollins called me with a pre-emptive offer of $200,000.

Multicultural literature, both fiction and nonfiction, makes my eyes light up. Books that have something important to say and characters with substance. Voice is everything to me in a novel. I'm fascinated by science and have sold many books by a variety of scientists and academics. Mainstream fiction, memoirs, biography, history, literary novels, those rare thrillers and mysteries that are truly original and gripping, world literature, politics, military, international affairs, women's issues, parenting, health, medicine. I am rightly known as an agent who welcomes new writers and the vast majority of books I've sold have been authored by new writers.

Subjects and categories writers shouldn't even bother pitching to you: No romances, religious, spiritual or inspirational books, no children's books, no erotic works, no science fiction, fantasy or horror.

What might you do if you weren't agenting: Writing. As most writers know, once the writing bug bites you, it's hard to get over. I was fortunate to have sold two novels to major New York houses but a writer always wants to do more. I am seriously considering writing a nonfiction book titled *Making It* which should be an interesting insider look at the publishing business from someone who started out as an outsider and had to battle their way inside, just like most of you reading this are doing.

What's the best way for fiction writers to solicit your interest: Be a gifted writer and a fantastic storyteller. Most literary fiction is focused on language and style. There's no compelling story. That's the main reason they get rejected. Sadly, most of the writers who come up with truly interesting plots don't write well enough for their books to sell.

What's the best way for nonfiction writers to solicit your interest: First, have a truly exciting story to tell that either hasn't been written about before or offers exciting new information on the subject. I expect every writer to have thoroughly researched the subject matter and to have a "platform." Publishers want writers with outstanding credentials which will attract reviewers and get media attention. The author should also have a well planned marketing and promotion strategy of their own which they'll use to generate sales.

Do you charge reading or any upfront fees: I do not charge any fees, upfront or later (not even submission fees).

Can you provide an approximation by % of what you tend to represent by category: 60% nonfiction, 25% YA/teen, 15% fiction. I might add this is not my choice. I would prefer 70% fiction and 30% the rest. The magic of fiction is that the author creates life. I love my brilliant scientists, doctors, and academics but a truly great novel is my passion. Commission structure: 15% in all cases except 20% for foreign sales or film/TV if it's placed through a sub agent. Number of titles sold last year: 45. Rejection rate: 99.5%.

In your experience, what are the most common pitching mistakes writers make: They don't think before they write. They just let it pour out. The result is illogical plots, inconsistent characters, clichéd, superficial writing and a bored agent. A writer should spend at least two hours of research for every hour of writing. They should know their characters as well as they know their secret thoughts. They should know everything about the situations they put their characters in, including what the streets they walk on look like.

Also, you're always off on the wrong foot when you get our name wrong. Form letters addressed to "agent" are sure losers. Query letters with misspelled words and bad grammar are instant rejects. But the most common mistake writers make is telling us how wonderful their book is. Never, ever try to sell us. Experience has taught us that the more modest the writer, the greater the talent, and vice versa. One of the funniest such letters I recently received informed me, "My book is a brilliant, compelling modern day version of Holden Caulfield's *Catcher in the Wheat*. Writers are told to keep their query letters short but one can overdo this as per the following: "Dear Agent, A woman takes her 12 year old daughter out of school and isolates her from the world. The novel is called Elizabeth. Sincerely,...." We do need more information than this. I invite writers to send along the opening 30 to 50 pages of their book with their query letter. This allows me to get a sense of the writing and the voice and greatly increases the author's chance of interesting me.

Describe the client from Hell, even if you don't have any: A client who emails or calls you every week after the first round of submissions has been mailed out—who falls apart emotionally when the first rejections come in—who acts as though they're the only client you have—who repeatedly asks what you're going to do after every rejection—who tries to make you feel you and only you are responsible for selling the book—the actual book they wrote has nothing to do with it.

What's your definition of a great client: Intelligent, appreciative, patient, a genuine grown-up who realizes a good agent works as hard as a writer and has enormous demands on their time from many areas.

How can writers increase the odds that you will offer representation: NEVER CALL ME ON THE PHONE WHEN I'VE NEVER HEARD OF YOU NOR SEEN ANY OF YOUR WRITING. Be honest, be professional, do your homework before you contact me, research your book, hone your writing craft, don't write for the market (meaning if you're written a book motivated simply by the desire to sell a book, go to some other agent). Write because you had to—because your story, fiction or nonfiction, was that important to you. If you've written a novel and not once during the time you wrote it did you feel excitement, fear, desire, hope desperation, curiosity, determination—if you never laughed or cried, then you never got inside your book. If you felt nothing, the reader will feel nothing.

Give me a bio that will get editors' attention. I cannot begin to tell you how many mss I've requested based solely on the bio info in the query letter. Here's an example: "The first chapter was a finalist in the Harcourt Brace Best New Voices in American Fiction 2007 contest and won the Katie O'Brien Scholarship for Fiction. I was subsequently awarded the Writer-in Residence at the Footpaths to Creativity Center in the Azores Island. I've worked for ten years as a wildlife biologist." However, nothing beats an opening description of the book that hooks me.

Why did you become an agent, and how did you become one: One of these days, I may really level and tell you why. Suffice it to say, I knew going in that I had absolutely no chance whatsoever of ever being successful. The odds were just so totally against me. In fact, I never expected a writer to actually contact me since none of the guide books responded to the listing I sent in. I had an ulterior motive. Then one day, to my shock, I found a ms in my mailbox. *Guide To Literary Agents* had listed me without telling me. I've always been cursed with an over developed sense of responsibility and that lone ms forced me to actually try and become a real agent. How I did it was through more work than I ever thought I was capable of. Most everything in my life has come easy to me. When I started my agency in late 1998, I was (and still am) living in La Jolla, California, 3000 miles from the heart of the publishing business. I didn't have a single writer or know a single editor. I'd never worked as an editor in a New York trade house. I knew nobody and nobody knew me. For the first six months I received nothing but the most ghastly imaginable mss, all of which I rejected. So the first step I took was to write advice columns for writers and convince some regional and national writers' magazines to publish them, in hopes of getting the attention of decent writers. Then I wrote the head of every major New York house (at this time I didn't even have a computer) and said I'd like to interview their editors. I will be grateful all my life to Sally Richardson at St. Martins and Emily Bestler at Simon and Schuster who out of the kindness of their hearts personally called me on the phone and offered me 5 or 6 of their editors. After that, everybody was willing to give me interviews.

The other thing I did was make what I hoped would be a short term sacrifice for a long term benefit. There are about 3000 people who call themselves agents in this country and I started out 3001. Major talented polished writers were not querying me. So I took the best of the raw talent and revised, edited and rewrote their MSS into salable books. There are a multitude of books out there with my writing sprinkled throughout them. Above all, I owe my success to New York editors, and I'm talking major editors for their unbelievable kindness. I had several writers who told me their previous agents never received a single response from editors when they sent submissions. That was the fate I feared. So I introduced myself. I wrote them about myself. They were so gracious! I'll never forget Jane Von Mehren, past VP Editor-in-Chief of Viking Penguin, now at Random House, calling me one day simply to ask how I was doing.

Carolyn Marino is a saint. She has cheered me on for years, never letting the fact she has yet to take one of my books deter her from encouraging me to keep sending. The brilliant editor of Ecco Press, Dan Halpren, has taken the time to write notes like, "I'm sorry this one won't work for Ecco but I remain hopeful." Michael Pietsch, Brian Tart and Wendy Lamb wrote wonderful recommendation letters to LMP so I could get listed with them (LMP only lists agents who are recommended by major editors), and I'd never even come close to selling them a book. I probably shouldn't start naming editors because there are so many others who reached out a helping hand. I founded my business on unpublished writers, the majority of whom had been rejected by everyone else for years. Now of course I'm also selling published writers but almost all are writers whose first books I sold and we're now placing their second and third books.

Describe to someone from another planet what you do as an agent: I make people's dreams come true.

How do you feel about editors and publishers: There's a common belief that editors don't really edit these days—they just acquire books. Nothing could be more wrong. Good editors (and most are) do enormous editing. When Robin Desser at Knopf bought *Train to Trieste*, it had gone through 5 edits—3 by me, one by the world famous author Sandra Cisneros and one by her personal editor. So what did Robin Desser do? She had the author rewrite the entire book from page one six times! I'd done so much editing on it that I knew the book by heart, but when I read it after Robin's editing, I was blown away. She made it extraordinary.

When Phoebe Yeh at HarperCollins bought *The Ghosts of War*, she sent me a copy of her first edit. There wasn't a single page and hardly a single line without her comments and changes. And this was a full ms! Since she does this with every book she buys, I can't imagine how she finds time to eat, sleep or have any personal life (and she's married with children). I hope every writer who reads this begins to see why they keep getting rejected. You can't just write a book and send it out. If it's worth anything at all, you need to rework and hone it time after time until it comes to life and glows. And when it's reached that stage, it will still be only halfway there but now professionals will take over and bring it to fruition. With rare exceptions, I love editors. They are so bright. Have gained so much knowledge (from their writers, actually), most really deeply care about books and they're all under such pressure all the time—they work enormously long hours and have demands on them writers can't even begin to imagine—yet they will always give new writers a chance. Regarding publishers: It saddens me that making money is so important to them that they'll publish really bad books because there's a celebrity attached or the writer has a

National Observer type story. I guess to stay in the business, they have to. But it didn't used to be that way before all the mergers and acquisitions with their companies going public and becoming beholden to Wall Street. I wish they'd reward writers who make money for them by considerably more generous royalties—they know what their break even point is—after that why not let the author share more fairly in the profits?

How do you feel about writers: My writers are all very special people to me. I consider them my friends. They share their personal life with me and I care about what happens to them. With the enormously gifted fiction writers in particular, I feel a sense of awe at their talent and great thankfulness that they chose me as their agent. As for the brilliant scientists I represent, I am in total awe of their knowledge and expertise. One of the greatest gifts being an agent has brought me is the chance to know such brilliant gifted people.

What do you see in the near future for book publishing: Most of us are very concerned about what's happening to the printed word. Newspapers have lost more than half their circulation. The internet is the new media and it becomes more powerful all the time. Kids don't read anymore. We may all end up representing bloggers.

What are your favorite books/TV shows/movies, and why: I work 15 hours a day, 7 days a week and before I became an agent, I read a minimum of 10 books a week and saw a movie at least once a week. Now I never see movies and never get to read real books. It's horrible, because I need to know what's out there. Thank God for *Publisher's Weekly* and editors who send me their writer's books so I can at least scan them. However, like most people, I am utterly fascinated by the presidential race and tape MSNBC and CNN during the day (do not care for FOX News), then sit up until 1AM watching. As for dramatic TV, I will watch anything Helen Mirren is in.

In your opinion, what do editors think of you: I'd rather let the editors tell you. From: Judith Gurewich at Other Press: "Dear Jodie, Please send us more manuscripts. I can see you understand my love for good writing and heartfelt stories." From Amy Gash at Algonquin: "Jodie, Your books are always so fascinating. I'm interested in this topic and would love to see the proposal. I'm so glad you keep sending projects my way!" From John Aherne at McGraw-Hill: "Hi Jodie, Boy, am I glad I asked to see this. My colleagues and I really liked and responded to this proposal. We all thought it was great! Thanks again for sending this wonderful proposal my way." From Bob Pigeon at Perseus Books: "Dear Jodie, Your query letter has certainly aroused my curiosity and kindled my interest. Please do send this proposal and sample chapter as soon as convenient. Please send it to me via email attachment. Have you sent the proposal to any other imprint in the Perseus Books Group? Looking forward to receiving the material."

On a personal level, what do you think people like about you and dislike about you: They are enormously grateful that I take chances on them as new and previously rejected writers, that I edit their material, that I continue to market it to multiple publishers after numerous rejections, knowing that I will probably never earn a penny from my work. They like knowing they can trust me and that selling their books is always more important to me than making money. This past year I sold books after 60, 72, 87 rejections and that's just for starters. I sold a book 3 *Minutes on Love* after representing it and fighting for it 3 years and recently sold it after 217 rejections. A debut novel by a Romanian author I took on 2 years ago, which received 132 rejections, was just pre-empted by Robin Desser at Knopf, won at auction by Doubleday in the UK with translation rights already sold to Italy, Germany, France, Holland, Greece, Serbia and Israel. It's currently at auction in Romania. I've had a few books that sell instantly but the majority of books I sell have gone through a minimum of 50 rejections. No wonder I have tendonitis. On the negative side, writers often find it hard to take my blunt criticisms. I don't have time to be polite and beat around the bush. If their writing sucks, I tell them. I also demand they be instantly available when I'm marketing their work and ready to provide editors with any and all material they request.

What are some representative titles that you have sold: *Freaked* by Jeanne Dutton (HarperCollins); *The Red Flag in American Bathrooms* by Dr. Wesley Jones (Penguin); *Diagnosis of Love* by Maggie Martin (Bantam); *Murder at Hotel Cinema* by Daniel Craig (Midnight Ink Five Star Mystery); *The Ring* by Kavita Daswani (HarperCollins); *Right Decisions* by Jim Stein (McGraw-Hill); *Choosing the Gender of Your Child* by Daniel Potter and Jennifer Thompson (Prometheus Books); *Messed Up* by Janet Lynch (Holiday House); *A Child's Journey Out of Darkness* by Leeann Whiffen (Sourcebooks); *The Ghosts of War* by Ryan Smithson (HarperCollins); *Seducing the Spirits* by Louise Young (The Permanent Press); *A Year With Cats and Dogs* by Margaret Hawkins (The Permanent Press); *Internal Affairs* by Connie Dial (The Permanent Press); *The Archivist* by M.F. Bloxan (The Permanent Press); *Does Israel Have a Future* by Connie Hilliard (Potomac Books); *Lessons from Baghdad* by Stephen O'Hern (Prometheus Books); *Hoodwinked* by Sherry Seethaler (Prentice Hall's Zoon's Trade Imprint); *America's Covert Military: The Inside Story of Private Contractors* by Shawn Engbrecht (Potomac); *The Truth About Our Energy Crisis* by Jim Mahaffey (Pegasus Books); *The Five Second Rule* by Anne Maczulak (Perseus/Da Capo); *How Math Can Save Your Life* by James Stein (John Wiley & Sons); *Murder at the Universe* by Daniel Craig (Midnight Ink Five Star Mystery); *The Root of Thought* by Andrew Koob (Prentice Hall's Zoon's Trade Imprint); *Pictures of the Mind* by Miriam-Boleyn Fitzgerald (Prentice Hall's Zoon's Trade Imprint); *A Matter of Gravity* by John Moffat (HarperCollins); *Salaam, Paris* by Kavita Daswanit (Putnam); *Mind Mapping* by Jamie Nast (John Wiley & Sons); *Inside the Crips* by Colton Simpson and Ann Pearlman (St. Martins); *Green Planet* by Stanley Rice (Rutgers University Press); *Critical Components of J.R.R. Tolkien* by Jay Ruud (Facts on File); *Understanding Biodiversity* by Julie Casper (Facts on File); *Computers, Internet and Society* by Robert Plotkin (Facts on File); *Makers of Modern Science: Chien-Shiung Wu* by Richard Hammond (Facts on File); *The Unknown Universe* by Richard Hammond (Career Press/New Page Books); *Microscopy* by Suzanne Bell (Taylor And Francis); *The Digital World* by Ananda Mitra (Facts on File); *The History of Nuclear Power* by Jim Mahaffey (Facts on File); *The Human Body* by Miriam Boleyn-Fitzgerald (Facts on File); *Encyclopedia of Environmental Studies* by Marc Menetrez (Facts on File); *Changing Eco Systems* by Julie Casper (Facts on File).

THE ANGELA RINALDI LITERARY AGENCY

P.O. Box 7877, Beverly Hills, California 90212-7877

310-842-7665   fax: 310-837-3143

www.rinaldiliterary.com   e-mail: amr@RinaldiLiterary.com

Agent's name: Angela Rinaldi

Career history or story: Executive Editor, NAL/Signet, Senior Editor, Pocket Books, Executive Editor, Bantam Books, Manager of book publishing for The Los Angeles Times. Taught publishing programs at UCLA. Member of the Literature Panel for the California Arts Council, AAR and PEN.

Subjects & categories you are interested in agenting, including fiction & non-fiction: Fiction: Mainstream and literary fiction, upmarket contemporary women's fiction, suspense, mysteries, thrillers, historical fiction. Non-fiction: Narrative non-fiction like Blink or Freakonomics—books that present a quirky aspect of the usual, memoir, women's issues/studies, current issues, cultural and social history, biography, psychology, popular reference, prescriptive and proactive self-help, health books that address specific issues, business, career, personal finance and books written by journalists, academics, doctors and therapists, motivational.

Subjects & categories writers shouldn't even bother pitching to you: Humor, techno thrillers, KGB/CIA espionage, drug thrillers, category romances, science fiction, fantasy, horror, westerns, cookbooks, poetry, young adult, children's, film scripts, magazine articles, religion, gift, how-to, Christian, religious, celebrity bios or tell alls.

What would you do if you weren't agenting: Editorial Consultant/freelance editor.

What's the best way for fiction writers to solicit your interest: Brief synopsis and the first three chapters. Do not send the entire ms. unless requested. Do not query by phone or fax. E-mail inquiries; please be brief, no attachments. Please tell me if I have your work exclusively or if it is a multiple submission. Include SASE. No metered mail or certified mail. UPS and Fedex will not deliver to a post office box. Please allow 4-6 weeks for response.

What's the best way for non-fiction writers to solicit your interest: Queries with detailed covering letter or proposal. Do not query by phone or fax. E-mail inquiries; please be brief, no attachments. Please tell me if I have your work exclusively or if it is a multiple submission. Include SASE. No metered mail or certified mail. UPS and FedEx will not deliver to a post office box. Please allow 4-6 weeks for response.

Do you charge reading or any upfront fees: No.

In your experience, what are the most common pitching mistakes writers make: Not knowing the genre they are writing in. Not researching the marketplace for similar titles. Pitching a novel that isn't finished and asking the agent to read incrementally. Pitching an undeveloped proposal. Pitching ideas that have been done many times over. Pitching more than one book at a time. Pitching novels and non-fiction at the same time. Not knowing the type of book I represent. Pitching to more than one agent and not letting each agent know. Mentioning that their previous agent died or is sick.

How can writers increase the odds that you will offer representation: Having a strong platform and knowing what that means. Being an expert in their field. Having stories published in journals. Big ideas, original ideas or noticing trends. Having ideas that explain the way we live. Having a "brand". Being able to get endorsements. Lovely writing. Good storytelling. Distinct voice. Writing a novel that combines literary writing with a commercial hook.

What are some representative titles that you have sold: *Who Moved My Cheese?* by Dr. Spencer Johnson; *Zen Golf: Mastering the Mental Game* by Dr. Joseph Parent (Doubleday); *Zen Putting: Mastering the Mental Game on the Greens* by Dr. Joseph Parent (Gotham Books); *Calling In "The One"* by Katherine Woodward Thomas (Three Rivers); *Welcome to the Real World* by Stacy Kravetz (Norton); *My First Crush* by Linda Kaplan (The Lyons Press); *Bone Lake* by Drusilla Campbell (Bookspan); *Blood Orange* by Drusilla Campbell (Kensington); *Rescue Me* by Megan Clark (Kensington); *The Starlite Drive-in* by Marjorie Reynolds (Morrow); *Blind Spot, Quiet Time* by Stephanie Kane (Bantam); *TWINS! Pregnancy, Birth and The First Year of Life* by Dr. Connie Agnew, Dr. Alan H. Klein and Jill Alison Ganon (HarperCollins); *The Thyroid Solution* by Dr. Ridha Arem (Ballantine); *Before Your Pregnancy* by Amy Ogle, M.S., R.D. and Dr. Lisa Mazzullo.

RIVERSIDE LITERARY AGENCY

41 Simon Keets Road, Leyden, MA 01337

www.riversideliteraryagency.com   e-mail: rivlit@sover.net

Agent's name: Susan Lee Cohen
Born: New York, New York.
Career story: I have been a literary agent for almost 30 years. I began my publishing career at Viking Penguin, and subsequently worked as a literary agent at Richard Curtis Associates and Sterling Lord Literistic before founding Riverside Literary Agency in 1990.

Subjects and categories writers shouldn't bother pitching to you: Genre fiction (romance, science fiction/fantasy, Westerns), children's books, poetry.

Do you charge fees separate from your commission, or offer non-agenting fee based services: No.

What are representative titles you have sold to publishers: *The Myth of Sanity* (Viking), *The Sociopath Next Door* (Broadway) and *The Paranoia Switch* (Farrar Straus & Giroux) by Martha Stout; *Reviving Ophelia* (Putnam/Ballantine), *The Shelter of Each*

Other (Putnam/Ballantine), *Another Country* (Putnam/Ballantine), *The Middle of Everywhere* (Harcourt), Letters to a Young Therapist (Basic Books), *Writing to Change the World* (Riverhead) and *Seeking Peace* (Riverhead) by Mary Pipher; *Pawprints of Katrina* by Cathy Scott (Wiley); *Right, Wrong and Risky* by Mark Davidson (Norton); *The Secret Magdalene* by Ki Longfellow (Crown); *Please Kill Me* by Legs McNeil and Gillian McCain (Grove/Atlantic); *Stop Running from Love* by Dusty Miller (New Harbinger); *Buddha is as Buddha Does* (HarperOne), *The Big Questions* (Rodale), *Awakening to the Sacred* (Doubleday), *Awakening the Buddhist Heart, Letting Go of the Person You Used to Be* (Doubleday), and *The Mind is Mightier than the Sword* (Doubleday) by Lama Surya Das.

RLR ASSOCIATES, LTD.

7 West 51st Street, New York, NY 10019

212-541-8641   fax: 212-541-6052

www.rlrliterary.net   e-mail: sgould@rlrassociates.net

Agent's name: Scott Gould; sgould@rlrassociates.net
Born: Baltimore, Maryland.
Education: New York University.
Career story: I began my career in the editorial department at Playboy Magazine, and later, handling rights at another agency before building my client list at RLR.

Subjects and categories you like to agent: I represent and am always on the look out for literary and commercial fiction (including genre fiction) and all kinds of well-written, narrative nonfiction, from history to pop science to humor.

Subjects and categories writers shouldn't bother pitching to you: I don't represent poetry or screenplays.

What's the most effective ways for writers to grab your attention: The best way to stand out is to email (or snail mail) a query letter that tells me everything about the project and you in an interesting and professional way, along with a few pages or more of the manuscript. Creativity counts, but in the end the book stands for itself, so don't kill yourself over a query letter.

Do you charge fees separate from your commission, or offer non-agenting fee based services: We follow the AAR guidelines and do not charge any reading or other fees.

What are representative titles you have sold to publishers: *Cash From Chaos: Creating and Building a Successful Gen X/Y Brand* by Eric Boyd and Sean Murphy (Prentice Hall/Pearson); *The Greatest Yankees Myths* by Peter Handrinos (Triumph Books); *Nathanael Greene: A Biography of the American Revolution* by Gerald Carbone (Palgrave Macmillan).

Why did you become an agent, and how did you become one: I became an agent because I love seeking out talent and making good books happen.

What are your favorite books, movies, TV shows, and why: Books: *Confederacy of Dunces, Jesus' Son, Lolita, Andy Kaufman Revealed!, Fear and Loathing in Las Vegas.* Movies and TV: *The Big Lebowski, The Wire, The Sopranos.*

You're welcome to share your thoughts and sentiments about the business of writing and publishing: This really is a business of relationships, which is generally a good thing because book people tend to be interesting people.

RITA ROSENKRANZ LITERARY AGENCY

440 West End Avenue, Suite 15D, New York, NY 10024-5358

212-873-6333

Agent's name: Rita Rosenkranz

Career history: Editor at various New York publishing houses before becoming an agent in 1990.

Categories/subjects that you are most enthusiastic about agenting: All areas of non-fiction, with emphasis on biography, business, parenting, cooking, current affairs, cultural issues, health, history, how-to, self-help, theater/film, popular culture, religious/inspirational, science, women's issues.

What you don't want to agent: Fiction, children's books, and poetry.

What's the best way for writers to solicit your interest: Send an outline/proposal with an SASE. I do not accept queries by e-mail or fax. I consider simultaneous queries and submissions.

Can you provide an approximation by % of what you tend to represent by category: Non-Fiction: 100%.

Please list representative titles you have sold: *The Confident Leader* by Larina Kase (McGraw-Hill); *National Baseball Hall of Fame and Museum* by Bert Sugar (Running Press); *Get Known Before the Book Deal* by Christina Katz (Writer's Digest Books); *Career Wisdom* by Michele Wright (Atria Books).

CAROL SUSAN ROTH LITERARY & CREATIVE

1824 Oak Creek Drive #416, Palo Alto, CA 94304

650-323-3795

e-mail: carol@authorsbest.com

Agent's name: Carol Susan Roth

Born: New Brunswick, New Jersey.

Education: B.A., New York University, M.A. Counseling and Psychotherapy, California Institute of Integral Studies, Professional Publishing Program, Stanford University, MegaBookMarketing Universities, Mark Victor Hansen.

Career history: Trained as a psychotherapist specializing in motivational seminars. More than a decade producing and promoting public events with the "who's who" in personal growth, spirituality and health (best selling authors including John Gray, Scott Peck, Bernie Siegal, Elizabeth Kubler-Ross, Thomas Moore). In 1987, produced the first business and spirituality conference, The Heart of Business, with Stanford University Graduate School of Business, Michael Ray. Literary agent since 1996.

Hobbies/personal interests: Horse whispering, Yoga, Hiking, Warm water sailing, meditation, the Dalai Lama.

Categories/subects that you are most enthusiastic about agenting: 100% Non-fiction. Pop culture, Humor, Health/Fitness, Business, Science, History, Herstory, Spirituality, Self-Help. Also, books (in series) or gifts that can be developed as a "brand."

What you don't want to agent: Sorry, no fiction/no channeling or book written by an author without credentials, ground breaking new content, charisma and dedication to making it a best seller.

If you were not an agent, what might you be doing instead: Book/gift product development and packaging. I enjoy working with bright, creative, caring people who want to make an important contribution by inspiring and empowering others. Raising and riding Arabian horses.

What's the best way for writers to solicit your interest: Send an email, pitch your idea, credentials and platform, (please no files) to me (carol@authorsbest.com) I'll get back to you immediately to request a proposal or not.

Do you charge any reading or management fees: No.

Can you provide an approximation by % of what you tend to represent by category: Fiction: 0%; Children's: 0%; Non-fiction: 90% pop culture, health, business , science, spirituality, self-help; Other: gift/audio 10%.

What are the most common mistakes writers make when pitching you: Not doing their homework on what an agent needs and wants to see in terms of pitch, query and proposal. (Please read Jeff Herman's *Write the Perfect Book Proposal*.)

How would you describe the client from Hell: Lack of integrity, lack of responsibility, lack of loyalty. I avoid them like the plague!

How would you describe the perfect client: My clients! Brilliant, big hearted, creative, cooperative, enthusiastic, hard-working, honest and loyal.

How would you describe to someone (or thing) from another planet what it is you do as an agent: As an agent, I work with experts to bring out the most valuable qualities in their work, the best way to position and then help sell their work from initial idea to the best seller book lists. Many times experts come to me with a book concept and together we make it even more appealing and marketable. I'm a visionary, confidante, coach, cheerleader, marketeer and matchmaker. I study the world of information/entertainment products to see what company is doing what. Prep and position my authors to have the greatest appeal to those who can compensate and promote them best.

Do you have any particular opinions or impressions about editors and publishers in general: They are the hearts and minds of the publishing industry. I admire great editors and enjoy their friendship and respect.

What do you think the future holds for writers, publishers and agents: This is the most challenging time I have seen for authors in the last twenty years. I also see it as the most promising time for new authors. I enjoy working with wonderful, brilliant, fun, creative experts to "break the code" to success in making their books best sellers. The secret is knowing your audience and using all the most cost-effective ways to reach them. All my authors actively market online, do traditional publicity (broadcast, cable and print). I also work with some of my authors to develop and produce PBS-TV programming.

Do you have any favorite (current) TV shows, films, or books that you especially like and how come: I enjoy "reality" TV; *The Apprentice, American Idol,* and *Survivor. Dr. Phil.* I loved *Wedding Crashers* and *Kundun.* The IMAX film *Everest.* I read lots of marketing, Tibetan Buddhism, biz, science, health books. I browse all sorts of books to find new ideas for my authors.

On a personal level, what do you think people like about you and dislike about you: Here are some of my favorite quotes: "Congratulations! Your agency has made it onto our Top 25 Agents list !"–Christine Mersch, Assistant Editor, *Writers Digest;* "Carol, You have such an amazing instinct for finding important commercial books! "–Jacqueline Murphy, Senior Editor, Harvard Business School Publishing; "I have a wonderful agent, Carol Susan Roth, who helped me develop my latest book, find a great publisher and secure an outstanding advance. I have worked with other agents in the past (one who is considered The Dean of Agents!) but, Carol stands head and shoulders above them all."–Michael Ray, Banc One Chair of Creativity, Stanford Business School and author, The Highest Goal; "I look forward to considering your future projects in personal growth, spirituality and holistic health."–Jackie Merri Meyer, Vice President, Warner Books; "Your marketing plan for Don Maruska's proposal is the BEST I have ever seen!"–Adrienne Hickey, Editorial Director, AMACOM (American Management Association Publishing).

What are representative titles you have sold to publishers: *Confessions of an Alien Hunter* and *The Immortals* (National Geographic Books); *Origins* (University Of California Press); *God in the Wilderness* (Doubleday); *Glimpses of Heaven* (Revell/Baker Books); *Living Wisdom With the Dalai Lama* (Soundstrue); *Healing Zen* (Viking/Penguin); *Yoga Rx* (Broadway Books); *Yoga Gems Calendar 2003-4* (Andrews Mcmeel); *The Chiropractic Way* (Bantam); *Heart Smart!* (John Wiley & Sons); *Pilates Fusion Book & Deck* (Chronicle Books); *Seasons of Change* (Conari/Red Wheel/Weiser); *Feng Shui for Dummies* (John Wiley & Sons); *Snooze or Lose!* (Joseph Henry Press/National Academies Press); *The Infertility Cure* (Little, Brown); *Bird Signs* (New World Library); *The Highest Goal* (Berrett/Koehler); *How Great Decisions Get Made!* (AMACOM); *Investing in Biotech* (Perseus); *Changewave Investing 2.0* (Currency/Doubleday); *Make It Big!!!* (John Wiley & Sons); *The Internship Advantage* (Perigee/ Prentice-Hall/Penguin); *10 Discoveries That Rewrote History* (Plume/Penguin); *Seven Stones That Rocked the World* (University Of California Press); *Hannibal* (Simon & Schuster).

Side: LITERARY AGENTS

REGINA RYAN PUBLISHING ENTERPRISES, INC.

251 Central Park West, New York, NY 10024

212-787-5589

www.publishersmarketplace.com/members/reginaryanbooks

e-mail: reginaryanbooks at rcn.com

queries: queryreginaryanbooks at rcn.com

Agent's name: Regina Ryan
Born: New York, New York.
Education: B.A. Trinity College, Washington D.C.; graduate work NYU and New School.
Career history: Editor: Alfred A. Knopf, Inc.; Editor-in-Chief, Macmillan Adult Books; founded firm as a book packaging and literary agency in 1977. Now, we are a literary agency only.
Hobbies/personal interests: Birding, mushroom hunting, wildflowers, cooking, gardening, ballet, modern dance, opera, reading, fine art.
Categories/subjects that you are most enthusiastic about agenting: Books that can change things for the better and/or open our eyes to something new and exciting. Areas of special interest include true adventure, memoir and well-written narrative non-fiction; also architecture, history, natural history (especially birds and wildflowers), politics, science, the environment, women's issues, parenting, cooking, psychology, health, wellness, diet, fitness, lifestyle, home improvement and design, business, leisure activities including sports, travel, gardening.
What you don't want to agent: No fiction or children's literature (other than those by clients I already represent), no poetry, movie scripts, or celebrity tell-alls, or

anything that involves vampires and/or demons or conspiracy theories.

If you were not an agent, what might you be doing instead: I would love to be a park ranger, a botanist, or an ornithologist but I suspect that in the real world I'd be a lawyer.

What's the best way for non-fiction writers to solicit your interest: I prefer a brief e-mail query or snail mail (with SASE) query describing the project, explaining why it is needed, an evaluation of the competition, and what his or her qualifications are. No telephone queries and no faxes. Please don't send by a method that requires a signature.

Do you charge reading or management fees: No.

What are the most common mistakes writers make when pitching you: They don't understand how to analyze the competition. They misunderstand the market for their books and often wildly exaggerate the possibilities to the point where it's useless. They don't get to the point but deliver too much preamble.

How would you describe the client from Hell: A client from hell can take several forms. There is the person who doesn't do what is asked of him or her; the person who turns in sloppy work; the person who calls on the phone for no real reason and/or talks endlessly; and finally the person who is never, ever satisfied.

How would you describe the perfect client: A great client is a really good writer who is a smart, hardworking pro who understands the business and who writes and promotes accordingly. My dream client is also polite, respectful and understands and appreciates what we've accomplished on his or her behalf.

How and why did you ever become an agent: I had been a book editor in publishing houses for many years before I went on my own, first as an out-of-house editor, then as a packager and agent. It was hard to do both packaging and agenting so I concentrated for some years on packaging. However, as a packager, most of my ideas came from my own head. I missed the variety of people and ideas that an editor is exposed to daily. Now, as a fulltime agent, I delight in the interesting people and ideas that come my way nearly every single day.

What, if anything, can a writer do to increase the odds of you becoming his or her agent: A great title and a good selling sentence that defines the book really helps. A writer should convince me that first of all, he or she is a really good writer. Then, the writer must show me that the subject is important, that there is a real need for it and a significant market for it. I want to be convinced that the book hasn't been done before and that the author has a good, strong platform.

How would you describe to someone (or thing) from another planet what it is that you do as an agent: The first thing I do is to find book projects to represent. This means I either read submissions or approach people who I'd like to see write a book. Once I've committed to a project, I guide the author in shaping a selling proposal using my strong editorial background and my understanding of the marketplace gained over my many years in the business. When the proposal is ready, I I bring it to the attention of the editors and publishers I think would be best for it. When a publisher makes an offer, I negotiate terms and review the contract. Then, once it is sold, I exploit whatever other rights are salable. I hover over the publishing process to help the book and author succeed out in the world in whatever way I can.

How do you feel about editors and publishers: I like editors and I respect them. They are usually overworked book lovers, just as I am. They work very hard in a very difficult, often frustrating publishing environment. Publishers – the "suits" – can be the cause of a lot of the above-mentioned frustration -- with their sometimes short-sighted view of the possibilities of some of my books, but in general, they too work hard and love books and try to do their best.

How do you feel about writers: I like writers. They are usually hard-working, creative, interesting and smart people. I know because I was married to one for 33 years.

What do you think the future holds for book publishing: I think it's going to get harder and harder to place books with the large publishers, unless non-fiction writers have a golden platform.

What are your favorite books, movies, TV shows, and why: I read fiction for my pleasure and recently I have developed a passion for Vladimir Nabokov *Pale Fire*. Also, Nikolai Bulgakov's, *The Master And Margarita*. My favorite movie of late is *Little Miss Sunshine*. I also loved *March Of The Penguins* and *The Devil Wears Prada*. On TV I like *Washington Week in Review, Book TV, Dog Whisperer, Top Chef, Project Runway, Nature, Nova, Antiques Road Show, Mystery*, and good movies on TV. Actually my favorite entertainment is listening to shows on WNYC, our local NPR talk radio station. I always learn something.

In your opinion what do editors think of you: I think they think of me as a pro, who understands the business and who represents quality projects.

On a personal non-professional level, what do you think people think of you: I think people think I'm fun, smart, a straight-shooter and a caring and loyal friend.

Please list representative titles you have sold: *Gilded Mansions: The Stately Homes of America's First Millionire Society*, Wayne Craven, W.W. Norton; *Chronicle: The 750 Year History Of An Eastern European Jewish Family*, Michael Karpin, John Wiley; *Return To The Middle Kingdom: One Family, Three Revolutionaries, and the Birth of Modern China*, Yuan-tsung Chen, Union Square Press; *Rain Before Rainbows: How Successful People Failed at First in Their Chosen Fields*, Darcy Andries, Sellers Publishing; *The Legacy: The Rockefellers and Their Museums*, Suzanne Loebl, Smithsonian Press; *Escaping Toxic Guilt: Five Proven Steps to Free Yourself from Guilt for Good*, Susan Carrell, McGraw Hill; *Mortality Bites: Living with Cancer in Your 20's and 30's*, Kairol Rosenthal, John Wiley; *Great Smoky National Park And Acadia National Park: FalconGuide Primers*, Randi Minetor, Globe Pequot Press; *151 Quick Ideas For Great Advertising On A Shoestring*, Jean Joachim, Career Press; *The Serotonin Power Diet: A Scientifically Proven Weight Loss Program That Uses Your Brain's Ability to Stop Your Overeating* by Judith Wurtman, Ph.D. and Nina Marquis, MD., Rodale; *The Bomb In The Basement: How Israel Got its Nuclear Option and What it Means for the World*, Michael Karpin, Simon and Schuster; *Anatomy of A Suicidal Mind* by Edwin Shneidman with an introduction by Judy Collins. Oxford University Press; *Escape From Saigon*, Andrea Warren. A Melanie Kroupa Book, Farrar, Straus and Giroux; *What Babies Say Before They Can Talk*, Paul Holinger, MD with Kalia Doner, Fireside Books. *The Altruist*, Walter Keady, MacAdam/Cage; *American Art: History And Culture*, Wayne Craven, McGraw Hill; *Beyond The Bake Sale: The Ultimate*

School Fund Raising Book, Jean Joachim, St. Martin's Press; *Lost In The Mirror: Borderline Personality Disorder*, Richard Moskovitz, MD, Taylor Publishing; *Surviving Hitler: A Teenager in the Nazi Death Camps*, Andrea Warren, HarperCollins Junior Books; *The Garden Primer*, Barbara Damrosch, Workman Publishing; *Thomas Eakins* by William Innes Homer, Abbeville Press; *Organize Your Office!* Ronni Eisenberg and Kate Kelly, Hyperion; *Pickups: Classic American Trucks* by Harry Moses, photographs by William Bennett Seitz, Random House; *Wildflowers In Your Garden*, Viki Ferreniea, Random House; *Living In Style Without Losing Your Mind*, Marco Pasanella, Simon and Schuster; *The Art Of The Table: Table Settings, Table Manners, Table Ware* by the Baronness Suzanne von Drachenfels, Simon and Schuster; *The Last Childhood: A Family's Memories of Alzheimer's*, Carrie Knowles, Three Rivers Press.

SCHIAVONE LITERARY AGENCY, INC.

236 Trails End, West Palm Beach, FL 33413-2135

561-966-9294

e-mail: profschia@aol.com

Jennifer DuVall: 3671 Hudson Manor Terrace, #11H, Bronx, NY 10463-1139

718-548-5332

www.publishersmarketplace.com/members/profschia

Agents' names: James Schiavone, Ed.D., CEO; Jennifer DuVall, President
Born: New York, New York.
Education: B.S., M.A., New York University; Ed.D. Nova University; Professional Diploma, Columbia University; Advanced studies: University of Rome, Italy.
Career history: Director of reading, Monroe County (FL) Public Schools; professor emeritus of developmental skills at the City University of New York; literary agent.
Categories/subjects that you are most enthusiastic about agenting: Celebrity biography, autobiography and memoirs, general fiction, mystery, romance, fantasy/science fiction, business/investing/finance, history, religious, mind/body/spirit, health, travel, lifestyle, children's (no picture books), African American, Latino, ethnic, science.
What you don't want to agent: Poetry, short stories, anthologies, or children's picture books. No scripts or screen plays. We handle film rights, options, and screenplays only for books we have agented.
If you were not an agent, what might you be doing instead: Teaching graduate courses in the psychology of reading, writing non-fiction.
What's the best way for writers to solicit your interest: Query letters only, one-page preferred (no phone or fax). For fastest response (usually same or next day) e-mail queries are acceptable and encouraged. For queries by post include SASE. No response without SASE. Do not send large envelopes with proposals, synopsis, sample chapters,

etc., unless specifically requested. Queries must be sent to the Main Office in West Palm Beach, except for those directed to Jennifer DuVall at the New York City branch office.

Do you charge reading or management fees: No reading fee.

Can you provide an approximation by % of what you tend to represent by category: Non-Fiction: 51%, Fiction: 41%, Children's: 5%, Textbooks: 3%.

What are the most common mistakes writers make when pitching you: Make initial contact via phone/fax; failure to query first before sending proposals, synopsis, etc.

How would you describe the perfect client: A published author who remains loyal to the author/agent partnership.

How and why did you ever become an agent: I have enjoyed a lifetime love of books and reading. I served as a reading specialist in schools and colleges and authored five trade books and three textbooks. I enjoy representing creative people and successfully working with them as partners in achieving and augmenting their career goals.

What, if anything, can a writer do to increase the odds of you becoming his or her agent: If a request is made for additional material, the author should prepare an outstanding, professionally written proposal along with sample chapters. For fiction, a brief well-stated synopsis accompanied by compelling initial chapters can make the difference in an offer of representation.

How would you describe to someone (or thing) from another planet what it is that you do as an agent: Sell creative work of authors/clients to major publishing houses; negotiate contracts; handle business details—enabling authors to concentrate on the craft of writing.

Do you have any particular opinions or impressions of editors and publishers in general: I have been fortunate in working with the best editors in the industry. Generally, they are conscientious, indefatigable, and sincere in bringing an author's work to press. Agenting would be impossible without them. Publishers are the backbone of the industry. I am grateful for the serious consideration they give to my highly selective submissions.

What do you think the future holds for writers, publishers, and agents: The future holds unlimited opportunities for all, especially the reading public.

On a personal level, what do you think people like about you and dislike about you: My clients tell me that they appreciate the unlimited contact they have with me. I am always available to discuss their need and concerns as writers. The editors I work with have always appreciated the time, care, and consideration I put into my submissions to them. While dislikes may exist, they haven't been expressed to me.

Please list representative titles you have sold: *A Brother's Journey* (Warner); *A Teenager's Journey* (Warner); *Inside: Life Behind Bars in America* (St. Martin's); *Tokyo Rose: An American Patriot* (Seaburn).

WENDY SCHMALZ AGENCY

Box 831, Hudson, NY 12534

518-672-7697   fax: 518-672-7662

e-mail: wendy@schmalzagency.com

Agent's name: Wendy Schmalz

Born: Willow Grove, Pennsylvania.

Education: B.A., Barnard College.

Career history or story: I started right out of college in the film department of Curtis Brown, Ltd. After a year, I went to Harold Ober Associates, where I continued to handle film rights, but also built my own list and represented the estates of F. Scott Fitzgerald and Langston Hughes. I opened my own agency in 2002.

Hobbies, interests: Woodworking, history.

Subjects & categories you are interested in agenting, including fiction & non-fiction: I represent adult and children's fiction and non-fiction.

Subjects & categories writers shouldn't even bother pitching to you: I don't represent genre fiction such as Sci-fi, romance or fantasy. I'm not looking for books for very young children and I'm not interested in taking on any new picture book writers. I don't handle self-help or Christian books.

What would you do if you weren't agenting: Forensic pathology.

What's the best way for fiction writers to solicit your interest: When I get a submission letter, I want to know the writer wants me specifically to represent him or her—that she isn't just fishing for an agent. I want the sense that they know what I represent and want me to represent them because they think I'd be right for the kind of writing they do.

What's the best way for non-fiction writers to solicit your interest: Same as above.

Do you charge reading or any upfront fees: No.

In your experience, what are the most common pitching mistakes writers make: In children's books everyone compares their books to *Harry Potter*. With adult books, too many authors describe their characters as being on a journey of self-discovery. Avoid clichés.

Why did you become an agent, and how did you become one: When I was a teenager I read Tennessee Williams's autobiography. He went on and on and how great his agent was. Before that, I didn't know what an agent was, but it sounded like a cool way to make a living.

What are some representative titles that you have sold: *Luna* (National Book Award Finalist) and *Between More and Jo* (Lambda Award winner) by Julie Anne Peters (Little Brown); *Buried* (Edgar Award winner) by Robin MacCready (Dutton); *Carolina Clay* by Leonard Todd (Norton); *The Koch Papers* by Edward I. Koch and Rafael Medoff (Palgrave); *The Horror Book of Lists* edited by Amy Wallace, Scott Bradley and Del Howison (HarperCollins); *Donuthead* and *Harry Sue* by Sue Stauffacher (Knopf).

SCOVIL CHICHAK GALEN LITERARY AGENCY, INC

276 Fifth Avenue, Suite 708, New York, NY 10001

212-679-8686   fax: 646-349-1868

www.scglit.com   e-mail: annaghosh@scglit.com

Agent's name: Anna Ghosh
Born: Bristol, United Kingdom.
Education: New School for Social Research, New York; Hampshire College, Massachusetts; Woodstock International School, India.
Career history: Agent at SCG since 1995.
Categories/subjects that you are most enthusiastic about agenting: Literary Non-fiction, Current Affairs, Investigative Journalism, History, Science, Social and Cultural Issues, Travel and Adventure.
What's the best way for writers to solicit your interest: Send a well written and thoughtful query letter.
Do you charge reading or management fees: No.
Can you provide an approximation by % of what you tend to represent by category: Non-Fiction: 70% nonfiction, Fiction: 30%.
Please list representative titles you have sold: *Last True Story I'll Ever Tell: An Accidental Soldier's Account of the War in Iraq* (Riverhead); *Ambitious Brew: The Story of American Beer* (Harcourt); *Living Cosmos* (Random House); *Churchill's Choice: Empire, War And The Great Bengal Famine* (Basic); *Reading Claudius* (Dial Press); *All Is Change: The Two Thousand Year Journey Of Buddhism To The West* (Little Brown); *Is Gluten Making Me Ill?* (Rodale); *Art of War for Women* (Doubleday).

SEBASTIAN LITERARY AGENCY

2160 Kenwood Way, Wayzata, MN 55391

952-471-9300

www.sebastianagency.com

Agent's name: Laurie Harper Markusen; laurie@sebastianagency.com
Born: September 1954.
Education: Business & finance, pre-law studies, Stanford Publishing Course.
Career story: I founded the Agency in 1985 in San Francisco, after closing my regional publishing company. I have authored two published books over the years, so I have been on many sides of the business. In 2000 I moved to Minneapolis to be near my family, and have never regretted it. I use my 25+ years of publishing experience and

network in both the Agency work and my consulting work for Author Biz Consulting.

Hobbies and special personal interests: Motorcycling (Suzuki Boulevard), sailing, movies, and almost any form of play. And of course, reading.

Subjects and categories you like to agent: Note: see the Web site for more specifics. Business & Finance (management, business narratives, financial); Health/Medicine/Nutrition (narratives from the field by professionals, leading edge research, disease/immunology/aging, nutrition guides); Women's Issues (personal growth, research & studies—across fields like communications, education, family and relationships, mental health, physical health, work and careers, aging, spiritual well-being) Psychology/Sociology/Personal Growth (this is for professionals writing from their private practices or client-based work, for the general trade audience, across a broad arena).

Subjects and categories writers shouldn't bother pitching to you: First novels, short story collections, poetry, screenplays, children's or YA books, scholarly or textbook, personal autobiographies, or personal story books about overcoming a particular disease.

What might you be doing if you weren't agenting: I would still happily work for the Authors Guild, and continue doing the consulting work I already do for writers. I enjoy it very much.

What's the most effective ways for writers to grab your attention: By email with no attachment, or snail mail—to tell me about your book and why you are the one to write it, as well as how you can market it once it is published.

Do you charge fees separate from your commission, or offer non-agenting fee based services: I do not offer any editing or critique services and if a project is not ready to go to publishers or to sell, I do not take it on. There are no reading fees, and I do not charge back U.S. postage or phone.

What are representative titles you have sold to publishers: *Stunned: The New Generation of Women Having Babies, Getting Angry, and Creating A New Women's Movement* by Karen Bridson (HCI); *Toxic Workplace: Managing Toxic Personalities and Their Systems of Power* by Mitch Kusy and Elizabeth Holloway (Jossey-Bass); *Secret Codebook of the High Achievers* by Sandra Naiman (Jist Publishing); *Career Chronicles* by Mike Glasgow (New World Library); *Money, Sex and Kids* by Tina Tessina (Adams Media); *The Warren Buffett Way*, 2nd Edition by Robert Hagstrom (John Wiley); *More Than You Know* by Michael Mauboussin (Columbia University Press); *Port in a Storm: How to Make a Medical Decision and Live to Tell About It* by Dr. Cole Giller (Lifelong Press/Regnery).

Why did you become an agent, and how did you become one: I was helping a couple of writers find publishers when I could not publisher their books, way back when, and that is how it happened. When I sold their books for them, I knew I had found the right work and the right place for me in this industry.

How would you describe "the writer from hell": One who expects to be paid a large advance before he or she has done the work to warrant it, which indicates a pattern of thinking and behavior that will sabotage everyone's efforts. It also shows a lack of knowledge or understanding about publishing. I also cannot work with an author who cannot or will not promote him or herself and market the book…This pretty much kills any possibilities for the author and the book.

What do you like best about your clients, and the editors and publishers you work with: The qualities I like best are: Intelligence, commitment, creativity, hard-working, good communicators, imagination, fascinating ideas, strong language skills, and good team players. It takes a strong and talented team to get the right book out in the right way and to have all the elements work successfully to accomplish its goals.

LYNN SELIGMAN, LITERARY AGENT

400 Highland Avenue, Upper Montclair, NJ 07043

973-783-3631

Agent's name: Lynn Seligman
Born: February 25, 1947 in New York City, New York.
Education: B.A., 1967, Goucher College; MA, 1968, Columbia University (French Literature); Graduate work for Ph.D. in French Literature except thesis, Columbia University.
Career history: Independent literary agent since 1985. Previously agent at Julian Bach Literary Agency, Inc. (1980-1985). Various subsidiary rights positions (1971-1980) at Simon & Schuster (Associate Director; Serial Rights Director), Doubleday (Foreign Rights Associate; Serial Rights Manager) and Thomas Y. Crowell. Books Editor at East/West Network (airline magazine group) in 1975.
Hobbies/personal interests: Reading, ballet, art, hiking and walking.
Categories/subjects that you are most enthusiastic about agenting: Nonfiction—memoir, psychology, health, medicine, science, women's issues and business. Fiction: literary, women's books and romance, horror, science fiction and fantasy.
What you don't want to agent: Children's books, with possible exception of young adult.
If you were not an agent, what might you be doing instead: International law? Veterinary medicine? These were areas I considered before I entered publishing, but I am very happy doing what I do. It lends itself to great change and adaptation within the field. And I am never bored.
What's the best way for fiction writers to solicit your interest: Write a great solicitation letter (no e-mail, and with SASE enclosed), including something about your background and interests. Include a sample of the book (about 10-20 pages), and a synopsis or summary so I can get a feel for the writing and story, if desired.
What's the best way for non-fiction writers to solicit your interest: Same as fiction, although the author's background and experience is more important here. Less important to have writing sample, except for memoir or narrative non-fiction.
Do you charge reading or management fees: No.

Can you provide an approximation by % of what you tend to represent by category: Non-Fiction: 70% (primarily parenting, health, medicine, psychology, memoir). Fiction: 30% (romance and women's fiction, horror, science fiction and fantasy, literary).

What are the most common mistakes writers make when pitching you: The most common mistake I can think of is telling me how much other editors, publishers, best friends, other writers, etc. loved the book. The latter two are not usually objective, and if the former ones loved it so much, it would have been bought before it landed on my desk.

How would you describe the client from Hell: I really cannot tolerate lying or verbal abuse, but I generally do not have these kinds of clients. I have a very small list and am pretty good at figuring out the people I can work with.

How would you describe the perfect client: Imaginative, intelligent, responsible, responsive and communicative.

How and why did you ever become an agent: I started out as an ESL teacher in the public schools. I loved the kids and hated teaching. But I know I loved publishing, so I began in editorial, then moved to subsidiary rights. Since I had gone about as far as I could in that area, I chose agenting, which combined my love of being close to the creative process with selling, which I also loved.

What, if anything, can a writer do to increase the odds of you becoming his or her agent: Write a great book that interests me!

How would you describe to someone (or thing) from another planet what it is that you do as an agent: I have no idea how to answer this question. Isn't what we do already being on another planet?

Do you have any particular opinions or impressions of editors and publishers in general: I think we all see how much harder it is to market books, and this trickles down to the publishers' and editors' behavior: the cult of the bestseller, the emphasis on platforms, the lack of support for a "smaller" book, etc. This issue is one for all retail businesses now, which publishing is, but when it involves creative people, it becomes more problematical for everyone to deal with. I think editors work very hard now to buy and sell books, and a lot less time on developing writers, so that job falls more and more to the agent.

How do you feel about writers: If I didn't love and respect writers and what they accomplish, I wouldn't be in this business.

What do you think the future holds for writers, publishers, and agents: Some of this answer is actually above, but I think the agent becomes even more important in the writer's career than ever before. The agent fills part of the role that the editor and publisher did. I also think that electronic publishing will be part of our future, in some kind of form, and I only hope that the rights of the creator will be protected. That role will be the responsibility of the agent as well.

What are your favorite books, movies, TV shows, and why: I have very eclectic tastes, in all respects. Two of my favorite TV shows are 24, for its excitement and unpredictability, and *Desperate Housewives*, for its biting sarcasm. Two of my favorite recently read books were *Truth and Beauty* by Ann Patchett, which is phenomenal view of friendship, insanity and the creative life, and *The Kite Runner*, which was beautifully written and gave a fascinating picture of another world. I love small quirky movies, mostly foreign and among my favorites were *Pan's Labyrinth* and *The Lives of Others*.

In your opinion, what do editors think of you: I really don't know exactly, but I think they pay attention when I send them projects, so it is a positive opinion for the most part.

On a personal level, what do you think people like about you and dislike about you: I think I am very honest and open (both a positive and negative trait!), sympathetic and caring about people close to me. On the negative side, I can be indecisive (seeing all sides at once—very Pisces) and try too hard to please everyone.

Please list representative titles you have sold: *Morbid Curiosity* by Deborah Le Blanc (Leisure Books); *Sinful Under the Sheets* by Barbara Pierce (St. Martin's); *My Father Before Me: How Fathers and Sons Influence Each Other Throughout Their Lives* by Dr. Michael Diamond (Norton); *Raising a Thinking Child* by Dr. Myrna Shure (Simon & Schuster/Pocket Books); *The New Professional Image* by Susan Bixler (Adams Media); *The Red Magician* by Lisa Goldstein (Tor Books, Starscape).

THE SEYMOUR AGENCY

475 Miner Street Road, Canton, NY 13617

315-386-1831

www.theseymouragency.com e-mail: marysue@twcny.rr.com

Agent's name: Mary Sue Seymour, AAR

Born: September 21, New York.

Education: B.S. from State University of New York plus thirty graduate hours mostly in education, hold New York State Teacher's certificate.

Career story: Began agency in 1992.

Hobbies and special personal interests: Hiking in the Adirondacks, walking my golden retriever, watching *American Idol*, going to church, reading my Bible, doing Sodoku puzzles, baking apple pies and homemade cinnamon rolls.

Subjects & categories you like to agent: Christian books of any type, especially historical Christian romance, category romance, and type of secular romance.

Subjects & categories writers shouldn't bother pitching to you: Fantasy romance, sci fi romance, erotica, short stories, poetry, general novels.

What might you be doing if you weren't agenting: Teaching art.

What's the most effective way for writers to grab your attention: A great query letter describing the project to a T—show me you can write.

Do you charge fees separate from your commission, or offer non-agenting fee based services: No.

What are representative titles you have sold to publishers: *Dump the Chump* by Catherine Dowda; *Everything Triathalon Book* by Brent Manley; *Everything Kids Spelling Book* by Shelley Sabga; *Everything Self Hypnosis Book* by Rene Bastarache; *Where Eagles Fly to Five Star* by Lisa Norato.

Why did you become an agent, and how did you become one: I was writing while teaching school. I had three agents—a couple of them were pretty bad and I wondered if I could be a successful agent. The first book I sent out sold a four book deal to Bantam so I believe it was meant to be. I quit teaching.

How do you feel about writers: I sympathize with them. There is a lot of room for error when you write a book yet writers have to have them perfect, and editors are so selective these days. Also the economy isn't that good and editors are buying more conservatively. It's a tough life and I have nothing but the greatest respect for authors. The key to being a happy author is to have other things you do simultaneously that you're good at. Then you will always have success in your life

What are your favorite books, movies, TV shows and why: I absolutely love *Walker, Texas Ranger* on the Hallmark Channel and I watch it whenever I can. It's so funny in some ways and of course the good guys always win. There are certain Christian undertones in the show that I like as well.

How would you describe "the writer from hell": I have never had one.

How would you describe the publisher and/or editor from hell: I have ne ver dealt with one. Editors are always professional or they wouldn't be editors.

What do you like best about your clients, and the editors and publishers you work with: They're nice, real people just like I try to be.

Do you wish to describe who you are: I love to travel to conferences and meet writers; I do about one conference a month. Conferences I plan to attend this year include one in Connecticut, RWA National in San Francisco, a Christian Writing Conference in Philadelphia, the Womens' Fiction Festival in Matera, Italy, Put Your Heart in the Book in New Jersey, and one in Lake Mary, Florida. I am really looking forward to being a faculty member on a Christian writing cruise in June 2009.

Will our business exist as we know it in 10 years or so from now: The advent of DVDs are taking over writing a little bit. I am anxious to see where the book industry will be in ten years.

WENDY SHERMAN ASSOCIATES, INC.

450 Seventh Avenue, Suite 2307, New York, NY 10123

212-279-9027 fax: 212-279-8863

Agents' names: Wendy Sherman, Emmanuelle Alspaugh, Michelle Brower
Born: Sherman: New York, New York; Brower: Berlin, New Jersey.
Education: Sherman: University of Hartford, Bachelors in Special Education;

Alspaugh: B.A. 1998, Sarah Lawrence College.; Brower: The College of NJ, B.A., and New York University, M.A.

Career history or story: Sherman: Opened this agency in 1999, was previously with the Aaron Priest Agency. Vice President executive director at Henry Holt, Vice President Associate publisher at Owl Books. Vice President sales and subsidiary rights (1998-1999). Also worked at Simon and Schuster and McMillan. Alspaugh: I started in publishing as an assistant at Fodor's, the travel division of Random House. I worked my way up to Editor and suddenly realized that I wanted to diversify the kinds of books I worked with. I decided agenting would be the best way to do that and I've never looked back. I worked at The Creative Culture agency for about a year before coming to Wendy Sherman Associates in the spring of 2007.

Hobbies, interests: Sherman: Reading, traveling; Alspaugh: Reading, traveling, anything French, film.; Brower: Brower: Crafting, cooking, film, animals..

Subjects & categories you are interested in agenting, including fiction & non-fiction: Sherman: Quality fiction, women's fiction, suspense, narrative non-fiction, psychology/self-help. Alspaugh: Women's fiction, romance, historical fiction, literary fiction, international/multicultural voices, YA, research-based non-fiction with a narrative or memoir element, journalism, business, science, biography, and memoir. Brower: Pop culture, music, humor, crafting, commercial fiction, thriller, literary fiction, narrative non-fiction, YA, and graphic novels. Books with elements of horror, fantasy, or science fiction that are for a mainstream audience.

Subjects & categories writers shouldn't even bother pitching to you: Science fiction, fantasy, horror, mysteries, and children's books. Alspaugh: Mystery, children's, dead-body-in-the-first-chapter thrillers. Brower: Cozies, children's picture books, category romance.

What would you do if you weren't agenting: Sherman: I could be back in corporate publishing, but choose not to pursue that career path. Alspaugh: Editing at a major house. Brower: I would probably be working in editorial.

What's the best way for fiction writers to solicit your interest: Query letter via regular mail to the agency, with a first chapter. Alspaugh: Send me a query either by e-mail or regular mail, including the first chapter of your manuscript. Brower: Query and first chapter, by e-mail or regular mail.

What's the best way for non-fiction writers to solicit your interest: Query letter via regular mail describing their book and credentials. Alspaugh: Send me a query either by e-mail or regular mail with your book proposal.

Do you charge reading or any upfront fees: No.

In your experience, what are the most common pitching mistakes writers make: The most common mistakes are not targeting the right agent and being unclear about your book in your query letter. Writers should do their research and find an agent who is a good fit for their material.

Describe the client from Hell, even if you don't have any: The client from Hell is unreasonably demanding and doesn't trust our judgment and experience.

What's your definition of a great client: The perfect collaboration between agent and author is one of mutual goals and respect.

How can writers increase the odds that you will offer representation: Have a fully polished book or proposal that's timely and well done.

Why did you become an agent, and how did you become one: Sherman: After leaving Henry Holt, I had the opportunity to work for the Aaron Priest Agency. I had thought about agenting for some time, and it seemed like the perfect way to make the change from working for a publisher to becoming an agent. Alspaugh: Joined Wendy Sherman Associates in 2007 after working at The Creative Culture literary agency, and as an Editor at Fodor's, the travel division of Random House. Brower: I started with Wendy Sherman Associates in 2004 after receiving my Masters degree in Literature, and I love working with clients to develop their ideas, shape their proposals, and take their fiction to the next level.

Describe to someone from another planet what you do as an agent: We bring writers to the attention of the best possible/most enthusiastic editor and publisher. We then do our best to ensure the book is published with the utmost enthusiasm. Alspaugh: I represent my clients' interests to a publisher. I work with them to hone their manuscripts and proposals, and I sell their work for the most I can get, then negotiate their contracts. I follow up with publishers for timely payments and marketing efforts. I protect my clients' rights to consult on book jacket art and other matters. I support, guide, and advise my clients, and help them to develop their careers.

How do you feel about editors and publishers: More than ever, editors have a very tough job. They not only have to find manuscripts they want to publish, but then convince in-house colleagues in editorial, marketing, and sales to support the acquisitions.

How do you feel about writers: We love writers, they are why we became agents. The best writers bring an immense amount of talent to the table and take direction well.

What are your favorite books/TV shows/movies, and why: *Watership Down* by Richard Adams; *A Tree Grows in Brooklyn* by Betty Smith; *The Glass Castle* by Jeannette Walls; All of Jane Austen and George Eliot; *Middlesex* by Jeffrey Eugenides. And so many more.

What are some representative titles that you have sold: Fiction: *Love in 90 Days* by Dr. Diana Kirschner (Center Street); *Kockroach* by Tyler Knox (William Morrow); *Marked Man* by William Lashner (William Morrow); *Souvenir* by Therese Fowler (Random House); *The Cloud Atlas* by Liam Callanan (Delacorte); *The Judas Field* by Howard Bahr (Henry Holt); *The Vanishing Point* by Mary Sharratt (Houghton Mifflin); *The Ice Chorus* by Sarah Stonich (Little, Brown); *Crawling at Night* by Nani Power (Atlantic Monthly Press). Nonfiction: *My First Five Husbands* by Rue McClanahan (Broadway); *Confessions of a Prep School Mommy Handler* by Wade Rouse (Harmony); *Why Men Fall Out of Love* by Michael French (Ballantine); *Cash In On Your Passion* by Jonathan Fields (Broadway); *Real Love* by Greg Baer (Gotham); *Feed The Hungry* by Nani Power (Free Press). Alspaugh: *Falling Under* by Danielle Younge-Ullman (Plume). Brower: *Oh, The Humanity!* by Jason Roeder (TOW Books); *Gag Reflex: A Paternity Memoir* by Cori Crooks (Seal Press). Brower: *Farm City: The Education of an Urban Farmer* by Novella Carpenter (Penguin Press); *Breathers: A Zombie's Lament* by S. G. Browne (Broadway Books); *Mixed Animal* by Richard Martin (MacAdam/Cage); *Slanted and Enchanted: Indie Culture in America* by Kaya Oakes (Henry Holt & Co).

THE ROBERT E. SHEPARD AGENCY

1608 Dwight Way, Berkeley, CA 94703-1804

510-849-3999

e-mail: mail@shepardagency.com

www.shepardagency.com

Agent' name: Robert Shepard

Education: B.A., M.A. in English, University of Pennsylvania

Career history: I've been an agent for 14 years and a part of the publishing world for more than two decades. Much has changed since I started out in the trade division of Addison-Wesley, a respected publisher that has since passed into history. But my background on the editorial, sales, and marketing sides gave me a good understanding of the "business" of publishing, including managing millions of dollars in sales and establishing excellent working relationships with scores of acquisitions editors. I bring all of that, a passion for nonfiction, and a healthy skepticism about the state of the publishing industry to bear in working with my clients. I enjoy helping them craft their proposals, sharing ideas with them as they write their books, helping them decide on the topics for their future works, and working with them to build their writing careers. I also enjoy the process of actually selling their books, and celebrating with my clients when the contract is signed and the advance check issued. The role of agents in the work of authors has become ever more critical. I'm proud of the close rapport I've established with authors and remain committed to the idea that books are the foundation of our culture; everything else springs from them. Since I love nonfiction, it's especially gratifying to see literary nonfiction works enjoying renewed success. This is an excellent time to be a nonfiction author, and I believe the works on my list have played a role in that.

Hobbies/personal interests: Hiking, biking, trains, raptors, and diagramming sentences.

Subjects that you would most love to agent: I represent only nonfiction, and under that heading I've cultivated two separate categories of books. The first consists of works driven by an exceptionally strong, unified literary narrative—books intended to make complex ideas accessible to a wider public; to shed new light on aspects of history, society, or popular culture; or to provide fresh insights into people, places, or concepts we may think of as commonplace. On this side of the practice, my subject headings include history, contemporary affairs and politics, science for laypeople, and topics in culture, sexuality, urbanism, and sports. The other general category of books I represent tends to be driven less by narrative and more by hard information; on this side, I have core interests in business, health, parenting, some topics in self-help, and occasional series-oriented works in such areas as music, science, and general reference. It's safe to say that I'm interested in neither the most commercial nor the most abstruse kinds of books, and that I'm rarely interested in works in spirituality or the metaphysical. On either side of the list, I'm happy to represent works that inform, that may change readers' minds, that may require a somewhat more intellectually curious audience, or about which someone might say "I never thought this would be an interesting subject, but I really loved reading this book." And I regularly digress. Sometimes, I represent a book simply because I think it will be fun.

Subjects that you definitely never want to agent: I never handle fiction, poetry, screenplays, or textbooks, and in general I'm not interested in memoirs, although occasionally books on my list may be written in the first-person or have an autobiographical component, especially when they relate to my regular categories. Robert E. Shepard Agency titles are usually aimed at a broad audience, so that highly specialized works (such as ones that examine religious writings in detail, or whose intended readers are mainly in a single profession) are not appropriate. As a general rule, I'm also not interested in spirituality (although historical works with some kind of religious overlay might be of interest), metaphysical subjects, or recovery.

If you were not an agent, what would you be doing: I'd probably be doing a lot more bicycling, preferably in Italy, conducting a symphony orchestra (after belatedly studying to do so for a couple of decades), or riding trains while on sabbatical from my job as the publisher of a distinguished literary non-fiction house. I'm not picky.

What's the best way for fiction writers to solicit your interest: I'm afraid they shouldn't—I don't represent fiction.

What's the best way for unsolicited writers to pitch you: Never call or fax; neither will speed consideration of your proposal. I encourage authors to mail a query letter or proposal, or to email a relatively brief query describing the proposed work, its intended audience, and the author's own credentials and reasons for writing on this subject. Don't just refer me to a Web site; I want to see how you present your ideas in the succinct form demanded by a query letter, whether by mail or email. Please do not attach any computer files to e-mail messages; for security purposes, they'll be deleted. If you use regular mail, always enclose a postage-paid return envelope capable of holding everything you sent me, without which you will not receive a reply.

Do you charge reading fees or try to sell non-agent services: No.

Do you require any kind of upfront payments from your clients: No.

Client representation by category: Non-Fiction: 100%.

Number of titles sold last year: 10. I've deliberately kept the practice small in order to devote time to my clients. I'm happy to see proposals from new authors, or from authors whose previous works may have been in genres other than general non-fiction. However, your credentials and expertise should be suited to the kind of book you're proposing.

Common mistakes writers make when pitching you: A big one is failing to share your proposal with a friend or another writer before you send it out. Authors who work in a vacuum risk losing perspective. In the many months you've been working on your book proposal—and very often they really do take that long to write—has your focus shifted inadvertently? Have you failed to discuss some aspect of your topic that an agent or editor might find fascinating—simply because you're too immersed in writing to realize you'd missed it? Have you made the strongest possible case that the audience for your book really exists, is large enough to interest publishers, and hasn't been inundated with competing books? Have you cited a date or name incorrectly, making yourself look careless even though you really do know your facts? A trusted adviser, particularly one with experience in writing books, can help you improve your proposal or even catch mistakes before you send it to agents. Not to sound like the English teacher I sometimes think I should have been, but bad spelling and grammar often guarantee rejection slips, too. Proofread your work, and if you don't trust your proofreading skills, find someone you do trust to help you. I also counsel authors to avoid proposal clichés. A big one is "there's no competition for my book." You should always try to find works that others might consider competitive, and then describe what's new, different, and better about yours. Another cliché is saying that you look forward to "partnering" with your publisher without saying, in detail, what you can do to help market your book. An author's "platform" is ever more important—critical, really, to the acquisitions process. Try to build up your portfolio. Send articles to op-ed pages and magazines, so you can include copies in your proposal packet. If you have experience on radio or television, or speaking in front of large audiences, cite it; if you don't, try to get some. Finally, there are two important housekeeping issues: Always enclose a return envelope large enough to hold your material, with the proper postage (without which you won't get a response); and always provide your return address!

Your description of the client from Hell: One with a great idea but without the inclination to write a super proposal, let alone a super book. Writing is tough and an agent wants to be your ally and work hard for you and for your book. But the hardest work of all must be yours.

How would you describe your dream client: Those who are passionate about writing, passionate about their subjects, and appreciative when things go right.

How can writers increase the odds that you will offer representation: Pay attention to other books, know how to differentiate your own from others, and take steps to build up your resume as a writer before you query. Write (and publish) articles and op-ed pieces. Try to get yourself in front of audiences if appropriate and on televeision and radio if possible—you don't have to be famous to be published, but you do have to be "marketable." And write a really outstanding query letter or proposal; it's critical to do your homework.

Why did you become an agent, and how did you become one: I love books and believe they can and should be central to our cultural life, even in an era when they're being joined by new sources of entertainment and information all the time. But the consolidations of leading publishers during the 1990s resulted in the loss of many editors, the very people who traditionally worked the closest with authors, helped them craft better books, and made sure that the marketing got done. The vast majority of today's editors are as talented and dedicated as ever, but find themselves with more books to edit and less time to spend with authors. So although authors create the intellectual property that fuels our culture, they can feel lost in the publishing shuffle, confused by business aspects of their writing careers, and even disillusioned by the paradoxical demand of publishers to write "fresh" books that nonetheless don't deviate much from the constraints of established categories. I see my role as an agent as that of a mentor and advocate for my clients and their work, as a diplomat who can moderate the author-publisher relationship, as a business adviser who watches over royalty statements, and, in the end, as someone who helps authors feel good about the writing experience, so they can write more books in the future. The bad news, unfortunately, is that an agent still spends a good part of his or her day saying "no." The good news is that, when everything works as it should, the wealth of media outlets available to us in the Internet age means books can be more rather than less influential.

Please list representative titles you have sold: *A Few Seconds of Panic* by Stefan Fatsis (Penguin Press), also the author of the bestselling *Word Freak* (Houghton Mifflin hardcover, Penguin paperback); *Night Draws Near* (Henry Holt & Co.), a Los Angeles Times Book Prize-winning work by Pulitzer Prize winner Anthony Shadid whose next book about Lebanon will be published by Holt; *The Foie Gras Wars* by Mark Caro (Simon & Schuster); *American Band* by Kristen Laine (Gotham); *Find Your Focus Zone* by Lucy Jo Palladino, Ph.D. (Free Press); *Your Symptoms Are Real* by Benjamin H. Natelson, M.D. (Wiley); *The Exhaustion Cure* by Laura Stack (Broadway Books), also the author of *Leave the Office Earlier* and *Find More Time*, both also from Broadway Books; *Champagne* by Don and Petie Kladstrup (William Morrow), also the authors of *Wine and War* (Broadway Books), an international bestseller published in 10 languages; *Women of Valor* by Ellen Hampton (Palgrave-MacMillan); *The Governmental Manual for New Superheroes* by Matthew David Brozik and Jacob Sager Weinstein (Andrews McMeel), also the authors of two other books in this series; *Coal: A Human History* by Barbara Freese (Perseus hardcover, Penguin paperback), a bestseller in the U.S. and published in several editions abroad; *The Rough Guide to Climate Change* by Robert Henson (Rough Guides/Penguin).

JACQUELINE SIMENAUER LITERARY AGENCY

Nonfiction: P.O. Box 770968, Naples, FL 34107-0968

Fiction: P.O. Box AG, Mantoloking, NJ 08738

Agents' names: Jacqueline Simenauer, bookagencies@gmail.com; Carole J. Greene, carnlar@gmail.com; Fran Pardi, agenteditor@gmail.com
The following information pertains to Jacqueline Simenauer:
Born: New York, New York.
Education: Fordham University.
Career story: After working as an articles editor for a national publication, I decided to start my own literary agency, and as a result of this, I coauthored a number of books with my clients. Some of the six books that I as involved with include the best selling *Beyond the Male Myth*, which was featured on Oprah, *Husbands and Wives*, *Singles: The New Americans*, which gained the attention of the White House, and *Not Tonight Dear*. They went on to sell over 200,000 copies. My work has also been featured in most

of the nation's magazines and newspapers including *Time, Readers Digest, Ladies Home Journal, The New York Times,* and *The Washington Post.* In addition, I have appeared in 100 radio/TV showings, including *Good Morning America* and the *Today Show.*

Hobbies and special personal interests: I have always worked so hard that I never found time to even think about a hobby. However, I do love classical concerts, I am a member o a wine society, love the Broadway theatre, and great fiction.

Subjects and categories you like to agent: I like a wide range of strong commercial nonfiction books that include medical, health, nutrition, popular psychology, how-to/self-help, parenting, women's issues, spirituality, men's issues, relaitonships, social sciences, beauty, controversial subjects.

Subjects and categories writers shouldn't bother pitching to you: This agency doesn't handle crafts, poetry, and children's books.

What might you be doing if you weren't agenting: You would probably find me cruising around the world.

What's the most effective ways for writers to grab your attention: Please write a really good query letter. This is so important. If you can't get your idea across effectively, then you've lost the agent.

Do you charge fees separate from your commission, or offer non-agenting fee based services: We do not charge a reading fee. The agency can draw on professionals to do book doctoring when requested, and the fee for that is currently $2.50 per page. In rare instances, we also offer ghostwriting servies (utilizing published writers on a contract basis). This represents a small part of our business—probably in the range of 5% or less.

What are representative titles you have sold to publishers: *The Insulin Resistance Diet* by Dr. Cheryle Hart and Mary Kay Grossman, R. D. (McGraw-Hill); *The Thyroid Guide* by Dr. Beth Ann Ditkoff and Dr. Paul Lo Gerfo (Harper); *Overcoming Anxiety Without Tranquilizers* by Dr. Edward H. Drummond (Dutton); *Decoding the Secret Language of Your Body* by Dr. Martin Rush (Fireside/Simon & Schuster); *Fasting and Eating for Health* by Dr. Joel Fuhrman (St. Martin's Press); *What To Do After You Say I Do* by Dr. Marcus J. Goldman and Lori Goldman (Prima); *Why Did it Happen* by Janice Cohn D.S.W. (Morrow); *The Mind Factor* by Dr. Jean Rosenbaum (Prentice Hall); *Bride's Guide to Emotional Survival* by Rita Bigel-Casher, Ph.D. (Prima); *Money Secrets the Pros Don't Want You to Know* by Stephanie Gallagher (AMACOM); *What is Fear* by Dr. Jean Rosenbaum (Prentice Hall); *Husbands and Wives* by Dr. Anthony Pietropinto; *The Healing Mind* by Eileen F. Oster (Prima); *The New Americans* (Simon & Schuster); *How to Avoid Divorce* by Dr. Jean Rosenbaum (Harper); *Biotypes* (Times Books); *The Joy of Fatherhood* by Dr. Marcus Goldman (Prima); *The Yankee Encyclopedia* by Mark Gallagher (Sagamore); *Every Woman's Guide to Investing* by Francie Prince and Douglas Pi (Prima); *Brave New You* by Mary Valentis, Ph.D. (New Harbinger Publications); *Beyond the Male Myth* by Dr. Anthony Pietropinto; *The Real Truth About Mutual Funds* by Herbert Rongold (American Management); *The Single Woman's Travel Guide* by Doris Walfield (Citadel Press); *Conquering Lonliness* by Dr. Jean Rosenbaum; *The Clinic* by Dr. Anthony Pietropinto; *Reenginering Yourself* by Dr. Daniel L. Araoz and Dr. William S. Sutton (Adams Media); *The Dream Girl* by Dr. Anthony Pietropinto (Adams Media);

Kleptomania by Dr. Marcus Goldman (New Horizon); *Is Your Volkawagon a Sex Symbol* by Dr. Jean Rosenbaum; *How I Sold A Million Copies of My Software* by Herbert R. Kraft (Adams Media); *Single's Guide to Cruise Vacations* (Prima).

Why did you become an agent, and how did you become one: I seemed to have always been involved with the publishing world, in one way or another. I had worked for a national publication as an articles editor, I was a freelance writer and coauthor. Agenting seemed the likely next step so I opened an agency. At first I was the only one. Then I was joined by my colleagues Fran Pardi and Carole Greene.

How do you feel about writers: I think my background as a freelance writer and coauthor makes me even more sympathetic to struggling writers. I understand what it feels like to see your name on a book jacket and appear on a major TV show, and if I can help you achieve your dream, then it becomes mine as well. But understand that it takes a great deal of perseverance to go from an idea to a proposal strong enough to get the attention of the publishing world. I hear good ideas all day long, yet few ever go anywhere.

How would you describe "the writer from hell": We agree with an stand with Carole. See below.

The following information pertains to Carole J. Green:

Born: Anderson, IN.

Education: Two degrees from Ball State University, Muncie Indiana; B.A. and M.A. in English.

Career story: After a career as a high school and college educator focusing primarily on composition and creative writing, I became a full-time freelance writer for 10 years and I wrote more than 700 articles for national and regional magazines. These encompoassed a wide range of topics including lifestyle, medical, business, finance, construction and home improvement, real estate, and golf. During that time, I also wrote award-winning advertising copy, marketing brochures, video scripts, newsletters, and press releases for clients. When I turned my attention to book projects, I became a ghost writer of three books, and edited books for private clients as well as a publihing company. After teaching, freelancing, ghosting, editing, and critiquing, the next logical step was becoming literary agent. Voila!

Hobbies and special personal interests: In addition to traveling the world with my hubby, I enjoy theatre, fine dining, golf, bridge, reading and music. Lots of reading. Someof it AFTER publication.

Subjects and categories you like to agent: As an agent, I find my tastes are quite eclectic, almost anything that is well written and has a chance of being salable. Nonfiction attracts me more than fiction. Send me a fascinating story, beautifully told with atention to expert use of the English language. I have a red pen and I'm not afraid to use it!

Subjects and categories writers shouldn't bother pitching to you: See above.

What might you be doing if you weren't agenting: When I'm not working with my authors, I am writing something from pro bono newsletters for groups I support to grocery lists. I am still tinkering with a novel I started many years ago. Maybe this year I'll finish it. Or maybe you'll keep me so busy I won't have time to work on it. Again.

What's the most effective ways for writers to grab your attention: Authors can best grab my attention by writing a query letter that demonstrates their grasp of language skills and their commitment to delivering the message in an interesting, professional manner. Just owning a computer with a word processing program is not enough to make you a writer, so forget the stylized graphics for your cover and concentrate on making that query letter so enticing that I salivate to take you on.

Do you charge fees separate from your commission, or offer non-agenting fee based services: See above.

What are representative titles you have sold to publishers: See above.

How do you feel about writers: How I feel about writers can be summed up by looking at my own career. I am totally supportive of the creative life. If you love to mess around with words and you have a story that would benefit others, I'll be the wind beneath your wings. The best writers through the ages have made the world a better place. If you aspire to that lofty goal, I'd like nothing better than to introduce you to the world. Will readers be glad they spent the time to read your book? That's what matters. If they'll toss it aside and mumble, "Waste of my time—I could have been herding the neighborhood cats" then please don't YOU waste MY time.

How would you describe "the writer from hell": I can't describe any writer, editor or publisher as "from hell" as long as they put forth sincere effort to produce a book that people will be glad to read. That goes for agents too, so don't bug me if you're my client. I'm putting forth sincere effort even if you don't hear from me for weeks!

You're welcome to share your thoughts and sentiments about the business of writing and publishing: One of my writing group friends once said, "Writing is the hardest work I ever loved." It IS difficult, much harder than most nonwriters comprehend. Getting your first book published can be daunting; however, every successful author had that "first" book. Don't ever let fear of failure stand in your way of attaining your goal of publishing your work. Changes in the publishing industry occur so fast—with e-books and Kindle, for example—that the wisest sage would have trouble foreseeing the future. Will people continue to read books? Absolutely. It's part of our DNA. How we'll do it will continue to evolve. As long as the marketplace desires good stories well told, whether fiction or nonfiction, I hope to do my bit in the process till someone has to pry my red pen out of my cold, still fingers.

The following information pertains to Fran Pardi:

Born: Pittsburgh, PA.

Education: B.A. in English, St. Francis University.

Career story: Before becoming an agent I worked as a teacher. Then I spent the next 20 years as a newspaper reporter for a daily paper, starting as a freelancer, then becoming a staff writer. My responsibilities at one of the state's major newspapers, included covering hard news. I worked in the features department for the last nine years. I have also worked as a freelance editor and writer, and I recently won an award for outstanding journalism.

Hobbies and special personal interests: Music, reading, dance, theatre.

Subjects and categories you like to agent: I specialize in fiction, but I do like cookbooks and medical books.

Subjects and categories writers shouldn't bother pitching to you: See above.

What might you be doing if you weren't agenting: Probably sitting on a beach or in front of a fireplace reading published books, as opposed to unpublished books.

Do you charge fees separate from your commission, or offer non-agenting fee based services: See above.

What are representative titles you have sold to publishers: See above.

Why did you become an agent, and how did you become one: I sort of fell into it.

How would you describe "the writer from hell": We agree with and stand with Carole. See above.

MICHAEL SNELL LITERARY AGENCY

P.O. Box 1206, Truro, MA 02666

508-349-3718

e-mail: snell.patricia@gmail.com

Agents' names: Michael Snell, Patricia Snell, Vice-President

Born: Michael: August 14, 1065, Denver, Colorado; Patricia: 1951, Boston, Massachusetts.

Education: Michael: B.A., Phi Beta Kappa, DePauw University; Patricia: FIT and Pratt Institute, New York.

Career history: Michael: 13 years as editor and executive editor for Wadsworth Publishing Company and Addison-Wesley (science, economics, English, computer science, business college textbooks); Patricia: Design offices in New York City's garment district and in Manhattan art galleries and museums. 12 years as partner in the Michael Snell Literary Agency.

Hobbies/personal interests: Michael: Golf, tennis, landscaping, shell fishing; Patricia: Gardening; landscaping; cooking; tennis; anything involving water (I'm a Pisces): swimming, surfing, fishing, shell fishing; movies, and all areas of design.

Categories/subjects that you are most enthusiastic about agenting: Michael: Any subject that lends itself to practical self-help and how-to presentation, especially business, management, leadership, entrepreneurship. Also health, fitness, psychology, relationships, parenting, pets, women's issues. Literary fiction. Science fiction, New Age, memoirs, children's books. Patricia: I have broad interests, from the practical to the sublime. Subjects that have the power to solve problems, enhance living, or transform lives gain my attention.

If you were not an agent, what might you be doing instead: Michael: Teaching; Patricia: Any number of things in design and the visual arts.

What's the best way for writers to solicit your interest: Michael: Write an enticing one-page query letter (with SASE), pitching your book/subject and establishing your credentials in the area. We'll tell you what we want to review (proposal, etc.);

Patricia: Write a brief, one-page query letter. Get to the point right away. Always include sufficient SASE.

Do you charge reading or management fees: Michael: No, though we do at times offer collaborative developmental and rewriting services, for which we charge additional commission points. We also represent a number of professional editors, rewriters, ghostwriters and developmental editors who can help content specialists bring their books to market; Patricia: No. But I may negotiate a higher commission on projects on which I agree to collaborate as developmental editor.

Can you provide an approximation by % of what you tend to represent by category: Michael: Adult Non-Fiction: 95%, Literary Fiction: 5%; Patricia: Adult Non-Fiction: 100%, mostly practical how-to and self-help.

What are the most common mistakes writers make when pitching you: Michael: A boring or lengthy query that does not get to the point quickly, identifying the subject and the author's credentials in a compelling way. Many new authors oversell their book, when their query letter should achieve one goal: to prompt the agent to ask to see a proposal or material. Also, too many new authors let their egos get in their way, selling too hard with too little humility. Since we only consider new clients on an exclusive basis, authors who have embarked on a fishing expedition, contacting and submitting material to many agents, put us off. Authors forget they're looking for a marriage partner, not a plumber or electrician. Tiny envelopes with insufficient postage create SASEs that will not accommodate feedback or our brochure on "How to write a book proposal" or our flyer offering a "Model proposal"; Patricia: Wasting my time with long, boring self-congratulatory letters. Failure to provide the proper return postage. I refuse to waste my time (and money) on those who cannot follow simple, clear directions.

How would you describe the client from Hell: Michael: Editors and agents avoid "High maintenance" authors, those who require constant communication, hand-holding, and reassurance. While agents do form strong bonds with their clients, they run a business that requires efficient, professional, respectful relationships. The worst clients can't see around their own egos: because they know everything about one thing (their subject), they think they know everything about everything. Poor students make poor clients; bad listeners make bad clients impatient people who want the publishing process to more quickly make agents' and editors' lives miserable. This is a slow way to make a fast buck: people in a hurry make too many mistakes; Patricia: Wasting my time, failing to follow directions, being a poor student in the long process of getting publishes, trying to rush what is an essentially slow process, failing to value my contribution or, worst of all, acting rudely (thankfully a rare occurrence).

How would you describe the perfect client: Michael: The ideal client possesses all the qualities of a good friend and business partner: knowledgeable, patient, humble, respectful, prompt, reliable, professional, perseverant, and funny. Nothing smoothes over the rough patches better than a sense of humor. The agent-author relationship is unique. Because the work involves a certain amount of "art," it engages strong emotions. The best clients don't let their passion for their work undermine a respectful and caring professional relationship with the people who will help them make their dreams come true: their agent and their editor. The quality of the relationship depends on trust: the ideal client trusts her agent's professionalism and listens carefully to guidance and advice. This becomes so crucial to the author-publisher relationship later on, the more an author develops trust with her agent, the better for everyone—not to mention the book's sales—later on; Patricia: The mirror opposite of the client from Hell. Those who behave professionally, valuing their time and mine. Those who show enthusiasm and express gratitude. Those who follow directions. Those who work hard throughout the whole process and realize that it is a long process with a long learning curve. Those who bring a good disposition and good manners to the work at hand, honoring the most important rule: We build a relationship before we build a book.

How and why did you ever become an agent: Michael: Having learned the art of book development as an editor for a book publisher, and having helped create dozens of bestsellers, I decided I'd rather make 15% commission on sales than keep taking home the measly salary publishers pay. I also got weary of the fact that editors were becoming less and less involved in the actual task of development (helping writers turn good ideas into great books). As an agent you can work closely with authors on their manuscripts, when necessary, and you can choose the people and projects that most attract you. I try to honor the same principles I coach my clients to practice: patience, perseverance, and professionalism. To those I'd add passion. I love books, have spent a lifetime overseeing their publication, and can think of no greater joy than opening that brand new baby book and smelling the ink on its pages; Patricia: I married into the business and, well, married my love of books with the opportunity to help create them.

What, if anything, can a writer do to increase the odds of you becoming his or her agent: Michael: Read this listing carefully and approach us with what you've learned about us in mind. When communicating with us, remember Pascal's apology: "I would have made it shorter, if I'd had the time." Time is priceless: don't waste it on long-winded queries and constant phone calls demanding a faster response. By the same token, take your time, pay attention to details when preparing submissions, and slow down. Nothing can kill an emerging relationship faster than hastily assembled material that arrives in our office incomplete and poorly organized. Did I mention patience? Did I mention approaching us like a good student? You can also request, with SASE, our brochure "How to write a book proposal"; you can read Michael Snell's book *From Book Idea to Bestseller*. And you can ask for information on how to buy a "Model proposal"; Patricia: Read all that I (and Michael) have said here, and take it all to heart.

How would you describe to someone (or thing) from another planet what it is that you do as an agent: We develop book ideas into bestsellers.

Do you have any particular opinions or impressions of editors and publishers in general: We love them. They pay our bills and help pay college tuition for our clients' children.

What do you think the future holds for writers, publishers, and agents: The market for good ideas, valuable information, and graceful communication will keep growing, no matter the form in which it gets packaged. Every ten years experts predict the death of the book, and every ten years the market has expanded.

Do you have any favorite (current) TV shows, films, or books that you espe-

cially like and how come: *The Sopranos, Rescue Me, 24, Capote, Crash*, and anything written by David James Duncan, or David Foster Wallace

On a personal level, what do you think people like about you and dislike about you: They like our honesty; they dislike our blunt criticism. They like our humor; they dislike our bad jokes. They like the money we make for them; they dislike the fact that we don't make them more.

Please list representative titles you have sold: *How Did That happen?: Holding People Accountable the Positive, Principled Way* by Roger Connors and Tom Smith (Viking/Portfolio); *The Art of Woo* by Richard Shell (Viking/Portfolio); *Women Leading in the New Era* by Birute Regine (Sourcebooks/Sphinx); *Stuck: Overcoming the Twelve Biggest Obstacles that Hold Women Back* by Sandra Ford Walston (Sourcebooks/Sphinx); *Global Trade for Entrepreneurs* by Larry Tuller (Entrepreneur Books); *Strategic Customer Service* by John Goodman (AMACOM); *Marketing for Rainmakers* by Phil Fragrasso (Wiley); *The Mortgage Minefield* by Barbara Osach and Richard Giannamore (AMACOM); *You, Him and Her: What to do When Your Husband Strays* by Paul Coleman (Adams Media); *Difficult Conversations With Your Kids* by Richard Heyman (Adams Media); *Difficult Convesations With Your Boss* and *Difficult Conversations With Your Employees* by Lynn Eisaguirre (Adams Media); *The Working Mom's Survival Guide* by Paula Peters (Adams Media).

STEELE-PERKINS LITERARY AGENCY

26 Island Lane, Canandaigua, NY 14424

585-396-9290

e-mail: pattiesp@aol.com

Agent's name: Pattie Steele-Perkins

Career history: Prior to becoming an agent Pattie Steele-Perkins was Creative Director for a Television Production Company. Prior to that she was a producer/director.

Categories/subjects that you are most enthusiastic about agenting: Romance and women's fiction all genres...category romance, romantic suspense, inspirational, multi cultural, paranormal, chick lit, lady lit.

What you don't want to agent: Non-Fiction and anything that does not meet the specific criteria of romance and women's fiction.

What's the best way for writers to solicit your interest: A brief e-mail query that includes a synopsis.

Do you charge reading or management fees: No.

Can you provide an approximation by % of what you tend to represent by category: Romance and women's fiction: 100%.

What are the most common mistakes writers make when pitching you: They don't research what I handle or they do research and pitch the story as if it were romance even though it isn't.

How would you describe the client from Hell: Clients that use foul language rather than just stet on copy edits. Clients that rant and rave on line about their editor or publishing house.

How would you describe the perfect client: Someone who loves to write and has stories to tell.

Do you have any particular opinions or impressions of editors and publishers in general: They are the smartest people I have ever met and they love books.

ROSEMARY B. STIMOLA

306 Chase Court, Edgewater, NJ 07020

voice/fax: 201-945-9353

www.stimolaliterarystudio.com   e-mail: info@stimolaliterarystudio.com

Agent's name: Rosemary B. Stimola

Born: November 6, 1952; Queens, New York.

Education: B.A. in Elementary Education/Theoretical Linguistics, Queens college; M.A. in Applied Linguistics, NYU; Ph.D. in Linguistic/Educational Psychology, NYU.

Career history or story: Professor of Language and Literature, children's bookseller, freelance editor, education consultant, literary agent.

Hobbies/personal interests: Beach combing, Latin dance, cockapoos.

Subjects & categories you are most enthusiastic about agenting: Preschool through young adult fiction/nonfiction; concept cookbooks.

What you don't want to agent: Adult fiction.

If you were not an agent, what might you be doing instead: Working in publishing, editorial, or marketing.

What's the best way for writers to solicit your interest: Referral through editors, clients, or agent colleagues always helps. See SUBMISSION GUIDELINES on Web site. Prefer e-mail queries, but no attachments please!

Do you charge reading or any upfront fees: No.

How do you feel about writers: I am in awe of good writers, and admire those less talented for their efforts.

How would you describe the writer from Hell: Desparate for money, has unrealistic expectations and a major ego, resistant to editor guidance and revision.

How would you describe the publisher or editor from Hell: Does not answer calls or respond to e-mails. Late with paperwork. Does not deliver what is promised in time or production.

Why did you become an agent, and how did you become one: It was an evolving state, allowing me to put the literary aesthetics I developed as an educator and the publishing knowledge I acquired as a bookseller to use in one role.

How would you describe to someone (or thing) from another planet what it is that you do as an agent: In the space between authors and publishing personnel, I serve as an advocate, facilitator, champion and trouble shooter all in the service of making the best possible book, one that I can then bring to foreign and film markets.

What do you like best about your clients, and the editors and publishers you work with: We are all lovers of story, dazzled by well-crafted written words and their ability to touch head and heart.

Will our business exist as we know it 10 years from now: Our business will certainly exist, but with world and technological changes, we must change as well. I couldn't say what the face of publishing will look like in future, but I would stake my life on its being an important force.

What are your favorite books/TV shows/movies, and why: *Harold and the Purple Crayon* (the perfect children's book); *Now, Voyager* (Bette Davis at her best!); *The Shawshank Redemption* (love this tale of friendship and triumph of spirit); *To Kill A Mockingbird* (read at 12 years of age, a life changing book for me); *Fried Green Tomatoes* (words and characters pull at my heart strings); *Starman* (attracted to the human element in this sci-fi tale); *Real Time with Bill Maher* (how else do we get through the madness?)

What are some representative titles that you have sold: *The Hunger Games Trilogy* by Suzanne Collins (Scholastic); *Soul Enchilada* by David Macinnis Gill (Greenwillow Press/Harper Collins); *The Adoration of Jenna Fox* by Mary Pearson (Henry Holt & Co/Macmillan); *Hurricane Song* by Paul Volponi (Viking Books); *Breathe My Name* by R.A. Nelson (Razorbill/Penguin); *Steinbeck's Ghost* by Lewis Buzbee (Feiwel & Friends/Macmillan); *Sandy's Circus* by Tanya Lee Stone (Viking Books); *Max and Pinky: Superheroes* by Maxwell Eaton III (Knopf/RH); *Nighty Night, Sleep Sleep* by Brian Anderson (Roaring Brook Press/Macmillan); *Swords, An Artist's Devotion* by Ben Boos (Candlewick); *Gourmet Gifting* by Dinah Corley (Harvard Common Press).

LES STOBBE

300 Doubleday Road, Tryon, NC 28782

828-808-7127   fax: 978-945-0517

e-mail: lstobbe@alltel.net

Agent's name: Les Stobbe

Career history or story: 1962-1970: Business magazine editor; 1970-1978: Editorial director, Moody Press; 1978-1982: VP and editorial director, Christian Herald

Books and Book Club; 1982-1985: Editor and director, Here's Life Publishing; 1985-1992: President, Here's Life Publishing; 1993-1996: Managing editor, Scripture Press Curriculum; 1996-2001: VP of communications, Vision New England; 1993-present: Literary agent; 2001-present: Editor-in-chief, Jerry B. Jenkins Christian Writers Guild.

Hobbies, interests: Boston Red Sox

Subjects & categories you are interested in agenting, including fiction & non-fiction: Adult Christian fiction and non-fiction.

Subjects & categories writers shouldn't even bother pitching to you: New age humanistic, children's books, young adult fiction.

What would you do if you weren't agenting: Writing books.

What's the best way for fiction writers to solicit your interest: Get editors at Christian Writers Guild conference to say, "Send me a proposal."

What's the best way for non-fiction writers to solicit your interest: See above.

Do you charge reading or any upfront fees: No.

In your experience, what are the most common pitching mistakes writers make: Sending documents with typos and grammatical mistakes.

What's your definition of a great client: One whose proposal is professionally prepared but is willing to improve the pitch.

How can writers increase the odds that you will offer representation: Attend a Christian writers conference and talk to editors.

Why did you become an agent, and how did you become one: Author friends insisted I represent them.

Describe to someone from another planet what you do as an agent: I open doors for clients at publishing houses.

How do you feel about editors and publishers: I was one of them.

How do you feel about writers: I love writers.

What do you see in the near future for book publishing: More consolidations, fewer titles.

In your opinion, what do editors think of you: I have a good reputation.

On a personal non-professional level, what do you think people think of you: A caring professional.

What are some representative titles that you have sold: *Hearing God's Voice* by Vern Heidebrecht (David C. Cook); *The Evidence* by Austin Boyd (Navpress); *Petticoat Ranch* by Mary Connealy (Barbour Publishing); *The Great American Supper Swap* by Trish Berg (David C. Cook); *Rolling Thunder* by Mark Mynheir (Multnomah-Waterbrook); *Pray Big* by Will Davis Jr. (Baker/Revell); *The 21 Most Effective Prayers of the Bible* by Dave Earley (Barbour Publishing); *From Jihad to Jesus* by Jerry Rassamni (AMG Publishing).

ROBIN STRAUS

229 East 79th Street, Suite 5A, NY, NY 10075

212-472-3282   fax: 212-472-3833

e-mail: robin@robinstrausagency.com

Agents' names: Robin Straus (President & Primary Agent); Erika Recordon (Junior Agent)

Education: Wellesley B.A., NYU School of Business M.B.A.

Career history: Started at publishing houses, doing editorial work at Little, Brown and subsidiary rights at Doubleday and Random House; VP Wallace & Sheil Agency for four years and started Robin Straus Agency, Inc. in 1983.

Categories/subjects that you are most enthusiastic about agenting: High quality literary fiction and non-fiction. Subject is of less importance than fine writing and research.

What you don't want to agent: Genre fiction such as science fiction, horror, romance, westerns; poetry; no screenplays or plays.

If you were not an agent, what might you be doing instead: Traveling the world; raising horses and dogs; going to medical school.

What's the best way for writers to solicit your interest: A great query letter and sample material that speaks for itself. Caution: we are a very small agency and unable to take on more than a few clients per year, so we would have to be completely smitten.

Do you charge reading or management fees: No.

Can you provide an approximation by % of what you tend to represent by category: Nonfiction: 60% (history, social science, psychology, women's interest, education, travel, biography, art history and many other fields); Fiction: 40%.

What are the most common mistakes writers make when pitching you: Bad grammar in letters, clichés, overstating claims for book being revolutionary. Asking us to download queries and manuscripts.

How would you describe the client from Hell: Being awakened every morning by a client's phone call.

How would you describe the perfect client: A captivating writer who can make any subject interesting; receptive to suggestions on how to improve work; appreciative that the publishing process is a collaborative effort; imaginative about ways to market self and books.

How and why did you ever become an agent: I started out my career working on manuscripts, but discovered I also liked the business end of publishing and moved into rights. Agenting seemed the best way to combine editorial and selling activities and be a strong advocate for authors.

What, if anything, can a writer do to increase the odds of you becoming his or her agent: Convince me with your arguments. Dazzle me with your prose. Make me fall in love with your characters.

How would you describe to someone (or thing) from another planet what it is that you do as an agent: When I want to represent an author, I work with him/her to help shape proposals and manuscripts to entice editors to make an offer. I submit material to publishers, negotiate contracts, vet royalty statements, sell translation, serial, film and audio rights on behalf of client. I generally act as the business manager for the author and intercede whenever necessary throughout the entire publishing process. I view my relationship with my clients as a continuum that extends over many books.

Do you have any particular opinions or impressions of editors and publishers in general: They do less editing than they used to, probably because they are under more pressure.

What do you think the future holds for writers, publishers, and agents: Even with all the competition for our time, books will always have an important place and publishers will continue to exist and figure out ways to stay central. With the rise of the Internet and other electronic media, there is a huge need for content and authors increasingly will find other venues and audiences for their work beyond paper over board volumes. The challenge will be in finding fair ways to compensate the writers while simultaneously protecting their work.

Please list representative titles you have sold: Fiction such as *The No. 1 Ladies Detective Agency* and other series, (Pantheon/Anchor); *The Ivy Chronicles* (Viking); *Coma* (Riverhead); *The Year of The French* (NY Review); *Crossways* (Ontario); *Who Do You Think You Are* (Touchstone); *The Time of Their Lives* (St. Martin's); *The Rose Labyrinth* (Atria), Nonfiction such as *Ideas* (HarperCollins); *The Fall of Berlin* (Viking); *Outfoxing Fear* (Norton); *Character Matters* (Touchstone); *A Writer at War* (Pantheon); *Mismatch* (Scribner); *Transatlantic* (HarperCollins); *Fishface* (Phaidon).

STROTHMAN AGENCY

6 Beacon Street, Suite 810, Boston, MA 02108

www.thestrothmanagency.com   e-mail: info@strothmanagency.com

Agents' names: Wendy Strothman, Dan O'Connell

Career story: Wendy Strothman, who led the turnarounds of two venerable Boston publishers, Beacon Press and Houghton Mifflin's Trade & Reference Division, has 30 years of publishing experience.

As Executive Vice President and head of Houghton Mifflin's Trade & Reference Division from 1996 through July 2002, she turned an unprofitable division into one of the most profitable in the industry. Strothman's efforts to publish books at the highest standards led the company to receive more literary awards than at any time in its history: two Pulitzer Prizes, one National Book Award, three Caldecott Medals, and two Newbery Medals, among many other honors.

At Houghton Mifflin, Strothman also acquired and edited books by key authors, including James Carroll (*An American Requiem*, winner of the National Book Award; *Constantine's Sword*, New York Times bestseller), Philip Roth (four novels, including *American Pastoral*, winner of the Pulitzer Prize, and *The Human Stain*, New York Times bestseller), John Kenneth Galbraith, Arthur M. Schlesinger Jr. (*A Life in the Twentieth Century*), and Paul Theroux. She vigorously pursued the defense in the lawsuit brought by the Margaret Mitchell estate to block publication of Alice Randall's *The Wind Done Gone*, a parody of *Gone with the Wind*.

From 1983-95, Strothman headed Beacon Press, a Boston publisher founded in 1854. She led Beacon to new prominence, publishing two New York Times bestsellers (*The Measure of Our Success* by Marian Wright Edelman and *Race Matters* by Cornel West) and one National Book Award winner, Mary Oliver's *New and Selected Poems*. Strothman began her career in 1973 at the University of Chicago Press where she launched the *Critical Edition of the Works of Giuseppe Verdi*.

Strothman is the Senior Fellow and the Secretary of the Brown University Corporation; at Brown she has funded the annual Wendy J. Strothman Faculty Research Award in the Humanities to facilitate research planned for publication. She has served on of the Board of Governors of Yale University Press and the Board of Trustees of the Cantata Singers in Boston, and now serves as a trustee of Deerfield Academy and on the board of the Friends of the Charlestown Navy Yard.

She has served as an expert witness on publishing matters and provides business consulting services to small non-profit publishers. In addition, she has led workshops in publishing for the American Academy of Arts and Sciences, the Nieman Foundation at Harvard University, and other institutions.

Known as an advocate for authors and freedom of expression and as a friend to independent booksellers, Ms. Strothman has received numerous awards, including the Publisher of the Year Award from the New England Booksellers Association, the Person of the Year Award for "permanent and significant contributions to the book industry" from the Literary Market Place, the 1994 PEN New England "Friend to Writers" Award, and a Doctor of Humane Letters from Meadville Lombard Theological School in Chicago and a Doctor of Human Letters from Brown. She is a frequent speaker at industry, library, and university events.

Career story: Dan O'Connell has devised and executed marketing and publicity campaigns for small presses, mid-sized publishers, and trade houses.

As Assistant Publicity Director at Houghton Mifflin's Trade & Reference Division, he worked with a range of distinguished authors including PEN Faulkner Award winner John Edgar Wideman (*Hoop Roots*), Harvard psychologist Daniel Schacter (*Seven Sins of Memory*), NBA finalist and science writer Steve Olson (*Mapping Human History, Count Down*), National Book Award winner James Carroll (*Secret Father*), and award-winning psychologist Pumla Gobodo-Madikizela of the University of Cape Town (*A Human Being Died That Night*). O'Connell devised brand-building campaigns for two of Houghton's most significant lines—*The American Heritage®* line of dictionaries and *The Peterson Field Guides*.

As Assistant Marketing Director at Beacon Press, O'Connell managed publicity campaigns for two national bestsellers, Cornel West's *Race Matters* and Marian Wright Edelman's *The Measure of Our Success*.

Before joining Beacon, O'Connell was Marketing Manager at Alyson Publications, the leading publisher of books for gay and lesbian readers. He began working in book publishing at The Brookings Institution in Washington DC where he handled subsidiary rights, among other marketing duties.

Subjects and categories you like to agent: We specialize in narrative non-fiction, memoir, history, science and nature, arts and culture, literary travel, current affairs, and some business. We have a highly selective practice in literary fiction and young adult literature.

Subjects and categories writers shouldn't bother pitching to you: We do not handle commercial fiction, romance, science fiction, picture books, gift books, poetry, or self help.

What's the most effective ways for writers to grab your attention: Fiction: Send a synopsis and two or three pages of your work, with a self-addressed stamped envelope. Nonfiction: We specialize in nonfiction. Send a query letter outlining your qualifications and experience, along with a synopsis of your work, and a self-addressed stamped envelope.

Do you charge fees separate from your commission, or offer non-agenting fee based services: We do not charge any upfront fees.

What are representative titles you have sold to publishers: A book of advice on "etiquette, ethics, and everything in between" by Robin Abrahams (Times Books); *The Sound of Freedom: Marion Anderson, the Lincoln Memorial, and the Democratic Imagination* by Ray Aresenault (Bloomsbury Press); *The Weeping Time: Anatomy of a Slave Auction* by Anne Bailey (HarperCollins); *Choke: What the Secrets of the Brain Reveal about Success and Failure at Work and at Play* by Sian Beilock (Simon &Schuster); *A Slave No More* by David W. Blight (Harcourt); *The Problem of Slavery in the Age of Emancipation* by David Brion Davis (Knopf); *Columbus and the Quest for Jerusalem* by Carol Delaney (Free Press); *The Race Card* by Richard T. Ford (Farrar, Straus & Giroux); *A Patent Lie and Errors* and *Omissions* by Paul Goldstein (Doubleday); *Addled: A Novel* by JoeAnn Hart (Little, Brown); *New Boy* by Julian Houston (Houghton Mifflin); *Kaufman Field Guide* series and *Flights against the Sunset* by Kenn Kaufman (Houghton Mifflin); *High Crimes: The Fate of Everest in an Age of Greed* by Michael Kodas (Hyperion); *Education's End: Why Our Colleges and Universities Have Given Up on the Meaning of Life* by Anthony T. Kronman (Yale); *Freedom for the Thought That We Hate: Biography of the First Amendment* by Anthony Lewis (Basic Books); *Stranger from Abroad: Hannah Arendt, Martin Heidegger and the Experience of Germans and Jews in the 20th Century* by Daniel Maier-Katkin (Norton); *Snow Falling in Spring: Coming of Age in China During the Cultural Revolution* by Moying Li (Farrar, Straus and Giroux); *Attack on the Liberty* by James Scott (Simon and Schuster); *Poisoned Profits: The Toxic Assault on Our Children* by Philip and Alice Shabecoff (Random House); *Sun & Shade: Three American Families Journey from Black to White* by Daniel Sharfstein (Penguin Press); *The Book of Getting Even and Tales Out of School* by Benjamin Taylor (Steerforth Press); *Backcast: Fly Fishing, Fatherhood, and a River Journey through the Heart of Alaska* by Lou Ureneck (St. Martin's); *Shell Game: Rogues,*

Smugglers, and the Hunt for Nature's Bounty by Craig Welch (HarperCollins); *Skipjack: Tracking the Last Sailing Oystermen* by Chris White (St. Martin's Press); *Riddled with Life: Friendly Worms, Ladybug Sex, and the Parasites that Make Us Who We Are* by Marlene Zuk (Harcourt).

THE TALBOT FORTUNE AGENCY, LLC.

John Talbot is located at: 180 E. Prospect Ave. #188, Mamaroneck, NY 10543

Gail Fortune is located at: 980 Broadway, Suite 664, Thornwood, NY 10594

www.talbotfortuneagency.com   e-mail: queries@talbotfortuneagency.com

Agents' names: John Talbot, Gail Fortune
The following information pertains to John Talbot.
Education: B.A., DePauw University.
Career history: John Talbot is a literary agent and former book editor with twenty-two years of publishing experience. Prior to becoming an agent he spent seven years with Putnam Berkley (now part of Penguin USA), where he rose to the rank of senior editor and worked with such major bestselling authors as Tom Clancy, W.E.B Griffin, and Jack Higgins, as well as rising literary stars such as Tom Perrotta. He published national bestsellers in hardcover, trade paperback, and mass market paperback, along with five New York Times Notable Books. He began his editorial career at Simon & Schuster.

Categories/subjects that you are most enthusiastic about agenting: I am most enthusiastic about representing narrative nonfiction of all types, commercial women's fiction, novels of suspense, and literary fiction. Narrative nonfiction can cover almost any subject, but history, current events, participatory journalism, sports, pop culture, business, and Christian spirituality are particular interests of mine. Newspaper and magazine experience is helpful; many books are generated from concepts first tried out in articles. A marketing platform, i.e. a Web site or Blog with a fan base in the tens of thousands or a list of corporate clients and customers, and a track record of speaking engagements and media apearances can be the deciding factor in getting a nonfiction sale.

In fiction, I am looking for the fresh and occasionally edgy voice, no matter the subject or genre. Writers with minority backgrounds and unusual experiences and perspectives interest me, as do writers of what Sue Miller calls domestic realism. Previous publication in literary journals and magazines is a plus. I'm also keenly interested in well-crafted thrillers with new or unusual hooks, and good genre fiction in growth categories such as paranormal romance.

What you don't want to agent: I do not represent children's books, science fiction, fantasy, Westerns, poetry, or screenplays.

What's the best way for writers to solicit your interest: Query via e-mail only.

Please see SUBMISSIONS GUIDELINES page.

Do you charge reading or management fees: We do not charge reading fees.

Can you provide an approximation by % of what you tend to represent by category: 50% fiction, 50% nonfiction.

What are the most common mistakes writers make when pitching you: Not following submission guidelines. Pitching multiple projects in one query letter. Sending queries that ramble. Using pressure tactics. Knocking published authors. Not trusting us or the business in general. Thinking someone's going to steal their idea. Relaying incomplete representation, submission, or publishing histories. Not being truthful or straightforward.

How would you describe the client from Hell: The client from Hell doesn't respect our time. They fail to recognize the publisher's justly proprietary attitude towards marketing, book design, and other facets of publication. They won't take suggestions for change, no matter how minor or well reasoned. They complain about writing and treat being published as a right instead of the opportunity and privilege it is.

How would you describe the perfect client: The perfect client respects our personal and professional lives. They trust us. They are open to input from their editor. They love to read and they love to write. They are enthusiastic about their ideas and about what they do.

How and why did you ever become an agent: Becoming an agent was a natural progression from being editors. The work is similar but we're able to spend less time in meetings and more time working with authors. We can also handle a more eclectic range of material, and we get to work with editors throughout the industry who share our passions and enthusiasms.

What, if anything, can a writer do to increase the odds of you becoming his or her agent: Please respect our time. Make sure your query is clear and succinct, and includes all of your contact information. Make sure your proposal (for nonfiction) or manuscript (for fiction) is complete and ready to go if we're interested. In general, approach publishing as a business and try to be as professional as possible right from the start. Of course, having a great project that's well researched and well executed goes a long way toward the above.

Do you have any particular opinions or impressions of editors and publishers in general: Editors are without a doubt the hardest working and most idealistic people in book publishing. Publishers represent the best opportunity for gifted writers to get wide distribution, readership, and money in what is often a difficult business.

Please list representative titles you have sold: Fiction: *Endwar* by Tom Clancy (Berkley); *24 Declassified: Vanishing Point* (HarperEntertainment); *Becoming Finola* (Pocket Books); *Under Darkness* (Signet Eclipse); *The Brothers Bishop* (Kensington); *If Wishing Made It So* (Signet Eclipse); *CSI: Nevada Rose* (Pocket Books); *Forgive the Moon* (NAL Accent); *French Pressed: A Coffeehouse Mystery* (Berkley Prime Crime). Nonfiction: *All Hands Down: The True Story of the Soviet Attack on the USS Scorpion* (Simon & Schuster); *Sundays in America: A Yearlong Road Trip in Search of Christian Faith* (Beacon);

While Europe Slept: How Radical Islam is Destroying the West from Within (Doubleday); *Last Flag Down: A Civil War Saga of Honor, Piracy and Redemption on the High Seas* (Crown).

The following information pertains to Gail Fortune.

Education: B.S., Northwestern University (Medill School of Journalism).

Career history or story: Gail Fortune is a literary agent and former book editor with eighteen years of publishing experience. Prior to becoming an agent she spent sixteen years at Putnam Berkley (now part of Penguin Group (USA)), where she rose from assistant to the Editor-in-Chief to Executive Editor. Her authors won six RITAs, and were nominated for Edgar and Anthony Awards. She published two Publishers Weekly Books of the Year. She edited many other national bestsellers in romance, mystery and narrative nonfiction.

Subjects & categories you are interested in agenting, including fiction & non-fiction: I am most enthusiastic about representing narrative nonfiction, commercial women's fiction, historical fiction, and romance novels. Narrative nonfiction can cover almost any subject, but history, food, travel and Christian spirituality are particular interests of mine. Newspaper and magazine experience is helpful; many books are generated from concepts first tried out in articles. In fiction, I am looking for a voice that grabs me and a narrative that keeps me turning the pages. I like original voices.

Subjects & categories writers shouldn't even bother pitching to you: I do not represent children's books, science fiction, fantasy, Westerns, poetry, prescriptive nonfiction or screenplays.

What's the best way for fiction writers to solicit your interest: Query via e-mail only. Please see SUBMISSION GUIDELINES page.

What's the best way for non-fiction writers to solicit your interest: Query via e-mail only. Please see SUBMISSION GUIDELINES page.

Do you charge reading or any upfront fees: We do not charge any reading fees.

In your experience, what are the most common pitching mistakes writers make: Not following the submission guidelines. Pitching multiple projects in one query letter. Sending queries that ramble. Using pressure tactics. Knocking published authors. Not trusting us or the business in general. Thinking someone's going to steal their idea. Relaying incomplete representation, submission, or publishing histories. Not being truthful or straightforward.

Describe the client from Hell, even if you don't have any: The client from hell doesn't respect our time. They fail to recognize the publisher's justly proprietary attitude towards marketing, book design, and other facets of publication. They won't take suggestions for change, no matter how minor or well reasoned. They complain about writing and treat being published as a right instead of the opportunity and privilege it is.

What's your definition of a great client: The perfect client respects our personal and professional lives. They trust us. They are open to input from their editor. They love to read and they love to write. They are enthusiastic about their ideas and about what they do.

How can writers increase the odds that you will offer representation: Please respect our time. Make sure your query is clear and succinct, and includes all of your contact information. Make sure your proposal (for nonfiction) or manuscript (for fiction) is complete and ready to go if we're interested. In general, approach publishing as a business and try to be as professional as possible right from the start. Of course, having a great project that's well researched and well executed goes a long way toward the above.

Why did you become an agent, and how did you become one: Becoming an agent was a natural progression from being editors. The work is similar, but we're able to spend less time in meetings and more time working with authors. We can also handle a more eclectic range of material, and we get to work with editors throughout the industry who share our passions and enthusiasms.

How do you feel about editors and publishers: Editors are without a doubt the hardest working and most idealistic people in book publishing. Publishers represent the best opportunity for gifted writers to get wide distribution, readership, and money in what is an often difficult business.

What are some representative titles that you have sold: *The Great Swim* by Gavin Mortimer (Walker Books); *Texas Princess* by Jodi Thomas (Berkley); *Twisted Creek* by Jodi Thomas (Berkley); *Married in Black* by Christina Cordaire (Madison Park Press); *A Notorious Woman* by Amanda Mccabe (Mills & Boon/Harlequin Historicals).

TALCOTT NOTCH LITERARY

276 Forest Rd., Milford, CT 06461

203-877-1146   fax: 203-876-9517

www.talcottnotch.net

Agent's name: Gina Panettieri, gpanettieri@talcottnotch.net
Born: June 8, 1960, Peekskill, New York.
Education: Long Island University Southampton, University of Virginia (double major Writing/Pre-med).
Career story: I came into agenting through one of the less common routes, by way of writing. I began as a freelance writer while still in college, writing anything from confession stories for Modern Romance to consumer protection and health articles. Later, I ran an ever-expanding critique group out of my home, and became very involved with writer support groups and organizations, and was represented myself by two well-known agents who taught me a great deal both about writing and about the business. But it was after assisting a number of writers in negotiating their own contracts that I became an agent myself and found my true calling. Within the last few years, I've begun writing again in addition to agenting, and am the author of *The Single Mother's Guide to Raising Remarkable Boys* (Adams Media 2008) and *Honey, We're Spoiling the Kids* (Adams Media 2009). Since most agents who write themselves either write about publishing, or

write novels, I suppose in becoming a parenting author I'm still sticking to the less common career routes!

Hobbies and special personal interests: I enjoy gardening (mind you, I didn't say I was particularly good at it, but the survival rate is improving), old movies (think *Royal Wedding* or *Arsenic and Old Lace*, NOT *Ferris Bueller's Day Off*), collecting cobalt glass and miniatures (houses, furniture, animals. I'm looking for a miniature cow if anyone knows a breeder). I love decorating for the holidays (Halloween is particularly fun). Researching for my own books keeps me reading a lot of psych, education and child development journals, which I actually enjoy. Finally, my own kids are a constant source of amusement and a limitless source of material for my books, to their great embarrassment.

Subjects and categories you like to agent: I primarily handle nonfiction, and my tastes are quite eclectic. I do a great deal of parenting, relationship, self-help, health, business/career, cooking, 'green' works, memoir and current events, as well as children's nonfiction. I'm not limited to those areas, though, and writers shouldn't hesitate to query me on nearly any nonfiction project. In fiction, I work mostly with mystery/suspense/thrillers and womens fiction, but I'll also do a bit of young adult and middle grade and some fantasy, action-adventure and science fiction.

Subjects and categories writers shouldn't bother pitching to you: Picture and board books, early readers, poetry, short stories.

What might you be doing if you weren't agenting: Probably writing full-time and continuing to be very involved in writing organizations.

What's the most effective ways for writers to grab your attention: Show you understand the market for your work, what's already been written on the subject and how your own work fills an existing need. Don't just use links to websites in lieu of writing a real query.

Do you charge fees separate from your commission, or offer non-agenting fee based services: No, never.

What are representative titles you have sold to publishers: *Fall* by Ron Franscell, winner of the 2007 Ippy for True Crime and the 2007 *Foreword Magazine* Book of the Year Award in True Crime (New Horizon, released in paper as *The Darkest Night* by St. Martin's Press); *The Connected Child* by Dr. Karyn Purvis, Dr. David Cross and Wendy Lyons Sunshine (McGraw-Hill); *Breaking the Co-Sleeping Habit* by Dr. Valerie Levine (Adams Media); *The Essential Supervisor's Handbook* by Brette and Terrence Sember (Career Press).

Why did you become an agent, and how did you become one: (The second half of this question was answered in an earlier question.) I love being an agent because it allows me to read so many fascinating works. I feel like I'm constantly learning. Agenting's an unending education. It's also terribly exciting to find something truly wonderful, important and meaningful, and be instrumental in bringing it to the world.

How do you feel about writers: I certainly respect what they do, and because I write myself, I can relate to many of their issues. I think that helps me present constructive criticism in ways that are more easily accepted, and also gives me a deeper perspective into the craft of writing. I also love their creative energy and the generosity of spirit of many writers. This is one industry where so many successful practitioners eagerly help new hopefuls.

What do you tell entities from other planets and dimensions about your job: I find new works that will help to enlighten people, enrich lives, and that entertain, comfort or possibly provoke the readers. Books make life vastly more interesting. I help bring those books to the people.

What are your favorite books, movies, TV shows, and why: I find reality programs like *The Deadliest Catch* and *Ice Road Truckers* to be interesting (for a while) because they make you aware of a different way of life, and also because they feature people who have not yet spurned the idea of a real challenge, hard work, testing their own limits, understanding self-sacrifice. Perhaps for the same reason, I love old movies and shorts, since they're often time capsules of earlier ways of life. I listen to old radio shows on CD (the most fascinating are the World War II era broadcasts), as well. In diving into what life was in America sixty years or seventy or even eighty years ago, again, you're learning, but this time about ourselves, and where we came from. It gives a new perspective on the present, on social roles, on the evolution of culture, on what's gone right, and wrong. With books, my tastes are eclectic and voracious, but again, I want to learn.

How would you describe "the writer from hell": Someone who has completely unrealistic expectations, such as instant success or that worrying about such trivial issues as spelling and grammar is 'what the editor is for', or someone who is unreasonably demanding of my time, since that would mean they're not respecting the time I must give to others.

How would you describe the publisher and/or editor from hell: Someone who pulls out all the stops to acquire a project and then loses steam afterward and doesn't continue to shepherd the project zealously. In those cases, everybody loses.

What do you like best about your clients, and the editors and publishers you work with: The exchange of ideas and energy.

You're welcome to share your thoughts and sentiments about the business of writing and publishing: This is an exciting, but challenging, time to work in publishing. The industry continues to meet new demands and pressures. From finding ways to 'go green' in what's traditionally been a huge-carbon-footprint business, to exploring new ways to promote and publicize works, to looking ahead to predict the needs of consumers in a changing economy, publishing is stimulating, stressful, joyous, frustrating, rewarding and exhausting. Never a dull moment.

Do you wish to describe who you are: Mom/agent/activist/tree-hugger/writer/helpmate/friend.

Will our business exist as we know it in 10 years or so from now: Yes, it will. It will continue to change to meet new demands and embrace new technology, but those things will occur in tandem and as a complement to the business as we know it today.

TESSLER LITERARY AGENCY, LLC

27 West 20th Street, Suite 1003, New York, NY 10011

www.tessleragency.com

Agent's name: Michelle Tessler

Education: Master's Degree in English literature and member of the Association of Author's Representatives.

Career history or story: Before forming her own agency, Michelle Tessler worked as an agent at Carlisle & Company, now part of InkWell Management. She also worked at the William Morris Agency and at the Elaine Markson Literary Agency. In addition to her agenting experience, Michelle worked as an executive of business development and marketing in the Internet industry. In 1994, just as the Internet was becoming a mainstream medium, she was hired by best-selling author James Gleick to help launch The Pipeline. She then went on to serve as Vice President of New Media at Jupiter Communications, and later at ScreamingMedia, before returning to traditional publishing. Her experience marketing content, products and services to appeal to both general and niche audiences is of great benefit to her authors as they look for creative and effective ways to get the word out on their books and grow their readerships.

Subjects & categories you are interested in agenting, including fiction & non-fiction: The Tessler Literary Agency is a full-service boutique agency. We represent writers of quality non-fiction and literary and commercial fiction. Our non-fiction list includes popular science, reportage, memoir, history, biography, psychology, business and travel. Committed to developing careers and building the readerships of the authors we represent, our agency offers personalized attention at every stage of the publishing process. Sharp editorial focus is given to clients before their work is submitted, and marketing support is provided along the way, as publishers begin to position the book in the marketplace through catalog copy, jacket designs, and marketing, promotion and launch strategies. We handle all domestic, foreign and subsidiary rights for our clients, working with a network of dedicated co-agents who specialize in film and translation rights.

What's the best way for fiction writers to solicit your interest: Please submit initial queries via the Webform at www.tessleragency.com.

What's the best way for non-fiction writers to solicit your interest: See above.

What are some representative titles that you have sold: *Flower Confidential* by Amy Stewart—A *New York Times* Bestseller—(Algonquin); *Body Clutter* by Marla Cilley (aka The Flylady) and Leanne Ely (aka The Dinner Diva)— A *New York Times* Bestseller—(Touchstone); *Presidential Doodles* from the creators of *Cabinet* Magazine (Basic); *A Sense of the World* and *The Extraordinary Journeys of James Holman* by Jason Roberts— Finalist For The National Book Critics' Circle Award—(Harpercollins); *Sixpence House: Lost in a Town of Books* by Paul Collins— A Booksense Bestseller—

(Bloomsbury); *How to be Lost* by Amanda Eyre Ward (Macadam Cage/Ballantine); *Saving Dinner* by Leanne Ely (Ballantine); *The Mommy Brain: How Motherhood Makes You Smarter* by Katherine Ellison (Basic); *Our Inner Ape: The Past and Future of Human Nature* by Frans De Waal— A *New York Times* Notable Book—(Riverhead); *Mediated* by Thomas De Zengotita (Bloomsbury); *Defining the Wind: The Beaufort Scale And How a 19th-Century Admiral Turned Science into Poetry* by Scott Huler (Crown); *Sink Reflections* by Marla Cilley (aka The Flylady) (Bantam); *Suburban Safari: A Year on the Lawn* by Hannah Holmes (Bloomsbury); *Forgive Me* by Amanda Eyre Ward (Random House); *In the Furnace of The Nation-Empires* by Michael Knox Beran (Free Press); *A Mid-Sized and Immodest Mammal: A Natural History of Myself* by Hannah Holmes (Random House); *The Fruit Hunters: Inside the Fruit Underworld* by Adam Gollner (Scribners); *The Miracle: The Epic Story of Asia's Quest for Wealth* by Michael Schuman (Harperbusiness); *A Nuclear Family Vacation: Travels in the World of Atomic Weaponry* by Sharon Weinberger and Nathan Hodge (Bloomsbury); *Vatican II: A People's History* by Colleen Mcdannell (Basic); *Bottomfeeder: An Ethical Eater's Adventures in a World of Vanishing Seafood* by Taras Grescoe (Bloomsbury); *The Day We Lost the H-Bomb: The True Story of a Missing Bomb and the Race to Find It* by Barbara Moran (Presidio).

S©OTT TREIMEL NY

434 Lafayette Street, New York, NY 10003

212-505-8353   fax: 212-505-0664

e-mail: st.ny@verizon.net, John M. Cusick: JMC.st.ny@verizon.net

Agents' names: Scott Treimel; John M. Cusick, Assistant
Born: San Diego, California.
Education: B.A. Antioch College, American History.
Career history or story: Curtis Brown, Ltd. (trained by Marilyn Marlow); Scholastic; World Features Syndicate; HarperCollins; founding director of Warner Bros. Worldwide Publishing.
Hobbies, interests: Theater, square dancing, dogs, politics, entertaining, history.
Subjects & categories you are interested in agenting, including fiction & non-fiction: We handle all categories of children's books, from board books through teen-novels. No adult projects.
Subjects & categories writers shouldn't even bother pitching to you: Religions/evangelical.
What would you do if you weren't agenting: Theatrical producer or beach bum.
What's the best way for fiction writers to solicit your interest: By post, not e-mail, notphone. A brief synopsis and the first several pages.
What's the best way for non-fiction writers to solicit your interest: By post, not e-mail, not phone. A proposal and detailed outline and a sample chapter.

Do you charge reading or any upfront fees: We do not charge a reading fee. We will invoice clients for photocopies and messengers.

In your experience, what are the most common pitching mistakes writers make: 1. Explaining the market to me; 2. Overselling themselves, not allowing their work to speak for itself.

Describe the client from Hell, even if you don't have any: One with unreasonable expectations, who is impatient with matters I can't control, and will not listen to advice, from with me or an editor. One who sends revised manuscripts in rapid succession and confuses our submissions to editors. One who writes "Have you heard from..." e-mails suggesting that we do not religiously inform clients of all goings-on as they happen.

What's your definition of a great client: Consistent, productive, passionate about craft, able to work well with the variety of personalities that contribute to making and marketing books. And a client who actively promotes his or her books.

How can writers increase the odds that you will offer representation: It is 99.9% about the content of the work. Therefore, to increase the odds, be original and writer brilliantly. That'll do it.

Why did you become an agent, and how did you become one: I worked on both sides, buying and selling intellectual property, and then I wanted to be closer to the key ingredient in the whole process: the creator. I am not beholden to corporate oversight and am able to advocate for the people who make the first and greatest contribution—the creators.

How do you feel about editors and publishers: We have many talented editors. I worry their publishers put so much pressure on them that they are unable to take chances, try new things. I like inependent vision, which the present committee-style publishing discourages.

What do you see in the near future for book publishing: 1. More focus on fewer titles; and 2. The increasing development of electronic distribution of literary work.

What are your favorite books/TV shows/movies, and why: I like cartoons, not the animated movies that always seem to wink at the adults in the audience, but cartoons on television. The old-style *Looney Tunes* and *Tom-and-Jerry* gag fests have been replaced with well-plotted story-telling—often solidly structured. I also dig the high visual style and experimenting. I watch *South Park*, *Futurama*, and *Sponge Bob*, but also *Camp Lazlo*, *Foster's Home for Imaginary Friends*, *The Grim Adventures of Bill and Mandy*, *Pokemon*, *Dexter's Laboratory*, *Robot Chicken*, *The Powerpuff Girls*. Writers for children can do well to tune in and discover the level of social sophistication and cultural references cartoon characters resource. My greatest disklike is a sentimentalized recollection of childhood. Cartoons source a more authentic point of view.

In your opinion, what do editors think of you: They think I am honest, direct, reasonable but not a softie. I believe they also think I have good taste and interesting projects.

On a personal non-professional level, what do you think people think of you: Straightforward, energetic, earnest, funny.

What are some representative titles that you have sold: *Right Behind You* by Gail

Giles (Little, Brown); *Please is a Good Word to Say* by Barbara Joosse (Philomel); *Megiddo's Shadow* by Arthur Slade (R-H/Wendy Lamb Books); *Comic Guy* by Timothy Roland (Scholastic); *My Life After Life* by Richard Scrimger (Tundra Books); *A is for Angst* by Barbara Haworth Attard (Harper Canada); *My Life as a Chicken* by Ellen Kelley (Harcourt); *The Ninja Who Wanted to be Noticed* by Julie Phillipps (Viking); *Kiki* by Janie Bynum (Sterling).

TRIDENT MEDIA GROUP

41 Madison Ave., New York, NY 10010

e-mail: JBent@tridentmediagroup.com

Agent's name: Jenny Bent

Born: November 23, 1969, New York, New York.

Education: B.A., M.A., English Literature with Highest Honors from Cambridge University, U.K.

Career history: Joined Trident three years ago after working at a variety of agencies. Began career as an assistant to top agent, Raphael Sagalyn in D.C.

Hobbies/personal interests: Yoga, bad television, my dogs, animal rescue.

Categories/subjects that you are most enthusiastic about agenting: High concept commercial women's fiction, quirky or funny literary fiction, high concept young adult, exceptional memoir, humor, fun women's lifestyle.

What you don't want to agent: Political books, new age, health/fitness, mysteries.

If you were not an agent, what might you be doing instead: Standing on the unemployment line.

What's the best way for writers to solicit your interest: Write a great, catchy query letter. See www.jennybent.com for an example.

Do you charge reading or management fees: No.

Can you provide an approximation by % of what you tend to represent by category: Commercial fiction (women's): 50%, Young Adult: 20%, Literary Fiction/Memoir: 10%, Humor: 10%, Lifestyle: 10%.

What are the most common mistakes writers make when pitching you: Being boring and long-winded. Also pitching books in a genre I don't represent.

How would you describe the client from Hell: Anyone who is nasty or abusive or refuses to communicate via e-mail.

How would you describe the perfect client: Prolific, low-maintenance, fun, talented.

How and why did you ever become an agent: Too long and boring to go into, but I couldn't really imagine doing anything else.

What, if anything, can a writer do to increase the odds of you becoming his or her agent: Have good credentials and write a great book.

What are your favorite books, movies, TV shows, and why: I love all kinds of trashy television—it's my guilty pleasure.

Please list representative titles you have sold: *Freshman* by Brent Crawford (Hyperion) (Young Adult); *Stop Dressing Your Six-Year-Old Like a Skank* by Celia Rivenbark (St. Martin's); *There's a (Slight) Chance I Might be Going to Hell* by Laurie Notaro (Random House); *How to be Cool* by Johanna Edwards (Berkley); *The Sweet Potato Queens First Big Ass Novel* by Jill Conner Browne with Karin Gillespie (Simon And Schuster); *Yellowcake* by Ann Cummins (Houghton Mifflin).

VERITAS LITERARY AGENCY

601 Van Ness Avenue, Opera Plaza Suite E, San Francisco, CA 94102

415-647-6964   fax: 415-647-6965

www.veritasliterary.com

Agents' names: Katherine Boyle, Katherine@veritasliterary.com; Megan O'Patry, Megan@veritasliterary.com

The following information pertains to Katherine Boyle.

Born: June 16th (Bloomsday!) 1969, Stanford, California.

Education: B.A., English and Psychology, Stanford University.

Career story: After graduation I worked at a variety of Bay Area independent presses and agencies while pursuing a publishing certificate at Berkeley. Veritas was established in 1995, and thereafter I joined the AAR and the Authors Guild.

Hobbies and special personal interests: Music and visual art addiction, foreign films, running, hiking, chapbook making, pet adoration, eating.

Subjects and categories you like to agent: Literary fiction, multi-cultural fiction, historical fiction, new fabulist and literary speculative fiction, southern fiction, literary thrillers and mysteries, narrative nonfiction, reportage, memoir, popular science, popular culture, natural history, current events and politics, women's issues, art and music-related biography.

Subjects and categories writers shouldn't bother pitching to you: New Age, romance, military history, westerns.

What might you be doing if you weren't agenting: It's a toss-up between whale scientist or London stage actress.

What's the most effective ways for writers to grab your attention: Well-written, concise queries.

Do you charge fees separate from your commission, or offer non-agenting fee based services: No.

What are representative titles you have sold to publishers: *Hedwig and Berti* by Frieda Arkin (St. Martins); *Sickened* by Julie Gregory (Bantam); *If I Am Missing or Dead* by Janine Latus (Simon & Schuster/Random House U.K.); *Free Burning* by Bayo Ojikutu (Crown); *I Was a Teenage Gumby* by Jean Gonick (Hyperion); *Sometimes the Soul* by Gioia Timpanelli (W.W. Norton/Vintage); *Deliberate Acts of Kindness* by Meredith Gould (Doubleday); *The Nature of Music* by Maureen McCarthy Draper (Riverhead/Putnam); *American Sideshow* by Marc Hartzman (Tarcher/Penguin); *65 Successful Harvard Business School Application Essays* by The Harbus (St. Martin's); *The Essential Nostradamus* by Richard Smoley (Tarcher/Penguin); *The Twins of Tribeca* by Rachel Pine (Miramax); *The Creative Writing MFA Handbook* by Tom Kealey (Continuum).

Why did you become an agent, and how did you become one: I've always loved books and great writing but I'm too fond of social interaction to thrive as a librarian. I couldn't ask for a better career to satisfy the introverted/extroverted poles of a Gemini personality.

How do you feel about writers: I adore them. It's a tough job and they're certainly doing more than their share to keep the culture on life support, generally earning a fraction of what video game designers make.

What do you tell entities from other planets and dimensions about your job: Storytelling is an ancient and universal art. Since dreams probably come from these other planes, it shouldn't be too hard to explain the field to an interested entity. All beings likely share the intuition that there's more wisdom embedded in a story than we'll ever know.

What are your favorite books, movies, TV shows, and why: Books: *Housekeeping, The Sea, The Restraint of Beasts* and anything by Alice Munro, William Maxwell and Italo Calvino. All of these authors can shift a reader's level of perception almost instantaneously. Movies: *I'm Not Scared, Dreams, The 400 Blows, Nights of Cabiria, The After Life*: all strange, beautiful, life affirming. T.V. *Flight of the Conchords* and *Prime Suspect*, because hilarity and Helen Mirren are also important.

How would you describe "the writer from hell": Someone who calls to pitch a "great idea" on the phone before they've even written a word.

How would you describe the publisher and/or editor from hell: Luckily I've been spared that circle so far.

What do you like best about your clients, and the editors and publishers you work with: I couldn't ask for a better cadre of kindred spirits. There's no greater rush than celebrating a book's success with a brilliant author and a wonderfully committed editor. Of course they're all individuals, but on the whole it's so reassuring to be surrounded by so many sane, thoughtful, intellectually curious, passionate, witty and good-natured people. I just wish that they weren't spread so far apart—we could throw some great parties.

Do you wish to describe who you are: "Trying to define yourself is like trying to bite your own teeth."—Alan Watts

Will our business exist as we know it in 10 years or so from now: While the tectonic plates are certainly shifting, books will always be beloved and necessary in this world. To sustain authors, however, it may be increasingly important to pursue alternate subrights arenas—pitching a historical fiction series to a video game producer, for example. A protean instinct will serve both authors and agents well, but the importance of craft, originality, and excellence will never disappear.

The following information pertains to Megan O'Patry.
Born: San Diego, California; 1984.

Education: B.A. in Pre-and Early Modern Literature, UC Santa Cruz; M.F.A. in Creative Writing, San Francisco State University.

Career story: A long time ago when the earth was green and there were more kinds of animals than you've ever seen...

Hobbies and special personal interests: Playwriting, black and white movies, teaching infants to swim.

Subjects and categories you like to agent: Literary fiction, narrative nonfiction, mainstream fiction, YA, to name a few.

Subjects and categories writers shouldn't bother pitching to you: Self-help, guide books.

What might you be doing if you weren't agenting: Working in Elmore Leonard's coffee shop.

What's the most effective ways for writers to grab your attention: A well-written query. Don't sell try to sell me a used car. I don't need a car, I live in the city. Please don't drop me into the middle of your story with aggressive adverbs, be honest and to the point. Always spell check.

Do you charge fees separate from your commission, or offer non-agenting fee based services: No.

Why did you become an agent, and how did you become one: It was a stage of evolution more or less. I followed Katherine Boyle home one day and lived under the dining room table for a while, next to a slush pile. The rest, as they say, is in development.

How do you feel about writers: Writers are like M&M's. They come in a variety of colors and you stuff them in your mouth, hoping for a hallucinatory effect. And sometimes you wake up on the side of the road in your underwear. I love writers!

What do you tell entities from other planets and dimensions about your job: I'm very tight-lipped. I communicate with bumper stickers. I pass on and receive a lot of intergalactic wisdom this way, such as: Go North for the cold beer.

What are your favorite books, movies, TV shows, and why: *A Hero of Our Time, The House of Leaves, Lolita, The West Wing, Deadwood, Weeds, The Last Unicorn, The Seven Faces of Dr. Lao* because of the writing, my friends, the writing!

How would you describe "the writer from hell": Someone who is unrealistic in their expectations, resistant to constructive criticism, and unacquainted with courtesies like please and thank you.

How would you describe the publisher and/or editor from hell: They love what they do and they come into any project with an open mind. We extend them the same necessity. At the end of the day, we may want different things but by the end of the week, we're all lined up.

What do you like best about your clients, and the editors and publishers you work with: They love what they do and they come into any project with an open mind. We extend them the same necessity. At the end of the day, we may want different things but by the end of the week, we're all lined up.

Will our business exist as we know it in 10 years or so from now: I have a bumper sticker somewhere that addresses this very issue...

MARY JACK WALD ASSOCIATES, INC.

111 East 14th Street, New York, NY 10003

Agent's name: Mary Jack Wald.

Born: Manhattan, New York.

Education: B.A., Union College.

Career history or story: Fourth grade teacher; permissions correspondent, Random House; editor, Random House; direct marketing, Random House, Western Publising; Managing editor, Golden Books, Western Publishing; Tori Mendez Agency.

Subjects & categories you are interested in agenting, including fiction & non-fiction: Not accepting new clients.

Subjects & categories writers shouldn't even bother pitching to you: Not accepting new clients.

What would you do if you weren't agenting: Write.

Do you charge reading or any upfront fees: No.

In your experience, what are the most common pitching mistakes writers make: Telling me how much their children, husband, friends loved their manuscript.

Describe the client from Hell, even if you don't have any: Call every day or worse; calls the editor you submitted to every day.

What's your definition of a great client: Talented, helpful, sense of humor.

Why did you become an agent, and how did you become one: Wanted to work directly with the author.

Describe to someone from another planet what you do as an agent: Try to find the right editor and publisher for the author. Then handle contract, royalty, reversion of rights.

What do you see in the near future for book publishing: More independent publishing houses.

In your opinion, what do editors think of you: Honest and understanding.

What are some representative titles that you have sold: Christopher Bahjalian, first three books (Carrall & Graf); Baxter Black (Crown Publishers); Yale Strom–too many to list; John Peel–too many to list; Denise Lewis Patrick–too many to list; Richie Tankerskey Cusick–too many to list; Gregg Loomis (Dorchester Publishing); Neil Johnson–too many to list.

WALES LITERARY AGENCY, INC.

P.O. Box 9428, Seattle, Washington 98109-0428

(For deliveries by UPS, DHL, Fed-Ex, all door-to-door couriers, contact the agency for the office street address.)

206-284-7114   fax: 206-322-1033

www.waleslit.com   e-mail: waleslit@waleslit.com

Agents' names: Elizabeth Wales, President; Neal Swain, Assistant Agent
The following information pertains to Elizabeth Wales.
Born: March 30, 1952.
Education: B.A., Smith College; graduate work in English and American Literature, Columbia University.
Career story: Worked in the trade sales departments at Oxford University Press and Viking Penguin; worked in city government and served a term on the Seattle school board; also worked as a Bookseller and Publisher's Representative.
Subjects and categories you like to agent: A wide range of narrative non-fiction and literary fiction. Especially interested in nonfiction projects that could have a progressive cultural or political impact. In fiction, looking for talented mainstream storytellers, both new and established. Occasionally interested in well-crafted psychological thrillers and speculative fiction. Especially interested in writers from the Northwest, Alaska, the West Coast, and what has become known as the Pacific Rim countries.
Subjects and categories writers shouldn't bother pitching to you: Children's books, how-to, self-help, and almost all genre projects (romance, true crime, horror, action/adventure, most science fiction/fantasy, techno thrillers).
Do you charge fees separate from your commission, or offer non-agenting fee based services: No reading fees.
What are representative titles you have sold to publishers: *Cold: An Untold Story in a Warming World* by Bill Streever (Little, Brown); *Unterzakhn: a Graphic Novel and Story of the Lower East Side* by Leela Corman (Schocken/Pantheon); *Wisdom of the Last Farmer, by David Mas Masumoto (The Free Press).*
Why did you become an agent, and how did you become one: For the adventure and the challenge; also, I am a generalist—interested in variety.

JOHN A. WARE LITERARY AGENCY

392 Central Park West, New York, NY 10025

Agent's name: John A. Ware

Education: A.B. in Philosophy, Cornell University, graduate work in English and American Literature, Northwestern University.

Career history: Editor, eight years, Doubleday; agent, one year, James Brown Associates/Curtis Brown Ltd.; founded John A. Ware Literary Agency.

Hobbies/personal interests: Running, mentoring, classical music and blues, Italy and Spain.

Categories/subjects that you are most enthusiastic about agenting: Biography and history, investigative journalism, social commentary and contemporary affairs, "bird's eye" views of phenomena, nature and Americana, literary and suspense fiction.

What you don't want to agent: Technothrillers and women's romance, men's action-adventures, how-to's (save the area of medicine and health), guidebooks and cookbooks, science fiction, reference, young adult and children's books, personal memoirs.

If you were not an agent, what might you be doing instead: Teaching philosophy, working as a sportswriter, or in some position in race relations.

What's the best way for writers to solicit your interest: Succinct query letter (only), with SASE.

Do you charge reading or management fees: No.

Can you provide an approximation by % of what you tend to represent by category: Fiction: 20%, Non-Fiction: 80%.

What are the most common mistakes writers make when pitching you: Overselling, instead of simply describing work, sending unasked for sample material.

How would you describe the client from Hell: Untrusting, discourteous, humorless.

How would you describe the perfect client: Professional about their writerly responsibilities, trusting, courteous, possesses a sense of humor.

How and why did you ever become an agent: I enjoy working with words, writers, and editors, and believe strongly in the permanent importance of the written word.

What, if anything, can a writer do to increase the odds of you becoming his or her agent: Covered above!

How would you describe to someone (or thing) from another planet what it is that you do as an agent: I try to do skilled, imaginative things with words and the writers who render them.

Do you have any particular opinions or impressions of editors and publishers in general: Smart, professional and, for the most part, prompt and courteous.

What are your favorite books, movies, TV shows, and why: *BBC News*, not much of a moviegoer, more, well, a reader.

Please list representative titles you have sold: Untitled on Afghanistan by Jon Krakauer (Doubleday); Untitled on the grace of basketball by Chris Ballard (Sports Illustrated/Simon & Schuster); *Spent: A Memoir of Shopaholism* by Avis Cardella (Little, Brown); *To Kill a Page: A Memoir of Illiteracy* by Travis Culley (Random House); *Inside the Minds of School Shooters* by Peter Langman (Palgrave/MacMillan); *W.C. Handy: A Biography* by David Robertson (Knopf).

TED WEINSTEIN LITERARY MANAGEMENT

307 Seventh Avenue, Suite 2407, New York, NY 10001

www.twliterary.com

(Agency accepts e-mail submissions only)

Agent's name: Ted Weinstein, AAR

Education: Bachelor's degree in Philosophy from Yale College, Master's degree in Public and Private Management from Yale School of Management.

Career history: Ted Weinstein has broad experience on both the business and editorial sides of publishing. Before founding the agency he held senior publishing positions in licensing, marketing, publicity and business development. Also a widely published author, Ted has been the music critic for NPR's "All Things Considered" and a commentator for the *San Francisco Chronicle* and many other publications.

Hobbies/personal interests: Politics, music, hiking, visual arts.

Categories/subjects that you are most enthusiastic about agenting: Wide range of intelligent nonfiction, especially narrative nonfiction, popular science, biography & history, current affairs & politics, business, health and medicine, food & cooking, pop culture and quirky reference books.

What you don't want to agent: Fiction, stage plays, screenplays, poetry, or books for children or young adults.

If you were not an agent, what might you be doing instead: I have so much fun as an agent that I can't imagine doing anything else. Whenever I retire (many decades from now) the only change will be I'll have time to read more fiction.

What's the best way for writers to solicit your interest: Best is by referral from someone I know and respect, but I also take on many clients who approach me unsolicited. For unsolicited queries, e-mail only – query or full proposal. See Web site for detailed submission guidelines.

Do you charge reading or management fees: NEVER! I'm an AAR member.

Can you provide an approximation by % of what you tend to represent by category: Non-Fiction: 100%.

What are the most common mistakes writers make when pitching you: Submitting a proposal for a type of work I do not represent. Sending a proposal that isn't polished, professional and typo-free. Telephoning the agency to query. Sending a mass e-mail cc-ing me and every other agent in the business.

How would you describe the client from Hell: Someone who doesn't act like a professional—missing deadlines, personalizing business issues. Publishing is a business and success is always more likely to come to those who are disciplined and hard-working and who treat the people they work with respectfully.

How would you describe the perfect client: Talented, professional, hard working—someone who treats his or her writing like a career (even if it isn't their only career).

How and why did you ever become an agent: Before becoming an agent I spent many years in different areas of publishing—editorial, marketing, business development, licensing—and agenting is an endlessly fun, fascinating and rewarding combination of all these areas.

What, if anything, can a writer do to increase the odds of you becoming his or her agent: Treat your writing as a long-term career, not just a one-book opportunity. Constantly improve your writing by getting feedback from writing groups, editors and other thoughtful coaches. Increase your public profile by publishing your words and ideas via newspapers, magazines and radio.

How would you describe to someone (or thing) from another planet what it is that you do as an agent: I'm a combination of editor, cheerleader, advocate, negotiator, marketing consultant, lawyer, accountant, career coach and therapist, in varying proportions depending on what each client needs from me to help them succeed.

Do you have any particular opinions or impressions of editors and publishers in general: They are smart businesspeople, without whom talented authors are unlikely to reach the audience they deserve, and they are some of the smartest readers anywhere. My clients and I carefully review every comment we receive from editors. No two editors will have the same reaction to any proposal, but the insights from each one are enormously valuable in helping my clients improve their work.

What do you think the future holds for writers, publishers, and agents: Authors increasingly need to think of themselves as CEOs of their own multimedia empires, promoting and publicizing themselves and their talents in every possible venue and looking to enhance and exploit the value of their insights and writing in every possible medium.

What are your favorite books, movies, TV shows, and why: I don't have enough time to read all the great books that are published every year, and I don't even own a TV.

On a personal level, what do you think people like about you and dislike about you: Professionalism-with-a-sense-of-humor, wide-ranging insights and creativity, forthrightness and integrity.

What are representative titles you have sold to publishers: *Inside Steve's Brain: The Leadership Secrets of Steve Jobs* by Leander Kahney (Penguin/Portfolio); *The Body Toxic* by Susanne Antonetta (Farrar Straus & Giroux); *The Unfinished Game: Pascal, Fermat and the Birth of Probability Theory* by Keith Devlin (Perseus/Basic); *Blank Spots on the Map: State Secrets, Hidden Landscapres, and the Pentagon's Black World* by Trevor Paglen (Penguin/Dutton); *The Autobiographer's Handbook: The 826 Valencia Guide to Writing a*

Memoir (Holt); *The New New Deal* (Penguin/Portfolio); *American Nightingale: The Story of Frances Stanger, Forgotten Heroine of Normandy* by Bob Welch (Simon & Schuster/Atria); *Ancient Wisdom, Modern Kitchen: Recipes from the East for Health, Healing and Long Life* (Perseus/Da Copa); *More than Human: How Biotechnology is Transforming Us and Why We Should Embrace It* (Random House/Broadway); *One-Letter Words: A Dictionary* by Craig Conley (HarperCollins); *American Chestnut: The Life, Death and Rebirth of a Perfect Tree* by Susan Freinkel (University of California Press); *Momma Zen: Walking the Crooked Path of Motherhood* by Karen Miller (Shambhala); *The Probiotics Revolution* by Sarah Wernick and Gary B. Huffnagle (Random House/Bantam).

WRITERS HOUSE

21 West 26th Street, New York, NY 10010

3368 Governor Dr, #224F, San Diego, CA 92122

www.writershouse.com

Agents' names: Albert Zuckerman; Dan Lazar; Steven Malk, smalk@writeshouse.com; Kenneth Wright; Josh Getzler, jgetzler@writershouse.com.
The following information pertains to Albert Zuckerman.
Born: Bronx, New York.
Education: A.B., Princeton; D.F.A. Yale Drama.
Career history or story: Naval officer; foreign services officer; assistant professor of playwriting and dramatic literature at Yale, winner of Stanley Drama Award for best play by a new American playwright; author of two novels published by Doubleday and Dell; writer for three daytime TV series, Broadway producer; founded Writers House in 1974; author of *Writing the Blockbuster Novel*.
Hobbies, interests: Tennis, movies, plays, reading wonderful books, working with talented writers.
Subjects & categories you are interested in agenting, including fiction & non-fiction: Great storytelling, fiction or non-fiction. Especially open to published novelists who are eager to move up a notch or several notches.
Subjects & categories writers shouldn't even bother pitching to you: Please, no how-to books.
What's the best way for fiction writers to solicit your interest: Write me an engaging and compelling letter. I subject one page in three paragraphs. 1.) What is fascinating and unusual about your book? How does it differ from others in its category? 2.) What is it about? Its story, theme, characters, special features. 3.) What is your writing experience and why are you the most qualified person to write it?
What's the best way for non-fiction writers to solicit your interest: Same as above.

Do you charge reading or any upfront fees: No.

What's your definition of a great client: Someone who has talent and craft but who also is willing to keep on revising until his or her work reaches its optimum condition.

Why did you become an agent, and how did you become one: I thought I could help writers more than the agents who had represented me. And I have.

How do you feel about editors and publishers: They have a tough job, and most of them do it well.

How do you feel about writers: Most of them are a great joy.

What do you see in the near future for book publishing: It will be with us as long as we're around.

In your opinion, what do editors think of you: I get the impression that I am liked and respected.

What are some representative titles that you have sold: *A Brief History of Time* by Stephen Hawking (Bantam); *The First Wives Club* by Olivia Goldsmith (Simon & Schuster); *The Pillars of the Earth* by Ken Follett (William Morrow); *Moneyball* by Michael Lewis (Norton); *The Religion* by Tim Willocks (Farrar Straus); *The Blue Day Book* by Bradley Trevor and Andrews McMeel (Greive).

The following information pertains to Dan Lazar.

Born: Jerusalem, Israel.

Career story: I started as an intern and worked my way up to senior agent.

Subjects and categories you like to agent: Literary and commercial fiction, women's fiction, historical fiction, thrillers, mysteries, gay and lesbian, young adult, middle grade, graphic novels or memoirs, Judaica, memoir, narrative nonfiction, pop-culture, humor.

Subjects and categories writers shouldn't bother pitching to you: Romance, picture books, cookbooks.

What's the most effective ways for writers to grab your attention: A great query letter and the first five pages of their manuscript.

Do you charge fees separate from your commission, or offer non-agenting fee based services: No fees.

What are representative titles you have sold to publishers: *Island of Lost Girls* by Jennifer McMahon (Harper); *Final Theory* by Mark Alpert (Touchstone); *Eve* by Elissa Aliott (Bantam); *Savvy* by Ingrid Law (Dial/Walden); *The Last Invisible Boy* (Ginee Seo/Atheneum); *Haiku Mama* (Quirk Books).

Why did you become an agent, and how did you become one: I loved books and reading. I applied for an internship at both publishers and agencies—Writers House hired me for the summer, and happily so! I've been here ever since.

What do you tell entities from other planets and dimensions about your job: You don't go to court without a lawyer, or buy a house without a real estate agent. Same for publishing—we're the author's champion and partner. Ideally (and more and more realistically) we're the one constant in the author's career, since editors move jobs and publishers are changing constantly.

What are your favorite books, movies, TV shows, and why: Favorite movies: *The*

Incredibles, Monsters Inc. Favorite TV shows: *The Daily Show, Will & Grace, DirtySexy-Money, Frasier, Freaks & Geeks.*

What do you like best about your clients, and the editors and publishers you work with: I love their books, and I admire their persistence and passion. Different tastes are what make this business tough and rewarding all at once, but we're all in it ultimately for the same reason.

Will our business exist as we know it in 10 years or so from now: The business as we know it changes every day! But it's not going anywhere.

The following information pertains to Steven Malk:

Born: Johannesburg, South Africa.

Education: B.A., Political Science and B.A., History, University of California San Diego.

Career story: Opened a West Coast office for Writers House in 1998. Worked for the Sandra Dijkstra Literary Agency prior to that.

Subjects and categories you like to agent: Books for children, middle-grade readers, and young adults.

Subjects and categories writers shouldn't bother pitching to you: Books that aren't intended for children, middle-grade readers, or young adults.

What might you be doing if you weren't agenting: Playing center field for the San Diego Padres (not really, but it's a nice thought).

What's the most effective ways for writers to grab your attention: Write a carefully thought-out, focused query that demonstrates a strong command of your work, and also explains why you're querying me, specifically.

Do you charge fees separate from your commission, or offer non-agenting fee based services: No.

What are representative titles you have sold to publishers: *The True Meaning of Smekday* by Adam Rex (Hyperion); *Clementine* by Sara Pennypacker, Illustrated by Marla Frazee (Hyperion); *King Dork* by Frank Portman (Delacorte Press); *Your Own, Sylvia: A Verse Portrait of Sylvia Plath* by Stephanie Hemphill (Knopf); *John, Paul, George, and Ben* by Lane Smith (Hyperion); *Reposessed* by A.M. Jenkins (Harpercollins); *Collect Raindrops: The Seasons Gathered* by Nikki Mcclure (Abrams); *Knucklehead: Tall Tales and Almost True Stories of Growing Up Scieszka* by Jon Scieszka (Viking); *The Secret Order of The Gumm Street Girls* by Elise Primavera (Harpercollins); *We Are the Ship: The Story of Negro League Baseball* by Kadir Nelson (Hyperion).

Why did you become an agent, and how did you become one: It allowed me to be involved in both the creative and business sides of the industry, and to work closely with and on behalf of authors I greatly admire. It was also the perfect outgrowth of bookselling for me, as I was able to apply everything I'd learned as a third-generation bookseller to my work as an agent.

What are your favorite books, movies, TV shows, and why: Books (not including books that I've represented, obviously): Anything by Barbara Cooney or Roald Dahl. Also *The Westing Game* by Ellen Raskin, *I'll Fix Anthony* by Judith Viorst, *The Carrot Seed* by Ruth Krauss, *Dear Genius: The Letters Of Ursula Nordstrom* by Leonard Marcus, and many, many more. Movies: *Hoosiers, Rushmore, Ghost World, Election, The Straight Story.*

The following information pertains to Kenneth Wright:

Education: B.A., University of Colorado, Boulder; M.A., Boston College.

Career story: Editor through publisher positions at Oxford University Press, Simon & Schuster, HarperCollins, Henry Holt, and Scholastic.

Subjects and categories you like to agent: Adult fiction and nonfiction; children's middle grade and YA fiction and nonfiction.

Subjects and categories writers shouldn't bother pitching to you: Fantasy. Romance. Genre. Picture books.

What's the most effective ways for writers to grab your attention: Make me laugh. Keep it short. Know your readers.

Do you charge fees separate from your commission, or offer non-agenting fee based services: No. Honest.

What are representative titles you have sold to publishers: David Macaulay (Roaring Brook/MacMillan); *The Lost Girls* by Amanda Pressner, Jennifer Baggett, and Holly Corbett (HarperCollins); *Why Santa Teleports* by Greg Mone (Bloomsbury).

The following information pertains to Josh Getzler.

Born: May 4, 1968, New York City.

Education: B.A., University of Pennsylvania, 1990; Radcliffe Publishing Course, 1990; M.B.A., Columbia Business School, 1995.

Career story: Started in editorial at Harcourt in 1991, then left to go to business school, expecting to get back into publishing after. Instead, I ended up owning and operating a minor league baseball team for 12 years (Staten Island Yankees), before selling in 2006 and returning to the world of books on the agency side. Apprenticed under Simon Lipskar and Dan Lazar, and now am also building a client list.

Subjects and categories you like to agent: Procedural mysteries (particularly, though by no means exclusively, period and foreign), thrillers, literary and commercial fiction, religion (not spiritual guidance—books about religious history or philosophy), sports, music.

Subjects and categories writers shouldn't bother pitching to you: Romance, picture books, religious fiction.

What might you be doing if you weren't agenting: Sports marketing, working on the business side of a publishing house, editing.

What's the most effective ways for writers to grab your attention: Clearly and concisely email a letter that tells me quickly what kind of book you are pitching. I want to know the genre; I want to know salient details about the story. I don't want to know that you think your book is important and groundbreaking, hilarious and a must-read. I want you to offer it up for evaluation, and I will respect your willingness to put it out there.

Do you charge fees separate from your commission, or offer non-agenting fee based services: NO.

What are representative titles you have sold to publishers: *Devil's Trill* by Gerald Elias, (St. Martin's Press).

Why did you become an agent, and how did you become one: When I was selling the baseball team, I was having a conversation with my wife, who told me that it was clear I needed to work in books again. Having 13 years of experience making deals and looking at contracts, I realized I could be suited to agenting. I decided to target existing agencies, rather than start a new one, and got lucky with timing that a position with Simon Lipskar and Dan Lazar at Writers House opened up.

What are your favorite books, movies, TV shows, and why: *Absalom, Absalom, The Caine Mutiny, The Day of the Jackal, The Tattooed Potato and Other Clues, O Jerusalem, Sherlock Holmes* (any of them, really). Movies: *Inherit The Wind, Bull Durham, My Cousin Vinny, Murder on the Orient Express, The Great Dictator*. TV Shows: *Taxi, Black Adder, Law and Order* (original), *MASH, Prime Suspect*.

Will our business exist as we know it in 10 years or so from now: Yes, I think so, although there will be a much greater emphasis on electronic rights. We will be even more in the business of representing intellectual property.

SUSAN ZECKENDORF ASSOCIATES, INC.

171 West 57th Street, New York, NY

Agent's name: Susan Zeckendorf

Born: New York.

Education: B.A., Wellesley College; M.Ed. Teacher's College Columbia.

Career history: Formerly counseling psychologist.

Hobbies/personal interests: Music, exercise.

Subjects & categories you are interested in agenting, including fiction & nonfiction: Literary fiction, historical fiction, mysteries, music, biography.

Subjects & categories writers shouldn't even bother pitching to you: Science fiction, fantasy, spiritual works.

What would you do if you weren't agenting: Psychologist.

What's the best way for fiction writers to solicit your interest: Query letter with SASE.

What's the best way for non-fiction writers to solicit your interest: Short, clear query letter with SASE.

Do you charge reading or any upfront fees: No.

In your experience, what are the most common pitching mistakes writers make: Sending complete manuscript unsolicited. Pitch too long.

Describe the client from Hell, even if you don't have any: Hostile, demanding.

What's your definition of a great client: Patient.

How can writers increase the odds that you will offer representation: Endorsements from well-known people.

Why did you become an agent, and how did you become one: I love books. Joined an agency.

Describe to someone from another planet what you do as an agent: Read, edit moderately, find appropriate publisher.

How do you feel about editors and publishers: Fine.

How do you feel about writers: Depends on the writer.

What do you see in the near future for book publishing: People will continue to read books.

What are your favorite books/TV shows/movies, and why: *The House of Mirth* by Edith Wharton.

In your opinion, what do editors think of you: Have no idea.

On a personal non-professional level, what do you think people think of you: They like me.

What are some representative titles that you have sold: *The Hardscrabble Chronicles* by Laurie Morrow (Berkley); *How to Write a Damn Good Novel Series* by James W. Frey (St. Martin's); *The True Life Story of Isobel Roundtree* (Pocket Books).

HELEN ZIMMERMANN LITERARY AGENCY

3 Emmy Lane, New Paltz, NY 12561

845-256-0977   fax: 845-256-0979

www.zimmermannliterary.com   e-mail: Helen@zimmagency.com

Agent's name: Helen Zimmermann
Born: 1964, Bronxville, New York.
Education: B.A. in English and Psychology, State University of New York, Buffalo.
Career history: 12 years in book publishing, most of them at Random House, then 5 years at an independent bookstore. I founded my agency in 2004.

Hobbies/personal interests: Climbing the 46 High Peaks in the Adirondacks (18 down, 28 to go), skiing, being an EMT, oh, and reading!

Categories/subjects that you are most enthusiastic about agenting: Memoir, pop-culture, women's issues, humor, nature, sports, accessible literary fiction, mysteries.

What you don't want to agent: Science fiction, horror, tales of male drinking habits, westerns, poetry, picture books.

What's the best way for writers to solicit your interest: By email. Please just send a detailed query letter to start. I will be in touch within 3 weeks (or sooner) if I want to see more material.

Do you charge reading or management fees: No.

Can you provide an approximation by % of what you tend to represent by category: Non-Fiction: 80%, Fiction: 20%.

What are the most common mistakes writers make when pitching you: Sending material that is sloppy or half-baked. If it's obvious you haven't done your homework, I won't be interested.

How and why did you ever become an agent: Working as the events director for an independent bookstore put me in contact with many aspiring writers. They would always ask, "How do I get published?" My answer was always "You need an agent." After about the 30th inquiry, I decided to become one myself.

How would you describe to someone (or thing) from another planet what it is that you do as an agent: If I met someone from another planet I would ask them if they needed an agent.

Do you have any particular opinions or impressions of editors and publishers in general: They are smart, hard-working folks in search of projects they deem worthy and will sell well. Never a good idea to forget that publishing is first and foremost a business.

What are your favorite books, movies, TV shows, and why: One of my all-time favorite books is *The River Why* by David James Duncan.

Please list representative titles you have sold: *Captain Freedom: A Superhero's Quest to Find the Celebrity He So Richly Deserves* by G. Xavier Robillard (HarperCollins); *My Private War: A WWII POW Memoir* by Normal Bussel (Pegasus Books); *Chosen by a Horse* by Susan Richards (Soho Press); *The Book Tour* by Susan Richards (Soho Press); *Truth Catcher* by Anna Salter (Pegasus Books); *101 Things NOT To Do Before You Die* by Robert Harris (Thomas Dunne Books); *The First Season: An NBA History* by Charley Rosen (McGraw Hill); *Cosmic Navigator* by Gahl Sasson (Red Wheel/Weiser); *The Mini Ketchup Cookbook and The Mini Mustard Cookbook* (Running Press).

ADVICE FOR WRITERS

Dear Reader,

The purpose of the Essay Section is to provide knowledge, and maybe even some wisdom. To most effectively utilize all the raw data in this book, I highly recommend that you fortify yourself with proven road maps. Eventually, your own experiences will serve as your best teacher. Until then, you will need to draw from what others might share.

Whenever I teach about how to get published, I ask my students to listen to everything I say and then forget it. Why? Because within anarchy can be found holiness. Information can be either empowering or entrapping. The human mind will "see," "feel" and "hear" whatever the environment "tells" it. It is difficult to re-direct the way an individual or an entire society perceives its reality. It has been said that the best way to hide something as outlandish as extraterrestrials would be to simply put them in the middle of Times Square, because the vast majority of people would "refuse" to perceive what "cannot" be there. Some people might report that they saw something quite odd, but most of them would probably be talked out of it by the non-silent majority that relies upon reason and good sense. In the end, some unsubstantiated and inconsistent rumors might filter into the supermarket tabloids about an ET invasion in Times Square. Once that happens, nobody who ever wants to be taken seriously again will admit to seeing anything out of the ordinary, and would likely convince themselves that it was all perfectly explainable. Of course, Times Square is a strange place anyway.

The greatest measure of everlasting success tends to belong to those who create something new and enduring. It could be an intangible idea that somehow alters the course of history. Or it could be a physical thing or process that makes humanity more capable of manipulating time and space (like the wheel, which was presumably invented by Mrs. Wheel). People who innovate are in a way the ultimate liberators and rule breakers. It's their frustration, hunger and lack of passive complacency that moves them to focus their energies for the purpose of changing what is. By nature, they are expansive. It's safe to assume that such individuals face tremendous opposition from the status quo. The vast majority of people are understandably threatened when confronted by the requirement to change, even when it is best for them to do so. All of us are capable of thinking beyond what already exists, and that approach to life will tend to be an asset when seeking to become a published writer. However, the risk of failure and rejection is always real, and can stand tall as the personal executioner of our dreams. To be eligible for success, a writer must be willing to endure all the pain that there might be.

Our nation's Puritan founders were fond of saying: *God is no respecter of persons.* That sentiment fit their belief system that human choices were mere manifestations of a pre-ordained universe. If you accept that as your truth, then it will be pointless to resist what your heart and soul ask of you. If you don't accept such a paradigm, then there is no excuse for you not to pursue what you see as your truthful path. There is also a middle ground, which is to accept that reality is indeed pre-determined, and yet live as if it is entirely your own free will that will bring you to tomorrow.

Writing, and the effort to become published, may at times resemble a dead end surrounded by the walls of a brutal confinement. But even then there is a path, and where there is a path there is a way. I hope that these essays will serve to strengthen you.

Jeff Herman

THE BATTLE OF THE "UNS"

(UNAGENTED/UNSOLICITED SUBMISSIONS)

JEFF HERMAN

Most major publishing houses claim to have policies that prevent them from even considering unagented/unsolicited submissions. "Unagented" means that a literary agent did not make the submission. "Unsolicited" means that no one at the publisher asked for the submission.

It's possible that you, or people you know, have already run into this frustrating roadblock. You may also be familiar with the rumor that it's more difficult to get an agent than it is to get a publisher—or that no agent will even consider your work until you have a publisher. On the surface, these negatives make it seem that you would have a better shot at becoming a starting pitcher for the Yankees or living out whatever your favorite improbable fantasy might be.

But, as you will soon learn, these so-called policies and practices are often more false than true, especially if you develop creative ways to circumvent them.

I have dubbed the previous obstacle course the Battle of the "UNs."

If you're presently unagented/unsolicited, you're one of the UNs.

Welcome! You're in good company.

Nobody is born published. There is no published author who wasn't at one time an UN. Thousands of new books are published each year, and thousands of people are needed to write them. You can be one of them.

In this chapter I'll show you how to win the Battle of the UNs. But first let me clarify an important distinction. When I use the word "win" here, I don't mean to say that you'll necessarily get your work published. What I mean is: You'll gain reasonable access to the powers-that-be for your work, and you'll learn how to increase the odds—dramatically—that your work will in fact be acquired.

Please be realistic. For every published writer, there are, at minimum, several thousand waiting in line to get published. "Many are called, but few are chosen."

It's completely within your power to maximize your chances of getting published. It's also within your power to minimize those chances. There are reasons why some highly talented people habitually underachieve, and those reasons can often be found within them. If you fail, fail, and fail, you should look within yourself for possible answers. What can you do to turn it around? If you find some answers, then you haven't failed at all, and the lessons you allow yourself to learn will lay the groundwork for success in this and in other endeavors.

Having an agent greatly increases the likelihood that you will be published. For one thing, on the procedural level, established agents can usually obtain relatively rapid (and serious) consideration for their clients. One basic reason for this is that editors view agents as a valuable screening mechanism—that is, when a project crosses the editor's desk under an agent's letterhead, the editor knows it's undergone vetting from someone in the industry who is familiar with the applicable standards of quality and market considerations.

I usually recommend that unpublished writers first make every attempt to get an agent before they start going directly to the publishers.

It's significantly easier to get an agent than it is to get a publisher—not the other way around. Most agents I know are always on the lookout for fresh talent. Finding and nurturing tomorrow's stars are two of our functions.

However, one of my reasons for writing and researching this book is to reveal to you that as a potential author, not having an agent does not necessarily disqualify you from the game automatically. Before I show you ways to win the Battle of the UNs, I'd like you to have a fuller understanding of the system.

YOU ARE THE EDITOR

Imagine that you're an acquisitions editor at one of America's largest publishing firms in New York City. You have a master's degree from an Ivy League college and you, at least, think you're smarter than most other people. Yet you're earning a lot less money than most of the people who graduated with you. Your classmates have become lawyers, accountants, bankers, and so forth, and they all seem to own large, well-appointed apartments or homes—whereas you, if you fall out of bed, might land in the bathtub of your minuscule New York flat.

On the other hand, you love your job. For you, working in publishing is a dream come true. As in other industries and professions, much of your satisfaction comes from advancement—getting ahead.

To move up the career ladder, you'll have to acquire at least a few successful titles each year. To find these few good titles, you'll be competing with many editors from other publishers and perhaps even with fellow editors within your own firm. As in any other business, the people who make the most money for the company will get the choice promotions and the highest salaries. Those who perform less impressively will tend to be passed over. (Of course, being a good editor and playing politics well are also important.)

There are two tried-and-true sources for the titles that publishers acquire: literary agents and direct solicitations.

LITERARY AGENTS

As an editor on the move, you'll cultivate relationships with many established literary agents. You'll want them to know what you like and what you don't like. And, by showing these agents you're disposed to acquiring new titles to build your position in the company, you'll encourage them to send you projects they think are right for you.

When you receive material from agents, you usually give it relatively fast consideration—especially if it's been submitted simultaneously to editors at other houses, which is usually the case.

When something comes in from an agent, you know it's been screened and maybe even perfected. Established agents rarely waste your time with shoddy or inappropriate material. They couldn't make a living that way because they'd quickly lose credibility with editors.

DIRECT SOLICITATIONS

If you're an ambitious editor, you won't just sit back passively and wait to see what the agents might bless you with. When you're resourceful, the opportunities are endless. Perhaps you'll contact your old American history professor and ask her to do a book showcasing her unique perspectives on the Civil War.

Or maybe you'll contact that young, fresh fiction writer whose short story you just read in a leading literary journal. You might even try reaching that veteran United States senator who just got censured for sleeping with his young aides.

One place you'll tend not to use is the "slush pile." This is the room (more like a warehouse) where all the unagented/unsolicited submissions end up.

Looking through the slush pile isn't a smart use of your limited time and energy. The chances that anything decent will be found there are much less than 1 percent. You have less-than-fond memories of your first year in the publishing business, when, as an editorial assistant (which was basically an underpaid secretarial job), one of your tasks was to shovel through the slush. Once in a great while, something promising could be found; but most of the stuff wasn't even close. At first, you were surprised by how unprofessional many of the submissions were. Many weren't addressed to anyone in particular; some looked as if they had been run over by Mack trucks; others were so poorly printed they were too painful for tired eyes to decipher—the list of failings is long.

No, the slush pile is the last place—or perhaps no place—to find titles for your list.

Now you can stop being an editor and go back to being whoever you really are. I wanted to show you why the system has evolved the way it has. Yes, though it's rational, it's cold and unfair, but these qualities aren't unique to publishing.

You're probably still wondering when I'm going to get to that promised modus operandi for winning the Battle of the UNs. Okay, we're there.

OUT OF THE SLUSH

The following steps are intended to keep you out of the infamous slush pile. Falling into the slush is like ending up in jail for contempt of court; it's like being an untouchable in India; it's like being Frank Burns on *M*A*S*H*. My point is that nobody likes the Slushables. They're everyone's scapegoat and nobody's ally.

Once your work is assigned to the slush pile, it's highly unlikely that it will receive effective access. Without access, there can be no acquisition. Without acquisition, there's no book.

Let's pretend that getting published is a board game. However, in this game you can control the dice. Here are several ways to play.

GET THE NAMES!

If you submit to nobody, it will go to nobody. Sending it to "The Editors," "Gentlemen," or the CEO of a $100-million publishing house equals sending it to no one.

Use the directory in this book to get the names of the suitable contacts.

In addition to using this directory, there are two other proven ways to discover who the right editors may be:

1. Visit bookstores and seek out recent books that are in your category. Check the acknowledgments section of each one. Many authors like to thank their editors here (and their agents). If the editor is acknowledged, you now have the name of someone who edits books like yours. (Remember to call to confirm that the editor still works at that publishing house.)

2. Simply call the publisher and ask for the editorial department. More often than not, a young junior editor will answer the phone with something like, "Editorial." Like people who answer phones everywhere, these people may sound as if they are asleep, or they may sound harried, or even as if they're making the most important declaration of their lives.
   Luckily for you, publishers plant few real secretaries or receptionists in their editorial departments, since it's constantly reconfirmed that rookie editors will do all that stuff for everyone else—and for a lot less money! Hence, real editors (although low in rank) can immediately be accessed.

Returning to the true point of this—once someone answers the phone, simply ask, "Who edits your business books?" (Or whatever your category is.)

You can also ask who edited a specific and recent book that's similar to yours. Such easy but vital questions will bring forth quick and valuable answers. Ask enough times and you can build a list of contacts that competes with this book.

DON'T SEND MANUSCRIPTS UNLESS INVITED TO DO SO!

Now that you're armed with these editors' names, don't abuse protocol (editors yell at me when you do—especially when they know where you've gotten their names). Initiate contact by sending a letter describing your work and encouraging the editor to request it.

This letter, commonly referred to as a query letter, is in reality a sales pitch or door-opener. (Please see the following chapter in this book about query letters for a full overview of this important procedure.) In brief, the letter should be short (less than $1\frac{1}{2}$ pages), easy to read and to the point, personalized, and well printed on good professional stationery. Say what you have, why it's hot, why you're a good prospect, and what's available for review upon request.

In addition to the letter, it's okay to include a resume/bio that highlights any writing credits or relevant professional credentials; a brief summary (2-3 pages) if the book is nonfiction, or a brief synopsis if it's fiction; a photo, if you have a flattering one; and promotional materials. Be careful: At this stage your aim is merely to whet the editor's appetite; you don't want to cause information overload. Less is more.

Also include a self-addressed stamped envelope (SASE). This is an important courtesy; without it, you increase your chances of getting no response. Editors receive dozens of these letters every week. Having to address envelopes for all of them would be very time-consuming. And at 37 cents a pop, it's not worth doing.

The SASE is generally intended to facilitate a response in the event of a negative decision. If the editor is intrigued by your letter, he may overlook the missing SASE and request to see your work—but don't count on it.

You may be wondering: If I have the editor's name, why not just send her my entire manuscript? Because you're flirting with the slush pile if you do. Even though you have the editor's previously secret name, you're still an UN, and UNs aren't treated kindly. An editor is inundated with reams of submissions, and her problem is finding good stuff to publish. If you send an unsolicited manuscript, you'll just be perceived as part of that problem. She'll assume you're just another slushy UN who needs to be sorted out of the way so she can go on looking for good stuff.

A bad day for an editor is receiving a few trees' worth of UN manuscripts; it deepens her occupational neurosis.

On the other hand, a professional letter is quite manageable. It is, at least, likely to be read. It may be screened initially by the editor's assistant, but will probably be passed upstairs if it shows promise.

If the editor is at all intrigued by your letter, she will request to see more material, and you will have earned the rank of being solicited.

Even if your work is not ultimately acquired by this editor, you will have at least challenged and defeated the UNs' obstacle course by achieving quality consideration. Remember: Many people get published each year without the benefits of being agented or initially solicited.

It's okay, even smart, to query several editors simultaneously. This makes sense because some editors may take a very long time to respond or, indeed, may never respond. Querying editors one at a time might take years.

If more than one editor subsequently requests and begins considering your work, let each one know that it's not an exclusive. If an editor requests an exclusive, that's fine—but give him a time limit (4 weeks is fair).

Don't sell your work to a publisher before consulting everyone who's considering it and seeing if they're interested. If you do sell it, be sure to give immediate written and oral notification to everyone who's considering it that it's no longer available.

The query-letter stage isn't considered a submission. You only need to have follow-up communications with editors who have gone beyond the query stage, meaning those who have requested and received your work for acquisition consideration. If you don't hear back from an editor within 6 weeks of sending her your letter, it's safe to assume she's not interested in your work.

If you send multiple queries, don't send them to more than one editor at the same house at the same time. If you don't hear back from a particular editor within 6 weeks of your submission, it's probably safe to query another editor at that house. One editor's reject is another's paradise; that's how both good and bad books get published.

We've just covered a lot of important procedural ground, so don't be embarrassed if you think you've forgotten all of it. This book won't self-destruct (and now, presumably, you won't either).

COLD CALLS BREED COLD HEARTS

One more thing: It's best not to cold-call these editors. Don't call them to try to sell them your work. Don't call them to follow up on query letters or submissions. Don't call them to try to change their minds.

Why? Do you like it when someone calls you in the middle of your favorite video to sell you land in the Nevada desert, near a popular nuclear test site?

Few people like uninvited and unscheduled sales calls. In some businesses, such as public relations, calling contacts is a necessary part of the process—but not in publishing. Furthermore, this business is based on hard copy. You may be the greatest oral storyteller since Uncle Remus, but if you can't write it effectively and engagingly, nobody will care. You'll end up soliciting their hostility. Of course, once they are interested in you on the basis of your hard copy, your oral and physical attributes may be of great importance to them.

On the other hand, some people are so skilled on the telephone that it's a lost opportunity for them not to make maximum use of it as a selling method. If you're one of these extremely rare and talented people, you should absolutely make use of whatever tools have proved to work best for you.

Everything I've said is my opinion. This is a subjective industry, so it's likely—no, it's for certain—that others will tell you differently. It's to your advantage to educate yourself to the fullest extent possible (read books, attend workshops, and so forth)—and in the end, to use your own best instincts about how to proceed.

I'm confident that my suggestions are safe and sound, but I don't consider them to be the beginning and the end. The more you know, the simpler things become; the less you know, the more complex and confusing they are.

BREAKING THE RULES

Taken as a whole, this book provides a structure that can be considered a set of guidelines, if not hard-and-fast rules. Some people owe their success to breaking the rules and swimming upstream—and I can certainly respect that. Often such people don't even know they're breaking the rules; they're just naturally following their own unique orbits (and you'll find a few illustrations of this very phenomenon elsewhere in these essays). Trying to regulate such people can often be their downfall.

On one hand, most of us tend to run afoul when we stray from established norms of doing business; on the other hand, a few of us can't succeed any other way (Einstein could have written an essay about that).

If you're one of those few, hats off to you! Perhaps we'll all learn something from your example.

Keep reading!

THE LITERARY AGENCY FROM A TO Z

HOW LITERARY AGENTS WORK

JEFF HERMAN

L iterary agents are like stockbrokers and real estate agents. They bring buyers and sellers together, help formulate successful deals, and receive a piece of the action (against the seller's end) for facilitating the partnership.

Specifically, literary agents look for talented writers, unearth marketable nonfiction book concepts, and discover superior fiction manuscripts to represent. Simultaneously, agents cultivate their relationships with publishers.

When an agent detects material she thinks she can sell to a publisher, she signs the writer as a client, perhaps works on the material with the writer to maximize its chances of selling, and then submits it to one or more appropriate editorial contacts.

HOW AGENTS WORK FOR THEIR CLIENTS

A dynamic agent achieves the maximum exposure possible for the writer's material, which greatly enhances the odds that the material will be published.

Having an agent gives the writer's material the type of access to the powers-that-be that it might otherwise never obtain. Publishers assume that material submitted by an agent has been screened and is much more likely to fit their needs than the random material swimming in the slush pile.

If and when a publisher makes an offer to publish the material, the agent acts on the author's behalf and negotiates the advance (the money paid up front), royalties, control of subsidiary rights, and many other important and marginal contract clauses that may prove to be important down the line. The agent acts as the writer's advocate with the publisher for as long as the book remains in print or licensing opportunities exist.

The agent knows the most effective methods for negotiating the best advance and other contract terms and is likely to have more leverage with the publisher than an un-agented writer does.

There's more to a book contract than the advance-and-royalty schedule. There are several key clauses that you, the writer, may know little or nothing about, but would accept with a cursory perusal in order to expedite the deal. Striving to close any kind of agreement can be intimidating if you don't know much about the territory; ignorance is a great disadvantage during a negotiation. An agent understands every detail of the contract and knows where and how it should be modified or expanded in your favor.

Where appropriate, an agent acts to sell subsidiary rights after the book is sold to a publisher. These rights can include: serial rights, foreign rights, dramatic and movie rights, audio and video rights, and a range of syndication and licensing possibilities.

THE AGENT'S PERSPECTIVE

No agent sells every project she represents. Even though authors are signed on the basis of their work's marketability, agents know from experience that some projects with excellent potential are not necessarily quick-and-easy big-money sales. And, yes, each and every agent has at least on occasion been as bewildered as the author when a particularly promising package receives no takers. Some projects, especially fiction, may be marketed for a long time before a publisher is found (if ever).

THE AUTHOR'S EXPECTATIONS

What's most important is that you, the author, feel sure the agent continues to believe in the project and is actively trying to sell it.

For his work, the agent receives a commission (usually 15 percent) against the writer's advance and all subsequent income relevant to the sold project.

Although this is an appreciable chunk of your work's income, the agent's involvement should end up netting you much more than you would have earned otherwise. The agent's power to round up several interested publishers to consider your work opens up the possibility that more than one house will make an offer for it, which means you'll be more likely to get a higher advance and also have more leverage regarding the various other contractual clauses.

The writer-agent relationship can become a rewarding business partnership. An agent can advise you objectively on the direction your writing career should take. Also, through her contacts, an agent may be able to get you book-writing assignments you would never have been offered on your own.

WHO'S THE BEST AGENT FOR YOU

There are many ways to get an agent. The best way to gain access to potential agents is by networking with fellow writers. Maybe some of your colleagues can introduce you to their agents or at least allow you to drop their names when contacting their agents. Most agents will be receptive to a writer who has been referred by a current and valued client.

This book features a directory of literary agencies, including their addresses, the names of specific agents, and their specialty areas, along with some personal remarks and examples of recent titles sold to publishers.

QUERY FIRST

The universally accepted way to establish initial contact with an agent is to send a query letter. Agents tend to be less interested in—if not completely put off by—oral presentations. Be sure the letter is personalized: Nobody likes generic, photocopied letters that look like they're being sent to everyone.

Think of the query as a sales pitch. Describe the nature of your project and offer to send additional material—and enclose a self-addressed stamped envelope (SASE). Include all relevant information about yourself—along with a resume if it's applicable. When querying about a nonfiction project, many agents won't mind receiving a complete proposal. But you might prefer to wait and see how the agent responds to the concept before sending the full proposal.

For queries about fiction projects, most agents prefer to receive story-concept sheets, plot synopses, or both; if they like what they see, they'll request sample chapters or ask you to send the complete manuscript. Most agents won't consider manuscripts for incomplete works of fiction, essentially because few publishers are willing to do so.

If you enclose an SASE, most agents will respond to you, one way or another, within a reasonable period of time. If the agent asks to see your material, submit it promptly with a polite note stating that you'd like a response within 4 weeks on a nonfiction proposal, or 8 weeks on fiction material. If you haven't heard from the agent by that time, write or call to find out the status of your submission.

CIRCULATE WITH THE FLOW

You're entitled to circulate your material to more than one agent at a time, but you're obligated to let each agent know that such is the case. If and when you do sign with an agent, immediately notify other agents still considering your work that it's no longer available.

At least 200 literary agents are active in America, and their individual perceptions of what is and isn't marketable will vary widely—which is why a few or many rejections should never deter writers who believe in themselves.

BUYER AND SELLER REVERSAL

When an agent eventually seeks to represent your work, it's time for her to begin selling herself to you. When you're seeking employment, you don't necessarily have to accept the first job offer you receive; likewise, you do not have to sign immediately with the first agent who wants you.

Do some checking before agreeing to work with a particular agent. If possible, meet the agent in person. A lot can be learned from in-person meetings that can't be gathered from telephone conversations. See what positive or negative information you can find out about the agent through your writers' network. Ask the agent for a client list and permission to call certain clients. Find out the agent's specialties.

Ask for a copy of the agent's standard contract. Most agents today will want to codify your relationship with a written agreement; this should protect both parties equally. Make sure you're comfortable with everything in the agreement before signing it. Again, talking with fellow writers and reading books on the subject are excellent ways to deepen your understanding of industry practices.

When choosing an agent, follow your best instincts. Don't settle for anyone you don't perceive to be on the level, or who doesn't seem to be genuinely enthusiastic about you and your work.

SELF-REPRESENTATION: A FOOL FOR A CLIENT?

Agents aren't for everyone. In some instances, you may be better off on your own. Perhaps you actually do have sufficient editorial contacts and industry savvy to cut good deals by yourself. If so, what incentive do you have to share your income with an agent?

Of course, having an agent might provide you the intangible benefits of added prestige, save you the hassles of making submissions and negotiating deals, or act as a buffer through whom you can negotiate indirectly for tactical reasons.

You might also consider representing yourself if your books are so specialized that only a few publishers are potential candidates for them. Your contacts at such houses might be much stronger than any agent's could be.

ATTORNEYS: LITERARY AND OTHERWISE

Some entertainment/publishing attorneys can do everything an agent does, though there's no reason to believe they can necessarily do more. A major difference between the two is that the lawyer may charge you a set hourly fee or retainer, or any negotiated combination thereof, instead of an agency-type commission. In rare instances, writer-publisher disputes might need to be settled in a court of law, and a lawyer familiar with the industry then becomes a necessity.

BOTTOM-LINE CALCULATIONS

The pluses and minuses of having an agent should be calculated like any other business service you might retain—it should benefit you more than it costs you. Generally speaking, the only real cost of using an agent is the commission. Of course, using the wrong agent may end up causing you more deficits than benefits, but even then you may at least learn a valuable lesson for next time.

Your challenge is to seek and retain an agent who's right for you. You're 100 percent responsible for getting yourself represented and at least 50 percent responsible for making the relationship work for both of you.

AN ALTERNATIVE INTRODUCTION TO LITERARY AGENTS

JEFF HERMAN

The title of this essay may be puzzling. I hope so, because it's meant to be. Let me explain. I wrote the essay preceding this one, also about agents, 20 years ago and have not changed it since. *Writer's Digest* magazine paid me $200 in 1987 to write that essay, and I have recycled it in this book through all 18 of its previous editions. My rationale was/is: *If it ain't broke, don't fix it.*

So is that essay broken? No, it's okay. Except it was written by a 20-something guy. Two decades since, that guy has morphed into me. What agents are and what we do has not changed too much over time, but I have. That's simply not the essay I would write today for numerous reasons. The No. 1 reason is that I am struggling every day to forget what I know, or at least pretend that I don't know it. What am I talking about?

At 27 I had a few years under my belt as a diversified publicist. I understood how to use the media to promote products, people and ideas. I had learned how to buy and wear a suit; how to keep my hair and face neat; how to function in an office; how to interact with other humans for the purpose of getting tasks done; how to work for jerks; and how to talk on a phone. I of course learned other things as well, but I have to stop the list somewhere.

A constellation of choices and circumstances brought me to the book business. Sensing that I had little to lose and an adventure to gain, I rented some office space and appointed myself a literary agent. It was the second half of the 1980s, disco was dead, and New York was still recovering from the humiliations of the '70s. I only had nominal experience and knowledge about the occupation that I had hired myself for, and I made the mistakes to prove it. Fortunately, the errors were to my own detriment and no one else's. But it was exciting. I was creating something and having fresh experiences along the way. I liked observing peoples' personalities and egos, and learning about their histories and the directions they chose. I was surprised to see how some of the most successful people were so clearly scared and self-doubting. And I was annoyed by the way some very gifted people could be so self-destructive and unwilling to own any accountability for their actions. I was especially intrigued by the way some people were able to make things happen for themselves and those who were with them. Native intelligence and formal education did not seem to matter as much as I expected. In the unstructured free-for-all entrepreneurial ways that are the emblem of our nation, those who may have spent their student careers in Special Ed classes could emerge from secret telephone booths as Masters of the Universe. People could be very interesting.

The passage of time and raw experience taught me what I know about the book business, and about people. Sometime in the mid-1990s I fell into a routine. My workload and commitments mushroomed. I would make decisions on the basis of other peoples' advice or the bottom-line calculations. The more visceral messages from my heart and gut lost their traditional primacy in the constitution of my life. I continued to succeed on the basis of hard work and intellect, and by riding the momentum that my earlier years established. But it was not so much of an adventure as it was a job. And that was changing me.

The changes were subtle. Looking back, I recall that I felt the urge to watch more TV; to eat more; to go out less; to be more fixed in my routines. I was inclined to think more and feel less. My time and energy belonged to the mounting tasks that my success generated. I was employed by what had to get done. I had essentially abdicated being the Master of my Domain. Of course, once I had a family to support, it could no longer be just about me. I didn't need much, but a family does. Like many people before me and since, I transitioned from being an explorer into being an expert. Explorers keep moving, looking, touching, consuming and discovering. Experts stand still and cultivate their crops. Each harvest is likely to follow the same template as the ones before, though the goal is to expand the bounty by making better use of the available resources. No accident that the root word for husband means farmer. A responsible farmer does not leave his land; he roots himself into the soil with every seed he sows, and conjures the earth's power to make food out of dirt, water and light.

Without experts, we'd all be nomads like our pre-historic ancestors. No steady homes; no security; no nuclear families; no settlements; no growers of wheat and barley, and no commerce between them. To this day, we would be herds of two-legged entities chasing after herds of the four-legged kind. But without the explorers our cars would have square tires. Without the explorers we might have nothing. In fact, we might be nothing. The experts probably held their ground as the fury of serial floods, droughts and ice ages swatted them into oblivion. To the contrary, the explorers instinctively shrugged off what was left behind, and discovered the future; our future. And that's still what they do every day. It is good for a society to have different kinds of people. Perhaps it's equally as good for each of us to embrace vast differences within our own beings, no matter how conflicted that may seem. Self-directed rejection and repression leads to decades of quiet desperation. Your bills may get paid, but you will owe yourself a fortune.

I digress. If you're still with me, let's talk about literary agents.

Actually, everything I said 20 years ago is still valid. Just read the essay that precedes this one. I did make a few revisions to reflect contemporary conditions.

WRITE THE PERFECT QUERY LETTER

DEBORAH LEVINE HERMAN
JEFF HERMAN

The query is a short letter of introduction to publishers or agents, encouraging them to request to see your fiction manuscript or nonfiction book proposal. It is a vital tool, often neglected by writers. If done correctly, it can help you to avoid endless frustration and wasted effort. The query is the first hurdle of your individual marketing strategy. If you can leap over it successfully, you're well on your way to a sale.

The query letter is your calling card. For every book that makes it to the shelves, thousands of worthy manuscripts, proposals, and ideas are knocked out of the running by poor presentation or inadequate marketing strategies. Don't forget that the book you want to sell is a product that must be packaged correctly to stand above the competition.

A query letter asks the prospective publisher or agent if she would like to see more about the proposed idea. If your book is fiction, you should indicate that a manuscript or sample chapters are available on request. If nonfiction, you should offer to send a proposal and, if you have them, sample chapters.

The query is your first contact with the prospective buyer of your book. To ensure that it's not your last, avoid common mistakes. The letter should be concise and well written. You shouldn't try to impress the reader with your mastery of all words over three syllables. Instead, concentrate on a clear and to-the-point presentation with no fluff.

Think of the letter as an advertisement. You want to make a sale of a product, and you have very limited space and time in which to reach this goal.

The letter should be only one page long if possible. It will form the basis of a query package that will include supporting materials. Don't waste words in the letter describing material that can be included separately. Your goal is to pique the interest of an editor who has very little time and probably very little patience. You want to entice her to keep reading and ask you for more.

The query package can include a short resume, media clippings, or other favorable documents. Do not get carried away, or your package will quickly come to resemble junk mail. Include a self-addressed stamped envelope (SASE) with enough postage to return your entire package. This will be particularly appreciated by smaller publishing houses and independent agents.

For fiction writers, a short (1- to 5-page), double-spaced synopsis of the manuscript will be helpful and appropriate.

Do not waste money and defeat the purpose of the query by sending an unsolicited manuscript. Agents and editors may be turned off by receiving manuscripts of 1,000+ pages that were uninvited and that are not even remotely relevant to what they do.

The query follows a simple format (which can be reworked according to your individual preferences):

1. lead;

2. supporting material/persuasion;

3. biography; and

4. conclusion/pitch.

YOUR LEAD IS YOUR HOOK

The lead can either catch the editor's attention or turn him off completely. Some writers think getting someone's attention in a short space means having to do something dramatic. Editors appreciate cleverness, but too much contrived writing can work against you. Opt instead for clear conveyance of thoroughly developed ideas and get right to the point.

Of course, you don't want to be boring and stuffy in the interest of factual presentation. You'll need to determine what is most important about the book you're trying to sell, and write your letter accordingly.

You can begin with a lead similar to what you'd use to grab the reader in an article or a book chapter. You can use an anecdote, a statement of facts, a question, a comparison, or whatever you believe will be most powerful.

You may want to rely on the journalistic technique of the inverted pyramid. This means that you begin with the strongest material and save the details for later in the letter. Don't start slowly and expect to pick up momentum as you proceed. It will be too late.

Do not begin a query letter like this: "I have sent this idea to 20 agents/publishers, none of whom think it will work. I just know you'll be different, enlightened, and insightful, and will give it full consideration." There is no room for negatives in a sales pitch. Focus only on positives—unless you can turn negatives to your advantage.

Some writers make the mistake of writing about the book's potential in the first paragraph without ever stating its actual idea or theme. Remember, your letter may never be read beyond the lead, so make that first paragraph your hook.

Avoid bad jokes, clichés, unsubstantiated claims, and dictionary definitions. Don't be condescending; editors have egos, too, and have power over your destiny as a writer.

SUPPORTING MATERIAL: BE PERSUASIVE

If you are selling a nonfiction book, you may want to include a brief summary of hard evidence, gleaned from research, that will support the merit of your idea. This is where you convince the editor that your book should exist. This is more important for nonfiction than it is for fiction, where the style and storytelling ability are paramount. Nonfiction writers must focus on selling their topic and their credentials.

You should include a few lines showing the editor what the publishing house will gain from the project. Publishers are not charitable institutions; they want to know how they can get the greatest return on their investment. If you have brilliant marketing ideas or know of a well-defined market for your book where sales will be guaranteed, include this rather than other descriptive material.

In rereading your letter, make sure you have shown that you understand your own idea thoroughly. If it appears half-baked, the editors won't want to invest time fleshing out your thoughts. Exude confidence so that the editor will have faith in your ability to carry out the job.

In nonfiction queries, you can include a separate table of contents and brief chapter abstracts. Otherwise, it can wait for the book proposal.

YOUR BIOGRAPHY: NO PLACE FOR MODESTY

In the biographical portion of your letter, toot your own horn, but in a carefully calculated, persuasive fashion. Your story of winning the third-grade writing competition (it was then that you knew you wanted to be a world-famous writer!) should be saved for the documentary done on your life after you reach your goal.

In the query, all you want to include are the most important and relevant credentials that will support the sale of your book. You can include, as a separate part of the package, a resume or biography that will elaborate further.

The separate resume should list all relevant and recent experiences that support your ability to write the book. Unless you're fairly young, your listing of academic accomplishments should start after high school. Don't overlook hobbies or non-job-related activities if they correspond to your book story or topic. Those experiences are often more valuable than academic achievements.

Other information to include: any impressive print clippings about you; a list of your broadcast interviews and speaking appearances; and copies of articles and reviews about any books you may have written. This information can never hurt your chances and could make the difference in your favor.

There is no room for humility or modesty in the query letter and resume. When corporations sell toothpaste, they list the product's best attributes and create excitement about the product. If you can't find some way to make yourself exciting as an author, you'd better rethink your career.

HERE'S THE PITCH

At the close of your letter, ask for the sale. This requires a positive and confident conclusion with such phrases as "I look forward to your speedy response." Such phrases as "I hope" and "I think you will like my book" sound too insecure. This is the part of the letter where you go for the kill.

Be sure to thank the reader for his or her attention in your final sentence.

FINISHING TOUCHES

When you're finished, reread and edit your query letter. Cut out any extraneous information that dilutes the strength of your arguments. Make the letter as polished as possible so that the editor will be impressed with you, as well as with your idea. Don't ruin your chances by appearing careless; make certain your letter is not peppered with typos and misspellings. If you don't show pride in your work, you'll create a self-fulfilling prophecy; the editor will take you no more seriously than you take yourself.

Aesthetics are important. If you were pitching a business deal to a corporation, you would want to present yourself in conservative dress, with an air of professionalism. In the writing business, you may never have face-to-face contact with the people who will determine your future. Therefore, your query package is your representative.

If editors receive a query letter on yellowed paper that looks as if it's been lying around for 20 years, they will wonder if the person sending the letter is a has-been or a never-was.

You should invest in a state-of-the-art letterhead—with a logo!—to create an impression of pride, confidence, and professionalism. White, cream, and ivory paper are all acceptable, but you should use only black ink for printing the letter. Anything else looks amateurish.

Don't sabotage yourself by letting your need for instant approval get the best of you. Don't call editors. You have invited them to respond, so be patient. Then prepare yourself for possible rejection. It often takes many nos to get a yes.

One more note: This is a tough business for anyone—and it's especially so for greenhorns. Hang in there.

QUERY TIPS

If you have spent any time at all in this business, the term *query letter* is probably as familiar to you as the back of your hand. Yet no matter how many courses you've attended and books you've read about this important part of the process, you may still feel inadequate when you try to write one that sizzles. If it's any consolation, you're far from being alone in your uncertainties. The purpose of the query letter is to formally introduce your work and yourself to potential agents and editors. The immediate goal is to motivate them to promptly request a look at your work, or at least a portion of it.

In effect, the letter serves as the writer's first hurdle. It's a relatively painless way for agents and editors to screen out unwanted submissions without the added burden of having to manhandle a deluge of unwanted manuscripts. They are more relaxed if their in-boxes are filled with 50 unanswered queries, as opposed to 50 uninvited 1,000-page manuscripts. The query is a very effective way to control the quality and quantity of the manuscripts that get into the office. And that's why you have to write good ones.

The term *query letter* is part of the lexicon and jargon of the publishing business. This term isn't used in any other industry. I assume it has ancient origins. I can conjure up the image of an English gentleman with a fluffy quill pen composing a most civilized letter to a prospective publisher for the purpose of asking for his work to be read and, perchance, published. Our environments may change, but the nature of our ambitions remains the same.

Let's get contemporary. Whenever you hear the term *query letter*, you should say to yourself "pitch" or "sales" letter. Because that's what it is. You need the letter to sell.

QUERY LETTER TIPS

- *Don't be long-winded.* Agents/editors receive lots of these things, and they want to mow through them as swiftly as possible. Ideally, the letter should be a single page with short paragraphs. (I must admit I've seen good ones that are longer than a page.) If you lose your reader, you've lost your opportunity.

- *Get to the point; don't pontificate.* Too many letters go off on irrelevant detours, which makes it difficult for the agent/editor to determine what's actually for sale—other than the writer's soapbox.

- *Make your letter attractive.* When making a first impression, the subliminal impact of aesthetics cannot be overestimated. Use high-quality stationery and typeface. The essence of your words is paramount, but cheap paper and poor print quality will only diminish your impact.

- *Don't say anything negative about yourself or your attempts to get published.* Everyone appreciates victims when it's time to make charitable donations, but not when it's time to make a profit. It's better if you can make editors/agents think that you have to fight them off.

WHY NOT SIMPLY SUBMIT MY MANUSCRIPT?

Q: Why can't I bypass the query hurdle by simply submitting my manuscript?
A: You may—and no one can litigate against you. But if you submit an unsolicited manuscript to a publisher, it's more likely to end up in the so-called slush pile and may never get a fair reading. If it's sent to an agent, nothing negative may come of it. However, most agents prefer to receive a query first.

Sending unsolicited nonfiction book proposals is in the gray zone. Proposals are much more manageable than entire manuscripts, so editors/agents may not particularly mind.

But you may want to avoid the expense of sending unwanted proposals. After all, the query is also an opportunity for you to screen out those who clearly have no interest in your subject.

Also, you shouldn't be overly loose with your ideas and concepts.

These pointers, in combination with the other good information in this book and all the other available resources, should at least give you a solid background for creating a query letter that sizzles.

THE KNOCKOUT NONFICTION BOOK PROPOSAL

JEFF HERMAN

ADVICE FOR WRITERS

The quality of your nonfiction book proposal will invariably make the difference between success and failure. Before agents and publishers will accept a work of fiction (especially from a newer writer), they require a complete manuscript. But, nonfiction projects are different: A proposal alone can do the trick. This is what makes nonfiction writing a much less speculative and often more lucrative endeavor (relatively speaking) than fiction writing.

You may devote five years of long evenings to writing a 1,000-page fiction manuscript, only to receive a thick pile of computer-generated rejections. Clearly, writing nonfiction doesn't entail the same risks.

On the other hand, writing fiction is often an emotionally driven endeavor in which rewards are gained though the act of writing and are not necessarily based on rational, practical considerations. Interestingly, many successful nonfiction writers fantasize about being fiction writers.

As you'll learn, the proposal's structure, contents, and size can vary substantially, and it's up to you to decide the best format for your purposes. Still, the guidelines given here serve as excellent general parameters.

An excellent model proposal is featured later in this chapter.

APPEARANCE COUNTS

- Your proposal should be printed in black ink on clean, letter-sized (8½″ x 11″), white paper.

- Letter-quality printing is by far the best. Make sure the ribbon or toner or ink cartridge is fresh and that all photocopies are dark and clear enough to be read easily. Publishing is an image-driven business, and you will be judged, perhaps unconsciously, on the physical and aesthetic merits of your submission.

- Always double-space, or you can virtually guarantee reader antagonism—eye-strain makes people cranky.

- Make sure your proposal appears fresh and new and hasn't been dog-eared, marked-up, and abused by previous readers. No editor will be favorably disposed if she thinks that everyone else on the block has already sent you packing. You want editors to suppose that you have lots of other places you can go, not nowhere else to go.

- Contrary to common practice in other industries, editors prefer not to receive bound proposals. If an editor likes your proposal, she will want to photocopy it for her colleagues, and your binding will only be in the way. If you want to keep the material together and neat, use a binder clip; if it's a lengthy proposal, clip each section together separately. Don't e-mail or send CDs unless the agent or editor consents to receiving that way.

THE TITLE PAGE

The title page should be the easiest part, but it can also be the most important, since, like your face when you meet someone, it's what is seen first.

Try to think of a title that's attractive and effectively communicates your book's concept. A descriptive subtitle, following a catchy title, can help to achieve both goals.

It's very important that your title and subtitle relate to the book's subject, or an editor might make an inaccurate judgment about your book's focus and automatically dismiss it.

For instance, if you're proposing a book about gardening, don't title it *The Greening of America.*

Examples of titles that have worked very well are:

How to Win Friends and Influence People by Dale Carnegie
Think and Grow Rich by Napoleon Hill
Baby and Child Care by Dr. Benjamin Spock
How to Swim with the Sharks Without Being Eaten Alive by Harvey Mackay

And, yes, there are notable exceptions: An improbable title that went on to become a perennial success is *What Color Is Your Parachute?* by Richard Bolles. Sure, you may gain freedom and confidence from such exceptional instances. By all means let your imagination graze during the brainstorming stage.

However, don't bet on the success of an arbitrarily conceived title that has nothing at all to do with the book's essential concept or reader appeal.

A title should be stimulating and, when appropriate, upbeat and optimistic. If your subject is an important historic or current event, the title should be dramatic. If a biography, the title should capture something personal (or even controversial) about the subject. Many good books have been handicapped by poorly conceived titles, and many poor books have been catapulted to success by good titles. A good title is good advertising. Procter & Gamble, for instance, spends thousands of worker-hours creating seductive names for its endless array of soap-based products.

The title you choose is referred to as the "working title."

Most likely, the book will have a different title when published. There are two reasons for this:

1. A more appropriate or arresting title (or both) may evolve with time; and

2. The publisher has final contractual discretion over the title (as well as over a lot of other things).

The title page should contain only the title; your name, address, and telephone number—and the name, address, and phone number of your agent, if you have one. The title page should be neatly and attractively spaced. Eye-catching and tasteful computer graphics and display-type fonts can contribute to the overall aesthetic appeal.

OVERVIEW

The overview portion of the proposal is a terse statement (one to three pages) of your overall concept and mission. It sets the stage for what's to follow. Short, concise paragraphs are usually best.

BIOGRAPHICAL SECTION

This is where you sell yourself. This section tells who you are and why you're the ideal person to write this book. You should highlight all your relevant experience, including media and public-speaking appearances, and list previous books, articles, or both, published by or about you. Self-flattery is appropriate—so long as you're telling the truth. Many writers prefer to slip into the third person here, to avoid the appearance of egomania.

MARKETING SECTION

This is where you justify the book's existence from a commercial perspective. Who will buy it? For instance, if you're proposing a book on sales, state the number of people who earn their livings through sales; point out that thousands of large and small companies are sales-dependent and spend large sums on sales training, and that all sales professionals are perpetually hungry for fresh, innovative sales books.

Don't just say something like "My book is for adult women and there are more than 50 million adult women in America." You have to be much more demographically sophisticated than that.

COMPETITION SECTION

To the uninitiated, this section may appear to be a set-up to self-destruction. However, if handled strategically, and assuming you have a fresh concept, this section wins you points rather than undermines your case.

The competition section is where you describe major published titles with concepts comparable to yours. If you're familiar with your subject, you'll probably know those titles by heart; you may have even read most or all of them. If you're not certain, check *Books in Print*—available in virtually every library—which catalogues all titles in print in every category under the sun.

Don't list everything published on your subject—that could require a book in itself. Just describe the leading half-dozen titles or so (backlist classics, as well as recent books) and *explain why yours will be different.*

Getting back to the sales-book example, there is no shortage of good sales books. There's a reason for that—a big market exists for sales books. You can turn that to your advantage by emphasizing the public's substantial, insatiable demand for sales books. Your book will feed that demand with its unique and innovative sales-success program. Salespeople and companies dependent on sales are always looking for new ways to enhance sales skills (it's okay to reiterate key points).

PROMOTION SECTION

Here you suggest possible ways to promote and market the book. Sometimes this section is unnecessary. It depends on your subject and on what, if any, realistic promotional prospects exist.

If you're proposing a specialized academic book such as *The Mating Habits of Octopi*, the market is a relatively limited one, and elaborate promotions would be wasteful.

But if you're proposing a popularly oriented relationship book along the lines of *The Endless Orgasm in One Easy Lesson*, the promotional possibilities are also endless. They would include most major electronic broadcast and print media outlets, advertising, maybe even some weird contests.

You want to guide the publisher toward seeing realistic ways to publicize the book.

CHAPTER OUTLINE

This is the meat of the proposal. Here's where you finally tell what's going to be in the book. Each chapter should be tentatively titled and clearly abstracted.

Some successful proposals have fewer than 100 words per abstracted chapter; others have several hundred words per chapter. Sometimes the length varies from chapter to chapter. There are no hard-and-fast rules here; it's the dealer's choice.

Sometimes less is more; at other times a too-brief outline inadequately represents the project.

At their best, the chapter abstracts read like mini-chapters—as opposed to stating "I will do… and I will show…" Visualize the trailer for a forthcoming movie; that's the tantalizing effect you want to create.

Also, it's a good idea to preface the outline with a table of contents. This way, the editor can see your entire road map at the outset.

SAMPLE CHAPTERS

Sample chapters are optional. A strong, well-developed proposal will often be enough. However, especially if you're a first-time writer, one or more sample chapters will give you an opportunity to show your stuff and will help dissolve an editor's concerns about your ability to actually write the book, thereby increasing the odds that you'll receive an offer—and you'll probably increase the size of the advance, too.

Nonfiction writers are often wary of investing time to write sample chapters since they view the proposal as a way of avoiding speculative writing. This can be a short-sighted position, however, for a single sample chapter can make the difference between selling and not selling a marginal proposal. Occasionally, a publisher will request that one or two sample chapters be written before he makes a decision about a particular project. If the publisher seems to have a real interest, writing the sample material is definitely worth the author's time, and the full package can then be shown to additional prospects, too.

Many editors say that they look for reasons to reject books and that being on the fence is a valid reason for rejecting a project. To be sure, there are cases where sample chapters have tilted a proposal on the verge of rejection right back onto the playing field!

Keep in mind that the publisher is speculating that you can and will write the book upon contract. A sample chapter will go far to reduce the publisher's concerns about your ability to deliver a quality work beyond the proposal stage.

WHAT ELSE?

There are a variety of materials you may wish to attach to the proposal to further bolster your cause. These include:

+ Laudatory letters and comments about you.

+ Laudatory publicity about you.

+ A headshot (but not if you look like the Fly, unless you're proposing a humor book or a nature book).

+ Copies of published articles you've written.

+ Videos of TV or speaking appearances.

+ Any and all information that builds you up in a relevant way, but be organized about it—don't create a disheveled, unruly package.

LENGTH

The average proposal is probably between 15 and 30 double-spaced pages, and the typical sample chapter an additional 10 to 20 double-spaced pages. But sometimes proposals reach 100 pages, and sometimes they're 5 pages total. Extensive proposals are not a handicap.

Whatever it takes!

MODEL SUCCESSFUL NONFICTION BOOK PROPOSAL

What follows is a genuine proposal that won a healthy book contract. It's excerpted from *Write the Perfect Book Proposal* by Jeff Herman and Deborah Adams (John Wiley & Sons) and includes an extensive critique of its strongest and weakest points. All in all, it's an excellent proposal and serves as a strong model.

The book is titled *Heart and Soul: A Psychological and Spiritual Guide to Preventing and Healing Heart Disease* and is written by Bruno Cortis, M.D. This project was sold to the Villard Books division of Random House.

Every editor who saw this proposal offered sincere praise. Ironically, several of these editors regretted not being able to seek the book's acquisition. From the outset I was aware this might happen. The past few years have given us numerous unconventional health and healing books—many of which are excellent. Most publishers I approached felt that their health/spirituality quota was already full and that they would wind up competing with themselves if they acquired any more such titles.

Experienced agents and writers are familiar with the market-glut problem. In many popular categories it's almost endemic. If you're prepared for this reality from the outset, there are ways to pave your own road and bypass the competition. Dedicated agents, editors, and writers want to see important books published, regardless of what the publishers' lists dictate.

Furthermore, it is not necessary for every publisher to want your book (though that is the proven way to maximize the advance).

In the end, you need only the right publisher and a reasonable deal.

Let's look first at the title page from the book proposal.

HEART AND SOUL

(This is a good title. It conjures up dramatic images similar to a soulful blues melody. And it has everything to do with what this proposal is about. The subtitle is scientific and provides a clear direction for the patients.)

Psychological and Spiritual Guide to Preventing and Healing Heart Disease
by
Bruno Cortis, M.D.
Book Proposal

The Jeff Herman Agency
PO Box 1522, 9 South Street
Stockbridge, MA
telephone: 413-298-8188

(The title page is sufficient overall. But it would have been better if the software had been available to create a more striking cover sheet. To a large degree, everything does initially get judged by its cover.)

OVERVIEW

(One minor improvement here would have been to shift the word "Overview" to the center of the page—or otherwise styling the typeface for such headings and subheadings throughout the proposal to make them stand out from the body text.)

Heart disease is the number-one killer of Americans over the age of 40. The very words can sound like a death sentence. Our heart, the most intimate part of our body, is under siege. Until now, most experts have advised victims of the disease, as well as those who would avoid it, to change avoidable risk factors, like smoking, and begin a Spartan regimen of diet and exercise. But new research shows that risk factors and lifestyle are only part of the answer. In fact, it is becoming clear that for many patients, emotional, psychological, and even spiritual factors are at least as important, both in preventing disease and in healing an already damaged heart.

(This is a powerful lead paragraph. The author knows a lot of books are out there about heart disease. The first paragraph of the overview immediately distinguishes this book proposal and draws attention to "new research." Anything that is potentially cutting edge is going to catch the eye of a prospective publisher.)

Like *Love, Medicine, and Miracles* by Bernie Siegel, which showed cancer patients how to take charge of their own disease and life, *Heart and Soul* will show potential and actual heart patients how to use inner resources to form a healthy relationship with their heart, actually healing circulatory disorders and preventing further damage.

(The preceding paragraph contains the central thesis for the project, and it is profoundly important. In retrospect, this could have worked exceedingly well as the first paragraph of the proposal, thereby immediately setting the stage. This is a clever comparison to a highly successful book. It indicates an untapped market that has already proved itself in a similar arena. Instead of merely making unsubstantiated claims based on the success of Dr. Siegel's work, the author shows what this book will do to merit the same type of attention.)

The author, Bruno Cortis, M.D., is a renowned cardiologist whose experience with hundreds of "exceptional heart patients" has taught him that there is much more to medicine than operations and pills.

(It is good to bring the author's credentials into the overview at this juncture. A comparison has been made with a highly successful and marketable doctor/author—which will immediately raise questions as to whether this author has similar potential. The author anticipates this line of editorial reasoning and here makes some strong statements.)

Dr. Cortis identifies three types of heart patients:

•　　Passive Patients, who are unwilling or unable to take responsibility for their condition. Instead, these patients blame outside forces, withdraw from social contacts, and bewail their fate. They may become deeply depressed and tend to die very soon.

•　　Obedient Consumers, who are the "A" students of modern medicine. Following doctors' orders to the letter, these patients behave exactly as they are supposed to, placing their fates in the hands of the experts. These patients tend to die exactly when medicine predicts they will.

•　　Exceptional Heart Patients, who regard a diagnosis of heart disease as a challenge. Although they may have realistic fears for the future, these patients take full responsibility for their situation and actively contribute to their own recovery. While they may or may not follow doctors' orders, these patients tend to choose the therapy or combination of therapies that is best for them. They often live far beyond medical predictions.

(This is an exceptional overview—especially where it defines the three patient types.)

It is Dr. Cortis's aim in this book to show readers how to become exceptional heart patients, empowering them to take responsibility for their own health and well-being.

(The remaining paragraphs of this overview section show a highly focused and well-thought-out plan for the book. The writing collaborator on this project had to condense and assimilate boxes and boxes of material to produce this concise and to-the-point overview that leaves no questions unanswered. Although it took a great deal of effort for the writer to write such a good proposal, there is no struggle for the editor to understand exactly what is being proposed and what the book is going to be about.)

Although Dr. Cortis acknowledges the importance of exercise, stress management, and proper nutrition—the standard staples of cardiac treatment—he stresses that there is an even deeper level of human experience that is necessary in order to produce wellness. Unlike other books on heart disease, *Heart and Soul* does not prescribe the same strict diet and exercise program for everyone. Instead it takes a flexible approach, urging readers to create their own unique health plan by employing psychological and spiritual practices in combination with a variety of more traditional diet and exercise regimens.

While seemingly revolutionary, Dr. Cortis's message is simple: You can do much more for the health of your heart than you think you can. This is true whether you have no symptoms or risk factors whatsoever, if you have some symptoms or risk factors, or if you actually already have heart disease.

MARKET ANALYSIS
Heart and Soul could not be more timely. Of the $1\frac{1}{2}$ million heart attacks suffered by Americans each year, nearly half occur between the ages of 40 and 65. Three-fifths of these heart attacks are fatal. While these precise statistics may not be familiar to the millions of baby boomers now entering middle age, the national obsession with oat bran, low-fat foods, and exercising for health shows that the members of the boomer generation are becoming increasingly aware of their own mortality.

(The writer would be well advised to ease off the use of the term baby boomer. It is so often used in book proposals that many editors are undoubtedly sick of it. It might have been better merely to describe the exceptional number of people in this pertinent age bracket—without attempting to sound trendy. Good use of facts, trends, and the public's receptivity to what some would characterize as an unorthodox treatment approach.)

This awareness of growing older, coupled with a widespread loss of faith in - doctors and fear of overtechnologized medicine, combine to produce a market that is ready for a book emphasizing the spiritual component in healing, especially in reference to heart disease.

Most existing books on the market approach the subject from the physician's point of view, urging readers to follow doctor's orders to attain a healthy heart. There is very little emphasis in these books on the patient's own responsibility for wellness or the inner changes that must be made for the prescribed regimens to work. Among the best known recent books are:

(Not a big deal in this instance—but ordinarily it would be better to have identified this portion of the proposal as the competition section, set it off under a separate heading.)

Healing Your Heart, by Herman Hellerstein, M.D., and Paul Perry (Simon & Schuster, 1990). Although this book, like most of the others, advocates proper nutrition, exercise, cessation of smoking, and stress reduction as the road to a healthy heart, it fails to provide the motivation necessary to attain such changes in the reader's lifestyle. Without changes in thinking and behavior, readers of this and similar books will find it difficult, if not impossible, to follow the strict diet and exercise program recommended.

In *Heart Talk: Preventing and Coping with Silent and Painful Heart Disease* (Harcourt Brace Jovanovich, 1987), Dr. Peter F. Cohn and Dr. Joan K. Cohn address the dangers of "silent" (symptomless) heart disease. While informative, the book emphasizes only one manifestation of heart disease and does not empower readers with the motivational tools needed to combat that disease.

(This section is termed the market analysis, which in this proposal actually departs from the approach of the typical marketing section of most proposals. Instead of telling the publisher how to sell the book, the writing collaborator [see the About the Authors section further on] shows special insight into the target audience. The key is that this analysis is not merely a statement of the obvious. This type of in-depth analysis of the potential reader can be very persuasive.)

The Trusting Heart, by Redford Williams, M.D. (Times Books, 1989), demonstrates how hostility and anger can lead to heart disease, while trust and forgiveness can contribute to wellness. While these are important points, the holistic treatment of heart disease must encompass other approaches as well. The author also fails to provide sufficient motivation for behavioral changes in the readers.

(The author does a good job of demonstrating the invaluable uniqueness of this particular project—especially important when compared with the strong list of competitors.)

The best book on preventing and curing heart disease is Dr. Dean Ornish's *Program for Reversing Heart Disease* (Random House, 1990). This highly successful book prescribes a very strict diet and exercise program for actually reversing certain types of coronary artery disease. This still-controversial approach is by far the best on the market; unfortunately, the material is presented in a dense, academic style not easily accessible to the lay reader. It also focuses on Dr. Ornish's program as the "only way to manage heart disease," excluding other, more synergistic methods.

(The writer collaborator directly analyzed the competition, highlighting the most relevant books on the market without listing each one directly. Although you do not want to present the editor with any unnecessary surprises, if there are too many similar books out in your particular subject area, you might want to use this approach. The writer confronts the heaviest competition directly by finding specific distinguishing factors that support the strength of his proposed project.)

APPROACH

Heart and Soul will be a 60,000- to 70,000-word book targeted to health-conscious members of the baby boom generation. Unlike other books on heart disease, it will focus on the "facts of the connection between the mind and the body as it relates to heart disease, showing readers how to use that connection to heal the heart." The book will be written in an informal but authoritative style, in Dr. Cortis's voice. It will begin with a discussion of heart disease and show how traditional medicine fails to prevent or cure it. Subsequent chapters will deal with the mind-body connection, and the role in healing of social support systems, self-esteem, and faith. In order to help readers reduce stress in their lives, Dr. Cortis shows how they can create their own "daily practice" that combines exercise, relaxation, meditation, and use of positive imagery. Throughout the book, he will present anecdotes that demonstrate how other Exceptional Heart Patients have overcome their disease and gone on to lead healthy and productive lives.

In addition to a thorough discussion of the causes and outcomes of coronary artery disease, the book will include tests and checklists that readers may use to gauge their progress, and exercises, ranging from the cerebral to the physical, that strengthen and help heal the heart. At the end of each chapter readers will be introduced to an essential "Heartskill" that will enable them to put the advice of the chapter into immediate practice.

Through example and encouragement *Heart and Soul* will offer readers a variety of strategies for coping with heart disease, to be taken at once or used in combination. Above all an accessible, practical book, *Heart and Soul* will present readers with a workable program for controlling their own heart disease and forming a healthy relationship with their hearts.

(This is a good summary statement of the book.)

ABOUT THE AUTHORS

Bruno Cortis, M.D., is an internationally trained cardiologist with more than 30 years' experience in research and practice. A pioneer of cardiovascular applications of lasers and angioscopy, a Diplomate of the American Board of Cardiology, contributor of more than 70 published professional papers, Dr. Cortis has long advocated the need for new dimensions of awareness in health and the healing arts. As a practicing physician and researcher, his open acknowledgment of individual spirituality as the core of health puts him on the cutting edge of those in traditional medicine who are beginning to create the medical arts practices of the future.

(This is a very good description of the author. The writing collaborator establishes Dr. Cortis as both an expert in his field and a compelling personality. All of this material is relevant to the ultimate success of the book.)

Dr. Cortis has been a speaker at conferences in South America, Japan, and Australia, as well as in Europe and the United States. His firm, Mind Your Health, is dedicated to the prevention of heart attack through the development of human potential. Dr. Cortis is the cofounder of the Exceptional Heart Patients program. The successful changes he has made in his own medical practice prove he is a man not only of vision and deeds, but an author whose beliefs spring from the truths of daily living.

(A formal vita follows in this proposal. It is best to lead off with a journalistic-style biography and follow up with a complete and formal resume—assuming, as in this case, the author's professional credentials are inseparable from the book.)

Kathryn Lance is the author of more than 30 books of nonfiction and fiction (see attached publications list for details). Her first book, *Running for Health and Beauty* (1976), the first mass-market book on running for women, sold half a million copies. *The Setpoint Diet* (1985), ghosted for Dr. Gilbert A. Leveille, reached the *New York Times* bestseller list for several weeks. Ms. Lance has written widely on fitness, health, diet, and medicine.

(Though she wasn't mentioned on the title page, Lance is the collaborator. This brief bio and the following resume reveal a writer with virtually impeccable experience. Her participation served to ensure the editors that they could count on the delivery of a high-quality manuscript. Her bio sketch is also strong in its simplicity. Her writing credits are voluminous, but she does not use up space here with a comprehensive listing. Instead she showcases only credits that are relevant to the success of this particular project. Comprehensive author resumes were also attached as addenda to the proposal package.)

HEART AND SOUL
by
Bruno Cortis, M.D.
Chapter Outline

(Creating a separate page [or pages] for the entire table of contents is a useful and easy technique to enable the editor to gain a holistic vision for the book before delving into the chapter abstracts. In retrospect, we should have had one here.)

(The following is an exceptional outline because it goes well beyond the lazy and stingy telegraph approach that many writers use, often to their own detriment. [Telegrams once were a popular means of communication that required the sender to pay by the word.] Here each abstract reads like a miniature sample chapter unto itself. It proves that the writers have a genuine command of their subject, a well-organized agenda, and superior skills for writing about it. Together they are a darn good team. Whatever legitimate reasons a publisher may have had for rejecting this proposal, it had nothing to do with its manifest editorial and conceptual merits. Some writers are reluctant to go this editorial distance on spec. However, if you believe in your project's viability and you want to maximize acquisition interest and the ultimate advance, you'll give the proposal everything you've got.)

Contents

Introduction: Beating the Odds: Exceptional Heart Patients
(See sample chapter.)

Chapter One
YOU AND YOUR HEART
Traditional medicine doesn't and can't "cure" heart disease. The recurrence rate of arterial blockage after angioplasty is 25-35 percent, while a bypass operation only bypasses the problem, but does not cure it. The author proposes a new way of looking at heart disease, one in which patients become responsible for the care and well-being of their hearts, in partnership with their physicians. Following a brief, understandable discussion of the physiology of heart disease and heart attack, further topics covered in this chapter include:

(This is a good technique for a chapter abstract. The writer organizes the structure as a listing of chapter topics and elaborates with a sample of the substance and writing approach that will be incorporated into the book. The editor cannot, of course, be expected to be an expert on the subject, but after reading this abstract will come away with a good sense of the quality of the chapter and the depth of its coverage.)

Heart disease as a message from your body. Many of us go through life neglecting our bodies' signals, ignoring symptoms until a crisis occurs. But the body talks to us and it is up to us to listen and try to understand the message. The heart bears the load of all our physical activity as well as our mental activity. Stress can affect the heart as well as any other body system. This section explores the warning signs of heart disease as "messages" we may receive from our hearts, what these messages may mean, and what we can do in response to these messages.

Why medical tests and treatments are not enough. You, the patient, are ultimately responsible for your own health. Placing all faith in a doctor is a way of abdicating that responsibility. The physician is not a healer; rather, he or she sets the stage for the patient's body to heal itself. Disease is actually a manifestation of an imbalance within the body. Medical procedures can help temporarily, but the real solution lies in the patient's becoming aware of his own responsibility for health. This may involve changing diet, stopping smoking, learning to control the inner life.

(Although the abstracts are directed to the editor who reviews the proposal, the writer incorporates the voice to be used in the book by speaking directly to the reader. This is an effective way to incorporate her writing style into the chapter-by-chapter outline.)

Getting the best (while avoiding the worst) of modern medicine. In the author's view, the most important aspect of medicine is not the medication but the patient/physician relationship. Unfortunately, this relationship is often cold, superficial, professional. The patient goes into the medical pipeline, endures a number of tests, then comes out the other end with a diagnosis, which is like a flag he has to carry for life. This view of disease ignores the patient as the main component of the healing process. Readers are advised to work with their doctors to learn their own blood pressure, blood sugar, cholesterol level, and what these numbers mean. They are further advised how to enlist a team of support people to increase their own knowledge of the disease and learn to discover the self-healing mechanisms within.

How to assess your doctor. Ten questions a patient needs to ask in order to assure the best patient-doctor relationship.

Taking charge of your own medical care. Rather than being passive patients, readers are urged to directly confront their illness and the reasons for it, asking themselves: How can I find a cause at the deepest level? What have I learned from this disease? What is good about it? What have I learned about myself? Exceptional heart patients don't allow themselves to be overwhelmed by the disease; rather, they realize that it is most likely a temporary problem, most of the time self-limited, and that they have a power within to overcome it.

Seven keys to a healthy heart. Whether presently healthy or already ill of heart disease, there is a great deal readers can do to improve and maintain the health of their hearts. The most important component of such a plan is to have a commitment to a healthy heart. The author offers the following seven keys to a healthy heart: respect your body; take time to relax every day; accept, respect, and appreciate yourself; share your deepest feelings; establish life goals; nourish your spiritual self; love yourself and others unconditionally. Each of these aspects of heart care will be examined in detail in later chapters.

Heartskill #1: *Learning to take your own pulse.* The pulse is a wave of blood sent through the arteries each time the heart contracts; pulse rate therefore provides important information about cardiac function. The easiest place to measure the pulse is the wrist: place your index and middle finger over the underside of the opposite wrist. Press gently and firmly until you locate your pulse. Don't use your thumb to feel the pulse, because the thumb has a pulse of its own. Count the number of pulse beats in fifteen seconds, then multiply that by four for your heart rate.

This exercise will include charts so that readers can track and learn their own normal pulse range for resting and exercising, and be alerted to irregularities and changes that may require medical attention.

(The inclusion of this technique shows how specific and practical information will be included in the book—important for a nonfiction book proposal. Editors look for what are called the program aspects of a book, because they can be used in promotional settings—and may also be the basis for serial-rights sales to magazines.)

Chapter Two
YOUR MIND AND YOUR HEART

This chapter begins to explore the connection between mind and body as it relates to heart disease. Early in the chapter readers will meet three Exceptional Heart Patients who overcame crushing diagnoses. These include Van, who overcame a heart attack (at age 48), two open-heart surgeries, and "terminal" lung cancer. Through visualization techniques given him by the author, Van has fully recovered and is living a healthy and satisfying life. Goran, who had a family history of cardiomyopathy, drew on the support and love of his family to survive a heart transplant and has since gone on to win several championships in an Olympics contest for transplant patients. Elaine, who overcame both childhood cancer and severe heart disease, is, at the age of 24, happily married and a mother. The techniques used by these Exceptional Heart Patients will be discussed in the context of the mind-body connection.

(The authors do not save the good stuff for the book. If you have interesting case studies or anecdotes, include them here: The more stimulating material you can include, the more you can intrigue your editor. In general, this chapter-by-chapter synopsis is exceptionally detailed in a simplified fashion, which is important for this type of book.)

How your doctor views heart disease: Risk factors v. symptoms. Traditional medicine views the risk factors for heart disease (smoking, high blood cholesterol, high blood pressure, diabetes, obesity, sedentary lifestyle, family history of heart disease, use of oral contraceptives) as indicators of the likelihood of developing illness. In contrast, the author presents these risk factors as *symptoms* of an underlying disease, and discusses ways to change them. Smoking, for example, is not the root of the problem, which is, rather, fear, tension, and stress. Smoking is just an outlet that the patient uses to get rid of these basic elements, which he or she believes are uncontrollable. Likewise high cholesterol, which is viewed by the medical establishment as largely caused by poor diet, is also affected by stress. (In a study of rabbits on a high-cholesterol diet, narrowing of arteries was less in rabbits that were petted, even if the diet remained unhealthful.) Other elements besides the traditional "risk factors," such as hostility, have been shown to lead to high rates of heart disease.

A mind/body model of heart disease. It is not uncommon to hear stories like this: They were a very happy couple, married 52 years. Then, suddenly, the wife developed breast cancer and died. The husband, who had no previous symptoms of heart disease, had a heart attack and died two months later. All too often there is a very close relationship between a traumatic event and serious illness. Likewise, patients may often become depressed and literally will themselves to die. The other side of the coin is the innumerable patients who use a variety of techniques to enlist the mind-body connection in helping to overcome and even cure serious illnesses, including heart disease.

Rethinking your negative beliefs about heart disease. The first step in using the mind to help to heal the body is to rethink negative beliefs about heart disease. Modern studies have shown that stress plays a most important role in the creation of heart disease, influencing all of the "risk factors." Heart disease is actually a disease of self, caused by self, and is made worse by the belief that we are its "victims." Another negative and incorrect belief is that the possibilities for recovery are limited. The author asserts that these beliefs are untrue, and that for patients willing to learn from the experience, heart disease can be a path to recovery, self-improvement, and growth.

The healing personality: tapping into your body's healing powers. Although the notion of a "healing personality" may sound contradictory, the power of healing is awareness, which can be achieved by anyone. The author describes his own discovery of spirituality in medicine and the realization that ultimately the origin of disease is in the mind. This is why treating disease with medicine and surgery alone does not heal: because these methods ignore the natural healing powers of the body/mind. How does one develop a "healing personality"? The starting point is awareness of the spiritual power within. As the author states, in order to become healthy, one must become spiritual.

Writing your own script for a healthy heart. Before writing any script, one must set the stage, and in this case readers are urged to see a cardiologist or physician and have a thorough checkup. This checkup will evaluate the presence or absence of the "risk factors" and assess the health of other body organs as well. Once the scene is set, it is time to add in the other elements of a healthy heart, all of which will be explored in detail in the coming chapters.

Making a contract with your heart. We see obstacles only when we lose sight of our goals. How to make (either mentally or on paper) a contract with one's heart that promises to take care of the heart. Each individual reader's contract will be somewhat different; for example, someone who is overweight might include in the contract the desire that in six months she would weigh so much. The point is to set realistic, achievable goals. Guidelines are provided for breaking larger goals down into small, easily achievable, steps. Creating goals for the future makes them a part of the present in the sense that it is today that we start pursuing them.

What to say when you talk to yourself. In the view of the author, the greatest source of stress in life is negative conversations we have with ourselves. These "conversations," which go on all the time without our even being aware of them, often include such negative suggestions as "When are you going to learn?" "Oh, no, you stupid idiot, you did it again!" When we put ourselves down, we reinforce feelings of unworthiness and inadequacy, which leads to stress and illness. Guidelines are given for replacing such negative self-conversation with more positive self-talk, including messages of love and healing.

Heartskill #2: *Sending healing energy to your heart.* In this exercise, readers learn a simple meditation technique that will help them get in touch with their natural healing powers and begin to heal their hearts.

Chapter Three
THE FRIENDSHIP FACTOR:
PLUGGING INTO YOUR SOCIAL SUPPORT SYSTEM

Heart disease is not an isolated event, and the heart patient is not an isolated human being. Among the less medically obvious "risk factors" involved in coronary disease are social isolation. In this chapter the author discusses the importance of maintaining and strengthening all the social support aspects of the patient's life, including family, friendship, community, and sex. He shows how intimacy and connection can be used not just for comfort but also as actual healing tools.

Sexual intimacy: the healing touch. Following a heart attack, many patients may lose confidence due to a fear of loss of attractiveness or fear of death. Citing recent studies, the author points out that there is a difference between making sex and making love. The desire for sex is a human need and is not limited to healthy people. Anybody who has had a heart problem still has sexual needs and ignoring them may be an additional cause of stress. Guidelines for when and how to resume sexual activity are offered. Other topics covered in this chapter include:

Keeping your loved ones healthy, and letting them keep you healthy
How you may be unwittingly pushing others out of your life
The art of nondefensive, nonreactive communication
Accepting your loved ones' feelings and your own
How to enlist the support of family and friends
Joining or starting your own support group

Heartskill #3: *Mapping your social support system*

Chapter 4
OPENING YOUR HEART:
LEARNING TO MAKE FRIENDS WITH YOURSELF

In addition to enlisting the support of others, for complete healing it is necessary for the patient to literally become a friend to himself or herself. This may entail changing old ways of thinking and responding, as well as developing new, healthier ways of relating to time and other external stresses. In this chapter the author explores ways of changing Type A behavior, as well as proven techniques for dealing with life's daily hassles and upsets. An important section of the chapter shows readers how to love and cherish the "inner child," that part of the personality that needs to be loved, to be acknowledged, and to have fun. Equally important is the guilt that each of us carries within, and that can lead not only to unhealthy behaviors but also to actual stress. The author gives exercises for learning to discover and absolve the hidden guilts that keep each of us from realizing our true healthy potential. Topics covered in this chapter include:

A positive approach to negative emotions
Checking yourself out on Type A behavior: a self-test
Being assertive without being angry
Keeping your balance in the face of daily hassles and major setbacks
Making a friend of time
Identifying and healing your old childhood hurts
Letting go of hurts, regrets, resentments, and guilt
Forgiving yourself and making a new start
The trusting heart

Heartskill #4: *Forgiveness exercise*

Chapter 5
IDENTIFYING AND ELIMINATING STRESS IN YOUR LIFE

The science of psychoneuroimmunology is beginning to prove that the mind and body are not only connected, but also inseparable. It has been demonstrated that changes in life often precede disease. Lab studies have shown that the amount of stress experienced by experimental animals can induce rapid growth of a tumor that would ordinarily be rejected. For heart patients, the fact of disease itself can become another inner stress factor that may worsen the disease and the quality of life. One out of five healthy persons is a "heart reactor," who has strong responses under stress that induce such unhealthful physiological changes as narrowing of the coronary arteries, hypertrophy of the heart muscle, and high blood pressure. In this chapter the author shows readers how to change stress-producing negative beliefs into constructive, rational beliefs that reduce stress. Included are guidelines to the five keys for controlling stress: diet, rest, exercise, attitude, and self-discipline.

Why you feel so stressed-out
Where does emotional stress come from and how does it affect your heart?
Your stress signal checklist
Staying in control
Calculating your heart-stress level at home and on the job
Stress management

Heartskill #5: *Mapping your stress hotspots*

Chapter 6
YOUR FAITH AND YOUR HEART

As the author points out, there are few studies in the field of spirituality and medicine, because physicians, like most scientists, shy away from what is called "soft data." Soft data are anything outside the realm of physics, mathematics, etc.: the "exact sciences." As a physician, the author has grown ever more convinced of the body's natural healing power, which is evoked through mind and spirit. No matter how "spirit" is defined, whether in traditional religious terms or as a component of mind or personality, the truth is that in order to become healthy, it is necessary to become spiritual.

In a 10-month study of 393 coronary patients at San Francisco General Hospital, it was proven that the group who received outside prayer in addition to standard medical treatment did far better than those who received medical treatment alone. Those in the experimental group suffered fewer problems with congestive heart failure, pneumonia, cardiac arrests, and had a significantly lower mortality rate. This chapter explores the possible reasons for this startling result and illuminates the connection between spirit and health.

The difference between spirituality and religion. A discussion of the differences between traditional views of spirituality and the new holistic approach that sees mind, body, and spirit as intimately connected and interdependent.

Faith and heart disease. The healing personality is that of a person who takes care of his own body. He may also use such other "paramedical" means to get well as physical exercise, a proper diet, prayer, meditation, positive affirmations, and visualization techniques. The author surveys these techniques that have been used for centuries to contribute to the healing of a wide variety of diseases. Other topics exploring the connection between faith and a healthy heart include:

> *Tapping into your personal mythology*
> *Forgiving yourself for heart disease*
> *Keeping a psychological-spiritual journal*

Heartskill #6: *Consulting your inner adviser*

Chapter 7
PUTTING IT ALL TOGETHER: HOW TO DEVELOP YOUR OWN DAILY PRACTICE FOR A HEALTHY HEART

Daily Practice as defined by the author is a personalized program in which readers will choose from among the techniques offered in the book to create their own unique combination of mental and physical healing exercises. Each component of the daily practice is fully explained. The techniques range from the familiar—healthful diet and exercise—to the more spiritual, including prayer, meditation, and visualization. Included are examples of use of each of these techniques as practiced by Exceptional Heart Patients.

> *The benefits of daily practice*
> *Meditation: how to do it your way*
> *Stretching, yoga, and sensory awareness*
> *Hearing with the mind's ear, seeing with the mind's eye*
> *The psychological benefits of exercise*
> *Healthy eating as a meditative practice*
> *The healing powers of silent prayer*
> *Creating your own visualization exercises*
> *Creating your own guided-imagery tapes*
> *Using other types of positive imagery*

Heartskill #7: *Picking a practice that makes sense to you*

Chapter 8
LEARNING TO SMELL THE FLOWERS

In our society, pleasure is often regarded as a selfish pursuit. We tend to feel that it is not as important as work. And yet the key element in health is not blood pressure, or cholesterol, or blood sugar; instead it is peace of mind and the ability to enjoy life. Indeed, this ability has been proven to prevent illness. In this chapter the author focuses on the ability to live in the moment, savoring all that life has to offer, from the simple physical pleasures of massage to the more profound pleasures of the spirit. Topics covered in this chapter include a discussion of Type B behavior, which can be learned. The secrets of this type of behavior include self-assurance, self-motivation, and the ability to relax in the face of pressures. The author shows how even the most confirmed Type A heart patient can, through self-knowledge, change outer-directed goals for inner ones, thus achieving the emotional and physical benefits of a Type B lifestyle. Other topics discussed in this chapter include:

Getting the most out of the present moment
Taking an inventory of life's pleasures
Counting down to relaxation
Hot baths, hot showers, hot tubs, and saunas
Touching; feeding the skin's hunger for human touch
Pets, plants, and gardens as healing helpers

Heartskill #8: *Building islands of peace into your life*

Chapter 9
CREATING YOUR FUTURE

The heart may be viewed in many different ways: as a mechanical pump, as the center of circulation, as the source of life. The author suggests viewing the heart above all as a spiritual organ, the center of love, and learning to figuratively fill it with love and peace. A positive result of heart disease is the sudden knowledge that one is not immortal, and the opportunity to plan for a more worthwhile, fulfilling life in the future. In this final chapter, Dr. Cortis offers guidelines for setting and achieving goals for health—of mind, body, and spirit. For each reader the goals, and the means to achieve them, will be different. But as the author points out, this is a journey that everyone must take, patients as well as doctors, readers as well as the author. No matter how different the paths we choose, we must realize that truly "our hearts are the same."

The Art of Happiness
Choosing your own path to contentment
Goals chosen by other exceptional heart patients

Developing specific action steps
Reinforcing and rethinking your life goals
Finding your own meaning in life and death

Heartskill #9: *Helping others to heal their hearts*

Recommended Reading

Appendix I
FOR FRIENDS AND FAMILY:
HOW TO SUPPORT AN EXCEPTIONAL HEART PATIENT

Appendix II
ON FINDING OR STARTING A SELF-HELP GROUP

Appendix III
ABOUT THE EXCEPTIONAL HEART PATIENT PROJECT

Authors Notes

Acknowledgements

Index

(Appendixes are always a valuable bonus.)

(It is great to be able to include an actual endorsement in your proposal package. Quite often, writers state those from whom they intend to request endorsements—but do not actually have them lined up. Perhaps unnecessary to say, but valuable to reiterate, is that editors and agents are not overly impressed by such assertions. They do, however, nod with respect to those authors who demonstrate that they can deliver on their claims. The inclusion of at least one such blurb creates tremendous credibility.)

GERALD G. JAMPOLSKY, M.D.
Practice Limited to Psychiatry
Adults and Children

April 1, 1998

Mr. Jeff Herman
The Jeff Herman Agency, Inc.
140 Charles Street, Suite 15A
New York, NY 10014

Dear Jeff:
You may use the following quote for Bruno's book:

> *"Dr. Bruno Cortis writes from the heart—for the heart. This is a much-needed and very important book."*

Gerald Jampolsky, M.D.
Coauthor of *Love Is the Answer*

With love and peace,
Jerry
Gerald Jampolsky, M.D.

(The author, Dr. Cortis, is very well connected in his field. He solicited promises from several prominent persons to provide cover endorsements like this one. Having these promises to provide such blurbs at the time I marketed the proposal further enhanced the agency's sales position.)

PROFOUND QUESTIONS & HUMBLE ANSWERS

JEFF HERMAN

In the course of my ongoing participation in publishing workshops, seminar presentations, and panels at writers' conferences, certain questions arise time and again. Many of these requests for information go straight to the heart of the world of book publishing.

The following questions are asked from the gut and replied to in kind. In order to be of value to the author who wishes to benefit from an insider view, I answer these serious queries in unvarnished terms, dispensing with the usual sugarcoating in order to emphasize the message of openness and candor.

Q: I have been at this for a long time, and can't get published. How come?
Well, your stuff may not be good. That's the easy answer, which probably applies to most of what gets written and, frankly, to some of what actually gets published. After all, books get published for many reasons, including the possibility that they are of high quality. But lack of quality is not, never has been, and never will be the only factor as to why books do or don't get published. That said, it's good to make your product the best it can be.

It's safe to say that everyone who works in publishing will agree that countless works of excellence don't make it to publication. That's unfortunate. But is it unfair? Who's to say?

Many works get published because the writer managed to get them to the right people at the right time. How and why did that happen?

Other fine works fail to "connect", in spite of the diligent efforts made by the writer to sell it. Why? I don't know. Why are some people very pretty, while others are very ugly? I don't know. Some consequences can be logically traced backwards to a cause or causes, or a lack of necessary acts.

But sometimes there is no apparent pathology behind what does and doesn't happen. And that's when we must simply surrender. There's an ancient Jewish saying, "Man plans, God laughs." Some things are left to our discretion and control, whereas other things obviously are not. It's possible that that may be why you did not sell your manuscript. But I don't know.

Q: Why are memoirs and autobiographies hard to sell?

Because the vast majority of us lead lives of quiet desperation that would bore even a 300-year-old turtle. None of us ever truly listen to each other. That's why a lot of us pay strangers $90 or more an hour to listen to us. Or at least we think they're listening.

So why should someone actually pay you to read about your life? If you can effectively answer that question, you may be qualified to write a book about YOU.

Now, there are ways to maneuver around this conundrum. For instance, you can place your life within the context of fascinating events. People do connect to events and situations that mirror their own lives and feelings right back at them.

You can think ahead by doing something notable or outrageous for the sole purpose of having a platform for writing about yourself. A lot of us do ridiculous things anyway, so why not do them in a planned conscious way? It's said that we all write our own script in life. So, if you are the designer of your own life, who do you have to blame for leading a boring life? Think about your life as a feature film, and start living it within that context. Pre-empt the cutting room floor whenever possible. Become someone that other people will pay to watch, read about, and listen to.

Even if you don't get anything sold, you may still end up with more friends.

Q: Why do editors, agents and some writers seem so snobby?

Because maybe they are. Why should you care? Because you want validation and snobs counter that. A long time ago, when I was young and a bit more stupid, I told a snobby editor to come clean my bathroom for me. He didn't. Neither did I; I hired a housekeeper. To this day I enjoy foiling people who think they are better then the rest. Sometimes, I think I'm better than the rest. But my better angels take care of that by hiding my car in a parking lot, or causing me to wash my mouth with shampoo. My list of due personal humiliations is infinite, and appreciated.

Snobbery is a burden, and a punishment unto itself. Let the snobs have their burden, and keep writing.

Q: Is it more difficult to get an agent than it is to get a publisher?

I believe it's substantially easier to get an agent than it is to get a publisher.

The primary reason for this is that no agent expects to sell 100 percent of the projects she chooses to represent. Not because any of these projects lack merit (though some of them may), but because only so many titles are published per year—and many excellent ones just won't make the cut. This is especially true for fiction by unknown or unpublished writers, or for nonfiction in saturated categories. As a result, many titles will be agented but never published.

Naturally, a successful agent prefers to represent projects that she feels are hot and that publishers will trample each other to acquire. But few, if any, agents have the luxury of representing such sure-bet projects exclusively. In fact, the majority of their projects may be less than "acquisition-guaranteed," even though they are of acquisition quality.

The agent assumes that many of these projects will eventually be sold profitably, but probably doesn't expect all of them to be. Every experienced agent knows that some of the best cash cows were not easily sold.

Make no mistake—it's not easy to get a reputable agent. Most agents reject 98 percent of the opportunities that cross their desks. They accept for representation only material they believe can be sold to a publisher. That is, after all, the only way for them to earn income and maintain credibility with publishers. If an agent consistently represents what a publisher considers garbage, that will become her professional signature—and her undoing as an agent.

But don't despair. This is a subjective business, composed of autonomous human beings. One agent's reject can be another's gold mine. That's why even a large accumulation of rejections should never deter you as a writer.

Some people get married young, and some get married later!

Q: Is there anything I can do to increase my odds of getting an agent?
Yes.

First consider the odds quoted in the previous answer. The typical agent is rejecting 98 percent of everything he sees. That means he's hungry for the hard-to-find 2 percent that keeps him in business.

If you're not part of that 2 percent, he'll probably have no use for you or your project. Your challenge is to convince him that you're part of that select 2 percent.

Q: What do agents and editors want? What do they look for in a writer? What can I do to become that kind of writer?
Let's back up a step or two and figure out why agents want to represent certain projects and why editors want to buy them. This industry preference has little to do with quality of writing as such.

Many highly talented writers never get published. Many mediocre writers do get published—and a number of them make a lot of money at it. There are reasons for this. The mediocre writers are doing things that more than compensate for their less-than-splendid writing. And the exceptional writers who underachieve in the publishing arena are (regardless of their talents) most likely doing things that undermine them.

In other words, being a good writer is just part of a complex equation. Despite all the criticism the educational system in the United States has received, America is exceedingly literate and has a mother lode of college graduates and postgraduates. Good, knowledgeable writers are a dime a dozen in this country.

Profitable writers, however, are a rare species. And agents and editors obviously value them the most. Once more: Being an excellent writer and a financially successful writer don't necessarily coincide. Ideally, of course, you want to be both.

To maximize your success as a writer, you must do more than hone your ability to write; you must also learn the qualifiers and the disqualifiers for success. Obviously, you wish to employ the former and avoid the latter. Publishing is a business, and agents tend to be the most acutely business-oriented of all the players. That's why they took the risk of going into business for themselves (most agents are self-employed).

If you wish, wear your artist's hat while you write. But you'd better acquire a business hat and wear it when it's time to sell. This subtle ability to change hats separates the minority of writers who get rich from the majority who do not.

In my opinion, rich writers didn't get rich from their writing (no matter how good it is); they got rich by being good at business.

Many good but not-so-wealthy writers blame various internal or external factors for their self-perceived stagnation. My answer to them is: Don't blame anyone, especially yourself. To lay blame is an abdication of power. In effect, when you blame, you become a car with an empty gas tank, left to the elements. The remedy is to fill the tank yourself.

Learn to view mistakes, whether they be yours or those of the people you relied upon, as inconvenient potholes—learning to move around them will make you an even better driver. Remember the old credo: Only a poor workman blames his tools.

Observe all you can about those who are successful—not just in writing, but in all fields—and make their skills your skills. This is not to insist that making money is or should be your first priority. Your priorities, whatever they are, belong to you. But money is a widely acknowledged and sought-after emblem of success.

If an emphasis on personal gain turns you off, you may, of course, pursue other goals. Many successful people in business find the motivation to achieve their goals by focusing on altruistic concepts—such as creating maximum value for as many people as possible. Like magic, money often follows value even if it wasn't specifically sought. If you're unfortunate enough to make money you don't want, there's no need to despair: There are many worthy parties (including charities) that will gladly relieve you of this burden.

Here are specific ways to maximize your ability to get the agent you want:

- *Don't start off by asking what the agent can do for you.* You're a noncitizen until the agent has reason to believe that you may belong to that exclusive 2 percent club the agent wants to represent. It's a mistake to expect the agent to do anything to sell herself to you during that initial contact. You must first persuade her that you're someone who's going to make good money for her business. Once you've accomplished that, and the agent offers you representation, you're entitled to have the agent sell herself to you.

- *Act like a business.* As you're urged elsewhere in this book, get yourself a professional letterhead and state-of-the-art office equipment. While rarely fatal, cheap paper and poor-looking type will do nothing to help you—and in this business you need all the help you can give yourself.
  Virtually anyone—especially the intellectually arrogant—is apt to be strongly affected on a subliminal level by a product's packaging. People pay for the sizzle, not the steak. There is a reason why American companies spend billions packaging, naming, and advertising such seemingly simple products as soap. We would all save money if every bar of soap were put into a plain paper box and just labeled "Soap." In fact, the no-frills section does sell soap that way—for a lot less. But few people choose to buy it that way. Understand this human princi-

ple, without judging it and use it when packaging yourself.

- *Learn industry protocol.* I never insist that people follow all the rules. As Thomas Jefferson wisely suggested, a revolution every so often can be a good thing. But you should at least know the rules before you break them—or before you do anything.

  For instance: Most agents say they don't like cold calls. I can't say I blame them. If my rejection rate is 98 percent, I'm not going to be enthusiastic about having my ear talked off by someone who is more than likely part of that 98 percent. Just like you, agents want to use their time as productively as possible. Too often, cold calls are verbal junk mail. This is especially true if you are a writer selling fiction; your hard copy is the foot you want to get through the door.

  Speaking for myself, most cold calls have a neutral effect on me (a few turn me off, and a few rouse my enthusiasm). I try to be courteous, because that's how I would want to be treated. I will allow the caller to say whatever he wants for about one minute before I take over to find out what, if anything, the person has in the way of hard copy. If he has some, I invite him to send it with an SASE. If he doesn't have any, I advise him to write some and then send it. Usually, I don't remember much about what he said on the phone; I may not even remember that he called. But that doesn't matter; it's the hard copy that concerns me at first. This is the way it works with most agents. We produce books, not talk.

  An agent's time is an agent's money (and therefore his clients' money). So don't expect any quality access until the agent has reason to believe you're a potential 2 percenter. If you're the CEO of General Motors, for instance, and you want to write a book, then all you need to do is call the agent(s) of your choice and identify yourself; red carpets will quickly appear. But the vast majority of writers have to learn and follow the more formalized procedures.

- *As explained elsewhere in this book, view the query letter as a sales brochure.* The best ones are rarely more than 1½-2 pages long and state their case as briefly and efficiently as possible.

Here are the most common query mistakes:

1. Long, unfocused paragraphs.

2. Pontificating about irrelevancies (at least, matters that are irrelevant from the agent's perspective).

3. Complaining about your tribulations as a writer. We all know it's a tough business, but nobody likes losers—least of all, shrewd agents. Always be a winner when you're selling yourself, and you'll be more likely to win.

Most agents are hungry for that golden 2 percent, and they dedicate a great deal of time shoveling through mounds of material looking for it. You must be the first to believe that you are a 2 percenter, and then you must portray yourself that way to others. Reality begins in your own head and is manifested primarily through your own actions—or lack thereof.

Every agent and editor has the power to reject your writing. But only you have the power to be—or not to be—a writer.

Q: Should I query only one agent at a time?
Some of my colleagues disagree with me here, but I recommend querying 5 to 10 agents simultaneously, unless you already have your foot in the door with one. I suggest this because some agents will respond within 10 days, while others may take much longer or never respond at all. Going agent by agent can eat up several months of valuable time before a relationship is consummated. And then your work still has to be sold to a publisher.

To speed up this process, it's smart to solicit several agents at a time, though you should be completely upfront about it. If you go the multiple-submissions route, be sure to mention in your query letters to each agent that you are indeed making multiple submissions (though you needn't supply your agent list).

When an agent responds affirmatively to your query by requesting your proposal or manuscript, it's fine then to give the agent an exclusive reading. However, you should impose a reasonable time frame—for instance, 2 weeks for a nonfiction proposal and 4 weeks for a large manuscript. If it's a nonexclusive reading, make sure each agent knows that's what you want. And don't sign with an agent before talking to all the agents who are reading your work. (You have no obligation to communicate further with agents who do not respond affirmatively to your initial query.)

Most agents make multiple submissions to publishers, so they should be sensitive and respectful when writers have reason to use the same strategy agents have used with success.

Q: How do I know if my agent is working effectively for me? When might it be time to change agents?
As I remarked earlier, agents don't necessarily sell everything they represent, no matter how persistent and assertive they may be. In other words, the fact that your work is unsold doesn't automatically mean that your agent isn't doing his job. To the contrary, he may be doing the best job possible, and it may be incumbent upon you to be grateful for these speculative and uncompensated efforts.

Let's say 90 days pass and your work remains unsold. What you need to assess next is whether your agent is making active and proper attempts to sell your work.

Are you receiving copies of publisher rejection letters regarding your work? Generally, when an editor rejects projects submitted by an agent, the work will be returned within a few weeks, along with some brief comments explaining why the project was declined. (In case you're wondering, the agent doesn't have to include an SASE; the editors want agent submissions.) Copies of these rejection letters should be sent to you on a regular basis as the agent receives them. While no one expects you to enjoy these letters, they at least document that your agent is circulating your work.

If you have received many such rejection letters within these 90 days, it's hard to claim that your agent isn't trying. If you've received few or none, you might well call the agent for a status report. You should inquire as to where and when your work has been submitted, and what, if anything, the results of those submissions have been. In the end, you will have to use your own best judgment as to whether your agent is performing capably or giving you the run-around.

If it ever becomes obvious that your agent is no longer seriously trying to sell your work (or perhaps never was), you should initiate a frank discussion with the agent about what comes next. If the agent did go to bat for you, you should consider the strong possibility that your work is presently unmarketable and act to preserve the agent relationship for your next project. Remember, if your work remains unsold, your agent has lost valuable time and has made no money.

If the evidence clearly shows that your agent has been nonperforming from day one, then your work has not been tested. You should consider withdrawing it and seek new representation.

Agent-hopping by authors is not rampant, but it's not uncommon either. Often the agent is just as eager as you—or more so—for the break-up to happen. One veteran colleague once told me that when he notices he hates to receive a certain client's phone calls, then it's time to find a graceful way to end the relationship.

The wisdom of agent-jumping must be assessed on a case-by-case basis. The evidence shows that many writers have prospered after switching, while others have entered limbo or even fallen far off their previous pace.

Before you decide to switch agents, you should focus on why you are unhappy with your current situation. It may be that if you appeal to your agent to discuss your specific frustrations—preferably in person, or at least by phone—many or all of them can be resolved, and your relationship will be given a fresh and prosperous start.

Agents are not mind readers. You only have one agent, but your agent has many clients. It is therefore mostly your responsibility as a writer client to communicate your concerns and expectations effectively to your agent. Your relationship may require only occasional adjustments, as opposed to a complete break-up.

Q: Who do agents really work for?
Themselves! Always have and always will.

True, agents serve their clients, but their own needs and interests always come first. Of course, this is the way it is in any business relationship (and in too many personal ones). You should never expect your lawyer, accountant, or stockbroker (and so on) to throw themselves into traffic to shield you from getting hit.

As long as the interests of the agent and the writer are in harmony, everything should work out well. However, on occasion the writer may have expectations that could be detrimental to the agent's own agenda (not to mention state of mind). Writers must never lose sight of the truth that publishers are the agent's most important customers. Only a foolish agent would intentionally do serious damage to her relationships with individual editors and publishing houses. It should be further noted that there is, therefore, a fine line that an agent will not cross when advocating for her clients.

Q: What do agents find unattractive about some clients?
Agents are individuals, so each will have his own intense dislikes. But, generally speaking, a certain range of qualities can hamper any and all aspects of an agent's professional association with a client—qualities that often have similarly negative effects in realms other than publishing. Here's a litany of displeasing client types and their characteristics.

- The Pest. Nobody likes a nag, whether at home or at the office. A squeaky wheel may sometimes get the grease—not that anyone likes the effect—but more often this person gets the shaft.

- The Complainer. Some people can never be satisfied, only dissatisfied. It seems to be their mission in life to pass along their displeasure to others. These folks are never any fun—unless you're an ironic observer.

- The BS Artist. These clients believe everything even remotely connected with themselves is the greatest—for example, their fleeting ideas for books should win them millions of dollars up front. Of course, if they actually produce the goods, then the BS part of the term doesn't apply to them.

- The Screw-Up. These clients miss trains, planes, and deadlines. Their blunders can create major hassles for those who count on them.

- The Sun God. Some people believe they are more equal than others and will behave accordingly. It's a real pleasure to see Sun Gods humbled.

- The Liar. Need I say more?

Sometimes these wicked traits combine, overlap, and reinforce themselves in one individual to create what an agent may rate as a veritable client from hell. Enough said on this subject for now, except that I would be remiss if I did not insist that no trade or professional class is immune to this nefarious syndrome—not even literary agents.

Q: How does someone become an agent?
For better or worse, anyone in America can declare himself an agent—at any time. But what people say and what they do are different things. Legitimate literary agents earn most or all of their income from commissions. The less-than-legitimate agencies most often depend on reading and management fees for their cash, with few, if any, actual book sales to their credit.

Most agents earn their stripes by working as editors for publishers. But that is by no means the only route, nor is it necessarily the most effective training ground. Good agents have emerged from a variety of environments and offer a broad range of exceptional credentials. What's most important is the mix of skills they bring to their agenting careers, such as:

1. Strong relationship skills—the ability to connect with people and earn their confidence.

2. Sales and marketing skills—the ability to get people to buy from them.

3. Persuasion and negotiating skills—the ability to get good results in their dealings.

4. An understanding of the book market and of what publishers are buying.

5. An ability to manage many clients and projects at the same time.

Q: Who owns book publishing?
Many decades ago, book-publishing entities were customarily founded by individuals who had a passion for books. Though they obviously had to have business skills to make their houses survive and thrive, money was not necessarily their primary drive (at least, not in the beginning), or they would have chosen more lucrative endeavors.

The vestiges of these pioneers can be found in the family names still extant in the corporate designations of most of today's publishing giants. But apart from the human-sounding names, these are very different companies today. Much of the industry is owned by multinational, multibillion-dollar conglomerates that have priorities other than the mere publication of books. The revenues from book operations are barely noticeable when compared with such mass-market endeavors as movies, TV/cable, music, magazines, sports teams, and character licensing. Stock prices must rise, and shareholders must be optimally satisfied for these firms to feel in any way stable.

Q: How does this type of ownership affect editors and the editorial-acquisition process?
This rampant corporate ownership translates into an environment in which book editors are pressured to make profitable choices if their careers are to prosper. At first look, that doesn't sound radical or wrongheaded, but a downside has indeed developed—editors are discouraged from taking risks for literary or artistic rationales that are ahead of the market curve or even with an eye toward longer-term development and growth of a particular writer's readership.

The bottom line must be immediately appeased by every acquisition, or the non-performing editor's career will crumble. The editor who acquires blockbusters that the culturally elite disdain is an editor who is a success. The editor whose books lose money but are universally praised by critics is an editor who has failed.

Of course, the previous comparison is extreme. Most editors are not single-minded money-grubbers and do their best to acquire meaningful books that also make commercial sense. Where the cut becomes most noticeable is for the thousands of talented fiction writers who will never write big money-makers. While slots still exist for them, large publishers are increasingly reluctant to subsidize and nurture these marginally profitable writers' careers. Commercially speaking, there are better ways to invest the firm's resources.

Q: What, if any, are a writer's alternatives?
Yes, the big kids are dominant on their own turf and intend to extend their claim to as much of book country as they can. But this isn't the end of the story. The heroes are the thousands of privately owned "Mom and Pop" presses from Maine to Alaska who only need to answer to themselves. Every year, small presses, new and old, make an important contribution to literate culture with books that large publishers won't touch. It's not uncommon for some of these books to become bestsellers. University presses also pump out important (and salesworthy) books that would not have been published in a rigidly commercial environment.

Q: Is there anything positive to say about the current situation?
I don't mean to imply that the corporate ownership of the bulk of the book industry is absolutely bad. Indeed, it has brought many benefits. Publishers are learning to take better advantage of state-of-the-art marketing techniques and technologies and have more capital with which to do it. The parent entertainment and communications firms enable the mainstream commercial publishers to cash in on popular frenzies, as with dinosaur mania, the latest and most salacious scandals, fresh interest in the environment or fitness, or celebrity and other pop-culture tie-ins, such as Gump and Madonna books.

The emergence of superstores enables more books to be sold. The stores create very appealing environments that draw much more traffic than conventional old-style bookstores. Many people who hang out at the superstores were never before motivated to go book shopping. But once they're in one of these well-stocked stores—whether at the bookshelves, ensconced in a reading-seat, or perched by a steaming mug at an in-store cafe—they're likely to start spending.

The unfortunate part is that many small independent bookshops cannot compete with these new venues. However, many others are finding clever ways to hang on, by accenting special reader-interest areas or offering their own individual style of hospitality.

Q: How profitable is publishing?
One way to measure an industry's profitability is to look at the fortunes of those who work in it. By such a measure, the book business isn't very profitable, especially when compared to its twentieth-century sisters in entertainment and information industries: movies, television, music, advertising, and computers. Most book editors require a two-income family if they wish to raise children comfortably in New York or buy a nice home. The vast majority of published authors rely upon their day jobs or spouse's earnings. A handful of authors make annual incomes in the six and seven figures, but it's often the movie tie-ins that get them there and in turn push even more book sales.

A fraction of book editors will climb the ranks to the point at which they can command six-figure incomes, but most never attain this plateau. Almost all of those writers just starting in the business earn barely above the poverty level for their initial publishing endeavors—if that.

A well-established literary agent can make a lot of money. The trick is to build a number of backlist books that cumulatively pay off healthy commissions twice a year, while constantly panning for the elusive big-advance books that promise short-term (and perhaps long-term) windfalls.

In many ways, the agents are the players best positioned to make the most money. As sole proprietors, they're not constrained by committees and can move like lightning. When everything aligns just right, the agent holds all the cards by controlling access to the author (product) and the publisher (producer).

The publishing companies themselves appear at least adequately profitable, averaging about 5 to 10 percent return on revenues (according to their public balance sheets). The larger companies show revenues of between $1 billion and $2 billion, sometimes nudging higher.

These are not sums to sneeze at. But most of those sales derive from high-priced nonbookstore products like textbooks and professional books. Large and midsize publishers alike are dependent upon their cash-cow backlist books for much of their retail sales. These books entail virtually no risk or investment, since their customer base is essentially locked in for an indefinite period, and the publisher has long ago recouped the initial investment. Many backlist books are legacies from editors and business dynamics that current employees may know nothing about.

The real risk for the current regime is their frontlist, which is the current season's crop. Large houses invest tens of millions of dollars to acquire, manufacture, market, and distribute anywhere from 50 to a few hundred "new" books. A small number of big-ticket individual titles will by themselves represent millions of dollars at risk. Most titles will represent less than $50,000 in risk on a pro-rata basis.

In practice, most of these frontlist titles will fail. The publisher will not recoup its investment and the title will not graduate to the exalted backlist status. But like the fate of those innumerable turtle eggs laid in the sand, it's expected that enough spawn will survive to generate an overall profit and significant backlist annuities well into the future.

In the fairness of a broader picture, it is known that most motion pictures and television shows fail, as do most new consumer products (such as soap or soft drinks) that have engendered enormous research-and-development costs. It's the ones that hit—and hit big—that make the odds worth enduring for any industry.

Q: What about attending writer's conferences?
Over the past 15 years I must have attended more than 100 writer's conferences in my role as an agent. I've gone to small towns, big cities, and luxury resorts. In all of them, I have discovered one common denominator: Writer's conferences are for writers what fertilizer is for crops.

It's invaluable for a writer to enter into communion with others of a like mind, at least once a year. The various classes about the usual subjects and the abundant networking opportunities are worthwhile bonuses. But the real benefit is what is received "between the lines". When does someone who writes actually become a writer? What is the initiation process? Most people who write can easily fall into an isolation zone.

Family members and friends may at best be indifferent about the person's passion for writing. At worst, they may belittle it as a wasteful self-indulgence that will never mean anything. Of course, once the writer starts accumulating impressive by-lines or has a book published, or best of all starts making a lot of money from writing, people may show more respect. But at any given moment most writers have not yet penetrated the ceiling that takes them into the world of actual publication, and those are the writers who need the most support and comfort. Writer's conferences are that special place where struggling writers can connect with fellow travelers, and meet those who have been "there" and suffered the same way before they arrived at greener pastures. A good conference experience will empower writers to be firmer in their identity and more determined to achieve their goals.

There are hundreds of writer's conferences each year and they are well spread out. Chances are there is at least one being given during the next 12 months within 150 miles from where you live. They are usually scheduled on weekends and sponsored by non-profit community based writer's clubs. The tuition is often quite modest and only intended to re-coup expenses. Ask your librarian or check the Internet for information about writer's clubs and conferences near you.

Q: Is there "ageism" in book publishing?
I have only been asked about racism in publishing once or twice. Each time I answered that I have neither witnessed it nor practiced it, but that does not mean that racism does not exist beyond my limited view. But there is a related question that I hear more frequently, which is: *Do book editors discriminate against elderly writers?* That question makes me uncomfortable because I have mixed feelings about how to answer it.

I can absolutely say that there is no organized program of discrimination against writers of a certain age. That said, there is the evidence of what does and does not get published, and the more subtle evidence of what agents and editors say to each other off the record. Now here I am going out on a limb, and I have not scientifically researched the facts. Nevertheless, I am suggesting that when it comes to fiction, that young unpublished writers have an edge over elderly unpublished writers. I do not believe that the same can be said for non-fiction. Why is this? Introducing new writers to the reading public is a tricky and risky business. The primary target market for new fiction tends to consist of younger readers who have not yet formed strong ties to existing authors. Because of their relative youth, they will be most attracted to themes and styles that they can personally relate to. We also see this emphasis on youth with new films, television shows, and consumer products. It follows that writers who look like and talk like the readers who are being targeted, will be the writers who are offered contracts. If you accept that this is the case, then yes, elderly writers are discriminated against, and to say otherwise is to be disingenuous or blind folded.

Assuming the above situation is a fact, is it a valid or immoral condition? Frankly, I don't know how to assess the morality of it for one big reason: The marketplace has its own morality. Look, the new fiction writer is as much a part of the product as anything that goes between the pages. Is it reasonable to expect that younger readers will gravitate to new fiction written by people who remind them of their parents or grandparents? Now I'll step-aside and let other people pick up the debate, assuming anyone has even read this deeply into the essay section of this book.

However, writers who are of a certain age should avoid making certain mistakes. For instance, when I read a query letter or author bio section, there usually is no reason why I need to be told how old the writers is, unless their age is somehow relevant to the material. Once writers start broadcasting how old they are, certain impressions will be formed in the eye of the reader, which can range from the positive to the negative. Why? Because that's what humans do, we form impressions, which get recalled by the information we are given. If your age is a variable of no consequence in the context of what you have written, then just keep it to yourself.

Q: Should I e-mail my query letters to agents?
I think you should, because I think that material that gets electronically delivered is easier to review and process then the submissions that get sent via hard copy. But like a lot of what I say, this is merely my impression. I have not scientifically evaluated what delivery methods are likely to achieve enhanced access, and I would also assume that a lot of it depends upon the preferences of the individual agent.

Q: What about agency fees?
Not that stupid question again. It keeps popping up wherever I meet writers. Clearly intelligent people describe the ridiculous abuses they get drawn into by people who claimed to be agents. If you pay a fee, especially to someone who has no documented track record of actually selling books to publishers, then you are making it possible for publishing scams to sustain and surpass the $50 million annual level that the FBI estimated several years ago.

THE AUTHOR-AGENCY CONTRACT

JEFF HERMAN

The author-agent relationship is first and foremost a business partnership. Like any business relationship, it is best to carefully and lucidly document what each party's respective responsibilities and due benefits are. Memories are short, but the written word is forever, assuming you don't lose the paperwork. If there is ever a disagreement or simple confusion about what's what, all you need to do is refer to the "contract". A good contract that anticipates all reasonably plausible circumstances, is the ultimate arbitrator, and will cost you no additional fees or aggravation.

Below is my agency's standard client contract. I consider it to be fair and liberal, and have had very few complaints about it over the years. To my knowledge, most agencies use contracts that are similar in content.

The key aspects to look for in the agency contract are as follows.

1. COMMISSIONS

Most agencies will charge a 15% commission against all advances and royalties they generate for the client. International and dramatization deals often require the agent to retain a co-agent, who has the necessary relationships in each respective country where a foreign rights deal might be made, or who has the requisite expertise to deal with the Hollywood jungle. When a co-agent is used, the two agents will evenly split the total commission, but this will require the overall commission to be increased to as much as 30%.

2. SCOPE OF REPRESENTATION

The contract should be clear about what properties are being represented at the current time, and perhaps into the future. The most liberal arrangement from the author's perspective will be to limit the scope only to the project "in-hand". It's best for the author to keep his options open regarding future books. Exceptions to this may be next works that are clearly derived from the first work, or an ongoing series.

3. DURATION OF CONTRACT

This is an area of variance for agency contracts. Some clearly state a six-month or longer term; others are completely open-ended. I prefer the latter. I believe that the agent or writer should be at liberty to end the whole thing whenever they feel compelled to do so. Obviously, the author will still be charged any due commissions that were earned prior to the termination, including any deals that result from the agent's pitches, even if consummated post-breakup.

4. FEES AND/OR REIMBURSABLE EXPENSES

As has been stated elsewhere in this book, a legitimate agent will only make money from the client if a book deal is entered into, thereby paying the agency its due commission. If the agency contract is structured in a way that enables the agency to show a profit even if the work is not sold to a publisher, then the author needs to be concerned. The ways this might show up include large upfront "management fees" or "retainers for expenses". If a so-called agency were to collect $500 five times a week, and never does anything to actually sell any of these works, it would be a very profitable scam, which is much more common than it ought to be. It is perfectly legitimate for an agency to track certain out-of-pocket expenses such as photocopying and shipping, and request reimbursement from the client at some point at cost.

5. REVIEWING AND NEGOTIATING THE AGENCY CONTRACT

It's the author's responsibility to understand and be comfortable with the contract before signing it. The author should not feel awkward about asking the agent to clarify items in the contract, and it is acceptable for the author to request that some reasonable revisions get made. Some authors prefer to have all their contracts vetted by their attorney. This is okay as long as the attorney understands the customs and protocols of the book publishing business. Otherwise, the attorney may go after certain provisions that are generally left alone, and end up wrecking the relationship before it can get off the ground. Assuming that the attorney does have some legitimate points for discussion, then the author should be willing to deal directly with the agency about them, and not turn the attorney lose on the agent.

SAMPLE LETTER OF AGREEMENT

This Letter of Agreement (Agreement) between The Jeff Herman Agency, LLC (Agency), and (Author), issued on 2008, will put into effect the following terms and conditions when signed by all parties to it.

REPRESENTATION

- The Agency is exclusively authorized to seek a publisher for the Author's work, referred to as the "Project", on a per-Project basis. The terms and conditions of this Agreement will pertain to all current and future Projects the Author explicitly authorizes the Agency to represent through written expression. Separate Agreements will not be required for future Projects, unless the terms and conditions differ from this Agreement and/or the Author requests a separate Agreement in each instance. The Agency cannot legally bind the Author to any Publisher contracts.

COMMISSION

- If the Agency sells the Project to a publisher, the Agency will be the Agent-of-Record for the Project's income-producing duration with the publisher, and will irrevocably receive and keep 15% of the Author's advance and royalty income relevant to sold Project received from the publisher. Unless otherwise stated, the Agency commission will also pertain to the Project's subsidiary rights, which commonly means dramatic, foreign, audio, video, merchandising and electronic adaptations of the primary Project. If the Agency uses a subagent to sell foreign or film rights, and the subagent is due a commission, the Agency commission for such will be 10% and the subagent's commission will not be more than 10%. The Agency will not be required to return any legitimately received commissions in the event the Author-Publisher' contract is terminated due to the Author's breach of contract, nor will the Agency bear any responsibility for errors and breaches committed by the Author. There will be an "Agency Clause" included in the body of the Author-Publisher contract memorializing the Agency's standing as a 'third party beneficiary", and providing for the Agency to receive due commission payments directly from the publisher and for the Author to receive due payments minus the commission directly from the publisher, the exact wording for which shall be subject to Author approval. These terms will be binding on the Author's estate in the event of his/her demise. In the event the Author's Project is placed with a publisher by the Agency, the Agency's status herein will extend to any subsequent contracts between Author and Publisher that pertain to a subsequent edition or revision of the Project, or are clearly derivative of the Project.

EXPENSES

- The Agency will be entitled to receive reimbursement from the Author for the following out-of-pocket expenses (at actual cost): Manuscript/proposal copying; necessary overnight deliveries; postage for submission of materials to publishers; foreign shipping and communications. An itemized accounting and records of such items will be maintained by the Agency and shown to the Author. No expense events in excess of $75.00 will be incurred without the Author's prior knowledge and consent.

PROJECT STATUS

- The Agency will forward to the Author copies of correspondence and documents received from Publishers in reference to the Author's Project(s).

REVISIONS

- This Agreement can be amended through written expression signed by all parties to the Agreement.

TERMINATION

- Any party to this Agreement can terminate it at any time following its execution by notifying the other parties in writing to that effect. However, the Agency shall remain entitled to all due commissions which may result from successful Agency efforts implemented prior to the termination. Termination of the Agency' representation of one or more Author Projects will not imply termination of this Agreement, unless such is specifically stated in writing.

Signatures below by the parties named in this Agreement will indicate that all parties concur with the terms and conditions of this Agreement, and will honor their respective responsibilities in good faith.

THE JEFF HERMAN AGENCY, LLC, JEFFREY H. HERMAN, PRESIDENT

Author's name:

Signature:_____

Specific Project(s) represented at this time ("working" or tentative title):

SECRETS OF GHOSTWRITING AND COLLABORATION SUCCESS

TONI ROBINO

Thousands of people in the world have valuable information to share or incredible stories to tell. But only a few of them have the ability or the time to write their own books. That's where you—the professional writer—come into the picture. If you're a strong, clear writer, have the ability to organize thoughts and ideas into a logical order, and can put your ego in the back seat, you may have what it takes to be a successful ghostwriter or collaborator.

The life of a professional writer has its share of pains, but it also has an ample amount of perks. To begin with, it provides a means of escape from the Monday through Friday, 9 to 5 grind. The pay is good, and as you improve your skills and broaden your network, it gets better. In addition to being paid to learn and write about interesting people, philosophies, and methods, being a professional writer puts you in touch with a wide array of fascinating people.

I've had the chance to interview some of the planet's most brilliant people and to explore the work of trendsetters and pioneers in the fields of business, psychology, health, fitness, relationship building, astrology, and metaphysics. I have been flown to Paris to meet with leaders in the field of innovation, wined and dined at some of New York's most exclusive restaurants, and collected agates on the Oregon coast, all in the name of "work." If this sounds appealing, keep reading.

WHAT'S THE DIFFERENCE BETWEEN GHOSTWRITING AND COLLABORATING?

One of the most common questions I'm asked is "What's the difference between a ghostwriter and a collaborator?" The answer can vary from project to project. But, typically, a ghostwriter gathers the author's original materials and research and turns them into a book, based on the author's specifications (if the book will be self-published) or the publisher's specifications (if the book has been sold through the proposal process.)

Theoretically, although ghostwriters do conduct interviews and undertake additional research, they do not contribute their own thoughts or ideas to the content of the book.

In reality, the boundaries of the ghostwriter are not always so clear. As a ghostwriter, I have created 80 percent of the exercises in a number of self-help books, provided many original ideas for content, and "given away" plenty of great title ideas. I don't regret these choices because they felt right and, in the cases mentioned, I was being fairly paid for my ideas, as well as for my services. My being generous with my contributions also made my clients happy and helped to build the foundation of my business. But don't take this too far. For one thing, it's not always a wise choice—particularly if you're giving away original ideas that are perfect for your own book. For another thing, the author you're working with may not appreciate this type of input from you. Do not overstep your boundaries as a ghostwriter by adding your own thoughts to a book, unless the author specifically asks you to do this.

In my more naïve days, and following two glasses of Chardonnay, I made the mistake of sharing my unsolicited input with the author of a health book that I was ghostwriting. In the midst of my enthusiasm, I started brainstorming ideas that she might use to illustrate some of the book's major points. Suddenly, she sprung out of her chair, pointed at me, and declared, "Let's get something straight. This is MY book!" Ouch! I was offering ideas without being asked, but on the other hand, I was only suggesting. Even so, take the word of an initiate and tread softly on your client's turf.

Nowadays, if an author wants me to contribute my own ideas and create original material to support the book, I work with that person as a collaborator and generally receive a coauthor credit, either on the cover or on the title page. Getting credit isn't the most important thing when you're starting out, but if you want to publish your own books in the future, stringing together a list of credits can give you a considerable advantage.

If a book cover says "by John Doe and Jane Smith," they were probably equal collaborators. That can mean:

- they're both experts and one or both of them wrote the book,

- they're both experts and they hired a ghostwriter to write the book, or

- the first author is the expert and the second is a professional writer.

If a book cover says "by John Doe with Jane Smith," Jane probably wrote the book. It could also mean that Jane was a contributor to the book.

Whether you will be serving as a ghostwriter or a collaborator should be clarified up front. Which way to go depends on the project and the people involved. Some of my clients want me to be a "ghost" because they want exclusive cover credit, or they want people to think they wrote their own book. (If this bothers you, now would be a good time to bail out.) Other clients say, "I'm not a writer. This is my material, but I don't want to pretend I wrote this book," or "You deserve credit for what you're doing." On the flip side of the coin, you may be willing to write some books that you don't want your name on. Let's hope this is not because you haven't done a good job! Perhaps you're trying to establish yourself in a particular field of writing and may not want to be linked with projects outside of your target area. That's a judgment call, and you're the best one to make it.

BEING "INVISIBLE" HAS ITS ADVANTAGES

Years ago, after signing my first contract to ghostwrite a book about personal development, I called a friend to share the great news. But instead of being happy for me, she said, "That's not fair. Why should you write a book and not get any credit for it? You teach that stuff in your seminars. Why don't you write the book yourself?" She was also upset that I wouldn't divulge the name of the "mystery author."

She had no way of knowing how challenging it can be to publish your first book flying solo. The author whom I was writing for was well-known and regularly spoke to huge crowds of people all around the world. He had created the perfect platform for this book and was in the prime position to make it a success. He had been previously published and his depth of knowledge in this topic was far greater than my own.

For me, it was a chance to learn more about one of my favorite topics from one of the best sources available. It was also a chance to slip into the publishing world through the back door. I dashed in and never looked back. Once I completed that book, the author referred me to a friend who hired me to write a book about her spiritual journey. She, in turn, introduced me to a professional speaker who wanted to self-publish a book on personal coaching, but could never find the time to write it. And so it goes. If you do a good job, one book can easily lead to the next.

Besides that, being invisible has its advantages. I can zip into the grocery store in purple sweatpants, hair in a ponytail on top of my head, and not a stitch of make-up, and nobody notices or cares! I can kiss my husband in public without camera flashes going off around us, and nobody shows up at my door uninvited, except my mother-in-law.

WHEN CREDIT IS DUE

After you've ghostwritten your first book or two, you'll have more confidence in yourself and your abilities. You will probably start fantasizing (if you haven't already) about seeing your name on the cover, instead of tucked into the acknowledgments section—if that! My name didn't even appear in the first few books that I wrote. Beginning with the fourth book, I asked for a credit in the acknowledgments. Since then, I've been thanked for being a wordsmith, editorial adviser, writing coach, editor, and a "great friend." At least, that was a step in the right direction. However, as much as I relish my anonymity, I also look forward to the day when I'm writing more of my own books than other people's! For that reason, most of the professional writing that I do now is as a collaborator/coauthor.

TEN STEPS TO SUCCEEDING AS A PROFESSIONAL WRITER

There are a number of things to consider before quitting your job and striking out as a professional writer. Writing is a constant process and no matter how good a writer may be, that individual can always get better. Another point to consider is that being a great writer doesn't ensure your success. Writing is a business, and the more you learn about running a business, the better off you'll be. If you're stagnating in a job you abhor, reframe your situation so that you see it as an opportunity to continue earning an income while you make the transition to your writing career. Meanwhile, focus on polishing your writing and interpersonal skills and learn as much about operating a business as you can. The more you learn now, the fewer mistakes you'll make later.

1. ASSESS YOUR WRITING SKILLS

Now is the time to be as objective about your writing as possible. Regardless of where you believe you could or should be along your writing path, what counts at the moment is where you are right now. What writing experience do you have? Have you taken any writing courses? Does your writing flow from one thought logically to the next, or does it need to be better organized? Is your writing smooth and conversational, or does it sound stiff or overly academic? What sorts of positive and negative comments have you received about your writing? Have you had anything published? If not, get going!

If you're too close to your writing to be objective, hire an editor, book doctor, or writing coach to give you some forthright feedback. This assessment will help you to learn where you excel and where you should focus your efforts for improvements. The good news is that there's a market for writers at all points on the professional spectrum. You may not be ready to take on your first book, but you could be qualified to ghostwrite an article, collaborate on a chapter, or polish someone else's work. Begin at your current skill level and commit to a path of improvement. By doing this, you will increase your abilities and your income.

2. MAKE YOUR FIRST LIST

Everyone knows at least a few experts. Whether the experts in your life are doctors, professors, psychologists, interior decorators, photographers, archaeologists, or magicians, chances are that some of them have a goal to write a book. Unless these people are good writers and have a lot of free time, which very few experts have, their book will remain on their "wish list" until someone like you shows up to help them. So begin to make a "potential author" list by answering the following questions. For each question, list as many names as you can think of.

Do you know people who are pioneers or experts in their field?
Do you know people who are famous, either in general or in their area of expertise?
Who are the experts, celebrities, or trendsetters whom your friends or associates know?

Once you've made your list, number the names, starting with number one for the person you would most like to work with. Resist the urge to contact these people until you have professionally prepared for your meeting, by learning more about them and taking Steps 3 and 4.

3. PREPARE A PROFESSIONAL PACKAGE

Put together a promotional package for yourself, or hire a professional to help you do it. This package should include your resume or bio, the services you offer, and a variety of writing samples, showing different styles and topics. You might also insert a page of testimonials from people you have helped with your writing skills or from teachers and coaches who can attest to your abilities. If you've been published, include clean copies of a few of your best clips. If you haven't, enclose a few essays that demonstrate your ability to write clearly and deliver a message effectively.

When you send out your promotional package, enclose a personal pitch letter.. Basically, you are telling people what you believe they have to offer the world through their experience or expertise. You're also telling them why you are the perfect person to write the article, manuscript, or book proposal.

4. SET YOUR RATES

Some writers enclose a rate sheet in their promotional package, but I don't recommend it. I do recommend that you make a rate sheet for your own reference. This will be your guide when you are deciding what to charge your clients. Since every project is a little different, don't commit to a price until you estimate how much time and money it will take for you to do the job well.

Calculate how fast you can write final copy, by keeping track of the actual hours spent writing, editing, and proofreading an article or sample chapter. When the piece is completed to your satisfaction, follow this formula:

Total number of words in final copy
Divided by
Total number of hours to complete final copy
Equals:
Your average speed per hour

The idea isn't to race. This exercise is designed to give you a reality check. If you don't know your average speed for producing final copy, you won't be able to create realistic deadline schedules and you'll have no idea how much you're earning for a day of work.

While you may be able to speed through a first draft, the chapter isn't finished until you've edited, polished, and proofread it.

In addition to estimating your actual writing time, build in time for research, interviews, and meetings with the author. You should also estimate the amount of postage, phone charges, faxes, audio tapes, transcription services, and anything else that will be money out of your pocket. Once you've done your homework, you can present the client with a Letter of Agreement (see Step 7) that includes what you will charge and what they will get for your fee.

Writers' rates vary wildly. I was paid $10,000 for the first few books that I ghost-wrote, and this is still a great starter rate for a nonfiction book ranging from 70,000 to about 85,000 words. You may not be able to charge this much the first time or two, but with each publication that you add to your list, you can inch up your price. When you reach the point where you are earning $15,000 or more on a book, you will be in the company of some of the most successful ghostwriters. The average fee to write a book proposal can range from $1,000 up to $8,000 or more. When you turn writing into a full-time adventure and write several proposals and books each year, while perhaps editing others, you'll be well on your way to ongoing financial and publishing success!

Many times, if you are working as a "writer for hire," you are paid a flat fee and do not receive royalties from book sales. If you are ghostwriting the book, you may be able to negotiate for royalties. (Royalties for ghostwriting can range from 10 percent of the author's royalties to 50 percent.) If you're a collaborator, in most cases you're entitled to a percentage of the book sales. However, many contracts state that the writer does not begin to receive royalties until the publisher has recouped the initial advance for the book. In some cases, the writer's royalties do not begin until the author has recouped the amount invested in the writer. The bottom line is that most ghostwriters don't receive a dime in royalties until thousands of books have been sold. I suggest that you charge what you're worth up front and think of royalties as icing on the cake.

5. POLISH YOUR INTERPERSONAL SKILLS

Unfortunately, some of the best writers are not comfortable talking to people or selling themselves to potential clients. If you see this as a possible pitfall in building your business, make it a priority to develop your interpersonal skills. Plenty of books, tapes, and seminars address personal development, communication skills, networking, and conflict resolution. Devote yourself to learning how to be more comfortable and effective in your interactions with others.

Practice listening closely to what your client is saying, without interrupting. Growing up in an Italian family with everyone talking at once, I had no problem paying attention to what my clients were saying. (If you can listen to three people at once, you can easily hear one at a time!) However, mastering the discipline to keep my mouth shut until it was my turn to talk was another matter entirely. While interjecting and simultaneous talking is considered par for the course in some settings, many people are offended by interruptions and consider them rude. If you have an exciting idea or pertinent question on the tip of your tongue, jot it down, and wait until your clients complete their thoughts, before chiming in.

Learn how to communicate with your clients in a way that is open and caring. For example, rather than telling an author that the file of notes she sent you was so disorganized that dealing with it was like "stumbling blindfolded through a maze," tell her you appreciate her ability to think of so many things at once. Then tell her what you want her to do. "Please put all of your notes under specific category headings, so I can keep all of your great ideas organized." The rule is to think before you speak. There are usually better ways to communicate a thought than the first words that pop into your head or out of your mouth!

Another skill that is essential for a ghostwriter and important for a collaborator is learning how to keep your ego in check. It's not uncommon for a writer to start feeling attached to a project and have a desire for greater freedom or control of the content or writing style. Remind yourself that this book is not yours. Your day will come, and working as a professional writer is paving the way for that to happen.

One of the surest ways to nip your ghostwriting career in the bud is to break the code of confidentiality that you have with the author of the book. Degrees of "invisibility" differ by project, but if the author doesn't want anyone to know you are writing the book, zip your lips. Other than perhaps your spouse, there is no one, and I mean no one, that you should tell. You can say you're writing a book, and you can divulge the general topic, but that has to be the end of the conversation. To this day, my best friends have no idea who I've ghostwritten books for—except in the cases where the authors have publicly acknowledged me for my participation.

Finally, one of the most beneficial interpersonal skills that a writer or anyone else can possess is a sense of humor. Things are bound to go wrong somewhere along the way, and being able to laugh together with your client will ease tension and stress and make the project a whole lot more fun. It's also valuable to learn to laugh at yourself. My father always said, "If you can look at yourself in the mirror at the end of the day and laugh, you'll make it in life." Oftentimes, when I write a book I create a blooper file, just for my own entertainment. This file contains all of the funny, startling, and obscene typos that I find when I proofread my work.

Keep in mind that there are scores of great writers in the world. Why would an author choose to work with someone who's cranky, arrogant, or self-absorbed if it's possible to work with someone equally talented who is also pleasant, down to earth, and fun?

6. KNOW WHEN TO RUN!

Some day, in the not too distant future, you will have a chance to write a book that you know in your gut is not a good match. This might be because it's a topic that bores your pants off, the point of view is in direct opposition to your own beliefs, or the material is leagues away from your scope of knowledge, experience, or ability for comprehension. In spite of all this, you may be tempted to leap into this "opportunity." Maybe your rent is due, the phone company is threatening to disconnect you, or maybe you just can't wait any longer to write your first book. Before you rationalize this decision or override your instincts, take a step back and think about it for at least two days before you commit. For instance, I should have failed algebra class, but my professor gifted me with the lowest passing grade. Even so, when I was offered a chance to ghostwrite *Understanding the Intrigue of Calculus*, I was tempted to do it. Fortunately, two bounced check notices (caused by my math errors) snapped me back to reality, and I graciously declined the offer.

Aside from making a good match with a topic, it is imperative that you feel good about the book's author. It usually takes about nine months to write a book and doing it with someone else can be compared to having a baby together—minus the sex. If you like each other, it can be a wonderful journey filled with creative energy. If you don't like each other, it can be a recurring nightmare that doesn't go away when you wake up.

Years ago, I took on the daunting task of "saving a book." The complete manuscript was due in three months and the author's writing team had mysteriously jumped ship. When I spoke with author for the first time, she was both friendly and enthusiastic, but she also seemed a little desperate. I ignored my instincts, and two days later I was sitting in her apartment discussing the book. Several things happened that day, and each one of them should have set off warning flares in my mind. To begin with, the author's materials were in complete disarray. (No problem, I told myself. I'm a great organizer.) Second, in between telling me how important it is to speak to our mates with respect, she was berating her husband for his lack of photocopying abilities and sundry other things that he couldn't do right to save his life. (She's just stressed out, I justified.) And third, as I leafed through the disheveled stacks of unnumbered pages, I came across a few very cryptic and angry-sounding notes from the writing team that had bailed out. (I reassured myself that even if others had failed, I would not.)

These rationalizations would soon come back to bite me. And not just once. As it turned out, nine writers had attempted to complete this manuscript before I was contacted. Four writers quit, one writer had a nervous breakdown, three of them disappeared into thin air, and another had his phone disconnected. Ironically, the week the book was released, I had the pleasure of meeting one of the writers who had wisely run for her life. We traded our "Crazy-Author Horror Stories" over steaming plates of fried rice and laughed until tears streamed down our cheeks. At that point it was funny, but not a moment before! If you connect with an author who enters the scene waving red flags, run for your life!

7. CLOSE THE DEAL

Verbal agreements are not enough. If you're working with a publishing house, the author or the author's agent will usually have a contract for you to sign. Make sure you understand this agreement before you sign it. Don't be afraid to ask questions. These contracts are written in "legalese" and can be daunting the first time you encounter one. If you're working with an author who plans to self-publish, create a "letter of agreement" that specifies exactly what services you are providing, the fees involved, the date of delivery, and any other considerations that should be put into writing. This document should be signed by both you and the author; it will help to prevent assumptions or other misunderstandings concerning your business agreement.

8. CAPTURE THE AUTHOR'S VOICE

Whether you're working as a ghostwriter or a collaborator, one of your jobs is to capture the voice of the author. Simply put, you want to write in a way that makes it sound like the author is talking. It shouldn't sound like another author whose style you admire, and it most certainly should not sound like you!

Practice reading a few paragraphs from a favorite book, and then write a few of your own, mimicking the author's voice. Do this with a wide variety of authors, and over time, you will develop an "ear" for others' voices.

One of the best ways to write in the author's voice is to conduct taped interviews with the author and have them transcribed onto computer disk. You can cut and paste the pertinent information into each chapter, in the author's own words, and then smooth it out and expand it as needed.

9. CREATE AND KEEP DEADLINES

There are nearly as many methods of meeting deadlines as there are writers. I tend to take a very methodical approach, dividing up the work into equal parts, circling my "days off," and carefully penciling each chapter deadline on my desk calendar. (I can't help it, I was born this way.) Other writers would go mad with this approach. One of the best writers I know creates 10 percent of the book the week she signs the contract and the other 90 percent the month before the manuscript is due. I couldn't even conceive of this approach and would never have believed it could be done if I hadn't witnessed it personally. The secret is to find out what works best for you. But don't kid yourself. Very few writers can write a great book in less than six months. At least until you settle into your own rhythm, pace yourself. Set reasonable deadlines and find a way to stay accountable to those dates.

Staying accountable to my own deadline schedule was initially much harder than I thought it would be. (There are so many tempting diversions in life!) Frequently, when I was supposed to be writing, I was toying with an art project, combing the forest floor in search of gourmet mushrooms, or just staring out the window. My sense of urgency wasn't ignited until my cash flow began to dwindle. That was when I discovered my motivation. Food, shelter, electricity. It may sound like common sense, but for me it was an "aha" moment. I do have some built-in motivation, but it's keeping my cash flow going that moves me from the sunroom to my office each day.

Linking your productivity with your payments works very well. Ask for one-third of your fee up front. This assures you that the author is serious and provides income so you can focus on the book. Schedule your second payment of one-third to coincide with turning in 50 percent of the manuscript. The final one-third is slated for the date you deliver the final manuscript to the author. If you feel you need more deadlines, divide your fee into four or more payments, each contingent on completing a certain amount of work.

10. ASK FOR REFERRALS

I don't have a business card that says "writer." I don't advertise my writing or editing services, and networking requires an hour's drive from the sanctuary of my forest home into the nearest city—which translates into: I rarely do it. By all sensible accounts, I shouldn't be making it as a ghostwriter. And yet I am, and have been for more than a decade. The secret to my success is word of mouth marketing. My clients are happy with my work and me, so they hire me again. They also tell their friends and associates about me, and the wheel continues to spin, seemingly of its own volition.

I know there are many more approaches to marketing, but I've learned that personal referrals usually provide clients whom I want to work with. It's possible for a satisfied client to refer you to an author whom you'd rather eat glass than work with, but most of the time, personal referrals increase your chances of connecting with authors and projects that are interesting and appealing.

When you've completed your work and satisfied your client, ask for referrals. If you've delivered the goods, they'll be happy to brag about you to their friends and associates who "just can't seem to find the right writer."

MAINTAIN YOUR BRIDGES

After the manuscript is complete, the author will be busy with promotional plans and getting back to regular business. You will be focusing on your next project. It's easy to get caught up in the day-to-day happenings and neglect to maintain the bridges that you've already built.

Make it a point to connect with satisfied clients from time to time. Hearing from you will help them think of you for future projects and will increase the likelihood that they'll remember to refer you to someone else. Every couple of months, send a card, a funny e-mail, or an upbeat fax. I phone previous clients only on occasion, and when I do, I call them at their office and keep it short. You want to be the person they look forward to hearing from, not the one who won't go away!

THE COLLABORATION AGREEMENT

JEFF HERMAN

Any book that is written by two or more writers is a collaborative effort. Such collaborative endeavors are predominately nonfiction works, though collaborative fiction is by no means unheard of (typically, a novel featuring a celebrity author that is for the most part written by someone else, or two bestselling novelists looking to synergize their reader base). There are several reasons why a writer might choose to collaborate with another, as opposed to writing the book alone.

The most common reasons are:

- A person may have the essential expertise, professional status, and promotability to author a book, but may lack time, ability, interest, or any combination of these, to do the actual writing. Therefore, retaining someone to do the writing is a sensible—even preferable—alternative.

- Some nonfiction projects, especially academic or professionally oriented ones, cover a broad range of material, and few individuals may have the requisite depth to write the book unilaterally. Therefore, two or more writers with complementary specializations may team up. For exceptionally technical books, such as medical texts, there can be several collaborators.

Many writers earn handsome incomes writing other people's books. When they are collaborative writers, their names are flashed along with the primary author of the project (and given second billing, usually preceded by "and," "with," or "as told to"). If they are true ghostwriters, they may well have the same level of input and involvement as collaborators, but will generally receive no public recognition for their work (other than perhaps a subtle pat on the back in the acknowledgments section).

WHAT ARE COLLABORATION AGREEMENTS?

As with any business relationship, it's wise for the collaborators to enter into a concise agreement (written in plain English) that spells out all the terms and conditions of the relationship—especially each party's respective responsibilities and financial benefits.

A collaboration agreement can run from 1 to more than 20 pages, depending on how much money is at issue and the complexity of the other variables. Most of the time we in the industry can keep these agreements down to an easy-to-read 2 pages. It's probably not necessary to go to the expense of retaining a lawyer for this task. If you have an agent, he can probably draw up an agreement for you or at least show you several samples.

The following is a sample collaboration agreement that is similar to ones used by many of my clients.

(Disclaimer: This sample collaboration agreement is intended only as a reference guide.)

SAMPLE COLLABORATION AGREEMENT

This Collaboration Agreement (Agreement) entered into on, 2008, by and between and will put into effect the following terms and conditions when signed by both parties.

1. _____will collaborate with _____ to write a book proposal for the purpose of obtaining a book contract for a nonfiction book based upon:
Subsequent to entering into a book contract, _____ and _____will collaborate on writing the entire manuscript.

2. The proposal will consist of conventional book proposal sections, including a full chapter outline and a sample chapter. Additional chapters will be generated if specifically requested by a prospective publisher who has interest in acquiring the book. Both the proposal and the subsequent manuscript will be entirely subject to review and consent prior to submission to a publisher.

3. _____shall be represented by The Jeff Herman Agency LLC.

4. _____will always be listed and referred to as the book's primary author and spokesperson, and his/her name will always appear first and be in larger print.

5. _____and _____ respective estates will be subject to the terms and conditions of this Agreement, in the event of either's demise.

6. It will primarily be _____ responsibility to provide the raw content and "voice" from which _____ will generate the editorial product.

7. This Agreement can be amended or expanded by attaching riders to it, if such riders are signed by _____ and _____, or their authorized successors.

8. No other claims or representations are made by either party; both agree that this Agreement fully and accurately integrates and expresses their respective intentions, responsibilities and commitments. No other representations, promises, or agreements are made except as may be in writing and signed by the party to be held responsible.

9. The division of the book's advance, royalties and subsidiary rights revenues shall be ___% to ___and ___% to___.

10. _____shall own the book's copyright.

11. _____will be responsible for paying out-of-pocket expenses relevant to the writing of the proposal and the manuscript, or will reimburse _____. Possible out of

pocket expenses might include: copying, postage/shipping, communications, travel. _____ will not make any unilateral expense decisions in excess of $25 without _____ prior consent.

12. In the event a deal is entered into with a publisher based upon the proposal written by _____, but _____ does not wish to continue as the collaborator to write the manuscript for any reason, then she shall be due a one time "kill fee" of $_____ from first proceeds in consideration of her work on the proposal. Thereafter, she shall have no additional claims or rights, and her engagement as expressed above shall be entirely terminated and concluded.

13. _____ and _____ warrant and represent that any material supplied by each party shall not infringe upon any common law or statutory copyright, shall not violate any right of privacy, shall not be libelous or violate any other right of any person. Each party agrees to indemnify the other against all liability, damage, cost and expense, including reasonable attorney fees, arising out of any breach of the foregoing representations and warranties.

14. _____ agrees that, without written consent, she will refrain from discussing, releasing, or causing to be released, any of the confidential information that _____ provides or causes to be provided, prior to it's publication in the book or otherwise publicized.

15. In the event no deal is entered into for the book by _____ 2008, then this Agreement will either be re-affirmed in writing by both parties, or it will automatically expire, and neither party will have any claims against the other. However, its expiration will not terminate or prejudice _____ rights and benefits as expressed above in the event her proposal is used to generate a book contract at a later date, unless she expressly and specifically abdicates them in writing.

The authorized signatures below will confirm that each party has reviewed the terms and conditions of this Agreement, and are hereby binding themselves to fulfill their respective tasks and comply with there respective obligations in good faith.

Agreed:

Agreed:

Q & A

Q: What about agent representation if it's a collaborative effort?
There are two possibilities:

1. The same agent will represent both parties. However, this requires the agent to be equal in her dealings with both parties. For instance, the agent should avoid tilting toward John while he's negotiating the collaboration agreement with Jane. What I do is provide both parties with accurate advice and then step aside as they—hopefully—work things out between themselves and then come back to me with all issues resolved.

    More important: the agent should not "double-dip." In other words, my commission will only pertain to the work's income. I will not touch any money that one collaborator may pay to the other, even if such payments exceed the work's advance.

2. Some collaborations can be coagented. Each collaborator may already have a different agent. Or it may be felt that there will be a conflict of interest for the same agent to represent both parties.

    When this happens, both agents will negotiate the collaboration agreement with each other in behalf of their respective clients. All parties will then work out a strategy to determine which agent is to be out front selling and negotiating the deal. Each agent will receive a commission only against her client's respective share.

As with any other business relationship, collaboration agreements generally have the best chance to produce a productive and successful outcome when they reasonably and realistically reflect the rights, responsibilities, special talents, and good interests of all involved parties.

WHEN THE DEAL IS DONE

HOW TO THRIVE AFTER SIGNING A PUBLISHING CONTRACT

JEFF HERMAN

Congratulations! You've sold your book to an established publishing house. You've gained entry to the elite club of published authors. You'll discover that your personal credibility is enhanced whenever this achievement is made known to others. It may also prove a powerful marketing vehicle for your business or professional practice.

Smell the roses while you can. Then wake up and smell the coffee. If your experience is like that of numerous other writers, once your book is actually published, there's a better-than-even chance you'll feel a bit of chagrin. Some of these doubts are apt to be outward expressions of your own inner uncertainties. Others are not self-inflicted misgivings—they are most assuredly ticked off by outside circumstances.

Among the most common author complaints are: (1) Neither you nor anyone you know can find the book anywhere. (2) The publisher doesn't appear to be doing anything to market the book. (3) You detest the title and the jacket. (4) No one at the publishing house is listening to you. In fact, you may feel that you don't even exist for them.

As a literary agent, I live through these frustrations with my clients every day, and I try to explain to them at the outset what the realities of the business are. But I never advocate abdication or pessimism. There are ways for every author to substantially remedy these endemic problems. In many cases this means first taking a deep breath, relaxing, and reaching down deep inside yourself to sort out the true source of your emotions. When this has been accomplished, it's time to breathe out, move out, and take charge.

What follows are practical means by which each of these four most common failures can be preempted. I'm not suggesting that you can compensate entirely for what may be a publisher's defaults; it's a tall order to remake a clinker after the fact. However, with lots of smarts and a little luck you can accomplish a great deal.

A PHILOSOPHY TO WRITE BY

Let me introduce a bit of philosophy that applies to the writer's life, as well as it does to the lives of those who are not published. Many of you may be familiar with the themes popularized by psychotherapists, self-awareness gurus, and business motivators that assert the following: To be a victim is to be powerless—which means you don't have the ability to improve your situation. With that in mind, avoid becoming merely an author who only complains and who remains forever bitter.

No matter how seriously you believe your publisher is screwing up, don't fall into the victim trap. Instead, find positive ways to affect what is or is not happening for you.

Your publisher is like an indispensable employee whom you are not at liberty to fire. You don't have to work with this publisher the next time, but this time it's the only one you've got.

There are a handful of perennially bestselling writers, such as John Grisham, Anne Rice, Mary Higgins Clark, and Michael Crichton, whose book sales cover a large part of their publisher's expense sheet. These writers have perhaps earned the luxury of being very difficult, if they so choose (most of them are reportedly quite the opposite).

But the other 99.98 percent of writers are not so fortunately invested with the power to arbitrate. No matter how justified your stance and methods may be, if you become an author with whom everyone at the publishing house dreads to speak, you've lost the game.

The editors, publicists, and marketing personnel still have their jobs, and they see no reason to have you in their face. In other words: Always seek what's legitimately yours, but always try to do it in a way that might work for you, as opposed to making yourself persona non grata till the end of time.

ATTACKING PROBLEM NO. 1: NEITHER YOU NOR ANYONE YOU KNOW CAN FIND THE BOOK ANYWHERE

This can be the most painful failure. After all, what was the point of writing the book and going through the whole megillah of getting it published if it's virtually invisible?

Trade book distribution is a mysterious process, even for people in the business. Most bookstore sales are dominated by the large national and regional chains, such as Waldenbooks, B. Dalton, Barnes & Noble, and Borders. No shopping mall is complete without at least one of these stores. Publishers always have the chain stores in mind when they determine what to publish. Thankfully, there are also a few thousand independently owned shops throughout the country.

Thousands of new titles are published each year, and these books are added to the seemingly infinite number that are already in print. Considering the limitations of the existing retail channels, it should be no surprise that only a small fraction of all these books achieves a significant and enduring bookstore presence.

Each bookstore will dedicate most of its visual space to displaying healthy quantities of the titles it feels are safe sells: books by celebrities and well-established authors, or books that are being given extra-large printings and marketing budgets by their publishers, thereby promising to create demand.

The rest of the store will generally provide a liberal mix of titles, organized by subject or category. This is where the backlist titles reside and the lower-profile newer releases try to stake their claims. For instance, the business section will probably offer two dozen or so sales books. Most of the displayed titles will be by the biggest names in the genre, and their month-to-month sales probably remain strong, even if the book was first published several years ago.

In other words, probably hundreds of other sales books were written in recent years that, as far as retail distribution is concerned, barely made it out of the womb. You see, the stores aren't out there to do you any favors. They are going to stock whatever titles they feel they can sell the most of. There are too many titles chasing too little space.

It's the job of the publisher's sales representative to lobby the chain and store buyers individually about the merits of her publisher's respective list. But here, too, the numbers can be numbing. The large houses publish many books each season, and it's not possible for the rep to do justice to each of them. Priority will be given to the relatively few titles that get the exceptional advances.

Because most advances are modest, and since the average book costs about $20,000 to produce, some publishers can afford to simply sow a large field of books and observe passively as some of them sprout. The many that don't bloom are soon forgotten, as a new harvest dominates the bureaucracy's energy. Every season, many very fine books are terminated by the publishing reaper. The wisdom and magic these books may have offered are thus sealed away, disclosed only to the few.

I have just covered a complicated process in a brief fashion. Nonetheless, the overall consequences for your book are in essence the same. Here, now, are a few things you may attempt in order to override such a stacked situation. However, these methods will not appeal to the shy or passive:

- Make direct contact with the publisher's sales representatives. Do to them what they do to the store buyers—sell 'em! Get them to like you and your book. Take the reps near you to lunch and ballgames. If you travel, do the same for local reps wherever you go.

- Make direct contact with the buyers at the national chains. If you're good enough to actually get this kind of access, you don't need to be told what to do next.

- Organize a national marketing program aimed at local bookstores throughout the country.

There's no law that says only your publisher has the right to market your book to the stores. (Of course, except in special cases, all orders must go through your publisher.) For the usual reasons, your publisher's first reaction may be "What the hell are you doing?" But that's okay; make the publisher happy by showing her that your efforts work. It would be wise, however, to let the publisher in on your scheme up front.

If your publisher objects—which she may—you might choose to interpret those remarks simply as the admonitions they are, and then proceed to make money for all. This last observation leads to ways you can address the next question.

ATTACKING PROBLEM NO. 2: THE PUBLISHER DOESN'T APPEAR TO BE DOING ANYTHING TO MARKET THE BOOK

If it looks as if your publisher is doing nothing to promote your book, then it's probably true. Your mistake is being surprised and unprepared.

The vast majority of published titles receive little or no marketing attention from the publisher beyond catalog listings. The titles that get big advances are likely to get some support, since the publisher would like to justify the advance by creating a good seller.

Compared to those in other Fortune 500 industries, publishers' in-house marketing departments tend to be woefully understaffed, undertrained, and underpaid. Companies like Procter & Gamble will tap the finest business schools, pay competitive salaries, and strive to nurture marketing superstars. Book publishers don't do this.

As a result, adult trade book publishing has never been especially profitable, and countless sales probably go unmade. The sales volumes and profits for large, diversified publishers are mostly due to the lucrative—and captive—textbook trade. Adult trade sales aren't the reason that companies like Random House can generate more than $1 billion in annual revenues.

Here's What You Can Do

Hire your own public relations firm to promote you and your book. Your publisher is likely to be grateful and cooperative. But you must communicate carefully with your publishing house.

Once your manuscript is completed, you should request a group meeting with your editor and people from the marketing, sales, and publicity departments. You should focus on what their marketing agenda will be. If you've decided to retain your own PR firm, this is the time to impress the people at your publishing house with your commitment and pressure them to help pay for it. At the very least, the publisher should provide plenty of free books.

Beware of this common problem: Even if you do a national TV show, your book may not be abundantly available in bookstores that day—at least, not everywhere. An obvious answer is setting up 800 numbers to fill orders, and it baffles me that publishers don't make wider use of them. There are many people watching Oprah who won't ever make it to the bookstore, but who would be willing to order then and there with a credit card. Infomercials have proved this.

Not all talk or interview shows will cooperate, but whenever possible you should try to have your publisher's 800 number (or yours) displayed as a purchasing method, in addition to the neighborhood bookstore. If you use your own number, make sure you can handle a potential flood.

If retaining a PR firm isn't realistic for you, then do your own media promotions. There are many good books in print about how to do your own PR. (A selection of relevant titles may be found in this volume's "Suggested Resources" section.)

ATTACKING PROBLEM NO. 3: YOU DETEST THE TITLE AND JACKET

Almost always, your publisher will have final contractual discretion over title, jacket design, and jacket copy. But that doesn't mean you can't be actively involved. In my opinion, you had better be. Once your final manuscript is submitted, make it clear to your editor that you expect to see all prospective covers and titles. But simply trying to veto what the publisher comes up with won't be enough. You should try to counter the negatives with positive alternatives. You might even want to go as far as having your own prospective covers professionally created. If the publisher were to actually choose your version, the house might reimburse you.

At any rate, don't wait until it's after the fact to decide you don't like your cover, title, and so forth. It's like voting: Participate or shut up.

ATTACKING PROBLEM NO. 4: NO ONE AT THE PUBLISHING HOUSE SEEMS TO BE LISTENING TO YOU

This happens a lot—though I bet it happens to certain people in everything they do. The primary reasons for this situation are either (1) that the people you're trying to access are incompetent; (2) that you're not a priority for them; or (3) that they simply hate talking to you.

Here are a few things you might try to do about it:

- If the contact person is incompetent, what can that person really accomplish for you anyway? It's probably best to find a way to work around this person, even if he begins to return your calls before you place them.

- The people you want access to may be just too busy to give you time. Screaming may be a temporary remedy, but eventually, they'll go deaf again. Obviously, their time is being spent somewhere. Thinking logically, how can you make it worthwhile for these people to spend more time on you? If being a pain in the neck is your best card, then perhaps you should play it. But there's no leverage like being valuable. In fact, it's likely that the somewhere else they're spending their time is with a very valuable author.

- Maybe someone just hates talking to you. That may be this person's problem. But, as many wise men and women have taught, allies are better than adversaries. And to convert an adversary is invaluable. Do it.

CONCLUSION

This essay may come across as cynical. But I want you to be realistic and be prepared. Many publishing success stories are out there, and many of them happened because the authors made them happen.

For every manuscript that is published, probably a few thousand were rejected. To be published is a great accomplishment—and a great asset. If well tended, it can pay tremendous dividends.

Regardless of your publisher's commitment at the outset, if you can somehow generate sales momentum, the publisher will most likely join your march to success and allocate a substantial investment to ensure it. In turn, the publisher may even assume all the credit. But so what? It's to your benefit.

FICTION DICTIONARY

JAMIE M. FORBES

In book publishing, people describe works of fiction as they relate to categories, genres, and other market concepts, which, coming from the mouths of renowned industry figures, can make it sound as if there's a real system to what is actually a set of arbitrary terminology. Categories are customarily viewed as reflecting broad sectors of readership interest. Genres are either subcategories (classifications within categories) or types of stories that can pop up within more than one category—though genre and category are sometimes used interchangeably.

For instance, suspense fiction (as a broad category) includes the jeopardy story genre (typified by a particular premise that can just as easily turn up in a supernatural horror story). Or, again within the suspense fiction category, there's the police procedural (a subcategory of detective fiction, which is itself a subcategory of suspense that is often spoken of as a separate category). The police procedural can be discussed as a distinct genre with its own special attributes; and there are particular procedural genre types, such as those set in the small towns of the American plains or in a gritty urban environment. As a genre-story type, tales of small-town American life also surface in the context of categories as disparate as literary fiction, horror stories, Westerns, and contemporary and historical romance.

As we can see, all of this yakety-yak is an attempt to impose a sense of order onto what is certainly a muddy creative playing field.

The following listing of commonly used fiction descriptives gives an indication of the varieties of writing found within each category. This is not meant to be a strict taxonomy. Nor is it exhaustive. The definitions associated with each category or genre are fluid and personalized in usage and can seem to vary with each author interview or critical treatise, with each spate of advertising copy or press release, or they can shift during the course of a single editorial conference. One writer's "mystery" may be a particular editor's "suspense," which is then marketed to the public as a "thriller."

Then, too, individual authors do come up with grand, original ideas that demand publication and thereby create new categories or decline to submit to any such designation. But that's another story—maybe yours.

ACTION-ADVENTURE

The action-oriented adventure novel is best typified in terms of premise and scenario trajectory. These stories often involve the orchestration of a journey that is essentially exploratory, revelatory, and (para)military. There is a quest element—a search for a treasure in whatever guise—in addition to a sense of pursuit that crosses over into thrillerdom. From one perspective, the action-adventure tale, in story concept if not explicit content, traces its descent from epic-heroic tradition.

In modern action-adventure we are in the territory of freebooters, commandos, and mercenaries—as well as suburbanites whose yen for experience of the good life, and whose very unawareness in the outback, takes them down dangerous trails. Some stories are stocked with an array of international terrorists, arms-smugglers, drug-dealers, and techno-pirates. Favorite settings include jungles, deserts, swamps, and mountains—any sort of badlands (don't rule out an urban environment) that can echo the perils that resound through the story's human dimension.

There can be two or more cadres with competing aims going for the supreme prize—and be sure to watch out for lots of betrayal and conflict among friends, as well as the hitherto unsuspected schemer among the amiably bonded crew.

Action-adventures were once thought of as exclusively men's stories. No more. Writers invented new ways to do it, and the field is now open.

COMMERCIAL FICTION

Commercial fiction is defined by sales figures—either projected (prior to publication, even before acquisition) or backhandedly through actual performance. Commercial properties are frontlist titles, featured prominently in a publisher's catalog and given good doses of publicity and promotion.

An agent or editor says a manuscript is commercial, and the question in response is apt to be: How so? Many books in different genres achieve bestseller potential after an author has established a broad-based readership and is provided marketing support from all resources the publisher commands.

Commercial fiction is not strictly defined by content or style; it is perhaps comparative, rather than absolute. Commercial fiction is often glitzier, more stylishly of the mode in premise and setting; its characters strike the readers as more assuredly glamorous (regardless of how highbrow or lowlife).

A commercial work offers the publisher a special marketing angle, which changes from book to book or season to season—this year's kinky kick is next year's ho-hum. For a new writer in particular, to think commercially is to think ahead of the pack and not jump on the tail-end of a bandwagon that's already passed. If your premise has already played as a television miniseries, you're way too late.

Commercial works sometimes show elements of different categories, such as detective fiction or thrillers, and may cut across or combine genres to reach out toward a vast readership. Cross-genre books may thus have enticing hooks for the reading public at large; at the same time, when they defy category conventions they may not satisfy genre aficionados. If commercial fiction is appointed by vote of sales, most popular mysteries are commercial works, as are sophisticated bestselling sex-and-shopping oh-so-shocking wish-it-were-me escapades.

CRIME FICTION

Related to detective fiction and suspense novels, in subject matter and ambiance, are stories centered on criminal enterprise. Crime fiction includes lighthearted capers that are vehicles in story form for the portrayal of amusingly devious aspirations at the core of the human norm. Crime stories can also be dark, black, noir, showing the primeval essence of tooth-and-nail that brews in more than a few souls.

Some of the players in crime stories may well be cops of one sort or another (and they are often as corrupt as the other characters), but detection per se is not necessarily the story's strong suit. It is just as likely that in the hands of one of the genre's masters, the reader's lot will be cast (emotionally, at least) in support of the outlaw characters' designs.

DETECTIVE FICTION

Varieties of detective fiction include police procedurals (with the focus on formal investigatory teamwork); hard-boiled, poached, or soft-boiled (not quite so tough as hard-boiled); and the cozy (a.k.a. tea-cozy mysteries, manners mysteries, manor house mysteries).

Detectives are typically private or public pros; related professionals whose public image, at least, involves digging under the surface (reporters, journalists, computer hackers, art experts, psychotherapists, and university academics, including archaeologists); or they may be rank amateurs who are interested or threatened via an initial plot turn that provides them with an opportunity (or the necessity) to assume an investigatory role.

The key here is that the detective story involves an ongoing process of discovery that forms the plot. Active pursuit of interlocking clues and other leads is essential—though sometimes an initial happenstance disclosure will do in order to kick off an otherwise tightly woven story.

The manifold denominations of modern detective fiction (also called mysteries, or stories or novels of detection) are widely considered to stem from the detective tales composed by the nineteenth-century American writer Edgar Allan Poe. Though mysterious tracks of atmosphere and imagery can be traced in the writings of French symbolists (Charles Baudelaire was a big fan of Poe), the first flowering of the form was in Britain, including such luminaries as Arthur Conan Doyle, Agatha Christie, and Dorothy L. Sayers. Indeed, in one common usage, a traditional mystery (or cozy) is a story in the mode initially established by British authors.

The other major tradition is the American-grown hard-boiled detective story, with roots in the tabloid culture of America's industrial growth and the associated institutions of yellow journalism, inspirational profiles of the gangster-tycoon lifestyle, and social-action exposés.

The field continues to expand with infusions of such elements as existentialist character conceits, the lucidity and lushness of magic-realists, and the ever-shifting sociopolitical insights that accrue from the growing global cultural exchange.

Occasionally, detective fiction involves circumstances in which, strictly speaking, no crime has been committed. The plot revolves around parsing out events or situations that may be construed as strange, immoral, or unethical (and are certainly mysterious), but which are by no means considered illegal in all jurisdictions.

FANTASY FICTION

The category of fantasy fiction covers many of the story elements encountered in fables, folktales, and legends; the best of these works obtain the sweep of the epic and are touched by the power of myth. Some successful fantasy series are set within recognizable museum-quality frames, such as those of ancient Egypt or the Celtic world. Another strain of fantasy fiction takes place in almost-but-not-quite archaeologically verifiable regions of the past or future, with barbarians, nomads, and jewel-like cities scattered across stretches of continent-sized domains of the author's imagination.

Fair game in this realm are romance, magic, and talking animals. Stories are for the most part adventurous, filled with passion, honor, vengeance—and action. A self-explanatory subgenre of fantasy fiction is termed sword-and-sorcery.

HORROR

Horror has been described as the simultaneous sense of fascination and terror, a basic attribute that can cover significant literary scope. Some successful horror writers are admired more for their portrayal of atmosphere than for attention to plot or character development. Other writers do well with the carefully paced zinger—that is, the threat-and-delivery of gore; in the hands of skilled practitioners, sometimes not much more is needed to produce truly terrifying effects.

The horror genre has undergone changes—there is, overall, less reliance on the religiously oriented supernatural, more utilization of medical and psychological concepts, more sociopolitical and cultural overtones, and a general recognition on the part of publishers that many horror aficionados seek more than slash-and-gore. Not that the readers aren't bloodthirsty—it is just that in order to satisfy the cravings of a discerning audience, a writer must create an augmented reading experience.

The horror itself can be supernatural in nature, psychological, paranormal, or techno (sometimes given a medical-biological slant that verges on sci-fi), or can embody personified occult/cultic entities. In addition to tales of vampires, were-creatures, demons, and ghosts, horror has featured such characters as the elemental slasher/stalker (conceived with or without mythic content), a variety of psychologically tormented souls, and just plain folks given over to splatterhouse pastimes. Whatever the source of the horror, the tale is inherently more gripping and more profound when the horrific beast, force, or human foe has a mission, is a character with its own meaningful designs and insights—when something besides single-minded bloodlust is at play.

At times, the horror premise is analogous to a story of detection (especially in the initial setup); often the horror plot assumes the outlines of the thriller (particularly where there is a complex chase near the end); and sometimes the horror-story scenario ascribes to action-adventure elements. However, rather than delineating a detailed process of discovery (as in a typical mystery) or a protracted hunt throughout (as in the thriller), the horror plot typically sets up a final fight to the finish (until the sequel) that, for all its pyrotechnics and chills, turns on something other than brute force.

LITERARY FICTION

The term literary describes works that feature the writer's art expressed at its most refined levels; literary fiction describes works of literature in such forms as the novel, novella, novelette, short story, and short-shorts (also known as flash fiction). In addition to these fictional formats, literary works include poetry, essays, letters, dramatic works, and superior writing in all nonfiction varieties, covering such areas as travel, food, history, current affairs, and all sorts of narrative nonfiction, as well as reference works.

Literary fiction can adhere to the confines of any and all genres and categories, or suit no such designation. A work of fiction that is depicted as literary can (and should) offer the reader a multidimensional experience. *Literary* can designate word selection and imagery that is careful or inspired or that affects an articulated slovenliness. A literary character may be one who is examined in depth or is sparsely sketched to trenchant effect. Literature can postulate philosophical or cultural insights and portray fresh ideas in action. Literary works can feature exquisitely detailed texture or complete lack of sensory ambiance.

Structurally, literary fiction favors story and plot elements that are individualistic or astonishingly new, rather than tried-and-true. In some cases the plot as such does not appear important, but beware of quick judgment in this regard: Plotting may be subtle, as in picking at underlying psychology or revelation of character. And the plot movement may take place in the reader's head, as the progressive emotional or intellectual response to the story, rather than demonstrated in external events portrayed on paper.

To say that a work is literary can imply seriousness. Nonetheless, many serious works are not particularly sober, and literary reading should be a dynamic experience—pleasurably challenging, insightful, riveting, fun. A work that is stodgy and boring may not be literary at all, for it has not achieved the all-important aim of being fine reading.

Obviously, a book that is lacking with respect to engaging characters, consciousness of pace, and story development, but that features fancy wordplay and three-page sentences, is hardly exemplary of literary mastery. Though such a work may serve as a guidepost of advanced writing techniques for a specialized professional audience, it is perhaps a more limited artifice than is a slice-and-dice strip-and-whip piece that successfully depicts human passion and offers a well-honed story.

Commercial literature, like commercial fiction in general, is essentially a back-definition; commercial literature indicates works of outstanding quality written by authors who sell well, as opposed to just plain literature, which includes writers and works whose readership appeal has not yet expanded beyond a small core. Noncommercial literary works are staples of the academic press and specialized houses, as well as of selected imprints of major trade publishers.

When a literary author attracts a large readership or manages to switch from the list of a tiny publisher to a mammoth house, the publisher might decide a particular project is ripe for a shot at the big-time and slate the writer for substantial attention, accompanied by a grand advance. If you look closely, you'll note that literary authors who enter the commercial ranks are usually not just good writers: Commercial literary works tap into the cultural pulse, which surges through the editorial avenues into marketing, promotion, and sales support.

In day-to-day commercial publishing discourse, to call a piece of work literary simply means it is well written. As a category designation, literary fiction implies that a particular book does not truly abide by provisos of other market sectors—though if the work under discussion does flash some category hooks, it might be referred to in such catch-terms as a literary thriller or literary suspense.

MAINSTREAM FICTION

A mainstream work is one that can be expected to be at least reasonably popular to a fairly wide readership. In a whim of industry parlance, to various people in publishing the label *mainstream* signifies a work that is not particularly noteworthy on any count—it's a work of fiction that's not literary, according to circumscribed tastes, and not something easily categorized with a targeted, predictable base of readership. Maybe not particularly profitable, either, especially if the publishing house is bent on creating bestsellers. A mainstream work may therefore be seen as a risky proposition, rather than a relatively safe bet.

Let this be a cautionary note: In some publishing minds, a plain-and-simple mainstream book signifies midlist, which equals no sale. In a lot of publishing houses, midlist fiction, even if it's published, gets lost; many commercial trade houses won't publish titles they see as midlist (see Midlist Fiction).

A mainstream work may be a good read—but if that's all you can say about it, that's a mark against its prospects in the competitive arena. When a story is just a good story, the publisher doesn't have much of a sales slant to work with; in publishing terms that makes for a dismal enough prognosis for an editor or agent to pass.

If a manuscript has to sell on storytelling merits or general interest alone, it most likely won't sell to a major publisher at all. If mainstream fiction is what you've got, you, the writer, are advised to return to the workshop and turn the opus into a polished piece with a stunning attitude that can be regarded as commercial, or redesign the story line into a category format such as mystery, suspense, or thriller. A mainstream mystery or mainstream thriller may contain characters who aren't too wacko and milieus that aren't overly esoteric. Such works are eminently marketable, but you might suppress the mainstream designation in your query and just call your work by its category or genre moniker.

If you've got the gifts and perseverance to complete a solid story, and you find yourself about to say it's a mainstream book and no more, you'll be farther along faster if you work to avoid the midlist designation. Think commercially and write intrepidly.

Please note: Many editors and agents use the term *mainstream fiction* more or less synonymously with commercial fiction (see Commercial Fiction).

MIDLIST FICTION

Midlist books are essentially those that do not turn a more-than-marginal profit. That they show a profit at all might testify to how low the author's advance was (usually set so the publisher can show a profit based on projected sales). Midlist books may be category titles, literary works, or mainstream books that someone, somewhere believed had commercial potential (yet to be achieved).

The midlist is where no one wants to be: You get little if any promotion, few reviews, and no respect. Why publish this kind of book at all? Few publishers do. A midlist book was most likely not intended as such; the status is unacceptable unless the writer is being prepped for something bigger and is expected to break through soon. When a writer or series stays midlist too long, they're gone—the publishers move on to a more profitable use of their resources.

If the publishers don't want you, and the readers can't find you, you're better off going somewhere else, too. (See Commercial Fiction or any of the other category designations.)

MYSTERY

Many people use the term *mystery* to refer to the detective story (see Detective Fiction). When folks speak of traditional mysteries, they often mean a story in the British cozy mold, which can be characterized—but not strictly defined—by an amateur sleuth (often female) as protagonist, a solve-the-puzzle story line, minimal body count (with all violence performed offstage), and a restrained approach to language and tone. Sometimes, however, a reference to traditional mysteries implies not only cozies, but also includes stories of the American hard-boiled school, which are typified by a private eye (or a rogue cop), up-front violence as well as sex, and vernacular diction.

On the other hand, mysteries are seen by some to include all suspense fiction categories, thereby encompassing police procedurals, crime capers, thrillers, and even going so far afield as horror and some fantasy fiction.

In the interests of clarity, if not precision, here we'll say simply that a mystery is a story in which something of utmost importance to the tale is unknown or covert at the outset and must be uncovered, solved, or revealed along the way. (See Crime Fiction, Detective Fiction, Fantasy Fiction, Horror, Suspense Fiction, and Thriller.)

ROMANCE FICTION

The power of love has always been a central theme in literature, as it has in all arts, in all life. For all its importance to the love story genre, the term *romance* does not pertain strictly to the love element. The field can trace its roots through European medieval romances that depicted knights-errant and women in distress, which were as much tales of spiritual quest, politics, and action as love stories. The Romantic movement of the nineteenth century was at its heart emblematic of the heightened energy lent to all elements of a story, from human passion, to setting, to material objects, to psychological ramifications of simple acts.

Thanks to the writers and readers of modern romances, they've come a long way from the days of unadulterated heart-stopping bodice-rippers with pampered, egocentric heroines who long for salvation through a man. Today's romance most often depicts an independent, full-blooded female figure in full partnership with her intended mate.

Modern romance fiction is most assuredly in essence a love story, fueled by the dynamics of human relationships. From this core, writers explore motifs of career and family, topical social concerns, detective work, psychological suspense, espionage, and horror, as well as historical period pieces (including European medieval, Regency, and romances set in the American West) and futuristic tales. Romance scenarios with same-sex lovers are highlighted throughout the ranks of vanguard and literary houses, though this theme is not a priority market at most trade publishers or romance-specialist presses.

Among commercial lead titles tapped for bestseller potential are those books that accentuate the appeal of romance within the larger tapestry of a fully orchestrated work. (See also Women's Fiction.)

SCIENCE FICTION

Take humankind's age-old longings for knowledge and enlightenment and add a huge helping of emergent technology, with the twist that science represents a metaphysical quest—there you have the setup for science fiction. Though the basic science fiction plot may resemble that of action-adventure tales, thrillers, or horror stories, the attraction for the reader is likely to be the intellectual or philosophical questions posed, in tandem with the space-age glitter within which it's set. In terms of character interaction, the story line should be strong enough to stand alone when stripped of its technological trimmings.

In the future fiction genre, the elements of science fiction are all in place, but the science tends to be soft-pedaled, and the story as a whole is character-based. In a further variation, the post-apocalyptic vision presents the aftermath of a cataclysm (either engendered by technology or natural in origin) that sets the survivors loose on a new course that demonstrates the often-disturbing vicissitudes of social and scientific evolution. Such scenarios are generally set in the not-too-distant future, are usually earth-based, or are barely interstellar, with recognizable (but perhaps advanced) technology as the norm.

Purity of genre is at times fruitless to maintain or define. Is Mary Shelley's *Frankenstein* a science fiction tale or a horror story, or is it primarily a literary work? Is Jules Verne's *20,000 Leagues Under the Sea* science fiction or a technothriller—or a futuristic action-adventure?

Stories of extraterrestrial exploration, intergalactic warfare, and other exobiological encounters are almost certain to be placed within the science fiction category, until the day when such endeavors are considered elements of realism.

SUSPENSE FICTION

Suspense fiction embraces many literary idioms, with a wide range of genres and subdivisions categorized under the general rubric of suspense. Indeed, in broad terms, all novels contain suspense—that is, if the writer means for the reader to keep reading and reading, and reading on…way into the evening and beyond.

Suspense fiction has no precise formula that specifies certain character types tied to a particular plot template. It is perhaps most applicable for a writer to think of suspense as a story concept that stems from a basic premise of situational uncertainty. That is: Something horrible is going to happen! Let's read! Within suspense there is considerable latitude regarding conventions of style, voice, and structure. From new suspense writers, editors look for originality and invention and new literary terrain, rather than a copycat version of last season's breakout work.

However, that said, writers should note that editors and readers are looking for works in which virtually every word, every scene, every blip of dialog serves to heighten suspense. This means that all imagery—from the weather to social setting, to the food ingested by the characters—is chosen by the writer to induce a sense of unease. Each scene (save maybe the last one) is constructed to raise questions or leave something unresolved. Every sentence or paragraph contains a possible pitfall. A given conversational exchange demonstrates edgy elementals of interpersonal tension. Everything looks rosy in one scene? Gotcha! It's a setup to reveal later what hell lurks underneath. Tell me some good news? Characters often do just that, as a prelude to showing just how wrong things can get.

The jeopardy story (or, as is often the case, a woman-in-jeopardy story) reflects a premise, rather than being a genre per se. A tale of jeopardy—a character under continuous, increasing threat and (often) eventual entrapment—can incorporate what is otherwise a psychological suspense novel, a medical thriller, an investigatory trajectory, or a slasher-stalker spree.

Additional subdivisions here include romantic suspense (in which a love relationship plays an essential or dominant role (see Romance Fiction), erotic suspense (which is not necessarily identical to neurotic suspense), and psychological suspense (see immediately following).

SUSPENSE/PSYCHOLOGICAL

When drifts of character, family history, or other psychodynamics are central to a suspense story's progress and resolution, the tale may aptly be typified as psychological. Sometimes superficial shticks or gimmicks suffice (such as when a person of a certain gender turns out to be cross-dressed—surprise!), but such spins work best when the suspense is tied to crucial issues the writer evokes in the characters' and readers' heads and then orchestrates skillfully throughout the story line.

There are, obviously, crossover elements at play here, and whether a particular work is presented as suspense, psychological suspense, or erotic suspense can be more of an advertising-copywriting decision than a determination on the part of editor or author.

THRILLER

The thriller category is exemplified more by plot structure than by attributes of character, content, or story milieu. A thriller embodies what is essentially an extended game of pursuit—a hunt, a chase, a flight worked fugue-like through endless variations.

At one point in the history of narrative art, thrillers were almost invariably spy stories, with international casts and locales, often set in a theater of war (hot or cold). With shifts in political agendas and technical achievement in the real world, the thriller formula has likewise evolved. Today's thriller may well involve espionage, which can be industrial or political, domestic or international. There are also thrillers that favor settings in the realms of medicine, the law, the natural environs, the human soul, and the laboratory; this trend has given rise to the respective genres of legal thriller, medical thriller, environmental thriller, thrillers with spiritual and mystical themes, and the technothriller—assuredly there are more to come.

The thriller story line can encompass elements of detection or romance and certainly should be full of suspense, but these genre-specific sequences are customarily expositional devices or may be one of many ambient factors employed to accentuate tension within the central thriller plot. When you see a dust jacket blurb that depicts a book as a mystery thriller, it likely connotes a work with a thriller plot trajectory that uses an investigatory or detective-work premise to prepare for the chase.

WESTERN FICTION

The tradition of Western fiction is characterized as much by its vision of the individualist ethic as it is by its conventional settings in the frontier milieu of the American West during the period from the 1860s to the 1890s, sometimes extending into the early 1900s. Though the image of the lone, free-spirited cowpoke with an internalized code of justice has been passed down along the pulp-paper trail, it has long been appreciated by historians that the life of the average itinerant ranch-hand of the day was anything but glamorous, anything but independent.

Whatever the historical record, editors by and large believe readers don't want to hear about the lackluster aspects of saddle tramps and dust-busting ruffians. Nevertheless, there have been inroads by books that display the historically accurate notions that a good chunk of the Western scene was inhabited by women and men of African American heritage, by those with Latino cultural affinities, by Asian expatriates, and by European immigrants for whom English was a second language, as well as by a diversity of native peoples.

Apart from the traditional genre Western, authors are equipped for a resurgence in a variety of novels with Western settings, most notably in the fields of mystery, crime, action-adventure, suspense, and future fiction. Among the newer Western novels are those replete with offbeat, unheroic, and downright antiheroic protagonists; and the standardized big-sky landscape has been superseded by backdrops that go against the grain.

Family sagas have long included at least a generation or two who drift, fight, and homestead through the Western Frontier. In addition, a popular genre of historical romance is set in the American West (see Romance Fiction).

Many contemporary commercial novels are set in the Western United States, often featuring plush resorts, urban and suburban terrain, as well as the remaining wide country. The wide variety of project ideas generated by writers, as well as the reader response to several successful ongoing mystery series with Western elements, indicates a lively interest out there.

WOMEN'S FICTION

When book publishers speak of women's fiction, they're not referring to a particular genre or story concept (even if they think they are). This category—if it is one—is basically a nod to the prevalence of fiction readers who are women. Women's fiction is a marketing concept. As an informal designation, women's fiction as a matter of course can be expected to feature strong female characters and, frequently, stories offered from a woman's perspective.

As for the writers of books in this category—many (if not most) are women, but certainly not all of them are; the same observation applies to readers. Men can and do read these works, too—and many professional male writers calculate potential readership demographics (including gender) as they work out details of story and plot.

In essence, what we've got is storytelling that can appeal to a broad range of readers, but may be promoted principally to the women's market. It makes it easier to focus the promotion and to pass along tips to the publisher's sales representatives.

Many women writers consider their work in abstract compositional terms, regardless of whom it is marketed to. Other women writers may be publicized as cultural pundits, perhaps as feminists, though they don't necessarily see their message as solely women-oriented. Are they women writers or simply writers? So long as sales go well, they may not even care.

Some women writers adopt the genderless pose of the literary renegade as they claw their way through dangerous domains of unseemly characterization, engage in breakthrough storytelling techniques, and explore emergent modes of love. (After all, how can a force of nature be characterized by sex?) Any and all of these female wordsmiths may find themselves publicized as women authors.

Romantic fiction constitutes one large sector of the women's market, for many of the conventions of romance tap into culturally significant areas of the love relationship of proven interest to women bookbuyers.

Descriptive genre phrases pop in and out of usage; some of them trip glibly from the tongue and are gone forevermore, while others represent established literary norms that endure: kitchen fiction, mom novels, family sagas, domestic dramas, historical romances, chick lit, lipstick fiction, erotic thrillers. When these popular titles are written, promoted, or both, in ways intended to pique the interest of women readers, whatever else they may be, they're automatically women's fiction.

SELF PUBLISHING

JEFF HERMAN

any books in print have sold hundreds of thousands of copies but will never appear on any lists, nor will they ever be seen in a bookstore, nor will the authors ever care. Why? Because these authors are self-publishers and make as much as a 90 percent profit margin on each copy they sell.

Their initial one-time start-up cost to get each of their titles produced may have been $15,000, but after that, each 5,000-copy print run of a hardcover edition costs about $1.25 per unit. The authors sell them for $25 each. When they do a high-volume corporate sale, they're happy to discount the books 20 percent or more off the $25 list price.

Now, we said that no bookstores are in the picture. Then how and where are the authors selling their books? The answer to this question is also the answer to whether it makes sense for you to self-publish. Here's what these authors do:

1. A well-linked Web site designed to sell and upsell.

2. A well-oiled corporate network, which translates into frequent high-volume orders by companies that distribute the book in-house as an educational tool or distribute them at large as a sales vehicle (customized printings are no problem).

3. Frequent public speaking events where backroom sales happen.

4. Frequent and self-generated publicity that's designed to promote the books and leads people to the Web site, a toll free number, or both.

Obviously, most of us don't have this kind of in-house infrastructure, which brings us back to the most important question: How will you sell copies of your self-published book? If you don't have a realistic answer in place, then self-publishing may not be a viable option after all, or at least your initial expectations have to be reoriented.

Why can self-publishers make so much money? Because they get to keep it. Here's how a conventional book publisher's deal gets divided up:

- Start with a trade paperback listed at $20.

- $10 goes to the retailer.

- $1.50 goes to the author.

- The first $15,000 goes to set the book up.

- $1.00 goes to printing each copy.

- $? Corporate overhead. (If the publisher overpaid on the advance, then this number goes higher.)

- $?? Publisher's profit. (This is a real wild card. If a publisher is an inefficient operation, than any profit may be out of reach. If too few books sell, there are only losses, no matter how lean and mean the publisher may be.)

A secondary source of no-overhead revenues for both publishers and self-publishers is ancillary rights, which includes exports, translations, and audio editions.

What's clear is that the published author makes a tiny fraction of the per-unit sale versus what the self-publisher makes. But the publisher also absorbs all the risks. And then there's the distribution factor…

WHAT'S DISTRIBUTION?

AND WHY DO SELF-PUBLISHERS HAVE A TOUGH TIME WITH IT?

Because everyone else does, too. Distribution is the process that gets books onto shelves, theoretically. Strong distribution does not ensure that bookstores will elect to stock the title. Too many books are published, compared to the quantity and quality of shelf space to accommodate them. You can have a big-name publisher and an invisible book. Distribution only generates the potential for the book to be available in stores, and nonexistent distribution deletes that potential.

All established book publishers have proven distribution channels in place, consisting of warehouses, fulfillment and billing operations, and traveling or regional salespeople who pitch the stores.

Smaller-sized presses may not be able to afford all of that, so they'll pay a 15 percent commission to a large house to handle it for them, or they will retain an independent distributor that does nothing but distribute for small presses.

Brick and mortar bookstores are not eager to open accounts with self-publishers. It's too much of a hassle. Same goes for independent distributors.

Several brilliant self-publishing consultants have devised ways to bypass these distribution obstacles. Look for their books in the "Suggested Resources" section of this book.

Vanity publishing is for morons. I don't mean to be insulting. It's just that you end up spending so much more than necessary, all for the illusion that you've been published in the conventional sense. In truth, the only thing you'll get out of the deal are boxes of expensive books that were probably not edited or well produced.

Hiring qualified editors, consultants, and so on, to help you make the best self-published book possible does not fall under the vanity label.

CAN SELF-PUBLISHERS SELL THEIR BOOKS TO CONVENTIONAL PUBLISHERS? SHOULD THEY WANT TO?

THE ANSWERS TO THE ABOVE QUESTIONS ARE: "YES" AND "MAYBE".

For the sake of clarity, a "conventional" publisher is a house that publishes books that are written by other people, as opposed to having been written by the same people who own or run the house. From hereon, I'll refrain from having to use the word conventional.

A self-published book may have sold as many as one million copies (a few actually have), but publishers may still deem the book as virtually unpublished. Why? Because publishers essentially focus on retail sales, and within retail sales, most of their focus is on bookstores. Few publishers have the capacity or mandate to sell books in other ways. Large non-store sales frequently happen, but generally because the buyers have come to the publisher to purchase or co-market the title in question, not because the publisher has been especially aggressive or innovative about generating such deals.

It follows that self-published books that have not penetrated bookstore shelves in any meaningful way, can still be seen as virgin meat by publishers, even if sales have been tremendous beyond the stores. As publishers see it, the bookstore represents an entirely new population of potential consumers who have not yet been tapped by whatever other sales activities the author has in place. Interestingly, consumers who purchase their books in stores are different then consumers who purchase books in other ways.

What's also interesting is just because a book is very successful outside the stores, does not necessarily mean that it will achieve the same or any success in the stores. The reverse is also true. Why? The answer should be obvious in a general sense: Consumers who buy books through infomercials, web sites, SPAMs, direct mail and at public events, may never go to bookstores. Conversely, consumers who go to bookstores may not be nearly as reachable through these other channels.

At a minimum, publishers evaluate self-published books as if they are untested raw manuscripts, and all consideration will be based upon the publisher's sense of the work's salability in bookstores. At a maximum, the publisher will take into consideration the self-published book's sales history and the author's ability to manifest those results. If it's believed that the author can duplicate her proven capacity to sell books once the product makes it into the stores, then that will add leverage to the kind of deal the author can make with a publisher.

Even if a self-published book did not sell very many copies, a publisher may still be very happy to pick it up if they can see that it has unfulfilled potential once it has distribution behind it. Publishers do not have any expectations that self-publishers can or should be able to succeed by themselves. But once again, even a successful self-publisher may not be able to interest a publisher, if the publisher does not think that the success can be transferred to bookstores.

Why would a successful self-publisher even want to give up his rights to a publisher? After all, the per-copy profit margin greatly surpasses the per-copy royalty. However, there are several good reasons why going over to the "other side" can be a shrewd move. Basically, the self-publisher would want to achieve the best of both worlds. She would want to be able to buy copies of the book from her publisher at a very high discount, so that she can still sell the copies through non-bookstore channels at an excellent margin. At the same time, the publisher would be selling the book in her behalf through bookstores, something she was unable to do by herself, thereby generating new revenues that would not have been earned otherwise.

If one of the self-published author's goals is to use the book as a medium for selling additional goods and services, then maximizing distribution may actually be more crucial than the per-copy profits, and bookstores are a wonderful way to "meet" quality consumers.

What all of this reveals is that self-publishers have to develop a flexible form of logic when it comes to understanding who buys books, and who conventional publishers know how to sell books to. Pretty much everyone buys certain kinds of food and clothing in predictable ways. But until you immerse yourself into the "laws" of the book market, you may be confused at what first appears to be the relative randomness of what books people buy, and how and where they get bought. If you are able to accept the apparent nonsense of it all, and open your mind to seeing through the dissonance into the way the book universe functions, then 2 + 2 will again equal 4, and you will also end up being a bit smarter than you were before.

THE AMAZON FACTOR

Over the last couple of years, many self-publishers have discovered clever ways for their books to reach the top 100 ranking on Amazon; a few have even managed to hit the #1 spot. The same is also true for some conventionally published authors.

Several highly paid consultants have made it their specialty to teach authors how to manipulate Amazon sales. It basically comes down to getting as many people as possible to buy the book from Amazon on a given day, which artificially spikes its ranking. Due to the growing prevalence of this strategy, it's not uncommon for an obscure book to abruptly become an Amazon Bestseller for a single day, and then revert to its natural stratospheric ranking.

The Amazon sales probably have nil impact on brick and mortar sales, and the marketing costs to drive the sales probably eat whatever extra revenues are generated.

So why do it? There are many valid reasons, such as: 1) Even fleeting visibility generated by a high ranking might attract lasting momentum and attention. 2) It's valuable and feels good to say and document that you were an Amazon Bestseller. 3) It might achieve specific professional benefits that go beyond simply selling a book.

THE GOOGLE FACTOR

Not only can none of us ever hide, but we can also make sure people find what we want them to.

Google has become the dominant search engine, to the extent that people now routinely say, "Google me/yourself/it/them". That could change, by the way. A few decades ago we used to say, "Make me a Xerox". I can't recall the last time I've seen a Xerox machine in person. Whatever the brand, search engines are obviously here to stay, and will become progressively more precise and invasive.

Like the Amazon Factor, many consultants have emerged who charge top dollar to help people achieve top Google rankings. You can also just pay Google a lot of money for high visibility. One common formula is to pay every time you get a "hit". However, this has been a big mistake for some entrepreneurs who ended up owing a lot of money for a huge surge of hits that failed to generate any actual sales. Everything has a learning curve, and we all try not to be the ones who get smashed into the curve while taking calculated risks. The bottom-line is that search engines, and the Internet in general, are still relatively new frontiers for creative "small fries", which includes self-publishers, to score out-sized results.

THE WRITER'S JOURNEY
THE PATH OF THE SPIRITUAL MESSENGER

DEBORAH LEVINE HERMAN

If you have decided to pursue writing as a career instead of as a longing or a dream, you might find yourself focusing on the goal instead of the process. When you have a great book idea, you may envision yourself on a booksigning tour or as a guest on a talk show before you've written a single word.

It's human nature to look into your own future, but too much projection can get in the way of what the writing experience is all about. The process of writing is like a wondrous journey that can help you cross a bridge to the treasures hidden within your own soul. It is a way for you to link with God and the collective storehouse of all wisdom and truth, as it has existed since the beginning of time.

Many methods of writing bring their own rewards. Some people can produce exceptional prose by using their intellect and their mastery of the writing craft. They use research and analytical skills to help them produce works of great importance and merit.

Then there are those who have learned to tap into the wellspring from which all genius flows. They are the inspired ones who write with the intensity of an impassioned lover. They are the spiritual writers who write because they have to. They may not want to, they may not know how to, but something inside them is begging to be let out. It gnaws away at them until they find a way to set it free. Although they may not realize it, spiritual writers are engaged in a larger spiritual journey toward ultimate self-mastery and unification with God.

Spiritual writers often feel as if they're taking dictation. Spiritual writing has an otherworldly feeling and can teach writers things they would otherwise not have known. It is not uncommon to read something after a session in "the zone," and question if indeed you had written it.

Writing opens you up to new perspectives, much like self-induced psychotherapy. Although journals are the most direct route for self-evaluation, fiction and nonfiction also serve as vehicles for a writer's growth. Writing helps the mind expand to the limits of the imagination.

Anyone can become a spiritual writer, and there are many benefits to doing so, not the least of which is the development of your soul. On a more practical level, it is much less difficult to write with flow and fervor than it is to be bound by the limitations of logic and analysis. If you tap into the universal source, there is no end to your potential creativity.

The greatest barrier to becoming a spiritual writer is the human ego. We treat our words as if they were our children—only we tend to be neurotic parents. Children are not owned by parents, but rather must be loved, guided, and nurtured until they can carry on, on their own.

The same is true for our words. If we try to own and control them like property, they will be limited by our vision for them. We will overprotect them and will not be able to see when we may be taking them in the wrong direction for their ultimate well-being. Another ego problem that creates a barrier to creativity is our need for constant approval and our tendency toward perfectionism. We may feel the tug toward free expression, but will erect blockades to ensure appropriate style and structure. We write with a "schoolmarm" hanging over our shoulders, waiting to tell us what we are doing wrong.

Style and structure are important to ultimate presentation, but that is what editing is for. Ideas and concepts need to flow like water in a running stream. The best way to become a spiritual writer is to relax and have fun. If you are relaxed and pray for guidance, you'll be open to intuition and higher truth. However, Writers tend to take themselves too seriously, which causes anxiety, which exacerbates fear, which causes insecurity, which diminishes our self-confidence and leads ultimately to mounds of crumpled papers and lost inspiration. You are worthy. Do not let insecurity prevent you from getting started and following through.

If you have faith in a Supreme Being, the best way to begin a spiritual writing session is with the following writer's prayer:

Almighty God (Jesus, Allah, Great Spirit, etc.), Creator of the Universe, help me to become a vehicle for your wisdom so that what I write is of the highest purpose and will serve the greatest good. I humbly place my (pen/keyboard/Dictaphone) in your hands so that you may guide me.

Prayer helps to connect you to the universal source. It empties the mind of trash, noise, and potential writer's blocks. If you are not comfortable with formal prayer, a few minutes of meditation will serve the same purpose. Spiritual writing as a process does not necessarily lead to a sale. The fact is that some people have more commercial potential than others. Knowledge of the business of writing will help you make a career of it. If you combine this with the spiritual process, it can also bring you gratification and inner peace. If you trust the process of writing and make room for the journey you will grow and achieve far beyond your expectations.

Keep in mind that you are not merely a conduit. You are to be commended and should take pride in the fact that you allow yourself to be used as a vessel for the Divine. You are the one who is taking the difficult steps in a world full of obstacles and challenges. You are the one who is sometimes so pushed to the edge that you have no idea how you go on. But you do. You maintain your faith and you know that there is a reason for everything. You may not have a clue what it is…but you have an innate sense that all of your experiences are part of some bigger plan. At minimum they create good material for your book.

In order to be a messenger of the Divine you have to be a vessel willing to get out of the way. You need to be courageous and steadfast in your beliefs because God's truth is your truth. When you find that your inner truth does not match that of other people, you need to be strong enough to stay true to yourself. Your soul, that inner spark that connects you to all creation is your only reliable guide. You will receive pressure from everywhere. But your relationship with your creator is as personal as your DNA. You will be a house divided if you accept things other people tell you to please them while sensing that it does not resonate with your spirit.

When you do find your inner truth your next challenge is to make sure that you do not become the person that tries to tell everyone else what to believe. When a spiritual writer touches that moment of epiphany it is easy to become God-intoxicated. There is no greater bliss than to be transformed by a connection to source of all Creation. It is not something that can be described. It is individual. This is why it is important for a spiritual writer to protect this experience for another seeker. The role of a spiritual messenger who manifests his or her mission through the written word, is to guide a person to the threshold of awakening. Bring them to the gate but allow God to take them the rest of the way. Your job is to make the introduction. From there the relationship is no longer your responsibility. Your task is to shine the light brightly for some other seeker to find it.

It is difficult to believe so strongly in something while feeling unable to find anyone to listen to you. If you try too hard you might find that there are others who will drain your energy and lifeforce, while giving nothing in return. They may ridicule you and cause you to step away from your path. You do not have to change the world by yourself. You need to do your part. Whether it is visible or as simple as helping someone know you care, you are participating in elevating the world for the better. Some people like it exactly as it is. There are those who thrive on chaos and the diseases of the soul. Your job as a spiritual writer is to protect your spirit as you would your own child. Do not give away your energy, make it available for those who truly want it and will appreciate it. When you write, expect nothing in return. While following the protocols of the business world, do not set your goal too high as needing to transform people's souls. If you do, you will elevate your responsibility beyond the capability of simple humans. If you do the groundwork, God will do the rest.

The world of the spiritual writer can be a very lonely place. It is easier to love God, creation and humanity, than it is to feel worthy of receiving the love in return. Those of us who devote our energy to wanting to make a difference through our writing forget that God has given us this gift as a reward for our goodness, faith and love. It is a two way street. What we give we can also receive. It maintains the balance. It replenishes our energy so we can continue to grow and fulfill our individual destiny. We are all loved unconditionally. God knows everything we have ever thought, done or even thought about doing. We judge ourselves far more harshly than God ever would. We come into this world to learn and to fix our "miss" takes. We only learn through object lessons. We have free will. Sometimes we have to burn our hands on the stove several times before we learn that it is too hot to handle. I personally have lived my life with the two by four on the head method. While not recommended, it is the only way I have been able to learn some of my more difficult lessons. I have often considered wearing a helmet.

When we connect with our inner truth we can become intoxicated with our own greatness. It is a very heady thing to write, especially if we are able to see our name in print. If we have people listening to what we have to say, we can believe that we are the message and forget that we are merely the messenger. Spiritual writers need to start every day praying for humility. If we don't, and there is danger that we are going to put ourselves before the purity of Divine truth, we will not be able to be the pure vessel that we had hoped to become. The universe has methods of protecting itself. We will experience humiliation to knock us down a few pegs to give us the opportunity to get over ourselves. I have experienced many instances of humorous humiliation such as feeling so amazed with myself only to literally splat on my face by tripping over air. No injury, except to my inflated pride. God has a sense of humor.

On a more serious note, spiritual messengers who are taken in by their own egos are vulnerable to negativity. The information they convey becomes deceiving and can help take people off their paths. This is why spiritual writers should always begin each session with a prayer to be a vessel for the highest of the high and for the greater good. While readers have the choice to discern the wheat from the chaff, in this time of rapid spiritual growth, it is important to help seekers stay as close to their paths as possible. There is no time for major detours. We all have a lot of work to do.

We are all here to improve the lives of each other. We are blessed with living in an information age where we can communicate quickly and clearly with one another. However, technology also serves to make us separate. We all cling to our ideas without respecting the paths of one another. We are all headed to the same place; the center of the maze where there is nothing and everything all at once. We are all headed for the place of pure love that binds all of us to one another. We don't want to get caught up with trivial arguments about who is right and who is wrong. Our goal right now needs to be how to foster everyone's path to his or her own higher truth. We share what we have so others can find it, without wasting time arguing the point to win them to our side. Too many battles have been fought over who is the most right. We all come from the same source.

When it comes down to it, spiritual writers are the prophets of today. You are here to give God direct access to our world in ways that we as human beings can understand. We need to listen to the essence of the message rather than focusing on who is the greater prophet. In the business of writing, there is no sin in profit. But in the mission of writing, one must not forget that we all answer to the same boss and serve the same master.

You are also a messenger. When you agree to be a spiritual writer, you are also agreeing to bring light into the world. This is no small commitment. Remember to keep your ego out of it. While it is important to learn to promote and support your work, you must not forget that you are the messenger and not the message. If you keep this at the center of your heart and remember that you serve the greater good, you are a true spiritual writer who is honoring the call. May God bless you and guide you always.

REJECTED...AGAIN

THE PROCESS AND THE ART OF PERSEVERANCE

JEFF HERMAN

ADVICE FOR WRITERS

Trying to sell your writing is in many ways similar to perpetually applying for employment, and it's likely you will run into many walls. That can hurt. But even the Great Wall of China has a beginning and an end—for it's simply an external barrier erected for strategic purposes. In my experience, the most insurmountable walls are the ones in our heads. Anything that is artificially crafted can and will be overcome by people who are resourceful and determined enough to do it.

Naturally, the reality of rejection cannot be completely circumvented. It is, however, constructive to envision each wall as a friendly challenge to your resourcefulness, determination, and strength. There are many people who got through the old Berlin Wall because for them it was a challenge and a symbol—a place to begin, not stop.

The world of publishing is a potentially hostile environment, especially for the writer. Our deepest aspirations can be put to rest without our having achieved peace or satisfaction. But it is within each of us to learn about this special soil and blossom to our fullest. No rejection is fatal until the writer walks away from the battle, leaving the written work behind, undefended and unwanted.

WHY MOST REJECTION LETTERS ARE SO EMPTY

What may be most frustrating are the generic word-processed letters that say something like: "not right for us." Did the sender read any of your work? Did that person have any personal opinions about it? Could she not have spared a few moments to share her thoughts?

As an agent, it's part of my job to reject the vast majority of the submissions I receive. And with each rejection, I know I'm not making someone happy. On the other hand, I don't see spreading happiness as my exclusionary purpose. Like other agents and editors, I make liberal use of the generic rejection letter.

Here's why: Too much to do, too little time. There just isn't sufficient time to write customized, personal rejection letters. To be blunt about it, the rejection process isn't a profit center; it does consume valuable time that otherwise could be used to make profits. The exceptions to this rule are the excessive-fee-charging operations that make a handsome profit with each rejection.

In most instances, the rejection process is "giveaway" time for agents and editors since it takes us away from our essential responsibilities. Even if no personal comments are provided with the rejections, it can require many hours a week to process an ongoing stream of rejections. An understaffed literary agency or publishing house may feel that it's sufficiently generous simply to assign a paid employee the job of returning material as opposed to throwing it away. (And some publishers and literary agencies do in practice simply toss the greater portion of their unsolicited correspondence.) Agents and editors aren't Dear Abby, though many of us wish we had the time to be.

Therefore, your generic rejection means no more and no less than that particular agent/editor doesn't want to represent/publish you and (due to the volume of office correspondence and other pressing duties) is relaying this information to you in an automated, impersonal way. The contents of the letter alone will virtually never reveal any deeper meanings or secrets. To expect or demand more than this might be perceived as unfair by the agent/editor.

KNOW WHEN TO HOLD, KNOW WHEN TO FOLD

It's your job to persevere. It's your mission to proceed undaunted. Regardless of how many books about publishing you've read, or how many writers' conferences you've attended, it's up to no one but you to figure out how and when to change your strategy if you want to win at the book-publishing game.

If your initial query results are blanket rejects, then it may be time to back off, reflect, and revamp your query presentation or overall approach. If there are still no takers, you may be advised to reconceive your project in light of its less-than-glorious track record. Indeed, there might even come a time for you to use your experience and newfound knowledge of what does and doesn't grab attention from editors and agents—and move on to that bolder, more innovative idea you've been nurturing in the back of your brain.

AN AUTHENTIC SUCCESS STORY

Several years ago, two very successful, though unpublished, gentlemen came to see me with a nonfiction book project. My hunch was that it would make a lot of money. The writers were professional speakers and highly skilled salespeople, so I arranged for them to meet personally with several publishers, but to no avail.

All told, we got more than 20 rejections—the dominant reason being that editors thought the concept and material weak. Not ones to give up, and with a strong belief in their work and confidence in their ability to promote, the authors were ultimately able to sell the book for a nominal advance to a small Florida publishing house—and it was out there at last, published and in the marketplace.

As of this writing, *Chicken Soup for the Soul*, by Jack Canfield and Mark Victor Hansen, has sold millions of copies and has been a *New York Times* bestseller for several years straight. Furthermore, this initial success has generated many bestselling sequels.

We all make mistakes, and the book rascals in New York are definitely no exception. Most important, Canfield and Hansen didn't take no for an answer. They instinctively understood that all those rejections were simply an uncomfortable part of a process that would eventually get them where they wanted to be. And that's the way it happened.

A RELENTLESS APPROACH TO SELLING YOUR BOOK

I once heard a very telling story about Jack Kerouac, one from which we can all learn something. Kerouac was a notorious literary figure who reached his professional peak in the 1950s. He's one of the icons of the Beat Generation and is perhaps best remembered for his irreverent and manic travel-memoir-as-novel *On the Road*.

SALES TALES FROM THE BEAT GENERATION

The story begins when Kerouac was a young and struggling writer, ambitiously seeking to win his day in the sun. He was a charismatic man and had acquired many influential friends. One day Kerouac approached a friend who had access to a powerful publishing executive. Kerouac asked the friend to hand-deliver his new manuscript to the executive, with the advice that it be given prompt and careful consideration.

When the friend handed the manuscript to the executive, the executive took one glance and began to laugh. The executive explained that two other people had hand-delivered the very same manuscript to him within the last few weeks.

What this reveals is that Kerouac was a master operator. Not only did he manage to get his work into the right face, but also he reinforced his odds by doing it redundantly. Some might say he was a manipulator, but his works were successfully published, and he did attain a measure of fame in his own day, which even now retains its luster.

...AND FROM THE BEATEN

I will now share a very different and more recent story. It starts in the 1940s, when a bestselling and Pulitzer Prize-winning young-adult book was published. Titled *The*

Yearling, this work was made into an excellent movie starring Gregory Peck. The book continues to be a good backlist seller.

In the 1990s, a writer in Florida, where *The Yearling*'s story takes place, performed an experiment. He converted the book into a raw double-spaced manuscript and changed the title and author's name—but the book's contents were not touched. He then submitted the entire manuscript to about 20 publishers on an unagented/unsolicited basis. I don't believe the submissions were addressed to any specific editors by name.

Eventually, this writer received many form rejections, including one from the book's actual publisher. Several publishers never even responded. A small house in Florida did offer to publish the book.

What is glaringly revealed by this story? That even a Pulitzer Prize-winning novel will never see the light of day if the writer doesn't use his brain when it's time to sell the work.

HOW TO BEAT YOURSELF—AND HOW NOT TO

People who are overly aggressive do get a bad rap. As an agent and as a person, I don't like being hounded by salespeople—whether they're hustling manuscripts or insurance policies. But there are effective ways to be heard and seen without being resented. Virtually anyone can scream loud enough to hurt people's ears. Only an artist understands the true magic of how to sell without abusing those who might buy. And we all have the gift to become artists in our own ways.

Here's an example of what not to do:

It's late in the day and snowing. I'm at my desk, feeling a lot of work-related tension. I answer the phone. It's a first-time fiction writer. He's unflinchingly determined to speak endlessly about his work, which I have not yet read.

I interrupt his meaningless flow to explain courteously that while I will read his work, it's not a good time for me to talk to him. But he will not let me go; he's relentless. Which forces me to be rude and cold as I say "Bye" and hang up.

I then resent the thoughtless intrusion upon my space and time. And I may feel bad about being inhospitable to a stranger, whatever the provocation.

Clearly, the previous scenario does not demonstrate a good way to initiate a deal. I'm already prejudiced against this writer before reading his work.

Here's a more effective scenario:

Same conditions as before. I answer the telephone. The caller acknowledges that I must be busy and asks for only 30 seconds of my time. I grant them. He then begins to compliment me; he's heard I'm one of the best, and so forth. I'm starting to like this conversation; I stop counting the seconds.

Now he explains that he has an excellent manuscript that he is willing to give me the opportunity to read and would be happy to send it right over. He then thanks me for my time and says good-bye.

I hang up, feeling fine about the man; I'll give his manuscript some extra consideration.

In conclusion, relentless assertiveness is better than relentless passivity. But you want your style to be like Julie Andrews's singing voice in *The Sound of Music*, as opposed to a 100-decibel boom box on a stone floor.

TRIBULATIONS OF THE UNKNOWN WRITER (AND POSSIBLE REMEDIES)

JEFF HERMAN

Many nations have memorials that pay homage to the remains of their soldiers who died in battle and cannot be identified. In a way, it seems that the legions of unpublished writers are the *Unknown Writers*. As has been expressed elsewhere in this book, it cannot be assumed that the unknown writer and her unknown work are of any lesser quality than those works that achieve public exposure and consumption, any more than those soldiers who died were less adept than those who got to go home. To the contrary, perhaps they were more adept, or at least more daring, and therefore paid the ultimate price.

No warrior aspires to become an unknown soldier, let alone a dead soldier. Every soldier prefers to believe that her remains would be known; would perhaps even explain what happened towards the end, and would be presented to her loved ones for final and proper farewells. It is much the same for the writer. No writer worth her ink wants to believe that her legacy of expression will be forever unknown. Even if her other accomplishments in life are magnificent, it is still those words on the pages that she wants revealed, preferably while she's still around to experience and enjoy it.

Obviously, in life and beyond, there are many unknown writers. That's just the way it is.

It may just be that the fear of living and dying as an unknown writer is the extra push you need to bring your work to the first step on the road to publication—getting your work noticed by a publishing professional, be it agent or editor. If you are still reading this essay, then it is absolutely true that you are willing to try harder to reach that goal. In recognition and respect for your aspirations and determination, I will provide additional insights and strategies to help you help yourself avoid the fate of the unknown writer.

But let's make sure that your goals, at least in the early stages of your publishing life, are reasonably measured. It is suitable to imagine yourself one day at the top of the publishing food chain. Why not? Genuine humans have to be there at any given moment, so why not you? However, it is improbable that you will arrive there in one step. Your odds will be enhanced through your dedication to learning, calculating, and paying the necessary dues. For the purposes of the lesson at hand, I will encourage you to focus on the more humble goal of simply transitioning to the realm of being a published writer. For sure, there is more to do after that, but we will leave those lessons for other places in this book, and for other books.

WAYS TO BE SEEN IN A CROWD

Established literary agencies, including yours truly's, are inundated with unsolicited query letters (both hard and digital), proposals, pieces of manuscripts, and entire manuscripts. This stream of relentless *in-take* easily runs from 50 to 150 uninvited submissions per week, depending on how visible the agency in question is to the world of writers at large. These numbers do not account for the many works that the agency has requested or were expecting from existing clients. Frankly, many successful agents are simply not hungry for more than what they already have, and make efforts to be as invisible and unavailable as possible.

The above scenario only tells of the agencies. It's likely that the publishers, both big and small, are receiving the same in even greater volumes, which is of dubious value since many publishers will simply not consider anything that is unsolicited or unrepresented, period.

How can your work go from being an unseen face in the crowd to a jack-in-the-box whose presence cannot be denied? Here are some suggested steps.

1. Don't merely do what everyone else is already doing. That doesn't mean that you should entirely refrain from doing what's conventional or recommended. After all, the beaten track is beaten for a reason: It has worked before and it will work again. But be open to the possibility of pursuing specific detours along the way. Look upon these excursions as a form of calculated wildcatting. If nothing happens, or if you end up puncturing the equivalent of someone's septic tank, then just take it as a lesson learned.

2. Make yourself be seen. A pile of No. 10 envelopes is simply that, and none of the component envelopes that form the pile are seen. Someone once sent me a letter shaped like a circle. It could not be grouped with that day's quota of query letters; it demanded to be seen and touched and dealt with, immediately. Another time I received a box designed as a treasure chest, which contained an unsolicited proposal. I did not appreciate receiving a bag of white powder with a certain proposal. The powder was flushed down the toilet and the manuscript returned without being read.

3. Be generous. Most submissions are actually a demand for time, attention and

energy. During a long day in the middle of a stressful week in the throes of a month in hell, none of those submissions will be seen as good faith opportunities from honorable people. To the contrary, they will feel like innumerable nuisances springing forth from the armpits of manic brain-eating zombies, with drool and odor. I can recall opening a package to find a handwritten card from a stranger telling me how much he appreciated my wonderful contributions to the business and how much I have helped him and others, etc., etc. I always remember those kinds of things; wouldn't you?

4. Don't be a nag, be a gift. Everyone likes gifts, and nobody likes nags. So why do so many aspiring writers (and others) act out like nags? It's counterintuitive. Of course, nature teaches us from the moment we are born that the noisy baby gets the tit. Passivity invites neglect. Noise attracts attention. What an interesting conundrum. Nagging is bad. Passivity leads to death. Noise can't be ignored. Well, all of that is equally valid, and none of it disqualifies the original point that you are a gift, so act like one.

5. Keep knocking, even after the door is opened. That does not make sense, and it might not be appreciated. But if someone were to keep knocking on my door even after I opened it, I would simply have to ask that person why he or she is doing that, and therein is the beginning of a conversation. Of course, it may all go down hill from there, but then it may not. What happens next depends on the nature of the conversation that has just been launched, regardless of its weird genesis.

6. Don't ask for anything, but offer whatever you can. If that is the energy projected throughout your communications, you will attract due wealth. However, the word due is rather crucial in this context. A well-intentioned worm may end up on the end of a fish hook, and a nasty frog may be well-fed all summer. Too often people stop at just being nice, and then they become prey. Is it fair that they are eaten for doing nothing at all? Actually, that's exactly what they asked for, to end up nourishing the needs of others. We must all serve a purpose, and we must all consume to survive. If you don't wish to be consumed, then don't present yourself for that. The universe is a layered place of lessons and challenges, and being a writer is just one of many ways to play the game. Don't just give yourself away, anymore than you would throw yourself away. If you value the gems you wish to share, you will discern with whom to grant them, and simply refuse to participate with others.

7. Know your gifts and appreciate them. I can tell right away when I am reading a query letter from a writer who believes in herself and the quality of her product, and I can see those who are not so sure that they should even be trying. Sometimes the writer is apologetic, or even goes as far as asking me if they should be trying. Ironically, the writer's quality as a writer cannot be predicted by their

native sense of self worth. In fact, great literature has emerged from the hearts of those who are seemingly committed to a life of losing. But there is a logical explanation for that: To each writer is assigned a muse. Some writers may hate themselves while loving their muse, and it shows.

WHEN NOTHING HAPPENS TO GOOD (OR BAD) WRITERS

AKA IGNORED WRITER SYNDROME (IWS)

JEFF HERMAN

"I will not be ignored!" screams Alex Forrest, the book editor played by Glenn Close, to her philandering lover played by Michael Douglas in the classic film, *Fatal Attraction*.

What perfect karma, a book editor being ignored, even though her job was not relevant to the conflict. Too bad about the rabbit, though.

It's an inalienable truth that any writer who aggressively pitches his or her work will encounter abundant rejections along the way. You know that. But what you may not have been prepared for was the big-loud-deafening nothing at all. You followed the given protocols; have been gracious, humble and appreciative; and have done nothing egregious. And you would never boil a rabbit. So what's your reward? Absolutely nothing; you have been ignored.

A document stating that your work has been rejected, even if clearly generic, may be a much more welcome outcome than the silence of an empty universe. At least that formal rejection letter reflects that you are part of a genuine process. True, you have been turned away at the gate, but it still seems that you belong to a fraternity of sorts. It's like you're an understudy, or simply wait-listed. Your existence is acknowledged even if un-welcomed, whereas to be ignored is proof of nothing. Nature abhors a vacuum, and any writer with nerve endings will understand why soon enough, if not already.

I write this essay because of the frequent feedback I receive from readers complaining about the non-responsiveness of editors and agents. I have carefully considered this phenomenon and how it must negatively affect the morale and stamina of those who are endeavoring in good faith to be published. I have decided that to be ignored deserves its own category in the travails of writing, and that it inflicts even more pain and frustration than the proverbial rejection. I shall designate it with a logical term: Ignored.

Why are so many writers ignored by editors and agents? I will respond to that with questions of my own. Why are so many children ignored? Why are so many of the poor and needy ignored? Why are so many social problems ignored? I could ask this question in countless ways, and the primary universal answer would essentially remain the same: It's far easier to do nothing.

Let's get back to our specific context. Agents and editors have demanding, often tedious, workloads that overwhelm the typical 40-hour work week (they tend to put in way more hours than that, even though they can rarely bill by the hour or receive extra pay). They are rewarded for generating tangible results, which is most often measured in the form of monetary revenues. Taking the time to respond to writers, even in a purely perfunctory manner, might be the courteous thing to do, but neither their businesses nor bosses will reward their kindness. You may feel such inaction is a misguided and shortsighted "policy," and you might be right, but it doesn't change the facts as they are.

Does being ignored mean that you have actually been read and rejected? This question can't be answered, because you're being ignored. It's possible that someone did read your work and rejected it, and then threw it out even if a SASE was attached. Why would someone do that? Because it's much easier to and they can't justify the time it would take to answer as many as 100 submissions per week. It's also possible that your submission has not been read and may never be read, because nobody is available to screen the "incoming" in any organized fashion. It's not out of the question that submissions will accumulate in numerous piles and boxes for several years before they are simply discarded, never to be opened. Does this strike you as harsh or ridiculous? Whatever; it is the way it is.

What is certain is that if your work is read and accepted, you will hear about it.

In closing, my message to you is that you not allow being ignored to diminish your dreams and goals. It's simply a part of the process and part of the emotional overhead you might encounter on your road to success. It's also a crucial reason why you should not put all of your manuscripts in one basket. To do so may be tantamount to placing your entire career into a bottomless pit. Making multiple submissions is reasonable and wise if you consider the possible consequences of granting an exclusive without any deadline or two-way communications. Please refer to the other essays and words of advice in this book to keep yourself from becoming a victim of Ignored Writer Syndrome (IWS).

MAKING IT HAPPEN

DEBORAH LEVINE HERMAN

Nothing is better than having your first book published. You may want to believe that spouses, friends, children, and world peace are more important, but when you see your name and your words in print it is nothing short of ego ecstasy. Your publisher gives you a release date and you wait expectantly for the fanfare, but unless you're well known already (and remember, this is your first book), chances are your publisher will devote only modest publicity to your book.

It will be exciting if you are asked to do radio or television interviews, but do not expect Oprah fresh out of the gate. There are exceptions, of course, but it's important for you to know that most books don't receive extensive publisher support. It may not seem logical that a publisher would take you all the way to the mountain and not help you climb your way to the top, but it is the reality of the business. The reality is that the destiny of your book remains largely in your hands. With the right combination of drive, know-how, and chutzpah, you can make it happen for yourself.

IDEAS FOR MAKING IT HAPPEN

Here are some ideas for making it happen.

You can always hire a publicist. If you have the means, there are many publicists who can help you promote your book and who will do a lot of the work for you. You will have many great bragging opportunities when you work it into conversations that your publicist is setting your book tour.

Publicists are expensive and don't always deliver. You may want to check out our book *Make It Big Writing Books* to become publicist-savvy. This book contains interviews with top publicists, as well as some great promotion ideas. You can also read about how some bestselling authors made it to the top.

If you don't take the publicist route, you can do many things for yourself. Work with your publisher's publicity department. Its staff members may not invest their time and resources, but they should support your efforts.

As soon as you know the approximate date your book will be released to the bookstores, start your campaign. Ask your publicity department for review copies of book and create a target list of possible magazines, newsletters, Web sites, and newspapers that might want to review your book. Don't sit on this. Magazines work months in advance. If your book is coming out in April, you should be contacting magazines as early as you possibly can; six months in advance isn't too soon. March is way too late. If you can't get review copies, you should still find ways to query the magazines. You may be able to get copies of your book covers and provide sample chapters.

It will be helpful for you to create an attractive publicity packet. You will need a biography of yourself, a good photograph, a copy of the book cover or the material your publisher uses to sell your book to the bookstores, a news release about your book, and any other relevant information. Do not forget to put in contact information. Book endorsements are also great, if you have them.

This packet can be used for magazines and any other print media, as well as for television and radio. If you want to spare some expense, create a one-page information sheet that you can fax to prospects whom you also contact by phone. Lists of radio stations are available in the reference department of your public library. Radio interviews can be done by phone. The key is to create a hook that will entice radio producers to use you on their shows. Think in terms of a short explanatory sentence that captures the essence of your book in as few words as possible.

For book signings, contact the promotions person at the bookstores you target. If you plan to visit various cities on a self-designed book tour, contact bookstores and local media well in advance so they can publicize the event. Maximize your visit to each city with a coordinated plan that will help promote your signing.

If your book is fiction, you can arrange for events in which you read portions of your book for an audience. Venues are available beyond the bookstores, but you will need to be creative in determining what they are.

If your book is nonfiction, create a topic stemming from your book that can be the subject of a workshop or lecture. Many venues are available that could help you publicize the event. Don't worry if you don't make money through lectures. If you are part of a seminar company, the exposure it will give your book in the promotional materials alone will be valuable.

Be creative. Don't let your ego trick you into believing you are above the hard work it takes to make a book successful. Roll up your sleeves. If you are passionate about your book, you are the one who can best "make it happen."

...G A WORKING WRITER

... HERMAN

Writing a book and becoming published does not have to be a dream unfulfilled. Quite often people who have great writing skill or who love to write are unable to be published because they never find the right vehicle.

Many times when I am screening query letters I see writers with interesting backgrounds and credentials. I get excited when I read a "good voice." However, more often than not I am disappointed with the book they are proposing. We are largely a non-fiction agency, so what we look for has a lot to do with the content and the uniqueness of the idea.

Another interesting dilemma is when I do happen to read a fiction synopsis and notice the person has very interesting credentials. When I determine that the novel is sub par, I am confused why the person didn't just stick to what he knows. It seems to me that there are many would be novelists who view writing as a hobby one begins upon retirement from something else. It is a glamorous thought to rent a house in the woods so as to have months in seclusion to write the next classic work of literature. The problem is, to fulfill this dream; you have to know how to write.

There are many opportunities to learn the craft. If you write, you are a writer. I wholeheartedly support writing as a spiritual journey of self- discovery. The process may be the end in itself. There are only so many books that will be published each year. It is important to savor the experience of creative expression rather than obsessively looking for the validation that you believe only a publishing contract can provide.

If, however, you want to be a published writer and you are not married to the subject matter or the need to be a novelist, there are many opportunities for you. Like it or not, there is a type of informal formula that enters into the decisions editors make in choosing books for their lists. Their job is to fill slots so that their publishing house can have a varied catalogue of "product" that will appeal to the sales force and ultimately to the booksellers. That is the fact of the matter. Books are products. You need to create one that people want to buy.

If you can write and are willing to work with other people to help them express themselves through the written word, there is a need for you. It may not fulfill your ego needs, but it will fill your wallet and will help you hone your craft. You can work as a collaborator, ghostwriter, editor or book doctor. If you have some moxy you can choose a subject you would like to write about and find a professional who will add strength to your credentials. If you have skill and creativity and are willing to work hard, you are needed in this business.

The key is your willingness to work hard. Being a working writer means not waiting for the muse. It means discipline. Ugh, the "d," word. It is certainly not one I would apply to myself in many areas of my life. We writers can allow some latitude. We are not always like other "normal," people. I can write feverishly for two hours and then have to stop when the well runs dry. I can usually pull myself back into the zone if I am under deadline, but I try to follow my own rhythms. But discipline is needed to be able to see the task to completion.

I know this will sound like one of those "back in the day I had to walk five miles in the snow to get to school" stories, but when I wrote my first book it was a straight ghostwritten work for hire. I did not really know what I was doing, but I had studied journalism and had written some magazine articles that had been published. I got the job because I was at the right place at the right time, depending how you looked at it. The book was a royal pain in the arse. By the time I handed it in I must have earned five cents per hour. The good news is I learned how to write a book.

As in any career path, you have to pay your dues. There are those few overnight successes, but as in Hollywood, more often than not, the overnight success has had many sleepless nights of struggle.

If you want to be a working writer, write. Then put yourself out there to literary agents and some of the organizations that work with writers who are looking for freelance assignments. Remember, it is important that you are at least a competent writer. The more experience you have the better you are. It is better to undersell yourself and over-deliver. You will be building a track record that will lead to bigger and better assignments. Your reputation is paramount.

Once you are known to be a reliable and competent writer you will probably have more work than you will know what to do with. This does not mean that you should give up your personal dreams of "writing your own stuff." Never do that. But if you want to be able to give up your day job, you have to replace it with something tangible. Writing is also networking. If you have publishing credits it can only add to your ability to maneuver through the publishing industry.

Whether or not you choose to take the road of the "writer for hire," you need to be willing to put in the time and energy it takes to earn your success.

TIME MANAGEMENT

DEBORAH LEVINE HERMAN

It is probably more difficult for writers who do not have a separate day job to manage time and to meet deadlines. If you are a full-time writer, you are not confined to a structured day and have to be self-disciplined and self-motivated.

If you are by nature a methodical writer who keeps an orderly home and an efficient calendar, is always prompt, and never misses appointments, I truly envy you. If you are like me, all of the above require great effort and are probably much more challenging than writing itself.

I love any kind of creative endeavor and am passionate about writing. I am also easily distracted. If I am not under deadline, I work at home and am just as likely to wallpaper my house as I am to write a book proposal, query letter, or fiction piece. As you know, there are many things writers can be doing between assignments to further their careers. You can write, research, plan, or promote existing projects. You can also promote yourself to gain a forum for your ideas and future projects. Unfortunately, I sometimes like to procrastinate to the point that I am not even aware of how much time I may be wasting.

I do not recommend the unofficial Deborah Herman method of kamikaze writing. As my career has developed, I have been learning to improve my time-management techniques. I am a work-in-progress, but I can share what works for me.

TIME MANAGEMENT TECHNIQUES

If writing is what you do, you need to treat it as a job. It is fine if you want to think about it all the time and define yourself by it. But it is important for you to delineate between the work of writing and your life. Otherwise, you will wind up looking at the basic activities of life management as something akin to playing hooky from what you really "should" be doing. There are even times when I view housework as a treat because I am stealing time from my work. For anyone who knows me, that is truly a pitiful concept.

You need to set up a schedule that allows you to leave your work behind. If you commit to a deadline, you must evaluate approximately how many work hours you will need to do the job. Some people write quickly and prolifically, and some write as if they are constipated. You have to be honest in determining how much time you will need for actual writing and how much time you will need to pace, twist your hair, or play solitaire on your PC until you are able to focus. You don't need to feel guilty if you have some writing rituals, but be sure to consider them part of your overall schedule.

It is best if you schedule your writing and writing-related activities at the same time every day. Writing is a very concentration-intensive activity so you may not be able to devote eight straight hours to it. If you can be productive for two hours, that may be enough time per day. If you need to do more, I suggest you work in two-hour blocks with a substantial break in between them.

You need to listen to your own writing rhythms. Sometimes I can work for 2 to 3 hours that seem like 1 hour, and other times 1 hour can seem like 10. As long as you set aside the same time each day, you will be consistently productive and will use your time well.

When you finish your writing or writing-related activities for the day or business week, forget about them. Have a life. Have fun. Get some exercise. Stretch. Take care of your home and laundry. Do the things everyone else does to create balance. Writing takes a lot out of you emotionally, physically, and mentally.

You do not want to use up your energy all at once, or you will become miserable and will no longer love to write. If you do not love to write, get out of the business. Writing is not glamorous. Sometimes it can be tedious and grueling. But if you can't imagine doing anything else with your life, make sure to be good to yourself so that you can be effective.

Do not wait for inspiration to strike before you write. If you have chosen writing as a profession, you need to be professional. You can't just wait for the right mood to strike before you get down to business. If you wake up feeling a little down, don't give into it. Kick yourself in the rear and get to your desk or computer.

Do not listen to your inner voice if it tells you your work stinks. Nothing will mess up your writing schedule more than your little inner demons. Go to work anyway, or you will never make any progress.

The unfortunate thing about writing is that we do not get the kind of instant feedback we would get at a standard job. If we do a good job, no one is there to tell us so, and we do not believe our friends and family anyway. If we do a bad job, we may not know it and will still not believe anyone who tells us so. We work in a vacuum. So plod along. You will get the feedback you need when you obtain contracts for your work or when you hand in the completed manuscripts to your publisher.

The irony about writing as a profession is that we need such strong egos and are probably among the least-secure members of the human population. So view yourself as a business producing a product. As long as it meets acceptable standards for the marketplace, do not worry if it is not perfect. Once you relax about the work, you will see how much more productive you can be.

You may even find you enjoy the process and produce higher-quality work. If you relax within the schedule you have created, you give yourself the chance to develop your craft and hone your skills and voice. Whether you are a ghostwriter, a novelist, or a specialist in nonfiction, you will develop a signature style. You can't do this if you are so uptight that you can't breathe.

So managing your time is really a state of mind. There are many books that will teach you specific techniques for organization, calendar usage, and time management to the minute. But for writers, the most important factor is how you feel about your writing, your career, and your life. If you seek balance and want to be productive, you will create a system that works for you. If you want to drive yourself crazy and wind up drinking yourself to an early grave so that you can be immortalized as an "arteest," let your time manage you.

I vote for balance. I love to be free-spirited and eccentric. It is my most comfortable persona. But when I am under deadline, I do not think the anxiety is worth it. I also do not think it is worth it if my house is ready to be condemned, my children are running away to Grandma's, and my husband is ready to commit justifiable homicide.

So take control of your time and see what a difference it will make.

THE STATE OF BOOK PUBLISHING

TODAY AND TOMORROW

JEFF HERMAN

For several years the big question for everyone in publishing has been: "How will the Internet affect the book business?"

I'm going to go out on a limb here and say that new technologies don't and won't matter, because it's all about delivery and production systems. It has nothing to do with the evolution of the creative process or the measure of America's appetite for reading books. Whether you're composing your verse with a chisel on a limestone tablet or orally dictating to a computer that will immediately generate your hard copy (or cyber copy), it's still all about creating.

Cassettes and LPs quickly disappeared when CDs appeared. But the producers, distributors, and artists remained the same. Napster did threaten to overthrow the status quo by enabling consumers to acquire products without having to pay, but that was obviously illegal and unsustainable.

One day consumers may routinely buy and read books without touching a piece of paper (*Star Trek*'s Captain Picard was deemed eccentric for his tendency to read books the "old fashioned" way). Yet what hasn't been clearly explained is why this, in and of itself, is revolutionary?

A revolution is when the existing power structure is abruptly overthrown and replaced by something much different. Do we see that happening? It's true that anyone with a computer can virtually self-publish his or her book in cyberspace. But then how do you get people to know about it and motivate them to buy it? Online self-publishing saves you the trouble and expense of printing and storing thousands of copies in your garage, all on spec, but one hundred thousand words written by WHO? is likely to be forever lost in cyberspace.

The only really important issue is working out a reasonable compensation structure for writers, as publishers shift their front- and backlists to electronic "books."

We need to pay closer attention to the fallout from the "globalization" of America's publishing infrastructure, which began more than 10 years ago and has managed to consolidate the largest piece of the publishing pie into a few hands, most of which are as American as a Volkswagen. Independently owned "boutique" houses will always emerge and thrive, but they can act only from the margins. The sky hasn't fallen, but the atmosphere is different.

In the past, most books were acquired not so much for their immediate success, but because it was hoped they would nourish the "backlist," which was the surest way for a publisher to bolster its existence into the future. But that isn't today's publishing model. The large houses and the bookstore chains want megaselling, supernova brands, not a smorgasbord of delicacies. You can almost see these words written across the proverbial transoms of editors' offices: "Only bestselling writers need apply."

This is not to suggest that the midlist book is dead; far from it. Publishers can't afford to kill the midlist. But they are disrespecting it by refusing to adequately support it. The race is on to consolidate resources and place bets on the Derek Jeters of publishing. That's what gets noticed and rewarded by the corporate overlords.

But here's a silly little secret: If large houses stopped betting the farm on flaky blockbusters and mostly concentrated on feeding their healthy backlists with smart midlist acquisitions, they would be much more profitable today and tomorrow, and many more writers could make decent money from writing. And there would be a lot more good books to sell, buy, and read.

Yet an even more systemic issue pre-exists today's regime: We are a nation of readers. Tens of millions of us avidly read *People* and many other mass-market publications each week. But only a tiny fraction of this dedicated readership routinely buys books. What a shame, especially for writers, since an expanding market would mean more book contracts.

Why? There are many reasons, but I believe the most important one is historical. Two hundred years ago only a few people could actually read, and the vast majority of the population was functionally illiterate. Furthermore, only a few people could actually afford to buy books. It follows that book publishing, at its very genesis, could and would only serve the nation's most affluent and educated layer, which formed a narrow slice of the whole.

Things are much different today, and most of us are decent and active readers. But publishing as an institution has never caught up with the fact that the "rest of us" now read and have a few bucks. In fact, the most profitable book sectors, like mass-market romance, are treated as proletarian baggage, even though they subsidize many of the million-dollar acquisition mistakes made by the "smart" people.

The day that book publishers can see the *National Enquirer* as a role model instead of a joke, editors will all be earning healthy six-figure incomes, bookstores will be as common as drugstores, and many more writers will actually be writing during the day.

7 INGREDIENTS FOR SUCCESSFUL PUBLISHING

JEFF HERMAN

There are many big-time winners in the world of writing, which is invariably measured by how much money they make combined with how much fame they attract. This is not meant to include writers who are merely successful, or individuals who can leverage their tremendous success in non-book endeavors to achieve huge book advances. We are speaking here of the extraordinarily successful one-per cent (probably less) of writers who achieve millionaire and celebrity status primarily as writers of books.

No mortal really knows the whole picture of why some people are super-successful. Even those who have made it to the top of the pyramid don't know why they are so successful. They may attribute their status to talent, or to a range of specific character traits they possess and opportunities they grasped, and everything they identify may be part of the picture; but it still won't be the entire picture. Someone else could perfectly replicate their entire "template for success" and end up with very different results, because like with a Stradavareus Violin some of the key ingredients remain unseen.

While there is no perfect model for how to make it big as a writer, there are definitely a range of traits and methodologies that can be learned and used to enhance success. They are briefly presented here.

TALENT

Being good at what you do will help a lot, and being great will help even more. How do you make it to Carnegie Hall? You can practice; practice and practice, or you can take the subway. It depends on whether you wish to be performing on the stage or be sitting in the audience. Frankly, either position is something of an achievement. Much of the time, it's not the best that beat the rest. Hunger and determination can be deployed to overwhelm individuals who are merely gifted. How often have you heard the legends about tiny children who have conjured the raw strength to lift cars off the bodies of their parents, and similar miracles? Perhaps such things do indeed happen.

RESPONSIBILITY

Unfortunately, the world is cluttered with individuals who blame other people, or just plain bad luck, for their frustrations in life. No doubt, we are not all presented with equal opportunities. Physical disabilities; racism; poor schooling; poverty; dysfunctional parents, are just a few of the obstacles that will challenge what people can achieve in their lifetimes. However, successful people have a strong tendency to find ways to maneuver around the obstacles that fate has put in their path. Their focus is on achieving their goals, as opposed to wailing against the walls that confront them. America may not be a perfect world, but there is a reason why so many people from other places strive to come here. It's because our culture encourages and rewards individuals who relentlessly strive to help themselves.

EVOLUTIONARY

This is not about Darwin or the fate of the Neanderthals.

Most successful people carry a portfolio of personal failures, humiliations and plain dumb decisions. The truly wise and modest ones know that what's behind them could just as easily be in front of them. What successful people possess in abundance is the ability to not only survive adversity, but to be transformed by it. They consume the pain and random upsets that define life, and then intrinsically recycle all of these forces to create their own results. The evidence shows that we exist in a dimension that literally kills stagnation and obsolescence, while giving birth to an endless stream of mutations. A mutation that emerged a mere hundred-thousand years ago is referred to as modern humans. While this species shares remarkable DNA and chromosome similarities with other contemporary life forms, its exact origins are a mystery. This transformative power that shapes everything in nature is surely there for all of us to draw from as we pass through our portion of life.

PLANNING

As a child, I would shuffle playing cards by tossing the deck high into the sky. The cards would scatter everywhere and I would then pick them up one at a time until the deck was re-established. This was much less efficient then conventional shuffling, but it did at least achieve my goal of reordering the cards. I had a valid plan. It's very easy to arrive somewhere when you don't have a destination in mind. But how do you know where you or why you are there, or anywhere? Some people deliberately choose amorphous paths because passivity makes no demands. But it's a fool's candy as they risk falling into a pit of desperation; and the deeper they plunge the more out-of-control they will feel. For sure, it's more tedious to structure an itinerary and then stick with it, but it is a way to reach a pre-determined result. Where there's a plan there is a will, and where there's a will there's a way. Each of us can design a personal Promised Land to strive for. But can we arrive? Better questions are: How do you intend to get there, and will you value each moment and adventure along the way?

SHOW UP

This one seems obvious, yet it's where most of us lose the game. Forfeiture is the biggest reason for frustration. It gives us a seemingly comfortable way to avoid failure (and success). Reasons to not even try are the deadliest weapons against a person's progress. There are many ways to do harm, with murder the most egregious. But to discourage yourself or others from trying to accomplish a good purpose, due to fear or envy, is a form of violence. Some of the best and the brightest will never try, which makes it easier for the rest of us to compete and prevail; but also deprives us of the opportunity to learn different, perhaps even superior, methods.

PASSION

It may sometimes appear as if super-successful people are somehow more alive then everyone else. This perception may be due to the fact that a certain percentage of highly successful people are unusually energetic and fast-paced. But the "silent" majority of high-achievers probably appear to be going through their days like everyone else. There's a powerful characteristic that may indeed differentiate successful people: Their tireless focus on what it is that they are doing. This is not to say that they must be devoid of a full life with families and hobbies, but there is always that one special fire that burns inside of them and acts like a locomotive. They are not living to simply get through another day. To the contrary, each day is a luscious opportunity to do what it is that they are driven to be. They have a juicy purpose that infuses each moment. They will sleep only because they have to. If unchecked, their passion can be so intense that it may become a jealous and all-consuming deity. There are limits to the commitments anyone should make. Dr. Frankenstein's passion was admirable, but his deeds were ultimately undesirable.

THE WILD CARD

Reasons for success are abundant and humans are complicated. There are people who possess a positive orientation in the context of business and money, and have achieved the success to prove it. But those same people may have a negative outlook regarding their relationships with others, and have bitter loneliness to show for it. What is the alchemy for being at one's best in all aspects of life? Why is it that the children of the proverbial shoemaker go barefoot? For those who know some Scripture, what has a man who sold his soul for all the kingdoms of the Earth? There are those who will build nations; those who build businesses; those who build breakthrough concepts, and those who will build families. All are builders. The Wild Card is that force within you and all around you that calls you.

BONUS INGREDIENT: CHARACTER

Character is largely a value judgment. How many of us actually see ourselves as others see us? Material and professional success in this world does not require personal morality. A reasonable measure of an individual's true contribution is an assessment of whether or not that person's deeds have been good or bad for the rest of us. On one extreme, people who have generated their success through the negative exploitation of other people and resources will leave an unfortunate legacy. A billionaire drug lord is an example of this kind of success.

Success is like a number. In of it itself it means nothing. But when you apply that number to illustrate a result, it will absorb a meaningful context and possess a genuine power to be creative or destructive.

THE INDEPENDENT EDITORS

Over the past few years, independent editors (aka "Book Doctors") have become much more numerous and are more frequently an important part of the publishing process. This relatively new and potentially indispensible utility player has earned a section all their own.

Simply stated, an independent editor is someone who is retained by a writer at a negotiated fee, for the purpose of helping to make the writer's proposal, pitch letter, marketing materials, story summary, chapters, entire manuscript, or any combination thereof, as professionally perfect as possible. These services are not to be confused with ghostwriting, collaborating or co-authoring, as it is not the editor's function to actually write anything, but to merely help the writer reach her best potential.

In-house editors may recognize an unpublished writer's rich potential, but lack the time or incentive to help chisel the raw product into a publishable form, and therefore reject it. In some cases the editor will conditionally reject it with the generous suggestion that if the writer can somehow make it better, he's welcome to re-submit it, which in turn opens the door for an independent editor. It's not uncommon for agents to do the same. Some writers decide to pre-empt or reduce the chance of rejection by retaining editorial support prior to pitching anything to anyone.

A significant trend, which has hopefully peaked, is the endemic downsizing that has plagued corporate publishing for more than a dozen years. Many excellent veteran editors were granted the proverbial "golden parachute" for the purpose of eliminating overhead. For obvious reasons, this brain drain hasn't been good for in-house quality, but that's for another essay. This displaced talent pool includes more than a few who have edited the most important and successful books that have been published over the past generation. These same editors are now available to help eligible writers reach their full potentials, for fees that are modest when compared to unrelated professional services.

The community of down-sized and retired editors lent itself to mutual support and combined marketing efforts. For instance, those who are best suited for memoirs can make referrals to those who specialize in romance. It can be inefficient and lonely to be an isolated freelancer, so forming loosely organized groups came naturally to those who had spent years in offices working with others. The initial groups didn't want to become too crowded or structured, so several new groups have been spawned to absorb the increasing supply of independent editors.

Presented here is verbatim information presented by each of the groups and their respective members. While I endorse the concept of using an independent editor when appropriate, and have confidence in the veracity and quality of everyone listed here, I do not specifically endorse any of them. In future editions, I hope to expand this section by including qualified independent editors who are not affiliated with a group. If you are one of them, feel free to contact me.

Jeff Herman

SCAMS AND BOOK DOCTORS

IN THAT ORDER

JEFF HERMAN

Publishing scams have become an epidemic. I read somewhere that writers are getting ripped off for more than $50 million a year, and some scam artists have even gone to jail.

Let's start by looking at ethics. I don't like ethics. They're like organized religion—prone to promoting arrogance, subjective judgment, and hypocrisy. I do like honesty. Honesty's best defense is the fast and consistent enforcement of consequences against those people who harm others.

The best defense is not to be a victim in the first place. Without becoming a paranoid lunatic, you must accept that bad deeds are hovering around waiting to happen. Sometimes, you may be tempted into being a perpetrator. That's why houses have glass windows and why the universe can't stay angry, or else we'd all have to go to Hell. It's more likely, however, that you'll be a victim, not a "do-er," on any given day; though it's hoped you'll be neither. Both extremes may be mostly, or completely, within your power to be or not to be. For instance, I'll never understand why women jog by themselves in Central Park when it's dark out. And I'll never understand why writers send fat checks to virtual strangers.

To what extent should society protect its citizens from making stupid choices? I've seen smart men and women date and marry morons, with predictably disastrous results. I've done enough stupid things in my life to qualify for the Infra-Mensa society many times over. How about you? Should someone have stopped us? And if we were stopped, might we not have been even more stupid the next time?

Basically, I'm praising stupidity as a natural right and gift. It's unnatural to overly protect people from themselves. We all see what happens to individuals who are excessively parented or to entire communities that are enabled to subsist in perpetual poverty and social decay.

So what about writers who get scammed? Well, they should stop doing it.

- They should stop sending money to get people to "read" their work, since there are several hundred real agents who will do that for free.

- They should stop smoking and stop eating other fat mammals.

- They should stop giving money to unproven strangers who promise to get them published, since there are several hundred real agents who will do that on a contingency.

- They should wear seatbelts, especially when in New York taxis.

- They should stop giving money to unproven strangers who promise to "fix" the work, especially since there are at least dozens of real former book editors who can genuinely fix your work.

- They should stop maintaining balances on their credit cards.

- They should always ask for evidence of ability whenever asked for money.

If we, as writers, walk the previous line, then parasitic acts could not exist and thrive. We would not need more laws, more people working for government, or any ethics. Such things only exist in the absence of honesty and in the dissonance that follows.

As a service, I have attached information about specific "Book Doctor" organizations and individuals that I'm familiar with and trust. These are people who either have deep experience working as real editors at real publishers, have "doctored" many manuscripts to the point of publication, or both. Retaining their skills will often make the difference between getting a deal or being a "close call."

I endorse none of these people or the expectations they might create. I simply want you to have a safe place to turn if you need help and are ready to receive.

The following is an actual pitch letter from a fee-charging agency, with only the names and other identifying information changed. Such correspondence is typical of the alluring invitations writers often receive in response to their agent submissions.

If a writer chooses to explore this route, I strongly advise following these preliminary steps:

1. Ask for references. You're being asked to shell out hundreds of dollars to a virtual stranger. Get to know those who would eat your money.

2. Ask for a list of titles sold. Find out whether the so-called agency actually has an agenting track record. Or is this particular operation just a high-priced reading service with an agency façade?

3. Better yet, call or write to non-fee charging agents and ask them to recommend book doctors, collaborative writers, or editorial freelancers whom they use to shape and develop their own clients' works, or see the "Book Doctor" section in this book. This may be a better place to spend your money.

BEWARE OF SHARKS!

The following correspondence is genuine, though all names and titles have been altered. My purpose for exposing these ever-so-slightly personalized form letters isn't to condemn or ridicule anyone. I simply wish to show how some subsidy publishers hook their clients.

SHARK HOUSE PUBLISHERS

Mr. Bourne Bate
Brooklyn Bridge
East River, NY 00000

Dear Mr. Bate:

Your manuscript *A Fish's Life* is written from an unusual perspective and an urgent one. In these trying economic times that have created despair and anguish, one must give thought to opportunities, and this upbeat and enthusiastic book makes us realize that those opportunities are out there! My capsule critique: Meticulous aim! With a surgeon's precision we're taught how to work through everything from raising money to targeting areas. There is a sharp eye here for all of the nuances, studded with pointers and reasoning, making it a crucial blueprint.

What can I say about a book like this? It stopped me in my tracks. I guess all I can do is thank you for letting me have the opportunity to read it.

The editors who read this had a spontaneous tendency to feel that it was imbued with some very, very good electricity and would be something very special for our list and saw such potential with it that it was given top priority and pushed ahead of every other book in house. The further problem is that publishing being an extremely rugged business, editorial decisions have to be based on hard facts, which sometimes hurt publishers as much as authors. Unfortunately, we just bought several new nonfiction pieces…yet I hate to let this one get away. Publishing economics shouldn't have anything to do with a decision, but unfortunately, it does and I was overruled at the editorial meeting.

Still I want you to know that this is a particularly viable book and one that I really would love to have for our list. Furthermore, this might be picked up for magazine serialization or by book clubs because it is so different. Our book *Enraptured* was serialized six times in *International Inquirer* and sold to Andorra. *The Devil Decided* sold well over 150,000 copies, and we have a movie option on it. *Far Away*, serialized in *Places* magazine and *Cure Yourself* was taken by a major book club.

I really want this book for our list because it will fit into all the areas that we're active in. Therefore, I'm going to make a proposition for you to involve yourself with us. What would you think of the idea of doing this on a cooperative basis? Like many New York publishers these days, we find that sometimes investors are interested in the acquisition of literary properties through a technique that might be advantageous under our tax laws. There is no reason that the partial investor cannot be the writer, if that person so chooses. Tax advantages may accrue.

I'd be a liar if I promised you a bestseller, but I can guarantee that nobody works as hard promoting a book as we do: We nag paperback, book clubs, magazines, and foreign publishers with our zeal and enthusiasm. We do our PR work and take it seriously because this is where we're going to make the money in the long run. One of our authors hired a top publicist on his own for $50,000. He came limping back to us, saying they didn't do the job that we did, and which we don't charge for. This made our office feel very proud of all our efforts.

I feel that your book deserves our efforts because it is something very special. Think about what I've written to you, and I will hold the manuscript until I hear from you. I truly hope that we can get together because I really love this book and believe it is something we can generate some good action for vis-à-vis book clubs, foreign rights, etc., because it is outstanding and has tremendous potential.

Sincerely,

Eda U. Live

Eda U. Live
Executive Editor

The writer of *A Fish's Life* wrote back to Shark House (all names have been changed) and informed the vanity press that he did not want to pay any money to the publisher to have his book published.

The vanity house responded with the following letter.

(This publisher has probably learned from experience that some exhausted writers will return to them with open wallets after fruitless pursuit of a conventional commercial publishing arrangement.)

SHARK HOUSE PUBLISHERS

Mr. Bourne Bate
Brooklyn Bridge
East River, NY 00000

Dear Mr. Bate:

I have your letter in front of me and I want you to know that I think very highly of the book. Before I go any further, I want to tell you that it is a topnotch book and it hits the reader.

In order for us to do a proper job with a book, there is a great deal of PR work involved and this is very costly. To hire an outside agent to do a crackerjack job would cost you upward of $50,000. Yet here we do not charge for it because it is part of our promotion to propel a book into the marketplace, and it is imperative that this be done. The author has to be booked on radio and TV, stores have to be notified, rights here and abroad have to be worked on, reviewers contacted, autograph parties arranged, and myriad details taken care of.

In view of this, why did I ask you to help with the project? I think the above is self-explanatory, especially when we are in the midst of a revolution between books and television. Publishers are gamblers vying for the same audience. Just because a publisher loves a book is no guarantee that the public is going to love it. In times when bookstores are more selective in the number of books they order, the best of us tremble at the thought of the money that we must put out in order to make a good book a reality.

Be that as it may, I have just come from another editorial meeting where I tried to re-open the case for us, but unfortunately, the earlier decision stands.

As a result, I have no choice but to return the manuscript with this letter. I would also like to tell you that you must do what the successful writers do. Keep sending it out. Someone will like it and someone will buy it.

I wish you every success. Live long and prosper.

Sincerely,

Eda U. Live

Eda U. Live
Executive Editor

NINE SIGNS OF A SCAM BOOK DOCTOR

JERRY GROSS

Working with an expert, ethical book doctor can often make the difference between being published or remaining unpublished. Conversely, working with an unqualified, unethical book doctor can often be hazardous—even fatal—to your career.

You've worked hard to save the money to hire a book doctor. Make sure that the book doctor you hire will turn out to be a good investment. Here are 9 signs that someone who claims to be a professional book doctor may be trying to scam you.

1. **A scam book doctor states that you can't get published unless you hire a book doctor.** You may hear that editors and publishers demand that a manuscript be professionally edited before they will consider it for publication, or that agents won't take on a client unless the writer first works with a book doctor to polish the manuscript.

   Not true. Agents and editors still take on manuscripts that need a lot of work, but, to be candid, they don't do it too often because they are usually overworked and overwhelmed by the volume of material submitted to them. That's why working with a good book doctor can at least improve your odds of being accepted by an agent and an editor.

2. **A scam book doctor guarantees, or at least implies, that his editing will get you accepted by an agent.**

   Not true! No reputable book doctor can make this statement because no book doctor can persuade an agent to represent a project that the agent does not like, believe in, or see as commercially viable. Beauty is in the eye of the beholder, and editors and agents often see a manuscript's potential through very different eyes.

3. **A scam book doctor guarantees, or strongly implies, that once she's edited your manuscript, an agent will definitely be able to sell it.**

   Not true. The vagaries, shifts of taste, and trends in the publishing marketplace are such that agents themselves cannot be sure which manuscripts will be salable.

4. **A scam book doctor admits (or you discover) that he has a "financial arrangement" with the person or company who referred you to him.** In plain English, this means that he kicks back part of his fee for the referral.

   This is inarguably unethical. There should be no financial relationship between the book doctor and the referring party. If one exists, it can adversely affect the honesty and integrity of his evaluation of your manuscript, or both.

5. **A scam book doctor does not guarantee that she will edit your manuscript personally.**

   Since you are hiring the editor for her specific expertise, insist that she guarantee in writing that she will edit the manuscript herself. If she won't do this, look elsewhere for an editor.

6. **A scam book doctor tells you that he can't take on your project, but will subcontract it.**

   However, he won't tell you who will edit it, and he won't provide you with that editor's background, samples of that editor's work, or any references. And he does not give you the right to accept or refuse the editor he suggests.

   If you do decide to work with another editor because the one you wanted is overbooked or otherwise unavailable, then you have every right to know as much about the person recommended by him as you know about the editor making the recommendation. You also have every right to decide whether you want to work with the editor whom he recommends.

7. **A scam book doctor won't provide references from authors or agents she's worked with.**

   Obviously, the editor won't provide you with names of dissatisfied clients, but you can learn a lot by gauging the enthusiasm (or lack of it) with which the client discusses working with the book doctor. Ask questions: "Was she easy and friendly to work with?"; "Was she receptive to ideas?"; "Was she available to discuss her approach to line-editing, critique of the manuscript, or both?"; "Did you feel that you got good value for your money?"

8. **A scam book doctor won't provide samples of his editing or critiques.**

   Engaging in a book doctor without seeing how he line-edits or problem-solves a manuscript is akin to buying oceanfront property in Arizona from a real estate salesman on the phone or on the Web. Talk is cheap, but good editing is expensive. Make sure you are buying the expertise you need; demand to see samples of the editor's work. If he balks, hang up the phone!

9. **A scam book doctor sends you an incomplete Letter of Agreement that does not specify all the costs you will incur, what she will do for each of her fees, a schedule of payment, and a due date for delivery of the edited or critiqued manuscript.**

Every one of your contractual obligations to each other should be spelled out clearly in the Letter of Agreement before you sign it. If changes are agreed upon during the course of the author-editor relationship, these changes should either be incorporated into a new Letter of Agreement that both parties sign or be expressed in rider clauses added to the Agreement that are initialed by both editor and author. There should be no hidden or "surprise" costs at the time of the final payment to the book doctor.

A final caution: Be convinced that you are hiring the right book doctor before signing the Letter of Agreement. Not only your money, but also your career is at stake!

Jerry Gross has been a fiction and nonfiction editor for many years, the last nineteen as a freelance editor/book doctor. He is Editor of the standard work on trade-book editing *Editors on Editing: What Writers Need to Know About What Editors Do*. He also creates and presents workshops and panels on editing and writing at writers' conferences. He can be reached at 63 Grand Street, Croton-on-Hudson, NY 10520-2518 and at jgross@bookdocs.com.

AN EDITOR OF ONE'S OWN

BY THE EDITORS OF WORDS INTO PRINT   (WWW.WORDSINTOPRINT.ORG)

A re book doctors really worth it? What do they do that agents and in-house editors might not? With all the help a writer can get on the journey from manuscript to published book, why hire an editor of one's own?

Before the Age of the Independent Editor, literary agents and publishing staff were the first publishing insiders to read a proposal or manuscript. Today, however, the focus on business interests is so demanding and the volume of submissions so great—agents alone take in hundreds of query letters a month—that a writer's work has to be white-hot before receiving serious consideration. In light of these developments, a writer may turn to an independent editor as the first expert reader in the world of publishing's gatekeepers.

WHAT ELSE DO INDEPENDENT EDITORS DO, AND HOW MUCH DO THEY CHARGE?

Services. Not every writer and project will call for the services of an independent editor. However, if you are looking for the kind of personalized and extensive professional guidance beyond that gained from workshops, fellow writers, online sources, magazines, and books, hiring an editor may well be worth the investment. An editor of your own can provide a professional assessment of whether or not your project is ready to submit, and to whom you should submit it; expert assistance to make your manuscript or book proposal as good as it should be; help with preparing a convincing submissions package; and an advocate's voice and influence to guide you in your efforts toward publication.

Another key role an independent editor plays is to protect writers from querying their prospects before their material is irresistible. Premature submissions cause writers needless disappointment and frustration. Your editor can zero in on the thematic core, central idea, or story line that needs to be conveyed in a way that is most likely to attract an agent and a publisher. In short, an editor of your own can identify the most appealing, salable aspects of you and your work.

Rates. "Good editing is expensive," our venerable colleague Jerry Gross prudently notes. What kind of editing is good editing and how expensive is it? The Internet and other sources quote a wide range of rates from a variety of editors. The numbers are not necessarily accurate or reliable. We've seen hourly rates ranging from about $25 to well above $200. Several factors account for this spread: the type of editing, the editor's level of experience, and the publishing venue. For example, rates for copyediting are lower than those for substantive editing. Moreover, standards in book publishing are particularly rigorous because books are long, expensive to produce, made to last, and vulnerable to the long-term impact of reviewer criticism.

Process. Book editors are specialists. Every book project arrives on the desk of an independent editor at a certain level of readiness, and the first task is to determine what the project needs. A deep book edit is typically a painstaking, time-consuming process that may move at the pace of only three or four manuscript pages per hour—or, when less intensive, eight to twelve pages per hour. Occasionally a manuscript received by an independent is fully developed, needs only a light copyedit, and may well be ready to submit as is. In other cases, the editorial process may require one or more rounds of revisions. If you are hiring an editor to critique your work, you should be aware that reading the material takes considerably more time than writing the critique. Sometimes a flat fee, rather than an hourly rate, may be appropriate to the project. Sometimes, as discussed below, editors will offer a consultation at no charge. A reputable independent book editor will be able recommend a course of action that may or may not include one or more types of editorial services, and give you a reliable estimate of the time and fees involved.

BUT WON'T THE IN-HOUSE EDITOR FIX MY BOOK?

Sometimes. Maybe. To an extent. Independents and in-house editors are, in many ways, different creatures. For starters, in-house editors spend much of the day preparing for and going to meetings. Marketing meetings. Sales meetings. Editorial meetings. Production meetings. The mandate for most of these in-house editors is to acquire new book projects and to shepherd those that are already in the pipeline. With so many extended activities cutting into the business hours, the time for actually working on a manuscript can be short.

Many in-house editors have incoming manuscripts screened by an already overworked assistant. (The days of staff readers are long gone.) The only quiet time the editor has for reading might be evenings and weekends. We have known editors to take a week off from work just to edit a book and be accessible to their authors. These days, too, the acquiring editor may not do any substantive work on a book project under contract, leaving that task to a junior editor. There is also a distinct possibility the acquiring editor may leave the job before that book is published, and this can occur with the next editor, too, and the next, threatening the continuity of the project. All of which doesn't mean that there aren't a lot of hard-working people at the publishing house; it means that editors have more to do than ever before and must devote at least as much time to crunching numbers as to focusing on the writer and the book.

Independent editors, on the other hand, spend most of their business days working exclusively with authors and their texts. They typically handle only a few manuscripts at a time and are free from marketing and production obligations. An independent editor's primary interest is in helping you to get your book polished and published. An editor of your own will see your project through—and often your next book, too.

WHAT DO AGENTS SAY ABOUT INDEPENDENT EDITORS?

"As the book market gets tougher for selling both fiction and nonfiction it is imperative that all submissions be polished, edited, almost ready for the printer. Like many other agents I do as much as possible to provide editorial input for the author but there are time constraints. So independent editors provide a very valuable service these days in getting the manuscript or proposal in the best shape possible to increase the chances of impressing an editor and getting a sale with the best possible terms." —Bill Contardi

"Agents work diligently for our clients, but there are situations in which outside help is necessary. Perhaps a manuscript has been worked on so intensively that objectivity is lacking, or perhaps the particular skill required to do a job properly is not one of an agent's strong suits. Maybe more time is required than an agent can offer. Fortunately, agents and authors are able to tap into the talent and experience of an outside editor. The outside editors I've worked with offer invaluable support during the editing process itself and for the duration of a project. Their involvement can make the difference between an author getting a publishing contract or having to put a project aside, or the difference between a less- or more-desirable contract."—Victoria Pryor

"The right editor or book doctor can make all the difference in whether a manuscript gets sold. A debut novelist, for example, may have a manuscript that is almost there, but not quite. With the input of a good editor, the novel can reach its full potential and be an attractive prospect to a potential publisher. Similarly, someone writing a memoir may have had a fascinating life but may not really have the God-given writing talent that will turn that life into a compelling and readable book. An editor can take that person's rough-hewn words and thoughts and turn them into a memoir that really sings on the printed page." —Eric Myers

"Occasionally a novel will land on my desk that I feel has talent or a good concept behind it but for whatever reason (the writing, the pacing) needs an inordinate amount of work. Instead of just rejecting it flat out I may then refer the author to a freelance editor, someone who has the time and expertise to help the author further shape and perfect their work." —Nina Collins

"I have had several occasions to use the help of freelance editors, and think they provide incalculable good service to the profession. In these competitive times, a manuscript has to be as polished and clean as possible to garner a good sale to a publisher. If it needs work, it simply provides an editor with a reason to turn it down. My job is to not give them any excuses. I do not have either the time or the ability to do the editorial work that may be required to make the manuscript salable. Paying a freelance professional to help shape a book into its most commercially viable form ultimately more than pays for itself." —Deborah Schneider

SO, HOW CAN I FIND THE RIGHT EDITOR?

You've searched online. You've looked in annual directories such as this one. You've asked around. A personal recommendation from a published writer-friend who has used an independent editor for his or her work may or may not do the trick. Every author has different needs, every author-editor dynamic a different chemistry.

Although sometimes an author and editor "click" very quickly, many editors offer free consultations, and it's fine to contact more than one editor at this stage. A gratis consult may involve an editor's short take, by phone or in writing, on sample material the editor asked you to send. But how to distinguish among the many independent editors?

Some editorial groups are huge, and they are open to all who designate themselves as editors; it might take some additional research to identify the members who are most reputable and best suited to your work. The smaller groups consist of editors who have been nominated, vetted, and elected, which ensures the high quality of the individual professionals. They meet with regularity, share referrals, and discuss industry developments. Your consultation, references offered, and the terms of any subsequent agreement can tell the rest.

Another way to find the right editor is to prepare your manuscript to its best advantage—structurally, stylistically, and mechanically. Jeff Herman's annual guide, for example, is filled with directions on manuscript preparation, and it is a good idea to follow them. Asking the opinion of one or more impartial readers—that is, not limiting your initial reviewers to friends and relatives—is a great strategy as well. If you have the benefit of a disinterested reader, you may be able to make some significant changes before sending an excerpt to an independent editor. One more element to consider: editors often will take your own personality and initial written inquiry into account as carefully as they do your writing. Seasoned independents do not take on every project that appears on the desk; they can pick and choose—and, working solo, they must.

TALES FROM THE TRENCHES

We hope we've given you a sense of what an editor of your own can do for you and where we fit into the publishing picture. But next to firsthand experience, perhaps nothing communicates quite as sharply as an anecdote. Here are a few of ours:

"A few years ago at Christmastime, a publisher hired me to reorganize, add text to, and edit a business manuscript by two high-profile authors. Over a year in the making, the very late manuscript was slated for publication the following fall. The delivered work was certainly thorough: about 500 pages worth of theories, including some very interesting brain and planet data. But despite a party of five's involvement (two authors, one marketing executive, one business journal publisher, one CEO), there was no clear definition of what the book was about. And that is perhaps one of the biggest reasons independent editors are hired: They are not usually part of the initial "team" and therefore bring fresh, unbiased opinions. In this case, I found the theme buried in a phrase on page 26.

"After that I met with the authors for two days in a hotel suite to restructure and organize the manuscript and figure out what had to be rewritten. The entire project was overhauled in two months. Once the premise was defined, everyone involved concentrated on it. But that would not have happened if an independent editor hadn't read the manuscript." —Susan Suffes

"An in-house editor called me with an unusual problem. He had signed up an acclaimed author for a new book project. She had written a number of stories—nonfiction narratives about her life in an exotic land. The problem was this: some of the stories had already been published in book form in England, and that collection had its own integrity in terms of theme and chronology; now she had written another set of stories, plus a diary of her travels. How could the published stories and the new ones be made into one book?

"I decided to disregard the structure of the published book altogether. As I reexamined each story according to theme, emotional quality, geographical location, and people involved, I kept looking for ways in which they might relate to each other. Eventually, I sensed a new and logical way in which to arrange them. I touched not one word of the author's prose. I did the same thing I always try to do when editing—imagine myself inside the skin of the writer. A prominent trade book review had this to say about the result: 'One story flows into the next…'" —Alice Rosengard

"A writer had hired me to help with his first book after his agent had sold it to a publisher because he wanted to expedite the revisions and final approval of his manuscript. As a result of our work together, the book came out sooner than anticipated; it also won an award and the author was interviewed on a major TV news program. The same author hired me a year later for his second book, purchased by a larger publisher, and this book, too, entailed some significant developmental editing. At that point we

THE INDEPENDENT EDITORS

AN EDITOR OF ONE'S OWN   929

learned the in-house editor had left the publisher and a new one had come aboard. This editor not only objected strongly to one whole section of the book; she also gave the author a choice: revise the section in one week or put the project on hold for at least six more months.

"From halfway across the world, the writer called me on a Friday to explain his publishing crisis, which was also coinciding with a personal crisis, and asked if we could collaborate closely on the fifty pages in question over the weekend. I agreed, cancelled my weekend plans, and we camped out at each end of the telephone and e-mailboxes almost nonstop for three days. He resubmitted the book on Tuesday, the book received all requisite signatures in-house, and a month later it went into production. This hands-on and sometimes unpredictable kind of collaboration with writers helps illustrate the special nature of independent editing." —Katharine Turok

"In August of 2005, a young woman who had just been fired from her very first job contacted me. She wanted my help writing a book about her experience. I asked if she'd written much before and I suppressed my groan when she said she hadn't, but what she lacked in credentials she made up for in energy and enthusiasm. She told me she had graduated at the top of her Ivy League college class and done everything right—good grades, great internships—to land a plum job at a consulting firm, but when she got there she quickly discovered that she didn't know how to have a job—she lacked the tools to deal with sexist bosses; she hadn't mastered PowerPoint; she believed her female coworkers would be supportive, not catty. She was determined to share what she'd learned to help other young women.

"As we worked together on her proposal, we not only structured her book but found ways to use her youth and inexperience in her favor—especially in terms of marketing. She built up her platform by writing for neighborhood papers, national newspapers, and eventually high-profile Web sites. All the pieces added up, the timing was right and she landed a great agent who secured a two-book deal." —Alice Peck

"My work on a book about a near-extinct species of birds was greatly enhanced when the author gave me a tour of a California estuary. Guided by his passion and on-site expertise, I was able to spot exquisite birds, hear bird-watching lingo, and see his high-end scope in action. Now I understood the thrill of what he was writing about, and was better able to help him communicate it.

"One of my most challenging assignments was to add action scenes to a memoir by an Olympic fencing champion. Here was a subject I knew nothing about. I tried to bone up in advance through reading, but my author had a better idea. Working his way across my living room floor, he sparred with an invisible opponent, demonstrating what he wished to describe in his book. I wrote down what I saw.

"As an independent editor, I have the time and freedom to work 'outside the book,' to literally enter the worlds my authors are writing about." —Ruth Greenstein

WORDS INTO PRINT

www.wordsintoprint.org

Words into Print is one of New York's top networks of independent book editors, writers, and publishing consultants. Founded in 1998, WiP is a professional alliance whose members provide editorial services to publishers, literary agents, and book packagers, as well as to individual writers. Members of WiP have extensive industry experience, averaging twenty years as executives and editors with leading trade book publishers. As active independent professionals, members meet individually and as a group with agents and other publishing colleagues; participate in conventions, conferences, panels, and workshops; and maintain affiliations with organizations that include PEN, AWP, the Author's Guild, the Women's National Book Association, the Modern Language Association, and the Academy of American Poets.

The consultants at Words into Print are committed to helping established and new writers develop, revise, and polish their work. They also guide clients through the publishing process by helping them find the most promising route to publication. WiP's editors and writers provide:

+ Detailed analyses and critiques of proposals and manuscripts

+ Editing, cowriting, and ghostwriting

+ Expert advice, ideas, and techniques for making a writer's project the best it can be

+ Assistance in developing query letters and synopses for literary agents and publishers

+ Referrals to literary agents, publishers, book packagers, and other publishing services

+ Guidance in developing publicity and marketing strategies

+ Project management—from conception through production

+ Inside information writers need to make their way successfully through the publishing world

Words into Print's editors offer top-tier assistance at competitive rates. Brief profiles appear below. For more information, please visit www.wordsintoprint.org.

Marlene Adelstein
e-mail: madelstein@aol.com

Thorough, constructive critiques, editing, advice on material's commercial potential and agent referrals when appropriate. Over twenty years' experience in publishing and feature film development. Specializes in commercial and literary fiction: mysteries, thrillers; women's fiction, romance, historical; young adult; memoir; nonfiction proposals; screenplays. Titles worked on include *Legally Blonde, Family Trust, Pilate's Wife, Ill-Equipped for a Life of Sex.*

Ruth Greenstein

e-mail: rg@greenlinepublishing.com

Twenty years of experience with literary fiction, biography/memoir, social issues, cultural criticism, arts, travel, nature, health, psychology, religion/spirituality, poetry, photography, media companions, reference. Cofounder of WiP; formerly with Harcourt and Ecco. Has worked with Alice Walker, Gary Paulsen, Sallie Bingham, John Ashbery, and Dennis Lehane. Offers a full range of editorial services, including synopsis writing and submissions guidance.

Alice Peck

e-mail: alicepeck@alicepeck.com

Edits, evaluates, and rewrites memoir, narrative, religion, spirituality, and fiction (especially first novels); writes and edits proposals. Acquired books and developed them into scripts for film and television (David Brown to MTV) before shifting her focus to editing in 1998. Authors include Tim Cockey (a k a Richard Hawke), Hannah Seligson, Slim Lambright, Susan McBride, Elaine Brown, Kim Powers, Laurence Klavan, and Jack Ross.

Alice Rosengard

e-mail: arosengard1@yahoo.com

Manuscript and proposal evaluation, developmental and structural editing, substantive editing and line editing for publishers, literary agents, and authors. Nineteen years in trade editorial department at HarperCollins Publishers; eighteen years as an independent editor. Concentrations: literary and mainstream fiction, history, memoir, biography, science, current events, cookbooks, poetry. Authors worked with include Stephen Mitchell, Martha Rose Shulman, and Larry Sloman.

Susan Suffes

e-mail: susuff@aol.com

Proposal evaluations, coauthoring, ghostwriting, rewriting, and editing. Over two decades of nonfiction manuscript acquisition for publishers including Warner Books. Concentrations: business, diet, health, finance, real estate, and self-help. Bestselling authors include John Sarno, M.D., Robert Kriegel, Sherman Silber, M.D., and Mark Sanborn. Written works published by Fawcett/Columbine, Gallup Press, and Rodale.

Katharine Turok

e-mail: kturok@wildblue.net

Manuscript evaluation; developmental, substantive, and line editing; rewriting; condensing. Literary and mainstream fiction, autobiography/memoir, biography, contemporary issues, film, history, nature, poetry, psychology, popular reference, theater, travel, visual arts, women's issues, translations. Over 20 years' international experience acquiring and editing works from new and established writers and published by major houses including Bloomsbury, Dutton, Folger Shakespeare Library, Scribner, and independent presses.

Michael Wilde
e-mail: michaelwildeeditorial@earthlink.net

Provides first-time and experienced authors with all manner of editorial services and help with writing. More than twenty years' experience working with leading authors and publishers in subjects ranging from scholarly and professional books to pop culture, literary and mainstream fiction, children's books, and young adult novels. Can assist in finding an agent when appropriate.

INDEPENDENT EDITORS GROUP

www.bookdocs.com

The Independent Editors Group is a professional affiliation of highly select, diverse, experienced freelance editors/book doctors who work with writers, editors, and agents in trade book publishing. They are: Sally Arteseros, Maureen Baron, Harriet Bell, Susan Dalsimer, Paul De Angelis, Michael Denneny, Joyce Engelson, Jerry Gross, Susan Leon, Richard Marek, James O'Shea Wade, Betty Sargent, and Genevieve Young.

Years of distinguished tenure at major publishing houses made them eminently qualified to provide the following editorial services on fiction and nonfiction manuscripts.

- In-depth evaluations and detailed critiques

- Problem-solving

- Plot restructure

- Developmental and line editing

- Reorganization, revision, and rewriting

- Book proposals and development

- Ghostwriting and collaborationIf any editor is unavailable, referrals will be made to other appropriate IEG members. Inquiries are welcomed; please do not send manuscripts. Fees, references, and resumes are available from editors on request.

Whenever you have a project calling for freelance editorial expertise, get in touch with the best editors in trade book publishing today to solve your manuscript problems.

Sally Arteseros
e-mail: SArteseros@cs.com
Edits all kinds of fiction; literary, commercial, women's, historical, contemporary, inspirational. A specialist in short stories. And in nonfiction: biography, autobiography, memoir, psychology, anthropology, business, regional books, and academic books. Editor at Doubleday for more than 25 years.

Maureen Baron
150 West 87th Street, #6C
New York, NY 10024
212-787-6260
Former Vice President/Editor in Chief of NAL/Signet Books continues to work with established and developing writers in all areas of mainstream fiction and nonfiction. Specialties: medical novels and thrillers; women's issues; health matters; African American fiction; biography; memoirs. Knows the market and has good contacts. Book club consultant.

Harriet Bell
315 E. 68th Street
New York, NY 10065
e-mail: harrietbell@verizon.net
www.bellbookandhandle.com
www.bookdocs.com
More than 25 years as editor and publisher at leading trade houses. Areas of interest and expertise: Nonfiction including business, cooking, crafts, diet, fitness, health and lifestyle, how-to, gastronomy, illustrated books, memoir, nonfiction narrative, popular psychology, reference and wine.

Susan Dalsimer
Editorial Consultant
320 West 86 Street
New York, NY 10024-3139
212-496-9164   fax: 212-501-0439
e-mail: SDalsimer124@aol.com
Edits fiction and non-fiction. In fiction edits literary and commercial fiction as well as young adult fiction. In non-fiction interests include the areas of memoir, spirituality, psychology, self-help, biography, theater, film and television. Authors worked with

include Paul Auster, Fredric Dannen, Thomas Farber, Annette Insdorf, Iris Krasnow, Padma Lakshmi, D.J. Levien, Anthony Minghella, John Pierson, Martin Scorsese, and Veronica Webb.

Paul De Angelis Book Development

273 Town Street
West Cornwall CT 06796
860-672-6882
e-mail: pdeangelis@bookdocs.com
www.bookdocs.com
Manuscript evaluations, rewriting or ghostwriting, and editing. Thirty years' experience in key positions at St. Martin's Press, E. P. Dutton, and Kodansha America. Special expertise in history, current affairs, music, biography, literature, translations, popular science. Authors worked with: Delany sisters, Mike Royko, Peter Guralnick, Barbara Pym, Alexander Dubcek.

Michael Denneny

459 Columbus Ave. Box 204
New York, NY 10024
212-362-3241
e-mail: MLDenneny@aol.com
34 years editorial experience at the University of Chicago Press, the Macmillan Company, St. Martin's Press and Crown Publishing. Works on both fiction and nonfiction manuscripts for publishers, literary agents and authors, doing editorial evaluations, structural work on manuscripts, and complete line editing, as well as helping with the preparation of book proposals. Published, among others, Ntozake Shange, Buckminster Fuller, G. Gordon Liddy, Linda Barnes, Joan Hess and Steven Saylor. Has won the Lambda Literary Award for Editing (1993), the Literary Market Place Editor of the Year Award (1994) and the Publishing Triangle Editor's Award (2002).

Joyce Engelson

1160 Fifth Avenue, #402
New York, NY 10029
Sympathetic, hands-on editing; goal: commercial publication. Forty years' experience. Concentrations: thrillers, mysteries, literary and first novels; health, psychology, mind/body, women's issues, American history, pop culture, sports, comedy ("best sense of humor in the biz"—try me!). Authors include Richard Condon, Norman Cousins, Gael Greene. And me.

Jerry Gross

63 Grand Street
Croton-on-Hudson, NY 10520-2518
e-mail: GrosAssoc@aol.com
More than 40 years of specific, problem-solving critiquing, line editing, restructuring,

and rewriting of mainstream and literary fiction and nonfiction manuscripts and proposals. Specialties: male-oriented escape fiction, popular psychology, and pop culture. My goal is to make the manuscript as effective and salable as possible.

Susan Leon
21 Howell Avenue
Larchmont, NY 10538
fax: 914-833-1429
Editor specializing in preparation of book proposals and collaborations, including two *New York Times* bestsellers. Fiction: All areas—commercial, literary, historical, and women's topics. Nonfiction: history, biography, memoir, autobiography, women's issues, family, lifestyle, design, travel, food. Also, law, education, information, and reference guides.

Richard Marek
240 Hillspoint Road
Westport, CT 06880
203-341-8607
Former President and Publisher of E. P. Dutton specializes in editing and ghostwriting. Edited Robert Ludlum's first nine books, James Baldwin's last five, and Thomas Harris' *The Silence of the Lambs*. As ghostwriter, collaborated on six books, among them a novel that sold 225,000 copies in hardcover and more than 2 million in paperback.

James O'Shea Wade
1565 Baptist Church Road
Yorktown Heights, NY 10598
voice/fax: 914-962-4619
With 30 years' experience as Editor-in-Chief and Executive Editor for major publishers, including Crown/Random House, Macmillan, Dell, and Rawson-Wade, I edit and ghostwrite in all nonfiction areas and specialize in business, science, history, biography, and military. Also edit all types of fiction, prepare book proposals, and evaluate manuscripts.

Betty Kelly Sargent
212-486-1531   fax: 212-759-3933
e-mail: bsargent@earthlink.net
Betty Kelly Sargent is a veteran book and magazine editor with over 30 years of experience in the publishing business. Most recently she was Editor-in-Chief of William Morrow and before that Books and Fiction Editor at *Cosmopolitan Magazine*. She has been an Executive Editor at large at Harper Collins, Executive Editor of Delacorte Press and started out as a Senior Editor at Dell Books. Now a writer and freelance editor she is co-author of *Beautiful Bones Without Hormones* with Leon Root, MD, *What Every Daughter Wants Her Mother To Know* and *What Every Daughter Wants Her Father To*

Know with Betsy Perry. She specializes in women's fiction as well as memoir, diet, health, lifestyle, self-help and general non-fiction.

Genevieve Young
30 Park Avenue
New York, NY 10016
fax: 212-683-9780
Detailed analysis of manuscripts, including structure, development, and line editing. Areas of special interest include biography, autobiography, medicine, animals, modern Chinese history, and all works with a story line, whether fiction or nonfiction.

THE CONSULTING EDITORS ALLIANCE

The Consulting Editors Alliance is a group of highly skilled independent book editors, each with a minimum of 15 years' New York publishing experience.

We offer a broad range of services, in both fiction and nonfiction areas. These services include development of book proposals, in-depth evaluation of manuscripts; project development; line editing and rewriting; "book doctoring"; and collaboration and ghostwriting.

We work with writers both published and unpublished, literary agents, packagers and editors at major publishers and at small presses across the country.

Arnold Dolin
212-874-3419   fax: 212-580-2312
e-mail: abdolin@consulting-editors.com
Specialties: Contemporary issues/politics, popular psychology, business, memoir/biography, literary fiction, gay fiction, theater, films, music. Arnold Dolin has held various editorial and executive positions during his nearly five decades in publishing. Most recently he was senior vice-president and associate publisher at Dutton Plume. He has edited a wide range of fiction and nonfiction, including *The Cause Is Mankind* by Hubert Humphrey, *On Escalation* by Herman Kahn, *Martha Graham: A Biography* by Don McDonagh, *With Child* by Phyllis Chesler, *Parachutes and Kisses* by Erica Jong, several books by Leonard Maltin, *Cures* and *Stonewall* by Martin Duberman, *Inside Intel* by Tim Jackson, *Defending the Spirit* by Randall Robinson, and *RFK* by C. David Heymann. His services are available as an editor and a consultant.

Moira Duggan
914-234-7937   fax: 914-234-7937-*51
e-mail: mduggan@consulting-editors.com
Specialties: Self-help, health, sports (especially equestrian), travel, nature, architecture, illustrated books, biography. Moira Duggan offers critique and solutions in all phases

of adult nonfiction book development: concept, presentation, writing style, factual soundness. Whether as an editor, collaborator or ghost, she aims for excellence of content and peak marketability in every project. Before turning freelance, she was managing editor at The Ridge Press, which conceived and produced quality illustrated books. She has written eight nonfiction titles, including *Family Connections: Parenting Your Grown Children* (coauthor), *The Golden Guide to Horses*, and *New York*. Her editorial philosophy: Respect and guide the writer; be committed, tactful and reliable; deliver on time.

Sandi Gelles-Cole
914-679-7630
e-mail: sgelles-cole@consulting-editors.com
Specialties: Commercial fiction and nonfiction. Other: First novels; "wellness" issues for women; general fiction or nonfiction on behalf of nonwriter experts or celebrities. Sandi Gelles-Cole founded Gelles-Cole Literary Enterprises in 1983, after eleven years as an acquisitions editor for major New York publishers. Strong points include: developing concept and integrating for fiction and nonfiction, concretizing concept and integrating it throughout the work; for fiction: structuring plot, developing subplot, deepening characterization, collaboration, rewriting, preparing proposals. Some authors Sandi Gelles-Cole has worked with: Danielle Steel, Alan Dershowitz, Victoria Gotti, Christiane Northrup, Rita (Mrs. Patrick) Ewing and Chris Gilson, whose first novel, *Crazy for Cornelia*, was sold in an overnight preemptive sale as a major hardcover and became a Los Angeles Times bestseller.

David Groff
212-645-8910
e-mail: dgroff@consulting-editors.com
Specialties: Fiction, biography/memoir, science, current affairs. David Groff is a poet, writer, and independent editor focusing on narrative. For the last eleven years, he has worked with literary and popular novelists, memoirists, journalists, and scientists whose books have been published by Atria, Bantam, HarperCollins, Hyperion, Little Brown, Miramax, Putnam, St. Martin's, Wiley, and other publishers. For twelve years he was an editor at Crown, publishing books by humorist Dave Barry, novelists Colin Harrison and Paul Monette, and journalists Patrice Gaines, Michael D'Antonio, and Frank Browning. He co-authored *The Crisis of Desire: AIDS and the Fate of Gay Brotherhood* by Robin Hardy, and *An American Family*, with Jon and Michael Galluccio. David's book *Theory of Devolution* was published in 2002 as part of the National Poetry Series.

Hilary Hinzmann
212-942-0771
e-mail: hhinzmann@consulting-editors.com
Specialties: History, science, technology, business, sports, music, political/social issues, biography/memoir and fiction. Formerly an editor at W.W. Norton, Hilary Hinzmann has edited *New York Times Book Review Notable Books of the Year* in both fiction

and nonfiction. Books he has worked on include *Winfield: A Player's Life* by Dave Winfield and Tom Parker (a *New York Times* bestseller), *Marsalis on Music* by Wynton Marsalis, *Virgil Thomson: Composer on the Aisle* by Anthony Tommasini, *The Perez Family* by Christine Bell, the Kevin Kerney mystery series by Michael McGarrity and *The Symbolic Species: The Coevolution of Language and the Brain* by Terrence W. Deacon. He is now assisting fiction and nonfiction writers with development of their work, editing manuscripts for publishers, ghostwriting and cowriting.

Judith Kern

212-249-5871   fax: 212-249-4954
e-mail: kernjt@aol.com
Specialties: Self-help, spirituality, lifestyle, food, health and diet. Other: Mysteries, women's fiction. Judith Kern was an in-house editor for more than twenty-five years, most recently a senior editor at Doubleday, before becoming an independent editor and writer. She has worked with well-known fiction writers including Charlotte Vale Allen, Jon Hassler, Bette Pesetsky, and Patricia Volk, and Edgar award-winning mystery writers Mary Willis Walker and John Morgan Wilson. Her bestselling and award-winning cookbook authors include Alfred Portale, Pino Luongo, Michael Lomonaco, and Madeleine Kamman. She has collaborated with Jennifer Workman on *Stop Your Cravings* (The Free Press); with Joe Caruso on *The Power of Losing Control* (Gotham); and with Dr. Jane Greer on *The Afterlife Connection* (St. Martin's Press). She also worked with Alan Morinis on *Climbing Jacob's Ladder* (Broadway); Dr. Arlene Churn on *The End Is Just the Beginning* (Doubleday/Harlem Moon); and Ivan Richmond on *Growing Up Zen in America* (Atria). She is a member of the Author's Guild, The James Beard Society, and the International Association of Culinary Professionals.

Danelle McCafferty

212-877-9416   fax: 212-877-9486
e-mail: dmccafferty@consulting-editors.com
Specialties: Thrillers, mysteries, women's contemporary and historical fiction, romances and inspirational novels. Other: Self-help, religion/spirituality, theater and true crime. A former senior editor at Bantam Books, Danelle McCafferty started her own editorial services business in 1990. She works on all stages of a manuscript, from outline and plot development to line editing and/or rewriting. Over the past twenty-five years, she has edited bestselling novels by Tom Robbins, Dana Fuller Ross, Peter Clement, Frank Perretti, Nora Roberts, Patricia Matthews and Janelle Taylor, among others. Nonfiction authors include Bill Ury (negotiating), Ed Jablonski (theater), and Eileen MacNamara (true crime). As editorial director for a packager, she oversaw six highly successful mystery series. The author of two nonfiction books and numerous articles, she is a member of the American Society of Journalists and Authors and the Editorial Freelancers Association.

Nancy Nicholas

e-mail: nnicholas@consulting-editors.com

Specialties: Fiction, including first novels, historical fiction, and mysteries; biographies and autobiographies, history, theatre, hobbies, and gay issues. Nancy Nicholas has worked at three book publishers and three magazines in a variety of roles. In eighteen years at Knopf, she worked on literary and popular fiction, serious nonfiction, and translations. At Simon & Schuster, she edited fiction and nonfiction by a number of celebrities, including Joan Collins, Marlene Dietrich's daughter Maria Riva, Jerry Falwell, Jesse Jackson, Shirley Conran, and Shelley Winters. At Doubleday, she worked on the revised Amy Vanderbilt etiquette book. She was also a senior editor at *Vogue*, *Mirabella*, and *Connoisseur* magazines. Since becoming a freelancer, Nicholas has handled projects for many publishers, from editing Nick Malgieri's baking books and Michael Lee West's "Crazy Lady" Southern fiction to riding herd on the project that became Bill Gates's *The Road Ahead* and writing *Cooking for Madam* with Marta Sgubin, Jacqueline Kennedy Onassis's cook.

Joan B. Sanger

voice/fax: 212-501-9352

e-mail: jsanger@consulting-editors.com

Specialties: Mainstream commercial fiction, primarily legal and medical thrillers, mysteries, contemporary women's fiction. Other: Structuring nonfiction proposals, biography and autobiography. Joan Sanger has been an independent editorial consultant for over ten years, primarily developing and editing commercial fiction. Her referrals come from agents, publishers and private clients. Her authors, who are published by Berkeley, Warner Books, HarperCollins, and Simon & Schuster, include Gary Birken, M.D., an author of medical thrillers who is working on his fourth novel, James Grippando, and Bonnie Comfort. Prior to setting up her consultancy she was a senior editor for fifteen years at Simon & Schuster, founder, vice-president and editor-in-chief of the hardcover division of New American Library, and vice-president and senior editor at G.P. Putnam. Among her bestselling authors are Irving Wallace, Kitty Kelley, Anne Tolstoi Wallach, Henry Fonda, and Arthur Ashe. She has been a member of the Women's Media Group for twenty years.

Carol Southern

e-mail: csouthern@consulting-editors.com

Specialties: Personal growth, relationships, spiritual/inspirational, health/beauty, women's issues, biography, memoir, lifestyle. Carol Southern is a consultant, editor, book doctor, and ghostwriter. Prior to starting her own business in 1998, she held editorial and executive positions at Crown and Random House, where she was publisher of her own imprint, Carol Southern Books. She has edited many successful authors, including Donald Kauffman, *Color*; Ron Chin, *Feng Shui Revealed*; Sonia Choquette, *The Psychic Pathway*; biographer Carol Brightman; and Pulitzer Prize winners Naifeh and Smith (*Jackson Pollock*), as well as bestselling lifestyle authors Martha Stewart, Lee Bailey, and Chris Madden.

Karl Weber

voice/fax: 914-238-6929

e-mail: kweber@consulting-editors.com

Specialties: Business, including management, personal finance and business narratives; also current affairs, politics, popular reference, and religious/spiritual. Karl Weber is a writer, book developer and editor specializing in nonfiction, with a focus on business-related topics. In fifteen years as an editor and publisher with McGraw-Hill, the American Management Association, John Wiley & Sons and Times Business/Random House, Weber edited many bestsellers in fields such as management, investing, careers, business narratives and memoirs. He helped to create Wiley's acclaimed *Portable MBA* book series, and, when *Worth* magazine in 1997 selected the fifteen best investment books of the past 150 years, two were titles edited by Weber. He also edited three best-selling books by former President Jimmy Carter, *Living Faith*, *Sources of Strength*, and *An Hour Before Daylight*.

THE EDITORS CIRCLE

www.theeditorscircle.com

We are a group of independent book editors with more than 100 years of collective experience on-staff with major New York book publishers. We have come together to offer our skills and experience to writers who need help bringing their book projects from ideas or finished manuscripts to well-published books.

As publishing consultants (or "book doctors"), we offer a variety of editorial services that include defining and positioning manuscripts in the marketplace; evaluating and critiquing complete or partial manuscripts and book proposals; editing, ghostwriting, or collaborating on manuscripts and proposals; offering referrals to agents and publishers; helping authors develop platforms and query letters; and consulting on publicity and marketing.

So if you need help refining your book idea, editing or restructuring your manuscript, or defining and positioning your project in the marketplace, the book publishing professionals of The Editors Circle can offer you the editorial services you seek, a successful track record of projects placed and published, and the behind-the-scenes, hands-on experience that can help you take your idea or manuscript wherever you want it to go.

The editorial professionals of The Editors Circle include:

Bonny V. Fetterman

Editing and consulting: Academic and popular nonfiction, with special expertise in Judaica and books of Jewish interest (Jewish history, literature, religion, culture, and Bible); General nonfiction (history, biography, memoirs); Works of scholarship (social sciences). Currently based: Jamaica, New York. Previous on-staff experience: Senior Editor of Schocken Books (15 years). Currently Literary Editor of *Reform Judaism* magazine.

Rob Kaplan

Editing, ghostwriting, and collaborating on nonfiction books and book proposals, including business, self-help, popular psychology, parenting, history, and other subjects. Currently based: Cortlandt Manor, New York. Previous on-staff experience: Amacom Books (American Management Association), Macmillan, Prentice Hall, Harper-Collins.

Beth Lieberman

Editing, collaborating, and proposal preparation: Parenting, psychology/motivational, women's issues, Los Angeles-interest, memoir, Judaica; commercial women's fiction, general fiction. Currently based: Los Angeles, California. Previous on-staff experience: New American Library (NAL), Warner Books, Kensington Publishing, Dove Books and Audio, NewStar Press.

John Paine

Commercial and literary fiction, including thrillers, women's suspense, historical, African American, and mystery. Trade nonfiction, including adventure, memoirs, true crime, history, and sports. Currently based: Montclair, New Jersey. Previous on-staff experience: Dutton, New American Library, Prentice Hall.

Susan A. Schwartz

Ghostwriting: fitness, memoirs, other nonfiction subjects. Nonfiction editing: popular health, parenting, business, relationships, memoirs; popular reference books (all subjects); book proposals, assessments, and evaluations; corporate marketing publications (histories, biographies, conference materials); website content. Fiction editing: women's fiction; medical, legal, and political thrillers; general categories. Currently based: New York, New York. Previous on-staff experience: Random House, Doubleday, Facts On File, NTC/Contemporary Books.

THE CREATIVE LITERARY ALLIANCE

www.creativeliteraryalliance.com

The Creative Literary Alliance is a group of independent New York City publishing professionals, offering clients worldwide a broad range of writing and editorial services. Each of us has at least 20 years' experience in the field, working with authors, literary agents and every major publisher. We are specialists in both fiction and nonfiction, and are accessible via telephone, email and/or in person.

Members of the Creative Literary Alliance can help you with:

- A detailed evaluation and critique of your manuscript or proposal

- Idea development

- Substantive editing, rewriting, and polishing of any written material

- Book collaboration, co-authoring, and ghostwriting

- Assistance with query letters and book synopses

- Coaching throughout the writing process

- Project management, from conception through production

- Guidance on self-publishing

- Advice on platform development and marketing strategies

- Referrals to literary agents, publishers, and other literary services

- Advice on all aspects of the publishing process

You may contact us collectively through our Web site, or any of us individually via email. We have helped many authors maximize their potential…we can help you!

Penelope Franklin
e-mail: penfrank@yahoo.com

Specialties — Nonfiction: animals/pets, art/architecture, biography/memoir/oral history, food/entertaining, health/fitness/nutrition, history/social sciences, humor, illustrated books, narrative nonfiction, natural history, paranormal, popular science, self-help/popular psychology, travel, women's issues/feminism.

Penelope Franklin is a versatile editor and writer with over 30 years of publishing experience. She has been associated with major publishers, including Reader's Digest Books, Columbia University, the United Nations, Oxford University Press, American Heritage magazine and *Current Biography* magazine. She has assisted many writers who use English as a second language. She works skillfully with first-time authors, as well as established ones, with an emphasis on preserving a client's unique voice throughout the writing process.

Janet Spencer King
e-mail: janet.s.king@verizon.net
Specialities — Nonfiction: health/fitness/nutrition, medical, narrative nonfiction, self-help/popular psychology, spritiuality/New Age, travel, women's issues/feminism. Fiction: commercial/mainstream

Janet Spencer King has been an editor and writer for more than 25 years. She was editor-in-chief and founding editor of three national magazines as well as the author or co-author of four books with major publishers. Janet has written hundreds of magazine articles and was for several years a book agent, placing both non-fiction and fiction with key publishing houses. Janet is also a certified holistic health counselor.

Diane O'Connell
e-mail: doconnell@nyc.rr.com
Specialties — Fiction: commercial/mainstream, thrillers/ mysteries/ suspense, young adult. Nonfiction: biography/memoirs, business, health/fitness/nutrition, social sciences, narrative nonfiction, self-help/popular psychology, spirituality/New Age, true crime.

An award-winning writer and editor with 25 years experience, Diane O'Connell has worked as an editor at Random House and Sesame Workshop, and is the author or co-author of five books, including the groundbreaking *Divorced Dads: Shattering the Myths* (Tarcher/Putnam), which was the subject of a 20/20 report. As editor, collaborator, and writing coach, Diane's approach helps authors find their voice and articulate their visions in published form. She specializes in working with first-time authors and those who are looking to take their career to the next level.

Olga Vezeris
e-mail: OVerzeris@aol.com
Specialties — Fiction: commercial/mainstream in areas of adventure, historical, sagas, thriller/mysteries/suspense, women's market. Nonfiction: adventure, animals/pets, art/architecture, business, crafts/hobbies, food/entertaining, gift books, health/fitness/nutrition, illustrated books, lifestyle/decorating, narrative nonfiction, self-help/popular psychology, spirituality/New Age, travel, true crime.

Olga Vezeris has some of the most extensive experience in the publishing industry, having had senior editorial and subsidiary rights positions in companies including Simon & Schuster, Grand Central Publishing (Warner Books), Workman, Harper-Collins and the Bertelsmann Book Club group, where she has acquired, edited or licensed many commercial fiction and non-fiction titles.

THE ELEVEN ESSENTIAL QUESTIONS FOR EVERY NON-FICTION AUTHOR

GERALD SINDELL

When I work with authors, as part of the book development process I have eleven basic questions that need to be addressed. Once we've worked through all of them authors can be fairly well assured they've reached the heart of their material, and that if the book is a success, it will be the success they actually want.

1. **Distinctions.** *What is new here? What are the new distinctions you have made that no one has seen before?*

   All new ideas are the result of making new distinctions. When we see something that no one else has seen, we are truly thinking and creating. The fundamental work of authors is making new distinctions and sharing those with their readers so that the reader, too, can see what is new.

2. **Identity.** *Who am I?*

   Each of us is inherently unique — we couldn't be like anyone else even if we spent our entire lives trying. I happen to believe that if anyone can get to the truth of who they are and get it written, they will have made a valuable contribution to the human condition.

   Before we can write authentically, we must understand who we are. We must discover our identity, the part of us that is immutable, the fingerprint of our soul. We can express our identity by asking ourselves, "What am I driven to do in this world?"

3. **Implications.** *Where do your ideas lead if taken to their extreme? In other words, what are their implications? Do your ideas agree with each other, forming a coherent whole, or is there conflict between your ideas? Can that conflict be resolved?*

   Even ideas that appear simple on the surface will have implications if applied elsewhere. Only by testing our ideas in a wide range of contexts can we discover if they are really what we mean, or whether we must continue to refine our thinking. For instance, if we express the notion that everyone should always obey the law, how do we justify the American Revolution? And if we discover there are exceptions to our beliefs, those exceptions can help us refine what we actually believe.

4. **Testing.** *What would prove your theories wrong? If you can describe the right test, your thinking and writing will be more readily accepted.*

    We are, of course, free to assert anything we want. Our readers, though, will often ask for some reasonable validation that what we are asserting is also true. The adoption of ideas will be greatly advanced if we can also offer the appropriate test that would show whether our assertions are true, or not. For instance, if we assert that high school students don't learn well until after 11:00 A.M., it would be valuable if we would also show how this has already been proven in the past, or could be tested in the future. If we can't figure out a convincing test, our ideas will be relegated to the scrapheap of pure conjecture.

5. **Precedent.** *Which writers and what ideas are your precedents? Are you clear how you fit into the great conversation of ideas?*

    Mortimer Adler described the history of thought in Western Civilization as being a Great Conversation. When we write non-fiction, we are automatically entering into dialogue with all of those who preceded us whether we are aware of it or not, so it would be valuable to find the leading writers both currently and in previous generations that have addressed the challenges that we are addressing. If we don't, we are risking appearing to be not well-informed. If we do discover our precedents, we will be much clearer about what is unique in our own thinking.

6. **Need.** *Who needs your knowledge? If you are writing to solve the problems of a small group, can you find others who would benefit from the same solutions? The second group might be larger than your initial target readership.*

    Most of us write to address our immediate audience that we know has a clear urgent need for what we have to say. It is frequently worthwhile to step back for a moment and ask if our work would benefit a wider group of people than just our core imagined readers. If it turns out that we have a much larger potential audience that would benefit from our work, it might be worthwhile to include their needs as we write. Our publisher will have a greater incentive to publish our book if we are writing for our largest prospective audience.

7. **Foundation.** *Is your thinking so new that it might represent a new body of law that can stand alone? If so, can you identity your underlying principles, and how they work together?*

Not every book can or ought to re-order the universe, but once in a while we might realize that we are defining a new field or a completely new way of organizing some area of thought. If we can discover the core underlying principles in our work we might add great value for our readers.

8. **Completion**. *Have you decided what the boundaries of your book are, and what it will take to be complete in and of itself?*
   Whether you are addressing your reader's desire to build a stone wall or understand the history of the Civil War, it is generally preferable to provide your reader with a single source solution for their needs — your book. If you cannot cover everything they will need to know, then you should consider providing the smallest possible list of the essential sources they will need.

9. **Connection**. *Once you know your target readers, have you thought about what voice will make it easiest for them to hear you? Have you structured your book in a way that will make it most easily grasped by your reader, as opposed to the way you might logically organize your ideas?*
   Most of us start out developing our books focused on what we have discovered and what we want to say. Our readers, generally, want to add to their knowledge and will benefit from a voice that seems to anticipate their questions and needs. It is helpful if authors can imagine several of their typical readers, and write with each of them in mind.

10. **Impact**. *Three years from now, if your book is successful, what will have changed in the world because of your work?*
    This question gets to the heart of why you're writing a book in the first place. Another way of getting to the same core question is asking yourself — if you had never lived, and what you knew to be true had never been heard by the world, what would have been lost? The answer to this question often takes the form of, "I want people to know that…" and whatever follows contains the essential part of your message, or your contribution.

    We can also ask ourselves, is there in existence a book that says what I want to say in pretty much the same fashion that I would want to say it? If so, we don't yet have a compelling reason for writing our book. If it would require a stack of books to pull together what it is we want to say, then we know we really need to write our own book.

11. **Advocacy**. *At first, only you can be a brilliant advocate for what you are creating. Have you crafted the language, metaphors, stories, and endorsements that will help others quickly and accurately understand the significance of what you have created?*
    If we ask others to take the first pass at defining us we run the overwhelming risk that they will get it wrong. We need to be brilliant at characterizing

what we have created, so that others can easily grasp the value of what is new here. Great authors are also great advocates for their work, which enhances the likelihood of reaching the audience that will benefit from it.

Gerald Sindell is an independent publishing consultant who works with his clients from the initial inception of their non-fiction books, to develop their strategy, and align that strategy with their business and personal goals. Sindell develops the book proposal with the author, supports the sale of the book with various agents, provides editorial support if required as the book is written. Sindell then coordinates the efforts of the author, publisher, and independent PR services in order to achieve the goals for success that were defined at inception. He can be reached at ThoughtLeadersINTL., www.thoughtleadersintl.com, 415-789-9040, 158 Saint Thomas Way, Tiburon, CA 94920.

WEB SITES FOR AUTHORS

WEB SITES FOR AUTHORS

O ne of the most valuable aspects of the World Wide Web for writers is that it provides the opportunity to explore the world of publishing. This annotated list of Web sites offers descriptions of some of the most useful sites for writers.

Now more than ever there's an infinite amount of resources available for writers on the internet in anything from membership/subscription sites to personal Web sites of authors who also list agents of the same genre.

New in this edition is a listing of blogs. The trend of blogging has spread among publishers – it is now common for trade and university publishers to keep a blog, or even separate blogs for different imprints. Publishing bloggers keep things mixed up with guest pieces by house authors, book reviews, interviews, links, industry news, current events, videos, and more. Publishers use blogs to keep the public aware of new releases, establish goodwill between press, authors, and customers, and as an outlet for interesting topical content related to their books.

Not only publishers keep blogs, though. The blogging trend has spread across the whole spectrum of the book world. Many literary agents keep blogs that give writers invaluable advice, critique mistakes, and lend crucial insights into their individual preferences and personalities. Writers keep blogs chronicling their own publishing experiences and hurdles. And others, from critics to businessmen, printers, and engineers, lend their own unique and valuable opinions about the publishing world.

We are aware that blogs sprout up quickly, and while a fairly large list has been gathered, it is far from comprehensive. Follow links, sample, and explore and you will learn much about what people are thinking and how to approach them.

Below is a sampling of what's available on the Web, grouped according to the following categories:

- Anthology Resources

- Blogging Resources

  - Literary/Industry Blogs

  - Literary Agent Blogs

  - Publisher Blogs

- University Press Blogs

- Children's Literature Resources

- E-Publishing Resources

- Funding Resources

- Horror Resources

- Mystery Resources

- Poetry Resources

- Romance Resources

- Science Fiction Resources

- Screenwriting Resources

- Western Resources

- General Resource Sites

ANTHOLOGY RESOURCES

ANTHOLOGIESONLINE

http://www.AnthologiesOnline.com

Writers will find more than great articles and frequent postings of calls for manuscripts. From *Chicken Soup* to Horror, anthology publishers post their calls for writers. Subscribers have advance notice of calls for manuscripts and may apply for a free promotional page.

The site has a comprehensive, up-to-date list of paying markets for writers of science fiction, fantasy, horror, and slipstream. One page lists all markets; other pages break out markets by pro, semi-pro, anthologies, and contests, as well as by print and electronic formats. Listings include summaries of guidelines and indications of markets' "aliveness," plus Web site URLs.

LITERARY/INDUSTRY BLOGS

BLOG OF A BOOKSLUT

http://www.bookslut.com/blog

Bookslut, the alias of eminent litblogger Jessa Crispin, features prolific magazine and book reviews, columns, interviews, essays, news, unusual links, history, book society, and much more.

BOOKDWARF

http://www.bookdwarf.com

The blog of Megan Sullivan, one of the frontlist buyers at the Harvard Book Store. She writes on books, reading reports, publishing news, film adaptations, humor, and opinion.

BOOKENDS, LLC

http://bookendslitagency.blogspot.com

Bookends is a literary agency focusing on fiction and nonfiction books for adult audiences. Their blog features publishing advice, views from the agent's perspective, industry opinions, book reviews, and inspiration.

BOOKNINJA

http://www.bookninja.com

Founded by Canadian editor and publisher George Murray, Bookninja is the premier Canadian literary site and is frequented by thousands of people from around the globe. It posts unusual publishing-related stories, hearsay, industry news, humor, and technology.

BOOKSQUARE

http://www.booksquare.com

The primary blog of Kassia Krozser. Honest, entertaining, and often hilarious writing on the publishing industry, technology, the Internet, markets, and writers.

CHEKHOV'S MISTRESS

http://www.checkovsmistress.com

Chekhov's Mistress, written by web developer, writer, and online publisher Bud Parr, is dedicated to discussing literature. Bud is also the organizer of Metaxucafe, the network "blog of literary blogs." Essays discuss literary classics, links, blogworld news, and literary history. Bud also runs an online Don Quixote discussion group, 400 Windmills (http://400windmills.com).

CONFESSIONS OF AN IDIOSYNCRATIC MIND

http://www.sarahweinman.com

Confessions of an Idiosyncratic Mind is the blog of Sarah Weinman, the Baltimore Sun's crime fiction columnist and writer of "Dark Passages," a monthly mystery and suspense column for the *Los Angeles Times Book Review*. It provides commentary on crime and mystery fiction, industry links, and genre news.

CONVERSATIONAL READING

http://esposito.typepad.com/con_read/

The blog of Scott Esposito, member of the National Book Critics Circle, reviewer and essayist, has been singled out by *The New York Times*, *The Village Voice*, and *Variety*, among others. It features literary news, interviews, reviews, rants, opinions, links, and more.

DEAR AUTHOR...

http://dearauthor.com/wordpress/

Six devoted readers serve up fiction book reviews (primarily romance and fantasy with some non fiction and manga thrown in) and provide honest commentary on the Romance genre and publishing industry.

THE ELEGANT VARIATION

http://www.marksarvas.blogs.com/

According to Fowler's, "The Elegant Variation" is a term for the inept writers pained efforts at freshness or vividness of expression. The acclaimed blog itself is the work of Mark Sarvas, writer, book reviewer, screenwriter, and newspaper editor. The posts feature quotes, marginalia, book reviews, contests, interviews, publishing news, book giveaways, and videos.

GALLEYCAT

http://www.mediabistro.com/galleycat/

Galleycat is an all-purpose literary weblog that features updates in the writing world, announcements, profiles, essays, interviews, events, industry and bookseller news, multimedia,

GOLDEN RULE JONES

http://goldenrulejones.com

This blog was started to cover literary events in Chicago, specifically fiction, poetry, and literary nonfiction.

LAILA LALAMI

http://www.lailalalami.com/blog

The blog of Laila Lamami, Moroccan born writer, novelist, Fulbright fellow, and professor. It features journal entries, news, commentary, links, photographs, and opinions.

LITBLOG CO-OP

http://www.lbc.typepad.com

The Litblog Co-Op is made up of a coalition of bloggers for the purpose of drawing attention to the best of contemporary fiction, authors, and presses. A variety of participating bloggers post their opinions about fiction, publishing news, reviews, and podcasts.

THE LITERARY SALOON

http://www.complete-review.com/saloon

The Literary Saloon offers opinionated commentary on literary matters, news, links, and tirades. Updated daily, it offers plenty on commentary and updates on the industry, both at home and internationally.

MAUD NEWTON

http://www.maudnewton.com

Brooklyn editor and writer Maud Newton's entertaining blog has been widely praised by publications as various as the *New York Times Book Review*, *Forbes*, *New York Magazine*, *The Washington Post*, and *Entertainment Weekly*. It features literary links, politics, humor, rants, recipes, essays, complaints, gossip, and more.

METAXUCAFÉ

http://www.metaxucafe.com

Metaxucafe aims to highlight the best content from the community of bloggers who write about books. Posts include litblog headlines – the 30 most recent posts from the "litblogosphere," member-posted content, editors choice section, a Flickr group, forums, and a blog-finding tool.

PUBLISHING FRONTIER

http://pubfrontier.com/about/

Started by Peter Brantley, the director of the Digital Library Federation, Publishing Frontier aims to conduct provocative public discussion of the publishing revolution and how it affects readers, society, economics, and fundamental values such as privacy. Posts follow on technology, popular culture, book printing, publishing practice, business, science, gadgets, and more.

PUBLISHING INSIDER

http://www.publishinginsider.typepad.com/publishinginsider

Written by Carl Lennertz of HarperCollins Publishers, Publishing Insider reflects a fascination with how and why books sell. Movies, music, and museums are also explored as he studies how word of mouth operates in larger society. Posts on style, songs, bestsellers, reissues, and marketing.

SLUSHPILE

http://www.slushpile.net

SlushPile features interviews, reviews of nonfiction, essays on publishing, advice for writers, industry news and commentary, pop-culture, and celebrity nonfiction.

THREE PERCENT

http://www.rochester.edu/College/translation/threepercent

Three Percent has the goal of becoming a destination for readers, editors, and translators interested in finding out about modern and contemporary international literature. The title is taken from the fact that only 3% of books published in the United States are works in translation (and for poetry and fiction the number is closer to 0.7%). The site is a part of the University of Rochester's translation program. It posts on translation exercises, international book series, reviews, magazines, international events, and publishing.

WOULDN'T YOU LIKE TO KNOW?

http://isabelswift.blogspot.com

The blog of Isabel Swift, a member of Harlequin's New Business Development team, it offers posts about publishing, editing, business, relationships, romance, and storytelling in the 21st century.

LITERARY AGENT BLOGS

AGENT IN THE MIDDLE

http://agentinthemiddle.blogspot.com

The blog of NY based literary agent Lori Perkins, AITM focuses on horror, social science fiction, dark fantasy, erotica, and pop culture. She posts on conventions, titles-I'd-like-to-see, erotica, romance, advice for writers, and agenting stories.

BOOKENDS, LLC

http://bookendslitagency.blogspot.com

Literary agent Jessica Faust posts on out-of-control clients, writing, submissions, frustrations, working with agents, reviews, revisions, genre, and breaking the "rules."

DYSTEL AND GODERICH LITERARY MANAGEMENT

http://knightagency.blogspot.com

The excellent Dystel and Goderich blog has posts on advances, insider publishing information, opinions, the business of writing, conferences, pitching, do's and don'ts, publicity, and essays.

THE EVIL EDITOR

http://www.evileditor.blogspot.com

The Evil Editor's blog features writing exercises, cartoons, fill-in-the-captions, feedback, horror, science fiction, obituaries, and plots.

THE KNIGHT AGENCY

http://knightagency.blogspot.com

The blog of the Knight Agency features member blogs, book reviews, news, recent deals, and manuscript submission.

LIT AGENT X

http://raleva31.livejournal.com

The blog of literary agent Rachel Vater, with Folio Literary Management. She posts on inspirational author tales, announcements, queries, blogs, websites, publicity, deals, and rejections.

LIT SOUP

http://litsoup.blogspot.com/

The blog of Jenny Rappaport, literary agent at the L. Perkins Agency. Posts on upcoming events, query rejections, interns, cat tales, advice for writers, and titles.

JANET REID, LITERARY AGENT

http://jereidliterary.blogspot.com/

Janet Reid is an agent with FinePrint Literary management and specializes in crime fiction. She writes on recent titles, advice for writers, funny experiences, crankiness, events, book covers, procrastination, and the more irreverent side of book agenting.

THE REJECTER

http://rejecter.blogspot.com/

This is the anonymous blog of an assistant at a literary agency. S/he writes: "On average I reject 95% of the letters immediately and put the other 5% on the 'maybe' pile. Here, I'll talk about my work." He posts on vanity presses, Amazon, podcasts, fiction, blogs, platforms, writer advice, and genres.

MISS SNARK

http://misssnark.blogspot.com

Although discontinued in May 2007, the archives of Miss Snark, the Literary Agent are definitely worth perusing, especially for the writer who wants an extremely candid view of how poor submissions are received. After receiving over 2.5 million hits, Writers ask questions about the various details of the submission process, courting an agent, how queries should be structured etc., and Miss Snark provides her very meticulous, professional, and uncensored opinions on what writers can do better.

PUB RANTS

http://pubrants.blogspot.com

The blog of Denver-based literary agent Kristin, PubRants, features advice for writers, opinions on details of query structuring, beginning writer mistakes, videos, journal entries, and music updates.

PUBLISHER BLOGS

THE ABBEVILLE MANUAL OF STYLE

http://www.abbeville.wordpress.com

The blog of Abbeville press, producer of fine art and illustrated books. Their posts feature interviews, photography, news, reviews, contests, videos, and opinions.

ADDENDA & ERRATA

http://www.ivpress.com/blogs/addenda-errata/

Addenda and Errata is a blog from the editors of InterVarsity Press and brings readers up to date on issues, trends, and news related to evangelical publishing program of IVP Academic.

ALYSON BOOKS

http://www.alyson.com

Alyson Book's Web site doubles as a blog with posts on new books, podcasts, a bookstore, submission calls, event announcements, literary awards, links, excerpts, and reviews.

AMISTAD CONFIDENTIAL

http://www.amistadconfidential.blogspot.com

An imprint of HarperCollins, Amistad Confidential publishes book by and for the people of the African Diaspora. Posts on writers, upcoming books, African and African American issues in publishing, & more.

ANDREWS MCMEEL PUBLISHING, LLC NEWS

http://andrewsmcmeelpublishing.blogspot.com

The Andrews McMeel blog has book reviews, print and Youtube interviews, publishing news, author press, and links.

BANTAM DELL NEWS

http://www.randomhouse.com/bantamdell/news

The Bantam Dell blog features free excerpts, links to audio readings, author awards, sweepstakes info, podcasts, and event announcements.

THE BEST WORDS IN THE BEST ORDER

http://www.fsgpoetry.com

The venerable publishing house Farrar, Straus, and Giroux has an excellent poetry blog that features giveaways, audio poetry readings, posts by FSG poets, reviews, and poetry links.

CHELSEA GREEN

http://www.chelseagreen.com

The front page of Chelsea Green's Web site doubles as a blog with posts on environmental news, new books, international events, podcasts, video interviews, Youtube, environmental events, profiles, green tips, and recipes.

CHRONICLE BOOKS BLOG

http://www.chroniclebooks.com/blog

The Chronicle Books blog's mission is to let visitors know "what we're reading, what we're publishing, what makes us laugh, and what excites us." It features giveaways, book release info, event announcements, design ideas, photographs, tips, and television reviews.

THE CONTEXT BLOG

http://www.dalkeyarchive.com/blogs/

The Dalkey Archive blogspace provides a place where the staff and friends of the Dalkey Archive can post about current issues in the literary (or non-literary) world.

DAVID R. GODINE, PUBLISHER

http://www.drgodine.blogspot.com/

The blog of David R. Godine, Publisher and Black Sparrow Books features upcoming titles, book reviews, articles, literary links, translations, blogs, bookstores, announcements, eulogies, and interviews.

ECO-COMPASS BLOG

http://www.blog.islandpress.org

The blog of environmentally oriented Island Press features posts by Island Press authors on current environmental issues, observations, opinions, essays, economics, public transportation, history, forests, fish, global warming, sustainability, and wildlife.

FALCON GUIDES

http://www.falcon.com/blog

Falcon Guides, an imprint of Globe Pequot, features blogs of travel logs, articles, book tours via kayak, news items, essays by travelers, expert blogs, and tips from experienced travelers.

FLOG!

http://www.fantagraphics.com/index.php?option=com_myblog

FLOG! the blog of Fantagraphics publisher of comic and art books, features doodles, art scans, convention coverage, cartoons, podcasts, interviews, sales, author and artist spotlights, and signings.

HAMPTON ROADS PUBLISHING INSIGHTS BLOG

http://www.hamptonroadspub.com/blog/

The blog of spiritual publisher Hampton Roads features posts on book reviews, novels, prizes, spiritualism, points of view from the editors, links, and op-eds.

HARLEQUIN'S PARANORMAL ROMANCE BLOG

http://paranormalromanceblog.wordpress.com/

This blog features frequent posts by Harlequin Paranormal Romance authors, talking about their books, writing experiences, inspirations, and personal stories. There are also interviews, and convention updates.

HARLEQUIN HISTORICAL AUTHORS BLOG

http://harlequinhistoricalauthors.blogspot.com/

Harlequin Historical authors discuss new releases, book excerpts, writing, and offers and promotions.

HARLEQUIN AMERICAN ROMANCE AUTHORS

http://harauthors.blogspot.com

The blog of authors who write Harlequin American Romance, the HAR blog features journal-style entries by authors on writing strategies and experiences, new releases, recipes, families, and pets.

HIPPOCRENE BOOKS LANGUAGE AND TRAVEL BLOG

http://hippocrenebooks.blogspot.com

This very interesting blog features free samples of language learning programs, travel writing, vocabulary, and language.

HOUSE/WORK BLOG

http://blogs.thomasnelson.com/thenelsonbuzz.do

This is the central blog hub of Thomas Nelson Publishers, housing the blogs of several Thomas Nelson editors, authors, and businessmen.

INTRIGUE AUTHORS BLOG

http://www.intrigueauthors.com/blog

Harlequin Intrigue authors write about romance, writing, sexy books, journal-style experiences, and new releases.

LONELY PLANET TRAVEL BLOG

http://www.lonelyplanet.com/blogs/travel_blog

Lonely Planet's 326 authors and 400 travel-loving staff use their blog network to bring the best in travel blogging – buzz-word events, breaking news, tough travel, odd corners, and the world's craziest kitsch.

THE MAC BLOG

http://www.foundry01.com/macmillan/

The blog of Macmillan family of publishers and imprints is written by a number of executives and influencers across the board, including adult trade, children's, college and academic, and magazine publishing.

NOLO BLOGS

http://www.nolo.com/blogs.cfm

The hub of Nolo legal publishing, it features numerous blogs on legal economics, divorce, estate planning, real estate, fundraising, patents, LLCs, law reform, and bankruptcy.

THE OLIVE READER

http://olivereader.com

The Olive Reader is the weblog of the Harper Perennial imprint of HarperCollins. It features posts on movies, a literary quote generator, info on books, the book world, event coverage and announcements, up-and-coming writers, amusing anecdotes, tattoos, pictures, and t-shirts.

ONE MISSION BLOG

http://blogs.augsburgfortress.com

The blog of Augsburg fortress contains "reflections on the ministry of publishing," worship, opinion, observations, announcements, book news, event information, and technology.

ORBIT BOOKS

http://www.orbitbooks.net

Orbit is a UK-based leading publisher of Science Fiction and Fantasy, recently established in the United States as an imprint of the Hachette Book Group USA. Their blog features items on Orbit books, info on author appearances, interviews, links, sci-fi related news, and movies.

O'REILLEY RADAR

http://radar.oreilly.com

The O'Reilly Radar features tech reviews and laments, guest bloggers, Internet, social networks, updates on the press, new books, statistical charts, and computer networks.

PANTHEON GRAPHIC NOVELS NEWS

http://www.randomhouse.com/pantheon/graphicnovels/news/

The blog of the Random House Graphic Novel imprint has updates on author appearances, comic book news, animated movies, reviews, event announcements, awards, and upcoming publications.

ROWMAN AND LITTLEFIELD PUBLISHERS BLOG

http://romanblog.typepad.com

The Rowman and Littlefield blog features lengthy, high quality articles and opinion by R&L authors, current events, political science, economics, literary updates, and education.

PENGUIN BLOG (USA)

http://www.us.penguingroup.com/static/html/blogs/

Reveals what life is like for Penguin editors, articles by Penguin authors and guest bloggers, podcasts, Penguin imprint news, and upcoming books.

SIMON AND SCHUSTER CANADA

http://canada.simonsaysblogs.com/

This eclectic blog features Youtube posts, new books, scandals, appearances, recipes, photographs, author appearances, contests, book expos, and technology.

GIBBS SMITH BOOKS BLOG

http://gibbs-smithbooks.blogspot.com/

Lifestyle and design publisher Gibbs Smith's blog has posts on new releases, author events, pictures, Youtube videos, kitchen tips, design tips, and interviews.

AN INDEPENDENT VISION

http://www.sourcebooks.com/independentvision/index.php

An Independent Vision provides the latest Sourcebooks news on their books and authors, conferences, and other activities.

SOFT SKULL

http://www.softskull.com/news

New York's premier alternative press. Features reviews, links to articles, video posts, art shows, publishing gossip, and technology

THE TYNDALE BLOG

http://www.tyndale.com/articles/blog/

The Tyndale Blog offers a closer look at Tyndale's products and its authors, including upcoming media interviews, information about publishing trend, and Tyndale corporate initiatives.

THE WINGED ELEPHANT

http://theoverlookpress.blogspot.com/

The book blog and book vlog of The Overlook Press, the Winged Elephant has posts on book reviews, new releases, literary essays, author profiles, and announcements.

ZONDERVAN BLOG

http://zondervan.typepad.com/zondervan

Zondervan's mission is to express the current evangelical POV as manifested in author commentary, book excerpts, interviews, trends analysis, stimulating links, news from behind the scenes, and user comments.

UNIVERSITY PRESS BLOGS

BEACON BROADSIDE

http://www.beaconbroadside.com

Beacon Press's blog features political writing, articles by Beacon authors, book updates, political links, opinion essays, interviews, and news.

BOOKMARK

http://www.uapress.blogspot.com

Bookmark, the blog of The University of Arkansas Press has reviews, announcements, links to UA author press, event info, and new books.

BROOKINGS PRESS BLOG

http://brookingspress.typepad.com/

The blog of The Brookings Institution has new and featured books, excerpts from Brookings Press authors, essays, links, and politics.

THE CHICAGO BLOG

http://pressblog.uchicago.edu/

The blog of the University of Chicago Press includes posts on author essays, interviews, excerpts, documentaries, book reviews, recent releases, current events, opinion, magazines, and links.

COLUMBIA UNIVERSITY PRESS BLOG

http://www.cupblog.org

The Columbia University Press Blog features posts on CUP titles, current events, reviews, politics, interesting books, posts by CUP authors, radio, and press.

DUKE UNIVERSITY PRESS

http://www.dukeupress.typepad.com

News from Duke University Press includes posts on current events, recent releases, videos, guest posts, reviews, and contests.

HARVARD UNIVERSITY PRESS PUBLICITY

http://www.harvardpress.typepad.com

HUP's blog features posts on book news and reviews, event notifications, current events, author interviews, and links.

ILLINOIS PRESS BOOK BLOG

http://www.press.uillinois.edu/wordpress/

As the tagline puts it, the UIP blog brings "author appreciation, broadcast bulletins, event ephemera, and recent reviews from the University of Illinois Press." Publishing news and links, trivia, amusements, and reviews.

INDIANA UNIVERSITY PRESS BLOG

http://iupress.typepad.com/blog/

The Indiana University Press blog features book reviews, feeds, history, Indiana-related material, choice links, catalogs, and Twitter updates.

LSU PRESS

http://lsupress.typepad.com/lsu_press_blog/

The Louisiana State University Press blog features interviews, release info, literature news, amusing videos, author events, essays, and photography.

MITPRESSLOG

http://mitpress.typepad.com/mitpresslog/

MIT Press features posts on technology, video games, international relations, academic news, environment, music, video, award news, the internet, blog watches, author links, architecture, math, philosophy, and more.

NEWS FROM THE UNIVERSITY OF GEORGIA PRESS

http://ugapress.blogspot.com/

The University of Georgia Press blog features book news, reviews, awards, press news, and info on UGAPress authors.

OUPBLOG

http://blog.oup.com

The blog of Oxford University Press USA features links, publishing updates, pop-culture articles, curious facts, words of the week, short biography, and much more eclectic material.

SAGE HOUSE NEWS

http://cornellpress.wordpress.com

Sage House News, the blog of the Cornell University Press, features author interviews, recent releases, links to articles, a Publicity Roundup, current events, blog reviews, podcasts, author news, and science.

THERE'S A HOLE IN THE BUCKET

http://holeinthebucket.wordpress.com/

The blog for The University of Alberta Press features posts by the editors, new books, reviews, event reports, awards, announcements, many photographs, info for authors, and links.

UNIVERSITY OF CALIFORNIA PRESS WEBLOG

http://uspress.typepad.com/ucpresslog/

The University of California Press Weblog features posts on book reviews, science, author posts, excerpts, press news, photographs, interviews, wine, podcasts, poetry, websites, awards, and current events.

UNIVERSITY OF HAWAI`I PRESS LOG

http://uhpress.wordpress.com

One the most respected publishers of Asian and Pacific studies in the world, the UHP blog includes posts on awards, recent releases, reviews, articles on Asian and Pacific history & current events, and Hawai`ian book event announcements.

UNIVERSITY OF NEBRASKA PRESS BLOG

http://www.nebraskapress.typepad.com/

This blog has info on new releases, Tuesday trivia, history, UNP author guest blogs, reviews, interviews, and event announcements.

UNIVERSITY OF PENNSYLVANIA PRESS LOG

http://pennpress.typepad.com/pennpresslog/

The UPenn Press blog features posts on new and forthcoming titles, excerpts, previews, interviews, links, current events, publishing updates, and commentary.

UNC PRESS BLOG

http://uncpressblog.com

The University of North Carolina Press blog has reviews, new releases, a Today in History feature, roadtrip journals, audio links, history, blogosphere updates, awards, and event reports.

UNIVERSITY OF WASHINGTON PRESS BLOG

http://uwashingtonpress.wordpress.com

Billing itself as a "forum for the exploration of Western and Environmental History," this press blog features podcasts, reviews, author info, book awards, and links to articles.

YALE PRESS LOG

http://yalepress.typepad.com/yalepresslog/

The Yale Press blog features recent releases, Yale Press author opinion, photocontests, podcasts, video, awards, eulogies, and summer reading lists.

CHILDREN'S LITERATURE RESOURCES

CHILDREN'S WRITING RESOURCE CENTER

http://www.write4kids.com/

"Whether you're published, a beginner, or just someone who's always dreamt of writing for kids," here you'll find a free library of how-to information, opportunities to chat with other children's writers and illustrators, links to research databases, articles, tips for beginners, secrets for success as a children's writer, message boards, a children's writing survey, the chance to ask questions of known authors, and the opportunity to register in the Web site's guestbook to receive free e-mail updates filled with news and tips. The site also features a listing of favorite books, Newberry Medal winners, Caldecott Award winners, current bestsellers, and a link to its own children's bookshop.

THE CHILDREN'S BOOK COUNCIL

http://www.cbcbooks.org/

"CBC Online is the Web site of the Children's Book Council—encouraging reading since 1945." It provides a listing of articles geared toward publishers, teachers, librarians, booksellers, parents, authors, and illustrators—all those who are interested in the children's book field.

THE SOCIETY OF CHILDREN'S BOOK WRITERS AND ILLUSTRATORS

http://www.scbwi.org/

This Web site "has a dual purpose: It exists as a service to our members, as well as offering information about the children's publishing industry and our organization to non-members." It features a listing of events, awards and grants, publications, information for members, information on how to become a member, and a site map.

VERLA KAY'S WEBSITE FOR CHILDREN'S WRITERS

http://www.verlakay.com

This site is packed with information to assist writers of children's stories. Whether you are a beginner or a multi-published writer, there is something here for you. A chat room with nightly chats with other children's writers, online workshops and transcripts of past workshops, a Getting Started page, and a Published Writers page are just some of the features of this award-winning Web site.

E-PUBLISHING RESOURCES

E-BOOKS CAFÉ

http://www.topzone.com/ebookscafe/

E-books Café is dedicated to helping fellow writers reach out and touch the world through words. It provides an assortment of books to the public in the e-book and POD format in all genres of fiction, as well as nonfiction. It also offers authors worldwide the opportunity to promote and sell their e-books and POD books for free at its site.

FUNDING RESOURCES

ART DEADLINE, THE

http://custwww.xensei.com/adl/

The Art Deadline is a "monthly newsletter providing information about juried exhibitions and competitions, call for entries/proposals/papers, poetry and other writing contests, jobs, internships, scholarships, residencies, fellowships, casting calls, auditions, tryouts, grants, festivals, funding, financial aid, and other opportunities for artists, art educators, and art students of all ages. Some events take place on the Internet."

AT-A-GLANCE GUIDE TO GRANTS, THE

http://www.adjunctadvocate.com/

The At-a-Glance Guide to Grants offers information about grants, including a glossary of terms in grant forms, sample contracts, links to grant-related sites, a database of funding opportunities, and related agencies, foundations, and organizations. The site also includes a tutorial section with information on how to write a proposal and how to win a grant.

FOUNDATION CENTER, THE

http://fdncenter.org/

The Foundation Center Web site is dedicated to assisting writers in finding grants. It offers "over 200 cooperating sites available in cities throughout the United States. Of particular note is its large online library, with a wonderful interactive orientation to grant seeking. You'll even find application forms for several funding sources here."

FUNDSFORWRITERS

http://www.fundsforwriters.com and
http://www.chopeclark.com/fundsforwriters.htm

FundsforWriters specializes in leading writers to grants, awards, contests, fellowships, markets, and jobs. The two Web sites and three newsletters provide a weekly abu ance of sources for writers to reference and put checks in the bank. The other sites teach you how to write. FundsforWriters tells you where to make a living doing it.

MICHIGAN STATE GRANT INDEX FOR WRITERS

http://www.lib.msu.edu/harris23/grants/3writing.htm

This index includes a list of Web sites containing information on poetry grants, award programs, science writing, screenwriting, contests, scholarships, fellowships, reference, and student writing. The Web site is divided into categories for easy browsing.

NATIONAL FOUNDATION FOR THE ARTS

http://www.nea.gov/grants/apply/Lit.html

The National Foundation for the Arts believes that through literature, a nation express its hopes and fears and tell its stories to its citizens and to the world. Their Web site includes information on grants for arts projects, literature fellowships, radio and television programs, and more.

NATIONAL WRITERS UNION

http://www.nwu.org/

The union for freelance writers working in U.S. markets offers grievance resolution, industry campaigns, contract advice, health and dental plans, member education, job banks, networking, social events, and much more.

SOUTHERN ARTS FEDERATION

http://southarts.org

The Southern Arts Federation, a non-profit regional arts organization founded in 1975, creates partnerships and collaborations; assists in the development of artists, arts professionals and arts organizations; presents, promotes and produces Southern arts and cultural programming; and advocates for the arts and arts education.

WESTERN STATES ARTS FEDERATION

http://www.westaf.org/

The WSAF is a "nonprofit arts service organization dedicated to the creative advancement and preservation of the arts. Focused on serving the state arts agencies, arts organizations, and artists of the West, WSAF fulfills its mission by engaging in innovative approaches to the provision of programs and services and focuses its efforts on strengthening the financial, organizational, and policy infrastructure of the arts in the West."

HORROR RESOURCES

DARK ECHO HORROR

http://www.darkecho.com/darkecho/index.html

Dark Echo Horror features interviews, reviews, a writers' workshop, dark links, and a newsletter. Articles relate to topics such as the perception and psychology of the horror writer, the "best" horror, and reviews of dark erotica. The site also offers information and links to fantasy writing.

HORROR WRITERS ASSOCIATION

http://www.horror.org/

The Horror Writers Association (HWA) was formed to "bring writers and others with a professional interest in horror together, and to foster a greater appreciation of dark fiction in general." Bestower of the Bram Stoker Awards, HWA offers a newsletter, late-breaking market news, informational e-mail bulletins, writers' groups, agents, FAQ, and links.

MASTERS OF TERROR

http://www.horrorworld.org

Masters of Terror offers information about horror fiction, book reviews, new authors, horror movies, author message boards, HorrorNet chat room, and a reference guide and critique of horror fiction that features some 500 authors and 2,500 novels. The site also includes exclusive author interviews, book and chapbook reviews, and horror news.

MYSTERY RESOURCES

CLUELASS HOME PAGE

http://www.cluelass.com

The ClueLass Home Page offers awards for mystery fiction and nonfiction, information about conferences and conventions, and mystery groups for writers and fans. It includes information about markets, other contests, reference material, and online support, as well as listings of mystery magazines and newsletters, an international directory of mystery booksellers and publishers, and factual links about crime, forensics, and investigation.

MYSTERY WRITERS OF AMERICA

http://www.mysterywriters.org

Mystery Writers of America "helps to negotiate contracts, watches development in legislation and tax law, sponsors symposia and mystery conferences, and publishes books." The site includes mystery links, awards, a calendar of events, writers' discussions, and a new online mystery every day. It was established to promote and protect "the interests and welfare of mystery writers and to increase the esteem and the literary recognition given to the genre."

SHORT MYSTERY FICTION SOCIETY

http://www.shortmystery.net

The Short Mystery Fiction Society "seeks to actively recognize writers and readers who promote and support the creative art form of short mysteries in the press, in other mystery organizations, and through awards." The site offers a newsletter and other resources.

SISTERS IN CRIME

http://www.sinc-ic.org

Sisters in Crime is a Web site that vows to "combat discrimination against women in the mystery field, educate publishers and the general public as to inequities in the treatment of female authors, raise awareness of their contribution to the field, and promote the professional advancement of women who write mysteries." The site includes information about local chapters of Sisters in Crime and offers mystery links and online bookstores.

POETRY RESOURCES

ACADEMY OF AMERICAN POETS

http://www.poets.org/index.cfm

The Academy of American Poets Web site offers news regarding contest opportunities and winners, an online poetry classroom, the first-ever poetry book club, events calendars, and a search feature to find a specific poet or poem. Users can also listen to an author read a poem in RealAudio. The "My Notebook" feature allows visitors to keep a file of favorite poems or readings from the site. There are also discussion group and literary links sections.

ELECTRONIC POETRY CENTER

http://wings.buffalo.edu/epc/

There are perhaps more poetry Web sites online than for any other literary genre, so picking one representative site is really quite pointless. But we do recommend the Electronic Poetry Center at the University of New York at Buffalo, which is the heart of the contemporary poetry community online, having been around since the early days of gopher space—practically the Dark Ages in computer time. Of particular note are the active and well-respected poetics mailing list, the large collection of audio files, and an extensive listing of small press poetry publishers.

POETRY SOCIETY OF AMERICA

http://www.poetrysociety.org/

The Poetry Society of America Web site includes information about the newest developments in the Poetry in Motion project, which posts poetry to seven million subway and bus riders in New York City, Chicago, Baltimore, Portland, and Boston. It also includes news about poetry awards, seminars, the tributes in libraries program, the poetry in public program, and poetry festivals.

POETS & WRITERS

http://www.pw.org/

Poets & Writers is an online resource for creative writers that includes publishing advice, message forums, contests, a directory of writers, literary links, information on grants and awards, news from the writing world, trivia, and workshops.

THE INTERNATIONAL LIBRARY OF POETRY

http://www.poetry.com

The International Library of Poetry Web site offers information about its writing competitions, which focus on "awarding large prizes to poets who have never before won any type of writing competition." The site also includes Internet links, a list of past winners, anthologies of winning poems, and chat rooms.

ROMANCE RESOURCES

ROMANCE WRITERS OF AMERICA

http://www.rwanational.org

Romance Writers of America (RWA) is a national nonprofit genre writers' association—the largest of its kind in the world. It provides networking and support to individuals seriously pursuing a career in romance fiction.

SCIENCE FICTION RESOURCES

SCIENCE FICTION AND FANTASY WRITERS OF AMERICA

http://www.sfwa.org

The official Web site of the Science Fiction and Fantasy Writers of America offers information about the organization, its members, affiliated publications, an art gallery, and various awards.

SFNOVELIST

http://www.sfnovelist.com/index.htm

SFNovelist is "an online writing group dedicated to novelists who write 'hard science' SF." It is a highly structured and organized system of the exchange of science fiction manuscripts for consideration by other writers. Its goals are to: "become in the marketplace a premier source of novelists who write believable/hard science" SF; garner the attention of SF publishers, SFWA, and other writers' organizations for SF novelists; and develop a cadre of strong novelists, most of whom become published. Behind every great writer is usually a group of fellow writers who are equally serious about their writing, establish a presence at major SF writer conferences and conventions, and provide services and information to members that will help them in their search for self-improvement and in getting published. This includes contacts with other known writers and publishers and sources of distribution and marketing.

STORYPILOT'S SCIENCE FICTION AND FANTASY MARKET ENGINE

http://www.storypilot.com

StoryPilot is a search engine that allows writers to search for paying markets to, customizable to fit their needs. Science Fiction and Fantasy writers can search by genre, pay rate, experience required, dates, and format.

SCREENWRITING RESOURCES

HOLLYWOOD CREATIVE DIRECTORY, THE

www.hcdonline.com

The Hollywood Creative Directory's mission is to be the preferred and preeminent source of professional and educational information to, for, and about the entertainment industry, not only to the current entertainment industry professional community, but to aspiring professionals as well. HCD publishes the *Producers Directory*, "the phone book to Hollywood," a must-have directory for screenwriters. HCD offers screenwriter and film directories in an online subscription database. The Web site maintains one of the best entertainment job boards for the industry. HCD also publishes many how-to screenwriting books under the imprint of Lone Eagle Publishing, including the best-selling *Elements of Style for Screenwriters* and *How Not to Write a Screenplay*.

HOLLYWOOD SCRIPTWRITER

http://www.hollywoodscriptwriter.com

Hollywood Scriptwriters is an international newsletter that offers articles on craft and business "to give screenwriters the information they need to work at their careers." The site includes low-budget and indie markets available for finished screenplays, as well as a listing of agencies that are currently accepting submissions from readers of Hollywood Scriptwriter. According to Hollywood Scriptwriter, "people like Harold Ramis, Francis Ford Coppola, and Larry Gelbart have generously given of their time, knowledge, and experiences to share with HS's readers."

SCREENWRITER'S RESOURCE CENTER

http://www.screenwriting.com

The Screenwriters Resource Center aims to "provide links to products and services for screenwriters, compiled by the staff at the National Creative Registry." It includes links to many screenwriting sites and offers advice and copyright words of warning for writers posting original work on the Internet.

SCREENWRITER'S UTOPIA

http://www.screenwritersutopia.com/

Screenwriter's Utopia includes "helpful hints for getting screenplays produced, script development services, and contest information." The site includes a screenwriters' work station, tool kit, agent listings, and creative screenwriting magazines. Interviews with the screenwriters of *Sleepless in Seattle*, *Blade*, and *The Crow: City of Angels* are featured, and other interviews are archived. The site also includes chat rooms, message boards, a writer's directory, and a free newsletter.

WESTERN RESOURCES

WESTERN WRITERS OF AMERICA, INC.

http://www.westernwriters.org

"WWA was founded in 1953 to promote the literature of the American West and bestow Spur Awards for distinguished writing in the Western field." The site offers information about Old West topics, a listing of past Spur Award winners, and opportunities to learn about WWA and the Spur Award, to apply for membership in WWA, to subscribe to *Roundup Magazine*, or to contact Western authors whose work interests you.

GENERAL RESOURCE SITES

1001 WAYS TO MARKET YOUR BOOKS

http://www.bookmarket.com/1001bio.html

1001 Ways to Market Your Books is a site that offers a book marketing newsletter, consulting services, and book marketing updates. Other topics include success letters, author bios, sample chapters, and tables of contents.

3AM MAGAZINE

http://www.3ammagazine.com

3am is a webzine dedicated to countercultural, radical, and the cutting edge of fiction, poetry, and nonfiction. It features author profiles, interviews, links, and samples of poetry and fiction.

ABSOLUTE WRITE

http://www.absolutewrite.com/

Absolute Write is the "one-stop Web home for professional writers." It offers specific resources for freelance writing, screenwriting, playwriting, writing novels, nonfiction, comic book writing, greeting cards, poetry, songwriting, and more. The site also features interviews, articles, announcements, and a newsletter.

AGENT QUERY

http://www.agentquery.com

Agent Query is meant to be the one-stop writer's resource on the web about literary agents and publishing. It aims to help writers navigate through the arcane world of book publishing and offers a free searchable database of over 900 agents and profile information.

AMERICAN BOOKSELLERS ASSOCIATION

http://www.bookweb.org

The American Booksellers Association is a trade association representing independent bookstores nationwide. The site links members to recent articles about the industry and features Idea Exchange discussion forums.

AMERICAN DIALECT SOCIETY

http://www.americandialect.org/

The American Dialect Society Web site offers discussion lists, a newsletter, and a contacts list. Writers will find the "Dialect in Literature Bibliography" useful, as well as CD-ROM dictionaries and style and grammar guides.

AMERICAN SOCIETY OF JOURNALISTS AND AUTHORS

http://www.asja.org/

The American Society of Journalists and Authors is "the nation's leading organization of independent nonfiction writers." It offers its members professional development aids, such as confidential market information, an exclusive referral service, seminars and workshops, and networking opportunities. The site offers all visitors a newsletter, legal updates from the publishing world, and professional links.

AMERICAN JOURNALISM REVIEW

http://www.ajr.org/

This redeveloped site includes more editorial content, updated links to news industry sites, an improved job search function called "The Employment Section," and other interactive features.

ASSOCIATED WRITING PROGRAMS, THE

http://www.awpwriter.org/

The Associated Writing Programs Web site offers information about the AWP annual conference, a list of writers' conferences, a list of AWP member schools, articles and information on writing and writing programs, and a sample of articles and news from the AWP magazine *The Writer's Chronicle*. Members of AWP enjoy an online conferencing system, career advice, career placement service, a subscription to *The Writer's Chronicle*, and notice of contests and awards.

AUTHOR NETWORK

http://www.author-network.com

Author Network is a flourishing international community for writers. The site includes articles, monthly columns, a newsletter, message board, discussion group, critique service, and thousands of links to other writing sites. The writer in residence, Paul Saevig, provides a regular supply of instructional essays that may help new writers or even established authors. Other material and articles are provided by regular contributors, who are generally published authors themselves. Author Network promotes individual writers and other sites of interest to writers, as well as competitions, conferences, and courses.

AUTHOR'S GUILD, THE

http://www.authorsguild.org/

For more than 80 years the Guild has been the authoritative voice of American writers...its strength is the foundation of the U.S. literary community. This site features contract advice, a legal search, information on electronic rights and how to join the organization, a bulletin index, publishers' row, a listing of board members, and current articles regarding the publishing field. There is also a link for Back-in-print.com, an online bookstore featuring out-of-print editions made available by their authors.

AUTHORLINK

http://www.authorlink.com/

This information service for editors, literary agents, and writers boasts more than 165,000 loyal readers per year. Features include a "Manuscript Showcase" that contains 500+ ready to publish, evaluated manuscripts.

BLACK WRITERS ALLIANCE

http://www.blackwriters.org/

The Black Writers Alliance is the "first literary arts organization to utilize the power of the online medium to educate, inform, support and empower aspiring and published black writers. The Black Writers Alliance (BWA) is dedicated to providing information, news, resources, and support to black writers, while promoting the Internet as a tool for research and fellowship among the cultural writing community." The site offers users access to its media kit, a forum, a directory of speakers, a photo album, mailing lists, and chat rooms. The Black Writers Alliance is the first online community that has hosted an annual conference for its members.

BOOKLIST

http://www.ala.org/booklist/index.html

Booklist is a "digital counterpart of the American Library Association's *Booklist* magazine." In the site is a current selection of reviews, feature articles, and a searchable cumulative index. Review topics include books for youth, adult books, media, and reference materials. The site also includes press releases, the best books list, and subscription information.

BOOKTALK

http://www.booktalk.com/

Want to find out how to click with the people who talk books? Booktalk is a site where writers and readers learn more about the publishing industry. Besides an extensive literary agent list, there are articles about how to get published, writing tips from authors, and a bulletin board. The host for many author home pages, Booktalk allows readers to interact with bestselling authors, learn about new releases, read book excerpts, and see what's upcoming. A slushpile section lists conferences and publishing links.

BOOKWIRE

http://www.bookwire.com/

Partners with *Publishers Weekly*, *Literary Market Place*, and the *Library Journal*, among others, BookWire is a site that offers book industry news, reviews, original fiction, author interviews, and guides to literary events. The site features publicity and marketing opportunities for publishers, authors, booksellers, and publicists, and it includes a list of the latest BookWire press releases.

BURRY MAN WRITERS CENTER, THE

http://www.burryman.com/

With members and visitors in 104 countries, the Burry Man truly is "a worldwide community of writers." Working professionals and beginning writers find exclusive articles on the craft and business of writing, an extensive list of freelance job resources, a vast section focusing on Scotland, and links to more than 3,000 primary sources of information, giving writers the chance to speak to one another and use the Internet to hone their skills.

ECLECTIC WRITER, THE

http://www.eclectics.com/writing/writing.html

This site is an information source for those interested in crime, romance, horror, children's, technical, screen, science fiction, fantasy, mystery, and poetry writing. It features articles, a fiction writer's character chart, resources by genre, reference materials, research, general writing resources, online magazines and journals, writing scams, awards, and a writing-related fun page.

EDITORIAL EYE, THE

http://www.eei-alex.com

The Editorial Eye Web site consists of a sampler of articles originally printed in the newsletter by the same name. The articles discuss techniques for writing, editing, design, and typography, as well as information on industry trends and employment. *The Eye* has been providing information to publication professionals for 18 years.

GRANTA

http://www.granta.com/

The *Granta* Web site offers information about the most current issue of this highly regarded literary journal. The introduction is an explanation and background info about the topic around which the issue is based. The contents of the issue are listed, and visitors to the site may read a sample from the issue, as well as obtain subscription and ordering information. It also offers similar information about back issues and a readers' survey.

HELIUM

http://www.helium.com

Helium is a community of writers who share expert information on virtually any topic. Helium welcomes essays and articles on subjects as diverse as cooking, traveling, and computers, rated and classified by the user community itself. Helium also features a Marketplace for Freelance Writers section where publishers advertise assignments and writers can submit their material.

HOLLYLISLE.COM

http://hollylisle.com/

HollyLisle.com offers a community of supportive writers helping each other reach their writing goals. Led by full-time novelist Holly Lisle, the community includes crit circles, discussion and research boards, workshops, free real-time writing classes with professional writers and people who can offer their expertise in areas of interest to writers, writing articles, free writing e-books and the award-winning free e-zine *Vision: A Resource for Writers*, plus chapters, cover art, works-in-progress, and surprises for readers.

LITERARY MARKET PLACE

tp://www.literarymarketplace.com/

The Literary Market Place Web site offers information about publishers, which are categorized by U.S. book publishers, Canadian book publishers, and small presses, as well as literary agents, including illustration and lecture agents. The site also offers trade services and resources.

MARKET LIST, THE

http://marketlist.com

The Market List was started in 1994 as an online ezine on AOL and Compuserve. The first comprehensive writers market guidelines online.

MIDWEST BOOK REVIEW

http:// http://www.midwestbookreview.com/

Responsible for *Bookwatch*, a weekly television program that reviews books, videos, music, CD-ROMs, and computer software, as well as five monthly newsletters for community and academic library systems and much more, the Midwest Book Review was founded in 1980. This site features its reviews.

NATIONAL ASSOCIATION OF WOMEN WRITERS—NAWW

http://www.naww.org/

The National Association of Women Writers—NAWW was founded to support, encourage, entertain, motivate, and inspire women writers. NAWW offers a *free* weekly inspirational/how-to e-magazine, an online Member Portfolio, a Member Publications page, a quarterly member publication ("*The NAWW Writer's Guide*"), a Discussion List, a Member Only Online Critique Group, Daily Inspiration, a Writer's Resource Library, and much more. The NAWW site was voted one of the Top Ten "Best Sites" by *Writer's Digest* for 2001.

NATIONAL WRITERS UNION, THE

http://www.nwu.org/

The National Writers Union is the trade union for freelance writers of all genres. The Web site provides links to various service of the union, including grievance resolution, insurance, job information, and databases.

PARA PUBLISHING

http://www.parapublishing.com/

The Para Publishing Book Publishing Resources page offers "the industry's largest resources/publications guide," a customized book writing/publishing/promoting information kit, as well as current and back issues of its newsletter. The site also includes research links, a listing of suppliers, and mailing lists.

PEN AMERICAN CENTER

http://www.pen.org/

PEN is an international "membership organization of prominent literary writers and editors. As a major voice of the literary community, the organization seeks to defend the freedom of expression wherever it may be threatened, and to promote and encourage the recognition and reading of contemporary literature." The site links to information about several PEN-sponsored initiatives, including literary awards.

PUBLISHER'S LUNCH

http://publisherslunch.com/

Publishers Lunch is the publishing industry's "daily essential read," read by more than 30,000 publishing people every day. It gathers together stories from all over the Web and print of interest to the professional trade book community, along with original reporting, perspective, and wisecracking.

PUBLISHER'S MARKETPLACE

http://publishersmarketplace.com/

Publishers Marketplace shares a brand and is run by the same people as Publishers Lunch, but is a different service. For a registration fee, Publishers Marketplace provides real-time information on book deals, profiles of agents and publishers, a publishing industry Job Board, Publisher's Lunch Deluxe and reviews.

PUBLISHERS WEEKLY ONLINE

http://publishersweekly.com/

Publishers Weekly Online offers news about the writing industry, as well as special features about reading and writing in general and genre writing. The site also includes news on children's books, book-selling, interviews, international book industry news, and industry updates.

PUT IT IN INK

http://www.putitinink.com

Put It In Ink brings you articles, tips, books, software, and information about the craft of writing and getting published. Find information about newsletters (both print and online), e-zines, self-publishing and traditional publishing, freelancing, freelance jobs/markets, marketing tips, article writing, ideas to write about, and more.

R. R. BOWKER

http://www.bowker.com/

R. R. Bowker is a site that offers a listing of books in print on the Web, books out of print, an online directory of the book publishing industry, a data collection center for R. R. Bowker publications, and a directory of vendors to the publishing community.

SHARPWRITER.COM

http://www.sharpwriter.com/

SharpWriter.Com is a practical resources page for writers of all types—a "writer's handy virtual desktop." Reference materials include style sheets, dictionaries, quotations, and job information. The Office Peacemaker offers to resolve grammar disputes in the workplace.

UNITED STATES COPYRIGHT OFFICE

www.copyright.gov

The United States Copyright Office site allows the user to find valuable information about copyright procedures and other basics. In addition, the user can download publications and forms, then link to information about international copyright laws.

WOMEN WHO WRITE

http://members.aol.com/jfavetti/womenww/www.html

Women Who Write is a "collage of women based all over the United States with a passion for writing." The site provides useful links and a large dose of encouragement to women writers of all experience levels.

WOODEN HORSE PUBLISHING

http://www.woodenhorsepub.com/

Wooden Horse Publishing is a complete news and resource site for article writers. Visitors get news about markets, including planned, new, and folding magazines; editor assignments; and editorial changes. The site features a searchable market database of over 3,000 U.S. and Canadian consumer and trade magazines. Entries include full contact information, writer's guidelines, and—only at Wooden Horse—reader demographics and editorial calendars. Newsletter describes new markets and industry trends.

WRITE FROM HOME

http://www.writefromhome.com/

Whether you're a freelance writer, author, or writing from home but employed by a publication, this site strives to offer work-at-home writers tips, information, and resources to help you balance your writing career and children under one roof. You'll also find lots of writing and marketing resources to help you achieve the success you desire. It features a chat room, e-mail discussion list, and a monthly e-zine, featuring articles, markets, guidelines, tips, and more.

WRITER'S MANUAL

http://www.writersmanual.com/

Writers Manual is an online writer-related information warehouse. It receives information from writers, publishers, and agents worldwide, which includes links, announcements, articles, book reviews, press releases, and more. The site features free writer-related articles, links and resources, recommended books, and a vast job board that lists jobs for traditional and online publishing markets, syndication markets, publishers, grants/fellowships, and contests. The site hosts contests on a monthly basis, including the Writer Critique Contest, in which a published author edits and critiques the writing of one winner.

WRITERS CENTER, THE

http://www.writer.org/center/aboutwc.htm

The Writers Center is a Maryland-based nonprofit that "encourages the creation and distribution of contemporary literature." The Web site provides information on the organization's 200+ yearly workshops and links to its publication *Poet Lore and Writer's Carousel*.

WRITERS GUILD OF AMERICA

http://www.wga.org/

The WGA West site provides information about the Guild and its services, such as script registration. Other links to writing resources are provided as well.

WRITERS NET

http://www.writers.net/

Writers Net is a site that "helps build relationships between writers, publishers, editors, and literary agents." It consists of two main sections, "The Internet Directory of Published Writers," which includes a list of published works and a biographical statement, and "The Internet Directory of Literary Agents," which lists areas of specialization and a description of the agency. Both are searchable and include contact information. It is a free service that hopes to "become an important, comprehensive matchmaking resource for writers, editors, publishers, and literary agents on the Internet."

WRITERS ON THE NET

http://www.writers.com/

"Writers on the Net is a group of published writers and experienced writing teachers building an online community and resource for writers and aspiring writers." A subscription to the mailing list provides a description and schedule of classes offered by the site and a monthly newsletter.

WRITERS WRITE

http://www.writerswrite.com/

This "mega-site" provides myriad resources, including a searchable database of online and print publications in need of submissions. The Writers Write chat room is open 24 hours a day for live discussion.

WRITERS-EDITORS NETWORK

http://www.writers-editors.com/

The Writers-Editors Network has been "linking professional writers with those who need content and editorial services since 1982." The site features agent listings, articles on marketing tools, and a database of over 10,000 e-mail addresses of editors and book publishers. The site also links to fabulous how-to e-books of dream jobs for writers.

WRITERSPACE

http://www.writerspace.com/

"Writerspace specializes in the design and hosting of Web sites for authors. We also provide Web services for those who may already have Web sites but wish to include more interactivity in the way of bulletin boards, chat rooms, contests, and e-mail newsletters." The site features an author spotlight, contests, workshops, mailing lists, bulletin boards, chat rooms, romance links, a guestbook, information on adding your link, Web design, Web hosting, its clients, and rates.

WRITERSWEEKLY.COM

http://www.writersweekly.com/

This is the home of the most current paying markets to be found online. WritersWeekly publishes a free weekly e-zine featuring new paying markets and freelance job listings. Serving more readers than any other freelance writing e-zine (60K, as of December 2001), it is dedicated to teaching writers how to make more money writing.

WRITING CORNER

http://www.writingcorner.com/

Writing Corner is dedicated to the reader and writer alike, providing a one-stop place for author sites, chats, and giveaways, along with articles on all aspects of writing. The weekly "JumpStart" newsletter is designed to motivate writers at every level, while the "Author's Corner" newsletter keeps readers apprised of author events. The site features market information, resource listings, book reviews, and vast archives of writing information for fiction, nonfiction, and corporate writers.

YOUCANWRITE

http://www.youcanwrite.com/

YouCanWrite is one of *Writer's Digest's* 101 Best Sites for Writers and is the brainchild of two long-time publishing professionals who know the business from the inside out. Aspiring nonfiction writers can get the real story on what agents and editors look for in a salable manuscript. The site offers a wealth of free information, and its Insider Guides are practical, fun to read e-books that cover all the bases—from agents to books proposals to contracts.

WRITERS FREE REFERENCE

http://www.writers-free-reference.com

Writers Free Reference is a very unique resource site with many eclectic features and links. Its most outstanding asset is a continuously updated list of literary agents and their e-mail addresses.

WRITING.ORG

http://www.writing.org

Writing.org is a very simple but very useful Web site. It includes links to articles and interviews with agents, tips on finding an agent, tips on avoiding scam artists, and other "no-nonsense" tips on being an aspiring writer. This site's creator is a published author, former editor, former agent, and has been helping writers online for almost ten years.

SUGGESTED RESOURCES

SUGGESTED RESOURCES

SELF-PUBLISHING RESOURCES

Aiming at Amazon: The New Business of Self-Publishing, or, How to Publish Books for Profit with Print on Demand
by Lightning Source
and *Book Marketing on Amazon.com*
by Aaron Shepard (Shepard Publications)
www.shepardpub.com

All-By-Yourself Self-Publishing
by David H. Li (Premier Pub Company)
PO Box 341267, Bethesda, MD 20827
e-mail: davidli@erols.com

Business and Legal Forms for Authors and Self-Publishers
by Tad Crawford (Allworth Press)
10 East 23rd Street, Suite 210, New York, NY 10010
212-777-8395

The Complete Guide to Self-Publishing: Everything You Need to Know to Write, Publish, Promote and Sell Your Own Book
by Tom Ross, Marilyn J. Ross (Writers Digest Books)
4700 E. Galbraith Road, Cincinnati, OH 45236
512-531-2690

The Complete Guide to Successful Publishing
by Avery Cardoza (Cardoza Pub)
132 Hastings Street, Brooklyn, NY 11235
800-577-WINS, 718-743-5229; fax: 718-743-8284
e-mail: cardozapub@aol.com

The Complete Self-Publishing Handbook
by David M. Brownstone, Irene M. Franck (Plume)
375 Hudson Street, New York, NY 10014
212-366-2000

The Economical Guide to Self-Publishing: How to Produce
and Market Your Book on a Budget
by Linda Foster Radke, Mary E. Hawkins, Editor (Five Star Publications)
PO Box 6698, Chandler, AZ 85246-6698
480-940-8182

Exports/Foreign Rights, Selling U.S. Books Abroad
by Dan Poynter (Para Publishing)
PO Box 8206-240, Santa Barbara, CA 93118-8206
805-968-7277; fax: 805-968-1379; cellular: 805-680-2298
e-mail: DanPoynter@aol.com, 75031.3534@compuserve.com

The Fine Print of Self-Publishing: The Contracts and Services of
45 Self-Publishing Companies Analyzed, Ranked, and Exposed
by Mark Levine (Bascom Hill Publishing Group)
212 3rd Ave. North, Suite 570, Minneapolis, MN 55401

How to Make Money Publishing from Home, Revised 2nd Edition:
Everything You Need to Know to Successfully Publish Books, Newsletters,
Web Sites, Greeting Cards, and Software
by Lisa Shaw (Prima Publishing)
3000 Lava Ridge Court, Roseville, CA 95661

How to Self-Publish & Market Your Own Book: A Simple Guide for Aspiring Writers
by Mark E. Smith, Sara Freeman Smith (U R Gems Group)
PO Box 440341, Houston, TX 77244-0341
281-596-8330

How to Self-Publish Your Book with Little or No Money!
A Complete Guide to Self-Publishing at a Profit!
by Bettie E. Tucker, Wayne Brumagin (Rainbow's End Company)
354 Golden Grove Road, Baden, PA 15005 US
724-266-2346; fax: 724-266-2346

Indie Publishing: How to Design and Publish Your Own Book
by Ellen Lupton (Princeton Architectural Press)
37 E. 7th Street, New York, NY 10003
212-995-9620; email: editorial@papress.com

Make Money Self-Publishing: Learn How from Fourteen Successful Small Publishers
by Suzanne P. Thomas (Gemstone House Publishing)
PO Box 19948, Boulder, CO 80308
800-324-6415

Perfect Pages: How to Avoid High-Priced Page Layout Programs or Book Design Fees and Produce Fine Books in MS Word for Desktop Publishing and Print-on-Demand
by Aaron Shepard
www.shepardpub.com

Print-on-Demand Book Publishing: A New Approach to Printing and Marketing Books for Publishers and Self-Publishing Authors
by Morris Rosenthal (Foner Books)
www.fonerbooks.com

The Publish It Yourself Handbook (25th Anniversary Edition)
by Bill Henderson (Introduction); (W. W. Norton & Company)
500 Fifth Avenue, New York, NY 10110
212-354-5500

Publish Your Own Novel
by Connie Shelton, Lee Ellison, Editor (Intrigue Press)
PO Box 27553, Philadelphia, PA 19118
800-996-9783

The Self-Publishing Manual: How to Write, Print & Sell Your Own Book
by Dan Poynter (Para Publishing)
PO Box 8206-240, Santa Barbara, CA 93118-8206
805-968-7277; fax: 805-968-1379; cellular: 805-680-2298
e-mail: DanPoynter@aol.com, 75031.3534@compuserve.com

A Simple Guide to Self-Publishing: A Step-by-Step Handbook to Prepare, Print, Distribute & Promote Your Own Book—3rd Edition
by Mark Ortman (Wise Owl Books)
PO Box 29205, Bellingham, WA 98228
360-671-5858; e-mail: publish@wiseowlbooks.com

Smart Self-Publishing: An Author's Guide to Producing a Marketable Book
by Linda G. Salisbury (Tabby House)
4429 Shady Lane, Charlotte Harbor, FL 33980-3024
941-629-7646; fax: 941-629-4270

The Well-Fed Self-Publisher: How to Turn One Book into a Full-Time Living
by Peter Bowerman (Fanove Publishing)
3713 Stonewall Circle, Atlanta, GA
770-438-7200

INDUSTRY RESOURCES

30 Steps to Becoming a Writer and Getting Published:
The Complete Starter Kit for Aspiring Writers
by Scott Edelstein (Writers Digest Books)
4700 E. Galbraith Road, Cincinnati, OH 45236
512-531-2690

1,818 Ways to Write Better & Get Published
by Scott Edelstein (Writers Digest Books)
4700 E. Galbraith Road, Cincinnati, OH 45236
512-531-2690

2009 Poet's Market
by Nancy Breen, Editor (Writers Digest Books)
4700 E. Galbraith Road, Cincinnati, OH 45236
512-531-2690

2009 Children's Writer's & Illustrator's Market
by Alice Pope (Writers Digest Books)
4700 E. Galbraith Road, Cincinnati, OH 45236
512-531-2690

2009 Novel & Short Story Writers Market
by Rachel McDonald (Writers Digest Books)
4700 E. Galbraith Road, Cincinnati, OH 45236
512-531-2690

2009 Writer's Market
by Robert Brewer (Writers Digest Books)
4700 E. Galbraith Road, Cincinnati, OH 45236
512-531-2690

Advice to Writers: A Compendium of Quotes, Anecdotes, and Writerly Wisdom
from a Dazzling Array of Literary Lights
by John Winoker, Compiler (Vintage Books)
299 Park Avenue, New York, NY 10171
212-751-2600

The American Directory of Writer's Guidelines:
What Editors Want, What Editors Buy (3rd ed.)
by John C. Mutchler (Quill Driver Books)
1831 Industrial Way, #101, Sanger, CA 93657
fax: 559-876-2170; e-mail: sbm12@csufresno.edu

The Art of the Book Proposal
by Eric Maisel, PhD. (Tarcher)
375 Hudson Street, New York, NY 10014-3657

The Art and Science of Book Publishing
by Herbert S. Bailey Jr. (Ohio University Press)
Scott Quadrangle, Athens, OH 45701

The Autobiographer's Handbook: The 826 Valencia Guide to Writing Your Memoir
by Jennifer Traig (Holt Paperbacks)
175 Fifth Avenue, New York, NY 10010
646-307-5151

Book Blitz: Getting Your Book in the News: 60 Steps to a Best Seller
by Barbara Gaughen, Ernest Weckbaugh (Best Seller Books)
7456 Evergreen Drive, Santa Barbara, CA 93117
800-444-2524

Book Business: Publishing: Past, Present, and Future
by Jason Epstein (W. W. Norton & Company)
500 Fifth Avenue, New York, NY 10110
212-354-5500; fax: 212-869-0856

Book Editors Talk to Writers
by Judy Mandell (John Wiley & Sons)
605 Third Avenue, New York, NY 10158-0012
212-850-6000; fax: 212-850-6088; e-mail: info@wiley.com

Book Proposals That Worked! Real Book Proposals That Landed 10K – 100K
Publishing Contracts
by Angela J. Hoy (Splinter Press)

The Book Publishing Industry
by Albert N. Greco (Allyn & Bacon)
75 Arlington Street, Suite 300, Boston, MA 02116
617-848-6000

Breaking into Print: How to Write and Publish Your First Book
by Jane L. Evanson, Luanne Dowling (Kendall/Hunt Publishing Company)
4050 Westmark Drive, PO Box 1840, Dubuque, IA 52004-1840
800-228-0810, 319-589-1000

Business and Legal Forms for Authors and Self-Publishers
by Tad Crawford (Allworth Press)
10 East 23rd Street, New York, NY 10010
fax: 212-777-8261; e-mail: groberts@allworth.com

The Career Novelist: A Literary Agent Offers Strategies for Success
by Donald Maass (Heinemann)
22 Salmon Street, Port Melbourne, Victoria 3207, Australia
e-mail: customer@hi.com.au

The Case of Peter Rabbit: Changing Conditions of Literature for Children
by Margaret MacKey (Garland Publishing)
29 W. 35th Street, New York, NY 10001-2299
212-216-7800; fax: 212-564-7854; e-mail: info@taylorandfrancis.com

Christian Writer's Market Guide 2008: The Essential Reference Tool for the Christian Writer
by Sally Stuart (WaterBrook Press)
12265 Oracle Blvd., Suite 200
Colorado Springs, CO 80921
719-590-4999

Complete Guide to Book Marketing
by David Cole (Allworth Press)
10 East 23rd Street, New York, NY 10010
fax: 212-777-8261; e-mail: groberts@allworth.com

The Complete Guide to Book Publicity
by Jodee Blanco (Allworth Press)
10 East 23rd Street, Suite 210, New York, NY 10010
212-777-8395

The Complete Guide to Writer's Groups, Conferences, and Workshops
by Eileen Malone (John Wiley & Sons)
605 Third Avenue, New York, NY 10158-0012
212-850-6000; fax: 212-850-6088; e-mail: info@wiley.com

The Complete Guide to Writing and Selling the Christian Novel
by Barbara Kipfer (Writer's Digest Books)
4700 E. Galbraith Road, Cincinnati, OH 45236
512-531-2690

A Complete Guide to Writing for Publication
by Susan Titus Osborn, Editor (ACW Press)
5501 N. 7th Ave., # 502, Phoenix, AZ 85013
877-868-9673; e-mail: editor@acwpress.com

The Complete Idiot's Guide to Getting Published
by Sheree Bykofsky, Jennifer Basye Sander (Alpha Books)
201 West 103rd Street, Indianapolis, IN 46290
317-581-3500

The Complete Idiot's Guide to Getting Your Romance Published
by Julie Beard (Alpha Books)
4500 E. Speedway, Suite 31, Tucson, AZ 85712
fax: 800-770-4329

Complete Idiot's Guide to Publishing Children's Books
by Harold D. Underdown, et al. (Alpha Books)
4500 E. Speedway, Suite 31, Tucson, AZ 85712
fax: 800-770-4329

The Copyright Permission and Libel Handbook:
A Step-by-Step Guide for Writers, Editors, and Publishers
by Lloyd J. Jassin, Steve C. Schecter (John Wiley & Sons)
605 Third Avenue, New York, NY 10158-0012
212-850-6000; fax: 212-850-6088; e-mail: info@wiley.com

Directory of Small Press/Magazine Editors & Publishers
by Len Fulton, Editor (Dustbooks)
PO Box 100, Paradise, CA 95967
530-877-6110, 800-477-6110; fax: 530-877-0222

Directory of Poetry Publishers 2007-2008
by Len Fulton (Dustbooks)
PO Box 100, Paradise, CA 95967
530-877-6110, 800-477-6110

Editors on Editing: What Writers Need to Know About What Editors Do
by Gerald Gross, Editor (Grove Press)
841 Broadway, New York, NY 10003
212-614-7850

The Fast Track Course on How to Write a Nonfiction Book Proposal
by Stephen Blake Mettee (Quill Driver Books)
1254 Commerce Ave, Sanger, CA 93657
559-876-2170; fax: 559-876-2180

The First Five Pages: A Writer's Guide to Staying Out of the Rejection Pile
by Noah T. Lukeman (Fireside)
1230 Avenue of the Americas, New York, NY 10020
212-698-7000

Formatting & Submitting Your Manuscript (Writer's Market Library Series)
by Jack Neff (Writers Digest Books)
4700 E. Galbraith Road, Cincinnati, OH 45236
512-531-2690

*From Book Idea to Bestseller: What You Absolutely, Positively Must Know
to Make Your Book a Success*
by Michael Snell, Kim Baker & Sunny Baker, Contributors (Prima Publishing)
3000 Lava Ridge Court, Roseville, CA 95661

Get Published: Top Magazine Editors Tell You How
by Diane Gage (Henry Holt)
115 West 18th Street, New York, NY 10011
212-886-9200; fax: 212-633-0748; e-mail: publicity@hholt.com

Get Known Before the Book Deal: Use Your Personal Strengths to Grow an Author Platform
by Christina Katz (Writers Digest Books)
4700 E. Galbraith Road, Cincinnati, OH 45236
512-531-2690

Getting It Published: A Guide for Scholars and Anyone Else Serious About Serious Books
by William Germano (University of Chicago Press)
1427 East 60th Street, Chicago, IL 60637
773-702-7700; fax: 773-702-9756

Get Your First Book Published: And Make It a Success
by Jason Shinder, Jeff Herman, Amy Holman (Career Press)
3 Tice Road, PO Box 687, Franklin Lakes, NJ 07417
201-848-0310

Getting Your Book Published for Dummies
by Sarah Parsons Zackheim (IDG Books Worldwide, Inc.)
919 E. Hillsdale Boulevard, Suite 400, Foster City, CA 94404-2112
800-762-2974

Guide to Literary Agents, 2009
by Chuck Sambuchino (Writer's Digest Books)
4700 E. Galbraith Road, Cincinnati, OH 45236
512-531-2690

How to Be a Literary Agent: An Introductory Guide to Literary Representation
by Richard Mariotti and Bruce Fife (Piccadilly Books)

How to Be Your Own Literary Agent: The Business of Getting a Book Published
by Richard Curtis (Houghton Mifflin Company)
222 Berkeley Street, Boston, MA 02116-3764
617-351-5000

How to Do Biography: A Primer
by Nigel Hamilton (Harvard University Press)
79 Garden Street, Cambridge, Massachusetts 02138
800-405-1619

How to Get Happily Published (5th ed.)
by Judith Appelbaum (HarperCollins)
10 East 53rd Street, New York, NY 10022-5299
212-207-7000

How to Write a Book Proposal
by Michael Larsen (Writers Digest Books)
4700 E. Galbraith Road, Cincinnati, OH 45236
512-531-2690

How to Write a Damn Good Novel
by James N. Frey (St. Martin's Press)
175 Fifth Avenue, New York, NY 10010
212-674-5151

How to Write and Sell Your First Nonfiction Book
by Oscar Collier, Frances Spatz Leighton (St. Martin's Press)
175 Fifth Avenue, New York, NY 10010
212-674-5151

How to Write Irresistible Query Letters
by Lisa Collier Cool (Writers Digest Books)
4700 E. Galbraith Road, Cincinnati, OH 45236
512-531-2690

How To Write Killer Fiction
by Carolyn Wheat (Perseverance Press)

How to Write & Sell Your First Novel
by Oscar Collier (Writers Digest Books)
4700 E. Galbraith Road, Cincinnati, OH 45236
512-531-2690

Immediate Fiction: A Complete Writing Course
by Jerry Cleaver (St. Martin's Press)

In the Company of Writers: A Life in Publishing
by Charles Scribner (Scribner)
1230 Avenue of the Americas, New York, NY 10020
212-698-7000

Inside Book Publishing
by Giles Clark (Routledge)
270 Madison Avenue, New York, NY 10016
212-216-7800   fax: 212-563-2269

The Insider's Guide to Getting an Agent
by Lori Perkins (Writers Digest Books)
4700 E. Galbraith Road, Cincinnati, OH 45236
512-531-2690

The Joy of Publishing
by Nat G. Bodian (Open Horizons)
PO Box 205, Fairfield, IA 52556

*Jump Start Your Book Sales: A Money-Making Guide for Authors,
Independent Publishers and Small Presses*
by Marilyn Ross, Tom Ross (Writers Digest Books)
4700 E. Galbraith Road, Cincinnati, OH 45236
512-531-2690

Keep It Real: Everything You Need to Know About Researching and
Writing Creative Nonfiction
by Lee Gutkind (W. W. Norton)
500 Fifth Avenue, New York, NY 10110
212-354-5500   fax: 212-869-0856

Kirsch's Guide to the Book Contract: For Authors, Publishers, Editors and Agents
by Jonathan Kirsch (Acrobat Books)
PO Box 870, Venice, CA 90294
fax: 310-823-8447

Kirsch's Handbook of Publishing Law: For Author's, Publishers, Editors and Agents
by Jonathan Kirsch (Acrobat Books)
PO Box 870, Venice, CA 90294
fax: 310-823-8447

Literary Agents: A Writer's Introduction
by John F. Baker (IDG Books Worldwide, Inc.)
919 E. Hillsdale Boulevard, Suite 400, Foster City, CA 94404-2112
800-762-2974

Literary Agents: The Essential Guide for Writers
By Debby Mayer (Penguin Books)

Literary Agents: What They Do, How They Do It, and How to Find
and Work with the Right One for You, Revised and Expanded
by Michael Larsen (John Wiley & Sons)
605 Third Avenue, New York, NY 10158-0012
212-850-6000; fax: 212-850-6088; e-mail: info@wiley.com

Literary Marketplace 2008: The Directory of the American
Book Publishing Industry with Industry Yellow Pages
by Karen Hallard (Information Today)
630 Central Avenue, New Providence, NJ 07974
888-269-5372; e-mail: info@bowker.com

Making It As a Freelance Writer: A Seasoned Pro Shows You How to
Skip Common Mistakes and Build the Career that You Want
by Sue-Elliot Sink (Silver Lake Publishing)

Making the Perfect Pitch: How to Catch a Literary Agent's Eye
by Katherine Sands (Watson-Guptill)
770 Broadway, New York, NY 10003
info@watsonguptill.com

Marketing Strategies for Writers
by Michael H. Sedge (Allworth Press)
10 East 23rd Street, Suite 210, New York, NY 10010
212-777-8395

Merriam-Webster's Manual for Writers and Editors
Merriam Webster
47 Federal Street, PO Box 281, Springfield, MA 01102
413-734-3134; fax: 413-731-5979; e-mail: mwsales@m-w.com

Negotiating a Book Contract: A Guide for Authors, Agents and Lawyers
by Mark L. Levine (Moyer Bell Ltd.)
Kymbolde Way, Wakefield, RI 02879
401-789-0074, 888-789-1945; fax: 401-789-3793
e-mail: sales@moyerbell.com

Nonfiction Book Proposals Anybody Can Write:
How to Get a Contract and Advance Before Writing Your Book
by Elizabeth Lyon (Blue Heron Pub)
1234 SW Stark Street, Suite 1, Portland, OR 97205
fax: 503-223-9474; e-mail: bhp@teleport.com

Novel & Short Story Writer's Market, 2009
by Rachel McDonald, (Writer's Digest Books)
4700 E. Galbraith Road, Cincinnati, OH 45236
512-531-2690

The Plot Thickens: 8 Ways to Bring Fiction to Life
By Noah Lukeman (St. Martin's Press)

Poet Power! The Practical Poet's Complete Guide to Getting Published (and Self-Published)
by Thomas A. Williams (Venture Press)
PO Box 1582, Davis, CA 95617-1582
530-756-2309; fax: 530-756-4790; e-mail: wmaster@ggweb.com

Poets Market 2009
by Nancy Breen (Writer's Digest Books)
4700 E. Galbraith Road, Cincinnati, OH 45236
512-531-2690

Publicize Your Books: An Insiders Guide to Getting Your Book the Attention It Deserves
by Jacqueline Deval (Perigee Trade)
375 Hudson Street, New York, NY 10014
212-366-2000

Publish to Win: Smart Strategies to Sell More Books
by Jerrold R. Jenkins, Anne M. Stanton (Rhodes & Easton)
35 Clark Hill Road, Prospect, CT 06712-1011
203-758-3661; fax: 603-853-5420; e-mail: biopub@aol.com

The Screenwriter's and Playwright's Market
by Sambuchino (Writer's Digest Books)
4700 E. Galbraith Road, Cincinnati, Ohio 45236
513-531-2690

Secrets of a Freelance Writer: How to Make $85,000 a Year
by Robert W. Bly (Henry Holt)
115 West 18th Street, New York, NY 10011
212-886-9200; fax: 212-633-0748; e-mail: publicity@hholt.com

Self-Editing for Fiction Writers
by Renni Browne, Dave King (HarperCollins)
10 East 53rd Street, New York, NY 10022-5299
212-207-7000

A Simple Guide to Marketing Your Book:
What an Author and Publisher Can Do to Sell More Books
by Mark Ortman (Wise Owl Books)
24425 Fieldmont Place, West Hills, CA 91307
818-716-9076; e-mail: apweis@pacbell.net

The Shortest Distance Between You and a Published Book
by Susan Page (Broadway Books)
841 Broadway, New York, NY 10003
212-614-7850

Telling Lies for Fun & Profit
by Lawrence Block, Sue Grafton (Introduction); (William Morrow & Company)
1350 Avenue of the Americas, New York, NY 10019
212-261-6500

This Business of Books: A Complete Overview of the Industry from Concept Through Sales
by Claudia Suzanne, Carol Amato & Thelma Sansoucie, Editors (Wambtac)
17300 17th Street, #J276, Tustin, CA 92780
800-641-3936; fax: 714-954-0793; e-mail: bookdoc@wambtac

What Book Publishers Won't Tell You:
A Literary Agent's Guide to the Secrets of Getting Published
by Bill Adler (Citadel Press)
3300 Business Drive, Sacramento, CA 95820
fax: 916-732-2070

Writer Tells All: Insider Secrets to Getting Your Book Published
by Robert Masello (Owl Books)
115 West 18th Street, New York, NY 10010
212-886-9200

Write the Perfect Book Proposal: 10 Proposals That Sold and Why
by Jeff Herman, Deborah M. Adams (John Wiley & Sons)
605 Third Avenue, New York, NY 10158-0012
212-850-6000; fax: 212-850-6088; e-mail: info@wiley.com

A Writer's Guide to Overcoming Rejection:
A Practical Sales Course for the As Yet Unpublished
by Edward Baker (Summerdale Publishing Ltd.)

Writer's International Guide to Book Editors, Publishers, and Literary Agents:
Make the Whole English-Speaking Publishing World Yours with This One-of-a-Kind Guide
by Jeff Herman (Prima Publishing)
3000 Lava Ridge Court, Roseville, CA 95661

The Writer's Market Companion
by Joe Feiertag, Mary Carmen Cupito (Writer's Digest Books)
4700 E. Galbraith Road, Cincinnati, Ohio 45236
513-531-2690

Writer's & Illustrator's Guide to Children's Book Publishers and Agents
by Ellen R. Shapiro (Prima Publishing)
3000 Lava Ridge Court, Roseville, CA 95661

The Writer's Legal Companion: The Complete Handbook for the Working Writer
by Brad Bunnin, Peter Beren (Perseus Press)
11 Cambridge Center, Cambridge, MA 02142
e-mail: info@perseuspublishing.com

The Writer's Legal Guide (2nd ed.)
by Tad Crawford, Tony Lyons (Allworth Press)
10 East 23rd Street, Suite 210, New York, NY 10010
212-777-8395

The Writer's Little Instruction Book: 385 Secrets for Writing Well and Getting Published
by Paul Raymond Martin, Polly Keener (Writer's World Press)
35 N. Chillecothe Road, Suite D, Aurora, OH 44202
330-562-6667; fax: 330-562-1216; e-mail: Writersworld@juno.com

Writing the Breakout Novel
by Donald Maass (Writer's Digest Books)
4700 E. Galbraith Road, Cincinnati, Ohio 45236
513-531-2690

Writing the Breakout Novel Workbook
by Donald Maass (Writer's Digest Books)
4700 E. Galbraith Road, Cincinnati, Ohio 45236
513-531-2690

Writing and Selling Your Novel
by Jack Bickham (Writer's Digest Books)

Writing Down the Bones: Freeing the Writer Within
by Natalie Goldberg (Shambhala Publications)
PO Box 308, Boston, MA 02117
617-424-0030; fax: 617-236-1563

*Writing Life Stories: How to Make Memories into Memoirs, Ideas into Essays,
and Life into Literature*
by Bill Roorbach (Writers Digest Books)
4700 E. Galbraith Road, Cincinnati, Ohio 45236
513-531-2690

Writing and Selling Your Novel
by Jack Bickham (Writer's Digest Books)
4700 E. Galbraith Road, Cincinnati, Ohio 45236
513-531-2690

Writing Successful Self-Help and How-To Books
by Jean Marie Stine (John Wiley & Sons)
605 Third Avenue, New York, NY 10158-0012
212-850-6000; fax: 212-850-6088; e-mail: info@wiley.com

Writing the Nonfiction Book
by Eva Shaw, Ph.D. (Rodgers & Nelsen Publishing Company)
PO Box 700, Loveland, CO 80537
970-593-9557

You Can Make It Big Writing Books:
A Top Agent Shows How to Develop a Million-Dollar Bestseller
by Jeff Herman, Deborah Levine Herman, Julia DeVillers (Prima Publishing)
3000 Lava Ridge Court, Roseville, CA 95661

Your Novel Proposal: From Creation to Contract: The Complete Guide to
Writing Query Letters, Synopses and Proposals for Agents and Editors
by Blythe Camenson (Writers Digest Books)
4700 E. Galbraith Road, Cincinnati, OH 45236
512-531-2690

E-PUBLISHING RESOURCES

The Columbia Guide to Digital Publishing
by William E. Kasdorf (Columbia University Press)

eBook Secrets Exposed: How to Make Massive Amounts of Money in Record Time
with Your Own eBook
by Jim Edwards and David Garfinkel (Morgan James Publishing)
1225 Franklin Avenue, Suite 325, Garden City, New York, 11530
516-620-2528

Electronic Publishing: Avoiding the Output Blues
by Taz Tally (Prentice Hall)

Electronic Publishing: The Definitive Guide
by Karen S. Wiesner (Avid Press)
5470 Red Fox Drive, Brighton, MI 48114
810-801-1177; e-mail: cgs@avidpress.com

ePublishing for Dummies
by Victoria Rosenborg (Hungry Minds, Inc.)
909 Third Avenue, New York, NY 10022

From Entrepreneur to Infopreneur: Make Money with books, E-Books, and Information Products
by Stephanie Chandler (Wiley)
111 River Street, Hoboken, NJ 07030-5774
201-748-6000

How to Get Your E Book Published
by Richard Curtis, W. T. Quick (Writers Digest Books)
4700 E. Galbraith Road, Cincinnati, OH 45236
512-531-2690

How to Publish and Promote Online
by M. J. Rose, Angela Adair-Hoy (Griffin Trade Paperback)
175 Fifth Avenue, New York, NY 10010
212-647-5151

How to Write a "How-to" Book (Or eBook): Make Money Writing About Your Favorite Hobby, Interest, or Activity
by Shaun Fawcett (Final Draft!)
803-746-4675

How to Write and Publish Your Own eBook in as Little as 7 Days
by Jim Edwards and Joe Vitale (Morgan James Publishing)
1225 Franklin Avenue, Suite 325, Garden City, New York, 11530
516-620-2528

Plug Your Book! Online Book Marketing for Authors, Book Publicity through Social Networking
by Steve Weber (Weber Books)
www.weberbooks.com

Poor Richard's Creating eBooks
by Chris Van Buren, Jeff Cogswell, Matt Wagner (Top Floor Publishing)

Real ePublishing, Really Publishing!: How to Create Digital Books by and for All Ages
by Mark W.F. Condon and Michael McGuffee (Heinemann)

Self-Publishing EBooks and PODS: One Step at a Time
by Timothy Sean Sykes (The Forager)

U-Publish.Com: How Individual Writers Can Now Effectively Compete with the Giants of Publishing
by Dan Snow, Danny O. Poynter (Unlimited Publishing)
PO Box 3007, Bloomington, IN 47402
e-mail: publish@unlimitedpublishing.com

Write Your eBook or Other Short Book – Fast!
by Judy Cullins, Dan Poynter, and Marshall Masters (Your Own World Books)
P.O. Box 67061, Scotts Valley, CA 95067
775-546-1472

Writing.Com: Creative Internet Strategies to Advance Your Writing Career
by Moira Anderson Allen (Allworth Press)
10 East 23rd Street, Suite 210, New York, NY 10010
212-777-8395

GLOSSARY

GLOSSARY

A

abstract A brief sequential profile of chapters in a nonfiction book proposal (also called a synopsis); a point-by-point summary of an article or essay. In academic and technical journals, abstracts often appear with (and may serve to preface) the articles themselves.

adaptation A rewrite or reworking of a piece for another medium, such as the adaptation of a novel for the screen. (*See also* **screenplay**.)

advance Money paid (usually in installments) to an author by a publisher prior to publication. The advance is paid against royalties: If an author is given a $5,000 advance, for instance, the author will collect royalties only after the royalty moneys due exceed $5,000. A good contract protects the advance if it should exceed the royalties ultimately due from sales.

advance orders Orders received before a book's official publication date, and sometimes before actual completion of the book's production and manufacture.

agent The person who acts on behalf of the author to handle the sale of the author's literary properties. Good literary agents are as valuable to publishers as they are to writers; they select and present manuscripts appropriate for particular houses or of interest to particular acquisitions editors. Agents are paid on a percentage basis from the moneys due their author clients.

American Booksellers Association (ABA) The major trade organization for retail book-sellers, chain and independent. The annual ABA convention and trade show offers a chance for publishers and distributors to display their wares to the industry at large and provides an incomparable networking forum for booksellers, editors, agents, publicists, and authors.

American Society of Journalists and Authors (ASJA) A membership organization for professional writers. ASJA provides a forum for information exchange among writers and others in the publishing community, as well as networking opportunities. (*See also* **Dial-a-Writer**.)

anthology A collection of stories, poems, essays and/or selections from larger works (and so forth), usually carrying a unifying theme or concept; these selections may be written by different authors or by a single author. Anthologies are compiled as opposed to written; their editors (as opposed to authors) are responsible for securing the needed reprint rights for the material used, as well as supplying (or providing authors for) pertinent introductory or supplementary material and/or commentary.

attitude A contemporary colloquialism used to describe a characteristic temperament common among individuals who consider themselves superior. Attitude is rarely an esteemed attribute, whether in publishing or elsewhere.

auction Manuscripts a literary agent believes to be hot properties (such as possible best-sellers with strong subsidiary rights potential) will be offered for confidential bidding from multiple publishing houses. Likewise, the reprint, film, and other rights to a successful book may be auctioned off by the original publisher's subsidiary rights department or by the author's agent.

audio books Works produced for distribution on audio media, typically audiotape cassette or audio compact disc (CD). Audio books are usually spoken-word adaptations of works originally created and produced in print; these works sometimes feature the author's own voice; many are given dramatic readings by one or more actors, at times embellished with sound effects.

authorized biography A history of a person's life written with the authorization, cooperation, and, at times, participation of the subject or the subject's heirs.

author's copies/author's discount Author's copies are the free copies of their books the authors receive from the publisher; the exact number is stipulated in the contract, but it is usually at least 10 hardcovers. The author will be able to purchase additional copies of the book (usually at 40% discount from the retail price) and resell them at readings, lectures, and other public engagements. In cases where large quantities of books are bought, author discounts can go as high as 70%.

author tour A series of travel and promotional appearances by an author on behalf of the author's book.

autobiography A history of a person's life written by that same person, or, as is typical, composed conjointly with a collaborative writer ("as told to" or "with"; *see also* **coauthor**; **collaboration**) or ghostwriter. Autobiographies by definition entail the authorization, cooperation, participation, and ultimate approval of the subject.

B

backlist The backlist comprises books published prior to the current season and still in print. Traditionally, at some publishing houses, such backlist titles represent the publisher's cash flow mainstays. Some backlist books continue to sell briskly; some remain bestsellers over several successive seasons; others sell slowly but surely through the years. Although many backlist titles may be difficult to find in bookstores that stock primarily current lists, they can be ordered either through a local bookseller or directly from the publisher.

backmatter Elements of a book that follow the text proper. Backmatter may include the appendix, notes, glossary, bibliography and other references, lists of resources, index, author biography, offerings of the author's and/or publisher's additional books and other related merchandise, and colophon.

bestseller Based on sales or orders by bookstores, wholesalers, and distributors, bestsellers are those titles that move the largest quantities. List of bestselling books can be local (as in metropolitan newspapers), regional (typically in geographically keyed trade or consumer periodicals), or national (as in *USA Today*, *Publishers Weekly*, or the *New York Times*), as well as international. Fiction and nonfiction are usually listed separately, as are hardcover and paperback classifications. Depending on the list's purview, additional industry-sector designations are used (such as how-to/self-improvement, religion and spirituality, business and finance); in addition, bestseller lists can be keyed to particular genre or specialty fields (such as bestseller lists for mysteries, science fiction, or romance novels, and for historical works, biography, or popular science titles)—and virtually any other marketing category at the discretion of whoever issues the bestseller list (for instance African-American interests, lesbian and gay topics, youth market).

bibliography A list of books, articles, and other sources, that have been used in the writing of the text in which the bibliography appears. Complex works may break the bibliography down into discrete subject areas or source categories, such as General History, Military History, War in the Twentieth Century, or Unionism and Pacifism.

binding The materials that hold a book together (including the cover). Bindings are generally denoted as hardcover (featuring heavy cardboard covered with durable cloth and/or paper, and occasionally other materials) or paperback (using a pliable, resilient grade of paper, sometimes infused or laminated with other substances such as plastic). In the days when cloth was used lavishly, hardcover volumes were conventionally known as clothbound; and in the very old days, hardcover bindings sometimes featured tooled leather, silk, precious stones, and gold and silver leaf ornamentation.

biography A history of a person's life. (*See also* **authorized biography**; **autobiography**; **unauthorized biography**.)

blues (or bluelines) Photographic proofs of the printing plates for a book. Blues are reviewed as a means to inspect the set type, layout, and design of the books pages before it goes to press.

blurb A piece of written copy or extracted quotation used for publicity and promotional purposes, as on a flyer, in a catalog, or in an advertisement (*See also* **cover blurbs**).

book club A book club is a book-marketing operation that ships selected titles to subscribing members on a regular basis, sometimes at greatly reduced prices. Sales of a work to book clubs are negotiated through the publisher's subsidiary rights department (in the case of a bestseller or other work that has gained acclaim, these rights can be auctioned off). Terms vary, but the split of royalties between author and publisher is often 50%/50%. Book club sales are seen as blessed events by author, agent, and publisher alike.

book contract A legally binding document between author and publisher that sets the terms for the advance, royalties, subsidiary rights, advertising, promotion, publicity—plus a host of other contingencies and responsibilities. Writers should therefore be thoroughly familiar with the concepts and terminology of the standard book-publishing contract.

book distribution The method of getting books from the publisher's warehouse into the reader's hands. Distribution is traditionally through bookstores but can include such means as telemarketing and mail-order sales, as well as sales through a variety of special-interest outlets such as health-food or New Age venues, sports and fitness emporiums, or sex shops. Publishers use their own sales forces as well as independent salespeople, wholesalers, and distributors. Many large and some small publishers distribute for other publishers, which can be a good source of income. A publisher's distribution network is extremely important, because it not only makes possible the vast sales of a bestseller but also affects the visibility of the publisher's entire list of books.

book jacket (*See* **dust jacket**.)

book producer or **book packager** An individual or company that can assume many of the roles in the publishing process. A book packager or producer may conceive the idea for a book (most often nonfiction) or series, bring together the professionals (including the writer) needed to produce the book(s), sell the individual manuscript or series project to a publisher, take the project through to manufactured product—or perform any selection of those functions, as commissioned by the publisher or other client (such as a corporation producing a corporate history as a premium or giveaway for employees and customers). The book producer may negotiate separate contracts with the publisher and with the writers, editors, and illustrators who contribute to the book.

book review A critical appraisal of a book (often reflecting a reviewer's personal opinion or recommendation) that evaluates such aspects as organization and writing style, possible market appeal, and cultural, political, or literary significance. Before the public reads book reviews in the local and national print media, important reviews have been published in such respected book-trade journals as *Publishers Weekly*, *Kirkus Reviews*, *Library Journal*, and *Booklist*. A gushing review from one of these journals will encourage booksellers to order the book; copies of these raves will be used for promotion and publicity purposes by the publisher and will encourage other book reviewers nationwide to review the book.

Books in Print Listings, published by R. R. Bowker, of books currently in print; these yearly volumes (along with periodic supplements such as Forthcoming Books in Print) provide ordering information, including titles, authors, ISBN numbers, prices, whether the book is available in hardcover or paperback, and publisher names. Intended for use by the book trade, Books in Print is also of great value to writers who are researching and market-researching their projects. Listings are provided alphabetically by author, title, and subject area.

bound galleys Copies of uncorrected typesetter's page proofs or printouts of electronically produced mechanicals that are bound together as advance copies of the book (compare **galleys**). Bound galleys are sent to trade journals (*see* **book review**) as well as to a limited number of reviewers who work under long lead times.

bulk sales The sale at a set discount of many copies of a single title (the greater the number of books, the larger the discount).

byline The name of the author of a given piece, indicating credit for having written a book or article. Ghostwriters, by definition, do not receive bylines.

C

casing Alternate term for binding (*see* **binding**).

category fiction Also known as genre fiction. Category fiction falls into an established (or newly originated) marketing category (which can then be subdivided for more precise target marketing). Fiction categories include action-adventure (with such further designations as military, paramilitary, law enforcement, romantic, and martial arts); crime novels (with points of view that range from deadpan cool to visionary, including humorous capers as well as gritty urban sagas); mysteries or detective fiction (hard-boiled, soft-boiled, procedurals, cozies); romances (including historicals as well as contemporaries); horror (supernatural, psychological, or technological); thrillers (tales of espionage, crisis, and the chase), Westerns, science fiction, and fantasy. (*See also* **fantasy**, **horror**, **romance fiction**, **science fiction**, **suspense fiction**, and **thriller**.)

CD or **computer CD**   High-capacity compact discs for use by readers via computer technology. CD-ROM is a particular variety; the term is somewhere between an acronym and an abbreviation (CD-ROMs are compact computer discs with read-only memory, meaning the reader is not able to modify or duplicate the contents). Many CDs are issued with a variety of audiovisual as well as textual components. When produced by publishers, these are sometimes characterized as books in electronic format. (*See also* **multimedia**.)

children's books   Books for children. As defined by the book-publishing industry, children are generally readers aged 17 and younger; many houses adhere to a fine but firm editorial distinction between titles intended for younger readers (under 12) and young adults (generally aged 12 to 17). Children's books (also called juveniles) are produced according to a number of categories (often typified by age ranges), each with particular requisites regarding such elements as readability ratings, length, and inclusion of graphic elements. Picture books are often for very young readers, with such designations as toddlers (who do not themselves read) and preschoolers (who may have some reading ability). Other classifications include easy storybooks (for younger school children), middle-grade books (for elementary to junior high school students), and young adult (abbreviated YA, for readers through age 17).

coauthor   One who shares authorship of a work. Coauthors all have bylines. Coauthors share royalties based on their contributions to the book. (Compare **ghostwriter**.)

collaboration   Writers can collaborate with professionals in any number of fields. Often a writer can collaborate in order to produce books outside the writer's own areas of formally credentialed expertise (for example, a writer with an interest in exercise and nutrition may collaborate with a sports doctor on a health book). Though the writer may be billed as a coauthor (*see* **coauthor**), the writer does not necessarily receive a byline (in which case the writer is a **ghostwriter**). Royalties are shared, based on respective contributions to the book (including expertise or promotional abilities as well as the actual writing).

colophon   Strictly speaking, a colophon is a publisher's logo; in bookmaking, the term may also refer to a listing of the materials used, as well as credits for the design, composition, and production of the book. Such colophons are sometimes included in the backmatter or as part of the copyright page.

commercial fiction   Fiction written to appeal to as broad-based a readership as possible.

concept   A general statement of the idea behind a book.

cool A modern colloquial expression that indicates satisfaction or approval, or may signify the maintenance of calm within a whirlwind. A fat contract for a new author is definitely cool.

cooperative advertising (co-op) An agreement between a publisher and a bookstore. The publisher's book is featured in an ad for the bookstore (sometimes in conjunction with an author appearance or other special book promotion); the publisher contributes to the cost of the ad, which is billed at a lower (retail advertising) rate.

copublishing Joint publishing of a book, usually by a publisher and another corporate entity such as a foundation, a museum, or a smaller publisher. An author can copublish with the publisher by sharing the costs and decision making and, ultimately, the profits.

copyeditor An editor, responsible for the final polishing of a manuscript, who reads primarily in terms of appropriate word usage and grammatical expression, with an eye toward clarity and coherence of the material as presented, factual errors and inconsistencies, spelling, and punctuation. (*See also* **editor**.)

copyright The legal proprietary right to reproduce, have reproduced, publish, and sell copies of literary, musical, and other artistic works. The rights to literary properties reside in the author from the time the work is produced—regardless of whether a formal copyright registration is obtained. However, for legal recourse in the event of plagiarism or other infringement, the work must be registered with the U.S. Copyright Office, and all copies of the work must bear the copyright notice. (*See also* **work-for-hire**.)

cover blurbs Favorable quotes from other writers, celebrities, or experts in a book's subject area, which appear on the dust jacket and are used to enhance the book's point-of-purchase appeal to the potential book-buying public.

crash Coarse gauze fabric used in bookbinding to strengthen the spine and joints of a book.

curriculum vitae (abbreviated **c.v.**) Latin expression meaning "course of life"—in other words, the **résumé**.

D

deadline In book publishing, this not-so-subtle synonym is used for the author's due date for delivery of the completed manuscript to the publisher. The deadline can be as much as a full year before official publication date, unless the book is being produced quickly to coincide with or follow up a particular event.

delivery Submission of the completed manuscript to the editor or publisher.

Dial-a-Writer Members of the American Society of Journalists and Authors may be listed with the organization's project-referral service, Dial-a-Writer, which can provide accomplished writers in most specialty fields and subjects.

direct marketing Advertising that involves a "direct response" (which is an equivalent term) from a consumer—for instance, an order form or coupon in a book-review section or in the back of a book or mailings (direct-mail advertising) to a group presumed to hold a special interest in a particular book.

display titles Books that are produced to be eye-catching to the casual shopper in a bookstore setting. Often rich with flamboyant cover art, these publications are intended to pique bookbuyer excitement about the store's stock in general. Many display titles are stacked on their own freestanding racks; sometimes broad tables are laden with these items. A book shelved with its front cover showing on racks along with diverse other titles is technically a display title. Promotional or **premium** titles are likely to be display items, as are mass-market paperbacks and hardbacks with enormous bestseller potential. (Check your local bookstore and find a copy of this edition of this *Guide*—if not already racked in "display" manner, please adjust the bookshelf so that the front cover is displayed poster-like to catch the browser's eye—that's what we do routinely.)

distributor An agent or business that buys books from a publisher to resell, at a higher cost, to wholesalers, retailers, or individuals. Distribution houses are often excellent marketing enterprises, with their own roster of sales representatives, publicity and promotion personnel, and house catalogs. Skillful use of distribution networks can give a small publisher considerable national visibility.

dramatic rights Legal permission to adapt a work for the stage. These rights initially belong to the author but can be sold or assigned to another party by the author.

dust jacket (also **dustcover** or **book jacket**) The wrapper that covers the binding of hardcover books, designed especially for the book by either the publisher's art department or a freelance artist. Dust jackets were originally conceived to protect the book during shipping, but now their function is primarily promotional—to entice the browser to actually reach out and pick up the volume (and maybe even open it up for a taste before buying) by means of attractive graphics and sizzling promotional copy.

dust-jacket copy Descriptions of books printed on the dust-jacket flaps. Dust-jacket copy may be written by the book's editor but is often either recast or written by in-house copywriters or freelance specialists. Editors send advance copies (*see also* **bound galleys**) to other writers, experts, and celebrities to solicit quotable praise that will also appear on the jacket. (*See also* **cover blurb.**)

E

editor Editorial responsibilities and titles vary from house to house (often being less strictly defined in smaller houses). In general, the duties of the editor-in-chief or executive editor are primarily administrative: managing personnel, scheduling, budgeting, and defining the editorial personality of the firm or imprint. Senior editors and acquisitions editors acquire manuscripts (and authors), conceive project ideas and find writers to carry them out, and may oversee the writing and rewriting of manuscripts. Managing editors have editorial and production responsibilities, coordinating and scheduling the book through the various phases of production. Associate and assistant editors edit; they are involved in much of the rewriting and reshaping of the manuscript and may also have acquisitions duties. Copyeditors read the manuscript and style its punctuation, grammar, spelling, headings and subheadings, and so forth. Editorial assistants, laden with extensive clerical duties and general office work, perform some editorial duties as well—often as springboards to senior editorial positions.

Editorial Freelancers Association (EFA)   This organization of independent professionals offers a referral service, through both its annotated membership directory and its job phone line, as a means for authors and publishers to connect with writers, collaborators, researchers, and a wide range of editorial experts covering virtually all general and specialist fields.

el-hi   Books for elementary and/or high schools.

endnotes   Explanatory notes and/or source citations that appear either at the end of individual chapters or at the end of a book's text; used primarily in scholarly or academically oriented works.

epilogue   The final segment of a book, which comes "after the end." In both fiction and nonfiction, an epilogue offers commentary or further information but does not bear directly on the book's central design.

F

fantasy   Fantasy is fiction that features elements of magic, wizardry, supernatural feats, and entities that suspend conventions of realism in the literary arts. Fantasy can resemble prose versions of epics and rhymes or it may be informed by mythic cycles or folkloric material derived from cultures worldwide. Fantasy fiction may be guided primarily by the author's own distinctive imagery and personalized archetypes. Fantasies that involve heroic-erotic roundelays of the death-dance are often referred to as the sword-and-sorcery subgenre.

film rights   Like **dramatic rights**, these belong to the author, who may sell or option them to someone in the film industry—a producer or director, for example (or sometimes a specialist broker of such properties)—who will then try to gather the other professionals and secure the financial backing needed to convert the book into a film. (*See also* **screenplay**.)

footbands   (*See* **headbands**.)

footnotes   Explanatory notes and/or source citations that appear at the bottom of a page. Footnotes are rare in general-interest books, the preferred style being either to work such information into the text or to list informational sources in the bibliography.

foreign agents   Persons who work with their United States counterparts to acquire rights for books from the U.S. for publication abroad. They can also represent U.S. publishers directly.

foreign market   Any foreign entity—a publisher, broadcast medium, etc.—in a position to buy rights. Authors share royalties with whoever negotiates the deal or keep 100% if they do their own negotiating.

foreign rights   Translation or reprint rights that can be sold abroad. Foreign rights belong to the author but can be sold either country-by-country or en masse as world rights. Often the U.S. publisher will own world rights, and the author will be entitled to anywhere from 50% to 85% of these revenues.

foreword An introductory piece written by the author or by an expert in the given field (*see* **introduction**). A foreword by a celebrity or well-respected authority is a strong selling point for a prospective author or, after publication, for the book itself.

Frankfurt Book Fair The largest international publishing exhibition—with five hundred years of tradition behind it. The fair takes place every October in Frankfurt, Germany. Thousands of publishers, agents, and writers from all over the world negotiate, network, and buy and sell rights.

Freedom of Information Act Ensures the protection of the public's right to access public records—except in cases violating the right to privacy, national security, or certain other instances. A related law, the Government in the Sunshine Act, stipulates that certain government agencies announce and open their meetings to the public.

freight passthrough The bookseller's freight cost (the cost of getting the book from the publisher to the bookseller). It is added to the basic invoice price charged the bookseller by the publisher.

frontlist New titles published in a given season by a publisher. Frontlist titles customarily receive priority exposure in the front of the sales catalog—as opposed to backlist titles (usually found at the back of the catalog), which are previously published titles still in print.

frontmatter The frontmatter of a book includes the elements that precede the text of the work, such as the title page, copyright page, dedication, epigraph, table of contents, foreword, preface, acknowledgments, and introduction.

fulfillment house A firm commissioned to fulfill orders for a publisher—services may include warehousing, shipping, receiving returns, and mail-order and direct-marketing functions. Although more common for magazine publishers, fulfillment houses also serve book publishers.

G

galleys Printer's proofs (or copies of proofs) on sheets of paper, or printouts of the electronically produced setup of the book's interior—the author's last chance to check for typos and make (usually minimal) revisions or additions to the copy (*see* **bound galleys**).

genre fiction (*See* **category fiction**.)

ghostwriter A writer without a byline, often without the remuneration and recognition that credited authors receive. Ghostwriters often get flat fees for their work, but even without royalties, experienced ghosts can receive quite respectable sums.

glossary An alphabetical listing of special terms as they are used in a particular subject area, often with more in-depth explanations than would customarily be provided by dictionary definitions.

H

hardcover Books bound in a format that uses thick, sturdy, relatively stiff binding boards and a cover composed (usually) of a cloth spine and finished binding paper. Hardcover books are conventionally wrapped in a dust jacket. (*See also* **binding; dust jacket.**)

headbands Thin strips of cloth (often colored or patterned) that adorn the top of a book's spine where the signatures are held together. The headbands conceal the glue or other binding materials and are said to offer some protection against accumulation of dust (when properly attached). Such bands, placed at the bottom of the spine, are known as footbands.

hook A term denoting the distinctive concept or theme of a work that sets it apart as being fresh, new, or different from others in its field. A hook can be an author's special point of view, often encapsulated in a catchy or provocative phrase intended to attract or pique the interest of a reader, editor, or agent. One specialized function of a hook is to articulate what might otherwise be seen as dry albeit significant subject matter (academic or scientific topics; number-crunching drudgery such as home bookkeeping) into an exciting, commercially attractive package.

horror The horror classification denotes works that traffic in the bizarre, awful, and scary in order to entertain as well as explicate the darkness at the heart of the reader's soul. Horror subgenres may be typified according to the appearance of were-creatures, vampires, human-induced monsters, or naturally occuring life forms and spirit entities—or absence thereof. Horror fiction traditionally makes imaginative literary use of paranormal phenomena, occult elements, and psychological motifs. (*See* **category fiction; suspense fiction.**)

how-to books An immensely popular category of books ranging from purely instructional (arts and crafts, for example) to motivational (popular psychology, self-awareness, self-improvement, inspirational) to get-rich-quick (such as in real estate or personal investment).

hypertext Works in hypertext are meant to be more than words and other images. These productions (ingrained magnetically on computer diskette or CD) are conceived to take advantage of readers' and writers' propensities to seek out twists in narrative trajectories and to bushwhack from the main path of multifaceted reference topics. Hypertext books incorporate documents, graphics, sounds, and even blank slates upon which readers may compose their own variations on the authored components. The computer's capacities to afford such diversions can bring reader and hypertext literature so close as to gain entry to each other's mind-sets—which is what good books have always done.

I

imprint A separate line of product within a publishing house. Imprints run the gamut of complexity, from those composed of one or two series to those offering full-fledged and diversified lists. Imprints also enjoy different gradations of autonomy from the parent company. An imprint may have its own editorial department (perhaps consisting of as few as one editor), or house acquisitions editors may assign particular titles for release on appropriate specialized imprints. An imprint may publish a certain kind of book (juvenile or paperback or travel books) or have its own personality (such as a literary or contemporary tone). An individual imprint's categories often overlap with other imprints or with the publisher's core list, but some imprints maintain a small-house feel within an otherwise enormous conglomerate. The imprint can offer the distinct advantages of a personalized editorial approach, while availing itself of the larger company's production, publicity, marketing, sales, and advertising resources.

index An alphabetical directory at the end of a book that references names and subjects discussed in the book and the pages where such mentions can be found.

instant book A book produced quickly to appear in bookstores as soon as possible after (for instance) a newsworthy event to which it is relevant.

international copyright Rights secured for countries that are members of the International Copyright Convention (*see* **International Copyright Convention**) and that respect the authority of the international copyright symbol, ©.

International Copyright Convention Countries that are signatories to the various international copyright treaties. Some treaties are contingent upon certain conditions being met at the time of publication, so an author should, before publication, inquire into a particular country's laws.

introduction Preliminary remarks pertaining to a piece. Like a foreword, an introduction can be written by the author or an appropriate authority on the subject. If a book has both a foreword and an introduction, the foreword will be written by someone other than the author; the introduction will be more closely tied to the text and will be written by the book's author. (*See also* **foreword**.)

ISBN (International Standard Book Number) A 10-digit number that is linked to and identifies the title and publisher of a book. It is used for ordering and cataloging books and appears on all dust jackets, on the back cover of the book, and on the copyright page.

ISSN (International Standard Serial Number) An 8-digit cataloging and ordering number that identifies all U.S. and foreign periodicals.

J

juveniles (*See* **children's books**.)

K

kill fee A fee paid by a magazine when it cancels a commissioned article. The fee is only a certain percentage of the agreed-on payment for the assignment (no more than 50%). Not all publishers pay kill fees; a writer should make sure to formalize such an arrangement in advance. Kill fees are sometimes involved in work-for-hire projects in book publishing.

L

lead The crucial first few sentences, phrases, or words of anything—be it a query letter, book proposal, novel, news release, advertisement, or sales tip sheet. A successful lead immediately hooks the reader, consumer, editor, or agent.

lead title A frontlist book featured by the publisher during a given season—one the publisher believes should do extremely well commercially. Lead titles are usually those given the publisher's maximum promotional push.

letterhead Business stationery and envelopes imprinted with the company's (or, in such a case, the writer's) name, address, and logo—a convenience as well as an impressive asset for a freelance writer.

letterpress A form of printing in which set type is inked, then impressed directly onto the printing surface. Now used primarily for limited-run books-as-fine-art projects. (*See also* **offset**.)

libel Defamation of an individual or individuals in a published work, with malice aforethought. In litigation, the falsity of the libelous statements or representations, as well as the intention of malice, has to be proved for there to be libel; in addition, financial damages to the parties so libeled must be incurred as a result of the material in question for there to be an assessment of the amount of damages to be awarded to a claimant. This is contrasted to slander, which is defamation through the spoken word.

Library of Congress (LOC) The largest library in the world is in Washington, D.C. As part of its many services, the LOC will supply a writer with up-to-date sources and bibliographies in all fields, from arts and humanities to science and technology. For details, write to the Library of Congress, Central Services Division, Washington, DC 20540.

Library of Congress Catalog Card Number An identifying number issued by the Library of Congress to books it has accepted for its collection. The publication of those books, which are submitted by the publisher, are announced by the Library of Congress to libraries, which use Library of Congress numbers for their own ordering and cataloging purposes.

Literary Market Place (LMP) An annual directory of the publishing industry that contains a comprehensive list of publishers, alphabetically and by category, with their addresses, phone numbers, some personnel, and the types of books they publish. Also included are various publishing-allied listings, such as literary agencies, writer's conferences and competitions, and editorial and distribution services. LMP is published by R. R. Bowker and is available in most public libraries.

literature Written works of fiction and nonfiction in which compositional excellence and advancement in the art of writing are higher priorities than are considerations of profit or commercial appeal.

logo A company or product identifier—for example, a representation of a company's initials or a drawing that is the exclusive property of that company. In publishing usage, a virtual equivalent to the trademark.

M

mainstream fiction   Nongenre fiction, excluding literary or avant-garde fiction, that appeals to a general readership.

marketing plan   The entire strategy for selling a book: its publicity, promotion, sales, and advertising.

mass-market paperback   Less-expensive smaller-format paperbacks that are sold from racks (in such venues as supermarkets, variety stores, drugstores, and specialty shops) as well as in bookstores. Also referred to as rack (or rack-sized) editions.

mechanicals   Typeset copy and art mounted on boards to be photocopied and printed. Also referred to as pasteups.

midlist books   Generally mainstream fiction and nonfiction books that traditionally formed the bulk of a publisher's list (nowadays often by default rather than intent). Midlist books are expected to be commercially viable but not explosive bestsellers—nor are they viewed as distinguished, critically respected books that can be scheduled for small print runs and aimed at select readerships. Agents may view such projects as a poor return for the effort, since they generally garner a low-end advance; editors and publishers (especially the sales force) may decry midlist works as being hard to market; prospective readers often find midlist books hard to buy in bookstores (they have short shelf lives). Hint for writers: Don't present your work as a midlist item.

multimedia   Presentations of sound and light, words in magnetically graven image—and any known combination thereof as well as nuances yet to come. Though computer CD is the dominant wrapper for these works, technological innovation is the hallmark of the electronic-publishing arena, and new formats will expand the creative and market potential. Multimedia books are publishing events; their advent suggests alternative avenues for authors as well as adaptational tie-ins with the world of print. Meanwhile, please stay tuned for virtual reality, artificial intelligence, and electronic end-user distribution of product.

multiple contract   A book contract that includes a provisional agreement for a future book or books. (*See also* **option clause/right of first refusal**.)

mystery stories or **mysteries**   (*See* **suspense fiction**.)

N

net receipts   The amount of money a publisher actually receives for sales of a book: the retail price minus the bookseller's discount and/or other discount. The number of returned copies is factored in, bringing down even further the net amount received per book. Royalties are sometimes figured on these lower amounts rather than on the retail price of the book.

New Age   An eclectic category that encompasses health, medicine, philosophy, religion, and the occult—presented from an alternative or multicultural perspective. Although the term has achieved currency relatively recently, some publishers have been producing serious books in these categories for decades.

novella A work of fiction falling in length between a short story and a novel.

O

offset (offset lithography) A printing process that involves the transfer of wet ink from a (usually photosensitized) printing plate onto an intermediate surface (such as a rubber-coated cylinder) and then onto the paper. For commercial purposes, this method has replaced letterpress, whereby books were printed via direct impression of inked type on paper.

option clause/right of first refusal In a book contract, a clause that stipulates that the publisher will have the exclusive right to consider and make an offer for the author's next book. However, the publisher is under no obligation to publish the book, and in most variations of the clause the author may, under certain circumstances, opt for publication elsewhere. (*See also* **multiple contract**.)

outline Used for both a book proposal and the actual writing and structuring of a book, an outline is a hierarchical listing of topics that provides the writer (and the proposal reader) with an overview of the ideas in a book in the order in which they are to be presented.

out-of-print books Books no longer available from the publisher; rights usually revert to the author.

P

package The package is the actual book; the physical product.

packager (*See* **book producer**.)

page proof The final typeset copy of the book, in page-layout form, before printing.

paperback Books bound with a flexible, stress-resistant, paper covering material. (*See also* **binding**.)

paperback originals Books published, generally, in paperback editions only; sometimes the term refers to those books published simultaneously in hardcover and paperback. These books are often mass-market genre fiction (romances, Westerns, Gothics, mysteries, horror, and so forth) as well as contemporary literary fiction, cookbooks, humor, career books, self-improvement, and how-to books—the categories continue to expand.

pasteups (*See* **mechanicals**.)

permissions The right to quote or reprint published material, obtained by the author from the copyright holder.

picture book A copiously illustrated book, often with very simple, limited text, intended for preschoolers and very young children.

plagiarism   The false presentation of someone else's writing as one's own. In the case of copyrighted work, plagiarism is illegal.

preface   An element of a book's frontmatter. In the preface, the author may discuss the purpose behind the format of the book, the type of research upon which it is based, its genesis, or underlying philosophy.

premium   Books sold at a reduced price as part of a special promotion. Premiums can thus be sold to a bookseller, who in turn sells them to the bookbuyer (as with a line of modestly priced art books). Alternately, such books may be produced as part of a broader marketing package. For instance, an organization may acquire a number of books (such as its own corporate history or biography of its founder) for use in personnel training and as giveaways to clients; or a nutrition/recipe book may be displayed along with a company's diet foods in non-bookstore outlets. (*See also* **special sales**.)

press agent   (*See* **publicist**.)

press kit   A promotional package that includes a press release, tip sheet, author biography and photograph, reviews, and other pertinent information. The press kit can be put together by the publisher's publicity department or an independent publicist and sent with a review copy of the book to potential reviewers and to media professionals responsible for booking author appearances.

price   There are several prices pertaining to a single book: The invoice price is the amount the publisher charges the bookseller; the retail, cover, or list price is what the consumer pays.

printer's error (PE)   A typographical error made by the printer or typesetting facility, not by the publisher's staff. PEs are corrected at the printer's expense.

printing plate   A surface that bears a reproduction of the set type and artwork of a book, from which the pages are printed.

producer   (*See* **book producer**.)

proposal   A detailed presentation of the book's concept, used to gain the interest and services of an agent and to sell the project to a publisher.

public domain   Material that is uncopyrighted, whose copyright has expired, or that is uncopyrightable. The last includes government publications, jokes, titles—and, it should be remembered, ideas.

publication date (or **pub date**)   A book's official date of publication, customarily set by the publisher to fall 6 weeks after completed bound books are delivered to the warehouse. The publication date is used to focus the promotional activities on behalf of the title—so that books will have had time to be ordered, shipped, and be available in the stores to coincide with the appearance of advertising and publicity.

publicist (**press agent**)   The publicity professional who handles the press releases for new books and arranges the author's publicity tours and other promotional venues (such as interviews, speaking engagements, and book signings).

publisher's catalog A seasonal sales catalog that lists and describes a publisher's new books; it is sent to all potential buyers, including individuals who request one. Catalogs range from the basic to the glitzy and often include information on the author, on print quantity, and on the amount of money slated to be spent on publicity and promotion.

publisher's discount The percentage by which a publisher discounts the retail price of a book to a bookseller, often based in part on the number of copies purchased.

Publishers' Trade List Annual A collection of current and backlist catalogs arranged alphabetically by publisher, available in many libraries.

Publishers Weekly (PW) The publishing industry's chief trade journal. *PW* carries announcements of upcoming books, respected book reviews, interviews with authors and publishing-industry professionals, special reports on various book categories, and trade news (such as mergers, rights sales, and personnel changes).

Q

quality In publishing parlance, the word "quality" in reference to a book category (such as quality fiction) or format (quality paperback) is a term of art—individual works or lines so described are presented as outstanding products.

query letter A brief written presentation to an agent or editor designed to pitch both the writer and the book idea.

R

remainders Unsold book stock. Remainders can include titles that have not sold as well as anticipated, in addition to unsold copies of later printings of bestsellers. These volumes are often remaindered—that is, remaining stock is purchased from the publisher at a huge discount and resold to the public.

reprint A subsequent edition of material that is already in print, especially publication in a different format—the paperback reprint of a hardcover, for example.

résumé A summary of an individual's career experience and education. When a résumé is sent to prospective agents or publishers, it should contain the author's vital publishing credits, specialty credentials, and pertinent personal experience. Also referred to as the curriculum vitae or, more simply, vita.

returns Unsold books returned to a publisher by a bookstore, for which the store may receive full or partial credit (depending on the publisher's policy, the age of the book, and so on).

reversion-of-rights clause In the book contract, a clause that states that if the book goes out of print or the publisher fails to reprint the book within a stipulated length of time, all rights revert to the author.

review copy A free copy of a (usually) new book sent to electronic and print media that review books for their audiences.

romance fiction or **romance novels**   Modern or period love stories, always with happy endings, which range from the tepid to the torrid. Except for certain erotic specialty lines, romances do not feature graphic sex. Often mistakenly pigeonholed by those who do not read them, romances and romance writers have been influential in the movement away from passive and coddled female fictional characters to the strong, active modern woman in a tale that reflects areas of topical social concern.

royalty   The percentage of the retail cost of a book that is paid to the author for each copy sold after the author's advance has been recouped. Some publishers structure royalties as a percentage payment against net receipts.

S

sales conference   A meeting of a publisher's editorial and sales departments and senior promotion and publicity staff members. A sales conference covers the upcoming season's new books, and marketing strategies are discussed. Sometimes sales conferences are the basis upon which proposed titles are bought or not.

sales representative (sales rep)   A member of the publisher's sales force or an independent contractor who, armed with a book catalog and order forms, visits bookstores in a certain territory to sell books to retailers.

SASE (self-addressed stamped envelope)   It is customary for an author to enclose SASEs with query letters, with proposals, and with manuscript submissions. Many editors and agents do not reply if a writer has neglected to enclose an SASE with correspondence or submitted materials.

satisfactory clause   In book contracts, a publisher will reserve the right to refuse publication of a manuscript that is not deemed satisfactory. Because the author may be forced to pay back the publisher's advance if the complete work is found to be unsatisfactory, the specific criteria for publisher satisfaction should be set forth in the contract to protect the author.

science fiction   Science fiction includes the hardcore, imaginatively embellished technological/scientific novel as well as fiction that is even slightly futuristic (often with an after-the-holocaust milieu—nuclear, environmental, extraterrestrial, genocidal). An element much valued by editors who acquire for the literary expression of this cross-media genre is the ability of the author to introduce elements that transcend and extend conventional insight.

science fiction/fantasy   A category fiction designation that actually collapses two genres into one (for bookseller-marketing reference, of course—though it drives some devotees of these separate fields of writing nuts). In addition, many editors and publishers specialize in both these genres and thus categorize their interests with catchphrases such as sci-fi/fantasy.

screenplay   A film script—either original or one based on material published previously in another form, such as a television docudrama based on a nonfiction book or a movie thriller based on a suspense novel. (Compare with **teleplay**.)

self-publishing A publishing project wherein an author pays for the costs of manufacturing and selling his or her own book and retains all money from the book's sale. This is a risky venture but one that can be immensely profitable (especially when combined with an author's speaking engagements or imaginative marketing techniques); in addition, if successful, self-publication can lead to distribution or publication by a commercial publisher. (Compare with **subsidy publishing**.)

self-syndication Management by writers or journalists of functions that are otherwise performed by syndicates specializing in such services. In self-syndication, it is the writer who manages copyrights, negotiates fees, and handles sales, billing, and other tasks involved in circulating journalistic pieces through newspapers, magazines, or other periodicals that pick up the author's column or run a series of articles.

serial rights Reprint rights sold to periodicals. First serial rights include the right to publish the material before anyone else (generally before the book is released, or coinciding with the book's official publication)—either for the U.S., a specific country, or for a wider territory. Second serial rights cover material already published, either in a book or another periodical.

serialization The reprinting of a book or part of a book in a newspaper or magazine. Serialization before (or perhaps simultaneously with) the publication of the book is called first serial. The first reprint after publication (either as a book or by another periodical) is called second serial.

series Books published as a group either because of their related subject matter (such as a biographical series on modern artists or on World War II aircraft) and/or single authorship (a set of works by Djuna Barnes, a group of books about science and society, or a series of titles geared to a particular diet-and-fitness program). Special series lines can offer a ready-made niche for an industrious author or compiler/editor who is up to date on a publisher's program and has a brace of pertinent qualifications and/or contacts. In contemporary fiction, some genre works are published in series form (such as family sagas, detective series, fantasy cycles).

shelf life The amount of time an unsold book remains on the bookstore shelf before the store manager pulls it to make room for newer incoming stock with greater (or at least untested) sales potential.

short story A brief piece of fiction that is more pointed and more economically detailed as to character, situation, and plot than a novel. Published collections of short stories—whether by one or several authors—often revolve around a single theme, express related outlooks, or comprise variations within a genre.

signature A group of book pages that have been printed together on one large sheet of paper that is then folded and cut in preparation for being bound, along with the book's other signatures, into the final volume.

simultaneous publication The issuing at the same time of more than one edition of a work, such as in hardcover and trade paperback. Simultaneous releases can be expanded to include (though rarely) deluxe gift editions of a book as well as mass-market paper versions. Audio versions of books are most often timed to coincide with the release of the first print edition.

simultaneous (or multiple) submissions The submission of the same material to more than one publisher at the same time. Although simultaneous submission is a common practice, publishers should always be made aware that it is being done. Multiple submissions by an author to several agents is, on the other hand, a practice that is sometimes not regarded with great favor by the agent.

slush pile The morass of unsolicited manuscripts at a publishing house or literary agency, which may fester indefinitely awaiting (perhaps perfunctory) review. Some publishers or agencies do not maintain slush piles per se—unsolicited manuscripts are slated for instant or eventual return without review (if an SASE is included) or may otherwise be literally or figuratively pitched to the wind. Querying a targeted publisher or agent before submitting a manuscript is an excellent way of avoiding, or at least minimizing the possibility of, such an ignoble fate.

software Programs that run on a computer. Word-processing software includes programs that enable writers to compose, edit, store, and print material. Professional-quality software packages incorporate such amenities as databases that can feed the results of research electronically into the final manuscript, alphabetization and indexing functions, and capabilities for constructing tables and charts and adding graphics to the body of the manuscript. Software should be appropriate to both the demands of the work at hand and the requirements of the publisher (which may contract for a manuscript suitable for on-disk editing and electronic design, composition, and typesetting).

special sales Sales of a book to appropriate retailers other than bookstores (for example, wine guides to liquor stores). This classification also includes books sold as premiums (for example, to a convention group or a corporation) or for other promotional purposes. Depending on volume, per-unit costs can be very low, and the book can be custom-designed. (*See also* **premium.**)

spine That portion of the book's casing (or binding) that backs the bound page signatures and is visible when the volume is aligned on a bookshelf among other volumes.

stamping In book publishing, the stamp is the impression of ornamental type and images (such as a logo or monogram) on the book's binding. The stamping process involves using a die with a raised or intaglioed surface to apply ink stamping or metallic-leaf stamping.

subsidiary rights The reprint, serial, movie and television, and audiotape and videotape rights deriving from a book. The division of profits between publisher and author from the sales of these rights is determined through negotiation. In more elaborately commercial projects, further details such as syndication of related articles and licensing of characters may ultimately be involved.

subsidy publishing A mode of publication wherein the author pays a publishing company to produce his or her work, which may thus appear superficially to have been published conventionally. Subsidy publishing (alias vanity publishing) is generally more expensive than self-publishing, because a successful subsidy house makes a profit on all its contracted functions, charging fees well beyond the publisher's basic costs for production and services.

suspense fiction   Fiction within a number of genre categories that emphasize suspense as well as the usual (and sometimes unusual) literary techniques to keep the reader engaged. Suspense fiction encompasses novels of crime and detection (regularly referred to as mysteries. These include English-style cozies, American-style hard-boiled detective stories, dispassionate law-enforcement procedurals, crime stories, action-adventure, espionage novels, technothrillers, tales of psychological suspense, and horror. A celebrated aspect of suspense fiction's popular appeal—one that surely accounts for much of this broad category's sustained market vigor—is the interactive element: The reader may choose to challenge the tale itself by attempting to outwit the author and solve a crime before detectives do, figure out how best to defeat an all-powerful foe before the hero does, or parse out the elements of a conspiracy before the writer reveals the whole story.

syndicated column   Material published simultaneously in a number of newspapers or magazines. The author shares the income from syndication with the syndicate that negotiates the sale. (*See also* **self-syndication**.)

syndication rights   (*See also* **self-syndication; subsidiary rights**.)

synopsis   A summary in paragraph form, rather than in outline format. The synopsis is an important part of a book proposal. For fiction, the synopsis portrays the high points of story line and plot, succinctly and dramatically. In a nonfiction book proposal, the synopsis describes the thrust and content of the successive chapters (and/or parts) of the manuscript.

T

table of contents   A listing of a book's chapters and other sections (such as the front matter, appendix, index, and bibliography) or of a magazine's articles and columns, in the order in which they appear; in published versions, the table of contents indicates the respective beginning page numbers.

tabloid   A smaller-than-standard-size newspaper (daily, weekly, or monthly). Traditionally, certain tabloids are distinguished by sensationalism of approach and content rather than by straightforward reportage of newsworthy events. In common parlance, "tabloid" is used to describe works in various media (including books) that cater to immoderate tastes (for example, tabloid exposé, tabloid television; the tabloidization of popular culture).

teleplay   A **screenplay** geared toward television production. Similar in overall concept to screenplays for the cinema, teleplays are nonetheless inherently concerned with such TV-loaded provisions as the physical dimensions of the smaller screen, and formal elements of pacing and structure keyed to stipulated program length and the placement of commercial advertising. Attention to these myriad television-specific demands are fundamental to the viability of a project.

terms   The financial conditions agreed to in a book contract.

theme   A general term for the underlying concept of a book. (*See also* **hook**.)

thriller A thriller is a novel of suspense with a plot structure that reinforces the elements of gamesmanship and the chase, with a sense of the hunt being paramount. Thrillers can be spy novels, tales of geopolitical crisis, legal thrillers, medical thrillers, technothrillers, domestic thrillers. The common thread is a growing sense of threat and the excitement of pursuit.

tip sheet An information sheet on a single book that presents general publication information (publication date, editor, ISBN, etc.), a brief synopsis of the book, information on relevant other books (sometimes competing titles), and other pertinent marketing data such as author profile and advance blurbs. The tip sheet is given to the sales and publicity departments; a version of the tip sheet is also included in press kits.

title page The page at the front of a book that lists the title, subtitle, author (and other contributors, such as translator or illustrator), as well as the publishing house and sometimes its logo.

trade books Books distributed through the book trade—meaning bookstores and major book clubs—as opposed to, for example, mass-market paperbacks, which are often sold at magazine racks, newsstands, and supermarkets as well.

trade discount The discount from the cover or list price that a publisher gives the bookseller. It is usually proportional to the number of books ordered (the larger the order, the greater the discount), and typically varies between 40% and 50%.

trade list A catalog of all of a publisher's books in print, with ISBNs and order information. The trade list sometimes includes descriptions of the current season's new books.

trade (quality) paperbacks Reprints or original titles published in paperback format, larger in dimension than mass-market paperbacks, and distributed through regular retail book channels. Trade paperbacks tend to be in the neighborhood of twice the price of an equivalent mass-market paperback version and about half to two-thirds the price of hardcover editions.

trade publishers Publishers of books for a general readership—that is, nonprofessional, nonacademic books that are distributed primarily through bookstores.

translation rights Rights sold either to a foreign agent or directly to a foreign publisher, either by the author's agent or by the original publisher.

treatment In screenwriting, a full narrative description of the story, including sample dialogue.

U

unauthorized biography A history of a person's life written without the consent or collaboration of the subject or the subject's survivors.

university press A publishing house affiliated with a sponsoring university. The university press is generally nonprofit and subsidized by the respective university. Generally, university presses publish noncommercial scholarly nonfiction books written by academics, and their lists may include literary fiction, criticism, and poetry. Some university presses also specialize in titles of regional interest, and many acquire projects intended for commercial book-trade distribution.

unsolicited manuscript A manuscript sent to an editor or agent without being requested by the editor/agent.

V

vanity press A publisher that publishes books only at an author's expense—and will generally agree to publish virtually anything that is submitted and paid for. (*See also* **subsidy publishing**.)

vita Latin word for "life." A shortened equivalent term for *curriculum vitae* (*see also* **résumé**).

W

word count The number of words in a given document. When noted on a manuscript, the word count is usually rounded off to the nearest 100 words.

work-for-hire Writing done for an employer, or writing commissioned by a publisher or book packager who retains ownership of, and all rights pertaining to, the written material.

Y

young-adult (YA) books Books for readers generally between the ages of 12 and 17. Young-adult fiction often deals with issues of concern to contemporary teens.

young readers or **younger readers** Publishing terminology for the range of publications that address the earliest readers. Sometimes a particular house's young-readers' program typifies books for those who do not yet read; which means these books have to hook the caretakers and parents who actually buy them. In certain quirky turns of everyday publishing parlance, *young readers* can mean anyone from embryos through young adults (and "young" means *you* when you want it to). This part may be confusing (as is often the case with publishing usage): Sometimes *younger adult* means only that the readership is allegedly hip, including those who would eschew kid's books as being inherently lame and those who are excruciatingly tapped into the current cultural pulse, regardless of cerebral or life-span quotient.

Z

zombie (or **zombi**) In idiomatic usage, a zombie is a person whose conduct approximates that of an automaton. Harking back to the term's origins as a figure of speech for the resurrected dead or a reanimated cadaver, such folks are not customarily expected to exhibit an especially snazzy personality or be aware of too many things going on around them; hence some people in book-publishing circles may be characterized as zombies.

INDEX

INDEX

RESOURCES FOR WRITERS

Norville, Andrea, 147
Novalis, 486
November, Sahryn, 128
Nuding, Micki, 45
Nyren, Neil, 123

O

Oblack, Linda, 398
O'Brien, Dorothy, 160
O'Brien, John, 205
O'Connor, Dr. Eugene, 407
O'Connor, Mike, 479
Octopus Books, 55, 66
O'Farrell, Anne Marie, 679, 681
O'Hayre, Meredith, 147
O'Hearn, Michael, 486
Ohio State University Press, 406-407
Ohlin, Peter, 408
O'Keefe, Shannon, 700
O'Keefe, Susan, 307
Oliver, Victor, 295
Oliveros, Chris, 467
Olsen, Jeff, 227
Olswanger, Anna, 542, 544
O'Malley, Janine, 74
O'Malley, Michael, 454
O'Neal, David, 343
O'Neill, Brendan, 147
O'Neill, Mary Ellen, 95
One World, 34, 36
Oolichan Books, 486-487
O'Party, Megan, 767, 769
Oram, Fern, 320
Orb, 89-90
Orbit, 55, 66-67
Orca Book Publishers, 487-488
O'Reilly Media, 303
Orjala, Todd, 432
Orman, Lindsay, 14
Osborne, Heather, 90
Osborne Media / McGraw Hill, 279, 283-284
O'Shea, Allen, See Allen O'Shea Literary Agency

Osman, Marion, 409
Osnos, Peter, 317
Ostashevsky, Ms. Luba, 79
O'Sullivan, Robert, 173
O'Sullivan, Wylie, 43
Oswald, Denise, 73
Ottaviano, Christy, 77
Ottewell, Wanda, 475
Oveis, Frank, 200
The Overlook Press, 304-305
Owen, Lorna, 19
Oxford University Press, 407-409

P

Pacheco, Lisa, 435
Padgett, Marvin, 204
Paladin Press, 305
Palgrave MacMillan, 68, 79
Panettieri, Gina, 760-762
Pantheon Books, 22, 24
Pardi, Fran, 742, 745-746
Parisi, Christina M., 154
Park Literary Group, LLC, The, 700-702
Park, Theresa, 700
Parris, Scott, 385
Parsley, John, 65
Parsons, Ed, 386
Parsons, Joseph, 429
Pastore, Julia, 13
Pathfinder Press, 306
Patnaik, Gayatri, 175
Patten, Amanda, 49
Patterson, David, 76
Patterson, Monique, 84
Patty, Ann, 232
Patty, Ms. P., 296
Paul, Joey, 294
Paul S. Levine Literary Agency, 657-658
Paulist Press, 306-307
Paulsen, Nancy, 131
Paumier, Jessica, 406
Pavia, Julian, 12, 14

THREE DOG
PRESS

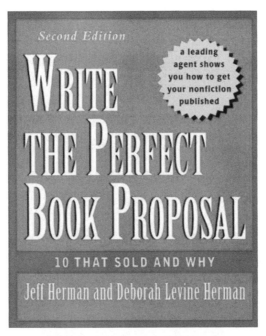

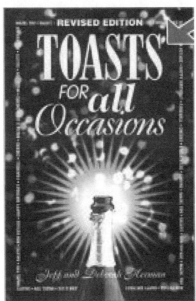

RFH Gets This title from the same scared and petrified to young man who wrote this story initially believing, after waking from a coma, into a new world so strange and unfamiliar and all so frightening not having remembering experiencing any of it before, overwhelmed with fear, the consumation of his entire life. This hell (reality) he was determined to overcome, Indeed we see with great effort, this young man JRiza learn as a survival Skill to overcome his reality and become a Ready man ready to take on anything this reality puts before him. In short, he believes he has already overcome hell and all its members, now he is ready and able to take on and indeed does take on - anything and everything this world throws at him

Deborah Herman's

GUIDE TO

SPIRITUAL
WRITING &
PUBLISHING

For all who are called
and wish to be
published.

FOR SALE SOON.

SEE OUR WEB SITE:

WWW.JEFFHERMAN.COM

AND DEBORAH HERMAN'S BLOG:

WWW.SPIRITUALWRITINGAGENT.COM